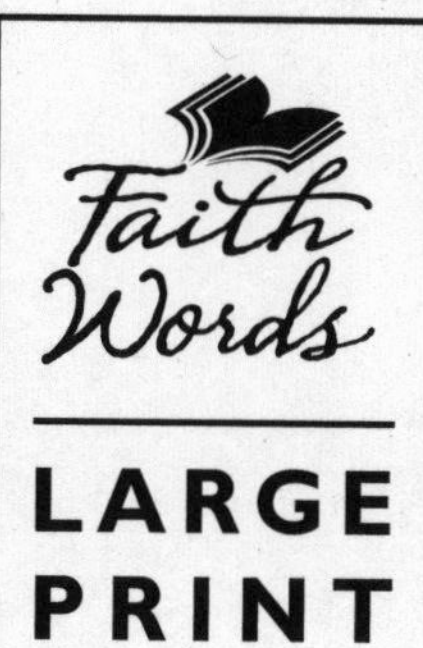
Faith Words
LARGE PRINT

The Power of Being Thankful

365 Devotions for Discovering the Strength of Gratitude

JOYCE MEYER

LARGE PRINT

FaithWords
Hachette Book Group
1290 Avenue of the Americas
New York, NY 10104

www.faithwords.com

Printed in the United States of America

RRD-C

First Large Print Edition: October 2014
10 9 8 7 6 5 4 3 2 1

FaithWords is a division of Hachette Book Group, Inc.
The FaithWords name and logo are trademarks of Hachette Book Group, Inc.

Library of Congress Cataloging-in-Publication Data
Meyer, Joyce, 1943–
The power of being thankful : 365 devotions for discovering the strength of gratitude / Joyce Meyer. — First Edition.
pages cm
ISBN 978-1-4555-1733-6 (hardcover)—ISBN 978-1-4555-3019-9 (large print hardcover)—ISBN 978-1-4789-8294-4 (audio download)—ISBN 978-1-4789-8293-7 (audiobook)—ISBN 978-1-4555-1734-3 (ebook) 1. Gratitude—Prayers and devotions. 2. Devotional calendars. I. Title.
BV4647.G8M49 2014
242'.2—dc23

2014008824

Introduction

I believe one of the most important things we can do is be thankful for our lives and all that God gives us and does for us. Too often, we focus on what we don't have or what we wish was different in our lives, and this focus causes us to go through life feeling dissatisfied and defeated. But when we stop and take the time to focus on what we already have and all the ways God has already blessed us, it gives us a new perspective—our mind is renewed, our attitude is affected, and our joy overflows.

That is why I'm excited about *The Power of Being Thankful*. This devotional is one year's worth of thankful thoughts compiled from some of my most popular books that will help you develop and maintain a heart of thanksgiving. Regardless of where you are in your journey with the Lord, I believe *The Power of Being Thankful* is going to help you begin enjoying your life with Him in a whole new way.

I pray that you will set aside the next year to pursue God with a thankful heart. Don't go through your life frustrated, miserable, and unhappy; God has something much better in store for you. Live each day with a thankful heart, grateful for every good thing—no matter how big or how small—that God has done in your life. As you begin to remember the good things God has done in your past and realize the blessings you have in the present, you can't help getting excited about what He is going to do in your future.

Be thankful and be ready...God has something amazing in store for your life!

Joyce Meyer

Thank [God] in everything [no matter what the circumstances may be, be thankful and give thanks], for this is the will of God for you [who are] in Christ Jesus [the Revealer and Mediator of that will].

1 THESSALONIANS 5:18

The Power of Being Thankful

The Best Way to Begin in Prayer

They are also to stand every morning to thank and praise the Lord, and likewise at evening.
1 CHRONICLES 23:30

No matter what we pray for, thanksgiving can always go with it. A good habit to develop is starting all of our prayers with thanksgiving. An example of this would be: "Thank You, Father, for all You have done in my life; You are awesome and I really love and appreciate You."

I encourage you to examine your life, to pay attention to your thoughts and your words, and to see how much thanksgiving you express. Do you murmur and complain about things or are you thankful?

If you want a challenge, just try to get through an entire day without uttering one word of complaint. Develop an attitude of thanksgiving in every situation. In fact, just become outrageously thankful—and watch as your intimacy with God increases and as He pours out greater blessings than ever before.

Prayer of Thanks

Thank You, Father, for the way You guide me in prayer. Help me to come to You in thanksgiving before I do anything else. Let gratitude be the foundation of my prayer life. I make the decision today to put aside complaining, being thankful in prayer instead.

Living at Peace

Peace I leave with you; My [own] peace I now give and bequeath to you. Not as the world gives do I give to you. Do not let your hearts be troubled, neither let them be afraid.

JOHN 14:27

Peace is one of the most important elements to enjoying your life.

A life of frustration and struggle, a life without peace, is the result of focusing on things you can't do anything about. When you worry about things beyond your control, stress and anxiety begin to creep into your life.

The apostle Paul said, "Be anxious for nothing, but in everything by prayer and supplication, with thanksgiving, let your requests be made known to God; and the peace of God, which surpasses all understanding, will guard your hearts and minds through Christ Jesus" (Philippians 4:6–7 NKJV).

Once we realize we are struggling with something and feel upset, we need to start praying and immediately turn the situation over to God, thankful He will provide according to His will and offer us peace. You and I are not called to a life of frustration and struggle. Jesus came so we could have righteousness, joy, and peace!

Prayer of Thanks

Father, I am grateful for peace. It is a wonderful gift that You have given me, and I ask for Your help to always be peaceful in every situation.

Let Your Light Shine

You are the light of the world. A city set on a hill cannot be hidden.

MATTHEW 5:14

As believers in Christ, we can be bubbling over with life. We can be vibrant, alive, active, energized, peaceful, and joy-filled.

It is our approach to God that determines our attitude and countenance. When we approach God with boldness, thankful for His grace and confident that He loves us and He is for us, we can't help but be full of life. However, a legalistic, religious approach to God steals life. It does not nourish it. Remember, Paul said, "The Law kills, but the Spirit makes alive" (2 Corinthians 3:6). When we follow the Spirit, we feel alive.

Each of us should ask ourselves the

question, *Would people want what I have by watching my life and looking at my countenance? Is my life reflecting a thankful, expectant heart, excited about what God is going to do each new day?*

We are to be the light of the world. Make sure your light is shining brightly today.

Prayer of Thanks

Father, I am thankful that I don't have to approach You through the law, but I can come boldly to Your throne because of Your amazing grace. Thank You that Your grace and joy brighten my life and allow me to be a light for the world to see.

Expect Something Good

May the God of your hope so fill you with all joy and peace in believing [through the experience of your faith] that by the power of the Holy Spirit you may abound and be overflowing (bubbling over) with hope.

ROMANS 15:13

One of the most powerful forces in the universe is hope. And as a child of God, you can have hope in unlimited measure. That's something to be thankful for!

Hope is the happy anticipation that something good is going to happen in your life. It's expecting something good. What are you expecting? Have you even thought about it? If you're expecting nothing, or if you are expecting just a little bit, you are going to get what you expect.

I always say, "I'd rather believe for a

whole lot and get half of it than believe for a little bit and get all of it."

God wants you to trust Him and have a happy expectation for something good. If you're in a tough situation today, expect it to change. If you're in a good situation today, expect it to get even better. God is a God of hope.

Prayer of Thanks

Lord, thank You for the power of hope in my life. Thank You that You are going to do something good, and I can trust You and hope for the best.

Practice Seeing the Positive

A happy heart is good medicine and a cheerful mind works healing, but a broken spirit dries up the bones.

PROVERBS 17:22

I encourage you to be a thankful, positive person. If you aren't it's just a matter of forming a new habit.

I was so negative at one time in my life that if I even tried to think two positive thoughts in succession my brain seemed to stop functioning. But now I am very positive and actually don't enjoy being with people who are negative.

If you have not formed the habit of being positive yet, you can begin today! Put reminders around your house or in your car, little signs that say, "Be positive." Ask the Holy Spirit to remind you if you are slipping into negativity. Ask your friends to help also. Set aside time during the day to focus on and be thankful for the good things God has blessed you with.

Positive, thankful thoughts don't happen by accident; you can choose to practice them. And remember, practice makes perfect.

Prayer of Thanks

Thank You, Father, for helping me think positive thoughts. I am grateful that I am not a prisoner to negative thinking and that I can choose to be happy and joy-filled.

Enjoy the Reward

Men will say, Surely there is a reward for the [uncompromisingly] righteous; surely there is a God Who judges on the earth.

PSALM 58:11

Taking time to enjoy the fruit of your labor is one of the main things that will keep you pressing on in difficult times.

God gave many men and women in the Bible difficult tasks to perform, but He always promised a reward. Looking to the reward helps us endure the difficulty. The Bible says in Hebrews 12:2 that Jesus despised the cross, but He endured it for the joy of obtaining the prize that was set before Him. He is now seated at the right hand of the Father.

I encourage you not to look merely at the work you do, but look also at the promise of the reward. Take time to be thankful for and enjoy the fruit of your labor and then you'll be energized to finish your course.

Prayer of Thanks

Thank You, Father, that I can always look forward to Your reward in my life. I am grateful that difficult times never last forever, but I can learn from them and expect Your goodness in my life.

The Importance of Right Thinking

For as he thinks in his heart, so is he.

PROVERBS 23:7

The mind is the leader or forerunner of all actions. The steps we take each day are a direct result of the thoughts we allow ourselves to think.

If we have a negative mind, we will have a negative life. On the other hand, if we renew our mind according to God's Word, we will experience "the good and acceptable and perfect will of God" for our lives (Romans 12:2).

So many people's struggles are rooted in wrong thinking patterns. Negative thinking can actually cause them to create the problems they experience in their lives; thankfully, though, we don't have to live captive to those thoughts. We can choose to line our thoughts up with the Word of God.

The mind is a battlefield. Decide to resist destructive, negative thinking and dwell on godly thoughts for your life instead. The more you change your mind for the better, the more your life will also change for the better.

Prayer of Thanks

Father, I'm thankful that I don't have to live as a captive to my thoughts. With Your help, I can change those negative thoughts that are affecting my life. I can win the battle of the mind by spending time in Your Word, meditating on Your promises, and making a conscious effort to think God-honoring thoughts over my life.

Keep On Keeping On

Let us not become weary in doing good, for at the proper time we will reap a harvest if we do not give up. GALATIANS 6:9 NIV

One of the most important truths you can be grateful for is that God has promised to never leave you—He is always by your side!

That's why it is important to remember this: No matter how difficult the circumstances may seem around you, don't give up! God is for you, and He is bigger than any trouble you may be facing.

You can regain the territory the devil has stolen from you. If necessary, regain it one inch at a time, being thankful for and always leaning on God's grace and not on your own ability to get the desired results. In Galatians 6:9, the apostle Paul simply encourages us to keep on keeping on! Don't be a quitter! Have an "I can do all things through Christ" attitude. God is looking for people who will go all the way through to the other side with Him.

Prayer of Thanks

Thank You, Father, that You give me the strength to never quit. I am grateful that You are always with me and that You fight my battles.

Discipline and Self-Control

Like a city whose walls are broken through is a person who lacks self-control.

PROVERBS 25:28 NIV

We can live a disciplined life filled with self-control. It is one of the keys to living a joyful life. The Bible teaches us in many places the importance of living a disciplined life.

If we don't discipline ourselves, our circumstances will eventually become situations we regret, but thankfully, God's Word teaches us to be temperate, which means to be marked by moderation, to hold ourselves within limits (to compromise between two extremes or find the middle ground).

Clearly we are to maintain balance. The area of finances is an example of where discipline is required. It is wrong to overspend, but it is also wrong to underspend.

God gives us money not to hoard, but to enjoy. Wisdom means saving some, spending some, and giving some away.

In every area of your life—relationships, finances, exercise, eating, career, thoughts, and words—ask God to help you live with discipline and self-control. Don't be led by emotional, in-the-moment thinking. Use the wisdom of God to live in balance and really enjoy your life!

Prayer of Thanks

Thank You, Father, that You have given me the fruit of self-control, and by Your grace, I can discipline myself. You give me strength and wisdom, and You guide me every step of the way.

Pursuing Peace

I have told you these things, so that in Me you may have [perfect] peace and confidence.

JOHN 16:33

Peace is one of the greatest blessings that God has given us, and we should thank Him for it daily. Simply desiring a life of peace is not enough. You have to pursue peace with God, peace with yourself, and peace with those around you. I have found that the more thankful I am, the more peaceful I am. Gratitude helps me focus on what I have instead of what I don't have, allowing me to stay focused on my blessings instead of worrying.

When walking in peace becomes a priority, you will make the effort needed to see it happen. I spent years praying for God to *give* me peace and finally realized He had *already* provided peace, but I had to choose it. Jesus said in John 14:27, "Peace I leave with you." Jesus has already provided your peace. Make the decision to walk in that peace today!

Prayer of Thanks

Father, thank You that You have provided everything I need to live at peace. Today, I choose to pursue that peace and live at rest, knowing You are greater than any trial or tribulation I may be going through. You are everything I need. You are my peace.

Taking the Time for Gratitude

At all times and for everything giving thanks in the name of our Lord Jesus Christ to God the Father. EPHESIANS 5:20

Throughout the Bible, we see people celebrating progress and victory in a variety of ways. One of those ways was to specifically take the time to give an offering to God and to thank Him. Noah did it. Abraham did it. And we can do it too.

We would quickly add a lot of celebration time to our lives if we would take the time to give thanks when God does amazing things for us. An attitude of gratitude shows a lot about the character of a person. It keeps God first, knowing that He is the source of every blessing we receive. Gratitude is never about feeling entitled—it's an attitude that says, "I know I don't deserve

God's goodness, but I am sure grateful for it."

Prayer of Thanks

Father, I am thankful that You have blessed me with so many good things in my life. Today, I take time to meditate on Your goodness and thank You for Your blessings.

There Is Always Time for Prayer

And they raised up their voices and called, Jesus, Master, take pity and have mercy on us!

LUKE 17:13

Whether you are a mother, a schoolteacher, an executive, a mechanic, or a brain surgeon, you are probably busy! You not only have the requirements of your job to fulfill, you may also have caretaking responsibilities with family or extended family. No matter how busy you are, be encouraged: God hears all prayers—even short ones—and that is something to be thankful for!

Prayer is something you can do throughout the day no matter how much you have on your to-do list. For example, if you are an exhausted stay-at-home mom who cleans up the house and changes diapers all day, then just take one minute to be still and say, "Oh, Jesus, I love You. Strengthen me right now. God, I need some energy. I am worn out."

It is okay to talk to God in a very simple way. By praying throughout the day in this simple, meaningful way, we invite God into every area of our lives, and that is exactly what He desires.

Prayer of Thanks

I thank You today, Father, that prayer doesn't have to be long and complicated. You hear even my short, heartfelt prayers. I am grateful that I can have a continuous conversation with You all through the day, and that You hear and answer me.

Living Beyond Your Feelings

When I am weak [in human strength], then am I [truly] strong (able, powerful in divine strength). 2 CORINTHIANS 12:10

On any given day, we may feel good or bad, happy or sad, excited or discouraged, and a thousand other things. Although feelings can be very strong and demanding, we do not have to let them rule our lives.

We can learn to manage our emotions rather than allowing them to manage us. This has been one of the most important biblical truths I have learned in my journey with God. It has also been one that allows me to consistently enjoy my life.

If we have to wait to see how we feel before we know if we can enjoy the day, then we are giving feelings control over us. But thankfully, we have free will and can make decisions that are not based on feelings. If we are willing to make right choices regardless of how we feel, God will always be faithful to give us the strength to do so.

Prayer of Thanks

Father, I thank You that I no longer have to let my feelings control me. I am so grateful that I don't have to wait to see how I feel every day before I know how to act. With Your help, I am going to live beyond my feelings—I'm going to live the joy-filled life Jesus came to give me!

Waiting Well

But let endurance and steadfastness and patience have full play and do a thorough work, so that you may be [people] perfectly and fully developed [with no defects], lacking in nothing.

JAMES 1:4

Patience is extremely important for people who want to glorify God and enjoy their lives. If we are impatient, the situations we encounter in life will certainly cause us to react emotionally.

The next time you have to wait on something or someone, instead of just reacting, try reminding yourself, *Getting upset will not make this go any faster, so I might as well enjoy the wait.* Then perhaps say out loud, "I am developing patience as I wait, so I am thankful in this situation." If you do that, you will be acting on the Word of

God rather than reacting to the unpleasant circumstance.

Remember, patience is a fruit of the Spirit that God wants to develop in your life. Don't merely think about how hard and frustrating it is, but think about how blessed you can be as you learn the art of waiting well.

Prayer of Thanks

Father, I am grateful that You have planted patience in my spirit and that through You, I can react properly to any situation. Help me today, and every day, to exercise patience in all things.

Getting Along with Difficult People

If possible, as far as it depends on you, live at peace with everyone. ROMANS 12:18

How do you react to people who are rude? Do you respond in love as the Word says we should, or do you join them in their ungodly behavior? I think there are a lot of rude and unpleasant people in the world today largely because of the stressful lives most people live.

We can be very thankful that we know the Word of God and have Him in our lives to help us and comfort us—to keep us from falling into the traps that stress can cause. But we must remember that a lot of people in the world who are difficult to get along with don't have that. Jesus said that we have done nothing special if we treat people well who treat us well, but if we are kind to someone who would qualify as an enemy, then we are doing well (see Luke 6:32–35).

People are everywhere, and not all of them are pleasant. Will you act on the Word of God and love them for His sake?

Prayer of Thanks

Father, when I am in a situation that requires me to deal with a hard-to-get-along-with person, let me pray for them rather than react to them emotionally. Thank You for giving me the grace to be kind to everyone—no matter how they act toward me.

Believing the Best of Others

Love bears up under anything and everything that comes, is ever ready to believe the best of every person, its hopes are fadeless under all circumstances, and it endures everything [without weakening].

1 CORINTHIANS 13:7

The Bible teaches us to always believe the best of every person.

However, if we merely let our thoughts lead us, they usually tend toward negativity. Sadly, the flesh without the influence of the Holy Spirit is dark and negative. Thankfully, we don't have to walk in the flesh, but we can choose to be led by the Spirit (see Romans 8:5). When we choose to let the Spirit lead us, we will see the best in other people, and we will be filled with life and peace in our souls.

I encourage you to begin seeing other people as children of God rather than as adversaries. Decide to look past their faults and see them as God sees them. Be grateful that the Spirit can help you see the best in every person in your life.

Prayer of Thanks

I thank You today, Father, that You forgive my sins and don't hold them against me. I ask You for Your strength in doing the same thing for others.

Trusting God

For You are my hope; O Lord God, You are my trust from my youth and the source of my confidence. PSALM 71:5

Trusting God allows us to enter His rest, and rest is a place of peace where we are able to enjoy our lives while being confident God is fighting our battles.

God cares for us; He will solve our problems and meet our needs, and thankfully, we can stop thinking and worrying about them. I realize this is easier said than done, but there is no time like the present to begin learning a new way to live—a way of living that is without worry, anxiety, and fear.

This is the time to begin believing and saying, "I trust God completely; there is no need to worry! I will not give in to fear or anxiety. God is the source of my confidence." The more you think about this truth, the more you will find yourself choosing trust over worry.

Prayer of Thanks

Father, thank You that I don't have to worry! I trust You to take care of me and to always be with me.

Loving Your Life

The thief comes only in order to steal and kill and destroy. I came that they may have and enjoy life, and have it in abundance (to the full, till it overflows).

JOHN 10:10

Do you believe God wants you to enjoy your life? Well, He does! In fact, part of God's will is for you to enjoy every moment of it. I know this is true because His Word says so in many places.

King Solomon, who is considered to have been very wise, wrote in Ecclesiastes 2:24: "There is nothing better for a man than that he should eat and drink and make himself enjoy good in his labor. Even this, I have seen, is from the hand of God."

Solomon said to make yourself enjoy the good of your labor. We should learn to value enjoyment because it is vital to being a balanced and healthy person. This does not mean that all of life becomes a huge party or a vacation, but it does mean that through the power of God we can learn to be thankful for and enjoy all of life.

Prayer of Thanks

Father, I am grateful that Jesus came so that I might have abundant life. When times are tough and my joy feels low, help me to remember that You have promised I can enjoy my life. Thank You for the joy, peace, and security I find in You.

The Bible Teaches Us to Be Thankful

I have inclined my heart to perform Your statutes forever, even to the end.

PSALM 119:112

Just as the Bible instructs us to praise God and to worship Him, it also gives us reasons to thank Him and teaches us how to offer our gratitude to Him, as shown in the Scriptures below:

- *We give praise and thanks to You,*
  O God, we praise and give thanks;
  Your wondrous works declare that
  Your Name is near and they who
  invoke Your Name rehearse Your
  wonders. Psalm 75:1
- *It is a good and delightful thing*
  to give thanks to the Lord,
  to sing praises [with musical

accompaniment] to Your name, O Most High... Psalm 92:1

- *Let us come before His presence with thanksgiving; let us make a joyful noise to Him with songs of praise!* Psalm 95:2
- *Enter into His gates with thanksgiving and a thank offering and into His courts with praise! Be thankful and say so to Him, bless and affectionately praise His name!* Psalm 100:4

Prayer of Thanks

Father, I am so thankful for the promises and instruction that I find in Your Word. Today, I choose to live a thankful life simply because You instruct me to in the Word of God. I will act in obedience and I believe that Your Word teaches me the best way to live.

Jesus Lived a Life of Thanksgiving

At all times and for everything giving thanks in the name of our Lord Jesus Christ to God the Father. EPHESIANS 5:20

Part of prayer's power is the power of thanksgiving...because there is not powerful living apart from a life of thanksgiving. During His earthly ministry, Jesus lived a life of thanksgiving. He gave thanks to the Father on many occasions and for many things.

For example, He gave thanks to God when He broke the loaves and fishes and fed the 4,000 people (see Matthew 15:36). He thanked God that He had heard His prayer concerning the raising of Lazarus from the dead (John 11:41–42). And He gave thanks to God when He gave the bread and wine to His disciples at the Last

Supper even though He knew His suffering and death were very close (see Mark 14:22–23).

If it was important for Jesus to live a life of thanksgiving, it should certainly be important for us to do the same thing.

Prayer of Thanks

Thank You, Father, for the example of Jesus and the thankful life He modeled for us. Help me to enter Your gates with thanksgiving every time I come to You in prayer. You are good and You are worthy of my thanksgiving and my praise.

A Matter of Focus

Looking unto Jesus, the author and finisher of our faith. HEBREWS 12:2 NKJV

It is very important to focus on the right things. This is why the Word of God instructs us to look away from all that distracts us and to look to Jesus, who is the Author and Finisher of our faith.

Whatever we focus on becomes magnified in our minds. When we focus on our problems, we continually roll them over and over in our minds, which is like meditating on them. The more we think and talk about our problems, the larger they become. A relatively small matter can grow into a huge issue merely because we focus on it too much.

Instead of meditating on our problems, we would be wise to meditate on God's

Word and His promises for our lives and to aggressively thank Him for them. When we do, we will see the faithfulness of God revealed, and our problems won't seem so big after all.

Prayer of Thanks

I am grateful, Father, that You are bigger than my problems, trials, and uncertainties. You are good and my heart is filled with thanksgiving for You and Your love.

Giving and Receiving Love

I give you a new commandment: that you should love one another. Just as I have loved you, so you too should love one another.

JOHN 13:34

Of all the things that we have to be grateful for in our lives, love is at the top of the list. Loving and being loved bring purpose and meaning to life. The world is looking for love, but they are really looking for God because God *is* love.

People look for fulfillment in life in many ways that may seem good at first but often leave them feeling frustrated, disappointed, and empty. Only by receiving God's love and walking in love (putting love into action by continually reaching out to others and making an effort to show them love through various acts of kindness) can they find the true fulfillment they are so desperately seeking.

Love will change your life! Ask God to help you receive and give love, and be thankful as you watch His love bring a fulfillment to your life you have never known.

Prayer of Thanks

Father, I am so thankful that You love me and that You have given me an ability to love others. Let Your love flow through me today in ways that will be a blessing to others.

Blessed to Be a Blessing

Let each of you esteem and look upon and be concerned for not [merely] his own interests, but also each for the interests of others.

PHILIPPIANS 2:4

Everyone needs a blessing. We all need to be encouraged, edified, complimented, and appreciated. And you have the ability to bless others. Be thankful that God not only blesses you, but that He has made you a blessing. We all get weary at times and need other people to let us know that we are valuable and appreciated.

I believe God blesses us so we can be a blessing—not only in a few places but everywhere we go. Look for people who are needy and bless them. Share what you have with those who are less fortunate than you are. And remember, everyone needs a blessing—even the successful people who appear to have everything.

When you live to meet needs and encourage those around you, you will find "joy unspeakable" in the process (see 1 Peter 1:8 KJV).

Prayer of Thanks

Father, I am so grateful for Your blessings in my life, and I am also grateful that You have enabled me to be a blessing. Help me reach out to others every day and focus on adding to their encouragement.

Prayer as the First Option, Not the Last Resort

For everyone who keeps on asking receives; and he who keeps on seeking finds; and to him who keeps on knocking, [the door] will be opened.

MATTHEW 7:8

One day I woke up with a throbbing headache. I walked around with that miserable headache almost all day, telling everybody I met about how terrible I felt—until I finally realized that I had complained most of the day and had never taken the time to simply pray and ask God to take the pain away.

Unfortunately, that response is rather typical for some of us. We complain about our problems and spend a majority of our time trying to figure out what we can do to solve them. We often do everything except the one thing we are told to do in the Word of God: ask, that we may receive and our joy may be full (see John 16:24 KJV).

Thankfully, God wants to provide for our every need. We have the awesome privilege of "asking and receiving," and we should always pray as a first response to every situation.

Prayer of Thanks

I thank You, God, in everything, no matter what the circumstance may be. I desire to be the most thankful person I can be, and I ask You to help me reach my goal.

Agreeing with God

Fight the good fight of the faith; lay hold of the eternal life to which you were summoned and [for which] you confessed the good confession [of faith] before many witnesses.

1 TIMOTHY 6:12

Take a step of faith and no matter how you feel, agree with God that He loves you. You are wonderfully made and have many talents and strengths. You are valuable, and as a believer in Jesus, you are the righteousness of God in Him. You have rightness before God instead of wrongness—be thankful for that amazing gift!

Begin to speak out against feelings of insecurity and say, "I belong to God and He loves me!" (see Ephesians 2:10). We believe more of what we hear ourselves say than what others say, so start saying something good and drown out the other voices that condemn you.

Fight for yourself! Fight the good fight of faith and refuse to live below the level at which Jesus wants you to live. His kingdom is righteousness, peace, and joy (see Romans 14:17). Don't settle for anything less.

Prayer of Thanks

I thank You, Father, that I can boldly declare in faith who I am in Christ. Thank You that You created me as one of a kind and You love me dearly. Today, I choose to believe that I am Your workmanship.

Just Do It

He said, Come! So Peter got out of the boat and walked on the water, and he came toward Jesus.
MATTHEW 14:29

Indecision wastes a lot of time, and time is too precious to waste. If you'll become a confident, decisive person, you'll accomplish a lot more with less effort.

No one learns how to hear from God without making mistakes. Don't be overly concerned about errors. Don't take yourself too seriously. You are a fallible, imperfect human being, but you can rejoice with thanksgiving because you serve an infallible, perfect God.

Learn from your mistakes, correct the ones you can, and trust God for His guidance and protection. If you feel that God is prompting you to give something away, help someone out, or make a change in your life, do it! Take some action and sow seeds of obedience. When you feel you have guidance from God, move in faith instead of stagnating in doubt and fear.

Prayer of Thanks

Father, I am thankful that I can trust You to help me learn from my mistakes. I don't have to worry or be afraid that I'll make the wrong decision, because I know You are with me. Thank You that You will lead and guide me—even through my mistakes.

Living Amazed

And they were amazed at His teaching, for His word was with authority and ability and weight and power. LUKE 4:32

I think that many times we let what should be extremely special to us—things we should be extremely grateful for—become too commonplace. Several years ago, I was "prayer murmuring" to the Lord (praying but kind of murmuring at the same time), and I said, "Lord, why don't I have those exciting, special things happen in my life like I used to when I first started to know You?"

And I'll never forget what the Lord spoke to my heart so clearly. He said, "Joyce, I still do the same things all the time, it's just that you've gotten used to it." *Ouch!*

I believe that if we'll stay amazed at the things God is doing in our lives—even the little things—we'll never be without hope. I encourage you to realize what you have, be thankful, and decide to live amazed… jaw-dropping, wide-eyed, "Wow! That was God!" amazed.

Prayer of Thanks

I am grateful that You are always doing special things in my life, Lord, and I pray that I will recognize them and be generous in my praise and gratitude. Help me live amazed.

Shelter in the Storm

He who dwells in the secret place of the Most High shall remain stable and fixed under the shadow of the Almighty [Whose power no foe can withstand]. PSALM 91:1

The best way to be safe during a natural storm is to take cover. If you do not seek shelter, the storm may harm you.

The Word of God gives us instructions on how to take cover when we face the spiritual storms of life. The first place you need to run when a storm hits in your life is to the secret place of the Most High, the presence of God. Meditate on His Word; pray; worship Him; thank Him and tell Him you trust Him as the winds of adversity blow. These are the spiritual disciplines no foe can withstand. When you practice these habits, you actually construct spiritual walls of protection around yourself. These walls will provide protection and enable you to stand strong in the midst of any storm.

Prayer of Thanks

Lord, I thank You that You are my shelter in the storm. When life's difficulties come my way, I don't have to be afraid because You are with me. I trust that You will calm the storms in my life and bring me safely through them. Thank You that You'll never leave me nor forsake me (see Hebrews 13:5).

Worry or Worship?

Give to the Lord the glory due to His name; worship the Lord in the beauty of holiness or in holy array. PSALM 29:2

Worry and worship are polar opposites, and we would be much happier if we learned to become worshippers instead of worriers. Worry creates an opportunity for the enemy to torment us, but worship (reverence and adoration of God) leads us into His presence, where we will always find peace, joy, and hope.

God created us to worship Him. He wants us to develop a deep, personal relationship with Him and an outrageous love for Him. This kind of love flows from a grateful heart, appreciative of who God is and what He has done.

Don't waste another day of your life

worrying. Determine what your responsibility is and what it is not. Don't try to take on God's responsibility. When we do what we can do, God steps in and does what we can't. So give yourself and your worries to God, worship Him, and begin enjoying the abundant life He has for you.

Prayer of Thanks

I thank You, Father, that I can choose to worship You rather than worry about my problems. Help me to see that You are greater than any obstacle I may face, and I can trust You to do in my life what I cannot.

Joyful in Every Circumstance

[After all] the kingdom of God is not a matter of [getting the] food and drink [one likes], but instead it is righteousness (that state which makes a person acceptable to God) and [heart] peace and joy in the Holy Spirit.

ROMANS 14:17

A wise person does not allow the moods of other people to alter theirs.

There is a story of a Quaker man who was walking down the street with a friend when he stopped at a newsstand to purchase a newspaper. The storekeeper was very rude and unfriendly. The Quaker man responded respectfully and was quite kind in his dealing with him. After paying for his paper and continuing to walk down the street, his friend asked, "How could you be so cordial to that man considering the terrible way he was treating you?" The Quaker man replied, "Oh, he is always that way; why should I let him determine how I am going to act?"

This is one of the amazing traits we see in Jesus—He changed people, they did not change Him. I encourage you to follow the example of Jesus. Do what God expects you to do and don't live under the tyranny of other people's moods and attitudes.

Prayer of Thanks

Father, I thank You that I can be joyful in every circumstance. Today, I choose not to let other people determine how I am going to live. With Your help, I am going to live in joy regardless of the circumstances around me.

No More Complaining

Bless (affectionately, gratefully praise) the Lord, all you His hosts, you His ministers who do His pleasure. PSALM 103:21

When we maintain an attitude of thanksgiving, we close the door to grumbling and complaining—which seem to be ever-present temptations in our lives. The truth is we don't develop a complaining attitude; we are all born with one. But with God's help, we can develop and nurture a thankful attitude.

If we practice regularly praising, worshipping, and thanking God, there will be no room for complaining, faultfinding, and murmuring. The Bible says in Philippians 2:14: "Do all things without grumbling and faultfinding and complaining..." Complaining opens the door for the devil to cause us trouble, but thankfulness opens the door for God to bless us.

Prayer of Thanks

I am grateful, Father, that with Your help I can develop a thankful attitude. I worship You for Your goodness, Your power, and Your might. I choose to be thankful for Your presence in my life rather than grumble and complain about things of the world.

Keep Life Fresh and Exciting

Delight yourself also in the Lord, and He will give you the desires and secret petitions of your heart. PSALM 37:4

It's good to occasionally (or perhaps frequently) do something that would be unexpected, something new or "out of the box." Do something that will surprise people and perhaps stretch you a bit. It will keep your life interesting, and you'll end up thanking God for your exciting new challenge or adventure.

We are not created by God to merely do the same thing over and over until it has no meaning left at all. God is creative. Just look at the amazing variety in His creation and you will have to agree that His creativity has no end.

In case you haven't noticed, God frequently changes things up in our lives.

Don't be afraid of change. Go ahead and do some of the things you would like to do but have kept putting off because you have never done them before.

Prayer of Thanks

I am grateful, Father, that You make my life fresh and exciting. Each day is a new challenge and an adventure. I thank You that I can be excited about the future ahead of me and I can live a fresh, bold, creative life in You.

The Key to Self-Acceptance

When they measure themselves with themselves and compare themselves with one another, they are without understanding and behave unwisely.

2 CORINTHIANS 10:12

Advertising is often geared to make people strive to look the best, be the best, and own the most. If you buy "this" car, you will really be number one! If you buy "this" particular brand of clothes, you will be just like "this" famous star and people will really admire you. The world constantly gives us the impression that we need to be something other than what we are.

Confidence begins with self-acceptance—which is made possible through a strong faith in God's love and plan for our lives. I believe it is insulting to God when we compare ourselves with others and desire to be what they are. Make a decision to be grateful for the person God made you to be, and then you will never again compare yourself with someone else. Appreciate others for who they are and enjoy the wonderful person you are.

Prayer of Thanks

Father, help me to love and appreciate the person You created me to be. I thank You that I don't have to compare myself to others in order to be accepted. You created me with a unique and wonderful purpose. I'm thankful that to You, I am special and beyond compare.

The Warfare of Love

Above all things have intense and unfailing love for one another, for love covers a multitude of sins [forgives and disregards the offenses of others]. 1 PETER 4:8

One of the most amazing things I've learned, something that still thrills my soul, is that love is actually spiritual warfare. This truth makes spiritual warfare fun, because loving people is very enjoyable.

First Peter 4:8 teaches us to have intense love for one another. The *King James Version* uses the word "fervent." The verb form of the Greek word translated *fervent* means "to be hot, to boil." Our love walk needs to be hot, on fire, boiling over, not cold and barely noticeable.

If we are hot enough with love, Satan won't be able to handle us. We might say we're "too hot to handle." Have you ever microwaved something for too long and couldn't get it out because it was too hot to handle? That's the way we should want to be.

On fire with love—and too much for the devil to handle!

Prayer of Thanks

I am grateful, Father, that You love me. Help me to follow Your example and love the people around me. Thank You that regardless of how people act toward me, I can love people with Your perfect, unconditional love.

Your Shield of Faith

Lift up over all the [covering] shield of saving faith, upon which you can quench all the flaming missiles of the wicked [one].

EPHESIANS 6:16

In years past, soldiers protected themselves with shields, and in Ephesians 6:16, the Bible speaks of "the shield of faith." Since shields provide protection, faith must be a way to protect ourselves when the enemy attacks. We can be grateful that God gives us a defense system. However, just like with an actual shield, His shield is only effective when it is raised up. It won't help a soldier if it is on the ground or by his side.

When the devil attacks us with unpleasant circumstances or thoughts that cause us to feel afraid, we should immediately lift up the shield of faith. The way we do that is by deciding that we will trust God instead of trying to figure out our own way to victory. It is helpful to say out loud, "I trust God in this situation!" Say it firmly with conviction. Jesus talked back to Satan by saying "It is written" and quoting Scripture (see Luke 4), and we can do the same.

Prayer of Thanks

Father, I thank You that Your Word is a powerful shield, and it is effective against everything the enemy tries to do in my life. My faith is based on Your Word and Your promises for my life.

The Fast Pace of Life

Come to Me, all you who labor and are heavy-laden and overburdened, and I will cause you to rest. [I will ease and relieve and refresh your souls.]

MATTHEW 11:28

We really do live in a time-crunched world; just about everything we do seems to be urgent. We live under incredible pressure and run from one thing to the next—to the point that we may neglect the things that are really important in life: family, our health, God, and building up our spiritual lives.

The truth is we cannot handle life apart from God. We cannot handle the pressure, the confusion, and the stress without Him. Our marriages will suffer, we will experience financial pressure, and our relationships won't thrive if we do not study God's Word and take time to pray.

But there is good news to be thankful for—God will strengthen us and enable us to handle life peacefully and wisely if we start praying about things instead of merely *trying* to get through the day. God will renew our strength and enable us to handle life and not be weary (see Isaiah 40:31).

Prayer of Thanks

Father, I am so thankful that You give me peace and rest even in the midst of a busy life. Help me to lean on You today and use wisdom in setting my schedule. You are the strength of my life and I totally depend on You.

Learning to Cope with Criticism

Rejoice and exult in hope; be steadfast and patient in suffering and tribulation; be constant in prayer. ROMANS 12:12

No matter what we do in life, at some point in time we will all face a level of criticism. But it is possible to learn how to cope with criticism and not let it affect your life.

We can be grateful for the example the apostle Paul set for us. Paul experienced criticism often, but he said that he was not concerned about the judgment of others. He knew he was in God's hands and that in the end he would stand before God and give an account of himself and his life. He would not stand before any man to be judged (see 1 Corinthians 4:3–4).

You may not always do everything right, but God sees your heart. If you're attempting to live for God and looking for ways to love others, God is pleased (see Matthew 22:37–40). Don't worry about the criticism of others; God loves you. His love and approval are all you need.

Prayer of Thanks

Father, I thank You that I don't have to listen to the criticism of others. You see my heart and You know my motives. I thank You that Your approval is greater than the approval of any person.

One of the Most Powerful Things You Can Do

By this shall all [men] know that you are My disciples, if you love one another [if you keep on showing love among yourselves].

JOHN 13:35

Purposely forgetting about ourselves and doing something for someone else—even while we are hurting—is one of the most powerful things we can do to overcome evil. And thankfully, God can help us do that.

When Jesus was on the cross in intense suffering, He took time to comfort the thief next to Him (see Luke 23:39–43). When Stephen was being stoned, he prayed for those stoning him, asking God not to lay the sin to their charge (see Acts 7:59–60). When Paul and Silas were in prison, they took time to minister to their jailer (see Acts 16:27–34).

If we will wage war against selfishness and walk in love, the world will begin to take notice. We will not impress the world by being just like them. But how many unsaved friends and relatives might come to know Jesus if we genuinely love them instead of ignoring, judging, or rejecting them? I believe it is time to find out, don't you?

Prayer of Thanks

Father, I pray that You will give me the ability to put the needs of others before my own. Thank You that Your love has the power to change lives. Help me demonstrate that power today.

Attitude of Gratitude

Do all things without grumbling and faultfinding and complaining [against God] and questioning and doubting [among yourselves].

PHILIPPIANS 2:14

You and I have many opportunities to complain on a regular basis. But complaining doesn't do any good; all complaining does is open the door for the enemy. It doesn't solve problems; it just creates a breeding ground for greater problems.

Instead of complaining, let's choose to respond to the Lord each day by developing an attitude of gratitude. This is not just an occasional expression of thanks, but a continual lifestyle of thanksgiving. The person who has developed an "attitude of gratitude" is one who is thankful and grateful for every single thing that God is doing in his or her life day by day.

Prayer of Thanks

Father, thank You for the way You provide for every area of my life. Instead of complaining about what I want or about what I don't have, I choose to be grateful for everything I do *have. You have been good to me—thank You for Your goodness.*

A New Level of Commitment

Commit your way to the Lord [roll and repose each care of your load on Him]; trust (lean on, rely on, and be confident) also in Him and He will bring it to pass. PSALM 37:5

God wants to take us to a new level of commitment. This is something to be excited about and grateful for because with commitment comes blessing. It's not always easy, but it is worth all it requires. We all fight battles and face the temptation to stop fighting and just give up, but commitment is the thing that enables us to resist that temptation.

When you are fiercely committed to God's purpose for your life, you will begin to experience all that He has for you. God loves you and He wants you to be in a committed relationship with Him—for life. I can't imagine anything more satisfying, more rewarding, or more adventurous. He has more in store for you than you have ever asked or imagined, but in order to see His plans become a reality in your life you will need to be 100 percent committed to Him and His will.

Prayer of Thanks

Father, I choose to commit my life fully to You. I thank You that You are leading me into the destiny You have for me. With Your help, I will focus on You and commit every part of my life to Your plan and purpose for me.

Living a Guilt-Free Life

Therefore, [there is] now no condemnation (no adjudging guilty of wrong) for those who are in Christ Jesus, who live [and] walk not after the dictates of the flesh, but after the dictates of the Spirit. ROMANS 8:1

We are not built for guilt. God never intended His children to be loaded down with guilt, so our systems don't handle it well at all. Had God wanted us to feel guilty, He would not have sent Jesus to redeem us from guilt. He bore, or paid for, our iniquities and the guilt they cause (see Isaiah 53:6 and 1 Peter 2:24–25).

As believers in Jesus Christ and as sons and daughters of God, we can be thankful that we have been set free from the power of sin (see Romans 6:6–10). That doesn't mean that we'll never sin, but it does mean that when we do, we can admit it, receive forgiveness, and be free from guilt. Our journey with God toward right behavior and holiness is progressive, and only when we stop dragging the guilt from past mistakes along with us will we really make progress toward true freedom and joy.

Prayer of Thanks

Father, I thank You that I don't have to carry guilt and shame around with me as I go through my life. Help me to let go of my past mistakes and walk in the freedom of Your grace and forgiveness.

Facing Fear Head-On

Those who trust in, lean on, and confidently hope in the Lord are like Mount Zion, which cannot be moved but abides and stands fast forever.
PSALM 125:1

One meaning of the word *fear* is "to take flight," so when we use the phrase "fear not," in a very real sense we are saying, "Don't run away from what frightens you." Remember, you don't have to do it in your own strength—God is with you. You can move forward with a grateful assurance in Him.

Whatever the situation is, face it; don't run from it. Don't try to hide from it; just meet it head-on, even when you feel like you'd rather not. Every man or woman who has ever been given the opportunity to do something great has had to face fear.

What will you do when you are tempted to be afraid? Will you run, or will you stand firm, thankful God is with you?

Prayer of Thanks

When I am in a situation where I begin to feel fear, help me, Father, to stand firm in Your strength. I am thankful that I do not have to flee. I can stand strong knowing that fear has no control over my life.

Making Each Day Extraordinary

...But David encouraged and strengthened himself in the Lord his God.

1 SAMUEL 30:6

No day will seem ordinary if we are thankful for the gift God is giving us at the start of each day. An extraordinary attitude can quickly turn an ordinary day into an amazing adventure. Jesus said He came so that we might have and enjoy life (see John 10:10). If we refuse to enjoy it, then it's no one's fault but our own.

I would like to suggest that you take responsibility for your joy and never again give anyone else the job of keeping you happy. You can control what you do, but you cannot control what other people do. So you may be unhappy a lot of the time if you depend on them as your source of joy.

The psalmist David said that he encouraged himself in the Lord, and if he can do it, then we can do it too.

Prayer of Thanks

Father, I am grateful for this new day that You have given me. Regardless of the actions or attitudes of others, I am going to enjoy this day because You are the source of my joy.

Responding to Encouragement

...For out of the fullness (the overflow, the superabundance) of the heart the mouth speaks.
MATTHEW 12:34

The more we encourage people, the better they respond. In fact, compliments actually help people perform better, while nagging makes them perform worse.

Choose a person who you would like to have a better relationship with and begin to sincerely and aggressively encourage and compliment them. I believe you will be amazed at how much better they respond to you. Your first concern might be, *If I ignore their faults, won't they just take advantage of me?* Of course, that can happen, but it usually doesn't.

What frequently happens is that the person being encouraged is so grateful for the encouragement, they have a change of heart and they work harder to do their part to make the relationship good. They are now doing it because they choose to and not because you are trying to force them.

Prayer of Thanks

Thank You, Father, that You encourage and build me up through the promises in Your Word. I pray that You will help me do the same for others. Thank You for showing me ways to encourage the people in my life today.

Enjoy the Fruit of Your Labor

There is nothing better for a man than that he should eat and drink and make himself enjoy good in his labor. Even this, I have seen, is from the hand of God.

ECCLESIASTES 2:24

It is not in God's plan for His children never to enjoy the fruit of their labor. It is good to work hard, but it is equally good to take time to enjoy life. Thankfully, God is El Shaddai, the God of more than enough. He is Jehovah Jirah, the Lord our Provider. He said that He was able to do exceedingly, abundantly, above and beyond all that we could ever dare to ask, think, or imagine (see Ephesians 3:20).

Certainly God wants and even commands us to serve and give to others generously—but God never intended that we feel guilty if we take time to enjoy the fruit of our labor. Hard work deserves reward, and we must not ever think that it doesn't. God rewards those who diligently seek Him (see Hebrews 11:6), so set aside some time to relax and enjoy the things He has rewarded you with.

Prayer of Thanks

Father, I thank You that I can enjoy the fruit of my labor. Help me find the balance between working hard and enjoying what I have worked for. Help me to enjoy what You have given me the strength to work for.

Grateful for Grace

Now Stephen, a man full of God's grace and power, performed great wonders and signs among the people.

ACTS 6:8 NIV

Grace can be of benefit to you in your everyday life. For example: When you get into a situation that begins to cause you to become frustrated, just stop and say, "O Lord, give me grace." Then believe in faith that God has heard your prayer, and be grateful that He is working out that situation simultaneously as you go about your daily routine.

Faith is the channel through which you and I receive the grace of God to meet our needs. The Bible says that grace is the power of God coming to us through our faith to meet our need. The next time you begin to feel frustrated, stop and choose to rely on the grace of God.

Prayer of Thanks

Father, I thank You for the power of Your grace in my life. Help me to rely on You today and not on my own strength. I thank You that You are with me and I can put my trust in You.

It's Okay to Be Different

The sun is glorious in one way, the moon is glorious in another way, and the stars are glorious in their own [distinctive] way; for one star differs from and surpasses another in its beauty and brilliance.

1 CORINTHIANS 15:41

We are all different. Like the sun, the moon, and the stars, God has created us to be different from one another, and He has done it on purpose. Each of us meets a need, and we are all part of God's overall plan.

Thankfully, we can be secure people, knowing God loves us and has a plan for our lives. We don't have to be threatened by the abilities of others. We can be free to love and accept ourselves and one another without feeling pressure to compare or compete.

When we struggle to be like others, not only do we lose ourselves, but we also grieve the Holy Spirit. God wants us to fit into His plan; He doesn't want us feeling pressured to fit into everyone else's plans. Different is okay; it is all right to be different.

Prayer of Thanks

Father, You have created me to be distinct and unique, and I thank You for that. With Your help I'm going to avoid the temptation to compare myself to others. I'm going to be secure in who You've created me to be today.

Rejoice and Be Glad

Rejoice in the Lord always [delight, gladden yourselves in Him]; again I say, Rejoice!

PHILIPPIANS 4:4

Many serious things are going on in this world, and we need to be aware of them and prepared for them. But at the same time, because of the Spirit of God in our lives, we can learn to relax and take things as they come without getting nervous and upset about them.

Thankfully, with God's help, we can learn how to enjoy the good life He has provided for us through the death and resurrection of His Son, Jesus Christ. Twice in Philippians 4:4–7, the apostle Paul tells us to rejoice. He urges us not to fret or have any anxiety about anything but to pray and give thanks to God in everything—not *after* every difficulty is over.

In spite of all the troubling things going on around us in the world, our daily confession can be, "This is the day the Lord has made; I will rejoice and be glad in it."

Prayer of Thanks

Father, no matter what goes on around me today, I thank You that I can rejoice and be glad. Thank You that my joy is not found in my circumstances—my joy is found in You.

The Leading of the Holy Spirit

But the Comforter (Counselor, Helper, Intercessor, Advocate, Strengthener, Standby), the Holy Spirit, Whom the Father will send in My name [in My place, to represent Me and act on My behalf], He will teach you all things. And He will cause you to recall (will remind you of, bring to your remembrance) everything I have told you. JOHN 14:26

The Holy Spirit acts somewhat like a traffic policeman inside of us. When we do the right things, we get a "green light" from Him, and when we do wrong things, we get a "red light." If we are about to get ourselves into trouble, but have not fully made a decision to proceed, we get a "caution signal."

The more we stop and ask God for directions, the more sensitive we become to the signals from the Holy Spirit within. Thankfully, He doesn't scream and yell at us; He simply whispers in the still, small voice (see 1 Kings 19:12) and lets us know we are about to make a mistake. Each time we listen and obey, it becomes easier to hear Him the next time. He will always lead us to newness of life and inner peace if we yield to Him.

Prayer of Thanks

Father, when I am in a situation where I'm not sure whether to proceed or not, help me to hear Your voice. I thank You that You have a clear direction for my life and that You will lead me and guide me into Your plan for my future.

Equipped to Meet the Needs of Others

And [God] Who provides seed for the sower and bread for eating will also provide and multiply your [resources for] sowing and increase the fruits of your righteousness [which manifests itself in active goodness, kindness, and charity].

2 CORINTHIANS 9:10

God blesses us so we can bless others. He wants us to have our needs met, and He wants us to be equipped to help people who are in need. This is one reason God promises to provide for us and to do so abundantly.

To help other people, we need strength, good health, and clarity of mind. We need money to help people who are struggling financially. We need clothes to be able to share with people who need them. We need joy to help those who are in despair.

God always provides these things—and more—as seed to a person who is willing to sow (see 2 Corinthians 9:9–10). This means, if you are thankful for what you have and willing to share with others, God will not only meet your needs, He will give you an abundance of supply so you will always be able to give. We can all win the battle against stinginess by simply practicing generosity.

Prayer of Thanks

I thank You, Father, that You bless me so I may bless others. Help me to see the needs around me, and help me to do my part to meet those needs. Thank You that there have been people who have helped me along the way. With Your help, I want to do the same for others.

Hearing, Receiving, and Obeying God's Word

Behold, I long for Your precepts; in Your righteousness give me renewed life... I will keep your law continually, forever and ever [hearing, receiving, loving, and obeying it]. And I will walk at liberty and at ease, for I have sought and inquired for [and desperately required] Your precepts.

PSALM 119:40, 44–45

Our joy is full when we gratefully receive God's promises for our lives and obey His commands. When we believe the Word and obey whatever Jesus puts in our hearts to do, we overcome the things that try to upset or frustrate us. Believing God's Word delivers us from struggling so that we may rest in the promises of God.

The Word says, "For we who have

believed (adhered to and trusted in and relied on God) do enter that rest" (Hebrews 4:3). If your thoughts have become negative and you are full of doubt, it may be because you have stopped hearing, receiving, and obeying God's Word. As soon as you start believing God's Word, your joy will return and you will be "at ease" again. Thankfully, that place of rest in God is where He wants you to be *every day* of your life.

Prayer of Thanks

Father, I am so grateful for Your Word. I know that the promises and instructions You give me are for my benefit. As I hear, receive, and obey the Word of God today, help me to experience the joy-filled, overcoming life Jesus came to give me.

Making a Trust Confession

The Lord is good, a Strength and Stronghold in the day of trouble; He knows (recognizes, has knowledge of, and understands) those who take refuge and trust in Him. NAHUM 1:7

When you choose to confess and meditate on the thought, *I trust God completely; there is no need to worry*, you will eventually form a new mind-set that will enable you to put your trust in God with ease. You will habitually look for what is good and magnify it, thanking God for each victory along the way. Life is very enjoyable when we decide to pray about everything and worry about nothing.

Don't be discouraged if forming mind-sets seems difficult in the beginning. You may have to say that you will trust God and not worry 1,000 times before you start to feel the effects of doing it. Just remember that each time you think and say the thing that agrees with God, you are making progress. Satan will relentlessly try to get you to give up, but if you will relentlessly decide to trust God, I guarantee that you will see the result in due time.

Prayer of Thanks

I thank You, Father, that You are trustworthy and I can depend on You in every area of my life. I trust that You can handle any and every problem I'm facing. I won't worry; I will trust in You.

Something God Responds To

That I may make the voice of thanksgiving heard and may tell of all Your wondrous works.

PSALM 26:7

Giving thanks is an important part of prayer because, like praise and worship, it is something God *responds* to. It's something God loves, something that warms His heart. Anytime we please God like that, our intimacy with Him increases—and that makes for a better prayer life.

Also, when we are thankful, we are in a position to receive more from the Lord. If we are not thankful for what we have, why should God give us something else to murmur or complain about? On the other hand, when God sees that we genuinely appreciate and are thankful for everything He gives us—the big things and the little things—He is inclined to bless us even more.

Prayer of Thanks

Father, thank You that I can have a personal relationship with You. I pray that You are blessed by my thanksgiving. I love You and I am so grateful for each thing that You have given me, no matter how big or how small.

Whose Opinion Is Right?

So shall My word be that goes forth out of My mouth: it shall not return to Me void [without producing any effect, useless], but it shall accomplish that which I please and purpose, and it shall prosper in the thing for which I sent it. ISAIAH 55:11

Opinions are very interesting because we all have different ones. You are entitled to your opinion, but that does not mean you should always give it to others. Most of the time people don't want our opinion; and even if they do ask for it, they hope we agree with the opinion they have already formed. Wisdom knows when to keep quiet and when to talk.

Not only should we be wise about how freely we give our opinion, we should also resist letting popular opinion become ours just because it is popular. Thankfully, God has given us His truths that can shape and form our opinions. If we'll decide to base our mind-sets and opinions on the unchanging Word of God, it doesn't matter what culture says or what seems popular at the time; God will reward you because His Word never returns void.

Prayer of Thanks

I thank You, Father, for the inspired Word of God that gives me truth to base my thoughts, mind-sets, and opinions on. Help me to know the difference between what is popular at the time and what is true and unchanging. Help me develop wise and encouraging opinions.

The Power of a Simple Prayer

Ask and keep on asking and you will receive, so that your joy (gladness, delight) may be full and complete. JOHN 16:24

I often tell people that one of the things they can do to enjoy their lives is to simplify their lives—that includes their prayer life too. Now when I say "simplify" your prayer life, I don't mean you should not pray often. The Bible says, "Pray without ceasing" (1 Thessalonians 5:17 NKJV). We can and should go to God frequently in prayer.

What I mean is that if you try to sound too eloquent, you can complicate your prayer life to the point of it being unbearable. It is good to know that we don't have to try to impress God with our prayers. Thankfully, we can just talk to Him like a friend; tell Him the way we truly think and feel. With God, you can always be sincere, and you can always be yourself. You don't have to put on religious airs. You can be real with God and simply enjoy spending time with Him.

Prayer of Thanks

Father, I thank You that talking with You is not a complicated process. I am so grateful that I can be myself with You and just pray what is on my heart. Help me to remember that prayer is a conversation and that I can come to you anytime throughout the day.

Waiting for a Breakthrough

Then David said, God has broken my enemies by my hand, like the bursting forth of waters. Therefore they called the name of that place Baal-perazim [Lord of breaking through].

1 CHRONICLES 14:11

There are many times when people give up just before a breakthrough—on the very brink of success. But don't give up! You can wait for 10 years and then suddenly, one day you wake up and everything has changed. Your dream has finally been fulfilled, the situation you lived in for so long is finally over, or you finally achieved the accomplishment for which you labored for years.

Be grateful that God has a plan for you and He has heard your prayers—you may not realize how close you are to your breakthrough. Even if you have to wait three, four, or five more years, if you will keep pressing on, thankfully, you will have the victory you need. Whatever you do, do not give up on the brink of your breakthrough. Do not stop hoping, believing, and obeying God. Instead say, "I will never quit; I will never give up."

Prayer of Thanks

Thank You, Father, that my breakthrough is on the way. I am not without hope and I am not on my own. You are with me, and You have a good plan for my life. I trust You, Lord, and I refuse to give up.

The Best Kind of Knowledge

For I resolved to know nothing while I was with you except Jesus Christ and him crucified.
1 CORINTHIANS 2:2 NIV

The apostle Paul possessed a lot of knowledge. He was a Pharisee of Pharisees, learned, educated. And before he was converted on the road to Damascus, he was very proud of what he knew. Isn't it interesting that sometimes the more people know, the more proud they become?

In 1 Corinthians 8:1, Paul said that knowledge puffs up. If we knew everything we think we would like to know, we wouldn't lean on God because we would be so proud and we'd think we didn't need Him.

Paul did a 180-degree turn from thinking he knew everything to saying that he had resolved to know nothing but Jesus Christ and Him crucified. I think Paul was saying, "All I know is Jesus, and I don't have to know anything more than that."

Jesus is the most important thing. Think about how much frustration you would save yourself if you gave up worrying and trying to figure everything out and were resolved to know nothing but Jesus. Thankfully, you can do exactly that!

Prayer of Thanks

I thank You, Father, that Jesus came to this earth and died for my sins. I may not have everything figured out, but I know the most important thing: my hope, peace, and joy are all found in Your love for me revealed in the sacrifice of Jesus.

Fellowship with the Lord

> *Then you will seek Me, inquire for, and require Me [as a vital necessity] and find Me when you search for Me with all your heart.*
>
> JEREMIAH 29:13

No matter how many principles and formulas you and I learn, we will never have lasting victory in our Christian life without spending time in personal, private fellowship with the Lord. The victory is not in methods; it is in God. If we are to live victoriously, we are going to have to look beyond ways to eliminate our problems and find the Lord in the midst of our problems.

The good news is that when we set aside time with God, He meets with us. We can be grateful, knowing that when we seek Him, we will find Him. God has a personalized plan for each of us, a plan that will lead us to victory. That is why principles, formulas, and methods are not the ultimate answer, because they do not allow for the individual differences in people. As good as all these things may be as general guidelines, they are not substitutes for personal fellowship with the Living God.

Prayer of Thanks

Thank You, Father, that I can meet with You at any time of the day or night. You're always here for me and You desire to spend time with me. Your Word says that when I seek You, I will find You. So help me, Lord, to find You in every part of my life today.

A Confident Person Avoids Comparison

But by the grace (the unmerited favor and blessing) of God I am what I am, and His grace toward me was not [found to be] for nothing. 1 CORINTHIANS 15:10

Confidence is not possible as long as we compare ourselves with other people. No matter how good we look, how talented or smart we are, or how successful we are, there is always someone who is better, and sooner or later we will run into them.

I believe confidence is found in knowing God loves us, realizing the gifts we have and being thankful for them—then we do the best we have with what God has given us to work with. Confidence is never found in comparing ourselves with others and competing with them.

Always struggling to maintain the number one position is hard work. In fact, it's impossible. Our joy should not be found in being better than others, but in being the best we can be for the Lord.

Prayer of Thanks

I thank You, Father, that I don't have to be better than others to be accepted by You. I am confident and secure because I know that You love me just as I am. Thank You for the peace that comes when I refuse to compare myself with others.

A New Nature

Therefore if any person is [ingrafted] in Christ (the Messiah) he is a new creation (a new creature altogether); the old [previous moral and spiritual condition] has passed away. Behold, the fresh and new has come!

2 CORINTHIANS 5:17

God's Word teaches us that when we receive Christ as our Savior and Lord, He gives us a new nature (see 2 Corinthians 5:17). He gives us His nature. He also gives us a spirit of discipline and self-control, which is vital in allowing us to choose the ways of our new nature. And He gives us a sound mind (see 2 Timothy 1:7). That means we can think about things properly without being controlled by emotion.

Every believer can be thankful that the way we once were passes away, and we have all the equipment we need for a brand-new way of behaving. With God's help we can choose spirit over flesh and right over wrong. Our renewed spirits can now control our souls and bodies or, to say it another way, the inner person can control the outer person. Then we can live out God's plan for our lives.

Prayer of Thanks

Father, I thank You that I am a new creation in You. I am so grateful for a fresh start and the new nature You have given me. Help me to leave the old ways behind today and live a brand-new, joy-filled life of victory in You.

Living Free of Regret

One thing I do [it is my one aspiration]: forgetting what lies behind and straining forward to what lies ahead.

PHILIPPIANS 3:13

Without God's help, we have difficulty doing things in moderation. We can eat too much, spend too much money, have too much entertainment, and talk too much. We are excessive in our actions because we behave emotionally. We feel like doing a thing, and so we do it, without any thought to the end result. After the thing is done and cannot be undone, we regret doing it.

But thankfully we do not have to live in regret. God gives us His Spirit to enable us to make right and wise choices. He urges us, guides us, and leads us, but we still have to cast the deciding vote. Forming new habits will require making a decision not to do what you feel like doing unless it agrees with God's will. With the help of the Holy Spirit, you can change your actions and live a life free of regret!

Prayer of Thanks

I thank You, Father, that I don't have to live stuck in regrets over my mistakes. You have forgiven me and made a new way for me. Help me to let go of yesterday's shortcomings and make better decisions today. Help me to live free of regret over my past and full of faith for my future.

Following God's Example

And God saw that the light was good (suitable, pleasant) and He approved it; and God separated the light from the darkness.

GENESIS 1:4

As believers, you and I have the same quality of life available to us that God has. His life is not filled with fear, stress, worry, anxiety, or depression. And thankfully, ours doesn't have to be either. Instead of worrying, God takes time to enjoy His creation, the works of His hands.

In the account of Creation as recorded in Genesis 1, Scripture frequently says that after God had created a certain portion of the universe in which we live, He saw that it was good (suitable, pleasant, fitting, admirable), and He approved it. (See verses 4, 10, 12, 18, 21, 25, 31.) It seems to me that if God took the time to enjoy each phase of His creation, His work, then you and I can also take time to enjoy our work. We can rejoice with gratitude knowing that God gives us the freedom to enjoy our accomplishments.

Prayer of Thanks

Father, thank You for the example You have set for me and for the life You have made possible for me to live. I don't have to live full of stress, fear, or worry. Help me to leave those things behind and enjoy the life You have given me.

Stepping Out into New Things

The wicked flee when no man pursues them, but the [uncompromisingly] righteous are bold as a lion. PROVERBS 28:1

God created you for an exhilarating life that often requires you to take bold steps of faith, and then see Him come through for you. So many people are unsatisfied with their lives simply because they won't step out into the new things they desire to do. They want to stay in "the safe zone," which may feel secure, but is not always where the joy and adventure of life can be found.

We can be thankful that God has a vibrant life in store for us. Don't let fear keep you from enjoying that life and destroying your destiny. As I like to say, "Feel the fear and do it anyway—do it afraid!"

I encourage you to include more variety in your life. Try new things; when you start feeling that life is getting stale and tasteless, add a little spice by doing something different. Start thinking and saying, "I will not live in fear."

Prayer of Thanks

Father, I pray that You will help me break out of ruts and boring, lifeless routines. I thank You that You have a vibrant, exhilarating life in store for me. And I thank You that new adventures are just around the corner. Help me enjoy each and every new thing that You bring my way.

Praise, Worship, and Thanksgiving

Sing to the Lord, O you saints of His, and give thanks at the remembrance of His holy name.
PSALM 30:4

Praise, worship, and thanksgiving are some of the simplest ways we can pray, and yet they are powerful spiritual dynamics. They are types of prayer because they are expressions of our hearts toward the Lord. When we praise, worship, or give thanks, we are talking to God—and that's all prayer really is.

Praise, worship, and thanksgiving enhance and empower our prayer lives because they keep our hearts focused on the Lord instead of on ourselves. They allow us to connect with God in passionate ways and to encounter His presence in our everyday lives. We do not need to wait for a church service or a corporate gathering in order to experience or express praise, worship, and thanksgiving; we can incorporate them into everything we do, all day long.

Prayer of Thanks

Father, I thank You that I can come to You in praise, worship, and thanksgiving all through the day. Help me to keep my heart focused on You instead of the circumstances around me. Thank You that You hear me and You are pleased with my praise.

Enjoy the Little Things

O give thanks to the Lord, for He is good; for His mercy and loving-kindness endure forever!
1 CHRONICLES 16:34

All it takes to begin to enjoy life to the fullest is a decision. And that decision affects everything—even the overlooked areas of our lives.

For example, you can decide to enjoy not only your work and your accomplishments, but even the commute to work in the mornings. Don't get so frustrated about traffic and have your mind on what you need to do when you arrive that you fail to enjoy the trip.

We can be grateful in traffic—grateful that we have a car, grateful that the car is running properly, grateful that we have a job, and grateful that we have a few extra minutes to spend time with God while we're stuck in traffic.

I encourage you to enjoy the little things today. Enjoy your home, your friends, your children . . . and yes, even the commute to work. Remember, all it takes is a decision.

Prayer of Thanks

Father, today I am deciding to be grateful for the little things and the overlooked things in my life. Help me have a heart of thanksgiving that chooses to see You and Your blessings in every situation.

Thank God for His Mercy

But I have trusted, leaned on, and been confident in Your mercy and loving-kindness; my heart shall rejoice and be in high spirits in Your salvation. PSALM 13:5

God is slow to anger and plenteous in mercy (see Psalm 103:8). It is impossible to deserve mercy, and that is why it is such a waste of time to try to pay for our mistakes with good works or guilt. We don't deserve mercy, but God gives it freely. This free gift is something to be thankful for!

Mercy overrides "the rules." You may have grown up in a home that had lots of rules, and if you broke any of them, you got into trouble. Although God does intend for us to keep His commands, He understands our nature and is ready to extend mercy to anyone who will ask for and receive it.

When we learn to receive mercy, then we will also be able to give it to others—and mercy is something many people seriously need.

Prayer of Thanks

Thank You, Father, for the way You extend mercy to me each and every day. I desire to please You in everything I do, but I thank You that when I fall short, You never fail to bless me with the free gift of Your love and mercy.

Contagious Generosity

Let all men know and perceive and recognize your unselfishness (your considerateness, your forbearing spirit). The Lord is near [He is coming soon]. PHILIPPIANS 4:5

With the help of the Lord, we can be a model of generosity for all those we come in contact with. If you are a giver rather than a taker in life, it won't take long before people realize you are quite different from what they are accustomed to. As they witness your joy, they will see that a thankful heart and a generous spirit make a person happier than being selfish.

Jesus encouraged us to let all men see our good and kind deeds so they would recognize and glorify God (see Matthew 5:16). Jesus did not mean that we should be show-offs or do things for the purpose of being seen; He was encouraging us to realize how much we do affect the people around us. Certainly, we can negatively affect others, but generosity also affects those around us in very positive ways, and makes us happy people.

Prayer of Thanks

Father, I thank You for the measure of influence You have given me. With Your help, I am going to use that influence to model a generous spirit. Help me, Father, to be a light in the darkness today.

Start Strong, Finish Well

[We pray] that you may be invigorated and strengthened with all power according to the might of His glory, [to exercise] every kind of endurance and patience (perseverance and forbearance) with joy.

COLOSSIANS 1:11

Everything we undertake in life has a beginning and an end. Typically, we are excited at the beginning of an opportunity, a relationship, or a venture; we're also happy when we can celebrate our achievement and have the satisfaction of a fulfilled desire. But between the beginning and the end, every situation has a "middle"—and the middle is where we often face our greatest challenges.

Between our beginnings and our endings we must develop the determination necessary to overcome the difficult circumstances we encounter in the middle. We can be people who finish what we begin. And we can be thankful that we don't have to do it alone—God will help us if we let Him.

You may be in the middle of something right now. Whatever you find yourself in the middle of, ask God for His strength and wisdom, discipline yourself a little while longer, and determine to see it all the way through to the finish.

Prayer of Thanks

I thank You, Father, that I am not alone in the middle of this situation. You are right here with me, and You are giving me the strength I need. With Your help, I am determined not to quit. I'm going to see this through and give You the glory with a successful finish!

God Loves You and Sees the Good in You

Are not two little sparrows sold for a penny? And yet not one of them will fall to the ground without your Father's leave (consent) and notice. But even the very hairs of your head are all numbered. Fear not, then; you are of more value than many sparrows.

MATTHEW 10:29–31

The Song of Solomon is an allegory of the love story between God and His people. Look closely at the following Scripture: "[He exclaimed] O my love, how beautiful you are! There is no flaw in you!" (Song of Solomon 4:7).

God loves you and sees the good in you. Isn't that wonderful? That is certainly something to be grateful for! God sees what you are becoming and will be; He is not overly concerned about your faults. He knew all of them when He invited you to be in an intimate relationship with Him.

All God wants is your love and a willingness to grow in Him. Your presence is a present to the world. You are unique and one of a kind. Do not ever forget, for even a day, how very special you are!

Prayer of Thanks

Father, I thank You that Your Word shows me just how much You love me. Regardless of what others may say, or even how I may feel myself, I choose to believe that I am deeply loved and wonderfully made by my heavenly Father.

Childlike Faith

Whoever will humble himself therefore and become like this little child [trusting, lowly, loving, forgiving] is greatest in the kingdom of heaven. MATTHEW 18:4

A child's faith is simple. A child doesn't try to figure everything out and make a detailed blueprint of exactly how he will get what he needs. He simply believes because his parents said they would take care of him.

Thankfully, the same can be true for us. As believers, our joy and peace are not based in doing and achieving—trying to figure everything out and fix it ourselves. They come with believing.

Joy and peace come as a result of building our relationship with the Lord. Psalm 16:11 tells us in His presence is fullness of joy. If we have received Jesus as our Savior and Lord, He, the Prince of Peace, lives inside us (see 1 John 4:12–15; John 14:23). We experience peace in the Lord's presence, receiving from Him and acting in response to His direction. Joy and peace come from knowing and believing—trusting in the Lord with a simple, childlike faith.

Prayer of Thanks

I am thankful that my joy and peace are not based on my abilities. Father, it is in You that I find everything I need. Today, I come to You with a childlike faith, trusting that You will take care of any problem in my life. Thank You, Father, that You are in control of my life, and my joy and peace are found in You.

Strength in the Waiting

I am looking and waiting for the Lord more than watchmen for the morning, I say, more than watchmen for the morning.

PSALM 130:6

If you have a problem, don't merely pray for the problem to go away, or that you will get something you need or desire; pray that God will strengthen you during your waiting period. Pray that you will have the grace to wait with a thankful attitude.

The Bible teaches us that when we pray, if we believe we have received and do not doubt, our prayer request will be granted (see Mark 11:22–24). But it does not say we will immediately get what we ask for.

Because God's timing is perfect, we can trust Him in the waiting process. I believe that the attitude we wait with partially determines how long we have to wait. An attitude of gratitude glorifies God and is a good witness of our faith to others.

Prayer of Thanks

Father, help me learn to wait with a thankful attitude. I thank You that You have a good plan and purpose for me, and You know exactly what I need and when I need it. So I trust in You with a grateful heart.

Patience and Wisdom Go Hand in Hand

For the Lord gives skillful and godly Wisdom; from His mouth come knowledge and understanding. PROVERBS 2:6

God wants us to use wisdom, and wisdom encourages patience. Wisdom says, "Wait a little while, until the emotions settle down, before you do or say something; then check to see if you really believe it's the right thing to do." Wisdom is grateful for what you already have and patiently moves into what God has for you next.

Emotions urge us toward haste, telling us that we must do something and do it right now! But godly wisdom tells us to be patient and wait until we have a clear picture of what we are to do and when we are to do it. We need to be able to step back from our situations and see them from God's perspective. Then we can make decisions based on what we *know* rather than on what we *feel*.

Prayer of Thanks

I thank You, Father, that patience is a fruit of the Spirit I can demonstrate in my life. With Your help, I am determined to make decisions today with wisdom and patience. Thank You for guiding me along the way.

Thankful and Enjoying Today

This is the day which the Lord has brought about; we will rejoice and be glad in it.

PSALM 118:24

Often young parents delay enjoying their child until he has reached a certain stage of growth. When he is an infant they say, "I'll be glad when he gets out of diapers (or stops cutting teeth or learns to walk)." Then they say, "I'll be glad when he's in kindergarten." Then it becomes, "I'll be glad when he is in school all day." Later they say, "I'll be glad when he graduates."

On and on it goes until the child is grown and gone, and the parents have never really enjoyed any stage of his life. They were always waiting to be glad *when*. Let me encourage you: Don't postpone being glad until everything is perfect—thank

God for every single stage along the way. Learn to rejoice and be glad in the Lord, this day and every day along the way in your life.

Prayer of Thanks

Father, I thank You for the stage of life I am in right now. Even when I face challenges and difficulties, help me remember that You have been good to me, and help me to be grateful for today.

True Prosperity

Beloved, I pray that you may prosper in every way and [that your body] may keep well, even as [I know] your soul keeps well and prospers.

3 JOHN 1:2

A person is never truly prosperous if all he has are things and money; real prosperity requires far more than that. The Bible gives a more complete approach to prosperity, and so should we.

When our bodies prosper, we are strong and physically healthy. Even if we currently have a physical ailment we can pray for and expect God to help us. True prosperity includes peace of mind and contentment. When our souls prosper, we flourish on the inside. We are at peace; we are full of joy; we live with a sense of purpose; we are growing spiritually; and we have strong, loving relationships with others.

Jesus said that He came so we could have and enjoy life in abundance and to the full (see John 10:10). God is a god of abundance, and He wants us to live abundant lives filled with thanksgiving and joy.

Prayer of Thanks

I thank You, Father, that You prosper my body and my soul. I pray today for the health and the peace that You promise in Your Word. Thank You that I am made whole in You.

Reach Your Full Potential

We are hard pressed on every side, but not crushed; perplexed, but not in despair.

2 CORINTHIANS 4:8 NIV

I fully believe that reaching your potential is linked to the way you handle adversity. Adversity isn't always bad. Actually, adversity can be something to be thankful for because God can use it to strengthen you. Winston Churchill said: "Difficulties mastered are opportunities won," and I wholeheartedly agree.

If you allow difficulties and challenges to frustrate, intimidate, or discourage you, you will never overcome them. But if you face them head-on and press through the adversities you encounter, refusing to give up in the midst of them and moving forward with a heart of gratitude, you will develop the skills and determination needed to be everything you were created to be and experience everything God intends for you.

Prayer of Thanks

I thank You, Father, that I don't have to give up when I face adversity—I can meet it head-on, knowing that You are always with me. Thank You for the promise that greater is He who is in me, than he who is in the world.

You Are Christ's Ambassador

So we are Christ's ambassadors, God making His appeal as it were through us. We [as Christ's personal representatives] beg you for His sake to lay hold of the divine favor [now offered you] and be reconciled to God.

2 CORINTHIANS 5:20

God has always said to His people and is still saying to us: "You and I are partners. You are My body in the earth today." We are the representation of Who God is. We are His mouth, His hands, His feet, His face. We are the ones who express His heart, demonstrate His love, and reveal His power to those around us. What an awesome privilege to be thankful for!

In humility, we should be moved to pray each day, "Father, thank You that I have the chance to be Your representative to the world today. Thank You for using me." We would be wise to also pray to access the wisdom and the resources of heaven for ourselves and for others. By the grace of God, we can partner with Him so that His purposes will come to pass in our lives and in the lives of those around us.

Prayer of Thanks

I thank You, Father, that You pour out Your treasure into earthen vessels. Thank You that You are using me to demonstrate Your love, kindness, power, and grace to the world around me. Help me to be Your ambassador to the world today.

Resting in God

And the Lord said, My Presence shall go with you, and I will give you rest.

EXODUS 33:14

We can be thankful that we don't have to worry about things, figure out everything, or carry heavy burdens in our lives. It is actually quite refreshing—and something to be grateful for—to realize that I don't need to have all the answers to my problems. We need to get comfortable with saying, "I don't know the answer to this dilemma, and I'm not going to worry about anything because God is in control and I trust Him. I'm going to rest in Him!"

When we're overloaded with the cares of life—struggling, laboring, and worrying—we need a mental and emotional vacation. Our minds need to rest from thinking about how to take care of problems, and our emotions need to rest from being upset. Worry isn't restful at all. In fact, it steals rest and the benefits of rest from us. So next time you feel you are carrying a heavy load in your mind or you find yourself worried and anxious, remember, you can put your trust in God and enjoy His rest.

Prayer of Thanks

Father, I am grateful that You give me rest. Thank You that I don't have to have all the answers all the time—I can trust in You and live a life of peace, contentment, and rest.

With all Your Heart

But if from there you will seek (inquire for and require as necessity) the Lord your God, you will find Him if you [truly] seek Him with all your heart [and mind] and soul and life.

DEUTERONOMY 4:29

When we think about how little time most people actually give God, we can understand why the Bible so strongly encourages us to seek Him. The fact is, we are missing the greatest thing in life if we never really get to know God personally.

The apostle Paul said that his determined purpose was to know God and the power that flowed out from His resurrection (see Philippians 3:10). The word *seek* is a very strong word. In its original language, it means "to crave; to pursue; to go after with all your might."

We can be thankful that our God is a wonderful God worth seeking. He is worth loving! He is worthy of all your passion and devotion. So don't wait until you find yourself in a desperate situation. Determine to seek and love God with all your heart from this moment on.

Prayer of Thanks

I thank You, Father, that I can seek You with all my heart and live in close relationship with You. Like Paul, I want to make it my determined purpose to know You. I thank You that You love me and that You reward me with Your presence when I seek after You.

Life Is a Journey

. . . But when the cloud was taken up, they journeyed; whether it was taken up by day or by night, they journeyed.

NUMBERS 9:21

Thankfully, our enjoyment in life is not based on always having enjoyable circumstances. It is an attitude of the heart, a decision to enjoy everything because all things—even little, seemingly insignificant things—have a part in the overall "big picture" of life.

Life is a journey. Everything in it is a process. It has a beginning, a middle, and an end. All aspects of life are always developing. Life is motion. Without movement, advancement, and progression, there is no life. In other words, as long as you and I are alive, we are always going to be going somewhere.

If you have not been enjoying the journey of your life, it is time to start. If you have been enjoying your life, then thank God and look for ways to enjoy it even more.

Prayer of Thanks

I thank You, Father, that my life is a journey. I'm not going to stay stuck in a difficult or trying situation forever—You are taking me through it. Help me to experience Your joy regardless of my surroundings. Help me to enjoy my life today!

Grateful and Aware of God's Love

Praise the Lord! (Hallelujah!) O give thanks to the Lord, for He is good; for His mercy and loving-kindness endure forever!

PSALM 106:1

God is always good to us, always faithful to us, always working so diligently in our lives. He is always doing something for us and acting in our best interest, so we need to respond by letting Him know we appreciate His abundant goodness.

For example, "Lord, thank You for a good night's sleep," or "God, I thank You that my visit to the dentist didn't hurt as much as I thought it might," or "Father, thank You for helping me make good decisions today," or "Lord, thank You for keeping me encouraged."

We can thank God silently in our

hearts, and we can also voice our thankfulness aloud because that helps us stay conscious and aware of God's love, which He demonstrates through His goodness to us.

Prayer of Thanks

I thank You, Father, that You are always faithful to me. Even when I can't see it, You are working on my behalf because You love me and You have a great plan for my life. Thank You for all the ways You demonstrate that love on a daily basis.

Harmony's Sweet Sound

So let us then definitely aim for and eagerly pursue what makes for harmony and for mutual upbuilding (edification and development) of one another.

ROMANS 14:19

While I was ministering in a church, God gave me a great illustration of what it means to live in harmony with each other.

I asked the entire worship team to return to the platform, and then I requested them to sing and play a song of their choice. I knew, of course, that they would all choose a different song because I had given no instructions on what song to sing or play. As they sang and played, the sound was horrible! There was no harmony. Then I asked them to play "Jesus Loves Me." It sounded sweet, soothing, and wonderfully comforting.

Disharmony is noise in God's ears. But when we live in harmony, we produce a sweet sound. When we learn the value of each other, we become thankful for each other and we learn to work together.

Prayer of Thanks

Father, I am grateful for the people You have put in my life. I want to live in harmony, not strife, so that my relationships will be a sweet sound to Your ear. Thank You for giving me the patience and wisdom I need to live in harmony with others.

The Greatest of These Is Love

But earnestly desire and zealously cultivate the greatest and best gifts and graces (the higher gifts and the choicest graces). And yet I will show you a still more excellent way [one that is better by far and the highest of them all—love].

1 CORINTHIANS 12:31

Where does love fit into your list of priorities? Jesus said, "A new commandment I give to you, that you love one another; as I have loved you" (John 13:34 NKJV). It seems to me that Jesus was saying love is the main thing on which we should concentrate. The apostle Paul states that "faith, hope, love abide...but the greatest of these is love" (1 Corinthians 13:13).

One of the greatest things we have to be thankful for is that God is love. So when we choose to walk in His love, we abide in Him. That is why love is the greatest thing in the world. It is the best thing to commit our life to, to seek to excel in.

I encourage you to do yourself a favor and show love to someone today. Love not only blesses others; it also blesses the one doing the loving.

Prayer of Thanks

Father, thank You that You love me and You demonstrate that love every day. Help me to receive Your love, and help me to turn around and share that love with others.

Refuse to Live in Fear

The Lord himself goes before you and will be with you; he will never leave you nor forsake you. Do not be afraid; do not be discouraged.

DEUTERONOMY 31:8 NIV

Fear is a spirit that produces feelings. When God told Joshua to not be afraid, He was not commanding him to not "feel" fear; He was commanding him to not *give in* to the fear he was facing.

I often encourage people to "do it afraid." That basically means when fear attacks you, you need to go ahead and do whatever God is telling you to do anyway. You may do it with your knees shaking or your palms sweating, but do it anyway. That's what it means to "fear not."

We can be thankful we have Scripture to meditate on when we feel afraid. God's promises strengthen us to keep pressing forward, no matter how we feel. The Word of God will give you the faith you need to overcome any feeling of fear.

Prayer of Thanks

Thank You, Father, that I don't have to give in to a feeling of fear. With Your help, I can press forward and do what You have called me to do regardless of my feelings. Thank You, Father, that I can do it afraid.

Letting God Have Control

Many plans are in a man's mind, but it is the Lord's purpose for him that will stand.

PROVERBS 19:21

If you haven't done a good job of running your own life, why not turn it over to the One who created you and knows more about you than you will ever know about yourself? If you start having trouble with an automobile, you take it back to the people who manufactured it to fix it. A similar principle is true with God. He created you and loves you very much. If your life is not satisfying to you, then take it to Him to fix it.

Your life will not change unless you make that very important decision to turn control of it over to God. And here is the good news: When you ask God to have

His way in your life, He says, "Yes." He will repair the damaged areas, give you direction to keep you safe as you travel through life, and give you a joy you've never known. With God in control, you can be grateful that your life has a new direction, purpose, and hope for the future.

Prayer of Thanks

Father, today I ask You to take absolute control of my life. Help me let go! Thank You that You can run things better than I ever could. I pray that You would heal, transform, and restore my life. I am grateful for the exciting new things in You that are in my future.

Dealing with Unresolved Issues

If possible, as far as it depends on you,
live at peace with everyone.

ROMANS 12:18

We all have days when we feel more emotional than other days. This can happen for many reasons, but sometimes we feel emotional because something upset us the day before and we didn't resolve it.

I remember a night when I was unable to sleep. Finally, around five in the morning, I asked God what was wrong with me. Immediately I recalled a situation from the day before in which I had been rude to someone. Instead of apologizing to them and asking God to forgive me, I rushed on to the next thing in my day. Obviously, my conduct was irritating my spirit. As soon as I asked God to forgive me and made a decision to apologize to the person, I was able to go to sleep.

If you feel unusually sad or as if you are carrying a heavy burden, ask God what is wrong. And when He shows you, be grateful that you have a chance to make the situation right.

Prayer of Thanks

I thank You, Father, that You want me to live in peace. If there are any unresolved issues that are causing me to feel anxious or burdened, I ask You to show them to me and give me the strength and wisdom to resolve them. I thank You that You will be with me every step of the way.

Invest in Your Healing

For you have need of steadfast patience and endurance, so that you may perform and fully accomplish the will of God, and thus receive and carry away [and enjoy to the full] what is promised. HEBREWS 10:36

What a blessing it is to know that the Holy Spirit helps us overcome our past. Thankfully, with faith and patience, you can recover from your past pain, from things that have been done to you, or from mistakes that you have made, but the recovery will require an investment of time on your part. You can either continue to invest in your misery, or you can begin to invest in your healing.

One of the ways you can deal with the past is by confessing God's promises instead of talking about negative, defeated feelings.

When you confess God's promises instead of your problems, you are exercising your faith and investing in your healing. This is a powerful way to really begin enjoying your life.

Prayer of Thanks

Father, I'm grateful that I can invest in my own healing by confessing Your Word over my life. Help me to focus on Your promises rather than my problems. Thank You that You have good things in store for my life.

The Power of Praise and Prayer

Enter into His gates with thanksgiving and a thank offering and into His courts with praise! Be thankful and say so to Him, bless and affectionately praise His name!

PSALM 100:4

The spiritual weapons that God gives us to use in our lives are tremendous blessings that we can be grateful for. One important weapon at our disposal is praise.

Praise defeats the devil, but it must be genuine heartfelt praise, not just lip service or a method being tried to see if it works. Praise and all other forms of prayer involve the Word. We praise God according to His Word and His goodness.

Prayer is born out of relationship with God. It is coming and asking for help, and always remembering to praise Him for all of His goodness. It is talking to God about something that bothers us. It is fellowship, friendship, and an opportunity to express gratitude for all that God is and does. If you want to have an effective prayer life, develop a good personal relationship with the Lord. Trust that He loves you, that He is full of mercy, and that He will help you when you ask.

Prayer of Thanks

Thank You, Father, for the power of praise and prayer in my life. I want to live each day in amazement of all that You have done for me. Help me to incorporate praise and prayer into my daily walk with You.

Staying Power

Looking away [from all that will distract] to Jesus, Who is the Leader and the Source of our faith [giving the first incentive for our belief] and is also its Finisher [bringing it to maturity and perfection].

HEBREWS 12:2

People who finish well in life are the ones with strong character. As believers, we can be grateful that the Holy Spirit is developing the character in us that we need to do what God calls us to do—we have "staying power." Jesus did not quit when His circumstances were rough, and He is our example. The Bible says we are to look away from all that distracts and look to Jesus instead.

I think most of us want to do and be everything God intends for us, and to enjoy it along the way. Great joy comes with finishing the race God has called you to run. Enjoy the journey and keep your eyes on the prize. One of the greatest testimonies you can have is *I'm still here.* When you speak those words, you are saying, "I did not quit. I did not give up. I am still here."

Prayer of Thanks

Father, I thank You that, with the help of the Holy Spirit, I have staying power. I make the decision today to keep going—to never give up. Help me to run my race with perseverance and discover the joy of finishing each task well.

Determined to Overcome

And He arose and rebuked the wind and said to the sea, Hush now! Be still (muzzled)! And the wind ceased (sank to rest as if exhausted by its beating) and there was [immediately] a great calm (a perfect peacefulness).

MARK 4:39

Thankfully, there is no storm in life that is greater than the power and purposes of God. When you refuse to allow your difficulties to *impress* you, then they will not *oppress* you or *depress* you either. If you put your focus on the Lord, you will hold steady in the storm and arrive safely at your God-appointed destination.

Any time we try to step out and do something for God, the enemy will oppose it. Paul certainly experienced this. He wrote in 1 Corinthians 16:9: "For a wide door of opportunity for effectual [service] has opened to me...and [there are] many adversaries."

Paul experienced opposition, and you will too. I encourage you to make up your mind that you're going to do what God is telling you to do. Don't be double-minded, second-guessing your decision. Determine to push through and refuse to turn back. Trust the Lord, be thankful for His strength, and press on no matter what.

Prayer of Thanks

Thank You, Father, that there is nothing too difficult for You. Help me to lean on You when there is a storm raging around me. I put my focus on You today, and I refuse to be impressed by my problem. I choose to be in awe of You instead.

Join the Party

A glad heart makes a cheerful countenance,
but by sorrow of heart the spirit is broken.

PROVERBS 15:13

When Jesus invited people to become His disciples and follow Him, He asked them if they wanted to join His party. I realize He was talking about His group, but I like to think that traveling with Jesus was probably a lot of fun as well as a lot of hard work.

Repeatedly throughout the gospels, we see Jesus invite people to leave their lifestyles and side with His party, and He is still issuing that invitation today. Yes, there is work to do for the kingdom of God, but thankfully we can have fun while we do it.

When we follow Jesus, we are not going to a solemn assembly or a funeral. We are joining His party that is full of life, peace, and never-ending joy!

Prayer of Thanks

Father, help me to lay aside the burdens and cares of this world and receive Your joy today. I thank You that You want me to have fun and enjoy the life You have given me. With Your help, I will celebrate Your goodness in my life today and every day.

More Than Partially Forgiven... Completely Forgiven

So if the Son sets you free, you will be free indeed. JOHN 8:36 NIV

Satan remembers every tiny thing we have ever done wrong and will do his best to remind us of those things every chance he gets. He is vigilant in his efforts to make us cower under the weight of our own shame. We all sin and come short of the glory of God. No person is without sin, and we all feel guilt at times, but when we keep that guilt long after we have been forgiven, it turns into shame.

Guilt and shame make us feel that God is angry, and so we withdraw from His presence and don't live the life God intended for us. We need to understand and be thankful that God forgives completely—not partially, or almost, but completely! The goodness of God is greater than any bad thing we have ever or could ever do. That should bring a feeling of thanksgiving and a sensation of joy sweeping through our souls!

Prayer of Thanks

Father, I am so thankful that You completely forgive me of my sins when I ask. Regardless of what I have done, forgiveness has been made possible through the sacrifice of Jesus. Thank You that I am righteous in Your sight.

Living with Confidence

Such is the reliance and confidence that we have through Christ toward and with reference to God. 2 CORINTHIANS 3:4

A person without confidence is like an airplane sitting on a runway with empty fuel tanks. The plane has the ability to fly, but without some fuel, it's not getting off the tarmac. Confidence is our fuel—and this is why the confidence we find in Christ is something to be grateful for.

Our confidence gets us started and helps us finish every challenge we tackle in life. Without confidence, we will live in fear and never feel fulfilled. Confidence allows us to face life with boldness, openness, and honesty. It enables us to live without worry and to feel safe. It enables us to live authentically.

When we know who we are in God, we

don't have to pretend to be somebody we're not because we are secure in who we are—even if we're different from those around us. Confidence allows us to live peaceful, joy-filled lives.

Prayer of Thanks

Father, I am thankful for the confidence I have in You. Thank You that I don't have to live an insecure, fearful, worried life. I can soar in my destiny because You give me the strength that I need.

Rejoicing in Progress

For You have been my help, and in the shadow of Your wings will I rejoice. PSALM 63:7

We can be thankful that God wants us to rejoice. In fact, the Bible discusses rejoicing at least 170 times. And if we study the Word, we find that rejoicing is the act of outwardly expressing an emotion.

We may clap our hands when our children show progress, we might shout when our goal is met, or we may laugh when we think about or talk of the goodness of God. We can also rejoice when we make progress in spiritual growth.

The Bible says that the path of the righteous grows brighter and brighter every day (see Proverbs 4:18). If you can look back and say, "I've improved over the last year. My behavior is a little bit better. I'm a little more patient. I'm more giving. I'm a tiny bit less selfish," then you can celebrate. Every improvement deserves some time for rejoicing!

Prayer of Thanks

Father, when I see a measure of progress in my life, help me remember to take some time to rejoice. Thank You for giving me a spirit of joy rather than a spirit of heaviness. I will celebrate and rejoice in You today.

The Power of Doing Good

. . . how God anointed Jesus of Nazareth with the Holy Spirit and power, and how he went around doing good and healing all who were under the power of the devil, because God was with him.

ACTS 10:38 NIV

I firmly believe that when we have problems, we should not worry, but we also need to continue doing the things we know to do. For example, if you have commitments, be sure to keep them. Quite often when people are encountering personal problems, they withdraw from normal life and spend all their time trying to solve the problem. All this unproductive activity prevents them from doing what they should be doing, which is "doing good."

Psalm 37:3 says that we should trust in

the Lord and *do good* and we will feed on His faithfulness. The faithfulness of God is something we can all be thankful for! I have discovered that if I continue my study of God's Word, continue praying, keep my commitments, and help as many people as I can, I experience breakthrough much faster. Helping others while we are hurting is actually a very powerful thing to do.

Prayer of Thanks

I thank You today, Father, that I am not subject to my problems. When I am going through something, I can respond by helping others around me. I am grateful that with Your help, I can do good for others; I can make a difference in this world.

A Natural Expression of Thanksgiving

O give thanks to the Lord, for He is good; for His mercy and loving-kindness endure forever!

PSALM 107:1

Thanksgiving can be a part of who we are deep down in our hearts; it is a type of prayer and it should flow out of us in a natural way that is simple and genuine.

Being thankful does not mean merely sitting down at the end of a day, trying to remember everything we need to be thankful for because we think we have to thank God in order to make Him happy, or to satisfy some spiritual requirement, or try to get Him to do something else for us.

Instead, it means having a heart that is sensitive to God's presence in our everyday lives, and just breathing out grateful prayers of thanksgiving every time we see Him working in our lives or blessing us.

Prayer of Thanks

Father, I am thankful that prayer is not some ritual or formula that I am required to follow. I am grateful that prayer is a comfortable, ongoing conversation with You based on an intimate relationship with You. I love You, Father, and I am excited to give You thanks all day long.

Receiving God's Love

Such hope never disappoints or deludes or shames us, for God's love has been poured out in our hearts through the Holy Spirit Who has been given to us.

ROMANS 5:5

Receiving is important in our relationship with God. When we receive from God, we actually take into ourselves what He is offering. As we receive His love, we then have love in us. Once we are filled with God's love, we can begin loving ourselves. We begin giving that love back to God and loving other people.

The Bible teaches us that the love of God has been poured out in our hearts by the Holy Spirit. That simply means that when the Lord comes to dwell in our hearts because of our faith in His Son Jesus

Christ, He brings love with Him, because God is love (see 1 John 4:8).

We all need to ask ourselves what we are doing with the love of God that has been freely given to us. Are we rejecting it because we don't think we are valuable enough to be loved? Or are we receiving His love with a thankful heart, believing that He is greater than our failures and weaknesses?

Prayer of Thanks

I am grateful, Father, that You love me and that Your love is perfect and unconditional. Help me learn to receive Your love by faith and go through each day knowing that I am valuable because I am loved by my heavenly Father.

The Source of Happiness

For You, O Lord, have made me glad by Your works; at the deeds of Your hands I joyfully sing.
PSALM 92:4

Focusing on our problems will prevent us from rejoicing and being glad. Look for the good in your life and your joy will increase. You might have a problem, but if you focus on what's good, then you will discover there are some good things in your life also. The world is full of people and situations that don't please us, so if we are waiting for perfect circumstances to make us happy, we will be waiting forever.

That's why we must learn to base our happiness and joy not on outward circumstances, but on the Lord's presence inside us. Thankfully, we can learn not to fret or have any anxiety about anything, but in everything to give thanks and praise to God. Then the peace that passes all understanding will be ours.

Prayer of Thanks

Father, thank You for the gifts of joy and contentment. Regardless of the circumstances around me, I choose to praise You and realize that You are the true source of my joy. Thank You for Your goodness in my life. I choose to put my hope in You.

God Says, "I Will Be with You"

. . . As I was with Moses, so I will be with you; I will not fail you or forsake you.

JOSHUA 1:5

The presence of God in our lives helps us overcome fear. If we know by faith that God is with us, we can be grateful for His presence and we can take on any challenge with confidence and courage. We may not always feel God's presence, but we can be thankful for His Word, remembering that He said He would never leave us or forsake us (see Hebrews 13:5).

In the Bible, the basis for not fearing is simply this: God is with us. And if we know God's character and nature, we know He is trustworthy. We do not have to know what He is going to do, when He is going to do it, or how He is going to do it. Simply knowing He is with us is more than enough.

Prayer of Thanks

Father, I am grateful that You have promised Your presence will never leave me. Thank You that no matter what things look like around me, I don't have to fear because You are with me and You will carry me through.

Access to God

In Whom, because of our faith in Him, we dare to have the boldness (courage and confidence) of free access (an unreserved approach to God with freedom and without fear).

EPHESIANS 3:12

Everything about our spiritual lives depends on our personal faith in God and our personal relationship with Him. We can enjoy that relationship because Jesus' death on the cross gives us free, unhindered access to our heavenly Father. And our faith makes it possible for us to have an intimate, dynamic relationship with Him.

Thankfully, we as ordinary human beings have free access to God at any time through prayer. It is exciting to know we can approach the Creator of the universe boldly without reservations, without fear—and with complete freedom. God loves you and wants a personal relationship with you—how awesome is that! Personal faith in God opens the door to unlimited help from Him.

Prayer of Thanks

Thank You, Father, that I can have a personal relationship with You. Today I come boldly before Your throne of grace, with more than just requests and petitions; I come to you full of gratitude for all that You have done in my life.

Love Shows Respect

Render to all men their dues... respect to whom respect is due, and honor to whom honor is due. ROMANS 13:7

Love respects the differences in other people. A selfish person expects everyone to be just the way he is and to like whatever he likes, but love appreciates the differences we all have.

Respecting individual rights is very important. If God wanted us to all be alike, He would not have given each of us a different set of fingerprints—we are all created equal, but we are still different.

We all have different gifts and talents, different likes and dislikes, different goals in life—these things make us unique, and we should be grateful for them. Love respects those differences. The person who loves has learned to give freedom to those he loves. Freedom is one of the greatest gifts we can give. It is what Jesus came to give us, and we must also give it to others.

Prayer of Thanks

I am thankful, Father, that You created us all uniquely. Help me to value the differences of others, and help me to love them just like You do.

Overcome Evil with Good

Do not let yourself be overcome by evil, but overcome (master) evil with good.

ROMANS 12:21

We must not use our personal problems as an excuse to be grouchy and unloving with other people. Always remember that we overcome evil with good. This is why it is so important that we trust God, and while we are waiting on a change in our circumstances, we should remember to do good, do good, and do good!

In the Bible, the apostle Paul shares how even in times when he was suffering, he believed that God would take care of those things that he entrusted to Him (see 2 Timothy 1:12–14). We can be grateful that, like Paul, we are called to give our problems to God and refuse to worry.

A simple formula for victory is trust God, don't worry, do good, and keep meditating on and confessing God's Word, because God's Word is the weapon we have been given by which we can overcome evil and do good.

Prayer of Thanks

Thank You, Father, that no matter what I may be going through, You give me opportunities to do good for those around me. I don't have to focus on myself; I can choose to help others. Let me be an encouragement and a blessing to someone today.

The Way God Created You to Pray

And when you pray, do not keep on babbling like pagans, for they think they will be heard because of their many words.

MATTHEW 6:7 NIV

Jesus not only loves to teach us—corporately—how to pray (see Matthew 6:9–13), He also loves to work with us as individuals. He wants to take us just the way we are, helping each of us discover our own rhythm of prayer and develop a style of prayer that maximizes our personal relationship with Him.

We can be grateful that God is far too creative to teach every person on earth to interact with Him through prayer in exactly the same way. He is the one who designed us all differently and delights in our distinctiveness.

Of course, there are "prayer principles" that apply to all believers, but God leads each of us as individuals. Don't feel pressure to pray exactly like someone else. If you pray as the Lord leads you, you'll be amazed at the change it will make in your prayer life.

Prayer of Thanks

Father, I'm depending on You to teach me how to pray. Thank You for gifting me with my own personal and distinct way of communicating. Help me to use what You have given me as I spend time with You in my daily prayer life.

You Don't Have to Defend Yourself

When He was reviled and insulted, He did not revile or offer insult in return; [when] He was abused and suffered, He made no threats [of vengeance]; but he trusted [Himself and everything] to Him Who judges fairly.

1 PETER 2:23

If we want to enjoy peaceful relationships, we will be wise to follow Jesus' example. He was accused of wrongdoing regularly, yet never once did He attempt to defend Himself. He wasn't bothered by what other people thought of Him; it did not disturb Him at all.

Jesus could do so because He knew who He was. He did not have a problem with His self-image. He was not trying to prove anything. He trusted His heavenly Father to vindicate Him, and, thankfully, we can do the same. It adds a lot of peace to our lives when we realize that God is our true defense, and we can remain calm while He deals with anyone who falsely accuses us.

Prayer of Thanks

Father, I desire to live in healthy, peaceful relationships. Thank You for the example of Jesus that shows me I don't have to defend myself. You are my vindication, and that is all I need.

Fuel for Even Greater Determination

For a righteous man falls seven times and rises again. PROVERBS 24:16

When people try something, but are unsuccessful, one of the primary reasons they give up is that they feel like "a failure." The truth is we are never a failure unless we give up. Even though we do our best, we all have times when things just don't work out the way we hope they will. We may fail at one thing, or even a few things, but that certainly does not make us failures in life.

Believe it or not, we should actually be grateful for the failures we encounter because they help prepare us for future success. Failing at some things humbles us and teaches us the lessons we need to learn for the next challenge ahead of us. You don't have to feel defeated from failure; think of failure as fuel for greater determination and success in the future.

Prayer of Thanks

Father, when I am in a difficult situation and tempted to give up, help me to remember that You are with me. Thank You that You give me the strength and determination to keep going. And thank You that no matter what happens, I know You have a good plan for my life.

Created for a Purpose

"For I know the plans I have for you," declares the Lord, "plans to prosper you and not to harm you, plans to give you hope and a future." JEREMIAH 29:11 NIV

As children of God, one of the things we can be grateful for is the knowledge that God has destined us to do great things. He created you for a purpose. He has opportunities He wants to give you and assignments He wants to entrust to you.

I'm sure you've realized by this point in your life that you will face opposition as you follow God. People who are called to greatness meet great challenges. God never promised us it would be easy. In fact, He guarantees we will have adversity in this world (see John 16:33). But He also promises to be with us through difficulties, to fight on our behalf, and to strengthen us to overcome any obstacle we confront.

No matter what comes your way, keep following the Lord in faith and with a grateful heart, knowing that He has destined you to do great things for His glory.

Prayer of Thanks

I thank You, God, that You have given me a hope and a future. Help me to follow Your leading and walk in my destiny. I trust Your guidance, and I am thankful for Your presence and power in my life.

Thankful for Peace

And let the peace (soul harmony which comes) from Christ rule (act as umpire continually) in your hearts [deciding and settling with finality all questions that arise in your minds, in that peaceful state] to which as [members of Christ's] one body you were also called [to live]. And be thankful (appreciative), [giving praise to God always].

COLOSSIANS 3:15

Peace is our inheritance from Jesus, and this is something to be thankful for. The Bible teaches that peace is to be the "umpire" in our lives, settling every issue that needs a decision. To gain and maintain peace in our hearts, we must choose to follow the guidance of the Holy Spirit and learn when to say no to certain things.

For example, if we don't feel peace about something, we should never go ahead and do it. And if we don't have peace *while* we are doing something, then we shouldn't expect to have peace *after* we have done it.

The presence of peace can help us decide and settle with finality all questions that arise in our minds. If you let the Word of God have its home in your heart and mind, it will give you insight, wisdom, and peace.

Prayer of Thanks

I thank You today, Father, that You have given me peace as my inheritance. Help me to let go of every worry and anxiety that would try to weigh me down. Instead, I choose to let peace guide me through all things in my life.

Being Who God Created You to Be

So God created man in His own image, in the image and likeness of God He created him; male and female He created them.

GENESIS 1:27

Most people are afraid to be different from everyone else. They are more comfortable following a crowd than daring to follow the leading of God's Spirit. When we follow the example of others, we may please people, but when we step out in faith and follow God's Spirit, we please Him.

There is a fulfillment that comes when we learn to untie the boat from the dock, so to speak, and let the ocean of God's Spirit take us wherever He wills. When we are in control, we strive to decide what will happen next, but when we let God's Spirit take the lead, we are in for a lot of God-ordained surprises in life.

We can be grateful that God has a unique, individual plan for each of us! Let's be determined to be ourselves and refuse to spend our lives feeling inferior just because we are different from someone else.

Prayer of Thanks

Father, thank You for my uniqueness. I am grateful that I don't have to follow the crowd in life—all I have to do is follow You. Today, I will look to You and not to others. Lead me and guide me as I follow You wholeheartedly.

The Source of Your Confidence

I have strength for all things in Christ Who empowers me [I am ready for anything and equal to anything through Him Who infuses inner strength into me; I am self-sufficient in Christ's sufficiency].

PHILIPPIANS 4:13

When we have confidence in God and choose to be secure in Him, we can progress to living confidently and enjoying the life He wants for us. Note that I said "confidence in God," not in ourselves. Usually, when people think of confidence, they think of self-confidence. There are many voices in society urging you to "believe in yourself!" That is what we *don't* want to do! Our confidence must be in Christ alone, not in ourselves, not in other people, and not in the world or its systems.

Thankfully, we can have a confidence rooted in Christ, knowing that He is everything we need—He is more than enough! The Bible states that we are sufficient in Christ's sufficiency (see Philippians 4:13). Another way to say it would be, "we have confidence only because He lives in us, and it is His confidence that we draw from." So go and live with confidence today—confident in Christ and His presence in your life.

Prayer of Thanks

I am grateful, Father, that I don't have to go through life with insecurity and a lack of confidence. Because of Your presence and power in my life, I can experience a new boldness and a joy like never before. Thank You for Your strength that empowers me.

It's Never Too Late

Be of good courage and let us behave ourselves courageously for our people and for the cities of our God; and may the Lord do what is good in His sight. 1 CHRONICLES 19:13

Are you doing what you really believe you should be doing at this stage in your life, or have you allowed fear to prevent you from stepping out into new things—or maybe higher levels of old things? If you don't like your answer, let me give you some good news: It is never too late to begin again!

Thankfully, you don't have to spend one more day living a narrow life that is controlled by your fears. You can make a decision right now that you will learn to live boldly, aggressively, and confidently. You don't have to let fear rule you any longer. It's important to note that you can't just sit around, waiting for fear to go away. There will be times when you have to feel the fear and take action anyway. Courage is not the absence of fear; courage is action in the presence of fear.

Prayer of Thanks

Father, I am thankful that I don't have to live in fear. I pray that You will fill me with Your strength and courage to press through and overcome any fear or uncertainty I may face today.

Set a Goal to Enjoy Every Part of Your Day

Therefore my heart is glad and my glory [my inner self] rejoices; my body too shall rest and confidently dwell in safety.

PSALM 16:9

There are dozens of things that happen during ordinary, everyday life, and we can enjoy them all if we just make a decision to do it.

Things like getting dressed, driving to work, going to the grocery store, running errands, keeping things organized, sending e-mails, taking the kids to practice, and hundreds of other things. After all, they are the things that life is made up of. Begin doing them with an attitude of gratitude and realize that, through the Holy Spirit, you can enjoy absolutely everything you do every day of your life.

Joy doesn't come merely from being entertained, but from a decision to appreciate each moment that you are given as a rare and precious gift from God.

Prayer of Thanks

Father, thank You for the gift of life, and thank You for every activity that comes with that gift. I pray that You will help me find joy in each part of my day as I live for You. I thank You that I can choose to enjoy even the average, routine parts of my day.

Overlooked Blessings

The lines have fallen for me in pleasant places;
yes, I have a good heritage.

PSALM 16:6

Have you stopped to think about how much you have to be thankful for?

If you woke up this morning with more body parts that don't hurt than those that do, you are blessed. If you have food, clothes, and a place to live, you are more secure than 75 percent of the world. If you have money in the bank, in your wallet, or spare change at home, you are among the top 8 percent of the world's wealthiest people. If you have never experienced the danger of battle, the loneliness of imprisonment, the agony of torture, or the pangs of starvation, you are ahead of 500 million people in the world. If you read this message, you are more blessed than two billion people in the world who cannot read.

Don't overlook any blessing—thank God every day for His goodness in your life.

Prayer of Thanks

Father, help me to realize just how blessed I am. Thank You for my health, my home, my family, the advantages I have been given, and the very air I breathe. I choose to focus on what I have rather than what I don't have. Thank You for my wonderful life.

Be Positive

We have thought of Your steadfast love,
O God, in the midst of Your temple.

PSALM 48:9

Positive minds—minds full of faith and hope—produce positive lives. Negative minds—minds full of fear and doubt—produce negative lives. In Matthew 8:13, Jesus tells us that it will be done for us as we have believed. This doesn't mean that you and I can get anything we want by just thinking about it. God has a perfect plan for each of us, and we can't control Him with our thoughts and words, but if we want His plan, we should think and speak in agreement with His will and plan for us.

I encourage you to think positively about your life and be thankful for the good things God is doing and going to do.

Practice staying positive in every situation that arises; even if you're going through a difficult situation, stand in faith, believing God will bring good out of it as He has promised in His Word.

Prayer of Thanks

Father, help me to keep my thoughts and my words focused on You. I thank You that You have good things in store for my life. I trust You today.

A Perfect Heart

And I will give them one heart [a new heart] and I will put a new spirit within them; and I will take the stony [unnaturally hardened] heart out of their flesh, and will give them a heart of flesh [sensitive and responsive to the touch of their God]. EZEKIEL 11:19

Although we don't behave perfectly all the time, it is possible for us to have a perfect heart toward God. That means that we love Him wholeheartedly, and we want to please Him and do what is right.

When we receive Jesus as the perfect sacrifice for our sins, He gives us a new heart and puts His Spirit in us. The heart He gives us is a grateful, pure, and perfect heart toward Him. I like to say that He gives us a new "want to." He gives us a desire to please Him.

All God really wants is for us to love Him, and out of that love, do the best we can to serve and obey Him. If we do the best we can each day, even though our best is still imperfect, God sees our hearts and views us as perfect anyway because of His grace (undeserved favor and blessing).

Prayer of Thanks

I thank You today, Father, that You see the attitude of my heart. I know that You have given me a new "want to," and with Your help, I am going to do my best to please You with my actions. I love You, Father, and I thank You for Your grace in my life.

Loving People, Trusting God

But Jesus [for His part] did not trust Himself to them, because He knew all [men]; and He did not need anyone to bear witness concerning man [needed no evidence from anyone about men], for He Himself knew what was in human nature. [He could read men's hearts.]

JOHN 2:24–25

Jesus loved people—we see that in His interaction with people, especially His disciples. He had great fellowship with them—traveled with them, ate with them, and taught them—but He did not trust Himself totally to them. Because He knew what was in human nature.

That does not mean He didn't trust them at all; He just didn't open Himself up and give Himself to them in the same way He trusted God and opened Himself up to His heavenly Father. He didn't expect them to be perfect toward Him and never disappoint Him.

We can be thankful for the example of Jesus because He shows us how we should live. We should love people, and we can trust them, but never give them the trust that belongs to God. He is always trustworthy, and He always has your best interest at heart.

Prayer of Thanks

Father, thank You for the example of Jesus. I love and trust the people close to me in life, but my ultimate dependence and trust is in You.

Equipped for Joy

The hope of the [uncompromisingly] righteous (the upright, in right standing with God) is gladness, but the expectation of the wicked (those who are out of harmony with God) comes to nothing.

PROVERBS 10:28

We can be thankful that it is God's will for us to enjoy the life He has provided. The joy of the Lord is our strength. With that knowledge, we can make the decision to enjoy life every day.

Enjoying life does not mean we have something exciting going on all the time; it simply means enjoying the simple, everyday things. Most of life is rather ordinary, but we are supernaturally equipped with the power of God to live ordinary, everyday life in an extraordinary way.

Yes, it takes God's power to enjoy life because all of life is not easy. Many things happen that we do not plan, and some of them are difficult. But Jesus said, "Cheer up, I have overcome the world and deprived it of the power to harm you" (see John 16:33).

Prayer of Thanks

Father, when I am faced with a difficult situation, help me to choose joy in spite of my circumstance. I thank You that Your joy is my strength each and every day.

What Do You Think About Yourself?

And I am convinced and sure of this very thing, that He Who began a good work in you will continue until the day of Jesus Christ [right up to the time of His return], developing [that good work] and perfecting and bringing it to full completion in you.

PHILIPPIANS 1:6

It is important that we have a healthy, scriptural view of ourselves. No one is perfect; we all have growing to do. But thankfully, we can know that we are loved and accepted by God while we are becoming the people He wants us to be.

These thoughts reflect the Bible-based self-image you can have in Christ:

1. I know God created me and He loves me (see Psalm 139:13–14; John 3:16).

2. I have faults and weaknesses, and I want to change. I believe God is working in my life, changing me little by little, day by day (see 2 Corinthians 3:18).
3. Everyone has faults, so I am not a failure just because I am not perfect (see 2 Corinthians 12:9).
4. No matter how often I fail, I will not give up, because God is with me to strengthen and sustain me (see Hebrews 13:5).
5. In myself I am nothing, and yet in Jesus I am everything I need to be (see John 15).
6. I can do all things I need to do—everything God calls me to do through His Son Jesus Christ (see Philippians 4:13).

Prayer of Thanks

Father, I am so thankful that I have a new identity in You. Regardless of what I have been told or how I feel on a given day, I will trust Your Word and believe that everything Your Word says about me is true.

Celebrate Change

Do not conform to the pattern of this world, but be transformed by the renewing of your mind. Then you will be able to test and approve what God's will is—his good, pleasing and perfect will.

ROMANS 12:2 NIV

As children of God, we can be thankful for the change God works in our lives. Throughout our journey here on earth, God's Spirit will be working with and in us, helping us change for the better. In order to make progress, we need to be open to God's work and be obedient to His guidance.

God wants us to see truth (reality) so we can agree with Him about any change that is needed, but we don't need to punish ourselves when we see our faults or to feel guilty and condemned. We can submit to God and learn to celebrate the changes that happen in our lives. Change and growth is a healthy process that God will continue as long as we are on earth in our human bodies. Transformation is something to be grateful for!

Prayer of Thanks

I thank You, God, that I don't have to be afraid of change, but that I can rejoice in it. Help me to be open to Your leading. I am grateful for Your work in my life.

The Best Way to Live

Some trust in and boast of chariots and some of horses, but we will trust in and boast of the name of the Lord our God.

PSALM 20:7

We can live by trying to take care of ourselves, or we can live by trusting God. Trusting God is the best and most peaceful way to live and, thankfully, it is an option available to us every day.

If you're under pressure because you're trying to take care of yourself, then choose to stop trying to make everything happen yourself, in your own timing, in your own way, according to your own plan. Instead, lean on God in every situation and pray:

Lord, whatever I may desire in life, if You don't want me to have it, I don't want it. If

You do want me to have it, I ask You for it and believe You will give it to me in Your time, in Your way, according to Your divine plan.

When you release yourself to God in this way, you will see marvelous things happen in your life.

Prayer of Thanks

Thank You, Father, that I can enjoy Your peace while You guide me and work Your will in my life.

Dealing with Emotional Pain

And after you have suffered a little while, the God of all grace [Who imparts all blessing and favor], Who has called you to His [own] eternal glory in Christ Jesus, will Himself complete and make you what you ought to be, establish and ground you securely, and strengthen, and settle you.

1 PETER 5:10

When we are hurting emotionally, we may feel angry, frustrated, or discouraged, but we do not have to let any of those feelings control us. We can manage our emotions with God's help, and we can be thankful we are not controlled by our feelings and emotions.

Many people are treated unjustly; they do not deserve the pain they experience. But we can be so glad that even when we go through ugly, painful things, we do have Jesus in our lives to help and strengthen us.

Perhaps you did not have a good start in life, but you can still have a good finish. Let go of the past and take a step into the good life that God sent His Son, Jesus, to purchase for you.

Prayer of Thanks

Father, thank You for helping me overcome any unjust treatment I may have or ever will experience in my life. I trust that You are my Vindicator and You always make wrong things right.

Living in God's Grace

But he said to me, "My grace is sufficient for you, for my power is made perfect in weakness."
2 CORINTHIANS 12:9 NIV

The truth that God wants you to enjoy your life is a blessing that every believer can be thankful for. But one of the main things that will keep you from enjoying your life is works of the flesh. A work of the flesh is our energy, our efforts trying to do what only God can do.

Trying to do God's job always leads to frustration. Trusting God to do what only He can do always leads to joy because "what is impossible with men is possible with God" (Luke 18:27).

The Bible says that God's grace is sufficient for us. Grace is God's undeserved favor and the power of God to meet our needs and solve our problems. We become frustrated when we try to achieve by works a life that God designed us to receive by grace. So rest in His grace today and be thankful for the joy that grace promises to bring.

Prayer of Thanks

I am grateful, Father, for Your grace in my life. Help me to always receive grace through faith in You and trust You to do what only You can do.

Look How Far You've Come

Yet, O Lord, You are our Father; we are the clay, and You our Potter, and we all are the work of Your hand. ISAIAH 64:8

It is easy for us to get caught up in looking at how far we have to go in reaching our goals instead of celebrating how far we have come. Think about it. How far have you come since you became a Christian? How much have you changed? How much happier are you? Are you more peaceful than you were before? Do you have hope? There is always plenty to celebrate if we look for it.

A thorough study of the Bible shows us that the men and women who God used in mighty ways always had the attitude of celebrating what God had done. They did not take His goodness for granted, but they openly showed appreciation and thankfulness for little things as well as big ones.

Prayer of Thanks

Father, today I choose to be full of thanksgiving for how far You have brought me. I may not be where I want to be yet, but I thank You that I'm not where I used to be.

Blessing Those Around You

. . . being mindful of the words of the Lord Jesus, how He Himself said, It is more blessed (makes one happier and more to be envied) to give than to receive.

ACTS 20:35

It is the will of God that we give thanks at all times and in everything (see 1 Thessalonians 5:18). Thanksgiving must have an expression in order to be complete. We can say that we are thankful, but do we show it? Are we expressing it? We say "thank you," but there are other ways of showing appreciation, and one of them is to bless others.

Giving to help others is one of the ways we can keep a continual cycle of blessing operating in our lives. God gives to us and we show appreciation by giving to someone else, and then He blesses us some more so we can do it all over again. What we give to others as a result of obedience to God is never lost. It leaves our hand temporarily, but it never leaves our life. We give it, God uses it to bless someone else, and we are blessed in return.

Prayer of Thanks

Thank You, Father, that You bless me so that I may be a blessing to others. Help me look for ways to give to those around me today. I am grateful for Your goodness, and I want to express that gratitude through my generosity to others.

A Key to Effective Prayer

I do not call you servants (slaves) any longer, for the servant does not know what his master is doing (working out). But I have called you My friends, because I have made known to you everything that I have heard from My Father. JOHN 15:15

One of the most important keys to effective prayer is approaching God as His friend. When we go to God believing that He sees us as His friends, new wonders are opened to us. We experience new freedom and boldness, which are both things to be extremely grateful for.

If we do not know God as a friend, we will be reluctant to be bold in asking for what we need. But if we go to Him as our friend, without losing our awe of Him, our prayers will stay fresh, exciting, and intimate.

A friendship involves loving and being loved. It means knowing that God is on your side, wanting to help you, cheering you on, and always keeping your best interest in mind. God loves you and desires your friendship!

Prayer of Thanks

Father, I am thankful that You have promised to be my friend. Help me to come to You in prayer, knowing that You love me and You are for me. Thank You, God, that I am never alone. You are my friend, and You are with me.

You Can Be as Close to God as You Want to Be

God has said, "Never will I leave you; never will I forsake you."

HEBREWS 13:5 NIV

Developing your friendship with God is similar to developing a friendship with someone on earth. It takes time. The truth is that you can be as close to God as you want to be; it all depends on the time you are willing to invest in the relationship. I encourage you to get to know Him by spending time in prayer and in the Word and by including Him in all that you do.

Your friendship with God will also deepen and grow as you walk with Him and as you experience His faithfulness. Form the habit of continual, simple, and loving conversation with God. He is always with you and always ready to listen. He is a friend who will never leave you or forsake you. One who is faithful, dependable, loving, and forgiving. That is a friend we can be thankful for!

Prayer of Thanks

Father, I thank You that my relationship with You is developing and growing stronger every day. Thank You that You are dependable and You will never let me down.

Burden-Free Living

Anxiety in a man's heart weights it down, but an encouraging word makes it glad.

PROVERBS 12:25

In this life, we will always have opportunities to be anxious, worried, and fretful. The devil will see to that, because he knows that anxiety weighs us down. When the devil tries to bring anxiety into our hearts, we can give that anxiety to the Lord in prayer with thanksgiving, making our requests known to Him. When we do that, we will experience the peace of burden-free living.

I encourage you to refuse to be weighed down with worry. Instead, turn to the Lord in prayer, rejoicing in the midst of every circumstance. The Lord is faithful, and He will give the peace and joy He has promised to all those who refuse to give in to worry and fear and instead turn to Him in simple faith and trust.

Prayer of Thanks

Father, when I begin to experience feelings of worry or anxiety, help me to cast my cares on You. Thank You that I don't have to live under heavy burdens any longer. Thank You that I can bring my worries to You so that I can live a life of peace.

The Gift of Right Now

So do not worry or be anxious about tomorrow, for tomorrow will have worries and anxieties of its own. MATTHEW 6:34

There is an anointing (God's presence and power) on today. In John 8:58, Jesus referred to Himself as "*I AM.*" If you and I, as His disciples, try to live in the past or the future, we are going to find life hard for us because Jesus is always in the present.

Jesus has plainly told us we don't need to worry about anything. All we need to do is seek Him and His ways, and He will add to us whatever we need, whether it is food or clothing or shelter or spiritual growth (Matthew 6:25–33). We don't need to be concerned about tomorrow. Instead, we can concentrate on today and thank God for today's blessings.

Calm down and lighten up! Laugh more and worry less. Don't ruin today by worrying about yesterday or tomorrow—neither of which you can do anything about. Enjoy today while you still can!

Prayer of Thanks

I am grateful, Father, for this day that You have given me. With Your help, I'm going to live in the present, not in the past or in the future. I thank You for what you have in store for me today.

What Choice Will You Make?

I call heaven and earth to witness this day against you that I have set before you life and death, the blessings and the curses; therefore choose life.

DEUTERONOMY 30:19

Jesus wants us to experience joy in our souls. It is important to our physical, mental, emotional, and spiritual health. This is why Proverbs 17:22 says, "a cheerful mind works healing." It is God's will for us to enjoy life!

It is time to decide to enter into the full and abundant life that God wills for us. We can be thankful that God allows us to choose what kind of life we want to live. Joy and enjoyment are available, just as misery and sadness are available. Righteousness and peace are available, but so are condemnation and turmoil. There are blessings and curses available, and that is why Deuteronomy 30 tells us to choose.

Make the right choice today. Choose Jesus. Choose joy. Choose peace. Choose life!

Prayer of Thanks

Father, I thank You that I can choose the quality of life I want to live for You. Help me to make wise decisions today. Help me to choose peace and joy. I know that You will give me wisdom and guide me every step of the way. Worry is useless and I choose not to waste my time on it!

The Spirit of a Conqueror

Yet amid all these things we are more than conquerors and gain a surpassing victory through Him Who loved us.

ROMANS 8:37

Are you living a victorious life in Christ? If you aren't, maybe today is the day for you to begin seeing yourself differently than you have in the past, to see yourself as one who overcomes adversities, not as someone who shrinks back in fear or feels overwhelmed every time a trial comes along.

You see, adversities are not optional, they are part of life, and it takes a conqueror to overcome them. Jesus Himself said that we would face trouble in this world (see John 16:33). Paul understood that obstacles were unavoidable and wrote in Romans 8:37 that we are "more than conquerors" and that we would "gain a surpassing victory."

To be more than a conqueror means that before you ever face adversity, before the battle against you even begins, you already know you will win as long as you trust God and don't give up. That's a promise to be grateful for—you are more than a conqueror in Christ Jesus!

Prayer of Thanks

Father, when I am in a situation that threatens to overwhelm or intimidate me, I will stand on Your Word that says I am more than a conqueror in You. Thank You that I will not be defeated because You are with me, and You are protecting me.

You Are Free from Your Past

It is for freedom that Christ has set us free. Stand firm, then, and do not let yourselves be burdened again by a yoke of slavery.

GALATIANS 5:1 NIV

Many people stay trapped in the past. But there is only one thing that can be done about the past, and that is to forget it. Thankfully, when you ask Him, God forgives and forgets your past…and you can too.

When we make mistakes, as we all do, we can simply ask God's forgiveness and move forward in the freedom Jesus provided for us. Like Paul, we are all pressing toward the mark of perfection, but no one has arrived.

I believe one of the reasons Paul enjoyed his life and ministry is because he made it a priority to leave his past in the past (see Philippians 3:13–14). Like us, he was pressing toward the mark of perfection, admitting that he had not arrived, but he had insight on how to enjoy his life while he was making the trip.

Let's follow Paul's example. Don't get stuck in the past—live in the freedom of forgiveness today!

Prayer of Thanks

I am thankful, Father, that my past is in the past. You have forgiven my sins and given me a fresh start. I accept Your forgiveness and I determine to live my present and my future for Your glory.

Victory over Dread

. . . Dread not, neither be afraid of them.

DEUTERONOMY 1:29

Dread is a close relative of regret. Dread places us in the future, whereas regret puts us in the past. Dread is also closely related to fear. People often dread doing something for fear of what might happen.

We know that God has not given us a spirit of fear (see 2 Timothy 1:7 KJV), and since He did not give us fear, we know that dread is not from Him either. Thankfully, we can reject feelings of dread, kicking them out of our lives once and for all.

Let this be a day of decision for you—a day when you decide to no longer operate in regret and dread. Become a *now* person. Live in the present, not the past or the future. God has a plan for your life now.

Trust Him today. Don't put it off another moment.

Prayer of Thanks

I believe it is Your will, Father, for me to live a life of peace and contentment. Thank You that I don't have to look back with regrets or look ahead with dread. I choose to live in the now *You have given me, making the most of each new day.*

Praising God all Day Long

Let everything that has breath and every breath of life praise the Lord! Praise the Lord! (Hallelujah!)

PSALM 150:6

One of the best things we can do throughout the day is to praise God while we work. No matter what you're trying to build—your home, your marriage, your business, financial security, an exercise plan, or an intimate relationship with God—do not forget to worship as you work.

Remember to praise God and thank Him for even small steps of progress. You don't have to make a production out of your praise; just keep a thankful heart and an attitude that says, "I love You, Lord. I worship You. I can't do this without You. I need Your help today. Thank You for giving me a goal to work toward and for helping me accomplish it."

Prayer of Thanks

I am grateful, Father, for even the smallest steps of progress You enable me to make in my life. I love You and I know that You are doing a good work in and through me. Thank You for everything You have done in my life and everything You are yet to do.

Jesus Showed Us the Way

Jesus Christ (the Messiah) is [always] the same, yesterday, today, [yes] and forever (to the ages).

HEBREWS 13:8

In every aspect of life, Jesus is our example—and Jesus always displayed emotional stability. The Bible actually refers to Him as "the Rock," and we can depend on Him to be solid, steady, and stable—the same—all the time. He's always faithful, loyal, mature, and true to His Word.

Jesus is not in one kind of mood one day and in another mood the next day. Thankfully, we can count on Him to be the same today as He was yesterday and the same tomorrow as He is today. Being able to depend on Jesus' stability and consistency is part of what makes a relationship with Him seem attractive to us. If we'll learn to be grateful for the example Jesus set, and follow His lead, we will be able to learn to be stable and enjoy life more.

Prayer of Thanks

I am grateful, Father, that I don't have to be ruled by my emotions. Thank You for the example of Jesus. Help me to be steady and solid no matter what is going on around me. Help me to be more like Jesus.

God Leads Us One Step at a Time

The steps of a [good] man are directed and established by the Lord when He delights in his way [and He busies Himself with his every step]. Though he falls, he shall not be utterly cast down, for the Lord grasps his hand in support and upholds him.

PSALM 37:23–24

As we go through this life, each of us is called to have an individual walk with God. Thankfully, God gives us the direction we need, showing us the way to go, and with His help we follow Him.

A walk with God takes place through one step of obedience at a time. Some people want the entire blueprint for their life before they will make one decision, but God does not usually operate that way; He leads us day by day. Not knowing everything the future holds requires us to live by faith, and that is what God desires.

By faith, we take each step God has shown us, and then He gives us the next one. At times we may fall down, but we can be grateful that God helps us get back up. We continue on by His strength and His grace, knowing that every time we need to make a decision, God will guide us because we have a personal relationship with Him.

Prayer of Thanks

I thank You today, Father, that You are guiding me one step at a time. I trust Your direction for my life. I thank You that Your plan for me is good and You will never lead me astray.

An Act of Love Endures Forever

If I [can] speak in the tongues of men and [even] of angels, but have not love (that reasoning, intentional, spiritual devotion such as is inspired by God's love for and in us), I am only a noisy gong or a clanging cymbal.

1 CORINTHIANS 13:1

Most of the things we devote our time and energy to are things that are currently passing away, things that will not last. We strive to make money, build businesses, achieve great accomplishments, be popular, own buildings, cars, and jewelry. We want to expand our minds and see the world, yet all of these things are temporal. They will all come to an end.

Only love never comes to an end. An act of love goes on and endures forever.

Thankfully, God allows us to have a

lasting impact when He asks us to love others. Henry Drummond says that "to love abundantly is to live abundantly, and to love forever is to live forever." In order to "love abundantly" and "love forever," I encourage you to first receive God's love for you...then you can walk in love toward everyone else.

Prayer of Thanks

Father, I am grateful that I can live my life in such a way as to have a lasting impact. Thank You for the power of love. Help me exercise that power and make an eternal impact by showing love to those around me today. Help me to always know what is truly important.

Enjoying Harmonious and Peaceful Relationships

...And you shall hold your peace and remain at rest. EXODUS 14:14

We were created to live in the love and enjoyment of harmonious relationships, free from dissension, confusion, and emotional trauma. God wants our lives to be free from division; He wants us to live in peace with each other; yet such a life often eludes many people. Instead, conflict wreaks havoc in their lives, leaving them wounded and alienated from one another.

But we can be thankful that Jesus gives us His peace. We don't have to live with broken, conflict-filled relationships. We can "hold our peace" in every situation. Psalm 34:14 says we can "crave peace and pursue it" and Matthew 5:9 says we can be "makers and maintainers of peace." As we remain peaceful, God works in our behalf.

Don't let relationship problems plague your life any longer. Determine to end the strife and do all that you can to pursue peace. If you decide to be a peacemaker, you'll be surprised what a difference it will make.

Prayer of Thanks

Father, help me to be a peacemaker in my relationships. I thank You that I no longer waste my time on petty arguments and foolish strife. As far as it depends on me, and with Your help, I am going to have peaceful, harmonious relationships.

God's Word Affects Every Area of Our Lives

Your word is a lamp to my feet and a light to my path. PSALM 119:105

While negative thoughts, words, emotions, and relationships can cause stress—and stress can cause sickness—positive thoughts, words, emotions, and relationships can bring health and healing. Consider the following Scriptures:

- *"A calm and undisturbed mind and heart are the life and health of the body…"* (Proverbs 14:30)
- *"My son, attend to my words…for they are life to those who find them, healing and health to all their flesh."* (Proverbs 4:20,22)

- *"Pleasant words are as a honeycomb, sweet to the mind and healing to the body."* (Proverbs 16:24)

We can be thankful for the power of God's Word in our lives. Meditating on Scripture and following God's instruction will cause us to think, speak, and live in a way that brings healing to every part of our lives.

Prayer of Thanks

Father, I thank You for Your Word and the healing it brings to my life. I am grateful that my thoughts, words, emotions, and relationships are all changed by the guidance You give me through Scripture.

Thankful for all God Has Done

Through Him, therefore, let us constantly and at all times offer up to God a sacrifice of praise, which is the fruit of lips that thankfully acknowledge and confess and glorify His name.

HEBREWS 13:15

Many people are familiar with the statement, "There is power in praise!" It's true, and when we praise God from our hearts, we exert power in the spiritual realm. God Himself inhabits the praises of His people (see Psalm 22:3).

Praise allows us to remember and express our joy and thanksgiving for all God has done for us…and everything He is going to do. It engages our hearts to focus on Him and our mouths to speak about Him.

Thankfully, we can tap into the power

that is released through praise—it gives us an opportunity to express how truly thankful we are. We do this because we love God, but also because praise and giving thanks are attitudes that God delights in. Praying with gratitude is the way to see prayer answered.

Prayer of Thanks

Father, I praise You because You are worthy to be praised. Thank You for everything You have done in my life and everything You are going to do in the future. I love You, and I praise You with everything I am.

Today Is a Perfect Day to Bless Others

And do not forget to do good and to share with others, for with such sacrifices God is pleased.

HEBREWS 13:16 NIV

The blessings of God in our lives are certainly something to be thankful for, but we must also remember that we are blessed in order to bless others.

Let me suggest an experiment today. Just think: *I am going to go out into the world today and I will be a blessing to others.* Then get your mind set before you ever walk out the door that you are going out as God's ambassador and that your goal is to be a giver, to love people, and to add benefit to their lives.

You can begin by smiling at the people you encounter throughout the day. A smile is a symbol of acceptance and approval—something most people in this world desperately search for. Deposit yourself with God and trust Him to take care of you while you sow good seed everywhere you go. Make a decision to let God work through you today!

Prayer of Thanks

I am so thankful for the blessings in my life, Father. Help me to use what You have given me to bless others. Today, I choose to spread Your love, Your joy, and Your blessings to the people I come in contact with.

Righteousness in Christ

I will greatly rejoice in the Lord, my soul will exult in my God; for He has clothed me with the garments of salvation, He has covered me with the robe of righteousness, as a bridegroom decks himself with a garland, and as a bride adorns herself with her jewels.

ISAIAH 61:10

Our righteousness in Christ is one of the greatest gifts we can ever be thankful for. Through faith in Christ we are placed in right-standing with God. And by faith, we are covered with His robe of righteousness. In other words, because we are trusting in Jesus Christ's righteousness to cover us, God views us as right instead of wrong. His righteousness becomes a shield that protects us from Satan.

In and of ourselves, we are less than

nothing; our righteousness is like filthy rags, for all have sinned and come short of the glory of God (see Isaiah 64:6; Romans 3:23). But we are justified and given a right relationship with God through faith. Knowing we are righteous through the work of Jesus brings peace and joy to our lives that no one can ever take away.

Prayer of Thanks

I thank You today, Father, that I have right standing with You and I am pleasing in Your sight because of the work of Jesus. I am grateful that I know I am accepted, loved, and approved by You.

Holding on to Hope

And now, Lord, what do I wait for and expect?
My hope and expectation are in You.

PSALM 39:7

God's Word says that He wants us to be blessed (see Deuteronomy 29:9). It states we can and will be blessed in every way when we walk in God's will. Satan wants to keep people fearful and hopeless. Hopelessness steals our God-given peace and joy.

The enemy tells people they will never have anything, their life will never change, and things will never get better. And when people believe his lies, they remain hopeless and discouraged. We receive what we believe, whether it is positive or negative, so it's vitally important for us to have faith in God constantly, like Mark 11:22–24 tells us to do.

Refuse to be hopeless and put your trust in God's Word. Be like Abraham, of whom it is said that although he had no reason to hope, he hoped in faith that God's promises would come to pass in his life. As he waited, he gave praise and glory to God, and Satan was not able to defeat him with doubt and unbelief (see Romans 4:18–20).

Prayer of Thanks

Father, thank You for the power of hope. I am grateful that no matter what the circumstances around me look like, I can place my hope in You and in Your Word. I am at peace today because You are the source of my hope.

Recognize Your Enemy

Be vigilant and cautious at all times; for that enemy of yours, the devil, roams around like a lion roaring [in fierce hunger], seeking someone to seize upon and devour.

1 PETER 5:8

John 10:10 states that "the thief comes only in order to steal and kill and destroy." The passage is referring to Satan and his system. Just as God has a system that He encourages us to live by, and He promises blessings if we do, Satan has a system and he wants us to live by it so he can steal our blessings.

Satan shows us a circumstance and then makes us afraid it will never change. God wants us to believe His Word is true even while we are still in the midst of the circumstance. That's why Scripture says, "Yet amid all these things we are more than conquerors…" (Romans 8:37).

In God's economy, we can believe before we see change or the good things we desire. Jesus gave us peace as our inheritance, but Satan does everything he can to rob us of it. Recognize your enemy, and stand aggressively against him in the peace and power of God.

Prayer of Thanks

Father, though I have an enemy who is trying to rob me of my joy, thank You that I don't have to fear him. You have already defeated the enemy, and Your Spirit lives within me. I recognize I have an enemy, but I thank You that the victory is already mine through Christ.

Relationship vs. Religion

For no person will be justified (made righteous, acquitted, and judged acceptable) in His sight by observing the works prescribed by the Law.
ROMANS 3:20

Jesus had much to say about religion, and none of it was good. Why? Because religion in His day was, and often still is, man's idea of what God expects. Religion is man trying to reach God through his own good works.

The Christian faith teaches that God has reached down to man through Jesus Christ. Thankfully, by placing our faith in Jesus, we receive the benefits from the work He has done for us. His work—not our own works of religion, not following rules and regulations man prescribes—justifies us and makes us right with God.

A Christian is not just someone who has agreed to follow certain rules and regulations and observe certain days as holy. A Christian is someone who has had his heart changed by faith in Jesus Christ.

Prayer of Thanks

I am grateful, Father, that I am free from man-made ideas of religion. I can relate to You in a personal, intimate way because of Jesus. Thank You for loving me and for living in a relationship with me.

When There Seems to Be No Way

Behold, I am doing a new thing! Now it springs forth; do you not perceive and know it and will you not give heed to it? I will even make a way in the wilderness and rivers in the desert.

ISAIAH 43:19

Have you ever faced a situation and said, "There is no way this can ever be"? Maybe some of these thoughts weigh on your mind:

- There is no way I can handle the pressure at work.
- There is no way I can pay my bills.
- There is no way to save my marriage.
- There is no way I can go back to college now.

With God's help, there is *always* a way. This is a beautiful truth to be grateful for. It may not be easy; it may not be convenient; it may not come quickly. You may have to go over, under, around, or through difficulty—but if you will simply keep on keeping on, you *will* find a way. Jesus said in John 14:6, "I am the Way and the Truth and the Life." He is the Way, and He will help you find a way even where there doesn't seem to be one.

Prayer of Thanks

Father, I thank You that You have "made a way in the wilderness." Help me to focus on You and not on my circumstances. Thank You that You are making a way for me today.

Love Never Gives Up

Love never fails [never fades out or becomes obsolete or comes to an end].

1 CORINTHIANS 13:8

Love never fails. In other words, it never gives up on people. We can be thankful that God never gives up on us, and we can have that same attitude toward others. The apostle Paul describes what love is in 1 Corinthians 13 and mentions that love always believes the best; it is positive and filled with faith and hope.

While Jesus was on earth, He gave a new commandment to His followers: that we love one another (see John 13:34). For this reason, walking in love should be the main goal of every Christian. God is love (see 1 John 4:8) and He never gives up on us. Let's choose to live with that same attitude. Believe in the power of love to change and transform anything and anyone. No person is beyond God's reach!

Prayer of Thanks

I am so thankful, Father, that Your love will never give up on me. Help me, Lord, to have that same attitude toward others. Help me to show Your love to the world around me.

How to Reach Your God-Given Goals

For which of you, wishing to build a farm building, does not first sit down and calculate the cost [to see] whether he has sufficient means to finish it? LUKE 14:28

Goals are important in life. Paul said that he pressed toward the goal (see Philippians 3:14). As believers, we can be thankful that God helps us set and reach healthy goals in our lives. Many people never accomplish their goals because they do not know how to set them. A popular and easy-to-remember acronym that has been successful in helping countless people reach their goals is the word *smart*:

Specific
Measurable
Attainable

Realistic
Timely

Specific: Make sure your goal is as specific as possible. **Measurable:** Goals that are hard to measure are goals that are hard to meet. **Attainable:** Make sure the goal itself is reachable. **Realistic:** It is important to dream big dreams and aim high, but don't set yourself up for disappointment by trying to reach an unrealistic goal. **Timely:** People who set goals without target completion dates rarely accomplish their objectives.

Prayer of Thanks

Father, I am thankful that I can meet the goals I set with Your help. I pray that You give me wisdom to set healthy goals for my life and the perseverance to reach every goal that I set.

A Time to Remember

And they [earnestly] remembered that God was their Rock, and the Most High God their Redeemer. PSALM 78:35

There are times to forget and things to forget. For example, when the apostle Paul said that he forgot what was behind, he was talking about not being condemned over past mistakes (see Philippians 3:13). In Isaiah, we are taught not to remember the things of old because God is doing a new thing. That simply means we are not to get stuck in the past.

We hear a lot of teaching about forgetting the past, and although there are times to do that, we should also be taught to remember with gratitude all the good things God has done in the past, passing that gratitude on to future generations. A thankful heart is a heart that remembers God's love and miraculous deeds and shares them with the world.

Prayer of Thanks

Father, I thank You for the amazing things You have done in my past. Help me to always remember Your goodness and use it to build my faith for even bigger and better things to come.

Seek the Giver, Not the Gift

Seek, inquire for, and require the Lord while He may be found [claiming Him by necessity and by right]; call upon Him while He is near.

ISAIAH 55:6

One of the many things we can be thankful for in our relationship with God is that He wants to be our friend (see John 15:15). But as you grow in your friendship with God, never forget that your relationship is based on who He is and not on what He can do for you. Keep seeking His presence, not His presents.

One of the hindrances to a vibrant, mature friendship with God is focusing on the benefits of friendship with God instead of focusing on *Him* as our friend. As human beings, we do not appreciate finding out that certain people want to be our friends just because we can get them something they want; we feel valued when we know people want to be friends with us simply because of who we are and because they actually like us—the same principle applies with God.

Prayer of Thanks

I thank You, God, that You love me and want to be in a relationship with me. Today, I seek You for who You are, not for what You can do for me. It is my heart's desire to know You more and more each day I follow You.

God Wants to Bless You

...They who seek (inquire of and require) the Lord [by right of their need and on the authority of His Word], none of them shall lack any beneficial thing.

PSALM 34:10

Some people have been taught that suffering and lack are virtues in the Christian life. Being able to maintain a good attitude during times of suffering is a virtue that is very important, but continually suffering is not God's will for anybody. We must never see God as a stingy God who would withhold something we need. Consider these verses:

- *"The Lord is my Shepherd [to feed, guide, and shield me], I shall not lack"* (Psalm 23:1).

- *"Let the Lord be magnified, Who takes pleasure in the prosperity of His servant"* (Psalm 35:27).
- *"He will bless those who reverently and worshipfully fear the Lord, both small and great"* (Psalm 115:13).

God is a good Father who loves to bless His children. God wants to bless you and see you enjoy your life! You can simply be thankful, receive it, and aggressively believe for God's best today.

Prayer of Thanks

Father, I thank You that You are good, You love me and want to bless me. Thank You that I don't have to be afraid because You will feed, guide, and shield me.

Praying Bold, Confident Prayers

Since we have such [glorious] hope (such joyful and confident expectation), we speak very freely and openly and fearlessly.

2 CORINTHIANS 3:12

God is looking for men and women who will pray bold prayers. One of the prayers I hear people pray often is what I call a "just" prayer. A "just" prayer sounds something like this: "Now, Lord, we *just* ask You to protect us," or "Oh, God, if You would *just* help us in this situation." These prayers make it sound as if we are afraid to ask God for very much.

When used this way, the word "just" means *barely enough to get by* or *by a narrow margin*. God wants to give us exceedingly, abundantly, above and beyond all that we can dare to hope, ask, or think (see

Ephesians 3:20)—that's something to be grateful for! God wants to hear bold, confident, faith-filled prayers prayed by truly thankful people who are secure in their relationship with Him. Don't be fearful of asking God for too much because He loves you and wants to do more for you than you can imagine.

Prayer of Thanks

Father, I am so thankful that You allow me to pray bold, confident prayers. I know You are not a God of just enough*—You are a God of* more than enough. *I take the limits off of You today, and I trust You to do something big in my life.*

Draw Near to God

Come close to God and He will come close to you. JAMES 4:8

Many times people draw away from God because of their sins and failures. Do you ever hear or study God's Word and end up feeling condemned? God's Word is meant to convict us of sin and convince us to do things God's way, but it is never intended to make us feel guilty or bad about ourselves.

When God reveals sin in your life, let it draw you to Him for help and forgiveness, never let it drive you away from Him. Remember, Jesus didn't die for perfect people who never make mistakes, but He died for sinners. He paid for our sins so we might receive His forgiveness and mercy and then actually learn from our mistakes.

We can be grateful and thankful that

the Lord didn't push us away because of our faults. Instead, He draws us to Him and begins to change us into what He wants us to be. All we have to do is be willing to be changed. Just ask Him and trust Him to do it. He is faithful. He will finish the work He has started in your life.

Prayer of Thanks

I thank You today, Father, that You draw me to Yourself despite my sins and my failures. Help me not to draw away from You when I make mistakes. Instead, help me choose to come to You in faith, believing that You love me and want to help me.

Thankful to Be Free from Confusion

For God is not the author of confusion but of peace, as in all the churches of the saints.

1 CORINTHIANS 14:33 NKJV

Confusion is not from God. When we are confused, it is because we are trying too hard to reason things out in our own minds instead of trusting Him. He offers us peace, not confusion. When you feel confused, you should realize that something about your approach to life is wrong. Perhaps you have moved out of grace and into your own works. That simply means you may be trying to solve your own problems instead of relying on God. But thankfully, you can give up your efforts and entrust yourself totally to the Lord, leaving your situation entirely in His hands.

Once you turn from your own efforts

and reasoning to the grace of God, you open a channel of faith through which He can begin to reveal to you what you need to know in order to handle that problem or situation. Enter God's rest, and then you will find the guidance you need.

Prayer of Thanks

I am grateful, Father, that You give me peace instead of confusion. I will live in Your grace each day, knowing that You can handle whatever situation or circumstance I may face. Thank You for Your peace—I receive it today.

A Life of Adventure

Whatever may be your task, work at it heartily (from the soul), as [something done] for the Lord and not for men.

COLOSSIANS 3:23

We were never created to live a boring life. God put a craving for adventure in us, and adventure means trying something we have never done before. If you are going to be adventurous, you may need to step out into something new. Don't sit on the sidelines of life and watch the brave people live exciting lives—join them. Step out of your "boat of safety" and see if you can walk on water as Peter did (see Matthew 14:26–31).

I assure you, if you are stepping out into God's will for you, He will make you able to succeed. You do not have to feel able, and you do not have to have experience.

All you need is the desire to be obedient to God, a thankful attitude, and a heart full of faith. God is not looking for ability; He is looking for availability. He is looking for somebody to say, "Here I am, God, send me. Here I am, use me. I want to serve You, God. I want to do all that You want me to do."

Prayer of Thanks

Father, I am thankful that You want me to enjoy an amazing, adventure-filled life. Whatever You have for me to do, I pray that You will make it clear. Thank You for the opportunities You are sending my way and the boldness You are giving me to make the most of them.

Be Assured of God's Love for You

And so we know and rely on the love God has for us. God is love. Whoever lives in love lives in God, and God in them.

1 JOHN 4:16 NIV

The key to trusting God is to know and believe you are loved by Him. To grow in God and be changed, we need to trust Him. Often He will lead us in ways that we cannot understand, but thankfully, even in those times, we can have a tight grip on His love for us—His never-ending love.

The apostle Paul was convinced that nothing would ever be able to separate us from the love of God in Christ Jesus (see Romans 8:38–39). We should and can have that same absolute assurance of God's never-ending love for us as individuals.

Accept God's love for you, and make that love the basis for your love and acceptance of yourself. Receive His affirmation, knowing that you are changing and becoming all that He desires you to be. Then start enjoying yourself—where you are—on your way to full spiritual maturity.

Prayer of Thanks

Father, thank You for the gift of Your love. No matter what happens, no matter what I may go through, knowing that You love me and You gave Your only Son for my salvation is all that I need. I am so grateful for Your love, and I love You in return.

Mighty to Save

Surely the arm of the Lord is not too short to save, nor his ear too dull to hear.

ISAIAH 59:1 NIV

Thankfully, God's arm can reach us no matter where we are, and we can have the joy of knowing that He delights in helping us. God hears us when we call on Him, and we have the privilege of trusting Him instead of trying to solve our own problems. Ephesians tells us that we should do what the crisis demands and then abide in Christ (see Ephesians 6:13).

When we attempt to do what only God can do, we end up frustrated and feeling miserable. For example, only God can change people, because only He has the ability to change a person's heart. I wasted many years trying to change myself, my husband, my children, and other relatives and friends, but nothing worked until I stopped trying in the flesh and began to trust God. You can believe and trust God, and while you do, He will work, and you can enjoy the wait.

Prayer of Thanks

Father, I thank You that You delight in helping me and that You are working in my life. Help me avoid my own fleshly effort and put my trust in You. I am grateful that the arm of the Lord is mighty to save in my life.

Following God's Lead

He refreshes and restores my life (my self); He leads me in the paths of righteousness [uprightness and right standing with Him—not for my earning it, but] for His name's sake. PSALM 23:3

God never leads us anywhere that He cannot keep us. If God is leading you to deal with some unpleasant situation in your life, don't run from it; trust that God is going to help you and be thankful that you are not alone. He promises to be with you at all times and never to leave you or forsake you.

Surrender can be frightening when we first begin to practice it, because we don't know exactly what the outcome will be if we yield ourselves to God's will. However, once we have surrendered and we begin to experience the peace that passes understanding, we learn quickly that God's way is better than any plan we could ever devise, and we are thankful for His leading. Cast your care on Him today, and let Him take care of you.

Prayer of Thanks

Father, when I am not sure what to do or where to go, I thank You that You have promised to lead me. I submit my will and my plans to You, and I will follow Your plan for my life wholeheartedly.

Safe and Secure

So we take comfort and are encouraged and confidently and boldly say, The Lord is my Helper; I will not be seized with alarm [I will not fear or dread or be terrified]. What can man do to me?

HEBREWS 13:6

A confident person feels safe. He believes he is loved, valuable, cared for, and protected by God's will for him. When we feel safe and secure, it's easy to step out and try new things.

During the initial construction on the Golden Gate Bridge, no safety devices were used, and twenty-three men fell to their deaths. For the final part of the project, however, a large net was used as a safety precaution. Twenty-five percent more work was accomplished after the net was installed. Why? Because the men had the assurance of their safety, so they were free to wholeheartedly serve the project.

When people feel safe, they are free to take a chance on failing in order to try to succeed. As children of God, we are safe and secure, knowing God loves us and has a good plan for our lives. Therefore, we can live with thanksgiving and confidence as we step out boldly each and every day.

Prayer of Thanks

I thank You, God, that You are always there to catch me when I fall. Today, I choose to live with confidence because I know I am safe and secure in Your love. I know nothing will happen to me that I can't handle because You are with me.

Developing the Habit of Being Thankful

Thank [God] in everything [no matter what the circumstances may be, be thankful and give thanks], for this is the will of God for you [who are] in Christ Jesus [the Revealer and Mediator of that will]. 1 THESSALONIANS 5:18

We all have many things to be thankful for in this life. The problem is that we get into the bad habit of taking them for granted, and sadly we often only see what we don't have.

Because we are so used to having plenty of clean water and healthy food, good clothes and nice homes, convenient transportation and excellent education, freedom and safety, and security, we forget that millions of people around the world do not enjoy these wonderful blessings.

I believe that maintaining an attitude of gratitude is something we need to do on purpose. Take time daily to think about your blessings and voice your gratitude to God for His continual goodness in your life. Make gratitude a habit!

Prayer of Thanks

Father, I pray that You will help me develop a habit of thankfulness. I don't want to take any blessing in my life for granted. Help me fully realize how You have blessed me, and I will be extremely grateful for You and Your provision in my life.

God Will Never Stop Loving You

Your mercy and loving-kindness, O Lord, extend to the skies, and Your faithfulness to the clouds.
PSALM 36:5

God is not angry and wrathful, just waiting to punish us for each of our mistakes. Aren't you grateful for that? If we spend our time believing that God is angry with us, we are focusing on what we have done wrong instead of what God has done right in sending His Son to pay for our sins. It is true that we all sin, and God doesn't like sin because of the damaging effects it has on His children. But we must always remember that God is good, kind, merciful, slow to anger, forgiving, faithful, and just.

If you receive God's love right in the midst of your imperfection, it will empower you to change your ways with His help.

God does love you. He has never stopped loving you and He never will.

Prayer of Thanks

I thank You today, Father, that You have always loved me and You always will. Let the truth of Your love guide me in every decision I make today. I thank You that I can enjoy my life, because I know that You are for me and Your love will never leave me.

Enjoying People

... You shall love your neighbor as [you do] yourself. MATTHEW 22:39

God has created all kinds of people with many different temperaments and personalities, and He enjoys them all. Variety seems to be something that God really delights in.

If you haven't given this any thought, take a little time and look around you. God created variety, and He says that what He has created is good; therefore, I urge you to accept those who are different from you and learn to enjoy them as God does.

We encounter a lot of people. Some of them by choice, but a lot of them just end up in our lives as we go through our day. If you want to enjoy each day of your life, be thankful for and choose to enjoy the people you interact with each and every day. If there is someone in your life you are struggling with, try to focus on the good things about them, and start thanking God for them instead of disliking them.

Prayer of Thanks

Father, help me to love and accept the people in my life the way that You do. Thank You that You have made us all different and yet You love us all the same. Today, I choose to appreciate and enjoy the people You bring across my path.

The Beautiful Truth

The Lord is merciful and gracious, slow to anger and plenteous in mercy and loving-kindness. PSALM 103:8

The promise that God is not mad at us is the most freeing truth we will ever find. God knows that we will sin, but He provided the forgiveness of our sins in Jesus. The beautiful truth is that when we no longer focus on our sin, we find that we do it less and less. As we focus on God's goodness, we become more and more like Jesus.

God, through Christ, has totally taken care of the problem of sin—that's something to be thankful for! God urges us not to sin, but He knew we would due to the weakness of our flesh, so He took care of the problem by sending His Son as the sacrifice for our sins.

Jesus paid for everything that we have done and ever will do wrong, and He opened up a new way for us to live and serve God. Not in fear or guilt, but in freedom, love, and intimacy. Receive God's love, mercy, and forgiveness today and be thankful for it!

Prayer of Thanks

Father, I am so grateful that You are not mad at me. I am thankful that You still love me even when I sin. And thank You for the sacrifice of Jesus, making it possible for me to be in relationship with You today.

How to Enjoy a Peaceful Life

For let him who wants to enjoy life and see good days... keep his tongue free from evil... Let him turn away from wickedness and shun it, and let him do right. Let him search for peace... [Do not merely desire peaceful relations with God, with your fellowmen, and with yourself, but pursue, go after them!]

1 PETER 3:10–11

If you want to walk in peace, 1 Peter 3:10–11 gives some helpful instruction. This passage shows four specific principles for those who want to enjoy life and live in peace.

- Keep your tongue from evil: God's Word clearly states that the power of life and death is in the mouth. We can bring blessing or misery into our lives with our words.

- Turn away from wickedness: We should take action to remove ourselves from any wicked environment.
- Do right: The decision to do right closes the door to doing wrong. Don't be weary in doing what is right, for in due season you will reap a harvest (see Galatians 6:9).
- Search for peace: Notice that we must search for it, pursue it, and go after it. Crave peace enough to make whatever changes are necessary to have it.

If you'll live by these principles and choose to be thankful for the peace God provides, then your relationships, attitude, and health will be transformed by the truth of God's Word.

Prayer of Thanks

Father, when I am in a situation that threatens to steal my peace, help me to remember that I can choose peace. I am thankful that You have given me Your peace and that it keeps me from being upset and frustrated.

Disappointed? Get Reappointed

A man's mind plans his way, but the Lord directs his steps and makes them sure.

PROVERBS 16:9

Disappointment occurs when our plans are thwarted by something we have no control over. We can be disappointed by unpleasant circumstances or by people who let us down. When we are disappointed, our emotions initially sink, and then sometimes they flare up in anger. But, thank God, we don't have to be led by emotions.

The next time you are disappointed, pay attention to the activity of your emotions, but instead of letting them take the lead, make the decision to manage them. There is nothing unusual or wrong about initial feelings of disappointment, but it is what we do from that point forward that makes all the difference in the world.

With God on our side, even though we will experience disappointments in life, thankfully, we can always get "reappointed." Trusting that God has a good plan for us and that He orders our steps is the key to preventing disappointment from turning into despair.

Prayer of Thanks

Father, I am so grateful that when I deal with a disappointment, I can trust that You have a better plan than mine. Thankfully, I can trust that You are working even when things don't work out the way I had planned.

God Is Your Reward

After these things, the word of the Lord came to Abram in a vision, saying, Fear not, Abram, I am your Shield, your abundant compensation, and your reward shall be exceedingly great.

GENESIS 15:1

In the world's system, you work hard and then you get your reward. When we follow God's plan and love and obey Him, we also get a reward. God does many wonderful things for us, but the greatest reward we get is an intimate relationship with Him. Trusting God always brings a wonderful reward.

When you get weary and doing what is right is difficult, just look forward to your reward. Jesus didn't look forward to what He would endure on the cross, but He didn't focus on His difficulty. Instead He focused on the good that would come in due time.

Look at Hebrews 12:2: "...*He, for the joy [of obtaining the prize] that was set before Him, endured the cross, despising and ignoring the shame, and is now seated at the right hand of the throne of God.*"

Prayer of Thanks

I thank You, God, that You are my reward. You are the One I turn to, and I know You will always make a way for me. In good times and bad, I will look to You.

It's Wise to Take a Break

The whole earth is at rest and is quiet; they break forth into singing. ISAIAH 14:7

God has created all things for our enjoyment and it begins by enjoying Him. He also wants us to enjoy one another and He wants us to enjoy ourselves. We can be thankful that God wants us to enjoy life, and we can allow that realization to affect how we go through our day.

Next time you have a desire to take a short break from your work and go for a walk in the park, go ahead and do it without feeling guilty or unspiritual. Your work will still be there when you return. If you have been working hard and feel you need a day off, then take it. You will be more fruitful if you take time to be refreshed. If you don't want to end up with all kinds of regret about things you wish you would have done, then get started today making every moment count. Work is good, but it does need to be balanced with rest and taking time to do things you enjoy.

Prayer of Thanks

I am grateful, Father, that You gave us the example of rest. When I'm feeling stressed out and overworked, help me to remember that it is wise to rest and be refreshed. Thank You for the peace and joy that comes when I choose to rest in You.

Know Who You Are

Namely, the righteousness of God which comes by believing with personal trust and confident reliance on Jesus Christ (the Messiah). [And it is meant] for all who believe.

ROMANS 3:22

God's Word assures us that we have tremendous value because of who we are—God's beloved children. What you do is not always perfect. But you can still know who you are—a child of God whom He loves very much. Your worth and value come from the fact that Jesus died for you, not because you do everything perfectly (see Romans 3:22–23; 4:5).

You are special to God, and He has a good plan for your life (see Jeremiah 29:11). You have been purchased with the blood of Christ (see Acts 20:28). The Bible refers to the "*precious blood of Christ,*" indicating that Christ paid a high price to ransom you and me (see 1 Peter 1:19). Believe that you are God's beloved child and never stop thanking Him that you are. That truth will bring healing to your soul and freedom to your life.

Prayer of Thanks

I am grateful, Father, that I have tremendous worth and value in Your sight. Thank You for the blood of Jesus that purchased my salvation. And thank You that I am forever Your child.

Count the Cost

For which of you, intending to build a tower, does not sit down first and count the cost, whether he has enough to finish it.

LUKE 14:28 NKJV

When we make a commitment to walk in love, it usually causes a shift in our lifestyle. Many of our ways—our thoughts, our conversation, our habits—begin to change. For instance, we may be accustomed to spending all our extra money on ourselves only to discover that walking in love requires that we spend some of it on others. We may also experience the same thing when it comes to how we use our time.

Love often requires sacrifice on our part, just as Jesus sacrificed in order to show His love for us. Love is tangible. It is not just an emotional feeling, a spiritual thing that cannot be seen or touched—love is evident to everyone who comes in contact with it. That's how God's love has always been for us. One of the greatest things we have to be grateful for is that God *demonstrated* His love for us (see Romans 5:8).

Prayer of Thanks

I thank You, Father, that You demonstrated Your love by sending Jesus to die for my sins—He paid the ultimate price. I pray that You will give me an opportunity to walk in love today by doing something helpful for someone else.

God's Mercy Is New Every Day

It is because of the Lord's mercy and loving-kindness that we are not consumed, because His [tender] compassions fail not. They are new every morning; great and abundant is Your stability and faithfulness.

LAMENTATIONS 3:22–23

One of the things we can praise God for daily with a heart full of gratitude is that He is determined to have an intimate relationship with each of us. The only way He can do that is if He extends grace, mercy, and forgiveness to us continually. And the only way we can have that relationship with Him is if we learn to continually receive His grace, forgiveness, and mercy.

In case you are wondering, you have not used up all of God's mercy for you. There is still an abundant amount available to you, and there will be as long as you live. God's mercy is new every day! And it is a gift that can only be enjoyed if it is received freely. So thank God for His mercy today, live boldly by His grace, and be all He created you to be.

Prayer of Thanks

Father, thank You for Your mercy, Your compassion, and Your loving-kindness that never fails. I celebrate Your goodness today, and I am so grateful that I can have a personal, intimate relationship with You.

Stable People Get Promoted

Not that I am implying that I was in any personal want, for I have learned how to be content (satisfied to the point where I am not disturbed or disquieted) in whatever state I am. PHILIPPIANS 4:11

Many people feel able and qualified to do a particular thing, and yet they live frustrated lives because the right doors don't seem to open. Why is that? The truth is they may be "able, but not stable." God has given them abilities, but perhaps they have not made the effort to mature in stability of character.

God must be able to trust us, and other people must be able to depend on us, in order for God to increase our level of responsibility. When we are stable and mature, our lives are marked by consistency and thankfulness. We continue to operate in the fruit of the Spirit even when we must endure situations or people that are not what we would like them to be.

Life is not problem-free, and it never will be. Let circumstances do what they will—but as far as you're concerned, be determined to remain stable and thankful in the Lord.

Prayer of Thanks

Thank You, Father, for the way You help bring strength and maturity to my life. Help me to be both "able and stable," so that I might accomplish all You have called me to do.

A Deeper Level of Prayer

...Not My will, but [always] Yours be done.

LUKE 22:42

Asking God for what we need and desire in the natural realm is definitely not wrong, but we should not major on those things. God's Word says that He knows what we need before we ask Him (see Matthew 6:8), so all we need to do is simply ask and let Him know that we are trusting Him to take care of everything that concerns us.

After we ask God for our daily physical needs, we can focus the majority of our prayer time on talking to Him about our spiritual needs, such as spiritual maturity, developing and displaying the fruit of the Spirit, obedience, and walking in love, to name a few. We also have the privilege of praying for other people and being part of their victories.

God is inviting you to a deeper walk with Him and that means you want His will even more than you want your own.

Prayer of Thanks

I thank You, Father, that You hear me every time I pray. Even though I have daily needs that I bring to You, help me to enter a deeper level of prayer. I pray that Your will would be done in my life and in the world around me.

No Longer a Victim

He heals the brokenhearted and binds up their wounds [curing their pains and their sorrows].

PSALM 147:3

You may have been a victim at one point in your life, but you don't have to remain one. You can be emotionally healthy and whole in your soul. The Word of God promises that God will heal your wounds. He will help you…He's waiting to help you.

We all have painful issues from the past that we need to deal with. Many of them were not our fault, and it isn't fair that we should suffer because of other people's behavior. Perhaps you were teased mercilessly as a child and still feel insecure or sensitive because of that old pain. Maybe someone you loved left you without explanation, or you may have been abused in some way. Whatever the source of your pain, be thankful that God loves you and wants to heal you. You don't have to spend your life as a victim; you can have victory and even help bring victory to others.

Prayer of Thanks

Father, I thank You that You are a healer. You have not left me to suffer in the pain of the past—You are healing my wounds and giving me the strength to move forward. Today is a new day, and I am going to enjoy every minute of it!

Our Thoughts Affect Our Attitude

[Let your] love be sincere (a real thing); hate what is evil [loathe all ungodliness, turn in horror from wickedness], but hold fast to that which is good. Love one another with brotherly affection [as members of one family], giving precedence and showing honor to one another.

ROMANS 12:9–10

If we allow our thoughts about a person to be negative, our attitude and behavior toward that person will also be negative. In order to love people, we must make a decision to think good thoughts about them.

God's Word teaches us to always believe the best of people. Our love should be sincere. If we are praying for an individual but thinking negative thoughts about what he is like and how he will probably never change, our prayers will be negated by our negative thinking.

It is important to have a loving attitude toward people, an attitude that is filled with mercy and kindness. A right attitude begins with right thinking. We can be grateful God has that attitude toward us, and we can be determined to have the same attitude toward others.

Prayer of Thanks

Father, I thank You that You love me enough to think good thoughts about me. Help me to have that same attitude when dealing with the people in my life. I want to be more like You today.

Love Displays Patience

Love endures long and is patient.

1 CORINTHIANS 13:4

Love is patient. It is not in a hurry. It always takes time to wait on God, to be grateful for His goodness, and to fellowship with Him. A person whose life is marked by love is patient with people. For example, he takes the time to listen to the elderly person who is lonely and wants to talk. He is willing to listen to the same story four or five times just to show kindness.

The patient person is long-suffering. He can put up with something uncomfortable for a long period of time without complaining. He has the power to endure whatever comes with a good attitude. Patience is a wonderful virtue, but it is a virtue than can only be developed under trial. In other words, we need something to be patient about in order to develop patience, so let's start thanking God each time we need to exercise patience instead of complaining about it.

Prayer of Thanks

Father, as I go through my day today, help me to be patient with those around me. Thank You that You give me the strength and ability to demonstrate godly character. Today, with Your help, I choose to be kind and patient every chance I get.

Because He Lives

We were buried therefore with Him by the baptism into death, so that just as Christ was raised from the dead by the glorious [power] of the Father, so we too might [habitually] live and behave in newness of life.

ROMANS 6:4

There is a popular song titled "Because He Lives," and it is about the fact that Jesus' death and resurrection give us the power and privilege to live life today in victory. Because He lives, we can face whatever comes our way, knowing that God will never allow us to go through more than we can bear, and that He always provides a way out.

Because Jesus lives, we can also have a new attitude toward ourselves. We can stop expecting ourselves to be perfect and learn to enjoy ourselves even in the midst of making mistakes. Jesus died for our mistakes and is alive today to help us grow in Him and be changed by His Word and Holy Spirit. Be grateful for the sacrifice of Jesus, and get a new attitude about yourself! Stop thinking that your failures and mistakes are too much for God. He has cast all of your sins behind His back (see Isaiah 38:17). He isn't looking at them, so you don't need to look at them either!

Prayer of Thanks

I thank You, Father, that Jesus is alive and that the same Spirit who raised Him from the dead dwells in me. Help me face every challenge in life boldly, put my guilt and sin behind me, and embrace Your mercy and forgiveness.

He's Done It Before, He Can Do It Again

David said, The Lord Who delivered me out of the paw of the lion and out of the paw of the bear, He will deliver me out of the hand of this Philistine. And Saul said to David, Go, and the Lord be with you!

1 SAMUEL 17:37

If we remember the miracles God has done in the past with awe and a thankful heart, we will not so easily fall into worry and fear when we have new challenges to face. When David was facing Goliath, he remembered the lion and the bear he had already slain with God's help. Because he remembered what God had done, he had no fear of his situation with Goliath.

Are you facing something right now that looks like a giant in your life? If so, remember God's goodness, be thankful for what He has done before, and choose to believe He can do it again. Write down three things that God has done for you in the past and focus on them instead of your problem. Nothing is impossible for God. Take some time to think about and talk about God's miraculous work. Then you will find courage filling your heart.

Prayer of Thanks

With all my heart, I thank You, Father, for the wonders You have done in the past. And today, I stand in faith, believing that You will work mightily in my life once again. Thank You for being the same yesterday, today, and forever.

God Does Not Forget You

. . . Yes, they may forget, yet I will not forget you. Behold, I have indelibly imprinted (tattooed a picture of) you on the palm of each of My hands; [O Zion] your walls are continually before Me. ISAIAH 49:15–16

Our faith increases when we understand that God remembers us. We can be grateful that we are never forgotten. He keeps one eye on us all the time. It doesn't matter if others have forgotten us or abandoned us; what really matters is that God never will. He remembers all of our prayers. He keeps our tears in a bottle, and does not forget the cry of the humble, poor, and afflicted (see Psalm 56:8; 9:12).

We may never understand why some difficult things happen the way they do, but no matter what happens, God is still

God and He has not forgotten you. He has your picture tattooed on the palm of His hand!

Prayer of Thanks

When I realize, Father, that You will never forget me, my heart is filled with gratitude. I'm thankful that I'm always on Your mind and that You have a wonderful plan for my life.

The Value of Self-Control

Live discreet (temperate, self-controlled), upright, devout (spiritually whole) lives in this present world. TITUS 2:12

As believers in Jesus Christ, God has given us a new nature, but at the same time, we also have to deal with the old nature. When we allow the old nature to rule, we follow feelings, when in reality, we should operate in self-control. Self-control is a fruit of our new nature and, thankfully, it is something that can be developed. Much like we build muscles by using them, we can develop self-control by using it.

Freedom in Christ is a gift to be thankful for, and exercising self-control is a form of freedom, not a type of bondage. You don't have to do what you feel like doing. You're free to do what you know is wise. Discipline and self-control will help you be what you say you want to be but never could be without the help of God's guidance and grace.

Prayer of Thanks

Father, I am so thankful that I don't have to be ruled by emotions or impulses. Thank You that, with Your help, I can live a self-controlled, overcoming life in Christ.

Your Emotions Don't Have a Vote

If any of you is deficient in wisdom, let him ask of the giving God [Who gives] to everyone liberally and ungrudgingly, without reproaching or faultfinding, and it will be given him.

JAMES 1:5

Learn not to ask yourself how you *feel* about things, but instead ask yourself if doing or not doing something is right for you. This is wisdom, and wisdom is a gift from God to be thankful for. You can choose to live by wisdom and decide to do what you know is right.

There may be a certain thing you want to do badly. It might be a purchase you want to make that you know you cannot afford. Your feelings vote yes, but your heart says no. Tell your feelings they don't get to vote. They are too immature to vote and will never vote for what is best for you in the long run. Don't let emotions rule your life and you will enjoy life more.

Prayer of Thanks

I am grateful, Father, that You give me the wisdom I need to make healthy, life-giving choices. Instead of giving my emotions the final say, I am going to look to You and to Your Word for direction in my life. Thank You that Your Word is a lamp unto my feet and a light unto my path.

Getting the Most Out of Your Marriage

Do to others as you would have them do to you.

LUKE 6:31 NIV

I wonder how many millions of people think, *I just don't feel the way I once did about my spouse. I wish I still felt excited about our marriage—that the romantic feelings would come back.* This is when we need to remember: wishing does not do any good; only action changes things.

If you don't feel you are getting anything out of your marriage, perhaps you are not putting enough into it. We usually give our spouses the unfair and unrealistic responsibility of making us happy rather than being grateful for them and choosing to make them happy. In the process, selfishness causes both of you to be unhappy. But you can change that! If you want your marriage or any other relationship to improve, just start being grateful for that person and try to bless them every chance you get.

Prayer of Thanks

Father, thank You for my spouse and for their unique gifts and abilities. Help me to appreciate them and focus on their strengths. Today, I choose to be a blessing and let You take care of everything else.

Let Peace Lead the Way

. . . To all of you that are in Christ Jesus (the Messiah), may there be peace (every kind of peace and blessing, especially peace with God, and freedom from fears, agitating passions, and moral conflicts). 1 PETER 5:14

The Bible teaches that God will lead us by the presence of peace. Thankfully, peace is the umpire in our lives that lets us know if we are in God's will or out of it. You will not experience peace if God is leading in one direction and you are pulling in another; you will feel frustrated and conflicted.

God will not force you to do what is right, but He will show you what to do if you seek Him and ask for His guidance. Then He will leave the choice to you. If you make right choices, you will reap good results that will cause you to be extremely grateful.

If you really want change in your life, take the step to follow God even if doing so is difficult for you. Be led by peace and trust that His plan for your life is better than you could even imagine.

Prayer of Thanks

Thank You, Father, for Your peace that passes all understanding. When I listen for Your voice and follow Your instruction in my life, I know that I will live with a peace and joy beyond compare.

Are You Distracted or Determined?

"Few things are needed—or indeed only one. Mary has chosen what is better, and it will not be taken away from her."

LUKE 10:42 NIV

In order to enjoy the present moment and the gifts it contains, we need to have balanced attitudes toward work. Luke 10:38–42 tells the story of Jesus' visit to the home of two sisters, Mary and Martha.

Martha was overly occupied and too busy (see Luke 10:40). But Mary sat down at Jesus' feet and listened to what He had to say. Martha was distracted with much serving; Mary was thankful Jesus was there and was determined not to miss the beauty of the present moment. And Jesus said that Mary made a better choice than Martha did.

Jesus did not tell Martha not to work; He told her not to be frustrated and have a bad attitude while she worked. Jesus wants us to work hard, but He also wants us to be wise enough to realize when we should stop all activity and not miss the miracle of the moment.

Prayer of Thanks

Thank You, Father, for the way You teach me to live my life in balance. Help me to do the work You have given me to do without letting it become a distraction to my relationship with You. Thank You that I can enjoy moments at Your feet each day.

The Beauty of Praise

I will recount the loving-kindnesses of the Lord and the praiseworthy deeds of the Lord, according to all that the Lord has bestowed on us, and the great goodness to the house of Israel, which He has granted them according to His mercy and according to the multitude of His loving-kindnesses. ISAIAH 63:7

One of the ways *Vine's Expository Dictionary of Old & New Testament Words* defines "praise" is *telling a tale* or *a narration.* In other words, praising God is simply recounting or telling aloud the great things He has done. Praise is beautiful because it magnifies the goodness of God and strengthens us and all those who hear us, enabling us to deal with some of the more unpleasant things in life.

If we are doing nothing more than

sitting at lunch with a friend and speaking about some wonderful things God has done with gratitude in our hearts, we are praising Him. In fact, the Bible says God likes those conversations, and when He hears them, He gets out His book of remembrance and records them (see Malachi 3:16). He does not record our murmuring, grumbling, or complaining, but He records the words we speak when praise is on our lips. Talk to someone today about something good God has done for you!

Prayer of Thanks

Father, I am thankful that my relationship with You is not a complicated list of religious rituals. I can praise You simply by telling others about Your goodness. Thank You for Your blessings in my life—I will praise You all day long.

Jesus Was Perfect for You

If we confess our sins, he is faithful and just and will forgive us our sins and purify us from all unrighteousness. 1 JOHN 1:9 NIV

Perfectionism is fueled with the tyranny of the *shoulds* and *oughts*. It is the constant nagging feeling of never being good enough. We think things like, *I should pray better, read the Bible more, and be kinder*. We instinctively want to be pleasing to God, and we are deeply afraid we aren't. As a result, we believe God is disappointed with us because we don't measure up.

But the pathway to God is not perfection. Some people in a crowd asked what they needed to do to please God, and the answer Jesus gave was, "Believe in the One Whom He has sent..." (John 6:29). More than anything, God wants us to trust Him and believe His Word. You can stop struggling to attain perfection and be thankful that you are righteous before God because of Jesus. You don't have to buy or earn God's love. It isn't for sale—it's free!

Prayer of Thanks

Father, help me to realize that I don't have to earn Your love or approval. I thank You that I am acceptable in Your sight because the sacrifice of Jesus has given me Your righteousness. I will live my life to please You today, not because I have to earn Your love, but because I want to show my love for You.

Growing in Maturity

Rather, let our lives lovingly express truth [in all things, speaking truly, dealing truly, living truly]. Enfolded in love, let us grow up in every way and in all things into Him Who is the Head, [even] Christ (the Messiah, the Anointed One).

EPHESIANS 4:15

God does not expect us to be perfect. In fact, it is precisely because we never could be perfect that He sent Jesus to save us and the Holy Spirit to help us in our daily lives. If we could do it by ourselves, we would not need help. Thankfully, Jesus came to forgive our imperfections and to wipe them away in God's sight. We actually are perfect through Jesus, but we can never be perfect in our own performance.

Jesus did say, "Be perfect, even as

your Father in heaven is perfect" (Matthew 5:48 NLT), but study of the original language reveals that He meant that we should grow into complete maturity of godliness in mind and character. God is not disappointed that we have not arrived at manifesting perfect behavior, but He does delight in finding us growing into maturity.

Prayer of Thanks

Father, I am so thankful that You help me grow into spiritual completeness and maturity. I'm not perfect, but because of Your work, I thank You that I'm okay and I'm on my way!

God Is Good . . . all the Time

. . . No one is [essentially and perfectly morally] good—except God only.

LUKE 18:19

God is good. Goodness is one of His many wonderful character traits to be grateful for. And because goodness is part of His character, we can expect Him to respond in that way every time. God is not good only sometimes; He is good all the time. He is good to people who don't deserve it. He helps us even when we have done dumb things, if we will just admit our mistakes and ask boldly for His help.

We can always ask God for help: "If any of you is deficient in wisdom, let him ask of the giving God [Who gives] to everyone liberally and ungrudgingly, without reproaching or faultfinding, and it will be given him" (James 1:5).

What good news! God will give us wisdom when we have trials—He will show us the way out. Thankfully, all we need to do is ask, and He will give without finding fault with us. Amazing!

Prayer of Thanks

Father, when I am in a situation where I need Your wisdom and Your provision, I ask that You will provide exactly what I need. I thank You that goodness isn't just something You display, it is Your very nature. I love You, and I thank You for Your goodness today.

The Apostle Paul's Thanksgiving List

Now thanks be to God for His Gift, [precious] beyond telling [His indescribable, inexpressible, free Gift]! 2 CORINTHIANS 9:15

Like Jesus, Paul thanked God for many things. He thanked Him that people received him as a minister. He thanked God for his partners. He thanked Him for the churches he founded. He thanked Him for the people in the churches.

In 2 Corinthians 2:14, Paul's grateful heart is on display when he says: *"But thanks be to God, Who in Christ always leads us in triumph [as trophies of Christ's victory] and through us spreads and makes evident the fragrance of the knowledge of God everywhere."*

Paul knew that it is by God's grace that we receive every good thing that He chooses to bestow upon us. We can follow

Paul's example and dedicate our lives to giving thanks to God that He has made us trophies of Christ's victory.

Prayer of Thanks

I thank You, Father, for Christ's victory that makes my salvation and my life in You possible. Like Paul, I want to live each day thankful for Your power and wonderful work in my life. Help me to never forget Your grace is poured out to me.

A Contented Heart Is a Grateful Heart

But godliness with contentment is great gain.
1 TIMOTHY 6:6 NIV

Being content and being grateful go hand-in-hand. People who are discontent have never developed a habit of being appreciative and thankful for the daily blessings in their lives. Think about this: If you were in the hospital right now, you would be content with something as simple as sitting in your own home in your favorite chair, but when you were at home in your chair, perhaps you were not content then either. We always think we will be content when...but why not choose to be content right now?

Even if you don't have what you want or need right now, keep a positive attitude and remain hopeful. Be content with what God has given you, refuse to focus on what you don't have, love others, and stay hopeful concerning every area of your life.

Prayer of Thanks

I thank You, God, that You have given me so many daily blessings. Help me to be content and not to take any of them for granted. Even as I wait on You for the things I am praying for, I choose to be grateful for the blessings I live in each and every day.

God Meets all Your Needs Abundantly

So Abraham called the name of that place The Lord Will Provide. And it is said to this day, On the mount of the Lord it will be provided.

GENESIS 22:14

It is important to develop an abundant mind-set—one that believes God will always provide whatever we need and is thankful in advance that He will do so.

All throughout Scripture, God promises to provide for His children. In fact, in the Old Testament, one of the Hebrew names of God is "Jehovah-Jireh," which means *The Lord Our Provider.* You and I are God's children. He is our Father, and He delights in providing for us just as natural parents delight in helping their children.

Clearly, all the resources of heaven and

earth are at our heavenly Father's disposal, so there is nothing we need that He cannot provide. He loves us and wants to take care of us. In fact, there is no one He would rather share His blessings with than His children. Start thanking God that everything you need is on its way to you right now!

Prayer of Thanks

Father, I am so thankful that You are Jehovah-Jireh. Regardless of how I feel or what my situation looks like, I will look to You and thank You in advance that You will provide for my every need in Your perfect timing.

Turning Any Situation Around for Good

As for you, you thought evil against me, but God meant it for good, to bring about that many people should be kept alive, as they are this day. GENESIS 50:20

Whatever may have happened to us in the past, it does not have to dictate our future. Regardless of what people may have tried to do to us, God can take it and turn it for good. Romans 8:28 (NIV) says, "In all things God works for the good of those who love him..."

In Genesis 37–50, Joseph's brothers meant evil against him. They devised a plan to destroy him by selling him into slavery in Egypt. But in the end, Joseph became second in command to Pharaoh and was used by God to save many lives.

Whatever happens in your life, remember that God is on your side. He will build your life, your reputation, your family, and your career. Be thankful that He is with you, put your confidence in Him, and prepare to be amazed at how He can turn every situation around for His glory!

Prayer of Thanks

I am grateful, Father, that You can turn any and every situation in my life around for good. Help me today to focus on You rather than my past. And thank You that You can take even the most painful parts of life and fashion something beautiful from them.

The Heart of an Eagle

That is why I would remind you to stir up (rekindle the embers of, fan the flame of, and keep burning) the [gracious] gift of God, [the inner fire] that is in you.

2 TIMOTHY 1:6

Do you ever feel like an eagle in a chicken yard? You know in your heart that there is much more within you than you are experiencing and expressing in your life right now. You feel certain God has a great purpose for your life—and you cannot escape or ignore the inner urge to "go for it."

I encourage you today to fan the flame inside you. Fan it until it burns brightly. Never give up on the greatness for which you were created, and never try to hide your uniqueness. Instead, be thankful for it, and be thankful that God has something special in store. Realize your hunger for adventure is God-given; wanting to try something new is a wonderful desire; and embracing life and aiming high is what you were made for. You are an eagle!

Prayer of Thanks

Father, thank You for the dreams and desires You have placed in my heart. Thank You that You have a destiny for me. Today, I will dare to dream of all the wonderful things You have in Your plan for my life.

Prayer Doesn't Have to Be Long

Call to me and I will answer you and tell you great and unsearchable things you do not know. JEREMIAH 33:3 NIV

The length of our prayers really makes no difference to God. All that matters is that we pray the way He is teaching us to pray and that our prayers are Spirit-led, heart-felt, thankful, and accompanied by faith. Throughout the Bible, there are incredibly brief, but powerful, prayers. Here are a few of them:

- Moses prayed for his sister: *"Heal her now, O God, I beseech You!"* (Numbers 12:13).
- Elijah prayed: *"O Lord my God, I pray, let this child's soul come back to him"* (1 Kings 17:21 NKJV).

- Jesus prayed: *"Father, forgive them, for they do not know what they do"* (Luke 23:34 NKJV).

There will be times when you'll pray longer prayers than others, but there is no correlation between how many minutes or hours we pray and whether God hears us. Just one word spoken to Him in faith from a sincere heart can reach His heart and move His hand.

Prayer of Thanks

Thank You, Father, that I can pray to You from my heart, no matter how long or short that prayer may be. I am grateful that I can just be myself when I'm with You.

The Awesome Power of God

Let be and be still, and know (recognize and understand) that I am God. I will be exalted among the nations! I will be exalted in the earth!

PSALM 46:10

If we aren't careful, it is easy to lose sight of the greatness of God. We tend to think of Him and His abilities from our limited perspective. But we must never forget that when the Lord rises up, every knee shall bow and every tongue confess that Jesus Christ is Lord, to the glory of God the Father (see Philippians 2:10–11).

We serve a great and mighty God, and we can be thankful that His greatness is at work in our lives. I encourage you to spend more time in worship and praise, and less time in planning and trying to tell God what He needs to do. Thank Him for His goodness and the fact that His power is at work in your life.

Prayer of Thanks

Father, help me to realize just how powerful and mighty You are. Thank You that no enemy can defeat You and nothing can stop Your work or Your plan in my life.

Listening When God Speaks

The sheep that are My own hear and are listening to My voice; and I know them, and they follow Me. JOHN 10:27

It's important that we don't think that prayer and fellowship with God is us doing all the talking. We can also spend time with Him listening. Prayer is a two-way street. Not only does God hear us, but thankfully, He speaks to us too.

A great exercise to practice while listening to God is to ask Him if there is anyone He wants you to encourage or bless—then be still and listen. You will be surprised at how quickly He responds. He will fill your heart with godly thoughts and goals. You will more than likely have some people come to mind and some creative ideas on how to bless and encourage them. These "ideas" and "thoughts" are God speaking to you. God speaks in many different ways, but one thing is for sure: We will miss His voice if we don't learn to listen.

God has ideas to present to you that you haven't even considered. Listen carefully to Him with a heart that is thankful for His presence. Then follow the advice given in John 2:5—"Whatever He says to you, do it."

Prayer of Thanks

Father, I thank You that You still speak to Your people. I pray that You will show me someone who needs encouragement today. Thank You for speaking to me and allowing me to be a blessing in someone's life.

A Beautiful Exchange

God made him who had no sin to be sin for us, so that in him we might become the righteousness of God.

2 CORINTHIANS 5:21 NIV

The beautiful exchange that takes place when we give our lives to God is something we can always be grateful for. Salvation means that we offer God what we have, and He gives us what He has.

He takes all of our sins, faults, weaknesses, and failures, and gives us His ability, His righteousness, and His strength. He takes our diseases, and sicknesses, and gives us His healing and health. He takes our messed-up, failure-filled past and gives us the hope of a bright future.

In ourselves we are nothing; our own righteousness is like filthy rags or a polluted garment (see Isaiah 64:6). But in Christ, we have a future to be thankful for—one worth looking forward to. The term "in Christ" very simply means that we have placed our faith in Him concerning every aspect of our lives. We are in covenant with Almighty God. What an awesome thought!

Prayer of Thanks

Father, when I am feeling inferior or condemned, help me to remember who I am in Christ. Thank You that I'm forgiven, accepted, righteous, strong, and able because I am found in You.

God Can Use the Most Unlikely of People

For God selected (deliberately chose) what in the world is foolish to put the wise to shame, and what the world calls weak to put the strong to shame. 1 CORINTHIANS 1:27

God often chooses those who are the most unlikely candidates for the job. By doing so, He has a wide open door to show how His grace and power can change human lives.

Each of us has a destiny, and there is absolutely no excuse not to fulfill it. We cannot use our weakness as an excuse, because God says that His strength is made perfect in weakness (see 2 Corinthians 12:9). We cannot use the past as an excuse, because God tells us old things have passed away and all things have become new (see 2 Corinthians 5:17).

How God sees us is not the problem; often it is how we see ourselves that keeps us from succeeding. If you'll see yourself as God sees you, grateful for His transforming power, no obstacle can stop you from His purposes. You are recreated in God's image and resurrected to a brand-new life. Your destiny is just waiting for you to claim it!

Prayer of Thanks

I thank You, God, that You choose the
weak things of the world to shame the wise.
Thank You that there is no excuse that can
keep me from fulfilling my destiny in You.
My life is Yours; have Your way through me.

Everybody Can Help Somebody

See that none of you repays another with evil for evil, but always aim to show kindness and seek to do good to one another and to everybody. 1 THESSALONIANS 5:15

Wishing for something does not produce the results we desire. Whatever God leads you to do, aggressively pursue what needs to be done to achieve those results.

I once heard a story about four people named Everybody, Somebody, Anybody, and Nobody. There was an important job to be done, and Everybody was sure Somebody would do it. Anybody could have done it, but Nobody did. Somebody got angry about that because it was Everybody's job. Everybody thought Anybody could do it, but Nobody realized that Everybody wouldn't do it. In the end, Everybody blamed Somebody when Nobody did what Anybody could have done.

The moral of the story is simple: If you see that something needs to be done and you have the ability to do it, be thankful for the opportunity God has given you and go be the change that everyone else is waiting for.

Prayer of Thanks

Father, I am so thankful for the strengths and gifts You have given me. Show me what You want me to do, and help me go after it with all my heart. With Your help, I know that I can make a difference.

Keep Moving Forward

Wait and hope for and expect the Lord; be brave and of good courage and let your heart be stout and enduring. Yes, wait for and hope for and expect the Lord. PSALM 27:14

If we are going to do anything great for God, and if we are determined never to give up on our dreams, we have to take chances; we have to be courageous. When we face situations that threaten or intimidate us, we need to pray for boldness and a courageous spirit. Feeling fear is never a problem as long as we have more courage than fear!

The spirit of fear will always try to keep us from going forward. For centuries, the enemy has used fear to try to stop people, and he is not going to change his strategy now. But thankfully, we can defeat fear.

We are more than conquerors through Him who loves us (see Romans 8:37). Courage is not the absence of fear; it is pressing forward while the feeling of fear is present. When you feel afraid, ask God to strengthen you, be thankful that He will, and move forward in His strength!

Prayer of Thanks

Thank You, Father, for the gift of boldness. I am grateful for the dreams You have given me and the determination to pursue them. I choose to never give up on the dreams You have placed in my heart.

Stronger and Stronger in the Lord

...I will strengthen and harden you to difficulties, yes, I will help you; yes, I will hold you up and retain you with My [victorious] right hand of rightness and justice.

ISAIAH 41:10

Consider your life. Are there situations you now handle well that would have previously made you feel fearful and anxious? Of course there are. As you have been walking with God, He has been strengthening you and hardening you to difficulties—you can be thankful that you are stronger than you used to be.

In the same way, I can assure and encourage you that some of the things bothering you right now will not affect you the same way in five years. We often struggle when we do certain things for the first time, but after gaining some experience, that struggle is no longer present. We can press through obstacles and never allow circumstances to control us. Instead, trust the Lord and know that He is working in your life in every situation.

Prayer of Thanks

Father, help me to learn from You in every situation I face. I thank You that I am stronger than I used to be, and I thank You that You are making me even stronger through my present circumstances. I put my trust in You, knowing that nothing is too difficult for You.

Grace and Thankfulness

For it is by free grace (God's unmerited favor) that you are saved (delivered from judgment and made partakers of Christ's salvation) through [your] faith. And this [salvation] is not of yourselves [of your own doing, it came not through your own striving], but it is the gift of God. EPHESIANS 2:8

It's difficult—if not impossible—to be truly grateful and thankful until we fully understand the grace of God. Grace is unmerited favor, but it is also God's power made available to us so we can do with ease what we could never do on our own. Once we grasp the fact that every good thing we have comes to us by the goodness of God, what is left for us but gratitude and thanksgiving?

It is hard to give credit to God when we

think that we deserve whatever we receive from Him. But it is hard not to give credit to God when we know that we do not deserve anything we receive from Him—it's all by His grace. Our lives should merely be a thankful response to that.

Prayer of Thanks

Father, I am thankful for Your grace. Without Your grace for my life, I would be without hope. But because of Your grace and power, I am grateful that I can accomplish the plans that You have for me.

The Opportunity to Show His Power

So he said to me, "This is the word of the Lord to Zerubbabel: 'Not by might nor by power, but by my Spirit,' says the Lord Almighty."

ZECHARIAH 4:6 NIV

I was at war with myself for many years. I did not like myself and tried to change myself continually. The more I struggled to change, the more frustrated I became, until the glorious day when I discovered Jesus accepted me just as I was. He, and only He, could make me what He wants me to be.

Don't rate yourself as unusable just because you have some weaknesses. God gives each of us the opportunity to be one of His successes. Our weakness gives Him the opportunity to show His power and His glory.

Instead of wearing yourself out trying to get rid of your weaknesses, give them to Jesus and be thankful that He is going to demonstrate His strength in you. Take your eyes off what you think is wrong with you and look to Him. Draw strength from His boundless might. Let His strength fill up your weaknesses. You cannot successfully change yourself, but you can trust God to do it for you.

Prayer of Thanks

I thank You, Father, that I don't have to be frustrated in life, trying to change myself in my own efforts. Help me today to release my weakness to You, knowing that in my weakness, You show Yourself to be strong.

Quick to Forgive

Be gentle and forbearing with one another and, if one has a difference (a grievance or complaint) against another, readily pardoning each other; even as the Lord has [freely] forgiven you, so must you also [forgive].

COLOSSIANS 3:13

The world is filled with pain and hurting people; and my experience has been that hurting people hurts others. The devil works overtime among God's people to bring offense, strife, and disharmony, but we can be thankful that God gives us a tool to disappoint and defeat the devil: We can be quick to forgive.

Forgiveness closes the door to Satan's attack so that he cannot gain a foothold that might eventually become a stronghold. It can prevent or end strife in our relationships with others. No wonder Scripture tells us over and over that we are to forgive those who hurt or offend us. Jesus made forgiveness a lifestyle, and He taught us to do the same. This is essential to living a joy-filled life.

Prayer of Thanks

Father, I am so thankful for the forgiveness You have given me through Jesus and for the grace to be able to forgive others. Regardless of what others have done to hurt or offend me, today I choose to forgive those who have caused me pain. Thank You for helping me to live out that forgiveness each new day.

Accept Your Children for Who They Are

Rear them [tenderly] in the training and discipline and the counsel and admonition of the Lord. EPHESIANS 6:4

Love and acceptance are the greatest gifts parents can give their children. Acceptance liberates our children and allows them to be who God designed them to be. Love sees the gifts in our children, thanks God for those gifts, and seeks to help them use those gifts for God's glory.

In order to have harmonious and positive relationships with our children, it is absolutely critical that—even when correcting them—we accept them for who they are and that we embrace their unique personalities. Love does not try to force our children to be what we want them to be.

It helps them be what God wants them to be, and to overcome their weaknesses and thrive in using their strengths.

Prayer of Thanks

I thank You today, Father, for the children You have given me and the unique gifts and personalities each one has. Give me wisdom to raise them to the best of my ability for Your glory. I am so grateful that You have placed them in my life.

Change and Transition

For I am the Lord, I do not change; that is why you, O sons of Jacob, are not consumed.
MALACHI 3:6

Everything changes except God—we can be thankful that He is the constant, unchanging source of our lives. Letting all the changes around us cause us to be upset won't keep changes from occurring. People change, circumstances change, our bodies change, our desires and passions change. One certainty in this world is change.

Most changes take place without our permission. But thankfully, with the help of the Holy Spirit, we can choose to adapt. If we refuse to make the transition in our minds and attitudes, then we are making a huge mistake. Our refusal to adapt doesn't change the circumstances, but it does steal our peace and joy. Remember, if you can't do anything about it, cast your care upon the Lord (see 1 Peter 5:7) and trust that He will take care of you.

Prayer of Thanks

I am grateful, Father, that when everything seems to be changing and unsure around me, I can trust that You will never change. Help me to look to You instead of my circumstance. I thank You that You are the foundation of my life.

Following God One Step at a Time

The steps of a [good] man are directed and established by the Lord when He delights in his way [and He busies Himself with his every step]. PSALM 37:23

If you want God to use you, do not let the fear of failure stop you from obeying Him as He leads you. Thankfully, God not only sees where you are, He sees where you can be. He not only sees what you have accomplished, He sees what you will do with His help. God is always leading us to greater things and wants us to look forward to the future. Don't fear the unknown because God knows everything, and you are safe with Him.

Following God is often like walking in a fog. We can only see one or two steps in front of us, but as we take those steps, the next ones become clear. As we trust the Lord, we will have an exciting journey that will make life adventurous and enjoyable—every step of the way.

Prayer of Thanks

Father, thank You that You are directing and establishing my steps. I trust You to lead me one step at a time into the destiny You have for me. Thank You that You have good things planned for my life.

Words Are Fuel for Emotions

He who guards his mouth and his tongue keeps himself from troubles.

PROVERBS 21:23

Words fuel good moods or bad moods; in fact, they fuel our attitudes and have a huge impact on our lives and our relationships. If we speak positive and good things, then we minister life to ourselves. We increase the emotion of joy. However, if we speak negative words, then we minister death and misery to ourselves; we increase our sadness and our moods plummet.

But, thankfully, we can control what words we speak and the quality of our lives. Why not help yourself first thing every day? Don't get up each morning and wait to see how you feel and then talk about every feeling you have to anyone who will listen. If you do that, you are giving your emotions authority over you. Instead, get up praising God for His goodness in your life. Let words of thankfulness fuel a life of peace and joy.

Prayer of Thanks

Father, thank You that I can choose what kind of attitude I am going to have by choosing to speak words of life each day. No matter how I feel or what is going on around me, I'm going to encourage and strengthen my spirit, not my flesh.

Thankful for the Process of Transformation

And all of us, as with unveiled face, [because we] continued to behold [in the Word of God] as in a mirror the glory of the Lord, are constantly being transfigured into His very own image in ever increasing splendor and from one degree of glory to another; [for this comes] from the Lord [Who is] the Spirit.

2 CORINTHIANS 3:18

Transformation doesn't happen overnight, and the process can seem very slow at times. But that doesn't change the fact that one of the benefits of living in a relationship with Jesus is the freedom to forget the past and move ahead into what God has for us.

When you are tempted to condemn yourself over the progress you think you should be making, turn your focus back on Jesus and be thankful that He is doing His work in your life in His perfect timing. Remind yourself, "God loves me and He has a good plan for my life. I haven't arrived yet, but I'm okay and I'm on my way!" Remember that through faith you have been made right with God, and even though you have not arrived at perfection, you are making progress.

Prayer of Thanks

Thank You, Father, that You are transforming my life in Your perfect timing. I trust You, and I choose not to feel condemned or frustrated anymore. You are at work in my life, and I am grateful for that.

God Has Good Things for You

He who did not withhold or spare [even] His own Son but gave Him up for us all, will He not also with Him freely and graciously give us all [other] things? ROMANS 8:32

Some people seem to have the idea that to be a Christian they have to give up everything they enjoy, but that is not true. God is love, He is good, and He wants us to enjoy good things. The Bible says God gives us all things ceaselessly to enjoy (see 1 Timothy 6:17). God loves us so much, He sent His Son, Jesus, to earth to take our sins and give us life, and life more abundantly (see John 3:16; 10:10). That's something to be forever grateful for! Anything God teaches us not to do is only for our benefit. We obey His commands for our own good according to the Word of God.

When we receive Jesus, we receive the kingdom of God within us, and that kingdom is righteousness, peace, and joy in the Holy Spirit (see Romans 14:17). We can choose to continue living with misery, depression, discouragement, fear, worry, anxiety, guilt, and condemnation, but Jesus wants us to receive freedom from those things. God doesn't want us carrying them around any longer. Through Jesus, we can live the joyful, overcoming, abundant life we were meant to live.

Prayer of Thanks

Father, help me to realize that You have nothing but good things in store for my life. Thank You that even when You correct and instruct me, You are showing me a better way to live. I am grateful for Your goodness and the joyful life I can experience in You.

Failure or Stepping-Stone?

Blessed (happy, to be envied) is the man who is patient under trial and stands up under temptation, for when he has stood the test and been approved, he will receive [the victor's] crown of life which God has promised to those who love Him. JAMES 1:12

No one sets out or wants to fail. But "failure" can be an important stepping-stone on the way to success. Failure certainly teaches us what not to do, which is often as important as knowing what we are to do! Making failure positive is all about how we look at it. We can learn to be thankful for our failures.

Many stories have circulated about how many times Thomas Edison failed before he invented the incandescent light bulb. I have heard he tried 700 times, 2,000 times, 6,000 times, and 10,000 times. No matter how many attempts he made, the number is staggering. But he never gave up. Edison is reported to have said that in all his efforts, he never failed—not once; he just had to go through many, many steps to get it right! It takes that kind of determination if you are really going to do anything worthwhile.

Prayer of Thanks

Father, I am thankful that You can take even the failures in my life and do something amazing with them. I believe in faith that You are doing something powerful in my life. I thank You in advance for what I'm learning, even in the tough times.

Developing Godly Courage

Seek the Lord and His strength; yearn for and seek His face and to be in His presence continually! 1 CHRONICLES 16:11

Giving in to a fear of failure will surely keep you from reaching your full potential in life. The good news is, you have no reason to fear failure. First of all, God is with you. And second, there is no such thing as failure if you simply refuse to quit.

Every time you are tempted to fear, be thankful for the times God has been with you and helped you in the past, and remember that He is with you now. He will not fail you or forsake you. He is your God; He will help you and hold you in His hand. He is hardening you to be able to face difficulties. He is building in you the strength, stability, and character you need to press through to the good things He has in store for you, and He is developing in you the courage to never give up.

God may allow us to go through difficulties in order to stretch and expand our capacity for faith. If you have great faith in God, you will be able to accomplish great things in your life.

Prayer of Thanks

Father, when I am in a situation where I begin to feel the fear of failure, I thank You that I don't have to give in to that feeling. I choose to stand firm instead of run. Thank You that You are with me and I have nothing to fear.

Getting Off the Performance Treadmill

In this the love of God was made manifest (displayed) where we are concerned: in that God sent His Son, the only begotten or unique [Son], into the world so that we might live through Him. 1 JOHN 4:9

As long as we are on what I call the "performance treadmill," we will inevitably suffer with disappointment in ourselves. We will feel that we have not performed as expected. We did not get an A on our spiritual tests, we fell short of our goals, we lost our tempers, and now we are disappointed with ourselves, and we are sure that God is disappointed too.

The truth that we can be grateful for is that God already knew that we wouldn't perform as expected when He chose to love us. And it is His love that is the basis for our relationship with Him, not our works. When our relationship with God is a solid foundation in our lives, we will be free to do the best we can, and not get stressed out about our imperfections. It's time to get off the treadmill and run in the freedom of His grace.

Prayer of Thanks

I thank You, Father, that You are not disappointed with me. You knew what You were getting when You chose me. Thank You for choosing me anyway and for loving me perfectly in the midst of my imperfections.

Taking a Peace Inventory

And He came and preached the glad tidings of peace to you who were afar off and [peace] to those who were near.

EPHESIANS 2:17

Do you enjoy a peaceful atmosphere most of the time? Are you thankful and able to keep your peace during the storms of life? Are you at peace with God? Are you at peace with yourself? These are important questions. It is good to take a "peace inventory," checking various areas of our lives to see if we need to make adjustments anywhere.

Jesus said He gave us His peace (see John 14:27). If He gives us His peace, we can gratefully walk in it and enjoy it. The minute we sense that we are losing our peace, we need to make a decision to calm down. I have found that the sooner I calm down, the easier it is to do so. If I allow myself to become extremely upset, it not only takes a toll on me emotionally, mentally, and physically, but it is more difficult to return to peace.

Jesus has provided peace for our lives, but we must appropriate it, not letting our hearts get troubled or afraid. We cannot just passively wait to feel peaceful. We are to pursue peace and refuse to live without it.

Prayer of Thanks

Father, thank You for the gift of peace that You have given me. As I do an inventory of my life, I choose to receive Your peace and live in it each day. I am so grateful that with Your help I can be at rest and enjoy Your peace.

The Gift of Repentance

If My people, who are called by My name, shall humble themselves, pray, seek, crave, and require of necessity My face and turn from their wicked ways, then will I hear from heaven, forgive their sin, and heal their land.

2 CHRONICLES 7:14

When I am headed in the wrong direction, I thank God for the ability to turn around and go in the right direction. That is actually what true repentance is. It is not just a feeling of being sorry, but also a decision to turn and go in the right direction from now on.

We get into trouble through making a series of wrong decisions, and with God's help, we will get our lives straightened out by a series of right decisions. It took more than a day to get into trouble, and it will take more than a day to get out.

Anyone who is ready and willing to make a real investment of time and right choices can see his or her life turn around for the better. God's mercy is new every day. He is waiting to give you mercy, grace, favor, and help; all you have to do is be thankful for that mercy and say "yes" to whatever God is asking of you.

Prayer of Thanks

Thank You, Father, for the new starts You provide in my life. Help me realize when I do wrong, then help me repent and begin again. I am so grateful for Your mercies that are new every morning in my life.

Let God Change You

Create in me a clean heart, O God, and renew a right, persevering, and steadfast spirit within me.

PSALM 51:10

When God shows us a fault, thankfully, He does not expect us to fix it in our own strength. He only wants us to acknowledge it, to agree with Him, to be sorry for it, and be willing to turn away from it. He knows—and we need to know—that we cannot change ourselves. But He will change us if we study His Word and cooperate with His Holy Spirit.

Change of all types is worth celebrating because it is required for progress. The process may not bring joy, but later on it will produce the peaceful fruit of righteousness that God desires and that we can enjoy (see

Hebrews 12:11). Give yourself permission to lighten up, and don't be so concerned about your own perfection. Do what you can do, and let God do what you cannot do.

Prayer of Thanks

Father, help me to be open to Your refining work in my life. I love You and I open my heart to receive Your instruction. Have Your way in my life today. Thank You for changing me to be more like You!

The Power of Laughter

In the world you have tribulation and trials and distress and frustration; but be of good cheer [take courage; be confident, certain, undaunted]! For I have overcome the world. [I have deprived it of power to harm you and have conquered it for you.]

JOHN 16:33

Praise God for laughter—what a wonderful gift! Laughter has tremendous power, and this is something everyone would be wise to do more of. We as Christians tend to be so anxious about everything—our sins, expecting perfection from ourselves, our personal growth, and trying to meet people's expectations. We can carry heavy burdens that Jesus never intended us to carry.

If we would just laugh a little more—*be of good cheer*, "cheer up"—we would find that a little bit of laughter makes our load much lighter. In the world we live in it is easy to find plenty to worry about, but we can choose to purposely find things to laugh about. Take every opportunity you can find to laugh and laugh and laugh!

Prayer of Thanks

Father, I thank You that Your joy is my strength and that laughter is a good medicine. Help me not to carry burdens that You never intended me to carry. Help me to relax and enjoy the power of laughter.

God Cares for You

Casting the whole of your care [all your anxieties, all your worries, all your concerns, once and for all] on Him, for He cares for you affectionately and cares about you watchfully.

1 PETER 5:7

God cares about everything that concerns you, and He wants to personally take care of you. Don't make yourself miserable worrying about things that God wants you to release to Him. When we are anxious today about what may happen tomorrow, or things that happened yesterday, we waste the day God has graciously given us.

The next time you are tempted to get anxious or upset about something—especially about something in the past or the future—think about something God has done for you lately and choose to be grateful. Learn from God's goodness in your past and prepare for your future, but live in the present, remembering that no matter what happens, He always loves you and wants what is best for you.

Prayer of Thanks

Father, I am so thankful that You love me and You care about my life. Today, I choose to not let worry ruin what You have planned for me. I am going to remain grateful that You are with me and You will never leave me.

Get Ready to Get Involved

But he answered, "You give them something to eat." MARK 6:37 NIV

One time, I was asking God to help a friend who was going through a very difficult time. She needed something, so I asked God to provide it. To my surprise, His answer to me was, "Stop asking Me to meet the need; ask Me to show you what you can do."

God wants us to be ready to get involved. He has blessed us with gifts, talents, and abilities. We need to not only be thankful for those things, but we need to use them to bless others.

As you go through your day, I encourage you to pray and watch for opportunities to do what you believe Jesus would do if He were still on earth in bodily form. If you are a Christian, Jesus lives in you now and you are His ambassador. Make sure you represent Him well. Be thankful for your blessings and look for ways to be a blessing to others around you.

Prayer of Thanks

Father, help me to see the needs of those around me. Thank You that You have blessed me in so many ways. Today I pray that You will show me ways I can share those blessings with others.

The Wonder of God's Mercy

Praised (honored, blessed) be the God and Father of our Lord Jesus Christ (the Messiah)! By His boundless mercy we have been born again to an ever-living hope through the resurrection of Jesus Christ from the dead.

1 PETER 1:3

The mercy of God toward each of us is something that we can always be thankful for. Charles Spurgeon once said, "God's mercy is so great that you may sooner drain the sea of its water or deprive the sun of its light or make space too narrow, than diminish the great mercy of God."

Wow! Think about that. Can any one of us drain the sea? We might be able to drain a bathtub or a pool . . . but not the sea! That gives you an idea of God's immense mercy toward us.

Although God does hate sin, and injustice makes Him angry, He is not an angry God! He is full of mercy, not holding our sins against us. We can never do so much wrong that there is no more mercy left for us. Thankfully, where sin abounds, grace does much more abound.

Prayer of Thanks

Father, I am thankful for Your mercy in my life. Even when You are displeased with my sin, I know that You love me and You hear my prayer. Thank You that You forgive my sins and stand ready to help me begin again.

Don't Get Stuck in a Moment

Restore to me the joy of Your salvation and uphold me with a willing spirit.

PSALM 51:12

Your future has no room for your past, and I encourage you not to get stuck in a moment or a time frame in your life that is over. Millions of people miss today because they either refuse to let go of the past or they worry about the future. Things in life like abuse and pain—things that happened to me and to millions of others—are unfortunate to say the least. Such abuses are traumatic and they do affect us, but we can recover.

God is a Redeemer and a Restorer—that's something we can be thankful for every day. He promises to restore our souls. There is a beautiful hope in knowing that if we invite Him in and cooperate with His healing process, God will restore us and give us a lifetime of new, joy-filled, divine moments with Him.

Prayer of Thanks

Father, I thank You that I never have to live stuck in the past. You are a Redeemer and a Restorer, and You want to bring healing in my life. Thank You that my past is over and I have a beautiful future to look forward to.

Your Perfect Heavenly Father

If you then, evil as you are, know how to give good and advantageous gifts to your children, how much more will your Father Who is in heaven [perfect as He is] give good and advantageous things to those who keep on asking Him! MATTHEW 7:11

If someone had an angry father, it is quite natural to view Father God as angry too. Hopefully you are one of the blessed ones who had an awesome earthly dad, but for many, that is not the case.

Children who grow up with angry, absent, or abusive fathers often don't feel safe. They have a feeling of impending doom or danger hanging over them most of the time. But, thank God, your heavenly Father is different from earthly fathers. If your father was absent, you need to know that God will never leave you. If your father was abusive or angry, your heavenly Father wants to give you a double reward for your former trouble (see Isaiah 61:7).

No matter how unfaithful your father may have been to you, I urge you not to let it ruin your life. Make a decision to believe the truth that your heavenly Father is faithful and loves you dearly.

Prayer of Thanks

Father, I thank You that I can look to You to be the parent I never had. Help me to forgive the injustices I endured as a child, and help me to move on to a new, happy, and peaceful life with You. I am grateful that You are a perfect heavenly Father.

Made to Encourage Others

Therefore encourage (admonish, exhort) one another and edify (strengthen and build up) one another, just as you are doing.

1 THESSALONIANS 5:11

One of the best things you can do for someone is encourage them and build them up. Say something positive to the people around you about who they are or how much you appreciate them. Or tell them how much God loves them and wants to bless them. Encouragement is powerful. It makes people feel better in every way.

I remember one time when I got a text message from my youngest son. All it said was, "I love you, Mommy!" At that moment, I literally felt refreshed by his words. They gave me the extra dose of strength I needed that day.

Think about the people you're going to be around today. Be thankful that they are in your life, and ask God to help you speak encouraging words to them. You might be surprised at what a difference it will make, not only for them, but for you too.

Prayer of Thanks

Father, as I am going through my day, I pray that You will show me ways I can encourage and build people up. Thank You for the opportunities You give me to make a difference in the lives of others. I want to seize my opportunities today.

Wisdom and Revelation

I keep asking that the God of our Lord Jesus Christ, the glorious Father, may give you the Spirit of wisdom and revelation, so that you may know him better. I pray that the eyes of your heart may be enlightened in order that you may know the hope to which he has called you, the riches of his glorious inheritance in his holy people, and his incomparably great power for us who believe. EPHESIANS 1:17–19 NIV

Rather than focus on negative things in life, the Bible teaches us to see good things in Christ with the "eyes of your heart." Ephesians 1:17–19 says that the Spirit of wisdom and revelation are important so we may:

- Have knowledge of God, or know God Himself. This is not knowledge gained through education, but revelation.

- Know the hope of our calling, the eternal plan of God and how we fit into it. We can be thankful that God has called us to be His sons and daughters, and as such, we have an inheritance.
- Know that revelation knowledge of God's power is available to us. We can do anything God asks us to do because of the greatness of His power.

Give thanks today that you can know God, have hope, and live in His power!

Prayer of Thanks

I thank You, Father, that You have given me hope in Christ Jesus. Today, I will focus on the good things in my life and listen for Your voice. Thank You that You lead and guide me in the wisdom and revelation of Your Word and Your Holy Spirit.

More Than Things

And my God will liberally supply (fill to the full) your every need according to His riches in glory in Christ Jesus.

PHILIPPIANS 4:19

Many times, we think of needs in terms of the basic necessities of life—food, shelter, clothing, and finances to purchase these things. These represent our physical needs, but God created us to need more than this. Our needs are varied.

We don't simply need money, nourishment, a roof over our heads, and clothes to wear. We also need wisdom, strength, health, friends, and loved ones; and we need the gifts and talents and abilities to help us do what we are supposed to do in life. We need many things, and thankfully, God is willing to meet *all* of our needs as we obey and trust Him. We must believe that He wants to provide for us and then develop an attitude of thanksgiving for what He has done and is doing.

Prayer of Thanks

Father, I thank You today for the gift of Your provision. You don't just meet some of my needs, You meet all of my needs. Thank You for Your complete and total provision that carries me through every day of my life.

Releasing the Weight of Worry

And who of you by worrying and being anxious can add one unit of measure (cubit) to his stature or to the span of his life?

MATTHEW 6:27

It is one thing to know that we should not worry, but it is quite another to be thankful for that truth and then actually stop worrying. One of the things that helped me let go of worry was finally realizing how utterly useless it is. Let me ask you: How many problems have you solved by worrying? Has anything ever gotten any better as a result of you worrying about it? Of course not.

The instant you begin to worry or feel anxious, give your concern to God in prayer. Release the weight of it and totally trust Him to either show you what to do or to take care of it Himself. Prayer is a powerful force against worry. I'm reminded of an old gospel chorus called "Why Worry When You Can Pray?" When you're under pressure, it's always best to pray about your need instead of fretting or complaining about it.

Prayer of Thanks

Father, I thank You that I don't have to live a life full of worry. I thank You that I can come to You in prayer the moment I begin to worry about something and I can cast my care on You. Help me make the wise choice to stop worrying and start trusting You today.

Winning the Battle of the Mind

[Inasmuch as we] refute arguments and theories and reasonings and every proud and lofty thing that sets itself up against the [true] knowledge of God; and we lead every thought and purpose away captive into the obedience of Christ (the Messiah, the Anointed One).

2 CORINTHIANS 10:5

Satan has declared war on God's children, and our minds are the battlefield in which the war is won or lost. Satan loves to put wrong thoughts into our minds—thoughts that are not in agreement with God's Word—hoping we will meditate on them long enough for them to become reality in our lives. We can cast down those wrong thoughts and bring every thought captive into the obedience of Jesus Christ.

Be thankful that you can choose your

own thoughts and that you are not a prisoner to whatever kinds of thoughts just fall into your mind. Think good things that agree with God's Word on purpose. Think about God's love for you and the good plan He has for your life. Think about how you can be a blessing to other people and how you can be a blessing to God by simply being available for Him to work through. Thinking right thoughts will close the door to wrong ones, and in the process, it also closes the door to the devil.

Prayer of Thanks

I thank You, Father, that I am Your child and I am greatly blessed. Today, I choose to think God-honoring thoughts, focusing on Your goodness in my life. I am grateful that I can choose what thoughts I am going to dwell on.

God Leads Us by Peace

Now may the Lord of peace Himself grant you His peace (the peace of His kingdom) at all times and in all ways [under all circumstances and conditions, whatever comes]. The Lord [be] with you all.

2 THESSALONIANS 3:16

People often do things they don't have peace about, and then they wonder why they have big messes in their lives. If we follow God's Word and are thankful for His direction and leading, we will enjoy blessed and peaceful lives. The Bible warns us that we will live in turmoil if we follow our own will and walk in our own ways (see Deuteronomy 28:15–33).

I hear people say things like this too often:

- "I know I shouldn't do this, but..."

- "I know I shouldn't buy this, but…"
- "I probably shouldn't say this, but…"

These words reflect an uncomfortable feeling deep inside, a "knowing" that the action they are taking is not right or good for them, but they won't surrender their wills to God's leading.

Thankfully, when we feel this lack of peace, we can decide to release our plans and submit to God's good plan for our lives.

Prayer of Thanks

I thank You, Father, that You lead me in peace. Help me be sensitive to the leading of Your Spirit as You set the course for my life. Thank You for the peace that comes with knowing You are in control and You have a good plan for me.

Learning to Expect God's Goodness

Every good gift and every perfect (free, large, full) gift is from above; it comes down from the Father.
JAMES 1:17

God delights in providing for His children. We must realize that He loves to bless us and simply learn to live with gratitude for His goodness. Here is a list of things to think and speak regarding God's provision in your life:

- All of my needs are met according to God's riches in Christ Jesus (see Philippians 4:19).
- God blesses me and makes me a blessing to others (see Genesis 12:2).
- I give and it is given unto me, good measure, pressed down,

shaken together, and running over (see Luke 6:38).

- God richly and ceaselessly provides everything for my enjoyment (see 1 Timothy 6:17).
- I serve God, and He takes pleasure in my prosperity (see Psalm 35:27).

Prayer of Thanks

Father, I am grateful for Your abundant provision in my life. I am thankful that You provide for my every need. Help me to trust Your goodness in my life and learn to look to You first to meet my every need.

Expressing the Unconditional Love of God

Hatred stirs up contentions, but love covers all transgressions. PROVERBS 10:12

Thankfully, God does not require us to earn His love, and we must not require others to earn ours. We must realize that love is something we are to become; it is not something we do and then don't do. We cannot turn it on and off, depending on whom we want to give it to and how they are treating us.

Sometimes we pray to be able to love the unlovely, and then do our best to avoid every unlovely person God sends our way. Some people are sent into our lives for the sole purpose of being sandpaper to us. Not only do others have rough edges, but so do we. Learning to walk in love with unlovely people is an important tool God uses to develop our spiritual maturity.

Believe it or not, we should be thankful for all the difficult people in our lives because they help us: they sharpen and refine us for God's use.

Prayer of Thanks

Father, I am grateful for the chance to love people in the same unconditional way that You love me. Help me to love everyone—even those people who are difficult to get along with. I thank You that You are using them to sharpen and refine me for Your use.

Prayer Is Just Like Breathing

Also [Jesus] told them a parable to the effect that they ought always to pray and not to turn coward (faint, lose heart, and give up).

LUKE 18:1

Prayer can be like breathing—regular, easy, second-nature—and we can pray our way through life as part of the way we live. In fact, just as our physical lives are sustained by breathing, our spiritual lives should be maintained by praying.

We can pray out loud or we can pray silently. We can pray sitting down, standing up, or lying on the floor. We can pray while we are moving or while we are being still. We can pray while we are shopping, waiting for an appointment, participating in a business meeting, doing household chores, driving, or taking a shower. These are good times to offer prayers of thanksgiving. We can pray things like, "Thank You, Lord, for everything You're doing," or, "Praise God, I know You're with me in this situation." Prayer is simply talking with God and expressing your heart to Him, and that can be done anytime, anywhere.

Prayer of Thanks

Father, thank You for the gift of prayer. Regardless of what my day looks like, I am so grateful that I can take a moment to pray in every situation, confident that You hear and answer me.

The One with You Is Greater

Be strong and courageous. Be not afraid or dismayed before the king of Assyria and all the horde that is with him, for there is Another with us greater than [all those] with him.

2 CHRONICLES 32:7

The attitude you and I can have in the face of our problems is one of peace and trust. Rather than looking at our past failures, our present difficulties, or our future fears, we can look to the Lord, thankful for His wisdom, strength, and power. We can remind ourselves that no matter how many problems may be facing us, the One who is with us is greater than all those opposing us.

If we depend totally on ourselves or on other people, we set ourselves up for failure and disappointment. The best thing we can do in any situation is lean on God. People may fail and disappoint us, but we can thank God that He will never fail us or forsake us.

Prayer of Thanks

I am grateful, Father, that You will never fail me or forsake me. Thank You for the relationships in my life, but help me to remember to come to You for help before I go to any person. You are my number one source of help and strength.

Grace, Grace, and More Grace

But where sin increased and abounded, grace (God's unmerited favor) has surpassed it and increased the more and superabounded.

ROMANS 5:20

We can never have a problem that is too big for the grace of God. If our problem gets bigger, thankfully, God's grace gets bigger too. If our problems multiply, so that we go from one to two to three or more, the grace of God also multiplies so that we are able to handle them.

No matter what our problems may be, or how many we are facing, we can put our faith in God to solve them. It just takes a grateful heart, confident that our God is big enough to handle whatever we face. What is impossible with man is possible with God.

If there is something that we are supposed to be doing, the Lord will give us the ability to do it. There is no way that He is going to lead us into a situation without empowering us to do what He has called us to do. Whatever you might be facing today, God's grace (enabling power) is yours, and you can do what is required through Christ Who is your strength.

Prayer of Thanks

Father, when I am faced with multiple problems at once, I thank You for Your grace that is sufficient for me. I am grateful that there is no problem, or amount of problems, too difficult for You.

How to Experience Real Change

Therefore we do not become discouraged (utterly spiritless, exhausted, and wearied out through fear). Though our outer man is [progressively] decaying and wasting away, yet our inner self is being [progressively] renewed day after day.

2 CORINTHIANS 4:16

Change does not come through struggle, human effort without God, frustration, self-hatred, self-rejection, guilt, or works of the flesh. Change in our lives comes as a result of having our minds renewed by the Word of God and by trusting God to work in us according to His will. God, Who began a good work in you, will complete it (see Philippians 1:6).

As we agree with God and really believe that what He says is true, it gradually begins to manifest in us. We begin to think differently, then we begin to talk differently, and finally we begin to act differently. This is a process that develops in stages, and we must always remember that while it is taking place, we can be thankful and have an attitude that says, "God is changing me little by little, and I can enjoy myself while He is working."

Prayer of Thanks

Father, thank You for changing me and making me what You want me to be. Thank You for completing the good work You have begun.

Finding God's Will

Therefore do not be vague and thoughtless and foolish, but understanding and firmly grasping what the will of the Lord is.

EPHESIANS 5:17

Most Christians want to know God's will for their lives. Let me share with you what at least a portion of God's will is. I cannot tell you whether or not His will is for you to move to Minneapolis, or where you are to send your children to school, or whether you are supposed to get the lead role in the Easter play at church. But I can give you one absolutely certain way to know and obey God's will for your life: Be thankful.

Be thankful—all the time, no matter what you are going through. That's right; just keep a grateful heart in every circumstance. Sometimes thanksgiving comes easily while other times it is difficult, but if you will develop and maintain an attitude of thanksgiving, you'll be in God's will. How can I be so certain? Because 1 Thessalonians 5:18 says, "In everything give thanks; for this is the will of God in Christ Jesus for you" (NKJV).

Prayer of Thanks

I thank You today, Father, that even while I wait for the specifics of Your will in my life, I can know Your broader will for my life—to always be thankful. Today I choose to live in Your will with a grateful heart, and I know You will reveal Your purposes for my daily life.

Joy with Each New Step

. . . If only I may finish my course with joy.
ACTS 20:24

The apostle Paul wanted to be all God wanted him to be, and he desired to do all God wanted him to do—but he wanted to do it with joy. We should learn to be joyful about our progress, not depressed about how far we still have to go or oppressed by a legalistic attitude about it. We can be thankful for everything God has done and everything He is still going to do. We can learn to look at the positive, not the negative.

One of the side effects of a legalistic approach to God is that people can never be satisfied unless they keep all of the Law. If they fail in one point, they are guilty of all (see James 2:10). Life is sometimes filled with failure, disappointment, and frustration. But one of the benefits of our New Covenant relationship with Christ is the fact that we can be led by the Holy Spirit instead of rules, and we can be joyful during the journey. Our joy is not to be found in our performance, but in Jesus Himself.

Prayer of Thanks

Father, I am thankful that You give me joy for the journey. Even as I am learning and growing in You, I can experience joy each new day. Thank You that I don't have to live under the Law; I am living in Your grace and Your joy every step of the way.

The Best Relationship You Can Have

Behold, I stand at the door and knock; if anyone hears and listens to and heeds My voice and opens the door, I will come in to him and will eat with him, and he [will eat] with Me.

REVELATION 3:20

We have the great privilege of developing a relationship with God and inviting Him to be a vital part of everything we do, every day. That starts with simple prayer—just talking to Him and sharing your life with Him as you go about the things you have to do. Be thankful that His presence is with you, and include Him in your thoughts, in your conversations, and in all your everyday activities.

When you let God out of the Sunday-morning box that many people keep Him in, letting Him invade your Monday,

Tuesday, Wednesday, Thursday, Friday, Saturday, and all day Sunday as well, you'll be amazed at what a difference it will make. Don't try to keep God in a religious compartment; He wants to have free access to every area of your life. He wants to be involved in every part of your life. He desires an intimate relationship with you.

Prayer of Thanks

I thank You, God, that You love me enough to want to be in relationship with me. I want to share every part of my life with You. Help me to remember that You are with me every minute of the day.

Secure Enough to Say "No"

Now am I trying to win the favor of men, or of God? Do I seek to please men? If I were still seeking popularity with men, I should not be a bond servant of Christ (the Messiah).

GALATIANS 1:10

Have you ever felt that you could not be everything that everybody wanted you to be? Have you ever known deep down inside that you really needed to say "no" to a lot of people—but the fear of displeasing them had your mouth saying, "I'll try," while your heart was screaming, "I can't do it!"?

Sometimes, insecure people say "yes," when they really mean "no." Those who succeed at being themselves don't allow others to control them. They are led by a bold heart that knows God loves them, not by the fear of displeasing others or being rejected by them.

We should not get angry at people because they place demands on us, because in reality it is our responsibility to order our lives. Thankfully, we can be secure in Christ and bold enough to say "no" to people when we know it is the right thing to do.

Prayer of Thanks

When I am in a situation, Father, where I am tempted to overcommit to something or someone even though I don't have a peace about it, help me to be secure enough to say "no." I thank You that my security is found in You, not in pleasing others.

Developing Great Faith

And Jesus, replying, said to them, Have faith in God [constantly]. MARK 11:22

Little faith can become great faith as we use it. As we take steps to trust God, we experience His faithfulness and that, in turn, encourages us to have greater faith. As our faith develops and grows, our problems have less power over us and we worry less—that's something to be grateful for.

We can choose to think about what God can do instead of what we cannot do. If we continually think about the difficulty of our situation, we may end up in despair, and that means we feel unable to find a way out. We feel trapped, and then it is easy to panic and begin to do irrational things that only make the problem worse. But the

Bible tells us that God always provides the way out (see 1 Corinthians 10:13). Even though you might not see the way out right now, one does exist and God will reveal it as you trust Him.

Prayer of Thanks

Father, I thank You that my faith can grow stronger as I put my trust in You. You are greater than any problem I will ever face. When I focus on You, I know that worry and despair will fade away. Thank You for Your faithfulness and Your work in my life.

What Does the Bible Say About It?

Now the Berean Jews were of more noble character than those in Thessalonica, for they received the message with great eagerness and examined the Scriptures every day to see if what Paul said was true.

ACTS 17:11 NIV

There are many things that influence our thoughts, and our own desire is one of them. I have discovered when I desire something in a strong way, it is easy for me to think God is telling me to get it. For this reason, we must always check to see if what we feel led to do lines up with the Word of God. God does often lead us by desire, but we want to be sure it is not merely fleshly desire.

Any idea, prompting, or thought that comes to us needs to be compared to the truth of Scripture. The Bible is written as a personal letter to each of us. God speaks to us, ministers to our needs, and directs us in the way we should go in His written Word. So if we think we have heard a word from God, we can check to see if it lines up with Scripture and be thankful that we have the infallible Word of God to live by.

Prayer of Thanks

Father, I am thankful for the truth of Your Word. When I feel a prompting in my spirit, I am grateful that I can make sure it lines up with Scripture. Today, I will listen for Your voice and live in accordance with what You tell me and what You have written in Your Word.

The Best Kind of Friends

The man of many friends [a friend of all the world] will prove himself a bad friend, but there is a friend who sticks closer than a brother. PROVERBS 18:24

We can love everybody, but we cannot be close friends with everybody. People who are upset with you for wanting to move on with God are often those who do not want to go on with Him themselves. Choose to form close relationships with other Christians who share the same values you have. A mature believer in Christ can help you reach new levels of maturity, but a carnal believer may be used as a temptation to cause you to compromise your faith.

God is faithful in all areas, and thankfully, we can ask Him to give us friends who will add to our lives instead of subtract from them. Always be thankful for good friends, for they are indeed a gift from God.

Prayer of Thanks

Father, when I find myself feeling lonely, help me to remember that You will provide the people in my life who will be an encouragement to me. I thank You that You provide everything I need, including friends.

The Gratitude That Comes with Grace

But by the grace (the unmerited favor and blessing) of God I am what I am, and His grace toward me was not [found to be] for nothing (fruitless and without effect).

1 CORINTHIANS 15:10

If you and I think that we deserve what we receive from God because we have earned it by our good works—our great amount of prayer, our daily Bible-reading, our giving—then we are not going to be thankful or grateful. On the contrary, we are going to think that whatever blessing we receive is proof of our own personal holiness.

But when we understand that every blessing we receive is only because of the grace of God, and never because we deserve it, our hearts are transformed. We are filled with gratitude for the goodness of God. There is nothing that can cause us to overflow with thanksgiving and praise more than a revelation of the grace of God that has been freely poured out upon our lives.

Prayer of Thanks

Father, I am grateful today for Your goodness in my life. I know that I haven't done anything to deserve it; You simply bless me because You love me. Thank You for Your perfect, unconditional love.

Let Your Light Shine

Let your light so shine before men that they may see your moral excellence and your praiseworthy, noble, and good deeds and recognize and honor and praise and glorify your Father Who is in heaven.

MATTHEW 5:16

Before we purchase something, we like to check its quality. As we shop, we read labels or we look for certain trademarks (brand names) that have a reputation for being of good quality. That is what people should be able to do with us as disciples of Christ. Love is the trademark (distinctive sign or characteristic) of a Christian. People should be able to identify us not only by what we say, but by how we behave.

As believers, we have a great opportunity to show the world who Jesus is. We do that by walking in His love—the love of the Father that was revealed and expressed in His Son Jesus and is now manifested in us. The Word says, "*Let your light so shine before men,*" and nothing shines brighter than love. Keep in mind that you have the privilege of personally representing Jesus, and be thankful that He will use you to draw people to Him.

Prayer of Thanks

Father, thank You for the example Jesus gave us of how to love others. And thank You for the opportunity I have to share Your love with everyone I come into contact with today. Help me shine brightly in a dark world.

But What if I Miss God?

And your ears will hear a word behind you, saying, This is the way; walk in it, when you turn to the right hand and when you turn to the left. ISAIAH 30:21

Sometimes we experience hesitation in life because we are afraid we might "miss God," or do something wrong as we try to follow Him. Let me encourage you by telling you that if you miss God's will for you somehow, you don't have to worry—He'll find you. I think we all get lost in life at times and need the mercy of God to show up and get us back on the right track. Today, you can thank God that He is faithful to straighten out any crooked path in front of you.

If you are afraid of making wrong decisions about your direction in life, all you have to do is remember how much God loves you and look at the testimonies of the people who have gone before you. The Bible is full of miraculous stories of God's guidance and provision.

When we take a step of faith after praying and seeking God, if we *do* make a mistake, then God will help us get back on track. Thankfully, God can make that so-called mistake somehow work out for our good.

Prayer of Thanks

I thank You, Father, that You see my heart. If I miss Your voice and Your direction in my life, I thank You that You'll find me and get me going in the right direction. I trust Your guidance and I choose today not to live in fear of missing You.

The Strength to Deal with Change

The name of the Lord is a strong tower; the [consistently] righteous man [upright and in right standing with God] runs into it and is safe, high [above evil] and strong.

PROVERBS 18:10

Many people don't like change. Former U.S. president Woodrow Wilson said, "If you want to make enemies, try to change something."

Often when we grow weary or simply become bored with a situation, we get restless and begin to pray: "Oh, God! Something has to change!" Then, when God tries to bring change into our lives, we say, "Lord, what are You doing? I don't think I can take this change!" We often find ourselves caught in the tension between wanting change and fearing change.

Thank God, He never changes. Because He is always the same, we can trust Him through any changing circumstances or situation (see Hebrews 13:8, Malachi 3:6). This should give us great courage and comfort when we face changes in our lives. We do not need to fear change; we can handle it, because God remains the same.

Prayer of Thanks

Father, I am so thankful that I don't have to fear change. You never change and You are my strong tower. I stand on the firm foundation of Your Word and I will live in peace, even when things are changing all around me.

Praying a "Right Now" Prayer

And this is the confidence (the assurance, the privilege of boldness) which we have in Him: [we are sure] that if we ask anything (make any request) according to His will (in agreement with His own plan), He listens to and hears us.

1 JOHN 5:14

We often hear about a prayer need or think about a situation and say to ourselves, *I need to pray about that later when I pray.* That thought is a stall tactic of the enemy. Why not pray right that minute? Procrastination is one of the major things that the devil uses to keep us from ever doing the right thing. Never put off until later what you can do right now!

Prayer would be easy if we just followed our hearts, but Satan wants us to procrastinate because he is hoping that we will forget the matter entirely.

A grateful heart is already focused on the Lord and ready to pray at any moment. Praying as we sense the desire or need to pray is easy to do, and it is the way we can pray continually and stay connected to God in every situation throughout the day.

Prayer of Thanks

Father, I thank You for the power of prayer. When there is a prayer need that comes to my attention, I'm going to talk to You about it immediately. Thank You that You are always ready to hear my prayer.

Humbly Leaning on the Lord

For God sets Himself against the proud (the insolent, the overbearing, the disdainful, the presumptuous, the boastful) [and He opposes, frustrates, and defeats them], but gives grace (favor, blessing) to the humble.

1 PETER 5:5

Humility is knowing we cannot succeed by trusting in ourselves and our own human effort. Instead, we trust in God, thankful that He does what we cannot. As we follow the leading of the Holy Spirit and lean on Him at all times, He always equips us to do what we should be doing. Most human failure comes from people trying to do things in their own strength without relying on God.

I have found that when I feel frustrated, it is because I am exerting fleshly effort trying to do something that only God can do. I suggest that when you feel frustrated that you stop and ask yourself if you are doing the same thing. Works of the flesh equal frustration, and works of the flesh mean that I am working without God.

We can live the joyful, overcoming life God has for us when we realize God helps those who know they cannot help themselves—those who realize they are totally dependent on Him and are grateful that He will provide everything they need.

Prayer of Thanks

Father, I am thankful that I do not have to depend on my own strength or best effort to get through life. Thank You that You are here to guide me and help me each day. I trust You and I place my life in Your hands.

Laying Down Your Life

Anyone who loves his life loses it, but anyone who hates his life in this world will keep it to life eternal. [Whoever has no love for, no concern for, no regard for his life here on earth, but despises it, preserves his life forever and ever.] JOHN 12:25

When we believe God is asking us to do something, we often begin with the questions: *What am I going to have to give up if I do this? If I do this, what will it cost me? If I do this, how uncomfortable am I going to be?*

The truth is that anything we do for God requires an investment. Part of loving Him involves a willingness to lay our lives down for Him. If God has been asking you to do something and you have been procrastinating because you know it will require sacrifice on your part, I urge you to go ahead and do it. Nothing feels better than knowing you have fully obeyed the Lord.

Do not be afraid of sacrifice when God calls you or puts something in your heart that He wants you to do. His plan for your life is greater than anything you can imagine. Be thankful that His plan is best and determine that you will pay the price and pass the test. I assure you, it is worth it.

Prayer of Thanks

I thank You today, Father, that no sacrifice I make for You will ever be without great benefit for my life. Fill me with the faith and strength to do all that You call me to do. I choose to obey Your voice in every single area of my life.

Going Through Is Better Than Getting Stuck

When you pass through the waters, I will be with you, and through the rivers, they will not overwhelm you. When you walk through the fire, you will not be burned or scorched, nor will the flame kindle upon you.

ISAIAH 43:2

We will all go through trying situations in life, some more difficult than others. Many times, we think the phrase "I'm going through something" is bad news, but if we view it properly, we realize *going* through is good; it means we are not stuck! We may be facing difficulties, but we can be thankful that at least we are moving forward.

We will face a variety of things, but those things we go through are the very circumstances, challenges, and situations that make us people who know how to overcome adversity. We do not grow or become strong during life's good times; we grow when we press through difficulties without giving up. When we do what we know is right even when it is difficult, uncomfortable, or inconvenient, we grow spiritually and we are strengthened.

Prayer of Thanks

I am grateful, Father, that even when times are tough, I can depend on You to carry me through. I am grateful that I can face any challenge because You are with me.

The Expectation of Joy

You will show me the path of life; in Your presence is fullness of joy, at Your right hand there are pleasures forevermore.

PSALM 16:11

Joy in life is a wonderful thing to have. We may want to see changes in our circumstances, but we don't have to allow unpleasant situations to make us miserable. We can be grateful that joy makes some of those less-desirable circumstances more bearable. Even when you are going through something that is difficult, you can release joy in your life by *expecting* something good to happen.

Joy can vary in intensity from calm delight to extreme hilarity. It is closely connected to our expectations (what we think and believe). One meaning of joy is: "The passion or emotion excited by the acquisition or expectation of good."* In other words, our joy is affected by how much we expect good things to happen to us. Don't fear or expect bad things to come your way. Pray, believe, and expect God's best for your life—then watch your joy increase.

Prayer of Thanks

Father, I thank You for Your joy. Today I will live in a faithful expectation of Your goodness in my life. I will rejoice in Your love and Your faithfulness.

---

* American Dictionary of the English Language, 1st ed. Facsimile of Noah Webster's 1828 edition, permission to reprint by G. & C. Merriam Company, copyright 1967, 1995 (renewal), by Rosalie J. Slater, s.v. "joy."

Exercising the Muscle of Self-Control

Make every effort to add to your faith goodness; and to goodness, knowledge; and to knowledge, self-control; and to self-control, perseverance; and to perseverance, godliness.

2 PETER 1:5–6 NIV

One of the biggest mistakes we make is to think we have no control over how we feel or what we do. God has given us a spirit of discipline and self-control, and it is called *self*-control because God gives us this tool to control ourselves. We all have it, but do we use it?

Anything we have but never use becomes dormant and powerless. Do you work out regularly? Why do you do that? You exercise to keep your bones and your muscles strong—to guard your health. Thankfully, God has given us self-control, and we can use it to guard our spiritual, emotional, and physical health. But we have to use that muscle in order for it to work properly. When we do, we begin to experience a new level of strength that only self-control can bring. Self-control is your friend, not your enemy. It helps you be the person you truly want to be.

Prayer of Thanks

Father, thank You that I have self-control. Help me to live a self-controlled life and follow Your Spirit rather than my flesh. Thank You that with Your help, I can have victory over the flesh and live in the freedom of Your Spirit.

Talk Yourself into a Better Mood

Death and life are in the power of the tongue, and they who indulge in it shall eat the fruit of it [for death or life].

PROVERBS 18:21

The words you say determine much of your attitude and outlook on life. If you will make a decision that you are going to say as little as possible about your problems and disappointments in life, they won't dominate your thoughts and your mood. It's time we stopped focusing on our problems and started focusing on the goodness of God.

If you talk as much as possible about your blessings and hopeful expectations with a thankful attitude, your frame of mind will match them. Be sure each day is filled with words that fuel love, peace, and joy, not anger, depression, bitterness, and fear. Talk yourself into a better mood! Find something positive to say in every situation, remaining thankful for the blessings of God that are all around you.

Prayer of Thanks

Thank You, Father, for every blessing You have given me. I choose to focus on You and Your provision in my life, rather than focusing on my problems or needs. I know that You are going to provide for me, and so I will keep my focus, my faith, and the words I speak centered around You.

The First Step in Planning

A man's mind plans his way, but the Lord directs his steps and makes them sure.

PROVERBS 16:9

Many times we make a plan, and then pray for it to work. But God wants us to pray first and ask Him for His plan. After we have His plan, then He wants us to trust Him to bring it to pass. We can live with an attitude of praise and thanksgiving, knowing that God's plans always succeed.

Activity birthed out of the flesh, our own effort without God, actually prevents God from showing Himself strong in our lives. The Bible describes that kind of activity as "works of the flesh." I've come to realize that works of the flesh are "works that don't work." That is not the way to live the higher life that God has prepared for us. Pray first, ask God for His plan, and trust Him to work in your life.

Prayer of Thanks

Father, thank You for the gift of prayer. Instead of leaning on my understanding today, I am going to come to You first and ask that You show me Your plan for today and for my life.

Refusing to Strike Out

What then shall we say to [all] this? If God is for us, who [can be] against us? [Who can be our foe, if God is on our side?]

ROMANS 8:31

The story is told of a little boy who was overheard talking to himself in his backyard. He was wearing a baseball cap and carrying a ball and bat: "I'm the greatest hitter in the world," he announced. Then he tossed the ball into the air, swung at it, but missed. "Strike one!" he yelled. He picked up the ball and said again, "I'm the greatest hitter in the world!" He tossed the ball into the air. He swung again and missed. "Strike two!" he yelled. He straightened his cap and said one last time, "I'm the greatest hitter in the world!" He tossed the ball up into the air and swung at it. He missed. "Strike three! Wow!" he exclaimed. "I'm the greatest *pitcher* in the world!"

A thankful, positive, never-give-up attitude will change your outlook and change your life.

Prayer of Thanks

Father, help me to see life in a new way. I thank You that because You are with me, I never have to feel like a failure again. You have a plan for my life. If I swing and miss, it just means that You have something better in store.

Standing Firm

Therefore put on God's complete armor, that you may be able to resist and stand your ground...and, having done all [the crisis demands], to stand [firmly in your place]. Stand therefore [hold your ground].

EPHESIANS 6:13–14

Faith stands firm, but fear takes flight and runs away. We are letting fear rule us if we run from what God wants us to confront. When the Israelites were afraid of Pharaoh and his army, God told Moses to tell them to "fear not; stand still...and see the salvation of the Lord" (Exodus 14:13).

We will never see or experience God's delivering power if we run from things in fear. Stand still and see what God will do for you. Trust Him, be thankful for His faithfulness, and give Him a chance to show His power and goodness to you.

When fear knocks on the door, send faith to answer. Don't speak your fears; speak faith. Say what God would say in your situation—say what His Word says, not what you think or feel.

Prayer of Thanks

Help me, Father, to stand firm when I feel anxious or afraid. I thank You that because You are with me, I have nothing to fear. Today, I will choose to stand firm rather than shrink back when I feel fear in my life.

Strength and Weakness

When the righteous cry for help, the Lord hears, and delivers them out of all their distress and troubles. PSALM 34:17

We all have some strengths and some weaknesses. This is true even of the people we read about in the Bible. Paul wrestled with his weaknesses (see 2 Corinthians 12:9), but he learned to be grateful for them because through them, he discovered Christ's strength and grace would be sufficient.

If we want to fully enjoy the life God has given us, we must realize Christ's grace is sufficient for our weaknesses too—and be grateful that it is! With the help of the Holy Spirit, we can know who we are in Christ and not be condemned because of our weaknesses. Lean on the Lord, and trust that His grace and strength are far greater than our weakness.

Prayer of Thanks

Father, I am so thankful that in my weaknesses You show yourself strong. Your strength and Your grace are sufficient for me just as they were for Paul. Thank You for Your daily strength in my life.

Don't Get Distracted, Simply Pray

You shall not need to fight in this battle; take your positions, stand still, and see the deliverance of the Lord... Fear not nor be dismayed. Tomorrow go out against them, for the Lord is with you.

2 CHRONICLES 20:17

Many times God tells us to do something or gives us an assignment and we begin doing it. But then the enemy comes against us, and when we turn to fight him, we turn away from God. Suddenly, the enemy has all our attention. We spend our time fighting him instead of praying and asking God to intervene.

I want you to know this: The enemy is really not your problem; he is God's problem. You will waste your time if you turn your attention away from your God-given assignments and opportunities and begin to focus on the enemy.

Satan knows that if he can distract you, he can ultimately defeat you. God is your defender; He promises to fight your battles for you. So when the enemy begins to stir up a storm in your life, be thankful God has the victory and do these simple things: pray and trust God.

Prayer of Thanks

Father, thank You for the power of prayer. Instead of trying to fight my own battles, I turn them over to You today. I am so grateful that, when the enemy comes in like a flood, I am more than a conqueror through You (see Romans 8:37).

The Resurrection Side of the Cross

I want to know Christ—yes, to know the power of his resurrection and participation in his sufferings, becoming like him in his death.

PHILIPPIANS 3:10 NIV

We can learn to live on the resurrection side of the cross. Jesus wasn't just crucified; thankfully, He was raised from the dead so that we might no longer be stuck in sin, living lowly, wretched, miserable lives.

Often we see a crucifix in a church with Jesus hanging on it. I know it is done to remember and honor Him, and I am not against it, but the truth is that He is not on the cross any longer. He is seated in heavenly places with His Father, and He is enjoying resurrection living.

We can thankfully celebrate that Jesus came to lift us out of the ordinary, out of negative thinking, guilt, shame, and condemnation. He came to take our sin to the cross and defeat it. It has no power over us any longer because we are forgiven—the penalty has been paid. We can live on the resurrection side of the cross and be seated in heavenly places with Him through faith.

Prayer of Thanks

Father, help me to experience the resurrection power of Jesus in my life. Thank You that Jesus conquered sin and death, and because Your Spirit lives in me, I can live an overcoming, victorious life too.

Happiest When Helping

And God is able to bless you abundantly, so that in all things at all times, having all that you need, you will abound in every good work.

2 CORINTHIANS 9:8 NIV

A study on the principle of the Golden Rule was conducted by Bernard Rimland, director of the Institute for Child Behavior Research. Each person involved in the study was asked to list 10 people he knew best and to label them as happy or not happy. Then they were to go through the list again and label each one as selfish or unselfish. Rimland found that all the people labeled happy were also labeled unselfish. "The happiest people are those who help others," he concluded.

God gives us the ability and opportunities to help others all throughout the day.

When we take the time to be a blessing, it causes us to focus less on what we don't have, feel grateful for what we do have, and experience a new level of joy in the process. Don't let a day go by without helping someone.

Prayer of Thanks

Father, I am thankful that You give me opportunities every day to be a blessing to others. You've blessed me with so much. I want to use what You have given me to bless someone else today.

God Is in Love with You

In this is love: not that we loved God, but that He loved us and sent His Son to be the propitiation (the atoning sacrifice) for our sins.

1 JOHN 4:10

The Bible is a record of God's amazing grace and love. The heroes we admire were people just like us. They failed miserably at times, and yet they found love, acceptance, forgiveness, and mercy as free gifts from God. His love drew them into intimate relationships with Him, empowered them to do great things, and taught them to enjoy their lives.

We can be grateful that just as they experienced that acceptance, we can experience it too. God doesn't approve of sin, but He does love sinners and will continue to work with us toward positive change.

Don't waste years living with a fear that God is angry with you. Thankfully, you can receive the amazing, passionate love of God and know that He is not disappointed with you as long as you continue to believe in Him. Your faith pleases Him, and it is what He requires (see John 6:28–29). God loves us because He chooses to and not because we deserve it. Be thankful today that you are loved unconditionally!

Prayer of Thanks

I thank You, Father, that You love and accept me. I can look into Your Word and see that You used men and women who were flawed and imperfect. If You could use them, I know that You can use me too.

A Believing Heart Is a Thankful Heart

Jesus replied, This is the work (service) that God asks of you: that you believe in the One Whom He has sent [that you cleave to, trust, rely on, and have faith in His Messenger].

JOHN 6:29

I think we all know—but need to be reminded on a regular basis—that God desires a thankful people, not a murmuring, grumbling, faultfinding people.

It is interesting to note as we study the history of the nation of Israel that this kind of negative attitude was a major problem that caused them to wander in the wilderness for 40 years before entering the Promised Land. We may call it by many names, but God called it "unbelief."

God's attitude is that if His people really believe Him, then no matter what happens in life, they will know that He is big enough to handle it and to make it work out for their good. Words of faith are filled with joyful expectation, and not with murmuring, faultfinding, and complaining. Joy and peace are the results of a thankful, believing attitude.

Prayer of Thanks

Father, I thank You that You are reminding me that there is blessing in a thankful, believing heart. Help me to trust in You no matter what the circumstances around me look like. I know You will provide for my every need.

Choosing Your Words Carefully

Even a fool when he holds his peace is considered wise; when he closes his lips he is esteemed a man of understanding.

PROVERBS 17:28

The book of Proverbs is filled with Scriptures about holding your tongue because there is wisdom in discretion. Sometimes the wisest thing you can say is nothing at all. Before you start talking about things you feel strongly about, ask yourself how much you really need to say. Get quiet and listen to what *God* is saying. You'll never regret saying what He wants you to say, the way He would say it.

I want to encourage you to concentrate on positive things and be thankful for these things. That will close the door to negative words and attitudes. As Romans 12:21

says, we overcome evil with good. In other words, if we stay busy doing right things, then there will be no room for the wrong ones. So make it your goal to do what is good before God, and enjoy the freedom and victory it brings to your life.

Prayer of Thanks

Father, I am so thankful that I can live in the wisdom You provide. Help me know when to speak up and when to be quiet. If it's a conversation I should stay out of, I thank You that You will help me exercise self-control and be disciplined enough to do so.

Desire Unity

Behold, how good and how pleasant it is for brethren to dwell together in unity!

PSALM 133:1

Bickering between God's people is nothing new. It was a problem in the early Church, just as it is now. Paul strongly encouraged and urged the church toward unity and wrote in Philippians 2:2: "Fill up and complete my joy by living in harmony and being of the same mind and one in purpose, having the same love, being in full accord and of one harmonious mind and intention."

Where there's unity, there's blessing and anointing. When people are thankful for each other and choose to live in unity, they will experience the power of agreement. But the power of God can't work in our lives if we stay bitter and angry toward people. His love can't flow through us if we're holding on to strife and resentment. Peace equals power, and no peace equals no power.

Prayer of Thanks

I thank You today, Father, for the power we can experience when we decide to come together in unity. Today, I choose to put aside strife and arguments in order to pursue peace and unity. I am grateful that You will help me do this in Your strength.

Carried in His Arms

I will say of the Lord, He is my Refuge and my Fortress, my God; on Him I lean and rely, and in Him I [confidently] trust!

PSALM 91:2

At various points in our lives, all of us feel we're getting "out of our depth" or "in over our heads." There are problems all around: A job is lost, someone dies, there is strife in the family, or a bad report comes from the doctor. When these things happen, our temptation is to panic because we feel we've lost control.

But think about it: The truth is that we've never been in control when it comes to life's most crucial elements. The only thing that holds us up—and the thing we can be most grateful for—is the grace of God, our Father, and that won't change.

God is never out of His depth, and therefore, we're safe when we're in life's "deep end" because we can trust that He will always carry us in His arms.

Prayer of Thanks

Thank You, Father, that You are a refuge for me. I know that because You are with me, I can feel safe and secure. Thank You that no matter how difficult life may seem, I can be at peace because You will never let me go.

An Attitude of Obedience

Sacrifice and offering You do not desire, nor have You delight in them; You have given me the capacity to hear and obey [Your law, a more valuable service than] burnt offerings and sin offerings [which] You do not require.

PSALM 40:6

God delights in our obedience. He wants to lead and guide us, but it does no good if we are not prepared to listen and obey. He has given us the capacity both to hear Him and to obey Him. God does not require a higher sacrifice than heartfelt obedience.

Some of what God asks you to do will be exciting, and some will not, but we should be equally prepared to follow Him either way. We can be thankful knowing that what He tells us to do will work out for good, if we will just do it His way.

If you want God's will for your life, I can tell you the recipe in its simplest form: *Pray and obey*. God has given you the capacity to do both.

Prayer of Thanks

Father, I am thankful that You speak to my heart and guide me in the way I should go. Regardless of how difficult it may seem, I want to obey Your voice and trust that Your plan for my life is best. Thank You for loving me and speaking to my heart.

Separating Your "Who" from Your "Do"

But God shows and clearly proves His [own] love for us by the fact that while we were still sinners, Christ (the Messiah, the Anointed One) died for us.

ROMANS 5:8

God wants us to be assured of His love and never allow anything to separate us from it. With a heart full of gratitude, we can rest in the knowledge that God loves us in the good times, and He loves us in the hard times. God loves us on the days we act right, and He loves us on the days we don't act right. Thankfully, God's love is unconditional.

He loves us based not on what we do, but on who we have become in Christ. In other words, we need to know that we are

God's beloved children, and how to separate our "who" from our "do." We won't *do* everything right all the time, but we are still in right-standing with God through Christ. God still loves us every moment of every day. That is something worth celebrating!

Prayer of Thanks

Father, I am grateful that Your love for me is based on who I am in Christ, not on what I do each day. Even though I want to please You with my actions, I thank You that Your love for me is deeper than that. You love me as Your child, and nothing can take away Your love.

The Best Friend You'll Ever Have

No one has greater love [no one has shown stronger affection] than to lay down (give up) his own life for his friends.

JOHN 15:13

Jesus is the best friend you will ever have. Whether or not you feel He is there, He is there for you to depend on in every area of your life. Lean on and trust Him with all your heart and mind. He will take you in the right direction and make your paths straight. You can talk to Him about everything.

Thank Him for the blessings He has given you—including the blessing of His presence. He always understands you and never rejects or condemns you. Nothing is too big for Him to handle, and for that matter, nothing is too small. Although we don't always *feel* God's presence, when we put our trust in Him, we see the result of Him working in our lives.

Prayer of Thanks

Thank You, Father, for the friend I have in Jesus. I believe that I am never alone and I have the best friend I could ever hope for in Christ Jesus. Thank You for Your daily love and presence in my life.

Let God In

For the eyes of the Lord run to and fro throughout the whole earth to show Himself strong in behalf of those whose hearts are blameless toward Him.

2 CHRONICLES 16:9

The closer you grow to God, the easier it is to develop a lifestyle of making the right choices. Philippians 2:12 says to work out your own salvation with fear and trembling. This means after your salvation when you are born again, you build your relationship with God by studying, learning, praying, and fellowshipping with God. You invite Him into every *area* of your life.

God is not willing to live in what I call a "Sunday morning box." He wants to invade every day of your life and be involved in everything you do. Be grateful that God is your partner in life. He delights in helping you, and He especially enjoys just being with you! Acknowledge God in all your ways and He will direct your steps (see Proverbs 3:6).

Prayer of Thanks

Father, I desire to give every part of my life to You. I thank You that Your power is too great to be confined to any one part of my life. Today, I choose to submit every part of my life and everything I have—my time, energy, talents, finances, relationships, and emotions—to You.

Refuse to Be Offended

Good sense makes a man restrain his anger, and it is his glory to overlook a transgression or an offense. PROVERBS 19:11

We have many opportunities every day to get offended; each time we must make a choice. If we choose to live by our feelings, we will never flow in the all-important facet of love called forgiveness. Forgiveness is the antidote for offense, and we can be very thankful that God has provided it as a way for us to keep our peace.

I once read that 95 percent of the time when people hurt our feelings, it was not what they intended to do. We always seem to assume people are attacking us, while the truth is, they are probably just being insensitive to how their behavior is affecting us. Rarely do people stay awake at night planning to be offensive to the people they meet the next day. Stress levels are high in the world today, and frequently people hurt us due to the pressure they feel inside themselves.

"Drop it, leave it, and let it go," is what *The Amplified Bible* says we are to do with offenses (see Mark 11:25). It is important to forgive quickly. Thankfully, the quicker we forgive, the easier it is to do. God is love, and He forgives and forgets. In order to be like Him, we can develop the same habit.

Prayer of Thanks

Father, I am thankful that You have forgiven me of all my sins. I pray that You will help me follow Your example and forgive those people who have hurt me. Thank You for Your strength that makes it possible for me to forgive others and live without offense.

It's Impossible for Love to Fail

But I tell you, Love your enemies and pray for those who persecute you.

MATTHEW 5:44

It is difficult to keep showing love to those individuals who take from us all we are willing to give and who never give anything back. But I want to encourage you not to give up. We are not responsible for how others act, only how we act.

The truth is that God did not give up on us. How could He? He is love, and love never quits—aren't you thankful for that? Love is always right there, doing its job. Love knows that if it refuses to quit, it will ultimately win the victory.

Some people may refuse to receive our love no matter what we do. But that does not mean that love has failed. Love upholds us. It gives us joy. It pleases God when we walk in love.

Prayer of Thanks

Father, when I am faced with a person who doesn't seem to receive love, help me to keep showing them love anyway. I know that no act of love is ever wasted. Thank You that love never fails.

Don't Worry About the Future

So do not worry or be anxious about tomorrow, for tomorrow will have worries and anxieties of its own. Sufficient for each day is its own trouble. MATTHEW 6:34

Worry, fear, and dread are classic "peace stealers." All of them are a total waste of energy; they never produce any good results. And we can resist each of them in the power of the Holy Spirit.

God has equipped us to handle life as it comes, but if we spend today worrying about tomorrow, we find ourselves tired and frustrated. God will not help us worry. Each day has enough for us to consider; we don't need to anticipate tomorrow's situations while we are still trying to live out today.

The only solution to worry is total abandonment to God and His plan. Even when unpleasant things happen, we can thank God that He has the ability to make them work out for our good if we continue to pray and trust Him (see Romans 8:28).

Prayer of Thanks

Father, I am so thankful that I can choose not to worry. Regardless of my circumstances, I can focus on You and trust Your plan for my life. Thank You that You are working all things together for my good.

God's Faithful Provision

Look at the birds of the air; they neither sow nor reap nor gather into barns, and yet your heavenly Father keeps feeding them. Are you not worth much more than they?

MATTHEW 6:26

God is faithful, and because faithfulness is embedded in His character, He cannot fail us or let us down. Experience with God gives us experience with His faithfulness. We all have needs, but we can be thankful that He meets those needs time and again. He may not always do what we would like, but He does do the right thing. He may not be early, but He is never too late.

I have seen God come through multitudes of times during the years I have been serving Him. I can truly say *God is faithful.* He has given me needed strength, answers that came just in time, right friends in right places, open doors of opportunity, encouragement, needed finances, and much more. And He will do the same for you! There is nothing we need that God cannot provide.

Prayer of Thanks

I thank You today, Father, that You are faithful. Your provision is always exactly what I need and exactly when I need it. Help me to look to You for provision in my life. Thank You that You are more than enough for me.

Keep Doing What Is Right

And as for you, brethren, do not become weary or lose heart in doing right [but continue in well-doing without weakening].

2 THESSALONIANS 3:13

History is filled with examples of people who are famous for doing great things—yet if we study their lives, we find that they failed miserably before they succeeded. Their real strength was not their talent as much as it was their tenacity. Consider these examples:

- NBA legend Michael Jordan was once cut from his high school basketball team.
- After his first audition, Fred Astaire received the following assessment: "Can't act. Slightly bald. Can dance a little."

- Best-selling author Max Lucado had his first book rejected by 14 publishers.
- Walt Disney was fired from a newspaper because he lacked ideas.

These people succeeded in a variety of different endeavors, but they had one thing in common: perseverance. A refusal to give up is one of the symptoms of confidence, and thankfully, confidence can be yours in Christ. Keep doing what you believe to be the right thing for you, and eventually you will enjoy the breakthrough you desire.

Prayer of Thanks

I am grateful, Father, that failure can be a learning tool. Help me today to have the confidence and perseverance needed to carry on, even through failure. I thank You that, with You in my life, I will always win as long as I don't quit.

The Free Gift of God's Love

For He foreordained us (destined us, planned in love for us) to be adopted (revealed) as His own children through Jesus Christ, in accordance with the purpose of His will [because it pleased Him and was His kind intent].

EPHESIANS 1:5

There is only one thing you can do with a free gift, and that is receive it and be grateful. I urge you to take a step of faith right now and say out loud, "God loves me unconditionally, and I receive His love!" You may have to say it a hundred times a day before it finally sinks in, but when it does, it will be the happiest day of your life.

To know that you are loved by someone is the best and most comforting feeling in the world. God not only loves you, but He also provides other people who will truly love you. When He does provide, be sure to remain thankful for those people. Having people who genuinely love you is one of the most precious gifts in the world.

Take time to thank God for His love and all the people who love you! It is His gift to you and, I believe, one of the most valuable gifts that you will ever receive.

Prayer of Thanks

Father, thank You for the free gift of Your love. I am grateful that You love me unconditionally and You have put people in my life who love me too. I don't take Your love for granted and, though I can never repay Your love, I want to live my life for You in return.

Faith over Fear

Now faith is the assurance (the confirmation, the title deed) of the things [we] hope for, being the proof of things [we] do not see and the conviction of their reality [faith perceiving as real fact what is not revealed to the senses].

HEBREWS 11:1

"I will not fear" is the only acceptable attitude we can have toward fear. That does not mean we will never feel fear, but it does mean we will not allow it to rule our lives. The Bible says that God has not given us a spirit of fear (see 2 Timothy 1:7).

Fear is not from God, but faith is! We should remember to do everything with a spirit of faith. Faith is confidence in God and a belief that His promises are true. Faith will cause a person to go forward, to try new things, and to be aggressive.

Be firm in your resolve to do whatever you need to do, even if you have to "*do it afraid*"! To "do it afraid" means to feel the fear and do what you believe you should do anyway. Stand in faith, be thankful for God's promises, and boldly pursue what God has put in your heart to do.

Prayer of Thanks

Thank You, Father, that I can live in faith and not in fear. Regardless of the difficulty of the situation I may be facing, I will choose to do what You have called me to do, even if I have to "do it afraid." Thank You for giving me the strength that I need.

Love Isn't Always Convenient

I will not sacrifice to the Lord my God burnt offerings that cost me nothing.

2 SAMUEL 24:24 NIV

If God wants us to help people, why doesn't He make it easy and inexpensive? Let me answer that question with another question. Did Jesus sacrifice anything to purchase our freedom from sin and bondage? Of course He did. He sacrificed everything—and we are eternally thankful for our salvation! One of the ways we can show our gratitude is by giving to help others.

I have learned that true giving is giving in a way that affects us. Giving away our clothes and household items that are old and we are finished with may be a nice gesture, but it is not sacrificial giving. Real giving occurs when we give somebody something that we want to keep, or something that will definitely cost us.

God gave us His only Son because He loves us, so what will love cause us to do? Don't let inconvenience or sacrifice keep you from truly loving others.

Prayer of Thanks

I am grateful, Father, that You loved me so much that You sent Your Son, Jesus, to die for my sins. Help me to remember that love is not self-serving, but it is selfless and sacrificial.

Simplicity and Decisions

But above all [things], my brethren, do not swear, either by heaven or by earth or by any other oath; but let your yes be [a simple] yes, and your no be [a simple] no, so that you may not sin and fall under condemnation.

JAMES 5:12

Decision-making can be simple if we refuse to be double-minded. After making a decision, stand firm, let your "yes" be "yes" and your "no" be "no." Indecision and double-mindedness not only bring confusion and complication, but, as James noted, they also cause condemnation (see James 5:12).

If we believe in our hearts that we should do something and then allow our heads to talk us out of it, it is an open door for condemnation. We often labor over decisions when actually we just need to decide.

Pray for God's wisdom and guidance, and then make decisions without worrying about them. Thankfully, you don't have to live in fear of being wrong. If your heart is right and you make a decision that is not in accordance with God's will and end up going astray, He will forgive you, find you, and get you back on course.

Prayer of Thanks

Father, help me to avoid complicating the process of decision-making. I thank You that You see my heart and You will correct my course if I take a wrong step. I thank You that I can simply follow what I believe You are leading me to do and trust You to protect me in the process.

Having a Childlike Approach to Life

Whoever will humble himself therefore and become like this little child [trusting, lowly, loving, forgiving] is greatest in the kingdom of heaven. MATTHEW 18:4

One thing we all know about children is that they enjoy life. A child can literally enjoy anything. A child can turn work into a game so he is able to enjoy it.

I recall asking my son to sweep the patio when he was about 11 or 12 years old. I looked outside and saw him dancing with the broom to the music playing on the headset he was wearing. I thought, *Amazing! He has turned sweeping into a game. If he has to do it, he is going to enjoy it.*

We should all have that attitude. We may not choose to dance with a broom, but we should choose an attitude of thanksgiving in everything we do and always enjoy all aspects of life.

Prayer of Thanks

When I am in a situation that doesn't seem like a lot of fun naturally, help me, Father, to make the most of it. I thank You that I can enjoy every part of my life, knowing that the joy of the Lord is my strength.

Strengthened Through Praise

Let them confess and praise Your great name, awesome and reverence inspiring! It is holy, and holy is He! PSALM 99:3

There is tremendous power in praise. We gain more and more strength, our faith increases, and the things that are coming to defeat us are destroyed as we praise God. Enjoying good praise and worship music is one of the tools we have available to help us live in an atmosphere of praise.

Every time we have an opportunity—even a minute or two while walking through a parking lot into a store, or waiting in line to pay for an item—take the opportunity to praise and worship God. After a while, praise becomes so natural that it flows out of us without a deliberate decision on our part. We find ourselves singing and thanking God as an automatic response to our awareness of His goodness, mercy, and grace.

Prayer of Thanks

Father, help me get to a place where my natural reaction is praise. Thank You that I can look to You and Your goodness rather than the cares of the world. I am grateful for Your presence and power in my life.

Partnering with God

Be unceasing in prayer [praying perseveringly].
1 THESSALONIANS 5:17

Prayer is the greatest privilege of our lives. It's not something we have to do; it's something we get to do! Prayer is one of the ways we partner with God to see His plans and purposes come to pass in our lives and in the lives of those we love. It is the means by which we human beings on earth can actually enter into the awesome presence and power of God.

Prayer allows us to share our hearts with God, to listen for His direction, to express our thanksgiving, and to know how to discover and enjoy all the great things He has for us. I have heard it said that "all failure is a failure to pray." Communicating with God is indeed the greatest privilege I know, and it is also the simplest privilege I know. Don't make prayer complicated or difficult. Keep it simple and enjoy every moment spent with the Lord in prayer.

Prayer of Thanks

Father, I thank You for the great privilege of coming to You in prayer. It is amazing to think that I can enter into Your presence with thanksgiving today. Thank You, Lord, for hearing my prayer and for guiding me as I go through my day today.

Shine On!

The Lord make His face to shine upon and enlighten you and be gracious (kind, merciful, and giving favor) to you.

NUMBERS 6:25

As you go through your day, ask the Lord to make His face shine upon you. Ask Him to lift up His countenance upon you and give you peace. Ask Him to shine His glory upon you, as He did with Moses. Then let that light so shine before others that they may see it and glorify your heavenly Father (see Matthew 5:16 KJV).

Letting your light shine can be as simple as putting a smile on your face. Practice smiling at others and you will find most of them smiling back. The light of God's glory is in you, but if you never show it outwardly, people won't be blessed. It is amazing what will happen if you will just be thankful, smile, and be nice to people. Show favor as often as you can to as many as you can. By so doing, you will receive favor, because we are told that whatever we sow is what we will reap (see Galatians 6:7).

Prayer of Thanks

I thank You, Father, for the opportunity I have to be a light in a dark world. Let Your light and Your life shine through me for others to see. I am grateful that with Your help, my life can be a blessing to others.

The Trap of Ingratitude

Let this same attitude and purpose and [humble] mind be in you which was in Christ Jesus: [Let Him be your example in humility.]

PHILIPPIANS 2:5

As human beings, we all struggle with selfishness and ingratitude. We can pray and believe God for something, and even be very thankful and grateful for it when we receive it. But it doesn't take us very long until we are no longer thankful and grateful for them, but actually come to think we are entitled to them.

If we aren't careful, we can even develop a demanding attitude in our relationship with the Lord. We can become upset and aggravated when the Lord doesn't give us everything we think we are entitled to. As His children, we do have an inheritance, but a humble attitude is necessary to receive it. A humble attitude pleases God and will keep our hearts grateful for every blessing we receive.

Prayer of Thanks

Father, I am so thankful for Your work in my life. Please help me to keep a humble attitude, never demanding Your goodness. Thank You that You pour out Your favor in my life, not because I've earned it, but simply because You love me and You want to bless me.

Great Expectations

I waited patiently and expectantly for the Lord; and He inclined to me and heard my cry.

PSALM 40:1

Sometimes we expect *nothing*; we merely wait to see what happens and *nothing* does because we have been expecting *nothing.* At other times, we may fall into the trap of expecting to be disappointed because we have been disappointed time and time again in the past, so we are afraid to hope for anything. However, God wants us to have a faith-filled expectation of His goodness, because He can do exceedingly, abundantly above all that dare to ask or think (see Ephesians 3:20).

Developing a very thankful attitude for God's present goodness in your life will open the door for God to do even more.

Let Him know that you expect to see His goodness in your life, not because you deserve it, but because He is good!

The Bible teaches us that God is waiting to bless people, but He is looking for someone who is expecting and believing for His favor (see Isaiah 30:18).

Prayer of Thanks

I thank You today, Father, that You promise in Your Word that You love me and You have a great plan for my life. I am grateful for Your abundant provision, and I stand in faith waiting with a positive expectation of Your goodness.

Staying in Peace

So repent (change your mind and purpose); turn around and return [to God], that your sins may be erased (blotted out, wiped clean), that times of refreshing (of recovering from the effects of heat, of reviving with fresh air) may come from the presence of the Lord.

ACTS 3:19

Peace with God is maintained by never attempting to hide sin. Because hiding sin just causes condemnation and guilt, and neither of those are productive in any way. God knows everything anyway, so it is useless to think we can hide anything from Him. When we make mistakes, we shouldn't withdraw from God, but we should come near to Him, thankful that He promises to restore us.

To repent means to turn away from sin

and return to the highest place. God is not surprised by our weaknesses and failures. Actually, He knew about the mistakes we would make before we made them. All we need to do is admit them because He is faithful to forgive us continually from all sin (see 1 John 1:9). God is waiting for you with open and outstretched arms—always run to Him!

Prayer of Thanks

I am grateful, Father, that You forgive my sins and You bring healing and restoration into my life. I choose to reject the condemnation of the enemy and come to You when I sin and fall short. Thank You that You forgive me and love me through it all.

God's Way Is Always Better

You will guard him and keep him in perfect and constant peace whose mind [both its inclination and its character] is stayed on You, because he commits himself to You, leans on You, and hopes confidently in You.

ISAIAH 26:3

We may not always get things our way in life, but we can trust that God's way is better. God is a good God, and He said that He has good things planned for His children: "For I know the thoughts and plans that I have for you, says the Lord, thoughts and plans for welfare and peace and not for evil, to give you hope in your final outcome" (Jeremiah 29:11).

We do not have to be afraid of harm, because God is not an angry judge; He is not mean. He is good. We can rejoice with thanksgiving, knowing that everything good in life comes from God. He wants us to trust Him, and when we take a step of faith to do so, we will see the goodness of God manifested in our lives. The more we surrender, the better life becomes.

Prayer of Thanks

Father, when I find myself disappointed by my circumstances, help me to remember that You are in control. I thank You that Your plan for my life is so much better than my own plan. I trust You and Your direction for my life.

You Have the Mind of Christ

For who has known or understood the mind (the counsels and purposes) of the Lord so as to guide and instruct Him and give Him knowledge? But we have the mind of Christ (the Messiah) and do hold the thoughts (feelings and purposes) of His heart.

1 CORINTHIANS 2:16

In 1 Corinthians 2:16, we are told we have the mind of Christ. This statement overwhelms many people. If these were not the words of the Bible, they wouldn't believe it. But Paul was not saying we're perfect or we'll never fail. He was telling us that we can think spiritual thoughts because Christ is alive within us. Thankfully, we no longer have to think the way we once did; we can begin to think as He does.

Another way to look at this is to point

to the promise God spoke through Ezekiel: "A new heart will I give you and a new spirit will I put within you, and I will take away the stony heart out of your flesh and give you a heart of flesh. And I will put my Spirit within you" (Ezekiel 36:26–27).

Your mind, heart, and spirit are new in Christ. You are growing spiritually and becoming more like Him each day—that's something to be thankful for!

Prayer of Thanks

Thank You, Father, that You have given me the mind of Christ. I no longer have to dwell on anxious, fearful, insecure thoughts. Because of Jesus, my mind is renewed and I can think positive, joyful, faith-filled thoughts about my life.

Fickle Feelings

And those who belong to Christ Jesus (the Messiah) have crucified the flesh (the godless human nature) with its passions and appetites and desires. GALATIANS 5:24

Feelings are very fickle. They are always changing; they come and go like the waves in the ocean. They are up, then down, and seem to be controlled by some unseen force that we don't understand. If we are wise, we don't go sailing in the ocean when it is wild with waves that appear dangerous, and neither should we follow our emotions when they are wildly changing.

Thankfully, we don't have to be controlled by our feelings. We can live submitted to the Word of God instead. The best thing to do when you're feeling overly emotional is wait for your feelings to settle before taking any action. Take the helm and sail your own ship. Don't just get into the boat with nobody at the helm and merely hope that the waves of life take you somewhere good. Instead of following feelings, trust God and follow His Word if you really want to experience a joyful life.

Prayer of Thanks

Father, I thank You for the gift of Your Word. I am grateful that I don't have to live controlled by my feelings. I choose instead to live according to the promises and instruction in the Word of God.

Condemnation or Conviction

For God did not send the Son into the world in order to judge (to reject, to condemn, to pass sentence on) the world, but that the world might find salvation and be made safe and sound through Him. JOHN 3:17

There is an important difference between condemnation (guilt) and true conviction from God.

Condemnation manifests as a heavy burden that requires us to pay for our faults and mistakes and pushes us down. Conviction is the work of the Holy Spirit, who is showing us that we have sinned and inviting us to confess our sins, to receive forgiveness and God's help to improve our behavior in the future. Condemnation makes the problem worse; conviction is intended to lift us out of the problem.

If you feel conviction, simply thank God for speaking to you, confess your sin to Him, and turn away from that sin. Then...receive God's forgiveness and let go of it! God forgives and forgets, and if you want to experience the joy of redemption that God wants us all to experience, you'll need to let go of it too.

Prayer of Thanks

Thank You, Father, that there is no condemnation in Christ Jesus. When You convict me of sin, help me to bring it to You in repentance without feeling burdened by guilt and condemnation. You have forgiven me, so I choose today to forgive myself as well.

The Wonderful Person God Says You Are

He has made everything beautiful.

ECCLESIASTES 3:11

When we receive Jesus as our Savior, He takes our sin and gives us His righteousness (see 2 Corinthians 5:21). I doubt that many of us understand the full impact of that. At no cost to us, we are made right with God. We can feel right instead of wrong!

Why not take a step of faith today and try saying or thinking something good about yourself. I am not encouraging a wrong kind of pride, but I am encouraging you to be bold enough to believe you are the wonderful person God says you are.

In Psalm 139, David confessed that

he knew God had made him, and then he said, "Wonderful are Your works, and that my inner self knows right well" (v. 14). David was thankful that he had been created by God in a wonderful way—you have been too! Be bold enough to believe that today.

Prayer of Thanks

Father, help me to experience the joy of knowing who I am in Christ. You have created me uniquely and saved me completely. I thank You that I am beautiful in Your sight.

Pray Without Ceasing

Pray at all times (on every occasion, in every season) in the Spirit, with all [manner of] prayer and entreaty. To that end keep alert and watch with strong purpose and perseverance, interceding in behalf of all the saints (God's consecrated people).

EPHESIANS 6:18

To pray at all times is to "pray without ceasing" (1 Thessalonians 5:17 NKJV), but how do we do that? We do it by keeping an attitude of thanksgiving and total dependence upon God as we go about our everyday lives, turning our thoughts toward Him in the midst of doing all the things we have to do.

I believe that God really wants us to live a lifestyle of prayer and that He wants to help us stop thinking about prayer as an event and begin to see it as a way of life, as an internal activity that undergirds everything else we do. He wants us to talk to Him and listen to Him continually—to pray our way through every day with our hearts connected to His.

Prayer of Thanks

Father, I am so grateful that You are always available. I can call on You in prayer all throughout the day, and I will never get a "busy" signal. Help me grow in prayer and let it be one of the greatest enjoyments in my life.

Thankful for God's Correction

Those whom I love I rebuke and discipline. So be earnest and repent.

REVELATION 3:19 NIV

God views conviction, correction, and discipline as something to be celebrated rather than something to make us sad or frustrated. Why should we celebrate when God shows us that something is wrong with us? Enthusiasm sounds like a strange response, but in reality, the fact that we can see something that we were once blind to is good news.

When we make enough progress in our relationship with God that we begin to sense when we are out of His will, then that is something to be thankful for. It is a sign of progress and should be celebrated joyfully. The longer we serve God and study

His ways, the more sensitive we become to His will. We eventually grow to the place where we know immediately when we are saying or doing something that is not pleasing to God, and we have the option of repenting and making a fresh start.

Prayer of Thanks

I am grateful, Father, that You love me enough to bring correction and instruction into my life. Thank You that You are transforming me and making me more like Your Son, Jesus.

Will I Have Enough?

Now to him who is able to do immeasurably more than all we ask or imagine, according to his power that is at work within us.

EPHESIANS 3:20 NIV

One of the strongest and most persistent fears that people experience is the fear that they won't have enough of what they need. We want to feel safe in every area of life. We want to be secure in our belief that we will have what we need when we need it. This fear can lead to an ungrateful heart, because it brings the feeling that there is never enough. It is best to ask God for what we want and need and then focus on what we do have instead of what we don't have.

God's Word says that we are not to fear because He is with us. It is just that simple: "Fear not [there is nothing to fear], for I am with you" (Isaiah 41:10). Thankfully, He has everything we need and He loves us. So like any loving parent, He will provide for us. He has promised to never leave or forsake us. We can be thankful that He never sleeps, He is ever-present, and He keeps watch over us with loving care.

Prayer of Thanks

Father, I am thankful that You provide all that I need and so much more. I refuse to live in fear, wondering if I will have enough. Thank You that You are a God who does immeasurably more than I could ask or imagine.

Sowing Seeds of Victory

Roll your works upon the Lord [commit and trust them wholly to Him; He will cause your thoughts to become agreeable to His will, and] so shall your plans be established and succeed.

PROVERBS 16:3

If you're not happy with the situation you're in right now, will you make the effort to change it? Do you want to be in the same situation this time next year? Or do you want something different? If you want to have something different, ask for the Lord's direction and then start moving that way. You can choose to pay the price on this end to have what you want later on.

You will have to spend some of this year moving toward your goals for next year. As you move forward, you'll need to make tough choices, and you'll come to some painful crossroads. But when you reach these places, press through. If you press through, you can be thankful that God is with you to help and strengthen you. If you begin working toward your goal now, you'll have the victory you long for later on.

Prayer of Thanks

Father, I pray that You will help me be disciplined enough each day to move toward my goals. I thank You that You have a good plan for my life, and if I'll do my part, You will always do Your part.

Victory Is Worth the Cost

For by You I can run through a troop, and by my God I can leap over a wall.

PSALM 18:29

Throughout the Bible, we find the commands of God always come with the promise of reward. God is not a taker; He is a giver. He never tells us to do anything unless it is for our ultimate benefit. I assure you: Everything God ever asks you to do, even if it is difficult, He asks because He has something great in mind for you—but in order to experience it, you will need to press through the hard place.

Don't think or say, "This is just too hard" when you know you need to do something. Be grateful that God never requires you to handle more than you can bear. With every difficulty, He always provides a way to overcome. You never have to say, "There is no way," because He *is* the way (see John 14:6) and He makes a way for you. You can do whatever God calls you to do in life! You have what it takes!

Prayer of Thanks

I am grateful, Father, that You won't ask me to handle more than I can bear. Today, as I press through the difficult areas in my life, I thank You that I am not pressing through alone—You are with me!

Thankful for Revelation from God

And they were completely astonished at His teaching, for He was teaching as One Who possessed authority, and not as the scribes.

MARK 1:22

It's sad to think that some people equate Christianity with just going to church and nothing more. In church, we are taught about God, but thankfully our life in Christ is more than just a weekly trip to church. Being a Christian is more than joining a church. It is a personal relationship with God through Jesus Christ.

To really know the Lord, we must be hungry for the type of knowledge that can only come from God Himself through revelation—this revelation is available through His Word and by His Holy Spirit in a personal and intimate way.

Revelation goes beyond what we think, see, or feel. It is an inner knowledge of God that cannot be taken from us. When we have this inner knowledge of God, we can be grateful and secure, knowing that nothing outward can sway us from our belief in God.

Prayer of Thanks

I am thankful, Father, that I can have a personal, intimate relationship with You. Today, I choose to listen for Your voice and follow Your leading. Thank You for Your revelation in my life.

Jesus Understands Your Weaknesses

For we do not have a High Priest Who is unable to understand and sympathize and have a shared feeling with our weaknesses and infirmities and liability to the assaults of temptation, but One Who has been tempted in every respect as we are, yet without sinning.

HEBREWS 4:15

The Word of God teaches that Jesus understands our weaknesses. He understands them because He took on human flesh in order to identify with us, and He was tempted in every respect as we are. And while He never sinned, He is not shocked when we fail.

It's okay to have weaknesses—it's only human. You are probably asking the same question I did when I dared to believe this freeing truth: "If I think I am free to have weakness, won't it just invite me to sin more?" The answer is no, it won't.

God's grace, and the freedom it offers, never entices us to sin more, but it does entice us to fall radically in love with Jesus. The more we realize that He loves us the way we are, the more grateful we become and the more we love Him. And that love for Him causes us to want to change for the right reason.

Prayer of Thanks

Father, thank You for the gift of grace. And thank You that You love me in spite of my failures and weaknesses. I know that You are strengthening me and making me more like Jesus. I am grateful for Your work, and I trust You every step of the way.

The Beauty of the New Covenant

For this is My blood of the new covenant, which [ratifies the agreement and] is being poured out for many for the forgiveness of sins.
MATTHEW 26:28

The new covenant is something to be forever grateful for. It is a better covenant that is far superior to the old. The old covenant was initiated with the blood of animals, but the new was initiated with the sinless blood of Jesus Christ. Under the new covenant, Jesus fulfilled or kept all of the Law of the old covenant and died in our place to pay for our sins and misdeeds.

Jesus took the punishment that we deserved and promised that if we would believe in Him and all that He did for us, He would forever stand in our place and our responsibility to keep the Law would be met in Him. The old covenant focused on what man could do, but the new covenant focuses on what God has done for us in Jesus Christ. (Read Hebrews 8 and 9 for more study in this area.)

Prayer of Thanks

I thank You, Father, that I can live in the powerful, freeing work of the new covenant. Thank You that You loved me enough to send Jesus to die for my sins. And thank You that I can live in an intimate, personal relationship with You.

When You Give God Your Best

Do your best to present yourself to God as one approved, a worker who does not need to be ashamed and who correctly handles the word of truth. 2 TIMOTHY 2:15 NIV

We can do our best for God, but we cannot offer Him perfection, and we don't have to feel pressure to do so.

I heard a story about a student who turned a paper in to his professor and the professor wrote on the bottom of it, "Is this the best you can do?" Knowing it was not his best, the student did the paper again, and once again the professor gave it back to him with the same phrase at the bottom. This went on for about three rounds and finally when the professor asked if it was the best he could do, he thought for a moment and answered, "Yes, I believe this is the best I can do." Then his professor said, "Good, now I will accept it."

All God wants is our best—He can work with that. We can be thankful that even though our best is not perfect, God can do something perfectly amazing with it!

Prayer of Thanks

Father, I am so thankful that You are pleased when I do my best for You, even though my best is far from perfect. Thank You that when I do my part, You are always faithful to do Your part with my life.

Are You Disappointed with God?

For as the heavens are higher than the earth, so are My ways higher than your ways and My thoughts than your thoughts.

ISAIAH 55:9

Perhaps you feel that God has let you down at some time in your life, or that one of His promises did not come true for you. If so, I urge you to realize that God doesn't always work within our time frame or in the ways that we would choose, but if you continue to trust Him, you will see the goodness of God in your life.

If you'll trust God each day, be thankful for the things He has done for you in the past, and decide to never give up, you will see Him doing amazing things in your life. God's faithfulness surrounds Him. It is part of His character, and we can count on Him to be with us and do all that He has promised to do. Don't let past disappointments hold you back—dare to trust God again today.

Prayer of Thanks

Father, help me to set aside my pain or disappointment and learn to trust You again. I realize that even when I don't understand Your plan, Your plan is still best. Thank You for Your faithfulness and Your love for me.

Faithful to Forgive

. . . Their sins and their lawbreaking I will remember no more.

HEBREWS 10:17

God is always faithful to forgive our sins just as He promised He would. Sometimes people won't forgive us, but God always forgives sin and then forgets it. And we can be thankful to know that there is no limit to God's forgiveness.

People often have limits to what they are willing to forgive or how often they are willing to do it, but God's forgiveness never runs out. People may say they forgive us, and then remind us of what we did that hurt them, but God never reminds us of our past sins, because He has forgotten them (see Hebrews 10:17).

When we are reminded of past sins, it

is not God bringing them to our remembrance; it is Satan, the accuser of God's people. Reject the lies of the enemy, and choose to receive the faithfulness of God to forgive.

Prayer of Thanks

I thank You today, Father, that You are always faithful to forgive. Regardless of how many times I mess up, I know that You love me and You are faithful to forgive my sins. I am grateful for Your forgiveness and I desire to live my best for You in response to Your goodness to me.

Your Unique Prayer

From His dwelling place He looks [intently] upon all the inhabitants of the earth—He Who fashions the hearts of them all, Who considers all their doings.

PSALM 33:14–15

Because God has fashioned our hearts individually, our prayers can flow naturally out of our hearts and be consistent with the way He has designed us. As we develop our individual styles of communication with God, we can learn from people who may be more experienced than we are, but we need to be careful not to make what others do our standard. Thankfully, Jesus is our standard, and He is the only standard we need.

Enjoy your time with the Lord. Don't try to force yourself to do what others do if you are not comfortable with that in your spirit. You don't have to keep up with others or copy their prayer styles. You can go before God with thanksgiving in your heart, knowing that He hears you and loves you just the way you are. You can pray as the "original" He has made you to be.

Prayer of Thanks

Father, I thank You that everything about me is unique—even the way I pray. Help me to shake off comparisons and just come to You with confidence as Your child. I love You, Father, and I love spending time with You.

Believing You Are a Disciplined Person

Rather, he must be hospitable, one who loves what is good, who is self-controlled, upright, holy and disciplined.

TITUS 1:8 NIV

I frequently hear people say, "I am just not a disciplined person," or, "I just don't have any self-control," and they name a certain area like eating, exercising, or keeping things organized. If you are one of these people who believe you are not disciplined, then I want to encourage you to change your thinking.

The apostle Paul stated that God hasn't given us a spirit of fear, but of power, love, and a sound mind, and a spirit of discipline and self-control (see 2 Timothy 1:7). Be thankful—God has already given you the discipline you need! It is time to start renewing your mind by meditating on this thought: *I am disciplined and self-controlled.*

You will never rise above what you believe, and as long as you believe you are not a disciplined person, then you won't be one. Instead, believe God's Word and live in its truth. You have self-control, and you are disciplined!

Prayer of Thanks

Father, I thank You that You have provided all of the discipline and self-control I need. Help me to renew my mind according to the truth of Your Word. I thank You that, with Your help, I can live a disciplined, overcoming life.

When It's Time for Something New

To everything there is a season, and a time for every matter or purpose under heaven.

ECCLESIASTES 3:1

When what you are doing no longer gives you joy—when there is no life in it for you anymore—that is a strong indication that God is finished with whatever He was doing through you. Prayer will help you find out if God is leading you to make changes.

Some individuals don't have any joy because they are trying to do things God is not calling them to do anymore. They are simply trying to ride a dead horse, so to speak. My advice is this: When the horse isn't moving, it is time to dismount!

Seek God's direction and have the boldness to say, "I did things a certain way for a long time, and I was grateful to have the chance to do it, but this isn't the way God is leading me now. I believe God is leading me to do something new."

Prayer of Thanks

Father, thank You for showing me when it is time to do something new. I trust You to lead and guide me, and I know that joy always comes with Your plan. I thank You in advance that You will make it abundantly clear which direction You want me to take.

The Joy of Spiritual Growth

He is the one we proclaim, admonishing and teaching everyone with all wisdom, so that we may present everyone fully mature in Christ.

COLOSSIANS 1:28 NIV

As your relationship with God matures, you will find yourself living less by guidelines, rules, and regulations, and more by the desires of your heart. As you learn more of the Word, you will find His desires fill your heart with thanksgiving and joy. God wants you to know His heart well enough that you will want to follow the prompting, leading, and guidance of the Holy Spirit.

Once you are free in Christ, stand fast in that liberty and do not become ensnared with the joy stealer of legalism, which is the yoke of bondage that you have put off (see Galatians 5:1). God wants to bring you into a new place that is full of freedom, so follow your heart, because that is where His law abides.

Prayer of Thanks

Thank You, Father, that the more time I spend in Your Word, the more I love it. I pray that Your Word would fill my heart so that my desires will begin to line up with Your instruction and direction for my life. Thank You that You are bringing me to maturity in You.

Just Believe

But I fear, lest somehow, as the serpent deceived Eve by his craftiness, so your minds may be corrupted from the simplicity that is in Christ.
2 CORINTHIANS 11:3 NKJV

God's plan for us is actually so simple that many times we miss it. Jesus has told us what to do to begin to discover God's plan: Believe! (See John 1:12; 3:16.)

When God says something to you in your heart, or when you read something in the Bible, you should say: "Thank You, Lord. I believe it. If God says He will prosper me, I believe it (see Jeremiah 29:11). If God says I will reap what I sow, I believe it (see 2 Corinthians 9:6). If He says to pray for my enemies, I believe it, and I am going to do it (see Matthew 5:44). If He says to call things that are not as though they were, I believe it, and I am going to do it (see Romans 4:17 KJV)."

If you choose to start believing God's Word, even before you see your circumstances change, then you will have joy. Simply believe God!

Prayer of Thanks

Father, help me to simplify things today by simply believing Your Word. Thank You for the promises You have given me as Your child. Today, I choose to simply believe that what You have said is true in my life.

Say "Yes" to What Is Really Important

But seek (aim at and strive after) first of all His kingdom and His righteousness (His way of doing and being right), and then all these things taken together will be given you besides.

MATTHEW 6:33

If you want to live a less complicated life, you may have to simplify it by not doing so much. Most people who are stressed and frustrated have become burned out because they try to squeeze too much into their schedules.

So learn to say "no" to a few things. Practice saying it: "No!" It's a simple word that becomes easier to say with each use. And learn to say "yes" only to what is really important in life—the things you truly believe to be God's will for you.

Spend time with your family and your friends. Enjoy God. Don't get too busy to enjoy all God has given you. Take time to laugh and be thankful for life.

Prayer of Thanks

Father, I am so thankful for the things that are truly important in my life. Today, I choose to focus on those things and let go of some of the other things that are distracting me. Thank You that with Your help I can really enjoy my life.

Conflict-Free Relationships

Remind [the people] of these facts and [solemnly] charge them in the presence of the Lord to avoid petty controversy over words, which does no good but upsets and undermines the faith of the hearers.

2 TIMOTHY 2:14

Peace is such an important ingredient to a happy life, but it is not enough to simply desire peace. We must actually pursue peace in our relationship with God and our relationships with others. Paul understood how elusive peace can be unless we diligently seek it, because in several of his letters, he urges believers to live in harmony.

To live in harmony, we should be thankful for each other, make allowances for each other, and overlook each other's mistakes and faults. We should be humble, loving, compassionate, and courteous. Always be willing to forgive quickly and frequently, and don't be easily offended.

Unity, harmony, and agreement are all peaceful, and we will experience them all if we seek them with our whole heart and are willing to be peacemakers as we go through life.

Prayer of Thanks

Father, when I am in a situation where I am tempted to bicker or argue, help me to be a peacemaker instead. I thank You for the fruit of self-control in my life. And thank You that I can live in harmony with those around me.

You Are Invited to a "Come as You Are" Party

It is through Him that we have received grace (God's unmerited favor)... and this includes you, called of Jesus Christ and invited ***[as you are]*** *to belong to Him.*

ROMANS 1:5–6 (EMPHASIS ADDED)

One of the first things we ask when we are invited to a party is, "How should I dress?" Most of us like it best when we feel that we can come as we are. We like it when we can relax and be ourselves. I love this Scripture because of the message of acceptance it brings.

God accepts us as we are and He works with us throughout our lives to help us become all that He wants us to be. Grace meets us where we are but, thankfully, it never leaves us where it found us.

God will work in you by His Holy Spirit and you will be changed! But you don't have to wait to come to Him. Thankfully, you can come right now just as you are. You don't have to stand off in the distance and only hear the music of the party; you are invited to attend.

Prayer of Thanks

I thank You, Father, that You love me just as I am. I know that You are working in my life to bring positive change, but I thank You that You still love me and accept me in the process. Thank You for Your grace that allows me to come to You just as I am.

Receiving an Inheritance

And if we are [His] children, then we are [His] heirs also: heirs of God and fellow heirs with Christ [sharing His inheritance with Him]; only we must share His suffering if we are to share His glory.

ROMANS 8:17

Our view of God, ourselves, and His plan for us is too small. God wants us to come out of smallness and see the greatness of His calling and our inheritance in Him. When we inherit something, it means that we get what someone else worked for. Jesus gained a prize for us. He worked for what we inherit, and all we can do is be grateful and receive it by faith. Nothing else is required.

One step of faith—simply believing and receiving God's goodness—will put you in the middle of the greatest inheritance ever passed from one person to another. That step of faith takes the struggle and frustration out of life. As 1 John 4:17 says, even "as He is, so are we in this world." That is good news to be thankful for!

Prayer of Thanks

Father, I am so thankful that I am Your child. Thank You for every gift and every provision that You have promised. And thank You that I have an inheritance of eternal life with You because of the work of Jesus on my behalf.

Doing Something Great with Your Life

I call heaven and earth to witness this day against you that I have set before you life and death, the blessings and the curses; therefore choose life, that you and your descendants may live.

DEUTERONOMY 30:19

I have often pondered why some people do great things with their lives while others do little or nothing at all. I know that the outcome of our lives is dependent not only upon God, but also upon something in us. Each of us must decide whether or not we will reach down deep inside and find the courage to press past fear, mistakes, mistreatment at the hands of others, seeming injustices, and all the challenges life presents. This is not something anyone else can do for us; we must do it ourselves.

I encourage you to take responsibility for your life and its outcome. Be grateful for God's blessings of the past and believe for even more in the future. What will you do with what God has given you? God gives everyone equal opportunity—you can choose life or death (see Deuteronomy 30:19). It is your choice, and I believe you will make the right one!

Prayer of Thanks

Father, I am thankful for the opportunity to do great things for You. I pray that You will help me make the most of each new day. Thank You that I can dream big. And because You are with me, nothing is impossible.

Becoming Good at Trusting God

The Lord is good, a stronghold in the day of trouble; and He knows those who trust in Him.

NAHUM 1:7 NKJV

We can spend all our time thinking and talking about what is wrong in the world or we can choose to concentrate on the good things. We can focus on what is wrong with a family member, friend, or coworker or we can purposely look for and highlight what is right.

If nine things are wrong and we only see two we feel are right, we can make the two seem larger than the nine—just by what we choose to concentrate on. This is a good time to remind yourself that you can choose your own thoughts. I have heard many people say, "I just can't control my thought life." The truth is that they chose to concentrate on the wrong thoughts.

Choose to concentrate on godly, faith-filled thoughts. Let your first response in any situation be to see the good, not the bad. Speak out loud and say, "I trust God completely. I know He has a plan. He is going to do something good in my life!"

Prayer of Thanks

Father, thank You that there are good things all around me to focus on. Help me see the best in people, not the worst. Thank You that I can choose my thoughts and I can enjoy the life You've given me.

What We Know (Part 1)

[And I pray] that the participation in and sharing of your faith may produce and promote full recognition and appreciation and understanding and precise knowledge of every good [thing] that is ours in [our identification with] Christ Jesus [and unto His glory].

PHILEMON 1:6

When you know the following scriptural truths, you can't help being thankful...

We know that we *are* children of God, and that we *are* called, anointed, and appointed by Him for greatness. We *are* destined to bring glory to God and be molded into the image of Jesus Christ. We *have* (not will have) righteousness, peace, and joy in the Holy Spirit. We *are* forgiven for all of our sins—even ones we haven't done yet—and our names are written in the Lamb's Book of Life. Jesus *has* gone before us to prepare a place for us, so that where He is, we may be also.

We know that until He returns for us, He *has* sent His Holy Spirit as our guarantee of the even greater good things that *are* to come. We *are* guaranteed an inheritance, for it *was* purchased with the blood of Jesus. We *have* a new covenant and *are* offered a new way of living!

Prayer of Thanks

I thank You today, Father, for these promises that I can declare with the authority of Scripture. I know that I am Yours and no one and nothing can separate me from Your love. Thank You for that assurance.

What We Know (Part 2)

[And I pray] that the participation in and sharing of your faith may produce and promote full recognition and appreciation and understanding and precise knowledge of every good [thing] that is ours in [our identification with] Christ Jesus [and unto His glory].

PHILEMON 1:6

When you know the following scriptural truths, you can't help being thankful...

We *are* made new creatures in Christ, old things *have* passed away and all things *have* become brand-new. We *can* let go of past mistakes and press toward the mark of perfection. We know that *God loves us* with an everlasting, unconditional love, and that His mercy endures forever. We know that all things *are* possible with God and we *can* do all things through Christ who is our strength.

We know that God never allows more to come on us than we can bear, but He *always* provides a way out, a safe place to land. We know that *all* things work together for good to those who love God and *are* called according to His purpose, and that what our enemies meant for harm, God intends for good. We know that He *is* our Vindicator, our Redeemer, and Restorer. He makes all things new!

Prayer of Thanks

Father, I pray that those words won't just be something I read, but they would take root deep in my heart. Thank You for Your promises. I believe them and choose to live in them today and from every day forward.

God Will Never Give Up on You

... Yes, I have loved you with an everlasting love; therefore with loving-kindness have I drawn you and continued My faithfulness to you. JEREMIAH 31:3

What your life amounts to is directly connected to what you think of yourself. We need to learn to think like God thinks. We must learn to identify with Christ and the new person He has made us to be.

In Scripture, God uses words such as "beautiful," "honored," "valued," and "precious" when He is speaking of His children. There is no doubt that we are far less than perfect, that we have faults and weaknesses, but God is God and He views us the way He knows we can be.

He sees us as a finished project while we are making the journey. He sees the end from the beginning and is not worried about what takes place in between. He is not pleased with our sin and bad behavior, but He will never give up on us and He always encourages us to press on. God believes in you!

Prayer of Thanks

I am grateful, Father, that You are a good Father who loves me unconditionally. Help me to see myself as You see me. Thank You that even though I am a work in progress, You already have the finished result in mind.

Listening for His Voice

Consequently, faith comes from hearing the message, and the message is heard through the word about Christ.

ROMANS 10:17 NIV

Learning to hear from God is very exciting. God wants to speak to us about the plan He has for our lives. His plan is a good plan, but we are in danger of missing it if we don't learn how to listen to and obey God's voice.

God speaks to us in many ways. He speaks to us through His Holy Spirit dwelling in us, through that "knowing" deep inside us, and through peace. He may also speak through other people, circumstances, wisdom, nature, and even through dreams or visions.

However, the two most prevalent ways God speaks to us are through His Word and the inward witness in our hearts. The Word of God is a valuable gift that we should be thankful for because it is God's direct message to us—it is unchanging and infallible. As you are learning to hear from God, always make sure the inward witness of your heart lines up with Scripture.

Prayer of Thanks

Father, thank You that You still speak to Your children. I pray that You will help me hear You and follow Your direction for my life. Thank You that You are teaching me how to follow Your leading in my life.

You Are the Home of God

Anyone who confesses (acknowledges, owns) that Jesus is the Son of God, God abides (lives, makes His home) in him and he [abides, lives, makes his home] in God.

1 JOHN 4:15

As believers, we have the life of God inside of us. *We are the dwelling place or home of God*. This truth is necessary for each of us to understand in order to enjoy close fellowship and intimacy with God. God takes up residence within us when we give our lives to Jesus, believing in Him as the only Savior and Lord. From that position, He, by the power of the Holy Spirit, begins a wonderful work in us.

We can be thankful that God loves us and chooses to make His home in us. He has the ability to do what He wants, and He chooses to make His home in our hearts. This choice is based not on any good deeds we have done or ever could do, but solely on the grace, mercy, power, and love of God. As believers in Christ, we become God's dwelling place (see Ephesians 3:17; 2 Timothy 1:14).

Prayer of Thanks

Thank You, Father, for the way You take up residence in my heart. You are not distant or out of reach. I thank You that You dwell in me and are involved in every area of my life.

Anger vs. Love

Beloved, let us love one another, for love is (springs) from God; and he who loves [his fellowmen] is begotten (born) of God and is coming [progressively] to know and understand God [to perceive and recognize and get a better and clearer knowledge of Him].

1 JOHN 4:7

Anger is a powerful emotion, but love is much stronger. And love is the model God has displayed for each of us.

- In anger we might criticize, but in love, we encourage.
- In anger we might turn away, but in love, we reach out.
- In anger we might withhold, but in love, we are generous.
- In anger we might glare, but in love, we smile.

- In anger we might blame, but in love, we forgive.

One of the best ways to show your gratitude for God's love is to share that love with others. Don't just be a recipient of God's love; be a dispenser of that love to all those you come in contact with.

Prayer of Thanks

Thank You, Father, for the display of love You have demonstrated for me to follow. I am grateful that You love me, and with Your help I am going to demonstrate that same love to others.

Honest and Heartfelt Prayers

The earnest (heartfelt, continued) prayer of a righteous man makes tremendous power available [dynamic in its working].

JAMES 5:16

If I could only emphasize one thing about prayer, I would tell people that it is so much easier than we think. Thankfully, God has not made prayer complicated; it really is simple. Sometimes people make prayer dry and difficult; sometimes our religious mind-sets and "systems" present prayer in such a way that it seems out of reach for many of us.

I tell you the truth when I say that God desires our prayer lives to be natural and enjoyable. He wants our prayers to be honest and heartfelt, and He wants our communication with Him unencumbered by rules, regulations, obligations, and legalism. He intends for prayer to be an integral part of our everyday lives—the easiest thing we do each day.

Prayer of Thanks

Father, I thank You that I can speak to You naturally and honestly. Thank You that I can talk to You like a friend, and I can know that You are always there when I need You.

Thankful for the Power of Prayer

To whom God was pleased to make known how great for the Gentiles are the riches of the glory of this mystery, which is Christ within and among you, the Hope of [realizing the] glory. COLOSSIANS 1:27

Short, simple prayers can be mighty beyond description, but that does not take away from the fact that prayer is also a grand mystery. Watchman Nee, a Chinese Christian who wrote many profound books while imprisoned for his faith, writes, "Prayer is the most wonderful act in the spiritual realm, as well as a most mysterious affair."

I believe the greatest mystery of prayer is that it joins the hearts of people on earth with God's heart in heaven. Prayer is spiritual and it goes into the unseen realm; it brings things out of that unseen realm into the realm we can see and into the world around us, right where we live.

We can thank God that prayer ushers spiritual blessings into our natural, everyday lives and brings spiritual power to bear on our earthly circumstances. We human beings are the only creatures in our known universe who can stand in the natural realm and touch the spiritual realm.

Prayer of Thanks

I thank You, Father, that You have entrusted to me the power of prayer. Help me to know that when I pray to You, I am not wasting words—I am connecting heaven to earth. Thank You, Lord, for the mystery and power of prayer.

The Little Things Are Important Too

Keep on asking and it will be given you; keep on seeking and you will find; keep on knocking [reverently] and [the door] will be opened to you. MATTHEW 7:7

It is difficult for our finite minds to grasp and believe that God wants to be involved in even the smallest details of our lives. But don't ever hesitate to take what you think are small things to God. After all, *everything* is small to God.

I remember a woman who came to me for prayer and wanted to know if it would be all right if she asked God for two things. If not, she assured me that she would only ask for one. It makes me sad when I hear people say things like that.

We can be thankful because God is generous and He wants to give even more than we know how to ask for. You have not because you ask not (see James 4:2), so go ahead and ask boldly, because it is God's will that you do so.

Prayer of Thanks

Father, I am thankful that there is no prayer request too big for You . . . and there is no prayer request too small for You. Today, I choose to bring every prayer need and declaration of thanksgiving to You, no matter how big or how small.

Following God's Direction

Direct me in the path of your commands, for there I find delight.

PSALM 119:35 NIV

It is vital to know what God's Word says about His role in your life, because it confirms His divine plan to be intimately involved with all that concerns you. God's Word says to acknowledge Him in all our ways and He will direct our paths (see Proverbs 3:6). To "acknowledge God" simply means to care what He thinks and to ask for His opinion.

Proverbs 3:7 says, "Be not wise in your own eyes." In other words, don't even think you can run your life and do a good job without God's help and direction. But, thank God, He *does* give us His direction so that we can discover all that He has for us as we follow Him! We can simply trust His leading and do what He tells us to do.

Prayer of Thanks

Father, when I am faced with a circumstance where I'm not sure what to do, I pray that You will give me clear direction. I thank You that I can acknowledge You and lean on Your Word to find guidance no matter what situation I am faced with.

Anytime, Anywhere Prayer

Bless (affectionately, gratefully praise) the Lord, O my soul; and all that is [deepest] within me, bless His holy name!

PSALM 103:1

Praying our way through the day is equally as important as devoting set-apart time to prayer. I believe God wants us to offer up acknowledgments of Him, make requests, and offer thanksgivings throughout each day. Learn to let prayer be as comfortable as breathing.

Just think about how you would feel if your children said, "I love you, Mom!" or "I love you, Dad!" every time they walked by you. When one of my children stops by the house or my office and says, "Hey, Mom, you're awesome! Just came by to tell you that," it makes my day.

Just letting people know you think they're great is the kind of communication that develops relationships. When we treat the Lord that way, our relationship with Him goes deeper and grows stronger, and we stay connected to Him through "anytime, anywhere" prayer. And He loves it.

Prayer of Thanks

I love You, Father, and I am thankful that You love me too. I want to take every opportunity to tell You how wonderful You are and how blessed I am. Thank You that I can come to You in prayer anytime, anywhere.

God Thinks You Are Amazing

I will praise You, for I am fearfully and wonderfully made; marvelous are Your works, and that my soul knows very well.

PSALM 139:14 NKJV

You may not feel like you're amazing or awesome, but God says that you are. Psalm 139 says that we are "fearfully and wonderfully made." Studying how the human body functions reveals that we are truly amazing creations.

When you receive Jesus Christ as your Lord and Savior, something happens to you on the inside. Paul writes that "the old [previous moral and spiritual condition] has passed away. Behold, the fresh and new has come!" (2 Corinthians 5:17)

You may not notice any difference when you look in the mirror; your behavior may not change overnight; your struggles may not suddenly disappear, but when you are "in Christ," a gradual and patient work of transformation is under way in your life. God sees the end of things from the beginning, and He sees you complete in Him. He sees you, through Jesus Christ, as new and completely righteous.

Prayer of Thanks

Thank You, Father, that I am fearfully and wonderfully made. Help me to see myself as You see me—righteous, complete, and dearly loved—through Christ!

Every Day Is Thanksgiving

Let us come before His presence with thanksgiving; let us make a joyful noise to Him with songs of praise! PSALM 95:2

Thanksgiving is not just a day to eat turkey and pumpkin pie, as we do in America. It was a day originally set aside to remember and give thanks to God for what He had done in protecting the first men and women who came to America, fleeing religious persecution in Europe. It was a type of harvest celebration like the one that the Jews celebrated; a day to give thanks for the crops they were able to harvest.

In addition to thanking God as we go through life, it is also a good idea to set aside special times of gratitude and giving thanks. Sometimes our family sits together and remembers where God has brought us from, and we thank Him for all He has done. Dave and I talk about our life when our children were all young and we lived in a tiny three-room apartment and had to cash in soda pop bottles to make it through until payday. I am sure you can recall times similar to those we had, and remembering them makes us thankful for how God brought us through them, and for all the progress we have made by His goodness.

Prayer of Thanks

Father, help me to realize that Thanksgiving is more than just a day on the calendar. I am grateful for all You have done in my life, not just today, but every day of the year.

Sometimes Love Is Just Being Friendly

This is My commandment: that you love one another [just] as I have loved you.

JOHN 15:12

God has blessed us with many things, and when our heart is right, we are thankful for each blessing. But we can do more than just be thankful. We can demonstrate that gratitude by deciding to use the blessings in our lives to be a blessing to others everywhere we go.

You can do this in big ways or in small ways, but doing it always blesses someone else. You'll be amazed at the results. One way you can be a blessing is just by being friendly. Make a real effort to be friendly with people everywhere you go and show a genuine interest in them. Try to make shy people feel comfortable and confident. Try giving a kind word to encourage someone who seems to be down. There are countless ways we can be a blessing if we think about it creatively. Don't let the sun set on any day without reaching out in some way to someone else.

Prayer of Thanks

Father, I am so thankful, not just for the countless blessings You have given me, but for the chance to share those blessings with others. I pray that You will show me new and creative ways to be friendly and encouraging to someone today.

Respect and Value Yourself

For we know, brothers and sisters loved by God, that he has chosen you.

1 THESSALONIANS 1:4 NIV

How we treat ourselves is often how we treat others. This is one reason why we need to be good to ourselves, and yet not be self-centered. We should respect and value ourselves.

Don't focus on your faults. We all have strengths and weaknesses. We should use our strengths and not stress out over our weaknesses, realizing that God's strength shows itself strong in them (see 2 Corinthians 12:9). After all, if we had no weaknesses, we would not need Jesus. He came for those who are imperfect and weak, and that is all of us.

You can enjoy peace with yourself, but

you will have to pursue it. Make a decision that since you are with you all the time, you should like yourself. God created you, and He does not make junk, so start being grateful for your strengths and stop stressing over your weaknesses.

Prayer of Thanks

I thank You today, Father, that You love me; You've chosen me and created me as a beautiful, unique individual. Help me see myself the same way You see me. Thank You that I can live in peace, knowing that I have been fearfully and wonderfully made by You.

Stress-Free Relationships

And become useful and helpful and kind to one another, tenderhearted (compassionate, understanding, loving-hearted), forgiving one another [readily and freely], as God in Christ forgave you. EPHESIANS 4:32

Do any totally stress-free relationships exist? I doubt it, but thankfully there are steps we can take to improve our relationships. Let me share four steps with you:

- Step 1: Develop and maintain peace with God and peace with yourself. Then and only then will you begin to develop a mindset that allows you to live in peace with others.
- Step 2: Don't expect people to be perfect, because they won't

be. This is an unrealistic expectation that will damage your relationships.

- Step 3: Don't expect everyone to be like you . . . because they aren't. Discovering that we are all uniquely different solves many relationship conflicts.
- Step 4: Be an encourager, not a discourager. Everyone loves to be with people who celebrate and notice strengths and choose to ignore weaknesses.

Prayer of Thanks

Father, I am grateful for the relationships I have with the people in my life. Let Your love flow through me as I purpose to strengthen these relationships. I thank You that I can do my part to build healthy, life-giving, stress-free relationships.

Living in the Present . . . and Loving It

Forget the former things; do not dwell on the past. ISAIAH 43:18 NIV

One of the beautiful things about life in Christ is that every day is a new beginning—a fresh start. We don't have to regret yesterday or dread tomorrow. We can celebrate today, thankful for God's presence in the moment.

There's a saying I love that goes like this: "Yesterday is history. Tomorrow is a mystery. Today is a gift; that's why it's called the present."

We can enjoy every moment of our lives and stay focused on the present. We shouldn't dwell on the past or look too far into the future, but we need to realize the present moment is God's gift to us *right now*. Let's make the decision to be grateful for today, live it to the full, and enjoy every part of it!

Prayer of Thanks

Father, thank You for the gift of today. Regardless of my past problems or my future challenges, I choose to celebrate my life with You in the present. Thank You that this is the day You have made; I will rejoice and be glad in it.

Boldly Facing Any New Challenge

David said to the Philistine, "You come against me with sword and spear and javelin, but I come against you in the name of the Lord Almighty, the God of the armies of Israel, whom you have defied."

1 SAMUEL 17:45 NIV

Many times we are far too fearful of trials and trouble. At the first sign of trouble, we begin to shrink back in fear. The believers who lived in past centuries seemed to display a different strength than most do today. We are rather accustomed to convenience and usually don't do well with suffering of any type; it frightens us.

Let's remember how David faced the giant Goliath and be joyful and thankful that we can defeat our enemies too. We can attack fear rather than letting it rule us. You are much more than your feelings. You are a powerful, wise, beloved child of God, and you can do whatever you need to do in life through Christ, who is your strength (see Philippians 4:13).

Prayer of Thanks

Thank You, Father, for the strength that I have because You are with me. No matter how difficult a challenge may seem, I will attack it with boldness because I know that nothing is impossible for You.

Are You Plugged In?

If you abide in Me, and My words abide in you, you will ask what you desire, and it shall be done for you. JOHN 15:7 NKJV

Faith is our plug into the grace and power of God. Think of a lamp. The lamp can give light only if it is plugged into a power source. If it is unplugged, it will not work, no matter how many times we turn the switch on and off.

I was once in a hotel room trying to get a lamp to work, and in frustration, thought, *Can't these hotels even provide a lamp that works?!* Then someone from the maintenance department came to my room, only to discover the lamp was unplugged.

Let me ask you, "Are you unplugged?" Have you let fear steal your faith? If you have, don't worry about it. Just decide right now that you are thankful for a new chance. Decide that you are going to have a new attitude, one that is filled with boldness, courage, and faith. "Plug in" and let your light shine.

Prayer of Thanks

Father, help me to plug into Your power today. I thank You for the faith that You have given me that simply needs to be activated. Today, I believe Your promises and I stand in faith ready to see them come to pass in my life.

Praying, Saying, and Doing

Think of yourself with sober judgment, in accordance with the faith God has distributed to each of you.

ROMANS 12:3 NIV

Faith is given to everyone, according to Romans 12:3, but that faith must be unleashed for it to do any practical good. It may sound spiritual to say, "I am full of faith," but are you using your faith? Faith is released by praying, saying, and doing whatever God asks us to do:

- Praying: We invite God to get involved in our situations through our prayers.
- Saying: It's important that we talk as if we truly believe God is working in our favor.

- Doing: The third ingredient in releasing your faith is to do whatever you believe God is asking you to do.

Be thankful for the faith God has given you and begin putting it to work in your life by praying, saying, and doing.

Prayer of Thanks

Father, I am thankful that I can release my faith by simply coming to You in prayer, speaking Your promises, and doing what You tell me to do. Help me to stand in faith when the circumstances are against me. I thank You that I can trust You completely.

Looking at the Whole Picture

If there is any virtue and excellence, if there is anything worthy of praise, think on and weigh and take account of these things [fix your minds on them].

PHILIPPIANS 4:8

When we focus on what has gone wrong in our lives, it can start to seem that nothing ever goes right, but that is simply not true. You may have had difficult things take place over the course of your life, but the mind-set of gratitude realizes that the good times have outnumbered the bad.

Look at your life as a whole rather than focusing on tragedies, trials, and disappointments. Looking at the good will give you courage to deal with the bad things and avoid living in fear. Realizing that God is with you, helping you along the way, provides the courage you need to face the future boldly, knowing that you truly can overcome any obstacle in the strength and power of the Lord.

Prayer of Thanks

Father, when I am feeling discouraged or overwhelmed by life, help me to see all the good things You have done. I thank You that the good outweighs the bad. And I thank You that there are many more good things to come.

Let God Help You

I am the Vine; you are the branches. Whoever lives in Me and I in him bears much (abundant) fruit. However, apart from Me [cut off from vital union with Me] you can do nothing.

JOHN 15:5

There have been times when we have all tried to handle our circumstances instead of trusting God to take care of them for us. It is not a sign of weakness to admit that we cannot help ourselves—it is the truth. You may be frustrated, struggling, and unhappy simply because you are trying to fix something you cannot do anything about. You may be trying to change something that only God can change.

While you are waiting for God to take care of the situation, I encourage you to be thankful that God is in control and to decide to enjoy the wait. That may be hard because it takes patience, but it pays marvelous dividends in the end. Waiting on God honors Him, and the Bible says that the person who honors God will be honored by Him (see 1 Samuel 2:30 NIV).

Prayer of Thanks

I thank You today, Father, that I don't have to handle my circumstances on my own, but that You are here to help me. While I wait on You, help me to enjoy the process, knowing that You have good things in store.

Changing the World Around You

And now these three remain: faith, hope and love. But the greatest of these is love.

1 CORINTHIANS 13:13 NIV

One of the best ways to get your mind off a problem or a troubling situation is to go help someone else. When you display love to others, it not only blesses you, but it changes the world around you. Those are two great reasons to start living in love.

We've all tried selfishness, discouragement, and self-pity—and we have seen the terrible fruit of that. The world has seen the results of those things too. But thankfully, genuine love is different!

Let's agree that we will live life God's way—in gratitude and love. Be mindful to be a blessing to others (see Galatians 6:10), put on love (see Colossians 3:14), and live like Jesus. Jesus got up daily and went about doing good (see Acts 10:38). If we will follow that example, we are sure to change the world.

Prayer of Thanks

I thank You, Father, that there is a better way to live my life than focusing on my problems. Today, I choose to go out and follow the example of Jesus by doing good to others. With Your help, I am going to be an agent of change in the world around me.

Joy Is a Decision

This is the day which the Lord has brought about; we will rejoice and be glad in it.

PSALM 118:24

Enjoying the abundant life Jesus died to give you is based on a decision you make, not on your circumstances. Thankfully, you can decide to be happy right where you are and to enjoy the life you have right now on the way to where you are going. You can make a firm decision to enjoy your journey.

You can begin by saying out loud, "I am going to enjoy my life." Until you get that thought established in your mind, every morning when you wake up, before you even get out of bed, I encourage you to declare out loud, "I am going to enjoy this day! I am seizing the day! I am taking authority over the devil—the joy thief—even before he tries to come against me. I have made up my mind that I am going to keep my joy today!" Having a right mind-set always helps in every situation.

Prayer of Thanks

I thank You today, Father, that I can choose to live in the abundant life Jesus died to give me. I don't have to live a miserable, unhappy life. I can choose to celebrate Your goodness and enjoy the life You have given me.

Choosing Positive Thinking

How precious and weighty also are Your thoughts to me, O God! How vast is the sum of them! PSALM 139:17

A confident person is a positive person. Confidence and negativity do not go together. They are like oil and water; they simply do not mix. I used to be a very negative person, but, thank God, He showed me that being positive is much more fun and fruitful.

When encouraged to think positively, people often retort, "That is not reality." But it has been said that 90 percent of what we worry about never happens. Why do people assume that being negative is more realistic than being positive?

Thinking positive thoughts is a simple matter of whether we want to look at things from God's perspective or Satan's. Are you doing your own thinking, choosing carefully to think thankful, positive thoughts—or are you passively thinking whatever kind of thoughts fill your mind? Thinking negatively makes you miserable. Why be miserable when you can be happy?

Prayer of Thanks

Father, I am so thankful that I can choose what thoughts to dwell on. With Your help, I can reject negative thinking, and I can focus on thoughts based on Your Word. Thank You that I can be a confident, positive person.

Discovering Your Destiny

> *The Lord will perfect that which concerns me; Your mercy and loving-kindness, O Lord, endure forever—forsake not the works of Your own hands.* PSALM 138:8

Many people are confused about what they are to do with their lives. They don't know what God's will is for them; they are without direction. If you are doing nothing with your life because you are not sure what to do, then I recommend that you pray, thank God that He has a destiny for you, and begin trying some things. It won't take long before you will feel comfortable with something. It will be a perfect fit for you.

Think of it this way: When you go out to buy a new outfit, you probably try on several things until you find what fits right, is comfortable, and looks good on you. Why not try the same thing with discovering your destiny? As we take steps of faith, our destinies unfold. A thankful person knows God is with him. He is not afraid to make mistakes, and if he does, he recovers and presses on.

Prayer of Thanks

I thank You today, Father, that You have a divine destiny for my life. As I step out in faith, help me discover Your good plan for my future. I am grateful that You walk with me as I seek to walk in Your path for my life.

New Beginnings

You were taught... to put off your old self, which is being corrupted by its deceitful desires; to be made new in the attitude of your minds; and to put on the new self, created to be like God in true righteousness and holiness.

EPHESIANS 4:22–24 NIV

One of the great things about a relationship with God that we can be grateful for is He always provides new beginnings. His Word says that His mercy is new every day. Jesus chose disciples who had weaknesses and made mistakes, but He continued working with them and helping them become all that they could be. Thankfully, He will do the same thing for you, if you will let Him.

The apostle Paul emphatically said that it was important to let go of what lies behind and press toward the things ahead (see Philippians 3:13). Don't be afraid of your past; it has no power over you except what you give it. Be thankful for all you have learned in the past, even from your mistakes, and also be thankful that today is a new beginning and that something good is going to happen to you today!

Prayer of Thanks

I am grateful, Father, that You have given me hope for the future. Thank You that each day is a new beginning, and I don't have to be controlled by my past any longer. I can receive Your mercy and believe for good things each new day.

Recovering from Pain

To grant [consolation and joy] to those who mourn in Zion—to give them an ornament (a garland or diadem) of beauty instead of ashes, the oil of joy instead of mourning, the garment [expressive] of praise instead of a heavy, burdened, and failing spirit—that they may be called oaks of righteousness.

ISAIAH 61:3

Recovering from pain or disappointment of any kind is not something that just happens to some people and not to others. It is a decision! You make a decision to let go and move on. You learn from your mistakes. You gather up the fragments of your life and give them to Jesus, and He will make sure that nothing is wasted (see John 6:12). You refuse to think about what you have lost; instead, you inventory what you have left and begin using it with a thankful heart.

In Christ, not only can you recover, but you can also be used to help other people recover. Be a living example of a thankful person who always recovers from setbacks no matter how difficult or frequent they are. Don't ever say, "I just cannot go on." Instead, say, "I can do whatever I need to do through Christ. I will never quit, because God is on my side."

Prayer of Thanks

Father, thank You that You bring healing in my life and You can create beauty from ashes. I pray that You will help me press on, refusing to quit. I want to use my experiences to help others find the same healing that I have found.

The Power of Planting Seed

Don't be misled—you cannot mock the justice of God. You will always harvest what you plant.

GALATIANS 6:7 NLT

There is great joy and benefit in the principle of planting a seed. When you give to others, the Lord blesses you in return—receive His blessings with a grateful heart.

I have learned to enjoy a variety of seed planting. I love to give to those in need and help bring them to a new level of joy, and I also love to give to those who enjoy a level of life that I would like to have.

If you want your ministry to grow, find a few larger ministries you respect and sow into them. If you want your marriage healed, sow into the life of someone who has a great marriage, releasing your faith with your seed for a harvest in that area. If you want to operate more fully in the fruit of the Spirit, find someone who is more advanced in that area than you are and sow into their life.

Actually, the possibilities are endless. When you start using what you have to be a blessing to others, your well will never run dry.

Prayer of Thanks

Father, I thank You that there is a harvest, or return, for every seed I sow. I pray that as I bless others and invest in their lives, You will do more with that seed than I ever could on my own. Thank You that giving to others can be a blessing in my life.

Choose Your Battles

Now may the Lord of peace Himself grant you His peace (the peace of His kingdom) at all times and in all ways [under all circumstances and conditions, whatever comes]. The Lord [be] with you all.

2 THESSALONIANS 3:16

I believe one of the best ways to enjoy the present moment and avoid undue stress is to refuse to let every little thing upset you. In other words, choose your battles, and don't make mountains out of molehills.

Before you devote time, energy, and emotion to an issue or a situation, ask yourself two questions. First, ask yourself how important it is; and second, ask yourself how much of your time, effort, and energy is really appropriate for you to put into it.

Know what really matters in life, be

grateful for these things, and focus on them. Learn to discern the difference between major matters and minor matters. Life has plenty of strain without adding anything more. When you are tempted to take on a project, step back first and decide if it's worth what it will require of you.

Prayer of Thanks

Father, I am thankful that You give me the wisdom to discern between things that really matter and things that don't. I pray that You will help me learn to let unimportant things go. Thank You that I can save my time and energy for those things that are truly important.

Two Kinds of Love

For I am persuaded beyond doubt (am sure) that neither death nor life, nor angels nor principalities, nor things impending and threatening nor things to come, nor powers, nor height nor depth, nor anything else in all creation will be able to separate us from the love of God which is in Christ Jesus our Lord.

ROMANS 8:38–39

To fully understand all the different facets of love, we must understand there are two kinds of love: the God-kind of love and man's love.

- Man's love fails, it gives up; but God's love never fails.
- Man's love is finite, it comes to an end; but God's love is infinite and eternal.

- Man's love is dependent on favorable behavior and circumstances; God's love is not based on our performance.
- People place conditions on their love, but God's love is unconditional.

This unfailing, infinite, unconditional love is the love God has for you every day! Be grateful for His love; celebrate His love; and be secure in life because you know you have the unconditional love and acceptance of your heavenly Father.

Prayer of Thanks

Father, help me to celebrate Your perfect, unconditional love for me today. I thank You that Your love is a higher love than man's love, and I am grateful that You extend that love to me every single day.

The Importance of Faith

But without faith it is impossible to please and be satisfactory to Him. For whoever would come near to God must [necessarily] believe that God exists and that He is the rewarder of those who earnestly and diligently seek Him [out]. HEBREWS 11:6

Faith is a powerful force that we have access to and should be very thankful for. When we live by faith, we release God to do amazing things for us and through us. Faith is the leaning of the entire human personality on God in absolute confidence in His power, wisdom, and goodness (see Colossians 1:4). We can come to God in childlike faith, simply believing His Word and placing our faith in Him to do what He has promised.

Some people say that they have no faith,

but that is not true. We all have faith, but we may not choose to put it in God. When you sit in a chair, you have faith that it will hold you up. When you deposit money in the bank, you have faith that you will be able to go back and get it when you need it. What, or whom, are you placing your faith in?

I urge you not to put your faith in something unstable and shaky, but put it in God Who is a solid Rock and never changes. He is faithful and will always do what He promises to do.

Prayer of Thanks

Father, I am thankful that You have given me a measure of faith. I release my faith in You and trust You to always meet my needs and take care of me. Thank You for Your goodness and Your love.

Ready for Battle

Do not be afraid of the enemy; [earnestly] remember the Lord and imprint Him [on your minds], great and terrible, and [take from Him courage to] fight for your brethren, your sons, your daughters, your wives, and your homes. NEHEMIAH 4:14

The verse above (Nehemiah 4:14) shows us Nehemiah as a strong and wise leader. Not only did he seek and rely on God, he also knew that the people needed to be ready to fight in the strength of the Lord.

I want to echo Nehemiah's words to you today: Fight for your home! Fight for your children! Fight for your right to live free from guilt and condemnation! Fight for your right to live under the grace of God and not be bound to legalism! Fight for your right to be happy! Fight for the dreams God has put in your heart! Fight for what is important to you! As Paul told Timothy, we need to fight the good fight of faith. That means to hold on, don't give up, and above all that you do, trust God because He is fighting for and with you.

Refuse to settle for anything less than everything God has for you, and be thankful that with God on your side, there is no way you can lose the fight.

Prayer of Thanks

Father, I am thankful that You give me the strength and courage to fight for what is important in my life. No matter how big the opposition may seem, I thank You that You will give me the victory in Christ Jesus.

The Word of God Is a Powerful Weapon

And take the helmet of salvation and the sword that the Spirit wields, which is the Word of God. EPHESIANS 6:17

God gives us the weapons we need to win every battle we face. God's Word is a sword for us, and we are able to wield it against the enemy. Our swords will not do any good if we keep them in their sheaths, just as a Bible won't help us if it just sits on a shelf gathering dust. To use our swords is to know, believe, and speak the Word of God.

If you wake up one morning and feel you want to give up, use your sword by saying: "I will not give up! I am thankful that God has plans to give me a future and a hope, and I am going to keep pressing on in faith so I can experience those plans" (see Jeremiah 29:11). God gives us weapons of warfare so we can use them. If you want to win, you will have to remain active. Passivity and wishing never win the battle.

Prayer of Thanks

I thank You, Father, that You have given me Your Word and that I can use it to win the victory. Help me to remember to lean on Your Word rather than my own strength. I am grateful for Your promises that sustain me through every battle.

Making a Thankful List

Enter into His gates with thanksgiving and a thank offering and into His courts with praise! Be thankful and say so to Him, bless and affectionately praise His name!

PSALM 100:4

To help you achieve and maintain a new level of contentment in your life, I encourage you to make a list of everything you have to be thankful for. Make it a long list, one that includes little things as well as big things. It should be long, because we all have *a lot* to be thankful for if we just look for it. I find new things daily to thank God for, and I am sure you will too.

Get out a piece of paper right now, or use your computer and start listing things you have to be thankful for. Keep the list and add to it frequently. Make it a point to think about the things that you're grateful for when you're driving the kids to an activity or waiting in line at the store. You can only learn the "power of thank you" by practicing it. The Bible says we are to be thankful and say so. Meditating on what you have to be thankful for every day and verbalizing it will be amazingly helpful to you.

Prayer of Thanks

Father, I thank You for the many provisions in my life You have blessed me with. I have so much to be grateful for because of Your overwhelming goodness. Help me never take any good thing—large or small—for granted.

Four Keys to Success

David acted wisely in all his ways and succeeded, and the Lord was with him.

1 SAMUEL 18:14

There are four keys to success in any endeavor you undertake. If these character traits and habits become part of the routine of your life, they'll enable you to move toward the success you long for.

- Commitment: Without commitment, people give up easily; they have no staying power at all.
- Determination: Determination enables us to achieve goals and pursue dreams that seem impossible.
- Waiting on the Lord: When success does not come easily, we

need to wait for the Lord and find our strength in Him.

- Be refreshed and renewed: We all need extended times of restoration and renewal to prepare us for new challenges ahead.

Examine your own life and ask yourself if you need to improve in any of these areas and be thankful that you don't have to do these things on your own. God is with you and, as you seek Him, He will give you the commitment, determination, the ability to wait on Him, and the renewal you need to succeed.

Prayer of Thanks

Father, when I am faced with a situation where success seems impossible, help me to remember to look to You for strength. I thank You that You will empower me to do what it takes to live a life of excellence.

Don't Sell Yourself Short

He is a double-minded man, unstable in all his ways.

JAMES 1:8 NKJV

Self-doubt makes us double-minded, and James 1:8 teaches us that a double-minded man is unstable. He really cannot go forward until he decides to believe in God and trust God's plan for his life.

I encourage you to take a big step of faith and stop doubting yourself. As the old saying goes, "Don't sell yourself short." You have more capabilities than you think you do. You are able to do a lot more than you ever did in the past. God will help you if you will put your trust in Him and stop doubting yourself.

Like everyone else, you will make mistakes. But thankfully, God will allow you to learn from them and will actually work them out for your good if you will decide not to be defeated by them. When doubt begins to torment your mind, start speaking the Word of God out of your mouth—you will win the battle.

Prayer of Thanks

Father, I am so thankful that You can take even my mistakes and turn them into something good. I pray that You will help me put doubt aside and trust You completely. Thank You that in Christ I have everything I need; I never have to doubt again.

Dare to Dream Big Dreams for God

Jabez cried to the God of Israel, saying, Oh, that You would bless me and enlarge my border, and that Your hand might be with me, and You would keep me from evil so it might not hurt me! And God granted his request.

1 CHRONICLES 4:10

I hope you have a dream or a vision in your heart for something greater than what you have now. Ephesians 3:20 (KJV) tells us that God is able to do exceedingly abundantly above and beyond all that we can hope or ask or think. If we are not thinking, hoping, or asking for anything, we are cheating ourselves.

We need to be thankful for the things God has done in the past, but still have the faith to think big thoughts, hope for big things, and ask for big things for the future. I always say, "I would rather ask God for a lot and get half of it than ask Him for a little and get all of it."

Prayer of Thanks

I thank You today, Father, that You want me to dream big for You. Help me to refuse to place limits on my life. I believe You have great things for me, and I thank You that You do exceedingly abundantly above and beyond all I could hope or ask or think.

Investing in Your Dream

The appetite of the sluggard craves and gets nothing, but the appetite of the diligent is abundantly supplied.

PROVERBS 13:4

Dreams for the future are possibilities, but not what I call "positivelies." In other words, they are possible, but they will not positively occur unless we do our part.

Far too many people take the "quick fix" method for everything. They only want what makes them feel good right now. They are not willing to invest for the future. But you can be different! If you are willing to pursue what God has placed in your heart, He will bless your pursuit. You can be thankful, knowing that when you do what God asks you to do, He will always do what only He can do.

There is a gold mine hidden in every life, but we have to dig to get to it. Be willing to dig deeper and go beyond how you feel or what is convenient in order to see your dreams come true.

Prayer of Thanks

I am grateful, Father, that with diligence and You at my side, my possibilities can turn into "positivelies." No matter how much work it requires, I am going to go after what You have placed in my heart. Thank You that when I do my part, You promise to do Your part too.

Purity Leads to Power

Therefore, since we are surrounded by such a great cloud of witnesses, let us throw off everything that hinders and the sin that so easily entangles. And let us run with perseverance the race marked out for us.

HEBREWS 12:1 NIV

In order to live in victory, it's important that we make up our minds to live for God no matter what. Hebrews 12:1 tells us to throw off every sin that entangles us. It is virtually impossible to be a spiritual success with known, willful sin in our lives. I don't mean to say that we must be absolutely perfect in order for God to use us, but I am saying that we must have an aggressive attitude about keeping sin out of our lives.

When God says something is wrong, then it is wrong. We don't need to discuss, theorize, blame, make excuses, or feel sorry for ourselves—we need to agree with God, thank Him for showing us, ask for forgiveness, and work with the Holy Spirit to get whatever it is out of our lives forever. Purity leads to power, and with God's help, we can live abundant, powerful lives.

Prayer of Thanks

Father, I thank You that You point out sin in my life so that I can move past that sin and live in victory. Today, I want to set aside any sin that entangles me and live a pure and holy life for You. Thank You that You will help me every step of the way.

What Is Real Success?

For what will it profit a man if he gains the whole world and forfeits his life [his blessed life in the kingdom of God]?

MATTHEW 16:26

Our real success and value in life is not found in climbing what the world thinks to be the ladder of success. It is not in a job promotion, a bigger house, a better-looking car, or being in the right social circles. Thankfully, true success is more simple than that…and more powerful.

True success is knowing God and the power of His resurrection. It is knowing that He loves you unconditionally and that you are made acceptable in Jesus, the Beloved Son of God, who died for you to pay for your sins. True success is found in living for God and His glory. Be a good steward of the abilities and resources that God has given you and you are sure to succeed, because He is with you every step of the way.

You never have to compare yourself with anyone else to determine if you are successful. Be the best version of you that you can be. You are a success!

Prayer of Thanks

Father, thank You that real success is found in You and not in anything the world has to offer. I am grateful that I have the gift of salvation and that You are with me always. As I do my best for You, I know that I am destined to succeed.

The Best Deal Ever

For God so greatly loved and dearly prized the world that He [even] gave up His only begotten (unique) Son, so that whoever believes in (trusts in, clings to, relies on) Him shall not perish (come to destruction, be lost) but have eternal (everlasting) life. JOHN 3:16

I have been offered once-in-a-lifetime deals from time to time, and I have found they are not always as good as they sound. They are usually intended to move us emotionally to make a quick decision so we don't miss this "marvelous, once-in-a-lifetime, never-to-be-repeated opportunity."

Thankfully, what God offers us in Christ is not a sales gimmick. It is available for anyone, any time they need it! Jesus, the substitutionary atonement, paid our penalty. He became guilty so that we could become innocent. He was guilty of no sin, yet He took on Himself the guilt of us all (see Isaiah 53:11). Live your life today thankful that your salvation is a free gift. There is no greater deal than that!

Prayer of Thanks

Father, I am thankful that I have the assurance of eternity in heaven with You. Thank You that Jesus took away my sins and gave me His righteousness. I will live every day grateful for my new life in Christ.

The Peace That Comes with Being Content

But if we have food and clothing, with these we shall be content (satisfied).

1 TIMOTHY 6:8

Nobody has a perfect life, and it is entirely possible that if you want someone else's life, they are busy wanting someone else's too; perhaps they even want your life.

Unknown people want to be movie stars, but movie stars want privacy. The regular employee wants to be the boss, but the boss wishes he did not have so much responsibility. A single woman wants to be married, but quite often, a married woman wishes she were single.

Contentment with life is not a feeling—it is a decision. Contentment does not mean that we never want to see change or improvement, but it does mean that we will do the best we can with what we have. It means that we are thankful for what God has given us and we are determined to enjoy the gift of life.

Prayer of Thanks

When I am tempted to be jealous of someone else's life, Father, I pray that You will help me to be content with who I am and what You have given me. I thank You that I have a purpose and destiny for my life. Today, I choose to be grateful and content.

Celebrating Life, Celebrating God

And they were continually in the temple celebrating with praises and blessing and extolling God. Amen (so be it). LUKE 24:53

Try beginning each day by saying, "I love my life!" Our own words have an effect on our mood, so it is best to say something that will help you feel good rather than something that will make you mad or sad. You can let staying happy be a fun challenge. See how many days you can go without getting into a bad mood or complaining.

Celebrating life is something we should do on purpose because we understand what a gift life is. God is life (see John 1:4), so in reality, when we celebrate life, we are celebrating God. Without Him there would be no life at all. Go ahead and try to create a better mood by saying, "I am thankful and I love my life!" If you really want to feel good, try this: "I love God, I love my life, I love myself, and I love people."

Prayer of Thanks

Thank You, Father, that I am not a victim of my own moods. I can speak positive, faith-filled words and improve my attitude and my day. I am thankful for the life You have given me, Father. I love my life!

Testimony Begins with T-E-S-T

Be assured and understand that the trial and proving of your faith bring out endurance and steadfastness and patience.

JAMES 1:3

I always love to hear a great testimony, but I also know that behind every extraordinary account of someone's life lies some kind of challenge or difficulty. No one ever has a testimony without a test.

We can pass all kinds of tests as we go through our lives, and passing them is part of never giving up. It's vital for us to understand the important role that tests and trials play in our lives, because understanding them helps us endure them and actually be grateful for the strengthening effect they provide.

Everything God permits us to go through will ultimately be good for us—no matter how difficult it is. When we encounter tests and trials, if we will embrace them and refuse to run from them, we will learn some lessons that will help us in the future.

Prayer of Thanks

Father, help me to experience Your peace even in the midst of a test I may be facing. I thank You that everything You permit me to go through will work out for my good. And I thank You that You give me the strength I need to overcome.

You Get to Decide

On the glorious splendor of Your majesty and on Your wondrous works I will meditate.

PSALM 145:5

Much of our thinking is habitual. If we regularly think about God and good things, godly thoughts become natural. Thousands of thoughts flow through our minds every day. We may feel we have no control over them, but we do. Although we don't have to use any effort to think wrong thoughts, we have to use much effort to think good thoughts, especially while we are forming new habits and renewing our minds.

God has given us the power to decide—to choose right thinking over wrong. But once we make that choice, we must continue to choose right thoughts. It's not a once-and-for-all decision, but it does get easier. The more we fill our lives with reading the Bible, prayer, praise, and fellowship with other believers, the easier it is to continue choosing thankful, faith-filled, godly thoughts.

Prayer of Thanks

Father, I am so thankful that though many thoughts might flow through my mind each day, I get to decide which thoughts to dwell on. Today, with Your help, I make a decision to choose right thinking over wrong thinking. Thank You that the more I do so, the easier it will become.

What Does the Future Hold?

The Lord is my Light and my Salvation—whom shall I fear or dread? The Lord is the Refuge and Stronghold of my life—of whom shall I be afraid? PSALM 27:1

The future holds a mixture of things we will enjoy and things we would rather do without, but both will come. In Philippians 4:11–12, Paul experienced times of being abased and times of abounding, but he also stated that he was able to be content in both, and we also have this option (and ability) as a gift from God. I am so thankful for the ability to be stable because I wasted many years being upset about things I could not control.

Jesus promised us that in the world we would have tribulation, but He told us to "cheer up" because He had overcome the world and deprived it of power to really harm us (see John 16:33). Make life as enjoyable as possible; be thankful for it, don't dread it. Face it with courage and say, "I will not fear, because greater is He that is in me than he that is in the world" (see 1 John 4:4).

Prayer of Thanks

I thank You today, Father, that I can have a positive, optimistic attitude about the future because I know I am not alone. No matter what obstacle I come up against, I can be of good cheer because You have overcome the world.

Choose to Bless the Lord at all Times

O give thanks to the Lord, call on His name; make known His doings among the peoples!

1 CHRONICLES 16:8

Our son once went on an outreach with a team that visits the homeless each weekend. After helping in this ministry, he called me and said, "If I ever complain again, please knock me down for being so stupid!" He was appalled over the things he had murmured about in the past once he saw, by comparison, how some people were living.

Think about it: Those without a place to live would love to have a house to clean, while we complain about cleaning ours. They would delight in having a car to drive, while we complain about how old ours are. It is easy to lose sight of how blessed we are, but we should work at keeping it in the front of our thinking. Be thankful for what you have been blessed with!

Choose to bless God all the time, no matter what is going on, as David did: "I will bless the Lord at all times; His praise shall continually be in my mouth" (Psalm 34:1).

Prayer of Thanks

I am grateful, Father, for Your blessings in my life. Please forgive me for the times I have taken Your goodness for granted. Today I choose to have a heart of gratitude for every blessing, no matter how small it may seem.

The Awesome Power of God Within You

And if the Spirit of Him Who raised up Jesus from the dead dwells in you, [then] He Who raised up Christ Jesus from the dead will also restore to life your mortal (short-lived, perishable) bodies through His Spirit Who dwells in you.

ROMANS 8:11

A group of pastors once asked me a question: Besides God Himself, what one thing helped me get from where I started in ministry to the level of success I currently enjoy? I immediately said, "I refused to give up!" There were thousands of times when I felt like giving up, thought about giving up, and was tempted to give up, but I always pressed on. I thank God for the determination He gives us.

Don't let life defeat you—face it with

boldness and courage, and declare that you will enjoy every aspect of it. You can do that because you have the awesome power of God dwelling in you. God is never frustrated or discouraged. He always has peace and joy, and since He lives in us and we live in Him, we can enjoy the same thing. We are empowered by God for difficult things, and with His help, we never need to give up!

Prayer of Thanks

Father, thank You that with Your help, I can be determined never to give up. I pray that You will give me the boldness and courage I need to keep pressing on to do what You have called me to do. Thank You that Your awesome power resides in me.

Don't Be Afraid of What People Think

The fear of man brings a snare, but whoever leans on, trusts in, and puts his confidence in the Lord is safe and set on high.

PROVERBS 29:25

We will never fulfill our destinies if we have undue concern over what people think. Let them think what they want. What someone thinks of us doesn't need to affect us at all because the truth is that their thoughts cannot hurt us if we don't worry about them. The only thing that should be important to us is what God thinks of us. It is not our reputation with people that is important, but it is our reputation in heaven that is important.

Don't worry about what other people think, because it won't change what they think anyway. Be thankful that God loves you and thinks highly of you—that's the only thing that matters! If you will break free from excessively caring about what other people think, you will instantly upgrade your level of living. You will increase your joy and your peace one hundred–fold.

Prayer of Thanks

Father, with Your help, I am going to stop worrying about what other people think about me. I thank You that You love me and You think good thoughts about me. Help me to realize that is all that matters.

You Can Be Confident

For in Him does our heart rejoice, because we have trusted (relied on and been confident) in His holy name. PSALM 33:21

God wants us to live with confidence and approach life boldly—and we can be thankful that He helps us do both. Make the choice today to start being more decisive. It may be a bold move for you if you have spent a lot of your life in fear and indecision, but it is necessary if you want to enjoy a life of peace. Indecision is not a peaceful place.

Put your confidence in Christ and who you are in Him, not in what people think of you. Know yourself! Know your heart, and don't wait for other people to dictate to you the truth about your value. Don't assume you are wrong every time someone does not agree with you. Believe that God's wisdom dwells inside of you. Believe you can make decisions. There is no point in believing something negative about yourself when it's just as easy to believe something positive—and it's certainly a lot more beneficial.

Prayer of Thanks

Father, I am thankful that my confidence is not in my own self or my abilities; my confidence is in Christ Jesus. I believe that I have Your wisdom and Your discernment. Today, I am going to live a bold, confident life.

Courageous People Wanted

Be strong (confident) and of good courage.

JOSHUA 1:6

Courage is a necessary quality if you intend to do great things for God. Leaders are not always the most gifted people, but they are people with courage. They are grateful for any new opportunity and they step out when others shrink back in fear. They take bold steps of faith. They may be wrong occasionally, but they are right enough of the time that it doesn't matter.

God expects us to increase, to be fruitful, and multiply (see Genesis 1:28). He admires courage; in fact, He demands it from those who work alongside of Him. The Lord told Joshua that he was to take Moses' place and lead the Israelites into the Promised Land, but there was one stipulation: He had to be strong and of good courage. The Lord was with Joshua to give him the courage he needed—and He is with you too.

Prayer of Thanks

Father, when I am in a situation that seems overwhelming, I thank you that You have already given me the courage I need. I thank You that You are with me and I have nothing to fear. Thank You that I can be strong and courageous.

Jesus' Prayer for You

And now I am coming to You; I say these things while I am still in the world, so that My joy may be made full and complete and perfect in them [that they may experience My delight fulfilled in them, that My enjoyment may be perfected in their own souls, that they may have My gladness within them, filling their hearts]. JOHN 17:13

When Jesus prayed to the Father in John 17:13, He actually prayed that we would have joy. He said, "I say these things... so that My joy may be made full and complete and perfect in them..." With Jesus Himself speaking and praying such powerful words about His desire for us to have joy, how could we ever doubt that God wants us to be happy and enjoy our lives?

If it is God's desire that we enjoy life, then why are so many people miserable and unhappy? Perhaps it is because we fail to set our minds to enjoy life. We can easily fall into a pattern of merely surviving and enduring rather than enjoying. But a new mind-set will release you to begin enjoying life like never before. The more you enjoy life, the more enjoyable you will be to be around, so get started today and don't delay.

Prayer of Thanks

I thank You, Father, that it is Your will for me to have joy. Regardless of what my circumstances look like around me, I will choose to live the kind of life You have for me. Thank You that I can have overwhelming, abundant joy every day of my life.

Living a Balanced Life

Let your moderation be known unto all men. The Lord is at hand.

PHILIPPIANS 4:5 KJV

Maintaining a life of balance is possibly one of the biggest challenges we have. I encourage you to regularly examine your life and ask yourself honestly if you have allowed any area to get out of balance. A lack of balance could be the root cause of not enjoying life as well as many other problems.

For example: Work is good, and we are grateful for the opportunity to work, but too much of it causes stress. Food is good, and we are certainly thankful we have food to eat, but as most of us know, too much of it is not good. It is possible to spend too much money, but it is also possible to not spend enough. Any area that is out of balance causes confusion and distress in our lives and steals our joy.

Balance every area of your life and all your activities. Do all things in moderation. That way, you'll avoid burnout and be able to enjoy everything.

Prayer of Thanks

Father, I am thankful for the blessings of provision in my life: work, food, and finances. Help me to keep things in proper perspective and live in moderation. Thank You that, with Your help, I can live with balance.

Putting God First

For from Him and through Him and to Him are all things. [For all things originate with Him and come from Him; all things live through Him, and all things center in and tend to consummate and to end in Him.] To Him be glory forever! Amen (so be it).

ROMANS 11:36

Everything God asks us to do is for our good. All of His instructions to us are intended to show us the way to righteousness, peace, and joy.

Jesus didn't die for us so we can have a religion, but so we can have a deep and intimate personal relationship with God through Him. He wants us to live with, through, and for Him. He created us for fellowship with Him—that is something to be thankful for!

The thing many people fail to realize is that they can never be fulfilled or have the satisfaction they desire apart from God. He created us for His pleasure and delight. He gives us life as a gift, and if we will freely offer it back to Him, then and only then can we live it fully and joyfully.

Prayer of Thanks

I thank You today, Father, for the gift of relationship with You through Christ Jesus. I am so grateful that everything You ask of me is for my benefit and good. Thank You that You have a wonderful plan for my life.

Faith, Gratitude, and Rest

So that your faith might not rest in the wisdom of men (human philosophy), but in the power of God. 1 CORINTHIANS 2:5

Faith allows us to rest—both mentally and emotionally. Even our will gets a rest when we have faith in God. We don't worry or reason, we are not upset or downcast, and we are not trying to make something happen that is not God's will—we are thankful that God is in control so that we can rest!

Paul sang praises to God while he was in jail. Jesus prayed for others while He was being crucified. Joseph decided that if he was going to be a slave, he would be the best slave his owner ever had. All throughout Scripture, we see the connection between faith, gratitude, and rest.

We need to be honest about what the real cause of our stress is. Is it really our circumstances in life, or is it the way we respond to the circumstances? There is a rest that comes with gratitude and faith. This is a rest we can live in every day.

Prayer of Thanks

I thank You today, Father, that I can live in rest. I don't have to worry or be downcast when I face challenges. Thank You that I can have faith, knowing that You are the One in control.

The Waste of Worry

Cast your burden on the Lord [releasing the weight of it] and He will sustain you; He will never allow the [consistently] righteous to be moved (made to slip, fall, or fail).

PSALM 55:22

Worry is totally useless. As I often say, it is like rocking in a rocking chair all day—it keeps you busy, but gets you nowhere. When we begin to look at worry in a realistic manner, we see what a complete waste it is. Our minds revolve endlessly around and around a problem, searching for answers that only God has. Pondering something in God's grace is peaceful, but worry is tormenting.

We can pray and ask God to help us not to worry, but ultimately, we must choose to put our thoughts on something other than our problems. A refusal to worry is proof that we trust God—it releases Him to go to work on our behalf. If you are willing to give up worrying, then you will be able to enter into an attitude of celebration and thanksgiving. You can trust God and enjoy life while He solves your problems. Give yourself permission to stop worrying.

Prayer of Thanks

Father, thank You for the gift of peace. Help me to focus on You rather than focusing on my problems. I thank You that I don't have to let worry rule my life; I can choose to live with peace by trusting in You.

Do Yourself a Favor

Then Peter came up to Him and said, Lord, how many times may my brother sin against me and I forgive him and let it go? [As many as] up to seven times? Jesus answered him, I tell you, not up to seven times, but seventy times seven! MATTHEW 18:21–22

As Christians, we should learn to be good at forgiving people, because we will be doing it all of our lives. The truth is, when we forgive, we are actually doing ourselves a favor. Thankfully, God has given us a way to free ourselves from the agony of anger and pain that come with unforgiveness—we can choose to forgive.

As long as we live, we will encounter people who hurt us, reject us, disappoint us, use the wrong tone of voice with us, fail to understand us, or let us down in times of need. Those experiences are part of human nature and they are part of the territory that comes with relationships. Why should we ruin our lives over other people's bad behavior? We can take the high road in Christ and forgive!

Prayer of Thanks

Father, I thank You that my peace and joy are not determined by the actions of others. With Your help, I can forgive those who offend or hurt me. Thank You, Father, that You have forgiven me and You give me the grace to forgive others.

About the Author

JOYCE MEYER is one of the world's leading practical Bible teachers. Her TV and radio broadcast, *Enjoying Everyday Life*, airs on hundreds of television networks and radio stations worldwide.

Joyce has written more than 100 inspirational books. Her bestsellers include *God Is Not Mad at You; Making Good Habits, Breaking Bad Habits; Do Yourself a Favor… Forgive; Living Beyond Your Feelings; Power Thoughts; Battlefield of the Mind; Look*

Great, Feel Great; The Confident Woman; I Dare You; and *Never Give Up!*

Joyce travels extensively, holding conferences throughout the year, speaking to thousands around the world.

Joyce Meyer Ministries U.S. & Foreign Office Addresses

Joyce Meyer Ministries

P.O. Box 655
Fenton, MO 63026
USA
(636) 349-0303

Joyce Meyer Ministries—Canada

P.O. Box 7700
Vancouver, BC V6B 4E2
Canada
(800) 868-1002

Joyce Meyer Ministries—Australia

Locked Bag 77
Mansfield Delivery Centre
Queensland 4122
Australia
(07) 3349 1200

Joyce Meyer Ministries—England

P.O. Box 1549
Windsor SL4 1GT
United Kingdom
01753 831102

Joyce Meyer Ministries—South Africa

P.O. Box 5
Cape Town 8000
South Africa
(27) 21-701-1056

r Books by Joyce Meyer

Ways to Simplify Your Life

ys to Finding Peace and Happiness

Any Minute

Approval Addiction

The Battle Belongs to the Lord

Battlefield of the Mind *

Battlefield of the Mind Devotional

Battlefield of the Mind for Kids

Battlefield of the Mind for Teens

Be Anxious for Nothing *

Beauty for Ashes

Being the Person God Made You to Be

Change Your Words, Change Your Life

The Confident Mom

The Confident Woman

The Confident Woman Devotional

Do Yourself a Favor... Forgive

Eat the Cookie... Buy the Shoes

Eight Ways to Keep the Devil Under Your Feet

Ending Your Day Right

Enjoying Where You Are on the Way to Where You Are Going

The Everyday Life Bible

Filled with the Spirit

Hearing from God Each Morning

How to Hear from God *

How to Succeed at Being Yourself

I Dare You

If Not for the Grace of God *

In Pursuit of Peace

The Joy of Believing Prayer

Knowing God Intimately

A Leader in the Making

Life in the Word

Living Beyond Your Feelings

Look Great, Feel Great

Love Out Loud

The Love Revolution

Making Good Habits, Breaking Bad Habits

Making Marriage Work (previously published as *Help Me—I'm Married!)*

Me and My Big Mouth! *

Never Give Up!

Never Lose Heart

New Day, New You

The Penny

Perfect Love (previously published as *God Is Not Mad at You)* *

The Power of Being Positive

The Power of Determination

The Power of Forgiveness

The Power of Simple Prayer

Power Thoughts

wer Thoughts Devotional

Reduce Me to Love

t Power of Speaking God's Word

he Secret to True Happiness

The Secrets of Spiritual Power

Seven Things That Steal Your Joy

Start Your New Life Today

Starting Your Day Right

Straight Talk

Teenagers Are People Too!

Trusting God Day by Day

Woman to Woman

The Word, the Name, the Blood

You Can Begin Again

Joyce Meyer Spanish Titles

Belleza en Lugar de Cenizas (Beauty for Ashes)

Cambia Tus Palabras, Cambia Tu Vida (Change Your Words, Change Your Life)

Como Formar Buenos Habitos y Romper Malos Habitos (Making Good Habits, Breaking Bad Habits)

Dios No Está Enojado Contigo (God Is Not Mad at You)

El Campo de Batalla de la Mente (Battlefield of the Mind)

Empezando Tu Día Bien (Starting Your Day Right)

Hazte Un Favor a Ti Mismo... Perdona (Do Yourself a Favor... Forgive)

Madre Segura de sí Misma (The Confident Mom)
Pensamientos de Poder (Power Thoughts)
Termina Bien tu Día (Ending Your Day Right)
Usted Puede Comenzar de Nuevo (You Can Begin Again)

* Study Guide available for this title

Books By Dave Meyer

Life Lines

NATIONAL STANDARDS FOR PHYSICAL EDUCATION*

1. Demonstrates competency in motor skills and movement patterns needed to perform a variety of physical activities.
2. Demonstrates understanding of movement concepts, principles, and tactics as they apply to the learning and performance of physical activities.
3. Participates regularly in physical activity.
4. Achieves and maintains a health-enhancing level of physical fitness.
5. Exhibits responsible personal and social behavior that respects self and others in physical activity.
6. Values physical activity for health, enjoyment, challenge, self-expression, and/or social interaction.

*National Association for Sport and Physical Education (NASPE), 2004.

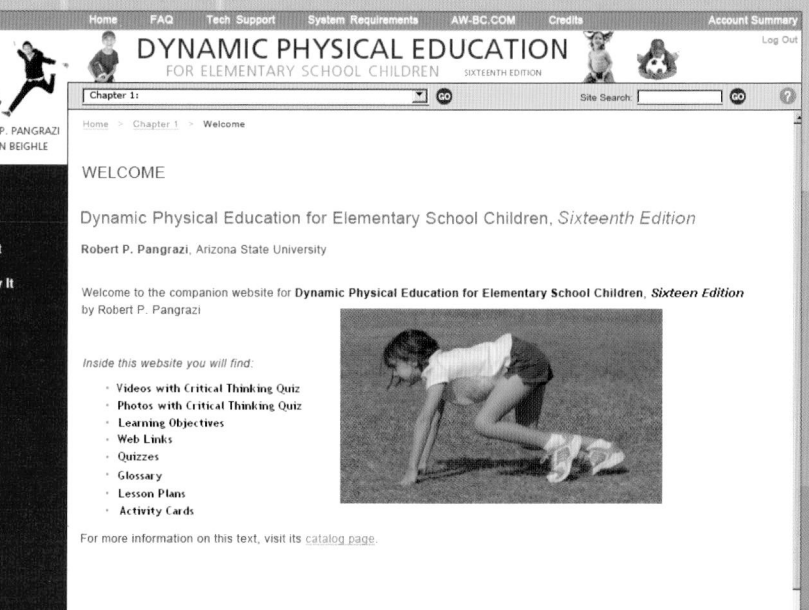

Put yourself on the path to **PE teaching success**

The Most Comprehensive Resource for Tomorrow's Teachers

Better Navigation through Chapters

Highlighted **Essential Components of Quality Programs** and **NASPE content** standards indicate which elements are emphasized to aid you in understanding why the information in each chapter is necessary and assist you in developing activities that will help children be active later in life. **Chapter summaries** and **stated outcomes** guide you through the chapters and help you identify key topics to integrate into your teaching behaviors.

ESSENTIAL COMPONENTS OF QUALITY PROGRAMS

I. Organized around content standards
II. Student-centered and developmentally appropriate
III. Physical activity and motor skill development form the core of the program
IV. Teaches management skills and self-discipline
V. Promotes inclusion of all students
VI. Focuses on process over product
VII. Promotes lifetime personal health and wellness
VIII. Teaches cooperation and responsibility and promotes sensitivity to diversity

FIGURE 3.6 Ready position.

Updated Design and Photo Program

More than 700 detailed photos and illustrations provide clearly referenced skills instruction. **The text contains more activities,** games, teaching strategies, and instructional cues than any other book on the market. **Updated design and photo program** features a new page layout to engage interest and help guide understanding.

Teaching Hints

1. Play two or more games simultaneously so students get to handle the ball more often.
2. Designate two teams to play each other. Both teams have "its" who wear different-colored pinnies. They are "it" when their team does not have the ball. When their team has the ball, they play offense with their teammates.

Birdies in the Cage

PLAYING AREA: Any smooth surface with circle marking

PLAYERS: 8 to 15 per team

SUPPLIES: A soccer ball, basketball, or volleyball

SKILLS: Passing, catching, intercepting

Players stand in circle formation with two or more children in the center of the circle. The goal is for the center players to try to touch the ball while circle players are passing it. After 15–20 seconds, choose new players to enter the circle. If scoring is desired, center players can count the number of touches they made. The ball should move rapidly. Passing to a neighboring player is not allowed. Play can be limited to a specific type of pass (bounce, two-hand, push).

Tips and Activities

Tips of practical ways to implement chapter ideas are featured throughout this edition. Teaching hints, safety tips, and numerous activities help you implement fun and educational lessons, and continue to aid you by providing valuable ideas and activity variations for use throughout your career.

Effective Preparation for Today's Students

Dynamic Physical Education Companion Website

www.pearsonhighered.com/pangrazi

New website organization makes learning to teach PE easy for you. Organized into four categories (See It, Read It, Review It, Do It), the website makes it easy to explore content and discover new activities that will help you succeed.

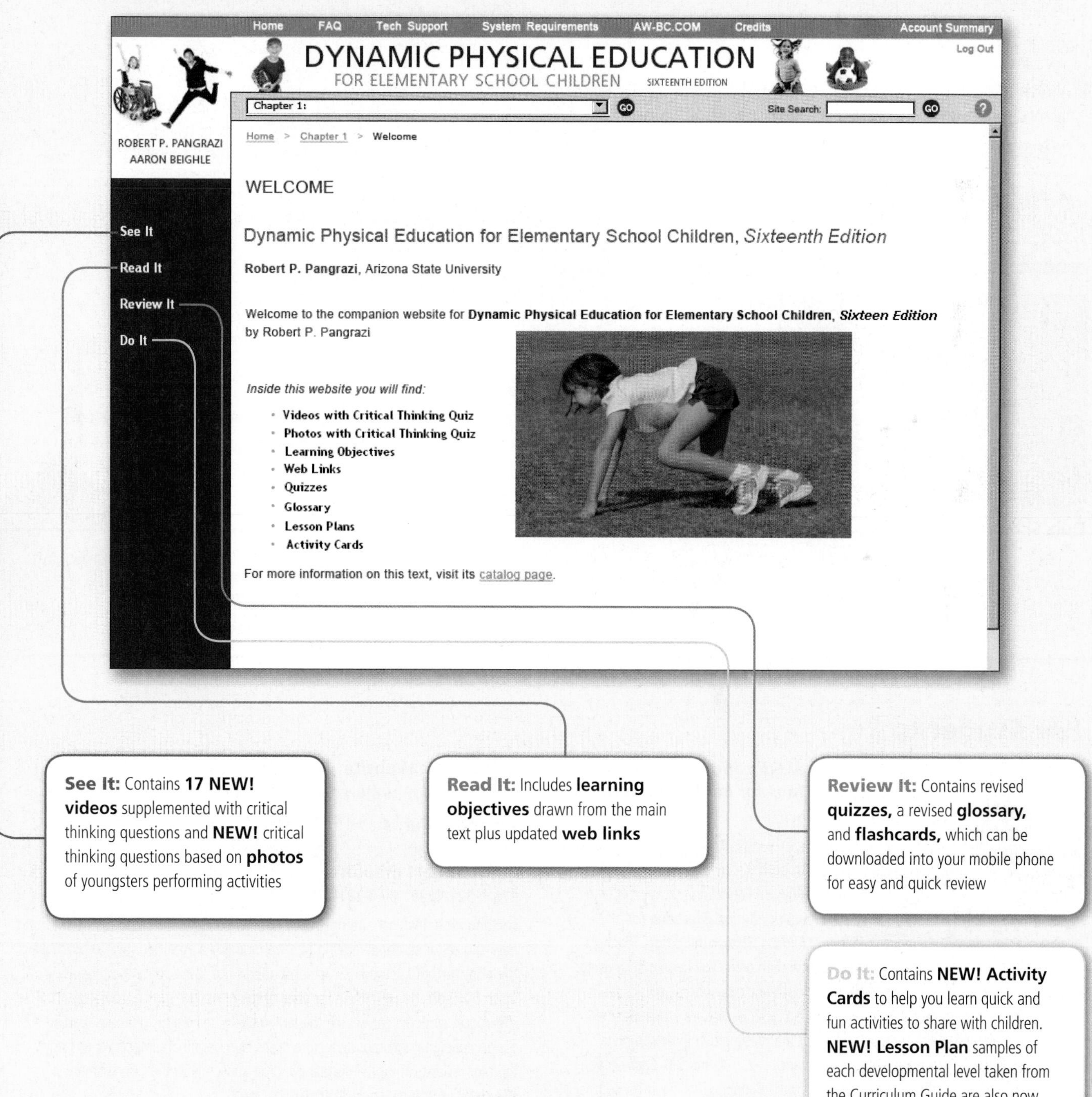

See It: Contains **17 NEW! videos** supplemented with critical thinking questions and **NEW!** critical thinking questions based on **photos** of youngsters performing activities

Read It: Includes **learning objectives** drawn from the main text plus updated **web links**

Review It: Contains revised **quizzes,** a revised **glossary,** and **flashcards,** which can be downloaded into your mobile phone for easy and quick review

Do It: Contains **NEW! Activity Cards** to help you learn quick and fun activities to share with children. **NEW! Lesson Plan** samples of each developmental level taken from the Curriculum Guide are also now available online for you.

All the **Resources You Need**

For Instructors

Instructor Resource DVD

978-0-321-60293-0 | 0-321-60293-5

This tool features:

- New PowerPoint® slide Lecture Outlines with integrated art from the book and links to new video clips
- A Quiz Show game for each section of the text
- Computerized Test Bank in TestGen®
- Microsoft Word® files of the Instructor's Resource Manual and Test Bank
- Additional DVD with full-screen closed captioned video clips demonstrating teaching techniques and students in action
- Seventeen new videos come in full-screen format (for viewing in class) with closed captioning and as links from the Lecture Outlines accompanied by discussion questions.

Instructional Videos:

- Management and Discipline Strategies for Physical Educators
- Teaching a Four-part Lesson
- Using Pedometers to Promote Physical Activity and Program Accountability
- Management Strategies for Teaching Classroom Activity Breaks

Activities Videos:

- Bubbles
- Dandy Dice
- Duo Balance
- Finger/Hand Wrestling
- Hand Signals
- Hi Low Jackpot
- High Medium Low
- In a Line
- Partner Mix
- Pass the Buck
- Pigs Fly
- Teacher Leader
- Throwing

Activity Videos

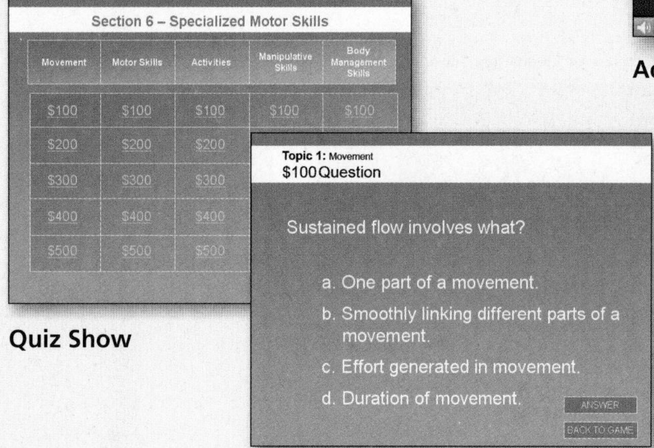

Quiz Show

Classroom Activity Breaks

- Activity breaks start and end quickly
- Reinforce students every step of the way
- Equipment adds excitement and skill learning to an activity
- Use games to teach social skills
- Effective management reduces the need for disciplinary action

PLAY *Video:* Teach Leader Activity

PowerPoint Lecture Outlines

For Students

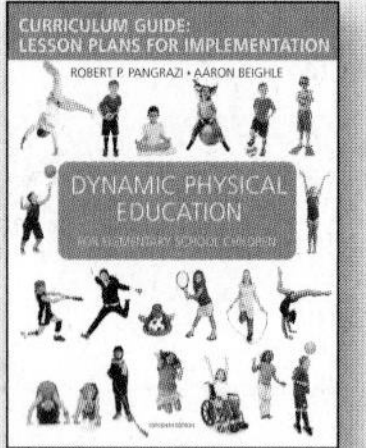

Dynamic Physical Education Curriculum Guide: Lesson Plans for Implementation

by Robert P. Pangrazi

978-0-321-56164-0 | 0-321-56164-3

A valuable reference for both the pre-service and in-service elementary Physical Education teacher, this text complements ***Dynamic Physical Education for Elementary School Children,* Sixteenth Edition.** Teachers of kindergarten through sixth grade will benefit from using these lesson plans as a guide for presenting movement experiences and skills in a sequential and well-ordered manner. Plans also include ideas for integrating academic content into daily classes. The lessons are presented in three complete sets that cover unique developmental levels, grades K-2, 3-4, and 5-6. Each section contains a year-long syllabus to assist teachers with planning. This newly revised text includes all the information necessary to present a comprehensive lesson.

Companion Website

www.pearsonhighered.com/pangrazi

See previous page for a full description.

CourseSmart e-book

978-0-321-62991-3 | 0-321-62991-4

Looking for a low cost alternative? CourseSmart Textbooks Online is an exciting new choice for students looking to save money. As an alternative to purchasing the print textbook, students can subscribe to the same content online and save up to 50% off the suggested list price of the print text. With a CourseSmart eTextbook, students can search the text, make notes online, print out reading assignments that incorporate lecture notes, and bookmark important passages for later review. For more information, or to subscribe to the CourseSmart eTextbook, visit **www.coursesmart.com**

DYNAMIC PHYSICAL EDUCATION

FOR ELEMENTARY SCHOOL CHILDREN

SIXTEENTH EDITION

ROBERT P. PANGRAZI

ARIZONA STATE UNIVERSITY

AARON BEIGHLE

UNIVERSITY OF KENTUCKY

Benjamin Cummings

San Francisco Boston New York
Cape Town Hong Kong London Madrid Mexico City
Montreal Munich Paris Singapore Sydney Tokyo Toronto

Senior Acquisitions Editor: Sandra Lindelof
Development Manager: Barbara Yien
Project Editor: Emily Portwood
Editorial Assistant: Jacob Evans
Senior Marketing Manager: Neena Bali
Production Supervisor: Dorothy Cox
Managing Editor: Deborah Cogan
Manufacturing Buyer: Jeffrey Sargent
Project Coordination: Progressive Publishing Alternatives
Composition: Progressive Information Technologies
Cover and Interior Design: Riezebos Holzbaur Design Group

Cover Photo Credits:
Front cover (from top, left to right): Chris Schmidt/iStockphoto; Elena Milevska/iStockphoto; Monika Adamczyk/iStockphoto; eva serrabassa/iStockphoto; Monika Adamczyk/iStockphoto; Robert Dant/iStockphoto; Julian Rovagnati/iStockphoto; Tammy Bryngelson/iStockphoto; Lawrence Sawyer/iStockphoto; iStockphoto; Thomas Perkins/iStockphoto; iStockphoto; Claudia Dewald/iStockphoto; Jiang Dao Hua/iStockphoto; Lev Olkha/iStockphoto; sparkmom/Fotolia; bonnie jacobs/iStockphoto; Nina Shannon/iStockphoto; Rich Legg/iStockphoto; jean schweitzer/iStockphoto; Lawrence Sawyer/iStockphoto

Back cover (from top, left to right): Serhiy Kyrychenko/shutterstock; Junial Enterprises/shutterstock; Image Source/Getty Images; Lawrence Sawyer/iStockphoto; Photodisc/Getty Images; Fotosearch; Thomas Perkins/iStockphoto; Jesus Cervantes/shutterstock; Photodisc/Getty Images; BLOOMimage/Getty Images

Endsheets (left to right): Jason Lugo/iStockphoto; Chris Fertnig/iStockphoto; Image Source/Jupiter Images; Serhly Kyrychenko/Shutterstock Images

Photo credits can be found on page 747.

Library of Congress Cataloging-in-Publication Data

Pangrazi, Robert P.
Dynamic physical education for elementary school children / Robert P. Pangrazi.—16th ed.
p. cm.
ISBN-13: 978-0-321-59253-8
ISBN-10: 0-321-59253-0
1. Physical education and training—Curricula—United States. 2. Physical education and training—Study and teaching (Elementary)—United States. 3. Physical education and training—Curricula—Canada. 4. Physical education and training—Study and teaching (Elementary)—Canada. I. Title.

GV365.P36 2009
372.86—dc22

2009003043

10 9 8 7 6 5 4 3 2 1—QWD—14 13 12 11 10

Benjamin Cummings
is an imprint of

www.pearsonhighered.com

ISBN-10: 0-321-59253-0
ISBN-13: 978-0-321-59253-8

DEDICATION

To my wife Deb whom I love and respect.

She is not only a valued professional colleague, but a special friend and companion who has enriched my life.

I regard Deb as a silent author who has contributed much to this textbook.

To my son and daughter, Charles and Connie, and their wonderful families.

I appreciate the joy and love they deliver on a regular basis.

To Dr. Victor P. Dauer, my late co-author, who taught and mentored me throughout my career and continues to guide my thinking and writing efforts.

ROBERT P. PANGRAZI

To my wife Barbara and daughters, Faith and Hope. Their energy, patience, and unconditional love amaze me every day.

To my parents, Ted and Sheila Beighle. Their love and devotion to family is truly inspirational. I am fortunate to call them Mom and Dad.

AARON BEIGHLE

ABOUT THE AUTHORS

ROBERT P. PANGRAZI, Ph.D., taught for 31 years at Arizona State University, Tempe, in the Department of Exercise Science and Physical Education, and is now Professor Emeritus. An AAHPERD Honor Fellow and a Fellow in the Academy of Kinesiology and Physical Education, he was honored by the National Association for Sport and Physical Education (NASPE) with the Margie Hanson Distinguished Service Award. He is a best-selling author of numerous books and texts, including multiple editions of *Dynamic Physical Education for Elementary School Children* and *Dynamic Physical Education for Secondary School Students,* with Paul W. Darst (Pearson Benjamin Cummings). He co-edited *Toward a Better Understanding of Physical Fitness and Activity: Selected Topics,* for the President's Council on Physical Fitness and Sports, with Chuck Corbin, and is a co-author of *Promoting Physical Activity and Health in the Classroom* (Pearson Benjamin Cummings, 2009). In addition to numerous other books and texts, he has written many journal articles and scholarly papers for publication, and he tours and lectures on a national level frequently.

AARON BEIGHLE, Ph.D., is a university instructor in Physical Education and Physical Activity for Youth courses. In addition to numerous scholarly articles and academic materials, including chapter contributions to a number of widely-used texts including previous editions of *Dynamic Physical Education for Elementary School Children* (15th ed., 14th ed.), he co-authored *Pedometer Power* (2nd ed., 2007, Human Kinetics), *Physical Activity for Children: A Statement of Guidelines for Children Ages 5–12* (2nd ed., 2004, NASPE), and *Promoting Physical Activity and Health in the Classroom* (Pearson Benjamin Cummings, 2009). His areas of research include physical activity promotion, specifically examining school-based physical activity programs, and the use of pedometers to encourage activity in young people. He is currently an Assistant Professor at the University of Kentucky, Lexington in the department of Kinesiology and Health Promotion.

BRIEF CONTENTS

PART I

Instruction and Program Implementation

PART II

Teaching the Objectives of Physical Education

CONTENTS

PART II

Teaching the Objectives of Physical Education

SECTION 4

Personal Health Skills

SECTION 5

Motor Skills

PREFACE

The sixteenth edition of *Dynamic Physical Education for Elementary School Children (DPE)* retains a strong emphasis on physical education for professional physical educators. Some have expressed concern that our profession is advocating physical *activity* rather than physical *education*. That is not the case with *DPE*; this edition retains its strong emphasis on skill development, activity promotion, and physical fitness behaviors. We want physical educators who use this text to be able to inspire students to live healthy, active lives and enjoy physical fitness throughout their lifespan. The New Features on the following pages continue to speak to the need for lifetime activity beginning at the elementary level, and will help new teachers effectively convey these concepts and activities to their young students.

GENERAL ORGANIZATION OF THE TEXT

The 30 chapters in *DPE* continue to be grouped into two major parts—*Instruction and Program Implementation* and *Teaching the Objectives of Physical Education.* Part I, *Instruction and Program Implementation,* contains the theory and requisite knowledge a teacher needs to develop a quality program. The chapters in Part I are separated into three sections that help students understand the need for quality physical education programs in schools, how to be a quality instructor, and an understanding of school procedures including the need for integrating academic content. When combined with the Internet websites included at the end of each chapter, the *Instructor's Resource Manual,* the *Instructor Resource DVD,* and new instructional videotapes, college and university instructors have a rich tool chest of ideas for helping pre-service and in-service teachers think, reflect, and improve the act of teaching.

Part I, *Instruction and Program Implementation,* contains the knowledge necessary to become an effective teacher. The chapters in this part are designed to teach students how to implement a comprehensive physical education program that meets the needs of all children.

Part I Instruction and Program Implementation

SECTION 1 Understanding the Need for Physical Education

CHAPTER 1 Elementary School Physical Education

CHAPTER 2 Teaching Children in the Physical Education Environment

SECTION 2 The Instructional Process

CHAPTER 3 Preparing a Quality Lesson

CHAPTER 4 Curriculum Development

CHAPTER 5 Improving Instructional Effectiveness

CHAPTER 6 Management and Discipline

CHAPTER 7 Children with Disabilities

SECTION 3 Program Implementation

CHAPTER 8 Evaluation

CHAPTER 9 Legal Liability, Supervision, and Safety

CHAPTER 10 Facilities, Equipment, and Supplies

CHAPTER 11 Integrating Academic Concepts

Section 1 offers a brief history of the profession and sets the framework for the entire text by listing and explaining the NASPE standards. Chapter 2 helps teachers understand children and their needs in a physical education setting.

Section 2 focuses on successful instruction. This section shows how to plan a quality lesson, view the importance of a curriculum, and teach it effectively. Management and discipline are always the constructs under which teachers will succeed or fail, and Chapter 6 offers much practical information for successfully teaching youngsters in an activity setting. Chapter 7 shows teachers how to adapt and modify activities to ensure inclusion and purpose for all students in their classes.

Part II, *Teaching the Objectives of Physical Education,* is filled with instructional activities. No text on the market offers teachers a greater variety of evidence-based activities, and even more activities have been added to this edition. This portion of the text is separated into four sections that are filled with activities and strategies designed to help teachers accomplish the NASPE standards that define a quality physical education program.

Part II Teaching the Objectives of Physical Education

SECTION 4 Personal Health Skills

CHAPTER 12 Promoting and Monitoring Physical Activity

CHAPTER 13 Physical Fitness

CHAPTER 14 Active and Healthy Schools

SECTION 5 Motor Skills

CHAPTER 15 Movement Concepts and Themes

CHAPTER 16 Fundamental Motor Skills and Introductory Activities

CHAPTER 17	Manipulative Skills
CHAPTER 18	Body Management Skills
SECTION 6	**Specialized Motor Skills**
CHAPTER 19	Rhythmic Movement Skills
CHAPTER 20	Gymnastic Skills
CHAPTER 21	Cooperative Skills
CHAPTER 22	Game Skills
SECTION 7	**Lifetime Activities and Sport Skills**
CHAPTER 23	Lifetime Activities
CHAPTER 24	Basketball
CHAPTER 25	Football
CHAPTER 26	Hockey
CHAPTER 27	Soccer
CHAPTER 28	Softball
CHAPTER 29	Track, Field, and Cross-Country Running
CHAPTER 30	Volleyball

Section 4 contains many activities and techniques for teaching personal health skills, including methods for teaching students how to develop and maintain an active and healthy lifestyle. This section includes chapters on the need to promote physical activity among students and how to create an active and healthy school environment.

Section 5 brings together methods and activities for teaching fundamental motor skills. Movement concepts, fundamental motor skills, and body management skills encompass the majority of content in this section. Now pre-service and in-service teachers can identify activities and strategies that will improve student competencies in this important skill area.

Section 6 is designed to improve specialized motor skills among students of diverse backgrounds. Chapters on manipulative skills, rhythmic movement skills, gymnastic skills, cooperative skills, and game skills offer in-depth coverage for the development of a personalized set of specialized skills.

Finally, Section 7 focuses on developing sport skills including skills for lifetime activities. These chapters contain many skills, drills, and lead-up activities. These chapters use the paradigm of teach the skill properly, practice it in a drill, and apply in a lead-up game that assures success.

As an added organizational aid, each section is color-coded for ease of reference. Each chapter in a section contains a tab in the outside margin that shows the chapter number and corresponds with the color code for that section. This makes it easy to find a desired section or chapter quickly.

DPE is written for classroom teachers and physical education teachers based on the authors' experience as physical education specialists. Material is written and illustrated with many examples that make it easy to understand. All activities in the text are listed in progression from the easiest activity to the most difficult. This enables teachers to plan a lesson that incorporates proper sequencing of skills. The accompanying lesson plan book, *Dynamic Physical Education Curriculum Guide: Lesson Plans for Implementation,* Sixteenth Edition, organizes the activities listed in *DPE* into a 36-week curriculum guide that features lesson plans for an academic year. The *Curriculum Guide* offers a section that identifies academic concepts that can be taught within a physical education lesson. This makes it easy for the physical educator to show classroom teachers and administrators how physical activities contribute to academic outcomes of the school. The NASPE content standards that are covered in each part of the lesson plans are included in the sixteenth edition. The *Curriculum Guide* offers three sets of plans for students at differing developmental levels. *DPE* and the *DPE Curriculum Guide* are used in a large number of schools as the foundation for a curriculum that is supplemented with local district materials and activities.

ESSENTIAL COMPONENTS OF QUALITY PROGRAMS AND NASPE NATIONAL STANDARDS FOR PHYSICAL EDUCATION

Across the country, a wide variety of differing areas of instructional emphasis characterize physical education programs. Some view these differences as an outcome of diverse and differing points of view while others think all programs should follow one model. Our point of view is that difference is part of the American culture. However, even when large differences exist, similarities mark quality programs. Therefore, in Chapter 1 we have identified eight key **essential components of quality programs.** Including these components allows programs to maintain their uniqueness while ensuring a quality program. These essential components are listed at the start of each chapter, and the components that are particularly relevant to each chapter are highlighted so it is possible to see how they contribute to a comprehensive physical education program.

With the age of accountability upon education, it has become vitally important to determine what should be taught and what youngsters should know when they leave the school environment. The American Alliance for Health, Physical Education, Recreation, and Dance (AAHPERD) and NASPE have done much to make physical educators aware of the need for content standards. The six **NASPE national standards for physical education** identified in Chapter 1 reflect the development of a program that stresses lifetime activity, competency in a wide variety of physical skills, the need for strong social and personal responsibility skills, and the knowledge needed to maintain personal wellness. These standards are placed at the start of each chapter to illustrate how they guide the content and development of this text. The standards that are particularly relevant to each chapter are highlighted.

The inclusion and integration of essential components and content standards are an important feature in this text. These features are designed to help pre-service and in-service teachers understand *why* they are teaching various skills and activities. Information and instructional activities in *DPE* are included only if they contribute to the standards or essential components found in Chapter 1.

NEW FEATURES

The first notable difference one finds in this edition is a new and exciting look. The entire text has been edited to make it more concise and easier to understand. The design of the book is entirely new and gives the text a fresh and inviting look. References, terminology, and some figures have been updated. A new section has been added to the end of Chapters 1–12 titled, "Applying What You Read." It is filled with questions and thoughts for future teachers to reflect on and discuss with peers and instructors.

The sixteenth edition of *DPE* reflects a number of significant changes based on feedback from peer reviewers and users of *DPE* and changes in the field of physical education. This edition of *Dynamic Physical Education for Elementary School Children* provides teachers with a sound foundation for establishing a well-rounded, comprehensive physical education program. What follows is a highlight of key changes and important chapter concepts in this edition:

- Chapter 4 focuses on developing a curriculum and a new section has been added on curriculum models. This chapter is sandwiched between the lesson planning (Chapter 3) and improving instructional effectiveness (Chapter 5) chapters. This makes it easy for teachers to see how these three chapters form the basis for planning and implementing a quality physical education program.
- Chapter 6 maintains its focus on the importance of knowing how to effectively manage and discipline students. This chapter helps teachers understand the difference between management strategies and the use of discipline when needed. A section on how to deliver corrective feedback without negative emotion has been added. Peer mediation is covered so students can help each other solve some of their interpersonal problems.
- Chapter 7 makes use of the STEPS model (space, task, equipment, people, safety) of modifying activities for inclusion. Continued emphasis has been placed on modifying activities to assure success for all students.
- Chapter 8 on Evaluation has new sections on student logs, peer assessment and authentic written tests. The second half of the chapter focuses on instructional analysis that can be performed by practicing teachers for self-improvement.
- Chapter 10 adds a new section on why constructing equipment is a process that needs to be carefully managed for safety and liability concerns.
- Chapter 11, Academic Integration, focuses on showing physical education teachers how they can integrate academic concepts into physical education lessons. The need for integrating concepts is discussed and a step-by-step approach is offered. A new section of multicultural activities has been added to help students understand the importance of diversity and respect for other cultures.
- Chapter 12, Promoting and Monitoring Physical Activity, is designed to help teachers learn how to combat student inactivity. Using pedometers to motivate students and monitor program outcomes is discussed in detail.
- Chapter 13 on physical fitness has been expanded to include some new activities for students such as Pilates and yoga. Evaluating the fitness levels of students with disabilities is also new in this edition. A section on how to measure and interpret body mass index (BMI) has been added to this chapter.
- Chapter 14, Active and Healthy Schools, shows how to change the environment of the school so students increase their activity levels and improve their nutrition and eating habits. A discussion on the impact of physical activity on cognitive development is new with research studies showing support for this hypothesis. Sun safety skills are also emphasized in this chapter since the incidence of skin cancer continues to increase.
- Cooperative activities appeal to elementary school youngsters. Chapter 21 explains how to present these activities to students. Parachute activities are included in this chapter because they demand a cooperative effort by students.
- For many adults, lifetime activities are the skills they use to stay active. Chapter 23 offers a number of activities that can be used to maintain an active lifestyle. This activity-based chapter includes walking, orienteering, tennis, bowling, badminton, and Frisbee units. The

coverage of tennis is expanded with many new games that can be taught in the gym. Bowling is all new and offers another opportunity for students to learn about an activity that is popular throughout the lifespan.

QUALITY CONTROL AND FIELD TESTING

A tradition that continues in this edition of *DPE* is to assure that all activities have been field-tested with children. We continue to teach elementary school children and evaluate new activities based in part on student reception and instructional effectiveness. A number of experts have been involved in evaluating and helping with this text to ensure the content is accurate and on the cutting edge. Don Hicks, St. Francis Episcopal Day School in Houston, has offered continuing feedback and evaluation of activities on a regular basis. Chapter 19, Rhythmic Movement Skills, was enhanced by Jerry Poppen, an expert physical educator; Paul James, Wagon Wheel Records; Dr. Barbara Cusimano, Oregon State University; and Deb Pangrazi, elementary school physical education resource teacher for the Mesa, Arizona, Public Schools. John Spini, current coach of the women's gymnastics team at Arizona State University, evaluated and contributed to Chapter 20, Gymnastic Skills. Dr. Carole Casten, California State University, Dominguez Hills, contributed the material for the section on rhythmic gymnastics. Dr. Virginia Atkins Chadwick, Fresno State University, and Dr. Julian Stein, George Mason University, evaluated and contributed to Chapter 7, Children with Disabilities. Jim Roberts, a Mesa, Arizona, physical education specialist, field-tested the materials for developing responsible behavior. In addition, the authors are indebted to the Mesa School District elementary school physical education specialists in Mesa, Arizona, who have field-tested the activities and offered numerous suggestions and ideas for improvement. Deb Pangrazi, Mesa Schools Supervisor of Elementary School Physical Education leads this stellar group of nearly 100 specialists. All these individuals have unselfishly contributed their energies and insights to assure that quality activities and teaching strategies are part of this textbook. The result of this continued field testing is a book filled with activities, strategies, and techniques that work.

SUPPLEMENTARY MATERIALS

Available with the sixteenth edition of *Dynamic Physical Education for Elementary School Children* is a complete package of supplements that offers students and instructors alike an integrated and comprehensive set of learning and instructional tools.

Physical Education Curriculum Guide: Lesson Plans for Implementation, Sixteenth Edition (0321561643) has been developed concurrently with the text and offers a framework for implementing a developmentally appropriate curriculum. The lesson plans are presented in three developmental levels, allowing for a greater range of activity and ensuring that presentations are closely aligned to the maturity and experience of students. The plans are filled with activities and outcomes that enable teachers to plan and understand *why* various activities are being taught. The lesson plans offer a framework for planning comprehensive lessons rather than preempting teachers from planning duties. As mentioned above, the curriculum guide offers sections on academic integration and content standards for each of the more than 110 individual lesson plans.

Lecture and Lesson Plan Videos: A number of videos have been developed for *Dynamic Physical Education for Elementary School Children,* including:

- **Pedometers and Accountability:** Features using pedometers in a physical education setting. How to use pedometers, a number of instructional activities for students, and how the pedometer can be used to increase program accountability are all covered in this video.
- **Implementing the Four-Part Physical Education Lesson Format:** Two four-part lessons taught by master teachers. Both a male and female master teacher participate so students have more than one model to emulate. Emphasis is placed on illustrating effective management techniques and quality instructional practices.
- **Management and Discipline in the Gymnasium:** Shows teachers effective ways to manage and group students through physical activity. Effective management strategies can increase the amount of activity students accumulate in physical education classes. Discipline without negative emotion is also discussed and illustrated in this video.

Videos from previous editions available on VHS include:

- **Active and Healthy Schools** (0-8053-0263-8) focuses on how to create an active and healthy school environment. This video shows the steps physical educators can implement to change the environment of an elementary school so increased physical activity and healthy eating habits are promoted. Schools that follow the illustrated steps will be able to meet the wellness plan that is mandated by the Child Nutrition and WIC Reauthorization Act of 2004.

- **Planning a Quality Lesson: How to Use the DPE Curriculum Guide** (0-8053-5708-4) shows how to plan an effective and fun lesson for your elementary school students.

Instructor Resource DVD (0321602935): This ancillary includes PowerPoint® lecture outlines for each chapter of the book, completely updated for the sixteenth edition by Mary Jo Sariscsany of California State University Northridge. The revised lecture outlines include art and photos from the book and video clips with discussion questions. Seven new Quiz Show games are also provided, as are JPEGs of all photos and illustrations from the book. All 17 new full-screen videos are included on an additional DVD, with optional close-captioning.

The **Instructor's Resource Manual** (0321602986), by Heather Erwin, University of Kentucky, is closely correlated to the text. For each chapter, it provides a chapter summary, desired student outcomes, a discussion of the main concepts of the chapter, ideas for presenting the content, discussion topics, suggested written assignments, and a cooperative learning project.

The **Test Bank,** extensively updated by Mary Jo Sariscsany, is now included with the Instructor's Resource Manual, and is available in a computerized format through TestGen© (0321602919), provided on the Instructor Resource DVD. It offers true/false, multiple-choice, matching, and essay questions for every chapter of the book. Answers and page references are provided. Utilizing the 1,500 test questions in the computerized test bank, instructors can create tests, edit questions, and add their own material.

Companion Website: Online content for students at www.aw-bc.com/pangrazi includes learning objectives, quizzes, critical thinking questions based on videos and photos, weblinks, sample lesson plans covering all developmental levels, new activity cards, and a glossary with flashcards. Access to password protected content is available by registering with the code provided in the front of the book.

ACKNOWLEDGMENTS

Useful textbooks are the result of cohesive teamwork among the publishing company, reviewers, and the author. I want to acknowledge the addition of a second author: Dr. Aaron Beighle, a faculty member at the University of Kentucky, played an important role in helping with this revision. His insight, hard work, and understanding of the instructional process have helped to make this edition more useful to teachers.

I am indebted to the professional group at Benjamin Cummings for their major contributions to this text. I am most appreciative of Sandy Lindelof, Senior Acquisitions Editor, for her ongoing support and encouragement. She offered excellent insight and direction for this edition and was the catalyst for the updated look and content. I am indebted to Emily Portwood, Project Editor, who coordinated the development and completion of this text with efficiency and thoughtfulness. She has an outstanding sense of organization and her hard work and enthusiasm are greatly appreciated. I also appreciate the efficiency and competency of Dorothy Cox, Production Supervisor. Sylvia Rebert, Project Manager, and all the others at Progressive Publishing Alternatives did a wonderful job handling the production of the text. To these and many other individuals at Benjamin Cummings who go unnamed, please accept a hearty thank you.

A sincere note of thanks goes to the following reviewers who provided valuable feedback that helped guide the author's efforts throughout the project: Dale Campbell, Vanguard University of Southern California; Bill Gordon, Oral Roberts University; Ingrid Johnson, University of Arizona; Michelle Grenier, University of New Hampshire; Tammy Schiek, Rockford College; and Lori Head, Idaho State University.

A thank you also to the following people who provided additional feedback on how they use *DPE* in their own courses: Bill Collman, William Penn University; Barbara Cusimano, Oregon State University; Kim Duchane, Manchester College; Melissa Evans, The University of Texas at Arlington; Randell Foxworth, Mississippi State University; Kim Gall, Calvin College; Allan Hodgert, Concordia University; Heather Hupke, Briar Cliff University; Joe Jones, Cameron University; Kathryn Kotowski, Cuyamaca College; Jodi Lord, Kishwaukee College; Arthur Miller, University of Montana; Sandra Nelson, Coastal Carolina University; Melissa Parks, Louisiana State University Alexandria; David Perron, Bluefield College; Lowell Pitzer, Missouri Baptist University; Moz Rahmatpanah, Central Methodist University; Bob Shannon, Lancaster Bible College; Terry Silver, Tennessee State University; Josey Templeton, The Citadel; Catherine Traister, Lock Haven University; Patty Vavra, Missouri Southern State University; Pat Whitley, Catawba College; and Elizabeth Zicha, Muskingum College.

Elementary School Physical Education

1

ESSENTIAL COMPONENTS OF QUALITY PROGRAMS

I. Organized around content standards
II. Student-centered and developmentally appropriate
III. Physical activity and motor skill development form the core of the program
IV. Teaches management skills and self-discipline
V. Promotes inclusion of all students
VI. Focuses on process over product
VII. Promotes lifetime personal health and wellness
VIII. Teaches cooperation and responsibility and promotes sensitivity to diversity

NATIONAL STANDARDS FOR PHYSICAL EDUCATION*

1. Demonstrates competency in motor skills and movement patterns needed to perform a variety of physical activities.
2. Demonstrates understanding of movement concepts, principles, and tactics as they apply to the learning and performance of physical activities.
3. Participates regularly in physical activity.
4. Achieves and maintains a health-enhancing level of physical fitness.
5. Exhibits responsible personal and social behavior that respects self and others in physical activity.
6. Values physical activity for health, enjoyment, challenge, self-expression, and/or social interaction.

*National Association for Sport and Physical Education (NASPE), 2004.

Physical education, as part of the general educational program, contributes to each child's total growth and development primarily through movement experiences. Program objectives provide the framework and direction for the physical education curriculum. Systematic and properly taught physical education can help achieve the major content standards, including movement competence, maintaining physical fitness, learning personal health and wellness skills, applying movement concepts and skill mechanics, developing lifetime activity skills, and demonstrating positive social skills. Modern physical education programs are influenced by cultural and educational factors related to games, sports, fitness, educational movement, perceptual–motor competency, federal mandates, value and attitude development, the Surgeon General's report, and the nationwide emphasis on physical activity.

Outcomes

- Justify the need for a quality physical education program in the elementary school setting based on the health benefits it can offer children.
- Cite the NASPE national standards for physical education.
- List program objectives and recognize the distinctive contributions of physical education.
- Describe the educational reasons for including physical education as part of the elementary school experience.
- Define *physical education* and its role in the elementary school experience.
- Explain how various pedagogical influences changed the course of elementary school physical education programs.
- Identify essential components of a quality physical education program.
- Verbally portray how various societal influences and federal mandates influenced elementary school physical education.

WHAT IS PHYSICAL EDUCATION?

Physical education means many things to many people. Physical education professionals often describe it as essential subject matter dedicated to learning in the psychomotor domain and committed to developing lifetime physical activity patterns. However, some people mistakenly think of physical education simply as athletics or competitive sports, and others see it as recess or free-time play. In short, to some people it is a meaningful pursuit, but others report having less than satisfactory physical education experiences—if they had physical education at all.

So, what is physical education? It is part of the total educational program that contributes, primarily through physical activity, to the total growth and development of all children. *Physical education* is defined as "education through movement." It is an instructional program that addresses all learning domains: psychomotor, cognitive, and affective. No other area of the curriculum is designed to help children learn to maintain an active lifestyle. This makes physical education a necessary component of the total school curriculum. It is not enough to educate children academically; they must also be educated physically. Too often, physical educators try to do all things for their students, including improving their academic skills. Certainly, whenever possible, it is important to do so. However, physical education programs must emphasize primarily the physical side of life. If students, particularly the inactive and unskilled, receive low-quality instruction in physical education, they most likely will mature into inactive adults. Unlike more physically skilled children, less skilled and inactive children often have little opportunity to participate in activities. For example, there are all types of opportunities for skilled children to participate in Little League, gymnastics clubs, and sport clubs. For other children, however, physical education may be the only part of the school curriculum that offers an opportunity to learn active skills. Thus a strong physical education program emphasizes helping all children succeed regardless of ability or skill level.

THE EVOLUTION OF ELEMENTARY SCHOOL PHYSICAL EDUCATION

Various concerns, historical events, and pedagogical influences have significantly affected elementary school physical education programs. Often these programs are created as responses to events publicized by the press and other interested parties. The many changes in elementary school physical education programs over the years clearly indicate how the public's needs and views shape the direction of U.S. education.

THE GERMAN AND SWEDISH INFLUENCE

During the 19th century in both Germany and Sweden, physical education systems focusing on body development were established in the schools. Around the middle of that century, German and Swedish immigrants to the United States introduced these concepts of physical education. The German system favored a gymnastic approach and required a good deal of equipment and special teachers. The Swedish system incorporated an exercise program into the activity presentations. The physical education program in many of the schools that adopted this system consisted of a series of structured exercises that children could perform in the classroom. The need for equipment and gymnasiums posed problems for the schools that followed these systems, and many economy-minded citizens questioned the programs. A combination of games and calisthenics evolved and became the first scheduled physical education activity offered in some U.S. schools. The Swedish system was structured and formal and often not suited to the needs of elementary school children.

THE EMPHASIS ON GAMES AND SPORTS

When about one-third of the American men drafted in World War I were rejected as physically unfit for military service, the result was a new demand for physical education in the schools. State educational authorities legislated minimum weekly time requirements for physical activity in school programs. In many states, these laws established physical education as part of the school curriculum. The laws were, however, quantitative in nature, and paid little attention to program quality.

Training programs designed for soldiers during World War I emphasized games and sports and proved more effective than calisthenics alone. This shift to using games and sports for physical development spawned school programs with similar emphasis. John Dewey, professor of philosophy at Columbia University, profoundly influenced educational theory in the mid-20th century. Two of Dewey's cardinal aims of education stressed attention to physical activities and gave impetus to the teaching of games and sports in schools. These aims, promoting health and effective use of leisure time, became school curricular responsibilities. Schools were charged with molding social change, and they placed a high value on games and sports.

Programs stressing sports and games appeared mostly in secondary schools. Elementary school programs were merely diluted models of these secondary programs; they literally can be described by answering the question, "What games are we going to play today?" During the Great Depression, equipment was difficult to secure and physical education teachers almost nonexistent. Physical education was relegated to a minor role, and many schools eliminated it entirely.

During World War II, many new training programs for special groups appeared. Research proved the efficacy of physical fitness development, hospital reconditioning programs, and other innovative approaches. Higher-quality physical education programs might have been expected after the war; but unfortunately, little positive effect trickled down to elementary school programs.

NATIONAL CONCERN ABOUT PHYSICAL FITNESS

A renewed emphasis on fitness occurred in the 1950s, after the publication of comparative studies (based on the Kraus-Weber tests) of fitness levels of U.S. and European children. A study by Kraus and Hirschland (1954) comparing strength and flexibility measurements of 4,000 New York–area school children with a comparable sample of Central European children had far-reaching results. The press became concerned about the comparative weakness of U.S. children; and because of this publicity, the fitness movement was born. One result of the uproar was the establishment of the President's Council on Physical Fitness and Sports, an agency established to promote physical fitness among school children as well as citizens of all ages. Recently, the council has focused on increasing children's activity rather than just promoting fitness. This focus is evident in an award program, the President's Challenge, for people who participate in regular physical activity and can maintain an ongoing physical activity regimen.

PEDAGOGICAL INFLUENCES

Teachers and professionals who see a need for different instructional methods and physical education programs can make changes. Such changes are often stimulated by dissatisfaction with the status quo and a desire to make physical education a more necessary part of the school curriculum. Following are some major approaches that have influenced the course of elementary school physical education.

Movement Education

Movement education originated in England and was incorporated into U.S. programs in the late 1960s. To some degree, it was a revolt against structured fitness programs, which included calisthenics done in a formal, command style. The demanding fitness standards advocated by the President's Council led some teachers to teach for fitness outcomes rather than presenting a balanced physical education program including skills and concepts. This practice created a backlash among some physical educators, who felt that creativity, exploration, and cognition should also be focal points of teaching.

Movement education programs shifted some of the responsibility for learning to children. The methodology featured problem solving and an exploratory approach. Adopting movement education led to the rejection of physical-fitness-oriented activities, especially calisthenics, which were labeled *training* and not education. Controversy arose over applying movement principles to the teaching of specific skills, particularly athletic skills. There was a tendency to apply the exploration methodology to all phases of instruction without examining its effectiveness. Regardless of the questions raised, movement education resulted in better teaching methodology and increased emphasis on instruction focused on the individual. Movement education also offered an opportunity for diversity of movement through creative instructional methods and allowed students of all ability levels to succeed.

Perceptual–Motor Programs

The focus of perceptual–motor programs was corrective; it attempted to remedy learning difficulties attributed to a breakdown in perceptual–motor development. Theorists held that children progressed in an orderly way through growth and developmental stages from head to foot (cephalocaudally) and from the center of the body outward (proximodistally). When disruptions, lags, or omissions occurred in this process, certain underlying perceptual–motor bases failed to develop fully and impaired the child's ability to function correctly in both the physical and the academic settings.

Perceptual–motor programs flourished due to concern for slow academic learners, sometimes called *slow* or *delayed* learners. Some children identified as academically subpar demonstrated motor problems involving such movement factors as coordination, balance and postural control, image of the body and its parts, and relationships involving time and space. Perceptual–motor programs attempted to remediate these shortcomings and gave physical education teachers hope that their profession would be viewed as integral to a child's academic success. But, when researchers examined the effectiveness of such programs, it was apparent that perceptual–motor activities did not improve academic achievement. Today, few perceptual–motor programs designed to replace physical education programs exist. However, the contribution of perceptual–motor programs in today's physical education programs is the integration of perceptual–motor principles into skill-learning sequences (such as using both sides of the body, practicing balance skills, etc.).

Conceptual Learning

Conceptual understanding (applying abstract ideas drawn from experience) plays an important part in physical education. In the process of movement, children learn to distinguish between near and far, strong and weak, light and heavy, and high and low. Physical education allows children to experiment with and establish an understanding of such movement concepts.

An example of a conceptual approach to physical education is the *Fitness for Life* program by Corbin and Lindsey (2005). Students spend time receiving information in a lecture situation and then use the information on themselves or on peers in a laboratory (physical education) setting. Information, appraisal procedures, and program planning are emphasized. Students are expected to understand the "how, what, and why" of physical activity and exercise. They learn to use diagnostic tests in areas such as cardiovascular endurance, muscular strength and endurance, flexibility, body composition, and motor ability.

Conceptual learning is an important part of the physical education program. However, some teachers believe that using an academic approach focused solely on knowledge and cognitive growth instead of on physical skills and activity will place physical education on par with other academic areas. Others believe that increasing student knowledge changes students' attitudes and behaviors and stimulates them to incorporate physical activity into their lifestyle. Neither of these beliefs has been proved to date. Increasing a person's knowledge does not ensure a change in behavior any more than reading and learning about how to play tennis makes a skilled tennis player. Students must experience and learn physical skills and understand their conceptual components. Physical activity is, and must remain, the core component of physical education because it is the only place in the school setting where physical skills are taught and learned.

Value and Attitude Development (Affective Domain Learning)

During the 1990s, the American public expressed concern about the lack of moral values among its youth. The political views of many U.S. leaders who emphasize law and order have created greater pressure on the schools to teach morals and values. In an annual Gallup Poll of the public's attitudes toward schools, lack of discipline often heads the list of major problems. Discipline problems also rank as a major concern of teachers. There is growing pressure on the schools to teach values, responsibility skills, and moral education.

Values, feelings, beliefs, and judgments have received more attention in the schools and in physical education classes in particular. Public concern about crime among professional athletes has also increased parents' demand for help with responsibility training. Such issues as alcohol and substance abuse, sex education, and AIDS awareness are being introduced in the elementary school years in an attempt to prevent students from developing problems later in life. Awareness programs are becoming more common in schools with physical educators, who are often called on to conduct appropriate district-approved programs.

FEDERAL MANDATES

Occasionally, citizens' concerns about their children have led to legislation affecting physical education curriculum and instruction. The following legislative mandates in particular continue to influence physical education programs throughout the United States.

Title IX: Equal Opportunity for the Sexes

Title IX of the Educational Amendments Act of 1972 has significantly affected most secondary school physical education programs. This federal law has less effect on elementary school physical education because most programs at this level have long been coeducational. Title IX rules out separation of sexes and calls for all offerings to be coeducational. The law is based on the principle that school activities and programs are of equal value for both sexes and that students should not be denied access to participation on the basis of gender. Legal ramifications have forced schools to provide equal access to physical education activities for boys and girls. Organizing separate competitions for the sexes is permissible, provided that mixed participation in an activity can be determined to be hazardous. In principle, the law also dictates that the most qualified teacher, regardless of gender, provides instruction.

Title IX also works to eliminate sexism and sex-role typing. Human needs and opportunities must prevail over traditional sexual stereotypes of masculinity and femininity. Segregating children by sex in elementary school physical education classes is indefensible because it takes away the opportunity for children to learn at an early age that gender differences are small in the desire to perform well athletically.

PL 94–142: Equal Rights for Students with Disabilities

Public Law 94–142 has given hope for a full education to the 3.5 to 4 million U.S. children with disabilities. This federal law mandates that all children have the right to a free and public education and are educated in the least restrictive educational environment possible. No longer can children with disabilities be assigned to segregated classes or schools unless a separate environment is determined by due process to be in the child's best interest. A 1990 amendment, Public Law 101–476 (also known as IDEA—Individuals with Disabilities Education Act), continues with the objective of providing handicapped individuals with the least restrictive environment in the school setting.

Mainstreaming is a term used for the practice of placing children with disabilities into classrooms with able children. These laws have resulted in degrees of mainstreaming (full or partial), allowing many children with disabilities to participate in regular physical education classes. PL 101–476, which is considered commendable and morally sound, often necessitates changing the school's structure and educational procedures as well as the viewpoints and attitudes of its personnel. Many teachers lack the educational background, experience, or inclination to handle children with disabilities in addition to children without disabilities. The answer is not to ignore the problem, but to provide teachers with knowledge and constructive approaches that allow them to successfully teach children who have disabilities. If children with disabilities are to function in society as adults, they deserve and need the opportunity to participate with able children.

Besides the mainstreaming of students with disabilities into regular education classes, PL 101–476 mandates that each such student receive a specific learning program, called an *individualized educational program* (IEP). Establishing the child's due process committee, developing the IEP, and monitoring that program in the student's best interest is a considerable challenge. IEPs, which help make education more personal and individual, can be used for able children as well.

Child Nutrition and WIC Reauthorization Act of 2004

Nationally, there is widespread concern about the health status of Americans—particularly related to physical activity and nutrition. The number of overweight Americans has increased rapidly in the past 15 years. Today, over 60% of Americans are overweight or obese (National Center for Health Statistics, 2004). Much of this increase is attributed to decreased physical activity patterns and increased amounts of calories consumed. Obviously, childhood problems with weight management and proper nutrition have put physical activity squarely in the public eye.

Physical education programs must focus on improving students' health status, particularly their eating habits and physical activity. In the Child Nutrition and WIC (Women, Infants, and Children) Reauthorization Act of 2004, the U.S. Congress established a new requirement that by the start of the 2006–07 school year, all school districts with a federally funded school meals program develop and implement wellness policies addressing nutrition and physical activity. This act offers physical educators an excellent opportunity to implement physical activity and eating behavior programs into their classes. Changing activity and eating behaviors takes the efforts of an entire community. Physical educators can make this an opportunity to change the school environment rather than focus on a minor curriculum change. Changing the school environment will require the efforts of parents, classroom teachers, administrators, and students. If implemented correctly, this mandate quite likely will lead physical education programs to a prominent role in the total school curriculum.

CONTEMPORARY SOCIAL INFLUENCES

A Nationwide Concern for Health and Wellness

The Surgeon General's report on *Physical Activity and Health* (U.S. Department of Health and Human Services [USDHHS], 1996) clearly outlined the health benefits of physical activity for all ages. The contributions of physical activity to health and wellness are widely known, and efforts are under way to promote physical activity among all segments of the population. Today's educators are increasingly focused on integrating physical activity into a healthful living style. This focus is pushing physical educators to develop programs that teach more than fitness and skill activities. *Wellness* is a broader concept than physical fitness. It is a dynamic state of well-being that implies living fully and deriving the most from life.

Eating wisely, controlling weight, dealing with tension, understanding body (muscular) movement, getting enough sleep, improving posture, keeping in shape, and dealing with future challenges (i.e., potential use of alcohol and drugs, and the risks of contracting AIDS or other infectious diseases) all affect wellness. The problem of weight control merits special attention in the elementary school. Unless their lifestyle changes at an early age, obese children usually become obese adults. Recent research shows that activity and inactivity track into adulthood—active children become active adults (Raitakari et al., 1994).

In teaching human wellness, physical education can have a lifelong impact on students. It is most effectively presented when classroom teachers and physical education specialists work together. Identifying wellness as a common goal for all school children makes physical education an integral, vital part of the total school curriculum. Wellness instruction teaches concepts that help students develop and maintain an active lifestyle. Understanding the principles of fitness, the importance of daily physical activity, and the benefits of physical fitness increases the odds that students will stay active throughout their lives (Dale, Corbin, & Cuddihy, 1998).

A Demand for "Back-to-Basics" Schools

Basic schools were designed in response to a perceived decline in academic performance. Basic schools stress discipline and cognitive learning, often at the expense of the arts and physical education. To increase academic rigor, the school day is lengthened; physical education and performing arts are dropped to allow more time for "the three Rs." A demand for uninterrupted academic time often makes it impossible to schedule physical education time for children. To combat this trend, physical education programs must demonstrate that they are instructional, of high quality, and a unique contribution to the school curriculum. In 1983, the National Commission on Excellence in Education presented a critical review of the entire U.S. educational process. Physical education was not included as part of a basic education. Whether the omission was intentional is open to question. In the past, other deliberations and reports have included physical education as a part of basic instruction. Perhaps the school experiences of commission members in the physical education area had taken an unorganized fun-and-games approach, so they perceived little need for such recreation. This attitude illustrates the importance of educating the public about the need for a quality physical education program in the quest to develop well-rounded students.

To conform to the concept of basic education, this text delineates fundamental content standards to be accomplished in physical education. It presents content standards in measurable terms, so that teachers and schools are held accountable for helping students reach a predetermined level of achievement. Though accountability is desirable, some abuse can occur when teachers are rewarded based solely on student achievement levels. Some teachers may turn to using memorization, drill, and rote learning and may encourage practice solely in areas where students will be tested. In physical education, this often means teaching only fitness test activities so students score well on a mandated physical fitness test. This approach can result in an inferior, narrow program that satisfies the school's accountability concerns but does little to give students a well-rounded education.

A National Focus on Physical Activity

Healthy People 2000: National Health Promotion and Disease Objectives (U.S. Public Health Service, 1990) stresses the role of physical activity in improving the health of all Americans. Most of the 300 physical activity target goals are specifically directed toward improving the health of U.S. children and youth, by decreasing health risks and emphasizing preventative approaches to a healthy lifestyle. Several of the physical activity objectives emphasize increased amounts of light to moderate activity (that is, activity similar in intensity to brisk walking) among children age 6 and older. For years, fitness goals and high-intensity activity were emphasized. The *Healthy People* report stresses moderate and regular physical activity. Much of the emphasis on improving the health status of youth is accomplished through a quality physical education program. The report focuses on the health benefits of exercise and activity for all students in contrast to systems that reward only physically gifted students.

Healthy People 2000 was followed by *Healthy People 2010* (USDHHS, 2000). Two major goals addressed in this report are to (1) increase the years of healthy life and (2) eliminate health disparities. These major goals are supported by enabling goals concerned with promoting healthy behaviors, protecting health, achieving access to quality health care, and strengthening community prevention. The objectives are grouped into various focus areas similar to those in *Healthy People 2000.* New focus areas include disability, low income, race and ethnicity, chronic diseases, and public health infrastructure.

The release of the Surgeon General's report on *Physical Activity and Health* (USDHHS, 1996) documented many health benefits achieved through moderate and regular activity. The report showed that people of all ages and both genders benefit from regular physical activity. Never before has a body of research been compiled to show the strong need for activity and fitness in the lives of youth. Activity programs are an absolute requisite for healthy children.

THE CURRENT STATUS OF PHYSICAL EDUCATION IN THE UNITED STATES

Educational outcomes of physical education have regularly been refocused. In fact, most trends have stayed in the public eye for 5 to 7 years and then, when interest wanes, a new trend surfaces. For example, the fitness push has surfaced three times in the last 50 years. Movement education was a backlash toward structured fitness, while perceptual–motor programs were designed to rectify learning disabilities. This profession has changed its focus so often that the public is not sure what physical education implies. When you say you are a physical education teacher, most people ask, "What do you coach?" Colleges and universities have compounded the problem by renaming their physical education departments—kinesiology, exercise science, sport studies, movement education, and so on. Again, most people find it hard to understand what competencies physical education brings to the educated child. Obviously, the authors believe that promoting physical activity and health are the outcomes that really matter for our inactive, overweight society. Physical education must be based on physical activity. It is time to stop being a moving target and encourage others to see the value of a quality physical education program.

Though professionals consider true physical education to be nothing less than a quality instructional program conducted by a physical education specialist, for many teachers this is not the actual experience. Most states and districts require physical education in their schools. However, the SHPPS 2006 report shows that when physical education requirements by grade are analyzed carefully, each grade shows a decline from about 50% in grades 1–5 to about 20% in grade 12 (Lee et al., 2007). Because many states and schools allow exemptions from physical education classes, the actual percentage of students receiving instruction is even lower. Few children in America receive daily physical education instruction. Only about 4% of elementary schools provide daily physical education all year for their students (Lee et al., 2007). When physical education is taught at these grade levels, a "specialist" often teaches it—though many people with this title do not hold valid credentials.

A common picture of elementary school physical education might look something like this: Children go to school and receive about 25 hours of overall instruction weekly. Out of the 25 hours, physical education may be scheduled for 30 to 60 minutes a week in a school that cares about physical education. This amounts to 2 to 4% of the total instructional time devoted to the health and wellness of students. Instruction may be carried out by a physical education specialist, classroom teacher, or paraprofessional. Often, up to four classes are sent to physical education at once, so the student–teacher ratio is 120 to 1 with one or two paraprofessionals sent to help. It is difficult for children to value physical activity if it is seldom taught. When class sizes are large, students are disciplined much more and the experience is less than satisfactory. Often, for young children, how they are taught is more important than what they are taught. Physical education teachers deserve the same respect and class sizes as classroom teachers.

THE NEED FOR PHYSICAL EDUCATION PROGRAMS

In the past decade, interest in the benefits of an active lifestyle has spawned a wide assortment of health clubs, a vast array of books and magazines about exercise and fitness, a weekly smorgasbord of distance runs and triathlons, streamlined exercise equipment, and apparel for virtually any type of physical activity. Unfortunately, most of this interest and lifestyle change has occurred among middle- and upper-class Americans. Little change in activity patterns has occurred in lower-middle- and lower-class families.

Children are products of their family environments. A 2003 national survey of children, sponsored by the Kaiser Family Foundation, showed that 8- to 14-year-olds watched an average of 3 hours and 16 minutes of television a day. However, adding videos, DVDs, computers, and video games to the TV time raises the total to more than 6 hours a day (Roberts, Foehr, & Rideout, 2005). Another study (Anderson et al., 1998) showed that children who watched 4 or more hours of television per day had significantly greater body mass index (BMI) than did children watching less than 2 hours per day. Health goals for the nation for the year 2010 (USDHHS, 2000) are based on increasing daily levels of physical activity. Many of the goals directly target schools, or programs that can take place within the school setting. These goals emphasize reducing inactivity and increasing light to moderate physical activity. The need is clear: implement physical education programs to teach students how to live an active and healthy lifestyle. What evidence is available that shows the benefits of a quality physical education program?

1. The percentage of overweight youth has more than tripled in the past 30 years (USDHHS, 2002). A recent study suggests that the prevalence of obesity is more strongly related to decreased energy expenditure than to increased energy intake (Jebb & Moore, 1999). The school environment discourages physical activity. Everywhere they go, students are asked to move slowly, sit still, and walk rather than run, resulting in decreased energy expenditure. A 30-minute physical education class can offer 1,200 to 2,000 steps of moderate to vigorous physical activity to counteract the effects of an inactive day (Beighle & Pangrazi, 2000; Morgan, Pangrazi, & Beighle, 2003). This exercise contributes substantially to the daily energy expenditure of students, particularly those who are inactive. For a student who is averaging 8,000 steps a day, a quality physical education class could increase the total number of steps by 20% and the accumulated steps to 10,000—a substantial increase in physical activity.
2. A positive experience in physical education encourages children to be active as adults. In a survey sponsored by the Sporting Goods Manufacturers Association (2000), 60% of respondents aged 18 to 34 reported that a positive experience in physical education classes encouraged them to be active later in life. On the other hand, of those respondents who said they were sedentary, only 10% said their physical education classes encouraged them to be active.
3. Overweight children grow into overweight adults. Studies (Guo et al., 1994; Must et al., 1992) show that adolescent weight is a good predictor of adult obesity. A study by Whitaker et al. (1997) showed that the risk of obesity persisting into adulthood is much higher among adolescents than younger children. The chance for childhood obesity persisting into adulthood increases from 20% at 4 years of age to 80% by adolescence (Guo & Chumlea, 1999). This supports the case for dealing with overweight children in elementary school, before the problem becomes much more difficult to rectify. Since a quality program encourages active behavior, it makes sense to have a program in place to help children understand the importance of proper weight management and an active lifestyle.
4. A quality physical education program educates students physically and can contribute to academic learning. However, taking time for physical education and recess does not detract from academic performance in school. An argument often used is that spending time on physical education will lower the academic performance of students because they have less time to study and learn. To the contrary, studies have shown that students who spend time in physical education classes do equally well or better in academic classes. Two major studies on this issue are the Three Rivers study (Trudeau et al., 1998) and a SPARK related activity program study (Sallis et al., 1999). In both cases, students received the health benefits of physical education without any negative impact on their academic performance.
5. Physical education gives students the skills they need to be active as adults. Unlike adults, children have time to practice and learn new skills. Few adults learn a new physical activity because they are busy and unwilling to start as a beginner. They often practice and use skills they learned earlier in childhood. Since many adults like to participate in activities having a requisite skill level (e.g., golf, tennis, racquetball, etc.), learning such skills during their school years makes them more likely to feel competent about participating in later life.
6. Physical activity (most often during physical education classes) gives children immediate and short-term health benefits (Bar-Or, 1995). For obese children, increased physical activity reduces the percentage of body fat. Additionally, increased activity reduces blood pressure and improves the blood lipid profile for high health-risk children. Finally, evidence shows that weight-bearing activities performed during the school years offer bone mineral density benefits that carry over into adulthood (Bailey, Faulkner, & McKay, 1996). Such activities can help prevent osteoporosis later in life.
7. Active children are more likely to become active adults. Telama et al. (1997) looked at retrospective and longitudinal tracking studies and concluded that the results "indicate that physical activity and sport participation in childhood and adolescence represent a significant prediction for physical activity in adulthood." Another

study (Raitakari et al., 1994) showed how strongly inactivity patterns track. In that study, the probability of an inactive 12-year-old remaining sedentary at age 18 was 51 to 63% for girls and 54 to 61% for boys. This clearly delineates the legacy we give to youth by placing them in an inactive family and school environment.

THE CONTENT OF PHYSICAL EDUCATION

Whether speaking of academic class settings or physical education, a key to providing proper education includes following agreed-upon guidelines, or standards, proven to ensure children obtain the right kind of education. Content standards are the framework of a program; they determine the focus and direction of instruction. Standards specify the content of the program—what students should know and be able to do. Standards express what knowledge students should possess and how they should demonstrate that knowledge when exiting a developmental level. Established standards can significantly contribute to the overall goal of school and U.S. society: developing a well-rounded individual capable of contributing to a democratic society. Quality programs are driven by standards that move children toward high-level achievement.

Physical education content standards are taught nowhere else in the school curriculum. If these standards are not accomplished in physical education classes, children will leave school without a well-developed set of physical skills. A positive result of efforts to identify standards is the general agreement among most professionals today about what a physical education program should accomplish. To describe a physically educated person, the National Association for Sport and Physical Education (NASPE, 2004a) has identified six major content standards for physical education. Generally, experts agree on the major content of the standards that constitute categories of emphasis for physical education instruction. Many school districts have developed similar sets of standards to allow for program individuality.

The standards give direction to instruction and form the framework for assessment and accountability in the program. The NASPE website (http://member.aahperd.org/template.cfm) also provides a series of assessment publications offering a wide range of strategies for identifying student progress toward the standards. The assessment series recommends a range of strategies including teacher observations, written tests, student logs, student projects, student journals, class projects, and portfolios. Assessment strategies offer teachers examples of many assessment styles, with the expectation that teachers will modify and select assessment tools appropriate to their own setting.

NASPE CONTENT STANDARDS FOR PHYSICAL EDUCATION

1

This section reviews each of the six NASPE national standards and refers to the chapters that offer instructional activities and strategies designed to reach these strategies. Each chapter in this text also opens with a table showing how activities in the chapter contribute to the desired standards. A detailed discussion of what teachers can expect students to learn follows each standard. Also included are two levels of outcomes for each standard: a set for children at Developmental Level I (see pages 11–15 for an in-depth discussion of developmental levels) and a set for youth at Developmental Levels II and III (grades 3–6).

Standard 1: Demonstrates competency in motor skills and movement patterns needed to perform a variety of physical activities.

Standard 1 focuses on skill competency. All people want to be skilled and competent performers. The elementary school years are an excellent time to teach motor skills because children have the time and predisposition to learn them. The range of skills presented in physical education should be unlimited; children need the opportunity to encounter and learn as many different physical skills as possible. Because children vary in genetic endowment and interest, they should have the opportunity to learn about their personal abilities in many types of skills and settings. Major areas of movement competence and motor skill development are described next.

Movement Concepts Skills

Students need to learn about the classification of movement concepts (Chapter 15) that include body and space awareness, qualities of movement, and relationships. Learning the skills is not enough; children need to explore them in a variety of settings. This standard ensures children will be taught how movement concepts are classified and is designed to give children an increased awareness and understanding of the body as a vehicle for movement while acquiring a personal vocabulary of movement skills.

Fundamental Motor Skills

Fundamental skills enhance the quality of life. This group of skills is sometimes labeled "basic" or "functional" skills. They are the skills children need to function fully in the environment. Fundamental skills are divided into three categories: locomotor, nonlocomotor, and manipulative skills.

Locomotor Skills

Locomotor skills (Chapter 16) are used to move the body from one place to another or to project the body upward,

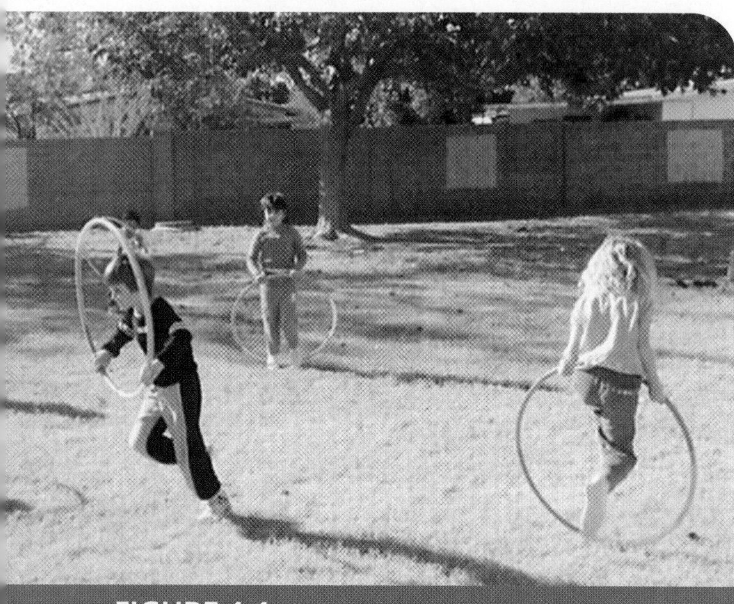

FIGURE 1.1 Developing manipulative skills.

as in jumping and hopping. These skills also include walking, running, skipping, leaping, sliding, and galloping.

Nonlocomotor Skills

Nonlocomotor skills (Chapter 16) are done in place, with little spatial movement. These skills, which are not as well defined as locomotor skills, include bending and stretching, pushing and pulling, balancing, rolling, curling, twisting, turning, and bouncing.

Manipulative Skills

Manipulative skills (Chapter 17) are developed by handling some type of object (Figure 1.1). Most of these skills involve the hands and feet, but other parts of the body also are used. Manipulation of objects leads to better hand–eye and foot–eye coordination, which are particularly important for tracking items in space. Manipulative skills are basic to many game skills. Propelling (throwing, striking, striking with an implement, kicking) and receiving (catching) objects are important skills that can be taught by using beanbags and various balls. Rebounding or redirecting an object in flight (e.g., a volleyball) is another useful manipulative skill. Continuous control of an object, such as a wand or a hoop, is also a manipulative activity.

Specialized Motor Skills

Specialized skills are used in various sports and other areas of physical education, including apparatus activities, tumbling, dance, and specific games. Specialized skills receive increased emphasis beginning with Developmental Level II activities. In developing specialized skills, progression is attained through planned instruction and drills. Many of these skills have critical points of technique, and teaching emphasizes correct performance.

Body Management Skills

Efficient movement of the body (Chapter 18) demands integration of various physical traits, including agility, balance, flexibility, and coordination (Figure 1.2). Students also need to develop an understanding of how to control their bodies while on large apparatus such as beams, benches, and jumping boxes.

Rhythmic Movement Skills

Individuals who excel in movement activities have a strong rhythmic ability. Rhythmic movement (Chapter 19) involves moving in a regular, predictable pattern. Being able to move rhythmically is basic to skill performance in all areas. A rhythmic program that includes dance, rope jumping, and rhythmic gymnastics offers a variety of activities to help students attain this objective. Early experiences center on functional and creative movement forms. Instruction begins with and capitalizes on locomotor skills that children already have: walking, running, hopping, and jumping. Rhythmic activities are a vehicle for expressive movement.

Gymnastic Skills

Gymnastic activities (Chapter 20) contribute significantly to children's overall physical education experience in elementary schools. Gymnastic activities develop body management skills without the need for equipment and apparatus. Flexibility, agility, balance, strength, and body control are outcomes that are enhanced by participating in gymnastics. Students learn basic gymnastic skills such as body rolling, balancing, inverted balancing, and tumbling in a safe and gradual way.

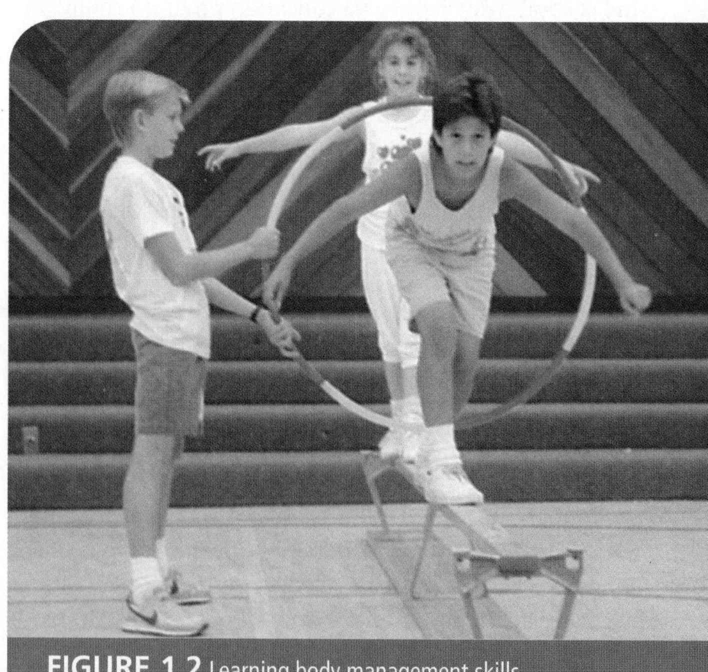

FIGURE 1.2 Learning body management skills.

Game Skills

Games (Chapter 22) provide children with the opportunity to apply newly learned skills in a meaningful way. Many games develop large muscle groups and enhance the ability to run, dodge, start, and stop under control while sharing space with others. Through games, children experience success and accomplishment. Social objectives encountered through games include developing interpersonal skills, accepting rule parameters, and increasing self-knowledge in a competitive and cooperative situation.

Sport Skills

Students learn sport skills (Chapters 24–30) in a context of application. They learn basic skills and then practice them in various drills. After learning and practicing the skills, students apply them in lead-up activities. Lead-up activities reduce the number of skills children must use to succeed, thus leading to successful participation. Sport skills require proper techniques, so the cognitive aspect of learning is also important.

Outcomes for Developmental Level I Students

a. Apply movement concepts such as body and space awareness, relationships, and qualities of movement to various locomotor and body management skills.

b. Move efficiently using various locomotor skills such as walking, running, skipping, and hopping.

c. Combine locomotor and nonlocomotor skills into movement themes (e.g., supporting body weight, forming bridges, and receiving and transferring weight).

d. Perform body management skills on the floor and on apparatus including benches, balance beams, individual mats, and jumping boxes.

e. Use various manipulative skills such as tossing, throwing, catching, and kicking.

f. Move rhythmically in various settings including fundamental rhythms, creative rhythms, and simple folk dances.

g. Perform simple gymnastic skills such as animal walks, body rolling, simple balances, and inverted balances.

h. Use various locomotor skills in low-organized game settings such as running, dodging, evading, and stopping.

Outcomes for Developmental Levels II and III Students

a. Perform specialized sport skills with mature form (e.g., throwing, catching, dribbling with foot and hand, kicking and striking, batting, punting, and passing).

b. Use sport skills in various activities such as volleyball pass, basketball dribble, and batting a softball.

c. Perform a wide variety of gymnastic skills including tumbling, inverted balances, individual stunts, and partner stunts.

d. Perform body management skills on a variety of apparatus including benches, balance beams, and climbing ropes.

e. Move rhythmically in various settings including folk, square, and line dances, rope jumping, and rhythmic gymnastics.

f. Apply a wide variety of locomotor and manipulative game skills in low-organized game settings.

g. Incorporate specialized sport skills in a variety of sport lead-up games.

Standard 2: Demonstrates understanding of movement concepts, principles, and tactics as they apply to the learning and performance of physical activities.

Standard 2 addresses developing knowledge about various aspects of physical activity. The school years are a time of opportunity—to experience and learn many different types of physical activities and skills. This standard gives students the opportunity to learn basic concepts of movement (Chapter 15). Movement concepts help students understand what, where, and how the body can move. Again, the emphasis is experiencing the diversity of human movement. Allied to this experience is learning the correct mechanics of skill performance (Chapter 3). Students leave school knowing about stability, force, leverage, and other factors related to efficient movement.

Instruction is focused on teaching students to be self-directed learners who can evaluate their performance and self-correct their skill technique. To become competent performers, they must understand that motor skills are learned only through repetition and refinement (two of the three R's of physical education). Because much adult activity is done alone, students need to learn how to warm up for activity and cool down when finished. Understanding simple principles of motor learning (Chapter 3) such as practice, arousal, and skill refinement will serve students well in future experiences.

Outcomes for Developmental Level I Students

a. Understand a vocabulary of basic movement concepts such as personal space, qualities of movement, body awareness, and the relationship of movements.

b. Understand words describing various relationships with objects, such as *around*, *behind*, *over*, *through*, and *parallel*.

c. Implement space awareness concepts and control of movements when performing locomotor movements in a group setting.

d. Understand basic mechanics of skill performance when doing specialized skills such as throwing, kicking, striking, and catching.

e. Appreciate the value of practice in learning motor skills.

Outcomes for Developmental Levels II and III Students

a. Collect information about improving skill performance, including asking friends and coaches, doing self-evaluation, and learning to monitor personal accomplishments.

b. Know the importance of repetition and refinement in learning specialized motor skills.

c. Understand how warm-up and cooldown prevent injuries.

d. Incorporate the mechanics of skill performance into various settings.

e. Use simple strategies when participating in various lead-up games (modified rules, equipment, and number of participants).

Standard 3: Participates regularly in physical activity.

Standard 3 is concerned with regular physical activity. Its basis is that active children mature into active adults (Raitakari et al., 1994). Specifically, learning how to monitor personal activity levels, plan meaningful activity programs, and make informed decisions about physical activity are important outcomes. The PLAY program (Arizona Department of Health Services, 2004) and the Activitygram (Cooper Institute, 2008) are designed to reward students for monitoring and participating in daily physical activity. Children need to learn where they can participate within their community and how they can join clubs, YMCAs, and sport programs. Chapter 12 offers information on these programs and ways to increase children's physical activity levels.

The basic considerations for lifetime activity are several. Sallis (1994) classifies the factors influencing people to be active: psychological, social, physical environmental, and biological. A major role of physical education is to foster those factors often referred to as *determinants of active living.* Psychological determinants are among the most powerful. For example, students must enjoy physical activity if they are expected to participate as adults. Enjoyment increases when there is an adequate level of proficiency in a favored activity. Since most adults do not participate in activities unless they feel competent in them, learning skills becomes a priority of childhood. Another psychological factor is the rational basis for play. This can be established through activity orientations that are transferable to other situations (e.g., various games suitable for small groups, and sports activities adapted to local situations).

Social and environmental influences also affect lifetime activity patterns. These factors include having family and peer role models, being encouraged by significant others, and having opportunities to participate in activities with others in one's social group. Physical environmental factors include adequate programs and facilities, adequate equipment and supplies, safe outdoor environments, and available opportunities near home and at school. Also included are adequate school opportunities such as recess, physical education, intramural games, recreation programs, and sports. Finally, biological factors include age, gender, and ethnic and/or socioeconomic status. For more details concerning determinants of physical activity, refer to Sallis's (1994) work.

A NASPE publication, *Physical Activity for Children: A Statement of Guidelines* (2004b), outlines why children need daily physical activity. It is the first document to recommend how much activity children need (at least 60 minutes per day). The publication discusses the physical activity pyramid and the importance of participating in different types of physical activity, including lifestyle activity, active aerobics, active sports and recreation, flexibility, and muscle fitness exercises. The guidelines offer support and direction for teachers who need to justify increasing their students' daily physical activity.

Outcomes for Developmental Level I Students

a. Show willingness to try different physical activities.

b. Understand how activities must be enjoyable for each individual if they are to be used throughout life.

c. Monitor the amount of time spent in short bouts of activity (e.g., "I played tag for 5 minutes").

d. Set aside time for play outside of school each day.

Outcomes for Developmental Levels II and III Students

a. Show willingness to try many different activities and to identify those activities best suited to them.

b. Demonstrate the ability to set physical activity goals for time and type of activity.

c. Find opportunities for play outside of school (e.g., after-school sports, intramurals, private clubs and organizations).

d. Use a pedometer to monitor daily activity in terms of steps or accumulated time.

e. Maintain an activity log showing the different types and amounts of physical activity accumulated each day.

Standard 4: Achieves and maintains a health-enhancing level of physical fitness.

Standard 4 is concerned with physical fitness. Physical fitness instruction (Chapter 13) for elementary school children concentrates on their participation in daily physical activity rather than the product of fitness (how many repetitions, how fast, or how far). Giving students an opportunity to offer input about their fitness program and make personal activity choices prepares them for a lifetime of activity. When students accept responsibility for participating in regular activity, fitness becomes an authentic learning experience that may last a lifetime. Positive experiences in physical activity are a must. Meeting this standard means helping students develop positive attitudes that carry over into adulthood. Little is gained if students develop high physical fitness levels in the elementary school years but leave school with a strong dislike of physical activity.

Teachers should devote part of each physical education period to having children learn about and experience fitness. But learning the facts of fitness is not enough; elementary school children must experience participation (Figure 1.3). Many people know the facts of fitness but do not stay active, because they have not learned the activity habit. The best way for students to learn the amount of effort necessary to maintain personal fitness is to experience it. Too often, fitness is seen solely as an aerobic experience. Today, it is clear that aerobics are important; but maintaining strength and flexibility is equally vital. Fitness routines that incorporate interval training (alternating aerobic activities with strength and flexibility activities) show students that the best lifetime fitness experience is a balanced one.

Meeting this standard also implies that students will leave elementary school understanding the basic facts of fitness. Such concepts as the FIT principle (frequency, intensity, and time) can be taught in short question-and-answer episodes. Because each individual has unique needs, and because programs must be developed according to these needs, an understanding of genetic diversity among people (such as differences in muscle type, cardiorespiratory endurance, and motor coordination) is required for helping students understand their physical capabilities. Understanding concepts such as how to exercise properly, how much activity is enough, and how to participate safely in activity helps give children a positive mind-set. Finally, students learn to personally evaluate their fitness levels in a semiprivate setting. By doing self-testing on health-related fitness and charting their physical activity, students can find out if they are in the healthy fitness zone on the Fitnessgram and Activitygram evaluations (Cooper Institute, 2008).

FIGURE 1.3 Fitness is a participatory experience.

Outcomes for Developmental Level I Students

a. Participate daily in at least 60 minutes of physical activity in and out of the school environment.

b. Monitor the basic physiological changes that occur when being active (increased rate of breathing, increased heart rate, and perspiration).

c. Participate in activities that develop muscular strength and endurance (e.g., climbing ropes, hanging activities, and supporting the body weight with arms and hands).

d. Perform a variety of flexibility activities.

e. Identify how personal body composition and different body types affect physical performance.

Outcomes for Developmental Levels II and III Students

a. Participate daily in at least 60 minutes of moderate to vigorous physical activity in and out of the school environment.

b. Engage in various activities that develop muscular strength, ranging from exercises to climbing.

c. Perform activities that increase and maintain flexibility.

d. Know basic elements of safe participation in activities (including safe exercises, overtraining, muscle soreness, and inherent risk of activities).

e. Monitor the intensity of exercise by counting heart and breathing rates.

f. Understand that all health-related fitness components (body composition, muscular strength and endurance, flexibility, and cardiorespiratory endurance) need to be given attention for total physical fitness.

g. Evaluate personal health-related physical fitness, and interpret the meaning of the results.

h. Understand the basic principles of training (i.e., frequency, intensity, and time).

Standard 5: Exhibits responsible personal and social behavior that respects self and others in physical activity.

Standard 5 addresses the need for responsible behavior. Physical education classes offer a unique environment for learning effective social skills. Children have the opportunity to internalize and practice the merits of participation, cooperation, competition, and tolerance. Some terms, such as *citizenship* and *fair play*, help define the desired social atmosphere. Through listening, empathy, and guidance, children learn to differentiate between acceptable and unacceptable ways of expressing feelings. Students must become aware of how they interact with others and how their behavior influences others' responses to them.

Responsible behavior (Chapter 6) implies behaving in ways that do not negatively affect others. Hellison (2003) and others have developed a methodology for teaching responsible behavior. It is generally accepted that if responsible behavior is to be learned, it must be taught through experiences where such behavior is continuously reinforced. Accepting consequences for one's behavior is learned and needs to be valued and reinforced by responsible adults. Responsible behavior occurs in a hierarchy of behavior that goes from being irresponsible to caring and behaving responsibly. Physical education classes are an excellent setting for teaching responsibility because most behavior is highly visible then. Children in a competitive setting may react in an openly irresponsible way, so instructors have a "teachable moment" to discuss such unacceptable behavior. Students must also learn to win and lose in an acceptable way and assume responsibility for their performances. Accepting the consequences of one's behavior is a lesson that arises regularly in a cooperative and/or competitive environment.

Conflicts must be solved nonviolently (Chapter 6) so all parties can maintain self-esteem and dignity. Physical education offers an excellent opportunity to apply conflict resolution skills. Students learn to solve conflicts and disagreements in a peaceful and nonthreatening manner. Many diversity and gender issues (Chapter 5) arise in activity settings, and insightful and caring instruction can help destroy negative stereotypes. Learning about the similarities and differences among cultures and how most people share common values and beliefs is an important outcome.

The lesson plan, the activities presented, the teachers' views of less successful students, and the treatment of children with disabilities send implied messages to students (the hidden curriculum). When teachers and parents respond to children in a caring way, the children learn they are loved, capable, and contributing people. If children believe they belong, they are loved and respected, and their successes outweigh their failures, they are on the road to developing a desirable self-concept.

Cooperation is an important behavior to teach in elementary physical education settings. Without cooperation, competitive games cannot be played. Competitive games demand cooperation, fair play, and respect for teammates; without these elements, the joy of participation is lost. Cooperative games teach children that all teammates are needed to reach group goals (Figure 1.4).

Outcomes for Developmental Level I Students

a. Participate in a variety of multicultural activities.

b. Understand how different individuals make a variety of contributions to the group.

c. Explain simple differences and similarities of activities played in different cultural and ethnic backgrounds.

d. Show empathy for the concerns and limitations of peers.

e. Resolve conflicts in an acceptable, nonviolent way.

f. Follow rules and procedures in physical activity settings.

g. Participate safely by observing safety procedures for equipment and apparatus.

h. Understand and follow the rules of low-organized games.

i. Cooperate in a group setting, and be willing to take turns and help others.

j. Show the ability to behave responsibly when differences of opinion occur.

k. Play willingly with all students regardless of race, gender, or disability.

Outcomes for Developmental Levels II and III Students

a. Understand how sports, games, and dance play a central role in modern-day cultures.

b. React positively to individuals who have cultural or ethnic differences, or who have limitations.

c. Demonstrate a willingness to participate with peers regardless of diversity or disability.

d. Enjoy and interact with peers in various physical activity settings.

e. Resolve conflicts in an acceptable, nonviolent way.

f. Show the ability to create or modify rules to better meet the group's needs.

g. Understand that cooperative skills must be developed before competitive games can be played.

h. Understand how sports and games affect issues of gender and diversity.

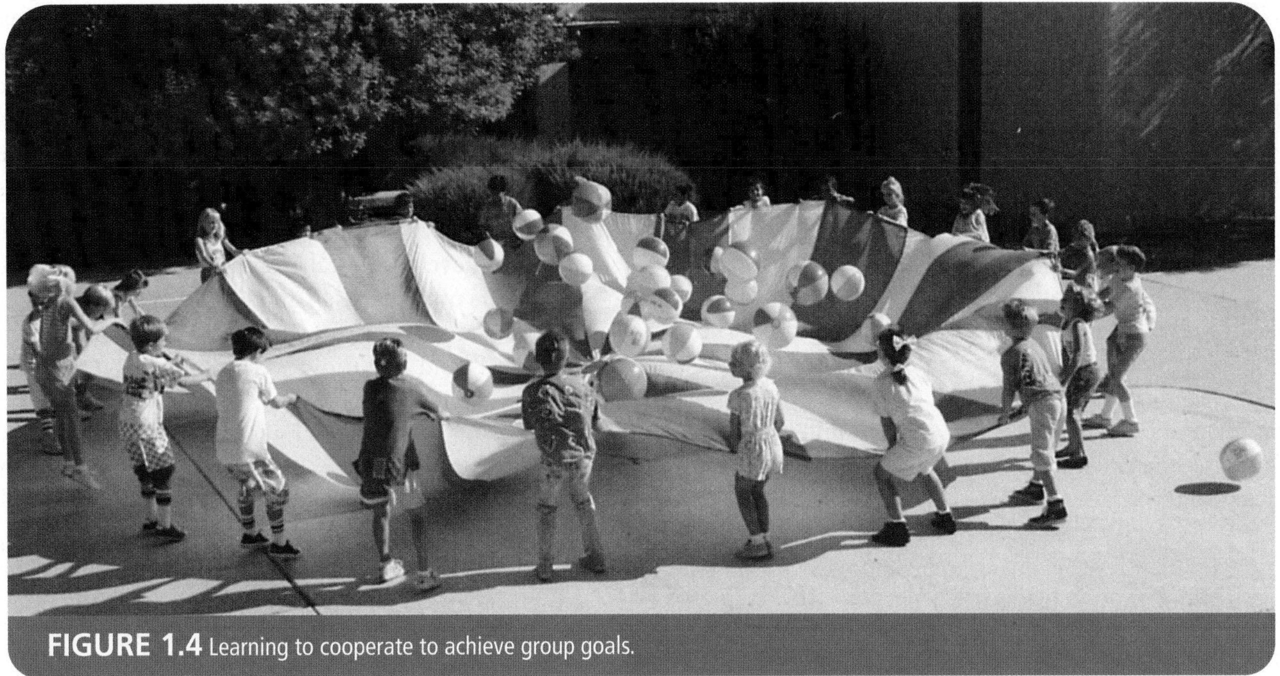

FIGURE 1.4 Learning to cooperate to achieve group goals.

i. Recognize the benefits (social and physical) of participating in group games and activities.

j. Show a willingness to follow rules, procedures, and safety guidelines in all physical activity settings.

k. Behave in a caring and helping way toward all peers.

Standard 6: Values physical activity for health, enjoyment, challenge, self-expression, and/or social interaction.

Standard 6 focuses on how much the student values physical activity, and whether the student has the knowledge needed to make thoughtful decisions affecting his or her health and wellness (Chapter 14). Meeting this standard does not have to turn physical education into a sedentary fact-learning experience. Instruction can be integrated into activity and skill development sessions. Simple principles about nutrition, stress, substance abuse, and safety can be woven into daily instruction to give children an opportunity to learn about healthy lifestyles.

Wellness implies developing a lifestyle that is balanced in all phases, with *moderation* the keyword. Wellness is based on developing a clear understanding of choices and alternatives that lead to making wise decisions. Students cannot make meaningful choices for wellness if they do not understand the consequences of their decisions. Wellness instruction involves studying the wisdom of past generations and integrating it into the lifestyles of current and future generations. In elementary school, basic wellness instruction covers how the skeletal, muscular, and cardiorespiratory systems function. Students also study lifestyle alternatives that affect wellness, including basic facts about nutrition, weight control, stress and relaxation, substance abuse, and safety.

Outcomes for Developmental Level I Students

a. Explain why physical activity is important for good health.

b. Try new activities, and persist in learning them.

c. Tell others how physical activity makes them feel good.

d. Know that everybody should be active at least 60 minutes a day.

Outcomes for Developmental Levels II and III Students

a. Make meaningful decisions about personal wellness by gathering information, considering the alternatives, and understanding the consequences accompanying such choices.

b. Know what types of physical activity are important for wellness.

c. Understand factors that are detrimental to good health (e.g., substance abuse and stress).

d. Understand how physical activity is important for weight management.

e. Understand the importance of safety, particularly in activity settings such as bicycling, swimming, playing sports, and walking.

f. Identify some examples of proper eating habits.

ESSENTIAL COMPONENTS OF A QUALITY PHYSICAL EDUCATION PROGRAM

Physical education teachers need to know the essential components of a quality physical education program. They must provide the critical elements that ensure students receive a quality physical education experience. The following components interlock to form a comprehensive physical education program that will be valued by parents, teachers, and students. Each component is described briefly here; in-depth coverage is offered in the chapters referenced under each point. Figure 1.5 illustrates the essential components of a quality physical education program.

I. **Quality physical education programs are organized around content standards that offer direction and continuity to instruction and evaluation.** A quality program is driven by a set of content standards. These standards are defined by various competencies that children are expected to accomplish. Standards are measurable so that both teachers and students know when progress has been made. Comprehensive physical education content standards are presented earlier in this chapter. Chapter 8 offers some evaluation strategies for teachers to see if they and their students are meeting the standards.

II. **Quality programs are student centered and based on the developmental urges, characteristics, and interests of students.** Children learn best when the skills and activities they must learn match their physical and emotional development. Including activities in the program because they match the teacher's competencies, but not the students' needs, is unacceptable. Teachers must teach new activities outside their comfort zone if they are going to present a comprehensive program. Chapter 4 discusses the urges, characteristics, and interests of children and how they affect the creation of a quality physical education program. Chapter 5 offers many ideas for understanding and teaching to the personal needs of students. A quality program focuses on the successes of students so that there is motivation to

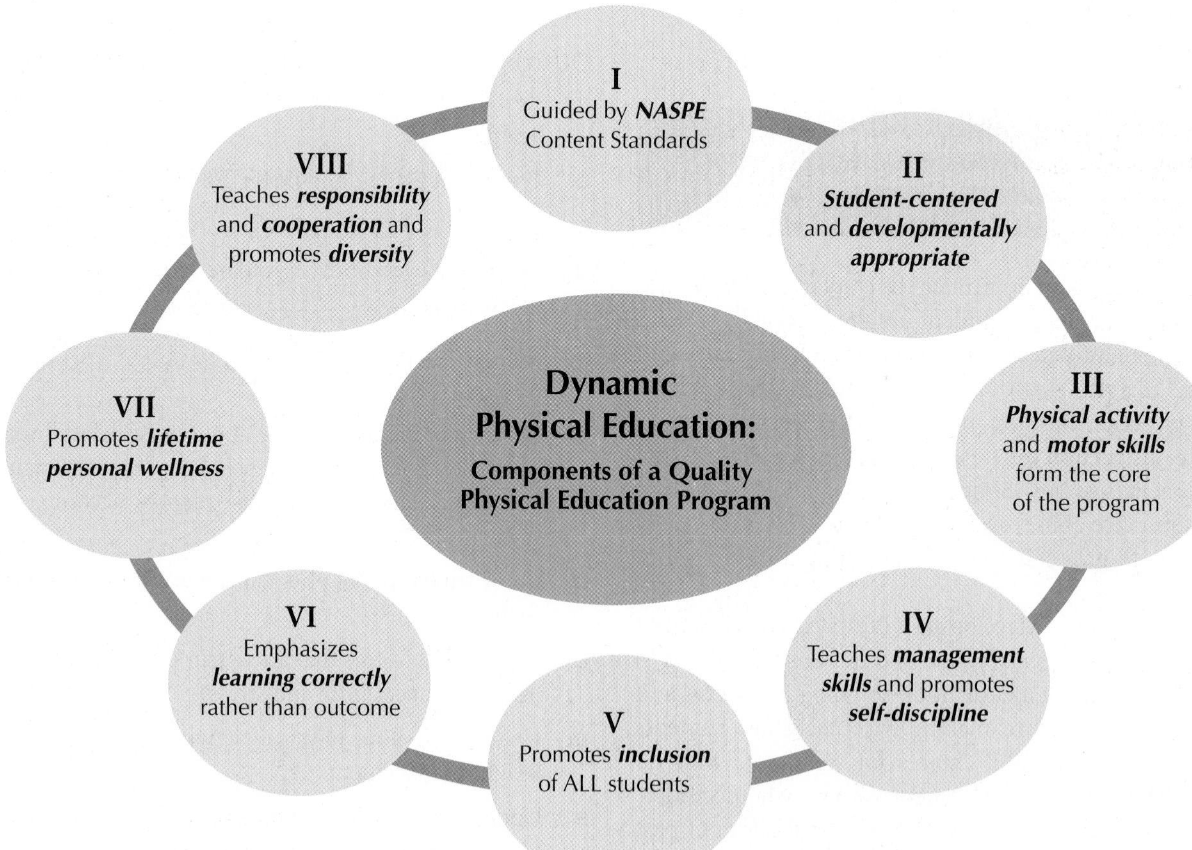

FIGURE 1.5 Essential components of a quality physical education program.

continue. Developing a positive set of behaviors toward physical activity is a key goal of physical education. Chapter 5 also discusses essential elements of teaching and how to give children positive reinforcement in learning situations.

III. Quality physical education programs make physical activity and motor skill development the core of the program. Physical education is the only place in the total school curriculum where students learn motor skills. In this unique discipline, it is mandatory that the physical education program focus on students' skill development and quality physical activity. Chapters 2 and 12 explain the importance of physical activity for children's optimal growth and development.

IV. Quality physical education programs teach management skills and self-discipline. Physical education teachers are often evaluated based on how students behave in their classes rather than on how much they know about physical education. Administrators and parents look to see that students are on task and receiving competent instruction. When a class is well managed and students work with self-discipline, the experience compares to classroom instruction, bringing credibility to the program. Chapter 6 offers many different methods for managing a classroom and promoting self-discipline.

V. Quality programs emphasize inclusion of all students. Instruction is designed for students who need help the most—less skilled students and children with disabilities. Students who are skilled and blessed with innate ability have many opportunities to learn. They have the confidence to take private lessons, join clubs, and play in after-school sports programs. Unskilled students or children with disabilities lack confidence and often cannot help themselves. Physical education is most likely the last opportunity children will have to learn skills in a caring, positive environment. Instructional progressions designed to facilitate less skilled and less motivated children will ensure a positive and successful experience. Students who are not naturally gifted must perceive themselves as successful if they are to enjoy and value physical activity. Chapter 7 focuses on dealing with children who have disabilities and modifying activities so all children can succeed.

VI. Quality physical education programs focus instruction on the process of learning skills rather than on the product or outcome of the skill performance. When students are learning new motor skills, performing the skill correctly is more important than the outcome of the skill. Children need to learn proper techniques first and then focus on the product of performing the skill. Put another way, it is more important to teach a child to catch a beanbag properly than worry about how many he catches or misses. Chapter 3 offers strategies for optimizing skill learning. Chapter 8 examines when to focus on the process or product evaluation of motor skills.

VII. Quality physical education programs teach lifetime activities that students can use to promote their health and personal wellness. Quality physical education programs prepare children to participate in activities they can perform when they become adults. If a program is restricted to team sports, the program will be of little value to most adults. Participation in sports activities declines rapidly with age. Less than 5% of adults above the age of 30 report playing a team sport (USDHHS, 1996). By far, walking is the activity most often reported in adulthood. Other activities such as stretching exercises, bicycling, strength development exercises, jogging, swimming, and aerobics are also popular with adults. Quality physical education looks to the future and offers activities that children can enjoy and use as adults. Chapter 12 offers information about the importance of teaching lifetime physical activity skills in a physical education setting. Chapter 14 explores instructional strategies for teaching wellness and developing a healthy lifestyle.

VIII. Quality physical education programs teach cooperation and responsibility and help students develop sensitivity to diversity and gender issues. Cooperative skills have to precede competitive skills. To enjoy group activities, students must agree to follow rules. Most fights and physical violence occur when children are in a physical activity setting. Physical education is an effective laboratory for students to learn to behave responsibly because behavior is so observable to others. Situations in physical activity give rise to the need to resolve conflicts peacefully. Chapter 6 presents ways to teach children responsible behavior and conflict resolution techniques. Students need to learn about similarities and differences between cultures. Competitive activities such as the Olympics often bring cultures together and offer students the opportunity to see different cultures compete with respect and dignity. Coeducational activities help students understand how activities cut across gender and stereotypes. When gender differences occur in physical activities, it is an excellent time to point out that individuals differ regardless of race or gender. Chapter 5 offers some strategies for dealing with gender and diversity issues.

APPLYING WHAT YOU READ

- The lessons you create as teachers will reflect your understanding of the definition of physical education, your physical education philosophy, and your knowledge of how the field has evolved.
- After developing a lesson, review the lesson and ask yourself: Does the lesson meet current mandates? Does the lesson reflect current philosophies in physical education?
- Physical educators are often asked to provide a rationale for their program. The section titled "The Need for Physical Education Programs" contains information needed for a presentation, paper, or report for administrators.
- Lessons in your program should allow you to address all NASPE standards. While preparing lessons, review the standards and ask yourself, "Am I meeting these?"
- Review your program regularly, referring to the "Essential Components of a Quality Physical Education Program." Are you addressing these components?

REFLECTION AND REVIEW

HOW AND WHY

1. How have your perceptions of physical education changed based on your understanding of its evolution?
2. How does physical education fit into a school's curriculum?
3. How can the nationwide focus on health, wellness, and physical activity influence children's lives?
4. How do the NASPE national standards help teachers?
5. Why is it important to understand the essential components of physical education?

CONTENT REVIEW

1. Are physical education programs and physical education teachers necessary? Defend your answer.
2. Why is physical education a unique component of the total school curriculum?
3. What has been the evolution of physical education?
4. What contributions have different pedagogical approaches made to the evolution of physical education?
5. How have federal mandates influenced physical education?
6. What are the content standards, and what role do they play in physical education?
7. What are the essential components of a quality physical education program, and what is the significance of each?

FOR MORE INFORMATION

REFERENCES AND SUGGESTED READINGS

Anderson, R. E., Crespo, C. J., Bartlett, S. J., Cheskin, L. J., & Pratt, M. (1998). Relationship of physical activity and television watching with body weight and level of fatness among children: Results from the Third National Health and Nutrition Examination Survey. *Journal of the American Medical Association, 279*, 938–942.

Arizona Department of Health Services. (2004). *PLAY: Promoting lifetime activity for youth.* Phoenix, AZ: Author.

Bailey, D. A., Faulkner, R. A., & McKay, H. A. (1996). Growth, physical activity, and bone mineral acquisition. *Exercise and Sport Science Reviews, 24*, 233–266.

Bar-Or, O. (1995). Health benefits of physical activity during childhood and adolescence. *Physical Activity and Fitness Research Digest, 2*(4), 1–6.

Beighle, A., & Pangrazi, R. P. (2000). The validity of six pedometers for measuring the physical activity of children. Unpublished manuscript.

Cooper Institute. (2008). *Fitnessgram/Activitygram test administration manual* (3rd ed.). Champaign, IL: Human Kinetics.

Corbin, C., & Lindsey, R. (2005). *Fitness for life* (5th ed.). Champaign, IL: Human Kinetics.

Dale, D., Corbin, C. B., & Cuddihy, T. F. (1998). Can conceptual physical education promote physically active lifestyles? *Pediatric Exercise Science, 10*, 97–109.

Guo, S. S., & Chumlea, W. C. (1999). Tracking of body mass index in children in relation to overweight in adulthood. *American Journal of Clinical Nutrition, 70*, 145S–148S.

Guo, S. S., Roche, A. F., Chumlea, W. C., Gardner, J. D., & Siervogel, R. M. (1994). The predictive value of childhood body mass index values for overweight at age 35 y. *American Journal of Clinical Nutrition, 59*(4), 810–819.

Hellison, D. (2003). *Teaching responsibility through physical activity* (2nd ed.). Champaign, IL: Human Kinetics.

Jebb, S. A., & Moore, M. S. (1999). Contribution of a sedentary lifestyle and inactivity to the etiology of overweight and obesity: Current evidence and research issues. *Medicine and Science in Sports and Exercise, 31*, S534–S541.

Kraus, H., & Hirschland, R. P. (1954). Minimum muscular fitness tests in school children. *Research Quarterly, 25*, 178–187.

Lee, S. M., Burgeson, C. R., Fulton, J. E., & Spain, C. G. (2007). Physical education and physical activity: Results from the School Health Policies and Programs Study 2006. *Journal of School Health, 77*, 435–463.

Morgan, C. F., Pangrazi, R. P., & Beighle, A. (2003). Using pedometers to promote physical activity in physical education. *Journal of Physical Education, Recreation & Dance, 74*(7), 33–38.

Must, A., Jacques, P. F., Dallal, G. E., Bajema, C. J., & Dietz, W. H. (1992). Long-term morbidity and mortality of overweight adolescents: A follow-up of the Harvard Growth Study of 1922 to 1935. *New England Journal of Medicine, 327*, 1350–1355.

National Association for Sport and Physical Education. (2004a). *Moving into the future: National standards for physical education* (2nd ed.). Reston, VA: Author.

———. (2004b). *Physical activity for children: A statement of guidelines* (2nd ed.). Reston, VA: Author.

National Center for Health Statistics. (2004). *Health, United States, 2004 with chartbook on trends in the health of Americans.* Hyattsville, MD: Centers for Disease Control and Prevention.

Raitakari, O. T., Porkka, K. V. K., Taimela, S., Telama, R., Rasanen, L., & Viikari, J. S. A. (1994). Effects of persistent physical activity and inactivity on coronary risk factors in children and young adults. *American Journal of Epidemiology, 140*, 195–205.

Roberts, D. F., Foehr, U. G., & Rideout, V. (2005). *Generation M: Media in the lives of 8–18 year olds.* Palo Alto, CA: Kaiser Family Foundation.

Sallis, J. F. (1994). Influences on physical activity of children, adolescents, and adults or determinants of active living. *Physical Activity and Fitness Research Digest, 1*(7), 1–8.

Sallis, J. F., McKenzie, T. L., Kolody, B., Lewis, M., Marshall, S., & Rosengard, P. (1999). Effects of health-related physical education on academic achievement: Project SPARK. *Research Quarterly for Exercise and Sport, 70*, 127–134.

Sporting Goods Manufacturers Association. (2000, May/June). *Fitness and sports newsletter.*

Telama, R., Yang, X., Laakso, L., & Viikari, J. (1997). Physical activity in childhood and adolescence as predictors of physical activity in young adulthood. *American Journal of Preventative Medicine, 13*, 317–323.

Trudeau, F., Laurencelle, L., Tremblay, J., Rajic, M., & Shephard, R. J. (1998). A long-term follow-up of participants in the Trois-Rivieres semi-longitudinal study of growth and development. *Pediatric Exercise Science, 10*, 366–377.

U.S. Department of Health and Human Services. (1996). *Physical activity and health: A report of the surgeon general.* Atlanta, GA: U.S. Department of Health and Human Services, Centers for Disease Control and Prevention, National Center for Chronic Disease Prevention and Health Promotion.

———. (2000). *Healthy people 2010: National health promotion and disease objectives.* Washington, DC: U.S. Government Printing Office.

———. (2002). *Prevalence of overweight among children and adolescents: United States, 1999.* Centers for Disease Control and Prevention, National Center for Health Statistics.

U.S. Public Health Service. (1990). *Healthy people 2000: National health promotion and disease objectives.* Washington, DC: U.S. Government Printing Office.

Whitaker, R. C., Wright, J. A., Pepe, M. S., Seidel, K. D., & Dietz, W. H. (1997). Predicting obesity in young adulthood from childhood and parental obesity. *New England Journal of Medicine, 337*, 869–873.

WEBSITES

American Alliance for Health, Physical Education, Recreation, and Dance
www.aahperd.org

American Heart Association
www.americanheart.org

Centers for Disease Control and Prevention
www.cdc.gov

The Presidential Active Lifestyle Program
www.presidentschallenge.org/pdf/ActiveLifestyle.pdf

Public Law 94–142
http://asclepius.com/angel/special.html

Title IX
www.ed.gov/pubs/TitleIX

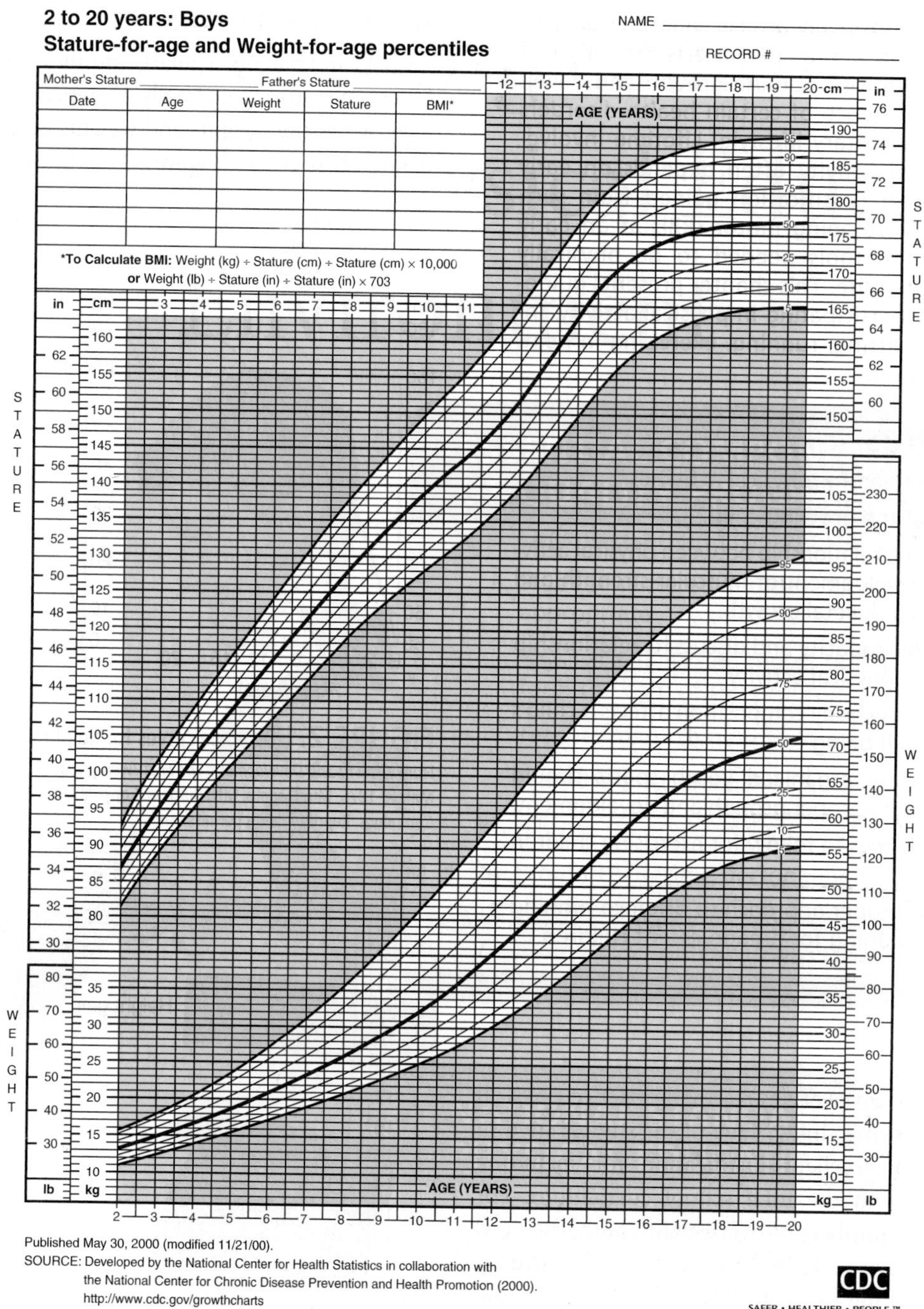

FIGURE 2.3 2 to 20 years: Boys' stature-for-age and weight-for-age percentiles.

Developed by the National Center for Health Statistics in collaboration with the National Center for Chronic Disease Prevention and Health Promotion (2000).

children are expected to be at a specific year of life. Another way to examine growth patterns is to look at a velocity curve, which reveals how much a child grows from year to year (Figure 2.2 on page 21). Children go through a rapid growth period from birth to age 5. From age 6 to the onset of adolescence, growth slows to a steady but increasing pattern. A general rule of thumb for motor learning is that when growth is rapid, the ability to learn new skills decreases. Because the growth rate slows during the elementary school years, this is an excellent window of time for children to learn motor skills.

During adolescence, children grow rapidly until reaching adulthood. In elementary school, boys are generally taller and heavier. Girls reach the adolescent growth spurt first, growing taller and heavier during sixth and seventh grade. This growth spurt is likely tied to girls reaching puberty earlier. In recent years, the average age when girls reach puberty has decreased. Research suggests

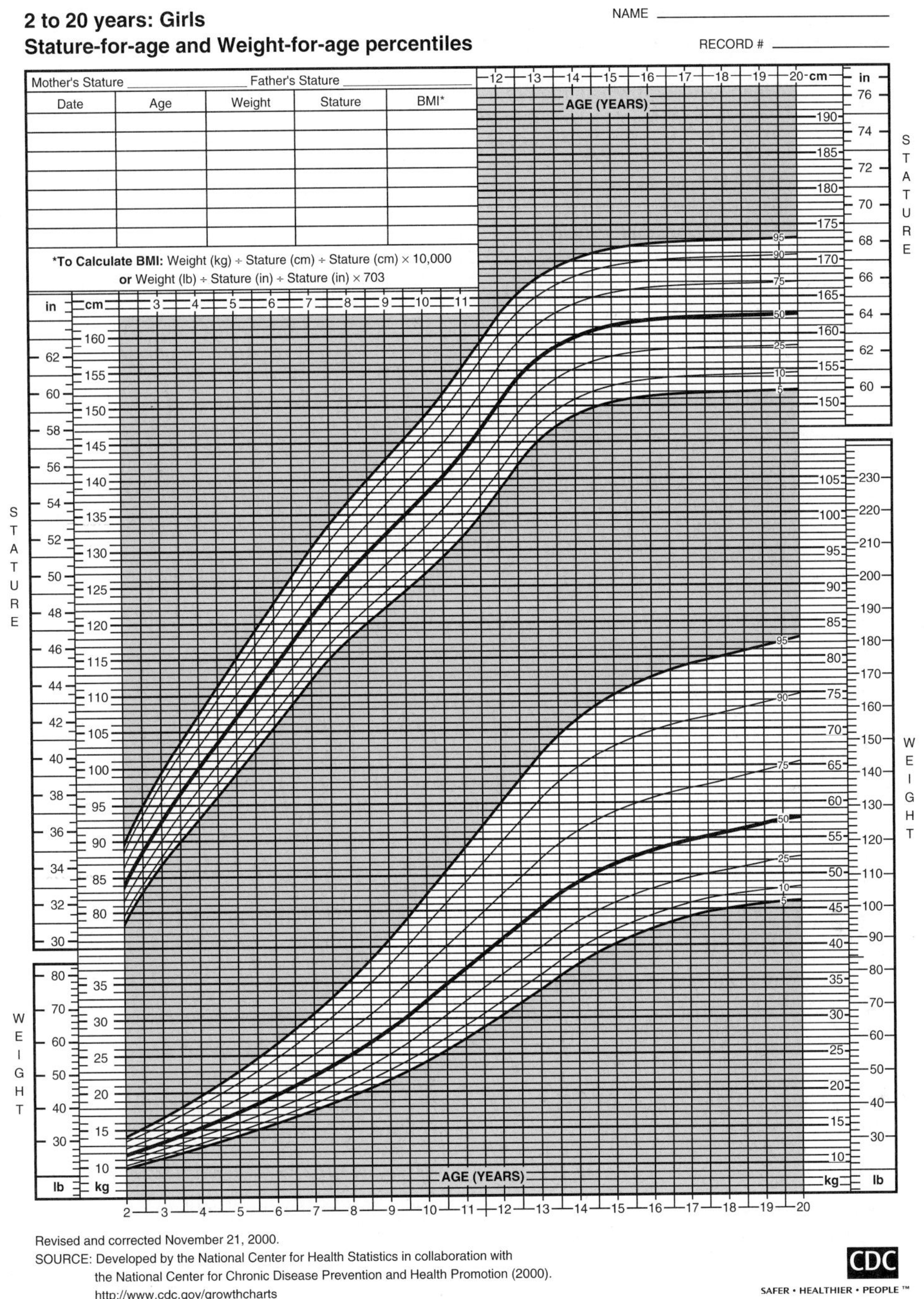

FIGURE 2.4 2 to 20 years: Girls' stature-for-age and weight-for-age percentiles.
Developed by the National Center for Health Statistics in collaboration with the National Center for Chronic Disease Prevention and Health Promotion (2000).

that, in part, the increased rate of childhood obesity, specifically in girls, has led to the earlier onset of puberty in girls (Lee et al., 2007). Boys quickly catch up and grow larger and stronger after puberty. The National Center for Health Statistics has developed growth charts based on a large sample of children (Figures 2.3 and 2.4,). These tables identify both stature (height) and weight percentiles for children ages 2 through 20. The tables offer an opportunity to visualize marked differences between children in a so-called normal population.

Young children have relatively short legs for their overall height. The trunk is longer in relation to the legs during early childhood. The ratio of leg length (standing height) to trunk length (sitting height) is similar for boys and girls through age 11. The head makes up one-fourth of the child's total length at birth and about one-sixth at age 6. Figure 2.5 (page 24) illustrates how body proportions change with growth. Because K–2 students have short legs in relation to their upper bodies, they are "top heavy" and fall more easily than adults do. This high center of

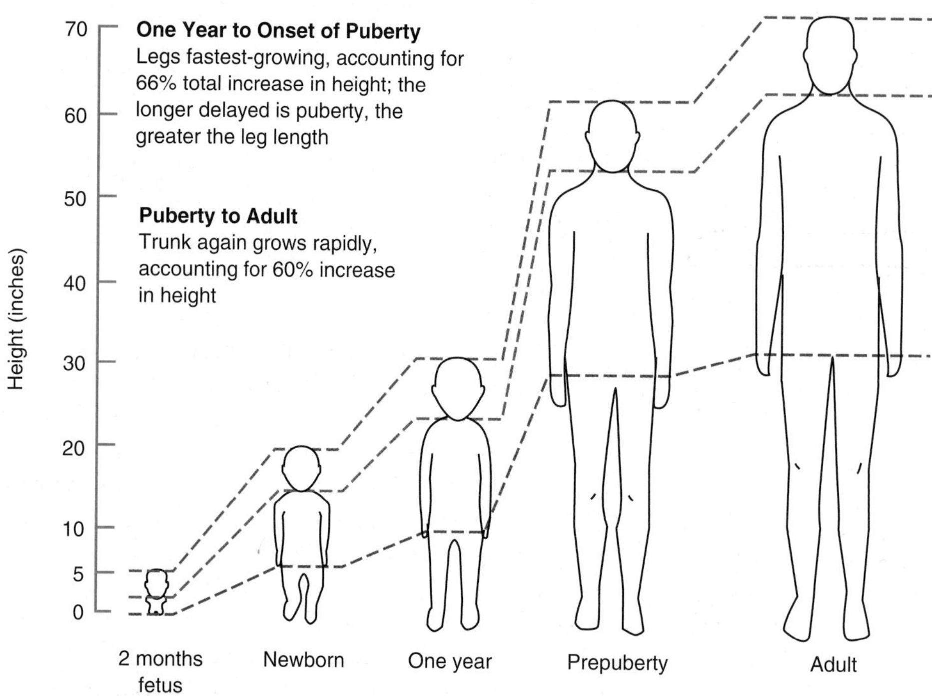

FIGURE 2.5 Changing body proportions from conception to adulthood.
From *Dynamics of Development: Euthenic Pediatrics* (p. 122), by D. Whipple, 1966, New York: McGraw-Hill.

gravity gradually lowers, giving children increased stability and balance.

BODY PHYSIQUE

A child's physique (somatotype) affects the quality of his or her motor performance. Sheldon, Dupertuis, and McDermott (1954) developed the original scheme for somatotyping, identifying three major physiques: *mesomorphy*, *ectomorphy*, and *endomorphy*. Rating is assessed from standardized photographs on a 7-point scale, with 1 being the least expression and 7 the most expression of the specific component. Rating each component gives a total score that identifies an individual's somatotype. A similar system of classification for children (Petersen, 1967) is available for teachers who are interested in understanding children's physiques.

In general, children with a mesomorphic body type perform best in activities requiring strength, speed, and agility, such as most team sports. The *mesomorph* is characterized as having a predominance of muscle and bone and is often labeled "muscled." The *ectomorph* is identified as being extremely thin, with a minimum of muscle development, and is characterized as "skinny." These children may be less proficient in activities requiring strength and power, but are able to perform well in aerobic endurance activities such as jogging, cross-country running, and track and field. The third classification is the *endomorph*, characterized as soft and round, with an excessively protruding abdomen. These children may perform poorly in many areas, including aerobic and anaerobic skill-oriented activities. The overweight child is generally at a disadvantage in all phases of physical performance. Somatotype classification illustrates how dramatically children differ in physique and requires that instruction accommodate individual differences.

SKELETAL MATURITY

Teachers often speak about students' *maturity*. Physical maturity strongly affects a student's performance in physical education. Maturity is usually measured by comparing chronological age with skeletal age. Ossification (hardening) of the bones occurs in the center of the bone shaft and at the ends of the long bones (growth plates). The rate of ossification accurately indicates a child's maturation rate. Maturation rate can be identified by x-raying the wrist bones and comparing the development of the subject's bones with a set of standardized X-rays (Gruelich & Pyle, 1959; Roche, Chumlea, & Thissen, 1988). A child whose chronological age is beyond her skeletal age is said to be a late (or slow) maturer. If a child's skeletal age is ahead of her chronological age, she is labeled an early (fast) maturer.

Studies examining skeletal age (Gruelich & Pyle, 1959; Krahenbuhl & Pangrazi, 1983) consistently show that in a typical classroom, the students display a 5- to 6-year variation in skeletal maturity. For example, a class of third graders who are all 8 years old chronologically usually range in skeletal age from 5 to 11 years. This means that some children are actually 5-year-olds skeletally and are trying to compete with others who are as mature as 11-year-olds. Effective programs offer activities that are developmentally appropriate and suited to children's level of maturity.

Early maturing children of both sexes are generally heavier and taller for their age than are average- or late-maturing students. Overweight children (endomorphs) are often more mature for their age than are normal-weight children and carry more muscle and bone tissue. However, these overweight children also carry a greater percentage of body weight as fat tissue (Malina, Bouchard, & Bar-Or, 2004), which decreases their motor performance. Boys' motor performance is related to skeletal maturity in that a more mature boy usually performs better on motor tasks (Clarke, 1971). For girls, however, motor performance seems to be unrelated to physiological maturity. These two findings suggest that motor development follows a different course for boys than for girls (Gidley Larson et al., 2007). Furthermore, Malina (1978) found that late maturation is commonly associated with exceptional motor performance. Physical education programs often ask students to learn at the same rate, although this practice may be detrimental to the development of students who are maturing at a faster or slower rate. Students do not mature at the same rate and are not at similar levels of readiness to learn (Figure 2.6). Offering a wide spectrum of developmentally appropriate activities helps ensure that children will succeed regardless of their maturity.

FIGURE 2.6 Children the same age vary in size and maturity.

MUSCULAR DEVELOPMENT AND STRENGTH

In the elementary school years, muscular strength increases linearly with chronological age (Beunen, 1989; Malina et al., 2004). A similar yearly increase occurs until adolescence, when a rapid increase in strength occurs. When differences in strength between the sexes are adjusted for height, there is no difference in lower-body strength from ages 7 through 17. When the same adjustment between the sexes is made for upper-body strength, however, boys have more strength in the upper extremity and trunk (Malina et al., 2004). Boys and girls can participate on somewhat even terms in activities demanding leg strength, particularly if their size and mass are similar. But in activities demanding arm or trunk strength, boys have an advantage, even if they are similar to the girls in height and mass. When pairing children for activities, do not partner students with someone who is considerably taller and heavier (or more mature) and thus stronger.

Muscle Fiber Type and Performance

People have a genetically determined number of muscle fibers. Muscles become larger when the size of each muscle fiber increases—that is, the size of the muscles is determined first by the number of fibers and second by their size. Our muscles are thus somewhat limited by our genetics.

Skeletal muscle tissue contains a ratio of fast-contracting fibers (fast twitch—FT) to slow-contracting fibers (slow twitch—ST; Saltin, 1973). The percentage of fast- versus slow-contracting fibers varies from muscle to muscle and among individuals. The percentage of each type of muscle fiber is determined during the first weeks of postnatal life (Dubowitz, 1970). Most individuals possess a 50–50 split; that is, half of the muscle fibers are FT and half are ST. A small percentage of people have a ratio of 60 to 40 (in either direction), and researchers have verified that some people have an even more extreme ratio.

What is the significance of variation in the ratio of muscle fiber type? ST fibers have a rich supply of blood and related energy mechanisms. This results in a slowly contracting, fatigue-resistant muscle fiber that is well suited to endurance (aerobic) activities. In contrast, FT fibers are capable of bursts of intense activity but are subject to rapid fatigue. These fibers are well suited to activities demanding short-term speed and power (for example, pull-ups, standing long jump, and shuttle run). ST fibers facilitate performance in the mile run or other endurance-oriented activities.

Surprisingly, elementary-age children who do best in activities requiring FT fibers also do best in distance running (Krahenbuhl & Pangrazi, 1983). Muscle fiber metabolic specialization does not occur until adolescence; this is a strong argument for keeping all children involved in varied physical activities throughout the elementary years. A child who does poorly in elementary school may do quite well during and after adolescence, when a high percentage of ST fibers will aid in the performance of aerobic activity. On the other hand, the same child may do poorly in a physical education program dominated by team sports that demand quickness and strength. Designing a program that incorporates activities using a range of physical attributes (that is, endurance, balance, and flexibility) is essential.

RELATIVE STRENGTH AND MOTOR PERFORMANCE

Strength is an important factor in performing motor skills. A study by Rarick and Dobbins (1975) identified and weighted factors contributing to children's motor performance. The factor identified as most important was strength in relation to body size (relative strength). High levels of strength in relation to body size helped predict which students were most capable of performing motor skills. Deadweight (fat) was the fourth-ranked factor in the study and was weighted negatively. Overweight children were less proficient at performing motor skills. Deadweight negatively affects motor performance because it reduces relative strength. Overweight children may be stronger than normal-weight children in absolute terms but are less strong when strength is adjusted for body weight. This lack of strength in relationship to body size causes overweight children to find a strength-related task (such as a push-up or pull-up) much more difficult than the task would seem to normal-weight children. The need for varied and personalized workloads is important to ensure all children can succeed in strength-related activities. Strength is an important part of a balanced fitness program and offers students a better opportunity for success in various motor development activities.

AEROBIC CAPACITY: CHILDREN ARE NOT LITTLE ADULTS

Maximal aerobic power is a person's maximum ability to use oxygen in the body for metabolic purposes. Oxygen uptake, all other factors being equal, determines the quality of endurance-oriented performance. Maximal aerobic power is closely related to lean body mass, which helps explain the differences in performance between boys and girls. When maximum oxygen uptake is adjusted per kilogram of body weight, it shows little change for boys (no increase) and a gradual decrease for girls (Rowland, 2005). This decrease in females is due to an increase in body fat and a decrease in lean body mass. When maximal oxygen uptake is not adjusted for body weight, it increases in similar amounts on a yearly basis for both boys and girls through age 12, although boys have higher values as early as age 5.

Adults interested in increasing endurance-based athletic performance train extensively to increase aerobic power. A frequently asked question is whether similar training will increase children's aerobic performance. A meta-analysis by Payne and Morrow (1993) analyzed 28 studies dealing with the impact of exercise on aerobic performance in children. The results showed that training caused little, if any, increase in aerobic power in prepubescent children. If young children's running performance improves, Rowland (2005) postulates that it may occur because they become more efficient mechanically or improve in anaerobic metabolism. Another theory is that young children are active enough to make intergroup differences negligible (Corbin & Pangrazi, 1992; Rowland, 2005).

Even though children demonstrate a relatively high oxygen uptake, they do not perform up to this level because they are not economical in running or walking activities. An 8-year-old child running at 180 meters per minute is operating at 90% of maximal aerobic power, whereas a 16-year-old running at the same rate is operating at only 75% of maximum. This explains why young children are less capable than adolescents and adults at competing over long distances, though they can maintain a slow speed for long distances (Rowland, 2005).

Children exercising at a certain workload perceive the activity to be easier than do adults working at a similar level. Children were asked to rate their perceived exertion at different percentages of maximal heart rate (Bar-Or & Ward, 1989) and usually rated the exertion as less stressful than did adults. Children also demonstrate a rapid recovery rate after strenuous exercise. This implies that teachers should not judge workloads for children based on their own perceptions of the difficulty of an activity. Teachers also should use a child's rapid recovery rate to full advantage. Exercise bouts can be interspersed with restful episodes of stretching and nonlocomotor movements. This type of interval training is a particularly effective training method to use with children because it allows them to exercise aerobically and then recover.

OVERWEIGHT CHILDREN AND PHYSICAL PERFORMANCE

Overweight children seldom perform physical activities on par with leaner children. In part, this is due to the greater metabolic cost of the overweight child's exercise. Overweight children require a higher oxygen uptake capacity to perform a given task. Being overweight takes a great toll on a child's aerobic power because such children must perform at a higher percentage of their maximal oxygen uptake (Figure 2.7). Usually, their maximal uptake values are lower than those of lean children. This gives overweight children less reserve capacity and causes them to perceive higher exertion (Bar-Or & Ward, 1989) when performing a task. These reactions contribute to the common perception among teachers that "overweight children don't like to run." Teachers must understand that asking overweight children to run as far and as fast as normal-weight children is unrealistic. Overweight children need adjusted workloads. There is no acceptable premise, physiological or psychological, for asking all children to run the same distance regardless of ability or body type.

Workloads should be based on time rather than distance. Lean and efficient runners should be expected to move farther than overweight students during a stipulated time period. All children *should not* have to do the same workload. Just as one would not expect kindergarten children to perform the same workload as that of fifth graders, it is unreasonable to expect overweight children to be capable of workloads similar to those of lean, ectomorphic children. *Exercise programs for overweight children should be designed to increase caloric expenditure rather than to improve cardiovascular fitness.* The intensity of the activity should be secondary to the amount of time the student is involved in some type of moderate activity.

FIGURE 2.7 Body composition affects physical performance.

TEACHING SPECIALIZED MOTOR SKILLS

Most children will participate in some type of sport activity, sometimes only because their parents want them to. Physical educators can offer expert advice to parents and community leaders. Since these programs may be administered by persons who have little understanding of young, immature children, it is important for teachers to step forward and share their knowledge.

ALLOW STUDENTS TO LEARN ALL SKILLS AND PLAY ALL POSITIONS

If the best athletes are always assigned to skilled positions, they gain skill at the other children's expense. Because all children deserve equal opportunity to learn sport skills, teachers must ensure that all children play all positions and receive similar amounts of practice time. Reinforcement schedules also need to be similar for children, regardless of their current skill level. Children participate in activities that offer them reinforcement; it is easy for them to become discouraged if they receive little encouragement and praise while trying to learn new skills and positions.

Teachers must understand that maturity plays an important role in dictating how students learn motor skills. Helping children learn all skills and play all positions will help them succeed when they reach maturity. For example, should the teacher identify a student as a pitcher or a right fielder, or as a lineman or a quarterback? Often, these questions are answered for students when teachers make judgments and force them to play a certain position. Many times, such judgments are based on the student's maturity rather than the actual skill level. In a study by Hale (1956), skeletally mature athletes were found to be playing in the skilled positions in the Little League World Series. Chronologically, all players were 11 years old, with a skeletal age range similar to that described earlier. The most mature were pitchers and catchers, and the least mature played at less skilled positions. This study points out how skeletally mature children receive more opportunity to throw at an early age (through pitching and catching). These children obviously have the chance to become better throwers due to the many opportunities they receive when throwing in games and practice. In contrast, children who are immature play right field and receive limited throwing or catching opportunities. Because these less mature children receive much less throwing practice, they are unlikely to ever close the skill gap and develop adequate skill competency.

ENSURE SUCCESS FOR ALL STUDENTS

The willingness to try new experiences and participate in activities is driven by how people feel about their ability level—their *perceived competence*. Perceived competence becomes more specific as students mature. Young students think they are good and competent at everything. As they become older (third or fourth grade), they start to realize that other students are better in some areas. Less able students receive less feedback, and expectations of them remain low. If these students are not given the chance to succeed in class, low perceived competence about their ability to perform physical skills results. This "learned helplessness" (Harter, 1978) eventually results in the students' disliking and dropping out of physical education and future physical activity. They are quite likely to leave school with negative feelings about developing an active lifestyle. Dropping out of physical education commonly occurs in middle school and high school, when students are able to make a choice. Unfortunately, however, the process of feeling incompetent likely begins in the elementary school years.

ASSUME ALL STUDENTS HAVE THE ABILITY TO ACHIEVE

Even though teachers and parents make early judgments about children's potential, it is difficult to identify outstanding athletes in the elementary school years. In a study by Clarke (1968), athletes identified as outstanding in elementary school were seldom outstanding in junior high school, and predictions based on elementary school performance were correct only 25% of the time. Most people would not risk discouraging a child if they knew they would be wrong 75% of the time. However, children are often labeled at an early age, even though three out of four such predictions are incorrect. Treat all children as if they have the potential to succeed. The goal of a physical education program is not to develop athletes, but to help *all* students develop their physical skills within the limits of their potential. The program should not be presented so that it allows the athletically gifted to excel at the expense of less talented children.

UNDERSTAND THAT STARTING YOUNG DOES NOT ENSURE EXCELLENCE

There is no evidence that having a child participate in sports at a young age will make her an outstanding athlete (Figure 2.8). In fact, many professional athletes did not play

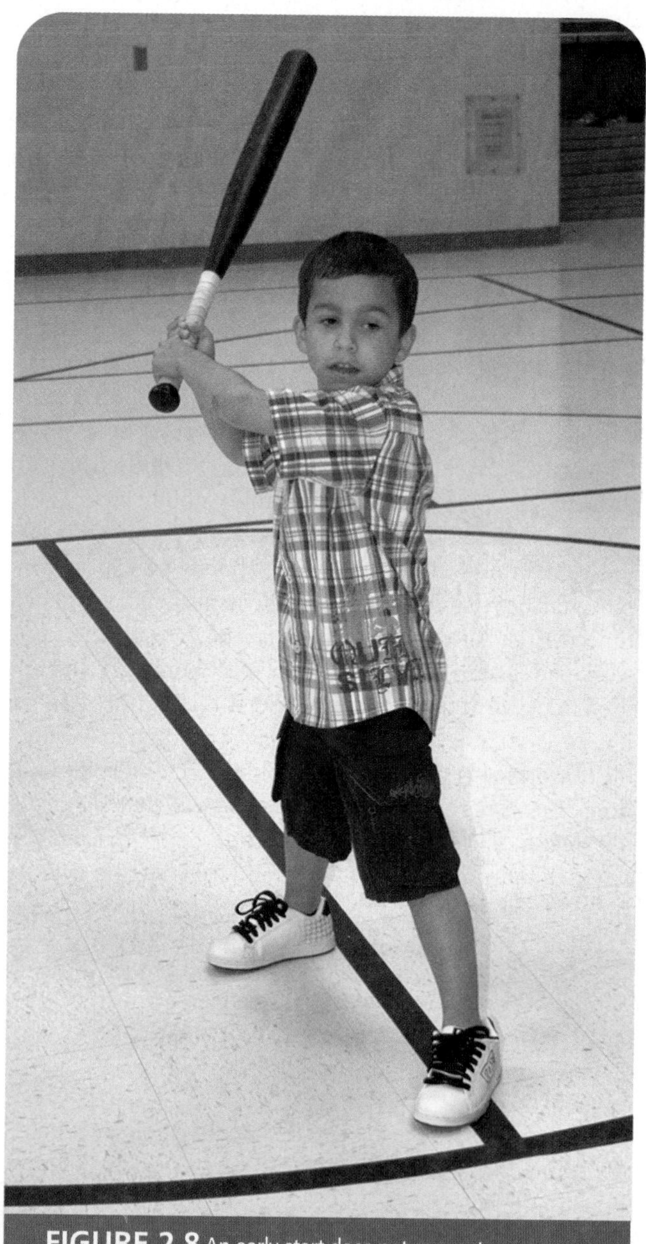

FIGURE 2.8 An early start does not guarantee success.

their sport of excellence until the high school years. Many parents and coaches push to have children start competing in a sport at an early age because this competition creates the perception that better athletes are developed by age 8 or 9. Participating children may seem extremely gifted compared with nonparticipants, because they have been practicing skills for 4 or 5 years. Naturally, "early starters" look advanced compared with children who have not been in an organized program. In most cases, however, a child who is genetically gifted quickly catches up to and surpasses the "early superstar" in 1 to 3 years. As Shephard (1984) states, "Any advantage that is gained from very prolonged training probably lies in the area of skill perfection rather than in a fuller realization of physical potential."

Children who have been in documented and competitive programs for many years may burn out at an early age. A documented program is one that offers extrinsic rewards (e.g., trophies, published league standings, ribbons, and excessive parental involvement). Evidence shows that extrinsic motivation (competition to win) may ultimately decrease intrinsic motivation, particularly in children aged 7 and older. Researchers (Thomas & Tennant, 1978; Whitehead & Corbin, 1991) found that younger children (age 5) perceived a reward as a bonus, thus adding to the joy of performing a throwing motor task. This effect decreased with age; by age 9, children saw the reward as a bribe and intrinsic motivation was undermined. There is no substitute for allowing young children to participate in physical activity for the sheer enjoyment and excitement involved in moving and interacting with peers.

If starting children early can create early burnout, why do parents feel pressured to force their child into a sport program? Some parents constantly compare their children to other children. They see other children participating and practicing sport skills in an organized setting. They worry that their children will be unable to "catch up" if they are not involved in a similar program immediately. Although this is not true, parents need reassurance, and they need facts. Physical educators can help parents find programs that minimize pressure and focus on developing skill. A key is to find programs that allow the child to participate regardless of ability, and to have fun while playing. Children consider having fun and improving their skills to be more important than winning (Athletic Footwear Association, 1990). Many children drop out of sport activities but would probably continue to participate if given the opportunity (Petlichkoff, 1992). Unfortunately, some programs become elitist and start eliminating and "cutting" less gifted players. It is difficult to justify this approach at the elementary school level. All children should have the opportunity to participate if they choose to.

Another reason parents start children at a young age is that children have free time. In their own lives, parents have little time to learn new skills. They feel their children have abundant free time for practice. Unfortunately, if the child shows promise, parents want to increase practice time "so all this talent is not lost." These parents need to be reminded that life includes more than athletic development and that many children have been maimed by stressing sports at the expense of their intellectual and social development. Participation in an activity should be self-selected and student-driven rather than externally motivated. Similarly, withdrawal from an activity should be child controlled rather than externally controlled (Gould, 1987). Participants should not be forced out of the program due to cost, limitation of participants, or injury.

GUIDELINES FOR EXERCISING CHILDREN SAFELY

As in most things, moderation is the key to ensuring that children are safe and grow up enjoying physical activity. Moderate exercise, coupled with opportunities to participate in recreational activity, develops a lasting desire to move. Some adults worry that a child may be harmed physiologically by too much activity. To date, there is no evidence that a healthy child is harmed through vigorous activity and exercise. Children can withstand a gradual increase in workload and are capable of workloads comparable to those of adults when the load is adjusted for height and size. Fatigue causes healthy children to stop exercising long before any health danger arises (Shephard, 1984). Further, the child's circulatory system is proportionally similar to an adult's and thus is not at a disadvantage during exercise.

During an outdoor lesson in the heat, build time into your lesson plan for students to take small-group trips to a water fountain, or provide jugs of water and cups to keep students hydrated.

EXERCISING IN THE HEAT

Use caution when exercising children in hot weather. Exercise does not stop when summer arrives, but teachers and parents should take certain measures to avoid heat-related illness. Children are not little adults. Physiologically, they do not adapt to temperature extremes as effectively as adults do (American Academy of Pediatrics [AAP], 2000; Bar-Or, 1983):

1. Children have higher surface area/mass ratios than adults do. This means children have more skin area for

heat to transfer into their bodies and, as noted in item 4, a decreased ability to remove the heat from their bodies.

2. When walking or running, children produce more metabolic heat per unit mass than adults do. Because children do not move efficiently, they generate more metabolic heat than do adults performing a similar task.
3. Sweating capacity is not as great in children as in adults, resulting in a lowered ability to cool the body.
4. The ability of the blood to convey heat from the body core to the skin is reduced in children due to a lower cardiac output at a given oxygen uptake. Young children do not pump as much blood per heartbeat, making it more difficult to get blood to the skin so heat can be dissipated. Combined with children's inefficient movement patterns, this is even more reason for caution.

These physiological differences give children a distinct disadvantage compared with adults when exercising in an ambient air temperature that is higher than the skin temperature. Individuals do acclimatize to warmer climates. However, children appear to adjust to heat more slowly (taking up to twice as long) than do adults (Malina et al., 2004). Also, children do not instinctively drink enough liquids to replenish fluids lost during exercise. The American Academy of Pediatrics (2000) offers the following guidelines for exercising children during hot days:

1. Reduce the intensity of activities that last 15 minutes or more whenever relative humidity and air temperature are above critical levels. Table 2.1 shows the relationship between humidity and air temperature and when activity should be moderated.
2. At the beginning of a strenuous exercise program or after traveling to a warmer climate, restrain the intensity and duration of exercise initially and then increase it gradually over a period of 10 to 14 days so students can adjust to the effects of heat. When this is not possible, decrease the students' participation time.
3. Be sure the children are hydrated 20 to 30 minutes before strenuous activity (Figure 2.9). During the activity, require periodic drinking (e.g., 150 milliliters per ½ cup of cold tap water every 20 minutes for a child weighing 40 kilograms, or 88 pounds).
4. Clothing should be lightweight and limited to one layer of absorbent material to facilitate evaporation of sweat and expose as much skin as possible. Replace sweat-saturated garments with dry ones. Never use rubberized sweat suits to produce weight loss.

FIGURE 2.9 Water is mandatory for participation in strenuous activity in the heat.

TABLE 2.1 Weather guide: When the humidity and air temperature exceed the corresponding levels, intense activity should be curtailed.

Humidity Level (%)	Air Temperature (°F)
40	90
50	85
60	80
70	75
80	70
90	65
100	60

The academy identifies children with the following conditions as being at a potentially high risk for heat stress: overweight, febrile (feverish) state, cystic fibrosis, gastrointestinal infection, diabetes insipidus, diabetes mellitus, chronic heart failure, caloric malnutrition, anorexia nervosa, sweating insufficiency syndrome, and mental retardation.

DISTANCE RUNNING

An often-asked question is how much and how far children should be allowed to run, particularly in a competitive or training setting. The answer is difficult to agree on because parents, teachers, and coaches seldom see the long-term effects of excessive running. The AAP recommends that although the research is not conclusive on acute running injuries resulting from training, any competitive running program involving young athletes must be supervised by a qualified adult (AAP, 2007). This supervisor should be trained in developing proper training schedules and qualified to educate runners and parents on issues related to running, including the effects of weather and hydration. Most importantly, as with any physical activity, the child must enjoy running, be free of injury, and have no fear of parental or peer pressure.

The International Athletics Association Federation (IAAF) Medical Committee states in part, "The danger certainly exists that with over-intensive training, separation of the growth plates may occur in the pelvic region, the knee, or the ankle. While this could heal with rest, nevertheless definitive information is lacking whether in years to come harmful effects may result." Due to these concerns, the committee asserts that training and competition for long-distance track and road-running events should not be encouraged. Up to the age of 12, it is suggested that children run no more than 800 meters (one-half mile) in competition. Increases in this distance should be introduced gradually—for example, a maximum of 3,000 meters (nearly 2 miles) in competition for 14-year-olds.

Fitness Testing Considerations

Teachers often test children at the start of the school year in the 1-mile run/walk or other high-effort aerobic tests. This practice should be discouraged, since many children may not have ample conditioning to participate safely in the activity. Further, in many parts of the country, the start of the school year is hot and humid, adding to the stress placed on the cardiovascular system. A recommendation is to test only at the end of the school year after students have had the opportunity to be conditioned. If this is not possible, at least give students 4 to 6 weeks to condition themselves. One recommendation is to start with a one-eighth-mile run/walk and gradually build to a 1-mile run/walk over a 4-week period.

A strongly recommended alternative is to eliminate the mile run and substitute the PACER aerobic fitness test (see page 145). The PACER can be administered indoors and does not require running to exhaustion. As a cardiovascular fitness measure, the PACER is as accurate as the mile run and produces much less emotional stress for participants.

RESISTANCE TRAINING

Educators are concerned about the use of resistance training for preadolescent children. Many worry about safety and stress-related injuries; others question whether such training produces significant strength gains. Accepted thinking for years was that prepubescents cannot make significant strength gains due to inadequate levels of circulating androgens. Evidence contradicting this viewpoint continues to build (Faigenbaum, 2003). A study by Cahill (1986) demonstrated significant increases in strength among 18 prepubescent boys. A study by Servedio et al. (1985) showed significant strength gains in shoulder flexion. Weltman et al. (1986) conducted a 14-week, 3-times-a-week program using hydraulic resistance training (circuit training using 10 different stations) in 6- to 11-year-old boys. Results showed an 18 to 37% gain in all major muscle groups. Strength can be increased through weight training in prepubescent students; however, prepubescent children gain strength differently from adolescents and adults (Tanner, 1993). In preadolescent children, strength gains seem to occur from motor learning rather than muscle hypertrophy. Children develop more efficient motor patterns and recruit more muscle fibers, but show no increase in muscle size (Ozmun, Mikesky, & Surburg, 1994).

Note that the term *resistance training* is used here to denote the use of barbells, dumbbells, rubber bands, or machines as resistance. This is in sharp contrast to *weight lifting* or *power lifting*, which is a competitive sport for determining maximum lifting ability. Many experts agree that weight *training* is acceptable for children, but weight *lifting* is highly undesirable and may be harmful. For strength training, the American Orthopaedic Society for Sports Medicine (AOSSM) (Duda, 1986) recommends that "(1) competition is prohibited, and (2) no maximum lift should ever be attempted." Further, AOSSM recommends a physical exam, proper supervision by knowledgeable coaches, and emotional maturity of the participating student. The AAP (2001) recommends that preadolescents and adolescents avoid competitive weight lifting, power lifting, bodybuilding, and maximal lifts until they reach skeletal maturity. Roberts, Ciapponi, and Lytle (2008) give an excellent review of research and guidelines for strength training in physical education classes for children and adolescents.

Safety and prevention of injury are paramount considerations for those interested in weight training for children. Weight training may not be an appropriate activity for a typical group of children in a physical education class. When injuries were reported, most were due to inadequate supervision, lack of proper technique, or competitive lifting. Most weight-lifting injuries were caused by the major lifts: the power clean, the clean and jerk, the squat lift, or the dead lift (Tanner, 1993). These lifts often are competitive and performed in an uncontrolled (ballistic) way; preadolescent children should not attempt them. To ensure an effective, safe program, teachers whose knowledge and expertise are limited should not conduct weight training programs for children.

The long-term effects of strength training in children have not been studied. Many experts also worry about highly organized training programs that emphasize relative gains in strength. A weight training program should be one component of a comprehensive fitness program for children. The National Strength and Conditioning Association (NSCA, 1996) recommends that prepubescent athletes' training include a variety of activities such as agility exercises (basketball, volleyball, tennis, and tumbling) and endurance training (distance running, bicycling, and swimming).

When children experience a variety of physical activities in elementary school physical education, they have little need for weight training. Children's strength can be enhanced in many ways besides using weights, which may present a safety issue (see Roberts et al., 2008). However, weight training is acceptable on an individual basis with parental approval in a club setting. If a weight training program for children is developed, it should be well researched and structured. Focus on the correct lifting technique, not the amount of weight lifted. Proper supervision and technique are key ingredients in a successful program. The following instructional guidelines are adapted from the National Strength and Conditioning Association position statement paper (available at www.nsca-lift.org).

- All workouts should be closely supervised by qualified adults, and the exercise environment should be safe and free of hazards. The exercise area should be large enough so the exercises can be performed correctly.
- Each child should be ready to follow instructions and adhere to training guidelines. Encourage students to ask questions, and praise them for participating.
- Students should warm up for 5 to 10 minutes before strength training.
- Students should start with one light set of 10 to 15 repetitions on several upper- and lower-body exercises. Starting with a light weight allows for appropriate adjustments. Realize that starting weights will vary depending on age, experience, and fitness level. Have students focus on learning the correct form and technique for each exercise.
- When the desired number of repetitions can be performed, increase the weight gradually (by about 1–3 pounds) and perform fewer repetitions.
- Progression may also be achieved by gradually increasing the number of sets, exercises, and training sessions per week. Depending on individual needs and goals, 1 to 3 sets of 6 to 15 repetitions performed on two to three nonconsecutive days per week are recommended.
- Whatever type of training equipment children use, remember that sound teaching methodologies and competent supervision are critical to the safety, effectiveness, and enjoyment of the youth weight training program.
- Remember that students enjoy activities that are fun and make them feel good about themselves.

APPLYING WHAT YOU READ

- All students develop and mature at different rates. When developing lessons and teaching, teachers absolutely must understand these concepts and treat students as individuals.
- When creating a lesson, be sure that the plan meets *all* students' needs. Are you considering the overweight children and their needs? What about students who have delayed skeletal development?
- The section on "Teaching Specialized Motor Skills" is important when you write lessons and while you are teaching. For example, while writing a lesson or teaching, ask yourself, "Am I allowing students to learn all skills and play all positions?" "Am I ensuring success for all students?"
- A clear understanding and implementation of information on exercise and children will assist you in teaching. You can then provide all students with a safe, fun physical education experience full of developmentally appropriate activities.

REFLECTION AND REVIEW

HOW AND WHY

1. How have your views of what is appropriate for children changed after reading this chapter?
2. Why is it important for physical education teachers to understand the growing child?
3. How might physical education be different for an overweight child as compared to a leaner peer?
4. Should children under 9 years old be allowed to play youth sports?
5. Is fitness testing in elementary physical education appropriate? Defend your answer.

CONTENT REVIEW

1. What impact do growth patterns, physique, and skeletal maturity have on skill acquisition and performance?

2. What is the importance of physical activity for children?
3. What are the influences of muscular development and strength on physical activity for children?
4. Is training designed to improve aerobic capacity appropriate for children? Explain.
5. What can be done to maximize the youth sport experience for all children?
6. What is the relationship between physical activity and intelligence?
7. How do adults and children differ in regard to exercising in the heat? Discuss guidelines for exercising students in the heat.

FOR MORE INFORMATION

REFERENCES AND SUGGESTED READINGS

American Academy of Pediatrics. (2007). Clinical Report: Overuse injuries, overtraining, and burnout in child and adolescent athletes. *Pediatrics, 119*(6), 1242–1245.

———. (2000). Policy statement: Climatic heat stress and the exercising child and adolescent. *Pediatrics, 106*(1), 158–159.

———. (2001). Policy statement: Strength training by children and adolescents. *Pediatrics, 107*(6), 1470–1472.

Athletic Footwear Association. (1990). *American youth and sports participation.* North Palm Beach, FL: Author.

Bar-Or, O. (1983). *Pediatric sports medicine for the practitioner.* New York: Springer-Verlag.

Bar-Or, O., & Ward, D. S. (1989). Rating of perceived exertion in children. In O. Bar-Or (Ed.), *Advances in pediatric sport sciences* (Vol. III). Champaign, IL: Human Kinetics.

Beunen, G. (1989). Biological age in pediatric exercise research. In O. Bar-Or (Ed.), *Advances in pediatric sport sciences* (Vol. III). Champaign, IL: Human Kinetics.

Cahill, R. R. (1986). Prepubescent strength training gains support. *The Physician and Sportsmedicine, 14*(2), 157–161.

Clarke, H. H. (1968). Characteristics of the young athlete: A longitudinal look. *Kinesiology Review, 3*, 33–42.

———. (1971). *Physical motor tests in the Medford boys' growth study.* Englewood Cliffs, NJ: Prentice-Hall.

Corbin, C. B., & Pangrazi, R. P. (1992). Are American children and youth fit? *Research Quarterly for Exercise and Sport, 63*(2), 96–106.

Dubowitz, V. (1970). Differentiation of fiber types in skeletal muscle. In E. J. Briskey, R. G. Cassens, & B. B. Marsh (Eds.), *Physiology and biochemistry of muscle as a food* (Vol. 2). Madison, WI: University of Wisconsin Press.

Duda, M. (1986). Prepubescent strength training gains support. *The Physician and Sportsmedicine, 14*(2), 157–161.

Faigenbaum, A. V. (2003). Youth resistance training. *Research Digest, 4*(3). Washington, DC: President's Council on Physical Fitness and Sports.

Gidley Larson, J. C., Mostofsky, S. H., Goldberg, M. C., Cutting, L. E., Denckla, M. B., & Mahone, E. M. (2007). Effects of gender and age on motor exam in typically developing children. *Developmental Neuropsychology, 32*(1), 543–562.

Gould, D. (1987). Understanding attrition in children's sport. In *Advances in pediatric sport sciences: Vol. 2. Behavioral issues.* Champaign, IL: Human Kinetics.

Gruelich, W., & Pyle, S. (1959). *Radiographic atlas of skeletal development of the hand and wrist* (2nd ed.). Stanford, CA: Stanford University Press.

Hale, C. (1956). Physiological maturity of Little League baseball players. *Research Quarterly, 27*, 276–284.

Harter, S. (1978). Effectance motivation revisited. *Child Development, 21*, 34–64.

International Athletics Association Federation. (1983). Not kid's stuff. *Sports Medicine Bulletin, 18*(1), 11.

Krahenbuhl, G. S., & Pangrazi, R. P. (1983). Characteristics associated with running performance in young boys. *Medicine and Science in Sports, 15*(6), 486–490.

Lee, J. M., Appugliese, D., Kaciroti, N., Corwyn, R. F., Bradley, R. H., & Lumeng, J. C. (2007). Weight status in young girls and the onset of puberty. *Pediatrics, 119*, e624–e630.

Malina, R. M. (1978). Physical growth and maturity characteristics of young athletes. In R. A. Magill, M. H. Ash, & F. L. Smoll (Eds.), *Children and youth in sport: A contemporary anthology.* Champaign, IL: Human Kinetics.

Malina, R. M., Bouchard, C., & Bar-Or, O. (2004). *Growth, maturation, and physical activity* (2nd ed.). Champaign, IL: Human Kinetics.

National Strength and Conditioning Association. (1996). Youth resistance training: Position statement paper and literature review. *Strength and Conditioning, 18*, 62–75.

Ozmun, J. C., Mikesky, A. E., & Surburg, P. R. (1994). Neuromuscular adaptations following prepubescent strength training. *Medicine and Science in Sports and Exercise, 26*(4), 510–514.

Pate, R. R., Dowda, M., & Ross, J. G. (1990). Associations between physical activity and physical fitness in American children. *American Journal of Diseases of Children, 144*, 1123–1129.

Payne, V. G., & Morrow, J. R., Jr. (1993). Exercise and VO_2 max in children: A meta-analysis. *Research Quarterly for Exercise and Sport, 64*(3), 305–313.

Petersen, G. (1967). *Atlas for somatotyping children.* The Netherlands: Royal Vangorcum Ltd.

Petlichkoff, L. M. (1992). Youth sport participation and withdrawal: Is it simply a matter of fun? *Pediatric Exercise Science, 4*(2), 105–110.

Rarick, L. G., & Dobbins, D. A. (1975). Basic components in the motor performances of children six to nine years of age. *Medicine and Science in Sports, 7*(2), 105–110.

Roberts, S. O., Ciapponi, T., & Lytle, R. (2008). *Strength training for children and adolescents.* Reston, VA: National Association for Sport and Physical Education.

Roche, A. F., Chumlea, W. C., & Thissen, D. (1988). *Assessing the skeletal maturity of the hand-wrist: Fels method.* Springfield, IL: Thomas.

Rowland, T. W. (1991). Effects of obesity on aerobic fitness in adolescent females. *American Journal of Disease in Children, 145*, 764–768.

———. (2005). *Children's exercise physiology.* Champaign, IL: Human Kinetics.

Sallis, J. F., & McKenzie, T. L. (1991). Physical education's role in public health. *Research Quarterly of Exercise and Sport, 62*, 124–137.

Saltin, B. (1973). Metabolic fundamentals of exercise. *Medicine and Science of Sports, 5*, 137–146.

Servedio, F. J., Bartels, R. L., Hamlin, R. L., Teske, D., Shaffer, T., & Servedio, A. (1985). The effects of weight training, using Olympic style lifts, on various physiological variables in prepubescent boys [Abstract]. *Medicine and Science in Sports and Exercise, 17*, 288.

Sheldon, W. H., Dupertuis, C. W., & McDermott, E. (1954). *Atlas of men: A guide for somatotyping the adult male at all ages.* New York: Harper & Row.

Shephard, R. J. (1984). Physical activity and child health. *Sports Medicine, 1*, 205–233.

Smoll, F. L., & Smoll, R. E. (1996). *Children and youth in sport.* Dubuque, IA: Brown and Benchmark.

Tanner, S. M. (1993). Weighing the risks: Strength training for children and adolescents. *The Physician and Sportsmedicine, 21*(6), 105–116.

Thomas, J. R., & Tennant, L. K. (1978). Effects of rewards on changes in children's motivation for an athletic task. In F. L. Smoll & R. E. Smoll (Eds.), *Psychological perspectives in youth sports.* New York: Hemisphere.

Trout, J., & Kahan, D. (2008). *Supersized PE: A comprehensive guidebook for teaching overweight students.* Reston, VA: National Association for Sport and Physical Education.

Weltman, A., Janney, C., Rians, C. B., Strand, K., Berg, B., Tippitt, S., Wise, J., Cahill, B. R., & Katch, F. I. (1986). The effects of hydraulic resistance strength training in pre-pubertal males. *Medicine and Science in Sports and Exercise, 18*, 629–638.

Whitehead, J. R., & Corbin, C. B. (1991). Effects of fitness test type, teacher, and gender on exercise intrinsic motivation and physical self-worth. *Journal of School Health, 61*, 11–16.

WEBSITES

Children and Physical Activity
www.cdc.gov/nccdphp/dash/presphysactrpt/index.htm
www.kidsource.com/kidsource/content4/promote.phyed.html
www.americanheart.org/presenter.jhtml?identifier=4596

Children's Health
www.aap.org

Fitness Tests
www.cooperinstitute.org/ourkidshealth/fitnessgram/index.cfm
www.presidentschallenge.org

Overweight
www.cdc.gov/nccdphp/dnpa/obesity/index.htm

The President's Challenge and the Presidential Active Lifestyle Award
www.presidentschallenge.org
www.presidentschallenge.org/pdf/ActiveLifestyle.pdf

Strength Training and Children
www.acsm.org/pdf/YSTRNGTH.pdf

Youth Sports
www.nays.org
http://kidshealth.org/parent/nutrition_fit
www.betterbodz.com/kid/myth.html

Preparing a Quality Lesson

3

ESSENTIAL COMPONENTS OF QUALITY PROGRAMS

I. Organized around content standards

▶ II. Student-centered and developmentally appropriate

III. Physical activity and motor skill development form the core of the program

▶ IV. Teaches management skills and self-discipline

V. Promotes inclusion of all students

▶ VI. Focuses on process over product

VII. Promotes lifetime personal health and wellness

VIII. Teaches cooperation and responsibility and promotes sensitivity to diversity

NATIONAL STANDARDS FOR PHYSICAL EDUCATION*

1. Demonstrates competency in motor skills and movement patterns needed to perform a variety of physical activities.

▶ 2. Demonstrates understanding of movement concepts, principles, and tactics as they apply to the learning and performance of physical activities.

3. Participates regularly in physical activity.

4. Achieves and maintains a health-enhancing level of physical fitness.

▶ 5. Exhibits responsible personal and social behavior that respects self and others in physical activity.

6. Values physical activity for health, enjoyment, challenge, self-expression, and/or social interaction.

*National Association for Sport and Physical Education (NASPE), 2004.

Effective teachers can use more than one style of teaching. In fact, they may use several styles during a single lesson. This chapter focuses on planning strategies associated with quality instruction. Before instructing a class, the teacher must make several decisions about the lesson. Knowing how to regulate instructional space and how to use formations helps teachers maximize students' learning. Instructors also need to understand the effect of developmental patterns, arousal, feedback, and practice on learning skills. A productive class environment demands consistently monitoring student performance, emphasizing safety, and developing a method for keeping students on task. This chapter offers a comprehensive lesson plan to encourage effective planning.

Outcomes

- Describe various teaching styles and the best time to use each style to increase student learning.
- Describe the role of planning in preparing for quality instruction.
- Understand the relationships between instruction and the developmental and experiential level of the students.
- List the pre-instructional decisions to be made before teaching a lesson.
- Know the basic mechanical principles involved in efficiently performing motor skills.
- Cite effective ways to use equipment, time, space, and formations in the instructional process.
- Understand how to optimize skill learning. Include discussions of developmental patterns, arousal, feedback, practice sessions, and skill progression.
- Understand the rationale for the four components of a lesson, and be able to describe each component.
- Know how to improve the quality of instructional presentations through reflection and critique.

PLANNING is a critical part of teaching that ensures a quality lesson. Pre-instructional decisions that determine how the lesson will be presented are discussed here and in Chapter 5. They include choosing a teaching style, using equipment effectively, utilizing class time, arranging for teaching space, and employing proper instructional formations. Planning also involves designing and implementing flexible, meaningful lesson plans. On an average day, teachers make many unexpected decisions. Their job is much easier when they make as many decisions as possible before presenting the actual lesson. Pre-instructional decisions are as important as the lesson content. Failing to carefully plan the lesson can diminish its effect.

Well-planned lessons tend to be carried out more smoothly. With planned, efficient transitions, student physical activity levels are likely to be higher and behavior problems are likely to decrease, giving the teacher more time for instruction. Effective lesson plans serve as a compass for daily instruction. Without a thoughtful plan, the lesson lacks direction and learning outcomes are difficult to achieve.

CHOOSE FROM A VARIETY OF TEACHING STYLES

One of the first steps to take when planning for instruction is to select the most effective teaching styles for each skill. A teaching style provides direction for presenting information, organizing practice, giving feedback, keeping students engaged in appropriate behavior, and monitoring progress toward goals or objectives. Teaching styles are usually defined in terms of planning and setup of the environment, the instructional approach used, the students' responsibilities during the lesson, and expected student outcomes. Successful instructors will incorporate a variety of teaching styles (Harrison, Blakemore, & Buck, 2007; Mosston & Ashworth, 2002; Rink, 2006; Siedentop & Tannehill, 2000).

There is no single "best" or universal teaching style. Some educators endorse their favorite approaches, but evidence suggests that no style is more effective than another. Using a repertoire of styles with different objectives, students, activities, facilities, and equipment is the mark of a master teacher. Selecting an appropriate teaching style involves many variables, including

1. Lesson objectives: skill development, activity promotion, knowledge, and social behaviors
2. Activities to be taught: body management skills, manipulative skills, or rhythmic movement skills
3. Students: individual characteristics, interests, developmental levels, socioeconomic status, motivation, and background
4. Class size
5. Equipment and facilities available for instruction
6. The teacher: unique abilities, skills, and comfort

Using a different teaching style in an appropriate setting often improves the environment for students and teachers and increases program effectiveness. A new or modified teaching style is not a panacea for all the ills of every school environment or setting, and a teaching style cannot be selected without considering a number of variables. Teachers can use combinations of styles in a lesson or unit plan. Figure 3.1 shows a continuum of teaching

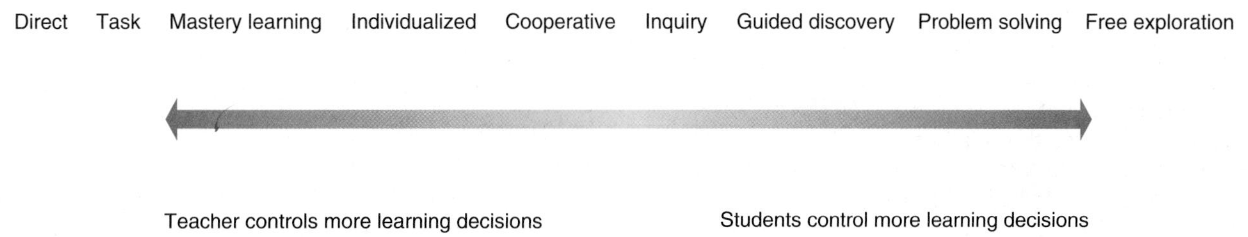

Direct Task Mastery learning Individualized Cooperative Inquiry Guided discovery Problem solving Free exploration

Teacher controls more learning decisions Students control more learning decisions

FIGURE 3.1 Continuum of teaching styles.

styles based on the degree of control and decision making exercised by the teacher and students. At one end of the continuum (Direct), only the teacher makes instructional decisions. At the other end (Free exploration), children make most of the decisions about their learning. Along the continuum there is a gradual shift in decision making and responsibility for learning.

DIRECT STYLE

The direct style is the most teacher-controlled approach. The teacher instructs either the entire class or small groups and guides their pace and direction. Direct teaching often begins with an explanation and demonstration of skills to be developed. Students are organized into partners, small groups, or squads for practice. While students practice, the teacher actively moves around the area correcting errors, praising, encouraging, and asking questions. Independent practice follows and is supervised by an actively involved teacher. Throughout the class, students can be brought together for evaluative comments and instruction, or to focus on another skill. Students spend most of the class time engaged in predetermined subject matter aimed at reaching established goals. Direct instruction makes the teacher the major demonstrator, lecturer, motivator, organizer, disciplinarian, director, and corrector of errors.

The direct teaching style is often compared to Mosston and Ashworth's (2002) command style, in which teachers use a signal or demonstration to command all actions performed by students. The direct teaching style has more flexibility and variations than the command style. The direct style, like any other, can be effective or ineffective depending on how it is used and administered. The direct style is effective for teaching physical skills—especially when students are inexperienced and the activity is inherently hazardous, as in racket skills, striking skills, and gymnastics. Because it gives the teacher more control, the direct style is useful when discipline is a problem. It is also useful for beginning teachers with new students, new content preparations, or large classes.

The direct teaching style emphasizes creating a controlled class environment that is safe for students. Effective use of the direct style minimizes time children spend passively watching, listening to a lecture–demonstration, or waiting in line. A challenge when using this style is offering activities that meet all students' needs. Higher- and lower-skilled students may be hindered when learning activities are too easy and unchallenging, or too difficult. This issue can be avoided, however, by offering learning tasks of varying difficulty.

TASK (STATION) STYLE

The task style of teaching involves arranging and presenting learning tasks at several learning areas or stations. Students rotate between learning stations. At each station, they practice a variety of tasks with a minimum of teacher direction. For example, students might spend 5 minutes at stations while practicing four or five defined tasks. When the time is up, the teacher cues them to rotate to a new station. This style offers more freedom than the direct approach because students can decide to practice different tasks.

Using the task style allows teachers to move away from being the central figure in the teaching process. Instruction focuses on visiting learning stations and interacting with students who need help. Less time is spent directing and managing the group as a whole. This approach requires more preparation time for planning and designing tasks. Adequate facilities, equipment, and instructional signs are necessary to keep students productive and working on appropriate tasks. Here are some guidelines for selecting, writing, and presenting tasks:

1. Select tasks that cover the basic skills of an activity.
2. Create tasks that are developmentally appropriate. Tasks should challenge the most skilled students and help the less skilled students succeed.
3. Avoid tasks that carry a high safety risk.
4. Tape task cards on the wall, strap them to boundary cones, or place them on the floor. Another alternative is to give each student a task sheet to carry station to station and take home for practice after school.
5. Write tasks so they are easy to comprehend. Use teaching cues or phrases that students already know. Effective task descriptions explain what the skill is and how to do it (Figure 3.2 on page 38). Periodically

Name ______________________ Class ______________ Grade ______________

Your expected outcome is to master 5 of the following individual rope-jumping steps. You must be able to complete at least 10 consecutive jumps when doing one of the steps. Please ask a friend to approve your performance before asking for instructor approval.

Approved by a friend	Approved by teacher	Skill to be completed
		Side Swing. Swing the rope, held with both hands, to one side of the body. Switch and swing the rope to the other side of the body.
		Double Side Swing and Jump. Swing the rope once on each side of the body. Follow the second swing with a jump over the rope. The sequence is swing, swing, jump.
		Running in Place. When the rope passes under the feet, shift the weight alternately from one foot to the other, raising the nonsupport foot in a running position.
		Spread Legs Forward and Backward. Start in a stride position with weight equally distributed on both feet. As the rope passes under the feet, jump into the air and reverse the position of the feet.
		Side Straddle Jump. Alternate a regular jump with a straddle jump. The straddle jump is performed with the feet spread to shoulder width.
		Cross Legs Sideways. When the rope passes underfoot, spread the legs in a straddle position (sideways) to take the rebound. As the rope passes underfoot on the next turn, jump up and cross the feet with the other foot forward. Then repeat with the other foot forward, continuing this alternation.
		Toe-Touch Forward. Swing the right foot forward as the rope passes under the feet and touch the right toes on the next count. Then alternate, landing on the right foot and touching the left toes forward.
		Toe-Touch Backward. Same as the Toe-Touch Forward, but touch the toes of the free foot to the back at the end of the swing.
		Shuffle Step. Push off with the right foot and sidestep to the left as the rope passes underfoot. Land with weight on the left foot and touch the right toes beside the left heel. Repeat in the opposite direction.

FIGURE 3.2 Task card: Advanced individual rope-jumping steps.

check that students understand and are practicing the tasks when unsupervised.

6. Select a combination of instructional equipment that offers feedback and motivation, such as targets, cones, hoops, ropes, and stopwatches.

The task style of instruction can involve a variety of grouping patterns. Students can work alone, with a partner, or in a small group. The partner or reciprocal grouping pattern is useful with large classes, limited amounts of equipment, and skills where partners can time, count, record, or analyze each other. For example, one partner dribbles through a set of cones while the other is timing and recording. In a group of three students, one student bounces and catches a ball off the wall, another analyzes the form with a checklist, and the third counts and records the number of catches. The social aspect of working on tasks with a partner or friend is a form of cooperative learning discussed later. Arrange learning tasks so students have many successes at first and then face some challenges. Objectives can be modified daily or repeated, depending on the progress of the class.

Some teachers are uncomfortable when first using the task style because it implies less order and control compared to direct instruction. With proper planning, organization, and supervision, however, the task style motivates students to practice a variety of tasks at their own pace. If students do not behave responsibly, teachers may require them to practice self-management skills focusing on freedom, flexibility, and opportunities to make decisions.

MASTERY LEARNING (OUTCOMES-BASED) STYLE

Mastery learning is an instructional style that takes a general program outcome and breaks it into smaller parts, providing a progression of skills. These subskills are the focus of learning and are written as tasks that students must master before attempting more complex skills. The number of subskills depends on the complexity of the outcome. If students do not achieve mastery, corrective activities can help them learn in different ways, such as alternative instructional materials, peer tutoring, or any other appropriate learning activity.

The mastery style involves the following steps:

1. Divide the outcome or movement competency into sequenced, progressive units.
2. Evaluate necessary (prerequisite) competencies.
3. Establish skill objectives for each of the successive learning units.
4. Have students informally evaluate themselves to determine if they are ready for formal testing by the teacher or a peer.
5. When a student is ready for formal evaluation, the teacher (or a peer) determines *pass* or *fail* for a particular outcome. Students who pass the evaluation move to the next learning unit.
6. Students who do not pass the evaluation continue practicing the skill, using alternatives or corrective measures the teacher provides.

The following outline demonstrates how a soccer lesson might be organized to teach the target outcomes for dribbling, trapping, and kicking using the mastery learning style.

Dribbling Outcomes

1. Dribble the ball a distance of 10 yards, three consecutive times, making each kick travel no more than 5 yards.
2. Dribble the ball through an obstacle course of six cones over a distance of 10 yards in 20 seconds or less.
3. With a partner, pass the ball back and forth five times while running for a distance of 20 yards, two consecutive times.

Trapping Outcomes

4. When the ball is rolled to you by a partner 5 yards away, trap it four of five times, using the instep method with the right and then the left foot.
5. Repeat outcome 4 using the sole of the foot.
6. With a partner tossing the ball, trap four of five shots using the chest method.

Kicking Outcomes

7. Kick the ball to your partner, who is standing 5 yards away, five consecutive times with the right and left inside-the-foot push pass.
8. Repeat outcome 7 using the instep kick. Loft the ball to your partner.
9. Kick four of five shots that enter the goal in the air from a distance of 10 yards.

Mastery learning is useful because students move at an individualized pace that lets them master preliminary skills needed to reach the outcomes. It offers a continuum of outcomes children can practice in their spare time. For this reason, the style is well suited for students with disabilities or those with low skills. However, because the style requires self-direction by the students, some may take longer to acquire the necessary discipline. Consider the amount of freedom, flexibility, and choice your students can handle and yet be productive. When introducing students to this style, use it sparingly and take time to teach the importance of self-management skills.

This style lends itself well to using small groups that rotate between learning stations. Another alternative is to have students rotate to any learning area they need to practice. Various grouping patterns (individually, with a partner, or with a small group) can be used depending on available facilities, equipment, objectives, and student choice. During the lesson, the teacher or peers can monitor successful completion of objectives. If class size is small, and the number of objectives also is small, a teacher may be able to do all of the monitoring. Otherwise, a combination of procedures is recommended. Student involvement in the monitoring process enhances their understanding of the objectives and shares learning responsibility. Monitors can use a performance chart to check objectives at each learning station or carry a master list from station to station. Another approach is to develop a performance sheet for each student that combines teacher and peer monitoring (Figure 3.3 on page 40). Peers monitor simple objectives while the teacher monitors more difficult ones. Students can also monitor themselves on the performance objectives. Try experimenting with several monitoring approaches based on the activity, number of objectives, students' abilities, class size, and available equipment and facilities.

INDIVIDUALIZED STYLE

The individualized style is based on the concept of student-centered learning through an individualized curriculum. This style uses various teaching strategies designed to allow students to progress at an individual rate. Each student's needs are diagnosed, and a program is prescribed to address those needs. Objectives are stated in behavioral terms. Students are required to learn cognitive factors before moving to psychomotor tasks.

Certain materials and hardware are necessary to establish the learning environment for individualized instruction,

Name: ____________________

Instructor approved	Peer reviewed	Skill
______	______	1. Toss and catch with both hands.
______	______	2. Toss and catch with right hand.
______	______	3. Toss and catch with left hand.
______	______	4. Toss and catch with the back of both hands (create soft home).
______	______	5. Toss, do a half turn, and catch with both hands.
______	______	6. Toss, do a heel click, and catch with both hands.
______	______	7. Place beanbag on foot, kick in the air, and catch.
______	______	8. Place beanbag on foot, kick in the air, and catch behind back.
______	______	9. Put beanbag between feet, jump up with beanbag, and catch.
______	______	10. Toss overhead, move to another spot, and catch.
______	______	11. Toss overhead, take three skipping steps, and catch.
______	______	12. Toss overhead, lie down, and catch with hands.

FIGURE 3.3 Performance objectives: Manipulative skills using beanbags.

such as reference books, wall charts, and cards for recording student progress. Other useful equipment includes slide and overhead projectors, cassette tape recorders, videotape players, screens, and chalkboards. Teachers can set up a learning center that includes materials, equipment, and software to direct the learning process (Figure 3.4). The individualized style of teaching follows five steps:

1. *Diagnosis.* The teacher determines each student's level of cognitive and psychomotor knowledge.
2. *Prescription.* Each student receives a learning package based on his or her current level of knowledge.
3. *Development.* Students work on tasks in the learning package until able to perform them. Self-testing goals are offered, and each student decides whether to proceed to final evaluation.
4. *Evaluation.* The teacher evaluates each student's psychomotor and cognitive progress. This step allows the teacher to counsel each student and reinforce critical points.
5. *Reinforcement.* If a student completes the tasks successfully, the teacher gives positive reinforcement, records the data on the student's progress chart, and prescribes a new learning package based on the student's needs. If the student does not perform the task successfully, the teacher offers possible alternatives for reaching the objective.

Learning packages form the core of the individualized style. The learning package is a student contract listing the skills students need to accomplish in a meaningful sequence. It consists of these parts:

1. The content classification statement describes the task or concept to be learned. This could be a psychomotor task (such as demonstrating the cartwheel) or a cognitive task (such as learning how to absorb force).
2. The purpose section explains what the package will do for the learner. For example, "This contract provides the activities that will enable you to perform a cartwheel."
3. The learning objectives identify what is to be learned, describe how the learning will take place, and explain how the student will perform when learning has occurred.
4. The diagnostic test (pretest) determines the student's knowledge and skill level. The student is given a cognitive test as well as psychomotor tasks to perform for assessment.
5. The learning activities section offers different ways to learn a skill, concept, or activity. Students can select any of the strategies to enhance learning. Learning strategies might include viewing and analyzing transparencies, listening to audiotapes for instruction in cognitive tasks, reading books (provided by the instructor) that describe the task, viewing videotapes that demonstrate and explain a skill to be performed, or studying charts that break down a skill into components. Students can ask other students who have successfully completed the activity to help them practice.
6. The self-test phase helps students decide if they are ready for a teacher's evaluation. Students can ask their peers to evaluate whether they are ready for the final test.
7. The final evaluation is an observable measure of the student's achievement. The teacher judges psychomotor achievements, and cognitive learning is measured by a written exam.

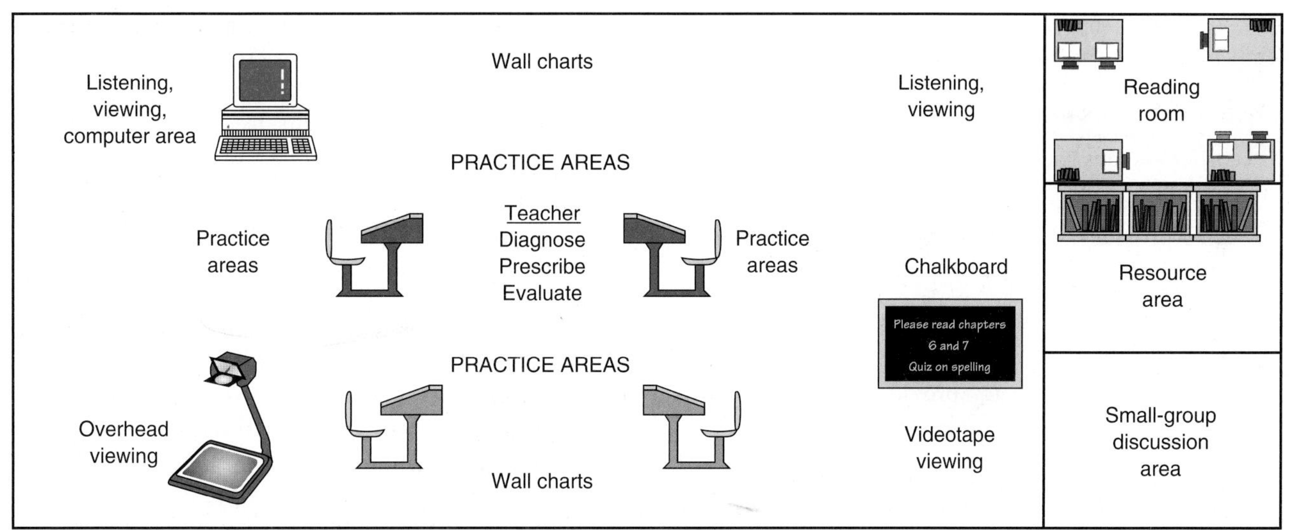

FIGURE 3.4 Organization of a learning center.

The individualized style allows students to control the rate of learning and to receive personalized feedback about progress. Teachers control the design of learning packages and the size of learning increments. Examining the learning process itself is a valuable experience that students can use later to learn new activities or skills. Individualized instruction has the following benefits:

- Students, parents, and administrators know exactly what is expected and accomplished by students.
- Self-direction enhances the motivational level of most students.
- Students at most competency levels find success and challenge with objectives.
- Students progress through the objectives at their own rate.
- Students choose and sequence learning activities.
- Students have some choice about the groupings for skill practice (such as alone, with a partner, or in a small group).
- Students accept more responsibility for learning.
- Teachers have greater freedom to give individual attention and offer feedback.

Despite its many advantages, the individualized style of instruction has some disadvantages. Most notably, preparation for this style can be time-consuming; a teacher must develop performance objectives for each student and revise them accordingly over the course of the class. The teacher also must develop an efficient system for monitoring student progress. Finally, incorporating the individualized style of instruction requires an adjustment period for teachers and students, who are often more comfortable with the direct approach.

COOPERATIVE LEARNING (RECIPROCAL) STYLE

When competing against each other for a grade or another measure of success, students strive for a goal that only a few can achieve. In competitive situations, students know that they can reach their goals only if other classmates fail (Johnson & Johnson, 2009). Cooperative learning is a style that focuses on the importance of people working together to accomplish common goals. In cooperative learning, students are in groups where each member works to reach common goals. In cooperative activities, individuals seek outcomes that are beneficial to themselves and to the group. Reciprocal teaching (Mosston & Ashworth, 2002) is another form of cooperative learning.

Cooperative learning helps foster constructive relationships among students. Teachers emphasize joint rather than individual outcomes, and peers have the opportunity to work with each other regularly. Because students are expected to foster their peers' success rather than wish for their failure, this style can enhance the students' social and psychological growth.

When using this style, teachers assign students a project or goal to complete as a team. Children are grouped heterogeneously (that is, by mixing race, ability, or socioeconomic level) so there is diversity within the team. Usually, two to five students are in each group. They work through the assignment until all group members understand and complete it. The very nature of cooperative learning helps students realize they cannot achieve the goal alone. A group is successful if the outcomes are meaningful and all members have cooperated and participated in reaching the goal. Group members can play various roles, including:

- Performer—does the skills or tasks
- Recorder—keeps track of statistics, trials, or key points made by the group
- Coach—provides skill feedback to the performer or times practice trials
- Presenter—communicates key points to the rest of the class
- Motivator—encourages and provides general and positive feedback to all group members

Cooperative learning is most successful when students switch roles often and the group tasks proceed from simple to complex. Teachers need to monitor the groups to ensure all members contribute, but the key to success is truly the students' ability to cooperate. Selected activities should require the knowledge and efforts of all group members. If students feel cooperation is not necessary to complete the task, the style is not effective. It must be clear that all members of the team are needed, even if in varying amounts of involvement. The tasks can be cognitive or psychomotor skills. Here are some class activities that could be used with the cooperative learning style:

- Design a fitness routine that requires each group member to create one or two exercises for inclusion. The overall routine must show balance (exercise all body parts) and be appropriate for the entire group.
- Modify a sport or game to make it more inclusive. The goal is to redesign the game so all students can play successfully.
- Have each group member design a drill that enhances skill learning and ensures that all group members improve. The drills must be cohesive and focus on a single skill to be learned (throwing, rope jumping, etc.).
- Break down a folk dance into various parts so that it is easier to learn. Each group member is responsible for teaching one of the parts. The group must determine how the parts will be put together (taught to the rest of the class).

See Chapter 21 for specific team and group challenges that are taught using the cooperative learning style.

INQUIRY STYLE

The inquiry style of teaching is process oriented rather than product oriented; thus, it emphasizes the learning process more than the final product or outcome. During this type of instruction, the teacher guides rather than commands students to solutions by using a combination of questions, problems, examples, and learning activities. For their part, students experience learning situations that require them to inquire, speculate, reflect, analyze, and discover answers on their own. The instructional environment is one of open communication where students feel comfortable experimenting and inquiring without fear of failure.

Advocates of the inquiry style feel it should have a more prominent place in educational methodology—including physical education—fearing that too many of today's approaches emphasize only listening, absorbing, and complying (Mosston & Ashworth, 2002). Proponents of this style believe it enhances students' ability to think, improves creativity, fosters a better understanding of the subject matter, enhances individual self-concept, and develops lifelong learning patterns. Critics of the inquiry method, specifically in physical education, point to these issues: too much time is spent on one subject or topic; a focus is on trivial or nonessential learning; most motor skills have a best way to be performed that should be quickly explained; students already know the answers; and the instruction is difficult to plan because each class has a wide range of knowledge and ability.

Regardless of the pros and cons, educators agree that students need to be involved in the learning process. Guided discovery and problem solving are two types of inquiry that give the learner more control over the direction and content of the learning process. These styles are effective when the goal is to immerse students in the process of uncovering new and better methods for performing motor skills.

GUIDED DISCOVERY (CONVERGENT) STYLE

Guided discovery is used when the teacher wants students to discover a single predetermined choice or result. Consider teaching the concept of opposition (e.g., a right-handed thrower should place the feet in a stride position with the left foot forward). Using guided discovery, students experiment with different foot patterns, with the goal of selecting the best pattern. They practice right-handed throwing with the following limitations: feet together, feet in a straddle position, feet in a stride position with the left foot forward, and feet in a stride position with the right foot forward. After practicing the four different foot positions, students choose the position with the best throwing potential.

Here are some skill techniques that students can explore to discover the best solutions:

1. Placement of the hands when catching
2. Angles of release for distance throwing with different implements such as the shot put, discus, football, and softball
3. Ready position for sport skills
4. Stopping and starting quickly
5. The best place to enter in long rope-jumping skills

PROBLEM-SOLVING (DIVERGENT) STYLE

The problem-solving style involves input, reflection, choice, and response. The problem is structured so that there is no one prescribed answer. A simple problem might be expressed as, "What are the different ways you can bounce a ball and stay in your personal space?" A best way may or may not be emphasized. A more complex problem involving deeper thought might be, "What is the most effective way to position and move your feet while guarding an opponent in basketball?" The solution could use an individual, partner, or group approach. Here are the steps in problem solving:

1. *Present the problem.* With no demonstration, give students a problem in the form of a question or statement that provokes thought and reflection.
2. *Determine procedures.* Ask students to think about the procedures required to arrive at a solution.
3. *Experiment and explore.* In experimentation, have students try different solutions, evaluate them, and make a choice. Self-direction is important, and the teacher acts in an advisory role—answering questions, helping, commenting, and encouraging, but not providing solutions.
4. *Observe, evaluate, and discuss.* Give all children the opportunity to offer a solution, either as an individual or small group, and to observe what others have discovered. Discussion centers on justifying a particular solution.
5. *Refine and expand.* After having the students observe solutions, give them the opportunity to rework their movement patterns, incorporating ideas from others.

Problem solving is useful when teaching concepts, relationships, strategies, and proper use of skills for specific solutions. A difficult step in the problem-solving style, however, is designing problems that students have not previously solved. This step may sound simple, but a student who knows the answer or secures the solution ahead of time may pass it on to the rest of the class, and the process of exploring and solving will be lost.

FREE-EXPLORATION STYLE

Free exploration is the most child-centered style of learning. In this style, teacher guidance is limited to selecting the instructional materials to be used and designating the area to be explored. Two directives might be: "Today, for the first part of the period, you may select any piece of equipment and see what you can do with it," or "Get a jump rope and try creating a new activity." No limits are imposed on children except those dictated by safety. If necessary, forewarn or remind students how to use equipment safely. This style is used effectively to introduce new equipment, concepts, and ideas to children so they generate new ideas and responses. It often works best with young children who are experiencing activities and situations for the first time.

With free exploration, the teacher avoids using demonstrations and praising certain results too early because these can lead to imitative and noncreative behavior. The teacher does stay involved, by moving among students to encourage, clarify, and answer individual questions. Concentrate on motivating effort, since the student is responsible for being a self-directed learner. It is wise to offer students the opportunity for self-direction in small doses, increasing the time as they become more disciplined. Give students many exploratory opportunities because this phase of learning takes advantage of the child's love of experimenting with movement and allows for free exercise of natural curiosity. Self-discovery is a necessary and important part of learning, and teachers can reinforce this concept by helping students experience the joy of creativity.

3

OPTIMIZE SKILL LEARNING

Helping students effectively learn motor skills requires teachers to understand a few basic principles of motor learning. Teaching motor skills is not a difficult task when teachers understand the basic tenets of proper performance techniques.

UNDERSTAND DEVELOPMENTAL PATTERNS

The learning and development of motor skills varies among children of similar chronological age. However, the *sequence* of skill development in children is similar and progresses in an orderly way. Three development patterns typify the growth of primary-grade children:

1. *Development generally proceeds from head to foot (cephalocaudal).* Coordination and management of body parts occur in the upper body before being observed in the lower. For example, children develop throwing skills before kicking competency.
2. *Development occurs from inside to outside (proximodistal).* Children control their arms before controlling their hands. They can reach for objects before they can grasp them.
3. *Development proceeds from general to specific.* Gross motor movements are learned before fine motor coordination and refined movement patterns. As children learn motor skills, nonproductive movement is gradually eliminated. When learners begin to eliminate wasteful, tense movements and can reproduce a smooth, consistent performance, motor learning is occurring.

Scrutinize activities you feel uncomfortable teaching to ensure all safety procedures have been implemented. If in doubt, discuss the activities with experienced teachers and administrators.

AVOID OVERSTIMULATING CHILDREN

Pressure to perform can positively or negatively affect motor performance. This external motivation to learn is also called *arousal* in motor learning terminology (Schmidt & Wrisberg, 2008). The key to proper motivation is to find the "just right" amount. With too little motivation, children are uninterested in learning. Too much arousal fills children with stress and anxiety, resulting in a decrease in motor performance. The more complex a skill, the more likely excessive stimulation is to disrupt learning. On the other hand, if a skill is simple, such as skipping or running, children can tolerate a greater amount of outside prompting without showing a reduction in skill performance. Optimally, children should be stimulated to a level at which they are excited and confident about participating.

Competition affects children's arousal level. When competition is introduced in the early stages of skill learning, stress and anxiety reduce a child's ability to learn. On the other hand, if competition is introduced after a skill has been overlearned, it can improve performance. Since most elementary school children have not overlearned skills, teachers should avoid highly competitive situations when teaching skills. For example, assume the objective is to practice basketball dribbling. The teacher places students in squads and runs a relay requiring them to dribble to the opposite end of the gym and return. The first squad finished is the winner. The result: instead of concentrating on dribbling form, students are more concerned about winning the relay. They are overaroused and determined to run as quickly as possible. They dribble poorly (if at all), the balls fly out of control, and the teacher is dismayed by the result. Unfortunately, the excessive desire to win overexcited the students, who had not yet overlearned dribbling.

OFFER MEANINGFUL SKILL FEEDBACK

Feedback is important in the teaching process because it affects what is to be learned, what should be avoided, and how the performance can be modified. Skill feedback is any kind of information about a movement performance. There are two types of skill feedback, intrinsic and extrinsic. *Intrinsic feedback* is internal, inherent in the performance of a skill, and travels through the senses such as vision, hearing, touch, and smell. *Extrinsic feedback* is external and comes from an outside source such as a teacher, a videotape, a stopwatch, and so on. Most elementary school students use extrinsic feedback (usually verbal) received from a teacher, peer, or parent. Skill feedback should be encouraging (or constructive), given frequently, delivered publicly so all students benefit, and based on performance or (preferably) effort.

In physical education, most of the feedback given to students should be process oriented. In the motor development literature, this concept is referred to as "knowledge of performance." When using process-based feedback, specific components of the learner's performance are used in the feedback. For example, "I like the way you kept your chin tucked," or "That's the way to step toward the target with your left foot." This type of feedback emphasizes the process and allows teachers to reinforce their teaching cues. In the preceding example, "chin tucked" is a teaching cue. Thus the teacher uses the instructional cue and then gives the child process feedback on the performance of that cue, or skill component.

An important aspect of this approach to giving specific, positive feedback is that it provides information about how to improve. Typically, students can succeed in performing at least one part of the skill (e.g., stepping in opposition), which leads to a greater feeling of success and enjoyment. When children become frustrated because they find it difficult to see improvement, process-oriented feedback gives them a lift and a resolve to continue practicing.

Make performance feedback short, content-filled, and concise. It should tell the child exactly what was correct or incorrect (e.g., "That was excellent body rotation"). Concentrate on one key point to avoid confusing the child. Imagine a young student who is told, "Step with the left foot, rotate the trunk, lead with the elbow, and snap the wrist on your next throw!" Such excessive feedback would confuse anyone trying to learn a new skill. If corrective feedback is needed, start by saying something positive about the performance. For example, "Andre, you sure are working hard today. Next time, try stepping with the other foot and see how that works."

With young children, focus your feedback on learning (process) rather than on skill performance (product). A child who manages to throw a ball into a basket (a product) might believe that the skill performance was done correctly even though the technical points of the throw were done incorrectly. The goal of elementary school physical education is to teach skills correctly, placing less emphasis on the outcome of the skill performance. In contrast, more emphasis is placed on product (performance) rather than on process (technique) when students enter the competitive world of athletics.

A final point about feedback: give students time to internalize the feedback. Often, teachers tell a child something and at the same time ask them to "try it again." The child will likely make the same mistake because he or she did not have time to concentrate on the feedback. Offer specific, positive, process-based feedback and then move to another child. Follow up on your feedback later. This gives the child a chance to relax, internalize the feedback, and modify future practice attempts.

DESIGN EFFECTIVE PRACTICE SESSIONS

Practice is a key part of learning motor skills. But students must receive more than the opportunity to practice; they must practice while focusing on quality of movement (practicing correctly). This section explains how to design practice sessions that optimize motor skill learning.

Focus Practice on Process

The emphasis of practice can go in two sometimes conflicting directions—product or process. Product- or performance-based practice has the teacher asking students to do the best they can and then reinforcing those who reach the desired outcome (product). Process-based practice, however, has the teacher encouraging students to learn the skill correctly without concern for the outcome. This leads to a product–process conflict. Students who think the teacher is interested in the product will be less willing to concentrate on proper technique. Focus practice on learning a skill correctly by emphasizing technique and encouraging experimentation. Emphasis on the outcome decreases a student's willingness to take risks and to learn new ways of performing a skill.

To minimize this conflict, make sure students know the focus of the practice session. In most cases, elementary school children will focus on technique since they are learning new motor patterns. Excessive pressure to perform without mistakes can stifle students' willingness to try (especially less gifted children). If it is necessary to evaluate a skill outcome, the teacher should tell students why the outcome is important and say, "We will practice doing our best today."

3

Use Mental Practice Techniques

Mental practice involves practicing a motor skill in a quiet, relaxed environment. The experience involves thinking about the activity and its related sounds, colors, and other sensations. Students visualize themselves doing the activity successfully and at regular speed. Images of failure should be avoided (Schmidt & Wrisberg, 2008). Mental practice stimulates children to think about and review the activity they are to perform. Some experience or familiarity with the motor task is required before students can derive value from mental practice. Mental practice is used in combination with regular practice, not in place of it. Before having students perform the task, prompt them to mentally review its critical factors and sequence.

Decide on Whole versus Part Practice

Skills can be taught by the whole or part method. The whole method involves learning the entire skill or activity in one dose. The part method breaks down a skill into a series of parts and then combines the parts into the whole skill. For example, in a rhythmic activity, each section of a dance is taught and then put together. A simple gymnastics routine might be broken into component parts and put back together for the performance.

Deciding whether to use the whole or part method depends on the complexity and organization of the skills to be learned. *Complexity* refers to the number of serial skills or components in a task. *Organization* defines how the parts are related to each other. *High organization* means the parts of the skill are closely related to each other, making separation difficult. An example of a highly organized and complex skill is throwing, which is difficult to practice without going through the complete motion. A low-organized skill is a simple folk dance, in which footwork and arm movements can be rehearsed separately. Generally, if the skills are high in complexity but low in organization, they can be taught in parts. If complexity is low but organization high, the skills must be taught as a whole. A final consideration is the duration of the skill. If the skill is of short duration, such as throwing, batting, or kicking, trying to teach the skill in parts is probably counterproductive. Imagine trying to slow down kicking and teach it part by part. The performer would not develop proper pattern and timing.

If they learn skill components separately, students then have to learn how to put the parts together. Practice time should be allowed for sequencing. For example, in a gymnastics routine, students might perform the activities separately, but find difficulty sequencing them because they have not learned how to modify each activity based on the previous one. Teaching a skill in parts is best used when it optimizes learning.

Determine the Length and Distribution of Practice Sessions

Short practice sessions usually produce more efficient learning than do longer sessions. This is due to both physical and mental fatigue (boredom). The challenge is to offer as many repetitions as possible within short practice sessions. Keep motivation high by varying approaches, challenges, and activities to develop the same skill. For example, using many different types of beanbag activities helps maintain motivation but still focuses on tossing and catching skills.

Another way to determine the length of practice sessions is to examine the tasks being practiced. If a skill causes physical fatigue, demands intense concentration, or has the potential to become tedious, keep practice sessions short and frequent, with adequate rest between intervals. Stop practice when students become bored or tired, and play a game until they are again ready to learn.

Practice sessions that are spread out over many days are usually more effective than sessions crowded into a short time. The combination of practice and review is effective for children because activities can be taught in a short unit and practiced in review sessions throughout the year. In the initial stages of skill learning, it is particularly important to schedule practice sessions in this way. Later, when success in skill performance increases motivational levels, teachers can lengthen individual practice sessions.

Use Random Practice Techniques

There are two ways to organize the presentation of activities to be taught. The first is *blocked practice*, where students complete all the trials of one task before moving on to the next task. Since blocked practice is effective during the first stages of skill practice, learners improve rapidly because they are repeatedly practicing the same skill. As a result, learners are often motivated to continue practicing. A drawback to blocked practice is that it makes learners believe they are more skilled than they actually are. When students try the skill in a natural setting, performance level lowers, and some children feel discouraged.

The other method is *random practice*, where the order of multiple task presentations is mixed and no task is practiced twice in succession. Goode and Magill (1986) showed that random practice was the most effective approach to use when learning skills. Blocked practice gave the best results during the acquisition phase of skill learning; however, students who learned a skill using random practice demonstrated much higher retention.

Random practice results in better retention because the students are mentally generating solutions. When they practice the same task over and over, children become bored, and they stop thinking about how to solve the problem. In contrast, students using random practice forget the motor program used and have to consciously re-create the solution to be successful, thus minimizing boredom.

Offer Variable Practice Experiences

Motor tasks are usually grouped into classes of tasks. For example, throwing involves a collection or class of movements. Throwing a ball in a sport can be done in many different ways; the ball can travel at different speeds, different trajectories, and varying distances. Even though throwing tasks are all different, the variations have basic similarities. Movements in a class usually involve the same body parts and have similar rhythm but can be performed with many variations. These differences create the need for variable practice in a variable setting.

Practice sessions for motor skills should include a variety of skills in a movement class, with a variety of situations and parameters in which the skill is performed, so students can respond to various novel situations. If a skill to be learned involves one fixed way of performing it (a "closed" skill), such as placekicking a football or striking a ball off a batting tee, variability is much less important. However, most skills are "open," and responses are somewhat unpredictable, which makes variability in practice the usual mode of operation (catching or batting a ball moving at different speeds and from different angles).

TEACH SKILLS IN PROPER PROGRESSION

Skill progression involves moving the learning process through ordered steps from the least challenging to the most challenging facets of an activity. Most motor skills can be ordered in an approximate hierarchy from simple to complex. Instructional progression includes reviewing previously learned steps before proceeding to new material and learning prerequisite skills before trying more difficult activities.

Developmental Levels and Progression

Children learn skills in a natural progression, but not at the same rate. Encourage students to progress at a rate that is best suited for them. This usually means that all children will be learning a similar class of skills (throwing or striking, for instance) but will progress at different rates and practice

TABLE 3.1 Equating developmental levels to grades and ages

Developmental Level	Grades	Ages
I	K–2	5–7
II	3–4	8–9
III	5–6	10–11

different skills within the category. This premise forms the basis for presenting a developmentally appropriate physical education program.

Placing activities into developmental levels makes it easier to present activities appropriate to students' maturity and abilities. Understand that placing activities in levels serves as a general guideline for instruction. Some students may be gifted or in need of special instruction. In that case, present activities that best suit the individual regardless of the recommended level. Schools group children by chronological age and grade rather than by developmental level; Table 3.1 shows how developmental levels roughly equate with grades and ages. To help plan lessons in which skills are presented in proper sequence, activities in Chapters 15–30 have been placed in order of difficulty, from beginning skills to the most advanced. For instructional and lesson planning purposes, the accompanying lesson plan book, *Dynamic Physical Education Curriculum Guide: Lesson Plans for Implementation* (Pangrazi, 2010), organizes the activities by developmental level.

Developmental Level I activities (used most often with kindergarten through second-grade children) are the least difficult and are the basis of more complex skills. Most of these skills are performed individually or with a partner to increase the success of primary-grade children. Examples are tossing and catching, striking a stationary object, and playing games that simply incorporate fundamental locomotor movements. The number of complex decisions to make while performing the skill is minimized so students can concentrate on the skill at hand. As students mature and progress into *Developmental Level II* (usually grades three through four), the tasks become more difficult; many are performed individually or in small groups. Environmental factors such as different speeds of objects, different sizes of objects, and games requiring locomotor movements and specialized skills (throwing, catching, and so on) are introduced at this level. In *Developmental Level III* (grades five through six), students use skills in various sport and game situations. Simple skills previously learned are sequenced into more complex motor patterns. Cognitive decisions about when to use a skill and how to incorporate strategy into the game are integrated into the learning experiences at this level. See Table 3.2 for a quick comparison of typical activities for the three developmental levels. The placement of activities into developmental levels is a general rule of thumb. *There will always be exceptions.* Expect to make exceptions to meet the developmental needs of students.

INTEGRATE MECHANICAL PRINCIPLES INTO INSTRUCTION

When planning for skill instruction, mechanical principles are an integral part of skill performance. It is best to teach young children the proper way to perform a skill so that they do not have to unlearn incorrect motor patterns later. Many teachers have experienced the difficulty of changing a performer's motor patterns after a skill has been learned incorrectly. Stability, force, leverage, motion, and direction are concepts best learned when they accompany a skill

TABLE 3.2 Characteristics of activities for Developmental Levels I, II, and III

Level	Typical Grades	Level of Difficulty	Individual or Group?	Examples and Characteristics
I	K–2	Least difficult; foundation for more complex skills; much concentration required to perform skills	Mostly individual; sometimes with a partner	Tossing and catching; striking a stationary object; games incorporating basic locomotor skills
II	3–4	More difficult; skills are performed more consistently; less concentration required	Often individual or in small groups; groups and teams introduced	Specialized skills and variation in environmental factors (e.g., speeds and size of objects)
III	5–6	Advanced individual and specialized skills and activities; skills often performed automatically without thinking; students able to perform well in group activities	Stress placed on playing with others and using skills in cooperative and competitive settings	Sport and game situations; involves cognitive decisions and strategies; more emphasis on manipulative activity, less on movement concept activities

being taught. A discussion of each is covered in the following sections.

STABILITY

Stability reflects balance and equilibrium, which affect the performance of many sport skills. A stable base is necessary when one applies force to a projectile or absorbs force. Instability is useful in some activities, such as when a rapid start is desired. Introduce these concepts:

1. For greater stability, increase the size of the base of support. The base must be widened in the direction of the force being applied or absorbed.
2. Move the body's center of gravity lower or closer to the base of support when stopping quickly or applying/absorbing force (as when pushing/pulling). Lower the center of gravity by bending the knees and hips (Figure 3.5).

FIGURE 3.5 Lowering the center of gravity while pulling.

3. Keep the center of gravity over the base of support (within the boundaries of the base) for stability and balance. When the center of gravity passes beyond the boundaries of the base of support, balance is lost. In most activities, students should keep the head up and eliminate excessive body lean. The ready position (Figure 3.6) is an example of a stable position used in many sport activities.
4. Use "free" or non-weight-bearing limbs as counterbalances to aid stability. The ready position and fast starts are used in many physical activity settings and illustrate how stability and instability (used in fast starts) can enhance performance.

FORCE

Force is a measure of the push or pull that one object or body applies to another. Force is necessary to move objects of various types and sizes. The larger the object to be moved, the greater the amount of force required to cause the movement. Generating large forces usually involves large muscle groups and a greater number of muscles than does the generation of a smaller force. Torque is the twisting or turning effect that force produces when it acts eccentrically with respect to a body's axis of rotation. Here are some concepts to remember when teaching children:

FIGURE 3.6 Ready position.

1. When resisting or applying force, the bones on either side of the major joints should form a right angle to each other. A muscle is most effective at causing rotation when it pulls at a 90-degree angle.
2. To generate greater force, activate the body parts in a smooth, coordinated way. For example, in throwing, rotate the hips and trunk first and then rotate (in sequence) the upper arm, lower arm, hand, and fingers.
3. Use more muscles to generate more force. Muscles can generate high levels of force when the contraction speed is low. For example, lifting a very heavy object rapidly is impossible.
4. Absorb force over a large surface area and for as long as possible. An example of absorbing force over a large surface area is a softball player rolling after a dive through the air to catch a ball. The roll absorbs the force with the hands and the large surface area of the body.
5. Use follow-through in striking and throwing activities to ensure maximum application of force and gradual

reduction of momentum. An example is the continued swing of the baseball bat after striking the ball.

LEVERAGE AND MOTION

Body levers amplify force into motion. Levers offer a mechanical advantage so that less effort is needed to accomplish tasks. Motion occurs after force has been applied or when force is absorbed. A simple lever is a bar or other rigid structure that can rotate about a fixed point to overcome a resistance when force is applied. Levers serve one of two functions: (1) they allow resistance greater than the applied force to be overcome, or (2) they serve to increase the distance or the speed at which resistance can be moved. Here are some characteristics of the body's levers and their effects on movement:

1. The body has first-, second-, and third-class levers (Figure 3.7). Most of these are third-class levers; they have the point of force (produced by the muscles) between the fulcrum (the joint) and the point of resistance (produced by the weight of the object to be moved).

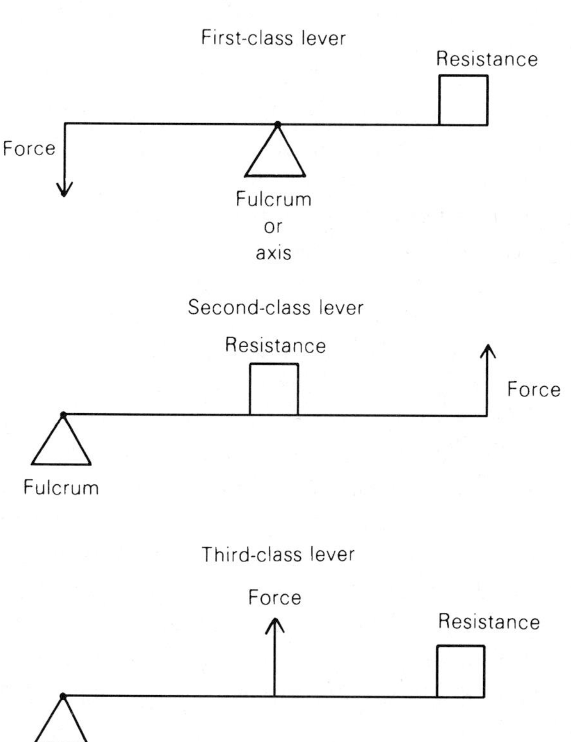

FIGURE 3.7 Types of levers.

2. Most of the body's levers are used to gain a mechanical advantage for speed, not to accomplish heavy tasks.
3. A longer force arm (distance from joint to point of force application) allows greater resistance to be overcome (Figure 3.8). This concept is useful when manipulating an external lever. For example, to pry open a paint can, force is applied to the screwdriver away from the rim rather than near the paint can. This allows the screwdriver to act as a longer lever.

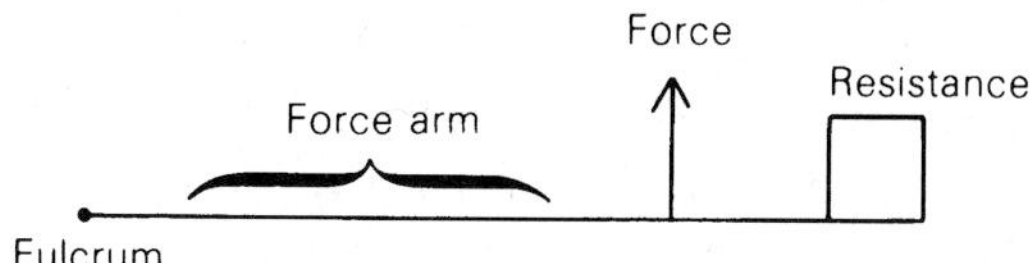

FIGURE 3.8 Longer force arm.

4. A longer resistance arm (distance from joint to point of resistance) allows greater speed to be generated (Figure 3.9). Rackets and bats are extensions of the arm; that is, they offer longer resistance arms for applying greater speed. The longer the racket or bat, therefore, the greater the speed generated. Longer levers are harder to rotate, which is why young baseball players are encouraged to choke up (grip higher on the bat) to make the bat easier to swing and control. Though the lever is shortened, bat velocity (at point of contact with the ball) is probably not reduced much. The important result is that performance improves through increased quality contacts.

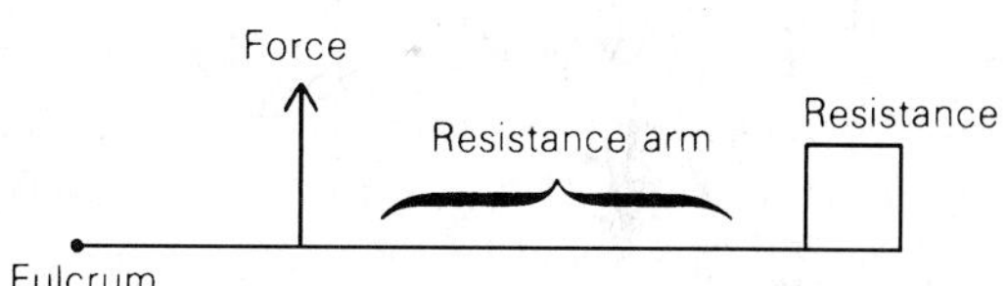

FIGURE 3.9 Longer resistance arm.

MOTION AND DIRECTION

In physical activities, most skills are associated with propelling an object. These concepts of motion and direction are basic to throwing, striking, and kicking skills learned in physical education:

1. The angle of release determines how far an object travels. Theoretically, the optimum angle of release is 45 degrees. The human body has limitations, however, that cause the optimum angle of release to be well below 45 degrees. For example, the angle of release for the shot put is 40 to 41 degrees; for the running long jump, it is 20 to 22 degrees.
2. A ball rebounds from the floor or from the racket at the same angle at which it is hit. However, various factors such as rotation applied to the ball, the type of ball, and the surface contacted by the ball can modify the rebound angle.
3. In most throwing situations, the propelled object should be released at a point tangent to the target.

During throwing, for example, the arm travels in an arc, and the ball must be released when the hand is in line with the target.

CONSIDER THE LEARNING ENVIRONMENT

The environment where students experience physical education can influence the effectiveness of instruction and learning. Factors such as space, equipment, and safety are important in planning a quality experience. Unlike student response and interest, environmental factors can be controlled entirely by the teacher. There is little excuse for not considering and planning for these variables.

PREDETERMINE YOUR SPACE NEEDS

A common error is to take a class to a large practice area, give students a task, and fail to define or limit the space where they are to perform it. In such a large area, the teacher cannot communicate with and manage the students, and many cannot see or hear what is being demonstrated. The skills being practiced and the teacher's ability to control the class will dictate the size of the space. As students become more responsive, the area can be enlarged. Regardless of its size, delineate the practice area. An easy way is to set up cones around the perimeter. Chalk lines, evenly spaced equipment, or natural boundaries can also serve as restraining lines.

The size of the practice area is also affected by the amount of instruction needed. When students are learning a closed skill and need constant feedback and redirection, it is important for them to stay near the instructor. Establish a smaller area where students can move in closer for instruction and then return to the larger area for practice.

Available space is often divided into smaller areas to maximize student participation. An example is a volleyball game where only 10 students can play on one available court. It is often more effective to divide the area into two courts so more students can play at once. A related consideration when dividing space is safety. If the playing areas are too close together, players from one area might run into those in the other area. A softball setting is unsafe if a player on one field can hit a ball into another play area.

USE EQUIPMENT EFFICIENTLY

Equipment can be a limiting factor. Before beginning the lesson, determine how much equipment is available since this will affect the lesson structure. For example, if there are only 16 paddles and balls for a class of 30, some type of sharing or station work will have to be organized. Know exactly what equipment is available and how much is in working condition. It is embarrassing to roll out a cart of playground balls only to find that half of them are not inflated.

FIGURE 3.10 Each student must have a piece of equipment.

How much equipment is enough? For individual-use equipment such as rackets, bats, and balls, each student should have one (Figure 3.10). For group-oriented equipment such as gymnastics apparatus, no more than four students should be waiting in line. Some teachers settle for less equipment because they teach as they have been taught. A common example is teaching volleyball with plenty of available equipment: Rather than having students work individually (each with a volleyball) against the wall or with a partner, the teacher divides the class into two long lines using one or two balls. Most of the equipment sits on the sidelines while students spend more time waiting in line than practicing skills.

If equipment is limited, adapt the instruction for the time being. Try not to accept the situation without voicing dissatisfaction. Some administrators characterize physical educators as good people who are always willing to "make do." Communicate with administrators regularly, and explain that instruction is much more effective when equipment is available. Speak with parent–teacher groups about having fund-raisers to buy needed equipment. Math teachers are not expected to teach math without books for each student, and physical educators cannot teach without adequate equipment. If you settle for less, you get less.

What are temporary alternatives when equipment is lacking? One solution is to teach using the task style—divide students into small groups so each group has enough equipment. In a softball unit, some students can practice fielding while others bat, others pitch, and so on. Another approach is to divide the class in half and have one group work on one activity while another works on an unrelated activity. If there is a shortage of paddles and balls, half of the class can practice racket skills while the other half plays half-court basketball. This approach is less educationally sound and increases teaching demands. Another solution is the peer review—one student practices an activity while a peer offers feedback and evaluation. They share equipment and take turns practicing and evaluating. A final solution is the most common—design drills that involve standing in line and waiting for a turn. This is unacceptable from an educational standpoint.

Effectively distributing equipment is a key component of a quality lesson; it reduces the time spent on tasks not related to learning. Distribute individual equipment by placing it around the perimeter of the area. This takes some setup time before the lesson, but it allows students to take a piece of equipment without confusion. Arrange large apparatus in the safest possible formation, so all pieces are visible from all angles.

Effective setup of equipment depends on the lesson. For example, lower the basket to focus on correct shooting form; lower the volleyball net to allow spiking. Place nets at different heights to allow different types of practice. Equipment and apparatus should always be modified to best suit the students' needs. There is nothing sacred about a 10-foot basket or a regulation-size ball. If modifying the equipment improves the quality of learning, do it.

ENSURE A SAFE ENVIRONMENT

Do not underestimate the importance of a safe environment. Injuries are inevitable in physical education classes, but if they are due to poor planning and preparation, you may be found liable (see Chapter 9). Teachers are expected to foresee hazardous situations that might result in student injury. Rules dictating safe and sensible behavior need to be taught and practiced. For example, if students are in a tumbling unit, they need instruction and practice in absorbing momentum and force. Have them practice safety procedures such as taking turns, spotting, and following directions.

Another component of a safe environment is a written curriculum for presenting lessons. A written curriculum offers evidence to a safety committee or court of law that the lesson activities were properly sequenced. An appropriate progression of activities also gives students confidence because they develop the skills needed to perform safely before moving on to the next level of difficulty.

Conduct safety inspections at regular intervals. If an apparatus has not been used for some time, inspect it beforehand to avoid having to stop a lesson and fix it. Keep tumbling mats, beanbags, and benches clean to prevent the spread of disease.

Despite the foregoing precautions, accidents can happen. All physical education activities have a certain degree of risk because students are moving. An important outcome of a physical education program is to offer students an opportunity to take calculated risks and overcome fear. When students feel adequate safety precautions are in place, they are more likely to try new activities that involve risk.

CHOOSE AN INSTRUCTIONAL FORMATION

Appropriate formations facilitate learning experiences. Different formations are needed for activities done in place (nonlocomotor), activities where children move (locomotor), and activities in which balls, beanbags, or other objects are thrown, kicked, caught, or otherwise received (manipulative). Select a formation based on ensuring maximum activity for all students. To minimize the amount of time students spend standing and waiting for a turn, limit squads to four students or less.

MASS OR SCATTERED FORMATION

The class scatters throughout the area so each student has a personal space. This formation is useful for in-place activities and when individuals need to move in every direction. Emphasize not bumping into, colliding with, or interfering with classmates. Scattered formation is basic to such activities as wands, hoops, individual rope jumping, and individual ball skills.

SQUAD FORMATION

In squad formation, members stand about 3 feet apart in a column. In extended squad formation, the squad column is maintained with more distance (10 to 15 feet) between members. Figure 3.11 shows regular and extended squad formations (L = leader).

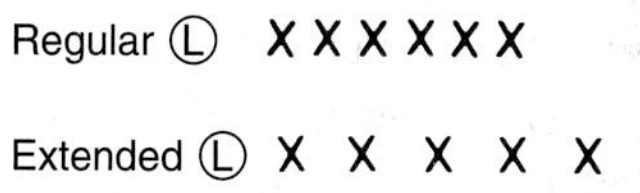

Regular Ⓛ XXXXXX

Extended Ⓛ X X X X X X

FIGURE 3.11 Regular and extended squad formations.

PARTNER FORMATION

Partner formation is useful for reciprocal teaching, where partners help each other learn new skills. Keep the pairs aligned if space is limited or objects are being caught and thrown (Figure 3.12).

FIGURE 3.12 Partner formation.

LANE OR FILE

The lane, or file, formation is commonly used with locomotor activity (Figure 3.13 on page 52). Students at the front of the lane move as directed and take their place at the rear of the lane.

X X X X
X X X X
X X X X
X X X X
X X X X
X X X X

FIGURE 3.13 Lane, or file, formation.

LINE AND LEADER

Line-and-leader formation (Figure 3.14) is often used for throwing and catching skills. The leader passes back and forth to each line player in turn. Place students in a semicircle-and-leader formation (Figure 3.15) so they are all the same distance from the leader.

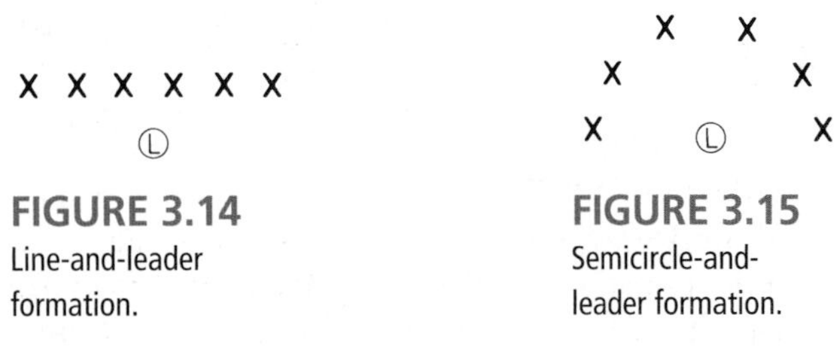

FIGURE 3.14 Line-and-leader formation.

FIGURE 3.15 Semicircle-and-leader formation.

DOUBLE LINE

The double-line formation is used for passing and kicking. Figure 3.16 shows a zigzag formation in which the ball is passed from one line to the next.

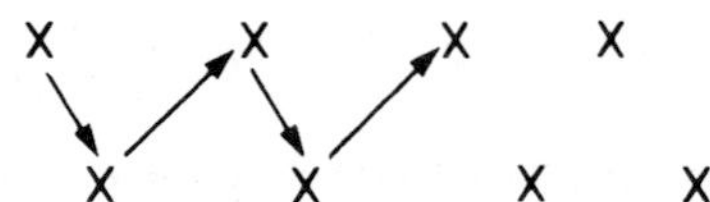

FIGURE 3.16 Double-line formation.

REGULAR SHUTTLE FORMATION

Try the regular shuttle formation (Figure 3.17) for practicing passing and dribbling skills on the move. It is often used for hockey, soccer, basketball, and football skills. The player at the head of one line dribbles toward, or passes to, the player at the head of the other line. Each player keeps moving forward and takes a place at the end of the other half of the shuttle.

FIGURE 3.17 Regular shuttle formation.

SHUTTLE TURN-BACK FORMATION

Shuttle turn-back formation (Figure 3.18) is used for passing, kicking, and volleying for distance. The player at the head of one shuttle line passes to the player at the head of the other. After passing, players go to the back of their line.

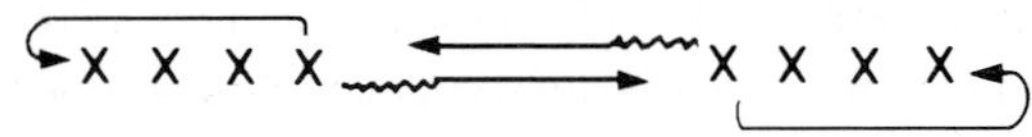

FIGURE 3.18 Shuttle turn-back formation.

SIMULTANEOUS CLASS MOVEMENT

Some activities require the entire class to move simultaneously. Without some structure and organization, this situation can become chaotic. For such activities, the following formations can be useful.

Children can start on opposite sides of the gym and exchange positions (Figure 3.19). On signal, they cross to the opposite side of the area, passing through the opposite line without contact.

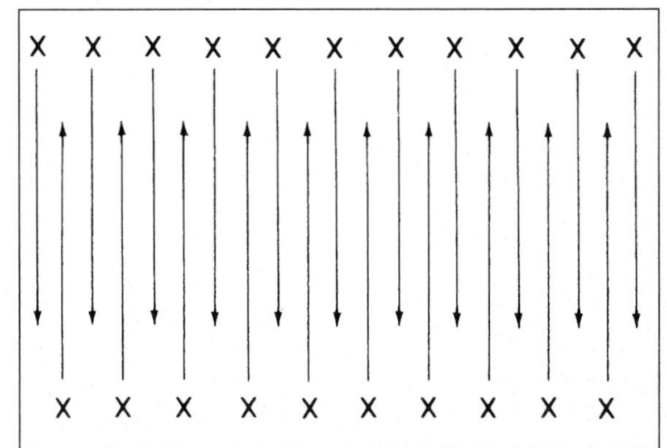

FIGURE 3.19 Exchanging positions on opposite sides.

Children can also start on opposite sides of the gym, move toward the center, and then go back. Form a dividing line with ropes, wands, or cones to mark the center (Figure 3.20).

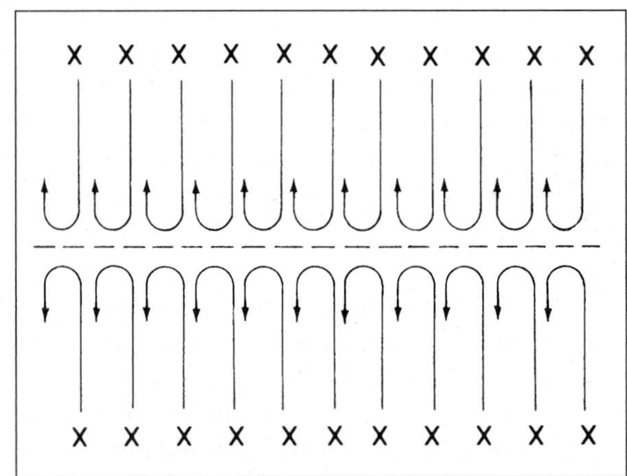

FIGURE 3.20 Moving to center and back on opposite sides.

Finally, children can start on each of four sides of the play area and alternately exchange sides (Figure 3.21). The children on one pair of opposite sides exchange first and then the others exchange. This formation is useful for class demonstrations—half of the class demonstrates while the other half observes and evaluates.

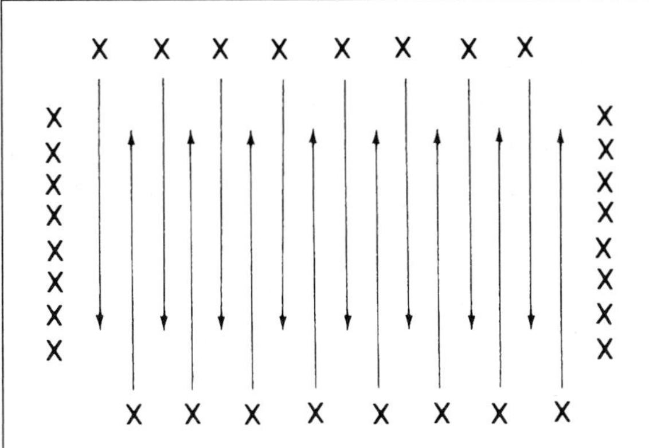

FIGURE 3.21 Exchanging on four sides.

DESIGN A LESSON PLAN

Written lesson plans vary in form and length, depending on the activity and the teacher's background. A written plan ensures that the lesson has been designed before children enter the activity area. It helps avoid hasty decisions that disrupt the unity and progression of instruction. Lesson plans give focus and direction, but they can and should be modified when needed. Students are more likely to make progress during a lesson when it is based on activities presented in earlier lessons. Teachers can write notes and changes on the lesson plans to suggest future modifications of the curriculum.

A standardized lesson plan allows teachers and substitute teachers to exchange plans within a school district. Include the following basic information in your lesson plan:

1. *Objectives.* Design and list instructional objectives for accomplishing content standards. See Chapter 4 for a discussion on writing effective objectives.
2. *Equipment required.* Identify amounts of materials and supplies required and how the equipment will be distributed.
3. *Instructional activities.* List actual movements and skill experiences to be taught. Place the activities in proper developmental sequence. You do not need to describe activities in detail, but give enough description so they can be easily recalled.
4. *Teaching hints.* Record organizational tips and important learning cues including equipment setup, student grouping, and teaching cues. If needed, list text and video references.

A common format is the four-part lesson plan. Figure 3.22 on pages 54–56 is a lesson plan taken from the accompanying curriculum guide by Pangrazi (2010). This curriculum contains a year's supply of lesson plans for Developmental Levels I through III. Each lesson includes an introductory or warm-up activity, fitness activities, lesson focus, and closing activity. Using four parts prepares students for the activity, ensures moderate to vigorous activity, teaches skills, and implements skills in a game setting.

Lesson planning takes time. Write them when you have ample time to plan and reflect. Lesson plans give direction to the day's lesson and may include many more activities than you can teach in a typical period. For quick reference, many teachers use a 4-by-6-inch card briefly describing the actual activities they are teaching. A lesson plan consists of four major parts, as described in the following sections.

INTRODUCTORY (WARM-UP) ACTIVITY

The introductory (warm-up) activity lasts 2 to 3 minutes and sets the tone for the rest of the lesson. If you can shape a class into a well-behaved group during the introductory activity, such behavior is easier to maintain for the rest of the lesson.

Starting a lesson is a difficult phase of teaching that can be made easier by practicing management skills such as stopping on signal, running under control, and so on. An effective rule of thumb is to run and freeze your class three times. If all students are with you after three freezes, begin teaching an introductory activity (Chapter 16). But, if students are not well managed at that point, skip the introductory activity and practice management skills. Remember that management skills take priority over physical development skills. You cannot teach children who are not paying attention to you. Learning to respect others takes top billing in any educational setting.

Movement Skills and Concepts (7)
Twisting, Turning, Stretching, and Relaxing Movements
Level I—Week 26

Objectives:

To apply movement concepts such as body and space awareness, relationships, and qualities of movement to a variety of locomotor and body management skills.

To combine locomotor and nonlocomotor skills into movement themes such as supporting body weight, bridges, and receiving and transferring weight.

NASPE Content Standards:

Introductory Activity: 1, 3, 5
Fitness Activity: 4
Lesson Focus: 1, 3, 6
Game: 1, 5

Equipment Required:

Music for animal movements

Teacher's choice of equipment for introductory activity and manipulative skills in the lesson focus

Instructional Activities	Teaching Hints

Introductory Activity—Creative and Exploratory Opportunities

Put out enough equipment so each child has a piece. Let them explore and create activities while moving. An alternative is to have students work with a piece of equipment with a partner or small group.

Teaching Hints: Ask students to move and be active without being told what to do. Encourage independent thinking.

Fitness Development Activity—Animal Movements and Fitness Challenges

1. Puppy Dog Walk—30 seconds.
2. Freeze; perform stretching activities.
3. Measuring-Worm Walk—30 seconds.
4. Freeze; perform abdominal development challenges.
5. Frog Jump—30 seconds.
6. Freeze; perform push-up position challenges.
7. Elephant Walk—30 seconds.
8. Freeze; do stretching activities.
9. Bear Walk—30 seconds.
10. Freeze; perform abdominal challenges.
11. Crab Walk—30 seconds.
12. Freeze and do stretching and relaxing activities.

Teaching Hints: Tape alternating segments (30 seconds each) of silence and music to signal duration of exercise. Students do animal movements when the music plays; they do fitness challenges when the music stops.

A variation is to place animal movement signs throughout the area and have students move from sign to sign, doing the appropriate animal movement each time they reach a new sign.

Lesson Focus—Movement Skills and Concepts (7)

Fundamental Skill: Twisting

1. Glue your feet to the floor. Can you twist your body to the right and to the left? Can you twist slowly? Quickly? Can you bend and twist at the same time? How far can you twist your hands back and forth?
2. Twist two parts of the body at the same time. Try three. More?
3. Twist one part of the body in one direction and another in a different direction.
4. Try to twist the upper half of your body without twisting the lower part. How about the reverse?
5. Sit on the floor, and see what parts of the body you can twist.
6. Try to twist one part of the body around another. Can you do this?
7. Balance on one foot and twist your body. Can you bend and twist in this position?
8. What different shapes can you make using twisted body parts?

Teaching Hints: Select a few activities from each category so students can practice a variety of skills. When possible, integrate manipulative skill activities with fundamental skill activities. A common error is to teach all the activities from one category. Teaching multiple groups of activities also enhances motivation.

Teach students the difference between a twist and a turn. Twisting is rotating a selected body part around its own long axis. Twisting involves movement around the body part itself. Turning focuses on the space in which the body turns and involves moving the entire body.

FIGURE 3.22 Example of a lesson plan.

Fundamental Skill: Turning

1. Turn your body left and right with quarter and half turns. Turn clockwise and counterclockwise.
2. (Post compass directions on the walls—north, south, east, and west.) Face the correct direction on call. Also face some other directions—northwest, southeast, etc.
3. Stand on one foot and turn around slowly; quickly; with a series of small hops.
4. Cross your legs with a turn and then sit down. Can you get up without moving your feet too much?
5. When you hear the signal, turn completely around once. Next time turn the other way. Now try with two full turns; three.
6. Lie on your tummy and turn yourself around in an arc. Try a seated position.

Stress maintaining balance while doing turning activities.

Perform twisting and turning movements in both directions. Also, try the movements in a sitting position or on tummy.

Fundamental Skill: Rocking

1. Rock in many different ways. Which part of your body can rock the highest?
2. Select a part of the body, and show me how you can rock smoothly and slowly. How about smoothly and quickly?
3. Rock like a rocking chair.
4. Lie on your back and rock. Point both hands and feet toward the ceiling and rock on the back.
5. Lie on your tummy and rock. Rock as high as you can. Hold your ankles and make giant rocks.
6. Rock in a standing position. Try forward, sideways, and diagonal rocking directions.
7. Select a position where you can rock and twist at the same time.
8. Lie on your back, with knees up, and rock side to side.

Make rocking a smooth and steady rhythm. It should be a controlled movement.

Rocking is usually best done when the body surface is rounded.

Discuss how the body can be rounded to make rocking easier.

Manipulative Skill: Student's Choice

Select one or more manipulative activities that need additional development regarding the children's needs and progress. During the week's work, a different activity might be scheduled each day.

Since equipment was placed out for the introductory activity, use it for the manipulative skill.

Movement Concept: Stretching and Curling

1. While on your feet, show me a stretched position. A curled position.
2. Go very slowly from your stretched position to the curled one you select. Go rapidly.
3. Keeping one foot in place (on a spot), show how far you can stretch in different directions.
4. Show me a straight (regular) curled position. A twisted curled position. A tightly curled position.
5. Select three different curled positions. On signal, go from one to the other rapidly. Repeat with stretch positions.
6. Explore and show the different ways your body can support itself in curled positions.

Stretching and curling are somewhat opposite movements.

Encourage stretching through the full range of movement. The stretch is done slowly and smoothly.

Encourage holding the stretch for 6 to 10 seconds.

Movement Concept: Tension and Relaxation

1. Make yourself as tense as possible. Now relax.
2. Take a deep breath; hold it tight. Release the air and relax.
3. Tense and reach as high as you can; slowly relax and drop to the floor.
4. Show how you can tense different parts of the body.
5. Tense one part of the body and relax another. Shift the tenseness to the relaxed part, and vice versa.
6. Press your fingers hard against your tensed abdominal muscles. Take your fists and beat lightly against the tensed position. Relax. Repeat.
7. Move forward, and stop suddenly in a tensed position. Relax. Repeat.

Relaxation activities are an excellent way to finish the lesson.

Help students learn to recognize when a limb and muscles are relaxed.

A quiet atmosphere facilitates relaxing. Soft voices encourage students to "wind down."

FIGURE 3.22 (Continued)

Closing Activity

Midnight

Supplies: None
Skills: Running, dodging

Establish a safety line about 40 feet from a den in which two or three players, the foxes, are standing. The other players stand behind the safety line and ask, "What time is it, Mr. Fox?" Choose one of the foxes to answer with various times, such as "one o'clock," four o'clock," etc. When the fox says a certain time, the class walks forward that number of steps. For example, if the fox says, "six o'clock," the class moves forward six steps. The fox continues to draw the players toward him. At some point, the fox answers the question by saying, "Midnight!" and chases the others back to the safety line. Any player who is caught becomes a fox in the den and helps to catch others.

Twins (Triplets)

Supplies: None
Skills: Body management

Have students scatter throughout the area with a partner (twin). Give commands such as, "Take three hops and two leaps," or "Walk backward four steps and three skips." When the pairs are adequately separated, the leader calls out, "Find your twin!" Players find their twin and stand frozen toe to toe. The goal is to avoid being the last pair to find each other and freeze. Students must move away from each other when following the commands. Alternatives are to find a new twin each time or to have twins start at opposite ends of the playing area.

Variation: The game is more challenging when played in groups of three (triplets). When using this variation, have students select new partners each time.

FIGURE 3.22 Example of a lesson plan. (Continued)

Introductory activities serve several purposes in the lesson format:

- Students engage in immediate activity upon entering the activity area. Children want to move right away rather than having to sit down, be quiet, and listen to instructions. Offer vigorous activity first; then give instructions or discuss learning objectives while they recover from vigorous activity.
- They serve as a physiological warm-up, preparing students for physical activity.
- This part of the lesson can be used for anticipatory set (Chapter 5, page 78) or to review previously learned skills. Anticipatory set previews the skill and cognitive objectives of the lesson.

PHYSICAL FITNESS AND ACTIVITY

The second part of the lesson is designed to enhance health-related fitness and promote lifetime physical activity. Include a variety of exercises so students experience the wide range of options available for maintaining an active lifestyle. This part of the lesson also teaches students the type and amount of activity necessary to maintain a healthy lifestyle. Discussing the importance of a healthy lifestyle is not enough; it must be experienced. Teach students how to determine their personal workloads, with an implied expectation that they will do their best. Forcing all students to do the same amount of activity fails to consider the genetic and personality differences inherent in a class of students. Physical fitness and activity are discussed in detail in Chapter 13.

LESSON FOCUS

Many adults use their physical skills as tools for participating in a physically active lifestyle. The lesson focus is designed to teach physical skills. It contains learning experiences to help students meet program content standards. Repetition and refinement of physical skills in a sequential and success-oriented setting characterize the lesson focus. This part of the lesson (15 to 25 minutes) emphasizes the process of performing skills correctly. It teaches students the skills required to function comfortably in a physically active lifestyle. Chapters 15–30 are filled with many instructional units presented in the lesson focus.

CLOSING ACTIVITY

The closing activity ends the lesson with an evaluation of the day's accomplishments—stressing and reinforcing skills learned, revisiting performance techniques, and checking cognitive concepts. The closing activity may be a game using skills developed in the lesson focus or simply a low-organized game or activity children enjoy (see Chapter 22 for a variety of games). If a lesson is demanding or spirited, focus closing activities on relaxing and winding down so students can return to the classroom in a calmer state of mind. Taking a few minutes to relax may calm teachers and students and create goodwill between classroom teachers and physical education specialists.

The closing activity may be minimized or deleted entirely. If a game or activity is the lesson focus, you may need more time for instruction. Whether a game is played or not, avoid disciplining a class by suggesting,

Planning

- Did I prepare ahead of time? Mental preparation ensures flow and continuity in a lesson.
- Did I understand the "whys" of my lesson? Knowing why you are teaching something enables you to present it with greater strength and conviction.
- Did I state my instructional goals for the lesson? Students are more focused if they know what they are supposed to learn.
- Did I plan the lesson so students can participate safely? Check that they have good areas for running; no slippery spots, broken glass, or objects to run into; adequate room for striking activities; and so on.

Equipment

- Was my equipment arranged before class? Proper equipment placement reduces management time and allows more time for instruction and practice.
- Did I use enough equipment to keep all students involved and assured of maximum practice opportunities?
- Did I notify the principal about equipment that needs to be repaired or replaced? On a regular basis, do I record areas where equipment is lacking or insufficient in quantity?
- Did I select equipment appropriate for the students' developmental level (i.e., proper size and types of balls, basketball hoop height, hand implements)?

Methodology

- Did I constantly move and reposition myself during the lesson? Moving allows you to be close to more students so you can reinforce and help them. It usually reduces behavior problems.
- Did I teach with enthusiasm and energy? Energy and zest rub off on students.
- Did I try to show just as much energy for the last class of the day as I did for the first class of the day? Did I work just as hard on Friday as I did at the start of the week?
- Did I keep students moving during lesson transitions? Did I plan my transitions carefully so it took little time to go to the next part of the lesson?

Instruction

- Was I alert for children who were having trouble performing the activities and needed some personal help? Children want to receive relevant but subtle help.
- Did I praise students who made an effort or improved? Saying something positive to children increases their desire to perform at a higher level.
- Did I give enough attention to each student's personalization and creativity? Everybody feels unique and wants to deal with learning tasks in a personal way.
- Did I teach for quality of movement, or just offer many activities in attempting to keep students on task? Repetition is a necessary part of learning new skills.

Discipline/Management

- Did I teach students to be responsible for their learning and personal behavior? Students need to learn responsibility and self-direction skills.
- Did I evaluate how I handled discipline and management problems? Did I preserve my students' self-esteem when correcting behavior? How could I have handled situations better?
- Did I make positive calls home to reinforce students who are really trying and working hard?

Assessment

- Did I bring closure to my lesson? This gives feedback about the effectiveness of instruction. It also allows students to reflect on what they have learned. Did I ask for answers in a way that lets me quickly check that all students understand?
- Did I evaluate the usefulness of activities I presented? Did I make changes as quickly as possible to ensure my lessons were improving and better meeting students' needs?
- Did I communicate with teachers and the principal about things that need to be improved or better understood? For example, did I say something about classes arriving late, teachers arriving late to pick up their class, schedule problems that cause excessive work, etc.?

FIGURE 3.23 Questions that aid the reflection process.

"We will not have a game if you don't quiet down." Closing activities are a useful part of the lesson and should not be used to bribe students to behave. Doing so may cause students to leave physical education classes with negative feelings.

REFLECTIVE TEACHING

Teaching is a full-time job. Teachers who excel and influence the lives of their students put a great deal of time and energy into their teaching. All who teach physical education work hard to reach physical education outcomes. But it is easy to identify a truly outstanding teacher who seems to get students to perform at a high level. One element apparent in all great teachers is their level of caring and thought. They spend a great deal of time thinking about the lessons they have presented, looking for new and better ways to get students to respond. This process is often referred to as *reflection*—sitting back and asking, "How could I have done better so students would have learned more?"

Many things make teaching difficult—the weather, teaching outside, having a limited amount of equipment, not knowing how some children will respond to your discipline techniques, and so on. There are no simple answers; what works one time may not work the next. Some teachers like to work from eight o'clock to three, and there had better not be anyone in their way at three o'clock. They teach the same way and the same thing year after year without change. It is often said that such teachers have been "teaching 20 years and have 1 year of experience." Their approach is the opposite of reflecting and trying to improve.

Quality teachers find time to reflect on all factors related to their lessons. Most teachers admit that their first lesson of the week is not as polished and effective as those near the end of the week. That first lesson does not include all the finer points learned through trial and error. Instruction improves when teachers reflect on why some things worked and others did not. Leave time at the end of the day to reflect and note ways to improve the lesson. Try keeping a journal related to inspiration and insight you uncover during the reflection process. Write down personal growth indicators and situations that show you are growing professionally. Continue to reflect; it is a dynamic, ongoing process. (Figure 3.23, page 57, lists questions that aid reflection.) Add other questions that are specific and related to your professional growth.

APPLYING WHAT YOU READ

- When developing a lesson, consider the most appropriate teaching style. Periodically reflect on the teaching styles you use most often. Although the most important consideration is what style fits the lesson, it is also important to use a variety of teaching styles throughout the curriculum.
- Do your lessons allow you to provide meaningful feedback? Be sure to create lessons that give you the opportunity to provide process-oriented feedback. That is, activities should allow students to practice cues (the process) with little emphasis on the product.
- To increase physical activity level and develop children's skills, create learning experiences that allow them to maximize the number of repetitions. The section on "Design Effective Practice Sessions" provides many strategies.
- Older students may enjoy learning the mechanical principles related to performing a physical activity. Integrating these concepts into lessons is easy and will not sacrifice physical activity time.
- Teachers have so many decisions to make when planning and teaching a lesson. To enhance lesson effectiveness, be sure to consider your equipment, space, and instructional formations before teaching a lesson.
- Quality lessons offer students a consistent structure that lets them know what to expect each time they come to physical education. The four-part lesson allows teachers to teach effectively and address meaningful outcomes.

REFLECTION AND REVIEW

HOW AND WHY

1. Why is it important for teachers to understand and use a variety of teaching styles?
2. How can knowledge of motor learning help teachers increase student learning in physical education?
3. Why are mechanical principles taught in elementary physical education? How might these principles help teachers and students?
4. How does the college learning environment differ from an appropriate learning environment for elementary physical education?
5. How did your elementary physical education learning environment differ from that advocated in this chapter?

CONTENT REVIEW

1. Identify the variables to consider when choosing a teaching style.
2. Describe the teaching styles used in physical education. Explain the effective use of each style.
3. Discuss the tenets of motor learning required to "optimize skill learning."
4. Explain several mechanical principles and how they are used in elementary physical education.
5. Describe four instructional formations. How can these formations be used?
6. Identify the four parts of a lesson. Discuss the characteristics and significance of each part.
7. State several issues that physical education teachers must address when preparing to teach.

FOR MORE INFORMATION

REFERENCES AND SUGGESTED READINGS

Byra, M., & Jenkins, J. (2000). Matching instructional tasks with learner ability: The inclusion style of teaching. Teaching style E. *Journal of Physical Education, Recreation, & Dance, 71*(3), 26–30.

Dyson, B., & Grineski, S. (2001). Using cooperative learning structures in physical education. *Journal of Physical Education, Recreation, & Dance, 72*(2), 28–31.

Gabbard, C. (2008). *Lifelong motor development* (5th ed.). San Francisco: Benjamin Cummings.

Gallahue, D. L., & Donnelly, F. C. (2003). *Developmental physical education for all children* (4th ed.). Champaign, IL: Human Kinetics.

Goode, S., & Magill, R. A. (1986). The contextual interference effects in learning three badminton serves. *Research Quarterly for Exercise and Sport, 57*, 308–314.

Graham, G., Holt/Hale, S. A., & Parker, M. (2007). *Children moving: A reflective approach to teaching physical education* (7th ed.). Boston: McGraw-Hill.

Harrison, J. M., Blakemore, C. L., & Buck, M. M. (2007). *Instructional strategies for secondary physical education* (6th ed.). Boston: McGraw-Hill.

Johnson, D. W., & Johnson, F. (2009). *Joining together: Group theory and group skills* (10th ed.). Upper Saddle River, NJ: Prentice Hall.

Metzler, M. W. (2000). *Instructional models for physical education.* Boston: Allyn & Bacon.

Mosston, M., & Ashworth, S. (2002). *Teaching physical education* (5th ed.). San Francisco: Benjamin Cummings.

Nichols, B. (1994). *Moving and learning: The elementary school physical education experience* (3rd ed.). St. Louis: McGraw-Hill.

Pangrazi, R. P. (2010). *Dynamic physical education curriculum guide: Lesson plans for implementation* (16th ed.). San Francisco: Benjamin Cummings.

Rink, J. E. (2006). *Teaching physical education for learning* (6th ed.). Boston: McGraw-Hill.

Rink, J. E. (2009). *Designing the physical education curriculum: Promoting active lifestyles.* Boston: McGraw-Hill.

Schmidt, R. A., & Wrisberg, C. (2008). *Motor learning and performance* (4th ed.). Champaign, IL: Human Kinetics.

Siedentop, D., & Tannehill, D. (2000). *Developing teaching skills in physical education* (4th ed.). Mountain View, CA: Mayfield.

WEBSITES

Physical Education Teaching and Curriculum Information
www.pecentral.com
www.pelinks4u.org
www.pe4life.org
www.masterteacher.com

Research for Education and Learning
www.mcrel.org

Research on Teaching Physical Education
www.UnlockResearch.com

Teaching Styles and Learning Styles
http://www4.ncsu.edu/unity/lockers/users/f/felder/public/Learning_Styles.html

3

4 Curriculum Development

ESSENTIAL COMPONENTS OF QUALITY PROGRAMS

- I. Organized around content standards
- II. Student-centered and developmentally appropriate
- III. Physical activity and motor skill development form the core of the program
- IV. Teaches management skills and self-discipline
- V. Promotes inclusion of all students
- VI. Focuses on process over product
- VII. Promotes lifetime personal health and wellness
- VIII. Teaches cooperation and responsibility and promotes sensitivity to diversity

NATIONAL STANDARDS FOR PHYSICAL EDUCATION*

1. Demonstrates competency in motor skills and movement patterns needed to perform a variety of physical activities.
2. Demonstrates understanding of movement concepts, principles, and tactics as they apply to the learning and performance of physical activities.
3. Participates regularly in physical activity.
4. Achieves and maintains a health-enhancing level of physical fitness.
5. Exhibits responsible personal and social behavior that respects self and others in physical activity.
6. Values physical activity for health, enjoyment, challenge, self-expression, and/or social interaction.

*National Association for Sport and Physical Education (NASPE), 2004.

This chapter offers a systematic approach for developing curriculum and suggests formats for organization and evaluation. A written curriculum gives direction to the instructional program. The steps for planning, designing, and implementing a comprehensive curriculum are given. The concepts of scope, sequence, and balance help ensure that the curriculum meets the needs of all students.

Outcomes

- Define *scope, sequence,* and *balance* as they relate to curriculum development.
- List common elements of a quality curriculum.
- Explain your philosophy of physical education for children.
- List environmental factors affecting curriculum development.
- Specify the seven-step approach in developing a quality curriculum.
- Specify the needs, characteristics, and interests of children, and explain how age and maturity factors affect program development.
- Describe the difference between content standards and student-centered objectives.
- Cite the three learning domains, and discuss characteristics of each.

CURRICULUM is a framework of child-centered physical activities that promote physical activity and skill development. A *curriculum* is a delivery system that gives sequence and direction to student learning experiences. The curriculum includes a set of beliefs and goals that evolve from a theoretical framework or value orientation. *Value orientation* is a set of personal and professional beliefs used in determining curricular decisions. Most often, physical educators have several value orientations, so physical education programs reflect a blend of values. This blending of value orientations results in the formulation of a teacher's instructional model. Metzler (2005) compares an instructional model for teachers to a blueprint for a builder.

In elementary physical education, several instructional models can be used to teach standards-driven content. This text uses a broad-based *multi-activity model* that focuses on promoting physical activity and developing students' physical skills. The multi-activity model uses units of physical activity or sport as the core curriculum. Units vary in length from 1 to 3 weeks, depending on program philosophy and student grade levels. The units are typically arranged with a balance of activities from categories such as lifetime activities, team sports, rhythmic activities, personal fitness activities, recreational activities, and low-organized games.

This model is popular because it allows for diversity and flexibility in meeting the changing interests and desires of today's students. Students have different competencies and interests, and they want to be able to participate in activities they enjoy. The multi-activity curriculum and short units ensure interesting activities for every student during the year.

As noted, there are other curriculum models. The sport education model centers on giving students a positive, "authentic" sport experience. The movement education model usually consists of educational dance, educational gymnastics, and education games that teach movement concepts. Hellison's model uses physical activity and the physical education environment to teach children skills that promote personal and social responsibility (2003). Teaching games for understanding (TGFU), also called the tactical games model, is a relatively new model in physical education. TGFU uses games as the context to teach the skills and knowledge needed to become competent. Other curriculum models include outdoor education, adventure education, health-related physical education, and conceptual physical education (see Kulinna, 2008, for descriptions of these models). Bear in mind that no model is the "right" model, and no model fits all needs. In practice, most physical education programs combine several models to teach desired outcomes.

When developing or revising a curriculum, the physical education staff must consider its value orientation toward the existing curriculum and the proposed changes. This process focuses on three major components: the subject matter to be learned, the students for whom the curriculum is being developed, and the society that has established the schools. Curriculums vary depending on the value orientations of the physical educators involved in the planning. Physical educators who place highest priority on mastering subject matter emphasize sports, dance, outdoor adventure activities, physical fitness activities, and aquatic activities. This orientation focuses on students learning skills and gaining knowledge so they can continue active participation for a lifetime. In contrast, instructors who favor a student-centered approach prize activities that develop the individual student. They emphasize helping students find personally meaningful activities. Other physical educators see student autonomy and self-direction as the most important goals. They focus instruction and curricula on lifetime sport skills and nontraditional activities, such as cooperative games and group activities, to foster problem-solving and interpersonal skills.

These examples illustrate only a few of the different value orientations of physical educators. Usually, most curricula are put together by committee and reflect several value orientations. To ensure consistent instructional goals, teachers need to know the value orientations driving their curriculum. Finding common ground among value orientations makes it easier for a staff to present lessons that teach common goals and objectives.

Before accepting a new teaching position, ask yourself these questions about the school's curriculum. (If you answer no to most of them, it may be difficult to work in such a setting because it conflicts with your value orientation.)

- Will the curriculum express a viewpoint about subject matter that is consistent with mine?
- Does the curriculum express a viewpoint about student learning that I believe?
- Does the curriculum express a viewpoint about the school's role in accomplishing social–cultural goals that is similar to my beliefs?
- Can I implement the instructional strategies I value within this model?

DESIGNING A QUALITY CURRICULUM

Figure 4.1 is a guide to constructing a meaningful, well-planned curriculum. The first four steps focus on designing a framework for selecting curriculum activities. These steps are often ignored because the focus is on activities that are easily implemented, even though they may not contribute to content standards. Designing a curriculum without a framework is like building a house without blueprints.

STEP ONE: DEVELOP A GUIDING PHILOSOPHY

The first step in curriculum design is to define a philosophy of physical education that reflects the educators' beliefs about how physical education fits into the total school curriculum and what it will accomplish for each student. Here is an example of a philosophical platform for physical education.

> Physical education is the part of a child's overall education that teaches and involves movement. Physical education must be largely an instructional program if it is to be a full partner in the child's overall education. Only high-quality programs based on developmental goals with demonstrable, accountable outcomes achieve this respect. The overriding goal of U.S. education—to develop an individual who can live effectively in a democracy—guides the development of this program. Although physical education stresses psychomotor goals, it also contributes to cognitive and affective learning domains. Three major and unique contributions of physical education to the total school curriculum are:
>
> 1. *To develop personal activity and fitness habits.* The program teaches children the conceptual framework under which personal fitness and lifetime activity habits are developed. This implies teaching the concept of human wellness (that is, teaching students how to maintain a vibrant and functional lifestyle throughout adulthood). Emphasis is placed on lifetime activity and personal habits that can be used in adulthood.
> 2. *To develop and enhance movement competency and motor skills.* Movement competency is rooted in developing a broad base of body management skills. The focus is on developing motor skills in a positive and nurturing environment. Personal competency in a wide variety of skills is an overriding theme of instruction.
> 3. *To gain a conceptual understanding of movement principles.* Moving efficiently requires learning basic concepts of movement and understanding anatomical and mechanical principles. Physical education instruction integrates knowledge and skill performance to develop students who know how to move.

STEP TWO: DEFINE A CONCEPTUAL FRAMEWORK FOR THE CURRICULUM

A conceptual framework is a series of statements characterizing the desired curriculum. These concepts establish criteria for selecting activities and experiences included in the curriculum. The framework directs the selection of activities and reflects beliefs about education and the learner. Here are some statements that define a child-centered, developmental curriculum:

- *Curriculum goals and objectives are appropriate for all children.* This statement implies a balanced curriculum

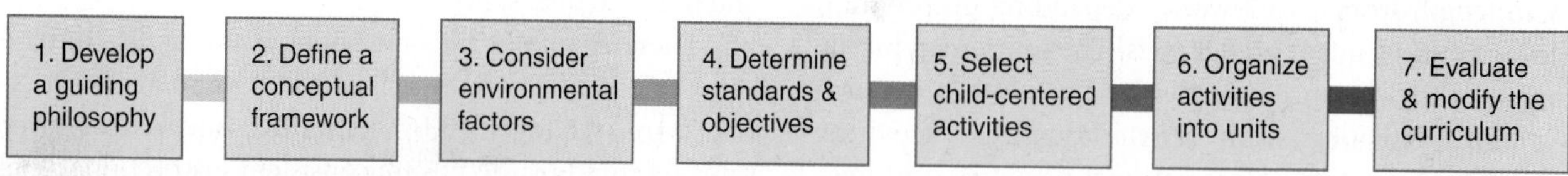

FIGURE 4.1 Steps for designing a quality curriculum.

covering fundamental skills, sport skills, games, rhythms and dance, gymnastics, and individual and dual activities. It focuses on developing a broad foundation of motor skills for all students.

- *Curriculum activities are chosen for their potential to help students reach national and local content standards.* The elementary school years are a time of experimentation, practice, and decision making with all movement possibilities. Activities are included in the curriculum not because teachers or students prefer them, but because they help students achieve national content standards.
- *The curriculum helps children develop lifelong physical activity habits and understand basic fitness concepts.* Regardless of the curriculum philosophy, it should be designed so children leave school with active lifestyle habits. The fitness program is experiential—students participate in fitness activities rather than just learning the facts of fitness. A meaningful curriculum offers varied, positive, and educational activities students can use throughout life.
- *The curriculum includes activities that enhance cognitive and affective learning.* Children are whole beings who need to learn more than just how to perform physical skills. They must understand skill performance principles and develop cognitive learning related to physical activity and wellness. Affective development—the learning of cooperative and social skills—can be fostered through group activities, and these skills are just as important as physical skills.
- *The curriculum provides experiences that help all children succeed and feel satisfaction.* Quality programs minimize failure and emphasize success. Activities that emphasize self improvement, participation, and cooperation encourage development-perceived competence, the feeling that "I am capable of performing well." Physical education instruction focuses on learning, without labeling students as winners or losers.
- *The curriculum is planned and based on an educational environment that is consistent with other academic areas in the school.* Like teachers in other disciplines, physical education teachers need good working conditions. They need class sizes similar to those of classroom teachers (20 to 35 students) and an assigned teaching area (a gym or multipurpose room). They need enough equipment for maximum activity and participation—meaning one piece of individual equipment for each youngster and ample apparatus to limit long lines and waiting for a turn. A daily program gives students maximum opportunity for learning and retention.
- *Activities in the curriculum are presented in an educationally sound sequence.* Progression is the soul of learning, and the curriculum should reflect progression vertically (between developmental levels) and horizontally (within each level and within each activity).
- *The curriculum includes an appropriate means of assessing student progress.* Student assessment includes health-related fitness, physical activity assessment, skill development, cognitive learning, and attitude development toward physical activity. Any assessment program should enhance curriculum effectiveness and help teachers individualize instruction, communicate with parents, and identify students with special needs.

STEP THREE: CONSIDER ENVIRONMENTAL FACTORS

Environmental factors are conditions in the community and school district that limit or extend the scope of the curriculum. These factors include the amount and type of equipment, budget size, and cultural makeup of the community. Other factors, such as the support of school administrators, can affect the scheduling or amount of required physical education in the school. Communities may value specific types of activities or experiences for their children. Environmental factors need to be examined carefully, but they should not restrict curriculum scope and sequence. Rather, they should give direction to the curriculum development process. A well-designed curriculum is a goal, direction, and destination for the future, a high road to instructional success. Consider various environmental factors, and use them to enhance curriculum creativity and scope.

The following environmental factors can sometimes be limiting, but they can be handled creatively to ensure that the curriculum is effectively implemented. Think big; develop a comprehensive curriculum that is as varied, broad, and creative as possible. Seek to expand and develop the curriculum beyond these limiting factors.

School Administrators

The support of school administrators significantly affects the curriculum, so it is important to inform them about program goals. Like the general public, administrators may have misconceptions about physical education and its contribution to the overall education of students. Most administrators will support physical education programs built on sound educational principles that are documented and evaluated.

The Community: People and Climate

Occupations, religions, educational levels, cultural values, and physical activity habits in the community are factors that can affect curriculum development. Parents have a strong influence on their children's activity interests and habits. The area's geographical location and climate of the area are also important factors. The terrain (mountains, deserts, etc.) and weather conditions affect people's activity interests. Extremely hot or cold climates strongly influence which activities are included in the curriculum and when they are scheduled during the year.

Facilities and Equipment

Available teaching facilities dictate which activities can be offered. Facilities include on-campus as well as off-campus areas in the neighboring community. Off-campus facilities might be a community swimming pool or park. Equipment must be available in quality and quantity. To learn at an optimum rate, each child needs a piece of equipment. Equipment can be purchased with school funds or with special funds raised through student performance programs. Some equipment can be built by school maintenance departments or as industrial arts projects. Another less desirable alternative is to ask students to bring equipment—such as jump ropes, soccer balls, and foam balls—from home. Once this precedent is set, administrators may fail to fund the program properly because they feel the physical educator can always find a way to "just get by."

Laws and Requirements

Laws, regulations, and requirements at the national, state, and local levels may restrict or direct a curriculum. Programs must conform to these laws. Examples of two national laws affecting physical education programs are Title IX of the Educational Amendments Act of 1972 and Public Law 94–142. Title IX enforces equal opportunities for both sexes, and PL 94–142 mandates equal access to educational services for students with disabilities (see Chapter 7). Individual states also may have laws that affect physical education programming.

Scheduling

The schedule or organizational pattern of the school affects curriculum development. How many times per week classes meet, how long class periods last, and who teaches the classes are factors to consider. Many scheduling alternatives exist: daily, two or three times per week, every other week, and so on. Regardless of the various parameters, most elementary schools have a scheduling committee that includes some classroom teachers, specialists in areas such as art and music, and the physical education teacher.

Consider several factors when developing schedules. Physical education classes typically are scheduled for 30 minutes. Some teachers prefer 40 minutes for upper grades, but this is a long period for primary-grade children. Conversely, classes can be too short. Some schools try to compress primary-grade classes to 20 minutes. A short class makes it difficult to present a balanced and complete lesson. Another important issue is how many periods a physical education teacher should teach per day. Physical education teachers should not be expected to have more contact time with students than classroom teachers do. Teaching physical education is demanding, and it is unfair to expect physical education specialists to teach all day without relief. An acceptable workload is eight or nine 30-minute periods per day with at least 5 minutes of passing time between classes so that teachers can rearrange equipment, talk to students, and take care of personal matters. Passing time also avoids the situation where a class has to wait for the current class to end.

Another important consideration is scheduling classes by developmental levels. Because physical education is equipment- and planning-intensive, scheduling by developmental level helps reduce the time needed for class area preparation and for setting up or removing equipment.

Budget and Funding

The funding allocated for purchasing new equipment and replacing old supplies affects curriculum quality. Physical educators deserve parity in funding with other school program areas. Students are not expected to learn to read and write without materials and supplies. Likewise, they cannot learn physical skills without the necessary equipment and facilities.

STEP FOUR: DETERMINE CONTENT STANDARDS AND STUDENT OBJECTIVES

Content standards determine the direction of the program as dictated and desired by the state, district, or individual school. Such standards are fixed goals for learning. They determine what students should know and be able to do upon completing their schooling. Student progress is dictated by how students compare to the fixed standards rather than how they compare to other students. Content standards determine the criteria for selecting instructional activities for the curriculum. The National Association for Sport and Physical Education (NASPE) has identified six national standards that guide the content of this textbook (see Chapter 1 for an in-depth discussion of each standard).

Write Student-Centered Instructional Objectives

After defining content standards, physical education teachers develop instructional objectives. Objectives dictate the specific activities students will need to learn throughout the school year. Student-centered objectives are usually written in behavioral terms. Behavioral objectives contain three key characteristics: (1) a desired behavior that is observable; (2) a behavior that is measurable; and (3) a criterion for success that can be measured. Objectives are written for all three learning domains—psychomotor, cognitive, and affective. A description of each domain follows.

1. *Psychomotor domain.* This domain (Corbin, 1976) is the primary focus of instruction for physical educators. The seven levels in psychomotor domain taxonomy are movement vocabulary, movement of body parts, locomotor movements, moving implements and objects, patterns of movement, moving with others, and movement problem solving. Students progress through these levels based on their own developmental level. They learn the vocabulary of movement before proceeding to simple body part movements. More complex movements are taught so children can participate in activities with others and solve personal movement dilemmas.
2. *Cognitive domain.* The cognitive domain was defined by Bloom (1956) and includes six major areas: knowledge, comprehension, application, analysis, synthesis, and evaluation. The cognitive domain for physical education focuses on knowing rules, health information, safety procedures, and so on, and being able to understand and apply that knowledge. As students mature, they learn to analyze different activities, develop personalized exercise routines (synthesis), and evaluate their fitness levels.
3. *Affective domain.* The affective domain (Krathwohl, Bloom, & Masia, 1964) deals with feelings, attitudes, and values. Major categories of learning in this area are receiving, responding, valuing, organizing, and characterizing. The affective domain changes more slowly than do the psychomotor and cognitive domains. How teachers treat students and the feelings students develop toward physical education are ultimately more important than the knowledge and skill developed in physical education programs.

Behavioral objectives are time-consuming to write. Some teachers become bogged down and discouraged because the number of objectives appears overwhelming. A text edited by Chepko and Arnold (2000) offers a wide variety of behavioral objectives and sample assessment activities based on content standards. This text expedites the task of writing a standards-based curriculum. The following are examples of behavioral objectives related to the NASPE content standards listed in Chapter 1.

Psychomotor Domain

1. Move efficiently using a variety of locomotor skills such as walking, running, skipping, and hopping.
2. Perform body management skills on various apparatus including climbing ropes, benches, and balance beams.

Cognitive Domain

1. Understand words that describe a variety of relationships with objects such as *around, behind, over, through,* and *parallel.*
2. Understand how warm-up and cooldown prevent injuries.

Affective Domain

1. Show empathy for the concerns and limitations of peers.
2. Demonstrate a willingness to participate with peers regardless of diversity or disability.

STEP FIVE: SELECT CHILD-CENTERED ACTIVITIES

Selecting activities for a child-centered curriculum requires a clear understanding of children's urges, characteristics, and interests. It makes little sense to gather activities for instruction if they are not developmentally appropriate or do not appeal to children. The major criterion to follow when selecting activities for the curriculum is, "Do the activities contribute to content standards and student-centered objectives?" This approach contrasts with selecting activities because they are fun or because you enjoy them. Some teachers fail to include activities in the curriculum if they lack confidence or feel incompetent to teach them. This situation results in a curriculum designed for the teacher's benefit rather than the students'. If an activity contributes to content standards, teachers need to develop the requisite instructional competency. Imagine a math teacher, due to feelings of incompetence, choosing not to teach fractions or multiplication tables to students. Teachers have a responsibility to learn how to teach new activities so students experience and learn requisite physical skills.

4

In the planning stage, gather as many activities as possible that contribute to content standards. The greater the number of activities considered, the more varied and imaginative the final program. In this step, emphasize brainstorming, creating, and innovating without restriction. The finished curriculum will be deficient if it is limited at this step. Later steps offer an opportunity to delete inappropriate activities.

Know the Basic Urges of Children

A basic urge is a desire to do or accomplish something. All children have similar urges, which are hereditary or environmentally influenced. Basic urges are linked closely to societal influences and are affected by teachers, parents, and peers. Usually, basic urges are similar among children of all ages and are not affected by developmental maturity. These urges provide direction for creating child-centered experiences.

The Urge for Movement

Children have an insatiable appetite for moving, performing, and being active. They run for the sheer joy of running. For them, activity is the essence of living. Design a physical education program that takes advantage of this craving for movement.

The Urge for Success and Approval

Children like to achieve and have their achievements recognized. They wilt under criticism and disapproval, whereas encouragement and friendly support can promote growth and development. Failure can lead to frustration, lack of interest, and inefficient learning. Successes should far outweigh failures, and students should achieve some success during each class period. Organize and present curriculum activities to ensure that students will feel successful.

The Urge for Peer Acceptance and Social Competence

Peer acceptance is a basic human need. Children want others to accept, respect, and like them. Teach and encourage peer acceptance in physical education and the overall school environment. Learning to cooperate with others, being a contributing team member, and sharing accomplishments with friends are important outcomes of the program for students.

The Urge to Cooperate and Compete

Children want to work and play with other children. They find satisfaction in being a needed part of a group and experience sadness when others reject them. Cooperation needs to be taught before competitive experiences since competition is impossible when people choose not to cooperate or follow the rules. Often, the joy of being part of a group far outweighs the gains from peer competition.

The Urge for Physical Fitness and Attractiveness

Boys and girls are eager to be fit, active, and attractive. Students who have any type of disability suffer much humiliation. The opportunity to improve personal skills often helps students overcome subpar strength, lack of physical skill, inadequate physical fitness, and obesity.

The Urge for Adventure

The drive to participate in something different, adventurous, or unusual impels children to try interesting new activities. When students ask, "What are we going to do today?" they hope for something new and exciting. This urge is one of the reasons that physical education units in elementary schools should be limited to 2 to 3 weeks in length.

The Urge for Creative Satisfaction

Children like to try different ways of doing things, experiment with different implements, and find creative ways of accomplishing goals. Finding new ways to express themselves physically satisfies the urge for creative action.

The Urge for Rhythmic Expression

Children's physical education should offer a variety of rhythmic activities that they can learn well enough to achieve satisfaction. Emphasize the natural rhythm involved in all physical activity, be it walking, running, or skipping. Many effective and beautiful sport movements can be done rhythmically, including shooting layups, jumping rope, and running hurdles.

The Urge to Know

Young people are naturally curious. They are interested in what they are doing and why they are doing it. Knowing why is a great motivator. It takes little time or effort to share with a class why they are performing an activity and how it contributes to their physical development.

Understand the Characteristics and Interests of Children

The urges of children represent broad traits that are typical of children regardless of age, sex, or race. In contrast, characteristics and interests are age- and maturity-specific attributes that influence learning objectives. Table 4.1 provides information that influences appropriate selection and sequencing of curriculum activities. The table analyzes the three learning domains—psychomotor, cognitive, and affective—and is grouped by developmental levels, which are discussed in the next section.

TABLE 4.1 Characteristics and interests of children

Characteristics and Interests	Program Guidelines
Developmental Level I	
Psychomotor Domain	
Noisy, constantly active, egocentric, exhibitionistic. Imitative and imaginative. Want attention.	Include vigorous games and stunts, games with individual roles (hunting, dramatic activities, story plays), and a few team games or relays.
Large muscles more developed; game skills not developed.	Challenge with varied movement. Develop specialized skills of throwing, catching, and bouncing balls.
Naturally rhythmic.	Use music and rhythm with skills. Provide creative rhythms, folk dances, and singing movement songs.
May suddenly become tired but soon recover.	Use activities of brief duration. Provide short rest periods or intersperse physically demanding activities with less vigorous ones.
Hand–eye coordination developing.	Give opportunity to handle different objects such as balls, beanbags, and hoops.
Perceptual abilities maturing.	Give practice in balance—unilateral, bilateral, and cross-lateral movements.
Pelvic tilt can be pronounced.	Give attention to posture problems. Provide abdominal strengthening activities.
Cognitive Domain	
Short attention span.	Change activity often. Give short explanations.
Interested in what the body can do. Curious.	Provide movement experiences. Pay attention to educational movement.
Want to know. Often ask *why* about movement.	Explain reasons for various activities and the basis of movement.
Express individual views and ideas.	Allow children time to be creative. Expect problems when children must line up and perform the same task.
Begin to understand the idea of teamwork.	Plan situations that require group cooperation. Discuss the importance of working together.
Sense of humor expands.	Insert some humor into the teaching process.
Highly creative.	Allow students to try new and different ways of performing activities; sharing ideas with friends encourages creativity.
Affective Domain	
No gender differences in interests.	Set up same activities for boys and girls.
Sensitive and individualistic; self-concept very important.	Teach taking turns, sharing, and learning to win, lose, or be caught gracefully.
Accept defeat poorly. Like small-group activities.	Use entire class group sparingly. Break into smaller groups.
Sensitive to feelings of adults. Like to please teacher.	Give frequent praise and encouragement.
Can be reckless.	Stress safe approaches.
Enjoy rough-and-tumble activity.	Include rolling, dropping to the floor, and so on, in both introductory and program activities. Stress simple stunts and tumbling.
Seek personal attention.	Recognize individuals through both verbal and nonverbal means. See that all have a chance to be the center of attention.
Love to climb and explore play environments.	Provide play materials, games, and apparatus for strengthening large muscles (e.g., climbing towers, climbing ropes, jump ropes, miniature challenge courses, and turning bars).
Developmental Level II	
Psychomotor Domain	
Capable of rhythmic movement.	Continue creative rhythms, singing movement songs, and folk dancing.
Improved hand–eye and perceptual–motor coordination.	Give opportunity for manipulating hand apparatus. Offer movement experience and practice in perceptual–motor skills (right/left, unilateral, bilateral, and cross-lateral movements).

(continued)

TABLE 4.1 Characteristics and interests of children (Continued)

Characteristics and Interests	Program Guidelines
Developmental Level II (Continued)	
More interest in sports.	Begin introductory sport and related skills and simple lead-up activities.
Sport-related skill patterns mature in some cases.	Emphasize practice in these skill areas through simple ball games, stunts, and rhythmic patterns.
Developing interest in fitness.	Introduce some of the specialized fitness activities to third grade.
Reaction time is slow.	Avoid highly organized ball games that require and place a premium on quickness and accuracy.
Cognitive Domain	
Still active but attention span longer. More interest in group play.	Include active big-muscle program and more group activity. Begin team concept in activity and relays.
Curious to see what they can do. Love to be challenged and will try anything.	Offer challenges involving movement problems and more critical demands in stunts, tumbling, and apparatus work. Emphasize safety and good judgment.
Interest in group activities; ability to plan with others developing.	Offer group activities and simple dances involving cooperation with a partner or a team.
Affective Domain	
Like physical contact and belligerent games.	Include dodging games and other active games, as well as rolling stunts.
Developing more interest in skills. Want to excel.	Organize practice in a variety of throwing, catching, and moving skills, as well as others.
Becoming more conscious socially.	Teach need to abide by rules and play fairly. Teach social customs and courtesy in rhythmic areas.
Like to perform well and be admired for accomplishments.	Begin to stress quality. Provide opportunity to achieve.
Essentially honest and truthful.	Accept children's word. Give opportunity for trust in game and relay situations.
Do not lose willingly.	Provide opportunity for children to learn to accept defeat gracefully and win with humility.
Gender difference still of little importance.	Avoid separation of genders in any activity.
Developmental Level III	
Psychomotor Domain	
Steady growth. Girls often grow more rapidly than boys.	Continue vigorous program to enhance physical development.
Muscular coordination and skills improving. Interested in learning detailed techniques.	Continue emphasis on teaching skills through drills, lead-up games, and free practice periods. Emphasize correct form.
Differences in physical capacity and skill development.	Offer flexible standards so all find success. In team activities, match teams evenly so individual skill levels are less apparent.
Posture problems may appear.	Include posture correction and special posture instruction; emphasize effect of body carriage on self-concept.
Sixth-grade girls may show signs of maturity; may not wish to participate in all activities.	Have consideration for their problems. Encourage participation on a limited basis, if necessary.
Sixth-grade boys are rougher and stronger.	Keep genders together for skill development but separate for competition in certain rougher activities.
Cognitive Domain	
Want to know rules of games.	Include instruction on rules, regulations, and traditions.
Knowledgeable about and interested in sport and game strategy.	Emphasize strategy, as opposed to merely performing a skill without concern for context.
Question the relevance and importance of various activities.	Explain regularly the reasons for performing activities and learning various skills.
Desire information about the importance of physical fitness and health-related topics.	Include in lesson plans brief explanations of how various activities enhance growth and development.

TABLE 4.1 (Continued)

Characteristics and Interests	Program Guidelines
Developmental Level III (Continued)	
Affective Domain	
Enjoy team and group activity. Competitive urge strong.	Include many team games, relays, and combatives.
Much interest in sports and sport-related activities.	Offer a variety of sports in season, with emphasis on lead-up games.
Little interest in the opposite gender. Some antagonism may arise.	Offer coeducational activities emphasizing individual differences of all participants, regardless of gender.
Acceptance of self-responsibility. Strong increase in drive toward independence.	Provide leadership and followership opportunities on a regular basis. Involve students in evaluation procedures.
Intensive desire to excel both in skill and in physical capacity.	Stress physical fitness. Include fitness and skill surveys to motivate and to check progress.
Respect for teammates a concern for both teachers and students.	Establish and enforce fair rules. With enforcement, include an explanation of the need for rules and cooperation if games are to exist.
Peer group important. Want to be part of the gang.	Stress group cooperation in play and among teams. Rotate team positions as well as squad makeup.

STEP SIX: ORGANIZE SELECTED ACTIVITIES INTO INSTRUCTIONAL UNITS

After selecting appropriate activities that contribute to content standards, design a delivery system that ensures all activities are taught. Activities are most often grouped by grade or developmental level. To allow for greater variation of skill development among students, this textbook groups activities and units of instruction by developmental level. Even though this developmental skill continuum is common to all students, there are large variations among children. This organization offers activities that are appropriate for the maturity and developmental levels of all students. Occasionally, it may be necessary to move to a higher or lower developmental level to accommodate students. Table 4.2 shows how developmental levels roughly equate with grades and ages. The following list describes learners at each level and identifies skills and competencies typical of children at those levels. Refer to Table 3.2 in Chapter 3 for a summary of activities at the three developmental levels.

TABLE 4.2 Equating developmental levels to grades and ages

Developmental Level	Grades	Ages
I	K–2	5–7
II	3–4	8–9
III	5–6	10–11

- *Developmental Level I.* For most children, activities used in Developmental Level I are appropriate for kindergarten through second grade. Most activities for younger children are individual in nature and center on learning movement concepts through theme development. Children learn about movement principles, and educational movement themes are used to teach body identification and body management skills. By stressing the joy and personal benefits of physical activity, teachers can help students develop positive behaviors that last a lifetime.
- *Developmental Level II.* Developmental Level II activities are usually appropriate for most third- and fourth-grade children. In Developmental Level II activities, students refine fundamental skills and begin to develop the ability to perform specialized skills. Practicing manipulative skills enhances visual–tactile coordination. At this level, children explore, experiment, and create activities without fear. While these activities do not stress conformity, children learn the how and why of activity patterns. Cooperation with peers receives more emphasis through group and team play. Initial instruction in sport skills begins in Developmental Level II, and a number of lead-up activities allow students to apply newly learned skills in a small-group setting.
- *Developmental Level III.* Developmental Level III activities place more emphasis on specialized skills and sport

activities. Most fifth- and sixth-grade students can perform activities at this level. Football, basketball, softball, track and field, volleyball, and hockey are added to sport offerings. Students learn and improve sport skills while participating in cooperative sport lead-up games. Less emphasis is placed on movement concept activities, and more of the instructional time is devoted to manipulative activity. Adequate time is set aside for the rhythmic program and for the program area involving apparatus, stunts, and tumbling.

After assigning activities to developmental levels, organize the activities in each instructional unit in order of difficulty, starting with the easiest to master and finishing with the most difficult. Organizing activities in progression (1) helps children be successful because the easiest activities are taught first, (2) ensures that safety and liability factors are met since the activities are presented in proper sequence, and (3) aids teachers in finding a starting point for their instructional presentation.

Another element to include in the instructional unit is a list of teaching hints that address safety, teaching for quality, dispersing equipment properly, and providing instructional cues to enhance motor skill development. An accompanying curriculum and lesson plan text by Pangrazi (2010) incorporates activities in this textbook and places them into lesson plans by developmental level. The lesson plans contain activity progressions, teaching hints, and learning objectives that help minimize the demands of planning. Besides the weekly lesson plans, a year-long curriculum is offered for each of the three developmental levels.

Table 4.3 illustrates the parallel listing of the four parts of the lesson in the yearly curriculum. This plan ensures that students learn many ways of warming up for activity and approximately 15 different types of fitness activity. In addition, they are exposed to 20 to 25 lesson activities that focus on skill development and 60 to 80 low-organized game activities.

Weekly Units

Organizing the curriculum into weekly activity units is a common approach. In this approach, instruction focuses on the same activity over an entire week. The weekly plan has three major advantages. First, one comprehensive lesson plan will suffice for the week and keep planning duties manageable. The objective is to move children along the path of learning at an optimal rate. What cannot be covered one day is taught in the next lesson. Second, less orientation instruction is needed after the first day. Safety factors, teaching hints, and key points need only a brief review each day; and equipment needs are similar from day to day. Third, progression and learning sequences are evident; both teacher and children can see improvement.

Activities in the "Lesson Focus" section of the lesson plans begin with skills all students can perform and progress to a point where further instruction and skill practice are necessary because students are challenged. Starting each lesson with basic activities ensures that all students begin with success. This outcome is critical for developing positive attitudes toward new activities. If the first thing children experience is failure, the rest of the unit will be a tough sell. Build instructional sequences for each day based on the preceding lesson. Limit the instructional units to 1 or 2 weeks so students do not become bored or discouraged. Long units force children who are unskilled or who dislike the activity to live with failure for a long time. If more time is needed for a specific unit, add another week or two later in the year. Use a game activity for a change of pace when the motivational level of the class (and of the teacher) seems to be waning.

Another approach to yearly planning is to use the movement theme approach. This approach takes a set of skills or movements and offers an array of activities for instruction related to the same skill. A wide variety of equipment is needed since the same skills are taught using different activities and equipment.

Check the Scope, Sequence, and Balance of the Curriculum

An important step in creating a quality program is to review and monitor the scope, sequence, and balance of the curriculum. These are important concepts for ensuring the curriculum is comprehensive and varied.

Scope is the yearly content of the curriculum. Scope is also referred to as the horizontal articulation of the curriculum. Monitoring the scope of the curriculum ensures that the entire content of the program is covered in a systematic, accountable way. In elementary school physical education, the scope of the curriculum is broad. Student interest wanes if units are too long, so many activities are presented rather than in-depth coverage of a few activities. Also, elementary school physical education is designed to help students learn about all the available types of physical activity.

Sequence, or vertical articulation, of the curriculum defines the skills and activities to be covered from year to year. Sequence ensures that students receive different instruction and activities at each developmental level. Of particular importance is the articulation of program material throughout elementary, middle, and senior high school programs.

Balance ensures that all objectives in the program receive adequate coverage. When reviewing curriculum scope and sequence, adhering to balance avoids a slant toward one particular area. To ensure balance, determine

TABLE 4.3 An example of a yearly plan: Developmental Level II

Week	Introductory Activity	Fitness Development Activity	Lesson Focus Activity	Game Activity
1	Move and freeze on signal	Teacher/leader movement challenges	Orientation	Back to Back Whistle Mixer
2	Fundamental movements and stopping	Teacher/leader exercises	Manipulative skills using wands and hoops	Hand Hockey Cageball Kickover Home Base
3	Move and assume pose	Teacher/leader exercises	Throwing skills (1)	Whistle Mixer Couple Tag Partner Stoop
4	Creative routines	Hexagon Hustle	Football-related activities	Football End Ball Five Passes
5	Four-corners movement	Hexagon Hustle	Manipulative skills using playground balls	Bounce Ball One Step
6	Run, stop, and pivot	Circuit training	Fundamental skills using tug-of-war ropes and relays	Nonda's Car Lot Indianapolis 500
7	European running	Circuit training	Stunts and tumbling skills (1)	Whistle Mixer Competitive Circle Contests Alaska Baseball
8	Magic number challenges	Astronaut drills	Soccer-related activities (1)	Circle Kickball Soccer Touch Ball Diagonal Soccer Soccer Take-Away
9	New leader	Astronaut drills	Soccer-related activities (2)	Soccer Touch Ball Diagonal Soccer Dribblerama Bull's-Eye
10	Group over and under	Aerobic fitness	Fundamental skills using parachutes	Nine Lives Box Ball
11	Bend, stretch, and shake	Aerobic fitness	PE games Recreational activities	Addition Tag Alaska Baseball Recreational activities
12	Fastest tag in the West	Walk, trot, and jog	Walking and jogging skills	Recreational activities
13	Jumping and hopping patterns	Challenge course fitness	Rhythms (1)	Whistle March Arches Home Base
14	Group tag	Walk, trot, and jog	Long-rope jumping skills	Fly Trap Trades Fox Hunt
15	Fleece ball fun	Challenge course	Stunts and tumbling skills (2)	Partner Stoop Crows and Cranes
16	Ball activities	Challenge course	Rhythms (2)	Fox Hunt Steal the Treasure Addition Tag
17	Partner leaping	Aerobic fitness and partner resistance	Basketball-related activities (1)	Birdie in the Cage Dribblerama Captain Ball Basketball Tag
18	Bridges by three	Aerobic fitness and partner resistance	Basketball-related activities (2)	Captain Ball Five Passes Around the Key

(continued)

TABLE 4.3 An example of a yearly plan: Developmental Level II (Continued)

Week	Introductory Activity	Fitness Development Activity	Lesson Focus Activity	Game Activity
19	Locomotor and manipulative activity	Exercise to music	Throwing skills (2)	In the Prison Snowball Center Target Throw Target Ball Throw
20	Yarnball fun	Exercise to music	Fundamental skills using benches	Cageball Kickover Squad Tag
21	Low organizational games	Continuity drills	Hockey-related activities (1)	Circle Keepaway Star Wars Hockey Lane Hockey Circle Straddleball
22	Following activity	Continuity drills	Hockey-related activities (2)	Modified Hockey Lane Hockey
23	Moving to music	Aerobic fitness	Manipulative skills using paddle and balls	Steal the Treasure Trees
24	Stretching activities	Stretching activities	Track and field skills (1)	Potato Shuttle Relay Shuttle Relays
25	Stretching activities	Stretching activities	Track and field skills (2)	Circular Relays Shuttle Relays One-on-one contests
26	Move and perform task	Walk, trot, and jog	Manipulative skills using beanbags	Crows and Cranes Galloping Lizzie
27	Long rope routine	Parachute fitness	Rhythms (3)	Jump the Shot Beachball Batball Club Guard
28	Squad leader movement	Parachute fitness	Stunts and tumbling skills (3)	Trades Beachball Batball
29	European running with equipment	Exercise to music	Individual rope jumping	Loose Caboose Wolfe's Beanbag Exchange Tag
30	Marking	Circuit training	Volleyball-related skills (1)	Beachball Volleyball Informal Volleyball
31	Tag games	Hexagon Hustle	Volleyball-related skills (2)	Beachball Volleyball Shower Service Ball
32	Combination movement patterns	Continuity drills	Rhythms (4)	Alaska Baseball Addition Tag
33	European running with variations	Aerobic fitness	Manipulative skills using Frisbees	Frisbee Keepaway Frisbee Golf
34	Tortoise and hare	Aerobic fitness	Fundamental skills using balance beams	Hand Hockey Nonda's Car Lot
35	Move and perform task	Parachute exercises	Softball-related activities (1)	Throw It and Run Two-Pitch Softball Hit and Run
36	Walk, trot, and sprint	Teacher/leader exercises	Softball-related activities (2)	Beat Ball Kick Softball In a Pickle

major areas of emphasis based on program objectives. These areas can be allotted a percentage of program time based on students' characteristics and interests. This determination reveals to administrators, teachers, and parents the direction and emphasis of the program. All areas have a proportionate share of instructional time that reflects the needs and characteristics of that area.

Another phase of balance is alternating units based on the type of student interaction required—that is, individual, dual (partner), and small-group or large-group activities. Team sports require organization in a large group, whereas a movement concepts lesson is individual in nature. Learning to catch is a partner activity, whereas a lead-up game requires small groups. The *Dynamic Physical Education Curriculum Guide* (Pangrazi, 2010) is balanced in this regard. Individual units are followed by small- or large-group activities, and so on. Balance ensures that children do not have to stay with one type of activity too long, so they can experience the types of physical activity they enjoy on a regular basis.

STEP SEVEN: EVALUATE AND MODIFY THE CURRICULUM

Evaluation schedules and suggested techniques for modifying the curriculum are an integral part of the curricular structure. Evaluative data are available from various sources: pupils, teachers, consultants, parents, and administrators. The type of data desired can vary. Achievement test scores can supply hard data to compare pre-assessments and post-assessments with those of other programs. Subjective assessments might include likes and dislikes, value judgments, problem areas, and needed adjustments. The evaluation schedule can select a limited area for assessment, or assessment can be broadened to cover the entire program. Collecting information is only the first step; the information must be translated into action. Modification of possible program deficiencies is based on sound educational philosophy. If the program has weak spots, identifying the weaknesses and determining the causes are important steps to take.

A pilot or trial project can be instituted if the new curriculum represents a radical change. One school in the district might be chosen to develop a pilot program. Site selection should offer the program a strong opportunity to succeed, for success depends largely on the school's educational climate. In some cases, the experimental program might be implemented with only one class in a school. Enthusiastic, skilled direction is necessary for such projects. Much information can be derived from this pilot process before implementing an entire program throughout the school system.

APPLYING WHAT YOU READ

- Your lessons will reflect your values. When writing a lesson, consider which of your values is affecting the model you are choosing for the lesson.
- A quality lesson should reflect your guiding philosophy and conceptual framework.
- As you write a lesson, be sure to consider all of the environmental factors (equipment, social norms, etc.) that may affect its effectiveness.
- During the curriculum development process, standards and objectives are identified. Every lesson you teach should address one to three of these objectives.
- One component of lesson writing is activity selection. Are the activities in your lesson the activities you selected during step 5 of the curriculum development process? Are they similar? Do they reflect the guiding philosophy?
- As part of the curriculum development process, activities are organized into instructional units. As you teach, be sure to reflect on their scope and sequence and make necessary changes to more effectively meet the needs of students and your program. Do the activities flow well? Are there weather issues that require the sequence to be modified?

REFLECTION AND REVIEW

HOW AND WHY

1. What is your value orientation for physical education? How will this influence your teaching?
2. Why have a curriculum?
3. Who should be involved in the curriculum development?
4. What issues must be considered by curriculum designers?
5. How are the needs, interests, and characteristics of elementary students today the same as, or different from, what they were 30 years ago?

CONTENT REVIEW

1. List and discuss the seven steps for designing a quality physical education curriculum.
2. State what environmental factors can affect a curriculum. Discuss your answers.
3. Define and discuss the importance of standards and student objectives.
4. Explain the importance of student-centered objectives.
5. Explain the role of the scope, sequence, and balance of a curriculum.
6. Discuss the three learning domains. Explain each domain.
7. List the common components of quality physical education curricula.
8. State what needs, characteristics, and interests of children must be considered when designing a physical education curriculum. Include comments on how age and maturity affect program development.

4

FOR MORE INFORMATION

REFERENCES AND SUGGESTED READINGS

Bloom, B. S. (Ed.). (1956). *Taxonomy of educational objectives, the classification of educational goals, handbook I: The cognitive domain.* New York: David McKay.

Chepko, S., & Arnold, R. K. (Eds.). (2000). *Guidelines for physical education programs, K–12: Standards, objectives and assessments.* Boston: Allyn & Bacon.

Corbin, C. B. (1976). *Becoming physically educated in the elementary school.* Philadelphia: Lea & Febiger.

Gabbard, C. (2008). *Lifelong motor development* (5th ed.). San Francisco: Benjamin Cummings.

Gallahue, D. L., & Donnelly, F. C. (2003). *Developmental physical education for all children* (4th ed.). Champaign, IL: Human Kinetics.

Graham, G., Holt/Hale, S. A., & Parker, M. (2007). *Children moving: A reflective approach to teaching physical education* (7th ed.). Boston: McGraw-Hill.

Hellison, D. (2003). *Teaching responsibility through physical activity* (2nd ed.). Champaign, IL: Human Kinetics.

Kelly, L. K., & Melograno, V. J. (2004). *Developing the physical education curriculum.* Champaign, IL: Human Kinetics.

Krathwohl, D. R., Bloom, B. S., & Masia, B. B. (1964). *Taxonomy of educational objectives, handbook II: Affective domain.* New York: David McKay.

Kulinna, P. H. (2008). Models for curriculum and pedagogy in elementary school physical education. *The Elementary School Journal, 108*(3), 219–227.

Lambert, L. T. (1999). *Standards-based assessment of student learning: A comprehensive approach.* Reston, VA: National Association for Sport and Physical Education.

Metzler, M. W. (2005). *Instructional models for physical education.* Scottsdale, AZ: Holcomb Hathaway.

Mosston, M., & Ashworth, S. (2002). *Teaching physical education* (5th ed.). San Francisco: Benjamin Cummings.

National Association for Sport and Physical Education (NASPE). (2004). *Moving into the future: National standards for physical education.* Reston, VA: American Alliance for Health, Physical Education, Recreation and Dance.

Pangrazi, R. P. (2010). *Dynamic physical education curriculum guide: Lesson plans for implementation* (16th ed.). San Francisco: Benjamin Cummings.

Rink, J. E. (2006). *Teaching physical education for learning* (6th ed.). Boston: McGraw-Hill.

———. (2009). *Designing the physical education curriculum: Promoting active lifestyles.* Boston: McGraw-Hill.

Siedentop, D., & Tannehill, D. (2000). *Developing teaching skills in physical education* (4th ed.). Mountain View, CA: Mayfield.

WEBSITES

Learning Domains

http://coe.sdsu.edu/eet/Articles/BloomsLD/index.htm
http://officeport.com/edu/blooms.htm

Physical Education Curriculum Information

www.pecentral.com
www.pelinks4u.org
www.pe4life.org
www.masterteacher.com

Improving Instructional Effectiveness

5

ESSENTIAL COMPONENTS OF QUALITY PROGRAMS

▶ I. Organized around content standards

II. Student-centered and developmentally appropriate

III. Physical activity and motor skill development form the core of the program

IV. Teaches management skills and self-discipline

▶ V. Promotes inclusion of all students

▶ VI. Focuses on process over product

VII. Promotes lifetime personal health and wellness

▶ VIII. Teaches cooperation and responsibility and promotes sensitivity to diversity

NATIONAL STANDARDS FOR PHYSICAL EDUCATION*

1. Demonstrates competency in motor skills and movement patterns needed to perform a variety of physical activities.
2. Demonstrates understanding of movement concepts, principles, and tactics as they apply to the learning and performance of physical activities.
3. Participates regularly in physical activity.
4. Achieves and maintains a health-enhancing level of physical fitness.
5. ▶ Exhibits responsible personal and social behavior that respects self and others in physical activity.
6. Values physical activity for health, enjoyment, challenge, self-expression, and/or social interaction.

*National Association for Sport and Physical Education (NASPE), 2004.

Some instructional elements in quality lessons cut across all presentations, regardless of the students' ages and grades or the lesson content. Diversity and gender particularly affect instruction in physical education. This chapter outlines some strategies for enhancing diversity and reducing gender stereotyping. Instructional effectiveness can be improved by using instructional cues, demonstration, modeling, and feedback. Communication with students clearly increases by offering one or two key points while demonstrating the desired behavior. Listening skills are as important as speaking skills in establishing meaningful relationships with students. Instructional cues—words or phrases—serve as quick, effective communication about proper technique in performing a particular skill or movement. Teachers can give students feedback in various ways—positive, negative, and corrective. Over time, positive feedback is the most effective way to develop positive attitudes toward activity. Instruction is best when it is personalized and offers something of value to each individual.

Outcomes

- Know how to teach for the promotion of diversity in physical education classes.
- Understand how gender stereotypes can be minimized.
- Identify various ways to communicate with children effectively in a physical education learning environment.
- Understand the procedures needed to develop effective instructional cues.
- Cite various ways to enhance communication between the teacher and the learner.

- Identify essential elements of instruction, and discuss how each element relates to the learning environment.
- Describe the value of nonverbal behavior in the physical education setting.
- Describe various demonstration and modeling skills that facilitate an environment conducive to learning.
- Understand how instructional cues can be used to increase student performance.
- Know techniques for giving students meaningful feedback about their performance.
- Describe various ways to personalize instruction in the physical education setting.

QUALITY instructors create a positive atmosphere for learning. They may not know more about skills and activities than less capable teachers do, but they can apply a set of effective instructional skills. This chapter deals with instructional techniques that all teachers can master. Becoming an effective teacher demands an inward look at your teaching personality and how it affects learning. The way teachers interact with students greatly influences how the students feel.

CHARACTERISTICS OF A QUALITY LESSON

An effective learning environment offers a set of instructional behaviors that occur regularly. These behaviors do not describe a specific method or teaching style, but allow for individual approaches to teaching content. The focus is less on what the teacher does and more on what students do. Any teaching style that produces high rates of student-engaged time and positive attitudes toward the subject matter is considered an effective learning environment. Evidence from teacher effectiveness research (Siedentop & Tannehill, 2000) indicates that, regardless of the teacher's instructional style, an educational environment is most effective when the following elements are present (Figure 5.1).

1. *Students are engaged in appropriate learning activities for a large percentage of class time.* Effective teachers use class time wisely. They plan carefully and insist on appropriate learning activities that deal with the subject matter. Students need time to learn; effective teachers ensure that students use class time to receive information and practice skills. Developmental learning activities are matched to students' abilities and contribute to overall class objectives.
2. *The learning atmosphere is success oriented, with a positive, caring climate.* Teachers who develop a supportive atmosphere foster learning and positive student attitudes toward school. Appropriate social and organizational behavior needs to be supported by teachers. Students and teachers must feel positive about working and learning in the physical education environment.
3. *Students are given clear objectives and receive high rates of information feedback from the teacher and the environment.* Students need to know what they are going to be held accountable for in the physical education class. Class activities are arranged so students spend large amounts of time learning the required objectives. Instructional activities are clearly tied to class objectives. Positive and corrective feedback is offered regularly, and students receive feedback on learning attempts even if the teacher is not available.
4. *Student progress is monitored regularly, and students are accountable for learning in physical education.* Students are expected to make progress toward class objectives. Students are able to assess and record their progress. They know exactly what is expected of them and how the expectations are tied to the accountability system.

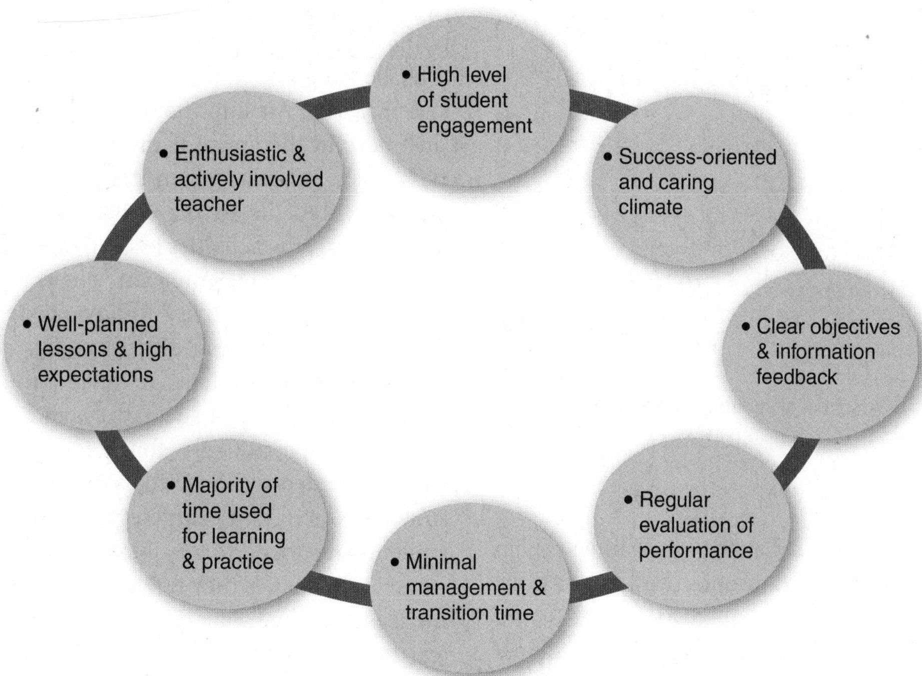

FIGURE 5.1 Characteristics of a quality lesson.

They are rewarded for small steps of progress toward larger goals.

5. *Low rates of management time and smooth transitions from one activity to another characterize the environment.* Effective teachers are good managers of students. Students move smoothly from one learning activity to another and spend little time waiting during instructional activities. Equipment is organized to facilitate smooth transitions. Instructional procedures are all tightly organized with little wasted time.
6. *Students spend a limited amount of time waiting in line or in other unproductive behaviors.* In effective instructional environments, students are engaged in subject matter most of the time. For physical education this means high rates of time spent practicing, drilling, and playing. Physical education is activity based, and students learn best when practice and learning times are maximized.
7. *Teachers plan their lessons and set high but realistic expectations for student achievement.* Effective planning implies that teachers have selected developmentally appropriate learning activities for students. Activities must not be too easy or too difficult. Students need success and challenge from learning activities, and a balance of both is critical to quality teaching. Expect students to learn, and hold them accountable for their progress.
8. *Teachers are enthusiastic about what they are doing and are actively involved in the instructional process.* Students need an enthusiastic model—someone who incorporates physical activity into his or her lifestyle. Active involvement means active supervision, enthusiasm, and high interaction rates with students. These characteristics enhance learning regardless of the teaching style used; they are important for ensuring student achievement and positive attitudes.

INCORPORATE ESSENTIAL ELEMENTS OF INSTRUCTION

Learning occurs when a well-planned curriculum is presented using a sound instructional style. Education is effective when a quality curriculum and able instruction are smoothly meshed. The curriculum is a vital component of the educational process, but a poorly taught curriculum limits students' progress. Hunter (1994) identified a set of essential elements for effective instruction, as shown in Figure 5.2 on page 78. This section takes Hunter's approach to instruction and adapts it to physical education.

DESIGN MEASURABLE STUDENT OUTCOMES

Educational outcomes give a lesson direction and meaning. When clearly stated, outcomes let learners know what they

Objectives

Anticipatory Set (hook)
Standards/expectations
Teaching
- Input
- Modeling/demo
- Direction giving (see below)
- Checking for understanding

Guided Practice
Closure
Independent Practice

FIGURE 5.2 Hunter's essential elements for effective instruction.
From: Hunter, M. C. (1994). *Mastery teaching.* Thousand Oaks, CA: Sage Publications.

are to accomplish. Learning is enhanced when students help select and set personal and group objectives. Discussions and teaching aids such as movies, videotapes, posters, and speakers can help teachers and students work toward objectives. Learning outcomes are characterized as follows:

- *Outcomes must define observable behavior.* Teachers and students must know when an outcome is reached. Attainment in physical education is easier than in some other areas because most activities are overt and easy to observe.
- *Objectives must identify clearly and specifically the content to be learned.* Teachers and students are comfortable when both parties clearly understand what is expected. Problems arise when students have to guess what the teacher wants them to learn. Students have a right to know what is expected and how they can reach the stated outcome. If outcomes are ambiguous or nonexistent, students have no way of knowing if they have improved or learned anything.

Develop outcomes for the three learning domains—psychomotor, cognitive, and affective. Psychomotor outcomes are defined most commonly in physical education and cover areas such as learning physical skills and developing health-related physical fitness. Cognitive outcomes for physical education involve knowledge and comprehension of skill performance principles related to fitness and activity. Affective outcomes focus on attitudes and behaviors, such as learning to cooperate with peers on a team or behave responsibly. Figure 5.3 provides examples of measurable student outcomes.

DETERMINE THE INSTRUCTIONAL ENTRY LEVEL

To determine the proper entry level for teaching, ask yourself, "At what skill level do I begin instructing my class?" Instruction in a new activity should begin with a successful experience, or students may be turned off and view the rest of the unit negatively. Selecting the skill level for instruction is challenging due to the wide variation in students' ability and maturity. An important step is to select an outcome (just beyond the grasp of the most skillful student in the class). Ask yourself, "When this lesson is over, where do I want the students to be?" Then, develop a sequence of essential learning activities leading to that outcome.

One way to determine entry level is to move through a series of activities (easy to advanced) until you notice several students having difficulty. This accomplishes two things: it allows students to review the skills they have learned (and thus feel successful), and it gives you a general idea of the students' ability levels. Another approach is to let students choose the entry level they feel is best suited for them. For example, use task charts listing skills students are to perform on the balance beam. Students can select activities they feel competent in performing and move at their own rate through the tasks. Instruction and learning are effective when students find an entry level that is appropriate for them.

USE ANTICIPATORY SET

Anticipatory set is a technique designed to focus students on an upcoming instructional concept. Often, students can be tentative about a new unit and need to be focused. Use anticipatory set to "mentally warm up" a class. Anticipatory sets are most effective when they tie into students' past learning experiences. In a basketball unit, asking students to identify why they are missing so many shots encourages them to think about technique. Instructional focus might involve discussing hand placement, keeping their eyes on the basket, or keeping their shooting elbow in. Anticipatory set also reveals the students' knowledge level. For example,

Psychomotor

"The student will demonstrate four ways to perform a forward roll."

"Using a jump rope, the student will be able to perform three consecutive forward crossover moves."

Cognitive

"The student will show an understanding of soccer rules by explaining when a corner kick is awarded."

"The student will demonstrate knowledge and understanding of rhythmic gymnastic routines by diagramming a sample floor routine for balls."

Affective

"After participating in physical activity, the students will be able to express their personal satisfaction in their accomplishments."

"The students will be able to share how they feel about participating in physical activities with friends."

FIGURE 5.3 Examples of measurable outcomes.

asking students, "What are three things we have to remember when tossing and catching beanbags?" reveals whether they know the basic catching skills. Identifying what students know is necessary for designing an effective lesson.

Another use for anticipatory set is to tell students the desired outcome. Explain what they are going to learn and why it is important. Few people care about learning if they do not know outcome or think it is unimportant. The more convinced students are about the importance of learning something, the more motivated they will be to participate.

Teachers do not always use anticipatory set, but they should have a reason for omitting it. If students already know the necessary information, taking time for anticipatory set has little value. On the other hand, at the beginning of a lesson, after an interruption, or when choosing to move to a new objective, teachers will find anticipatory set useful. Examples of anticipatory sets are shown in Figure 5.4.

DELIVER MEANINGFUL SKILL INSTRUCTION

Instruction is the cornerstone of learning; it is how teachers share information with students. Such information can include defining the skill, describing the elements of the skill, and explaining when, why, and how to use the skill. Here are some suggestions for effective instruction:

1. *Limit instruction to one or two key points.* It is difficult to remember a series of instructions. Giving students several points related to skill performance leaves them unsure and frustrated, and most learners remember only the first and the last points. Emphasizing one or two key points makes it easier for students to focus their concentration.
2. *Refrain from lengthy skill descriptions.* When instructions last longer than 30 seconds, students become listless because they cannot comprehend and remember all of the input. Develop a pattern of short, concise presentations alternated with practice sessions. Short practice sessions allow students to refocus on key points of a skill many times. If you need to instruct for longer than 30 seconds, break it into small segments. Allow students to apply your instructions after each segment.
3. *Present information in its most basic, easily understood form.* If a class does not understand the presentation, you—not your students—have failed. Check to see if students understand the material (discussed further in the next section).
4. *Separate the management and instructional episodes.* Consider these instructions, given while presenting a new game: "In this game, we will break into groups of five. Each group will get a ball and form a small circle. On the command 'Go,' the game will start. Here is how you play the game . . ." (a long discussion of game rules and conduct follows). Because the instructions are long, students forget what they were asked to do earlier. Or, they think about the group they want to be in rather than the game rules. Instead, move the class into groups of five in circles (management) and then discuss the activity to be learned (instruction). This approach reduces the length of the instructional episode, and it makes it easier to learn how the game is played.

- "On Monday we practiced the skills of passing, dribbling, and shooting layups. Yesterday we used those skills in a game of three-on-three. Take a few moments to think about the problems you had with dribbling or passing skills. (Allow time for thought and discussion.) Today we are going to use some drills that will help you improve in these areas."
- "Think of activities that require body strength and be ready to name some when called upon. (Allow time for thinking and discussion.) This week we are going to learn some activities that will help us become stronger."
- "What is it called when we move quickly in different directions? Think of as many activities as you can that require agility, and be ready to share with the class. (Allow time for thinking and discussion.) This week we are going to learn how to do Tinikling. This rhythmic activity will improve your agility level."

FIGURE 5.4 Examples of anticipatory sets.

"Does everybody understand?" rarely garners adequate responses from students, and you will not know if students completely understand safety instructions. Instead, ask questions that can be answered by a thumbs up or by a hand raised if they think a demonstration is correct. Also use peer-checking methods.

ACTIVELY MONITOR STUDENT PERFORMANCE

Active monitoring ensures that students stay on task and practice activities correctly. Teachers must stand where they can make eye contact with all students. Students generally stay on task when they know someone is watching them. Try to be unpredictable when moving around the teaching area. If students know where you like to stand while teaching and observing, some of them will move away from you; others will stay nearby. Random positioning ensures contact and proximity with all students in the class.

Teachers commonly assume they must move to the same area when giving instructions. They believe that students listen only when the teacher is at or near this "instructional spot." This belief is incorrect, and it sometimes results in some rather negative consequences. Students who choose to exhibit deviant or off-task behaviors usually move as far away from the instructor as possible. If you always instruct from the same place, some of these students will find a position that is hard to observe. Further, by staying in one place, you will not be near students who need or want attention. Deliver instruction from the perimeter of the area, and vary your location regularly.

Teacher movement coupled with effective observation keeps students on task. Positioning yourself to observe skill performance enhances your ability to improve student learning. If you are observing kicking, stand to the side rather than behind the student. When observing student performance, avoid staying too long with a single group of students or the rest of the class will begin to move off-task. Give a student one or two focus points and then move to another student.

Because teacher movement affects instructional effectiveness, it needs to be planned. To facilitate coverage, divide the instructional area into four (or more) equal areas and deliberately move into the far corner of each area a certain number of times. Try to give instructions and reinforcement from all four quadrants of the area. Ask a student to chart your movement if you are interested in reaching a personal goal. (See Figure 8.15, page 153, for a chart for recording different teacher behaviors.)

USE INSTRUCTIONAL CUES

Instructional cues are keywords that quickly and efficiently communicate proper technique and performance of skills and movement tasks. Children require a clear understanding of critical skill points because they develop motor learning and cognitive understandings at the same time. Teaching activities without instructional cues can result in ineffective learning if students do not clearly understand proper technique and key points of performance. When using instructional cues, consider the following points.

Develop Precise Cues

Make cues short, descriptive phrases that call attention to key points of skill technique. Cues must be precise and accurate. They should guide learners and enhance the quality of learning. Cues make it easier for learners to remember a sequence of new motor patterns. Study an activity, and design cues that focus student learning on correct skill technique.

All teachers occasionally must teach activities they know little about. Developing cues in areas of less expertise requires some research. Many textbooks and media aids outline key points of skills. For example, *Teaching Cues for Basic Sport Skills for Elementary and Middle School Students* (Fronske & Wilson, 2002) offers teaching cues for a wide variety of physical activities. Other resources are teachers who have strengths in different activities. Videotape an activity, and analyze points of performance where students are having the most difficulty.

Use Short, Action-Oriented Cues

Effective cues are short and to the point. To avoid confusing and overwhelming the learner, present only a few cues during each lesson. Design cues that contain keywords and are short. Meaningful cues encourage the learner to focus on one phase of a skill during practice. If a student is learning to throw, offer a cue such as, "Begin with your throwing arm farthest from the target." This cue reminds the student not to face the target, which precludes trunk rotation in later phases of the throw. Other examples of throwing cues are

"Step toward the target."

"Keep your eye on the target."

"Shift your weight from the rear to the front foot."

To examine the effectiveness of cues, see if they communicate the skill as a whole. Have all the critical points of throwing been covered, or is the skill incorrect in certain phases? Most skills can be broken down into three parts: preparation, action, and recovery. Focus on only one phase of a skill since most people can best concentrate on one thing at a time. Action-oriented words are effective with children, particularly if the words sound exciting. For example, "*Pop up* at the end of the forward roll," "*Twist* the body during the throw," or "*Explode* off the starting line." In other situations, let the voice influence the effectiveness of the cue. For example, if a skill is to be done smoothly and softly, speak softly and ask students to "let the move-

FIGURE 5.5 Effective teachers demonstrate skill techniques.

- Students are in partners spread out about 20 yards apart; one partner has a football. "When kicking the football, take a short step with your kicking foot, a long step with the other foot, and kick *(demonstrate)*. Again, short step, long step, kick *(teaching cue)*."
- "Listen to the first verse of this schottische music. I'll do the part of the schottische step we just learned starting with the second verse *(demonstrate)*. Ready, step, step, step, hop *(teaching cue)*. When I hit the tambourine, begin doing the step."
- "Today we are going to work on developing fitness by moving through the challenge course. Move through the course as quickly as you can, but do your best at each challenge; quality is more important than speed. Travel through the course like this *(demonstrate)*. Move under the bar, swing on the rope, and so forth *(teaching cue)*. When I say go, start at the obstacle nearest you."

FIGURE 5.6 Combining demonstration and teaching cues.

ment *floooow*" or to "move *smoooothly* across the balance beam." The most effective cues use voice inflections, body language, and action words to signal the desired behavior.

Integrate Cues

Integrating cues involves putting the parts of a skill together so that learners can focus on the skill as a whole. Integrated cues depend on prior cues used when presenting a skill and assume the understanding of concepts from earlier phases of instruction. Here are some examples of integrated cues:

"Step, rotate, throw."

"Run, jump, and forward roll."

"Stride, swing, follow through."

The first cue listed reminds students to sequence parts of the skill. The second cue helps young children remember a sequence of movement activities. Integrated cues help learners remember proper sequencing of skills and form mental images of the performance.

ENHANCE INSTRUCTION BY DEMONSTRATING SKILLS

A fast, effective way to present a physical activity is to demonstrate it (Figure 5.5). Effective demonstration accentuates critical points of performance. While demonstrating, simultaneously call out key focal points so students know what to observe. Teachers and students can demonstrate instructional activities. No matter who does it, the demonstration must be clear and unambiguous in the early stages of learning.

Teachers cannot be expected to demonstrate all physical activities. Even skilled teachers need an alternative plan for teaching activities they cannot perform. By reading, studying, and analyzing movement, you can develop an understanding of how to present activities. If performing an activity is impossible, know what key points of the activity should be emphasized. Use visual aids and media to enhance instruction.

If possible, slow down the demonstration and present it step-by-step. Many skills can be videotaped and played back in slow motion. Stop the replay at critical places so students can emulate a position or technique. For example, in a throwing unit, freeze at a point that illustrates the arm position. Have students imitate moving the arm into proper position based on the stop-action pose. Figure 5.6 offers examples for combining teaching cues and demonstration.

USE STUDENTS TO DEMONSTRATE SKILLS

If you cannot demonstrate a skill, find a student who can help. Be sure students can correctly demonstrate the desired skill, so they will not be embarrassed in front of the class. You can usually find a capable student by asking the class to perform the desired skill. Identify a student who is correctly performing the skill during the practice session, and ask if he or she is willing to demonstrate. Most students will not volunteer to demonstrate unless they feel able. While the student demonstrates the skill, identify key points of the action.

Student demonstration brings original ideas into the lesson sequence (Figure 5.7). It also helps build children's self-esteem. At opportune times, stop the class and let

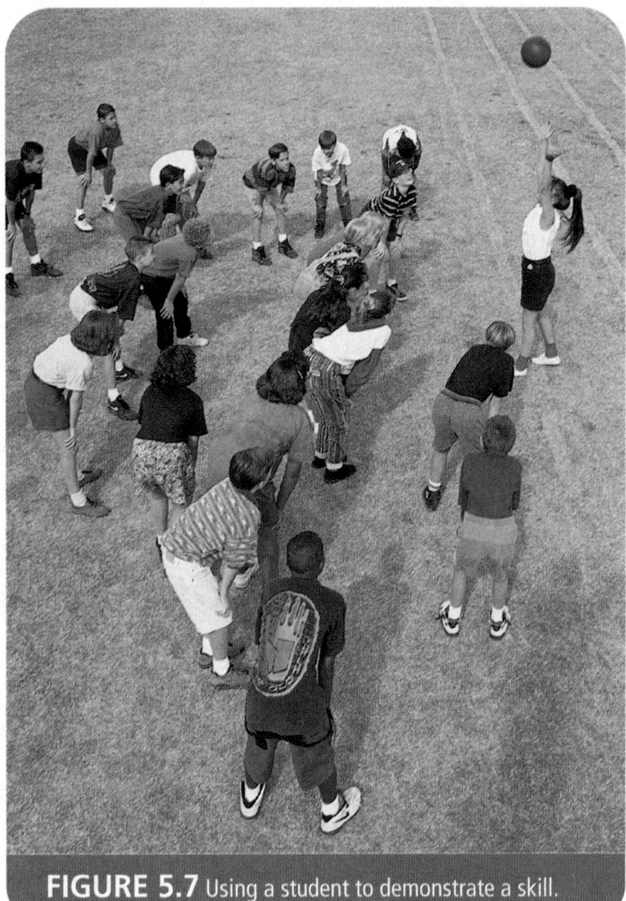

FIGURE 5.7 Using a student to demonstrate a skill.

children volunteer to show what they have done. Make positive comments about demonstrations. If you are unsure about students' abilities to demonstrate, ask them to try the activity while all other students are engaged. If they are successful, have them demonstrate. If not, let them know you will call on them at another time. Go on to another child without comment or reprimand, saying only, "Thank you, Janet. Let's see what Carl can do." Or redirect the class to continue practicing. Ensure that all students who want to be selected are given an opportunity at one time or another.

CHECK FOR UNDERSTANDING

To monitor student progress, check to see if they comprehend instructional content. Students may act like they understand even when they do not. Some teachers have a common (but poor) habit of asking periodically, "Does everybody understand?" They appear to be checking for understanding, but this seldom is the case. Such teachers often do not even wait for a response—and in any case, it takes a brave and confident student to admit to not understanding in front of the entire class. To avoid embarrassing students in front of their classmates, teachers need a quick, easy way to check for understanding. Some suggestions follow.

1. *Use hand signals.* Examples might be: "Thumbs-up if you understand," or "If you think this demonstration is correct, balance on one foot," or "Raise the number of fingers to signal whether you think student 1, 2, or 3 did a correct forward roll." If the teacher then moves on quickly and without comment, students will learn to signal without embarrassment. If the situation is touchy or embarrassing, students can signal with their heads down and eyes closed.
2. *Ask questions that can be answered in choral response.* Some students may mouth an answer even though they do not know the correct response. A strong response by the class indicates that most students understand.
3. *Direct a forthcoming check to the entire class rather than to a specified student.* For example, "Be ready to demonstrate the grapevine step." This encourages all members of the class to focus on the activity, knowing they may be called on to demonstrate. This approach does not ensure that everyone understands, but it motivates students to think about the skill check.
4. *Use peer-checking methods.* Have students pair up and evaluate each other's performance using a checklist you have designed. To ensure the validity of scoring, students can be evaluated by one or more students.
5. *Use tests and written feedback to monitor cognitive concepts.* For example, use written tests to see if students can diagram and explain the options of an offense or a defense. Asking students to list safety precautions for an activity ensures student understanding. Use some restraint when administering written instruments—too many can take time away from skill practice. Use these instruments when the information cannot be gathered more efficiently with other methods.

OFFER GUIDED PRACTICE

Guided practice helps ensure that students are performing a skill correctly. Practice does not necessarily make perfect if it is incorrect practice. Correct practice develops correct skill patterns, whereas incorrect practice ingrains mistakes. During the early phases of guided practice, small amounts of information are presented. New skills build on previously learned skills, so students can see the importance of prerequisite learning.

Offer practice sessions as quickly as possible after students have received instruction. Let them get a "feel" for the skill as a whole before they work on parts of it. In guided practice sessions, monitor group responses and offer feedback to encourage learning new activities. Make feedback specific, immediate, and focused on the skill being practiced. Ensure that drills and lead-up activities guarantee all students the same amount of practice. If anyone has to receive less practice, make it the skilled performer.

BRING CLOSURE

Closure is a time to review learning that has taken place during the lesson. Closure helps increase retention because students have to think about what they have learned. Focus closure discussions on what students have learned rather than on just naming activities practiced. Closure is not simply a recall of activities that were completed, but a discussion of the skills and knowledge learned through practice.

Closure can be an opportunity to show similarities between movement patterns in different skills. Students may not realize that a new movement pattern is parallel to one learned earlier. Discussing what was learned focuses students on what they should be learning through practice. Closure is also a time to remind children to tell their parents and others what they have learned. How many times do parents ask, "What did you learn at school today?" only to hear the reply, "Nothing"? Here are some prompts for closure discussions:

"Describe two or three key components of skill performance to your partner."

"Demonstrate the proper skill when I (or a peer) give you a verbal cue."

"Use a closing activity that requires implementation of learned skills."

"Describe and demonstrate a key point for a new skill learned in the lesson."

A caution about closure is in order here. Often, before conducting closure, teachers line up students in preparation for returning to the classroom. Unfortunately, this leaves students standing close to each other, giving them an opportunity to disrupt the class by talking and bothering others. Keep the class spaced out and sitting in the teaching area while you conduct closure.

PROVIDE INSTRUCTIONAL FEEDBACK

Delivering student feedback is an important part of instruction. Used properly, feedback enhances a student's self-concept, improves the focus of performance, increases the rate of on-task behavior, and improves student understanding. Consider the following points to enhance the quality of your instructional feedback.

TYPES OF FEEDBACK

Much of the feedback teachers deliver is corrective, focusing on rectifying or improving student performance. Avoid giving negative feedback (such as, "That was a lousy throw"). Students expect some corrective feedback, but when it is the only feedback offered, it creates a negative environment. A danger of overusing corrective feedback is that it creates a climate where students worry about making errors for fear the instructor will embarrass or belittle them. Further, many children surmise that no matter what they do correctly, their efforts are seldom recognized.

Try to focus feedback on positive student performance. A positive atmosphere motivates students to accept a challenge and risk errors or failure. Positive feedback also helps teachers feel upbeat about students because it focuses on their strengths. Corrective feedback does have its place; Siedentop and Tannehill (2000) recommend a 4-to-1 ratio of positive to corrective feedback. Teachers commonly teach like they were taught. If your physical education teacher overused corrective feedback, you may do the same. Most teachers need to increase positive feedback and decrease negative feedback.

USE MEANINGFUL FEEDBACK STATEMENTS

It is easy to develop positive, yet habitual patterns of interaction. Teachers often overuse statements such as, "Nice job," "Way to hustle," "Much better," "Right on," and "Great move." Students may "tune out" these repetitious comments and fail to feel their positive effect. General comments also offer little specific information or value, thus allowing for misinterpretation. Suppose that after a student does a forward roll, you say, "Nice job." You are pleased with the performance because her head was tucked; she thinks you are pleased because her legs were bent. Nonspecific feedback can easily reinforce an incorrect behavior.

FIGURE 5.8 Delivering meaningful feedback.

Adding specific information or value to feedback improves desired student behavior (Figure 5.8). The value content of a feedback statement tells students why it is important to perform a skill in a certain way. Students clearly understand why their performance was positive and can build on the reinforced behavior. Examples of feedback with value content are:

"Good throw. When you look at your target, you are much more accurate."

"Excellent catch. You bent your elbows while catching, which created a soft home for the ball."

"That's the way to stop. When you bend your knees, you always stop under control."

Here are some examples of feedback with specific content:

"That's the way to tuck your head on the forward roll."

"Wow! Everybody was dribbling the ball with their heads up."

"I'm impressed with the way you kept your arms straight."

DISTRIBUTE FEEDBACK EVENLY

Feedback should be evenly distributed to all students by moving systematically from student to student, assuming there are no major discipline problems. This approach fosters contact with students several times during the lesson. It also keeps students on task because they know the teacher is moving and "eyeballing" everybody regularly. If skills are complex and refinement is a goal, it is better to take more time with individual students. This involves watching a student long enough to offer specific and information-loaded feedback. The result is high-quality feedback to fewer students.

When offering instructional feedback to a student, avoid watching the student after giving the feedback. Many students become tense if you tell them how to do something and then wait to see if they do it exactly as you instructed. It takes time to change skill performance, and students will often repeat the same mistake before learning the desired technique. Observe carefully, offer feedback, move on to another student, and recheck progress later.

EFFECTIVE FEEDBACK: POSITIVE, FOCUSED, AND IMMEDIATE

Often feedback is group oriented; that is, the entire class receives it. This method is efficient, but it leaves the most room for misinterpretation. Some students may not understand the feedback; others may not listen because it does not seem relevant. When giving individual feedback, do not do so within other students' hearing. Instead, avoid humiliating a student and making him or her resent the feedback (and you) by directing negative or corrective feedback quietly so that only the student hears it.

Focus feedback on the desired refinement of a task. For example, if you want students to "give" while catching a ball thrown by a partner, avoid giving feedback about the quality of the throw. If catching is the focus, feedback should be on catching, as in, "Rachel is reaching out and giving with her hands when she catches the ball." Students do not have to see each other accomplish the desired outcome. Observing other students is effective only if the performer can show the skill correctly. If this approach is used exclusively, less skilled (or shy) performers will never have an opportunity to receive class feedback. Instead, tell the class how well a student is doing and move on; for example, "Mike always keeps his head up when dribbling." Although students in Developmental Levels I and II are willing to be praised in front of other students, some older students will dislike being singled out. In this case, make feedback personal in nature.

Offer feedback to students as soon as possible after a correct performance. When feedback is delayed, allow students to practice immediately so they can apply the feedback. Little is gained if students are told how to improve but have no chance to practice before leaving class. Few students remember points made in previous classes. If the class is almost over, consider limiting feedback to situations that students can practice immediately. If not, write down points of emphasis that you want to teach at the next class meeting.

NONVERBAL FEEDBACK

Nonverbal feedback is effective because students usually interpret it easily and often view it as meaning more than words. Beginning teachers may have a difficult time coordinating their feelings and words with body language. They may be pleased with student performance, yet display a less-than-pleased response (e.g., by frowning and putting their hands on their hips). They may want to be assertive but take a submissive stance. For instance, when undesirable behavior occurs, an unsure teacher might place his hands in his pockets, slouch, and back away from the class. These nonverbal behaviors signal anything but assertiveness and send students a mixed message.

Many types of nonverbal feedback can be used to encourage a class: thrusting a finger into the air to signify "You're number 1," thumbs-up, high fives, shaking hands, and so on (Figure 5.9). In contrast to positive nonverbal behaviors, negative nonverbal behaviors may include putting hands on the hips, finger to the lips, frowning, and staring. Effective use of nonverbal feedback increases the validity and strength of verbal communication.

When using nonverbal feedback, find out how the customs and mores of different cultures affect children's response to different types of gestures. For example, only

FIGURE 5.9 Using nonverbal communication.

parents and close relatives may touch Hmong and Laotian children on the head. A teacher who pats the child on the head for approval is interfering with the child's spiritual nature. The okay sign, touching thumb and forefinger, indicates approval in the United States. However, in several Asian cultures it is a "zero," indicating the child is not performing properly. In many South American countries, the okay sign has a derogatory sexual meaning. Ask for advice when using nonverbal gestures with children from other cultures.

To make nonverbal feedback more convincing, practice it by displaying various emotions in front of a mirror. Or, try displaying different emotions to someone who does not know you well. If they can identify the emotions and see them as convincing, you are an effective nonverbal communicator. Video recorders are effective tools for self-analysis. Analyze how you look when under stress, when disciplining a student, when praising, and so on. You may find that you exhibit distracting or unassertive nonverbal behaviors such as playing with the whistle, slumping, putting your hands in your pockets, or shuffling your feet. Just as verbal feedback must be practiced and critiqued, so must nonverbal behavior.

CONSIDER THE PERSONAL NEEDS OF STUDENTS

If teaching involved only presenting physical activities to students, it would be a rather simple endeavor. The uniqueness of each student in a large class is a factor that makes teaching complex and challenging. This section focuses on ways to make instruction meaningful and personal. Teachers who can make each student feel important will influence those children's lives. Understanding the diversity of classes, encouraging student creativity, and allowing students to make educational decisions are some ways to make a lesson feel as if it were specifically designed for each student.

TEACH FOR DIVERSITY

Multicultural education allows all students to reach their potential regardless of the diversity among learners. Four major variables of diversity influence how teachers and students think and learn: race/ethnicity, gender, social class, and ability. Multicultural education creates an educational environment in which students from varying backgrounds and experience come together to experience educational equality (Manning & Baruth, 2009). Multicultural education assumes that children come from different backgrounds and helps them make sense of their everyday lives. It emphasizes the contributions of various groups that make up our country and focuses on how rather than what to learn.

Current population trends in the United States are changing our classrooms. Children who were previously excluded from classes because of language, race, economics, and abilities are now learning together. Teaching now requires a pluralistic mind-set and the ability to communicate across cultures. Educators have a responsibility to teach children to live comfortably and to prosper in this diverse and changing world. Students must celebrate their own culture while learning to appreciate the world's diversity. For most students, classroom interaction between teachers and students is the major part of multicultural education they will receive. Here are some things teachers can do to teach and value diversity:

1. Help students learn about the similarities and differences among cultures.
2. Encourage students to understand that people from similar cultures share common values, customs, and beliefs.
3. Make children aware of acts of discrimination, and teach them ways to deal with inequity and prejudice.
4. Help children develop pride in their family's culture.
5. Teach children ways to communicate effectively with other cultures and races and with the other gender.
6. Instill respect for all people regardless of race/ethnicity, gender, social class, and ability.

How teachers perceive students strongly affects their performance. Teachers who effectively teach for diversity hold high expectations for all students, including ethnic minority children and youth. Research shows that teachers tend to have lower expectations for ethnic minority youth (Vasquez, 1988). These low expectations are seen in interpersonal interactions and in the opportunities students receive for enrichment and personal growth. At-risk youth need a rich curriculum that allows no room for failure and provides the necessary support for success.

Teachers who lack knowledge about other cultures must educate themselves so they better understand the needs of all students. Diversity implies differences within and between cultures. Learning about other cultures increases the teacher's understanding of each student's early experiences and worldview. The focus should be on understanding the cultures as well as the individuals. This contrasts with learning about a culture and then stereotyping its members as "all the same." Fuller (2001) offers some questions to seek answers for when working with a different group or culture:

1. *What is their history?* Certainly, few teachers can become experts in the history and cultures of all the students they teach. However, they can recognize and be familiar with major events and important names within the cultures.

2. *What are their important cultural values?* Different cultures interact and discipline students in different ways. Ask parents and students how they work with children and what values are particularly important in their households.

3. *Who are influential individuals in their group?* Students will identify with local individuals who are held in high esteem in their community. Knowing the role models their students admire will give teachers insight into those students.

4. *What are their major religious beliefs?* Many groups belong to similar religions that drive many of their beliefs. These beliefs also influence the values of children in a community.

5. *What are their important political beliefs?* Important political issues are often discussed at home. By making an effort to learn about these issues, teachers show they are interested in how their students live in their community.

6. *What political, religious, and social days do they celebrate?* Students will discuss these important days and expect teachers to understand why they celebrate them. Talking about these days with students creates goodwill and makes students feel like their culture is valued.

Increasing instructional focus on cooperative learning is strongly recommended. This offers students the opportunity to work together toward common goals and feel positive about each group member's different contributions. Diversity can also be increased through discussion sessions. The more participants there are, the better the chances for diverse viewpoints. When students are involved in discussions, they are usually attentive and participating in the learning process. Students are motivated by different approaches because they come from varied backgrounds. Getting to know students will increase the possibility of being able to effectively help them learn.

Here are some teaching tips that can help increase instructional effectiveness in a diverse setting:

- At the start of the school year (and at regular intervals thereafter), talk to students about the importance of encouraging and respecting diversity.
- For group activities, insist that groups be diverse in race, gender, and nationality.
- Be aware of how you speak about different groups of students. Do you refer to all students in the same way? Do you address boys and girls differently? Develop a consistent style for addressing all students regardless of their differences.
- Encourage all students to participate in discussions. Avoid allowing some students from certain groups to dominate interaction. Call on students randomly so everyone has an equal chance of contributing.
- Treat all students with respect, and expect them to treat each other with dignity. Intervene if a student or group of students is dominating.
- When a difficult situation arises over an issue with undertones of diversity, take a time-out and ask students to evaluate their thoughts and ideas. Give all parties time to collect their thoughts and plan a response.
- Make sure evaluations and grades are written in gender-neutral or gender-inclusive terms.
- Encourage students to work with different partners every day. By getting to know each other, children can learn to appreciate their differences.
- Invite to class guest speakers who represent diversity in gender, race, and ethnicity even if they are not speaking about multicultural or diverse issues.
- When students make sexist or racist comments, ask them to restate the ideas in a way that does not offend others. Teach students to express their opinions, but not in an inflammatory way.
- Rotate the leaders when using groups. Give all students the opportunity to learn leadership skills.

Gender Differences

Teachers greatly influence how children learn to behave. Adults model gender-specific behaviors for children and youngsters, who in turn copy the behavior. Research shows that teachers tend to treat boys and girls differently (Grossman & Grossman, 1994). For example, teachers pay more attention to boys and encourage them more. Teachers give more praise for achievement to boys and call on girls less often than they call on boys. Teachers also respond to inappropriate behavior from boys and girls in different ways. Aggression is tolerated more in boys than in girls. However, disruptive talking is tolerated more in girls than in boys. Boys are reprimanded more than girls, and teachers use more physical means of disciplining boys.

A teacher's expectations for boys and girls strongly affect his or her interactions with them. For example, many teachers expect boys to be more active, more precocious, and not as good academically. Consequently, teachers pay closer attention to boys; and when boys do well, they are more likely to get positive attention. Girls, on the other hand, are expected to be more reserved and to do well academically, so they tend to be overlooked when they are doing "what they are supposed to do." When girls misbehave, teachers see it as an aberration and are more negative to the female than they might be to the male. This is a common, yet unacceptable, pitfall among teachers. It takes a concerted effort to overcome these biases.

Some physical education teachers believe that girls cannot perform at a level similar to boys, even though research shows otherwise. Particularly in elementary school, differences in strength, endurance, and physical skills are minimal. An effective physical education environment helps all children find success. Using the following teaching behaviors minimizes stereotyping by gender:

- Reinforce the performances of all students regardless of gender.
- Provide activities that are developmentally appropriate and allow all students to find success.
- Design programs that ensure success in coeducational experiences. Boys and girls can challenge each other to achieve higher levels if the atmosphere is positive.
- Do not use—and do not accept—students' stereotypical comments such as, "You throw like a girl."
- Include activities in the curriculum that cut across typical gender stereotypes so students learn, for example, that rhythms are not just for girls, and football is not just for boys.
- Arrange activities so the more aggressive and skilled students do not dominate. Little is learned if students are taught to be submissive or to play down their ability.
- Arrange practice sessions so that all students receive equal amounts of practice and/or opportunity to participate. Practice sessions should not give more practice opportunities to the skilled while the unskilled stand aside and observe.

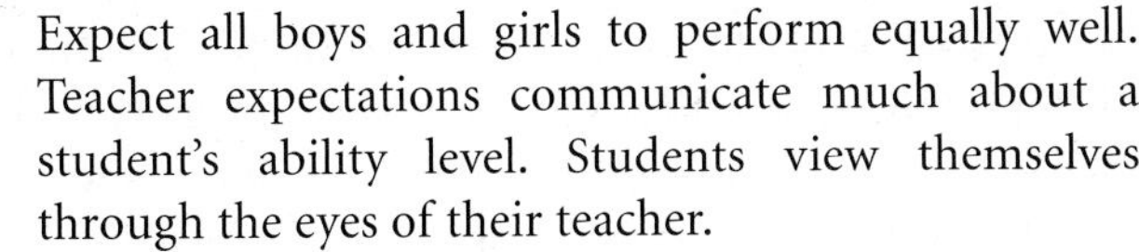

- Expect all boys and girls to perform equally well. Teacher expectations communicate much about a student's ability level. Students view themselves through the eyes of their teacher.

ENCOURAGE CREATIVE RESPONSES

An effective lesson includes more than planned experiences. Giving students an opportunity to create and modify new experiences is an important part of the total learning environment. Effective lessons include opportunities for creative expression and student input regarding lesson implementation.

By encouraging creativity in the classroom, a teacher helps students develop habits of discovery as well as reflective and abstract thinking. Self-discovered concepts are often better retained and retrieved for future use. To encourage creativity, set aside time for students to explore (Figure 5.10). For example, offer a hoop and the challenge, "See how many movements you can do with it." Offer creative opportunities during appropriate segments of the instructional sequence. Ask children to add on to a movement progression just presented or to expand it in a new direction. Make the lesson plan flexible enough to allow for creativity at teachable moments. Stimulate creativity with a show-and-tell demonstration. After a period of exploration, have students demonstrate movement patterns they have created.

ALLOW STUDENTS TO MAKE EDUCATIONAL DECISIONS

Decision making is a large part of behaving responsibly, but responsibility is a learned skill that takes practice. The decision-making process involves learning the consequences of decisions, including their effect on others. Cognitive development of students can be enhanced by allowing them to be an integral part of the lesson—choosing content, implementing the lesson, and assessing each other's techniques and development. When students are allowed to make decisions at a young age, incorrect decisions result in much less serious consequences and offer an opportunity to learn.

FIGURE 5.10 Creating different movement variations.

If children are always told how to behave when they are young, they may not know how to make serious decisions affecting their future as they age. Give them the opportunity to make decisions and choose from various alternatives, even if they make poor choices. The following strategies can help students learn to make decisions in a safe environment:

1. *Limit the number of choices.* This strategy retains ultimate control for the teacher, but gives students a chance to decide, in part, how the outcome is reached. Use this technique when learners have had little decision-making opportunity. If you have a new class and know little about the students, limit their choices. For example, give students the choice of practicing either a drive or a pass shot in a hockey unit. The desired outcome is that students practice striking skills, but they can decide which striking skill to practice.
2. *Let students modify activities.* This strategy reduces pressure because the teacher no longer has to make exceptions and listen to student complaints that "It's too hard to do" or "I'm bored." Modification allows learners to change activities to suit their personal skill level. There are many ways to modify activities, for example:
   a. Use a slower-moving family ball rather than a handball.
   b. Increase the number of fielders in a softball game.
   c. Lower the basket in a basketball unit.
   d. Decrease the length of a distance run or the height of hurdles.
3. *Offer open-ended tasks.* This approach offers wide latitude for making decisions about the content of the lesson. You decide the educational outcome, and students determine how to reach it. For example:
   a. "Develop a game that requires four passes before a shot on goal."
   b. "Plan a floor exercise routine that contains a forward roll, a backward roll, and a cartwheel."
   c. "Design a rope-jumping routine that involves a long rope, four people, and two pieces of manipulative equipment."

The problem-solving approach has no predetermined answers. Students apply principles they already know and transfer them to new situations. Ultimately, the problem is solved through a movement response that has been guided by cognitive involvement.

DEVELOP POSITIVE AFFECTIVE SKILLS

The performing arts (physical education, music, and drama) offer opportunities for affective domain development. These include learning to share, express feelings, set personal goals, and function independently. Teamwork—learning to be subordinate to a leader, as well as being a leader—is learned. Effective instruction includes teaching the whole person rather than just physical skills. It is disappointing to hear a teacher say, "My job is just to teach skills. I'm not going to get involved in developing attitudes. That's someone else's job." Physical education offers an opportunity to develop positive attitudes and values. Much is lost when students leave physical education with well-developed physical skills but negative attitudes toward physical activity and participation. Ponder these situations:

1. A teacher asks everyone to run a mile, knowing overweight students will run slowest. Many faster students who finish first will hurry the slower students to finish—an embarrassing situation. Obese students cannot change the outcome of the run even if they want to. Whenever they run, these students experience failure and belittlement—small wonder they hate physical activity.
2. Students are asked to perform skills in front of the class. Lesser skilled students feel unsure and perform more poorly because of the pressure. Many of them vow never to perform these skills again.
3. A student pitches in a softball game only to find she is unable to throw strikes. The teacher refuses to remove her from the situation, admonishing her to "concentrate!" This student may never want to pitch again.

Few people have positive feelings about an activity if they are embarrassed or fail miserably. How students feel about a subject affects their motivation to learn. So, when planning, analyze whether the lesson will result in experiences that help students develop positive attitudes and values.

Students have to sense that you care about their feelings and that you try to avoid placing them into embarrassing situations. It is not a sign of weakness to care about students. Knowingly placing students into embarrassing situations is never justified and results in negative student attitudes. The teacher's attitude, not the lesson plan, fosters positive feelings toward activity. The attitudes and values that students form are based partly on how their teachers and peers treat them. To enhance the affective domain, how you teach is as important as what you teach. Your students are human beings with needs and concerns; treat them with courtesy and respect. Discover how students feel by asking them. If you ask, however, be aware that the feedback may not be positive. Learn to listen without taking it personally or making negative judgments about students when they are honest. Concern for others' feelings creates an atmosphere that fosters positive attitudes and values.

PERSONALIZE INSTRUCTION

Though most instruction is conducted as a group activity, it is obvious that student's ability levels vary widely. As students mature, the range of ability increases because many students participate in extracurricular activities such as Little League baseball, YBA basketball, and private tutoring in gymnastics. In physical education classes, this range of experiences demands that tasks be modified so all students find success. Here are some ways to personalize instruction and accommodate developmental differences among students:

1. *Modify the conditions.* Adjust tasks and activities to help all children succeed. If students are learning to catch, move partners closer together, have them use a slower-moving object such as a beach ball or a balloon, use a larger target, change the size of boundaries or goal areas, let students toss and catch individually, or use a larger-striking implement. Try to minimize error and maximize success for the activity. When students find little success, they exhibit off-task behavior to draw attention away from their subpar performance. Such behavior indicates that the error rate is too high and learning is stymied.
2. *Use self-competition.* As surprising as it sounds, if the success rate is too high, students become bored. Ask students to set personal goals—for example, to see if they can beat their personal best performance. Challenge students by asking them to accomplish higher levels of performance, using a faster-moving object, increasing the distance to the goal, or decreasing its size. Students respond best to challenges that are personal and slightly above their current skill level. Try to avoid holding all students to a single standard of performance.
3. *Offer different task challenges.* During the lesson, allow students to work on different tasks. Task cards and station teaching help students learn at an optimum rate. Present several tasks of varying complexity so that students can find personal challenges. For example, students with limited upper body strength will have difficulty with inverted balances. Include some activities using the legs so all students can achieve some success as they work on balance skill challenges.

EMPLOY EFFECTIVE COMMUNICATION SKILLS

Communicating with learners is critical, and communication skills can always be improved. For children to learn essential information, the teacher must communicate in a way that encourages students to listen. Quality instructors seem able to create a positive atmosphere for learning. They may not know more about skills and activities than less able teachers do, but they often know how to communicate effectively. Meaningful feedback helps students learn when skills are performed correctly and when they need refinement.

Students want to communicate openly and honestly with adults. Behavior used in talking to students can help keep relationships strong. When talking with students, assume a physical pose that expresses interest and attention. Kneel at times, so children do not always have to look up. Check to see if your facial and verbal cues reinforce your interest and concern. The following suggestions can help teachers establish a positive bond with students and create a learning environment enjoyed by everyone.

1. *Focus on specific behavior of students rather than making general comments that are personal and insulting.* Here is an example of speaking about a student's behavior: "Talking when I am talking is unacceptable behavior." Such feedback identifies behavior that can be improved upon and avoids questioning the student's self-worth. This approach helps students feel you are interested in helping rather than belittling them. In contrast, saying something like, "Why are you always talking and acting foolish?" negatively reflects on the child's character and undermines his or her self-esteem. It is also nonspecific, so the student does not know what behavior you are reprimanding. Identify the specific misbehavior, and then state the type of behavior you expect.
2. *Understand the child's viewpoint.* Imagine if someone embarrassed you in front of a class. How would you feel if you were inept and trying to learn a new skill with others watching? These and other emotions make listening difficult for youngsters. Unrestrained feedback can stress a youngster and increase behavior problems. When suggesting ways to improve performance, do so privately (so other students cannot hear you) and allow the student to practice without scrutiny. Asking students to try something new and then watching over them until they do it correctly can be intimidating and cause resentment.
3. *Identify your feelings about the learner.* Teachers sometimes send their students mixed messages. You may be unhappy with a student because of a previous incident, yet be unwilling to confront her. As a result of these pent-up feelings, you might then offer the student unkind or sarcastic feedback about a skill performance. Usually, when you have negative feelings toward a student, that student cannot understand your unhappiness. Communicate how you feel (even if it is negative), but make sure such communication is directed at specific, correctable behavior in a caring manner.

5

4. *Accentuate the positive.* When teaching key instructional points of a skill, accent positive performance points rather than incorrect actions. For example, stress that children "land lightly," rather than saying, "Don't land so hard." An easy way to emphasize key points positively is to say, "Do this because. . . ." If there are several different and acceptable ways to perform movement patterns, be explicit with your points.
5. *Optimize speech patterns.* Avoid giving sermons at the least provocation. Sermons seldom work in the teaching environment. Acquire a broad vocabulary of effective phrases to indicate approval and good effort. A common list circulated among teachers shows one hundred ways to say, "Good job." Also, a period of silence can be effective; it gives students time to digest the information.
6. *Conduct lengthy discussions in a classroom setting.* Students expect to move around in the activity area, whereas they have learned to sit and interact cognitively in the classroom. Presenting lengthy explanations in the classroom before students go to the activity area makes maximum use of activity time. Explain rules, outline procedures and responsibilities, and draw formations on the chalkboard. In the activity area, try to limit discussions to 30 seconds.
7. *Respect student opinion.* Avoid humiliating a child who gives a wrong answer. Teachers can deal with this issue in several ways. Pass over inappropriate answers by directing attention to more appropriate responses. Or, suggest that the student has offered a good answer, but the question was not asked correctly. Ask the student to "save that answer" and then go back to that student when the answer is correct for another question. When injecting your personal opinion into the question-and-answer process, label it as such and avoid making it sound more valuable than student opinion. Try not to be surprised or offended if children comment negatively in response to a query asking for candid opinions about an activity or procedure. When opinions are honest, some are bound to be negative.

BE AN EFFECTIVE LISTENER

Effective listening skills are harder to learn than speaking techniques. Teachers are trained to impart knowledge to students and have practiced speaking for years. Many students view teachers as people who speak but do not listen. Poor communication often occurs because of a breakdown in listening. There is truth in the adage, "You were given two ears and one mouth so you could listen twice as much as you speak." These suggestions promote effective listening skills:

1. *Be an active listener.* Active listeners convince the speaker they are interested in what the speaker is saying. Much of this interaction occurs through nonverbal behavior such as eye contact, nodding the head in agreement, facial expressions, and moving toward the speaker (Figure 5.11).
2. *Listen to the hidden message of the speaker.* Young children sometimes find it difficult to express their feelings clearly. The words expressed may not signal what the child is actually feeling. For example, a child may say, "I hate P.E." Most children do not hate all phases of physical education, and most likely a more current activity (such as jumping rope) is the problem. Try acknowledging their feelings with a response such as, "You sound angry; are you having a problem you want to discuss?" This helps students realize that their feelings are important and gives them an opportunity to clarify concerns. It prevents the teacher from internalizing students' anger (or frustration) and responding in an emotionally charged manner, such as "I don't want to hear that; now get back on task!"
3. *Paraphrase what the student said.* Paraphrasing is restating in your own words what was said to you, including your interpretation of the other person's feelings. For example, you might respond, "Do I hear you saying you are frustrated and bored with this activity?" If the paraphrasing is correct, it makes the student feel validated and understood. If the interpretation is incorrect, the student has an opportunity to restate his or her concern.
4. *Let students know you value listening.* Teachers who listen to students learn about their students' feelings. Let students know you will listen, and then do something

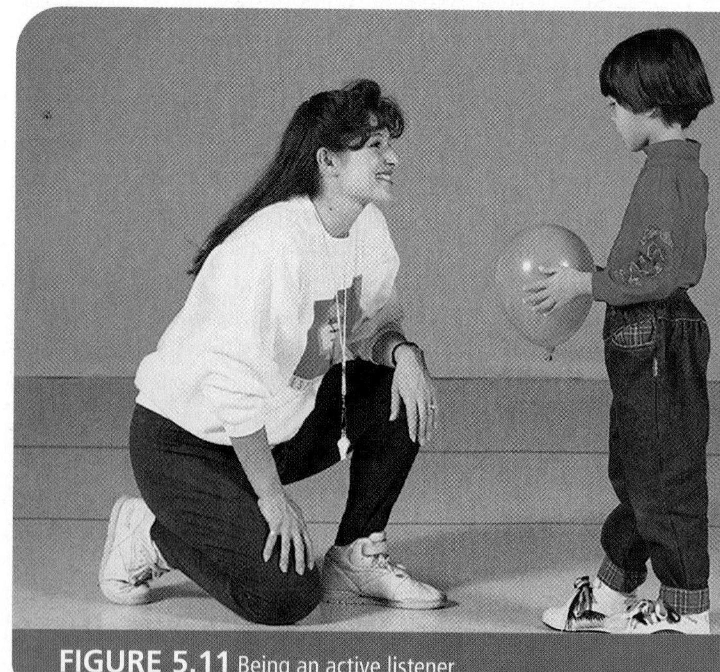

FIGURE 5.11 Being an active listener.

about what they say. If you are a good listener, you will hear things that are not always positive. For example, students may honestly tell you which activities they do not enjoy. They may express how they felt when they were criticized. If not taken personally, this communication can be constructive. It may not be valid criticism of the program or your procedures, but it opens the door to good communication. A word of caution: if you find it difficult to accept such feedback, it is best to ask students to keep their comments to themselves. Avoid such interactions if the feedback will affect your confidence.

APPLYING WHAT YOU READ

- Before writing and implementing effective lessons, review and become familiar with the section, "Characteristics of a Quality Lesson." These points will help you develop effective, quality lessons.
- As you write a lesson, be sure to create outcomes and objectives that can be measured efficiently. Can you quickly assess the outcome and determine if the lesson was a success?
- When organizing a lesson, you must make some key decisions. How will you teach a specific skill? How will the class move from one activity to another? How will you scan and monitor students? What cues can you use? How will you piece together instruction to make sure you do not talk too long? Who will demonstrate the skill?
- Videotaping a lesson is an excellent way to evaluate your instructional effectiveness. As you watch a video of yourself, pay close attention to the types of feedback you provide. Is it generic? Meaningful? Specific? Do you give more feedback to boys? Girls? Skilled students?
- Quality instruction utilizes principles of motivation. While teaching, ask yourself if you are applying those principles.

REFLECTION AND REVIEW

HOW AND WHY

1. State whether the characteristics of a quality lesson were present for all students in your elementary physical education classes as a child.
2. Using teacher talk, list five meaningful feedback statements. Use statements other than those presented in this chapter, and discuss why your statements are meaningful.
3. Describe how you can promote diversity in your classes. Why is this important?
4. Discuss your strengths and weaknesses when communicating.

CONTENT REVIEW

1. List and explain the characteristics of a quality elementary physical education program.
2. Explain the importance of several essential elements of instruction.
3. State the key components of instructional feedback. Discuss each component.
4. Describe ways to make instruction personal and meaningful for students.
5. Discuss several important communication skills for teachers.

FOR MORE INFORMATION

REFERENCES AND SUGGESTED READINGS

Banks, J. A. (2009). *Teaching strategies for ethnic studies* (8th ed.). Boston: Allyn & Bacon.

Bennett, C. L. (2007). *Comprehensive multicultural education: Theory and practice* (6th ed.). Boston: Allyn & Bacon.

Buck, M. M., Lund, J. L., Harrison, J. M., & Blakemore, C. L. (2007). *Instructional strategies for secondary physical education* (5th ed.). Boston: McGraw-Hill.

Cushner, K. H. (2006). *Human diversity in action: Developing multicultural competencies for the classroom* (3rd ed.). Boston: McGraw-Hill.

Fronske, H. (2005). *Teaching cues for sport skills for secondary school students* (3rd ed.). San Francisco: Benjamin Cummings.

Fronske, H., & Wilson, R. (2002). *Teaching cues for basic sport skills for elementary and middle school students.* San Francisco: Benjamin Cummings.

Fuller, M. L. (2001). Multicultural concerns and classroom management. In C. A. Grant & M. L. Gomez (Eds.), *Campus and classroom: Making schooling multicultural.* Upper Saddle River, NJ: Prentice Hall.

Grossman, H., & Grossman, S. H. (1994). *Gender issues in education.* Boston: Allyn & Bacon.

Hunter, M. C. (1994). *Mastery teaching.* Thousand Oaks, CA: & Sage.

Kelly, L., & Melograno, V. (2004). *Developing the physical education curriculum.* Champaign, IL: Human Kinetics.

Koppelman, K., & Goodhart, L. (2008). *Understanding human differences: Multicultural education for a diverse America* (2nd ed.). Boston: Allyn & Bacon.

Manning, M. L., & Baruth, L. G. (2009). *Multicultural education of children and adolescents* (5th ed.). Boston: Allyn & Bacon.

Mosston, M., & Ashworth, S. (2004). *Teaching physical education* (5th ed.). San Francisco: Benjamin Cummings.

Pang, V. O. (2005). *Multicultural education: A caring-centered, reflective approach* (2nd ed.). Boston: McGraw-Hill.

Rink, J. E. (2006). *Teaching physical education for learning* (4th ed.). Boston: WCB/McGraw-Hill.

Siedentop, D., & Tannehill, D. (2000). *Developing teaching skills in physical education* (4th ed.). Mountain View, CA: Mayfield.

Tiedt, P. L., & Tiedt, I. M. (2006). *Multicultural teaching: A handbook of activities, information, and resources* (7th ed.). Boston: Allyn & Bacon.

Vasquez, J. (1988). Contests of learning for minority children. *Educational Forum, 52*(3), 243–253.

5

Wardle, F., & Cruz-Janzen, M. I. (2004). *Meeting the needs of multiethnic and multiracial children in schools.* Boston: Allyn & Bacon.

WEBSITES

Activity Cues
www.pecentral.org/climate/monicaparsonarticle.html

Communication
http://crs.uvm.edu/gopher/nerl/personal/comm/e.html
http://nonverbal.ucsc.edu
www.pecentral.org/climate/monicaparsonarticle.html
www.bizmove.com/skills/m8g.htm

Elements of Instruction
www.humboldt.edu/~tha1/hunter-eei.html

Enhancing Teacher Effectiveness
www.hcc.hawaii.edu/intranet/committees/FacDevCom/guidebk/teachtip/enhance.htm

Multicultural Education
www.ncrel.org/sdrs/areas/issues/educatrs/leadrshp/le4pppme.htm

Management and Discipline

ESSENTIAL COMPONENTS OF QUALITY PROGRAMS

I. Organized around content standards

II. Student-centered and developmentally appropriate

III. Physical activity and motor skill development form the core of the program

► IV. Teaches management skills and self-discipline

V. Promotes inclusion of all students

VI. Focuses on process over product

VII. Promotes lifetime personal health and wellness

► VIII. Teaches cooperation and responsibility and promotes sensitivity to diversity

NATIONAL STANDARDS FOR PHYSICAL EDUCATION*

1. Demonstrates competency in motor skills and movement patterns needed to perform a variety of physical activities.
2. Demonstrates understanding of movement concepts, principles, and tactics as they apply to the learning and performance of physical activities.
3. Participates regularly in physical activity.
4. Achieves and maintains a health-enhancing level of physical fitness.
5. ► Exhibits responsible personal and social behavior that respects self and others in physical activity.
6. Values physical activity for health, enjoyment, challenge, self-expression, and/or social interaction.

*National Association for Sport and Physical Education (NASPE), 2004.

Management and discipline are vital to effective instruction. Management requires designing and implementing a preventive approach to discipline. This chapter presents effective class management skills that improve the efficiency and productivity of instruction. Dealing with behavior involves two major parts: (1) modifying and maintaining acceptable behavior, and (2) an approach to decreasing unacceptable behavior. Procedures such as time-out, reprimands, and removing privileges are described. Ways to minimize the use of criticism and punishment are reviewed, and specific recommendations are listed.

Outcomes

- Describe the role of the teacher as it pertains to managing children in a physical education setting.
- Implement management and discipline skills that result in a positive and constructive learning environment.
- Identify techniques used to start and stop the class; organize the class into groups, formations, and squads; and prepare students for activity.
- Cite acceptable and recommended procedures for dealing with inappropriate behavior.
- Describe techniques to increase or decrease specific behaviors.
- Explain the role of teacher reaction in shaping and controlling student behavior.
- Design or modify games that are effective in changing student behavior.
- Know the shortcomings of criticism and punishment when used to change and improve student behavior.
- Understand the legal consequences of expelling a student from school.

SUCCESSFUL teachers effectively manage student behavior. Management skills may vary among teachers in emphasis and focus, but collectively they characterize quality teaching. Effective teachers make three assumptions: teaching is a profession; students are in school to learn; and the teacher's challenge is to promote learning. These assumptions imply a responsibility to teach a diverse group of students—those who accept instruction and those who do not. Competent teachers maintain faith in students who have not yet found success and expect them to do so eventually. Most children in a class are relatively easy to teach, but being able to help low-aptitude and indifferent students make appreciable gains is the result of effective instruction.

EFFECTIVE MANAGEMENT AND DISCIPLINE: A COORDINATED APPROACH

Managing student behavior is not easy. Teachers often question their ability to control and manage a classroom. A class of children is a group of individuals, each requiring unique treatment and understanding. Some teachers question the importance of effective management and discipline. The most basic reason for management and discipline is to help children learn effectively without infringing on other children's rights. U.S. society is based on freedom partnered with self-discipline. Americans have much personal freedom as long as they do not encroach on the rights of others. Likewise, children can enjoy freedom as long as their behavior is consistent with educational objectives and does not prevent other students from learning.

Most children choose to cooperate and participate with teachers. In fact, the learner is largely responsible for allowing the teacher to teach. No one can be taught who chooses not to cooperate. Effective management of behavior means maintaining an environment in which all children have the opportunity to learn. Students who choose to be disruptive and off task compromise the rights of students who choose to cooperate. When a teacher has to spend a great deal of time working with children who are disorderly, students who want to learn are shortchanged.

A smoothly functioning class is a joy to watch. Teachers behave in ways that promote positive student behavior; in turn, students perform in a positive, caring way. Management and discipline techniques are interrelated; one affects the other. Throughout this chapter, *management* is defined as "organizing and controlling the affairs of a class." It refers to how students are organized, started and stopped, grouped, and arranged during class. Effective management means that students are moved quickly, called by their names, and moved into instructional formations, taught efficiently, and so on. *Discipline* is defined as "modifying student behavior when it is unacceptable." When things do not go smoothly, and some students decide not to follow the teacher's management requests, discipline techniques are required to create a constructive teaching environment.

It is unrealistic to believe that it is possible to work with children without having some type of discipline problem. But teachers can take these steps to develop a well-managed and disciplined class:

1. Use proper teaching behaviors.
2. Define class procedures, rules, and consequences.
3. Incorporate efficient management skills.

4. Teach acceptable student behavior.
5. Use behavior management to increase acceptable behavior.
6. Decrease unacceptable behavior with discipline.

USE PROPER TEACHING BEHAVIORS

In a well-managed class, teacher and students assume dual responsibility for learning. Presentations and instructional strategies used are appropriate for the capabilities of students and the nature of activity sequences. How teachers teach, more than their particular teaching style, determines what students learn. Effective class management and organizational skills create an environment that gives students freedom of choice, in harmony with class order. When a skillful instructor prevents problems before they occur, less time is spent dealing with deviant behavior.

Understand how your behavior can influence students. What students learn reflects your personality, outlook, ideals, and background. Recognize your personal habits and attitudes that affect students negatively. Try to model the behavior you desire from students. This means hustling if you demand that students hustle. It means listening carefully to students or performing fitness activities from time to time. Modeling acceptable behavior strongly affects students. The phrase "Your actions speak louder than your words" has significant implications.

DEVELOP AN ASSERTIVE COMMUNICATION STYLE

It is important to hear yourself speak to students. Taping a class session will help you identify the approach you take when interacting with your class. Your communication style is often revealed when you are under pressure or unsure of yourself. At that point, teachers who are not assertive may become aggressive or passive in trying to get students "back in line." Generally, a teacher communicates in three ways when dealing with management and discipline scenarios. Each style is discussed in detail here, the goal being for teachers to learn to develop and use an assertive style of communication when dealing with management and discipline issues.

Passive Communicator

To avoid becoming upset at students, a passive teacher "hopes" to make all children happy. *Passive* means "trying to avoid all conflict and please others." Directly or indirectly, the passive teacher is constantly saying, "Like me, appreciate what I do for you." Many passive teachers want to be perfect so everybody will like them, and their students will behave perfectly. When students behave like students and go off task, Mr. Passive becomes upset and angry. The passive teacher typically lets behavior slide until "he can't take it anymore." Then he loses composure and lashes out at the class in anger. When the anger subsides, Mr. Passive wants to make up and again starts the cycle of letting things go and trying to be liked. This cycle is frequently repeated.

Passive teachers often turn over their power to students, particularly the least cooperative students. They will say things like, "We are not going to start until everyone is listening!" Interpreted concretely, students may hear, "This is great. We don't have to start until we are finished with our conversation." Passive teachers also ignore unacceptable behavior and hope it will disappear. Ignoring seldom causes behavior to disappear; rather, it becomes worse over time. Passive teachers often say things but never follow through. For example, "If you do that one more time, I am going to call your parents." When there is no follow-through or it is impossible to follow through, the words are empty and meaningless, and students soon learn disrespect for the teacher. Another common trait of a passive teacher is asking questions that result in useless information: "What did you do that for?" or "Why are you doing this?" or "Don't you know better than that?" These questions only make the teacher frustrated and angry at all of the "I don't know" responses.

Aggressive Communicator

An aggressive teacher wants to overpower students by coming on strong. Aggressive people feel that discussions are a form of competition that they must win at all costs. A common trait of aggressive communicators is that they use the word "You" all the time. These statements keep students feeling defensive and attacked: "You never listen to me; you are always the one in trouble; you are the problem here; you are always talking." Aggressive responders often think they have all the answers and try to express others' viewpoints. They may say to a student, "You think that because you did that last year in Mr. Jones's class, you can do it in my class." Obviously, no one knows what another person is thinking, and it serves no purpose to communicate this way.

Aggressive teachers often use the words *always* and *never*. These are labeling words. They make students feel as if they are bad people who always behave in certain ways or never do anything right. Words that generalize and label create problems in communication and often result in alienation rather than respect for a teacher. Aggressive teachers often see students as personally attacking them and focus on labeling the student rather than dealing with the behavior. Typically, they do not reveal how they feel about things and are unwilling to express their own thoughts. If students never know how a teacher feels, they will likely not develop much empathy for their instructor. A good rule of

6

thumb is this: any statement about the student other than your own feelings or thoughts will give your communication an aggressive quality.

Assertive Communicator

An assertive teacher does not beg, plead, or threaten. Rather, he or she expresses feelings and expectations straightforwardly. Assertive people are not afraid to say what they want and do not worry about what others will think of them. Teachers who want to be liked are quite concerned about what their students think. An assertive teacher wants what is best for students and does not worry about what they think. Assertiveness comes across to students as a no-nonsense approach that needs to be followed. The approach is clear, direct, and concrete (requiring little interpretation by students). For example, an assertive teacher might say to a student who has been talking out of turn, "It upsets me when you talk while I am talking." This teacher is expressing feelings and making it clear what the unacceptable behavior is. Now the teacher follows that statement with an assertive statement that expresses the acceptable behavior: "That is your second warning; please go to time-out." Assertive communication emphasizes clarity without anger. Assertive responding does not involve high emotion, which turns assertion into aggressiveness.

An excellent way to make messages more assertive is to use the word *I* instead of *you*. Talking about your own feelings and emotions will make the messages sound much more reasonable and firm: "When you are playing with your equipment while I am talking, it bothers me and makes me forget what I planned on saying. Please leave your equipment alone when I talk." Such messages always identify the disrupting or annoying behavior, offer how you feel, and direct the student to behave properly. An excellent reference on assertive discipline is *Conscious Discipline* by Becky Bailey (2001).

CREATE A PERSONAL BEHAVIOR PLAN

A key element of an effective management approach is to understand and plan for how you will behave when disciplining students. Serious misbehavior can cause some teachers to become angry, others to feel threatened, and others to behave tyrannically. Personal behavior plans usually include the following points:

1. *Maintain composure.* Students do not know your "hot buttons" unless you reveal them. If you "lose it," students lose respect for you and believe you are an ineffective teacher.
2. *Acknowledge your feelings when student misbehavior occurs.* Do you feel angry, threatened, challenged, or fearful? How do you typically respond when a student defies you?
3. *Design a plan for yourself when such feelings occur.* For example, count to 10 before responding, or take five deep breaths. Avoid dealing with a student's misbehavior until you know how you feel.
4. *Know the options you have for dealing with the deviant behavior.* Talking with students is best done after class if it will take more than a few seconds. When time is limited, some options are to quietly warn the student; quietly remove the student from class; or quietly send another student for help if the situation is severe.

BE A LEADER, NOT A FRIEND

Students want a teacher who is knowledgeable, personable, and a leader. They are not looking for a new friend; in fact, most students feel uncomfortable if they think you want to be "one of them." Let students know what they will learn during the semester. Do not try to be a part of their personal discussions. There must be a comfortable distance between you and your students. You can still be friendly and caring; it is important to be empathetic toward students as long as you express concern in a professional way. Being a leader means knowing where to direct a class. You are responsible for what is learned and how it is presented. Student input is important, but ultimately, it is your responsibility to lead a class to acceptable objectives.

COMMUNICATE HIGH STANDARDS

Students respond to your expectations. If you expect students to perform at high levels, most of them will strive to do so. A common and accurate expression is, "You get what you ask for." If you expect students to perform to the best of their abilities, they likely will do so. On the other hand, if you seemingly do not care whether they try, many students will do as little as possible.

UNDERSTAND WHY STUDENTS MISBEHAVE

Students misbehave for various reasons, some of which are presented in Figure 6.1. Understanding these reasons and being able to identify them when the misbehaviors occur will help you anticipate and prevent many behavior problems. Students sometimes misbehave because they did not understand the instructions. Give instructions and then proceed with the activity. If some students are not performing correctly, perhaps they still did not understand. Clarify the instructions and proceed. This two-tiered approach usually ensures that directions are clear and that ample opportunity is given for all to understand.

- The student may be testing the teacher.
- The student may have some type of learning disability that causes the behavior problem.
- The student may be looking for reinforcement from the teacher.
- The student may have low self-esteem, which causes the student to misbehave while trying to become the center of attention.
- The student may not understand the directions given.
- The student may be bored and unchallenged by the activities.
- Performing the activities may result in continuous failure, so the student misbehaves to avoid revealing a lack of ability.
- Parents may deal with their children in a manner completely unlike the methods used in physical education.
- The teacher may not like the student, thus forcing the student to be combative and angry.
- Failure in other subjects may carry over to physical education.

FIGURE 6.1 Typical causes of misbehavior.

DELIVER NEGATIVE AND CORRECTIVE FEEDBACK INDIVIDUALLY

When you deliver negative and corrective feedback, do so privately and personally to individual students. Few people want to have negative or corrective comments delivered globally for others to hear. Besides, not all students should be punished for the behavior of a few misbehaving classmates. Negative feedback directed to a group can have contrary results. If you criticize the entire group, you will likely lose the respect and admiration of students who were behaving properly.

AVOID FEEDBACK THAT OFFERS THE POSSIBILITY FOR BACKLASH

Some verbal types of interactions may work in the short term but have long-term negative consequences. The following types of feedback often work immediately but cause greater problems over the long haul. If students become resentful, they may tend to be deviant when the teacher is not around. Here are some approaches you will want to avoid:

- *Preaching or moralizing.* The most common example of moralizing is telling students they "should know better than that!" Students make mistakes because they are young and learning. A part of learning is making mistakes. Correct mistakes in a quiet and caring way.
- *Threatening.* Threats are ultimatums that attempt to terminate unacceptable behavior, even though you know the threat will be impossible to carry out. For example, the ultimatum, "If you do not stop that, I'm going to kick you out of class" sounds tough but is usually impossible to enforce. You are not in a position to expel students, and some students know you cannot carry out the threat. If students hear enough idle threats, they will start to tune out, and their respect for you will gradually wane.
- *Ordering and commanding.* If you are bossy, students begin to think they are nothing more than pawns to be moved around the area. Request that students carry out tasks. Courtesy and politeness are requisites for effective teacher–student relationships.
- *Interrogating.* When a problem arises (such as a fight between students), an initial reaction is to find out who started the fight rather than dealing with the combatants' feelings. Little is gained by trying to solve "who started it." Students often shirk the blame and suggest it was not their fault. Try calmly saying, "You know fighting is not accepted in my class. You must have been very angry to place yourself in this situation." This encourages students to talk about their feelings rather than place blame. It also communicates a caring and concerned attitude toward children even when they do something wrong.
- *Refusing to listen.* This approach commonly manifests itself as, "Let's talk about it some other time." At times, during instruction, this response is necessary to keep students focused. But, if you always refuse to listen, students will avoid interacting with you and believe you do not care.
- *Labeling.* Labeling is characterized by telling children, "Stop acting like babies" or "You're behaving like a bunch of first graders." On an individual level, such feedback might sound like, "You're always the troublemaker." Using labels is degrading and dehumanizes children. Teachers who use labeling often think it will improve performance. In reality, it is usually destructive and leaves students with negative feelings.

DEFINE CLASS PROCEDURES, RULES, AND CONSEQUENCES

Effectively managing a class depends on letting students know what you expect of them. They want to know what routines they are going to follow. Without guidelines and routines, students have to guess what the teacher wants every day. This situation makes students uneasy. As an example of the need for guidance, consider these students who are outside in a physical education lesson. Their teacher tells them not to get too far away so they can hear all the directions. Sure enough, some students stray beyond a distance the teacher deems acceptable, and they are disciplined. Unfortunately, the wrong party was disciplined; the teacher was at fault because he did not set up clear guidelines. How can students judge what is too far away? What if they felt they could hear the directions, but the teacher did not think so? Can the teacher be consistent in applying this rule when even he does not know how far is too far? If he had set up cones at the perimeter of the area and asked the students to stay inside them, he could have eliminated the problem entirely. Carry out the following steps at the start of the school year, and reinforce them throughout the year.

STEP ONE: DETERMINE ROUTINES FOR STUDENTS

Being assertive is important. Students feel best when they know your expectations, and they expect to follow established routines. Explain your routines so that students understand why you are using them. Here are some routines that teachers often use:

1. How students are supposed to enter the teaching area.
2. How the teaching area is defined.
3. Where and how they should meet—in sitting squads, moving and freezing on a spot, in a semicircle, and so on.
4. What they should do if equipment is located in the area.
5. What signal is used to "freeze" a class.
6. How they procure and put away equipment.
7. How they will be grouped for instruction.

After establishing and practicing these routines, teachers and students can work together comfortably.

STEP TWO: DETERMINE RULES AND PROCEDURES FOR THE SCHOOL YEAR

Rules are an expected part of the school environment. School administrators typically judge teachers' effectiveness by how well they manage students rather than what they know about subject matter. Teachers want students to show respect—to teachers and to other students. It is reasonable to expect students to behave. If you cannot manage students, you cannot teach them. When creating your rules, select general categories rather than specific behavior. For example, "Respect your neighbor" means many things, from not pushing to not swearing at another student. Post rules in the teaching area where all students can easily read them. Here are some examples of general rules:

- *Stop, look, and listen.* This involves freezing on signal, looking at the instructor, and listening for instructions.
- *Take care of equipment.* This includes caring for equipment and distributing, gathering, and using it properly.
- *Respect the rights of others.* This covers behavior such as not pushing others, leaving others' equipment alone, not fighting or arguing, and not physically or emotionally hurting others.

To avoid seeming too strict, try not to make too many rules. Keep in mind that it is hard for students to remember all the details of more than three to five general rules. Too many rules can cause students to become "rule-specific." A child may choose to chew gum in the multipurpose room because the rule is "No gum-chewing in the halls." When students become rule-specific, they do not learn to think about right and wrong and the spirit of the rule; rather, they look for exceptions to the rule. Rules are general guidelines for acceptable behavior rather than negative statements telling students what they cannot do. Consider these points when designing rules:

- Select major categories of behavior rather than a multitude of specific rules.
- Identify observable behavior. This makes it easy to determine whether a student is following a rule and does not involve subjective judgment.
- Make rules reasonable for the students' age level. Meaningful rules cut across all ages and can be used throughout the elementary school years.
- Limit the number of rules (three to five).
- State rules briefly and positively. It is impossible to write a rule that covers all situations and conditions. Make the rule brief, yet broad.

STEP THREE: DETERMINE CONSEQUENCES WHEN RULES ARE NOT FOLLOWED

When rules are broken, students must learn to accept the consequences of their misbehavior. List and post consequences in a prominent place in the teaching area. Discuss the rules and consequences with students to make sure they understand and see the need for behavior guidelines. Having agreed-upon rules and consequences involves students in developing the classroom environment. One of the best ways to earn students' respect is to treat them all in a fair and caring way. Most students are willing to accept the consequences of their misbehavior if they think their treatment will be consistent with and equal to that of other students. Animosity occurs when students sense that you play favorites. Physical education teachers commonly favor gifted athletes and students who are physically attractive. Be aware of such behavior, and prevent its occurrence. One reason for defining consequences before misbehavior is that it allows you to administer the consequences equitably. When a student chooses to break a rule, apply the consequences without judging her character or making a derogatory statement about her. It is the student's misbehavior, not you, that has triggered the consequences.

STEP FOUR: SHARE YOUR RULES WITH PARENTS, TEACHERS, AND ADMINISTRATORS

It is not enough to share your rules with students. If there is truth in the saying, "It takes a village to raise a child," it makes sense to be sure all parties know and understand your rules. A newsletter to parents at the start of the year explaining your program and your approach to class management will set the tone for students immediately. Parents will have little complaint if their child has a problem; routines, rules, and consequences were clearly explained in the newsletter. Post your rules and consequences in your teaching areas so students, parents, and teachers can see them. Sharing your rules with classroom teachers and administrators also helps clarify your expectations. Classroom teachers will then be able to reinforce your approach. Principals will also clearly understand what you expect, and it will be easier to work together to achieve common goals.

STEP FIVE: HAVE THE CLASS PRACTICE RULES SYSTEMATICALLY

Rules stipulate expected class behavior. If there is a rule for proper care of equipment, give students the opportunity to practice how you want equipment handled. If a rule requires students to stop and listen, practice such behavior and reinforce a proper response. Student behavior is not always correct, regardless of rules. It is common to hear teachers tell students, "I told you before not to do that." This assumes that telling students once will result in perfect adherence to rules. Obviously, this is not the case. Continue to allow time for students to practice acceptable behavior throughout the school year.

INCORPORATE EFFICIENT MANAGEMENT SKILLS

Class management skills are prerequisites to effective instruction. To move and organize students quickly and efficiently, teachers must understand various techniques and students must accept them. If a class is unmanageable, it is unteachable. Most students enjoy a learning environment that is organized, efficient, and devotes nearly all of the class time to learning skills.

Teach class management skills like you teach physical skills. All skills need to be learned through practice and repetition until they become second nature. Viewing class management skills in this light makes it easier to have empathy for students who do not perform well. Just as students make mistakes when performing physical skills, some will perform management skills incorrectly. A simple, direct statement such as, "It appears that you have forgotten how to freeze quickly; let's practice," is much more constructive than indicting a class for its carelessness and disinterest.

6

DELIVER INSTRUCTION EFFICIENTLY

If students are not listening when instructions are given, little learning occurs. Deliver instructions in small doses, focusing on one or two points at a time. Instructions should be specific and seldom last longer than 20 to 30 seconds. An effective approach is to alternate short instructional episodes with periods of activity. This contrasts with the common practice of delivering long, involved technical monologues on skill performance only to find that many students have forgotten most of the information by the time practice begins. In a series of spoken items, people usually remember only the first and the last; thus, most students will be able to integrate and concentrate on only one or two points during skill practice. Minimizing the amount of content per instructional episode helps eliminate students' frustration and allows them to focus on stated goals. This is not to suggest that information should not be delivered to students, but that the "tell it all at the start" style should be replaced by the more effective "input, practice, feedback" model.

When giving instructions, tell students *when* to perform an activity before stating *what* the activity is. An effective way to implement "when before what" is to use a keyword, such as *Begin!* or *Start!* to start an activity. For example, "When I say *Start!* I'd like you to . . ." or, "When I say *Go!* I want you to jog to a beanbag, move to your own space, and practice tossing and catching." The keyword is not given until all directions have been issued, so students must listen to all instructions before starting.

STOP AND START A CLASS CONSISTENTLY

The most basic and important management skill is being able to stop and start a class. Use a loud audio signal to stop a class and a voice command to start the class (see the previous discussion). After choosing your signals, use them consistently. Many teachers like to have students assume a

FIGURE 6.2 Class in freeze position.

specific position when they stop (Figure 6.2). Freezing in the ready position with hands on knees helps keep students' hands in their own space so they do not distract other students. Using both an audio signal (e.g., a whistle) and a visual signal (raising the hand overhead) is effective because some children may not hear the audio signal when engrossed in activity. If children do not respond to the signal to stop, take time to practice the procedure. Reinforce students when they perform management behavior properly. Often, skill performance is reinforced but correct management behavior is not. Any behavior that is not reinforced regularly will not be performed well.

Expect 100% compliance when students are asked to stop. If only some students stop and listen to directions, class morale degenerates. Students begin to wonder why they have to stop but other students do not. Scan the class to see if all students are stopped and ready to respond to the next set of directions. If you settle for less than full attention, students will fulfill those expectations.

MOVE STUDENTS INTO GROUPS AND FORMATIONS QUICKLY

Teachers must regularly move students into small groups and instructional formations. Simple techniques can be used to help students enjoy this process and do it quickly. Any grouping technique should require students to match up with someone near them rather than running and looking for their best friend. Place some rubber marking spots in the center of the area and call them the "friendship spots." Students who need a partner run to a friendship spot and raise their hands. After finding a partner, they move out of the friendship spot area. This approach keeps students from feeling "left out."

Finding Partners

Use the activity Toe-to-Toe (see page 548) to teach children to find partners quickly. The goal of the game is to get toe-to-toe with a partner as fast as possible. Other challenges are to get elbow-to-elbow or shoulder-to-shoulder or look into a partner's eyes. Students without a partner must go to the friendship area (described earlier) and find someone else without a partner. To keep children from looking for a favorite friend or refusing to be someone's partner, tell them they must quickly find the nearest person. If students insist on staying near a friend, have the class move around the area and find a different partner each time you call, "Toe-to-toe!" This technique will help children meet many more students.

Other suggestions for finding partners are to ask students to find a partner who is wearing the same color, whose birthday is during the same month, whose phone number has two of the same numbers in it, and so on. To arrange students in equal-sized groups, place an equal number of different-colored beanbags or hoops on the floor. Ask students to move throughout the area and, on signal, to sit on a beanbag. All students with a red beanbag are in the same group, those with green beanbags make up another group, and so on.

Dividing a Class in Half

To divide a class into two equal groups, have students get toe-to-toe with a partner. For Developmental Level I students, have one partner sit down while the other remains standing. Those standing are asked to go to one area, after which those sitting are then moved to the desired location. With students in Developmental Levels II and III, have one partner raise a hand. Move the students with their hands up to one side of the area.

Creating Small Groups

Another activity for arranging students in groups of a selected size is Whistle Mixer (see page 561). When the whistle is blown a certain number of times, students form groups corresponding to that number and sit down to show that their group has the correct number. Students left out go to the friendship area, find the needed number of members, and move to an open area. After mastering this skill, students will be able to move quickly into groups with the correct number of students. Teachers can use hand signals along with the whistle to show the desired number of students per group.

Creating Circles or Single-File Lines

An effective technique for moving a class into a single-file line or circle is to have students run randomly in the area until a signal is given. On the signal to "fall in," students continue jogging, move toward the perimeter of the area, and fall in line behind someone. Everyone jogs in the same direction as the teacher. As long as students continue to move behind another person, a circle forms automatically. Either you or a student leader can lead the line into an acceptable formation or position.

Another method of moving a class into formation is to ask students to get into various formations without talking. They can use visual signals but cannot ask someone verbally to move. Have groups hustle to see how quickly they can form the acceptable formation. Another method is to hold up a shape drawn on a large card to signal the acceptable formation. Young students learn to visualize shapes through this technique.

Use Squads to Expedite Class Organization

Some teachers find that placing students into squads helps them manage a class effectively. Squads offer a place for students to meet, keep certain students from being together, group students into prearranged teams of equal ability, and make it easier to learn students' names. Here are some guidelines for using squad formation to maximize teaching effectiveness:

1. Squads or groups should be selected so that a child who might be chosen last is not embarrassed. In all cases, avoid using an "auction" approach, where student leaders look over the group and pick their favorites. A fast way to form squads is to use the Whistle Mixer technique described earlier.
2. Designate a location for assembling students into squad formation. On signal, children move to the designated area, with squad leaders in front and the rest of the squad behind.
3. Use squad leaders so that students have an opportunity to learn leadership and following skills among peers. Examples of leadership activities are moving squads to a specific location, leading squads through exercises or introductory activities, and appointing squad members to certain positions in sport activities.
4. The composition of squads can be predetermined. It may be important to have equal representation of the sexes on each squad. Squad makeup may be determined by ability level so that you can quickly organize games with teams of similar ability. Squads can also be used to separate certain students so they will not disrupt the class. Change squad members regularly so students can work with all students in the class.
5. In most cases, an even number of squads should be formed. This allows the class to be broken quickly into halves for games. Dividing a class of 30 students into 6 squads of 5 members ensures a small number of students for each piece of apparatus and minimizes waiting in line for group activities.
6. Using squads should be an exciting activity that encourages movement and creativity. For example, place numbered cones in different locations around the activity area. Write the numbers in a different language, or hide them in a mathematical equation or story problem. When students enter the gym, instruct them to find their squad number and assemble. Another method is to distribute task cards specifying how the squads are arranged. The first squad to follow instructions correctly can be awarded a point or be acknowledged by the rest of the class. Examples of tasks for squads might be arranging the members in a circle, sitting with their hands on their heads, or assuming crab positions in a straight line facing northwest. Task cards can also be used to specify an introductory activity or tell students where to move for the fitness development activity.
7. An effective way to use squads is "home base." Place a number of marking spots on the floor throughout the area. When the teacher calls "home base," the captains quickly find the closest spot, and their squad members line up behind them. If an even number of squads has been created, half of the spots can be put in each half of the area. When "home base" is called, the class quickly divides in half. This is handy for station teaching as well; place a spot at each of the teaching stations and call "home base" to line up a squad at each station.

KNOW STUDENTS' NAMES

Effective class management requires learning the names of your students. Praise, feedback, and correction go unheeded when students are addressed as, "Hey, you!" Develop a system to help you learn names. One approach is to memorize three or four names per class period. Write the names on a note card, and identify those students at the start and throughout the period. At the end of the period, identify the students again. Each time the class meets, continue in this way until you know everyone's name.

Tell students you are trying to learn their names. Ask them to say their name before performing a skill or answering a question. After learning a student's name, you can use it during activities; for example, say, "Mary, it's your turn to jump."

Another approach to learning names is to photograph each class, in squads, and identify students by matching names to the picture. Before class, identify a few students whose names you know and a few you do not know. Set personal goals by calculating the percentage of students whose names you know after each period.

ESTABLISH PRE- AND POST-TEACHING ROUTINES

Children appreciate the security of knowing what to do from the time they enter the instructional area until they leave. Effective teaching demands routine handling of certain procedures. The following situations occur before and after teaching and need to be planned for before the lesson.

Nonparticipation

An efficient system should be devised for identifying children who cannot participate in the lesson. This decision is best made before children arrive at the lesson area and by someone (nurse or classroom teacher) other than the physical education teacher. This avoids a situation in which the physical education teacher encourages students to participate even though they are not supposed to do so because of a medical problem. A note from the classroom teacher or school nurse, listing the names and health problems of those who are to sit out or to take part in modified activity, can be delivered as children enter the room. Accept the information at face value. This avoids the time-consuming procedure of questioning students on the sidelines to determine what the problem is and what the solution should be. A student with a note from home or from a physician should never be allowed to participate without parental permission.

Entering the Teaching Area

Nothing is more difficult than trying to start a class when the children have entered the teaching area in a loud, disorderly way. Meet your class at the door. Explain how students should enter the area and what they are supposed to do. Another successful approach is to have the class enter the area and begin jogging around. On the signal to freeze, students stop and listen as the day's activities are described. Another, less desirable method is to have students enter the area and sit in squads behind their cones or floor markers. Instruction starts when all students are in position. Regardless of the method used, students should enter the area under control and knowing where they are supposed to meet.

When a classroom teacher lets students straggle in late, or brings the entire class in late, it disrupts the instructional process. Discuss the problem of tardiness with the teacher and try to find a solution. Try designating a couple of responsible students in each class to remind the classroom teacher that physical education begins in 5 minutes. Another solution is to designate an area away from the teaching area where classes can assemble, and request that they line up at the gym door as soon as the entire group is ready. Resolve this problem quickly even if it requires asking the school's administrator to intervene.

Starting the Lesson

Students enter the activity area expecting to move. Take advantage of their urge to move by engaging them in some activity before discussing the lesson. Students are more willing to listen after they have participated in vigorous activity. Let them try an activity before instructing them on points of technique; this also gives you an opportunity to assess their performance level. Many students listen to instruction better after trying an activity and finding it difficult to perform correctly.

Closing the Lesson

Following a regular routine for closing the lesson is beneficial. It allows time for closure of the instructional content as well as a procedure for leaving the teaching area. A closing routine helps calm and quiet students and is appreciated by classroom teachers picking up their class. Another way to calm students is to take a few minutes for relaxation activities.

Equipment Procedures

Make students responsible for securing the equipment they use. Teach students how you want them to get the equipment and return it at the end of the lesson. This minimizes the amount of equipment rearrangement you will have to do. Place your equipment around the perimeter of the teaching area so all students have easy access. Using students to assist in distributing and gathering equipment before and after school allows an opportunity to work closely with students who need special attention.

Dealing with Student Behavior Problems

Children who misbehave during class need to be talked with after class. This makes it critical to schedule a minimum of 5 minutes of passing time between classes. Scheduling classes back-to-back makes it impossible to talk with students, rearrange equipment, and take care of personal matters. If time between classes is not available, give a "meeting appointment" form to the classroom teacher and student. This reminds both parties of the student's obligation to meet with you at the end of the school day.

USE EQUIPMENT EFFECTIVELY

When using small equipment such as balls, hoops, and jump ropes, be sure that every student has a piece for personal use. For large equipment or apparatus, establish as many stations or groups as possible. A class of 30 requires a minimum of six benches, mats, or jumping boxes to keep waiting time short. One way to cut students' waiting time is to use return activities (see Chapter 18) so students can perform a task or tasks while returning to their squad.

Teach students where to place the equipment during instruction. Equipment should be in the same (home) position when the class is called to attention. For example, beanbags are placed on the floor, basketballs between the feet, and jump ropes folded and placed behind the neck. Placing the equipment in home position avoids the problem of children striking one another with the equipment, dropping it, or practicing activities when they should be listening. To keep students from playing with the equipment when it is placed on the floor, ask them to take a giant step away from it.

Distribute equipment to students as rapidly as possible. When they have to wait in line for a piece of equipment, time is wasted and behavior problems occur. Many teachers assign student leaders to get the equipment for their squad, but this approach results in many students sitting and waiting. A better and faster method is to have the equipment placed around the perimeter of the area (Figure 6.3). On signal, students move to acquire a piece of equipment, take it to their personal space, and begin practicing an assigned skill. This approach takes advantage of the natural urge to try the equipment and reinforces students who procure equipment quickly.

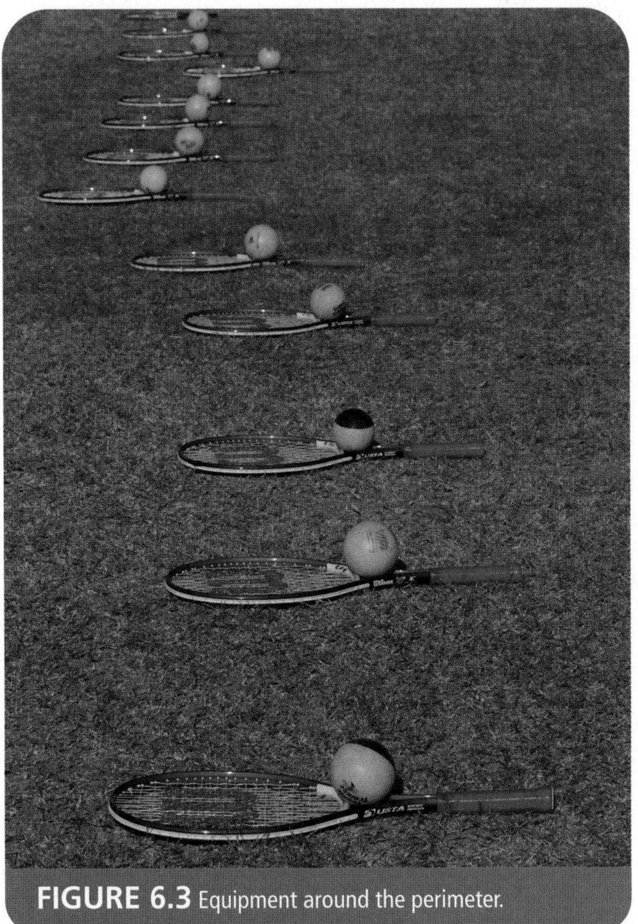

FIGURE 6.3 Equipment around the perimeter.

Use the reverse procedure to put equipment away. Certainly, any method beats the often-used practice of placing the equipment in the middle of the area in a container and having students "run and get a ball." This approach raises children's chances of being aggravated or hurt.

However you have students acquire equipment, clearly explain what to do with the equipment after they get it. Waiting for all students to get equipment before anybody starts using it allows the slowest and least cooperative students to set the pace. Do not make students who have hustled to get their equipment wait for the slowpokes. Let students start practicing as soon as they get their equipment. Interact with those students who are slow and less cooperative while the others are practicing.

TEACH ACCEPTABLE STUDENT BEHAVIOR

There are several ways to teach children socially acceptable behavior. Teaching acceptable behavior has always been a basic reason that societies developed schools in the first place. By implementing a program that focuses on behavior, a school shows parents and students this is an important school outcome. This section outlines several programs used in the physical education setting that focus on acceptable and responsible behavior.

RESPONSIBILITY THROUGH PHYSICAL ACTIVITY

Concern about student behavior and lack of discipline has increased the need to teach responsible behavior to students. Hellison (2003) developed strategies and programs for teaching responsibility skills in a physical education setting. A premise for learning responsible behavior is that it must be planned for, taught, and reinforced. Responsible behavior takes time and practice to learn, much like any other skill.

Levels of Responsible Behavior

Hellison (2003) suggests a hierarchy consisting of five levels of responsible behavior students can learned. The hierarchy, with examples of typical student behavior at each level, is as follows.

Level 0: Irresponsibility

Level 0 students are unmotivated and undisciplined. Their behavior includes discrediting other students' involvement and interrupting, intimidating, manipulating, and verbally or physically abusing other students and perhaps the teacher.

Behavior examples

- At home: Blaming brothers or sisters for problems; lying to parents.
- On the playground: Calling other students names; laughing at others.
- In physical education: Talking to friends when the teacher is giving instructions; pushing and shoving when selecting equipment.

Level 1: Self-Control

Students at this level do not participate in the day's activity or show much mastery or improvement. These students control their behavior enough that they do not interfere with other students' right to learn or the teacher's right to teach.

Behavior examples

- At home: Refraining from hitting a brother or sister even though angry.
- On the playground: Standing and watching others play; not getting angry at others because they did something to upset them.
- In physical education: Waiting until an appropriate time to talk with friends; having control and not letting others' behavior bother them.

Level 2: Involvement

These students show self-control and are involved in the subject matter or activity.

Behavior examples

- At home: Helping clean up the dishes after dinner; taking out the trash.
- On the playground: Playing with others; participating in a game.
- In physical education: Listening and performing activities; trying even when they dislike an activity; doing an activity without complaining or saying, "I can't."

Level 3: Self-Responsibility

Level 3 students take responsibility for their choices and for linking these choices to their own identities. They are able to work without direct supervision, eventually taking responsibility for their intentions and actions.

Behavior examples

- At home: Cleaning up without being asked.
- On the playground: Returning equipment after recess.
- In physical education: Following directions; practicing a skill without being told; trying new activities without encouragement.

Level 4: Caring

Students behaving at this level are motivated to extend their sense of responsible behavior by cooperating, giving support, showing concern, and helping.

Behavior examples

- At home: Helping take care of a younger brother or sister or a pet.
- On the playground: Asking others (not just friends) to join them in play.
- In physical education: Helping someone who is having trouble; helping a new student feel welcome; working with all students; showing that all people are worthwhile.

Responsible behavior is taught by using various strategies. Post the levels of responsibility in the teaching area. Explain the different levels of behavior, and identify acceptable behaviors at each level. Finally, implement the program by reinforcing acceptable behavior and redirecting inappropriate behavior. The program is based on this two-pronged approach: (1) catch students using responsible behavior and reinforce them; and (2) redirect students behaving at level 0 by asking, "At what level are you performing, and what level would be more acceptable?" An example is the following discussion between teacher and student:

You see a student behaving at level 0 and open dialogue with the student in a nonconfrontational and nonadversarial manner:

"Johnny, it appeared you were making fun of someone."

"I wasn't making fun of anyone!"

"Maybe not, but if you were, what level of behavior would it be?"

"Zero!"

"Is that the kind of person you want to be or the level of behavior you want to show?"

"No!"

"If you were at level 0, do you think you could make some changes? Perhaps you could move to level 1 and have self-control even if someone else makes you mad or even if you do not like that person."

Strategies for Increasing Responsible Behavior

Teacher feedback forms the core of the responsibility approach, but there are many ways to increase responsible behavior in the instructional setting. Here are some strategies that can be used:

- *Model acceptable behavior.* How you interact with students encourages responsible behavior. Students do not care about how much you know until they know how much you care. Treat children with dignity and respect, and follow through with responsible action and words. In return, expect students to treat you and others with the same dignity and respect.

- *Use reinforcement.* Give students specific feedback about the quality of their behavior. When giving corrective feedback, make sure it identifies the acceptable level of behavior. If you are reinforcing acceptable behavior, explain why the behavior is acceptable and say that you appreciate it. In some cases, it may be beneficial to identify a super-citizen or give a "happy-gram" for special behavior.
- *Offer time for responsibility and reflection.* Give students time to think about the attitudes and behaviors associated with each of the levels. Ask them to fill out a self-responsibility checklist (Figure 6.4) at different times of the year.
- *Allow student sharing.* Let students give their opinions about responsible behavior. Accept all students' feelings as important. Focus on ways to encourage higher levels of responsible behavior. Brainstorming with your students to identify consequences of high and low behavior is effective. Another practice is to ask different students to give examples of responsible behavior at different levels. Give students time to share how they feel when someone uses a high- or low-level behavior around them.
- *Encourage goal setting.* Help students set goals for responsible behavior they want to exhibit. This can be done at the start of the lesson by asking students to tell a partner the behavior they want to use today. At the end of the lesson, partners evaluate each other to see if the behavior was exhibited. Examples of behaviors are listening, hustling, following directions, being courteous, and complimenting others.
- *Offer opportunities for responsibility.* Students often can be given responsibility in a class setting. Being a group leader, team captain, referee, score keeper, rule maker, or dispute resolver are roles that encourage students to exhibit high-level behavior. Since responsible positions affect other students, effective leaders have to behave responsibly.
- *Allow student choice.* Responsible behavior is best learned when students make choices. The natural consequences of self-selected choices are often the best teachers. Students can choose games, decide on fitness activities, and select partners. Discussion about how to make meaningful health choices (see Chapter 14) is an important phase of learning to make responsible choices.

My Self-Responsibility Checklist

Name: ____________________
Date: ____________________

Self-control:

__________ I did not call others names.
__________ I had self-control when I became mad.
__________ I listened when others were talking.
__________ Other (describe) __________

Involvement:

__________ I listened to all directions before starting.
__________ I was willing to try all activities.
__________ I tried activities even when I didn't like them.
__________ Other (describe) __________

Self-Responsibility:

__________ I followed directions without being told more than once.
__________ I did not blame others.
__________ I worked on activities by myself.
__________ Other (describe) __________

Caring:

__________ I helped someone today.
__________ I said something nice to someone.
__________ I asked someone to do something with me.
__________ Other (describe) __________

FIGURE 6.4 Example of a responsibility checklist.

TEACHER-DIRECTED CONFLICT RESOLUTION

Conflict between students can result in aggression and violence. About one in seven children is either a bully or a victim (Beane, 1999). Nobody wants to create a world where the strong dominate and the weak live in fear and submission. Conflict is a part of daily life, and children should understand that they must deal with it effectively. Students can learn ways to respect others' opinions and feelings while maintaining their own worth and dignity.

Conflicts are solved in various ways, but the most common methods involve three types of behavior—dominating, appeasing, and cooperating. Students who use the dominating style are often unsure about their standing in the group. They want things done their way but are afraid others will reject them. They often lack confidence and try hard to get others to accept their way of doing things. Students who are appeasers lack confidence but want to be accepted by others. They do not like conflict and are willing to set aside their feelings to placate others.

Neither the dominating nor the appeasing approach for solving conflicts is effective in the long run. No one likes to be dominated or put in the position of having to appease others. Conflict resolution can help students learn to solve conflicts peacefully and with no apparent losers. This strategy takes a cooperative approach to solving problems. Cooperation often builds positive feelings between students and leads to better group cohesiveness. The following steps are typically used to resolve conflicts, and they are effective with younger children or children inexperienced in conflict resolution. If children are experienced in conflict resolution, they may be able to carry out the steps without instructor intervention.

1. *Stop the aggressive behavior immediately.* Separate students in conflict immediately, and give them an opportunity to cool down. Time-out boxes are an excellent place to send students to relax and unwind.
2. *Gather data about what happened, and define the problem.* Ask what happened, who was involved, and how each child is feeling. Ask open-ended questions such as, "What happened?" and "How did you feel about . . . ?" to help students talk freely about the problem.
3. *Brainstorm possible solutions.* Keep in mind that brainstorming is a nonjudgmental process that accepts all solutions regardless of their perceived value. Encourage students to think of as many options as possible by asking open-ended questions such as, "How could we solve this problem?" or "What other ways could we deal with this?"
4. *Test the solutions generated through brainstorming.* Ask a question such as, "What solutions might work best?" Help students understand the implications of the solutions and how the solutions can be implemented. Accept solutions that may differ from your way of solving the problem.
5. *Help implement the plan.* Walk students through the solution to help them understand the approach. Guide them through the steps by asking, "Who goes first?" and "Who will take the next step?" As the solution is implemented, it may need to be changed. Any changes can be agreed on by the involved students.
6. *Evaluate the approach.* Observe to make sure the plan is accomplishing the accepted outcome. Encourage students to change the plan again if necessary.

The conflict resolution process takes practice and time. It demands certain behaviors from the instructor and an objective approach to resolution. Good listening to both parties is necessary. Both sides of the problem must be explored, and students must feel as though the process was equitable. This process does not place blame, which only encourages defensive behavior such as appeasing or being aggressive. Students must trust that the process will be equitable and objective and that they will get a fair shake if they deal with the issue cooperatively.

PEER MEDIATION

Peer mediation is similar to conflict resolution except that it is student directed. Students resolve their own disputes and conflicts, and a neutral peer acts as moderator. In peer mediation, the goal is to work out differences constructively. Mediation gets students involved in the problem-solving process, either as mediators or disputants, and teaches them a way of handling conflicts. A text by Cohen (2005) is an excellent resource for a step-by-step approach to student peer mediation.

Students are trained to help their classmates identify the problems behind the conflicts and find solutions. Peer mediation is not about who is right or wrong. Instead, students are encouraged to move beyond the immediate conflict and learn to get along with each other. Peer mediators ask the disputing students to tell their stories and ask the students questions for clarification.

A key component to any mediation process is letting all students tell their own story, so they feel as if someone understands their perspective. Common situations involving name calling, spreading rumors, bumping into students in the hallways, and bullying are often best resolved through peer mediation. There are two parts to the mediation process: establishing ground rules and following the steps of mediation.

Ground Rules

All parties (including the mediator) participate in reviewing, and agreeing to follow, the ground rules. When agreement is reached, mediation begins. Students must agree to these basic ground rules:

- *The problem will be solved.* Participants must agree that a solution will be found in the session. It is not acceptable to leave without solving the problem.
- *The truth will be told.* Students must agree to tell the truth regardless of its effect on the situation. Since students are solving the problem without adult supervision and the session is confidential, telling the truth will not result in negative consequences.
- *The full story will be heard without interruption.* Both parties must be able to tell their side of the story without interruption. Each person should feel that their side of the story is completely and fairly presented.
- *All parties will act in a respectful manner.* Students need to learn to state their case without excessive emotion and anger.
- *All discussion will be confidential.* Both the arbitrator and the parties in conflict agree not to discuss the situation with nonparticipants.
- *The solution will be implemented.* Both parties will carry out the agreement regardless of whom the solution favors.

Mediation Steps

When the ground rules are agreed on, mediation led by a trained peer begins. The problem is not discussed while reviewing ground rules. The mediation steps are about solving the actual problem and doing so in a manner dictated by the ground rules students agreed to follow. Here are the steps to finding a mediated solution:

- *Tell your story or grievance.* Both students have a chance to tell their side of the story. This should be an opportunity to "lay it on the table" and feel that the problem is clearly understood by both the other party and the mediator.
- *Verify the story.* The mediator and the other party have the opportunity to ask questions to clarify and verify the story. The mediator is responsible for finding out exactly what happened and how each party feels.
- *Discuss the conflict.* The mediator conducts a discussion about the situation and the emotions involved.
- *Brainstorm solutions to the problem.* All parties discuss various ways to solve the problem. The mediator emphasizes the need to find solutions that resolve the situation for both parties.
- *Discuss and implement the agreed-upon solution.* Both parties have already agreed to follow the ground rules. One rule was to solve the problem, so it is not acceptable to leave without a solution.
- *Sign a contract.* After agreeing to a solution, the offended parties must sign a contract agreeing to carry out the solution.

USE BEHAVIOR MANAGEMENT TO INCREASE ACCEPTABLE BEHAVIOR

Positive discipline focuses on reinforcing acceptable behavior by acknowledging a child's positive attributes. Increasing positive behavior may help reduce negative behavior because the student receives more feedback and attention. Lavay et al. (2006) provide an excellent resource for taking a systematic approach to positive behavior management. This section presents an action plan for modifying and maintaining acceptable behavior. The program involves three phases: (1) increasing acceptable behavior; (2) prompting acceptable behavior; and (3) sharing acceptable behavior. One note here: It is usually best to think of behavior as *acceptable* and *unacceptable* rather than *positive* and *negative*. *Unacceptable* and *acceptable* speak only to the behavior, not the child. Positive and negative behavior can easily be interpreted by the child as good and bad. This starts to characterize the child as good or bad, which is never an effective or constructive approach for improving student behavior.

INCREASE ACCEPTABLE BEHAVIOR

"Catch them doing what you want them to do" is one secret to increasing acceptable behavior. Behavior that is followed by appropriate positive reinforcement will occur more often in the future. This principle is the key for increasing acceptable behavior. Its strength is that it focuses on positive, acceptable educational outcomes. Key points for implementing the principle lie in deciding what to use as reinforcers, selecting those that effectively reinforce individuals, and properly using the reinforcers.

Social Reinforcers

Teachers most often use this class of reinforcers when students perform acceptable behavior. Well before starting school, most children experience an environment filled with social reinforcers. Parents use praise, physical contact, and facial expressions to acknowledge children's acceptable behavior. Here are some reinforcers that can be used with students in a physical education setting:

Words of Praise

Great job.	Nice going.
Exactly right.	I really like that job.
Perfect arm placement.	That's the best one yet.
Way to go!	Nice hustle.

Physical Expressions

Smiling	Holding a clenched fist overhead
Nodding	Clapping
Giving thumbs-up	
Winking	

Physical Contact

Handshake	High five

Find out what type of social reinforcers students are accustomed to responding to in the school setting. Certain reinforcers may embarrass students or make them uncomfortable. For example, some students may not want to be touched, even to the point of receiving a high five. Students, particularly those of the opposite sex, may incorrectly interpret a hug or pat on the back. If you are unsure, ask the school administrator to clarify which social reinforcers can be used.

Activity Reinforcers

Various types of activities that children enjoy can be used as reinforcement. To determine activities that can be used as reinforcers, see what children do during their free time. Activities that will reinforce a class include offering free time to practice a skill, the opportunity to play a game, and extra time in physical education class. Also consider having some children help administer equipment, act as teacher's aides, be peer teachers in a cross-aged tutoring situation, or serve as team captains. Students might receive special privileges such as being "student of the day," getting to choose the game to play, or having lunch with the teacher.

Token Reinforcers

Because physical education is closely related to athletic competition, where winners often receive awards and trophies, many teachers feel a need to offer some type of token as a reinforcer. The less favorable aspect of giving tokens (points, ribbons, or certificates) is that when only the winners get them, other students are less likely to be motivated to perform in the future. Some teachers give participation certificates or ribbons to all students; however, this gives the token little reinforcement value. In addition, some studies show that extrinsic rewards may actually decrease a child's intrinsic desire to participate (Greene & Lepper, 1975; Whitehead & Corbin, 1991). Token reinforcers work best with primary-grade children, who are motivated by receiving the tokens. However, after the age of 9, students begin to see tokens as a form of bribery to behave in a certain manner. Generally, it is best to use token reinforcers only if it appears that social reinforcers are ineffective.

Selecting Reinforcers

Teachers frequently ask, "How do I know what will be reinforcing to my students?" Fortunately, most children respond to praise, attention, smiles, games, free time, and privileges. A practical way to identify effective reinforcers is to observe children during free time, analyzing the things they enjoy doing. Another simple solution is to ask them what they would like to do. Most children will tell you that they would like more recess, free time, or other enjoyable activity.

Using Social Reinforcers

Effective use of social reinforcers requires giving praise and making positive statements. You may feel uncomfortable when learning to offer students positive reinforcement because such behavior feels inauthentic. Teachers learning how to reinforce often say, "I do not feel real, and children think I'm not sincere." Any change in communication patterns feels uncomfortable at first. Trying new ways of communicating with a class requires a period of adjustment. New patterns of praise and reinforcement often feel contrived and insincere (fortunately, most students do not know the difference), and there is no way to avoid the discomfort. Teachers who are unwilling to experience the uneasiness of learning usually do not change. Do not assume that patterns of speech you learned as a child are effective in an instructional setting. Teachers are made, not born; success comes with hard work and dedication. If practiced regularly, new behavioral patterns can become a natural part of your repertoire.

Praise is effective when it refers to specific behavior exhibited by a student. Avoid using general statements such as, "Good job" or "You are an excellent performer." Nonspecific statements do not tell a student what he did well. They leave the student wondering what you meant. If the student's thoughts do not align with your intent, incorrect behavior may be reinforced. To improve the specificity and effectiveness of feedback, describe the behavior to be reinforced rather than judging it. This reinforces the student and tells the other students what behavior you expect. For example, compare these statements.

> *Describing:* "I saw your excellent forward roll, James; you tucked your head just right."
>
> *Judging:* "That's not how I told you to do it. You can do better."

In the first example, the student is identified and the specific behavior performed is reinforced. In the second situation, it is impossible to identify what the behavior is or who is getting the feedback. In most cases, if a question can be asked about delivered praise or criticism (such as what was good, or why the performance was incorrect), the feedback is nonspecific and open to misinterpretation. To increase acceptable behavior, verbally or physically describe what made the performance effective, good, or noteworthy. This reinforces the student and communicates to the rest of the class what behavior is expected by the instructor.

The Premack Principle

The Premack principle (Premack, 1965) is often used unknowingly to motivate students. This principle states that a highly desirable activity can be used to motivate students to learn an activity they enjoy less. In practice, this principle allows students to participate in a favorite activity after performing a less enjoyable one. The Premack principle is often called the "Eat your peas if you want dessert" rule. Here are some examples of the Premack principle in use:

- "You may shoot baskets [preferred] after you complete the passing drill [less desirable]."
- "When everybody is quiet [less desirable], we will begin the game [preferred]."
- "Those who raise their hand [less desirable] will be selected to answer the question [preferred]."

PROMPT ACCEPTABLE BEHAVIOR

Prompts are used to remind students to perform acceptable behavior. They encourage development of new patterns of behavior. Here are some common ways to prompt children in the physical education setting.

1. *Modeling.* You or a student performs the acceptable behavior with the expectation that the other students will respond similarly. For example, placing your piece of equipment on the floor when stopping a class reminds the class to do likewise. Modeling is an effective prompt for acceptable behavior because young students emulate their teacher.
2. *Verbal cues.* Using cues like "Hustle" and "Keep going" reminds students about acceptable behavior. Verbal cues can help maintain the lesson pace, increase the performance level, or motivate students to stay on task.
3. *Nonverbal cues.* Many physical cues are given through body language to communicate concepts like "Hustle," "Move over here," "Great performance," "Quiet down," and so on. When learning skills, students can take nonverbal physical cues to move into proper position, follow the correct pattern, or properly align body parts.

Avoid using prompts so much that students will not perform without them. The process of gradually removing the prompt so that behavior is self-motivated is called *fading.* Though you are likely to keep giving some prompts, use the weakest (least intrusive) prompt possible to stimulate the behavior. Instead of a prompt, you could give students a long lecture about the importance of staying on task; but lectures are time-consuming, unsuited for repetitive use, and ineffective in the long run. Select a short, distinctive cue that students can easily identify with the acceptable skill.

Also be sure that the prompt identifies the task being prompted. If you prompt the class to "hustle" and the prompt is not tied to an acceptable behavior, there may be confusion. Some children may think your prompt means to perform the skill as fast as possible; others may think it means to stop what they are doing and hustle to the teacher. So students clearly understand your prompt, use it consistently to stimulate the desired behavior.

Create colorful posters that clearly outline your safety procedures and post them in the activity space. Review the rules as necessary with your students through warm-up activities and games.

SHAPE ACCEPTABLE BEHAVIOR

When behavior is unacceptable, use shaping techniques—extinction and reinforcement—to create new behavior. Two steps are followed when shaping behavior.

1. *Use differential reinforcement to increase the incidence of acceptable behavior.* Reinforce responses that reach a predetermined criterion, and ignore those that do not meet the criterion (extinction). For example, suppose you want students to put their equipment on the floor within 5 seconds after a signal. Using differential reinforcement, reinforce the students whenever they meet the 5-second criterion and ignore their performance when it takes longer than 5 seconds.
2. *Expand the criterion that must be reached for reinforcement to occur.* This step involves gradually shifting the criterion toward the desired goal. If the acceptable behavior is for the class to get quiet within 5 seconds after receiving a signal, you may have to start with a 12-second interval. Why the longer interval? It is unreasonable to expect an inattentive class to quiet down quickly. If you start with a 5-second interval, you and your students will most likely fail to meet the criterion. What's more, students will not often achieve this stringent standard of behavior, giving you few opportunities to reinforce them. Consequently, you and the class feel unsuccessful. To avoid this outcome, expand the criterion by starting with a 12-second interval. When the class reaches this goal, shift to 10 seconds and ask the class to perform to this new standard. Repeat the process gradually until the class reaches the 5-second interval.

Changing behavior can be accomplished in a similar way by taking a systematic approach to behavior modification. Figure 6.5 on page 110 offers a step-by-step plan for changing unacceptable behavior.

6

DECREASE UNACCEPTABLE BEHAVIOR WITH DISCIPLINE

Corrective feedback and the use of consequences can be effective in decreasing unacceptable behavior. Consequences are actions that follow misbehavior and teach students that their behavior results in some action from the environment, peers, or teacher.

USE CORRECTIVE FEEDBACK

First, as described earlier, try using positive reinforcement to increase acceptable behavior so it will replace unacceptable behavior. If a skilled student is always criticizing less able children, ask him to help others and serve as a student assistant. The intent is to teach him to deliver positive, constructive feedback rather than criticism. An effective rule of thumb before using corrective feedback is to reinforce the acceptable (desired) behavior twice. For example, assume a child is slow to stop on signal, while most other students are stopping and listening properly. Ask the class to move and freeze again. Reinforce students who are on task. (With older students, reinforce the class as a whole rather than

Changing behavior can be done if teachers are willing to experiment and be patient. Teachers want to change behavior quickly and on the spot and at times make incorrect decisions because they don't have time to think of an effective solution. In-class misbehavior can be temporarily stopped, but may often go unchanged for the future. Realize that change will require long-term action that must be planned ahead of time. The following steps can be used to develop a plan for changing behavior:

- Identify a single behavior that needs to be changed, improved, or strengthened. Don't pick more than one behavior as it will make it much more difficult to monitor change.
- Identify a behavior that will be substituted for the behavior to be changed.
- Determine what positively reinforces the student. Have a discussion with the student to see what is reinforcing.
- Decide whether a negative reinforcer is needed to give momentum to the change process.
- Develop a plan for getting the desired behavior to occur. This will generate a behavior that can be reinforced and used to replace the undesirable behavior.
- Put the plan into effect and set a time frame for evaluation of the plan. Decide what modifications are needed to make the plan more effective. This modification may demand a different set or schedule of reinforcers or negative consequences. If an entirely different plan is needed (because the behavior hasn't decreased or changed), make such changes and proceed.
- Continue evaluating and modifying the plan.

FIGURE 6.5 A plan for changing misbehavior.

individuals.) If the result is not acceptable, try it again. In primary-grade classes, misbehaving students frequently emulate those who are being reinforced. If not, you may have to use corrective feedback.

Corrective feedback should be clear and specific. Students must know exactly what behavior they are to stop and what acceptable behavior they are to start. Use corrective feedback as soon after the misbehavior as possible, and deliver positive reinforcement immediately following the acceptable behavior.

After being disciplined or corrected—especially if such feedback is not delivered correctly—students may respond negatively and disrupt the class. Whether delivering corrective feedback or consequences, use these steps to avoid teacher–student conflicts that embarrass students and yourself.

1. *Do not address the student publicly.* Raising your voice at a student and calling her out across the room seldom improves things. Buy some time to talk with the student privately by giving the class a task to perform. It may be as simple as jogging around the area or quickly asking them to pick their equipment and practice a task. While they are engaged, you are in control and have time to discuss the situation quietly with the misbehaving student.
2. *Isolate the student and yourself.* Do not correct a student where others can hear what you are saying. The problem is a private matter between you and the student.
3. *Deal with one student at a time.* Often, a few students are misbehaving together. Separate them and deal with their unacceptable behavior one-on-one. If you do not separate them, they may form a consensus of opinion about what happened that disagrees with your perceptions.
4. *State your position once; repeat it once if you believe the student did not understand.* Do not argue or try to prove your point. Take no more than 10 or 15 seconds to tell the student the unacceptable behavior and state the acceptable behavior you would like to see.
5. *Deliver and move away.* Avoid glaring at a student when delivering corrective feedback. Such behavior is confrontational to older students. Walk up behind them and softly deliver your feedback. Walk away after you have delivered the feedback. By walking away, you show the offenders that you are not interested in discussing what they have to say. Do not eyeball a student after reprimanding him—you may see things you don't want to see. Get yourself back on track by positively reinforcing one or two students who are performing the acceptable behavior.
6. *Do not threaten or bully the student.* This tactic builds resentment in students and may cause greater problems in the future.
7. *Avoid touching the student when correcting behavior.* Even if you have positive intentions, touching can send mixed messages. Some students do not want to be touched and will aggressively pull away and make a scene in front of the class.
8. *Do not curse or raise your voice excessively.* Avoid using sarcasm. Instead, clearly state the acceptable behavior you expect the student to exhibit.

When corrective feedback fails to change unacceptable behavior, students need to understand that such behavior brings negative consequences. Becoming responsible for one's behavior may be the most important social behavior learned from the school experience. Consequences of unacceptable behavior include reprimands, removal of positive consequences, and time-out.

Try Reprimands

Reprimands are commonly used to decrease unacceptable behavior. If given in a caring and constructive way, they can serve as effective reminders to behave.

- Identify the unacceptable behavior, state briefly why it is unacceptable, and communicate to students what behavior is acceptable. For example, "You were talking while I was speaking. It is unacceptable behavior and bothers me and other students, so please listen to me."

- Do not reprimand in front of other students. It embarrasses students and can diminish their self-esteem. When students feel belittled, they may lash out and behave even more unacceptably.
- Speak about behavior, not the person, when reprimanding. Ask that the behavior stop rather than telling a student that "You are always causing problems in this class." Avoid general and negative statements related to the student's personality.
- After reprimanding and asking for acceptable behavior, reinforce it when it occurs. Be vigilant in looking for the acceptable behavior since reinforcing such behavior will cause it to occur more often in the future.

Remove Positive Consequences

Parents often use this tactic when their children misbehave, so many students are familiar with it. The idea is to remove something positive from the student when misbehavior occurs. For example, have students who misbehave give up some of their free time, lose grade points, or sit out an activity they enjoy. This approach is not effective unless students really value the privilege or activity removed. Here are a few key principles for using this technique:

- *Be sure that the magnitude of the removal fits the crime.* Children who commit a minor infraction should not have to miss recess for a week.
- *Be consistent in removal, treating all students and occurrences the same.* Students believe teachers are unfair if they are more severe with one student than another. In addition, a student penalized for a specific misbehavior should receive the same penalty for a later repetition.
- *Make sure students understand the consequences of their misbehavior before receiving the penalties.* This avoids applying penalties in an emotional, unthinking way. Students who know the consequences are choosing to accept the penalty for misbehaving.
- *Chart a student's misbehavior to see if the frequency is decreasing.* Regardless of the method used, if the behavior is not decreasing—or is increasing—change methods until a decrease in frequency occurs.

Use Time-Out from Reinforcement

The time-out procedure is an equitable technique for dealing with children in a manner consistent with social values. Rules are clearly posted, and consequences are clear and easy to comprehend. Teachers find time-out effective for dealing with unacceptable behavior that occurs randomly on an individual basis. During time-out, students who misbehave leave the class setting and go to a designated area for a specific time. *Time-out* means "time out from reinforcement." It does not mean the student is a "bad person," only that she has behaved unacceptably and needs a time-out to reconsider and redirect the misbehavior. When placing students in time-out, tell children they are acceptable individuals, but their misbehavior is unacceptable.

Most students receive time-out because they have disrupted the class and must be removed so the class can continue without interruption. Children also can voluntarily use the time-out area as a "cooling off" spot when they become angry, embarrassed, or frustrated. Students who are on time-out for fighting or arguing should be at opposite ends of the area so the behavior does not escalate. After the time-out, they should stay in their half (or quadrant) of the teaching area for the rest of the class period. This prevents recurring agitation between the two combatants and the possibility of increased hostility.

6

Discuss your time-out plan with students so they know exactly what constitutes acceptable and unacceptable behavior as well as the consequences of misbehaving. Be sure to post a list of acceptable behavior (rules) and consequences for unacceptable behavior. A point here is necessary: some teachers want to have students stay in the time-out area for 5 minutes before returning. That is fine if you have a way to keep track of the time. However, it is difficult to manage when several children go to time-out at different times. Some teachers use the "You can return when I say you can" method. The problem with this approach is that it is arbitrary, and you may leave a student in time-out longer than you had planned. Also, if a student is a chronic offender, you may leave her in time-out longer for the same behavior than you would a student who seldom misbehaves. This sends a message that you have favorites and like some students better than others. An effective behavior management system should be fair and consistent.

Time-out does not change behavior if the child is reinforced by this consequence. Time-out means receiving *as little* reinforcement as possible. If class participation is a negative experience for students, taking them out of class will be a positive consequence. The physical location for time-out must be considered to make it effective. If the teacher—thinking it is a good location for time-out—sends a misbehaving student to the office, the student may find some of her friends there. The student thus avoids participating in class, and she gets to visit with friends. Another example: in our society, being a spectator is highly reinforcing. People will pay high prices to watch others play sports or act. For some students, sitting at the side of the teaching area and looking on as a spectator may be more reinforcing than participating in class activities. If you put someone in time-out, make sure he is not facing the class and interacting with

FIGURE 6.6 Student assigned to time-out.

peers (Figure 6.6). *Remember—if students do not enjoy being in class, time-out does not work.*

Consequences for Unacceptable Behavior

Just as with rules, consequences for unacceptable behavior should be listed and posted in the area. Discuss each of the consequences until you reach general class consensus that the rules are fair and necessary. A possible set of consequences for unacceptable behavior follows.

First Misbehavior The student is warned quietly that the unacceptable behavior must stop. Students are not always aware that they are bothering others, and a gentle reminder will refocus them. A private conversation with the student might be as follows: "John, you were talking while I was talking. That is unacceptable behavior. I will appreciate you listening in the future. This is your first warning."

Second Misbehavior The student goes to a time-out spot and stays there until ready to return and behave acceptably. Place time-out stations in each of the four corners of the instructional area. When outdoors, delineate the instructional area with four cones and place a time-out sign on each cone. It is acceptable for the student to go to the time-out area and return immediately to physical education class, but the assumption is that the student has agreed to behave properly.

Third Misbehavior The student goes to the time-out area for the rest of the period. Each time a student starts a new class, he should receive a fresh start on the consequences. It is fairly common to hear a teacher tell a student at the start of class, "If you do one thing wrong, you are going to time-out for the rest of the period." This student is then treated differently from all the other students. It is hard to establish a positive relationship with a student if he feels you are unfair or uncaring.

If the unacceptable behavior continues each time the class meets, most schools have an in-school suspension program to deal with severe behavior. In-school suspension requires the student to leave her class of students and move into another room of students (of a different grade level). This ensures that she receives little, if any, reinforcement. The foregoing steps assume that you have communicated with the student about her unacceptable behavior and how she is expected to behave.

If these consequences are ineffective, the next alternative is to talk with the principal about more serious consequences. The last alternative is to call in the parents for a conference with you and the principal. Use discretion when deciding to call parents. Doing so may further alienate you from the student because of parental pressure and punishment at home. Another possibility is that parents will disagree with your assessment. If parents cannot or will not support you, dealing with the behavior in a school setting may be a better option. Along the same lines, do not ask the principal to solve all your problems with misbehaving students. The principal will soon come to believe that you cannot effectively manage students. Ultimately, your behavior will erode the principal's confidence in your teaching ability.

Safety Tip

Avoid using physical activity, such as running laps, for punishment. You may not be aware of a student's health issues that could be triggered by excessive or unusual activity.

IMPLEMENT BEHAVIOR CONTRACTS WITH OLDER STUDENTS

A behavior contract is a written statement specifying certain student behaviors that must occur for students to earn certain rewards or privileges. The contract is drawn up after a private conference to decide on appropriate behaviors and rewards. It is agreed upon and signed by the student and teacher. This approach allows students to make decisions that will improve their own behavior.

The behavior contract may be a successful strategy for intermediate-grade students with severe behavior problems. Every attempt should be made to find activities in physical education class (such as Frisbee play, jump-rope games, aerobics, or basketball) that are naturally rewarding. If this is not possible, different types of rewards may have to be used. For example, a student who is interested in music could be allowed to spend some time selecting CDs or tapes to be used for class during the next week. As behavior improves and the student's attitude becomes more positive, rewards should be switched to physical education activities. The contract is gradually phased out as the child gains control of the behavior and can participate in normal class environments.

Contracts can be written for a small group of students or for an entire class with similar problems, but teachers must be careful about setting up a reward system for too many students. The system can become too complex or time-consuming to supervise properly. The contract is best used with a limited number of students who have severe problems. Examples of behavior contracts are shown in Figures 6.7 and 6.8. The contract in Figure 6.8 can be used with an individual, a small group, or an entire class of students.

INCORPORATE BEHAVIOR GAMES FOR OVERALL CLASS BEHAVIOR

Behavior games are an effective strategy for changing class behavior in the areas of management, motivation, and discipline. These activities use the shaping technique and are useful in changing whole-class behavior (in contrast to individual student behavior). If you are having problems in any of these areas, a well-conceived behavior game may quickly turn the situation around. These games can be organized so a group of students compete against each other or against an established criterion. The goal of the game is to use group contingencies to develop behaviors that enhance the learning environment and to eliminate behaviors that detract from the environment.

The following behavior game was used successfully with sixth graders in an effort to improve management behaviors.

1. Divide the class into four to six squads. Each squad has a designated color for identification. Mark a starting area by arranging four boundary cones in appropriate colors.
2. The rules of the game are as follows:
   - **a.** Each squad member must be ready for activity and in proper position at a designated starting time. *Reward:* 2 points.
   - **b.** Each squad member must move from one activity to another activity within the specified time (10, 20, or 30 seconds) and begin the appropriate behavior. *Reward:* 1 point for each activity.
   - **c.** Each point earned is rewarded with 1 minute of free activity time on Friday. Free activity time includes basketball, Frisbee playing, rope jumping, or any other activity popular with students.
   - **d.** The squad with the most points for the week earns a bonus of 5 points.
3. Explain the allotted time for each management episode (10, 20, or 30 seconds), and give a "go" signal. At the end of the time, give the signal for "stop" and award points for appropriate behavior.
4. Successful squads are praised and their points recorded on a small card. Unsuccessful squads are not hassled or criticized, just reminded that they did not earn a point.
5. On Fridays, award the appropriate squads the special free-time activities while the other squads continue with the regularly scheduled class activities.

Date:__________

I, ____________________, agree to follow the rules listed below:

1. Listen when the teacher is talking.
2. Do not touch others during class.

If all the rules are followed during physical education class, I will earn 10 minutes of basketball activity for myself and a friend after school on Thursday anytime between 3:00 and 3:45.

Signed: ______________________________, Student

Signed: ______________________________, Teacher

FIGURE 6.7 Individual behavior contract.

Group Behavior Contract

Our squad agrees to follow the rules listed below:

1. Listen when the teacher is talking.
2. Take care of the equipment.
3. Treat others as we would like to be treated.

One point is earned each time the music stops and every member of the squad is following the rules. No points are awarded if one or more members of the squad are not following the rules. Each point is worth 1 minute of free activity time to be awarded every other Friday.

Signed: Squad Number ________________ ________________

______________________________ ________________

______________________________ ________________

______________________________ ________________

FIGURE 6.8 Group behavior contract.

6. Slowly phase out (fade) the game as students begin to manage themselves more quickly.

Research used to evaluate behavior games showed these results:

- The use of group contingencies and free-time activities reduced overall class management time.
- The free-time activities were within the physical education curriculum objectives and served as a break from regular activities.
- The free-time activities gave the teacher an opportunity to interact with students on a personal level.
- Students enjoyed the competition and the feeling of success when they behaved appropriately.
- Students enjoyed the free times with novelty activities.
- The positive approach of the game seemed to improve the overall teaching–learning atmosphere. Students were more attentive and cooperative.
- Teachers estimated that more time was available for instruction due to decreased management time.

When designing behavior games, be sure to structure them so that any student or squad is able to win the game. Each game need not generate one winner and many losers. Be aware that one or two students may find it reinforcing to cause their team to lose the behavior game. They will try to break every game rule to make sure that their team loses consistently. In these cases, hold a special team discussion with a vote to eliminate those students from the team and the game. These students are then sent to a time-out area or to in-school suspension. They can be asked to sit out the rest of the behavior game.

Another effective behavior game can be used to help students persist at learning activities in a station-type approach. Often, four to six learning stations are used for instruction. Performance objectives or learning tasks are posted at each station for students to practice. However, some students may not be motivated and will not use their time productively until you rotate to the station where they are working. Overall, this environment is unproductive, and you will quickly tire of hassling unmotivated students. A possible solution to this situation is the following game:

1. Divide the class into four to six squads. Let the students pick a name for their squad.
2. Set up the learning stations with the activities to be practiced. Each squad needs its own learning station.
3. Program a cassette tape with popular music. Intersperse short gaps of silence throughout the tape.
4. Inform students that if everyone in their squad is properly engaged in practicing the appropriate task, the squad will earn a point at each gap in the music. If one or more persons are not engaged, the point will not be awarded.
5. Exchange points for minutes of time in selected activities such as Frisbee play, juggling, or rope jumping. Fridays can be designated as reward days, when the accumulated time is used.
6. Change the music regularly. Also change and slowly increase the intervals between gaps until the gaps are eliminated. The music then serves as a discriminative cue for future practice time.

Students enjoy exercising and practicing skills while listening to music. The music enhances the motivational level and productivity of the environment. Students can be allowed to bring their own music as a special reward for productive behavior. (Make sure the music is not offensive to others due to sexual, ethnic, or religious connotations.)

USE CRITICISM SPARINGLY

Use criticism and punishment with caution and good judgment. Criticism is sometimes used with the belief that it will improve student performance. Some teachers make scolding and criticism the behavior control tools of choice because these tools give the impression that the results are effective and immediate. Usually, misbehavior stops and the teacher assumes the situation has been rectified. Unfortunately, this is not always the case. Criticism and punishment lend a negative air to the instructional environment and negatively affect both student and teacher. The old saying, "It hurts me more than you" often applies. Most teachers feel uncomfortable when they must criticize or punish students. It makes them feel that they cannot handle students and that the class is incorrigible. This feeling of incompetence leads to a destructive cycle where students feel negative about the instructor and the instructor feels negative about the students. In the long run, this is the debilitating impact of criticism and punishment.

As mentioned, another negative aspect of criticism is that it does not offer a solution. In one study (Thomas et al., 1968), a teacher was asked to stop praising a class. Off-task behavior increased from 8.7% to nearly 26%. When the teacher was asked to increase criticism from 5 times in 20 minutes to 16 times in 20 minutes, students demonstrated more off-task behavior. On some days the percentage of off-task behavior increased to more than 50%. When teachers criticize off-task behavior and do not praise on-task accomplishment, off-task behavior increases dramatically. Using criticism makes teachers feel effective (students respond to the request of the criticism), but students do not actually change. In fact, the students are reinforced (they receive attention from the teacher) for their off-task behavior. Further since their on-task behavior is not praised, it decreases. The net result is exactly the opposite of what is desired.

MAKE PUNISHMENT A LAST RESORT

Deciding whether to use punishment in an educational setting is a difficult issue. Punishment can have negative side effects because fear is the primary motivator. Consider the long-term need for punishment. If the long-term effects of using punishment are more beneficial than not using it, it is unethical not to use punishment. In other words, if a child is going to be in a worse situation because punishment was not used to deter self-destructive behavior, it is wrong not to use it. It may be necessary to punish a child for protection from self-inflicted harm (for example, using certain apparatus without supervision). It may be necessary to punish children so that they learn not to hurt others. Punishment in these situations will cause discomfort to teacher and child in the short run, but it may allow the student to participate successfully in society later.

Most situations in the educational setting do not require punishment, because they are not as severe as those just described. A major reason for avoiding punishment is that it can have negative side effects. When children are punished, they learn to avoid the source of punishment. It forces them to be more covert in their actions. They spend time finding ways to avoid being caught. Instead of encouraging students to discuss problems with teachers and parents, punishment teaches them to avoid these individuals for fear of retribution. Punishment also teaches children to be aggressive toward others. Children who have been physically or emotionally punished by parents treat others the same way. The result is a child who is secretive and aggressive with others—certainly less than desirable traits. Finally, if punishment is used to stop certain behavior, as soon as the punishment stops the behavior will return. Thus, little has been learned; the punishment has just led to short-term change.

If it is necessary to use punishment, remember these points:

1. *Be consistent and make the punishment "fit the crime."* Students quickly lose respect for a teacher who treats others with favoritism. They view the teacher as unfair if punishment is extreme or unfair. Peers quickly side with the student who is treated unfairly, causing a class morale problem for the instructor.
2. *Offer a warning signal, as discussed previously.* This may prevent excessive use of punishment, as students often behave after receiving a warning. In addition, they probably view the teacher as caring and fair.
3. *Do not threaten students.* Offer only one warning. Threats have little impact on students and make them feel that you cannot handle the class. One warning gives students the feeling that you are not looking to punish them and are fair. Follow through; do not challenge or threaten students and then fail to deal with the behavior.
4. *Make sure the punishment follows the misbehavior as soon as possible.* When delayed, punishment is much less effective and more often viewed as unfair.
5. *Punish quietly and calmly.* Do not seek revenge or be vindictive. If you expect responsible behavior from students, be sure you reprimand and punish in a responsible way. Studies (O'Leary & Becker, 1968) show that quiet reprimands are more effective than loud ones.

6

Try to avoid developing negative feelings toward a student because you internalize the misbehavior. Being punitive when handling deviant behavior destroys any chance for a worthwhile relationship with the student. Handle misbehavior in a manner that contributes to the development of responsible, confident students who understand that people who function effectively in society must adjust to certain limits. Forget about past bouts of deviant behavior, and approach the student with a positive mind-set at the start of each class. If you do not, students will feel labeled and changing their behavioral will be more difficult. Students may also learn to live up to the teacher's negative expectations.

If you use punishment, make sure that it applies only to those students who misbehave. Punishing an entire class for the deviant behavior of a few students is unfair and may trigger unacceptable side effects. Students become hostile toward those who caused the loss of privileges, and this peer hostility lowers the level of positive social interaction with the students who have misbehaved.

EXPULSION: LEGAL CONSIDERATIONS

If serious problems occur, discuss them with the classroom teacher and principal. Deviant behavior frequently is part of a larger, more severe problem that is troubling a child. A cooperative approach may provide an effective solution. A group meeting involving parents, classroom teacher, principal, counselor, and physical education specialist may open avenues that encourage understanding and increase productive behavior.

Legal concerns involving the student's rights in disciplinary areas are an essential consideration. While minor infractions may be handled routinely, expulsion and other substantial punishments can be imposed on students only after due process. The issue of student rights is complicated, and most school systems have established guidelines and procedures for dealing with students who have been removed from the class or school setting. Students should be removed from class only if they are disruptive to the point of interfering with the learning experiences of other children and if all other means of altering behavior have not worked. Sending a child out of class is a last resort and means that both teacher and student have failed.

APPLYING WHAT YOU READ

- To become an effective classroom manager, you must first determine the type of communicator you are. Use the information under "Develop an Assertive Communication Style" to determine your communication style.
- Before you begin teaching, identify key teaching behaviors demonstrated by effective classroom managers.
- Effective teachers have a firm understanding of why students misbehave. Becoming familiar with Figure 6.1 will help you as you teach.
- At the start of the school year, follow the steps delineated under "Define Class Procedures, Rules, and Consequences." This will get you off on the right foot for establishing an effective learning environment.
- As you evaluate and reflect on your teaching, what management skills are you incorporating?
- Many strategies for teaching acceptable behavior are presented. These strategies will prove valuable when you begin teaching and working to shape student behavior.

REFLECTION AND REVIEW

HOW AND WHY

1. How would you respond to a child who consistently misbehaves?
2. How does it make you feel when a professor knows your name?
3. How might pre- and post-teaching routines change depending on the school?
4. Why is it important for teachers to know their own trigger points? What are your trigger points?
5. What rules would you have in your classes?
6. What types of emotions might you feel when placing a child in time-out?
7. As an adult, how does criticism make you feel?

CONTENT REVIEW

1. What class management skills are necessary to be an effective teacher?
2. What is the importance of using efficient instruction, a consistent stop signal, and moving students into formation quickly in an effective lesson?
3. How can knowing the names of students help teachers?
4. What types of routines do successful teachers establish?
5. What is the effective use of equipment?

FOR MORE INFORMATION

REFERENCES AND SUGGESTED READINGS

Bailey, B. A. (2001). *Conscious discipline.* Oviedo, FL: Loving Guidance.

Beane, A. (1999). *The bully free classroom.* Minneapolis, MN: Free Spirit Publishing.

Canter, L., & Canter, M. (1997). *Assertive discipline: Positive behavior management for today's classroom.* Santa Monica, CA: Lee Canter and Associates.

Charles, C. M. (2008). *Building classroom discipline* (9th ed.). Upper Saddle River, NJ: Prentice Hall.

———. (2008). *Today's best classroom management strategies: Paths to positive discipline.* Upper Saddle River, NJ: Prentice Hall.

Cohen, R. (2005). *Students resolving conflict.* Tucson, AZ: Good Year Books.

Fields, M. V., & Fields, D. M. (2006). *Constructive guidance and discipline: Preschool and primary education* (4th ed.). Upper Saddle River, NJ: Prentice Hall.

Greene, D., & Lepper, M. R. (1975). Turning play into work: Effects of adult surveillance and extrinsic rewards on children's internal motivation. *Journal of Personality and Social Psychology, 31*, 479–486.

Hellison, D. (2003). *Teaching responsibility through physical activity* (2nd ed.). Champaign, IL: Human Kinetics.

Lavay, B. W., French, R., & Henderson, H. L. (2006). *Positive behavior management in physical activity settings* (2nd ed.). Champaign, IL: Human Kinetics.

O'Leary, K. D., & Becker, W. C. (1968). The effects of intensity of a teacher's reprimands on children's behavior. *Journal of School Psychology, 7*, 8–11.

Premack, D. (1965). Reinforcement theory. In D. Levine (Ed.), *Nebraska symposium on motivation.* Lincoln, NE: University of Nebraska Press.

Siedentop, D., & Tannehill, D. (2000). *Developing teaching skills in physical education* (4th ed.). Mountain View, CA: Mayfield.

Thomas, D. R., Becker, W. C., & Armstrong, M. (1968). Production and elimination of disruptive classroom behavior by systematically varying teachers' behavior. *Journal of Applied Behavior Analysis, 1*, 35–45.

Whitehead, J. R., & Corbin, C. B. (1991). Effects of fitness test type, teacher, and gender on exercise intrinsic motivation and physical self-worth. *Journal of School Health, 61*, 11–16.

WEBSITES

Classroom Management

www.pecentral.org/climate/index.html
www.honorlevel.com/techniques.html
www.consciousdiscipline.com
http://maxweber.hunter.cuny.edu/pub/eres/EDSPC715_MCINTYRE/AssertiveDiscipline.html
www.positivediscipline.com

7

Children with Disabilities

ESSENTIAL COMPONENTS OF QUALITY PROGRAMS

- ▶ I. Organized around content standards
- ▶ II. Student-centered and developmentally appropriate
- III. Physical activity and motor skill development form the core of the program
- IV. Teaches management skills and self-discipline
- ▶ V. Promotes inclusion of all students
- ▶ VI. Focuses on process over product
- VII. Promotes lifetime personal health and wellness
- ▶ VIII. Teaches cooperation and responsibility and promotes sensitivity to diversity

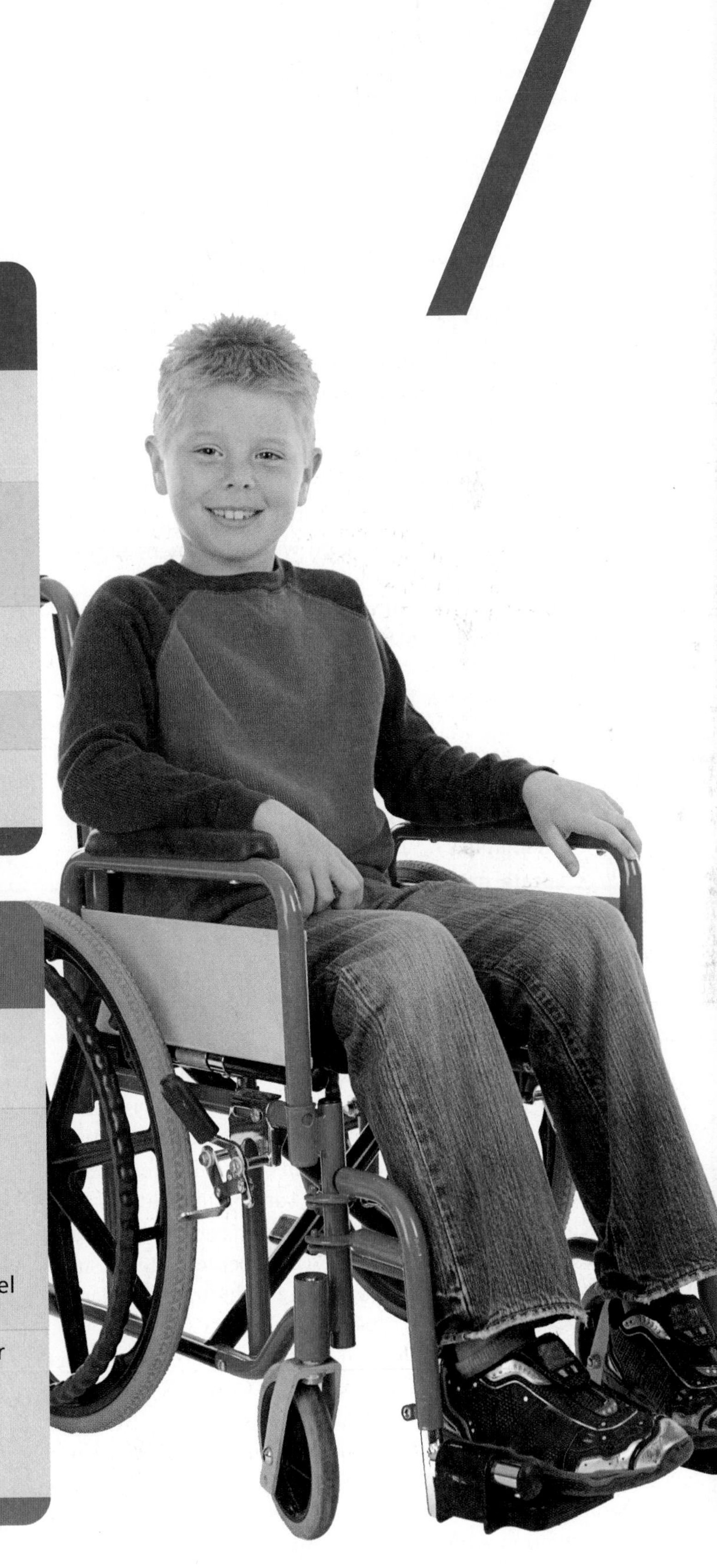

NATIONAL STANDARDS FOR PHYSICAL EDUCATION*

- ▶ 1. Demonstrates competency in motor skills and movement patterns needed to perform a variety of physical activities.
- 2. Demonstrates understanding of movement concepts, principles, and tactics as they apply to the learning and performance of physical activities.
- 3. Participates regularly in physical activity.
- 4. Achieves and maintains a health-enhancing level of physical fitness.
- ▶ 5. Exhibits responsible personal and social behavior that respects self and others in physical activity.
- ▶ 6. Values physical activity for health, enjoyment, challenge, self-expression, and/or social interaction.

*National Association for Sport and Physical Education (NASPE), 2004.

Federal law requires every state to develop a plan for identifying, locating, and evaluating all children with disabilities. Due process for students and parents is an important requisite when conducting formal assessment procedures. Mainstreaming involves the practice of placing children with disabilities into classes with able children. Moving a child to a less restrictive learning environment is based on achievement of specified competencies that are required for moving into the new environment. The most common types of disabilities and ways to modify activities for successful participation are discussed. Programs for children with weight problems, motor deficiencies, and postural problems are detailed step-by-step.

Outcomes

- Understand the implications of PL 94–142 and IDEA for physical education.
- Explain due process guidelines associated with assessment procedures.
- Develop a plan for identifying, locating, and evaluating all children with disabilities.
- Cite standards associated with assessment procedures for special children.
- Identify essential elements of an individualized education program, and list the stages of development.
- List guidelines for successful inclusion of students.
- Describe ways of modifying activities for inclusion.
- Describe characteristics of specific impairments and ways to modify learning experiences in physical education to accommodate children with disabilities.
- Locate nationally validated programs to assist in the screening, assessment, and curriculum development for children with special needs.

PROVIDING a quality educational experience for all students is the responsibility of the educational system. All professionals should view this responsibility as an ethical and professional duty rather than something required by law. It is the appropriate thing to do for all children—and all children come to school with varying ability levels, disabled or not. Dr. Claudine Sherrill in her text (2004) states that "in a sense, all good physical education is adapted physical education."

The Education for All Handicapped Children Act (Public Law 94–142) was passed by Congress in 1975. It was the 142nd act of legislation passed by the 94th Congress. This legislation introduced new requirements, vocabulary, and concepts into physical education programs across the United States. These concepts include individualized education programs (IEPs), mainstreaming, least restrictive environments, zero reject, and progressive inclusion. The purpose of the law is clear and concise:

> It is the purpose of this act to assure that all handicapped children* have available to them . . . a free appropriate public education which emphasizes special education and related services designed to meet their unique needs, to assure that the rights of handicapped children and their parents or guardians are protected, to assist States and localities to provide for the education of all handicapped children, and to assess and assure the effectiveness of efforts to educate handicapped children.

In short, the law requires that all youth with disabilities, ages 3 to 21, receive a free and appropriate education in the least restrictive environment. The law includes students in public and private care facilities and schools. Youth with disabilities who can learn in regular classes with the use of supplementary aids and services must be educated with children in the regular class. Physical education is the only specific area mentioned in PL 94–142. The law indicates that the term *special education* "means specially designed instruction, instruction in physical education, home instruction, and instruction in hospitals and institutions." A 1997 amendment, Public Law 105–17 (also known as IDEA—Individuals with Disabilities Education Act), continues with the objective of providing handicapped individuals with the least restrictive environment in the school setting. The Individuals with Disabilities Education Act states, "Physical education services, specially designed if necessary, must be made available to every child with a disability receiving a free appropriate public education." Autism and traumatic brain injury have been added to the list of handicapping conditions that should receive the least restrictive environment. IDEA provides that an individual transition plan be developed no later than age 16 as a component of the IEP process. Rehabilitation and social work services are included as related services.

To comply with PL 94–142, schools must locate, identify, and evaluate all students who might have a disability. A screening process must be followed by a formal assessment procedure. An assessment must be made and an IEP developed for each student before placement into a special program can be made. The law states who will be responsible for developing the IEP and what the IEP will contain.

The passage of PL 94–142 shows that a strong commitment has been made to equality and education for all

* The term *handicapped* is used in PL 94–142 to include children who are mentally retarded, hard of hearing, deaf, speech impaired, visually handicapped, seriously emotionally disturbed, orthopedically impaired, other health impaired, deaf-blind, multihandicapped, or specific learning disabled. The phrase *students with disabilities* is used throughout this chapter to identify children with such conditions.

Americans. Before 1970, these students had limited access to schools. They certainly did not have an equal opportunity to participate in school programs. The government also ensured that funding would be made available to provide quality instruction. The law authorizes a payment to each state of 40% of the average per pupil expenditure in U.S. elementary and secondary schools, multiplied by the number of children with disabilities who are receiving special education and related services. The federal mandate reveals public concern for comprehensive education programs for all students regardless of disability.

LEAST RESTRICTIVE ENVIRONMENT

PL 105–17 uses the term *least restrictive environment* to help determine the best placement arrangement of students with disabilities. This concept refers to the idea that not all individuals can do all of the same activities in the same environment. However, the concept of zero reject entitles everyone of school age to some aspect of the school program. No one can be totally rejected because of a disability. All students, regardless of ability level, must have access to physical education. The focus should be on placing students into settings that offer the best opportunity for educational advancement. It is inappropriate to place a child in an environment where success is impossible. However, it would be debilitating to put a student into a setting that is more restrictive than necessary. Special educators speak about many experiences that offer children a variety of opportunities, from participating in general physical education classes to physical education in a full-time special school (Figure 7.1).

The least restrictive environment also varies depending on the unit of instruction and the teaching style. For example, for a student in a wheelchair, a soccer activity might be very restrictive, whereas in basketball or Frisbee activities, the environment would be less restrictive. For a student with emotional disabilities, the direct style of instruction might be the least restrictive environment, while a problem-solving method with group cooperation may be too difficult and would end up being more restrictive. Consistent and regular judgments need to be made since curriculum content and teaching styles change the type of environment the student enters. It is shortsighted to place students into a situation and then forget about them. Evaluation and modification of environments need to be ongoing. The concept of "progressive inclusion" focuses on the idea that students make progress as a result of educational experiences. Thus, students with disabilities should have the opportunity to

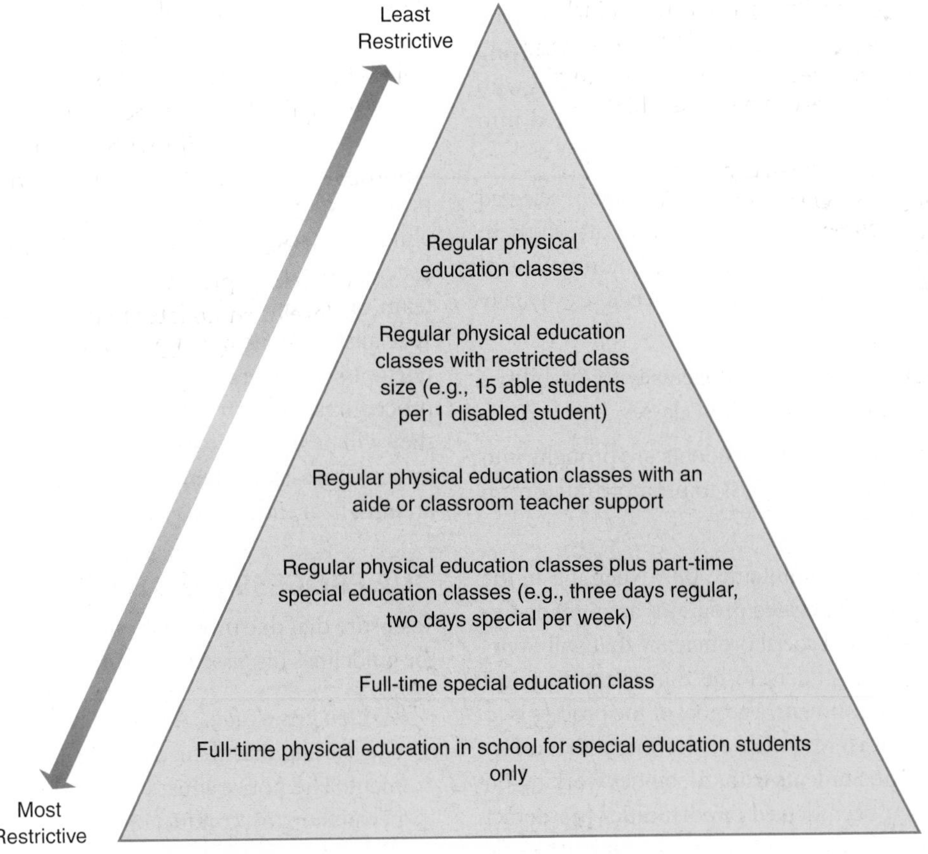

FIGURE 7.1 Physical education inclusion options, least to most restrictive environments.

progress to the least restrictive environments and experience more and more of the mainstream of our schools and their programs.

MAINSTREAMING/INCLUSION

Physical educators usually speak in terms of mainstreaming rather than least restrictive environments. *Mainstreaming* means that students with disabilities must have opportunities to integrate with other students in public schools. Prudent placement in a least restrictive educational environment means that the setting must be as normal as possible (normalization) while ensuring that the student can fit in and achieve success in that placement. The placement may be mainstreaming but is not confined to this approach. There are several categories of placement relative to physical education classes.

1. *Full mainstreaming.* Students with disabilities function as full-time members of a regular school routine. They go to all classes with able students. Within the limitations of their disability, they participate in physical education with able peers. An example may be auditory-impaired students who with a minimal amount of assistance are able to participate fully.
2. *Mainstreaming for physical education only.* Students with disabilities are not members of the regular academic classes in the schools but can still participate in physical education with able peers. This setting may include students with emotional disabilities who are grouped in the classroom and are separated into general physical education classes.
3. *Partial mainstreaming.* Students participate in selected physical education experiences but do not attend them full-time because they can be successful in only a few of the offerings. Their developmental needs are usually met in special classes.
4. *Special developmental classes.* Students with disabilities are in segregated special education classes.
5. *Reverse mainstreaming.* Able students are brought into a special physical education class to promote intergroup peer relationships.

Segregation should be maintained only when it is in the student's best interests. Segregated programs are intended to establish a level of skill and social proficiency that will eventually enable the special student to be transferred to a less restricted learning environment. The goal of the process is to place students in the least restrictive environment that offers them the most benefit. Students with disabilities working on their own have often been denied opportunities to interact with peers and become a part of the social and academic classroom network.

Students with disabilities need contact with support personnel during mainstreaming. The physical education teacher is responsible for the mainstreamed students during class time, but these students may still require access to special education teachers, school psychologists, and speech therapists. Though these support personnel may view physical education as a time to get rid of their students, they are a source of information and support for the physical education teacher in charge.

Be sure that students with disabilities understand what is to be accomplished before an activity begins, especially when working with children who have an intellectual disability or an auditory impairment.

SCREENING AND ASSESSMENT

The screening process involves all students in a school setting and is part of the "child find" process. It is often conducted at the start of the school year and is performed district-wide. The physical educator usually conducts screening tests, which may include commonly used test batteries (such as the Fitnessgram). In most situations, screening tests may be administered without parental permission and are used to initially identify students who may need special services.

Assessment is conducted after screening evaluations have been made. Assessment is usually conducted after child find screening by referring identified students to special education directors. Assessment is performed by a team of experts that may include the physical education specialist. Due process for students and parents is an important requisite when conducting formal assessment procedures. Due process assures parents and children that they will be informed of their rights and that they have the opportunity to challenge educational decisions they feel are unfair or incorrect.

DUE PROCESS GUIDELINES

To ensure that due process is offered to parents and students, the guidelines discussed here must be followed:

- *Written permission.* A written notice must be sent to parents stating that their child has been referred for assessment. The notice must explain that the district requests permission to conduct an evaluation to determine if their child requires special education services. Also included in the permission letter must be the reasons for testing and the titles of the tests to be used. Before assessment can begin, the letter must be signed by the parents and returned to the district.

- *Interpretation of the assessment.* The assessment results must be interpreted in a meeting with parents. Persons who are knowledgeable about the test procedures must be present to answer questions parents may ask. At the meeting, parents must be told whether their child has any disabilities and what services will be provided for the child.
- *External evaluation.* If parents are not satisfied with the assessment results, they may request an evaluation outside the school setting. The district must provide a list of agencies that can perform such assessment. If the results differ from the school district evaluation, the district must pay for the external evaluation. However, if the results are similar, parents must pay for the external testing.
- *Negotiation and hearings.* If parents and the school district disagree on the assessment results, the district must try to negotiate the differences. When negotiations fail, an impartial hearing officer listens to both parties and renders an official decision. This is usually the final review; however, both parties have the right to appeal to the state department of education, which must render a binding and final decision. Civil action through the legal system can be pursued should the district or parents still disagree with this action. However, few cases reach this level of long-term disagreement, and educators should not hesitate to serve the needs of children with disabilities based on this concern.
- *Confidentiality.* As usual, only parents of the child or authorized school personnel can review the student's records. Review by other parties can occur only if the parents of the child under review give their written permission.

PROCEDURES FOR ENSURING ASSESSMENT STANDARDS

PL 94–142 requires that assessment is held to certain standards to ensure fair and objective results. The following areas are specifically delineated.

Selection of Test Instruments

Test instruments used must be valid examinations that measure what they purport to measure. Thus, when selecting instruments, it must be clear to all parties how the tests were developed and how they will correctly measure the area of possible disability. More than one test procedure must be used to determine the student's status. Both formal and informal assessment techniques should be used to ensure that the results measure the student's impairment rather than simply reflect the student's shortcomings.

It is unfortunate that children must be labeled as disabled in order to reap the benefits of a special education program. The stigmatizing effect of labels and the fallibility of various student testing methods create a dilemma that must be faced. Although current pedagogical practices discourage labeling, it is double-talk because school districts have to certify the disability (to receive funding) for which the child is classified.

Administration Procedures

Many disabilities interfere with standard test procedures. For example, many students have communication problems, so any testing must be sure to measure their motor ability rather than their lack of communication skills. Many students have visual and hearing disabilities that prevent educators from using tests that rely on these senses.

A probability of misdiagnosis and incorrectly classifying children as mentally retarded can occur among certain ethnic groups such as Native Americans, African Americans, and Spanish-speaking children. Some of these children may be victims of a low standard of living and be only environmentally retarded and in need of cultural enrichment. This is subtle discrimination, but it must be replaced with the understanding that children differ because of culture, poverty, migrancy, and language. Many of the tests are based on white middle-class standards. Minority children should be carefully assessed to determine the validity of the testing procedure.

Team Evaluation

Various experts should be used for assessment. Providing a multidisciplinary team helps ensure that all facets of the child are reviewed and evaluated. Evaluation professionals must be well trained and qualified to administer the various tests. The school district is responsible for ensuring that a proper evaluation occurs.

DEVELOPING AN INDIVIDUALIZED EDUCATION PROGRAM

PL 94–142 requires that an IEP be developed for each child with a disability receiving special education and related services. The IEP must be developed by a committee, as stipulated by the law. The committee must include a local education association representative who is qualified to provide and supervise the administration of special education, the child's parents, the teachers who have direct responsibility for implementing the IEP, and, when appropriate, the student. Other individuals may be included at the discretion of the parents or the school district.

This program identifies the child's unique qualities and determines educationally relevant strengths and weaknesses. A plan is then devised based on the diagnosed strengths and weaknesses. Figure 7.2 is an example of a comprehensive IEP form. The IEP must contain the following material:

1. Current status of the child's level of educational performance.
2. A statement of long-term goals and short-term instructional objectives.
3. A statement of special education and related services that will be provided to the child, and a report describing the extent to which the child is able to participate in regular educational programs.
4. The dates for initiation of services and anticipated duration of the services.
5. Appropriate objective criteria for determining on an annual basis whether the short-term objectives are being reached.

INDIVIDUALIZED EDUCATION PROGRAM

☐ Initial Placement
☐ Re-evaluation
☐ Change of Placement
☐ Review

A. **STUDENT INFORMATION:**
Student Name ______ (Last First Middle) Student No. ______ Home School ______
Date of Birth ______ Chronological Age ___ (M___ or F___) Present Placement/Grade ______
Parent/Guardian Name(s) ______ Receiving School ______
Home Address ______ (Street City/State Zip) Program Recommended ______
Home Phone ______ Work Phone ______ Starting Date ______
Emergency Phone ______ Three (3) Year Re-evaluation Due Date ___/___/___
Primary Language (Home) ______ (Child) ______ Interpreter Needed: Yes ___ No ___

B. **VISION SCREENING RESULTS:** Pass ___ Fail ___
Date: ______ Comments: ______
HEARING SCREENING RESULTS: Pass ___ Fail ___
Date: ______ Comments: ______

C. **REQUIRED OBSERVATION(S):** (All categories other than regular teacher)
______ (Date(s)) By: ______ (Name(s)) ______ (Date(s)) By: ______ (Name(s)) ______ (Date(s)) By: ______ (Name(s))

D. **SUMMARY OF PRESENT LEVELS OF PERFORMANCE:**
Educational: ______

Behavioral: ______

E. Additional justification. See comments ______ (Initial) See addendum ______ (Initial)

F. **PLACEMENT RECOMMENDATION INDICATING LEAST RESTRICTIVE ENVIRONMENT:**
Related services needed: Yes ______ No ______ (*List below.)

Placement Recommendation	Person Responsible	Amount of Time (Range)	Entry Date On/About	Review Reports On/About	Projected Ending Date	IEP Review Date
Primary:						
*Related Services:						

Transportation Needed? Yes ______ No ______ (If Yes, submit MPS Special Education Transportation Request Form.)

Describe extent student will participate in regular program: ______

Page 1 of ______

FIGURE 7.2 Example of an individualized education program (IEP).

Developing and sequencing objectives for the student are the first steps in formulating the IEP. Short- and long-range goals should be delineated, and data collection procedures and testing schedules established to monitor the child's progress. Materials and strategies to be used in implementing the IEP should also be established. Finally, the committee selects evaluation methods for monitoring student progress as well as program effectiveness. The student may be moved to a less restrictive environment upon achieving the specified competencies required to function in the new environment.

The IEP must contain a section determining whether specially designed physical education is needed. If not, the child should be held to the same expectations as the peer group. A child who needs special physical education might have an IEP with specified goals and objectives and might be mainstreamed in general physical education with goals that do not resemble those of classmates.

INDIVIDUALIZED EDUCATION PLAN

REPORT OF MULTIDISCIPLINARY CONFERENCE
Date Held ______

Student Name ______ Student No. ______

G. **PROGRAM PLANNING:**

Long-Term Goals: ______

Short-Term Objectives (Goals): ______

H. **EVALUATION:**

Evaluation criteria are described in the Individual Implementation Plan (IIP) which is available in the classroom file.

I. **PLACEMENT COMMITTEE:**

The following have been consulted or have participated in the placement and IEP decisions:

Names of Members	Position	Present (Initial)	Oral Report	Written Report	Signatures
	Parents/Guardian				
	Parents/Guardian				
	School Administrator				
	Special Ed Administrator				
	School Psychologist				
	Nurse				
	Teacher(s) Receiving				
	Teacher(s) Referring				
	Interpreter				

Dissenting Opinion: Yes ______ No ______ If Yes, see comments ______ (Initial) See addendum ______ (Initial).

J. **PARENT (OR GUARDIAN) STATEMENT:**

We agree to the placement recommended in this IEP. Yes ______ No ______

We give our permission to have our child counseled by the professional staff, if necessary. Yes ______ No ______

We understand that placement will be on a continuing trial basis and we will be contacted if any placement changes are contemplated. We are aware that such placement does not guarantee success; however, in order to help our child, we accept the responsibility to cooperate in every way with the school program. We acknowledge that we have been notified of and have received a copy of our due process rights pertaining to Special Education placement and have a basic understanding of these rights. We acknowledge that we have received a copy of the completed IEP Form.

______ Parent or Guardian Signature ______ Date

COMMENTS: ______

Page 2 of ______

FIGURE 7.2 (Continued)

Continued and periodic follow-up of the child is necessary. Effective communication between special and regular teachers is essential, because the child's progress needs careful monitoring. After the designated time period or school year, a written progress report is filed along with recommendations for action during the coming year or time period. A program for the summer months can be an excellent prescription to ensure that improvement is maintained. Records should be complete so that information is always available about the child's problem and the effects of long-term treatment.

A SYSTEMATIC APPROACH TO SUCCESSFUL MAINSTREAMING

Mainstreaming and integrating children into an environment where they can succeed is a moral issue. Educators are responsible for ensuring that all students have the opportunity to take part in activity and related social experiences. All parents desire the best experiences for their children, and the goal of teachers is to help facilitate this desire. The issue is not whether to mainstream, but how to mainstream effectively (Figure 7.3). The physical educator must teach many students, some with disabilities and diverse impairments. Learning strategies that the instructor is familiar with and has been using successfully may not be appropriate for students with disabilities. Attitudinal change is important since the teacher must accept the student as a full-fledged participant and assume the responsibilities that go along with special education. Few disagree that mainstreaming increases the difficulty of offering instruction for all students, but teachers who support it show their concern for the human spirit regardless of a student's condition.

DETERMINE HOW TO TEACH

The success or failure of the mainstreaming process depends largely on the interaction between the teacher and the student with a disability. There is no foolproof, teacher-proof system. Purposes and derived goals may be more important to students with disabilities than to so-called normal peers. Proper levels of fitness and skill are vital for healthful living and enable students with disabilities to compete with peers.

It is important to accept responsibility for meeting the needs of students, including those with disabilities that permit some degree of mainstreaming. Teachers need to be able to judge when referral for special assistance or additional services is in order. Physical education teachers must be able to (1) analyze and diagnose motor behavior of students with disabilities, (2) provide appropriate experiences for remediation of motor conditions needing attention, and (3) register data as needed on the student's personal record. Record keeping is important. Set aside a short period, perhaps 5 minutes between classes, to accomplish the task promptly. When time between classes is short, the teacher can use a portable tape recorder for recording evaluative comments during class time.

To work successfully with students with disabilities, teachers have to understand specific impairments and how they affect learning. Teachers also must know how to assess motor and fitness needs and how to structure remediation to meet those needs. Keep some alternative strategies in reserve in case the original method fails.

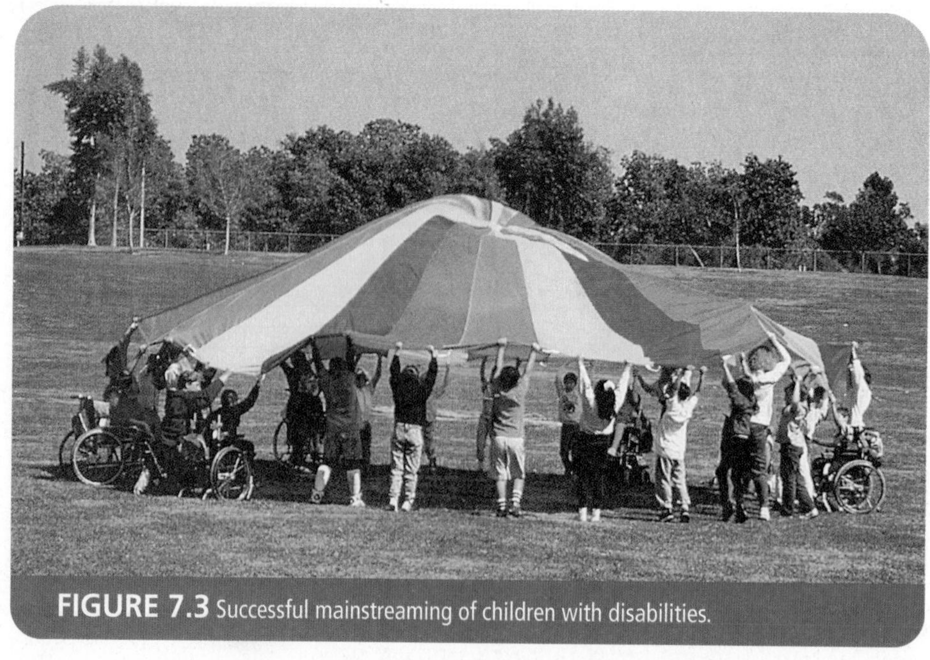

FIGURE 7.3 Successful mainstreaming of children with disabilities.

Make use of the special education specialist when possible because he or she sees the child in various settings. When giving explanations and directions, be sure all students understand. Check that students with disabilities understand what is to be accomplished before the learning experiences begin, especially when working with the hearing impaired. Concentrate on finding activities where students can excel. Avoid placing students with disabilities in situations where they could easily fail. Offer participative opportunities that make the best use of their talents. Stress the special objectives of those with disabilities. Obvious increments of improvement toward terminal objectives are excellent motivators for both students and teachers. Let students know that you as a teacher are vitally interested in their progress.

DETERMINE WHAT TO TEACH

This step involves reviewing the existing physical education curriculum and determining how it will affect students who have differing needs. An important consideration is whether certain activities completely exclude certain students. Many students with disabilities have severe developmental lags that will work against successful integration if the curriculum is not modified. On the other hand, if the student is going to be included, he must be able to accomplish a portion of the program. It also may be that certain activities are limiting and inclusion is not in the student's best interest. A compromise must be reached where the physical education teacher has made changes in their curriculum and mainstreamed students realize that some activities are not suited to their participation. It should be the teacher's intent and responsibility to individualize activities as much as possible so children with disabilities are smoothly integrated.

FIND WAYS TO MODIFY INSTRUCTION AND ACTIVITIES FOR STUDENT SUCCESS

Students may need additional consideration when participating in group activities, particularly when the activity is competitive. Much depends on the student's physical condition and the type of disability. Students like to win in a competitive situation, and resentment may result if a team loss is attributed to the presence of a student with a disability. Equalization helps reduce this source of friction. Rules can be changed for everyone, so the student with a disability has a chance to contribute to group success. On the other hand, all students need to recognize that everyone has a right to play.

Be aware of situations that devalue the student socially. Avoid using the degrading method of having captains choose teams from a group of waiting students. Elimination games should be changed so that points are scored instead of players being eliminated. Determine the most desirable involvement for students with disabilities by analyzing participants' roles in game and sport activities. Assign a role or position that will make the experience as natural or normal as possible.

Students with disabilities have to build confidence in their skills before they will want to participate with others. Individual activities give them a greater amount of practice time without the pressure of failing in front of peers. The aim is to make students with disabilities less conspicuous and not set apart from able classmates. Using students with disabilities as umpires or score keepers should be a last resort. Being overprotective benefits no one and prevents the special student from experiencing challenge and personal accomplishment. Avoid the tendency to underestimate students' abilities.

Many instructional modifications can be made that are not obvious to other students but will improve the opportunity for special students to succeed. For example, factors such as teaching styles, verbal instructions, demonstrations, and the elimination of distractions might easily be manipulated in a manner that improves the lesson for all.

A Reflection Check

Modifying the lesson affects many people: the students with differing needs, the other students in the class, and the teacher. It is relatively easy to modify activities, but it can be quite difficult to make modifications that add to the total environment rather than create unsafe conditions or reduce the educational value of the experience. When thinking about ways to accommodate all students, take some time to reflect on the total experience. As you formulate modifications, consider these questions:

1. Do the changes allow the student with differing needs to participate successfully yet still be challenged?
2. Does the modification make the setting unsafe for the student with differing needs as well as for those students without disabilities?
3. Does the change negatively affect the quality of the educational experience? Is learning seriously hampered because of the change that was made?
4. Does the change cause an undue burden on the teacher? This is important; many teachers come to resent students with differing needs because they feel the burden is too great.

Certainly, change needs to be made, but it has to be reasonable for all parties.

Activities need to be modified because all students have differing needs. In fact, when teachers seldom or never modify activities, they probably are not meeting the needs of many students. Effective teachers always examine an activity and know that it is their responsibility to make the environment better for all students. "Doing the most good for the most students" is a good concept to follow. One strategy to assist teachers in making appropriate modifications is to use the STEPS (space, task, equipment, people, and safety) concept. Figure 7.4 gives an overview of this model and its components. The rest of this section provides ways to modify activities for a variety of ability limitations using principles of the STEPS model.

Modifications for Students Lacking Strength and Endurance

1. *Decrease or increase the size of the goal.* In basketball, lower the basket; in soccer, the goal might be enlarged.
2. *Modify the tempo of the game.* Adapt games to use brisk walking rather than running. Another way to modify tempo is to stop the game regularly for substitution. Using autosubstitutions can be an excellent method: students determine when they are fatigued, and they ask a predetermined substitute to take their place.
3. *Reduce the weight and/or modify the size of the projectile.* A lighter object moves more slowly and inflicts less damage upon impact. A larger object is easier for students to track visually and catch.
4. *Reduce the distance that a ball must be thrown or served.* Options are to reduce the dimensions of the playing area or to add more players to the game. In serving, others can help make the serve playable. For example, in volleyball, other teammates can bat the serve over the net as long as the ball does not touch the floor.
5. *In games played to a certain number of points, reduce the number required for a win.* For example, volleyball games could be played to 7 or 11 points, depending on the players' skill and intensity.
6. *Modify striking implements by shortening and reducing their weight.* Rackets are much easier to control when they are shortened. Softball bats are easier to control when the player "chokes up" and uses a lighter bat.
7. *If possible, slow down the ball by letting out some air.* This change reduces the speed of rebound and makes the ball easier to control in a restricted area. It also keeps the ball from rolling away from players when it is not under control.
8. *Have students play the games in a different position.* Some games may be played in a sitting or lying position, which is easier and less demanding than standing or running.
9. *Provide matching or substitution.* Match a student on borrowed crutches with a student in braces. Two players can be combined to play one position. A student in a desk chair with wheels can be matched against a student in a wheelchair. Permit substitute runners.
10. *Allow students to substitute skills.* For example, if a student can strike an object but lacks the mobility to run, select another student to run.

Successful Experiences for All Children

Space
- Alter the activity space
- Lower baskets
- Increase or decrease goal size
- Move shooting lines forward or backward
- Decrease size of field

Task
- Modify rules
- Allow more bounces in games like tennis or volleyball
- Change position roles
- Change speed of movement

Equipment
- Use larger or smaller equipment
- Change the weight of the equipment

People
- Change the size of teams
- Alter teams often
- Use small-sided games and switch team matchups often

Safety
- Always ensure activity modifications maintain high levels of safety for all students

FIGURE 7.4 STEPS model for adapted activities.

Modifications for Students Lacking Coordination

1. *Increase the size of the goal or target.* Enlarging a basketball hoop increases the opportunity for success. Another alternative is to offer points for hitting the backboard near a hoop. Since scoring is self-motivating, modification should occur until success is ensured.
2. *Offer protection when appropriate.* Students who lack coordination are more susceptible to injury from a projectile. Use various types of protectors (such as glasses, chest protectors, or face masks).
3. *When teaching throwing, allow students to throw at maximum velocity without concern for accuracy.* Use small balls that can be grasped easily. Fleece balls and beanbags are easy to hold and release.
4. *Use a stationary object when teaching striking or hitting.* Use a batting tee, or a tennis ball fastened to a string, to

FIGURE 7.5 Modifying an activity for successful participation.

help students find success. Also permit them to use a larger racket or bat and to choke up on the grip.

5. *Make projectiles easily retrievable.* Students who must spend a lot of time on recovering the projectile will receive few practice trials and feel frustrated. Place them near a backstop or use a goal that rebounds the projectile to the shooter.
6. *When teaching catching, use a soft, lightweight, slow-moving object.* Beach balls and balloons are excellent for beginning catching skills since students can track their movement visually. In addition, foam rubber balls eliminate a student's fear of being hurt by a thrown or batted projectile.

Modifications for Students Lacking Balance and Agility

1. *Increase the width of rails, lines, and beams when having students practice balance.* Having students carry a long pole will help minimize rapid shifts of balance and is a useful lead-up activity.
2. *Have students increase the width of their base of support.* Teach students to keep their feet spread at least to shoulder width.
3. *Emphasize use of many body parts when teaching balance.* The more body parts that are in contact with the floor, the easier it is to balance the body. Beginning balance practice should emphasize controlled movement using as many body parts as possible.
4. *Have students increase the surface area of the body parts in contact with the floor or beam.* For example, walking flat-footed is easier than walking on tiptoe.
5. *Have students lower their center of gravity.* This gives the children more stability and greater balance. Emphasize bending the knees and leaning slightly forward.
6. *Make sure that surfaces offer good friction.* Floors and shoes should not be slick, or students will fall. Carpets or tumbling mats help increase traction.
7. *Provide balance assistance.* A barre, cane, or chair can be used to keep the student from falling.
8. *Teach students how to fall.* Students with balance problems will inevitably fall. Offer practice in learning how to fall so that they gradually learn how to absorb the force.

DETERMINE WHAT SUPPORT AND AID ARE NECESSARY

When a student is deemed ready for placement, consultation between the physical education teacher and the special education supervisor is of prime importance. In a setting where emotions and feelings run high, it is important to ensure that communication and planning occur regularly. The reception and acceptance of students cannot be left to chance. A scheduled plan has to be instituted before mainstreaming the student. Special and physical education professionals must discuss the needs of the student as well as the physical education teacher and develop realistic expectations. Quite possibly, the special education teacher will have to participate in the physical education class to ensure a smooth transition. The discussion should center on what students can do rather than on what they cannot do. Any approach that has lowered expectations when treating students is dehumanizing.

Safety Tip

Student abilities can change throughout the school year. You may need to modify your lesson plans to ensure the physical education environment is still safe and appropriate for students with disabilities as the year progresses.

Full information about the student's needs must be in the physical education teacher's hands before the student participates. Physical education teachers must feel able to tell the support personnel what kind of help they need and not feel as though they are burdening the support personnel. At times, the physical education teacher may need to be direct and tell the support person exactly what to do to assist the

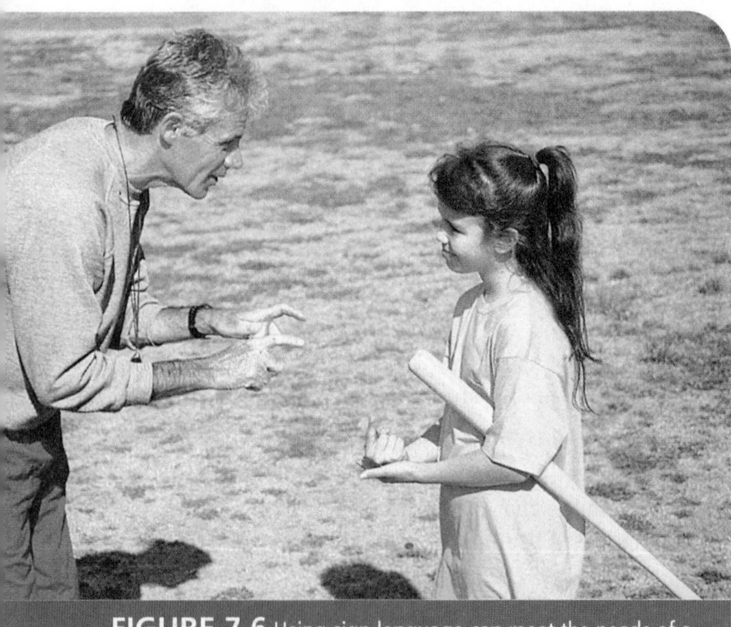

FIGURE 7.6 Using sign language can meet the needs of a student with an auditory impairment.

child. The support person and the physical education teacher must work together to provide assistance that is best for the child. If the physical educator feels that students with differing needs were dropped into her class before she was asked what kind of help she required to integrate them properly, she will have negative feelings about those students. The agreed-on procedure should also be implemented when the student moves from one mainstreaming situation to another. Both able students and students with disabilities need opportunities to make appropriate progress.

TEACH TOLERANCE TO ALL STUDENTS

All students must learn and respond to issues related to being disabled. Fully able students must learn to understand, accept, and live comfortably with persons with disabilities. They should recognize that students with disabilities are functional and worthwhile individuals who have innate abilities and can make significant contributions to society. The concept of understanding and appreciating individual differences merits positive development and should concentrate on three aspects:

1. Recognizing the similarities among all people—their hopes, rights, aspirations, and goals.
2. Understanding human differences and focusing on the concept that all people are disabled in various ways. Some people's disabilities are severe enough to interfere with normal living.
3. Exploring ways to deal with those who differ without overhelping them, and stressing the acceptance of all students as worthwhile individuals. People with disabilities deserve consideration and understanding based on empathy, not sympathy.

INTEGRATE STUDENTS WITH DIFFERING NEEDS INTO THE CLASS SETTING

Once the mainstreamed student, able students, and teacher have received preliminary preparation, consideration can be given to integrating the disabled child into the learning environment. When correctly implemented, mainstreaming allows the student to make educational progress, achieve in those areas outlined in the IEP, learn to accept limitations, observe and model appropriate behavior, and become socially accepted by others. Guidelines for successfully integrating students with disabilities into physical education follow.

1. Help students with disabilities meet target goals specified in the IEP and participate in the regular program of activities. This may call for resources beyond the physical education class, including special work and homework.

FIGURE 7.7 Children with disabilities can find the joy of participation.

2. Build ego strength; stress abilities. Eliminate established practices that unwittingly contribute to embarrassment and failure.
3. Foster peer acceptance by treating each student as a functioning, participating member of the class.
4. Concentrate on the student's physical education needs and not on the disability. Stress fundamental skills and physical fitness qualities.
5. Provide continual monitoring, and periodically assess the student's target goals. Anecdotal and periodic record keeping are implicit in this guideline.
6. Be constantly aware of students' feelings and anxiety concerning their progress and integration. Provide positive feedback as a basic practice.

APPLYING WHAT YOU READ

- Before teaching any lesson, it is crucial that teachers understand PL 94–142 and IDEA. Reviewing this section earlier in the chapter will ensure that your program and school are appropriately meeting the needs of all students.
- At the beginning of the year, teachers should review student files to determine which students have IEPs, if they are making appropriate progress, and how they are being assisted.
- Effective lesson planning includes reflecting on appropriate practices and instruction for students with disabilities. All teachers should ask themselves, "Am I making appropriate modifications?" This chapter offers many modification strategies for meeting the needs of all students.
- Teaching students with special needs requires appropriate support and aid. Before teaching, determine if these resources are available.

REFLECTION AND REVIEW

HOW AND WHY

1. How do you feel about teaching individuals with disabilities?
2. Why is it important for children with disabilities to participate in physical education?
3. Do all children have disabilities? Explain your answer.
4. How can teachers generate parental and social support for children with disabilities?

CONTENT REVIEW

1. Identify the implications of PL 94–142 and IDEA for physical education teachers.
2. Discuss the screening and assessment procedures for evaluating students.
3. Describe how individualized education programs are developed. Include comments on who is involved and what the IEP contains.
4. Describe inclusion and mainstreaming. Discuss guidelines for successful inclusion.
5. Identify methods of modifying activities for inclusion.
6. Identify several disabilities and techniques for modifying activities to accommodate these disabilities.

FOR MORE INFORMATION

REFERENCES AND SUGGESTED READINGS

Auxter, D., Pyfer, J., & Huettig, C. (2005). *Principles and methods of adapted physical education and recreation* (10th ed.). Boston: McGraw-Hill.

Bennett, T., Bruns, D., & Deluca, D. (1997). Putting inclusion into practice: Perspectives of teachers and parents. *Exceptional Children, 64*(1), 115–132.

Block, M. E. (2000). *A teacher's guide to including students with disabilities in regular physical education* (2nd ed.). Baltimore: Paul H. Brookes.

Block, M., Oberweiser, B., & Bain, M. (1995). Using classwide peer tutoring to facilitate inclusion of students with disabilities in regular physical education. *The Physical Educator, 52*(1), 47–56.

Block, M., & Vogler, E. V. (1994). Inclusion in regular physical education: The research base. *Journal of Health, Physical Education, Recreation, and Dance, 65*(1), 40–44.

Bouchard, C., Tremblay, A., Despres, J. P., Nadeau, A., Lupien, P. J., & Theriault, G., et al. (1990). The response to long-term overfeeding in identical twins. *New England Journal of Medicine, 322*, 1477–1482.

Brustad, R. J. (1993). Who will go out and play? Parental and psychological influences on children's attraction to physical activity. *Pediatric Exercise Science, 5*, 210–223.

Burton, A., & Miller, D. (1998). *Movement skill assessment.* Champaign, IL: Human Kinetics.

Cooper Institute. (2004). *Fitnessgram activitygram test administration manual* (3rd ed.). Champaign, IL: Human Kinetics.

Davis, R. W. (2002). *Inclusion through sports: A guide to enhancing sport experiences.* Champaign, IL: Human Kinetics.

DePauw, K., & Goc Karp, G. (1994). Integrating knowledge of disability throughout the physical education curriculum: An infusion approach. *Adapted Physical Activity Quarterly, 11*, 3–13.

Dobbins, D. A., Garron, R., & Rarick, G. L. (1981). The motor performance of educable mentally retarded and intellectually normal boys after covariate control for differences in body size. *Research Quarterly, 52*(1), 6–7.

Dunn, J. M. (1997). *Special physical education: Adapted, individualized, developmental.* Madison, WI: Brown & Benchmark.

Education for All Handicapped Children Act of 1975, Pub. L. No. 94–142.

Epstein, L. H., Woodall, K., Goreczny, A. J., Wing, R. R., & Robertson, R. J. (1984). The modification of activity patterns and energy expenditure in obese young girls. *Behavior Therapy, 15*(1), 101–108.

Foster, G. D., Wadden, T. A., & Brownell, K. D. (1985). Peer-led program for the treatment and prevention of obesity in the schools. *Journal of Consulting and Clinical Psychology, 53*(4), 538–540.

Harter, S. (1985). *Manual for the self-perception profile for youth.* Denver: University of Denver.

7

Horvat, M., Eichstaedt, C. B., Kalakian, L. H., & Croce, R. (2002). *Developmental/Adapted physical education: Making ability count* (4th ed.). San Francisco: Benjamin Cummings.

Jansma, P., & French, R. (1994). *Special physical education: Physical activity, sports, and recreation.* Englewood Cliffs, NJ: Prentice Hall.

Lavay, B., & DePaepe, J. (1987). The harbinger helper: Why mainstreaming in physical education doesn't always work. *Journal of Health, Physical Education, Recreation, and Dance, 58*(7), 98–103.

Lieberman, L., & Houston-Wilson, C. (2002). *Strategies for inclusion: A handbook for physical educators.* Champaign, IL: Human Kinetics.

Lohman, T. G. (1987). The use of skinfold to estimate body fatness on children and youth. *Journal of Physical Education, Recreation, and Dance, 58*(9), 98–102.

Sherrill, C. (2004). *Adapted physical activity, recreation and sport* (6th ed.). Boston: WCB/McGraw-Hill.

Simon, J., & Smoll, F. (1974). An instrument for assessing youth's attitude toward physical activity. *Research Quarterly, 45*(4), 407–415.

Ulrich, D. A. (1983). A comparison of the qualitative motor performance of normal, educable, and trainable mentally retarded students. In R. L. Eason, T. L. Smith, & F. Caron (Eds.), *Adapted physical activity.* Champaign, IL: Human Kinetics.

U.S. Department of Health and Human Services. (1995). *Asthma & physical activity in the school* (NIH Publication No. 95-3651). Washington, DC: National Institutes of Health.

Vogler, E. W. (2003). Students with disabilities in physical education. In S. Silverman & C. Ennis (Eds.), *Student learning in physical education.* Champaign, IL: Human Kinetics.

Winnick, J. P. (2005). *Adapted physical education and sport.* (4th ed.). Champaign, IL: Human Kinetics.

Winnick, J. P., & Short, F. X. (1999). *The Brockport physical fitness test manual.* Champaign, IL: Human Kinetics.

Yun, J., Shapiro, D., & Kennedy, J. (2000). Reaching IEP goals in the general physical education class. *Journal of Physical Education, Recreation, and Dance, 71*(8), 33–37.

WEBSITES

Adapted Physical Education
www.pecentral.org
www.palaestra.com
www.pelinks4u.org/sections/adapted/adapted.htm
www.twu.edu/inspire

Adapted P.E. Assessment Tools
www.pecentral.org/adapted/adaptedinstruments.html

Children's Disabilities Information
www.childrensdisabilities.info

Inclusion Programs That Work
www.ed.gov/pubs/EPTW/eptw12/index.html
www.palaestra.com/Inclusion.html
http://clerccenter.gallaudet.edu/kidsworlddeafnet/

Legal Issues
www.ed.gov/offices/OSERS/Policy/IDEA/the_law.html

National Standards
http://apens.org

Evaluation

ESSENTIAL COMPONENTS OF QUALITY PROGRAMS

- ▶ I. Organized around content standards
- ▶ II. Student-centered and developmentally appropriate
- ▶ III. Physical activity and motor skill development form the core of the program
- IV. Teaches management skills and self-discipline
- ▶ V. Promotes inclusion of all students
- ▶ VI. Focuses on process over product
- ▶ VII. Promotes lifetime personal health and wellness
- VIII. Teaches cooperation and responsibility and promotes sensitivity to diversity

NATIONAL STANDARDS FOR PHYSICAL EDUCATION*

1. ▶ Demonstrates competency in motor skills and movement patterns needed to perform a variety of physical activities.
2. Demonstrates understanding of movement concepts, principles, and tactics as they apply to the learning and performance of physical activities.
3. Participates regularly in physical activity.
4. Achieves and maintains a health-enhancing level of physical fitness.
5. Exhibits responsible personal and social behavior that respects self and others in physical activity.
6. Values physical activity for health, enjoyment, challenge, self-expression, and/or social interaction.

*National Association for Sport and Physical Education (NASPE), 2004.

There are many types of evaluation, but all evaluation is done to improve instruction and increase learning. Ways to evaluate student learning include checklists, logs, tests, and scoring rubrics. A grading system that communicates student progress to parents is difficult to design. There are many reasons for giving grades and just as many reasons for avoiding grading in elementary schools. A student progress report helps parents understand their child's progress in physical education. Growth in instructional effectiveness occurs when teachers choose to self-evaluate their instruction. A program checklist can be used to score the total physical education setting.

Outcomes

- Differentiate between formal and informal evaluation.
- Explain and understand the differences between process and product evaluation.
- Cite several ways to assess student learning.
- Know the advantages of a progress report for parents.
- Describe arguments for and against grading in physical education.
- Identify methods of instructional analysis of teacher behavior.
- Identify ways to self-evaluate instructional behavior.
- Recognize the key elements of an effective physical education evaluation form.

ASSESSMENT AND EVALUATION

The purpose of evaluation is to determine whether progress is being made toward objectives. Evaluation should review all phases of education, including pupil progress, teacher performance, and program effectiveness. Evaluation can be formal or informal and can focus on individual or group progress. For clarity, this chapter looks at evaluation as a multifaceted approach that includes *assessment* (student performance), *institutional evaluation* that evaluates whether the school (or district or state) is reaching desired student outcomes, and *instructional effectiveness* as measured by quantifying teacher behavior. A related area to be evaluated is the actual physical education program, and an instrument for this purpose is included at the end of the chapter.

ASSESS STUDENT PERFORMANCE

Assessment is defined as the collection of information about student performance. Traditionally, assessment in physical education has been directed at functions of compliance (i.e., participation, attendance, effort) and not on components that reflect student learning. Even when performance is considered, it is done in ways that are suspect in recording true learning. Hopple (2005) suggests the use of ongoing assessment as a tool to improve planning, evaluate learning, and maximize teaching effectiveness. The purpose of assessment in this chapter is to help teachers obtain knowledge about student performance that can be used for grading and measuring student accountability. As professionals, physical education teachers tend to perform informal assessments daily when they help students improve skill performance. The important issue becomes how they use this information to evaluate or even grade students. Furthermore, it is essential that teachers use the assessments as instructional tools to assist in planning lessons and modifying instruction in an effort to maximize student learning.

In the field of physical education, assessment is a difficult issue. Classes are often bigger than traditional classroom settings, the area covered is more expansive, and there is often no permanent record of work completed (like a written example of work for an English class) for teachers to take home and thoroughly inspect. Faced with such obstacles, what can physical education teachers do to produce a quality assessment routine for students? The assessment process is crucial in providing feedback to students, teachers, and parents. Collecting data allows teachers to make judgments about student performance based on certain criteria.

Many components are evaluated in physical education. A major part of assessment is examining the skill learning and development that occur through the instructional process. Even though skill development is a primary focus of physical education, it is not enough; students need to learn about strategy, skill performance techniques, and positive attitudes toward physical activity. Written exams can be used to evaluate whether students have requisite knowledge for successful participation. The area of attitudes and values is important to the program. Students will choose not to participate if their attitudes and values have not developed concurrently with skills and knowledge. Assessment instruments serve various purposes (Hopple, 2005). Here are some common reasons for assessment.

- *Grading.* Performance on established instruments offers objective data for grading. Communicating with students and parents is more effective when an objective, systematic tool has been used for assessment. Parents and students can see how the students compare to others and are given a realistic view of their performance in relation to other students or established criteria. Grades based on objective data carry more credibility and respect both inside and outside the profession.

- *Motivation.* Nothing motivates individuals more than improvement. When improvement can be documented through assessment, it shows that effort has been rewarded. The extent (or lack) of improvement is not clear if assessment is not a part of the program. Another factor that motivates students is setting reachable goals. Students who are unaware of their performance level and ability have difficulty identifying goals they can achieve.
- *Diagnosis.* Assessment often reveals problems or deficiencies. When teaching an entire class, teachers find it difficult to gauge each student's ability and progress. Often, the teacher expends more energy monitoring student behavior than observing student performance. Assessment focuses that energy on progress of individual students and reveals those students who are deficient or performing skills incorrectly.
- *Placement and equalization.* At times, it is beneficial to group students homogeneously—that is, placing students with equal ability in groups. On the other hand, if assessment reveals some students who are skilled and others who are having problems, the teacher can use a peer-tutoring method (skilled helping less skilled). Student assessment helps teachers place students with peer helpers and equalizes small groups to enhance learning.
- *Program assessment.* Student assessment can reveal program effectiveness and the relevancy of objectives. If all students pass the assessment, the program goals may be too low. If many fail, the quality of instruction may be inadequate or the standard of performance may be too high. Over time, student assessments can give direction to the program as objectives and instructional strategies are modified to increase student success.
- *Program support.* Results of regular assessment can be used to defend and support the program. The data gained through assessment can reveal what students are expected to learn and how effectively they are learning. *Accountability* is a buzzword among educators; to gain public support, schools must document what students are learning. When making cutbacks in programs, administrators usually ask faculty members to justify continuation of their programs.

ASSESSMENT: PROCESS OF LEARNING OR PRODUCT OUTCOMES?

Physical education is different from academic areas because it demands physical rather than mental performance. In academia, once a student masters a skill, she no longer thinks about that skill and focuses on new skills. Once mastered, the ability to add numbers or read words stays with people throughout life. In physical education, however, skills are lost if not practiced. Thus physical education calls for a slightly different perspective.

Two types of outcomes pertain to students: (1) process of learning and (2) product (performance). *Process of learning outcomes* relate to performing movement patterns and skills with emphasis on correct technique. The form used to execute the movement, not the outcome of the skill performed, is the point of assessment. In contrast, *product outcomes* focus on performance in measurable increments of what learners accomplish. When applying product outcomes to ball skills, the teacher might emphasize how many times the ball is caught without a miss. On the other hand, process outcomes would focus on the techniques of catching properly. In thinking about the outcomes you want for your students, consider these key questions.

8

DEVELOP ATHLETES OR TEACH ALL STUDENTS?

Should elementary school physical education focus on product outcomes, or should it emphasize the process of learning skills correctly? Should physical education experiences be designed to develop high-quality performers, or should they focus on teaching all students the correct way to perform skills? Physical education has a unique role in the elementary school curriculum. Nowhere else can students receive skill instruction and the opportunity to learn the benefits of lifetime activity. Academics can teach character, knowledge, social skills, and the like, but only physical education can accomplish unique physical skill and activity outcomes. Physical education does not have to be like academics; in fact, it is important because it is different.

IS PERFECTION POSSIBLE IN PHYSICAL EDUCATION?

Physical education has no absolute and exact product. Cognitive knowledge is based on the building-block theory—that new learning is based on previously acquired facts. For example, basic math facts are necessary to perform higher-level math manipulations. Physical education differs in that the same set of skills is learned and refined throughout the school years. For instance, the skill of throwing is taught in elementary school and continues to be repeated and refined each year thereafter. After students learn the basic skill, teachers emphasize repetition and refinement of the skill.

Perfection (of skill performance) does not occur in physical education, or in sport for that matter. This idea contrasts with academic areas, which demand accuracy and correctness. New knowledge is based on previously learned information, which is based on a commonly accepted body of information. This is not so with physical education, because correct performance is impossible to predict and errors are expected. Even the best athletes miss half of the baskets they shoot or make an out in baseball about 70% of the time. However, sometimes physical educators teach as though reaching perfection is realistic and reasonable. In response, their students believe that focusing on the outcome (such as making a basket) is more important than performing the skill correctly. Teachers encourage such thinking when they reinforce skill attempts that are correct while failing to comment on a student's quality of performance.

Encourage students when they excel in physical activity, but avoid pressuring them beyond their developmental readiness. You may end up turning them off the activity or push them to injure themselves.

SKILL REFINEMENT OR SKILL PERFORMANCE?

Refining a skill is not the same as improving performance. Teachers have been taught to evaluate the effectiveness of their teaching based on how many students reach product benchmarks, such as making a certain number of baskets or jumping rope a number of times without a miss. Many teachers have written such outcomes, thinking they will be able to get all students to reach them. Unfortunately, they promise a product that may not be achievable. For example, creditable golf pros assure their adult pupils that they can improve their swing, which, over time, *may* result in improved golf scores. They do not guarantee improved scores, because they cannot control the client's genetic makeup or psychological willingness to change, practice, and improve. The golf pro guarantees that she will teach with enthusiasm, be knowledgeable of the latest techniques, and devote the time and energy necessary to help refine her client's skills. Teachers can teach students how to perform skills properly, but they cannot guarantee that all students will be high-level performers.

WINNING OR FEELING GOOD?

The ultimate goal of physical education is to graduate students who feel competent and willing to perform skills throughout a lifetime of activity. Knowing how to live an active lifestyle may be more important for students than being able to make 10 to 15 free throws or hit 20 successful tennis serves. Students also benefit from learning to value effort more than victory. Something is lost for many participants when winning dictates success. The process of doing one's best is an important issue in physical education. It is possible, but not common, to find students who participate in an activity without worrying about winning and losing. Many areas of the school curriculum emphasize cooperative learning. Physical education can benefit by such an approach. Evidence shows that cooperative learning improves self-esteem and attitude toward school and can temper the negative aspects of competition (Johnson, Johnson, & Holubec, 1998). Activity and participation can be enhanced through the joy of working together.

Consider the product–process conflict and how it relates to a teacher's view of the instructional environment. A product-oriented teacher usually focuses on skill performance and shows less concern for students' feelings about the learning experience. In a game of Frisbee Golf, for example, the focus is on the outcome of the game—the score, winning or losing. The process-oriented teacher, on the other hand, is more concerned that students develop proper techniques of skill performance and positive attitudes toward the activity. Winning or losing is secondary to the learning experience. Most teachers find themselves somewhere between the two viewpoints and place varying amounts of emphasis on process and product. A reminder is in order here: physical education teachers should not act as coaches (who are expected to focus on winning) in the physical education setting. They are coaches when they work in the athletic arena. Quality teachers and coaches are able to separate the two different professions to ensure that proper outcomes are reached in both arenas.

ASSESS STUDENT OUTCOMES

Student performance can be assessed in many different ways. Informal assessment often occurs on the spot when a teacher corrects or reinforces a student's performance. Several more formal, yet alternative assessments are becoming popular because teachers are expected to assess and report student progress toward program standards (Chepko & Arnold, 2000; Hopple, 2005).

Many of the following techniques can be used to measure learning in the three major learning domains. The domains are briefly described here; see Chapter 4 for more information.

1. *Psychomotor domain.* This area is related to learning motor skills. Students are most often assessed in this domain because physical education focuses on skill development. Figure 8.1 is an example of a way to evaluate skills in the psychomotor domain.
2. *Cognitive domain.* This area focuses on understanding concepts of movement performance and related fitness and activity knowledge. It is most often evaluated

Student Name	Elbows are flexed in preparation to catch.	Hands adjust to the flight of the ball.	Contact is made with the hands. Elbows are flexed.	Force of the ball is absorbed by the hands and arms.
Jon				
Mike				
Mary				
Aaron				
Deb				

FIGURE 8.1 Checklist rubric for scoring catching skills.

with written tests. Figure 8.2 is an example of a knowledge test related to pedometers.

3. *Affective domain.* This area involves responsibility and attitudes toward physical education and physical activity—how a student feels and how a student behaves. This domain deals with a set of internal feelings, so it is often best to allow students to evaluate themselves. It is important to know how students feel about the physical education experience. Figure 8.3 on page 136 is an example of an instrument that Developmental Level II students can use to show their attitudes toward physical education activities.

Student assessment tools are not standardized instruments for evaluating the institutional effectiveness of the program. For most student assessment tools, individual teachers decide what elements to include. A rubric or checklist is not effective unless the teacher does much work and testing to make it valid and reliable. A valid instrument

Pedometer Knowledge Test

Name: ______________________________

1. Pedometers measure physical activity. What two ways do the pedometers we use in class measure our physical activity?

2. Where should the pedometer be placed to ensure that it will measure accurately?

3. What are the two rules we learned about using pedometers in physical education?

4. What types of physical activity will a pedometer measure?

5. If two people are walking together and one person is tall and the other is short, who will have the most steps on their pedometer when they reach the end of their walk?

FIGURE 8.2 Evaluating the cognitive domain: Pedometer knowledge.

How I Feel about Activities in Physical Education

Name: ______________________________

The following are some activities we have learned in our physical education class. Please show how you feel about each of the activities by drawing a happy or sad face on the face next to each of the activities.

- Team activities such as basketball, football, and volleyball.
- Individual activities such as juggling, rope jumping, and animal walks.
- Fitness activities such as jogging, push-ups, and sit-ups.
- Gymnastic activities such as forward rolls, log rolls, and cartwheels.
- Using pedometers to measure physical activity.
- Playing simple games like tag, Home Base, Busy Bee, and Crows and Cranes.
- Activities that use equipment such as balance beams, benches, and jumping boxes.
- Activities I can do at home by myself such as walking, riding my bike, and swimming.

FIGURE 8.3 Evaluating the affective domain: How I feel.

accurately measures what it purports to measure, and its validity must be tested in various settings. A reliable instrument measures the same behaviors accurately over and over, yielding the same results when the same student is tested. Student assessment tools do have value; they are an inventory of skills and behaviors each teacher believes students should learn. They give teachers a systematic way to collect information that lets students and their parents know whether expected outcomes have been met.

CHECKLIST RUBRICS

A checklist rubric is a rating scale that lists multiple criteria related to a task or motor skill performance. This rubric is most often used to evaluate skill performance outcomes. The criteria are techniques students should use when performing skills. A basic question common to most assessments is, "Can the child perform the stated motor pattern using proper techniques?" Teachers using this type of assessment require accurate knowledge of the critical elements of the skills. Videotaping is useful for viewing the skill performance several times and in slow motion. For example, a 9-year-old child at the expected developmental level should be able to demonstrate all four components when catching. If a child of this age exhibits only two of the components, a developmental deficiency is indicated. Figure 8.1 is an example of a checklist rubric for catching skills. This rubric lists four critical elements required for all catching skills. In most cases, the quality of behavior is not judged; the behavior is simply marked as present or absent.

OBSERVATION CHECKLISTS

An observation checklist is another means of assessing student progress. Observation checklists are commonly used for assessing skill performance. Criteria governing proper technique for the motor skills are listed, and the child's performance is checked against these criteria. Limiting coverage to two or three critical techniques is usually best. For ease of recording, criteria can be rated on a 3-point scale: above developmental level (3 points), at developmental level (2 points), or below developmental level (1 point). The record sheet can also be organized so that achievement levels are listed and the evaluator circles the appropriate number. Figure 8.4 is an example of an observation checklist for some fundamental locomotor skills.

Class ______________________ Grade ______________ Date ______________

Scoring: 3 = above developmental level 2 = at developmental level 1 = below developmental level	Running			Jumping			Hopping			Skipping		
	Arm Action	Leg Action	Composite	Arm Action	Leg Action	Composite	Arm Action	Leg Action	Composite	Arm Action	Leg Action	Composite
Student's Name												

FIGURE 8.4 Observation checklist for locomotor skills.

RATING SCALES

Rating scales have long been used as a system for reporting progress to students and parents. A class roster with skills listed across the top of the sheet is a common way to record class progress. It is a graphic indication of those students who may require special help. If grading is based on the number of activities students master, the checklist can deliver this information. Rating scales are usually most effective when skills are listed in the order they should be learned. In this way, instruction is designed to address diagnosed needs. To avoid disrupting the learning process, it is best to record student progress informally while students are practicing. Figure 8.5 is a sample checklist for rope jumping.

ANECDOTAL RECORD SHEETS

To assess children's progress in physical education, teachers can use anecdotal record sheets that list student names and provide room for comments. Such records can be reinforcing to both student and teacher since it is often difficult to remember how much progress has been made. Anecdotal records enable teachers to inform students of their initial skill level compared with their present performance.

Another use for anecdotal record sheets is to monitor behavior in the affective domain. For example, teachers may have behavior expectations of students who exhibit behavior problems. Teachers can write short notes about how these students behaved each day. This leads to a documented record of how long the behavior has occurred and when it started to improve (or not improve). The teacher can then share this information with parents or students.

A tape recorder is useful for recording anecdotal information. Comments can be recorded during observation and transcribed later, thus making it easier to learn students' names and behavior patterns and leading to greater understanding of student performance. Observations should be recorded at the start of the unit and compared with observations made later in the semester. A sample anecdotal record sheet is illustrated in Figure 8.6.

STUDENT LOGS

Intermediate-grade students are capable of maintaining a log that indicates their progress toward a goal over time. Assume students want to increase the amount of physical activity they accomplish each day. Teacher and students can cooperatively design goals to help the students become more active. Another approach is to ask students to develop behaviors they need to accomplish to reach their goals. The log should include goal behaviors they have accomplished over time—decisions and choices made, time spent on goal behaviors, and a reflection area to record their perceptions of the experience.

Students can share their experiences and feelings about things they have tried. The logistics of activities each student has tried can be shared. Examining how well the stated outcomes were reached is the most common way to evaluate logs. For example, for students who wanted to increase their activity outside of school, a high score would go to children who were active for 30 minutes 5 days a week. An

Rope-Jumping Checklist

Student	Jump in Place	Jump, Turn Both Ends	Jump, Pendulum Swing	Slow Time	Fast Time	Alternate-Foot Step	Swing Step Forward	Rocker Step	Spread Legs, Forward	Toe-and-Heel Touch	Shuffle Step	Cross Arms	Cross Arms, Backward	Double Jump	

FIGURE 8.5 Sample skill checklist.

Anecdotal Record Sheet

Class Ms. Massoney Date 2/14

Bob: Is making progress on the backward jump. Sent a jump rope home with him for practice.

Gene: Seems to be discouraged about rope jumping. Called parents to see if there is a problem outside of school.

Linda: Discussed the need for helping others. She is going to be a cross-aged tutor for next two weeks, as her performance in batting is excellent.

FIGURE 8.6 Sample anecdotal record sheet.

acceptable score would go to students who were active 3 days a week. An unacceptable score would go to those who were active 1 day or less.

Classroom teachers particularly like student logs because they encourage students to write—a major emphasis in the classroom. But without appropriate planning, student logs may take away time from physical activity. To avoid this issue, physical education teachers can collaborate with the classroom teacher to allow time for writing in the classroom following physical education. This may require the development of writing prompts for students, but it is worth the time. If this approach is not possible, teachers must develop routines for students to retrieve writing materials, do the writing, and return the materials. Since maximizing physical activity is a critical component of physical education, limit writing time to 3 to 4 minutes, use it sporadically throughout the school year, and confine it to use in fourth through sixth grades.

PEER AND SELF-ASSESSMENTS

Students in the intermediate grades are capable of self-evaluation and peer assessment. For self-assessment, they can review lists of performance objectives and make judgments about their achievement (Figure 8.7 on page 140). If more objectivity is desired, students can evaluate each other, or groups of two or three students can evaluate one another. Self-evaluation reduces teacher evaluation time, allowing more time for instruction. The ability to evaluate oneself and the desire to be evaluated are important outcomes of any effective program.

Student self-assessments are particularly useful for affective domain behavior. Use them to monitor how students feel about certain activities or about their behavior. Having students assess themselves forces a look inward that may help both the teacher and student understand why the behavior is occurring. It is also possible to learn about activities students enjoy and how they behave when they do not like an activity.

Peer assessment can be another way of teaching students how to recognize quality performances. Students must be taught how to evaluate and know what is expected of them before they begin the process. Peer assessment takes practice and feedback from teachers and peers. A good way to teach the evaluation process is to have the class observe a skill performance by a similarly aged student. In most cases, it is better to use a video of someone the students do not know. This allows for honest input about the skill performance without fear of hurting a fellow student. Upper-grade students can examine the performance and determine what should be assessed and how success should be defined. Discussion should follow to help peers understand how they would communicate their evaluation scores to fellow students.

Students can also benefit from using rubrics or checklists to guide their assessments. At first these tools can be provided by the instructor; once the students have more experience, they can develop the rubrics. Checklists should remind peer evaluators to comment primarily on the skill performance rather than on items unrelated to the skill.

For peer evaluation to be effective, the learning environment in the activity area must be supportive and positive. Students must feel comfortable and trust one another in order to provide honest and constructive feedback. Instructors who use group work and peer assessment can help students develop trust by forming small groups and letting them work together for several weeks. Allowing students to become more comfortable with each other leads to better peer feedback.

WRITTEN TESTS

Written tests are administered to check the cognitive learning that has accompanied physical skill learning. Use true/false or multiple-choice tests to minimize sedentary time and simplify correction. One approach is to use exit

Responsible Behavior Checklist

Name: ______________________________

Please rate yourself on your personal behavior during the times you were playing in games this week. Answer the questions fairly and as accurately as possible.

My Level of Responsible Behavior*	**0**	**1**	**2**	**3**	**4**
1. I encouraged others and said things such as, "Nice job," "Good hustle," "Excellent catch," etc. Explain why you gave yourself this rating:					
2. I won or lost gracefully. I didn't get angry or put down others. Explain why you gave yourself this rating:					
3. I followed the rules without trying to cheat. I was willing to abide by the referee's decisions. Explain why you gave yourself this rating:					
4. I did my best to get all my teammates involved in the game. Explain why you gave yourself this rating:					
5. I was willing to play in games even when it wasn't my favorite activity. Explain why you gave yourself this rating:					
*0 indicates you never behaved this way. 4 indicates you always behaved this way.					

FIGURE 8.7 Student self-assessment. Evaluating the affective domain: Responsible behavior.

slips (Figure 8.8). After a lesson, students quickly retrieve an exit slip and pencil, complete the items, and return the slips to the teacher. By offering only one to three items focusing on the key cognitive concepts of the day, you can check student learning while minimizing interference with activity time. On the other hand, short-answer or essay questions encourage students to apply knowledge to different situations. When composing tests, consider the students' reading level to ensure that you are testing for knowledge, not comprehension. Oral questions are often best for younger students. It may seem obvious, but remember that written tests give little to no indication of how a child will perform a motor skill. Be careful not to grade just on written tests that examine cognition, since physical education is primarily based on becoming skilled physically.

GRADING

Physical education grading policies in elementary schools vary widely, ranging from no grading at all to grading with letter grades as in high school classes. So, is it better to grade or not to grade? Each system has its merits, and there is no definitive answer. If a decision is made to grade, a more difficult question arises: What grading system should be used? For an in-depth review of grading systems and ideas for evaluation, see the text by Lacy and Hastad (2007).

POINTS AGAINST USING A GRADING SYSTEM

- Grades can vary between teachers and schools. A single-letter grade means one thing to one teacher and another to a different teacher. When a student moves to a different school, the meaning of the grade might not transfer, and teachers at the new school may view it differently.
- Physical education does not emphasize content and product. Rather, it judges success by improvement on skills. Grades in academic areas reflect achievement and accomplishment; because grades in physical education reflect improvement and effort, they may be interpreted incorrectly.
- Often, physical education classes in elementary schools meet only once or twice a week. Regularly testing for

1. In the F.I.T.T. Principle, the "I" stands for:

    A. Index

    B. Injury

    C. Intensity

    D. Immune

2. Frequency refers to how long you are physically active.

    A. True

    B. False

FIGURE 8.8 Exit slip.

grade requirements is time-consuming. Physical educators in this setting are trying to squeeze as much learning as possible into the class period, and grading reduces their instructional time.

- Physical education is diverse and broad. Instruction covers all three learning domains—skill development, attitude formation, and content knowledge. Trying to grade all three domains is difficult and time-consuming. Further, which of these three domains is most important, and can any of them be overlooked?
- Grading usually occurs in areas where standardized instruments have been developed. Fitness testing is the major area in elementary physical education where such tests have been developed. Due to the lack of standardized tests in other areas, teachers may give excessive attention to fitness testing.
- Physical education emphasizes physical fitness and skill performance. Performance in these areas is strongly controlled by genetics, making it difficult for every child to achieve, even when he "gives it his best effort." Also, when grades are given for physical fitness performance, some students feel discouraged because they trained and still did not reach standards of high performance.

POINTS FOR USING A GRADING SYSTEM

- When grades are not given, academic respect is lost. Physical education already suffers from the misguided perception that physical educators do not teach anything, they just "roll out the ball." Lack of a grading system may make others think that little learning is occurring.
- Grades inform parents about their child's performance. Parents have a right to know how their children perform in physical education. Grades are used by teachers in other areas and are easily understood and interpreted by parents; therefore, they should be used in physical education.
- A grading system provides accountability. When grades are given, administrators and parents often assume that teaching and student accomplishment have occurred.
- A grading system rewards skilled students. Students are rewarded in academic areas for their intelligence and performance and should be similarly rewarded for accomplishment in physical education settings.

IF YOU CHOOSE TO GRADE, CONSIDER THE FOLLOWING . . .

If you decide to implement a grading system, more difficult issues follow. There are different ways to grade, and many issues have to be examined before developing a grading approach. Consider the following points when determining how you will assign grades.

8

Educational Outcomes versus Administrative Tasks

It is generally agreed that physical education should help students achieve in various areas including skill development, personal values, and cognitive development. Some grading systems assign weight to each of these areas when compiling a grade. Regardless of the emphasis each area receives, the final grade depends on accomplishment of educational objectives. This contrasts with grading on completion of administrative tasks, where students earn some or all their grade by attendance, participation, and attitude. This latter approach grades students on tasks that have little to do with accomplishing physical education objectives. Furthermore, these tasks are usually documented at the beginning of the period and have little effect on holding students accountable for their in-class performances.

Consider the conflicts arising when students are graded on achieving educational objectives versus accomplishing administrative tasks. Assume a student in a math class regularly forgets to bring a pencil and is tardy but earns an A grade on all math exams. Does this student earn a final grade of A, or is the student penalized for doing poorly on administrative tasks (tardiness and so on) and given a C grade? Reverse the situation and assume the student has an outstanding attitude, is never tardy, and always brings the proper supplies to class. At the end of the semester, the student has earned a C grade on exams yet performed all administrative tasks at a high level. Does this student receive a final grade of A? If grades in other curricular areas of the school are earned by accomplishing educational objectives or performing administrative tasks, it is probably wise to follow suit in the physical education area.

Attitude versus Skill Performance

Another area of concern when grading is whether attitude or skill performance should be the focal point. Those who emphasize attitudes stress the importance of students leaving school with warm, positive feelings toward physical activity. These educators often say, "I am not concerned about how many skills my students learn; I just want them to walk out of my class with positive feelings about physical activity." They assume that students who feel positive about physical activity will be willing to be active throughout their lifetimes. These teachers assign grades based on the process of trying rather than on reaching skill outcomes. Students who receive higher grades may not be the most skilled but have shown good behavior and a positive attitude throughout the semester.

Teachers who reside in the product camp focus primarily on student accomplishment and see effort as something that is laudable but not part of the grading process. They would say, "I don't really care whether students like me or physical education. What is ultimately important is their performance. After all, the students who are best in math earn the highest grades, so why should it be any different in physical education?" Teachers who focus on performance give the highest grade to the best performer, regardless of other factors. Less skilled students, no matter how hard they try, will not receive an above-average grade.

This is a difficult, hotly debated problem to resolve in physical education. One viewpoint is that students should learn from the grading system how society works. People are rewarded in life for their performance, not for how hard they try. For example, if real estate agents try hard but never sell a house, they make no money. The payoff is for selling houses, not for trying hard to sell houses. An opposing viewpoint is that many people in society are rewarded for effort, so "doing your best" should be rewarded.

A solution to consider is to grade on performance while focusing the instruction on students' attitudes toward physical activity and skill learning. Much is to be said for teaching that helps students develop a positive attitude toward activity. Attitude development depends largely on how teachers present the material rather than on how students perform skills. Help students understand that they also perform differently from each other in math or science and receive a respectively higher or lower grade.

Relative Improvement

Some physical educators believe that effort, or "just doing the best that you can," should be the most important factor in assigning grades. To reward effort, these teachers base student grades on how much a student improves. This involves pre-testing and post-testing to determine the amount of progress made throughout the grading period. This approach contrasts with basing the grade on absolute performance; the best performer in the class quite possibly will not receive the highest grade because of less improvement.

Grading on improvement is time-consuming and requires that the same test be given at the beginning and end of the semester or unit. The test may or may not accurately reflect what has been learned in the class, and it may not be sensitive enough to reflect improvement made by both poor and outstanding performers. Testing at the beginning of a unit can be discouraging and demoralizing if a student performs poorly in front of peers. It can also be hazardous in activities such as gymnastics or archery that require intensive instruction to prevent accident or injury.

Another consideration is the issue of performing for a grade. Students learn quickly to perform at a low level on the pre-test in order to demonstrate a higher degree of improvement on the post-test. A related problem is that improvement is sometimes easier at beginning levels of skill than at high levels of performance. Most teachers are aware of the rapid improvement beginners make before reaching a learning plateau. A skilled performer may be at a level where improvement is difficult to achieve. Lack of improvement in this situation results in a skilled performer receiving a lower grade than a beginner.

Grading on Potential or Effort

Some teachers choose to grade on whether students reach their potential. Such teachers decide what a student's potential performance level should be and then assign a grade based on whether the student reached that level. The grade a student receives depends on the teacher's subjective perception of that student's genetic abilities and limitations. How can any teacher really know a student's absolute potential? Students who are graded this way are being rated on an unknown factor: potential.

This approach often depends on the teacher's feelings about the student in question. It is based on intangibles, and a student may receive a grade because she is "just like her brothers or sisters." When grades are based on a teacher's subjective beliefs rather than on criteria that are measured and evaluated, they are difficult to defend. How would a parent react to a teacher's statement that "Your child received a failing grade because he just didn't live up to his potential"? To be defensible, grading systems need to be based on tangible data gleaned from observable behavior and performance.

Negative versus Positive Grading

To make the grading system defensible and concrete, some teachers have used point systems. In most point systems, both performance objectives and administrative factors are listed as grade components. A student earns a grade through performance, attitude, and knowledge. Point systems can become a negative influence if handled incorrectly. For example, some teachers give students 100 points at the start of the semester and then "chip off" points for various unsatisfactory levels of performance. A student may lose points for not trying, not performing, or not knowing answers on a test. Students soon realize that they need to concentrate on negative behaviors that lose points rather than on educational objectives.

In contrast, some teachers use a point system that rewards positive behavior. Students receive points for performing well, and they can earn their grades through self-direction. In a negative system, teachers make all the judgments about points lost and receive in turn the negative feelings of the student. In a positive system, students can behave in a positive way to earn points. Teachers are constantly rewarding positive behavior, which fosters positive feelings toward physical education and teachers. Rewarding positive behavior makes students feel that the teacher cares about their welfare and growth.

A negative system tends to focus teachers on what students cannot do, rather than on what they should or can do. Energy is spent on "policing" students and threatening to take away points if they do not behave. Students respond poorly to this approach, since losing points does not require an immediate change in behavior and a redirection. The loss of points results in a lower final grade, a consequence that is usually 6 to 9 weeks away. Few students respond positively to grade leverage through a negative system. Students who care about their grades are performing well in the first place. Threatening to lower the grade of a student who does not like physical education or school in general only further alienates the student and is based on a system of negative reinforcement. The grading system should positively encourage students to perform.

Letter Grades versus a Student Progress Report

Letter grades tell parents very little about their children's performance in physical education. Frequently, the grade reflects the student's behavior while the parents interpret it as an indicator of their student's physical skill level. A letter grade does not communicate progress or performance related to other students at a similar developmental level. A student progress report takes more time to compile but gives parents much more information and helps communicate program goals.

Figure 8.9 on page 144 is an example of a progress report that could be used to share information with parents. The seven areas of evaluation represent the six major content standards of the program (see Chapter 1). If desired, some of the specific benchmarks under each standard could also be included. Note that program standards are divided into two major areas: (1) physical education skills and (2) social skills and responsible behavior. Most teachers want an opportunity to separate behavior and skill performance when grading. This progress report allows students to be rewarded for effort and proper behavior regardless of their skill and physical ability. Evaluating a student based on developmental level gives parents an idea of how their child is performing compared to others of similar development and maturity. This report helps parents understand the skill performance of other children who are similar developmentally or who are above, at, or below their child's skill level. Such feedback may help temper unrealistic expectations of parents and coaches who do not have the perspective of seeing many children at similar developmental levels.

Completing a progress report takes more time than assigning letter grades, so a progress report cannot be sent home as often as a simple letter grade. Most elementary school teachers are responsible for 350 to 600 or more students, so completing a progress report for each student four times a year would be an unrealistic expectation. A solution is to offer a comprehensive, meaningful progress report once a year or once every second or third year. This approach alerts teachers to students they will have to grade for the forthcoming year and gives them time to review these students in detail throughout the year.

EVALUATE INSTITUTIONAL OUTCOMES

Institutional outcomes are goals that the state, school district, superintendent, school board, and parents want to reach. They are also referred to as "accountability outcomes" or developed as answers to the question, "What should the physical education program contribute to the total school environment?" To evaluate institutional goals, it is necessary to use a test that is valid and respected within as well as out of the school setting. The best examples of tests for measuring institutional outcomes in schools today are the "high-stakes" tests used for measuring math, science, and reading outcomes. In some cases, students are not allowed to graduate without passing these exams. It is a poor reflection on the institution if a large number of students do not pass, so the tests become an important catalyst for change.

HEALTH-RELATED FITNESS

Physical fitness testing has occurred for decades in physical education. Some experts argue for emphasizing fitness testing less and activity evaluation more (Ernst, Beighle,

Progress Report for Physical Education

Student: ______________________ **Class:** ______________________

Students are expected to learn a wide variety of skills in physical education. The following areas reflect major program standards. Expectations are that your child will perform at or above developmental level (compared with other students the same age). If you are interested in discussing the progress of your child, please arrange a meeting with the physical education instructor.

Physical Education Assessment

Program Standards	**Developmental Level Performance**		
	Above	**At**	**Below**
Exhibits motor skills and movement competence			
Is able to monitor and maintain physical fitness			
Understands human movement principles			
Uses lifestyle habits that foster wellness			
Possesses lifetime physical activity skills			

Social Skills and Responsible Behavior Assessment

Students are graded on social skills and responsible behavior in physical education classes. Rewards and consequences are recorded daily. Grades are based on how students perform in these areas.

O = Outstanding Exhibits effort and a positive attitude about participating in physical activities on a regular basis. Cooperates with classmates and receives no more than one behavior consequence during the 9 week grading period.

S = Satisfactory Willingly attempts activities. Puts forth average effort, displays a positive attitude, cooperates with classmates, and receives two to five behavior consequences during the 9 week grading period.

N = Needs Improvement Consistently exhibits off-task behavior and/or a negative attitude. Has difficulty cooperating with classmates. Parents are notified by midterm of the grading period if their child is in jeopardy of receiving a grade of "N."

Program Standards	**O**	**S**	**N**
Develops quality social skills			
Exhibits responsible behavior			

Instructor's Comments

FIGURE 8.9 Sample progress report.

Corbin, & Pangrazi, 2006). Currently the Fitnessgram system (Cooper Institute, 2008) is a popular test used to measure health-related physical fitness and is the recommended test for the American Alliance for Health, Physical Education, Recreation, and Dance (AAHPERD). The test items have been checked for validity and reliability. The Fitnessgram offers a variety of fitness test items so teachers can develop a customized test battery. The Fitnessgram focuses on teaching students the importance of activity for good health. Students are not compared to one another but receive feedback about their fitness and whether it meets the minimum standard for good health.

The Fitnessgram is based primarily on exercise behaviors rather than on students' attempts to demonstrate that they are the "best." The Fitnessgram program acknowledges and commends performance, but its highest priority is developing and reinforcing health-related behaviors that are attainable by all students. The behavior programs are used to commend participants for various activities: completing exercise logs, achieving specific and personalized goals, and fulfilling a contractual agreement (with a responsible adult). A helpful text for understanding fitness and activity topics is *Toward a Better Understanding of Physical Fitness & Activity: Selected Topics, Volume II* (Corbin, Pangrazi, & Franks, 2004).

Fitnessgram Test Items

This section briefly describes suggested test items in the Fitnessgram. The manual includes other test items to give teachers a choice of designing a different test battery. A comprehensive test administration manual, related materials, and software can be ordered from Human Kinetics, P.O. Box 5076, Champaign, IL 61825-5076 (www.Fitnessgram.net).

Aerobic Capacity

The PACER (Progressive Aerobic Cardiovascular Endurance Run) test is an excellent alternative to the mile run—it involves a 20-meter shuttle run and can be performed indoors. This progressive test starts at a level that allows all students to succeed and gradually increases in difficulty. The test objective is to run back and forth across the 20-meter distance within a specified time limit that gradually decreases. The 20-meter distance does not intimidate students (compared to the mile) and avoids the problem of teaching students to pace themselves rather than run all-out and fatigue rapidly.

Body Composition

Body composition is evaluated using percentage of body fat, which is calculated by measuring the triceps and calf skinfolds or body mass index (calculated using height and weight).

Abdominal Strength

The curl-up test uses a cadence (one curl-up every 3 seconds). The maximum limit is 75. Students lie faceup with their knees bent at a 140-degree angle. The hands are placed flat on the mat alongside the hips. The objective is to gradually sit up and move the fingers down the mat a specific distance.

Upper Body Strength

The push-up test is done to a cadence (one every 3 seconds) and is an excellent substitute for the pull-up. A successful push-up is counted when the arms are bent to a 90-degree angle. The push-up test allows many more students to experience success. Other alternative test items are the modified pull-up, the pull-up, and the flexed-arm hang.

Trunk Extensor Strength and Flexibility

The trunk lift test is done from a facedown position. This test involves lifting the upper body 6 to 12 inches off the floor using the muscles of the back. The position must be held until the measurement can be made.

Flexibility

The back-saver sit and reach test is similar to the traditional sit-and-reach test, but it is performed with one leg flexed so that students avoid hyperextending. Measurement is made on both the right and left legs.

Criterion-Referenced Health Standards

A major reason for health-related fitness evaluations is to provide students, teachers, and parents with information about good health. The Fitnessgram (Cooper Institute, 2008) uses *criterion-referenced health standards* that represent good health instead of traditional percentile rankings. These standards represent a fitness level that offers some degree of protection against diseases resulting from sedentary living. The Fitnessgram uses an approach that classifies fitness performance into two categories: needs improvement and healthy fitness zone (HFZ). All students are encouraged to score in the HFZ, but there is little advantage to scoring beyond this zone. Unlike percentile rankings, criterion-referenced health standards do not compare students against each other. Instead, students are taught to be concerned with personal fitness and minimizing possible health problems by trying to score in the HFZ.

Criterion-referenced health standards for aerobic fitness are based on a study by Blair et al. (1989). A significant decrease in risk of all-cause mortality occurred when people were active enough to avoid being classified in the bottom 20% of the population. The risk level continues to decrease as fitness levels increase, but not significantly when compared to moving out of the least active group. The aerobic performance minimums (mile run or PACER) for the Fitnessgram HFZ require achieving a fitness level above that for the least active portion (bottom 20%) of the population.

Criterion-referenced health standards for percentage of body fat are calculated from equations reported by Slaughter et al. (1988). Detailed information on the development of these equations and other issues related to measuring and interpreting information on body composition is available in Lohman (1992). Williams et al. (1992) reported that students with body fat levels above 25% for boys and 30–35% for girls are more likely to exhibit elevated cholesterol levels and hypertension. The lower limit for the Fitnessgram HFZ corresponds to these levels of body fat. In other words, students who have higher levels of body fat may be at risk for future health problems.

Criterion-referenced health standards have not been established for abdominal strength, upper-body strength, or flexibility. For example, it is difficult to determine whether a lack of upper-body strength is important for quality health. Instead, criterion-referenced training standards are used for these areas of fitness. These standards reflect a reasonable expectation for students who are sufficiently active.

Effective Uses of Fitness Tests

Fitness tests are designed to evaluate and educate students about the status of their physical fitness. Despite continued research and improvement, fitness tests—particularly field-based tests—have limitations and usually show low validity (i.e., they do not measure what they purport to measure). Therefore, how the tests are used becomes an important issue. Fitness tests can be used in three major ways: (1) to teach personal self-testing, (2) to establish personal-best fitness performances, and (3) to evaluate institutional fitness goals. The personal self-testing program is most strongly advocated in the elementary school physical education program. It takes the least amount of time, is educational, and can be done in an unthreatening way. Little instructional time is lost, and students learn how to evaluate their fitness—a skill that will serve them for a lifetime. Many people have experienced fitness testing many times, but few people ever learn how to evaluate their personal fitness level.

Personal Self-Testing

The personal self-testing program is student centered, concerned with the process of fitness testing, and emphasizes learning to self-evaluate. Students can work on this program individually or with a friend. Partners evaluate each other and develop their own fitness profiles. The goal is to learn the process of fitness testing so that students will be able to evaluate their health status during adulthood. Students are asked to do their best, but the teacher does not interfere in the process. The results are the student's property and are not posted or shared with other students. The personal self-testing program is an educational endeavor; it also allows for more frequent evaluation because it can be done quickly, privately, and informally.

Figure 8.10 shows a self-evaluation Fitnessgram form for student use. Students check the "HFZ" column to indicate they have met the minimum criterion-referenced health standard for each test item. Recording the data helps students learn to self-evaluate without the stigma of others viewing or knowing about it. A final note: It is acceptable for some students to choose not to be tested on a certain item because they fear embarrassment (skinfolds) or failure (PACER). It is worse for them to be tested and embarrassed than not to be tested at all. Morgan, Beighle, Pangrazi, & Pangrazi (2004) offer a detailed description of implementing fitness self-testing.

Personal-Best Testing

The personal-best testing approach appeals to gifted performers and to motivated students. The objective is to achieve a maximum score in each of the test items. This approach has been used for years with most fitness tests. In addition, several awards (President's Council on Physical Fitness and Sports, 2008) are issued to high-level performers. Unlike the self-testing approach discussed earlier, this is a formal testing program. Test items must be performed correctly, following test protocol to the letter. Testing also requires a considerable amount of time to administer.

Personal-best testing is an elective program that requires maximal performance and usually is not motivating to less capable students. Some students are threatened and fear the embarrassment of failing to perform well in front of peers. To avoid embarrassing these students, administer the test outside of class time. Offer testing opportunities after or before school and on a weekend when school is not in session. As another elective option, some city recreation departments offer fitness testing opportunities outside the physical education program. This approach is much less threatening; students can choose to participate in the personal-best testing session or decide to forgo it entirely.

Institutional Evaluation

The institutional evaluation program involves examining students' fitness levels to see if the institution (school) is reaching its desired objectives. Institutional objectives are closely tied to the physical education curriculum. If the curriculum is adequate and the goals are meaningful, most students should be able to reach institutional goals. A common approach for institutional goal setting is to establish a percentage of the student body that must

My Personal Fitness Record

Name ________	**Age** ____	**Grade** ____	**Room** ____	
	Score		**HFZ***	
Body Composition				
Calf (leg) Skinfold				
Triceps (arm) Skinfold	+			
Total (leg and arm)	=			
Cardiovascular Endurance PACER				
Abdominal Strength Curl-Ups				
Upper Body Strength Push-Ups				
Back Strength Trunk Lift				
	L	R		
Lower Back Flexibility Sit and Reach				
	L	R		
Upper Body Flexibility Shoulder Stretch				

* HFZ means you have scored in the Healthy Fitness Zone. You have achieved or passed the minimum fitness standard requiredfor good health and feeling good. Regardless of whether you scored in the HFZ for all the tests, you must maintain an active lifestyle for good health. Try to accumulate at least 60 minutes of activity every day.

You do not have to share the results of your personal fitness record. It is for your information and should help you determine your health status. Ask your teacher if you need ideas for increasing your physical activity level. You are learning the process of evaluating your fitness. The scores recorded may not be accurate.

FIGURE 8.10 Fitnessgram form: My Personal Fitness Record.

meet or exceed criterion-referenced health standards for a fitness test.

Since this type of testing affects teachers and programs, it is done in a formal, standardized way. A common approach is to train a team of parents to administer tests throughout the system. This ensures accuracy and consistency across all schools in the district. Each test item is reviewed separately, since objectives may be reached for some but not all of the items. To avoid testing all students every year, some districts evaluate only during entry-level years (i.e., the seventh and ninth grades). This minimizes the amount of formal testing students have to endure during their school career.

PHYSICAL ACTIVITY

Another way to evaluate the effectiveness of the institution is to monitor the amount of physical activity students accumulate daily. Fortunately, accurate instruments are now available for measuring the amount of physical activity students accumulate (for an in-depth discussion of physical activity monitoring and promotion, see Chapter 12). Using pedometers to measure children's physical activity levels is now an accepted instructional and research methodology (Beighle, Pangrazi, & Vincent, 2001; Crouter, Schneider, Karabulut, & Bassett, 2003; Kilanowski et al., 1999). Many pedometers have a function that measures total hours and minutes of activity time accumulated throughout the day.

Every time a person moves, the pedometer starts accumulating time. When the person stops moving, the timing function stops. This function is useful for students and parents because most activity recommendations are expressed in minutes per day (see Chapter 12).

There are a number of ways to gather institutional data with pedometers. Research has shown that data on 4 days of physical activity will accurately indicate student's average activity level. A set of pedometers can be rotated between classrooms to establish the average level of activity for each classroom. Goals for classes and schools can be established using this objective data set. Physical activity is a more achievable outcome measure (as compared to physical fitness outcomes) for elementary school students. Students can be monitored for 4 days at the start of the school year and again near the end of the year. An excellent outcome of monitoring physical activity is that all students can become more active. Contrast this with physical fitness, where most of the performance in elementary school students is controlled by their genetic endowments and physical growth. Most pre-test/post-test fitness gains shown in elementary school are due to children becoming 8 to 9 months older.

Another spin-off of monitoring physical activity is that an award system for active children can be implemented. The President's Council on Physical Fitness and Sports has developed an award for students who accumulate at least 60 minutes of physical activity almost every day for 6 weeks. The award, called the Presidential Active Lifestyle Award, looks like the Presidential Physical Fitness Award (President's Challenge, 2008). Students can sign up and log their activity into the website each day at www.presidentschallenge.org. This is an excellent way to promote physical activity outside the school day.

CHILDREN'S ATTRACTION TO PHYSICAL ACTIVITY (CAPA)

The Children's Attraction to Physical Activity (CAPA) instrument is used to assess the attraction of children ages 8 to 12 to physical activity (Brustad, 1995). The CAPA has been used for research purposes and validated by Brustad (1995). It is a 15-item pencil-and-paper instrument that assesses the extent of children's interest in physical activity by having them consider two opposing viewpoints. Children first choose the point of view that describes them and then select the strength of that feeling ("sort of true" or "really true") for each of the 15 items. The instrument is scored on a scale of 1 to 4 points, with 4 reflecting the most positive attraction to physical activity. Figure 8.11 on pages 149–150 shows the CAPA instrument.

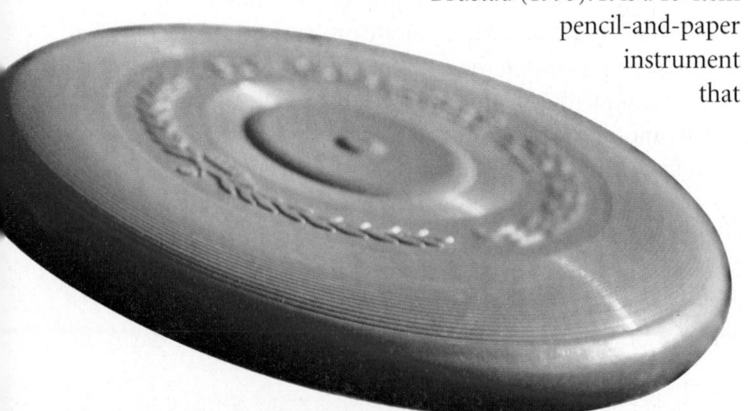

Since the CAPA is a standardized instrument, schools can use the results to see if the physical education program is positively influencing the students' affective domain. Schools and classrooms can be compared to see how students feel about physical activity. If attitudes toward physical activity are low, teachers and parents can develop strategies to improve the students' feelings.

EVALUATE INSTRUCTIONAL EFFECTIVENESS

Obtaining meaningful feedback about your own instructional behavior is vital to improved teaching ability. But it is often difficult to find someone capable of offering evaluative feedback. Principals and curriculum supervisors may be too busy to evaluate teaching regularly, or they may lack the skills to systematically evaluate teaching behavior. This situation accentuates the importance of finding ways for self-evaluating teaching as a primary avenue for improvement. Without regular and measurable means of evaluation, it is nearly impossible to improve the quality of teaching. Teachers have long been told to talk less, move more, praise more, learn more names, and increase student practice time—all without documented methods of measurement. This section offers methods for evaluating teaching behavior that are observable and therefore measurable. For in-depth information on this topic, the texts *Developing Teaching Skills in Physical Education* (Siedentop & Tannehill, 2000) and *Analyzing Physical Education and Sport Instruction* (Darst, Zakrajsek, & Mancini, 1989) are excellent resources.

The do-it-yourself approach to evaluation is recommended because feedback you can review in the privacy of your office is easier to digest and less threatening. You can set personal goals and chart your performance privately. When you choose to evaluate your teaching procedures, you are making a commitment to change. This attitude is in contrast to the resistance that some teachers feel when principals and supervisors evaluate them and dictate change. Instructors often doubt the validity of the latter process and find reasons for not changing.

What I Am Like

Please look at the sample question first. Choose only one answer to each question. There are no right or wrong answers. Simply choose the statement you think is most true for you.

Sample

	Really true for me	Sort of true for me				Really true for me	Sort of true for me
	A	B	Some kids like to eat ice cream more than anything else.	BUT	Other kids like other foods more than ice cream.	C	D

	Really true for me	Sort of true for me				Really true for me	Sort of true for me
1.	A	B	Some kids have more fun playing games and sports than anything else.	BUT	Other kids like doing other things.	C	D
2.	A	B	Some kids don't like to exercise very much.	BUT	Other kids like to exercise a whole lot.	C	D
3.	A	B	Some kids get told by other kids that they are not very good at games and sports.	BUT	Other kids are told that they are good at games and sports.	C	D
4.	A	B	Some kids get teased by other kids when they play games and sports.	BUT	Other kids don't get teased when they play games and sports.	C	D
5.	A	B	Some kids think that the more exercise they get the better.	BUT	Other kids think that it is not good to get too much exercise.	C	D
6.	A	B	Some kids don't enjoy exercise very much.	BUT	Other kids enjoy exercise a whole lot.	C	D
7.	A	B	Some kids try hard to stay in good shape.	BUT	Other kids don't try hard to stay in good shape.	C	D
8.	A	B	Some kids don't like getting out of breath when they play hard.	BUT	Other kids don't mind getting out of breath when they play hard.	C	D

FIGURE 8.11 Children's Attraction to Physical Activity (CAPA) instrument.

8

	Really true for me	Sort of true for me				Really true for me	Sort of true for me
9.	A	B	Some kids think it is very important to always be in good shape.	BUT	Other kids don't think it is so important to always be in good shape.	C	D
10.	A	B	For some kids, games and sports is their favorite thing.	BUT	Other kids like other things more than games and sports.	C	D
11.	A	B	Some kids are popular with other kids when they play games and sports.	BUT	Other kids are not very popular with others when they play games and sports.	C	D
12.	A	B	Some kids look forward to playing games and sports.	BUT	Other kids don't look forward to playing games and sports.	C	D
13.	A	B	Some kids really don't like to exercise.	BUT	Other kids do like to exercise.	C	D
14.	A	B	Some kids feel bad when they run hard.	BUT	Other kids feel good when they run hard.	C	D
15.	A	B	Some kids don't like to run very much.	BUT	Other kids do like to run a whole lot.	C	D

Source: From Attraction to physical activity in urban school children: Parental socialization and gender influences, *Research Quarterly for Exercise and Sport,* 67 (pp. 316–323) by R. J. Brustad, 1996. Copyright 2007 by Pearson Benjamin Cummings. Reprinted with permission.

FIGURE 8.11 Children's Attraction to Physical Activity (CAPA) instrument. (Continued)

The first steps to self-improvement are deciding what teaching behavior to evaluate and finding the best possible way to record and monitor the data. Start by evaluating a single teaching behavior since recording more than one variable at a time can be frustrating and confusing. After determining the behavior to change, design a coding form to facilitate recording the data.

Coding sheets are best designed for a specific teaching behavior. Areas on the sheet are provided for recording teacher's name, the date, the lesson focus and content, the grade level and competency of the students, the duration of the lesson, and a short description of the evaluation procedure. Maintaining a consistent format for the coding sheets will make it easier to compare your performance throughout the year. The next section offers appropriate coding forms for gathering data on various teaching behaviors. These forms are examples that can be modified to meet your specific needs. Effective teachers usually make self-evaluation an ongoing, integral part of their teaching.

There are many ways to gather data about your teaching. For example, students who are not participating can gather the data; another teacher can gather the data easily; or the data can be gathered from an audiotape or a videotape. Most teachers feel comfortable evaluating their own teaching performance. Because daily teaching behavior is least affected when outside observers are not present, self-evaluation techniques are more likely to reveal actual instructional patterns.

INSTRUCTIONAL TIME

It is important to know the amount of instruction you offer students. To analyze instructional time, record the number of instructional episodes and the length of each episode. The average length of an instructional episode can be evaluated as well as what percentage of the lesson was used for instruction. Generally, episodes should be short and frequent, with a goal of limiting each episode to 30 seconds or less.

How To Do It

1. Design a form for duration recording (Figure 8.12).
2. Have a colleague or a nonparticipating student turn on the stopwatch every time you begin an instructional episode; or record the lesson using an audiotape recorder and time the instructional episodes at the end of the day. Establish consistency in identifying the difference between instructional and management episodes.
3. Total the amount of time spent on instruction.
4. Convert the amount of time to a percentage of the total lesson time by dividing the total lesson time into the time spent on instruction. The average length of an instructional episode can be determined by dividing the amount of instructional time by the number of instructional episodes.

MANAGEMENT TIME

Management time includes episodes that occur when students are moved into various formations, when equipment is gathered or put away, and when directions are given relative to these areas. Disciplining a class is another example of time used for management. As a rule of thumb, if you are talking and not giving instructions, you are managing students.

An observer can record the length of each episode. These data are useful for analyzing how much of the lesson time is devoted to management. You may be alerted to inefficient organizational schemes or realize that students are not responding quickly to explanations and requests.

How To Do It

1. Design a form to gather the desired data (Figure 8.13 on page 152).
2. Record the lesson with an audiotape recorder. Time the episodes of management, and note the length of each episode on the form.
3. Total the amount of management time and divide it by the length of the period to determine the percentage of management time in the lesson.

8

Instructional Time

Teacher Charlene Darst Observer B. Pangrazi

Class 1st period Grade 5th Date and Time 3/22 - 9:05

Lesson focus Basketball Comments 1st class meeting of unit

Starting time 9:30 Ending time 10:00 Length of lesson 30 min

15	10	8	35	17	1:03	31	9	8
14	21	10	21	43	7			

Total instruction time 5 min 12 sec

Percentage of class time devoted to instruction 17%

Number of episodes 15 Average length of episodes 31.5 sec

FIGURE 8.12 Sample form for calculating instructional time.

Management Time

Teacher Don Hicks Observer Connie Orlowicz

Class 6th period Grade 3rd Date and Time 10/29 - 1:30

Lesson focus Manipulative skills Comments

Starting time 1:30 Ending time 2:00 Length of lesson 30 min

55	10	21	20	35	18	29	10	10	21	9	19	21
11												

Total management time 4 min 49 sec

Percentage of class time devoted to management 16%

Number of episodes 14 Average length of episodes 20.6 sec

FIGURE 8.13 Sample form for calculating management time.

4. Total the number of episodes and divide this number into the amount of time devoted to management to find the average length of a management episode.

PRACTICE TIME (TIME ON TASK) AND DEAD TIME

To learn physical skills, students must have an opportunity for productive skill practice. Physical education programs have a finite amount of scheduled time per week. Practice time, or time on task, has also been referred to as academic learning time in physical education (ALT-PE). Practice time is the amount of time students spend practicing skills that result in accomplishment of program objectives. Gathering data to show the amount of time students are involved in productive, on-task activity can reveal whether students have enough time to learn skills. In a well-regarded school district, the author found that the average amount of activity time per 50-minute period was only 9 to 12 minutes. More learning might occur if practice time were increased.

Duration recording is best for evaluating practice time. A student or fellow teacher observes the lesson and times when students are involved in practicing skills. Figure 8.14 shows the results of a duration recording for practice time. Strive to increase the amount of time devoted to skill practice by using more equipment, implementing drills that limit standing in line, or streamlining verbal instructions.

The amount of dead time in a lesson also can be measured. Dead time occurs when students are off task or doing something unrelated to practice, management, or

Teacher: Debbie Massoney
School: Whittier Elementary

Parts of the lesson	Practicing	Inactive, off-task, listening
Introductory activity	1.5 min	0.5 min
Fitness development	6.5 min	1.5 min
Lesson focus	10.0 min	4.0 min
Game	5.0 min	1.0 min
Total	23.0 min	7.0 min

FIGURE 8.14 Results of a duration recording for practice time.

Practice Time

Teacher Eugene Petersen Observer P. W. Darst

Class 2nd period Grade 4th Date and Time 11/15 - 9:15

Lesson focus Gymnastics skills Comments week two

Starting time 9:25 Ending time 10:00 Length of lesson 35 min

35	10	2:04	25	29	1:39	17	55	34
43	1:55	1:01	33	10	10	18	1:17	4:50
24	39	31	34					

Total practice time 20 min 13 sec

Percentage of class time devoted to practice 57.8%

Number of episodes 22 Average length of episodes 55.1 sec

FIGURE 8.15 Sample form for collecting data on practice time.

instruction. Examples might be waiting in line for a turn, doing nothing because instructions were not understood, or waiting for the ball to come to them during game play.

How To Do It

1. Design a form for collecting the data (Figure 8.15).
2. Identify a student who will be timed when practicing. This is a critical step. The student chosen should be neither exceptional nor below par and should give a realistic picture of the amount of practice time allotted. Record the dead time by timing when that student is not involved in on-task practice, management, or instructional activity. Another way to calculate dead time is to subtract the combined amounts of time used for practice, management, and instruction (assuming all have been timed) from the total length of the lesson.
3. Turn on the stopwatch when the student is involved in practice (or dead) activity. Stop the watch when the student stops (or starts) practicing. Record the amount of practice (or dead) time. Time all practice (or dead) episodes.
4. Total the amount of time devoted to student practice (in minutes), and divide it by the length of the lesson. This is the percentage of practice time in a lesson. To compute the percentage of dead time, total the amount of dead time and divide it by the length of the lesson.

RESPONSE LATENCY

Response latency, the amount of time it takes for students to respond to commands or signals, occurs when students are instructed to begin or stop an activity. An observer records the amount of time that elapses between the moment a command is given to start or stop an activity and the moment the students actually begin or stop. The amount of elapsed time is the response latency.

The average duration of response latency can be calculated. A certain amount of response latency should be expected, but most instructors feel strongly about how much they are willing to tolerate. After more than a 5-second response latency, teachers usually become uneasy and expect the class to stop or start.

How To Do It

1. Develop a form for gathering the data (Figure 8.16 on page 154).
2. Have a nonparticipating student or colleague time the response latency that occurs when the class is asked to

Response Latency

Teacher Jim Roberts Observer Bob Pangrazi

Class 2nd period Grade 2nd Date and Time 2/5 - 9:00

Lesson focus Movement concepts Comments

Starting time 9:05 Ending time 9:35 Length of lesson 30 min

Starting Response Latency

3	7	5	9	15	3	3	4	9	7	5	3	
2	4	10	7									

Stopping Response Latency

10	12	9	8	8	15	8	6	2	9	10	11	15
14	5	5	13									

Total amount of starting response latency 1 min 42 sec

Percentage of class time devoted to response latency 5.7%

Number of episodes 16 Average length of episodes 6 sec

Total amount of stopping response latency 2 min 41 sec

Percentage of class time devoted to stopping response latency 8.9%

Number of episodes 17 Average length of episodes 9.5 sec

FIGURE 8.16 Sample form for evaluating response latency.

stop (or start). The clock should run from the time a command is given until the next command is given, or until the class is involved in productive behavior. Starting and stopping latency are two separate behaviors that must be recorded separately.

3. Calculate the average episode length by tallying the number of response latency episodes and dividing this number into the total amount of time devoted to response latency.

STUDENT PERFORMANCE

Some classes have a greater percentage of students performing at optimum level than others do. The percentage of students performing the desired task is an excellent indicator of a well-managed class. The placheck (planned activity check) observation technique (Siedentop & Tannehill, 2000) is an excellent way to monitor the percentage of students who are on task.

Placheck recording is a technique used to observe group behavior at different times during a lesson. At regular intervals, the observer scans the class from the left to the right side of the instructional area and records the number of students who are not performing the predefined behavior. (Recording the smaller number of students exhibiting a behavior is easier. For example, if you are interested in identifying the percentage of students on task, generally it is easier to record the number of students *not* on task.) Each student in the class is observed only once during a scan. The observer does not go back and change the decision, even if the student changes behavior during the interval. Intervals should last for 10 seconds and be randomly spaced throughout the lesson, with 8 to 10 observation intervals. Signals to scan the class should be recorded on a tape recorder at random intervals to cue the observer.

The placheck is used to monitor behavior that is "yes or no" in nature—students either are performing the desired behavior or they are not. Examples of areas that might be evaluated are on task behavior, active behavior, or effort in performing an activity. Once the results are determined, a goal can be set to increase the percentage of students involved in the desired observable behavior.

How To Do It

1. Design a form for recording the desired data. The sample form in Figure 8.17 can be used to identify three different types of student performance. The data gathered indicate on-task and off-task student behavior.
2. Place 8 to 10 "beeps" at random intervals on a tape recording to signal when to conduct a placheck.
3. Have the observer scan the area in a specified, consistent direction from left to right each time the tape-recorded signal is heard. The class is scanned for 7 to 10 seconds while the observer records the number of students engaged in the desired behavior.
4. Convert the data to a percentage by dividing the total number of students into the number of unproductive students and then multiplying the result by 100. Four

Student Performance

Teacher Albert Santillan Observer Ms. Estfan

Class 8th period Grade 6th Date and Time 5/5 - 2:30

Lesson focus Rhythmic movement skills Comments

Starting time 2:30 Ending time 3:00 Length of lesson 30 min

Active/Inactive

On-Task/Off-Task

5	4	12	7	3	3	2	5	6	5
4	3								

Effort/Noneffort

Number of plachecks 12

Total number of students 30

Average number of students not on desired behavior 4.9

Average percentage of students not on desired behavior 16%

FIGURE 8.17 Sample form for placheck observation.

to six plachecks spaced throughout a class period will yield valid information about class conduct.

INSTRUCTIONAL FEEDBACK

Feedback given to students strongly affects the instructional presentation. Feedback can be defined and measured so that meaningful goals for improvement can be established. The process of changing interaction patterns can create some discomfort, but ultimately it pays dividends. The following areas can be evaluated to give direction for implementing useful change.

Praise and Criticism

When students are involved in activity, give them feedback related to their performance. Feedback can either be positive and constructive, or negative and critical. It is easy to ask a student or peer to record the occurrence of praise and criticism. The results can be tallied and evaluated at the end of the day. The number of instances and the ratio of positive to negative comments are then calculated. With this information, goals can be set for increasing the number of comments per minute and modifying the ratio of positive to negative comments.

General versus Specific Feedback

Feedback to students can be general or specific. "Good job," "Way to go," and "Cut that out" are examples of general feedback. General feedback can be positive or negative; it does not specify the behavior being reinforced. In contrast, specific feedback identifies the student by name and reinforces an actual behavior; it also might be accompanied with a valuing statement. An example is, "Michelle, that's the way to keep your head tucked! I really like that forward roll!" To evaluate this area, tally general and specific feedback instances. Feedback can be positive or negative, and this distinction can be recorded (Figure 8.18).

Using first names is important in personalizing feedback and directing it to the proper individual. The number of times first names are used can be totaled. Valuing statements can also be evaluated. Data gathered in these categories are divided by the length of the lesson (in minutes) to render a rate per minute.

Corrective Instructional Feedback

Effective teachers inspire students to achieve higher levels of performance. Part of this process involves giving performers

Instructional Feedback

Teacher ____________ Observer ____________

Class ____________ Grade ________ Date and Time ____________

Lesson focus ____________ Comments ____________

Starting time ________ Ending time ________ Length of lesson ________

Interactions unrelated to skill performance	+								
	−								
General instructional feedback	+								
	−								

Corrective instructional feedback

First names

Nonverbal feedback	+								
	−								

Ratio + to −/nonskill related ____________

Ratio + to −/skill related ____________

FIGURE 8.18 Sample form for feedback observation.

meaningful corrective feedback. Corrective feedback focuses on improving the student's performance. Corrective instructional feedback should be specific so that students know what they must correct. An example of corrective instructional feedback is, "You struck the soccer ball much too high. Try to strike it a little below center." This type of feedback tells the student what was incorrect about the skill attempt and how to perform the skill correctly.

Nonverbal Feedback

Much performance feedback is given nonverbally. Nonverbal communication is meaningful to students and may be at least as effective as verbal forms of communication. Examples of nonverbal feedback after a desired performance are a pat on the back, a wink, a smile, a nod of the head, the thumbs-up sign, and clapping the hands. Nonverbal feedback can also be negative: a frown, shaking the head in disapproval, walking away from a student, and laughing at a poor performance.

A student or another instructor can tally the number of positive and negative nonverbal behaviors exhibited by a teacher. Students are often better at evaluating the instructor in this domain, because they are keenly aware of the meaning of the instructor's nonverbal mannerisms.

How To Do It

1. Design a form to collect the data (see Figure 8.18).
2. Audiotape a lesson to play back and evaluate later.
3. Record the data to be analyzed. At first, it is best to take one category at a time. For example, analyze the use of first names during the first playback, and then play the tape again to evaluate corrective feedback.
4. Convert the data to a form that can be generalized from lesson to lesson (i.e., rate per minute, rate per lesson, or ratio of positive to negative interactions).

ACTIVE SUPERVISION AND STUDENT CONTACT

Effective instructors actively supervise students by moving among them and offering personalized feedback. The number of times an instructor becomes personally involved with a student can be counted. One-on-one feedback differs from total class interaction and offers insight into each student's behavior and concerns.

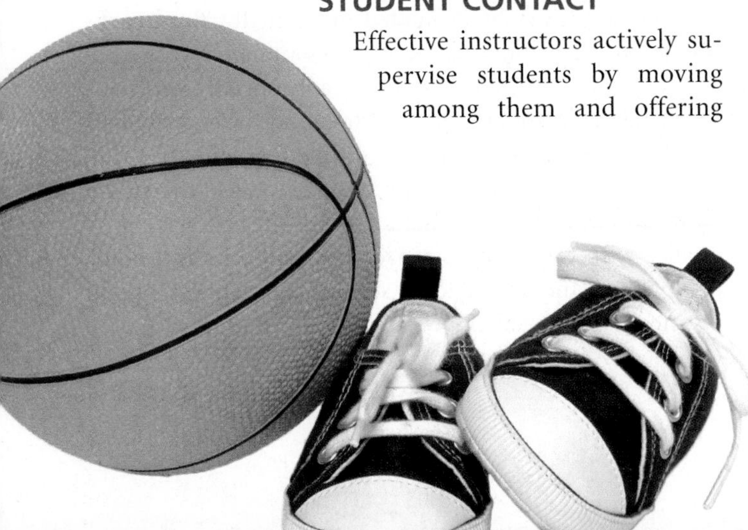

Allied to this area is the relationship between teacher movement and active supervision. Many instructors establish an area in the gymnasium where they feel most comfortable teaching. Before instruction begins, they move to that area. This consistent movement pattern can cause students to drift to different areas, depending on their feeling about the activity or the instructor. Students who like the instructor will move closer, whereas students who dislike the teacher or are uneasy about the activity may move as far away as possible. As a result, the better performers typically are near the instructor and students who may be somewhat less able are farther away and harder to observe.

The teacher can avoid these problems by moving throughout the teaching area. A way to evaluate movement is to divide the area into quadrants and tally the number of times you move into each quadrant. A tally in the quadrant is made when you speak to a student or the class as a whole. Simply passing through a quadrant does not count. The amount of time spent in each quadrant can also be evaluated. Try to spend similar amounts of time in each area. When students cannot predict where you will be next, they have a greater tendency to remain on task.

Movement related to the use of lesson time can be determined by the amount of time the teacher stays in a quadrant. The amount of time a teacher spends in each quadrant can be recorded in corresponding locations on the form and analyzed at the end of the lesson. Another technique is to code the type of behavior that occurs each time the instructor moves into a new quadrant. For example, an "M" might signify management activity, an "I" instructional activity, and a "P" practice time. This approach reveals the location and amount of time spent on each behavior.

How To Do It

1. Develop a coding form similar to the one in Figure 8.19 on page 158.
2. Ask a nonparticipating student or a colleague to record the desired data on active supervision. An alternative is to videotape the lesson and evaluate it later.
3. Evaluate the data by calculating the number of moves per lesson and the number of moves during instruction, management, and practice.

8

Teacher Movement

Teacher Alan Scarmazzo Observer Debbie Pangrazi

Class 5th period Grade 1st Date and Time 3/17 - 1:05

Lesson focus Movement concepts Comments

Starting time 1:15 Ending time 1:45 Length of lesson 30 min

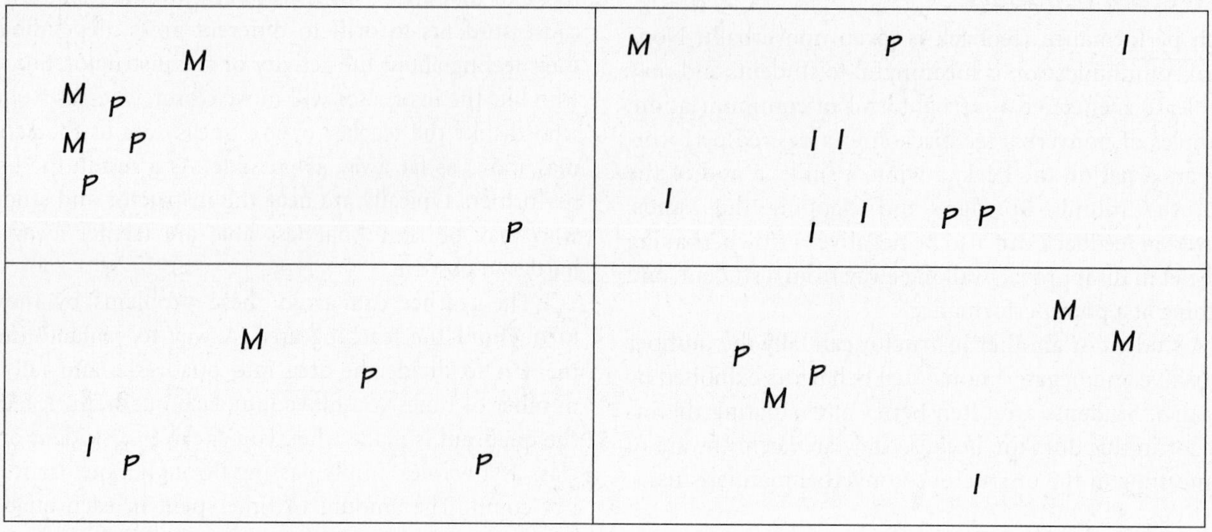

M M P M P P P	M P I I I I I P P I
M P I P P	M M P P M I

Total number of moves 28

Number of moves (I) 8 (M) 8 (P) 12

Average number of moves per minute .93

FIGURE 8.19 Sample form for evaluating active supervision and student contact (M = management activity, I = instructional activity, P = practice time).

EVALUATE YOUR PROGRAM

Your program should be evaluated regularly to ensure that it is achieving stated program goals. Evaluation instruments reflect program philosophy and objectives of individual districts. Figure 8.20 (pages 159–161) is a sample instrument that may be adapted for your own use, depending on district needs and goals. This instrument can be used to expose serious program deficiencies and operational difficulties. The results, including program strengths and weaknesses, can be shared with administrators or used by teachers to evaluate a program they have developed. The instrument can also be used to compare programs or to identify effective programs.

In the sample instrument, evaluative statements are written as a set of standards that, when met, ensure an effective program. The four areas evaluated are (1) program philosophy, (2) instructional procedures, (3) curricular offerings, and (4) facilities, equipment, and supplies. The entire instrument can be used, or any of the four areas can be evaluated individually. Read each statement, determine the level of compliance with the accepted standard, and circle the appropriate score on the rating scale. Include any comments at the end of each section. Rate and assign points on the following basis: 2 indicates full compliance (the program meets the standard fully without deficiencies), 1 indicates partial compliance with room for improvement, and 0 indicates no compliance (the deficiency is serious and detrimental to an effective program).

Physical Education Program Evaluation

Program Philosophy

1. Physical education is regarded by the administration as an integral part of the total curriculum and is dedicated to the same curricular goal, the fullest possible development of each pupil for living in a democracy. 0 1 2
2. A written and up-to-date sequential curriculum is available and used by all instructors. 0 1 2
3. Lesson plans are developed from the course of study and are used as the basis for instruction. 0 1 2
4. A meaningful progression of activities is evident between developmental levels. 0 1 2
5. Students are scheduled in the physical education program on a regular basis. 0 1 2
6. Music, field trips, and extracurricular activities are not accepted as substitutes for physical education. 0 1 2
7. Students are excused from physical education on a long-term basis only when they can submit a physician's statement indicating the medical condition and the duration of the excuse. 0 1 2
8. Appropriate arrangements are made for students with medical, religious, or temporary health excuses. 0 1 2
9. A nurse, teacher, or staff member with suitable first aid training is available in case of accident. 0 1 2
10. The budget specified for physical education equipment and supplies is adequate. 0 1 2
11. Physical education demonstration programs are offered regularly for purposes of public relations and general information. 0 1 2
12. The minimum amount per class of time allotted for physical education activity is 30 minutes. 0 1 2
13. Each class receives physical education instruction a minimum of three times per week, excluding recess and supervised play. 0 1 2
14. Class sizes are the same as those allotted to classroom teachers. 0 1 2
15. Program activities are coeducational in nature. 0 1 2
16. Classroom teachers do not keep students from physical education classes for disciplinary reasons. 0 1 2

Comments:

Instructional Procedures

1. The teacher is prepared prior to the class. A written set of instructional activities is carried into the lesson on a small note card. 0 1 2
2. Equipment is correctly arranged around the perimeter of the activity area prior to class. 0 1 2
3. Proper procedures are used for acquiring and putting away equipment. 0 1 2
4. The instructor constantly moves and repositions him-/herself so all students are in the line of sight. Instruction is conducted from different areas in the activity area. 0 1 2
5. Children in need receive special help during the lesson. The level of instruction is geared to the needs of students who lack skill. 0 1 2
6. Students understand why they are practicing skills. 0 1 2
7. There is an adequate level of teacher enthusiasm and energy. Teacher movement and personal involvement are evident. 0 1 2
8. Positive encouragement is given to all students. Youngsters are encouraged to do their best. 0 1 2
9. Students are directed to be responsible for their learning and personal behavior. Content instruction is stopped when there is a need to improve behavioral skills. 0 1 2

FIGURE 8.20 Sample evaluation form for physical education program (0 = no compliance; 1 = partial compliance; 2 = full compliance).

10. Instruction is focused on developing quality skills rather than on changing activities often in an attempt to keep students on task. Adequate opportunity is given for repetition and refinement of skills.	0	1	2
11. Closure of the lesson is a positive experience. Students are encouraged to evaluate their level of responsibility. The pitfall of nagging students about their poor class performance is avoided.	0	1	2
12. Discipline and management problems are handled effectively. The self-esteem of students is preserved during behavior correction episodes.	0	1	2
13. Disciplinary measures in physical education instruction do not include physical punishment.	0	1	2
14. Procedures for dealing with accidents, including administration of first aid, reporting, and follow-up, are in written form.	0	1	2
15. Knowledge of liability concerns related to physical education instruction and programming is evident.	0	1	2
16. Facilities, equipment, and activity areas that could be liabilities are reported in writing to appropriate administrators.	0	1	2
17. Bulletin boards, charts, pictures, and other visual materials are posted and used in the instructional process.	0	1	2
18. Teaching aids such as instructional signs, videotapes, and posters are used to enrich and supplement instruction.	0	1	2

Comments:

Curricular Offerings

1. The physical education program provides learning experiences to help each child attain the following:			
a. Refinement of motor skills and movement competence	0	1	2
b. Development of lifestyle habits that foster wellness	0	1	2
c. Ability to monitor and maintain physical activity	0	1	2
d. Understanding and applying human movement principles	0	1	2
e. Enjoyment of a lifetime of physical activity	0	1	2
f. Acquisition of quality social skills	0	1	2
g. Ability to demonstrate responsible behavior	0	1	2
2. All children are considered important and the program is adjusted to suit the maturity and skill levels of youngsters.	0	1	2
3. Each lesson has a portion of time (7 to 10 minutes) devoted to physical fitness activities.	0	1	2
4. The physical education program emphasizes and allocates enough time at the appropriate grade level for each of the following areas:			
a. Educational movement concepts	0	1	2
b. Fundamental skills, including locomotor, nonlocomotor, manipulative, and specialized skills	0	1	2
c. Rhythmic activities	0	1	2
d. Gymnastics activities	0	1	2
e. Games and relays	0	1	2
f. Sports and lead-up activities	0	1	2
5. Both indoor and outdoor teaching stations are available for physical education instruction.	0	1	2
6. Units of instruction last no longer than 3 weeks and include skill instruction.	0	1	2

Comments:

FIGURE 8.20 Sample evaluation form for physical education program (0 = no compliance; 1 = partial compliance; 2 = full compliance). (Continued)

Facilities, Equipment, and Supplies

1. Facilities include teaching stations that allow all students a minimum of three classes per week.	0	1	2
2. Outdoor facilities include the following:			
a. A physical education instructional area that is isolated from playground activities	0	1	2
b. Areas where different age groups can play without interference from each other	0	1	2
c. Areas for court games	0	1	2
d. Cement or asphalt spaces marked with a variety of game patterns	0	1	2
e. Backstops and goals for softball, soccer, and basketball	0	1	2
f. Suitable fencing for safety and control	0	1	2
g. Outdoor playground equipment, including climbing apparatus, turning bars, and tetherball areas	0	1	2
3. The outdoor area is free from rocks, sprinkler heads, and other hazards that might cause injury.	0	1	2
4. Indoor facilities meet the following standards:			
a. Clean, sanitary, and free from hazards	0	1	2
b. Well lighted, well ventilated, heated, cooled, and treated for proper acoustics	0	1	2
c. Surfaced with a nonslip finish and painted game area lines	0	1	2
5. There is periodic inspection of all facilities and equipment, both indoor and outdoor, and a written report is filed with appropriate administrators.	0	1	2
6. Storage facilities are adequate for supplies and portable equipment.	0	1	2
7. An office that is located near the instruction area is provided for the physical education instructor.	0	1	2
8. Basic supplies are sufficient in the following areas:			
a. Manipulative equipment (one piece for each child): fleece balls, small balls, beanbags, wands, hoops, and jump ropes	0	1	2
b. Sport and game balls: softballs, footballs, volleyballs, basketballs, soccer balls, floor hockey sticks and pucks, tetherballs, and cageballs in sufficient numbers	0	1	2
c. Sport and game supplies: cones, pinnies, track and field standards, jumping pits, and hurdles	0	1	2
d. Testing equipment: measuring tapes, stopwatches, calipers to measure skinfold thickness, and specialized apparatus	0	1	2
9. Sufficient materials are available for a varied rhythmic program: CD/tape player, tapes and CDs, tom-toms, and tambourines.	0	1	2
10. Capital-outlay items for the indoor facility include the following:			
a. Minimum of six tumbling mats (4 by 8 feet or larger)	0	1	2
b. Individual mats (one per student)	0	1	2
c. Sufficient climbing apparatus so that at least one-half of the class can be active at one time. Apparatus should include wall bars, chinning bars, horizontal bars, climbing ropes on tracks, and ladders.	0	1	2
d. Balance-beam benches (at least six)	0	1	2
e. Jumping boxes (at least eight)	0	1	2
f. Basketball goals, volleyball nets, hockey goals	0	1	2
g. Equipment carts (at least two)	0	1	2

Comments:

FIGURE 8.20 (Continued)

8

APPLYING WHAT YOU READ

- Integrate assessment, either formal or informal, in all lessons. Plan assessments to avoid interfering with physical activity and instruction time.
- When planning a lesson, it is important to select the tool that best assesses the outcomes you are focusing on and meets your students' needs.
- Thoughtful consideration of your grading system is essential and must be aligned with the school and physical education program objectives.
- Appropriate use of physical fitness testing makes testing educational for both student and teacher. Carefully plan how you will efficiently implement physical fitness testing. How will you avoid embarrassing students? How can you conduct fitness testing in a shorter period of time?
- Successful teachers self-evaluate their instruction. This chapter offers many teaching behaviors and lesson components to assess. Evaluating your instruction will prove invaluable as you move forward in your career.

REFLECTION AND REVIEW

HOW AND WHY

1. In a music or art class, would you want to be evaluated based on the product or the process? Why? How does this relate to your grading as a physical education teacher?
2. How is giving a child on-the-spot feedback about his or her performance a form of evaluation?
3. How are you evaluated as a college student? Do you feel you are evaluated fairly? Explain.
4. How can progress reports be more effective tools for communicating with parents?
5. Would you rather self-evaluate a lesson using videotape or have a peer evaluate you during the lesson? Why?
6. Why might the ability to be self-critical be important for physical education teachers and physical education curriculum designers?

CONTENT REVIEW

1. Discuss the significance of focusing on the process in physical education. Comment on how physical education and other academic areas differ regarding evaluation.
2. Identify and describe several methods of assessing performance outcomes.
3. Describe advantages and disadvantages of a grading system and the steps for implementing one.
4. Explain how teachers can use self-evaluation.
5. Explain four areas of teaching that can be evaluated; describe how to assess the specific areas.

FOR MORE INFORMATION

REFERENCES AND SUGGESTED READINGS

Beighle, A., Pangrazi, R. P., & Vincent, S. D. (2001). Pedometers, physical activity, and accountability. *JOPERD, 72*(9), 16–19.

Blair, S. N., Kohl, H. W., Paffenbarger, R. S., Clark, D. G., Cooper, K. H., & Gibbons, L. W. (1989). Physical fitness and all-cause mortality: A prospective study of healthy men and women. *Journal of the American Medical Association, 17*, 2395–2401.

Block, M. E., Lieberman, L. J., & Connor-Kuntz, F. (1998). Authentic assessment in adapted physical education. *Journal of Physical Education, Recreation, and Dance, 69*(3), 48–55.

Brustad, R. J. (1995). Who will go out and play? Parental and psychological influences on children's attraction to physical activity. *Pediatric Exercise Science, 5*, 210–223.

———. (1996). Attraction to physical activity in urban schoolchildren: Parental socialization and gender influences. *Research Quarterly for Exercise and Sport, 67*, 316–323.

Chepko, S., & Arnold, R. K. (Eds.). (2000). *Guidelines for physical education programs: Grades K–12 standards, objectives, and assessments.* Boston: Allyn & Bacon.

Cooper Institute. (2008). *Fitnessgram/Activitygram test administration manual* (3rd ed.; M. Meredith & G. Welk, Eds.). Champaign, IL: Human Kinetics.

Corbin, C. B., Pangrazi, R. P., & Franks, B. D. (Eds.). (2004). *Toward a better understanding of physical fitness & activity: Selected topics, Vol. 2.* Scottsdale, AZ: Holcomb Hathaway.

Crouter, S. C., Schneider, P. L., Karabulut, M., & Bassett, D. R., Jr. (2003). Validity of 10 electronic pedometers for measuring steps, distance, and energy cost. *Medicine and Science in Sports and Exercise, 35*(8), 1455–1460.

Darst, P. W., Zakrajsek, D. B., & Mancini, V. H. (1989). *Analyzing physical education and sport instruction* (2nd ed.). Champaign, IL: Human Kinetics.

Ernst, M., Beighle, A., Corbin, C. B., & Pangrazi, R. P. (2006). Appropriate and inappropriate uses of Fitnessgram: A commentary. *Journal of Physical Activity and Health, 3*(suppl 2), S90–S100.

Hopple, C. J. (2005). *Elementary physical education teaching and assessment: A practical guide* (2nd ed.). Champaign, IL: Human Kinetics.

Johnson, D. W., Johnson, R. T., & Holubec, E. J. (1998). *Circles of learning: Cooperation in the classroom.* Edina, MN: Interaction.

Kilanowski, C. K., Consalvi, A. R., & Epstein, L. H. (1999). Validation of an electronic pedometer for measurement of physical activity in children. *Pediatric Exercise Science, 11*, 63–68.

Lacy, A., & Hastad, D. (2007). *Measurement and evaluation in physical education and exercise science* (5th ed.). San Francisco: Benjamin Cummings.

Lambert, L. T. (1999). *Standards-based assessment of student learning: A comprehensive approach.* Reston, VA: National Association for Sport and Physical Education.

Lohman, T. G. (1992). *Advances in body composition.* Champaign, IL: Human Kinetics.

Morgan, C. F., Beighle, A., Pangrazi, R. P., & Pangrazi, D. (2004). Using self-assessment for personal fitness evaluation. *Teaching Elementary Physical Education, 15*(1), 1–3.

President's Council on Physical Fitness and Sports. (2008). *The President's Challenge handbook.* Washington, DC: Author.

Siedentop, D., & Tannehill, D. (2000). *Developing teaching skills in physical education* (4th ed.). Mountain View, CA: Mayfield.

Slaughter, M. H., Lohman, T. G., Boileau, R. A., Horswill, C. A., Stillman, R. J., Van Loan, M. D., & Benben, D. A. (1988). Skinfold equations for estimation of body fatness in children and youth. *Human Biology, 60*, 709–723.

Williams, D. P., Going, S. B., Lohman, T. G., Harsha, D. W., Webber, L. S., & Bereson, G. S. (1992). Body fatness and the risk of elevated blood pressure, total cholesterol and serum lipoprotein ratios in children and youth. *American Journal of Public Health, 82,* 358–363.

Wood, T. M., & Zhu, W. (Eds.). (2006). *Measurement practice and theory in kinesiology.* Champaign, IL: Human Kinetics.

Zhu, W., Safrit, M. J., & Cohen, A. (1999). *FitSmart test user manual.* Champaign, IL: Human Kinetics.

WEBSITES

Assessment Ideas and Grading
www.pecentral.org/assessment/assessment.html
www.pelinks4u.org
www.pe4life.org

Fitnessgram/Activitygram
www.fitnessgram.net

President's Council on Physical Fitness and Sports
www.fitness.gov
www.presidentschallenge.org

Self-Assessment/Reflection
www.utexas.edu/academic/cte/getfeedback
www.coe.ufl.edu/school/proteach/pathwiselesson/pathwise.htm

Video as an Assessment Tool
http://teaching.berkeley.edu/bgd/videotape.html

8

9 Legal Liability, Supervision, and Safety

ESSENTIAL COMPONENTS OF QUALITY PROGRAMS

I. Organized around content standards
II. Student-centered and developmentally appropriate
III. Physical activity and motor skill development form the core of the program
IV. Teaches management skills and self-discipline
V. Promotes inclusion of all students
VI. Focuses on process over product
VII. Promotes lifetime personal health and wellness
VIII. Teaches cooperation and responsibility and promotes sensitivity to diversity

NATIONAL STANDARDS FOR PHYSICAL EDUCATION*

1. Demonstrates competency in motor skills and movement patterns needed to perform a variety of physical activities.
2. Demonstrates understanding of movement concepts, principles, and tactics as they apply to the learning and performance of physical activities.
3. Participates regularly in physical activity.
4. Achieves and maintains a health-enhancing level of physical fitness.
5. Exhibits responsible personal and social behavior that respects self and others in physical activity.
6. Values physical activity for health, enjoyment, challenge, self-expression, and/or social interaction.

*National Association for Sport and Physical Education (NASPE), 2004.

This chapter explains the various legal terms and situations associated with physical education as well as instructional and administrative procedures common to the responsible and prudent conduct of the physical education program. It is a teacher's legal responsibility to create a safe environment that minimizes risk and the opportunity for injury and to provide a standard of care that any reasonable and prudent professional with similar training would apply under the given circumstances. Safety instruction is designed to prevent accidents and should be included in lesson plans to ensure coverage. A comprehensive safety checklist is included to be sure that beginning teachers understand how to establish an accident-free environment.

Outcomes

- Define *tort, negligence, liability, malfeasance, misfeasance, nonfeasance,* and other terms common to legal suits brought against educators.
- List major points that must be established to determine teacher negligence.
- Explain how to examine all activities, equipment, and facilities for possible hazards and sources of accidents.
- Identify common defenses against negligence.
- Describe supervisory responsibilities expected of all teachers.
- List guidelines for the proper supervision of instruction, equipment, and facilities.
- Describe aspects of sport programs that often give rise to lawsuits.
- Understand how to ensure safety, focusing on prevention.
- Outline an emergency care plan.

SCHOOL DISTRICT personnel, including teaching and nonteaching members, are obligated to exercise ordinary care for student safety. This duty is manifested as the ability to anticipate reasonably foreseeable dangers and the responsibility to take necessary precautions to prevent problems from occurring. Failure to do so may make the district the target of lawsuits.

Compared with other subject matter areas, physical education is particularly vulnerable to accidents and resultant injuries. More than 50% of all accidents in the school setting occur on the playground and in the gymnasium. Even though schools cannot be held financially accountable for costs associated with treatment of injuries, they can be forced to pay these expenses if the injured party sues and wins judgment. Legal suits are conducted under respective state statutes. Principles underlying legal action are similar, but certain regulations and procedures vary among states. You should acquire a copy of the legal liability policy for your district. Districts usually have a written definition of situations in which teachers can be held liable.

All students have the right to freedom from injury caused by others or by participating in a program. Courts have ruled that teachers have the duty to protect their students from harm. Teachers must exercise the teaching skill, discretion, and knowledge that members of the profession in good standing normally display in similar situations. When citizens believe this standard of care was not exercised, lawsuits may result.

Liability is the responsibility to perform a duty to a particular group. It is an obligation to perform in a particular way that is required by law and enforced by court action. Teachers are bound by contract to carry out their duties reasonably and prudently. Liability is always a legal matter. Before one can be held liable, it must be proved in a court of law that negligence occurred.

9

TORTS

In education, a *tort* is concerned with the teacher–student relationship and is a legal wrong that results in direct or indirect injury to another individual or to property. *Black's Law Dictionary* (Garner, 2004) defines a tort as

> a private or civil wrong or injury, other than breach of contract, for which the court will provide a remedy in the form of an action for damages. Three elements of every tort action are: existence of legal duty from defendant to plaintiff, breach of duty, and damage as proximate result.

As the result of a tort, the court can award money for damages that occurred. The court can also award money for punitive damages if a breach of duty can be established. Usually, the court awards the offended individual for damages that occurred due to the negligence of the instructor or other responsible individual. Punitive damages are much less common.

NEGLIGENCE AND LIABILITY

Liability is usually concerned with a breach of duty through negligence. To determine liability, lawyers can examine a situation that led to injury. Four major points are examined in deciding if a teacher is liable due to negligence.

DETERMINATION OF LIABILITY

1. *Duty.* The first point considered is that of duty owed to the participants. Did the school or teacher owe students a duty of care that implies conforming to certain standards of conduct? To determine a reasonable standard, the court compares the conduct of other teachers who are members of the profession in good standing.

2. *Breach of duty.* A teacher must commit a breach of duty by failing to conform to the required duty. After it is established that a duty was required, it must be proved that such duty was not performed. Two situations are possible: (a) the teacher did something that was not supposed to be done (e.g., putting boxing gloves on students to resolve their differences), or (b) the teacher did not do something that should have been done (e.g., failing to teach an activity using proper progressions).
3. *Proximate cause.* The teacher's failure to conform to the required standard must be the proximate cause of the resulting injury. It must be proved that the injury was caused by the teacher's breach of duty as well as by his or her failure to provide a reasonable standard of care. The plaintiff's expert tries to convince the court that a requisite standard was not met, while the defendant's expert tries to show that the teacher met the proper standard of care.
4. *Damages.* Actual harm must occur if liability is to be established. If no injury or harm occurs, there is no liability. It must be proved that the injured party is entitled to compensatory damages for financial loss or physical discomfort. Actual damages can be physical, emotional, or financial, but the court offers only financial awards.

FORESEEABILITY

A key to the issue of negligence is foreseeability. Courts expect a trained professional to foresee potentially harmful situations. Could the teacher have anticipated the danger of the harmful act or situation and used appropriate measures to prevent it? If the injured party can prove that the teacher should have foreseen the danger involved in an activity or situation (even in part), the teacher will be found negligent for failing to act reasonably and prudently. This potential outcome underscores the need to examine all activities, equipment, and facilities for possible hazards and sources of accident.

TYPES OF NEGLIGENCE

Negligence is defined by the courts as conduct that falls below a standard of care established to protect others from unreasonable risk or harm. This section examines several types of negligence.

MALFEASANCE

Malfeasance occurs when a teacher does something improper by committing an unlawful and wrongful act with no legal basis (often referred to as an *act of commission*). Malfeasance can be illustrated as follows: A male student frequently misbehaves. In desperation, the teacher gives him a choice of punishment—a severe spanking in front of the class or running many laps around the field. He chooses the former and suffers physical and emotional damage. Even though the student chose the punishment of spanking, the teacher is still liable for any physical or emotional harm caused.

MISFEASANCE

Misfeasance occurs when a teacher follows proper procedures but does not perform according to the required standard of conduct. Misfeasance is usually the subpar performance of an act that might otherwise have been lawfully done. An example would be a teacher's offering to spot a student during a tumbling routine and then not doing the spotting properly. If the student is injured due to a faulty spot, the teacher can be held liable.

NONFEASANCE

Nonfeasance is based on lack of action in carrying out a duty. This is usually an *act of omission*—the teacher knew the proper procedures but failed to follow them. Teachers can be found negligent if they act or fail to act. Understanding and carrying out proper procedures and duties in a manner befitting members of the profession are essential acts. In contrast to the misfeasance example, nonfeasance occurs when a teacher knows that he must spot certain gymnastic routines but fails to do so. Courts expect teachers to behave

A Case of Foreseeability?

A common game (unfortunately) in many school settings is bombardment, or dodgeball. During the game, a student is hit in the eye by a ball and loses vision in that eye. Was this a foreseeable accident that could have been prevented? Were the balls being used capable of inflicting severe injury? Were students aware of rules that might have prevented this injury? Were the students' abilities somewhat equal, or were some able to throw with such velocity that injury was predictable? Were all students forced to play the game? These questions would likely be considered in court in attempting to prove that the teacher should have predicted the overly dangerous situation.

Does Student Size Make a Difference?

Students are playing a game of Diagonal Soccer. On signal, three students from each team run to the center, trying to get the ball first and gain scoring advantage. One of the students is small and weighs about 70 pounds. A student on the other team is mature and weighs nearly 160 pounds. As they approach the ball, the large student runs over the small student, knocking him down and causing a head injury. Within 2 weeks the student has a seizure, and the parents plan to sue. Should the students have been matched for size? For maturity and ability? Does gender make a difference? Could the game have been modified to avoid this injury? Is the teacher guilty of malfeasance?

with more skill and insight than parents do because teachers are educated to give students a higher standard of professional care than are parents.

CONTRIBUTORY NEGLIGENCE

The situation is different when the injured student is partially or wholly at fault. Students are expected to exercise sensible care and to follow directions or regulations designed to protect them from injury. When improper behavior by the injured party causes the accident, it is usually ruled to be *contributory negligence* because the injured party contributed to the resulting harm. This responsibility is directly related to the child's maturity, ability, and experience. Most states have laws specifying that a child under 7 years of age is incapable of contributory negligence (Baley & Matthews, 1988).

COMPARATIVE OR SHARED NEGLIGENCE

Under the doctrine of comparative negligence, the injured party can recover only if found to be less negligent than the defendant (the teacher). Where statutes apply, the amount of recovery is generally reduced in proportion to the injured party's participation in the circumstances leading to the injury.

COMMON DEFENSES AGAINST NEGLIGENCE

Negligence must be proved in a court of law. Teachers are frequently negligent in carrying out their duties, yet the injured party does not take the case to court. If a teacher is sued, some of the following defenses are used to show that the teacher's action was not the primary cause of the accident.

ACT OF GOD

The act of God defense places the cause of injury on forces beyond the teacher's or the school's control. The defense claims that it was impossible to predict an unsafe condition; but through an act of God, the injury occurred. Typical acts would be a gust of wind that blew over a volleyball standard or a cloudburst of rain that made a surface slick. The act of God defense can be used only in cases where the injury would have occurred even if reasonable and prudent action had been taken.

PROXIMATE CAUSE

The defense of proximate cause attempts to prove that the accident was not due to teacher negligence. The breach of duty by the teacher and the injury must be closely related.

I Told Them, But They Did It Anyway!

A physical education instructor teaching a class of fourth-grade students has thoroughly covered softball hitting and related safety rules and marked out clearly visible restraining lines. During class, students are engaged at various softball stations. One student runs through the restricted area and is hit by an aluminum baseball bat. Who is to blame? Was the student old enough to know better? Were too many stations being taught at the same time? Should the teacher have foreseen that an accident might happen even if students were warned? Are aluminum or wood bats an appropriate choice for physical education classes? Is there an assumption of risk in all physical education activities that these situations occasionally will occur?

This is a common defense in cases dealing with proper supervision. Suppose a student is participating in an activity supervised by a teacher. When the teacher leaves the playing area to get a cup of coffee, the student is injured. The defense lawyer will try to show that the accident would have occurred regardless of the teacher's location.

ASSUMPTION OF RISK

Clearly, physical education is a high-risk activity when compared with most other curriculum areas. When choosing to be part of an activity, participants assume the accompanying risk. Physical education teachers seldom use the assumption of risk defense because they typically do not give students a choice between participating or not. An instructor for an elective program who allows students to choose desired units of instruction might find this a better defense than one who teaches a totally required program. Athletic and sport club participation is by choice, and players must assume a greater risk in activities such as football and gymnastics.

CONTRIBUTORY NEGLIGENCE

The defense often claims contributory negligence in attempting to convince the court that the injured party acted in a manner that was not typical of students of similar age and maturity. The defense attempts to demonstrate that the activity or equipment in question had been used for years with no record of accident. A case is made based on how students were taught to act safely and on the premise that the injured student acted outside the parameters of safe conduct. A key point in this defense is whether the activity was suitable for the participants' age and maturity level.

AREAS OF RESPONSIBILITY

A two-tiered approach for analyzing injuries is useful for determining responsibility. The first tier includes duties the administration must assume in support of the program. The second tier defines duties of the instructor or staff member charged with teaching or supervising students. Each party has a role to fill, but some overlap occurs. The following example illustrates the differences.

A student is hurt while performing a tumbling stunt. A lawsuit ensues, charging the teacher with negligence for not following safe procedures. The administration could also be included in the suit, being charged with negligence for hiring an incompetent (unqualified) instructor. Three levels of responsibility should be considered when delegating responsibility because:

1. They identify different functions and responsibilities of the teaching staff and administration.
2. They provide a framework for reducing injuries and improving safety procedures.
3. They provide perspective for following legal precedents.

The following sections consider both administrative and instructional duties for the responsibilities described.

SUPERVISION

All activities in a school setting must be supervised, including recess, lunchtimes, and field trips. For supervision to function properly, the school's responsibilities are critical.

Administration

Two levels are identified in supervision: general and specific. General supervision (e.g., playground duty) refers to broad coverage when students are not being controlled directly by a teacher or designated individual. A supervision plan should exist, designating the areas to be covered and including where and how the supervisor should rotate. This plan, kept in the principal's office, covers rules of conduct governing student behavior. Rules should be posted prominently on bulletin boards, especially in classrooms. Besides the plan, administrators must select qualified personnel, provide necessary training, and monitor the plan properly.

The general supervisor is concerned primarily with student behavior, focusing on the student's right to a relaxing recreational experience. Supervisors observe the area, looking for breaches of discipline, particularly when an individual or group "picks on" another child. The supervisor needs to look for protruding sprinkler heads, broken glass, and debris on the play area. Before leaving the area, the supervisor must find a qualified substitute to keep supervising the area.

Instructional Staff

General supervision is necessary during recess, before and after school, during lunch break, and during certain other sessions when instruction is not offered. The supervisor should know the school's supervision plan as well as emergency care procedures in case of an accident. Supervision is an overt act; supervisors are actively involved and moving throughout the area. The number of supervisors depends on the type of activity, size of the area, and number and age of the students.

Specific supervision requires the instructor to be with a certain group of students (a class). An example is spotting students engaged in challenging gymnastic activities. If certain pieces of apparatus require special care and proper use, post rules and regulations near the apparatus (for upper-grade children). Make students aware of the rules and give them appropriate instruction and guidance in applying the rules. When rules are modified, rewrite them in proper form. There is no substitute for documentation when the need to defend policies and approaches arises.

When teaching, arrange and teach the class so that all students are in view. This implies supervising from the perimeter of the area. Standing at the center of the student group with many students behind you makes it impossible to supervise a class safely and effectively. Never leave equipment and apparatus unsupervised when it is accessible to students in the area. An example is leaving equipment on the playing field between classes. If other students in the area have easy access to the equipment, they may use it unsafely, and the teacher can be found liable if an injury occurs.

Do not agree to supervise activities for which you are unqualified to anticipate possible hazards. If this situation arises, send a written memo to the department head or principal stating this lack of insight and qualification. Maintain a copy for your files.

Merriman (1993) offers five recommendations to ensure that adequate supervision occurs:

1. The supervisor must be in the immediate vicinity (within sight and hearing of the students).
2. If required to leave, the supervisor must have an adequate replacement before departing. Adequate replacements do not include paraprofessionals, student teachers, custodial help, or untrained teachers.
3. Supervision procedures must be planned and incorporated into daily lessons.
4. Supervision procedures should include what to observe and listen for, where to stand for the most effective view, and what to do if a problem arises.
5. Supervision requires that participants' age, maturity, and skill ability always be considered, as well as the inherent risk of the activity.

INSTRUCTION

Instructional responsibility rests primarily with the teacher, but administrative personnel have certain defined functions as well.

Administration

The administration should review and approve the curricular plan. The curriculum should be reviewed regularly to keep it current. Be sure the curriculum includes activities that meet program objectives and contribute to students' growth and development. It makes little sense in a court of law to say that an activity was included "for the fun of it" or "because students liked it."

Administrators are obligated to support the program with adequate funding. The principal and higher administrators should visit the program periodically. Familiarity with program content and operation ensures that all practices receive adequate administrative supervision.

Instructional Staff

During instruction, teachers have a duty to protect students from unreasonable physical or mental harm. This includes avoiding any acts or omissions that might cause such harm. Teachers are educated, experienced, and skilled in physical education and must foresee possibly harmful situations.

The major area of concern involving instruction is whether all students are adequately instructed before or during participation in an activity. Adequate instruction means (1) teaching children how to perform activities correctly and use equipment and apparatus properly, and (2) teaching students necessary safety precautions. If instructions are not given correctly and understandably, and they do not cover proper technique, the instructor can be held liable. The risk involved in an activity must be communicated to the learner.

Students' ages and maturity levels play an important role in activity selection. Younger students require more care, simple instructions, and clear restrictions in the name of safety. Some students lack appropriate fear, and the teacher must be aware of this when discussing safety factors. A very young child may have little concern about performing a high-risk activity if an instructor is nearby.

I Know We Had a Supervisor Out There!

At lunch, students have free time to play on the activity field or in the gymnasium. One teacher is assigned to supervise the students on the playing field and one supervises the gym. The playing field is large, and an injury occurs opposite where the teacher is standing. She hustles to help the student. While busy attending the injured student, the teacher does not notice a fight that breaks out. A larger student severely beats a smaller student. Is the teacher liable because she did not see the fight? Can one teacher adequately supervise a playground full of students? Is the administrator responsible because only one teacher was assigned to supervise? Did the teacher have a way to communicate with the front office to ask for additional help?

This places much responsibility on the teacher to give adequate instruction and supervision.

Careful planning is a must. Written curriculum guides and lesson plans can offer a well-prepared approach that other teachers and administrators gladly support. Lesson plans should include proper sequence and progression of skill. Teachers are on defensible grounds if they can show their progression of activities was based on presentations designed by experts and followed carefully when teaching. District and state guidelines enforcing instructional sequences and restricted activities should be checked and followed closely.

Proper instruction demands that students not be forced to participate. If a child is required to perform an activity unwillingly, his teacher may be open to a lawsuit. In a lawsuit dealing with stunts and tumbling (Appenzeller, 1970), the court held the teacher liable when a student claimed she was forced to try a stunt called a "roll over two" before being adequately instructed in how to perform it. Gymnastics and tumbling are areas of frequent lawsuits due to inadequate instruction. Posting the proper sequence of skills and lead-up activities may be useful to ensure these skills were presented properly. Tread the line carefully between offering encouragement and forcing students to try new activities.

The following points help ensure safe instruction:

1. Sequence all activities in units of instruction and develop written lesson plans. Problems occur when snap judgments are made under the daily pressure and strain of teaching.
2. Scrutinize high-risk activities to ensure that all safety procedures are implemented. If in doubt, discuss the activities with experienced teachers and administrators.
3. Make sure activities used in the curriculum are appropriate to the wide range of maturity and development of students in a class.

Safety Tip

When you modify safety rules or rules of familiar games, clearly communicate the revisions to your students so everybody is aware of safe use of space.

4. When students' grades are based on the number of activities they participate in, some students will feel forced to try all activities. Make it clear to students that it is their choice to participate. When they are afraid of getting hurt, they can elect not to perform an activity.
5. Include in written lesson plans necessary safety equipment. The lesson plan should detail how equipment is arranged, how the mats are placed, and where the instructor carries out supervision.
6. If a student claims injury or brings a note from parents asking that the student not participate in physical activity, honor the request. Teachers almost always receive excuses at the start of the period, when they are busy with many other duties (getting equipment ready, taking roll, and opening lockers). It is difficult to make a thoughtful judgment during this time. The school nurse is qualified to make these judgments when they relate to health and should be expected to make such decisions. If the excuses continue for a long time, the teacher or nurse should schedule a conference with the parents to rectify the situation.
7. Make sure the instruction includes activities that are in line with available equipment and facilities. An example is the amount of space available. A soccer lead-up activity may no longer be safe and appropriate if it is brought indoors due to inclement weather.

The Need for a Curriculum and Lesson Plan

A former gymnast who is now an elementary school physical education teacher decides to teach her classes gymnastics. The school has no curriculum guide, and the teacher does not write lesson plans. She decides to have students try a headspring over a tumbling mat. A student is seriously hurt (severe neck injury that causes paralysis), and his parents file a $1.5 million lawsuit. What argument would you use to defend yourself in this situation? Would it help if you could say that gymnastics was part of the school curriculum? What if the plaintiff's lawyer brings in an expert witness who says the instructional sequence was inappropriate? Can you show your written lesson plan that delineates the proper instructional sequence based on what expert instructors recommend? Can you be an expert in every activity you teach, or do you need to rely on other experts for the proper sequence of activities to teach?

8. If spotting is required for safe completion of activities, make sure the instructor or trained students always perform the spotting. Teaching students how to spot is as important as teaching them physical skills. Safe conduct is learned.
9. If students are working independently at stations, distribute carefully constructed and written task cards to help eliminate unsafe practices.
10. Have a written emergency care plan posted in the gymnasium. This plan should be approved by health care professionals and followed to the letter when an injury occurs.

Teachers who incorporate punishment into the instructional process should carefully examine its consequences before using it. Physical punishment that leads to permanent or long-lasting damage is certainly indefensible. The punishment used must be in line with the physical maturity and health of the student involved. A teacher's practice of having students perform laps when they have misbehaved might go unchallenged for years. But what if an asthmatic student or a student with congenital heart disease is asked to run and suffers injury or illness? What if the student is running unsupervised and is injured from a fall or suffers heat exhaustion? In these examples, it is hard to defend such punitive practices. Making students perform physical activity for misbehavior is indefensible under any circumstance. If a child is injured while performing physical punishment, teachers are usually found liable and held responsible for the injury.

SAFETY

The major thrust of safety is to prevent situations that cause accidents. Studies estimate that more than 70% of injuries in sport and related activities can be prevented through proper safety procedures. On the other hand, some accidents occur despite precautions, and proper emergency procedures should be established for such situations. The U.S. Consumer Product Safety Commission conducted a comprehensive study of injuries received in sport and related activities (2008) that involved a network of computers in 119 hospital emergency rooms that channeled injury data to a central point. The sports and activities that produced the most injuries were, in order, football, touch football, baseball, basketball, gymnastics, and skiing. The facility that produced the most disabling injuries was the swimming pool.

Learning to recognize potential high-risk situations is an important factor in preventing accidents. Teachers must clearly understand the hazards and potential dangers of an activity before they can establish controls. Instructors must not assume that participants are aware of the dangers and risks involved in various activities, but instead thoroughly inform students before participation. See the "Guidelines for Creating a Safe Environment" box on page 172 for specific guidelines and recommendations.

THE SAFETY COMMITTEE

Safety should be publicized regularly throughout the school. Students, parents, and teachers also need a process for voicing concerns about unsafe conditions. A safety committee can meet regularly to establish safety policies, rule on requests to allow high-risk activities, and analyze serious injuries that have occurred in the school district. This committee should develop safety rules that apply district-wide to all teachers. It may determine that some activities are too high-risk for the return in student benefit. The committee may establish acceptable criteria for sports equipment and apparatus.

Include one or more high-level administrators, physical education teachers, health officers (nurses), parents, and students on the safety committee. School administrators are usually indicted when lawsuits occur; because they are held responsible for program content and curriculum, their representation on the safety committee is important. Students on the committee may be aware of possible hazards, and parents may often voice concerns overlooked by teachers.

Running for Punishment—The Right Choice?

Children participating in a physical education class are unruly. They talk when they shouldn't and generally do not cooperate. The teacher, in a fit of controlled anger, has two students run laps around a large field until they decide to behave. It is a hot fall day and, after 15 minutes of running, one student falls and goes into convulsions on the far side of the field (one-third of a mile away from the teacher). The teacher doesn't see the child go down until a student tells him about it. Is this malfeasance? Is running an acceptable choice for punishment? Were the weather conditions considered? Did the youth have a preexisting health condition? Were the students under the teacher's watchful eye or out of sight? Could you defend yourself in this situation?

9

Guidelines for Creating a Safe Environment

1. **Conduct in-service sessions in safety.** Experienced, knowledgeable teachers should lead these sessions. Department heads may be responsible for the training, or outside experts can be employed and assigned responsibility. Give in-district credit to participating teachers to demonstrate the district's concern for using proper safety techniques.
2. **Review medical records.** Reviews should occur at the start of each school year. Identify students with disabilities, and note them within each class listing before the first instructional day. If necessary, the classroom teacher or school nurse can call the doctors of students with disabilities or students with activity restrictions to inquire about the situation and discuss special needs. The classroom teacher or school nurse should notify physical education teachers about students who have a special condition such as epilepsy or temporary problems caused by taking medication.
3. **Provide student safety orientations.** Throughout the school year, safety discussions should cover potentially dangerous situations, class conduct, and rules for proper use of equipment and apparatus. Teachers should urge students to report any condition that might cause an accident.
4. **Discuss safety rules.** At the start of each instructional unit, cover specific safety issues. Post rules and regularly bring them to students' attention. Posters and bulletin boards can promote safety in an enjoyable and stimulating way.
5. **Train students to serve as instructional aides.** Aides must be properly instructed before being part of the educational process. Supervise student aides carefully, because teachers are still responsible even if an aide is the one performing a duty incorrectly.
6. **Monitor instructional practices for possible hazards.** For example, match students in competitive situations by size, maturity, and ability. Supply instruction required for safe participation before an activity begins. Give instructors a competence check to ensure they are adequately trained to offer instruction in various activities. Prepare the instructional area for safe participation; if the area lacks necessary apparatus and safety devices, modify instruction to meet safety standards.
7. **Include a safety checklist with the inventory of equipment and apparatus.** Whenever necessary, send equipment needing repair to proper agents. If the repair cost is more than 40% of the replacement cost, discarding the equipment or apparatus is usually a more economical choice.
8. **Record and report injuries in student files.** Also file an injury report by type, such as ankle sprain or broken arm. To facilitate analysis at regular intervals, a report should list the activity and the conditions. Analysis may show that injuries occur regularly during a specific activity or on a certain piece of equipment. This process can give direction for creating a safer environment or for defending the safety record of a sport, activity, or equipment type.
9. **Ensure that teachers have up-to-date first aid and CPR certification.** Administrators should be sure that teachers meet these standards and should provide training sessions when necessary.

THE EMERGENCY CARE PLAN

Before any emergency arises, teachers should prepare themselves by learning about special health and physical conditions of students (Gray, 1993). Most schools have a method for identifying such students. If a student has a problem that may require treatment, a consent-to-treat form should be on file in case the parent or guardian is unavailable. Keep necessary first aid materials and supplies available in a readily accessible kit.

Establishing procedures for emergency care and notification of parents in case of injury is of utmost importance in providing a high standard of care for students. To plan properly for emergency care, all physical education teachers should have first aid training. *First aid* is the immediate and temporary care given at an emergency before a physician is available. Its purposes are to save life, prevent aggravation of injuries, and alleviate severe suffering. If there is evidence of life-threatening bleeding or if the victim is unconscious or has stopped breathing, the teacher must administer first aid. Do not move already-injured persons unless further injury may result if they are not moved. As a general rule, however, do not move an injured person unless absolutely necessary. If a back or neck injury is indicated, immobilize the victim's head and do not move him or her without using a spine board. Remember, the purpose of first aid is to save life. The emergency care plan should consist of the following steps:

1. *Administer first aid to the injured student as the first priority.* Treat only life-threatening injuries. Immediately

call the school nurse to the scene of the accident. Emergency care procedures should indicate whether the student can be moved and in what fashion. It is critical that the individual applying first aid avoid aggravating the injury.

2. *Notify parents as soon as possible when emergency care is required.* Each student's file should list home and emergency telephone numbers where parents can be reached. If possible, the school should have an arrangement with local emergency facilities so that a paramedic unit can be called immediately to the scene of a serious accident.
3. *Release the student to a parent or a designated representative.* Policies for transporting injured students should be established and documented.
4. *Promptly complete a student accident report while the details of the accident are clear.* Figure 9.1 is an example of an accident form covering the required details. The principal and the nurse should each retain copies, and the physical education teacher should receive a copy.

EQUIPMENT AND FACILITIES

School responsibility for equipment and facilities is required for both noninstructional and class use.

ADMINISTRATION

The principal and the custodian oversee the fields and playground equipment used for recess and outside activities. Instruct students to report broken and unsafe equipment, as well as hazards (glass, cans, rocks), to the principal's office. If equipment is faulty, remove it from the area. Have the physical education specialist regularly (perhaps weekly) inspect equipment and facilities. If a specialist is not employed, either the principal or custodian can do the inspection. File the inspection results by formal letter with the school district safety committee. Replace sawdust, sand, or other shock-absorbing material regularly. For use in recording safety inspections, administrators should have a written checklist of equipment and apparatus. Note the date of inspection, and be sure that inspection occurs regularly. If a potentially dangerous situation exists, post rules or warnings to inform students and other teachers of the risk. Even if the safety inspection is not your responsibility, if you see a problem, immediately report it to administrators by memo or letter. If an accident occurred and it was discovered that you had not reported an unsafe situation, you might be held liable for the accident.

Proper installation of equipment is critical. Have a reputable firm that guarantees its work install climbing equipment and other equipment that must be anchored. When examining apparatus, inspection of the installation is important. Maintenance of facilities is also important. Keep grass cut short, and inspect the grounds for debris. Fill any holes in the ground, and remove loose gravel. Repair or eliminate hazards found on playing fields. On indoor floors, use a proper finish that prevents excessive slipping. Shower rooms should have a roughened floor finish to prevent falls when the floors are wet.

Safe participation in an activity can be enhanced by the selection of equipment and facilities. Base the choice of apparatus and equipment on the students' growth and developmental levels. For example, allowing elementary school children to use a horizontal ladder that was designed for high school students may result in a fall that causes injury. The legal concept of an *attractive nuisance* implies that some piece of equipment or apparatus, usually left unsupervised, was so attractive to children that they could not be expected to avoid using it. When an injury occurs, even though students may have been using the apparatus incorrectly, teachers and school administration are often held liable because the attractive nuisance should have been removed from the area when unsupervised.

INSTRUCTIONAL STAFF

Indoor facilities are of primary concern to physical education instructors. Even though the administration is charged with overall responsibility for facilities and equipment, including periodic inspection, instructors should regularly inspect the safety of the instructional area. If corrective action is needed, notify the principal or other designated administrator in writing. Verbal notification is not enough to legally protect the instructor.

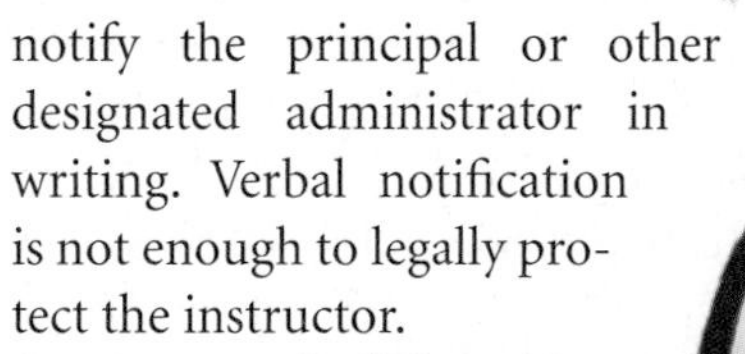

Arrange facilities with safety in mind. Often, the side- and endlines of playing fields for sports such as football, soccer,

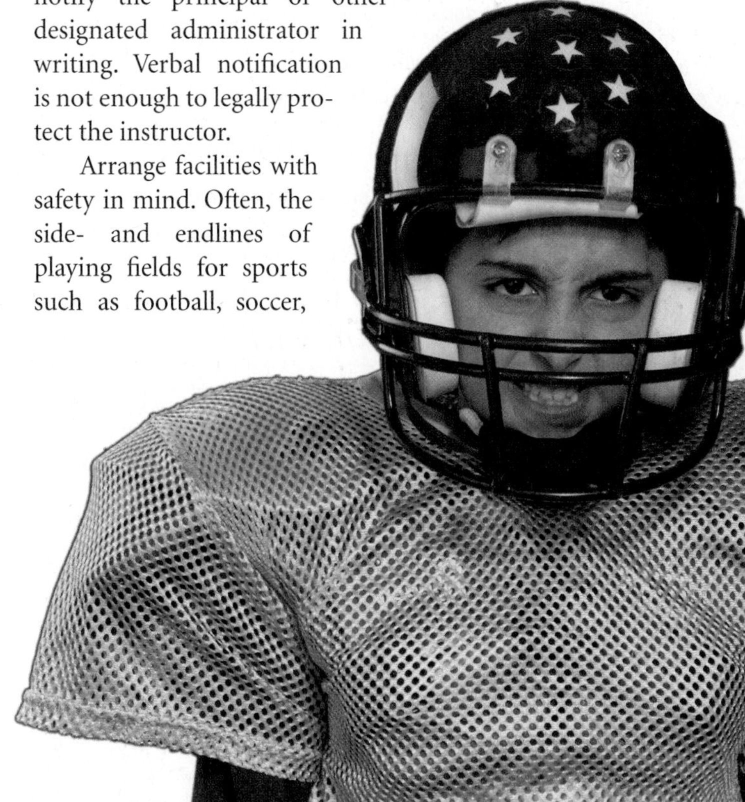

Student Accident Report

____________________ **School**

In all cases, this form should be filed through the school nurse and signed by the principal of the school. The original will be forwarded to the superintendent's office, where it will be initialed and sent to the head nurse. The second copy will be retained by the principal or the school nurse. The third copy should be given to the physical education teacher if the accident is related.

Name of injured ____________________ Address ____________________

Phone _______________ Grade __________ Home room ____________ Age ________

Parents of injured ______________________________

Place of accident ____________________ Date of accident ____________

Hour ____________ A.M. P.M. Date reported ____________ By whom ____________

Parent contact attempted at ____________ A.M. P.M. Parent contacted at ____________ A.M. P.M.

Describe accident, giving specific location and condition of premises ____________________

____

Nature of injury ______________________________
(Describe in detail)

Care given or action taken by nurse or others ____________________

____

Reason injured person was on premises ____________________
(Activity at time—i.e., lunch, physical education, etc.)

Staff member responsible for student supervision at time of accident ____________________

____

Is student covered by school-sponsored accident insurance? __________ Yes __________ No

Medical care recommended __________ Yes __________ No

Place taken after accident ______________________________
(Specify home, physician, or hospital, giving name and address)

By whom __________ **At what time** ____________ A.M. P.M.

Follow-up by nurse to be sent to central health office

Remediative measures taken ______________________________
(Attach individual remarks if necessary)

School ____________________ Principal ____________________

Date ____________________ Nurse ____________________

On the back of this sheet, list all persons familiar with the circumstances of the accident, giving name, address, telephone number, age, and location with respect to the accident.

FIGURE 9.1 Sample accident report form.

and field hockey are placed too close to walls, curbs, or fences. Adjust the boundaries to allow adequate room for deceleration, even though the size of the playing area is reduced. In the gymnasium, do not have students run to a line that is close to a wall. Another common hazard is placing basketball hoops too close to the playing area. Be sure the poles that support the baskets are padded.

Proper use of equipment and apparatus is important. Regardless of the condition of equipment, if it is misused, it may result in an injury. Instruct students on how to use equipment and apparatus before they are used. To ensure that all points are covered, include all safety instruction in the written lesson plan.

Equipment should be purchased based on quality and safety as well as potential use. Many lawsuits occur because of unsafe equipment and apparatus. The manufacturer may be held liable for such equipment, but this has to be proved. Thus the teacher must state, in writing, the exact specifications of the desired equipment. The process of bidding for lower-priced items may result in the purchase of less safe equipment. If teachers have specified proper equipment in writing, however, the possibility of their being held liable for injury is reduced.

PERSONAL PROTECTION: MINIMIZING THE EFFECTS OF A LAWSUIT

Despite proper care, injuries do occur, and lawsuits may be initiated. Two courses of action are necessary to minimize the effects of a suit.

LIABILITY INSURANCE

The school district's liability insurance may cover its teachers, but most often teachers buy their own policy. Many physical education professionals join the American Alliance for Health, Physical Education, Recreation, and Dance (AAHPERD) and purchase liability insurance at a reasonable cost. Members can obtain a group liability policy for a modest amount. Most policies provide for legal services to contest a suit and will pay indemnity up to the limits of the policy (liability coverage of $500,000 is most common). Most policies give the insurance company the right to settle out of court. Unfortunately, when this occurs, some people may infer that the teacher was guilty even though the circumstances indicate otherwise. Insurance companies usually settle out of court to avoid the excessive legal fees required to try the case in court.

RECORD KEEPING

The second course of action in minimizing lawsuits is to keep complete records of *all* accidents. Teachers may fail to document an accident because they perceive it to be "minor." A look through the legal literature shows many cases that began as a minor bump on the head that led to problems later. Besides, many lawsuits occur months or even years after the accident, when memory of the situation is fuzzy. Fill out accident reports immediately after an injury occurs. Take care to provide no evidence, oral or written, that others could use in a court of law. In the report, do not try to make a diagnosis or define the supposed cause of the accident. Simply record what happened by completing the Student Accident Report (see Figure 9.1).

If newspaper reporters probe for details, avoid describing the accident beyond the basic facts. When discussing the accident with administrators, focus on only the facts recorded in the accident report. Remember that school records can be subpoenaed in court proceedings. The point here is not to dissemble, but to be cautious and avoid self-incrimination.

SAFETY AND LIABILITY CHECKLISTS

Use the following checklists to monitor the physical activity (physical education, recess, and playground) environment. Immediately rectify any situations that deviate from safe and legally sound practices.

Supervision and Instruction

1. Are teachers adequately trained in all the activities they are teaching?
2. Do all teachers and recess supervisors have evidence of a necessary level of first aid training?
3. When supervising, do personnel have access to a written plan of areas to be observed and responsibilities to be carried out?

4. Have students been warned of potential dangers and risks and advised of rules and the reasons for the rules?
5. Are safety rules posted near areas of increased risk?
6. Are lesson plans written? Do they include provisions for proper instruction, sequence of activities, and safety? Are all activities that are taught listed in the district curriculum guide?
7. When introducing a new activity, do teachers always instruct the class in safety precautions and instructions for correct skill performance?
8. Are the activities taught in the program based on sound curriculum principles? Could the activities and units of instruction be defended based on their educational contributions?
9. Do the methods of instruction recognize individual differences among students, and are the necessary steps taken to meet all students' needs regardless of gender, ability, or disability?
10. Are substitute teachers given clear and comprehensive lesson plans so they can maintain the scope and sequence of instruction?
11. Is the student evaluation plan based on actual performance and objective data rather than on favoritism or arbitrary and capricious standards?
12. Is appropriate dress required for students? This does not imply wearing uniforms, only dress (including shoes) that ensures the safety of all students.
13. When necessary for safety, are students grouped according to ability level, size, or age?
14. Is the class left unsupervised when the teacher visits the office, lounge, or bathroom? Is one teacher ever asked to supervise two or more classes at once?
15. If students are used as teacher aides or to spot other students, are they properly instructed and trained?
16. Are playground supervisors appropriately trained?
17. Is adequate supervision taking place? Is the supervisor-to-student ratio adequate?

Equipment and Facilities

1. Is all equipment (physical education and recess/playground) inspected regularly, and are the inspection results recorded on a form and sent to the proper administrators?
2. Is a log maintained recording the regular occurrence of inspections, the equipment in need of repair, and the times repairs were made?
3. Are "attractive nuisances" eliminated from the gymnasium, playing field, and playground?
4. Are specific safety rules posted on facilities and near equipment?
5. Are the following inspected periodically?
   a. Playing field for the presence of glass, rocks, and metal objects
   b. Fasteners holding equipment such as climbing ropes, horizontal bars, baskets, or swings
   c. Goals for games such as football, soccer, and field hockey, to be sure they are fastened securely
   d. Padded areas, such as goal supports
6. Are mats placed under apparatus from which a fall is possible?
7. Are playing fields arranged so participants will not run into each other or be hit by a ball from another game?
8. Are landing pits filled and maintained properly?

Emergency Care

1. Is there a written procedure for emergency care?
2. Is a person who is properly trained in first aid available immediately following an accident? Are cell phones or walkie-talkies available for physical education teachers and recess supervisors?
3. Are emergency telephone numbers readily accessible?
4. Are parents' telephone numbers available?
5. Is an up-to-date first aid kit available? Is ice immediately available?
6. Are health folders listing restrictions, allergies, and health problems of students maintained?
7. Are health folders routinely reviewed by instructors?
8. Are students who participate in extracurricular activities required to have insurance? Is the policy number recorded?
9. Is there a plan for treating injuries that involve the local paramedics?
10. Are accident reports filed promptly and analyzed regularly?

Transportation of Students

1. Have parents been informed that their students will be transported off-campus?
2. Are detailed travel plans approved by the site administrator and kept on file?
3. Are school vehicles used whenever possible?

4. Are drivers properly licensed and vehicles insured?
5. If teachers or parents use their own vehicles to transport students, are the students, drivers, and car owners covered by an insurance rider purchased by the school district?

THE SPORTS PROGRAM

Often physical educators participate, either as a coach or league/program supervisor, in youth sports. For this reason, they must understand the legal issues associated with such programs. One common problem with elementary school sports programs for school administrators is providing qualified coaches. The administration should set minimum requirements for coaches and ensure that incompetent individuals are removed from coaching duties. When students are involved in extracurricular activities, teachers (coaches) are responsible for the safe conduct of activities. The following areas often give rise to lawsuits if not handled carefully.

MISMATCHED OPPONENTS

If an injury occurs, the instructor is liable even when competitors are the same gender and choose to participate. The question that courts examine is whether an effort was made to match students according to height, weight, and ability. Courts are less understanding about mismatching in the physical education setting compared with an athletic contest, but mismatching is to be avoided in any situation.

WAIVER FORMS

Require participants in extracurricular activities to sign a responsibility waiver form. The form should explain the risks involved in voluntary participation and discuss briefly the types of injuries that have occurred in the past during practice and competition. Supervisors should remember that waiver slips do not waive the rights of participants, and that teachers and coaches still can be found liable if injuries occur. The waiver form should communicate clearly the risks involved and may be a strong "assumption of risk" defense.

MEDICAL EXAMINATIONS

Participants must have a medical examination before participating. Keep records of the examination on file and mark them prominently when physical restrictions or limitations exist. It is common to "red dot" the folders of students with a history of medical problems. Students must not be allowed to participate unless they purchase medical insurance, and evidence of such coverage should be kept in the folders of athletic participants.

PRESEASON CONDITIONING

Preseason conditioning should be undertaken systematically and progressively. Starting the season with a mile run for time makes little sense if students have not been preconditioned. Be aware of guidelines dealing with heat and humidity. For example, in Arizona, guidelines advise avoiding strenuous activity when the temperature exceeds 85°F and the humidity exceeds 40%. When these conditions are exceeded, running is curtailed to 10 minutes and active games to 30 minutes. Students should be hydrated before activity, and drinking water made available on demand.

TRANSPORTATION OF STUDENTS

Whenever students are transported, teachers are responsible for their safety both en route and during the activity. Transportation liability can be avoided by having participants arrange their own transportation to the event (Pittman, 1993). If the school must provide transportation, it should always use licensed drivers and school-approved vehicles. Travel plans should include official approval from the appropriate school administrator. One special note: Drivers who are paid or reimbursed for the trip dramatically increase the possibility of their being held liable for injury. To make matters worse, many insurance policies do not cover drivers who are compensated for transporting students. Teachers who transport students and receive reimbursement should purchase a special insurance rider that provides liability coverage for this situation.

9

APPLYING WHAT YOU READ

- To properly carry out your duties as a physical educator, you must have a basic understanding of the legal terms that help define those duties.
- Your responsibilities as a teacher fall under the areas of supervision and instruction. Do you know what your responsibilities are?
- Safety is an issue in physical education. As you write lessons and prepare your program, be sure to consider the guidelines for safety provided in this chapter.
- As you prepare for each school year, take time to reflect on your emergency plan, student accident report, and steps you have taken to minimize the effects of a lawsuit.

REFLECTION AND REVIEW

HOW AND WHY

1. Should teachers have professional insurance?
2. How can effective classroom management help teachers avoid legal issues?

3. How can teachers protect themselves from lawsuits?
4. Why is a safety and liability checklist important?

CONTENT REVIEW

1. Define a *tort.*
2. Identify four major points that must be established to determine if a teacher is negligent. Also, discuss the importance of foreseeability.
3. List and explain types of negligence.
4. Describe common defenses against negligence.
5. Discuss the importance of supervision and instruction when examining responsibility.
6. Identify who is responsible for equipment and facilities. Explain your answer.
7. List some issues related to sports programs that often result in lawsuits.
8. Briefly describe several guidelines for safety in physical education.
9. Explain the importance of an emergency care plan, and discuss the steps in the plan.

FOR MORE INFORMATION

REFERENCES AND SUGGESTED READINGS

Appenzeller, H. (1970). *From the gym to the jury.* Charlottesville, VA: Michie Company Law Publishing.

———. (1993). *Managing sports and risk management strategies.* Durham, NC: Carolina Academic Press.

———. (Ed.). (1998). *Risk management in sport: Issues and strategies.* Durham, NC: Carolina Academic Press.

———. (2003). *Managing sports and risk management strategies* (2nd ed.). Durham, NC: Carolina Academic Press.

Baley, J. A., & Matthews, D. L. (1988). *Law and liability in athletics, physical education, and recreation.* Boston: Allyn & Bacon.

Carpenter, L. J. (2000). *Legal concepts in sport: A primer* (2nd ed.). Champaign, IL: Sagamore Publishing.

Dougherty, N. J. (Ed.). (2002). *Principles of safety in physical education and sport* (3rd ed.). Reston, VA: AAHPERD.

Dougherty, N. J., Golberger, A. S., & Carpenter, A. S. (2007). *Sport, physical activity, and the law* (3rd ed.). Champaign, IL: Sagamore Publishing.

Garner, B. A. (Ed.). (2004). *Black's law dictionary* (8th ed.). St. Paul, MN: West Group.

Gray, G. R. (1993). Providing adequate medical care to program participants. *Journal of Physical Education, Recreation, and Dance, 64*(2), 56–57.

Hart, J. E., & Ritson, R. J. (2002). *Liability and safety in physical education and sport: A practitioner's guide to the legal aspects of teaching and coaching in elementary and secondary schools* (2nd ed.). Reston, VA: AAHPERD.

Merriman, J. (1993). Supervision in sport and physical activity. *Journal of Physical Education, Recreation, and Dance, 64*(2), 20–23.

Pittman, A. J. (1993). Safe transportation—A driving concern. *Journal of Physical Education, Recreation, and Dance, 64*(2), 53–55.

U.S. Consumer Product Safety Commission. (2008). *Public safety playground handbook.* Washington, DC: U.S. Government Printing Office.

van der Smissen, B. (1990). *Legal liability and risk management of public and private entities.* Cincinnati, OH: Anderson.

WEBSITES

Legal Issues and Physical Education

www.kin.sfasu.edu/finkenberg/kin511/Liability.html

Playgrounds

www.cpsc.gov/CPSCPUB/PUBS/playpubs.html
www.playdesigns.com
www.peacefulplaygrounds.com

School Safety and Security

www.schoolsecurity.org
www.sasked.gov.sk.ca/docs/physed/safe/gym.html

Facilities, Equipment, and Supplies

10

ESSENTIAL COMPONENTS OF QUALITY PROGRAMS

I. Organized around content standards

▶ II. Student-centered and developmentally appropriate

III. Physical activity and motor skill development form the core of the program

IV. Teaches management skills and self-discipline

V. Promotes inclusion of all students

VI. Focuses on process over product

VII. Promotes lifetime personal health and wellness

VIII. Teaches cooperation and responsibility and promotes sensitivity to diversity

NATIONAL STANDARDS FOR PHYSICAL EDUCATION*

1. Demonstrates competency in motor skills and movement patterns needed to perform a variety of physical activities.
2. Demonstrates understanding of movement concepts, principles, and tactics as they apply to the learning and performance of physical activities.
3. Participates regularly in physical activity.
4. Achieves and maintains a health-enhancing level of physical fitness.
5. Exhibits responsible personal and social behavior that respects self and others in physical activity.
6. Values physical activity for health, enjoyment, challenge, self-expression, and/or social interaction.

*National Association for Sport and Physical Education (NASPE), 2004.

Chapter 10 presents procedures associated with the design, purchase, maintenance, and construction of physical education facilities, equipment, and supplies. *Equipment* refers to items that are rather fixed in nature. Equipment has a relatively long life span, needs periodic safety checks, and requires planned purchasing. Supplies are nondurable items with a limited period of use. When resources are limited, much equipment can be constructed. This chapter has a comprehensive section on how to build equipment and supplies.

Outcomes

- Identify standards to follow in constructing outdoor and indoor physical education facilities.
- Understand that safety is an essential consideration in facility design.
- Illustrate floor lines and markings that enhance management potential and increase ease of instruction.
- List essential equipment and supplies for physical education in the elementary school.
- List recommended equipment for outdoor and indoor physical education areas.
- Outline a systematic plan for storing physical education equipment and supplies.
- Describe procedures for the care and repair of physical education equipment and supplies.
- Be able to construct selected physical education equipment and supplies.

PHYSICAL EDUCATION facilities are logically divided into two categories: outdoor and indoor. Outdoor space usually provides enough room for several classes to work at once. When weather conditions require frequent use of indoor space, a minimum of one indoor teaching station for every eight classrooms is needed. Further, to meet the needs of students with disabilities (as required by Public Law 94–142), another indoor play area, separate from but close to the regular indoor facility, is needed.

Physical education facilities should be planned for the maximum projected enrollment. Too often, planning is done for the present situation. Later, when the school adds classrooms, the physical education areas are not changed. What once was an adequate arrangement becomes a scheduling problem. Adding physical education facilities is difficult because of generally escalating costs and the relatively high cost of physical education facilities in comparison to the cost of adding regular classroom space.

OUTDOOR FACILITIES

Outdoor areas should include field space for games, a track, hard-surfaced areas, apparatus areas, play courts, age-specific play areas, covered play space, and a jogging trail. Fields should be leveled, drained, and turfed because grass is the most usable field surface. An automatic sprinkler system is desirable, but sprinkler heads must not protrude and become safety hazards. Automatic installations permit sprinkling during the evening and night so the fields are not too soggy for play the next day.

Mark a hard-topped area for various games such as tetherball, volleyball, and basketball. Other markings for this area might include four-square courts, hopscotch layouts, and circles for games. Simple movement pattern courses can also be marked. Some research suggests that painting playground surfaces with bright, attractive art (e.g., castles, dragons) may help increase activity levels during recess (Stratton & Mullan, 2005). Some administrators prefer a hard surface for the entire play area because it eliminates the mud problem and the need for sprinkling and lowers maintenance costs. Hard surfaces are used when play space is limited and when the number of students makes it difficult to maintain a turf surface.

As a minimum, the outdoor facility should have a track, located where it will not interfere with other activities. If a permanent installation is not practical, a temporary track can be laid out each spring (see page 699).

In the planning, designate separate play spaces for different age groups. These areas should contain apparatus designed for each age group. Locate the play area for primary-level children well away from areas where footballs and softballs are used. Place small, hard-surfaced play courts near the edges of the outdoor area, thus spreading out the play groups. These courts, approximately 40 by 60 feet, can be equipped for basketball, volleyball, or both. A covered shed can be divided for use by different age groups. Climate conditions would dictate the need for such facilities.

A walking/jogging trail can stimulate interest in walking or jogging. Small signs indicating the distances covered and markers outlining the trail are all that are needed. Stations with exercise tasks can be placed at intervals. For example, a station could instruct students to accomplish a specified number of push-ups or sit-ups. Such a circuit is popularly called a *parcourse* or *fitness stations course.*

An area set aside as a developmental playground is an important part of the total play space. The area should contain equipment and apparatus and be landscaped to have small hills, valleys, and tunnels for children. A recommended approach is to divide the playground into various developmental areas so that children must use different body parts in different areas of the play space. One area might contain a great deal of climbing equipment to reinforce arm–shoulder girdle development, and another area might challenge the leg and trunk regions. Equipment and apparatus should be abstract, leaving creation and imagination to the children. Apparatus can be manipulated and changed to suit children's needs and desires.

SAFETY ON THE PLAYGROUND

Studies by the U.S. Consumer Product Safety Commission (2008) show that most injuries (79%) are caused when children fall from apparatus and strike the underlying surface. The surface under the equipment is a major factor affecting the severity of injuries associated with falls from apparatus. Injuries range from minor bruises to skull fractures, concussions, and brain damage. Falls onto paved surfaces result in a disproportionately high number of severe injuries. Some deaths also have resulted from such falls.

The choice of materials needs to be based on local conditions and the availability of funds. Concrete, asphalt, and other paved surfaces under apparatus require little maintenance, which is why they are used. But hard surfaces do not soften the impact of accidental falls and thus are unsuitable for playground use. Organic materials such as pine bark nuggets, pine bark mulch, shredded hardwood bark, and cocoa shell mulch are recommended. Other materials are wood chips, shredded tires, and sand. If hard surfaces are already in place, outdoor interlocking tiles or dense synthetic turf may be laid over them.

If loose, organic materials are used, provide at least a 6-inch layer of material to cushion the impact of falls. Continuous, proper maintenance is as important as selecting the proper material. Because children will move the material away from the area, it requires frequent leveling, grading, and replacement. Also screen the material to eliminate insects, animal excrement, and concealed sharp objects. Unfortunately, organic materials decompose, become pulverized and dusty, and mix with dirt, thus losing their cushioning properties. In rainy or humid weather, they can absorb moisture and pack down, resulting in a loss of resiliency. Select materials that do not harden during freezing temperatures. Allied to maintenance is the need for a checklist of procedures to be followed and filled out regularly.

OUTDOOR APPARATUS AND EQUIPMENT

The emphasis on promoting physical activity should dictate the selection of outdoor equipment. Equipment that offers "sit-and-ride" experiences (swings, merry-go-rounds, and teeter-totters) does not meet this criterion. A second criterion is safety. Each piece of equipment should minimize the potential for injury. In general, if equipment has moving parts, its potential for injury increases. This section offers suggestions for equipment based on their potential to develop various components of fitness. Remember that safety is the highest priority with playground equipment because it is often left unsupervised. If a playground is not restricted during nonschool hours, it may be best to stick to traditional equipment. An excellent website on Adventure Playgrounds covers this topic in greater detail (http://adventureplaygrounds.hampshire.edu/index.html).

EQUIPMENT FOR UPPER-BODY DEVELOPMENT

Most children lack the opportunity to develop upper-body strength. To develop arm–shoulder girdle strength on the playground, students need the opportunity to climb, swing, and elevate their bodies. Climbing is important for physical development and for helping children learn to overcome the fear of new situations. The following equipment can be used to develop arm–shoulder girdle strength:

- Large telephone cable spools, fastened securely so they will not move or tip over. Children can climb on and jump off the spools.
- Climbing poles placed next to platforms that children can reach by climbing the poles.
- Logs and clean railroad ties, positioned vertically, with handholds or handles placed in strategic locations for climbing.
- Tires attached to telephone poles or logs for climbing through and around.
- Jungle gyms attached securely.
- Horizontal ladders in various combinations and forms. Arched ladders are quite popular and allow children to reach the rungs easily. Uniladders, consisting of a single beam with foot pegs on each side, give children a different ladder challenge.
- Logs anchored vertically with handholds for climbing.

EQUIPMENT FOR LOWER-BODY DEVELOPMENT

Equipment and apparatus for enhancing lower-body development should encourage children to use locomotor movements throughout the available space. Allow enough distance and area to ensure movement. Here are suggestions for developing lower-body strength:

- Provide large spaces, which encourage free movement and running games.
- Anchor railroad ties vertically at varying heights and distances to encourage children to walk, run, hop, and jump from one to the other.

- Fasten used automobile tires to the ground in different patterns to stimulate moving in and out, around, and over the tires using different movements.
- Construct stairways and platforms for climbing on and jumping off.
- Offer stepping stones to encourage movement patterns. Create a design that leads to oppositional patterning while moving.
- Design miniature challenge courses containing tires to move over and through, sand pits to run and jump into, and poles or cones for moving around and dodging.

EQUIPMENT FOR BALANCE SKILLS

Balance is improved through regular practice. Many pieces of equipment can be used to challenge students' balance skills. Encourage children to move under control while practicing balance. Here are some suggestions for balance challenges:

- Balance beams made of 4-by-4-inch beams can be permanent installations. Arrange them in various patterns, but no more than 12 to 18 inches above the ground.
- Logs, anchored securely, can be used as balance beams.
- Provide balance beams that start at 6 inches wide and progress in difficulty to 1½ inches.
- Wooden ladders secured 6 inches above the ground can offer students opportunities to walk on the rungs and rails.

EQUIPMENT FOR SPORT SKILLS

Basketball Goals

Outdoor basketball goals may or may not be combined with a court. Children play a lot of one-goal basketball, which does not require a regulation court. The goals should be in a surfaced area, however. For elementary school use, place outdoor baskets 8 to 9 feet above the ground. The lowered height sometimes poses a problem because children can jump up and grasp the front of the rim, sometimes damaging or pulling off the basket. Strong construction that withstands such abuse is one solution. Some schools have reverted to the 10-foot-high basket, thus putting it out of reach of most children.

Volleyball Standards

Volleyball standards should have flexible height adjustments, including a low height of 30 inches for use in paddleball.

Softball Backstops

Softball backstops can be either fixed or portable.

Tetherball Courts

Tetherball courts should have fastening devices for the cord and ball so that they can be removed from the post for safekeeping.

Track and Field Equipment

Jumping standards, bars, and pits should be available. These must be maintained properly.

INDOOR FACILITIES

The gymnasium must be well planned for maximum use. The combination gymnasium–auditorium–cafeteria facility leaves much to be desired and creates more problems than it solves. Although it may be labeled a "multipurpose room," a better description is probably "multiuseless." The cafeteria poses a particular problem. The gymnasium must be vacated before the lunch hour so that chairs and tables can be set up, and the facility is not available again for physical education activities until it has been cleaned, which usually involves mopping. This eliminates noontime recreational use and leaves little play area for children during inclement weather. In extreme cases, a lack of help postpones gymnasium use for the early part of the afternoon, until the custodian has completed cleaning chores. Special programs, movies, and other events requiring chairs and the use of the area also complicate the situation.

Ideally, the gymnasium is located in a separate wing, connected to the classrooms by a covered corridor. It provides ready access to play areas. Isolating the gym from the rest of the school minimizes the noise problem and allows after-school and community groups to use the facilities without access to other parts of the school. The indoor facility is planned so that athletic contests can be scheduled there at times, but its primary purpose is not to be an athletic facility. Consideration for spectators is not a major planning concern. Only after basic physical education needs have been met are the needs of spectators considered.

The gymnasium floor has markings and boundaries outlining convenient areas for common activities. The markings are painted on the floor after applying the first or second sealer coat. A finish coat is then applied on top of the markings. Figure 10.1 shows how floor markings can maximize a facility's usefulness.

Temporary lines needed occasionally during the year can be applied with pressure-sensitive tape. These tapes are, however, difficult to remove completely and are likely to take off the finish when removed. A hardwood (preferably maple) floor is recommended for the gymnasium. Other surfaces limit community use and create safety and maintenance problems.

For safety reasons and for rebound practice, gym walls have a smooth surface at a distance of 8 to 10 feet up from the floor. Walls and ceilings have acoustical treatment. Exposed beams should be available for attaching apparatus. When planning a new facility, include a recess for each set of ropes on tracks. Insulation conforms to modern health standards, and older buildings should be scrutinized for unacceptable insulation materials such as asbestos fibers and certain formaldehyde-based plastics.

The gym should be well lit, with fixtures recessed to prevent damage. Arrange lights so they can be serviced from the floor. All walls should have electrical outlets. A permanent overhead public address system is desirable, as well as a record, tape, or CD player for easy access.

In a new facility, place windows high on the long sides of the gymnasium. Include protection from glare and direct sun.

If baskets and backboards need to be raised and lowered often, a motor-driven system eliminates laborious hand cranking. The system switch should be activated with a key.

The facility's storage space must be carefully planned. Equipment and instructional supplies require much storage space, and they must be readily available.

One problem frequently associated with a combination auditorium–gymnasium facility is the use of the physical education storeroom for bulky auditorium equipment such as portable chairs on chair trucks, portable stages, lighting fixtures, and other paraphernalia for dramatic productions. Unless the storage facility

10

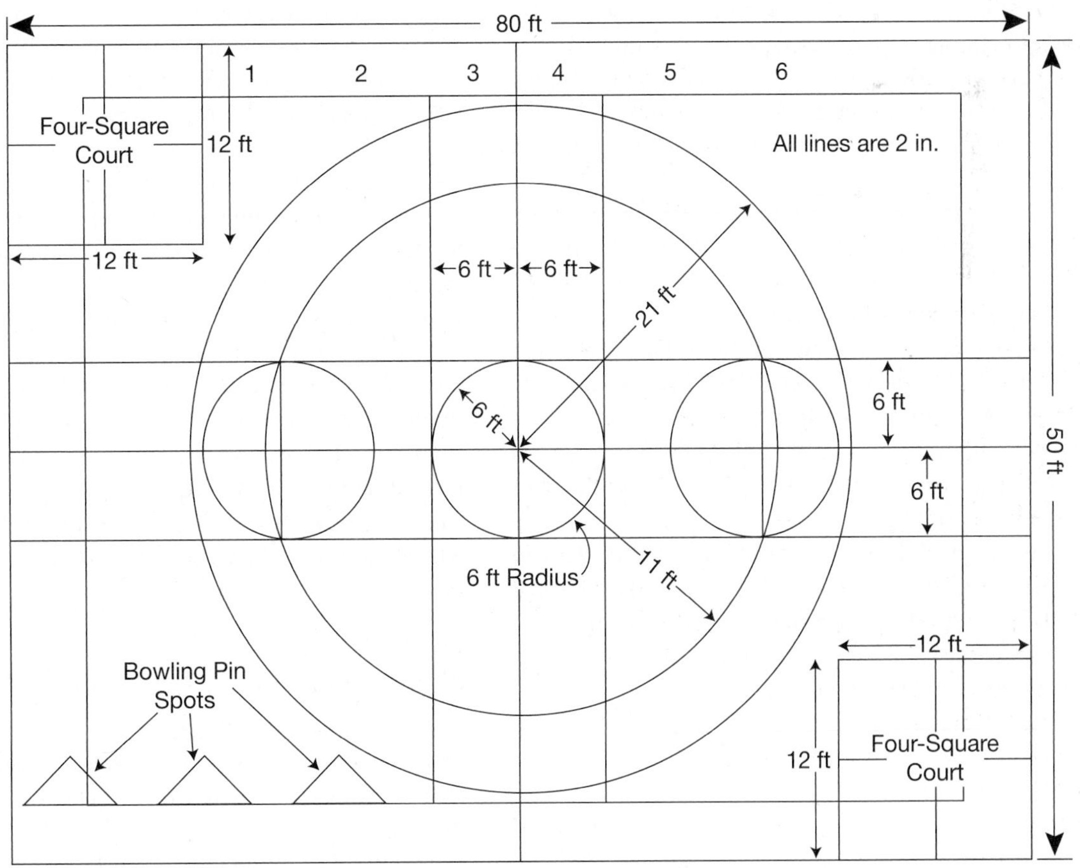

FIGURE 10.1 Floor markings to maximize gymnasium use.

is quite large—and most are not—an unworkable and cluttered facility is the result. The best solution is two separate storerooms for the dual-purpose facility, or at least one very large storeroom. Figure 10.2 shows an ideal physical education storage area.

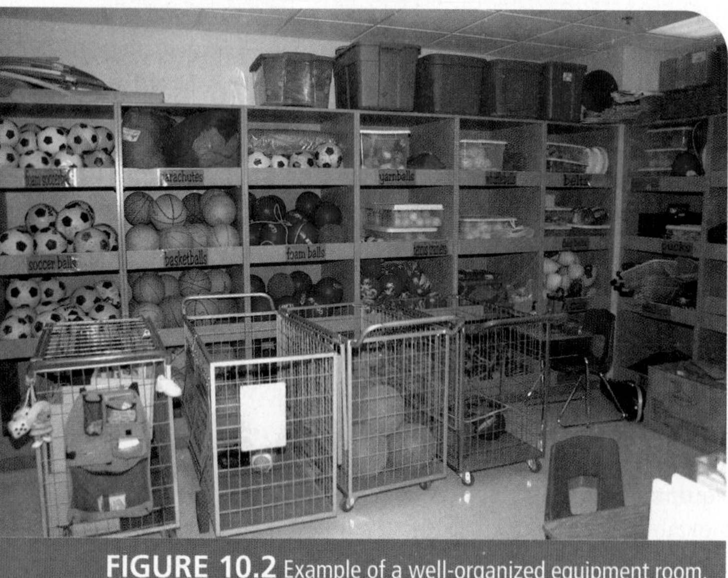

FIGURE 10.2 Example of a well-organized equipment room.

A separate storage area of cabinets is essential for outside groups who use the facility. These groups do not have access to the regular physical education supply room. If they are permitted to use school equipment, the equipment is checked out to the group and later checked in again.

Many storage areas in European schools have doors on tracks, similar to U.S. overhead garage doors. This design has several advantages, especially that the overhead opening simplifies the handling of large apparatus.

Most architects are unaware of the storage needs of a modern physical education program. Teachers can only hope that the architects designing new schools will be persuaded to allow for sufficient storage. For the physical education specialist, an office–dressing room with toilet and shower is desirable.

If contract or task styles of teaching are important in the instructional process, an area that houses instructional materials is useful. Children can go to this area, search through materials, and view loop films and videotapes as they complete their learning packets.

EQUIPMENT AND SUPPLIES

As mentioned, *equipment* refers to more or less fixed items, and *supplies* are nondurable items with a limited life span. For example, a softball is listed under supplies, but the longer-lasting softball backstop is in the equipment category. Equipment needs periodic replacement, and budget planning must consider the life span of each piece of equipment. Supplies generally are purchased once a year. It is important to have adequate financing for equipment and supplies and to spend funds wisely.

To meet physical education program objectives, sufficient instructional materials must be available. Be sure there is enough equipment that children can use practice time well rather than waiting in line.

Safety Tip

If you don't have enough equipment or supplies, use peer coaching so equipment is shared, students practice taking turns, and you don't need to split your focus and risk incidents happening through lack of supervision.

Policies covering the purchase, storage, issuance, care, maintenance, and inventory of supplies are required to make optimum use of the program budget. Decide on program features first and then implement a purchasing plan based on these features. Having a minimal list of instructional supplies stabilizes the teaching process.

Consider having the school staff build some equipment. Quality must not, however, be sacrificed. Articles from home (including empty plastic jugs, milk cartons, old tires, and the like) should be regarded as supplementary materials. The administration must be careful not to look for the cheap or no-cost route to securing supplies, thus sacrificing valuable learning experiences when the program requires an appreciable investment.

Some articles—yarn balls, hoops, Lummi sticks, balance beams, and bounding boards, for instance—can be made satisfactorily by school staff, by parents, and sometimes by students. For other articles, remind the administration that homemade equipment is usually a temporary solution only, undertaken in a program's early phases when equipment costs are high and cannot all be met immediately.

PURCHASING POLICIES

Purchasing supplies and equipment involves careful study of need, price, quality, and material. The safety of the children who will use the equipment is paramount. Quantity buying by pooling the funds of an entire school district generally results in better use of the tax dollar. However, cooperative purchasing may require compromises on equipment type and brand to satisfy different users in the system. If bids are requested, careful specifications are necessary. Request bids for specified items only, and do not accept "just as good" merchandise in their place.

Make one person at the school responsible for obtaining physical education supplies and for keeping records of equipment, supplies, and purchasing. Needs will vary from school to school, and it is practical for school district authorities to deal with a single person at each school. This system allows for prompt attention to repair and replacement of supplies. The person designated can also be responsible for testing various competing products to determine which ones give the best service over time. Some kind of labeling or marking of materials is needed to accomplish such testing.

An accurate inventory of equipment is required at the start and end of each school year. A sound inventory system tracks the durability of equipment and supplies and accounts for lost or misplaced supplies. Order supplies and equipment by the end of the school year, or earlier, if possible. To allow time for checking orders and making any necessary adjustments before the school year begins, specify an early delivery date.

Most equipment of good quality lasts 7 to 10 years, thus keeping replacement costs to a minimum. School district purchasing agents who select low-cost items with little regard for quality are applying financially unsound policy. Budgetary practices should include an allotment for the yearly purchase of instructional supplies as well as for major replacement and procurement costs for large items, which are usually staggered over several years. After obtaining sufficient equipment and supplies, the program's budget considerations will be for replacement and repair only.

INDOOR EQUIPMENT

Several principles govern the choice of indoor equipment. First, a reasonable variety and amount of equipment should be available to keep children active. Include items to facilitate arm–shoulder girdle development (for example, climbing ropes, climbing frames, ladders, and similar apparatus). A criterion for selection is that most, if not all, indoor equipment be of the type that children can carry, assemble, and disassemble. A regular trampoline, for example, does not meet this criterion.

MATS FOR TUMBLING AND SAFETY

Mats are basic to any physical education program. Enough mats—at least eight—must be available to provide a safe floor for climbing apparatus. Light, folding mats are best because they are easy to handle and store (Figure 10.3). They stack well and can be moved on carts. Mats should have fasteners so that several can be joined. Plastic covers allow for easy cleaning. (The one objection to plastic covers is that they are not as soft as the type of mat cover used for wrestling.) Mats should be 4 feet wide and 7 or 8 feet long. Heavy hand-me-down mats from the high school program may prove difficult for younger students to handle and bulky to store.

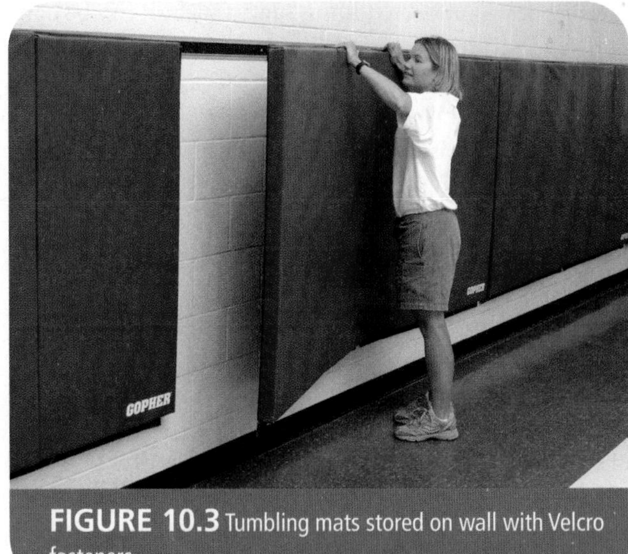

FIGURE 10.3 Tumbling mats stored on wall with Velcro fasteners.

Other mats that might be considered are thick, soft mats (somewhat like mattresses) and inclined mats. Soft mats are generally at least 4 inches thick and may entice the timid to try activities they otherwise would avoid. Inclined mats are wedge-shaped and provide downhill momentum for rolls.

INDIVIDUAL MATS

The primary-level program requires a supply of 30 to 35 individual mats. The mats, which can be 20 by 40 inches or 24 by 48 inches, are useful for practicing many movement experiences and introductory tumbling activities.

TAPE/CD PLAYER

A portable combination tape and CD player with remote control is the most affordable and versatile choice for the physical education program.

BALANCE-BEAM BENCHES

Balance-beam benches have double use. They can serve as regular benches for many types of bench activity, and, when turned over, they can be used for balance-beam activities. Wooden horses or their supports can serve as inclined benches. Six benches are a minimum for class activity.

BALANCE BEAMS

A wide beam (4 inches) is recommended for kindergarten and first grade. Otherwise, a 2-inch beam can be used.

Balance beams in two widths (2 and 4 inches) can be constructed from common building materials.

CHINNING BAR

The chinning bar is especially useful for physical fitness testing and in body support activities. A portable chinning bar, installed in the gym doorway, is an acceptable substitute.

CLIMBING ROPES

Climbing ropes are essential to the program. At least eight ropes are required, but having more than eight allows for better group instruction. Climbing ropes on tracks are the most efficient to handle (Figure 10.4). With little effort or loss of time, the ropes can be pulled out for activity.

Quality climbing ropes made of synthetic fibers are now available. The best are olefin fiber ropes that are nonallergenic and have nonslip qualities, thus forestalling the problem of slickness—a characteristic of plastic ropes and even of older cotton ropes. Ropes should be either $1\frac{1}{2}$ or $1\frac{3}{4}$ inches in diameter. Climbing ropes on tracks and other large apparatus can be purchased from Gopher Sport, 220 24th Avenue NW, P.O. Box 998, Owatonna, MN 55060-0998; phone: 1-800-533-0446 or www.gophersport.com.

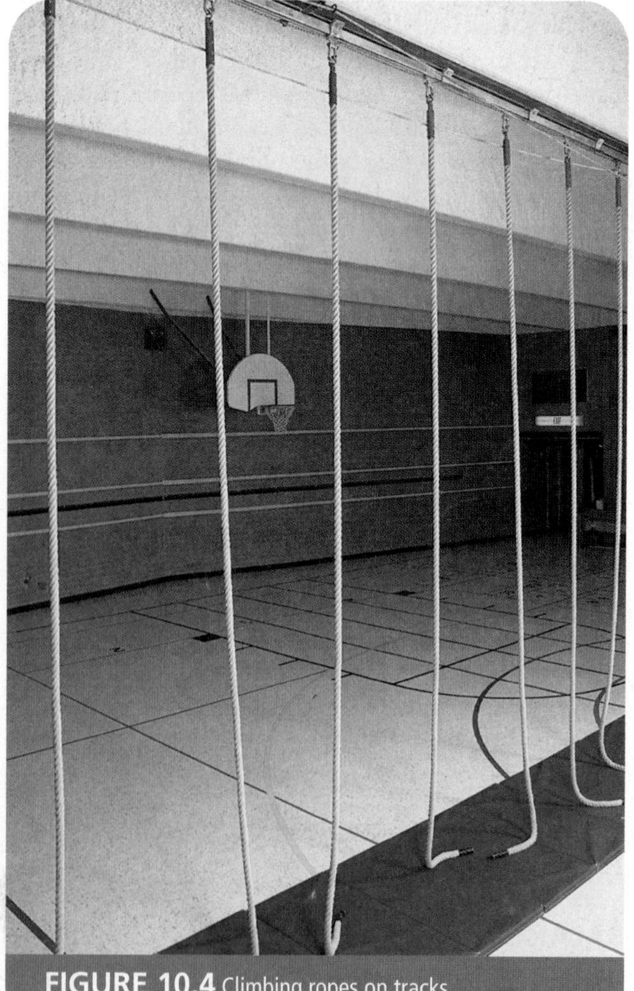

FIGURE 10.4 Climbing ropes on tracks.

VOLLEYBALL STANDARDS

Volleyball standards should adjust to various heights for different grade levels and games.

SUPPLY CART

A cart to hold supplies is desirable. Other carts can be used for the audio equipment and for regular and individual mats.

JUMPING BOXES

Small boxes used for jumping and related locomotor movements extend students' opportunities to work on basic movement skills. Boxes should be 8 and 16 inches high. If the boxes are made by staff, specify about 16 by 16 inches with a skidproof rubber surface on the bottom for stability. Holes drilled through the sides provide fingerholds for ease of handling. Eight boxes, four of each size, are a minimum number for the average-sized class. Jumping boxes also can be purchased from Gopher Sport.

HORIZONTAL LADDER SETS

Horizontal ladders that fold against the wall make an excellent indoor equipment addition. The ladder may be combined with other pieces of apparatus in a folding set.

OTHER INDOOR ITEMS

A portable chalkboard is desirable, as is a wall screen for displaying visual aids. To display announcements or notes, hang a large bulletin board and a wall chalkboard near the gym's main door. An audiovisual cart or stand for projectors is helpful. Be sure it includes enough electrical cord to reach wall outlets.

Rebound nets for throwing and kicking have excellent utility. They are, however, hard to store. Substitute goals for basketball and related games can be designed. One suggested goal is 4 feet square, with the rim 5 feet above the ground. Beginners can find success with this goal design. The frame can be made of 1-inch pipe or plastic (PVC) tubing.

EQUIPMENT AND SUPPLIES FOR PHYSICAL EDUCATION

Knowing what equipment to obtain for your program and where to find it can be an obstacle, but it need not be a major obstacle. Figure 10.5 identifies the equipment, supplies, and capital-outlay items needed to teach a quality physical education program. The items are listed by priority based on cost, need, and versatility of the equipment. The first piece of equipment listed (playground balls) can be

Priority	Material and Supplies	Quantity
1	8½ in. inflatable rubber playground balls	36
1a	8 in. foam balls (can be substituted for playground balls)	36
1b	8 in. polyurethane-coated foam balls (A substitute for playground balls; they are much more durable and give a true bounce. They can be used for all types of sport activities.)	36
2	6 in. × 6 in. beanbags, assorted colors	72
3	Jump ropes (plastic segments for beginners and speed ropes for experienced jumpers)	
	7 ft length	36
	8 ft length	36
	9 ft length	18
	16 ft length (long rope-jumping)	12
4	Hoops (solid or segmented)	
	30 in. diameter	36
	36 in. diameter	36
5	Wands (36 in. length, ¾ in. diameter hardwood)	36
6	Game cones (12 in. bright orange vinyl)	20
7	Tambourine, single head, double ring	1
8	Plastic racquets (sized for elementary children)	36
9	Foam balls for racquet skills (2½ in.)	36
10	Fleece balls (3–4 in. diameter)	36
11	Floor hockey sticks and pucks—36 of each	36
12	Whiffle balls (use for throwing, hockey, softball, etc.)	36
13	Individual mats (23 in. × 48 in. × ½ in.)	36
14	Partner tug-of-war ropes (handles on both ends made with nylon webbing or garden hose and ⅜ in. nylon rope)	18
15	Juggling scarves	108
16	Beach balls (18 in. to 20 in. diameter)	36
17	Soccer balls (junior size or trainers)	18
18	Basketballs (junior size)	18
19	Footballs (junior size or foam rubber)	18
20	Volleyballs (lightweight trainer balls)	18
21	Softballs (extra soft)	18
22	Softball bats (wood or aluminum)	3
23	Frisbees (9–10 in. diameter)	36
24	Magic stretch ropes	12
25	Cageball (24 in.)	1
26	Pinnies (four colors—12 each)	48
27	Ball bags (nylon see-through mesh)	12
28	Team tug-of-war rope (¾ in. × 50 ft nylon with sealed ends)	1
29	Stopwatches (digital)	6
30	Batons (for track and field relays)	12
31	Scooterboards, 12 in. with handles	18
32	Bowling pins	30
33	Lummi sticks	72

FIGURE 10.5 Basic equipment and supplies needed for quality physical education.

Priority	Capital-Outlay Items	Quantity
1	Tumbling mats (4 ft × 8 ft × 1¼ in. thick; four sides of Velcro fasteners)	12
2	Cassette tape player	1
3	Parachute and storage bag (28 ft diameter)	1
4	Electric ball pump	1
5	Heavy-duty equipment (ball) carts	4
6	Balance-beam benches (12 ft length)	6
7	Jumping boxes (8 in. height)	6
8	Jumping boxes (16 in. height)	6
9	Audiovisual cart with electrical outlet (for tape player, etc.)	1
10	Sit-and-reach box (measure flexibility)	2
11	Utility gym standards (for volleyball nets, etc.)	2
12	Field marker (for chalking lines)	1

FIGURE 10.5 Basic equipment and supplies needed for quality physical education. (Continued)

used to teach the most units, so it has the highest priority. The quantity of equipment is also listed to ensure that the proper amount is ordered to facilitate a normal class size. Some of the equipment can be constructed rather than purchased, as described later in this chapter.

Most of the equipment listed is available from Gopher Sport (www.gophersport.com). The author has worked closely with this company to develop a *Dynamic Physical Education* equipment list. This list offers all the equipment and teaching materials needed for a high-quality program. Equipment has been field-tested and is shipped quickly with an unconditional lifetime guarantee. For a current catalog or more information, call 1-800-533-0446 or fax a request to 1-800-451-4855.

STORAGE PLANS

When a class goes to the gymnasium for physical education, the teacher has a right to expect enough supplies to be available to conduct the class. A master list stipulating the kinds and quantities of supplies in storage should be maintained. A reasonable turnover is to be expected, and supply procedures must take this into account. Supplies in the storage facility should be available for physical education classes and for organized after-school activities. These supplies are not to be used for games played during recess or for free play periods; each classroom has its own supplies for such purposes. Establish a system for storing equipment and supplies. "A place for everything and everything in its place" is the key to good housekeeping. Label bins, shelves, and other assigned areas where supplies and equipment are to be kept.

Teachers and students must accept responsibility for maintaining order in the storage facility. Squad leaders or student aides can assume major responsibility. At the end of each week, the teacher in charge of the storage area can assign older children to help tidy the area, put any stray items back in place, and repair or replace articles as needed. Principals are more favorably inclined toward purchase requests when obvious care is taken of instructional materials.

Some schools use small supply carts, as pictured in Figure 10.6. The carts, which hold the most frequently used supplies, take up some additional space but save students time in accessing needed items. The carts can be built inexpensively to meet specific needs, or they can be purchased from a commercial manufacturer. A cart for audio equipment and carts that store and move mats and balls are helpful.

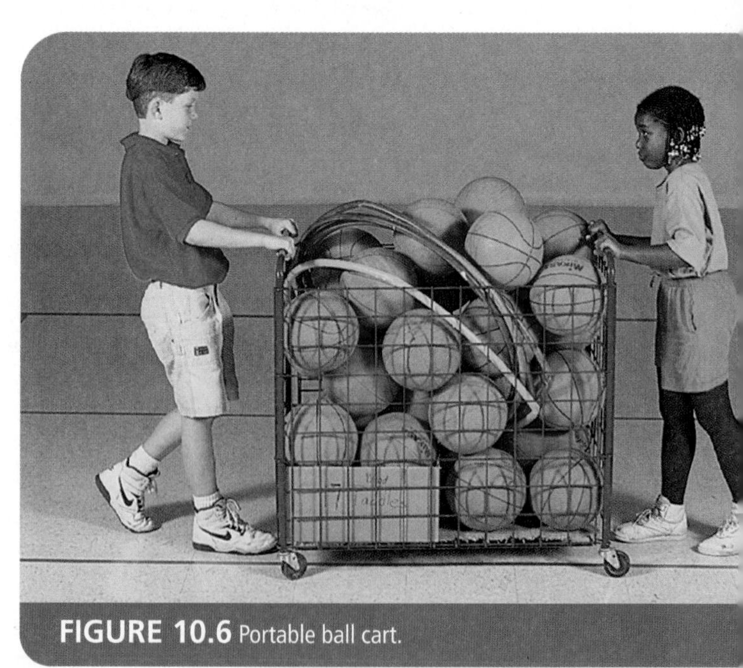

FIGURE 10.6 Portable ball cart.

Establish an off-season storage area for equipment not in present use, and keep this area locked. It is important to know who has keys to the storage area so that if equipment goes missing, it is possible to identify those with access to the area.

CARE, REPAIR, AND MARKING

A definite system should be developed for repairing supplies and equipment. A quick decision must be made whether to repair an item locally or send it out. If the repair will take too long and cost too much, just use the item as long as possible. Establish an area for equipment needing repair, so that all these articles are evident at a glance.

Balls must be inflated to proper pressures. This means using an accurate gauge and checking the pressures periodically. Moisten the inflation needle before inserting it into the valve. Instruct children to kick only those balls made specifically for kicking (soccer balls, footballs, and playground balls).

Repair cuts, abrasions, and breaks in rubber balls immediately. Some repairs can be made with a vulcanized patch, like those used to repair tire tubes. For other repairs, a hard-setting rubber preparation is of value. When repair is beyond the scope of the school, send the ball out for repair.

For off-season storage, deflate balls somewhat, leaving just enough air in them to retain their shape. Clean leather balls with an appropriate conditioner.

Mats are expensive and need proper care if they are to last. Establish a place where they can be stacked properly; or if the mats have handles or Velcro, hang them (see Figure 10.3 on page 185) to serve as padding for the walls. A mat truck is another storage option if there is space for the truck. Periodically clean the newer plastic or plastic-covered mats with a damp, soapy cloth.

For small items, clean plastic ice-cream buckets are adequate storage receptacles. Most school cafeterias have these and other containers that can be used in the storage room to keep order. Small wire or plastic baskets also make good storage containers.

Mark all equipment and supplies. This is particularly important for equipment issued to different classrooms. Use indelible pencil, paint, engraver, or stencil ink for marking. Few marking systems are permanent, however, and re-marking at regular intervals is necessary. Sporting goods stores have marking sets. An electric burning pencil works well when used carefully to avoid damaging the equipment.

Rubber playground balls come in different colors, and their assignment to classrooms can be based on the color. A code scheme with different-colored paints also can be used. A color system designating the year of issue is another idea that offers the opportunity to document equipment usage and care.

CONSTRUCTING EQUIPMENT AND SUPPLIES

This section is divided into two parts. The first part offers recommendations for sources and materials needed to construct equipment and supplies. The second part provides diagrams and specifications for building equipment economically. If the recommended equipment can be described adequately without an illustration, it is included in the first part.

RECOMMENDATIONS FOR CONSTRUCTING EQUIPMENT AND SUPPLIES

The supply of balls can be augmented with tennis balls or sponge balls. Discarded tennis balls from the high school tennis team are useful. Poke holes in the tennis balls if they are too lively for young children to handle. Sponge balls are inexpensive and, with care, last indefinitely.

A good supply of ropes for jumping is essential. The newer, plastic-link jump ropes are recommended; these

Author's Note: The next section shows how to construct equipment because doing so can be a short-term solution when starting a new program or unit of instruction. However, this text does not actively promote self-constructed equipment, for several reasons.

- Constructed equipment is usually second rate and does not last long. It also gives teachers and students a feeling of being second-rate citizens because little money is spent for their teaching and learning tools.
- Constructed equipment is often a rough equivalent of the commercial product. This means less skilled students are using the lowest-quality equipment to learn, whereas more advanced (generally high school) athletes have the best quality. Obviously, unskilled students need the benefit of the best possible equipment if they are to succeed.
- Safety and liability can become problems depending on who constructed the equipment and whether it meets minimal safety standards. If an accident occurs, and it can be proved that the constructed equipment does not meet safety standards of commercially built equipment, the school may be held liable for the injury.
- If you show your building administrator that you can get by without a budget because you are willing to construct your equipment, you will never have an adequate budget.

Homemade equipment should be a last resort and a short-term solution.

ropes have good weight, come in attractive colors, can be shortened easily (by removing links), and can be purchased with color-coded handles. The handles provide good leverage for turning. However, ropes can also be made from cord. Heavy sash cord or hard-weave polyethylene rope is suitable. The ends should be whipped, heated, or dipped into some type of hardening solution to prevent unraveling. The lengths can be color-coded with dye or stain. Developmental Level I students use mostly 7-foot ropes, with a few 6- and 8-foot ropes. Developmental Levels II and III students use mostly 8-foot ropes, with a few 7- and 9-foot ropes. Instructors will require 9- or 10-foot ropes.

Enough ropes should be available in the suggested lengths for each child to have a rope of the correct length. The supply of ropes should include 8 to 10 long (14- to 16-foot) ropes for long-rope jumping activities. A jump-the-shot rope can be made by tying an old, completely deflated volleyball to one end of a rope.

Beanbags are made easily. High-quality, bright-colored muslin is suitable as a covering. Some teachers have asked parents to save the lower legs of worn-out denim jeans; this material wears extremely well and is free. Other instructors prefer a beanbag with an outer liner that snaps in place to allow for washing. Another idea is to sew three sides of the beanbag permanently. The fourth side is used for filling and has an independent stitch. The beans can be removed through this side when the bag is washed. Beanbags should be about 4 by 4 inches or 6 by 6 inches and can be filled with dried beans or peas, wheat, rice, or even building sand.

For games requiring boundary markers, use pieces of rubber matting; small sticks or boards, painted white, are also excellent. A board 1 by 2 inches across and 3 or 4 feet long makes a satisfactory marker.

Tetherballs should have a snap-on fastener for easy removal.

Schools near ski areas may be able to get discarded towropes. These make excellent tug-of-war ropes.

Bowling pins or clubs can be turned in the school shop, or suitable substitutes can be made. For example, pieces of 2-by-2-inch lumber cut short (6 to 10 inches) stand satisfactorily. Lumber companies usually have dowels 1 to 1½ inches in diameter. Sections of these dowels make a reasonable substitute for clubs. Broken bats also can be made into good substitute clubs.

White shoe polish has many marking uses and can be removed from the floor with a little scrubbing.

Three-pound coffee cans make excellent targets. Empty half-gallon milk cartons also have a variety of uses.

Inner tubes can be cut in strips and used as resistance exercise equipment. The tube should be cut crosswise into 1-inch-wide strips.

Old bowling pins can be obtained from most bowling alleys free of charge. Because the standard pins are too large for children to handle easily, cutting 2 to 4 inches off the bottom is recommended. Parallel cuts through the body of the pin provide shuffleboard disks. For kindergarten and first-grade children, make improvised balls from crumpled newspaper bound with cellophane tape. Papier-mâché balls are also useful. Light foam-rubber cubes can be trimmed to make interesting objects for throwing and catching.

Bamboo for making tinikling poles can sometimes be procured from carpet stores, which use the poles for supporting the center of a carpet roll. Plastic tinikling sticks are available commercially.

DIAGRAMS AND SPECIFICATIONS FOR CONSTRUCTING EQUIPMENT AND SUPPLIES

Safety standards should apply to all school-constructed equipment; be sure the construction and the materials used do not create safety hazards. The design must be educationally sound and utilitarian.

Balance Beam

The balance beam is used for many kinds of activities. Two types of stands for a 2-by-4-inch beam are shown in Figure 10.7. The beam can be placed with the wide or the narrow side up, depending on the student's skill. If the beam is longer than 8 feet, place a third stand in the middle. To prevent splintering and cracking, carefully sand the beam and then apply multiple coats of finish.

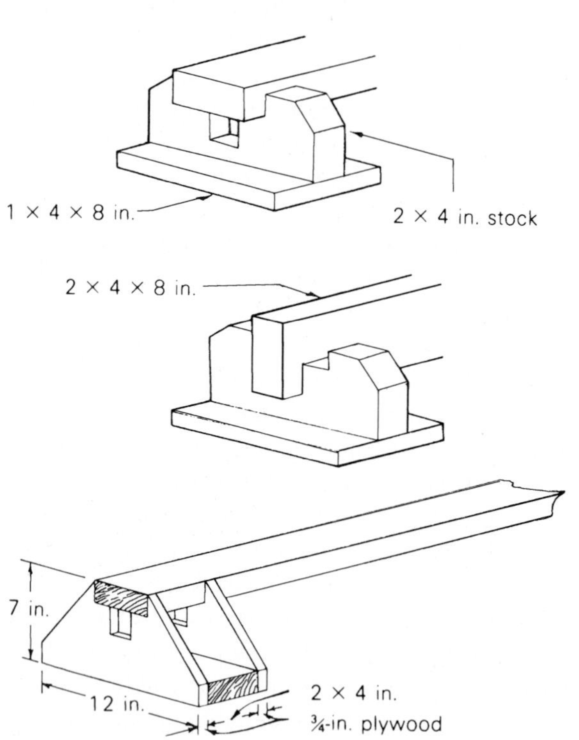

FIGURE 10.7 Balance beam with stand.

Balance-Beam Bench

The balance-beam bench is a versatile piece of equipment. Its dimensions can be modified depending on the students' age (Figure 10.8). It should be made of hardwood or hardwood plywood and be well finished.

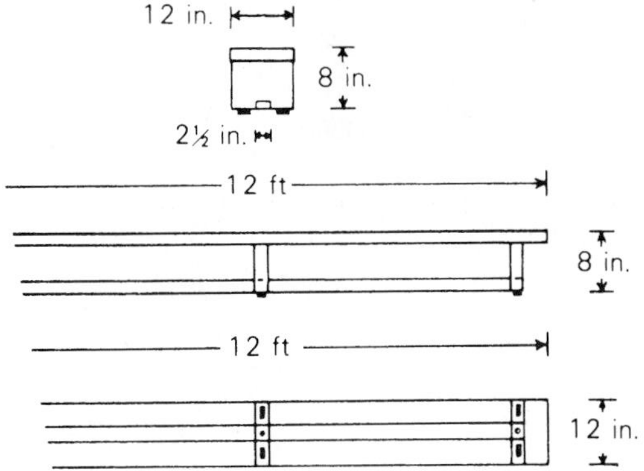

FIGURE 10.8 Balance-beam bench.

Balance Boards

Many styles of balance board can be constructed, depending on the materials available and individual needs (Figure 10.9). Glue a piece of rubber matting to the top of the board to prevent slipping, and place it on an individual mat or on a piece of heavy rubber matting. A square board is easier to balance than a round one, because its corners touch the floor and give more stability.

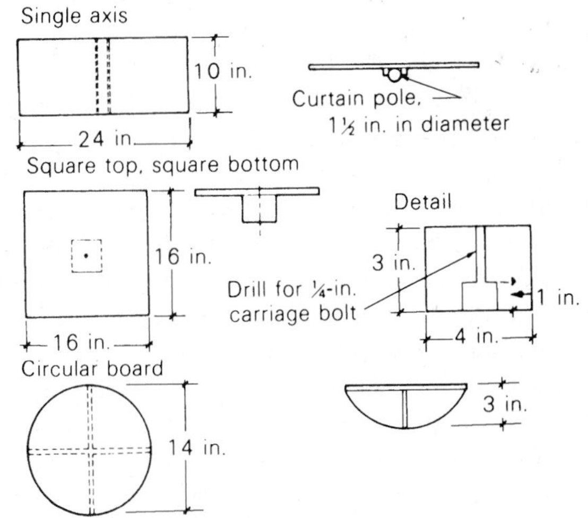

FIGURE 10.9 Styles of balance board.

Batting Tee

Ideally, the batting tee should be adjustable to accommodate batters of various heights (Figure 10.10). Constructing an adjustable tee takes time, however, and the results are not always satisfactory. An alternative is to make several non-adjustable tees of different heights.

Materials:

One piece of 1-inch pipe, 24 to 28 inches long

One piece of radiator hose, 8 to 12 inches long, with an inside diameter of 1½ inches

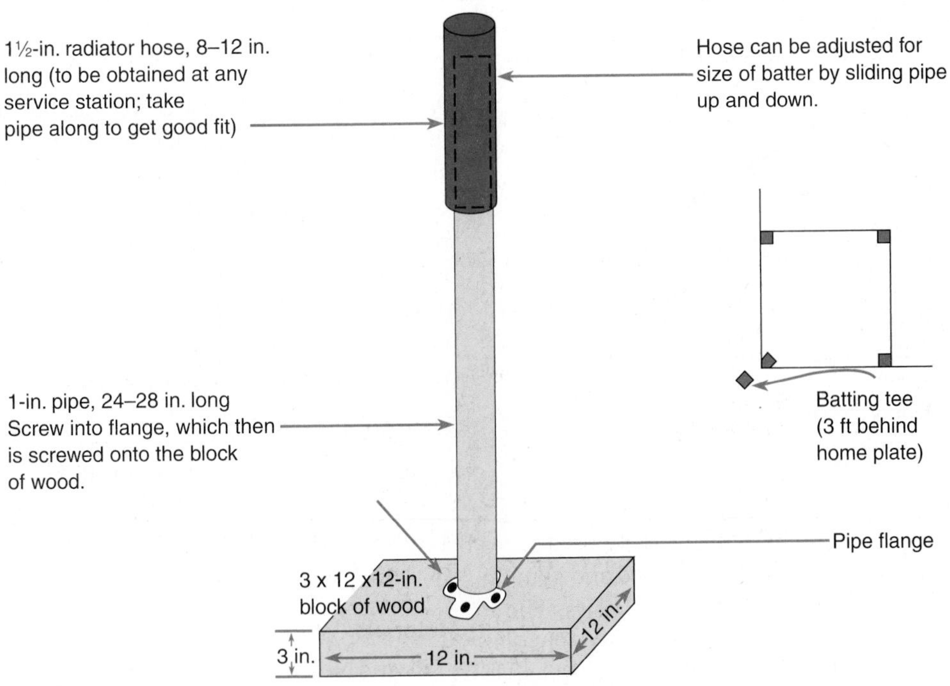

FIGURE 10.10 Batting tee construction.

10

One block of wood, 3 by 12 by 12 inches

One pipe flange for 1-inch pipe, to be mounted on the block

Screws and hose cement

Directions: Mount the flange on the block and screw the pipe into the flange. Place the radiator hose on the pipe. Paint as desired. To secure a good fit for the radiator hose, take the pipe to the supply source. If the hose is to remain fixed, then secure it with hose cement.

An alternative method is to drill a hole in the block and mount the pipe directly in the hole with mastic or good-quality glue. Note that 1-inch pipe has an outside diameter of approximately 1 inch, allowing the hose to fit properly over it.

Blocks and Cones

Blocks with grooves on the top and on one side are excellent for forming hurdles with wands. A 4-by-4-inch board cut in lengths of 6, 12, and 18 inches yields several hurdle sizes. Cones can be notched and used in place of the blocks (Figure 10.11).

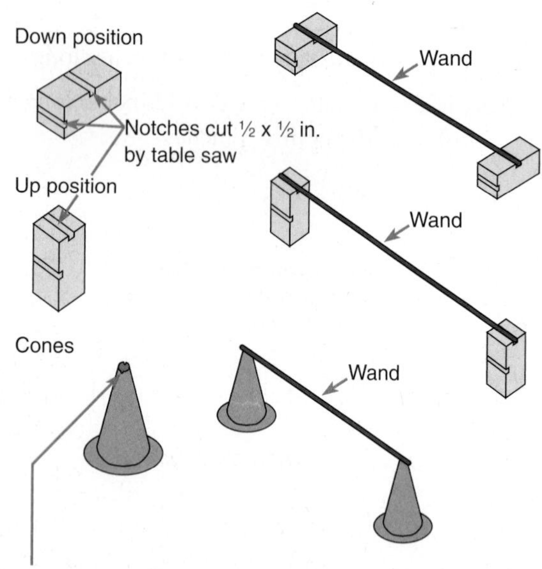

FIGURE 10.11 Blocks and cones.

Bowling Pins

Bowling alleys give away old pins, which can be used for many purposes. Some suggested uses are as field and gymnasium markers, for bowling games, and for relays. The bottom 2 inches of the pin should be cut off, and the base sanded smooth (Figure 10.12). Pins can be numbered and decorated with decals, colored tape, or paint.

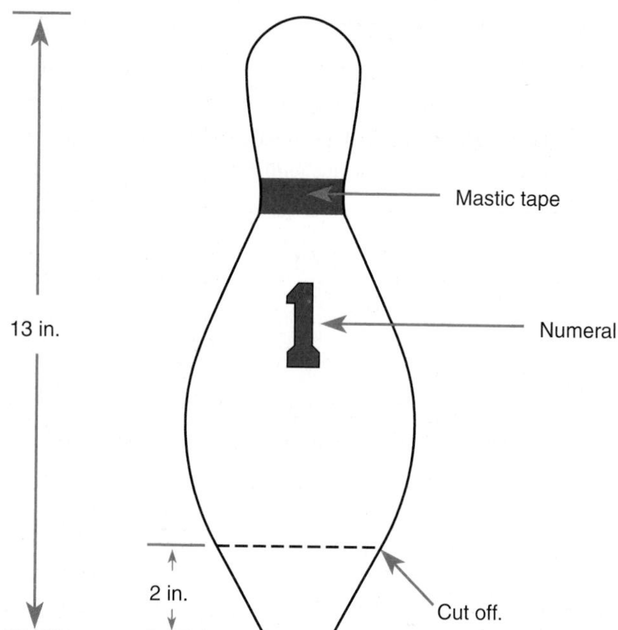

FIGURE 10.12 Bowling pin.

Conduit Hurdles

Conduit hurdles are lightweight and easy to store. Because they are not weighted and fall over easily, children have little fear about hitting them. The elastic bands can be moved up and down to create different heights and different challenges. Conduit can be purchased at most electrical supply houses.

Materials:

One piece of ½-inch electrical conduit pipe, 10 feet long

One piece of 1-inch stretch elastic tape

Wood dowel, ½-inch diameter

Directions: Bend the piece of conduit to the following dimensions: uprights are 30 inches high, the base is 30 inches wide, and the sides of the base are 15 inches long. A special tool for bending the conduit usually can be purchased from the supply house where the conduit was bought. Sew loops on each end of the elastic tape so the tape slides over the ends of the hurdles with a slight amount of tension. If necessary, put short pieces of dowel into the ends of the conduit to raise the height of the hurdle (Figure 10.13).

Footsies

Footsies can be made economically by the children and provide an excellent movement challenge. The activity requires coordination of both feet to keep the footsie rotating properly.

Materials:

Plastic bleach bottle, half-gallon size

One piece of ⅛-inch clothesline rope

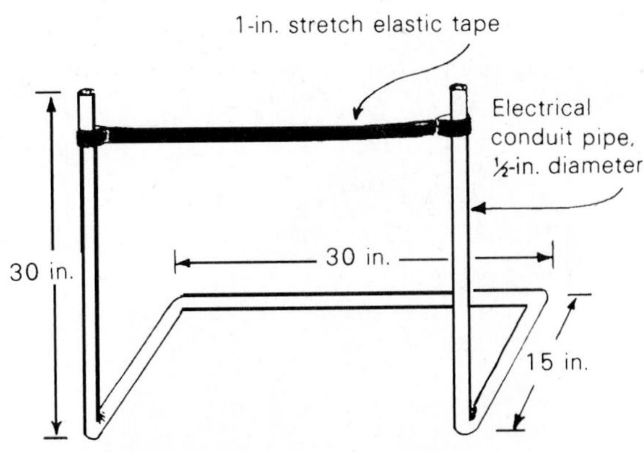

FIGURE 10.13 Conduit hurdle construction.

Old tennis ball

Large fishing swivel, preferably with ball bearings

Directions: Cut a circular strip about 2 inches wide out of the bottom of a bleach bottle. Cut two holes in the strip about 1 inch apart. Thread a 3-foot piece of clothesline through the holes, and tie a knot on the outside of the strip. Cut the clothesline in half and tie the swivel to each end of the cut cord. The swivel prevents the rope from becoming twisted.

Puncture the tennis ball with an ice pick, making two holes directly across from each other. Thread the line through the holes with a piece of wire or a large crochet hook. Tie a large knot near the outer hole so the line cannot slip back through (Figure 10.14).

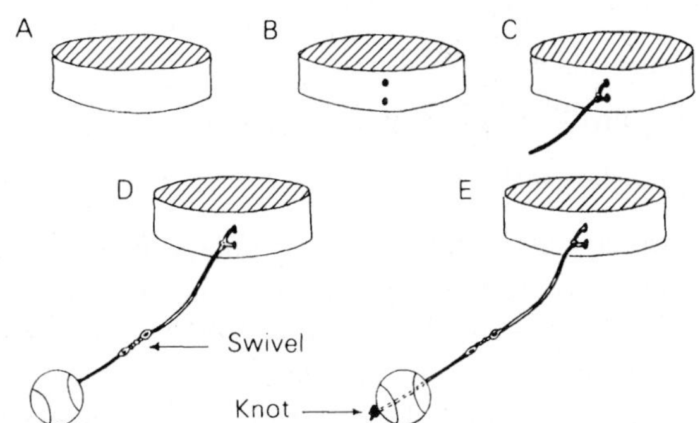

FIGURE 10.14 Footsie construction.

Gym Scooters

Scooters are easily constructed from readily available materials and can be made in many sizes and shapes. The casters should be checked to make sure they do not mark the floor. Scooters have many activity applications and can be used to move heavy equipment.

Materials:

One piece of 2-inch yellow pine board, 12 by 12 inches

Four ball-bearing casters with 2-inch wheels of hard rubber

Protective rubber stripping, 4 feet long

Cement

Screws and paint

Directions: Actual dimensions of the board are around $1\frac{5}{8}$ by $11\frac{5}{8}$ inches. Two pieces of ¾-inch plywood glued together can be substituted. Cut and round the corners, smoothing them with a power sander. Sand all edges by hand, and apply two coats of paint. Fasten the four casters approximately $1\frac{1}{2}$ inches diagonally in from the corners. A rubber strip fixed around the edges with staples and cement (Figure 10.15) will cushion the impact of the scooter on other objects.

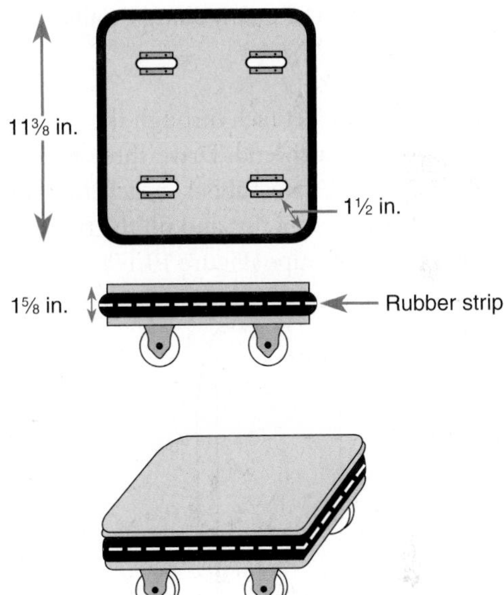

FIGURE 10.15 Gym scooter construction.

Hoops

Hoops can be constructed from ½-inch plastic water pipe (PVC), which unfortunately is available in drab colors only. The cost savings of using the pipe are, however, great. Hoops can be constructed in different sizes. A short piece of dowel, fixed with a power stapler or tacks, can be used to join the ends together (Figure 10.16 on page 194). An alternative joining method is to use special pipe connectors. Weather-stripping cement helps make a more permanent joint.

Hurdle and High-Jump Rope

The weighted hurdle and high-jump rope is ideal for beginning hurdlers and high jumpers who may fear hitting the bar. The rope can be hung over the pins of the high-jump standards; the weights keep the rope fairly taut.

Materials:

One piece of ⅜-inch rope, 10 feet long

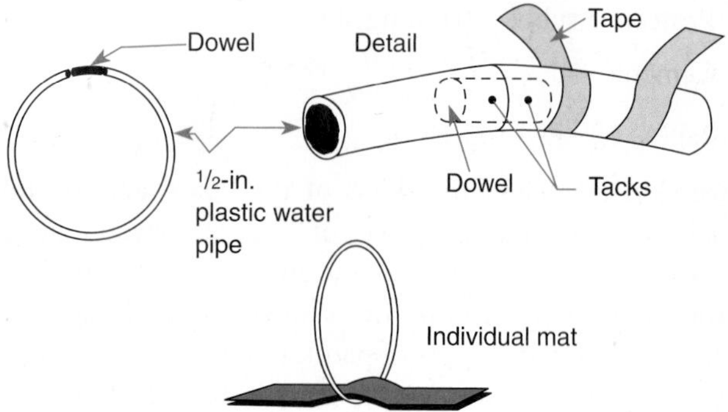

FIGURE 10.16 Hoop construction.

Two rubber crutch tips (number 19)

Tacks (number 14) and penny shingle nails

Sand

Directions: Drive a carpet tack through the rope approximately 3/4 inch from each end. Drive three nails into the bottom of each of the two rubber crutch tips. Place the rope ends inside the crutch tips and fill the tips with sand. Tape shut the top of the tips (Figure 10.17).

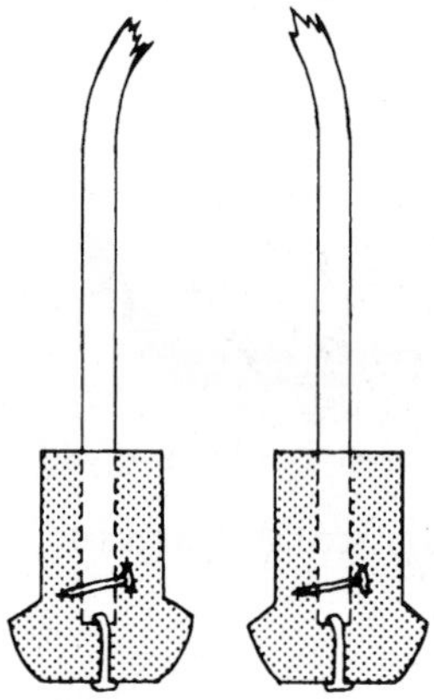

FIGURE 10.17 Weighted hurdle and high-jump rope construction.

Individual Mats

Individual mats can be made from indoor-outdoor carpeting with a rubber backing. This prevents the mat from sliding on the floor and offers some cushion. The mats also can be washed easily when they become soiled. Mats of different colors are preferable, because they can be used for games, for color tag, and for easily dividing the class by mat color. Carpet stores often have small pieces and remnants that they will sell cheaply or give away.

Another type of individual mat is designed to fold (Figure 10.18). These mats are useful for aerobic dance classes because they are lighter and easier to handle than carpet mats. The major drawback is that folding mats are more expensive.

FIGURE 10.18 Folding individual mat.

Jumping Boxes

Jumping boxes are used to develop a wide variety of body management skills. The dimensions can be varied to satisfy individual needs, but 8- and 16-inch boxes seem to be the most useful.

Materials:

3/4-inch marine plywood

Wood screws, paint, and glue

Carpet pad remnants

Naugahyde or similar material to cover box top

Upholstery tacks

Directions: Cut the four sides to similar dimensions and then sand them together to make sure they are exactly the same size. Use a countersink and drill the screw holes, apply glue at the joints, and screw the sides together. When the box is assembled, sand all edges to remove any sharpness. Paint the boxes, preferably with a latex-based paint because it chips less than oil-based enamel does. If handholds are desired, drill holes and then cut them out with a saber saw (Figure 10.19). Covering is optional. If desired, cut a carpet pad remnant the size of the top of the box, and cover it with Naugahyde. The Naugahyde should overlap about 4 inches on each side of the box so that it can be folded under to make a double thickness and then tacked down.

Jumping Standards

Jumping standards are useful for hurdling, jumping, and over-and-under activities. Many shapes and sizes are possible (Figure 10.20).

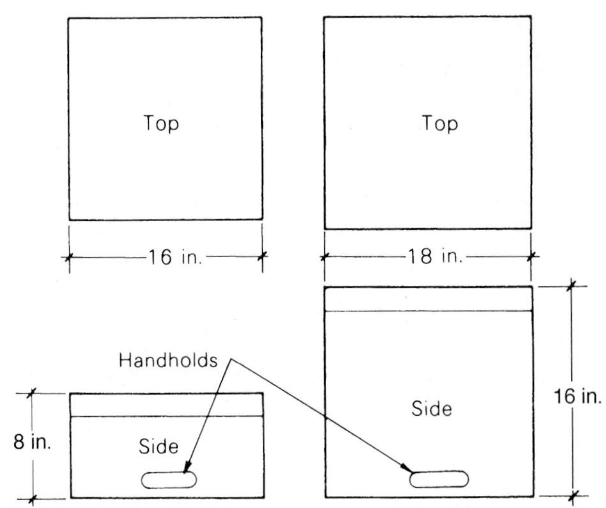

FIGURE 10.19 Jumping box construction.

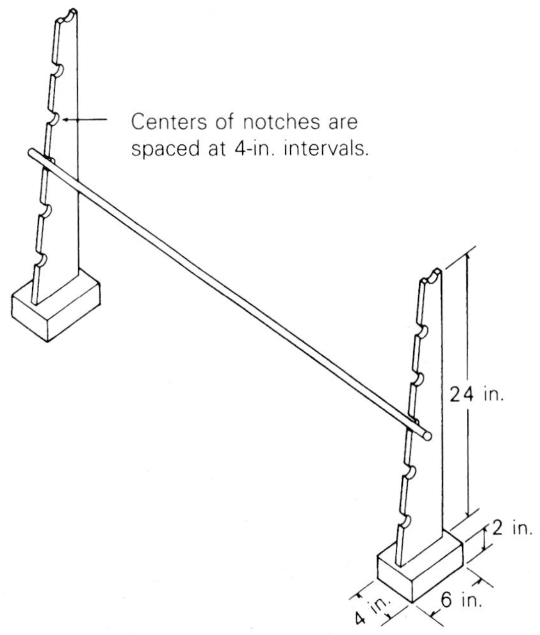

FIGURE 10.20 Jumping standard construction.

Materials:

Two pieces of ¾-inch plywood 25 inches long, cut as shown

Two blocks of wood, 2 by 4 by 6 inches

Glue and paint

Broomstick, 48 inches long

Directions: Mortise the wood blocks lengthwise, about 1 inch deep. After cutting the uprights to form, set them with glue into the blocks—making sure the uprights are plumb. Paint as desired. For quick positioning of the crosspiece, mark corresponding notches of the uprights with small circles of the same color.

Ladder

A ladder laid on the floor or on a mat provides a floor apparatus for various movement experiences and has value in remedial programs and programs for exceptional children. Sizes may vary (Figure 10.21).

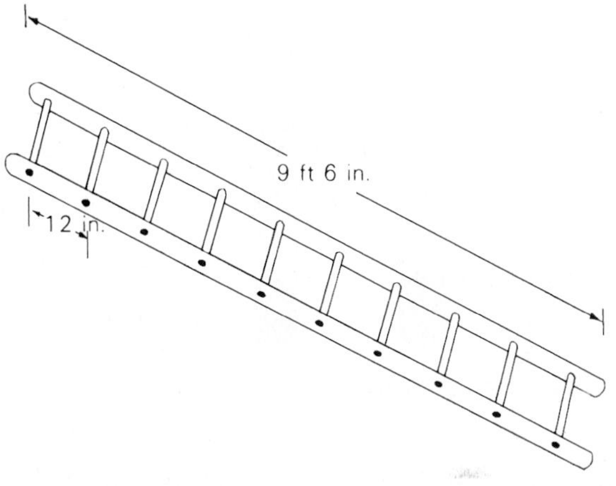

FIGURE 10.21 Ladder construction.

Materials:

Two straight-grained 2-by-4-inch timbers, 9½ feet long

Ten 1¼-inch or 1½-inch dowels, 20 inches long

Glue

Paint or varnish

Directions: Round the ends and sand the edges of the timbers. Center holes for the ladder rungs 12 inches apart, beginning 3 inches from one end. Cut the holes for the rungs 1/16 inch smaller than the diameter of the rungs. Put glue in all the holes on one timber, and drive in all the rungs. Next, glue the other timber in place. Varnish or paint the ladder.

Lummi Sticks

Lummi sticks are excellent tools for developing rhythmic skills. The sticks can also be used as relay batons.

Materials:

1-inch dowel, in 12-inch lengths

Paint and varnish

Directions: Notches and different colors are optional, but these decorations do make the sticks more attractive. If desired, use a table saw to cut notches ⅛ inch wide and ⅛ inch deep. Round off the ends and sand the entire stick. Paint and varnish the stick as shown in Figure 10.22 on page 196.

Magic Ropes/Jump Bands

Magic ropes or jump bands can be made by stringing together 25 to 30 large rubber bands. Common clothing elastic

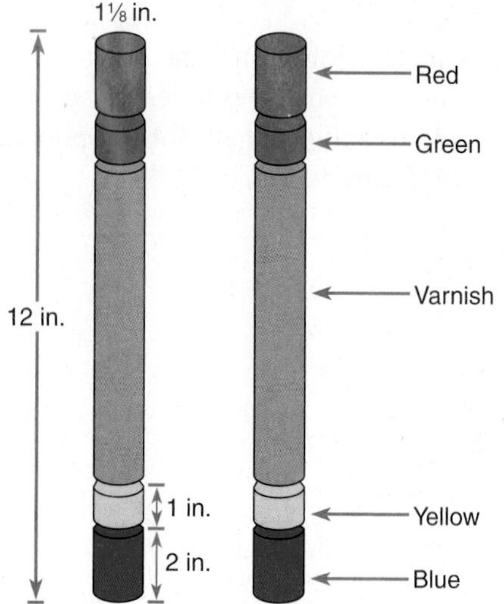

FIGURE 10.22 Lummi stick construction and decoration.

also can be used to make the ropes (Figure 10.23). Some teachers have had success with shock cord, which usually can be purchased at a boating marina or hardware store. Bungee cord of the proper length may also be used. Like shock cord, it can be found at many sports equipment outlets.

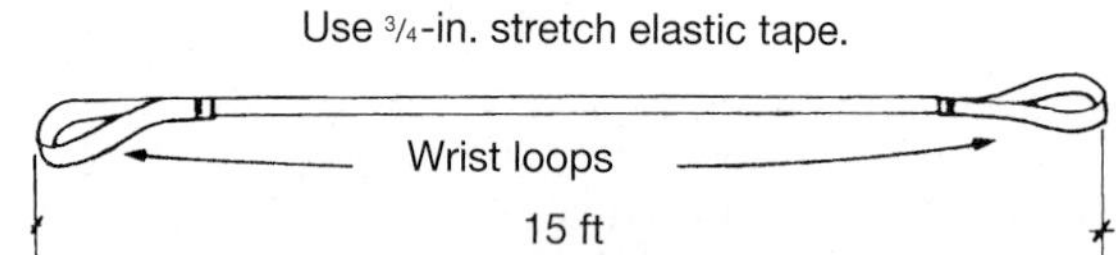

FIGURE 10.23 Magic rope construction.

Outdoor Bases

Bases for softball, baseball, and so on can be made in many ways. Use heavy canvas, folding it over three or four times and stitching it together. Cut heavy rubber matting to size. For more permanent bases, cut and paint pieces of outdoor plywood (Figure 10.24).

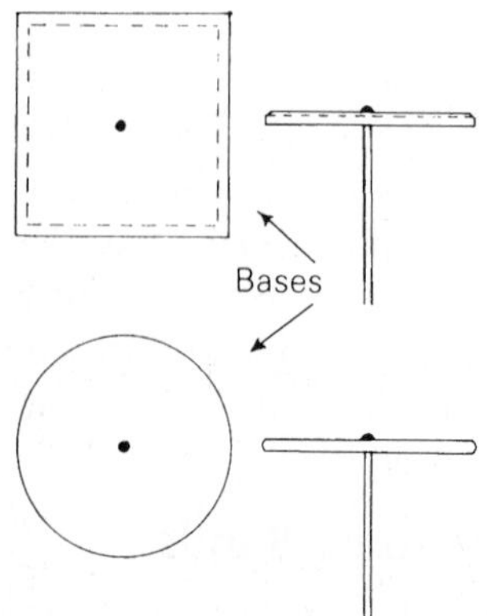

FIGURE 10.24 Outdoor base construction.

Materials:

Exterior ¾-inch plywood

One ½-inch carriage bolt, 14 inches long

Paint

Directions: Cut the plywood into 12-by-12-inch squares. Bevel and sand the top edges. Drill a ½-inch hole in the center of the base and then paint the base. When the paint dries, place the carriage bolt into the center hole and drive it into the ground. To make the base more secure, use more holes. Large spikes can be substituted for carriage bolts.

Paddles

Paddles can be made in many sizes and with different thicknesses of plywood (Figure 10.25). Usually, ¼-inch plywood is recommended for kindergarten through grade 2, and ⅜-inch plywood for grades 3 through 6. Paint or varnish the paddles, and tape the handles for a better grip. Drill holes into the paddle area to make it lighter and decrease air resistance. Good-quality plywood, perhaps marine plywood, is essential.

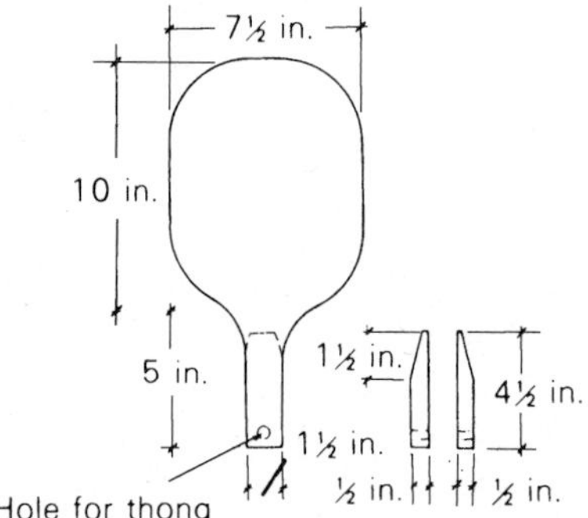

FIGURE 10.25 Paddle construction.

For hitting foam-rubber or newspaper balls, nylon-stocking paddles work well. They are lightweight and do not cause injuries, so they are excellent for primary-grade use. Students can use a badminton birdie with the paddle for activities such as hitting over a net and for many individual stunts.

Materials:

Old nylon stocking

Wire coat hanger

Masking tape or athletic tape

String or wire

Directions: Bend the hanger into a diamond shape. Bend the hook into a loop, which becomes the handle of the paddle (Figure 10.26). Pull the stocking over the hanger,

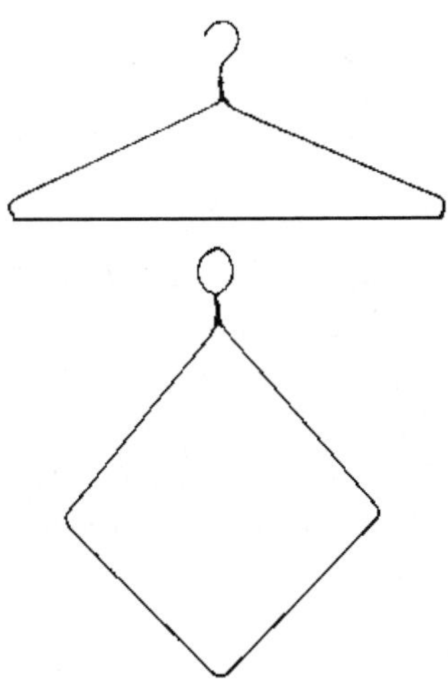

FIGURE 10.26 Frame for nylon-stocking paddle.

beginning at the corner farthest from the handle, until the toe of the nylon is as tight as possible against the corner point of the hanger. Hold the nylon at the neck of the hanger and stretch it as tight as possible.

Tie the nylon securely with a piece of heavy string or light wire. Wrap the rest of the nylon around the handle to make a smooth, contoured surface. Complete the paddle by wrapping tape around the entire handle to prevent loosening.

Paddle Tennis Net Supports

Paddle tennis net supports can be made to stand by themselves on the floor and still provide proper net tension. The stands come apart easily and quickly and can be stored in a small space. For lengths up to 8 feet or so, use a single center board with holes on each end, thus eliminating the need to bolt two pieces together (Figure 10.27).

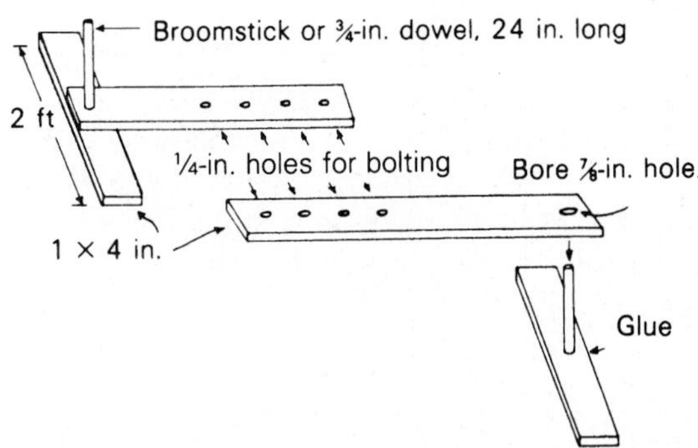

FIGURE 10.27 Paddle tennis net support construction.

Materials:

Two broomsticks or ¾-inch dowels, 2 feet long

Two 1-by-4-inch boards, 2 feet long

One or more additional 1-by-4-inch boards

Glue

Directions: For the upright supports, drill a ¾-inch diameter hole in the center of each 1-by-4-inch board. Drive the dowel into the hole, fixing it with glue. Notch the dowels at intervals for different net heights.

The crosspiece length depends on the court width. For a single crosspiece, bore holes into each end. Make the holes big enough (⅞ inch) for the dowel to slide through easily. If the crosspiece is in two sections, use ¼-inch bolts to join the sections (see figure).

Partner Tug-of-War Ropes

Partner tug-of-war ropes can be made from garden hose and ropes (Figure 10.28). Cheaper, plastic garden hose (⅝-inch in diameter) works much better than more expensive rubber hose. Plastic hose creases less and protects the hands better than rubber hose does. White, soft, braided nylon rope (⅜-inch diameter) is strong enough and much easier to handle than other types of rope. Use a bowline knot that does not slip and tighten around the hands. To prevent the rope ends from fraying, melt them over a flame.

10

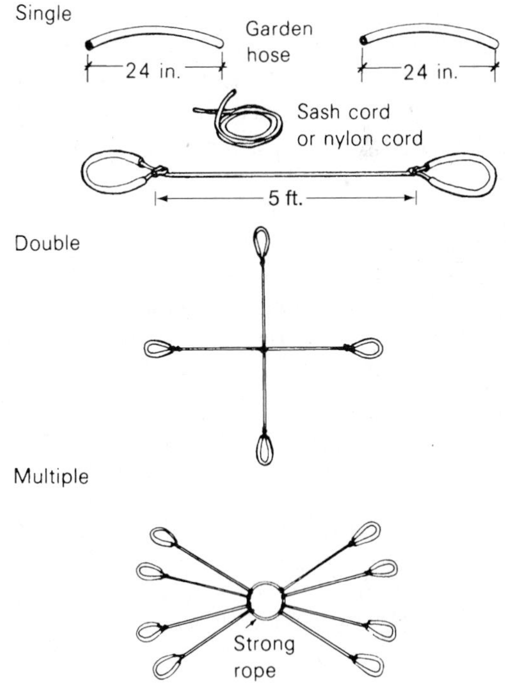

FIGURE 10.28 Partner tug-of-war construction.

Plastic Markers and Scoops

One-gallon plastic jugs filled halfway with sand and recapped make fine boundary markers. Paint the markers different colors to signify goals, boundaries, and division lines. The jugs also can be numbered and used to designate different teaching stations. Plastic bottles can be cut down to make scoops (Figure 10.29) for use in many activities.

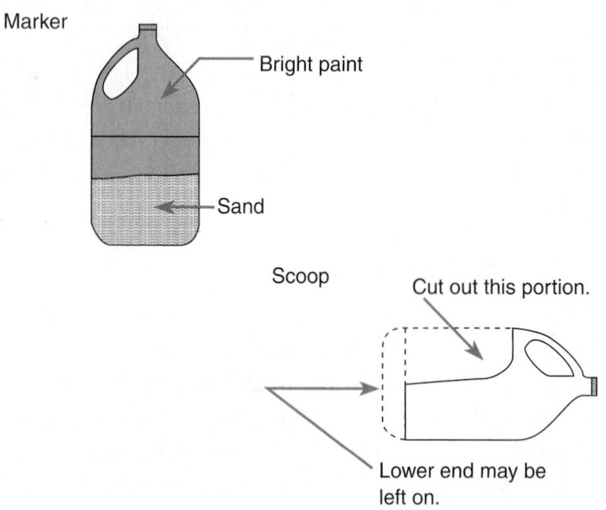

FIGURE 10.29 Plastic marker and scoop.

Rings, Deck Tennis (Quoits)

Deck tennis is a popular recreational net game that requires only a ring as basic equipment. Students can easily make the rings and use them in playing catch and for target throwing. They can be made from heavy rope by braiding the ends together, but the method shown in Figure 10.30 is easier. Weather-stripping cement helps strengthen the joints.

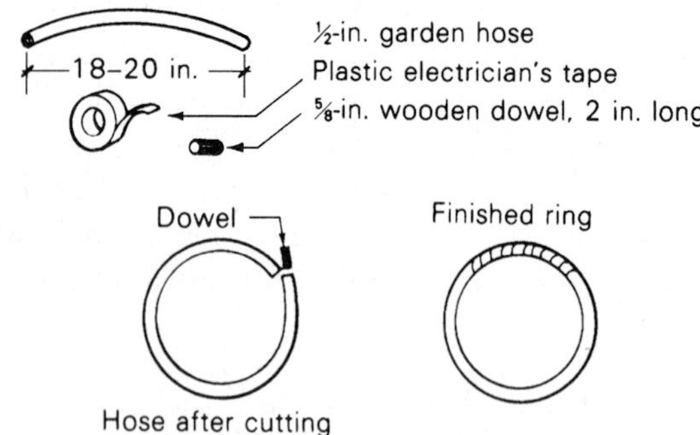

FIGURE 10.30 Ring construction.

Ringtoss Target

Many ringtoss targets can be made from a piece of 1-by-4-inch lumber or an old broom handle. Targets can either be hung on the wall or placed flat on the ground. The quoits constructed from garden hose are excellent for throwing at the targets. To signify different point values, paint the target pegs in different colors.

Materials:

Two 1-by-4-inch boards, 18 to 20 inches long

Five pegs, 6 inches long (old broom handles)

Screws and paint

Directions: Glue and screw the 1-by-4-inch boards together, as shown in Figure 10.31. Bore holes in the boards with a brace and bit, and glue or screw the pegs into the holes. Screw two small blocks under the ends of the board placed on top so that the target stands level. Paint the base and the sticks, and, if desired, number the sticks to show point values.

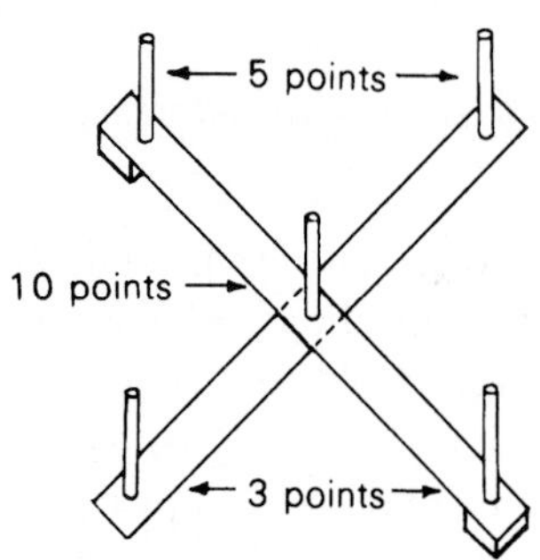

FIGURE 10.31 Ringtoss target construction.

Sit-and-Reach Box

Sit-and-reach boxes are used for measuring flexibility in the Fitnessgram (Figure 10.32). The basic sit-and-reach box is a 12-inch cube with a top 21 inches long. Sit-and-reach boxes for the Fitnessgram require the top of the box to be marked in inches. The 9-inch mark lines up with the side of the box where the feet are placed.

FIGURE 10.32 Sit-and-reach box.

Tire Stands

Tire stands keep tires in an upright position (Figure 10.33). The upright tires can be used for movement problems, over-and-through relays, vaulting activities, and as targets.

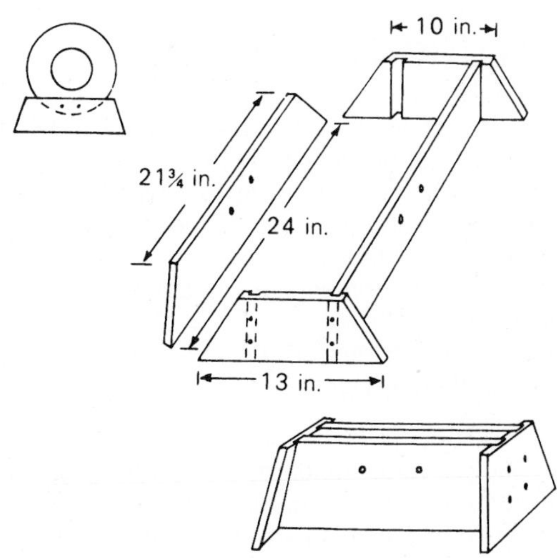

FIGURE 10.33 Tire stand construction.

Tires are much cleaner and more attractive when they are painted both inside and out.

Materials:

Two 1-by-6-inch boards, 24 inches long, for side pieces

Two 1-by-6-inch boards, 13 inches long, for end pieces

Four 3/8-inch carriage bolts, 2 inches long

Glue, screws, and paint

One used tire

Directions: Cut the ends of the side boards at a 70-degree angle. Dado each end piece with two grooves 3/4 inch wide and 1/4 inch deep. The distance between the grooves depends on the width of the tire. Round off the board corners and sand the edges. Glue and screw the stand together. Install the tire in the frame by drilling two 3/8-inch holes in each side of the frame and in the tire. Secure the tire inside the frame with the bolts. Paint both the tire and the frame a bright color. For better stability when using large tires, increase the overall stand size.

Track Starter

The track starter simulates a gun report. Provide many starters so the children can start their own races.

Materials

Two 2-by-4-inch boards, 11 inches long

Two small strap hinges

Two small cabinet handles

Directions: Cut the boards to size, and sand off any rough edges. Place the two blocks together, and apply the two hinges with screws. Add the two handles on the outsides of the boards. Open the boards and then slam them together quickly to create a loud bang (Figure 10.34).

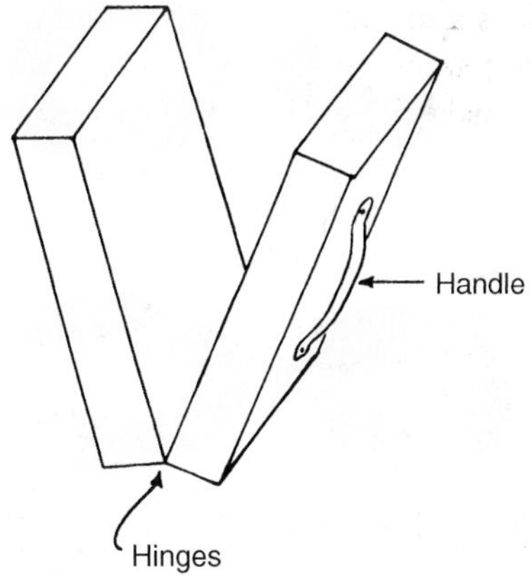

FIGURE 10.34 Track starter.

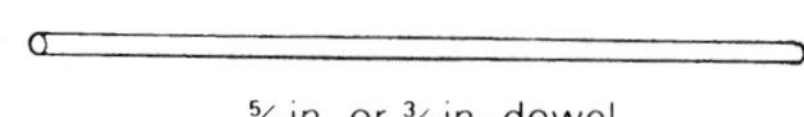

Lengths: grades K–1 = 30 in., 2–3 = 36 in., 4–6 = 42 in. or 1 m

FIGURE 10.35 Wand dimensions.

Wands

Handles from old brooms make excellent wands (Figure 10.35). The handles may have different diameters, but this is not important. Sand the ends, and paint the wands in different colors. If noise is a concern, place rubber crutch tips on the wand ends.

Yarn Balls

Yarn balls can be used to enhance throwing and catching skills as well as for many games. Yarn balls do not hurt when they hit a child, and they can be used in the classroom or in other areas of limited space. Older children or the PTA can make yarn balls. Two construction methods are offered here; both work well. When possible, use wool or cotton yarns because the balls will shrink and become tight when soaked in hot water or steamed. Nylon and other synthetic yarns do not shrink and bond.

Materials for Method One:

One skein of wool or cotton yarn per ball

One piece of box cardboard, 5 inches wide and about 10 inches long

Strong, light cord for binding

Directions for Method One: Wrap the yarn 20 to 25 times around the 5-inch-wide dimension of the cardboard. Slide the yarn off the cardboard, and bind it in the middle with the cord to form a tied loop of yarn. Continue this procedure until all of the yarn is used up and tied in looped

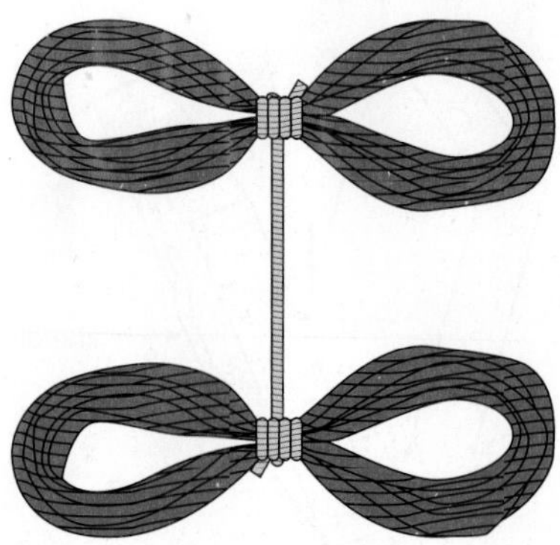

FIGURE 10.36 Yarn ball, method one.

bunches. Next, take two of the tied loops and tie them together at the center, using several turns of the cord. This forms a bundle of two tied loops, as illustrated in Figure 10.36. Continue tying the bundles together until all are used. Now cut the loops carefully so the yarn lengths are quite even, and trim the formed ball.

Materials for Method Two:

Two skeins of yarn per ball

Two cardboard doughnuts, 5 or 6 inches in diameter

Strong, light cord for tying

Directions for Method Two: Make a slit in the doughnuts so that the yarn can be wrapped around the cardboard (Figure 10.37). Holding strands from both skeins, wrap the yarn around both doughnuts until the center hole is almost completely filled with yarn. Lay the doughnut of wrapped yarn on a flat surface, insert a pair of scissors between the two doughnuts, and cut around the entire outer edge. Carefully insert a double strand of the light cord between the two doughnuts and catch all of the individual yarn strands around the middle with the cord. Tie the cord as tightly as possible with a double knot. Remove the doughnuts, and trim the ball if necessary.

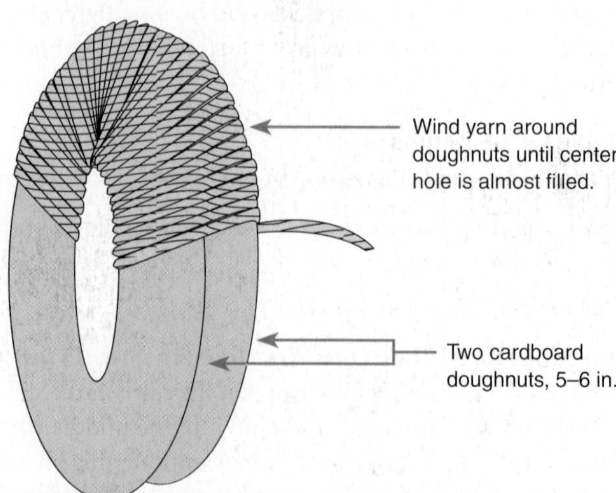
Wind yarn around doughnuts until center hole is almost filled.
Two cardboard doughnuts, 5–6 in.

FIGURE 10.37 Yarn ball, method two.

REFLECTION AND REVIEW

HOW AND WHY

1. Do the school facilities in your area meet the standards of outdoor facilities?
2. How might teachers have to adapt because of the many "non-PE" uses of the indoor physical education facilities?
3. Why would "homemade" equipment be necessary for some schools?
4. How can teachers ensure appropriate maintenance of equipment?

CONTENT REVIEW

1. Present several standards for outdoor facilities. Include comments regarding playgrounds.
2. Identify four pieces each of outdoor equipment for upper-body development, lower-body development, and balance skills.
3. Discuss the standards for indoor facilities for physical education.
4. Discuss the difference between equipment and supplies. Provide examples of each.
5. List equipment primarily used indoors.
6. Discuss the importance of purchasing policies, storage plans, and maintenance for equipment.

FOR MORE INFORMATION

REFERENCES AND SUGGESTED READINGS

Carpenter, L. J. (2000). *Legal concepts in sport: A primer* (2nd ed.). Champaign, IL: Sagamore Publishing.

Dougherty, N. J., Golberger, A. S., & Carpenter, A. S. (2007). *Sport, physical activity, and the law* (3rd ed.). Champaign, IL: Sagamore Publishing.

Dougherty, N. J. (Ed.). (2002). *Principles of safety in physical education and sport* (3rd ed.). Reston, VA: AAHPERD.

Hart, J. E., & Ritson, R. J. (2002). *Liability and safety in physical education and sport: A practitioner's guide to the legal aspects of teaching and coaching in elementary and secondary schools* (2nd ed.). Reston, VA: AAHPERD.

Hinson, C. (2001). *6 steps to a trouble-free playground.* Hockessin, DE: PlayFit Education, Inc.

Raatma, L. (1999). *Safety on the playground.* Mankato, MN: Bridgestone Books.

Stratton, G., & Mullan, E. (2005). The effect of multicolor playground markings on children's physical activity level during recess. *Preventive Medicine, 41*, 828–833.

U.S. Consumer Product Safety Commission. (2008). *Handbook for public playground safety* (Publication No. 325). Washington, DC: Author.

WEBSITES

Equipment
www.gophersport.com

Making Physical Education Equipment
www.pecentral.org/preschool/prekhomemadeequipmentmenu.html
http://igreen.tripod.com/gerpe/id18.html

Playground Safety
www.cpsc.gov/CPSCPUB/PUBS/playpubs.html
www.playgroundsafety.org
www.ndparks.com/recreation/grants/lwcf/playgrounds.pdf

Integrating Academic Concepts

11

ESSENTIAL COMPONENTS OF QUALITY PROGRAMS

- ▶ I. Organized around content standards
- ▶ II. Student-centered and developmentally appropriate
- ▶ III. Physical activity and motor skill development form the core of the program
- IV. Teaches management skills and self-discipline
- ▶ V. Promotes inclusion of all students
- VI. Focuses on process over product
- VII. Promotes lifetime personal health and wellness
- VIII. Teaches cooperation and responsibility and promotes sensitivity to diversity

NATIONAL STANDARDS FOR PHYSICAL EDUCATION*

1. Demonstrates competency in motor skills and movement patterns needed to perform a variety of physical activities.
2. ▶ Demonstrates understanding of movement concepts, principles, and tactics as they apply to the learning and performance of physical activities.
3. Participates regularly in physical activity.
4. Achieves and maintains a health-enhancing level of physical fitness.
5. Exhibits responsible personal and social behavior that respects self and others in physical activity.
6. Values physical activity for health, enjoyment, challenge, self-expression, and/or social interaction.

*National Association for Sport and Physical Education (NASPE), 2004.

Integrating academic concepts into physical education involves incorporating concepts learned in the classroom into the physical education lesson in an effort to reinforce the concepts or teach them from a different perspective. Though research findings do not suggest that increasing children's physical activity levels increases their academic performance, integrating academic content into physical education may help clarify concepts students are having difficulty with or simply strengthen their understanding of a concept. In addition, by assisting classroom teachers through integrating academic content, physical education teachers build goodwill with classroom teachers and improve the overall climate of the schools to the extent that all teachers are working toward the betterment of all students.

Outcomes

- Define *integrating academic concepts*, and explain its importance.
- Understand the role of integrating academic concepts in physical education.
- Explain the benefits and limitations of integrating academic concepts in physical education.
- Discuss the relationship between physical activity and learning.
- Present models of integration of academic concepts, and discuss how they can be used.
- Describe several activities that integrate either math, language arts, science, and/or social studies into a quality physical education lesson.

INTEGRATING ACADEMIC CONCEPTS INTO PHYSICAL EDUCATION

During their time in school, students are often taught concepts that combine two seemingly unrelated academic areas. Reading about the habitats of animals combines reading (language arts) and biology (science). Students calculating the distance from their town to the state capital use concepts from both math and social studies. Instruction designed to integrate two or more concepts from different areas to enhance learning is referred to as *integration*. Other terms to describe this process are *interdisciplinary, multidisciplinary,* and *cross-disciplinary*. Although each term has a specific definition, for the purpose of this chapter and book, the term *integration* is used throughout.

Physical education offers an outstanding setting for integration of academic concepts with minimal impact on the integrity of the physical education curriculum. For instance, teachers often have students time their stretching exercises by counting from 1 to 10. To integrate a foreign language, teachers can have students count in that language; to integrate spelling, students can spell out vocabulary words for the week; and to integrate math, students can skip-count by fours. All of these examples are simple adjustments to common instructions that physical education teachers use. However, these adjustments do require planning.

While it is clear that academic concepts can be integrated into a quality physical education curriculum, physical education instruction should not be centered on academic integration. Academic integration is a secondary outcome for physical education in contrast to the six primary NASPE outcomes discussed in Chapter 1. It is important to remember that physical education is the only area in the school where children are taught how to care for their bodies. Integrate academic concepts as much as possible, but not at the expense of physical activity and student health.

When integrating academic concepts, plan a series of instructional activities that ensures physical education outcomes are reached, and then determine the academic concepts that can be integrated into the physical activities. For example, math relays are commonly used when integrating physical education and math. In this activity, teams of 5 to 6 students, one student at a time, run the length of the gym, retrieve a flash card, and bring it back to the team. After all members finish, the class uses the numbers from the flash cards and creates the largest number possible. When integrating academic content into the physical education curriculum, maintain the integrity of the physical education program. In addition, integration should occur *after* establishing a solid, well-planned, quality physical education program.

WHY INTEGRATE ACADEMIC CONCEPTS?

Education is always seeking strategies and research to support methods for effectively teaching concepts. One such method is integration. Studies by Purcell-Cone, Werner, Cone, and Woods (1998) support the use of integration in a variety of subjects, but the research has shown mixed results. Thus more research in this area is needed before absolute conclusions can be drawn. Relatively few studies clearly support integration through physical education as an effective strategy for teaching academic content, but many teachers believe this practice should be promoted. To this end, countless journals, books, and workshops have highlighted activities and ideas for integration. Several of these are listed in the "References and Suggested Readings" section at the end of this chapter.

If the research is not definitive, why incorporate academic concepts into the physical education lesson? In an era of accountability that places great pressure on classroom teachers to increase academic achievement by increasing high-stakes test scores, physical educators can support classroom teachers by offering to supplement the classroom content. This shows classroom teachers that physical educators are team players concerned with student learning. Integrating also motivates classroom teachers to observe or visit the physical education setting to see how concepts are being integrated. Lastly, if physical educators are integrating academic content and showing an interest in the classroom, classroom teachers may be inclined to integrate physical activity into their classroom instruction. If this situation arises, the physical educator should assist classroom teachers with ideas and strategies for teaching physically active students (Pangrazi, Beighle, & Pangrazi, 2009). Specifically, classroom teachers may need assistance with management strategies and equipment.

Integration in physical education has benefits and limitations. The benefits include building goodwill in the school, helping students who are kinesthetic learners, teaching content in a new setting through a different method, demonstrating that physical educators are educators too, and increasing students' activity level when classroom teachers integrate physical activity into their instruction. The limitations most often cited are finding time to develop the lessons, planning for integration that does not sacrifice the physical education lesson, and feeling uncomfortable teaching outside an area of expertise. These are legitimate concerns; but with some practice and the belief that integration can supplement classroom learning, physical education teachers can create effective integration activities.

TYPES OF INTEGRATION

Several models can be used when planning academic integration activities. These models range from the physical education teacher working alone to a group of teachers working together to develop learning experiences in various settings. The individual model involves the physical education teacher working to develop ideas for integrating academic content. For example, the teacher may want to integrate concepts related to levers during a throwing lesson. This idea requires reviewing information on levers and how they relate to throwing and deciding how to integrate the concepts into the lesson without sacrificing time for activity and the learning of throwing skills.

When using the partner model, the physical education teacher collaborates with a classroom teacher. This collaboration can be as simple as the physical education teacher asking the classroom teacher for that week's vocabulary words. The model can also be more complex. Two teachers might develop a yearly calendar that teaches similar concepts during the same time—a physical education lesson involving a Mexican folk dance could be taught during the same week as a geography lesson on Mexico. For the physical education lesson, the teacher could use Spanish terms during instruction and have students count in Spanish while stretching. Such changes do not compromise the physical education curriculum; they enrich the educational experience and reinforce academic concepts learned in other areas.

The group collaboration model usually involves a group of classroom teachers from a common grade level and the physical educator. This model involves a fair amount of planning that usually centers on a theme. Teachers take the theme and generate learning activities that cut across academic areas. For example, during a set period, most of the student activities can be related to an Olympics theme. Each class chooses a specific country to represent. In social studies, students learn about the cultures, geography, economy, people, and/or government of their country and the others being represented. For math, students calculate distances between cities and the population of the countries involved. This activity is followed by calculating the average population of the countries and graphing the number of Olympic medals each country earned. During language arts, students read about their country and write a summary of their readings, write letters to pen pals in that country, and learn common phrases from their country's language. For science, concepts associated with the environment of all the countries, their weather, plants and animals, and inventions are covered. The technology teacher helps students research their country online. The music teacher teaches songs, anthems, and dances from each country while the art teacher helps students create the country's flags or draw posters advertising the Olympics. A school assembly can serve as the opening ceremonies where students report about their countries, sing their national anthems, and display their flags. During physical education, students participate in activities related to the Olympics and discuss the history of these activities in the Olympics. Other examples involving the group model are a Viking theme, a Civil War theme, and an ancient Rome theme. Although planning is necessary, the result can be an exciting, educational experience that students will likely remember for a lifetime.

HOW TO INTEGRATE ACADEMIC CONTENT

As stated earlier, integrating academic content must be carefully and thoughtfully planned to ensure that the activity is a quality learning experience and to maintain the integrity of the physical education curriculum. The following topics are a series of steps for initiating integration in physical education, learning what to integrate, and learning how to enhance the effectiveness of the integration activities.

DECIDE ON THE INTEGRATION MODEL

The individual model involves a fair amount of research to determine what to teach, at what level it should be taught, how to teach it, and what lessons to teach it in. The partner model requires you to choose a potential teacher to partner with. It is important that the partner teacher be equally interested in what is being taught in physical education. Ideally, the classroom teacher will also be interested in strategies for teaching academic concepts through physical activity in the classroom. Choosing the group model requires you, the physical education teacher, to select teachers who are generally interested in all of the activities, not just those they are teaching.

ASK TEACHERS WHAT CONCEPTS THEY WILL BE TEACHING

Take an interest in what concepts classroom teachers are teaching. Doing so makes you seem like an interested, supportive teacher who wants to help their students reach academic outcomes. Many classroom teachers will provide a calendar containing concepts being taught in the coming weeks. From this calendar, you can generate integration ideas. The classroom teachers often can mention concepts that could be taught through physical education.

ASK HOW CONCEPTS ARE BEING TAUGHT

Once the academic concepts to be integrated are established, it is important for you to find out how these concepts are being taught. Using key terms or similar ideas and slightly modifying them may be helpful when teaching the integrated material. Conversely, teaching a concept differently than how the classroom teacher teaches it may help some students learn the concept better. Approach the classroom teacher to find out what concepts students are having trouble with in the classroom. It may be that physical education offers an excellent opportunity to teach the same concepts with a different strategy, namely, teaching the concepts with movement. If this is the case, discuss it with the classroom teacher. In some cases, teaching the same concept with two different methodologies or perspectives may confuse children rather than help them learn.

SHOW CLASSROOM TEACHERS WHAT IS BEING TAUGHT DURING PHYSICAL EDUCATION

Invite the classroom teacher to a lesson involving integration. This serves two purposes. First, the classroom teacher can provide feedback concerning the integration activity that you might use to make the activity more effective. Inviting the classroom teacher also exposes the teacher to physical education. Often, classroom teachers have little knowledge of what is being taught during physical education. Having them observe a lesson will show them that physical education is educational and makes an important contribution to the school curriculum.

REFLECT

When reflecting about your lessons, it is important to evaluate integration activities as well. Ask yourself these questions: Did the integration activity sacrifice any of the activity planned for the physical education lesson? Could I have integrated the concept with less interference? Did the students understand the academic content? How could I change the integrated activity to make it more effective? Would the integrated concept fit better in another part of the lesson or in another lesson?

ACADEMIC INTEGRATION ACTIVITIES

The rest of this chapter presents ideas for integrating academic concepts into physical education instruction. All of the activities are designed to be implemented with the *Dynamic Physical Education Curriculum Guide* (Pangrazi, 2010) lessons. They teach a variety of academic concepts while maintaining physical education outcomes. In fact, many of the activities are simple modifications to traditional activities. Each state and academic area has standards for what students should learn. In addition, because each class, student, and teacher learns academic content in a different way, presenting all the activities that could be implemented to teach each of the objectives in each academic area is not possible. Also keep in mind that the purpose of integrating academic content into physical education is to supplement and enhance what is being taught in the classroom rather than replace it.

Instructional activities in this chapter are organized into five areas: math, language arts, science, social studies, and multicultural. These are the primary academic content areas in most elementary school curricula. Each academic area is then subdivided into "Integration Tips" and "Activities." Integration tips are simple strategies that teachers may use to teach academic content in physical education. For example, rather than saying, "Freeze," a teacher might say, "Fifteen degrees Fahrenheit" to signal a freeze and to reinforce that water freezes when below 32 degrees Fahrenheit. Integration tips are not specific to a lesson; they can be used in various lessons. For each integration activity that follows, these four components are listed: the academic concept, the PE concepts, the PE lesson part where the concept should be integrated, and the supplies necessary to teach the concept. "Academic Concept" is the general concept (or concepts) being taught or reinforced through the activity. For specific standards and objectives related to the four academic areas, refer to the websites at the end of the chapter. "PE Concept" states the general physical education concepts being taught during the activity. "PE Lesson Part" shows where the integration activity can be taught during a four-part lesson. If the activity is part of a lesson focus, ideas for the types of lessons are provided. For more information about these lessons and ideas for integration, see the *Dynamic Physical Education Curriculum Guide* (Pangrazi, 2010) that accompanies this text.

MATH

During the early elementary years, students learn math concepts such as number recognition and meaning, counting, shapes, addition, subtraction, measuring, and patterns. As they progress through the grades, students learn numbers through 1 million, multiplication, division, fractions, percent, degrees, geometry, and statistics. To familiarize themselves with elementary math, physical educators can read elementary school math books and examine the *Principles and Standards for School Mathematics,* published by the National Council of Teachers of Mathematics (2000). This provides mathematics standards and expectations and is comparable to the National Association for Sport and Physical Education's *National Standards for Physical Education* (2004).

Integration Tips

Counting (Skipping Numbers)

Any time counting is used during a lesson (e.g., keeping score, timing a stretch), instruct students to count by a given number. For example, rather than saying that one goal equals 1 point, say that each goal is worth 3 points. Thus, as the number of goals accumulates, students must count by threes.

Math Terms

Many mathematical terms such as *diameter* and *perimeter* can easily be integrated into many physical education lessons. For example, rather than instructing students, "Jog around the outside of the gym floor," tell them, "Jog around the perimeter of the gym." When discussing the influence the size of a ball has on throwing, instead of saying, "Is a bigger ball easier to throw or harder to throw?" say, "If a ball has a larger diameter, is it easier to throw? Remind me what *diameter* means before you answer." These examples allow math terms to be integrated without interfering with the physical education lesson.

Degrees and Fractions

In many physical education lessons, students are told, "Turn facing away from the teacher" or "Turn all the way around." Early in physical education experiences, these basic terms are necessary; but as students become older, you can use more challenging directions to teach math concepts. For example, have students turn "360 degrees" or "180 degrees" before catching a beanbag or when dismounting from a balance bench. Similarly, incorporate fractions by having students make a half turn or a three-quarter turn. For further challenge, you could instruct students to make a $^{4}/_{4}$ turn or a $^{36}/_{72}$ turn.

Estimating

Because numbers are often used during physical education, estimating can be naturally integrated into many lessons. Here are just two examples. Messy Back Yard is a game in which students try to rid their backyard (side of the court) of yarn balls by throwing them over the net to the other team's side. Meanwhile, the other team tries to rid its side as well. After a set amount of time, the teacher stops the game, and yarn balls on each side are counted. To teach estimation, before counting the number of balls on each side, instruct children to estimate how many balls are on each side and keep that number in their heads. When you announce the actual number, the children then self-assess their estimates. Another example is to ask students to estimate how many times they can toss their beanbags a certain height and catch them in 30 seconds. Repeat this activity two or three times to allow students to make adjustments to their estimates.

Measurement

Measurement is often included during the physical education lesson. Concepts related to measuring distance, height, weight, and time can all be integrated into physical education lessons. During a jumping lesson, ask students to jump as far as they can and then quickly measure the distance of their jump using tiles on the floor (Figure 11.1 on page 206). Floor tiles are generally 12 inches square. Track and field lessons also offer many opportunities for students to measure. Students can time each other in a run, measure the length of a person's long jump, or measure the height of a high jump.

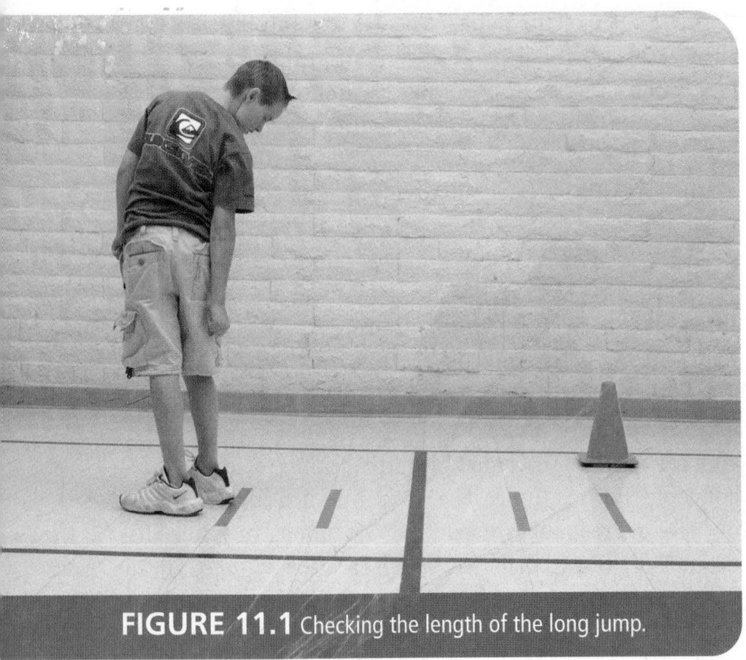

FIGURE 11.1 Checking the length of the long jump.

8 Skips

3 Gallops

11 Hops

FIGURE 11.2 Number challenge sign.

Activities

Mystery Number

MATH CONCEPTS: Number recognition, number sequencing

PE CONCEPTS: Locomotor skills, spacing, sequencing skills

PE LESSON PART: Introductory activity

SUPPLIES: Laminated signs with numbers or sequences of numbers

Hold one of the laminated signs in the air so the students can see it and you cannot. Instruct students to perform their favorite locomotor skill the same number of times indicated on the sign. When they finish, they should stop and then pick a different locomotor skill and perform it the same number of times. For example, if the sign has the number 8 on it, a child may choose to walk eight steps, stop, and then skip eight times. The teacher, by watching the students, tries to determine the mystery number.

For older students, a sequence of numbers is placed on the sign. For example, a sign could read "7, 3, 15." For each number, students choose a locomotor movement and perform it. One student may choose to gallop 7 times, walk 3 steps, and jump 15 times. When these are completed, the students start over with a different sequence of 7, 3, 15. Again, the teacher tries to determine the number sequence on the card. If desired, specific locomotor movements can be provided for each number, as shown in Figure 11.2.

Shapes

MATH CONCEPT: Shape recognition

PE CONCEPTS: Locomotor skills, low-organized games

PE LESSON PART: Game activity

SUPPLIES: Different-colored laminated circles, squares, triangles, and rectangles

Each student stands in a circle with a laminated shape on the floor in front of him or her. When you call out a specific shape, all students with that shape step back out of the circle and begin running around the circle in a designated direction. Their goal is to get back to their shape as quickly as possible. As soon as all runners have returned to their position, you call out another shape. While the runners are running, the rest of the class is responsible for running in place and cheering on the runners. To add some challenge for older students, rather than say, "Triangle," use the number of sides of the shape ("Three") as the signal. As a variation, rather than shapes, use the color of the shape. When you say, "Red," all students with a red shape are runners. Because this activity involves movement of light intensity, it works well as a game following a vigorous activity such as individual rope jumping.

Symmetry Asymmetry

MATH CONCEPTS: Symmetric and asymmetric balance

PE CONCEPTS: Nonlocomotor skills, balance, body awareness

PE LESSON PART: Lesson focus (gymnastics)

SUPPLIES: Tumbling mats

During a gymnastics lesson, students are often asked to perform balances while meeting various challenges (e.g., balancing on two body parts; balancing on three body parts, one being a hand; etc.). For this activity, ask students to perform a symmetric or asymmetric balance with a specific challenge. Examples include a symmetric balance with only three body parts touching the mat or an asymmetric balance with both feet flat on the mat.

Body Numbering

MATH CONCEPT: Number recognition

PE CONCEPTS: Nonlocomotor skills

PE LESSON PART: Lesson focus (movement concepts)

SUPPLIES: None

Using nonlocomotor skills, ask students to make the shape of a number with their bodies. This can be accomplished while lying on the floor or standing. Students can also work together to form a larger number.

Human Pencil (Shapes and Numbers)

MATH CONCEPT: Number recognition

PE CONCEPTS: Spacing, locomotor skills

PE LESSON PART: Lesson focus (movement concepts)

SUPPLIES: None

Tell students that the gym floor is one big piece of paper and they are human pencils. Ask students to walk and make a circle, a triangle, and a square. Following this activity, ask questions such as, "How many turns did you make to create a triangle?" Since they already know how to make a circle, as a transition to making numbers, ask students to skip and make the number 0. Next, have them make numbers or a sequence of numbers using various locomotor skills. For an added challenge, give number problems such as 2 + 2 and have the students "write" the answer as human pencils.

11

Pedometer Recording

MATH CONCEPT: Place values

PE CONCEPTS: Importance of physical activity, measuring physical activity, logging physical activity

PE LESSON PART: Lesson focus

SUPPLIES: Pedometers, pedometer recording card, pencils

One effective use of pedometers is to have students record their physical education steps. Using the card in Figure 11.3, students record their data and learn the place values of the numbers. Although the

Name: ____________ **Teacher:** ____________

Day: **Pedometer Steps:**

	Thousands	Hundreds	Tens	Ones
____________	☐	☐	☐	☐
____________	☐	☐	☐	☐

FIGURE 11.3 Pedometer data card with place values.

number of steps children accumulate will vary depending on the lesson, in a 30-minute physical education lesson, most students will accumulate between 1,500 and 2,000 steps. By recording their data on a place-value card, students learn ones, tens, hundreds, and thousands.

Computing Average Number of Steps

MATH CONCEPT: Computing an average

PE CONCEPT: Tracking physical activity

PE LESSON PART: Lesson focus

SUPPLIES: Pedometers, pedometer recording card, pencils

For older children, after they have recorded several days of physical education data, ask them to compute the average number of steps they take during physical education. Because this activity is sedentary, it is best either to coordinate with the classroom teacher so he can complete the activity in the classroom or to use this activity as one station in a circuit. When students reach this station, they compute their average of previous physical education classes and then begin working on a task assigned by the teacher or the station sign.

Number Wizard

MATH CONCEPTS: Positive and negative numbers

PE CONCEPTS: Locomotor skills, low-organized games

PE LESSON PART: Game activity

SUPPLIES: None

Have the entire class stand on a line in the middle of the teaching area, and explain that the gym floor is going to be their number line. The line they are standing on is zero. One child, designated the "Number Wizard," stands in the middle of the line. The Number Wizard calls out either a positive or a negative number. For a positive number, all students take that many steps forward. For a negative number, all students take that many steps backward. Throughout the game, the entire class stays in a straight line. When the Number Wizard yells, "Zero," the class tries to get back to zero before being tagged by the Number Wizard. Children who are tagged join the Number Wizard.

Odds

MATH CONCEPTS: Odd and even numbers

PE CONCEPTS: Chasing, fleeing, locomotor skills, spacing, low-organized games

PE LESSON PART: Introductory activity or game activity

SUPPLIES: None

Partners stand facing each other on a line. One partner is designated "odd" and the other "even." As in the Rock, Paper, Scissors game, students place one fist in the palm of the other hand. The game is played one-on-one and begins with both players hitting the palms of their hands twice and saying, "Math rocks." On the third strike, rather than a fist they extend from 1 to 5 digits. Both partners should have one hand out in front. The partners quickly count the number of fingers on both hands. If the total is odd, the person designated "odd" chases her partner. If she can tag him before he takes three steps, she gets a point. If the total number of fingers is even, the "even" person becomes the chaser.

Odds and Evens

MATH CONCEPTS: Odd and even numbers

PE CONCEPTS: Low-organized games, chasing, fleeing, locomotor skills

PE LESSON PART: Game activity

SUPPLIES: Large die (optional)

This game is played with the same rules as Crows and Cranes (page 556) except that teams are "Odds" and "Evens." To start, the teacher calls out a team name to identify who will be chased. For added challenge, the teacher also calls out actual numbers and students must decide if they are odd or even (or, the teacher can roll a large die to determine the numbers). Finally, the teacher calls out math equations. Students must then solve the equation and decide if the solution is odd or even.

Five Dollars

MATH CONCEPT: Counting money

PE CONCEPTS: Throwing, catching, scoring, cooperation, rolling

PE LESSON PART: Game activity

SUPPLIES: One tennis ball

This game is played outside in groups of three to four students. One person is designated the "Bank Teller," and the rest of the group stands 30 to 50 feet away. The Bank Teller throws a ball into the air toward the group. If the ball is caught in the air, the person who catches it gets one dollar. Catching the ball after one bounce is worth 75 cents; after two bounces, 50 cents; after three bounces, 25 cents. If the ball is rolling, no money is awarded. Once the ball is caught or picked up after rolling, it is rolled to the Bank Teller, who throws the ball again. This process continues with each person counting his or her money. The first person to earn five dollars becomes the Bank Teller. As in softball, players should be encouraged to call for the ball to avoid collisions.

Beanbag Math

MATH CONCEPTS: Addition, subtraction, multiplication, division

PE CONCEPT: Tossing

PE LESSON PART: Lesson focus (movement concepts), game activity

SUPPLIES: Beanbags, Frisbees

The Frisbees are marked and set up as in Figure 11.4, about 5 feet from the tossing line. Students work with a partner to create a math equation that results in a specific number (goal), which the teacher designates. Alternating beanbag tosses, the first toss is to a numbered Frisbee. Next, the second partner tosses to a Frisbee marked with a math operation sign to determine what math operation will be used. The third toss goes to a numbered Frisbee. For example, if the first toss lands in a Frisbee numbered 9, the second in the "×" Frisbee, and the third in a Frisbee numbered 5, the partners would earn 45 points. If the teacher sets the goal at 50 points, the easiest way to get to 50 would be to toss to the "+" Frisbee and then the "5" Frisbee. Depending on the length of the game, the teacher may pick a large or a small goal. Students must reach the designated goal exactly. Moving the tossing line back will add difficulty to the activity, particularly as the partners approach the goal. Offer further challenge by making the goal a negative number. It is important to review cues and give instruction in tossing during this activity.

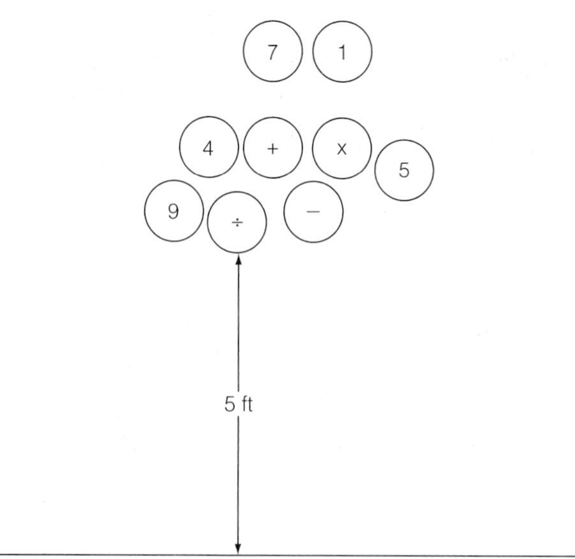

FIGURE 11.4 Beanbag Math Frisbee setup.

LANGUAGE ARTS

In the elementary years, students explore language and learn to express ideas by writing, speaking, listening, and communicating nonverbally. Concepts such as giving and following directions, reading, learning vocabulary, thinking critically, taking notes, spelling, and interacting with others are taught. The National Council of Teachers of English and the International Reading Association have published the *National Standards for English Language Arts* (2004), an excellent source of concepts being taught in language arts in elementary schools.

Integration Tips

Reading

Reading is just one language arts area that can be integrated into physical education. An effective strategy for integrating reading without sacrificing activity time is to use instruction signs. Figures 11.5 through 11.7 are examples of instruction signs that require reading. Figure 11.5 on page 210 involves simple word recognition. After reading the word, students perform the skill while moving to one of the many other signs placed on the floor throughout the teaching area. Figure 11.6 on page 210 requires reading and comprehension of several sentences. These types of signs work well at stations. At each station, students must read the sign and then do the activity. Figure 11.7 on page 211 requires reading and following more complex instructions. Again, in station format, students move from station to station reading and following instructions. The effective use of instructional signs efficiently integrates reading into physical

FIGURE 11.5 Word recognition.

education and allows the teacher to move about the teaching area, helping those who need assistance. The instructional signs shown here (and many more) are available from DeLynn Designs, 7435 S. Rita Lane, Tempe, AZ 85283 (dlpangra@hotmail.com).

Spelling

Often in physical education, students are asked to count to a given number to determine the length of time to stretch. This activity can be used to teach skip-counting as discussed earlier; it can also be a great time to teach the spelling of physical education terms or terms being used in the classroom (e.g., spelling words or vocabulary words from a specific content area). Instructions to implement spelling could be, "Fourth graders, choose your favorite lower body stretch that we have learned in physical education. Instead of counting today, we are going to spell words as we stretch. I checked with Ms. Panko, and I know you are studying Antarctica, so let's spell it." The teacher then slowly starts the class spelling with a counting tempo.

Parts of Speech

Because physical education is full of action words like *skip, run, throw, roll,* and *tap*, it is an excellent way to

Alternate Forearm Pass
& Overhand Pass
Work by yourself

1. Overhead pass to yourself and catch it.
Practice this skill.

2. Make two passes before catching the ball.
Practice this skill.

3. Alternate an overhand pass with a forehand pass and catch it.
Practice this skill.

FIGURE 11.6 Volleyball sign.

Push-Ups
upper body strength
Partner or Individually
Use a mat!
1. Begin by lying on the mat with hands under the shoulders. Keep your back straight.
Then, push up until your arms are straight.
2. Lower your body until your elbows make a 90-degree angle and upper arms are parallel to the floor.
The push-ups must be performed to the rhythm on the CD.
3. You may count your own push-ups, or you may have a partner count them. Count each time your elbows bend to a 90-degree angle.
4. Stop after two consecutive misses such as:
You are unable to stay with the rhythm on the CD.
You do not bend your arms to a 90-degree angle.
Your back is not straight.
Your knees touch the floor.

FIGURE 11.7 Fitness self-testing sign.

teach students about verbs. An effective strategy is to quiz students following a bout of instructions. After saying, "Everyone jump," briefly stop and ask, "What was the verb in that sentence?" If the students do not immediately respond with "Jump," quickly say, "It was *jump*; remember, verbs show action." The key to this strategy is to give students no more than 5 seconds to call out the verb. As this process continues, students learn which words are verbs and begin responding quickly. Use the same process to teach other parts of speech (nouns, adverbs, adjectives, etc.).

Antonyms and Synonyms

Physical education offers many contrasting and similar words, so it is an excellent opportunity for teaching antonyms and synonyms. During a locomotor lesson, you can ask students to skip at a slow level. Next, ask them to skip at the level that is the antonym for *slow*. As part of a nonlocomotor activity in which you tell students, "Stretch to make yourself large," ask for examples of synonyms for *large*. If students have not learned the words *antonym* and *synonym*, use the words *opposite* and *same*.

Using Foreign Languages

Because many students are kinesthetic learners, reinforcing terms they are learning in a foreign language class may be effective in helping them learn those terms. Students can count in different languages. Key terms for the lesson such as *ball, bounce, roll,* or *jump* can be translated and used during instruction. Rather than say, "Hustle and get a tennis ball," you could say, "Hustle and get a *pelota de tenis.*" Also, use the foreign language term for the activity (e.g., *gymnastics* is *gymnastique* in French and *gymnasia* in Spanish) when introducing the activity and referring to it during the lesson. By working with the foreign language teacher, you can integrate key terms being learned in the classroom into your physical education instructions. For example, if students are learning the terms in a foreign language for the English words *above, below, in front of,* and *behind,* you can easily include them in physical education instruction.

Peer Teaching

For Developmental Level III students, peer teaching can be an effective tool to help students learn the language

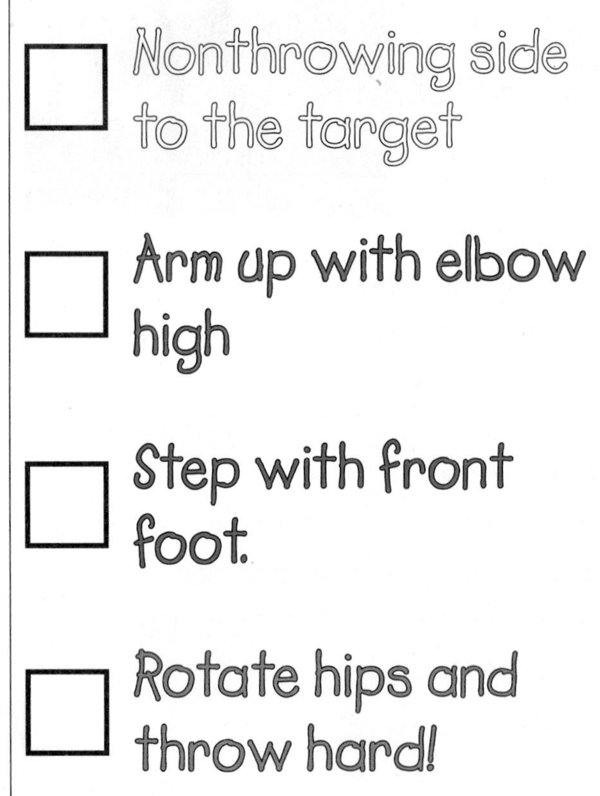

Nonthrowing side to the target
Arm up with elbow high
Step with front foot.
Rotate hips and throw hard!

FIGURE 11.8 Peer teaching sheet.

concepts of listening and verbal instruction. Peer teaching simply involves one student teaching another a skill using the cues and strategies learned in class. At the end of a softball unit, for example, you might ask one student to teach his partner how to throw using the cues discussed in class. Students can also assess their teaching skills by using a self-assessment sheet (Figure 11.8). This process requires partners to use their listening and speaking skills.

Activities

Body Spelling

LA CONCEPT: Spelling

PE CONCEPTS: Spacing, nonlocomotor skills

PE LESSON PART: Lesson focus (movement concepts, gymnastics), game activity

SUPPLIES: None

Working in groups of 4 to 5, students must use their bodies to make letters to spell out words the teacher provides. Students can make the words while standing or lying on the ground (Figure 11.9). For younger students, use short words and have each child form one letter of the word. For

FIGURE 11.9 Making letters.

example, to spell *dog,* one child would be the *D,* one the *O,* and one the *G.* With older students, use longer words; but the entire group may have to make each letter. That is, to spell *locomotor,* the entire group would make an *L,* then an *O,* and so on. Classroom vocabulary words or physical education terms work well for this activity.

Alphabet Freeze

LA CONCEPT: Letter recognition

PE CONCEPTS: Body awareness, spacing, nonlocomotor skills

PE LESSON PART: Introductory activity, game activity

SUPPLIES: None

Students begin the activity by moving about the teaching area. When the teacher says, "Alphabet freeze," the students select a letter and freeze in that shape. The activity continues, with students forming a different letter for each freeze. You may also choose the letter by saying, "Alphabet freeze—*A*," and all students freeze while forming an *A.* You may also instruct students to freeze either in a standing position or on the ground.

Letter Tag

LA CONCEPT: Letter recognition

PE CONCEPTS: Body awareness, spacing, nonlocomotor skills

PE LESSON PART: Introductory activity, game activity

SUPPLIES: None

This game is similar to Frozen Tag (page 549). If a child is tagged, she freezes in the shape of any letter.

To unfreeze her, a classmate must either say the letter or make the letter with her. The teacher can also call out the letter shape that students must form; in that case, the student must make the letter to unfreeze a classmate.

Spelling Toss

LA CONCEPT: Spelling

PE CONCEPT: Tossing

PE LESSON PART: Lesson focus (movement concepts), game activity

SUPPLIES: Frisbees or Poly spots marked with various letters, beanbags

Place the letters 5 to 10 feet away from the tossing line (see Figure 11.10). Students then spell words by tossing their beanbags onto the letters in the correct order. If *T, S, P, I,* and *E* are the letters available, students can spell *steps, pet, step, pie, pies, sit,* or *pit.* Be sure to reinforce safe tossing techniques.

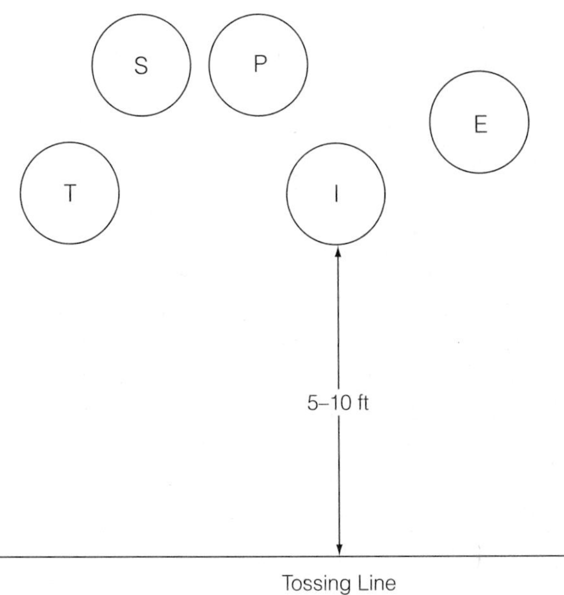

FIGURE 11.10 Spelling Toss Frisbee diagram.

Human Pencil (Spelling)

LA CONCEPT: Spelling

PE CONCEPTS: Locomotor skills, spacing

PE LESSON PART: Lesson focus (movement concepts)

SUPPLIES: None

Instruct students to spell a specific word using locomotor skills. They are pencils and the entire teaching area floor is their paper. Teachers can lead into the activity with these instructions: "Show me how you would walk to make an *O.*" "Now show me how you would walk to spell *cat.*" "Okay, now show me how you can skip and spell *education.* I know that's one of your spelling words this week."

Nouns and Verbs

LA CONCEPT: Parts of speech

PE CONCEPTS: Chasing, fleeing, locomotor skills, low-organized games

PE LESSON PART: Game activity

SUPPLIES: None

This game is similar to Crows and Cranes (page 556), but the teams are called "Nouns" and "Verbs." To help students learn the game, begin by simply using *noun* or *verb* as the chase word. Then call out other nouns or verbs as the chase word. Use caution when choosing chase words. Many words such as *jump* can be either a noun or a verb. Students who skateboard are likely to think of a jump, whereas other students may think of jumping as an activity. Early on, when calling out the chase word, you may want to point in the direction students should be moving to help those who cannot decide if a word is a noun or a verb.

In a Line

LA CONCEPT: Alphabetizing

PE CONCEPT: Cooperation

PE LESSON PART: Game activity

SUPPLIES: None

The activity begins with the entire group standing on a line. Challenge the students to get in alphabetical order by first name, and add that everyone in the group must have at least one foot on the line at all times. Once students achieve this, challenge them to get into alphabetical order by their last names without speaking. They may use gestures, but they must keep one foot on the line at all times. During this activity, students can become creative by using letters on their shirts, shoes, or jewelry. However, it is important to let them develop their own strategies.

11

Language Lion Says

LA CONCEPTS: Listening, following directions

PE CONCEPTS: Nonlocomotor skills, locomotor skills, manipulative skills, fitness challenges

PE LESSON PART: Introductory activity, game activity

SUPPLIES: None

This game is played like Simon Says, but with "Language Lion" as the leader. Use only commands that tie in physical education movements. Typically, in Simon Says, the students stay in one place. For Language Lion Says, students are moving throughout the teaching area. As the game ends, you can briefly comment, "When most students think of language arts, they think of words that we write or say. But an important part of language is being able to listen, and playing Language Lion Says helped everyone practice their listening skills."

SCIENCE

Because elementary students are often fascinated by science, they are receptive to teaching concepts such as the senses, animals, the environment, the solar system, climate, matter, energy, force, and plants. By reviewing the *National Science Education Standards* (1996) published by the National Research Council, physical education teachers can learn the content being taught in elementary science and more effectively generate creative ways to integrate science concepts into physical education.

Integration Tips

Freeze Signal

Successful teachers have an effective signal that freezes the class. One strategy for teaching Developmental Level III students about temperature is to use "Thirty-two degrees Fahrenheit" as the freeze signal since water freezes at 32 degrees (or at 0 degrees Celsius). Once students learn this concept, teachers can say any number less than 32 degrees Fahrenheit or 0 degrees Celsius to signal the students to freeze. For example, "Eleven degrees Fahrenheit" means to freeze.

Body Part Identification

In science, students learn to identify body parts. Since taking care of the body through physical activity is an important theme of physical education, body part identification can be integrated. Some teachers simply have students copy them by saying, "Touch your eyes, your nose, your femur, your triceps." This activity teaches body parts and develops listening skills. Also, touching a specific body part can be the "Go" signal. For example, you can say, "When I touch my humerus bone, hustle to the line on the east side of the gym," and then immediately touch your humerus (or, to check for student understanding, touch other bones).

Influence of Physical Activity on the Body

During a vigorous lesson such as jogging/walking or individual rope jumping, children often need short breaks. These breaks are a great time to teach the influence of physical activity on the body. Concepts such as increased heart rate and why it happens, sweating and why it happens, why we get tired, and many others can quickly be discussed during short breaks. Using this strategy throughout the year can be an effective way to teach these concepts.

Activities

Muscle and Bone Tag

SCIENCE CONCEPTS: Muscle and bone identification

PE CONCEPTS: Fleeing, chasing, locomotor skills, low-organized games

PE LESSON PART: Introductory activity, fitness development, game activity

SUPPLIES: None

This tag game starts with 5 students, chosen by the teacher as taggers. If they tag someone, they "give up the tag," and the tagged person becomes the tagger. Before the game, the teacher chooses a bone or muscle that is the "base." If a child touches that bone or muscle and repeats its name three times, he is safe from being tagged for 5 seconds. He may use his base only once per game, and taggers cannot stand by him waiting for the 5 seconds to expire. This is called the "no guarding" rule.

Ponies in the Stable

SCIENCE CONCEPT: Animal habitats

PE CONCEPTS: Locomotor skills, low-organized games, spacing

PE LESSON PART: Game activity

SUPPLIES: One Poly spot per student

Students are in scattered formation with a Poly spot at their feet. On signal, they begin galloping around the teaching area. When the teacher says,

"Ponies in a stable," they quickly find a spot and stand on it. To teach other animal habitats, call the game "Frogs on a Lily Pad," "Rabbits in a Burrow," or "Gorillas in the Jungle." For each of these games, the children's locomotor movement should mimic the animal's.

Palm Push

SCIENCE CONCEPTS: Force, pushing, pulling

PE CONCEPTS: Balance, body awareness

PE LESSON PART: Introductory activity, fitness development, lesson focus (gymnastics), game activity

SUPPLIES: None

Players face each other, standing about 12 inches apart. They place the palms of their hands together and must keep them together throughout the game. The object of the game is to get the opponent to move one of her feet. After a few rounds, the teacher asks a few brief questions: "How does force affect this game?" "Is it better to have a lot of force or not much?" "How could you use a little bit of force and still move your opponent off balance?"

Finger Fencing

SCIENCE CONCEPTS: Force, pushing, pulling

PE CONCEPTS: Balance, body awareness

PE LESSON PART: Lesson focus (gymnastics), game activity

SUPPLIES: None

Partners start balanced on one foot, facing each other with index fingers hooked. The object is to push or pull the opponent off balance. If a student causes her opponent to lose his balance, she receives a point and they start over. After a few minutes of play, the teacher stops the class to discuss strategies related to pushing and pulling. "Is pushing better or is pulling the best?" "Can you use both?" Be sure that partners are matched by size for this game.

Levers

SCIENCE CONCEPTS: Levers, force

PE CONCEPTS: Throwing, striking with a racquet, cooperation

PE LESSON PART: Lesson focus (throwing skills, racket activities, tennis, softball, soccer)

SUPPLIES: Rackets, yarn balls, playground balls

Since many motions and activities used in physical education involve levers, the concept of levers can easily be integrated into lessons. As a break from skills involving throwing, kicking, or racket skills, have students get a partner and assume the wheelbarrow position. Ask questions such as: "What part of your body is making a lever?" "What part was making a lever when we were throwing? Or kicking? Or using the racket?" Have students perform various skills they have learned in physical education and then ask, "What type of levers are those?" A large picture similar to Figure 11.11 on page 216 may help students answer this question.

11

Science of Throwing

SCIENCE CONCEPTS: Trajectory and distance, weight and distance

PE CONCEPTS: Cooperation, throwing

PE LESSON PART: Lesson focus (throwing skills, softball)

SUPPLIES: Tennis balls, yarn balls

Introduce three trajectories that a ball can take—such as straight up, straight out, or up and out. In an open space, have students experiment with the distance a tennis ball travels when thrown at these three different trajectories. Then challenge the students to throw the yarn balls using the three trajectories (Figure 11.12 on page 216). Follow this activity by briefly discussing the influence of trajectory and ball weight on distance traveled. After the discussion, allow time for more throwing so that students can experiment.

It "Matters"

SCIENCE CONCEPTS: Changes in matter, states of water

PE CONCEPTS: Locomotor skills, spacing

PE LESSON PART: Introductory activity

SUPPLIES: None

Students begin by moving around the teaching area. Challenge the class to keep moving, but in half of the space while trying not to touch anyone. Further

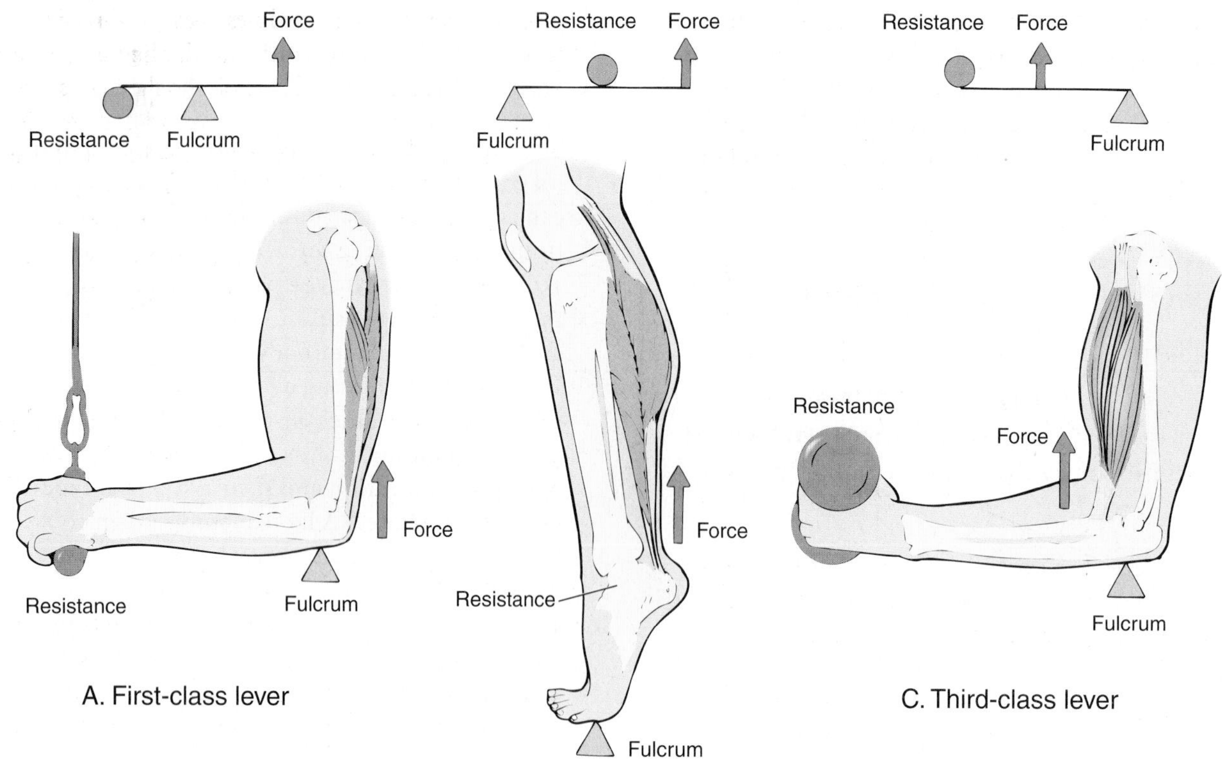

FIGURE 11.11 Types of levers in human joints.

challenge the class to move in half of that space (one-quarter of the original space). Remind students not to touch anyone. Next, ask them to recall what they know about molecules of water when it is in a solid, liquid, or gas state. Finally, have the class move like gas molecules, solid molecules, and liquid molecules.

Bounce Rebounce

SCIENCE CONCEPTS: Forces, influence of weight on reaction, action and reaction

PE CONCEPTS: Volleying, bouncing, dribbling, catching, passing

PE LESSON PART: Lesson focus (playground ball activities, basketball, volleyball)

SUPPLIES: 1 playground ball and 1 balloon per student

First ask students to bounce or dribble a playground ball in general space. Ask them to experiment by applying different forces to the ball to see how they affect the bouncing. After briefly discussing how greater force makes the ball bounce higher, have students trade their playground balls for balloons.

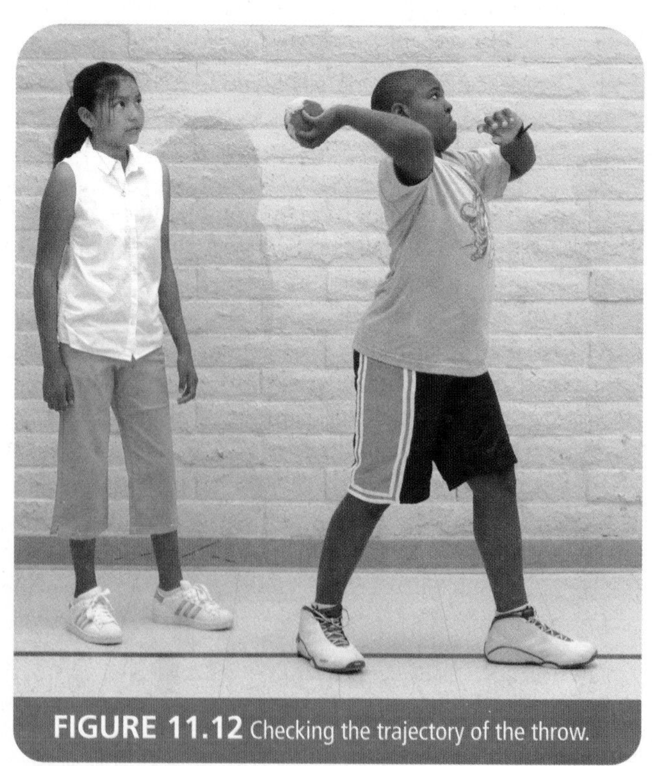

FIGURE 11.12 Checking the trajectory of the throw.

Next have students volley the balloon using different amounts of force. Challenge students to bounce the balloon as if it were the playground ball. Freeze the class and ask would happen if they struck the playground ball with the same force, and why. Ask: "Why does the playground ball bounce back up better than the balloon?" Next, have partners stand side by side while bouncing the ball off the wall to each other. After each pass, have them take one step away from each other. Ask them: "What happens to your pass? What happens if you pass it like you did when you were close together?" Conclude with the idea that the ball bounces off the wall and the floor at the same angle that it hits them. This concept is particularly important when teaching a bank shot and dribbling during a basketball unit.

Animals Move

SCIENCE CONCEPT: Animal locomotion

PE CONCEPTS: Animal movements, spacing

PE LESSON PART: Introductory activity

SUPPLIES: None

Start the game by choosing a leader to call out different animals and a method of movement. For instance, the leader might call out, "Horses fly. Birds crawl. Salmon swim." When the leader states a correct relationship, the class must move accordingly. In this example, students make a swimming movement. The children do not move when the leader gives an incorrect relationship. Keep games short so that all children have a chance to lead.

SOCIAL STUDIES

Social studies includes geography, history, government, economics, and other areas. At the elementary level, students learn concepts such as directions, family, rules and laws, the geography of different regions, U.S. history, state history, political systems, cultures, and community. These and many other concepts taught in social studies are presented in *Expectations of Excellence: Curriculum Standards for Social Studies* (National Council for Social Studies, 1994).

Integration Tips

Directions

Directions are an important part of geography and can easily be taught throughout a physical education curriculum. The first step is to place large north, south, east, and west signs on the appropriate walls. Early in the curriculum, teachers can simply refer to lines using a direction. For instance, "When I say, 'Go', hustle to the line by the south wall." At first it may be helpful to point to the line as well. As students mature, instruction can refer to the "southwest wall" or "the cone closest to the northeast basket." If teaching outside, students can be taught to use the sun to determine direction. To do this, students need to know only the time of day and from which direction the sun rises. These concepts are especially useful if orienteering is taught later in the year to older students.

Games from Other Countries

The physical education curriculum is filled with activities from other countries. When teaching these activities, simply take a few minutes to discuss the country, show where it is on a map, and talk about the languages spoken there.

Class Greeting

Prepare a list of the greetings used in other countries. Each week, select a greeting of the week to use when the class arrives. The students should then try to determine which country uses that greeting. Gestures such as bowing or handshaking can also be used.

11

Conversation

Often in physical education, students work on skills with partners. During these activities, remind students to concentrate on the skills, but also teach them how to have conversations. Discuss appropriate questions, how to ask questions, or what to say if you say something wrong. These skills, often assumed to be learned by children, are often neglected. Social time during physical education is important, and physical education is a great time to teach social skills.

Cooperative Activities

Cooperation is an important component of community, family, and relationships. See Chapter 21, "Cooperative Activities," for many activities that teach cooperative skills such as communicating, sharing, and listening.

Activities

Rules

SS CONCEPT: The need for rules and laws

PE CONCEPTS: Classroom management skills

PE LESSON PART: Introductory activity

SUPPLIES: None

Early in the school year, rules for physical education are established. This is an excellent time to discuss the importance of rules outside of physical education and outside of school. During the activity, discuss the importance of following directions. To practice this skill, students can follow a series of instructions that then lead to a game. Here is an example:

"When I say, 'Toe-to-toe,' quickly get toe-to-toe with the person closest to you. Toe-to-toe (pause). Thank you for doing that quickly. Now one partner remains standing while the other sits. If you are standing, please report to the line by the south wall. If you are sitting, please report to the line by the north wall."

After giving these directions, have the class play a game. When the game ends, ask, "What would have happened if the class had decided not to follow directions?" It is important to teach students early in the year that following rules leads to more enjoyment for everyone.

Going on a Trip

SS CONCEPTS: Urban, suburban, rural, and state history; geography of the world

PE CONCEPTS: Spacing, locomotor movements, manipulative skills

PE LESSON PART: Lesson focus (movement concepts), game activity

SUPPLIES: Vary

This activity is limited only by the imagination. Teachers can lead students on trips through a city, county, region, state, country, continent, or geographic location such as the mountains or a jungle. If exploring Kentucky, students can pretend to move like horses over rolling hills by galloping at different levels. On a jungle expedition, students can move like gorillas, panthers, monkeys, and birds. When visiting an urban area, students must read street signs (made by the teacher), know where to cross the street, and obey street crossing rules. Students can also learn traffic laws while driving their cars (scooter boards) on a predetermined path.

Moving across the United States (or State or County)

SS CONCEPTS: Geography, history, famous people

PE CONCEPTS: Jumping rope, locomotor skills, tracking physical activity

PE LESSON PART: Lesson focus (individual rope jumping, long-rope jumping, walking and jogging skills)

SUPPLIES: Pedometers, jump ropes, maps, tracking sheets

One important use of pedometers in physical education is teaching students to track their physical activity levels across several different lessons. Using step cards (Figure 11.13), students track their number of strides during each lesson. Then, based on their stride length, they calculate the distance they traveled in miles. The teacher totals the distance traveled by the entire class. Before teaching this activity, the teacher determines a route across a given area and tracks the class's progress on a map. It may be best to start with the school's town or county and then progress to larger areas such as states or well-known trails. As the class moves across the route, discuss historic facts related to students' present location, teach a dance that originated in a nearby town, or study historic figures from the area. To plan the activity, the route must be predetermined, and the physical education teacher should collaborate with other teachers in the school. Because calculating distance traveled may take students more than a few minutes, this assignment can be completed in the classroom. The book *Pedometer Power* (Pangrazi, Beighle, & Sidman, 2007) gives more examples of this activity.

How Do I Get There?

SS CONCEPTS: Travel, evolution of transportation, rural and urban settings

PE CONCEPT: Locomotor skills

PE LESSON PART: Introductory activity, lesson focus (movement concepts)

SUPPLIES: None

For this activity, ask students to demonstrate how they would travel to a specific place if they lived during a given time in history. For example, you could say, "If I lived in the 1700s and wanted to get to my neighbor's house, can you show me how I could get there?" The teacher then points out students who are walking, jogging, skipping, or galloping like a horse, which would have been methods of travel during that time. Depending on their age, some students will pretend to drive a car. This is a teachable moment for discussing the modes of

Pedometer number 8			PE Steps		
Teacher	Day 1	Day 2	Day 3	Day 4	Day 5
Edmondson					
Brockhagen					
Casson					
Yniguez					
Panko					
Jackson					
Jones					

FIGURE 11.13 Physical education step card.

transportation and the distances between neighbors in the 1700s. Use this activity throughout the year to correspond with historic periods being studied in the classroom.

Greetings

SS CONCEPTS: Cultures, courtesy

PE CONCEPT: Locomotor movements

PE LESSON PART: Introductory activity

SUPPLIES: None

Introduce students to different cultures by having them learn and use their greetings. As students move about the teaching area, the teacher calls out a method of greeting (e.g., shaking hands, bowing, curtsying, or giving a high five). The students then move about performing this greeting with as many people as possible before the teacher gives another locomotor movement. The teacher briefly tells students which countries use the various greetings. For older children, the teacher simply calls out the country and has the class respond with the appropriate greeting.

Courtesy Tag

SS CONCEPT: Citizenship

PE CONCEPTS: Low-organized games, body management, locomotor skills, chasing, fleeing

PE LESSON PART: Introductory activity, game activity

SUPPLIES: None

This game is like Frozen Tag (page 549). Designate several students as taggers. When tagged by a tagger, the tagged person must freeze. While frozen, the student stands with his hands raised, calling out, "Please help me!" He must say, "Please." When not frozen, players move around giving high fives to the players who are frozen. After getting a high five, the frozen player must say, "Thank you," and the other player must say, "You're welcome," before the frozen player can reenter the game. To add variety to the game, designate a specific greeting (see the previous activity) that frozen students must perform with unfrozen students before reentering the game. As with all tag games, the game is stopped often and new taggers are selected.

Trades

SS CONCEPT: Occupations and their roles in the community

PE CONCEPTS: Low-organized games, fleeing, chasing, locomotor skills

PE LESSON PART: Game activity

SUPPLIES: None

This game, described on page 562, is an excellent way to teach students about different occupations. After each round, teachers can quickly discuss the selected occupations and how those occupations contribute to the community.

MULTICULTURAL ACTIVITIES

We live in a diverse world. For this reason, it is essential to help students understand the importance of diversity and respect for various cultures. To combine learning with fun activities, teach these concepts by having students explore the games played in other cultures. The following games and activities are from countries from around the world.

Ball in the Air (Balone en el Aire)

MC CONCEPT: Argentina

PE CONCEPTS: Low-organized games, manipulative skills, running

PE LESSON PART: Introductory activity, game activity

SUPPLIES: One ball

The game begins with Team A standing on an endline and Team B standing in a circle in the middle of the teaching area. On signal, all students on Team A run around Team B to a cone on the other side of the teaching area and back to their line. At the same time, Team B is passing the ball around the circle. When all Team A members return to their starting line, they yell "Parar" ("stop" in Spanish), to signal Team B to stop passing the ball. Team B then counts the number of people who passed the ball. Teams change roles and play another round.

Great Wall of China

MC CONCEPT: China

PE CONCEPTS: Low-organized games, chasing, fleeing, and dodging

PE LESSON PART: Introductory activity, game activity

SUPPLIES: None

The middle third of the teaching area is designated "The Great Wall." One player stands "on the wall" and is designated the guard. The other players stand on one endline. The guard then calls out "Cross my wall," signaling players to run to the other endline. As players run, the guard tags as many players as possible but may not leave the wall area. Players who are tagged move to the wall and become guards. This process continues until only one player remains. That player becomes the guard for the next game.

Da Ga

MC CONCEPT: Ghana

PE CONCEPTS: Low-organized games, chasing, fleeing, dodging, locomotor skills

PE LESSON PART: Introductory activity, game activity

SUPPLIES: None

Da Ga means "boa constrictor." One player is the boa, who stays in a small area marked and designated as the boa's house. The rest of the class spreads out in the teaching area. Play begins when the boa leaves her house to tag other players. Tagged players join hands with the boa and go back to the house. These players then leave the house, still holding hands, to tag other players. Play continues with the boa increasing in length until only 3 or 4 players remain. If the boa breaks, all students forming the snake must return to the house and rejoin hands.

Skyros

MC CONCEPT: Greece

PE CONCEPTS: Low-organized games, throwing, catching, locomotor movements

PE LESSON PART: Game activity

SUPPLIES: Two 6- to 8-inch balls per group of 20

Two teams scatter throughout the area with two goal lines created 20 to 30 feet apart. Teams score points by passing the ball to a teammate over the other team's goal line. The player with that ball may not move but teammates can, and the opponents can play defense. The player with the ball may not be touched, and the ball may not be stolen from him. If Team A drops the ball or throws the ball and it hits the ground, Team B gets the ball. When one team scores, the other team immediately gets the ball and play continues.

Hora

MC CONCEPT: Israel

PE CONCEPTS: Rhythmic skills

PE LESSON PART: Introductory activity, game activity

SUPPLIES: "Hava Nagila" music in 4/4 time

The national dance of Israel, this dance uses the following steps:

1. Small step with left foot to the left
2. Kick right foot in front of left leg
3. Small step with right foot to the right
4. Kick left foot in front of right leg
5. Small step with left foot to the left
6. Right foot over left foot
7. Small step with left foot to the left
8. Right foot behind left foot

Mexico Kick Ball

MC CONCEPT: Mexico

PE CONCEPTS: Low-organized games, kicking, passing

PE LESSON PART: Game

SUPPLIES: One ball and six markers (cones, spots, etc.) per group of 6

Spread the markers throughout the area, and have each player stand by one. Depending on the size of the teaching area, the spots should be at least 5 feet apart. Player 1 kicks the ball toward the marker by Player 2. Player 2 must then guide the ball around the marker in as few kicks as possible. Once the ball goes all the way around the marker, Player 2 kicks it toward the marker by Player 3. The goal is to get the ball around all six markers and back to the first marker in the fewest number of kicks. Upon accomplishing this, the team is challenged to develop a strategy for decreasing the number of kicks and then to test the strategy.

Same or Different

MC CONCEPT: Pakistan

PE CONCEPTS: Low-organized games

PE LESSON PART: Introductory activity, game activity

SUPPLIES: None

Three players stand forming a triangle. To begin, all players jump two times together. On the third jump, each player puts one foot forward. The player who puts forward a different foot than the other two players did gets a point. If all three players put the same foot forward, no points are scored.

HEALTH ACTIVITIES

More elementary physical educators are being asked to teach health content. Fortunately, many health concepts can easily be integrated into the physical education curriculum and taught using physical education. Here are just a few examples of games and activities physical educators can use to integrate health content into their lessons. Pangrazi, Beighle, and Pangrazi (2009) offer many other activities related to nutrition, sun safety, and various other health concepts.

Grab a Meal

HEALTH CONCEPT: The importance of a balanced diet

PE CONCEPTS: Game skills, locomotor skills, cooperation

PE LESSON PART: Game activity

SUPPLIES: Plastic food, hoops

This game is quite similar to Barker's Hoopla (page 564). In this game, the hoop is the team's plate. Rather than using beanbags, they use plastic food, which can be purchased at most toy stores. First, challenge the teams to accumulate as much food as possible on their "plates." On signal, students move to another team's plate and pick up a single piece of food. They then return to their plate and place the food on it. They continue until getting the signal to stop. It is important that students do not "guard" their plates, and that all food is placed on the plates, not tossed or thrown. Here are other challenges for the teams:

- Accumulate the least amount of food.
- Gather a balanced meal.
- Gather an unhealthful meal.
- Accumulate only fruits (or some other type of food) on your plate.

Anytime and Sometimes

HEALTH CONCEPT: The difference between healthful and unhealthful foods

PE CONCEPTS: Chasing, fleeing, simple game skills, locomotor skills

PE LESSON PART: Game activity

SUPPLIES: Pictures of healthful and unhealthful foods

The game is played like Crows and Cranes (page 556) but uses the chase words *anytime* and *sometimes*. *Anytime* foods are fruits, vegetables, whole grains, and so on—foods that can be eaten anytime. *Sometimes* foods are candy, cake, soda, and potato chips—that can be eaten only sometimes. For added challenge and to test students' understanding of the terms, rather than saying the type of food, call out a specific food (e.g., strawberries or candy bars) as the chase word. The students must decide if the food is a sometimes food or an anytime food and then move in the appropriate direction.

Stress

HEALTH CONCEPT: The impact of stress on health

PE CONCEPTS: Chasing, fleeing, simple game skills, locomotor skills

PE LESSON PART: Game activity

SUPPLIES: Stress balls or beanbags

Choose 3 to 4 students as taggers or stressors. Students who are tagged by stressors freeze. After 30 to 45 seconds, stop the game and ask, "What is a stressor?" After mentioning a few examples, explain that as in the game, stressors slow us down and affect our health. Select new stressors and play another round for 30 to 45 seconds. Next, explain that physical activity can help relieve stress, and choose 3 to 4 students to be stress relievers. Stress relievers carry a stress ball. Now, when a student is tagged, she freezes and raises her hand. If a stress reliever tags her, she is unfrozen and continues playing. Teachers may choose to have more stressors than stress relievers to demonstrate the importance of balancing stress and stress relief.

Hygiene Movement

HEALTH CONCEPT: Various ways to maintain good hygiene

PE CONCEPTS: Locomotor skills, following instructions

PE LESSON PART: Introductory activity

SUPPLIES: None

Students begin by moving in scattered formation and freeze on signal. You then tell them, "For this activity, the 'Go' signal is when I pretend to wash my hands like you should do before eating, after playing outside, and after using the bathroom." You then say, "When I give the 'Go' signal, let's see you gallop," and then pretend to wash your hands. Use other signals such as flossing your teeth, brushing your teeth, combing your hair, and taking a bath. To see if students are listening, pretend to brush your teeth before pretending to wash your hands.

Royal Cholesterol

HEALTH CONCEPT: The risks of excess cholesterol in the blood

PE CONCEPTS: Chasing, fleeing, simple game skills, locomotor skills

PE LESSON PART: Game activity

SUPPLIES: None

The class (representing the blood) stands on one endline, and the entire teaching area is the blood vessel. Select one student to be King/Queen Cholesterol and stand in the center of the area. On signal, the blood attempts to move to the other endline without being tagged by King/Queen Cholesterol. If tagged, students move to the middle and join hands with other cholesterol. After a few rounds the blood vessel becomes crowded, making it hard for the blood to get through without being stopped. You can then briefly discuss the importance of maintaining healthy cholesterol levels via diet and physical activity.

Senses

HEALTH CONCEPT: The importance of all senses

PE CONCEPTS: Manipulative skills

PE LESSON PART: Game activity

SUPPLIES: Balls and blindfolds (optional)

One partner begins by teaching the other partner to throw. As students begin working together, add some challenges like these:

- The teaching partner may only speak; no moving or modeling.
- The throwing partner is blindfolded.
- The teaching partner may not speak, but may use modeling.
- The teaching partner may not speak or model, but can teach by moving her partner's arm and body through the throwing motion.

Students then reverse roles, and try a new skill. Locomotor skills work for this activity as well.

APPLYING WHAT YOU READ

- When preparing your lessons, consider if you can integrate academic concepts into lessons without interfering with your physical education objectives.
- Consider teaching strategies, such as counting in Spanish or spelling words while stretching, that you can easily integrate into your teaching.
- Teachers can use several strategies to integrate academic concepts. Be sure to consider all these strategies, and select the one that works best for each situation.

REFLECTION AND REVIEW

HOW AND WHY

1. Why should physical education teachers integrate academic concepts into their lessons?
2. How can physical education teachers go about integrating academic content?
3. Why might physical education teachers be apprehensive about integrating academic content?

CONTENT REVIEW

1. Discuss the models of integration available to physical educators.
2. Explain some of the issues a physical educator should consider when deciding whether to integrate academic content.
3. List and discuss strategies teachers should use when integrating academic content into physical education.
4. Discuss several ways to integrate math into physical education.
5. Explain three strategies or activities that can be used to integrate science into physical education.
6. List four ways to integrate language arts into physical education.
7. Describe several methods of integrating social studies into physical education.

FOR MORE INFORMATION

REFERENCES AND SUGGESTED READINGS

Blaydes-Madigan, J. (2004). *Thinking on your feet* (2nd ed.). Murphy, TX: Action Based Learning.

Christie, B. A. (2000). Topic Teamwork: A collaborative integrative model for increasing student-centered learning in grades K–12. *Journal of Physical Education, Recreation, and Dance, 71*(8), 28–32.

Jensen, E. (2000). *Brain based learning.* San Diego, CA: Brain Store Publishing.

National Association for Sport and Physical Education. (2004). *Moving into the future national standards for physical education.* Reston, VA: McGraw-Hill.

National Council for the Social Studies. (1994). *Expectations of excellence: Curriculum standards for Social Studies.* Alexandria, VA: Scorpio Educational Communications.

National Council of Teachers of English and International Reading Association. (2004). *Standards for the English language arts.* www.ncte.org/store/books/standards/105977.htm.

National Council of Teachers of Mathematics. (2000). *Principles and standards for school mathematics.* http://standards.nctm.org/.

National Science Teachers Association. (1996). *National science education standards.* www.nsta.org/standards.

Pangrazi, R. P. (2010). *Dynamic physical education curriculum guide: Lesson plans for implementation* (16th ed.). San Francisco: Benjamin Cummings.

Pangrazi, R. P., Beighle, A., & Pangrazi, D. P. (2009). *Promoting physical activity and health in the classroom.* San Francisco: Benjamin Cummings.

Pangrazi, R. P., Beighle, A., & Sidman, C. (2007). *Pedometer power* (2nd ed.). Champaign, IL: Human Kinetics.

Placek, J. H. (2003). *Interdisciplinary curriculum in physical education: Possibilities and problems.* In S. J. Silverman & C. D. Ennis (Eds.), *Student learning in physical education: Applying research to enhance instruction* (pp. 255–271). Champaign, IL: Human Kinetics.

Purcell-Cone, T., Werner, P., Cone, S. L., & Woods, A. M. (1998). *Interdisciplinary teaching through physical education.* Champaign, IL: Human Kinetics.

Werner, P. (Ed.). (2003). Interdisciplinary learning [Special section]. *Teaching Elementary Physical Education, 14*(4).

———. (2003). The integrated curriculum [Special section]. *Teaching Elementary Physical Education, 10*(1).

WEBSITES

Health Standards
www.aahperd.org/AAHE/

Language Arts Standards
www.ncte.org

Math Standards
http://standards.nctm.org

Science Standards
www.nap.edu/catalog.php?record_id=4962

Social Studies Standards
www.socialstudies.org/standards

12 Promoting and Monitoring Physical Activity

ESSENTIAL COMPONENTS OF QUALITY PROGRAMS

- ▶ I. Organized around content standards
- ▶ II. Student-centered and developmentally appropriate
- ▶ III. Physical activity and motor skill development form the core of the program
- IV. Teaches management skills and self-discipline
- ▶ V. Promotes inclusion of all students
- VI. Focuses on process over product
- ▶ VII. Promotes lifetime personal health and wellness
- VIII. Teaches cooperation and responsibility and promotes sensitivity to diversity

NATIONAL STANDARDS FOR PHYSICAL EDUCATION*

1. Demonstrates competency in motor skills and movement patterns needed to perform a variety of physical activities.
2. ▶ Demonstrates understanding of movement concepts, principles, and tactics as they apply to the learning and performance of physical activities.
3. ▶ Participates regularly in physical activity.
4. ▶ Achieves and maintains a health-enhancing level of physical fitness.
5. Exhibits responsible personal and social behavior that respects self and others in physical activity.
6. ▶ Values physical activity for health, enjoyment, challenge, self-expression, and/or social interaction.

*National Association for Sport and Physical Education (NASPE), 2004.

This chapter explains the differences between physical fitness and physical activity and explores how students choose one outcome over the other based on their personal needs. The Physical Activity Pyramid shows students how they can plan for and incorporate physical activity into their daily lives. The focus is on adding at least 60 minutes of moderate to vigorous activity to their daily routine.

Pedometers are an important tool for teachers and students in promoting physical activity. Pedometers are accurate if students learn the best placement point on their body. Goals can be easily set using pedometers that measure steps or activity time. Students can set achievable personal goals to ensure continued motivation. Guidelines for teachers are offered for using pedometers in physical education classes. Finally, teachers are urged to use pedometers to measure the effectiveness of their physical education programs. Showing an increase in physical activity outside the school environment may be among the most positive aspects of a quality physical education program.

Walking is the "real" lifestyle activity. It can be done nearly anywhere, and most students can walk for activity. Walking is also effective in teaching students to deal with weight management issues. Some schools implement a school-wide walking program to help create an "active school." This chapter presents many walking activities for use in any setting.

Outcomes

- Describe why activity is just as effective as fitness for ensuring health.
- Know the importance of the different levels for optimal health and how to teach those concepts to students.
- Understand how to identify moderate to vigorous physical activity.
- Know how to incorporate pedometers into physical education lessons.
- Help students learn where to place the pedometer for highest accuracy.
- Help students design personal goals for activity.
- Understand why pedometers can be used to measure program activity outcomes.
- Express the role of physical activity in maintaining proper body weight.
- Implement a school-wide walking program.

PHYSICAL ACTIVITY or physical fitness? Which of these outcomes should physical education focus on in the quest to serve students? The answer depends on each student's needs and desire. Physical educators have long known that fitness is best for all students regardless of their condition, age, maturity, or ability. In the 1950s, youth fitness became a national concern. As is often the case, educational leaders focused on testing, specifically fitness testing, to solve the problem of low fitness levels. Fitness testing was mandated; most adults remember having their fitness levels evaluated twice a year. The issue was simple: tests showed that children were unfit, and getting them fit would result in a fit and healthy society. Fifty years later, when asked to show a measure of accountability for their programs, most teachers fall back on fitness testing.

Sadly, this approach for children and their health has failed. Today's youth are showing the same (sometimes larger) deficits in personal health as their parents did. The percentage of overweight youth has more than tripled in the past 30 years (Hedley et al., 2004), and fitness levels show little to no improvement. Physical education often does not help those who need it most—children who are inactive, overweight, and not interested in physical fitness activities. Could it be that fitness testing these youth in front of others twice a year and labeling those with inadequate scores as "unfit" is undermining their desire to be active? Are schools failing the students we want to help the most?

It is clear that students have different needs and different personal goals. Some students (particularly adolescents) want to develop their personal fitness to the highest level possible to improve their skill performance (skill-related fitness). Others want to improve their appearance. But most elementary school students want to enjoy moderate to vigorous activity and do not care about achieving a high fitness level. They may be better served by developing a lifestyle that includes daily physical activity. To separate these areas, this text presents physical fitness and physical activity in separate chapters. *Physical activity* is defined as bodily movement produced by the contraction of skeletal muscle and substantially increasing energy expenditure (National Association for Sport and Physical Education [NASPE], 2004). Physical activity is an umbrella term that looks at the process of moving in various ways such as exercise, sports, and leisure activity. This chapter focuses on moderate to vigorous physical activity that people of all ages and abilities can perform throughout life.

In contrast, *physical fitness* is a set of attributes that people have or achieve in relation to their ability to perform physical activity (USDHHS, 1996). Physical activity is a process-oriented outcome related to behavior and lifestyles; physical fitness is a product-oriented outcome that emphasizes achieving a higher state of being. Physical fitness has a strong genetic component that limits the level of fitness a person can achieve. Most adults do not pursue a high level of physical fitness but are interested in living an active lifestyle and maintaining health-related fitness. Similarly, most students who are nonathletes are not interested in the product of physical fitness but are open to learning to enjoy their bodies through lifetime physical activities. Chapter 12 focuses on the process of being physically active for good health, while Chapter 13 helps students learn to develop skill-related physical fitness. Being physically active is a goal for the masses; becoming more physically fit is pursued by a much smaller group.

PHYSICAL ACTIVITY FOR CHILDREN

National Association for Sport and Physical Education (NASPE) activity guidelines for elementary school children (2004) call for 60 minutes or more of physical activity (total volume) on most days of the week. More recently, Strong and colleagues (2005) conducted a systematic review of literature and developed evidence-based physical activity recommendations for youth. These scholars recommended the same activity level as the NASPE guidelines. Adult recommendations (30 minutes a day), based primarily on the energy expenditure needed to reduce risk of chronic disease, are associated with what is commonly called "aerobic or cardiovascular fitness." It is important that students gain experience in all areas of physical activity and for all parts of health-related physical fitness, not just aerobic or cardiovascular fitness. Such a recommendation requires a greater time commitment. The four major NASPE activity guidelines are summarized below. For in-depth detail about the physical activity guidelines for children, see the NASPE report (2004).

Guideline 1: **Children should accumulate at least 60 minutes, and up to several hours, of *age-appropriate* physical activity on all or most days of the week. This daily accumulation should include moderate and vigorous physical activity that is primarily intermittent.**

It is becoming clear that students need much more than 60 minutes of activity. For example, using data collected with a pedometer that measures activity time and steps, 60 minutes of physical activity equates to not quite 5,000 steps. The President's Council on Physical Fitness and Sports (2008) has established the Presidential Active Lifestyle Award daily threshold of 11,000 steps for girls and 13,000 for boys. Clearly, 60 minutes is a minimal level for children to achieve each day. Physical activity minutes accumulated each day should include some moderate activity, such as brisk walking, and some activity more vigorous than brisk walking. Most children are active in intermittent bursts, ranging from a few seconds to several minutes, alternated with rest periods. Continuous vigorous physical activity lasting several minutes *should not* be expected for most children, nor should it be a condition for meeting the guidelines.

Guideline 2: **Children should participate in several bouts of physical activity lasting 15 minutes or more each day.**

Much of a child's daily activity is accumulated throughout the waking hours. However, if optimal benefits are to accrue, much of the activity should be as described in Guideline 2. Examples of physical activity bouts are recess, physical education, play periods, and sports practices. A key point of this guideline is that a 15-minute recess is vital to children's health and development. Eliminating recess and time for physical activity is indefensible—but all too common in today's schools. To be clear, these bouts of 15 minutes or more are not expected to be continuous activity such as jogging around a track. Instead, they should include physical activity and opportunity for social development.

Guideline 3: **Children should participate each day in a variety of age-appropriate physical activities designed to help them achieve optimal health, wellness, fitness, and performance benefits.**

Different levels of physical activity are described in the Physical Activity Pyramid (Figure 12.1 on page 229). It is recommended that children select from all of the first three levels of activities in the pyramid each week. A section on the types of physical activity follows later in the chapter.

Guideline 4: **Extended periods (2 hours or more) of inactivity are discouraged for children, especially during the daytime hours.**

Research suggests that people (including children) who watch excessive amounts of television, play computer games, work on computers for extended periods of time, or engage in other low-energy activities likely fail to meet Guidelines 1, 2, and 3 (Gordon-Larsen, McMurray, & Popkin, 2000). In general, extended periods of sedentary behavior (in and out of school) are discouraged. Because many positive activities are sedentary (homework; studying; learning to read, write, and think; and family time), children have some periods of relative inactivity in a typical day. Research shows that reducing the average amount of daily sedentary time is effective in counteracting weight problems in children (Epstein et al., 1995). Children must be active when opportunities are available, such as before and after school, at appropriate times during school, and on weekends.

MODERATE TO VIGOROUS ACTIVITY

Experts roughly agree on what constitutes light, moderate, and vigorous physical activity. Metabolic equivalent (MET), the ratio of work metabolic rate to resting metabolic rate, is a measure of activity. One MET equals calories expended at rest (resting metabolism), 2 METS is activity that is twice as intense as being at rest, 3 METS is three times as intense, and so on. Activities of 3 METS or fewer are considered to be light activities. Examples are strolling (slow walking), slow stationary cycling, stretching, golfing with a motorized cart, fishing (sitting), bowling, carpet sweeping, and riding a mower (Pate et al., 1995). Moderate activities range in the area of 4 to 6 METS. Examples of moderate activities are shoveling, sweeping, and walking at 2.5 miles per hour. Activity that expends more than six times the energy expended at rest (more than 6 METS) is considered vigorous (high intensity). Examples of activity at this level are brisk walking, running, stair climbing, and rope jumping. A study by Harrell et al. (2005) showed that children burn more calories at rest and while exercising than do adults. If you are using a standard adult MET table, increase the values somewhat to compensate for the energy expenditure differences between adults and children.

Students and adults are healthier when they engage in moderate to vigorous activity of all types. For years people have been told that to feel the benefits, we must perform aerobic activity in one long, continuous bout. Now we know that activity can be beneficial even if accumulated in several shorter bouts throughout the day. For example, 15 minutes of walking and 15 minutes of aerobic dance done at different times of the day, or three 10-minute intervals of continuous cycling done throughout the day, meet the physical activity prescription. Table 12.1 shows differences between intermittent and continuous physical activity.

TABLE 12.1 Different types of physical activity

Intensity of Activity	Intermittent	Continuous
Moderate	Playing one-wall handball	Walking to a destination at 2.5 mph
	Playing catch with a friend	Hiking
	Raking the leaves or vacuuming	Riding a bike
	Playing four-square	Skateboarding
Vigorous	Playing tag games	Jogging
	Rope jumping	Track activities
	Playing softball or football	Soccer
		Swimming

TABLE 12.2 Lifestyle activity prescription for children

Frequency	Daily, with frequent activity sessions (three or more) per day
Intensity	Moderate to vigorous activity. Alternating bouts of vigorous activity with rest periods as needed, or moderate continuous activity such as walking or riding a bike to school. Examples of activity include walking, playing running games, doing chores at home, and climbing stairs.
Time	Duration of activity necessary to expend more than 6 to 8 kcal/kg/day. Equal to calories expended in 60 minutes or more of active play or moderate sustained activity, which may be distributed over three or more activity sessions.

Expending calories in activity that equals 60 minutes of moderate to vigorous effort (walking briskly) each day (1,000 to 2,000 kcal per week) achieves health benefits similar to performance-related fitness training (see Chapter 13). The lifestyle activity prescription for children (Table 12.2) covers a broad range of moderate to vigorous activities including those that students can do as part of work or normal daily routines as well as of free time. Lifestyle activity recommendations are measured in frequency, intensity, and time; but they are not a physical fitness prescription, which requires high-intensity activity (training zone heart rates). Although they do not require intense physical activity, lifestyle activities have health benefits. Many people remain sedentary or stop exercising because they believe that only vigorous, high-intensity exercise is beneficial. The new recommendations make it easier for sedentary people to see the value in participating in moderate activity.

THE PHYSICAL ACTIVITY PYRAMID

The Physical Activity Pyramid (Figure 12.1) is a prescription model for good health that helps students understand how much and what type of activity they need. The activity pyramid, a visual approach to activity prescription, is useful because people have become confused in recent years by scientific reports about the amount of physical activity needed for health and fitness benefits. The Physical Activity Pyramid helps students understand the different categories of activity. Each category is required for good health and total body fitness.

The pyramid is divided into six categories and four levels that emphasize the benefits of each activity type. Activities with broad general health and wellness benefits for many people are at the base of the pyramid.

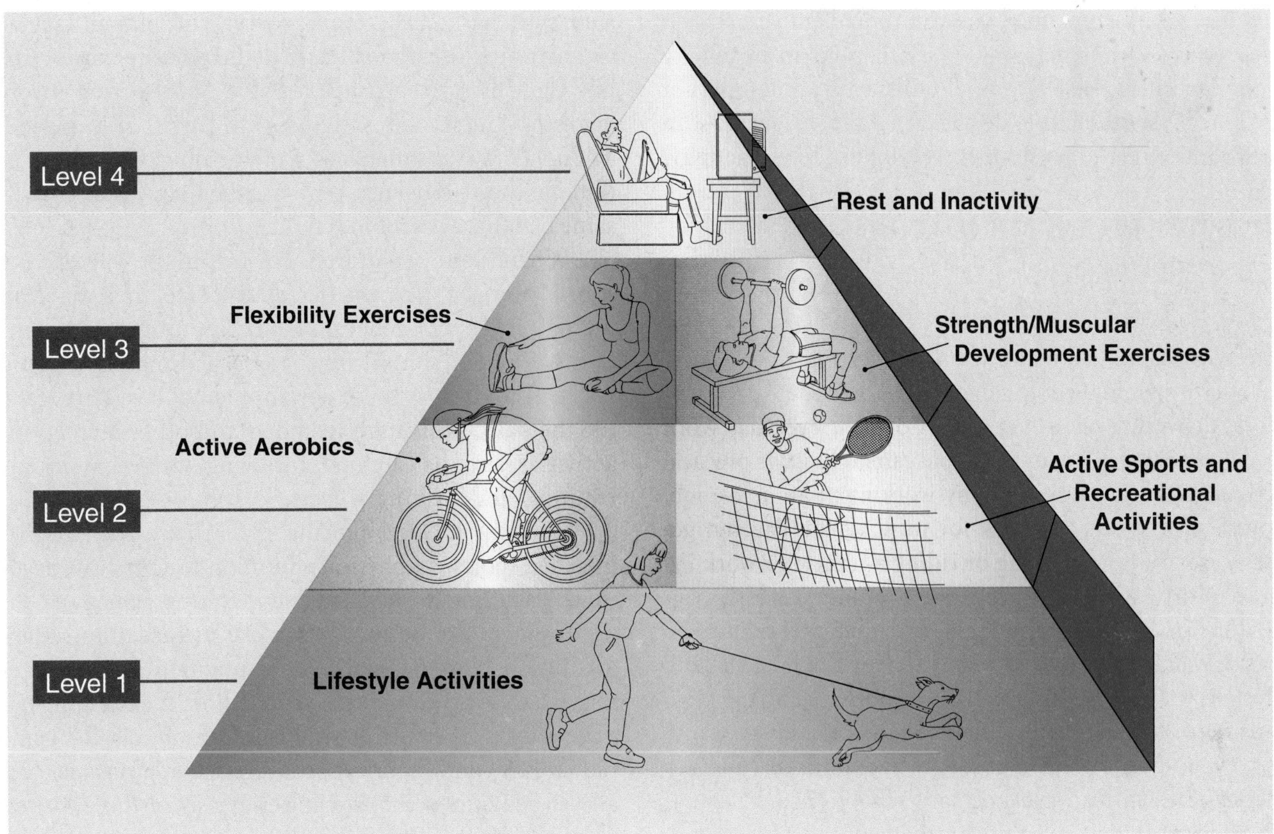

FIGURE 12.1 The Physical Activity Pyramid.

Lifestyle activity is at the base of the pyramid because scientific evidence indicates that inactive people who begin regular exercise have the most to gain. The Surgeon General's report on physical activity and health (USDHHS, 1996) points out that our nation could reap great health and economic benefits if the 24% of the U.S. population who are totally sedentary began getting modest amounts of regular physical activity. Further, those who are only occasionally active can benefit by meeting the standards for lifestyle activity suggested in level 1 of the pyramid. Benefits at this level are wide ranging and include a reduced risk of diseases such as heart disease, diabetes, and cancer. The extra calories expended in doing these activities are also useful in controlling body fat and reducing the risk of obesity. Wellness benefits include increased functional capacity and improved quality of life.

Level 2 contains more vigorous activities. Scientific reports suggest that for already active people, active aerobics as well as active sports and recreation offer additional health and fitness benefits. For people with little free time, regular activity from level 2 can substitute for lifestyle activity, though participation at both levels is encouraged. Like lifestyle activities, the activities at this level offer broad general health benefits. Note that the more vigorous nature of level 2 activities makes them difficult for some people, so they may be less appealing than level 1 activities are.

Level 3 exercises are designed to build flexibility and muscle fitness. Performing exercises of either type builds physical fitness that contributes to improved performance in various jobs and in active sports. Muscle fitness has also been associated with reduced risk of osteoporosis (Shaw and Snow-Harter, 1995), and both types of exercises when prescribed and performed correctly may contribute to reduced rate of injury and less risk of back problems (Plowman, 1993).

Rest and inactivity are at the top of the pyramid (level 4). In general, they do not provide physical activity benefits, but rest does contribute to health.

A secondary basis for the location of activities in the pyramid is their frequency. As the level increases, the frequency of participation decreases. Activities at level 1 should be performed daily; those at levels 2 and 3 can be performed fewer days per week; and inactivity (level 4), not rest, should be limited on all days of the week.

The Physical Activity Pyramid can also be used as a teaching tool. Place a poster version of the pyramid in the teaching area so you can refer to it during lessons. For example, while students do flexibility exercises, you can point to that section on the pyramid and remind them what level 3 activities are and how often they should be done. You can also use the pyramid (placed by the exit door) as a quick review before students leave class. When students are familiar with the pyramid, you can quiz them verbally on the levels of various activities or ask them to do an activity from a specific level. For example, during the fitness part of the lesson, ask students to do a level 3 activity. Quickly scan the room to check that students are doing a level 3 activity.

ACTIVITY RECOMMENDATIONS FOR CHILDREN

Level 1: Lifestyle Physical Activities

Lifestyle physical activities form the base of the Physical Activity Pyramid. People can do these activities (e.g., yard work, delivering mail, etc.) as part of their everyday work or daily routine. Of course, people can do lifestyle physical activities in other ways than by working at an active job. Someone who sits at a desk for most of the day can get lifestyle activity by walking or riding a bicycle to work instead of driving a car. Other lifestyle physical activities can be done in or around the home. For example, raking the leaves, walking to the store, and carrying the groceries are lifestyle activities. Housework that requires using the large muscles of the body is also lifestyle physical activity.

Typically, the greatest portion of accumulated minutes of physical activity for elementary school children comes from lifestyle activities. Lifestyle activities for this age include active play and games involving the large muscles. Climbing, tumbling, and other activities that require lifting the body or relocating the body in space are desirable activities when they can be done safely. Activities are typically intermittent rather than continuous. These activities normally involve few rules and little formal organization. Lifestyle activities such as walking to school, when possible, and helping with chores at home are also appropriate.

Level 2: Active Aerobics

Pyramid level 2 includes aerobic activities. Active aerobics are performed at a pace for which the body can supply enough oxygen to meet the demands of the activity. Because lifestyle activities meet this criterion, they are aerobic. Examples of popular moderate to vigorous active aerobics are jogging, brisk walking, moderate to vigorous swimming, and biking. Participation in some aerobic activities is appropriate as long as children are not expected to participate in them continuously for a long time. More appropriate are intermittent aerobic activities like recreational swimming, family walking, or aerobic activities in the lifestyle activity category (walking or bicycling to school or in the neighborhood).

Level 2: Active Sports and Recreational Activities

Active sports and recreational activities are also at level 2 of the Physical Activity Pyramid. Some examples of active sports are basketball, tennis, soccer, and hiking. Like active aerobics, this type of activity is typically more vigorous than lifestyle physical activity. Sports often involve vigorous bursts of activity with brief rest periods. Though they are often not truly aerobic, when they are done without long rest periods, they have many of the same benefits as aerobic activities.

When young children choose to be involved in sports, the sports must be modified to their developmental level. In general, children at Developmental Levels I and II should not be engaged mainly in active sports. Children at these developmental levels are learning the basic skills used in sports and other recreational activities, such as catching, throwing, walking, jumping, running, and striking objects.

Children at Developmental Level III are often involved in active sports, so physical education teachers can devote more class time to such activities. Lead-up games and skill development are necessary to make the activities suitable for this age. Emphasizing sports conditioning is unnecessary for this age group; most of the time spent in this type of activity is dedicated to skill learning and playing games rather than conditioning. Encourage age-appropriate recreational activities with a lifetime emphasis, or those that can be done with family and friends.

Level 3: Flexibility Exercises

Physical activity describes virtually all types of games, sports, and exercises. *Exercise* most commonly describes the type of physical activity done especially to build physical fitness. Flexibility exercises are included at level 3 of the pyramid. They are referred to as "exercises" because they are done specifically to build the part of physical fitness called *flexibility*. Flexibility is the ability to use joints through a full range of motion as a result of having long muscles and elastic connective tissues. There are, no doubt, some activities from levels 1 and 2 of the pyramid that help build flexibility to some extent. Still, developing this part of fitness requires doing special flexibility exercises that involve stretching the muscles and using the joints through their full range of normal motion. For this purpose, stretching exercises are best.

In general, the amount of time children at Developmental Levels I and II spend on flexibility exercises should be minimal. Because they are more flexible than adults, most children find this type of exercise relatively easy. Teaching some stretching exercises is important for illustrating the importance of flexibility. Active play activities such as tumbling and climbing are encouraged for flexibility development. Children at Developmental Level III should spend more time learning and performing flexibility exercises. Children, especially boys, begin to lose flexibility at this age. Some regular stretching is recommended, either in the form of age-appropriate flexibility exercises or activities that promote flexibility (e.g., tumbling and stunts).

Level 3: Strength and Muscular Development Exercises

Pyramid level 3 includes exercises and physical activities designed and performed specifically to increase strength (the amount of weight one can lift) and muscular endurance (the ability to persist in muscular effort). Some activities at lower levels may help develop these parts of muscle fitness, but even the most active people often need extra exercises to build strength and muscular endurance.

Participation in some strength exercises as part of a physical education class or a regular family fitness program is appropriate for students. But as long as they are accumulating adequate daily amounts of activities from lower pyramid levels, children do not need to spend much time in routinely performing organized calisthenics. Modified fitness activities (see pages 254–257) are an excellent way to help children learn about exercises. Formal resistance training is usually not recommended, particularly in a group setting.

Children at Developmental Level III participate in strength development activities that require them to move and lift their body weight. Active play and games and sports that require muscle overload are desirable for these students. Exercises using body weight are appropriate when teachers offer alternative exercises so all children can succeed. It is important to show children the relevance of these exercises. Formal exercises and conditioning programs as part of youth sports or other activity programs typically should not form a major part of activity periods, though highly motivated children may benefit from these activities. Children of this age can develop modest gains in strength and muscular endurance using resistance training (see Chapter 2). However, other activities are generally better suited to most children's needs, particularly in a class setting.

Level 4: Rest and Inactivity

At the top of the pyramid are rest and inactivity. Some types of inactivity are not necessarily detrimental to health. For example, adequate amounts of sleep are needed, and rest is important after vigorous exercise. Children need some private time to be involved in play of types other than in activities using the large muscles. Sedentary activities such as classroom learning also have benefits. Even so, the Physical Activity Pyramid is designed to provide information about the benefits of regular physical activity. Sedentary living is not typical of healthy children and is discouraged as a lifestyle. Long periods of inactivity during the day should be limited. Youth who sit and watch television or spend their free time playing video games are not getting the activity they need for good health.

USING PEDOMETERS TO MONITOR PHYSICAL ACTIVITY

Pedometers are a natural fit for a chapter on monitoring and promoting physical activity. They offer an objective measure of a person's daily amount of physical activity. Most pedometers do not measure the intensity of physical activity, only the quantity of physical activity in step and time. (Recently, Gopher Sport released a new pedometer called the *FITstep* that does monitor the intensity of physical activity.) Electronic pedometers detect movement by recording vertical acceleration at the hip. Pedometers are small and fasten easily to a belt or waistband. In their most basic form, pedometers measure the number of steps a person takes. Counting steps is an effective way to measure how much activity students accumulate. Because pedometers are not waterproof, they cannot measure swimming activity; nor can they accurately measure activities on wheels, such as bicycling, skateboarding, and inline skating. Most of the physical activity people accumulate (about 90%) is over land, so pedometers are still one of the best ways to measure physical activity for young and old alike. Using pedometers to measure children's physical activity levels is now an accepted instructional and research methodology (Beighle, Pangrazi, & Vincent, 2001; Crouter et al., 2003; Kilanowski, Consalvi, & Epstein, 1999).

When purchasing pedometers for physical education, teachers have several issues to consider. First and foremost is the accuracy of the pedometers. This is a critical issue, discussed in detail below. The pedometer features must also be considered. Several pedometers on the market have features other than counting steps. Many pedometers have a function that measures activity time. Every time a child moves, the pedometer starts accumulating time. When the child stops moving, the timing function stops. This function shows the total hours and minutes of time accumulated while wearing the pedometer. Most pedometers measure distance covered and caloric expenditure. To measure distance covered, enter the length of a child's step into his pedometer. The pedometer then calculates distance covered by multiplying the step length times the number of steps. To measure energy expenditure, enter factors such as weight and stride length into the pedometer. Based on the number of steps taken, pedometers calculate the number of kilocalories expended. Rather than taking time to enter each child's stride length and weight, physical education teachers can simply measure steps and activity time. These two variables alone provide valuable, and likely the most useful, data in the physical education setting.

THE ACCURACY OF PEDOMETERS

Activity recommendations based on daily minutes of physical activity for youth (NASPE, 2004) and adults (USDHHS,

2000) have created an interest in accurately measuring personal movement. When people are asked to recall and self-report all their activity during the previous day, most find it difficult to quantify how active they were. Besides, recall may have been done on an atypical day, thus resulting in an under- or overestimation of physical activity (Sallis, 1991). For children, an objective measuring tool is helpful for documenting activity levels because it avoids depending on recollection and reading of questionnaires. The pedometer is an objective way to measure physical activity, and its validity and reliability have been studied by several researchers. A recent study (Crouter et al., 2003) evaluated the validity of 10 different electronic pedometers and found them "most accurate." A similar study (Schneider et al., 2003) examined the reliability and accuracy of 10 pedometers over a 400-meter walk with similar results.

Pedometers are less accurate when people move slowly (less than 4 kilometers per hour) or walk with an uneven gait (Crouter et al., 2003). Pedometers depend on a fairly consistent up-and-down motion with each step, and an uneven or slow gait may not create enough movement for the pedometer to measure. Pedometers overestimate distance covered at slower speeds and underestimate actual distance at higher speeds. Caloric expenditure is most often overestimated (Crouter et al., 2003). These errors in distance and energy expenditure are not surprising, since they are all based on consistency of step length and walking speed. Throughout a day of activities, both step length and walking speed most likely will vary. Another factor contributing to the error is that some pedometers require the stride length to be entered in 3-inch intervals, thus resulting in over- or underestimating distance covered.

Pedometer placement on overweight students also may cause undercounting errors. On these students, excess body fat around the waist may force the pedometer orientation away from the vertical plane of the body. If the pedometer is not parallel to the body, its accuracy is affected, and it stops counting when the angle is too far from vertical. The next section explains how to find an accurate placement point for difficult cases.

TEACHING STUDENTS ABOUT PEDOMETER PLACEMENT AND ACCURACY

Pedometers are designed to be worn in front, at the waistline, directly in line with the midpoint of the thigh and kneecap. This positioning is accurate for most users, but it is not always the best placement for 20% to 30% of users. Therefore, students first need to locate a placement point on their waistline where the pedometer measures most accurately. Here is how to ensure that the pedometer measures accurately.

1. Place the pedometer on the waistband in line with the midpoint of the thigh and kneecap. The pedometer must be parallel with the body and upright. If it is angled in any direction, it will not measure accurately. Teach students to open their pedometer (without removing it from the waistband) and reset it to 0 steps. Have them walk at their normal pace while counting the number of steps they are taking. Ask them to stop immediately when 30 steps are reached. Open the pedometer and check the step count. If the step count is within plus or minus 2 steps of 30, this placement is an accurate location for the pedometer. If the step count is less accurate, try step 2.
2. Move the pedometer along the waistband toward the belly button or the hip. Placing the pedometer slightly in front of the hip works best for some students. Open the pedometer, clear it, and have the student take 30 steps as described in step 1. Again, if the step count is within plus or minus 2 steps of 30, this new placement is accurate and the user should always attach the pedometer there. If not, try another placement and repeat the step test.
3. If finding an accurate measuring position is difficult, remember that pedometers must remain in an upright plane (with the pedometer display parallel to the body) in order to accurately register step counts. Loose-fitting clothing affects accuracy because the clothing absorbs the slight vertical force that occurs with each step. Excess body fat may also tilt the pedometer and negate accuracy. In such cases, placement at waist level behind the hip and on the back may offer an accurate measurement. Another alternative is to use a Velcro belt to ensure that the pedometer stays upright. Attach the Velcro belt above waist level if necessary to keep the pedometer vertical. Repeat the 30-step process until an accurate placement is found. One caveat here: If Velcro belts are used, have all students in the class use them to avoid embarrassing any student. Gopher Sport (www.gophersport.com) offers Velcro belts in different colors that also can serve to designate teams for games and sports.

PEDOMETERS AND PERSONAL GOAL SETTING

A common approach in physical education uses the idea that "one standard fits all." It is based on a single standard and assumes that one goal will fit all types of students regardless of age, gender, or health. This practice of mass prescription often turns off students who need activity the most. For example, an often-referenced standard is 10,000 steps per day (Hatano, 1993). This goal was intended for cardiovascular disease prevention but has grown to be a popular standard for pedometer-measured activity for people of all ages. A recently developed goal for youth is 11,000 steps a day for girls and 13,000 steps a day for boys. This standard is used for the Presidential Active Lifestyle Award (President's Council, 2008), which is awarded to students who meet these daily standards over a 6-week period.

The problem with a *single-standard goal* is that it does not account for the substantial individual differences among people of all ages and gender. Some students may be predisposed to be active and will easily reach the step criteria; others may find it next to impossible because they are naturally less active. How many steps *should* be set as a standard? Should it be set high, so only those who are already active can reach it? Should it be set low, so most people can reach it? Should it be set high enough to offer a proven health-related benefit? If you accumulate more than 11,000 steps, is there any point in moving beyond the 11,000-step threshold? If you accumulate 4,000 steps each day, does 11,000 steps seem an impossible goal? Setting one goal that benefits everyone in a large population is a difficult proposition at best.

The approach recommended here is the *baseline and goal-setting* technique (Pangrazi, Beighle, & Sidman, 2007). This method requires everyone to identify their average daily activity (baseline) level. For preadolescent youth, 4 days of monitoring step counts (or activity time) are required to establish an average activity level (Trost et al., 2000). Baseline data can be entered in a chart like the one in Figure 12.2 on page 234.

After establishing the baseline level of activity, each student has a reference point for setting a personal goal. The personal goal is established by taking the baseline activity level and adding 10% more steps (or time in whole minutes) to that level. For example, assume a baseline of 6,000 steps per day. The personal goal for the first 2 weeks is 6,000 steps plus 600 more steps for a total of 6,600 steps. If the goal is reached on most days in this 2-week period, another 10% (600 steps) is added to the goal and the process repeated. For most people, a top goal of 4,000 to 6,000 steps above their baseline level is a reasonable expectation. Using the example of 6,000 baseline steps here, a final goal of 10,000 to 12,000 steps would be the goal.

This baseline and goal-setting approach allows for individual differences. It gradually increases personal goals so they seem achievable to even inactive individuals. Most people are interested in establishing their baseline levels of activity, and this strategy helps motivate students to increase their current activity levels.

A third way to establish step levels for youth is to define a healthy activity zone (HAZ). This method sets no one standard for each child to reach and has been utilized by the Fitnessgram (Cooper Institute, 2008) to specify a range of scores (the healthy fitness zone) where students should score on fitness test items. Some of the Fitnessgram test items (e.g., PACER run and skinfolds) are based on health-related criteria, and others are based on improvement due to training. For physical activity, a range of steps (or activity time) can be established for each gender and can serve as the HAZ. This method requires further research, but it may be acceptable for establishing a range of scores that apply to most children and adults. Ultimately a combination of methods, such as baseline/goal setting and HAZ standards, may be the best solution.

USING P233ERS IN A CLASS SETTING

The physical education teacher's first step after deciding to use pedometers is to obtain them. A set of 36 pedometers costs between $400 and $800, depending on the type and features. Many schools have asked parent–teacher groups to fund pedometers. Create interest by making a presentation to the group and asking for support. Another approach is a "shareware" program where pedometer companies sell to schools at a reduced price. Schools, in turn, sell the pedometers to parents and others to raise money. Selling pedometers is a much healthier fund-raising activity than selling candy or cookie dough.

Using pedometers in physical education requires teaching students how to use them. Teachers quickly become frustrated with students who fuss with their pedometers because they have no process to follow. The following procedure seems to minimize pedometer handling time, resulting in maximum instructional time. Number each pedometer, and store no more than six pedometers in each container (Figure 12.3 on page 235). Make sure that each container has the same number of pedometers so you can easily see when a pedometer is missing (and which student has it).

Teaching students to secure, fasten, and put away the pedometers is critical to successfully integrating pedometers into the program. Teach students to enter the teaching area, pick up their assigned pedometer, and put it on while moving around the area. When all students have their pedometers on, freeze the class and have students reset their pedometers (Figure 12.4 on page 235). Class then begins as usual. After class, students remove their pedometers, put them into the proper container, record their steps or activity time on the sheet next to their container, and prepare to exit class. A few basic rules will help maintain minimal disruptions when using pedometers: (1) "You shake it, we take it," and (2) "You take it off your waist, we take it." When a student takes off his pedometer, he loses the privilege to use it that day. Students who remove their pedometers and open them during the normal routine distract their classmates

Step 1: Calculate Your Baseline Step Counts

Name: ____________

Date: ____________

Day 1 Step Count: ______

Day 2 Step Count: ______

Day 3 Step Count: ______

Day 4 Step Count: ______

Total Step Count: ______ divided by 4 equals ______. This number is your average **baseline step count** and will be used to determine your personal activity goal.

Step 2: Calculate Your Step Count Goal

The next step is to calculate your personal step count goal. A couple of examples are shown below. The first person discovered that she had a baseline step count of 4,000 steps. After 10 weeks her step count goal increases to 6,000 steps. For the person who has a baseline of 6,000 steps, her step count goal will increase to 9,000 steps by the final weeks. Thus, both individuals will increase their number of steps by one-third.

Baseline	Personal Goal (10 percent of your baseline plus your baseline)	Weeks	Total Step Counts
4,000 steps	4,000 × 0.10 = 400; 400 + 4,000 = 4,400 Every 2 weeks thereafter, the goal will be increased by 400 steps.	1 & 2	4,400
		3 & 4	4,800
		5 & 6	5,200
		7 & 8	5,600
		9 & 10	6,000
6,000 steps	6,000 × 0.10 = 600; plus 6,000 = 6,600 Every 2 weeks thereafter, the goal will be increased by 600 steps.	1 & 2	6,600
		3 & 4	7,200
		5 & 6	7,800
		7 & 8	8,400
		9 & 10	9,000
	______ × 0.10 = ______; plus ______ = ______ Every 2 weeks thereafter, the goal will be increased by ______ steps.	1 & 2	
		3 & 4	
		5 & 6	
		7 & 8	
		9 & 10	

FIGURE 12.2 Setting personal activity goals using pedometers.

and irritate the teacher. Pedometers also are more likely to be dropped and broken when removed from the waistband.

Another important point about using pedometers is the novelty phase. If the pedometers are not carefully monitored, especially in the introductory phase, many of them will be damaged. One way to overcome the high-interest/novelty period is to follow this schedule: For the first 6 to 8 weeks of school, use the pedometers in physical education classes only. From then until the winter break, use the pedometers to evaluate how much activity students get during the school day. Students put the pedometers on in the morning and return them at the end of the school day. After winter break, students can use the pedometers to carry out 24-hour monitoring. Each morning, they put on the pedometers and clear them. The next morning, in class, students record their activity and reset the pedometers. Recording is conducted only from Monday through Friday morning because accurate weekend readings are hard to obtain, and more pedometers are lost when students take them home for the weekend. Once they become a part of each student's lifestyle, fewer pedometers are lost or misplaced. Many schools develop a replacement policy before letting students take pedometers out of the school environment. Each student's family receives a letter explaining the activity program and the use of

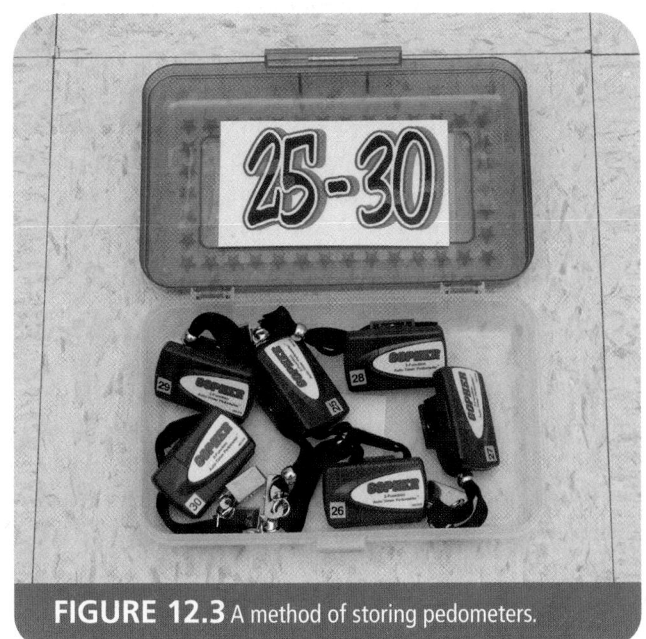

FIGURE 12.3 A method of storing pedometers.

pedometers. Pedometers that are lost must be replaced for a fee.

Pedometers are valuable tools for testing hypotheses. Teachers can challenge students to answer questions such as, "Are students more active than parents?" or "Do you take more steps during a football class or an ultimate Frisbee class?" Students can modify or invent a game based on pedometer-determined steps. Students also can use pedometers to determine their leisure-time physical activity with an aim of establishing personal goals (as described earlier) or engaging in daily physical activity.

The following activities illustrate various ways to use pedometers in a school setting. They are explained in more detail in the resource book *Pedometer Power* (Pangrazi, Beighle, & Sidman, 2007).

FIGURE 12.4 Students resetting their pedometers.

Moving across the State or United States

Students accumulate steps and measure their stride length to find out how far they have traveled across a state or U.S. map. As students reach different checkpoints, conduct class discussions about foods, art, and various cultural sites. A number of interactive Web-based programs are designed to promote physical activity and to allow students to log their steps each day.

Active or Inactive

Students can participate in various physical education lessons and try to predict which lessons are high activity and which are low activity. An enjoyable related activity is to have students guess how many steps they will take in the activity. With time, they will begin to understand the activity value of different sports and games.

A Safe Walk to School

Walking to school can add 1,000 to 2,000 steps each day to a student's activity level. This activity teaches students about walks that are safe, walks that increase in distance (and steps), and walks that avoid traffic.

School Steps Contest

All classes participate in this school-wide contest. Each class adds the step counts of all students and the teacher, and then divides the total count by the number of students. Finding the average number of steps for the entire class makes this a group competition and avoids focusing on less active students. A gentle reminder here: Let students decide whether to reveal their step count. A sensitive approach is to have the students place their step counts anonymously on a tally sheet.

The President's Council on Physical Fitness and Sports sponsors the Presidential Active Lifestyle Award (PALA; www.presidentschallenge.org). At this website, students can log their activity time or steps. By accumulating 60 minutes or from 11,000 steps (girls) to 13,000 steps (boys) on most of the days of the week for 6 weeks, students can earn a PALA patch. If 35% of the students in a school earn the PALA twice or more during the year, the school can become an "Active Lifestyle Model School."

These schools receive a certificate and are recognized on the website.

Estimation, or How Many Steps Does It Take?

Mark off a distance of exactly 1/8 or 1/4 mile. Students put on their pedometers, clear them at the starting line, and walk at a normal pace to the end of the distance. Depending on the distance they walked, they multiply the number of steps they accumulated by 8 or 4. That is the number of steps it takes them to walk 1 mile.

PEDOMETERS AND PROGRAM ACCOUNTABILITY

A common issue for physical education teachers is finding criteria they can be held accountable for. Many teachers have chosen fitness or skill development as outcomes they are willing to use as a measure of their success. But before choosing fitness or skill development as their success criterion, teachers may want to consider several issues. Fitness is most commonly used because tests have long been used in the school setting. However, such tests may not be a good choice, because the increase in obesity among today's youth decreases fitness test performance. Common sense indicates that aerobic endurance and various strength measures are directly affected by the increase in body fat among youth. Besides, genetics strongly influences children's ability to respond to training (Bouchard, 1999), and some children will show little or no improvement. Growth also confounds fitness results; it is hard to tell if students' performance improved due to the training or to the fact that they grew older and stronger. Another problem in using fitness as an outcome is the amount of time currently available for physical activity during the school day. Students' chances of improving their fitness are limited to an extent measurable by fitness testing. Many students will improve their fitness test scores purely by maturing, but this result does not account for the teacher's contribution to student fitness. Using fitness as the main indicator of teaching success may be inviting failure.

Skill development is an important assessment outcome for physical education. However, a large part of skill performance also is genetically endowed. Physical skills also can be difficult to evaluate due to time constraints and the large number of students seen by the physical education teacher. Physical skills are never perfected; even the world's best basketball and soccer players miss as many shots as they make. Baseball players strike out 3 in 10 times at bat. Rugby players fumble the ball and miss kicks. Skills do need to be emphasized or assessed, but since their performance will always be imperfect, it is asking a lot of teachers to base program success on their students' skill performance. Also, for evaluating skill development, few instruments are valid, reliable, and easy to administer in a limited time. Teachers also know that taking a lot of time to assess skill performance leaves little time to teach those skills.

Why not base program success on a school increase in physical activity? What could be more important for health and wellness than increasing the amount of activity students accumulate daily? All students can move and be physically active both in and out of school. Barring physical disability, all students can monitor their physical activity levels using pedometers. Most parents are delighted when their children are learning to live an active lifestyle. That might be one of the best legacies of a physical education program.

When the school year starts, use pedometers to evaluate the students' baseline activity levels. Follow this with regular monitoring several times during the school year. Students, regardless of genetic predisposition, can raise their goals for increasing daily physical activity. Physical education teachers can establish goals for various subgroups including classes, grade levels, and gender. School administrators might accept a 2% increase in physical activity, accumulated as a school-wide goal over an 18-week period. Use activity levels both in and out of school as separate outcomes. Out-of-school activity can be regarded as physical education homework. A program designed to increase the amount of physical activity students accumulate each day is a valuable contribution to all students' health.

WALKING: THE "REAL" LIFETIME ACTIVITY

Why is walking the "real" lifetime activity? Figure 12.5 presents criteria for identifying activities that people have the most likelihood of participating in for a lifetime. These criteria are not all-inclusive, but for the most part they help people understand the meaning of *lifetime physical activity*. Only one activity meets all the criteria, resulting in a "yes" answer to every question: walking.

Almost everyone can walk. In fact, walking is the basis for all lifetime physical activity. People who have trouble walking feel negative effects on their quality of life. Thus physical education should focus on teaching the joy of moving and walking to accumulate physical activity. Students can learn to maximize the number of steps they take rather than trying to accomplish movement tasks in the fewest possible steps. Teachers can emphasize the many benefits of being a walker. Walking has so many

Lifetime Physical Activity Criteria

Activity ______________________________

1. Can the activity be performed at various intensities? yes/no
2. Can the activity be modified to provide enjoyment for participants of varying levels? yes/no
3. Can the activity be done with 1–2 participants? yes/no
4. Is the activity costly? yes/no
    a. Does the activity require extensive amounts of equipment? yes/no
    b. Does the activity require a membership? yes/no
    c. Does the activity require a specific playing field/surface/court? yes/no
5. Can the activity be participated in with minimal risk of injury? yes/no

FIGURE 12.5 Lifetime physical activity criteria.

health-related benefits that if it could be taken as a pill, it would be a best seller at health stores. Walking has few side effects and many benefits:

- *Weight management.* When combined with a healthy approach to eating, walking is a lifetime approach to weight management. Proper weight management decreases the risks of many hypokinetic (low activity) diseases such as type 2 diabetes, heart disease, stroke, cancer, and osteoarthritis.
- *Blood pressure management.* Physical activity strengthens the heart and makes it more efficient so that it pumps more blood with less effort. This decreases pressure on the arteries and vital organs. Walking appears to be as effective as some medications in reducing high blood pressure.
- *Boosting high-density lipoproteins (HDL).* HDL helps reduce low-density lipoproteins (LDL) or "destructive cholesterol." LDL increases plaque buildup in the arteries, which is a major cause of heart attacks.
- *Reducing the risk of type 2 diabetes.* Type 2 diabetes is increasing at an alarming rate among young people. People at high risk of diabetes can cut their risk in half by combining walking with lower fat intake and a 5% to 7% decrease in weight.
- *Decreasing the risk of heart disease.* Walking for 3 hours a week is associated with a 30% to 40% lower risk of heart disease in women.

Walking requires no special equipment and has a low injury rate. Walking, probably more than any other activity, continues when students reach adulthood. Its simplicity makes walking valuable in staying healthy. For the best health results, walk at least five times per week for 30 minutes or more per session. Certainly, any amount of time for walking is beneficial. The 30 minutes can be accumulated in three bouts of at least 10 minutes, but a 30-minute walk is recommended for children. To realize the benefits of walking, students need to remember just a few things:

1. Walk at a brisk pace with a comfortable stride and a good arm swing.
2. If you cannot walk and talk at the same time, slow the pace slightly. For most school children, this is not a problem; the opportunity to socialize may be more important than the walk itself. The most important outcome is to enjoy the experience and realize the benefits of walking.
3. The walking program in school is a great place to coordinate pedometer use. Students can begin to see how many steps they typically gather in a specified amount of time. The Walk4Life pedometers can measure both walking time and steps. All things being equal, the more steps gathered in a specified time, the higher the intensity of the walk.

12

WALKING AND WEIGHT MANAGEMENT

Currently, an estimated 16% of youth are overweight. Another 15% are at risk for becoming overweight (Beals, 2003). Because about 70% of overweight adolescents grow up to be overweight adults, it is important to increase their activity in the elementary school years. Unfortunately, over the last 10 years energy expenditure through physical activity has decreased while energy intake (calories) has increased. Large servings of fast-food meals and high-fat foods certainly contribute to this increase in caloric consumption. Weight management always deals with both caloric intake and expenditure, and people who successfully maintain healthy body weight have usually learned to balance their food intake and physical activity. Various studies show that if people manage their weight only through diet, they usually regain the weight as soon as they stop dieting. Certainly, restricting diet in a highly controlled setting causes weight loss; but if not coupled with a new and more active lifestyle, successful weight management is short lived.

Walking is probably the activity of choice for overweight students. It is easy on the joints, does not overly stress the cardiovascular system, and is not painful to perform. The old adage "No pain, no gain" makes no sense for overweight students. Many of these students already have a negative view of physical activity. Students who were forced to be active when young will push back to a sedentary lifestyle when they are old enough to make personal decisions. To rekindle the joy of activity for these students, parents and teachers must be encouraging and kind. Using their own pedometers often helps students find a new interest in being active.

People often ask, "Does walking really make a difference in weight management?" The answer is yes, it makes a difference—unless you eat more calories than you burn. Consider this: The number of calories burned during exercise depends on several factors, most importantly the speed of walking and body size. Table 12.3 shows the number of calories burned during a 30-minute walk based on body weight.

Assume an 80-pound student takes a 30-minute walk at a moderate pace and burns about 86 calories. To reward himself, he decides to eat a typical-size candy bar. Without looking at the nutrition label, he eats the candy bar and quickly ingests 300 to 350 calories—a net gain of over 200 calories. Depending on energy intake and expenditure balance, about 3,500 calories equals a pound of weight gained or lost. Within 2 to 3 weeks, if this student continues to walk 30 minutes a day but adds a candy bar to his normal daily food intake, he will gain a pound of weight. This shows why it is necessary to balance physical activity and diet. It also illustrates how easy it is to gain weight even when adding daily physical activity. One thing about increasing physical activity and decreasing sedentary behavior is that most people do not eat when they are active. Just being active may make it easier to decrease caloric expenditure.

TABLE 12.3 Approximate calories burned in 30 minutes of walking

Body Weight in Pounds	Approximate Calories Burned
40	43
50	54
60	64
70	75
80	86
90	96
100	107
110	118
120	129
130	139
140	150
150	161
160	172

Walking (or trekking) poles (used like ski poles) are in vogue today, and they may be a boon for Developmental Level III students who are overweight. People in Scandinavian countries have used walking poles for years, and studies show that walkers using poles burn 25% to 30% more calories than when walking without poles (Church, Earnest, & Morss, 2002). The poles increase heart rate by 10 to 15 beats and put more than 90% of the body's muscle mass to work. They also help absorb some of the impact on the knees and ankles, thus increasing upper body strength and decreasing hip, knee, and foot injuries. Adding walking poles to a physical education program is another way to motivate students, reduce joint injuries in overweight children, and help students realize greater results from their walking. Excellent websites on using and purchasing walking poles are www.walkingpoles.com or www.trekkingpoles.com.

IMPLEMENTING A SCHOOL WALKING PROGRAM

As always, safety is vital. When initiating a walking program, instruct students to walk where they are all within the teacher's view. For most people, walking around a track or field gets boring. With the administration's approval, teachers can design walking courses around the school neighborhood so students can try many different paths and learn the time required to walk them. Before allowing students to use a path, teachers need to drive along it, write directions, and map the mileage. Set up safety guidelines that are integrated into each path. Here are some safety guidelines to consider:

- Make sure students always use the sidewalk. If there is no sidewalk, have students walk on the left side of the roadway facing traffic.
- Stipulate that students must walk with another person or in a small group. If someone is injured or needs help, one member of the group can return to the school for help.
- Because running from aggressive dogs only makes the problem worse, teach students to stop, face the dog, and give it a stern, "No!"
- Have students sign out and specify the path they will walk. If students are missing, it will be much easier to track them.
- Make sure the school nurse clears students who have serious health problems. These students must wear "medical tags" in case of an accident requiring emergency care.
- Encourage parents to get their children walking or running shoes with reflective tape built into them. Students wearing these shoes are more visible to automobile drivers.

- Have students warm up before the walk, and teach them to cool down afterward. After they walk a short distance, have them stop and stretch their arms, legs, and back (see Chapter 13 for suggested stretches). When they have finished the walk, have them stretch again.
- Make sure students drink plenty of water, whether it is cold or hot. They should drink 8 ounces of water 15 minutes before the walk. If it is hot and dry, have them drink 5 ounces every 15 to 20 minutes during the walk. At the end of the walk, have them drink another 8 to 16 ounces of water. Waiting for the thirst signal as a reminder to drink may be too late. Thirstiness usually occurs after the body needs water.
- In cold weather, teach students about layering clothing so they can remove a layer if they are too hot. Layers of lighter clothing are much more useful than one heavy layer. Students should wear a hat, gloves, and scarf if necessary. In hot weather, have them wear loose, light-colored clothing, a hat, and sunglasses. Emphasize that to avoid skin damage due to ultraviolet light from the sun, students must apply sunscreen when they will be outside for more than a few minutes—in any weather.

Safety Tip

Establish a protocol for students to sign out with their name and the path on which they will be walking when participating in pedometer walking activities. Because you have timed the route ahead of time, you will know when students should return.

SUGGESTED WALKING ACTIVITIES

I Spy

On their walk, students take with them a scorecard that has a challenge on it. For example, "Identify as many different makes of cars as possible." Or, "List as many different birds and animals as you can." Design different cards to create varying challenges. After their walks, students can discuss the items they have identified.

Mixed-Up Walks

For short periods, add some walking variations (backward, sideways slide leading with left shoulder and then right shoulder, skipping, galloping). For example, have students start with backward walking for 1 minute, then regular walking for 1 minute, then skipping for 1 minute, then regular walking, and so on. Tasks assigned also can include challenges like, "Complete your walk by making 10 left turns on your route." Be sure to document where students make a turn.

Interval Walk

Set up a walking circuit that includes stretching and strength activities at each corner of the football field. For example, instruct students to walk a lap, then do a standing stretch for 30 seconds, then walk half a lap to a sitting stretch, then walk another lap, then do some abdominal activities, and then walk to a push-up station.

Cross-Country Walking

Set up a cross-country walking race with teams from the class. Draw a map that offers a nice variety of walking areas. Students try to walk as quickly as possible and receive a number at the finish line. The team with the lowest number of points wins. This is a competitive activity, but it can be approached in a positive and fun way.

Walking Golf

Set up a walking "golf" tournament around your teaching space with hula hoops for holes, cones for the tees, and a tennis ball for each student to throw. Students throw the ball and then walk with their group to the hoop. Students use a scorecard to keep track of the number of throws needed at each hole.

Treasure Hunt

Set up a walking course with a set of clues to follow to get to 10 sites. At the sites, tape a set of words that students can later arrange in order to spell a popular saying or jingle. Clues might include "a place for extra points on the south side"; "a place for H_2O"; "fans sit here on the west side"; "long jumpers take off here"; "stand under this for the score of the game"; "a place for trash."

Poker Walk

Set out several decks of cards at various locations around the teaching area. Students walk to each deck and pick up one card without looking at it. They walk to as many decks as possible within a time limit and then add up the points. Give a prize for high and low point totals. Set it up so that anyone can win just by walking to the card areas, picking up the cards, and adding up the points at the end of the game.

Know Your Community

Have the class take different walks and identify different types of businesses and professional offices along their route. Challenge students to find various businesses or locations.

Weekly Walking Calendar

Each week, give students a 5-day calendar that lists various things to do on their walk. For example: Monday: Walk with a friend. Tuesday: Walk with walking poles. Wednesday: Walk, stop, and stretch periodically. Thursday: Walk 15 minutes in one direction and return to the starting spot by retracing your path. Friday: Walk and use a pedometer to count your steps.

Learn about Your Friend

Give students a series of questions on a card that will help them get to know a friend better. Challenge them to walk and discover new things about a friend while moving.

Off-Campus Walks

Students can gain extra credit by taking walks outside of the school day. This can be an excellent opportunity for them to use pedometers to track their walks. They can record their steps and activity time and report to the class on both measures.

APPLYING WHAT YOU READ

- Quality lesson plans teach students while promoting lifelong physical activity. As you write lessons, be sure to convey that message during each class.
- Do your lessons help students understand the physical activity pyramid and guidelines?
- Pedometers are a great tool to teach students about physical activity, help them learn goal setting, and give you valuable data to assist in improving instruction. Have students use pedometers as much as possible.
- Walking activities are great additions to a physical education lesson because they require minimal equipment, and children can use them outside of physical education class.

REFLECTION AND REVIEW

HOW AND WHY

1. Why is walking often called the "real" lifetime activity?
2. How can walking play an important role in weight management?
3. What are the basic steps to follow when implementing a walking program in physical education?
4. What can be done to encourage students' physical activity outside of the school environment?

CONTENT REVIEW

1. What is the effect of adding at least 60 minutes of daily physical activity to your lifestyle?
2. What are the levels of the Physical Activity Pyramid? How much time should be spent on the components each week?
3. What level in the Physical Activity Pyramid forms the foundation for good health? How can students be taught to change their activity habits to meet the minimum activity requirements?
4. What can pedometers measure? Which of the measurements is most accurate and useful for most students? Why?
5. What are the steps to follow when teaching students to develop personal goals? When should the goals be reset?
6. What are the three most common areas physical educators use to establish the accountability of their programs? Which of these might be most meaningful as a program outcome?
7. What are three walking activities that can be assigned to students for after-school physical activity?

FOR MORE INFORMATION

REFERENCES AND SUGGESTED READINGS

American College of Sports Medicine. (2005). *ACSM's guidelines for exercise testing and prescription* (7th ed.). Philadelphia: Lippincott, Williams, & Wilkins.

Beals, K. A. (2003). Addressing an epidemic: Treatment strategies for youth obesity. *ACSM Fit Society Page*, Spring 2003, 9–11.

Beighle, A., Pangrazi, R. P., & Vincent, S. D. (2001). Pedometers, physical activity, and accountability. *JOPERD, 72*(9), 16–19.

Bouchard, C. (1999). Heredity and health related fitness. In C. B. Corbin & R. P. Pangrazi, (Eds.), *Toward a better understanding of physical fitness and activity.* Scottsdale, AZ: Holcomb Hathaway.

Church, T. S., Earnest, C. P., & Morss, G. M. (2002). Field testing of physiological responses associated with Nordic walking. *Research Quarterly for Exercise and Sport, 73*(3), 296–300.

Cooper Institute. (2008). *Fitnessgram/Activitygram test administration manual* (3rd ed.). Champaign, IL: Human Kinetics.

Corbin, C. B., & Pangrazi, R. P. (1992). Are American children and youth fit? *Research Quarterly for Exercise and Sport, 63*(2), 96–106.

Crouter, S. C., Schneider, P. L., Karabulut, M., & Bassett, D. R., Jr. (2003). Validity of 10 electronic pedometers for measuring steps, distance, and energy cost. *Medicine and Science in Sports and Exercise, 35*(8), 1455–1460.

Decker, J., & Mize, M. (2002). *Walking games and activities.* Champaign, IL: Human Kinetics.

Epstein, L. H., Valoski, A. M., Vara, L. S., McCurley, J., Wisniewski, L., & Kalarchian, M. A., et al. (1995). Effects of decreasing sedentary behavior and increasing activity on weight change in obese children. *Health Psychology, 14*(2), 109–115.

Gordon-Larsen, P., McMurray, R. G., & Popkin, B. M. (2000). Determinants of adolescent physical activity and inactivity patterns. *Pediatrics, 105*, E83.

Harrell, J. S., McMurray, R. G., Baggett, C. D., Pennell, M. L., Pearce, P. F., & Bangdiwala, S. I. (2005). Energy costs of physical activities in children and adolescents. *Medicine and Science in Sports and Exercise, 37*(2), 329–336.

Hatano, Y. (1993). Use of the pedometer for promoting daily walking exercise. *International Council for Health, Physical Education and Recreation, 29*, 4–28.

Hedley, A. A., Ogden, C. L., Johnson, C. L., Carroll, M. D., Curtin, L. R., & Flegal, K. M. (2004). Overweight and obesity among U.S. children, adolescents, and adults, 1999–2002. *JAMA, 291*, 2847–2850.

Kilanowski, C. K., Consalvi, A. R., & Epstein, L. H. (1999). Validation of an electronic pedometer for measurement of physical activity in children. *Pediatric Exercise Science, 11*, 63–68.

Morgan, C. F., Jr., Pangrazi, R. P., & Beighle, A. (2003). Using pedometers to promote physical activity in physical education. *JOPERD, 74*(7), 33–38.

National Association for Sport and Physical Education. (2004). *Physical activity for children: A statement of guidelines* (2nd ed.). Reston, VA: Author.

Pangrazi, R. P., Beighle, A., & Sidman, C. L. (2007). *Pedometer power: Using pedometers in school and community* (2nd ed.). Champaign, IL: Human Kinetics.

Pate, R. R., Pratt, M., Blair, S. N., Haskell, W. L., Macera, C. A., & Bouchard, C., et al. (1995). Physical activity and public health. *JAMA, 273*(5), 402–407.

Plowman, S. A. (1993). Physical fitness and healthy low back function. *Physical Activity and Fitness Research Digest, 1*(3), 1–8.

President's Council on Physical Fitness and Sports. (2008). *The president's challenge handbook.* Washington, DC: Author.

Sallis, J. F. (1991). Self-report measures of children's physical activity. *Journal of School Health, 61*, 215–219.

Sallis, J. F., & Patrick, K. (1994). Physical activity guidelines for adolescents: Consensus statement. *Pediatric Exercise Science, 6*(4), 302–314.

Schneider, P. L., Crouter, S. E., Lukajic, O., & Bassett, D. R., Jr. (2003). Accuracy and reliability of 10 pedometers for measuring steps over a 400-m walk. *Medicine and Science in Sports and Exercise, 35*(10), 1779–1784.

Shaw, J. M., & Snow-Harter, C. (1995). Osteoporosis and physical activity. *Physical Activity and Fitness Research Digest, 2*(3), 1–8.

Strong, W. B., Malina, R. M., Blimkie, C. J. R., Daniels, S. R., Dishman, R. K., & Gutin, B., et al. (2005). Evidence based physical activity for school-age youth. *Journal of Pediatrics, 146*(6), 732–737.

Trost, S. G., Pate, R. R., Freedson, P. S., Sallis, J. F., & Taylor, W. C. (2000). Using objective physical activity measures with youth: How many days of monitoring are needed? *Medicine and Science in Sports and Exercise, 32*(2), 426–431.

U.S. Department of Health and Human Services. (1996). *Physical activity and health: A report of the Surgeon General.* Atlanta, GA: Centers for Disease Control and Prevention, National Center for Chronic Disease Prevention and Health Promotion.

———. (2000). *Healthy People 2010. National health promotion and disease objectives.* Washington, DC: U.S. Government Printing Office.

Vincent, S. D., & Pangrazi, R. P. (2002). Does reactivity exist in children when measuring activity levels with pedometers? *Pediatric Exercise Science, 14*(1), 56–63.

WEBSITES

Pedometers

http://walking.about.com/cs/measure/bb/bybpedometer.htm
http://walking.about.com/cs/measure/tp/pedometer.htm
www.pecentral.org/pedometry
www.walk4life.com

Videos and Instructional Materials

www.walkingpoles.com
www.trekkingpoles.com

Walking Programs

www.accustep10000.org
www.americaonthemove.org
www.steptracker.com
www.10k-steps.com

13 Physical Fitness

ESSENTIAL COMPONENTS OF QUALITY PROGRAMS

I. Organized around content standards
II. Student-centered and developmentally appropriate
III. Physical activity and motor skill development form the core of the program
IV. Teaches management skills and self-discipline
V. Promotes inclusion of all students
VI. Focuses on process over product
VII. Promotes lifetime personal health and wellness
VIII. Teaches cooperation and responsibility and promotes sensitivity to diversity

NATIONAL STANDARDS FOR PHYSICAL EDUCATION*

1. Demonstrates competency in motor skills and movement patterns needed to perform a variety of physical activities.
2. Demonstrates understanding of movement concepts, principles, and tactics as they apply to the learning and performance of physical activities.
3. Participates regularly in physical activity.
4. Achieves and maintains a health-enhancing level of physical fitness.
5. Exhibits responsible personal and social behavior that respects self and others in physical activity.
6. Values physical activity for health, enjoyment, challenge, self-expression, and/or social interaction.

*National Association for Sport and Physical Education (NASPE), 2004.

The value and the importance of teaching lifetime physical fitness is discussed in this chapter. An understanding of the difference between health- and skill-related fitness helps clarify the need for emphasizing lifetime activity. High-level fitness performance is no longer an objective for most children. Instead, the goal is to increase the activity and general fitness level of all students to improve their health status. Fitness activities for children can be moderate in intensity and still offer many health benefits. This chapter includes suggestions for developing a fitness module, motivating children to maintain fitness, and developing positive attitudes toward activities. Also described are some exercises and proper performance techniques for inclusion in a health-related program that meets all students' needs.

Outcomes

- Differentiate between skill- and health-related physical fitness.
- Describe the fitness status of youth in the United States.
- Explain the role that a broad program of physical fitness and activity plays in the elementary school curriculum.
- Identify the various components of health- versus skill-related physical fitness.
- List guidelines for developing and maintaining physical fitness.
- Develop a fitness module.
- Cite strategies and techniques for motivating children to maintain physical fitness.
- Discuss the importance of fitness testing, and cite several tests that can be used to measure fitness in children.
- Categorize various exercises by the muscle group involved.
- Characterize isotonic, isometric, and isokinetic exercises.
- Identify harmful physical activities and exercises.
- Plan and demonstrate many activities and exercises that can improve the physical fitness of children.

DEFINITIONS OF PHYSICAL FITNESS

Physical activity is a process that involves accumulating a wide variety of movement. Many experts believe that if people accumulate enough physical activity, physical fitness will take care of itself. Physical fitness is often measured to see if an adequate standard is in place to ensure good health. The general definition of *physical fitness* is "a set of attributes that people have or achieve relating to their ability to perform physical activity" (U.S. Department of Health and Human Services—USDHHS, 1996). An alternative definition is "a state of well-being with a low risk of premature health problems and energy to participate in a variety of physical activities" (Howley & Franks, 2007).

The two types of physical fitness most often identified are health-related physical fitness and skill-related physical fitness. The difference between *physical fitness related to functional health* (health related) and *physical performance related to athletic ability* (skill related) makes it easier to develop proper fitness objectives and goals for children. Health-related physical fitness is a subset of skill-related fitness (Figure 13.1).

Health-related fitness is characterized by moderate to vigorous physical activity, as discussed in Chapter 12. People who are generally unwilling to exercise at high intensities should aim for health-related fitness. Health-related fitness activities can be integrated into everyday activities that are often characterized as lifetime activities. In contrast, skill-related physical fitness includes the health-related components; but it also covers components related to genetic limitations that control physical performance. Skill-related fitness is the right choice for people who *can* and *want* to perform at a high level, but it is less acceptable to most people because it requires training and exercising at high intensities.

13

HEALTH-RELATED PHYSICAL FITNESS

Teaching health-related fitness should be a priority in physical education. Health-related fitness benefits all students by improving their health status through daily physical activity. Health-related fitness is one of the few areas where all students can succeed regardless of ability level and genetic

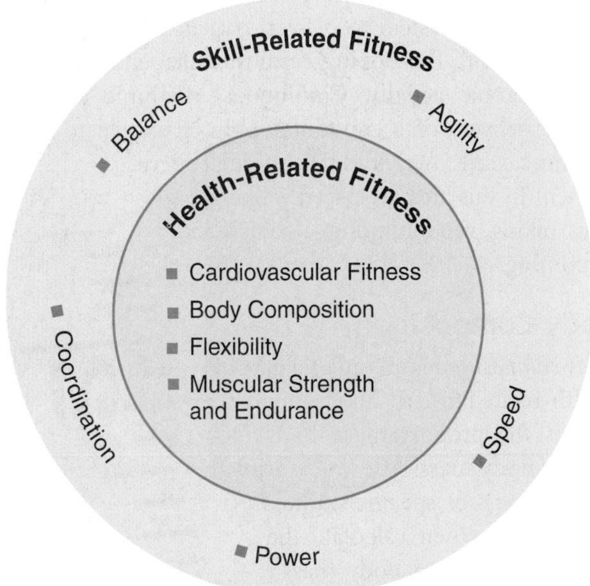

FIGURE 13.1 Components of physical fitness.

limitations. Students learn that if they are willing to be active, they will be healthier. This contrasts with skill-related fitness, which is performance oriented and influenced by genetic traits and abilities. A primary reason for teaching health-related fitness is to help students develop positive lifetime activity habits.

Health-related physical fitness includes aspects of physiological function that protect students from diseases related to a sedentary lifestyle. Such fitness can be improved and/or maintained through regular physical activity. Specific components include cardiovascular endurance, body composition (ratio of leanness to fatness), flexibility, muscular strength and endurance, and flexibility. These components are all measured in the Fitnessgram test (Cooper Institute, 2008) as described in Chapter 8. The Fitnessgram (Cooper Institute, 2008) uses criterion-referenced health standards that represent good health instead of the traditional percentile rankings often found in skill-related fitness tests. These standards specify a level of fitness that helps protect students against diseases resulting from sedentary living. The Fitnessgram classifies fitness performance into two categories: needs improvement and healthy fitness zone (HFZ). All students are encouraged to score in the HFZ, but there are few benefits in scoring beyond the HFZ. Criterion-referenced health standards are not designed to compare students. The goal is for all students to achieve and move their personal performance into the HFZ. The following sections describe major components of health-related fitness.

Cardiovascular Endurance

Aerobic fitness offers many health benefits and is often seen as the most important element of fitness. *Cardiovascular endurance* is the ability of the heart, the blood vessels, and the respiratory system to deliver oxygen efficiently for an extended time. Developing cardiovascular endurance requires aerobic activity. Continuous, rhythmic activities require delivery of a constant supply of oxygen to the muscle cells. Activities that stimulate development in this area are paced walking, jogging, biking, rope jumping, aerobics, and swimming.

Body Composition

Body composition is an integral part of health-related fitness. Body composition is the proportion of body fat to lean body mass. After measuring the thickness of specific skinfolds, teachers can then calculate the percentage of lean body mass for each student (using formulas developed using other, more accurate methods of measuring body composition). The percentage of lean body mass is easier to communicate to parents than the more involved methods.

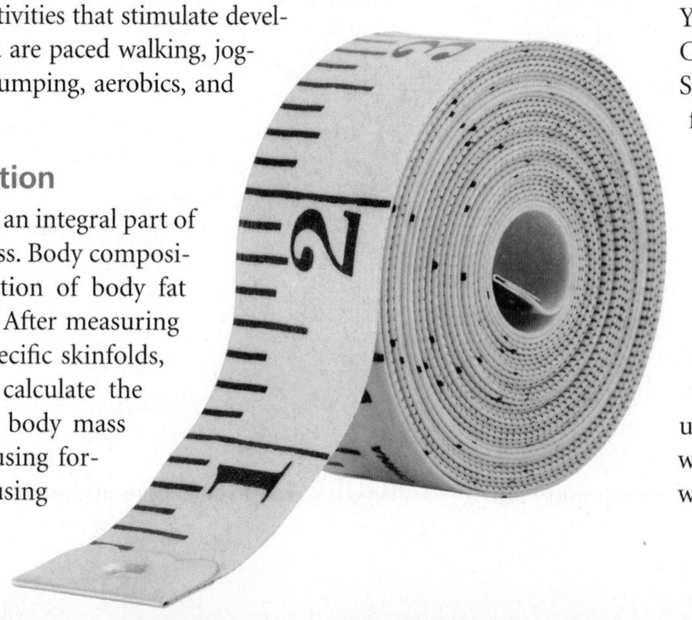

Flexibility

Flexibility is the range of movement through which a joint or sequence of joints can move. Inactive individuals lose flexibility, whereas frequent movement helps retain the range of movement. Stretching activities increase the length of muscles, tendons, and ligaments. The ligaments and tendons retain their elasticity through constant use. Flexibility is important to fitness; a lack of flexibility can create health problems for individuals. People who are flexible usually have good posture and may have less low-back pain. Many physical activities demand a range of motion to generate maximum force, such as serving a tennis ball or kicking a soccer ball.

Muscular Strength and Endurance

Muscular strength is the ability of muscles to exert force. Most activities do not build strength in areas where it is needed—the arm–shoulder girdle and the abdominal–trunk region. *Muscular endurance* is the ability to exert force over an extended period. Endurance postpones the onset of fatigue so that activity can continue for longer. Sport activities require muscular endurance because participants must perform throwing, kicking, and striking skills many times without fatigue.

SKILL-RELATED PHYSICAL FITNESS COMPONENTS

Skill-related fitness includes physical qualities enabling a person to perform in sport activities. For years, the primary fitness test for teachers was the American Alliance for Health, Physical Education, Recreation, and Dance (AAHPERD) Youth Fitness Test (AAHPERD, 1987). Today this test is known as the President's Challenge Youth Fitness Test (President's Council on Physical Fitness and Sports—PCPFS, 2008). Skill-related fitness is closely related to athletic ability. Speed, agility, coordination, and so on are the basis of excelling in sports. Because skill-related fitness is strongly influenced by a child's natural or inherited traits, it is difficult for most students to achieve. In contrast to health-related tests, skill-related fitness tests often use norm-referenced standards, which compare students based on where they rank among their peers.

For some students, the goal becomes trying to do better than other students rather than learning to do the best they can regardless of peer scores.

Skill-related fitness components are useful for performing motor tasks related to sport and athletics. The ability to perform well on skill-related tests depends largely on a child's genetic endowment. All students can perform adequately in health-related fitness activities, but only a few children excel in them. Asking students to "try harder" only adds to their frustration if they lack natural ability, because they see their more skilled friends perform well without effort. When teaching skill-related fitness, offer an explanation of why some students perform well with little effort while others, no matter how hard they try, never excel. Offer many examples that illustrate genetic differences such as speed, jumping ability, strength, and physical size in individuals. Understand that a few students will want to work hard to improve their fitness performance, but most will be satisfied to play, be active, and enjoy their bodies in a less demanding way. For less skilled students, health-related fitness is an important outcome.

Skill-related physical fitness includes the health-related factors just listed as well as the following traits:

- *Agility* refers to the body's ability to change position rapidly and accurately while moving in space. Sports requiring agility include wrestling and football.
- *Balance* refers to the body's ability to maintain a state of equilibrium while either stationary or moving. Maintaining balance is essential to all sports and especially important in gymnastic activities.
- *Coordination* is the body's ability to perform more than one motor task at a time. In football, baseball, tennis, soccer, and other sports that require hand–eye and foot–eye skills, coordination can be developed by repeatedly practicing the skill to be learned.
- *Power* is the ability to transfer energy explosively into force. Developing power requires performing strength activities with maximum force and as quickly as possible. Skills requiring power include high jumping, long jumping, shot putting, throwing, and kicking.
- *Speed* refers to the body's ability to move rapidly. Usually associated with running forward, speed is essential for success in most sports and general locomotor movement skills.

ARE CHILDREN FIT?

Many physical education teachers believe that today's youth are less fit than they were in the past. This opinion is often used to justify more physical education time in the schools. Comparative research (Corbin & Pangrazi, 1992) suggests that the fitness of today's children has not degenerated; they perform at a level similar to that of students 40 years ago. In the last four national surveys (1957 to 1985) of youth fitness conducted by AAHPERD and/or the President's Council on Physical Fitness and Sports, the only test items included in all four surveys were pull-ups and the flexed-arm hang. When these two items were compared over four decades, both boys and girls showed increased upper-body strength. Unfortunately, other areas of fitness are harder to compare due to variation in survey test items.

Youth have shown a serious and documented decline in body composition. From 1999 to 2002, 16% of youth ages 6 through 19 years were overweight, and another 31% were at risk for becoming overweight (85th percentile of sex-specific BMI-for-age growth charts; Hedley et al., 2004). This large increase in obesity takes its toll on fitness scores. Common sense dictates that if a student can do 50 push-ups at normal weight, putting 20 pounds of sand on her back will decrease the number of push-ups she performs. Body fat is dead weight that does not contribute to muscular or cardiovascular performance. Thus, all strength and aerobic performance scores decrease as obesity increases rapidly among youth.

WHY CAN'T ALL CHILDREN MEET FITNESS STANDARDS?

Is it realistic to expect all children to reach specified fitness standards? What factors control fitness performance, and how much control do children have over their fitness accomplishments? Payne and Morrow (1993) reviewed 28 studies examining training and aerobic performance in children and concluded that improvement is small to moderate in prepubescent children. The relatively small to moderate increase in pre- to post-aerobic improvement and the weak relationship between a training program and its effect led these researchers to question traditional practices involving children and their fitness. Are we expecting too much from traditional physical education or fitness programs? Have award structures, designed to motivate children using these programs or test batteries, been appropriately designed when children appear to show only small improvements in aerobic capacity? Clearly, curriculum planners, teachers, fitness directors, exercise physiologists, and physicians need to carefully consider the ramifications of these findings.

Much of fitness test performance is explained by heredity (Bouchard, 1999; Bouchard et al., 1992). Other factors such as environment, nutrition, and maturation affect fitness performance as well, as reflected in physical fitness test scores. Research shows that heredity and maturation strongly affect fitness scores (Bouchard, 1999; Bouchard et al., 1992; Pangrazi & Corbin, 1990) and may have more to do with youth fitness performance than does activity level. Some children have a definite advantage on tests due to certain attributes such as leg length, lung capacity, or body type. Even when untrained, these children score better than others do.

Beyond heredity lies another factor that predisposes some children to high (or low) performance. Recent research has shown that differences in "trainability" are strongly influenced by genetic predisposition (Bouchard, 1999; Bouchard et al., 1992). *Trainability* refers to the idea that some individuals benefit from training (regular physical activity) more than others do. Suppose that two children perform the same workload throughout a semester. Child A quickly improves dramatically; child B does not. Child A simply responds more favorably to training than does child B; child A inherited a body that responds to exercise. Child A improves her fitness and scores well on the test, and she concludes, "The activity works—it makes me fit." Child B scores poorly, receives negative or no feedback, and concludes, "Activity doesn't improve my fitness, so why bother?" Child B's fitness actually may improve (but less than child A's), though it will take longer to show. Due to genetic limitations, child B will probably never achieve child A's fitness level.

Another factor influencing fitness performance is physical maturation. Teachers know that some children mature faster than others. If two students are the same age and sex, but one is physiologically older (advanced skeletal maturation), the more mature student usually performs better on tests than does the less mature child. Examining fitness norms shows that performance levels increase as children grow older. Because age does not accurately reflect physical maturity, an immature, active child might score lower than a more mature, less active child of the same age. Maturation can override the effects of activity among young children. Age also plays a role in fitness performance (Pangrazi & Corbin, 1990). As little as 3 months' difference in age helps students perform better than younger children, regardless of training. Expect older students in the same class with younger children to perform better.

Many teachers and parents believe that children's fitness primarily reflects the amount of activity and exercise they perform regularly. These adults assume that students who score high on fitness tests are active and those who score low are inactive. This assumption is often wrong. Physical activity is an important variable in fitness development for adults; but for children, other factors are at least as important. Studies indicate a low relationship between physical fitness and physical activity among children (Pate, Dowda, & Ross, 1990; Pate & Ross, 1987; Ross et al., 1987). Teachers who make the mistake of assuming that children are inactive because they earned low scores on a fitness test will create misunderstanding among students.

Children want to succeed. They try to behave in ways that please the teacher and impress their friends. When the teacher says fitness scores can be improved by working hard each day, most children believe him. Students who have been exercising regularly expect to do well on the fitness tests—and, of course, teachers expect the same. But if their scores are lower than expected, students can be disappointed. They are discouraged if the teacher concludes that their low fitness scores reflect inactivity and lack of exercise. Such conclusions as, "You weren't as fit as some of your peers, so you must not have worked hard enough" can be destructive. They may damage self-esteem and harm respect between student and teacher. Conversely, it can be incorrect to assume that students who score high on fitness tests are active. Students who are genetically gifted may be inactive, yet still perform well on fitness tests. If teachers do not teach otherwise, these students incorrectly develop the belief that they can be fit and healthy without being active.

WHY ARE MOST CHILDREN LABELED UNFIT?

For years, the only available fitness test for teachers was the Youth Fitness Test (AAHPER, 1976; AAHPERD, 1987), which is currently available as one component of the President's Challenge (PCPFS, 2008). This test measures skill-related fitness and awards the presidential fitness award to students performing at the 85th percentile or better in all test items. Data from the National School Population Fitness Survey (Reiff et al., 1987), funded by the President's Council on Physical Fitness and Sports, showed that only one-tenth of 1% of boys and three-tenths of 1% of girls could pass a battery of six tests at the 85th percentile. Why are the standards so high? One explanation is that it compares with academic standards, and test developers felt that physical education standards should be set at a similar level.

Because many physical educators and parents felt that the 85th percentile standard was unrealistically high, a second award was created—the National Fitness Award. To earn this award, students must pass the same battery of test items at the 50th percentile or better. Unfortunately, when using a battery of tests, most students fail at least one item, causing them to lose the award and be identified as unfit. Only 15% of boys and 19% of girls are able to pass all items at the 50th percentile standard. Using a battery of tests to define fitness is a way to fail most children. Even at this lowered standard, over 80% of students fail. Common sense suggests that if students pass five out of six test items, they should be declared fit rather than unfit. For teachers, it is important to discuss children's successes on fitness test items, rather than declaring them unfit because they failed one item.

The definition of physical fitness has changed over the years, giving people other reasons to believe that children are unfit. Newer fitness tests are focusing on health-related fitness and its relationship to good health and well-being. High performance on fitness test items is not necessary for good health. Studies find that moderate amounts of health-related physical fitness also contribute to good health (Blair et al., 1989; USDHHS, 1996). When health-related fitness test items are used to evaluate fitness, many children perform as well as those did in years past.

Finally, in making a strong case for physical education, many physical education teachers may choose to believe that children are unfit. This belief is not based in fact, because children's fitness has been measured over a 40-year period and shows little improvement or decline (Corbin & Pangrazi, 1992). Accept the fact that preadolescent youth are nonresponders to training (see Chapter 2) and unlikely to show fitness improvement even with training regimens. An important issue is the increasing body weight observed in youth. Daily physical activity is critical for successful weight management. Teachers must focus on educating youth about fitness concepts, the effort they require, and the need for increased physical activity. The ultimate goal is for students to have positive feelings about lifelong physical activity and fitness.

FITNESS TESTING ISSUES

In fitness testing for children, the overriding consideration is to make the experience positive and educational. Children can learn about improving personal fitness and developing a lifestyle that maintains good health without being turned off by the testing experience. Imagine the embarrassment of children when their fitness test results are announced to the class. Because many schools test children twice a year, every year, some students are labeled unfit for an entire school career. How could this practice possibly encourage inactive children who need the most motivation?

SKILL-RELATED OR HEALTH-RELATED FITNESS TEST?

Students need to know the differences between the types of fitness so they understand their purposes. Skill-related fitness helps improve performance in motor tasks related to sport and athletics. The ability to perform well on skill-related tests is strongly influenced by predetermined genetic skills. If skill-related fitness is encouraged in elementary school, teachers need to explain why some people perform well while others, no matter how hard they try, never reach high levels of performance. Many obvious examples such as individual differences in speed, jumping ability, strength, and physical size illustrate genetic differences.

In contrast, health-related physical fitness focuses on how much activity is required for good health. Teachers emphasize the processes of activity and participation rather than the product of high-level physical skill performance. Usually, health-related fitness batteries use criterion-referenced health standards (see page 243), in contrast to skill-related fitness tests that use percentile scores. Criterion-referenced standards relate to the minimum amount of activity required for good health. Performance exceeding the minimum requirement is laudable but not essential to good health. This approach teaches students the importance of maintaining a personal level of fitness through regular activity rather than comparing their fitness level with others.

REPORTING BODY MASS INDEX TO PARENTS

Some states now require each student's body mass index (BMI) to be calculated and sent home to parents. The point of this practice is to inform parents about the status of their child's weight. BMI scores, which are calculated from a child's weight and height, are controversial among professionals. BMI is a reliable indicator of body fat for most, but not all, children and teens. BMI does not measure body fat directly, but research has shown that BMI correlates to direct measures of body fat, such as underwater weighing. Because it is inexpensive and easy to do, BMI is used as an alternative to direct measures of body fat.

For children, the BMI is age- and sex-specific; it is often referred to as BMI-for-age. The easiest way to determine BMI is to use the Centers for Disease Control and Prevention's (CDC) Calculator for Teens and Children at http://apps.nccd.cdc.gov/dnpabmi/Calculator.aspx. The calculator requires date of birth, date of measurement, sex, and height and weight without shoes and heavy clothes. The calculator reports the BMI and the BMI-for-age percentile and their weight status category as shown in Table 13.1. Percentiles are the most commonly used indicator to

TABLE 13.1 CDC weight status categories with BMI age for percentile rankings

Weight Status	CDC Age for Percentile Ranking
Underweight	Less than the 5th percentile
Healthy Weight	5th percentile to less than the 85th percentile
At Risk of Overweight	85th percentile to less than the 95th percentile
Overweight	Equal to or greater than the 95th percentile

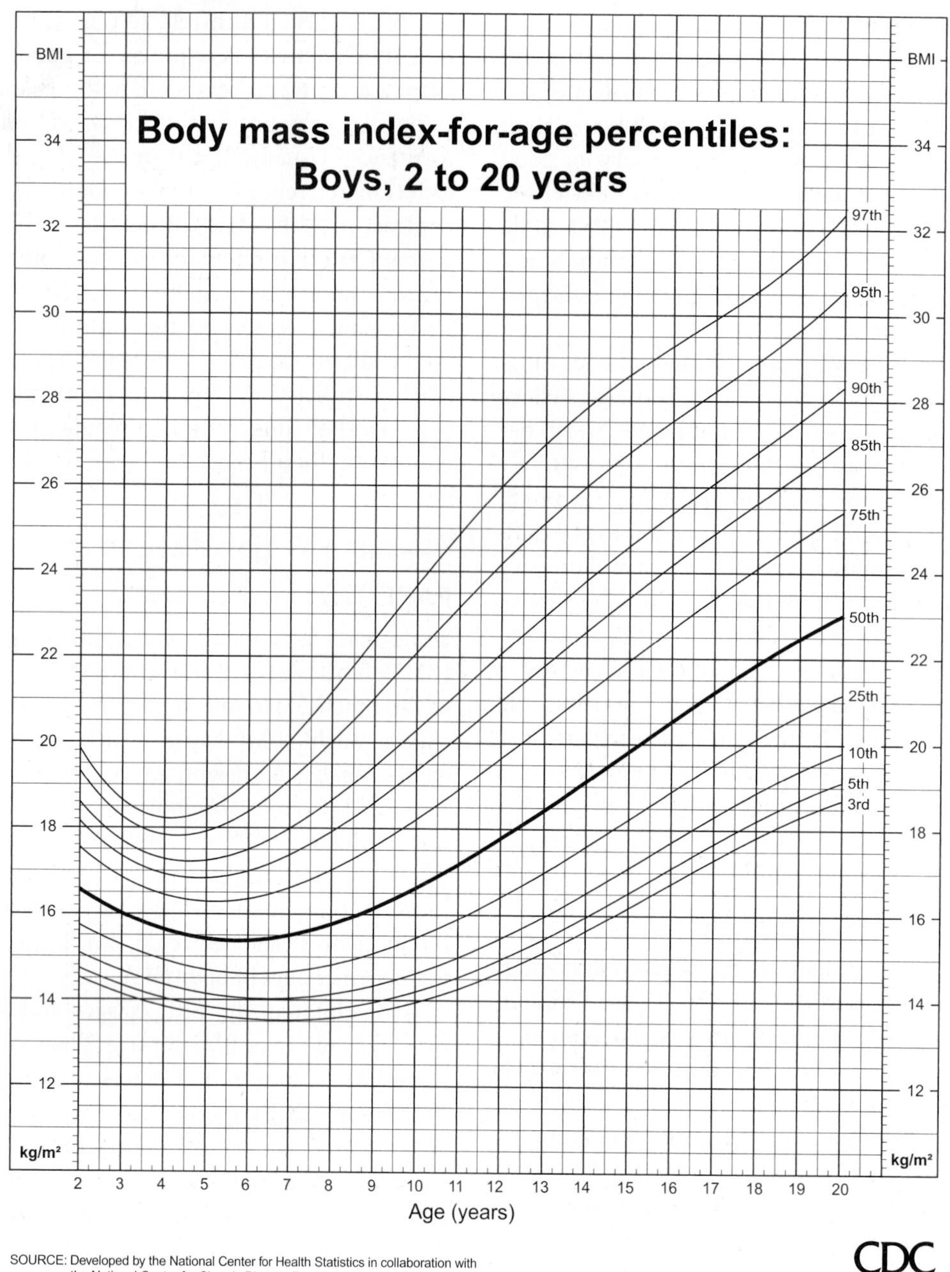

FIGURE 13.2 Boys' body mass index-for-age percentiles: 2 to 20 years.

assess the size and growth patterns of individual children in the United States. The percentile indicates the relative position of the child's BMI number among children of the same sex and age.

Teachers can use the CDC's BMI age for percentiles charts to show parents how their child's BMI score compares to those of other students the same age and sex (Figures 13.2 and 13.3). Parents can see if their child falls into healthy weight percentiles or decide whether they want to consult a professional if their child falls into the other categories. The teacher must remember that the BMI is an estimate, and health professionals need to do further analysis and use different methods to see if other issues need to be addressed. The major purpose of sharing BMI with parents is to alert them to potential issues.

SHOULD PERFORMANCE RECOGNITION AWARDS BE USED?

For years, award systems have been used to recognize students who demonstrate high levels of fitness performance. Originally, award systems were meant to motivate students to improve their fitness level; but research shows that performance awards usually motivate only students who

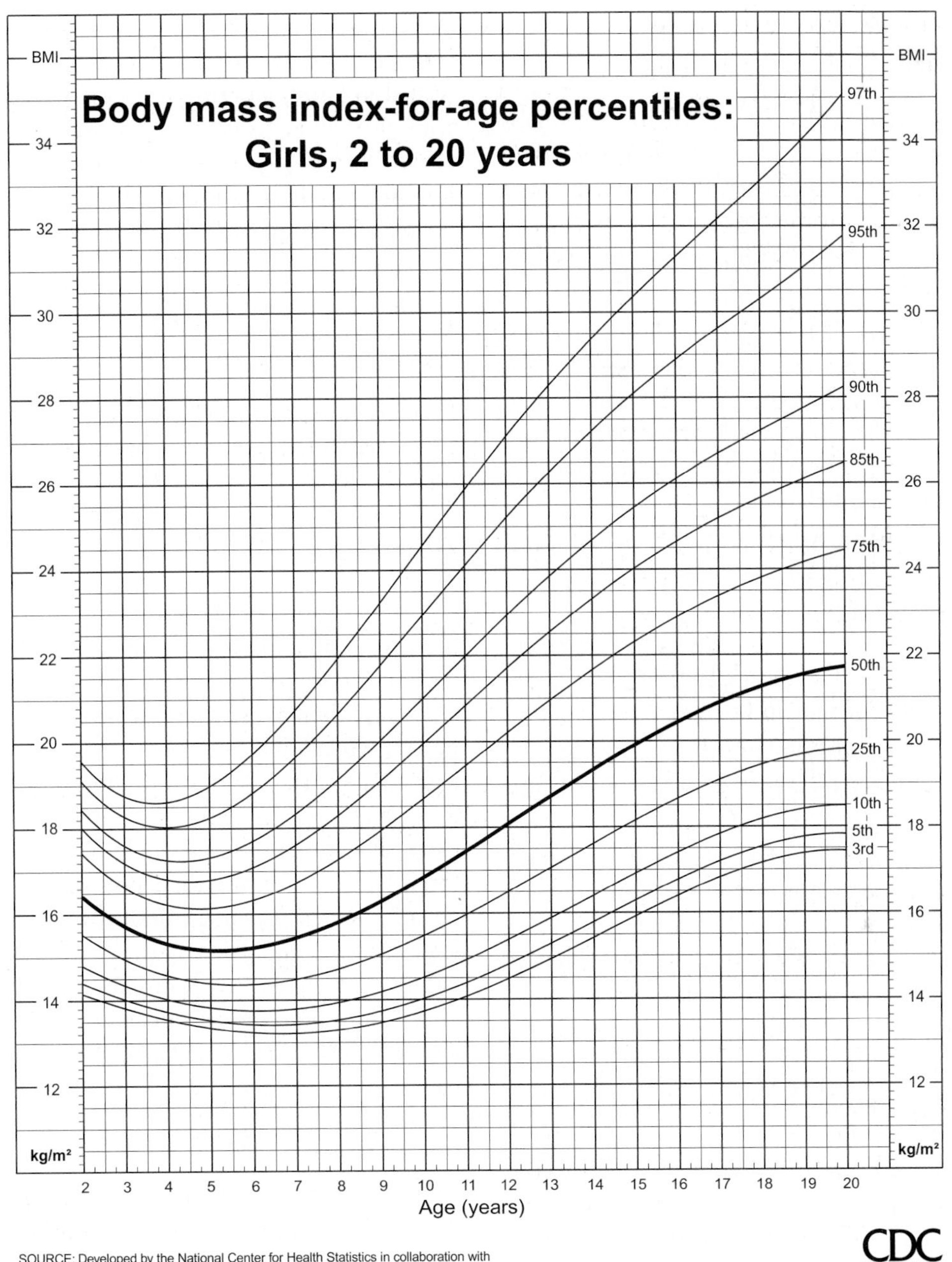

FIGURE 13.3 Girls' body mass index-for-age percentiles: 2 to 20 years.

believe they can earn them (Corbin et al., 1990; Corbin, Lovejoy, & Whitehead, 1988). Many students find it impossible to earn such awards and often feel there is no use in trying. Fitness awards focus on a single episode of accomplishment, making the act of participating in daily activity less important than earning an award. Students learn that the only thing that counts with fitness is performance on the yearly test.

Reward systems that focus on improvement look at short-term changes. Fitness award systems ask students to look at their immediate health status. Studies show that students who achieve at an elite level do so because they are genetically gifted (Bouchard et al., 1992). Gifted students who can pass the test without training start to believe they do not have to exercise regularly. If awards are used, it is best to reward participation in regular activity (behavior) rather than fitness performance. The physical education teacher's role is to encourage lifelong behavior. When the focus is on long-term behaviors, instruction emphasizes participation in regular and moderate activity.

Awards are not recommended. They are extrinsic and not available to all children, and children need to be taught in a way that does not undermine their intrinsic motivation. If for some reason awards are used, try to consider and incorporate these points:

1. Base awards on achievement of challenging, yet attainable goals (Locke & Lathan, 1985). Difficult goals fail to elicit effort from students (Harter, 1978). Students least likely to try for an award are those with low self-esteem; they are probably the students who most need to achieve such goals.
2. If fitness goals do not seem attainable to students, "learned helplessness" sets in (Harter, 1978). This phenomenon occurs when children believe there is no use in trying to reach the goals. Learned helplessness often occurs when performance rather than participation or effort is rewarded.
3. If children's activity is being motivated by an award system, phase it out as soon as possible. Awards do motivate primary-grade children; however, by age 9 or 10, children start to see the rewards as bribery to do something (Whitehead & Corbin, 1991). Gradually removing awards helps students learn that participation should be done for intrinsic and personal reasons.
4. Develop an alternative, long-term approach that focuses on behavior rather than a single outcome by giving awards that recognize students for regular participation in activity. All students can earn these awards, which help establish lifelong activity habits. This approach also supports research cited in the Surgeon General's report on the benefits of moderate to vigorous physical activity (USDHHS, 1996).

EVALUATING STUDENTS WITH DISABILITIES

If there is a school-wide fitness testing program, it makes sense to assure that students with disabilities also have the same opportunity. The Surgeon General's report on Physical Activity and Health (USDHHS, 1996) points out that people with disabilities are less likely to engage in regular moderate physical activity than are people without disabilities, yet they have similar needs to promote health and prevent unnecessary disease. For most children with disabilities, the Fitnessgram test (Cooper, 2008) meets their needs for identifying health-related fitness. However, if the Fitnessgram is unsuitable for specific students, other alternatives are available—such as the Brockport Physical Fitness Test by Winnick and Short (1999). This test has been standardized for students with intellectual disabilities, spinal cord injuries, and visual impairments. An excellent resource covering these issues in more depth is the text by Horvat, Block, and Kelly (2007). The authors examine assessment issues related to motor development and motor skill performance, physical fitness, posture and gait, and behavior and social competencies.

Certainly, this topic requires more coverage than the present text can offer. Regardless of the fitness test used, all students must receive equal treatment and consideration related to health and fitness issues. A final caveat: Children with disabilities usually fail to accumulate enough daily activity. Increasing their daily physical activity may be more important than evaluating fitness levels because physical activity is a lifestyle change that will serve them throughout life.

CREATE POSITIVE ATTITUDES TOWARD FITNESS

Fitness activity is neither good nor bad. The way you teach fitness activities determines how your students feel about making fitness a part of their lifestyles. Here are some strategies for making physical activity a positive learning experience.

PERSONALIZE FITNESS ACTIVITIES

Students who cannot perform exercises are not likely to develop a positive attitude toward physical activity. For example, children in grades 1–5 are top heavy. Their oversized heads (in relation to their bodies) make it difficult to do fitness activities such as push-ups or sit-ups. (The abdominal and upper-body strength activities later in this chapter will allow all children to succeed.) To develop positive attitudes toward activity, fitness experiences should allow children to determine their personal workloads. Use time as the workload variable, and ask children to do the best they can within a time limit. People dislike and fear experiences they view as forced on them from an external source. Voluntary long-term exercise is more likely when individuals are internally driven to do their best.

EXPOSE CHILDREN TO A VARIETY OF FITNESS ACTIVITIES

By offering children a variety of fitness opportunities, teachers can decrease the monotony of doing the same routines week after week and help students discover the fitness activities they enjoy. Students are willing to accept activities they dislike if they know they will soon experience some they enjoy. A yearlong routine of calisthenics and 1-mile runs forces children, regardless of ability and interest, to participate in the same routine. Systematically changing fitness activities is a significant way to help students feel positive about fitness.

GIVE STUDENTS POSITIVE FEEDBACK ABOUT THEIR EFFORT

Teacher feedback contributes to the way children view fitness activities. Immediate, accurate, and specific feedback regarding effort encourages continued participation. When offered in a positive way, feedback can stimulate children to extend their participation beyond the gym. Reinforce all children, not just those performing at high levels. All children need feedback and reinforcement even if they cannot perform at an elite level.

TEACH PHYSICAL SKILLS AND FITNESS

Physical education has two major objectives: fitness and skill development. Skills are the tools that many adults use to maintain personal fitness. These people maintain fitness through skill-based activities such as tennis, badminton, swimming, golf, basketball, aerobics, bicycling, and so on. People who feel competent in an activity are much more likely to participate as adults. Some states mandate fitness testing, leading teachers to worry that their students will not pass. Unfortunately, some teachers sacrifice skill development to gain more time for teaching fitness. School programs must graduate students with requisite entry skills in a variety of activities.

BE A ROLE MODEL

Appearance, attitude, and actions speak loudly about teachers and their values regarding fitness. Teachers who display physical vitality, take pride in being active, participate in activities with children, and are physically fit will positively influence children to maintain an active lifestyle. It is unreasonable to expect teachers to complete fitness routines 9 times a day, 5 days a week. However, teachers periodically must exercise with a class to show their willingness to do what they ask students to do.

Students love to see their teachers demonstrate skills. As much as you may want to impress them with a hard kick or throw, slow a demonstration and present it step-by-step, accounting for any safety cues they may need to be aware of when performing the movement themselves.

CARE ABOUT CHILDREN'S ATTITUDES

Attitudes dictate how students participate in activity. Too often, adults want to force fitness on children in an effort to make them all physically fit. This results in insensitivity to the feelings of participants. Training does not result in lifetime fitness. When students are trained without concern for their feelings, the result will be fit children who may hate physical activity. A negative attitude is difficult to change. Students should not avoid fitness activity, but they must enjoy the experience. Do not funnel all students into one type of fitness activity. Running may harm the health of obese children; lean, uncoordinated students may not enjoy contact activities.

The fitness experience works best when it is a challenge rather than a threat. A *challenge* is an experience that participants feel they can accomplish. A *threat* is a task that seems impossible no matter what the student does. The student, not the teacher, decides whether an activity is a challenge or a threat. Listen carefully to students rather than telling them they "should do it for their own good."

START EASY, AND PROGRESS SLOWLY

Developing fitness is a journey, not a destination. No teacher wants students to become fit and then quit being active. A rule of thumb is to have students start at a level they can *accomplish* successfully. This usually means self-directed workloads within a specific time frame. Do not force students into heavy workloads too soon. Start easy, ensure success, and gradually increase the workload. This approach prevents the discouragement of failure and excessive muscle soreness. When students successfully accomplish activities, they develop a system of self-talk and feel positive about their exercise behavior. Students thus minimize self-criticism and the feeling that they are not living up to their own or others' standards.

USE LOW-INTENSITY ACTIVITY

Make activity appropriate to the child's developmental level. The amount of activity needed for good health is dictated by two variables—intensity and duration. Most children participate in high-volume–low-intensity activity because they have several opportunities for activity each day. This naturally occurring activity is consistent with their developmental level. In contrast, most adults are involved in low amounts of high-intensity–low-volume activity because they have little time for activity each day. This contrast of activity styles leads adults to believe that children need to participate in high-intensity activities to receive health benefits.

Adults often think children are unfit because they do not like to participate in high-intensity fitness activities. This focus on high-intensity activity can discourage some children and burn them out at an early age. Children are the most active segment of society (Rowland, 1990), and it is important to maintain and encourage this trait through moderate to vigorous activity. When teachers and parents reinforce regular, low-intensity activity, fitness follows to the extent possible for each child, given heredity and maturation level.

DEVELOP AN UNDERSTANDING OF PHYSICAL FITNESS PRINCIPLES

Physical education instruction should teach habits that carry over to out-of-school activities. No matter how often students participate in physical education, they need to learn the principles of physical fitness as well as the practice of physical activity. When students are not taught fitness activities, they learn that such activities are unimportant or not valued by teachers and the school. Children are experiential; they learn by participating, and they develop perceptions based on those experiences. If physical activities are taught in school, students begin to learn the role of daily activity in a healthy lifestyle. Children are taught at a tender age how to brush their teeth, so they learn the habit of protecting their teeth for a lifetime. It is just as important to teach children the habit of being active so their physical health does not decay.

Teaching students different ways to develop and maintain fitness (even if only 1 day per week) demonstrates that the school values health and exercise as part of a balanced lifestyle. What better outcome than to teach students how to maintain a balanced fitness program for life? Consider these suggestions for integrating fitness concepts into the physical education program.

1. Provide basic explanations of rudimentary anatomy and kinesiology. Children can learn the names and locations of major bones and muscle groups, including how they function in moving various joints.
2. Provide an understanding of how fitness is developed. Explain the value of the procedures followed in class sessions so children understand the purpose of all fitness development tasks. Also teach children the components of a lifelong personal fitness program.
3. Bring the class together at the end of a lesson to discuss key fitness points to help students understand why fitness is important. Learning to value being physically fit, to apply the principles of exercise, and to see how fitness can be part of their lifestyle can positively alter students' views of physical activity. To share cognitive information, teachers can establish a muscle of the week, construct educational bulletin boards to illustrate fitness concepts, or send home handouts on principles of fitness development.
4. Develop cognition of the importance of fitness to health. Help students understand how and why to perform fitness activities. They need to know the benefits of maintaining a minimal fitness level.
5. Place bulletin boards in the teaching area to explain components of the physical education program to parents and students. Bulletin boards can feature skill techniques, motivational reminders, and upcoming fitness activities. Classroom teachers are required to develop bulletin boards for their classes; physical education teachers can enhance their credibility by designing visual aids for the gymnasium.
6. Use music to accompany fitness routines and motivate the students. Exercise videotapes are an excellent medium for beginning a new fitness activity.
7. Help children understand the values of physical fitness and the physiology of its development and maintenance. Homework dealing with the cognitive aspects of fitness development communicates to parents that their children are gaining knowledge for a lifetime.
8. Emphasize self-testing programs that teach children to evaluate personal fitness levels (see page 139) without concern that others may be judging them. Fitness and activity are personal matters for most adults, and children should receive the same consideration.

AVOID HARMFUL PRACTICES AND EXERCISES

The following points contraindicate certain exercise practices and should be considered when offering fitness instruction. For in-depth coverage of contraindicated exercises, see Corbin, Lindsey, and Welk (2007).

1. The following techniques (Macfarlane, 1993) should be avoided when performing abdominal exercises that lift the head and trunk off the floor:
   - Avoid placing the hands behind the head or high on the neck. This may cause hyperflexion and injury to the discs when the elbows swing forward to help pull the body up.
   - Keep the knees bent. Straight legs cause the hip flexor muscles to be used earlier and more forcefully, making it difficult to maintain proper pelvic tilt.
   - Do not hold the feet on the floor. Having another student secure the feet places more force on the lumbar vertebrae and may lead to lumbar hyperextension.
   - Do not lift the buttocks and lumbar region off the floor. This also causes the hip flexor muscles to contract vigorously.
2. Two types of stretching activities have been used to develop flexibility. Ballistic stretching (strong bouncing movement), once the most common method, has been discouraged for many years because it was thought to increase delayed-onset muscle soreness. The other method, static stretching, involves increasing the stretch to the point of discomfort, backing off slightly until the position can be held comfortably, and stretching for an extended time. Static stretching has been advocated because it is thought to reduce muscle soreness and prevent injury. One study (Smith et al., 1993) disputed the muscle soreness and tissue damage theory with findings that both ballistic and static stretching produce increases in muscle soreness. In fact, static stretching actually induced significantly more soreness than did ballistic stretching. Static stretching is an excellent choice, but ballistic stretching is probably not as harmful as once thought.

3. If forward flexion is done from a sitting position in an effort to touch the toes, the bend should be from the hips, not from the waist, and it should be done with one leg flexed. In response to this concern, the Fitnessgram backsaver sit-and-reach test item is now done with one leg flexed to reduce stress on the lower back.
4. Straight-leg raises from a supine position should be avoided because they may strain the lower back. The problem can be somewhat alleviated by placing the hands under the small of the back, but it is probably best to avoid such exercises altogether.
5. Deep knee bends (full squats) and the duck walk should be avoided. They may damage the knee joints and have little developmental value. Flexing the knee joint to 90 degrees and returning to a standing position is more beneficial.
6. When stretching from a standing position, students should not hyperextend their knees. The knee joint should be relaxed rather than locked. It is often effective to have students do their stretching with bent knees; this reminds them not to hyperextend the joint. In all stretching activities, allow students to judge their own range of motion. Expecting all students to be able to touch their toes is unrealistic. If you are concerned about touching the toes from this position, have them do so from a sitting position with one leg flexed.
7. Avoid activities that place stress on the neck. Examples of such activities include the Inverted Bicycle, Wrestler's Bridge, and abdominal exercises with the hands behind the head.
8. Do not have students perform the so-called hurdler's stretch. This activity is done in the sitting position with one leg forward and the other leg bent and to the rear. This stretch places undue pressure on the knee joint of the bent leg. Substitute a stretch using a similar position with one leg straight in front and the other leg bent with the foot placed in the crotch area.
9. Avoid stretches that demand excessive back arching. An example: In a prone position, the student reaches back and grabs the ankles. By pulling and arching, the exerciser can hyperextend the lower back. This stresses the discs and stretches the abdominal muscles, which most people do not need to stretch.

IMPLEMENT A YEARLONG FITNESS PLAN

Developing a yearlong plan of fitness instruction helps ensure that students have a variety of experiences. It also allows for progression and offers a well-rounded program of instruction. Plan physical fitness instruction like you would plan skill development sequences. The *Dynamic Physical Education Curriculum Guide: Lesson Plans for Implementation* (Pangrazi, 2010) offers a yearlong sequence of fitness units for children at all three developmental levels.

When organizing a yearlong plan for fitness instruction, consider these points. Fitness units should vary in length depending on the students' age. Children need to experience a variety of routines that maintain a high level of motivation. During the elementary school years, trying different types of activities is more important than following progressive, demanding fitness routines. Adhere to one principle: *No single method of developing fitness is best for all children.* Offer a variety of routines and activities so students learn that fitness is not lockstep and unbending. The yearlong plan should offer activities that allow all children to succeed at one time or another during the school year.

The yearlong plan reveals that routines contain more structured activities as children grow older. Most of the activities listed for Developmental Level I children are unstructured and allow for wide variation of performance. For children in Developmental Levels II and III, emphasis on proper technique and performance increases. However, do not expect every student to do every activity exactly the same. It is unrealistic to think that an obese child will be able to perform at a level similar to that of a lean child. Allow for variation in performance while emphasizing the importance of "doing your best."

13

IMPLEMENTING FITNESS ROUTINES

Fitness routines are exclusively dedicated to presenting a variety of fitness activities. Here are some suggestions for successfully implementing fitness routines.

1. Precede fitness instruction with a 2- to 3-minute warm-up period. Introductory activities are useful for this purpose because they allow students to prepare for strenuous activity.
2. Be sure the fitness part of the daily lesson, including warm-up, lasts only about 10 to 13 minutes. Some will argue that more time is needed to develop adequate fitness, but

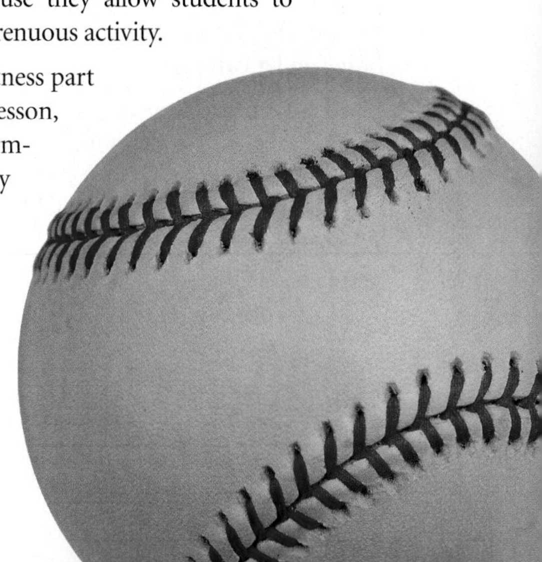

most teachers have only a 20- to 30-minute instruction period. Because skill instruction is part of a balanced physical education program, compromise is necessary to ensure that all phases of the program are covered.

3. Use activities that exercise all body parts and cover the major fitness components. Children are capable performers when workloads are geared to their age, fitness level, and abilities.
4. Use a variety of fitness routines comprising sequential exercises for total body development as a recommended alternative to a yearlong program of regimented calisthenics. To replace the traditional approach of doing the same routine day in and day out, offer a diverse array of activities appealing to the children's interests and fitness levels.
5. Assume an active role in fitness instruction. Children respond positively to role modeling. Teachers who actively exercise with children, hustle to assist students having difficulty, and make exercise fun can instill in children the value of an active lifestyle.
6. When determining workloads for children, remember that the available alternatives are time or repetitions. Base the workload on time rather than on a specific number of repetitions, so students can adjust their workload within personal limits. Beginning dosages for exercises should start at a level where *all* children will succeed. The best way to ensure success is to allow students to adjust the workload to suit their capabilities. Using a specific amount of time per exercise allows less gifted children to perform successfully. Do not expect all children to perform exactly the same workload.
7. Take advantage of interval training with students. Alternate stretching and strength development exercises with aerobic exercises. This permits students to recover from an aerobic activity while stretching. It also allows for recovery time after strength development activities. Most routines are effective in 30-second intervals; any longer, and students become fatigued or bored and go off task.
8. Use audiotapes to time fitness activity segments so you are free to move throughout the area and offer individualized instruction. The easiest way to time segments is to alternate 30-second intervals of music and silence. When music is playing, it signals that students are to perform an aerobic activity. The silence interval signals stretching or strength development activity.
9. *Never* use fitness activities as punishment. Students must not view push-ups and running as things you do when you misbehave. The opportunity to exercise should be a privilege as well as an enjoyable experience. Think of the money adults spend to exercise. Take a positive approach, and offer students a chance to jog with a friend when they do something well. This allows them to visit and to exercise with a positive feeling. Be an effective salesperson; sell your students on the joy of activity and the benefits of physical fitness.

FITNESS ACTIVITIES FOR DEVELOPMENTAL LEVEL I

Fitness activities for young children can teach components of physical fitness as well as exercise various body areas. All the fitness routines that follow alternate strength and flexibility activities with cardiovascular activity. Most routines include strength and flexibility activities. Together, the introductory and fitness activity offer broad coverage by including activities for each of these five areas: arm–shoulder girdle, trunk, abdomen, legs and cardiorespiratory system, and flexibility.

MODIFIED FITNESS ACTIVITIES THAT ENSURE A SUCCESSFUL EXPERIENCE

Too often, students are asked to take on an impossible fitness load. For example, look at the developmental characteristics of 5- through 8-year-old children. Their heads are about 90% of adult size, their trunks are 50% of adult size, and their legs are short (30–40% of adult size). There is no way for these top-heavy, short-legged little people to succeed at doing push-ups and sit-ups. Yet, time and again, teachers ask children of this age to do these important exercises—only to see them fail. Small wonder that most children enter the intermediate grades hating push-ups and sit-ups. The following fitness activities are modifications that can help ensure a successful experience. Present the activities early in the year to students in all grades. Then, when push-ups or abdominal activities are assigned, students can select any of the modified activities they feel they can perform successfully.

Students must be able to select activities they enjoy. The student, not the teacher, must dictate workload. No teacher knows how many repetitions of an activity a child can perform. Allowing each student to do his or her best is ideal. Fitness is not effective when forced down a student's throat. Most people will avoid future activity if they feel pressured and unsuccessful in their early experiences with fitness activities.

Alternate stretching and flexibility activities with aerobic activities to avoid fatiguing students. When pushed too hard aerobically, children show their fatigue in many different ways (i.e., complaining, quitting, misbehaving, or sitting out). Be aware of how far to push and when to ease up.

Arm–Shoulder Girdle Strength Activities

Here are some activities to help students develop arm–shoulder girdle strength. They precede the push-up activities and should be practiced first. All the challenges encourage students to support their body weight with the arms and shoulders.

1. Practice taking your weight completely on your hands.
2. In crab position, keep your feet in place and make your body go in a big circle. Do the same from the push-up position.
3. In crab position, go forward, backward, and to the side. Turn around, move very slowly, and so on.
4. Successively from standing, supine, and hands-and-knees positions: Swing one limb (arm or leg) at a time, in different directions and at different levels.
5. Combine two limb movements (arm-arm, leg-leg, or arm-leg combinations) in the same direction and in opposite directions. Vary the levels.
6. Swing the arms or legs back and forth and go into giant circles. In supine position, make giant circles with the feet.
7. In a bent-over position, swing the arms as if swimming. Try a backstroke or a breaststroke. What does a sidestroke look like?
8. Make the arms go like a windmill. Turn the arms in different directions. Accelerate and decelerate.
9. Show other ways you can circle your arms.
10. Pretend that bees are swarming around your head. Brush them off and keep them away.

Push-Up Lead-Up Activities

The push-up (Figure 13.4) and crab positions are excellent for developing upper-body strength. Allow students to rest with one knee on the floor in the up position rather than lie on the floor. Let students select a challenge they feel able to accomplish rather than being forced to fail at doing push-ups. Many of the directives listed for the push-up position also can be done in the crab position. As students develop strength, they make a controlled descent to the floor from the up position. The following activities can be done with one knee down (beginning) or in the regular push-up (more challenging) position.

FIGURE 13.4 Push-up position.

1. Hold your body off the floor (in push-up position).
2. Wave at a friend. Wave with the other arm. Shake a leg at someone. Do these challenges in the crab position.
3. Lift one foot high. Now lift the other foot.
4. Bounce both feet up and down. Move the feet out from each other while bouncing.
5. Inch the feet up to the hands and go back again. Inch the feet up to the hands and then inch the hands out to return to the push-up position.
6. Reach up with one hand and touch the other shoulder behind the back.
7. Lift both hands from the floor. Try clapping the hands.
8. Turn over so that your back is to the floor. Now complete the turn to push-up position.
9. Walk on your hands and feet. Try two hands and one foot. Walk in the crab position (tummy toward the ceiling).
10. With one knee on the ground, touch your nose to the floor between your hands. As you get stronger, move your head forward a little and touch your nose to the floor. (The farther the nose touches the floor in front of the hands, the more strength is demanded.)
11. Lower your body an inch at a time until your chest touches the floor. Return to the up position any way possible.
12. Pretend you are a tire going flat. Gradually lower yourself to the floor.

Abdominal Strength Lead-Up Activities

The basic position for exercising the abdominal muscles is supine on the floor or on a mat. Challenges should lift the upper and lower portions of the body from the floor, either singly or together. Since young children are top heavy, they find it difficult to perform most abdominal exercises. Therefore, begin early abdominal development with students lying on the floor and lifting the head. Have students progress to a sitting position and gradually lower (with head tucked) the upper body backward to the floor.

1. Lift your head from the floor and look at your toes. Wink your right eye and wiggle your left foot. Reverse.
2. In a supine position, "wave" a leg at a friend. Use the other leg. Use both legs.
3. Lift your knees up slowly, an inch at a time.
4. Pick up your heels about 6 inches off the floor; swing them back and forth. Cross your feet and twist them.
5. Sit up any way you can and touch both sets of toes with your hands.
6. Sit up any possible way and touch your right toes with your left hand. Do it the other way.
7. In a sitting position, lean the upper body backward without falling. How long can you hold this position?
8. From a sitting position, lower your body slowly to the floor. Vary the positions of your arms (across the tummy, the chest, and above the head).
9. From a supine position, curl up by pulling up on your legs.
10. From a supine position, hold your shoulders off the floor.
11. From a supine position, lift your legs and head off the floor.

Trunk Development Activities

Movements that include bending, stretching, swaying, twisting, reaching, and forming shapes help develop trunk strength. No particular sequence exists, but the activity should move from simple to more complex. Vary the position the child is to take: standing, lying down, kneeling, or sitting.

Bending

1. Bend in different ways.
2. Bend as many parts of your body as you can.
3. Make different shapes by bending 2, 3, and 4 parts of your body.
4. Bend the arms and knees in different ways and on different levels.
5. Try different ways of bending your fingers and wrist of one hand with the other. Use some resistance (explain *resistance*). Add body bends.

Stretching

1. Keep one foot in place and stretch your arms in different directions; move with the free foot. Stretch at different levels.
2. Lie on the floor; stretch one leg different ways in space. Stretch one leg in one direction and the other in another direction.
3. Stretch as slowly as you can and then snap back to original position.
4. Stretch with different arm-leg combinations in several directions.
5. See how much space on the floor you can cover by stretching.
6. Combine bending and stretching movements.

Swaying and Twisting

1. Sway your body back and forth in different directions. Change the position of your arms.
2. Sway your body, bending over.
3. Sway your head from side to side.
4. Select a part of your body and twist it as far as you can in one direction and then in the opposite direction.
5. Twist your body at different levels.
6. Twist two or more parts of your body at the same time.
7. Twist one part of your body while untwisting another.
8. Twist your head to see as far back as you can.
9. Twist like a spring. Twist like a screwdriver.

10. Stand on one foot and twist your body. Untwist.
11. While seated, make different shapes by twisting.

Leg and Cardiorespiratory Development Activities

Leg and cardiorespiratory development activities include a range of movement challenges in general space or in place. Children fatigue and recover quickly. Take advantage of this trait by alternating cardiorespiratory activities with strength and flexibility exercises.

Running Patterns

Running in different directions

Running in place

Ponies in the Stable (page 329)

Tortoise and Hare (page 329)

European Rhythmic Running (page 331)

Running and stopping

Running and changing direction on signal

Jumping and Hopping Patterns

Jumping in different directions back and forth over a spot

Jumping or hopping in, out, over, and around hoops, individual mats, or jump ropes laid on the floor

Jumping or hopping back and forth over lines, or hopping down the lines

Rope Jumping

Individual rope jumping—allow choice

Combinations

Many combinations of locomotor movements can be used to motivate students. Here are some possible challenges.

1. Run in place. Do some running steps in place without stopping.
2. Skip or gallop for 30 seconds.
3. Slide all the way around the gymnasium.
4. Alternate hopping or jumping for 30 seconds with 30 seconds of rest.
5. Jump in place while twisting your arms and upper body.
6. Do 10 skips, 10 gallops, and finish with 30 running steps.
7. Hold hands with a friend and do 100 jumps.
8. Jump rope as many times as possible without missing.
9. Hop back and forth over a line from one end of the gym to the other.
10. Try to run as fast as you can. How long can you keep going?

ANIMAL MOVEMENTS

Animal activities are enjoyable for Developmental Level I children, who enjoy mimicking animal sounds and movements. Most of the animal movements are done with the body weight on all four limbs, which helps develop the arms and shoulders. Challenge students to move randomly throughout the area, across the gym, or between cones set at a specific distance. Increase workload by extending the distance or the amount of time students do each animal walk. To avoid excessive fatigue, alternate the animal movements with stretching activities. Here are some animal movements that can be used. See Chapter 20 for descriptions of more animal movements.

- *Puppy Walk.* Move on all fours (not the knees). Keep the head up and move lightly.
- *Lion Walk.* Move on all fours while keeping the back arched. Move deliberately and lift the "paws" to simulate moving without sound.
- *Elephant Walk.* Move heavily throughout the area, swinging the head back and forth like an elephant's trunk.
- *Seal Walk.* Move by using the arms to propel the body. Allow the legs to drag along the floor, like a seal would move.
- *Injured Coyote.* Move using only three limbs. Hold the injured limb off the floor. Vary the walk by specifying which limb is injured.
- *Crab Walk.* Move on all fours with the tummy facing the ceiling. Try to keep the back as straight as possible.
- *Rabbit Jump.* Start in a squatting position with the hands on the floor. Reach forward with the hands and support the body weight. Jump both feet toward the hands. Repeat the sequence.

FITNESS GAMES

Fitness games are highly motivating and excellent for cardiovascular endurance. Instruct all students to keep moving during the game. A great way to be sure this occurs is to play games that do not eliminate players. A player who tags someone is no longer "it," and the person tagged becomes the tagger. This makes it difficult for players to tell who the tagger is, and it ensures that players cannot stop and stand when the tagger is somewhere nearby. If various games stipulate a "safe" position, allow players to maintain this position for only 5 seconds. Because fitness games primarily focus on cardiovascular fitness, alternate the games with strength and flexibility activities. The following are some games that can be played.

- *Stoop Tag.* Players cannot be tagged when they stoop.
- *Back-to-Back Tag.* Players are safe when they stand back-to-back. Other positions can be designated (toe-to-toe, knee-to-knee, etc.).
- *Train Tag:* Form groups of 3 or 4 and make a train by holding the hips of the other players. Three or four players are designated as "it" and try to hook onto the rear of the train. If they are successful, the player at the front of the train becomes the new it.
- *Color Tag.* Players are safe when they stand on a specified color. Leaders may change the "safe" color at any time.
- *Elbow-Swing Tag.* Players cannot be tagged as long as they are performing an elbow swing with another player.
- *Balance Tag.* Players are safe when they are balanced on one body part.
- *Push-up Tag.* Players are safe when they are in push-up position. Other exercise positions, such as bent knee curl-up, V-up, and crab position, can be used.
- *Group Tag:* Players are safe from being tagged only when they are all in a group (its size specified by the leader) and holding hands. For example, the number might be "4," which means that students holding hands in groups of four are safe.

MINIATURE CHALLENGE COURSES

Miniature challenge courses (Figure 13.5) can be set up indoors or outdoors. The distance between the start and finish lines depends on the type of activity. A good starting point is a distance of about 30 feet, but this can be adjusted. Mark the course boundaries with cones.

Each child performs the specified locomotor movement from the start to the finish line and then jogs back to the start. Movement is continuous. Give directions in advance so that no delay occurs. Limit the number of children on each course to normal squad size or fewer. The following movements can be specified:

- All types of locomotor movements: running, jumping, hopping, sliding, and so on

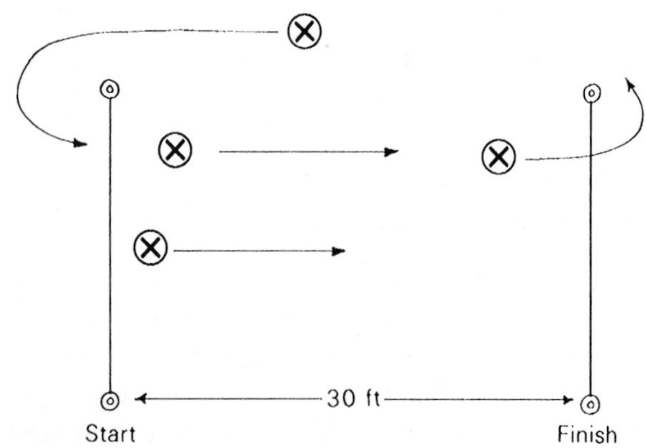

FIGURE 13.5 Miniature challenge course.

- Movements on the floor: crawling, Bear Walk, Seal Crawl, and the like
- Movements over and under obstacles or through tires or hoops

Sample Routine

1. Crawl under a wand set on two cones.
2. Roll down an inclined mat.
3. Logroll up an inclined mat.
4. Move up and down on jumping boxes. Climb on the last box, jump, and roll.
5. Crawl through hoops or bicycle tires held by individual mats.
6. Walk a balance beam.
7. Pull the body down a bench in prone position.
8. Leap over five carpet squares.
9. Move through a tunnel created by four jumping boxes (or benches) covered with a tumbling mat.
10. Hang on a climbing rope for 10 seconds.
11. Crab-walk from one cone to another and back.
12. Run and weave around a series of five cones.

PARACHUTE FITNESS ACTIVITIES

The parachute has long been a popular item in elementary physical education. Usually used to promote teamwork, provide maximum participation, stimulate interest, or play games, the parachute also can be a tool for developing physical fitness. Teachers can develop exciting fitness routines by combining vigorous shaking movements, locomotor circular movement, and selected exercises while holding onto the chute.

Parachute Fitness Activities

1. Jog while holding the chute in the left hand. (music)
2. Shake the chute. (no music)
3. Slide while holding the chute with both hands. (music)
4. Sit and perform curl-ups. (no music)
5. Skip. (music)
6. Freeze, face the center, and stretch the chute tightly. Hold for 8 to 12 seconds. Repeat 5 to 6 times. (no music)
7. Run in place while holding the chute taut at different levels. (music)
8. Sit with legs under the chute. Do a seat-walk toward the center. Return to the perimeter. Repeat 4 to 6 times. (no music)
9. Place the chute on the ground. Jog away from the chute and return on signal. Repeat. (music)
10. Move into push-up position holding the chute with one hand. Shake the chute. (no music)
11. Shake the chute and jump in place. (music)
12. Lie on back with feet under the chute. Shake the chute with the feet. (no music)
13. Hop to the center of the chute and return. Repeat. (music)
14. Sit with feet under the chute. Stretch by touching the toes with the chute. Relax with other stretches while sitting. (no music)

✔ Teaching Hints

1. Tape alternating segments (20 seconds each) of silence and music to signal duration of exercise. Music segments indicate aerobic activity with the parachute; intervals of silence signal using the chute to enhance flexibility and strength development.
2. Space students evenly around the chute. Have them use different hand grips (palms up, down, mixed). Make sure all movements are done under control. Instruct the faster and stronger students to moderate their performance.

WALK, TROT, AND JOG

Four cones outline a square or rectangular area 30 to 40 yards on a side. (Indoors, use the circumference of the gym.) Children are scattered around the perimeter, all facing the same direction. Use a whistle to give signals. On the first whistle, children begin to walk. On the next whistle, they change to a trot. On the third whistle, they jog faster but still under control. Finally, on the fourth whistle, they walk again. Repeat the cycle, allowing faster-moving students to pass on the outside.

Another way to signal change is by drumbeat. One beat signals walk, 2 beats signal trot, and 3 beats signal run. The three movements can be presented in random order. For variation, try other locomotor movements such as running, skipping, galloping, and sliding. At regular intervals, stop students and have them perform various stretching activities and strength development exercises. This allows short rest periods between bouts of activity. Examples of activities are one-leg balance, push-ups, curl-ups, touching the toes, and any other challenges.

Walk, Trot, and Jog

Move to the following signals:

1. One drumbeat—walk.
2. Two drumbeats—trot.
3. Three drumbeats—jog.
4. Whistle—freeze and perform exercises.

Perform various strength and flexibility exercises between bouts of walking, trotting, and jogging. Exercises might include:

- Bend and Twist
- Sitting Stretch
- Push-up Challenges
- Abdominal Challenges
- Body Twist
- Standing Hip Bend

✔ Teaching Hints

1. Tape alternating segments (30 seconds each) of silence and music to signal duration of exercise. Music segments indicate walking, trotting, and jogging activities. Intervals of silence signal performance of the strength and flexibility exercises.
2. Any exercises can be substituted. Try to have students exercise all body parts.

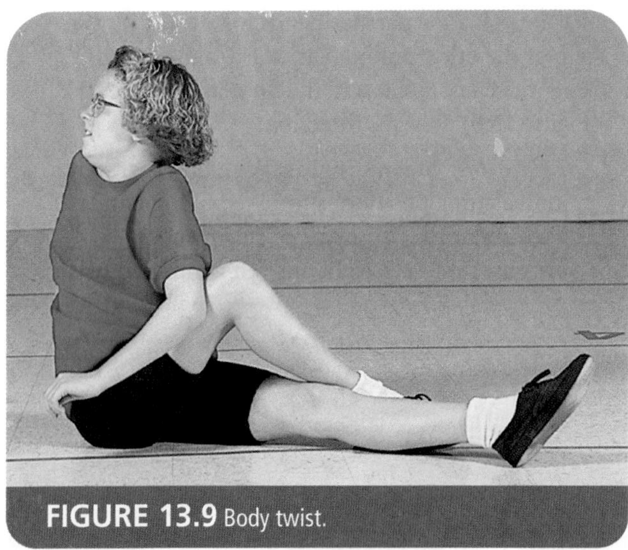

FIGURE 13.9 Body twist.

MOVEMENT: Rotate the upper body toward the right hand and arm. Reverse the position and stretch the other side of the body.

Standing Hip Bend

STARTING POSITION: Stand with the knees slightly flexed, one hand on the hip, and the other arm overhead.

MOVEMENT: Bend to the side with the hand resting on the hip. The arm overhead should point and move in the direction of the stretch with a slight bend at the elbow. Reverse and stretch the opposite side.

Arm–Shoulder Girdle Exercises

Arm–shoulder girdle exercises for this age group include both arm-support and free-arm activities.

Push-Ups

STARTING POSITION: Assume the push-up position (see Figure 13.4 on page 255), holding the body straight from head to heels.

MOVEMENT: Keeping the body straight, bend the elbows and touch the chest to the ground; then straighten the elbows, raising the body in a straight line.

IMPORTANT POINTS: The movement is in the arms. The head is up, with the eyes looking ahead. The chest touches the floor lightly, without receiving the weight of the body. The body remains in a straight line throughout, without sagging or humping.

VARIATION: Some students develop a dislike for push-ups because they are asked to perform them without any modification. Allow students to judge their strength and choose a push-up challenge (page 255) they feel able to accomplish. Instead of asking an entire class to perform a specific number of push-ups, personalize the workload by allowing each child to accomplish as many repetitions as possible of a self-selected push-up challenge in a specified amount of time.

Controlled movement is a goal; speed is not desirable. Push-ups are done at will, allowing each child to achieve individually within a specific time limit.

Reclining Pull-Ups

STARTING POSITION: One student lies in supine position. Her partner is astride, with feet alongside the reclining partner's chest. Partners grasp hands with interlocking fingers, with some other suitable grip, or with an interlocked wrist grip.

MOVEMENT: The student on the floor pulls up with her arms until her chest touches the partner's thighs. The body remains straight, with weight resting on the heels (Figure 13.10). Then she returns to position.

IMPORTANT POINTS: The supporting student keeps the center of gravity well over the feet by maintain-

FIGURE 13.10 Reclining pull-ups.

ing a lifted chest and proper head position. The lower student maintains a straight body during the pull-up and moves only the arms.

VARIATION: Raise as directed (count 1), hold the high position isometrically (counts 2 and 3), return to position (count 4).

Triceps Push-Up

STARTING POSITION: Assume the inverted push-up position with the arms and body held straight.

MOVEMENT: Keeping the body straight, bend the elbows and touch the seat to the ground; then straighten the elbows and raise the body.

IMPORTANT POINTS: The fingers point toward the toes or are turned in slightly. The body is held firm with movement restricted to the arms.

Arm Circles

STARTING POSITION: Stand erect, with feet apart and arms straight out to the side.

MOVEMENT: Do forward and backward circles with palms facing forward, moving arms simultaneously. The number of circles executed before changing can be varied.

IMPORTANT POINTS: Avoid doing arm circles with palms down (particularly backward circles) as it stresses the shoulder joint. Maintain correct posture, keeping the abdominal wall flat and holding the head and shoulders back.

Crab Kick

STARTING POSITION: Crab position, with the body supported on the hands and feet and the back parallel to the floor. The knees are bent at right angles. For all crab positions, keep the seat up and avoid body sag.

MOVEMENT: Kick the right leg up and down (counts 1 and 2; Figure 13.11). Repeat with the left leg (counts 3 and 4).

Crab Alternate-Leg Extension

STARTING POSITION: Assume crab position.

MOVEMENT: On count 1, extend the right leg forward so that it rests on the heel. On count 2, extend the left leg forward and bring the right leg back. Continue alternating.

FIGURE 13.11 Crab kick.

Crab Full-Leg Extension

STARTING POSITION: Assume crab position.

MOVEMENT: On count 1, extend both legs forward so the weight rests on the heels. On count 2, bring both feet back to crab position.

Crab Walk

STARTING POSITION: Assume crab position.

MOVEMENT: Move forward, backward, sideways, and turn in a small circle right and left.

Flying Angel

STARTING POSITION: Stand erect, with feet together and arms at sides.

MOVEMENT: In a smooth, slow, continuous motion, raise the arms forward with elbows extended and then upward, at the same time rising up on the toes and lifting the chest, with eyes following the hands (Figure 13.12 on page 264). Lower the arms sideways in a flying motion and return to starting position.

IMPORTANT POINTS: Keep the abdomen flat throughout to minimize lower back curvature. The head is back and well up. The exercise is done slowly and smoothly, under control.

VARIATION: Move the arms forward as if doing a breaststroke. Then slowly raise the arms, with hands in front of the chest and elbows out, to full

FIGURE 13.12 Flying Angel.

overhead extension. Otherwise, the movement is the same as the Flying Angel.

Abdominal Exercises

For most exercises stressing abdominal development, start from the supine position on the floor or on a mat. When lifting the upper body, begin with a roll-up (curling) action, moving the head first so that the chin touches the chest, thus flattening and stabilizing the lower back curve. Bend the knees to better isolate abdominal muscles and avoid stressing the lower back. When doing abdominal exercises, avoid moving the trunk up to the sitting position (past 45 degrees) since it may cause pain and exacerbate back injury in susceptible individuals (Macfarlane, 1993).

Some children develop a dislike for abdominal work in the early school years. This occurs because they are top heavy and unable to successfully lift their upper body off the floor. To ensure success, allow students to choose an abdominal challenge they feel able to accomplish. Instead of asking an entire class to perform a specified number of curl-ups, personalize the workload by allowing students to accomplish as many repetitions as possible in a specific amount of time using a self-selected abdominal challenge.

Reverse Curl

STARTING POSITION: Lie on the back with the hands on the floor and to the sides of the body.

MOVEMENT: Curl the knees to the chest. The upper body remains on the floor. As abdominal strength increases, the child should lift the buttocks and lower back off the floor.

IMPORTANT POINTS: Roll the knees to the chest and return the feet to the floor after each repetition. The movement is controlled, emphasizing the abdominal contraction.

VARIATIONS:

1. Hold the head off the floor and bring the knees to the chin.
2. Instead of returning the feet to the floor after each repetition, hold them 1 or 2 inches off the floor. This activity requires greater abdominal strength because there is no resting period (feet on floor).

Pelvis Tilter

STARTING POSITION: Lie on the back with feet flat on the floor, knees bent, arms out in wing position, and palms up.

MOVEMENT: Flatten the lower back, bringing it closer to the floor by tensing the lower abdominals and lifting up on the pelvis. Hold for 8 to 12 counts. Tense slowly and release slowly.

Knee Touch Curl-Up

STARTING POSITION: Lie on the back with feet flat, knees bent, and hands flat on top of thighs.

MOVEMENT: Leading with the chin, slide the hands forward until the fingers touch the kneecaps and gradually curl the head and shoulders until the shoulder blades are lifted off the floor (Figure 13.13). Hold for 8 counts and return to position. To avoid stress on the lower back, do not curl up to the sitting position.

Curl-Up

STARTING POSITION: Lie on the back with feet flat, knees bent, and arms on the floor at the side of the body with palms down.

MOVEMENT: Lift the head and shoulders to a 45-degree angle and then back in a 2-count pattern.

FIGURE 13.13 Curl-up.

The hands should slide forward on the floor 3 to 4 inches. The curl-up can also be done as an 8-count exercise, moving up on count 1, holding for 6 counts, and moving down on count 8.

IMPORTANT POINTS: Roll up, with the chin first. The hands remain on the floor.

Curl-Up with Twist

STARTING POSITION: Lie on the back with feet flat and knees bent. Arms are folded and placed across the chest with hands on shoulders.

MOVEMENT: Do a partial curl-up and twist the chest to the left. Repeat, turning the chest to the right (Figure 13.14).

VARIATIONS:

1. Touch the outside of the knee with the elbow.
2. Touch both knees in succession. The sequence is up, touch left, touch right, and down.

FIGURE 13.14 Curl-up with twist.

Leg Extension

STARTING POSITION: Sit on the floor with legs extended and hands on hips.

MOVEMENT: With a quick, vigorous action, raise the knees and bring both heels as close to the seat as possible (Figure 13.15). The movement is a drag with the toes touching lightly. Return to position.

VARIATION: Alternate bringing the knees to the right and left of the head.

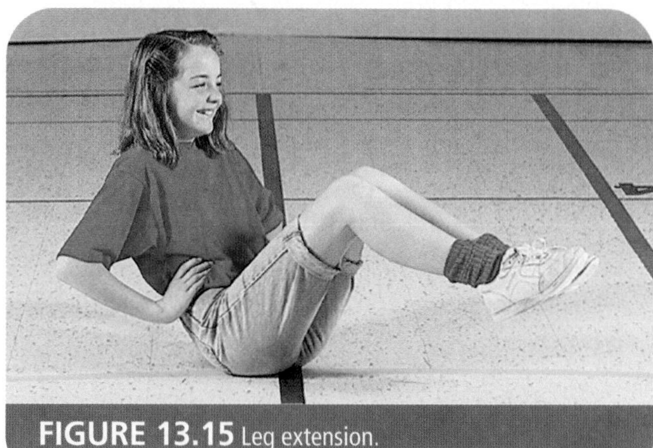

FIGURE 13.15 Leg extension.

13

Abdominal Cruncher

STARTING POSITION: Lie in supine position with feet flat, knees bent, and palms of hands cupped over the ears (not behind the head). An alternate position is to fold the arms across the chest and place the hands on the shoulders.

MOVEMENT: Tuck the chin and curl upward until the shoulder blades leave the floor. Return to the floor with a slow uncurling.

VARIATION: Lift the feet off the floor and bring the knees to waist level. Try to touch the right elbow to the left knee and vice versa while in the crunch position.

Leg and Agility Exercises

Running in Place

STARTING POSITION: Stand with arms bent at the elbows.

MOVEMENT: Run in place. Begin slowly, counting only the left foot. Speed up somewhat, raising the knees to hip height. Then run at full speed, raising the knees hard. Finally, slow down. The run should be on the toes.

VARIATIONS:

1. Tortoise and Hare. Jog slowly in place. On the command "Hare," double the speed. On the command "Tortoise," slow the tempo to the original slow jogging pace.
2. March in place, lifting the knees high and swinging the arms up. Turn right and left on command while marching. Turn completely around to the right and then to the left while marching.
3. Fast Stepping. Step in place for 10 seconds as rapidly as possible. Rest for 10 seconds and repeat five or more times.

Jumping Jack

STARTING POSITION: Stand at attention.

MOVEMENT: On count 1, jump to a straddle position with arms overhead. On count 2, recover to starting position.

VARIATIONS:

1. Begin with the feet in a stride position (forward and back). Change feet with the overhead movement.
2. Instead of bringing the feet together when the arms come down, cross the feet each time, alternating the cross.
3. Upon completing each set of 8 counts, do a quarter turn right. (After four sets, the child is facing in the original direction.) Do the same to the left.
4. *Modified Jumping Jack.* On count 1, jump to a straddle position with arms out to the sides, parallel to the floor, and palms down. On count 2, return to position.

Treadmill

STARTING POSITION: Assume push-up position, except that one leg is brought forward so that the knee is under the chest (Figure 13.16).

MOVEMENT: Reverse the position of the feet, bringing the extended leg forward. Change back again so the original foot is forward. Continue rhythmically alternating feet.

IMPORTANT POINTS: The head is kept up. A full exchange of the legs is made, with the forward knee coming well under the chest each time.

FIGURE 13.16 Treadmill.

Power Jumper

STARTING POSITION: Begin in a semi-crouched position, with knees flexed and arms extended backward.

MOVEMENT: Jump as high as possible and extend the arms upward and overhead.

VARIATIONS:

1. Jump and perform different turns (quarter, half, full).
2. Jump and perform different tasks (such as click heels, slap heels, clap hands, catch an imaginary pass, snare a rebound).

Trunk-Twisting and Bending Exercises

Trunk Twister

STARTING POSITION: Stand with feet shoulder width apart and pointed forward. The hands are cupped and placed loosely over the shoulders, with the elbows out and the chin tucked.

MOVEMENT: Bend downward, keeping the knees relaxed. Recover slightly. Bend downward again and simultaneously rotate the trunk to the left and then to the right (Figure 13.17). Return to original position, pulling the head back, with chin in.

Bear Hug

STARTING POSITION: Stand with feet comfortably spread and hands on hips.

MOVEMENT: Take a long step diagonally right, keeping the left foot anchored in place. Tackle the right leg

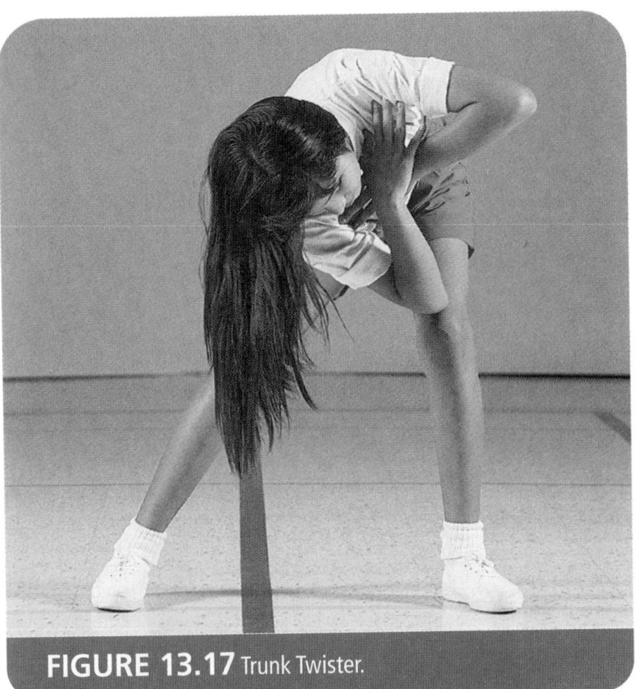
FIGURE 13.17 Trunk Twister.

around the thigh by encircling the thigh with both arms. Squeeze and stretch (Figure 13.18). Return to position. Tackle the left leg. Return to position.

IMPORTANT POINT: The bent leg must not exceed a right angle.

Side Flex

STARTING POSITION: Lie on one side with lower arm extended overhead. The head rests on the lower arm. The legs are extended fully, one on top of the other.

MOVEMENT: Raise the upper arm and leg diagonally (Figure 13.19). Repeat for several counts and then change to the other side.

FIGURE 13.18 Bear Hug.

FIGURE 13.19 Side Flex.

VARIATION: Side Flex, supported. Similar to the regular Side Flex but more demanding. Student maintains a side-leaning rest position throughout (Figure 13.20).

FIGURE 13.20 Side Flex, supported.

Body Circles

STARTING POSITION: Stand with feet shoulder width apart, hands on hips, and body bent forward.

MOVEMENT: Make a complete circle with the upper body. Perform a specific number of circles to the right and the same number to the left.

VARIATIONS:

1. Circle in one direction until told to stop and then reverse direction.
2. Try placing the hands on the shoulders and spreading the elbows wide. Otherwise, the exercise is the same.

Lotus Pose

Sit with legs crossed and spine erect as in Figure 13.25. With the hands on the knees, close the eyes and slowly inhale and exhale deep breaths.

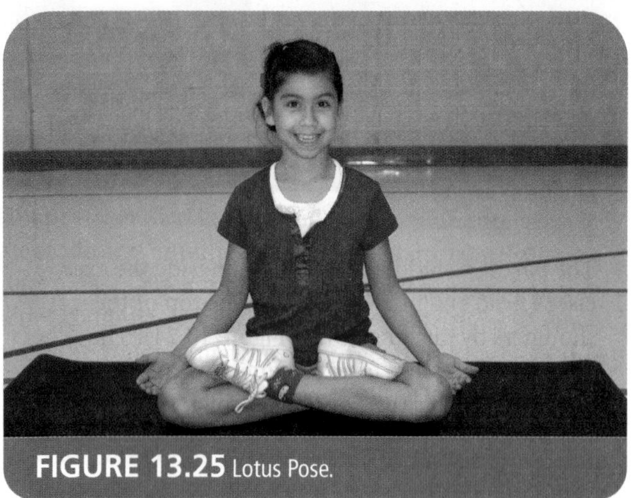

FIGURE 13.25 Lotus Pose.

Sunrise and Sunset

Begin by standing tall and taking three deep breaths. Next, inhale and lift the arms overhead while pressing the feet into the ground. Reach to the sky for 3 to 5 seconds at the top. For the sunset, slightly bend the knees. While exhaling, bend forward from the hips as far as is comfortable. Focus on maintaining appropriate posture and a flat back. Finally, inhale, bringing the arms above the head, and exhale, bringing palms together and down to chest height with fingers pointing upward. In yoga, this is the namaste ("NAH-mah-stay") position.

Tree Pose

Start in namaste position. Lift the right foot and hold it against the inside of the left thigh (or calf). Raise both arms high and spread them like the branches of a tree (Figure 13.26). After holding this pose for three breaths, return to the starting position. Do the same posture, this time lifting the left foot.

Up Cat

Start on all fours with fingers facing forward. Place the knees below the hips and the hands below the shoulders. While inhaling, assume the posture seen in Figure 13.27. The key is to move the tailbone and

FIGURE 13.26 Tree Pose.

shoulders up while moving the center of the torso downward into a backbend. Complete the posture by looking slightly up.

FIGURE 13.27 Up Cat pose.

Down Cat

This posture is typically combined with the Up Cat. From the Up Cat position, inhale deeply and take the position seen in Figure 13.28. The spine is rounded with the middle of the back pressed "as high as possible." Tuck the head and look backward between the knees.

Fish

Begin on the back with legs straight, arms close to the body, and palms down. Slowly slide the arms under the body while inhaling and raising the chest upward. After two deep breaths, exhale and slowly move to the starting position. Once there, slowly bring the knees to the chest and hug them (Figure 13.29).

FIGURE 13.28 Down Cat pose.

FIGURE 13.29 Fish pose.

Child's Pose

Start by sitting on the heels. Bend at the hips and move downward while slightly opening the knees so the stomach is on the thighs. Bring the arms back to the feet with palms up and rest the forehead on the ground. A continuation of this pose involves moving the arms forward with palms down (Figure 13.30).

FIGURE 13.30 Child's Pose.

Downward Facing Dog

Begin on the hands and knees. Inhale deeply and then exhale while lifting the knees and pushing the toes into the floor. As the legs move backward, the bottom moves upward toward the sky and the head hangs down loosely, like fruit from a tree. Straighten the arms and legs and try to place the heels on the ground to stretch the hamstrings. This pose is typically followed immediately by the Child's Pose.

Pilates Activities

Pilates, like yoga, has quickly become a popular fitness activity that attracts individuals of varying abilities. The program, which originated in Germany, focuses on breathing, good posture, and controlled exercises that strengthen and stretch muscles. Pilates movements are usually performed in sequence; but at the elementary school level, when the exercises are just being learned, teach them as individual exercises and until students are comfortable with them.

Stretch with Knees Sway

Start in a supine position and slowly bring the knees to the chest and hug the knees. Flatten the entire back to the ground and hold the position. Slowly sway the knees from side to side, holding for a second on each side.

13

Spinal Rotation

Sit in a straddle position with good posture and extend the arms out to the side. Rotate the upper body to one side and hold; then rotate to the other side and hold.

Rolling Ball

In a seated position on the floor, bring the knees to the chest and hug the ankles. From this position, roll backward while maintaining the curved spine.

Plank

This position is similar to a push-up, but the weight is placed on the elbows rather than the hands. The forearms and hands are pointed forward. Depending on strength, students may wish to have their knees resting on the ground rather than their feet. Keeping the abdominal muscles tight and back and bottom in a straight line, try to balance in this position for as long as possible.

Star Positions

Similar to a yoga posture, the Star 1 exercise begins with the student in the Plank (see above) position. The first movement is to put all the weight on the right elbow and rotate the hips so the left hip is higher and both feet are on the ground with the left hand raised in the air.

The Star 2 position requires raising the left leg off the ground and maintaining balance only on the right elbow and right foot. The third and final step in the Star sequence is to start in a traditional push-up position and move to the Star 1 position by balancing on the right hand. Next, move to the Star 3 position.

EXAMPLES OF FITNESS ROUTINES

When planning fitness routines, establish variety in activities and include different approaches. This plan minimizes the inherent weaknesses of any single routine. The routines should exercise all major parts of the body. When placing fitness activities into a routine, avoid overloading the same body part with two similar exercises. For example, if push-ups are being performed, the next exercise should not be crab-walking, since it also stresses the arm–shoulder girdle.

Measure exercise dosage for students in time rather than repetitions. It is unreasonable to expect all students to perform the same number of exercise repetitions. As discussed earlier, fitness performance is controlled by several factors, including genetics and trainability, which make it impossible for all children to do the same workload. When time is used to determine the workload, each child can personalize the amount of activity performed within the time constraints. It is reasonable to expect a gifted child to perform more repetitions in a certain amount of time than a less genetically endowed child does. An obese child may not be able to perform as many push-ups as a leaner peer can. Develop positive attitudes toward activity by asking students to do the best they can within the time allotted.

Student Leader Exercises

Students enjoy leading their peers in single exercises or an entire routine. Students need time to practice before leading their peers effectively in a stimulating exercise session. Do not force children to lead; this can result in failure for the child as well as the class. The following routine is an example of student leader exercises.

Student-Led Routine

Encourage students to do the best they can within the specified time limit.

Arm circles	30 seconds
Push-up challenges	30 seconds
Bend and twist	30 seconds
Treadmill	30 seconds
Sit-up challenges	30 seconds
Single-Leg Crab Kick	30 seconds
Knee-to-Chest Curl	30 seconds
Run in place	30 seconds
Spinal Rotation	30 seconds

Conclude the routine with 2 to 4 minutes of jogging, rope jumping, or other aerobic activity.

Squad Leader Exercises

Squad leader exercises give students an opportunity to lead exercises in a small group. This is an effective method for teaching students how to lead others and helping them learn to put together a well-balanced fitness routine. A student from each squad is given a task card that has exercises and activities grouped by how they affect different parts of the body (Figure 13.31). After leading the exercise for the desired amount of time, the first student passes the card to another squad member, who becomes the next

Task Card for Squad Leader Exercises

Aerobic Activities	**Abdominal Strength Exercises**
Running in Place	Reverse Curls
Jumping Jacks	Pelvis Tilters
Treadmill	Knee Touch Curl-ups
Power Jumper	Curl-ups
Rhythmic Jumping	Curl-ups with Twist
	Plank
Flexibility Activities	**Upper Body Strength Exercises**
Bend and Twist	Star 1
Stretch with Knee Sway	Reclining Pull-ups
Partner Rowing	Triceps Push-ups
Lower Leg Stretch	Arm Circles
Achilles Tendon Stretch	Crab Kicks
Body Twist	Crab Full-leg Extensions
Standing Hip Bend	Crab Walk

FIGURE 13.31 Sample task card for squad leader exercises.

leader. To ensure a balanced routine, each new leader must select an exercise from a different group. The following is an example of how exercises and activities are grouped for the squad leader exercise routine.

If there is a delay in starting an exercise, advise the squad to walk or jog rather than stand in place.

Squad Leader Relay

Divide the class into groups of 4 or 5 students. Give each group a task card listing 8 to 10 exercises. One of the group members begins as the leader and leads the group through an exercise. Each time an exercise is completed, the card is passed to a new leader.

Use alternating intervals of music to signal exercising (30 seconds) and silence (5 to 8 seconds) to indicate passing the card.

Exercises to Music

Exercises to music add another dimension to developmental experiences. Many commercial CD sets with exercise programs are available. Use a homemade tape with alternating intervals of silence and music to signal time for exercises and aerobic activity. For example, if doing Random Moving, students could run/walk while the music is playing and stretch during the silent interval. Using tapes frees you from keeping an eye on a stopwatch. Many exercise modules work well with music, including circuit training, aerobic fitness routines, continuity exercises, astronaut exercises, squad leader exercises, and rope-jumping exercises. A set of prerecorded music intervals on CD is available from Human Kinetics, P.O. Box 5076, Champaign, IL 61825-5076 (800-747-4457) or www.humankinetics.com. The CDs are titled *Physical Education Soundtracks, Vol. 1 and Vol. 2.* A routine using music follows.

Sample Routine

Crab Kicks	25 seconds
Rope Jumping	30 seconds
Windmills	25 seconds
Walk and do arm circles	30 seconds
Abdominal Crunchers	25 seconds
Jumping Jack variations	30 seconds
Side Flex	25 seconds
Two-Step or Gallop	30 seconds
Triceps Push-ups	25 seconds
Aerobic Jumping	30 seconds
Push-Up challenges	25 seconds
Leg Extensions	30 seconds
Walking to cool down	30 seconds

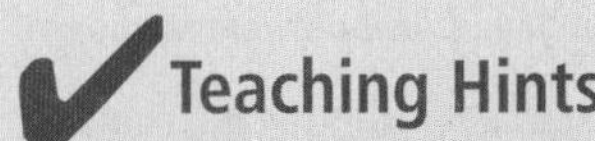

1. Select music with a strong rhythm and distinct beat. When the music is on, students perform aerobic activities (for 30 seconds). During the silent interval, students perform the strength development and flexibility exercises (for 25 seconds).
2. Use scatter formation.

Circuit Training

Circuit training incorporates several stations, each with a designated fitness task. Students move from station to station, generally in a prescribed order, completing the designated fitness task at each station. Exercises for the circuit focus on developing all parts of the body. Activities also will involve the various components of physical fitness (strength, power, endurance, agility, and flexibility).

Instructional Procedures

1. Each station provides an exercise task to perform without assistance. Exercises that directly follow each other must make demands on different parts of the body. This ensures that one task does not cause fatigue and affect students' ability to perform the next task.
2. Assign an equal number of students to each station. This keeps demands on equipment low and activity high. For example, if there are 30 children for a circuit of six stations, start 5 children at each spot.
3. Use prerecorded music, whistle signals, and even verbal directions to signal students to the next station. The tape provides time control and consistency to the circuit, and it allows you to help students without worrying about timing.
4. The number of stations can vary, but ideally should be between six and nine (Figures 13.32 and 13.33 on page 274).

Signs at the different stations can include the name of the activity and any necessary cautions or stress points for execution. When children move between lines as limits (as

1 Running in place	2 Curl-ups	3 Arm circles
6 Crab Walk	5 Trunk Twister	4 Agility Run

Supplies and equipment: Mats for Curl-ups (to hook toes)
Time needed: 4 minutes—based on 30-second activity limit, 10 seconds to move between stations

FIGURE 13.32 Sample six-station circuit training course.

1 Rope Jumping	2 Push-ups	3 Agility Run	4 Arm circles
8 Windmill	7 Treadmill	6 Crab Walk	5 Reverse Curl
9 Hula-Hooping (or any relaxing "fun" activity)			

Supplies and equipment: Jumping ropes, mats for knee push-ups (if used), hoops (if used)
Time needed: 6 minutes—based on 30-second activity limit, 10 seconds to move between stations

FIGURE 13.33 Sample nine-station circuit training course.

in the Agility Run), traffic cones or beanbags can be used to mark the designated boundaries.

Timing and Dosage

Setting a fixed time limit at each station is the easiest way to administer circuit training. Children do their personal best during the time allotted at each station. Give students a 10-second interval to move from one station to the next. Later, reduce the interval to 5 seconds. Students start at any station, as designated, but follow the established station order. A second method of timing is to sound only one signal for the change to the next station. With this plan, all students cease activity at their station, move to the next, and immediately begin the task at that station without waiting for another signal.

The activity demands of the circuit can be increased by making the exercises more strenuous. For example, a station could specify knee or bench push-ups and later change to regular push-ups, a more demanding exercise. Another method of increasing intensity is to have each child run a lap around the circuit area between station changes. Cardiovascular endurance can be enhanced by dividing the class into halves. One half exercises on the circuit while the other runs lightly around the area. On signal to change, the runners go to the circuit and the others run.

Another method of organizing a circuit is to list several activities at each station. The circuit then can be made more than once, and students will do a different exercise each time they return to the same station. If students make the circuit only once, they can perform their favorite exercise from those listed. Exercises at each station should emphasize development of the same body part. A sample circuit training routine follows.

Sample Routine

Ask students to do the best they can for 30 seconds at each station. This implies that students will not perform similar workloads. Fitness is a personal challenge.

Rope Jumping
Triceps Push-ups
Agility Run
Body Circles
Hula-Hooping
Reverse Curls
Crab Walk
Tortoise and Hare
Bend and Twist

Conclude circuit training with 2 to 4 minutes of walking, jogging, rope jumping, or other self-paced aerobic activity.

Teaching Hints

1. Tape alternating segments of silence and music to signal duration of exercise. Music segments (begin at 30 seconds) indicate activity at each station; intervals of silence (10 seconds) announce it is time to stop and move to the next station.
2. Use signals such as start, stop, and move up to ensure rapid movement to the next station.
3. Ask students to do their personal best. Expect workloads to differ.

Alternate Toe Touching

Begin on the back with arms extended overhead. Alternate by touching the right toes with the left hand, and vice versa. Bring the foot and the arm up at the same time and return to the flat position each time.

Continuity Exercises

Children are scattered, each with a jump rope. They alternate between rope jumping and exercises. The rope-jumping episode is timed. At the signal to stop rope jumping, children drop the ropes and take the beginning position for the exercise selected. Many of the exercises use a 2-count rhythm. When children are positioned for the exercise, the leader says, "Ready!" The class completes one repetition of the exercise and responds, "One, two!" This is the response for each repetition. For increased enjoyment, the leader can say, "P.E.!" and the class performs the exercise and responds with, "is fun!" Try other brief phrases, such as "Work hard! Keep fit!" To enable a successful experience for children, modify the push-up and abdominal challenges (pages 254–257). A sample routine of continuity exercises follows.

Sample Routine

Rope jumping—forward	25 seconds
Double Crab Kick	30 seconds
Rope jumping—backward	25 seconds
Knee touch curl-up	30 seconds
Jump and turn body	25 seconds
Push-ups	30 seconds
Rocker Step	25 seconds
Bend and Twist	30 seconds
Swing-Step forward	25 seconds
Side Flex	30 seconds
Free jumping	25 seconds

Relax and stretch for a short time.

Teaching Hints

1. Make a tape that alternates music segments (25 seconds) with silent segments (30 seconds). While the music plays, students jump rope; when silence occurs, students do a flexibility and strength development exercise.
2. Allow students to adjust the workload to their level. This implies resting if the rope jumping is too strenuous.

Hexagon Hustle

Using six cones, form a large hexagon. Students do the "hustle" by moving around the hexagon, changing their movement patterns every time they reach one of the six points in the hexagon. On signal, the hustle stops and students do selected exercises.

Instructional Procedures

1. To create a safer environment, have children move in the same direction around the hexagon.
2. Inform children of the new activity to be performed by placing laminated posters with colorful illustrations by the cones.
3. Instruct faster children to pass to the outside of slower children.
4. Change the direction of the hustle after every exercise segment.

Sample Routine

Tape alternating segments of silence and music to signal duration of exercise. Music segments (25 seconds) indicate moving around the hexagon; intervals of silence (30 seconds) announce flexibility and strength development activities.

Hustle	25 seconds
Push-up from knees	30 seconds
Hustle	25 seconds
Bend and Twist (8 counts)	30 seconds
Hustle	25 seconds
Jumping Jacks (4 counts)	30 seconds
Hustle	25 seconds
Curl-ups (2 counts)	30 seconds
Hustle	25 seconds
Crab Kick (2 counts)	30 seconds
Hustle	25 seconds
Sit and stretch (8 counts)	30 seconds
Hustle	25 seconds

Power Jumper	30 seconds
Hustle	25 seconds
Squat Thrust (4 counts)	30 seconds

Conclude the Hexagon Hustle with a slow jog or walk.

Astronaut Exercises

Astronaut exercises are performed in circular or scatter formation. Routines are developed by moving using various locomotor movements, alternated with stopping and performing exercises in place. The following movements and tasks can be used in the routine.

1. Various locomotor movements such as hopping, jumping, running, sliding, skipping, taking giant steps, and walking high on the toes.
2. Movement on all fours—forward, backward, or sideways—with respect to the direction of walking. Repeat backward and forward using the Crab Walk.
3. Stunt movements such as the Seal Walk, Gorilla Walk, and Rabbit Jump.
4. Upper-body movements and exercises that can be done while walking, such as Arm Circles, bending right and left, and body twists.
5. Various exercises performed in place when the music stops. Include a balance of arm–shoulder girdle and abdominal exercises.

Astronaut exercises can be adapted successfully to any developmental level. The movements selected will determine the intensity of the routine. More active children pass on the outside. Enjoyment comes from being challenged by a variety of movements.

Sample Routine

Walk, do arm circles	35 seconds
Crab Full-Leg Extension	30 seconds
Skip sideways	35 seconds
Body Twist	30 seconds
Slide; change lead leg	35 seconds
Jumping Jack variations	30 seconds
Crab Walk	35 seconds
Curl-ups with Twist	30 seconds
Hop to center and back	35 seconds
Four-count push-ups	30 seconds
Gallop Backward	35 seconds
Up Cat; Down Cat	30 seconds
Grapevine Step (Carioca)	35 seconds
Trunk Twisters	30 seconds
Power Jumper	35 seconds

Cool down with stretching and walking or jogging for 1 to 2 minutes.

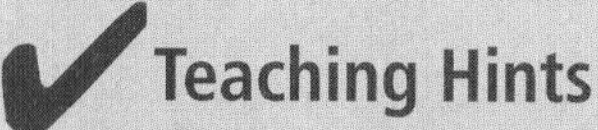

1. Tape alternating segments of music and silence to signal duration of exercise. Music segments indicate aerobic activity; intervals of silence announce flexibility and strength development activities.
2. Use scatter formation; ask students to change direc-tions from time to time to keep spacing. Allow stu-dents to adjust the workload pace. Allow them to move at a pace that is consistent with their ability level.

Challenge Courses

Challenge courses are popular as a tool for fitness development in the elementary schools. Students move through the course with proper form rather than run against a time standard. The course is designed to exercise the entire body through a variety of activities. Equipment such as mats, parallel bars, horizontal ladders, high-jump standards, benches, and vaulting boxes can make effective challenge courses (Figure 13.34). An array of courses can be designed, depending on course length and tasks included. Some schools have established permanent courses.

Here is the equipment list for the sample course shown in Figure 13.34:

- Three benches (16 to 18 in. high)
- Four tumbling mats (4 by 8 ft)
- Four hoops
- One pair of high-jump standards with magic rope
- One climbing rope
- One jumping box
- Five chairs or cones

Aerobic Fitness Routines

Aerobics is a fitness activity that helps people of all ages develop cardiorespiratory fitness, strength, and flexibility. A leader is designated to perform a series of movements that the other students follow. There are few limits to the range of activities a leader can present. Manipulative equipment (including balls, jump ropes, hoops, and wands) can be integrated with movement activities.

Instructional Procedures

1. Base movement patterns on units of 4, 8, or 16 counts.
2. Vary movements so stretching and flowing movements are alternated with the more strenuous aerobic activities.
3. Keep steps relatively simple. Focus on activity rather than developing competent rhythmic performers. Stress

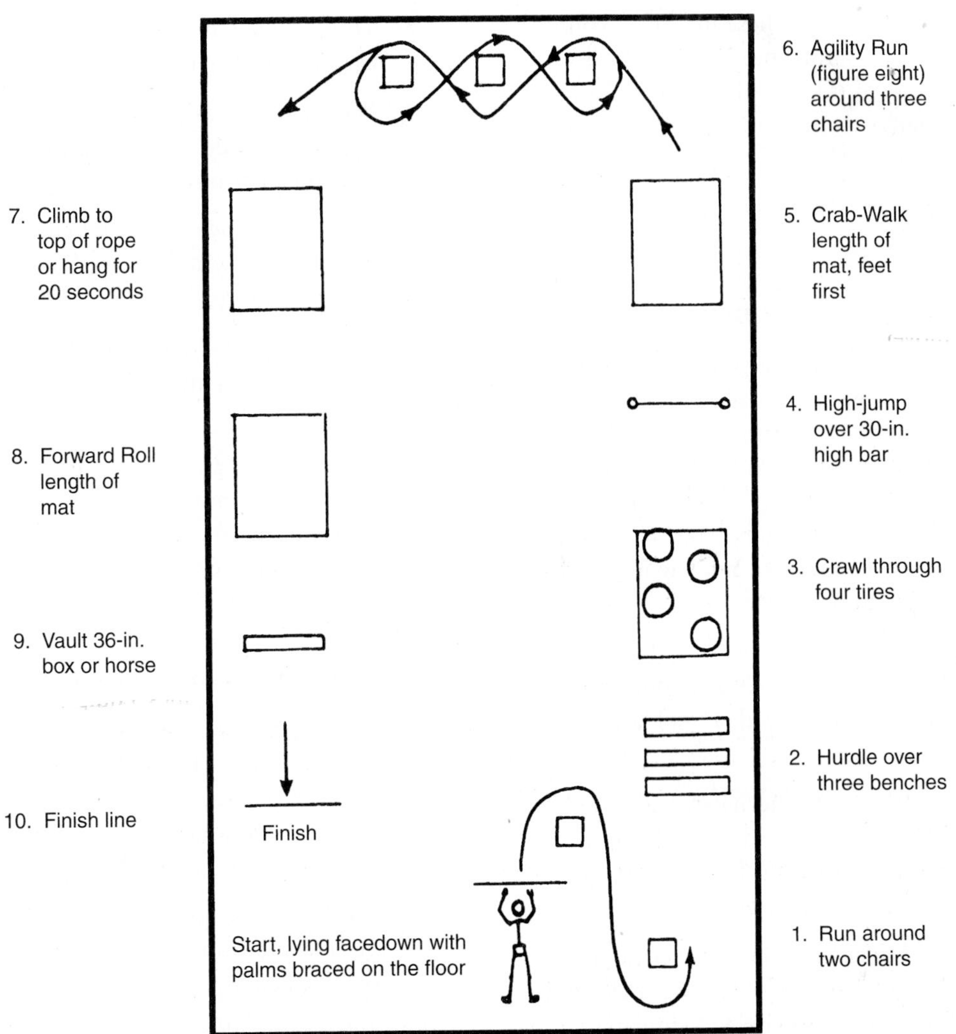

FIGURE 13.34 Indoor challenge course.

continuous movement (moving with the flow) rather than perfection of routines. Running and bouncing steps are easily followed and motivating.

4. Remember that routines are best when they are not rigid. Students should not have to worry about being out of step.
5. Establish cues to help students follow routines (e.g., "Bounce," "Step," "Reach," and "Jump").

Basic Steps

Here are some basic steps and movements for use in developing a variety of routines. Most steps are performed to 4 counts, although the count can vary.

Running and Walking Steps

1. *Directional runs*—forward, backward, diagonal, sideways, and turning.
2. *Rhythmic runs with a specific movement on the fourth beat.* Examples are knee lift, clap, jump, jump-turn, and hop.
3. *Runs with variations.* Run while lifting the knees, kicking up the heels, or slapping the thighs or heels; or run with legs extended, as in the goose step.
4. *Runs with arms in various positions*—on the hips, in the air above the head, and straight down.

Movements on the Floor

1. *Side leg raises.* Do these with a straight leg while lying on the side.
2. *Alternate leg raises.* While on the back, raise one leg to meet the opposite hand. Repeat, using the opposite leg or both legs.

3. *Rhythmic push-ups.* Do these in 2- or 4-count movements. A 4-count would be as follows: halfway down (count 1), touch nose to floor (count 2), halfway up (count 3), and fully extend arms (count 4).
4. *Crab Kicks and Treadmills.* Do these to 4 counts.

Upright Rhythmic Movements

1. *Lunge variations.* Perform a lunge, stepping forward on the right foot while bending at the knee and extending the arms forward and diagonally upward (counts 1 and 2). Return to starting position by bringing the right foot back and pulling the arms into a jogging position (counts 3 and 4). Vary the lunge by changing its speed, depth, and direction.
2. *Side bends.* Begin with the feet apart. Reach overhead while bending to the side. This movement is usually done to 4 counts: bend (1), hold (2 and 3), and return (4).
3. *Reaches.* Reach upward alternately with each arm. Reaches can be done sideways also and are usually 2-count movements. Fast alternating 1-count movements can be done, too.
4. *Arm and shoulder circles.* Make arm circles with one or both arms. Vary the size of the circles and the speed. Do shoulder shrugs in a similar way.

Jumping Jack Variations

1. *Jump with arm movements.* Alternately extend upward and then pull in toward the chest.
2. *Side Jumping Jacks.* Use regular arm action while the feet jump from side to side or forward and backward together.
3. *Feet variations.* Try different variations such as forward stride alternating, forward and side stride alternating, kicks or knee lifts added, feet crossed, or heel-toe movements (turning on every 4th or 8th count).

Bounce Steps

1. *Bounce and clap.* This is like a slow-time jump-rope step. Clap on every other bounce.
2. *Bounce, turn, and clap.* Turn a quarter or halfway with each jump.
3. *Three bounces and clap.* Bounce three times and bounce and clap on count 4. Add some turns.
4. *Bounce and rock side to side.* Transfer the weight from side to side, or forward and backward. Add clapping or arm swinging.
5. *Bounce with body twist.* Hold the arms at shoulder level and twist the lower body back and forth on each bounce.
6. *Bounce with floor patterns.* Bounce and make different floor patterns such as a box, diagonal, or triangle.
7. *Bounce with kick variations.* Perform different kicks such as knee lift and kick; double kicks; knee lift and knee slap; and kick and clap under knees. Combine the kicks with 2- or 4-count turns.

Activities with Manipulative Equipment

1. *Jump ropes.* Perform basic steps such as forward and backward with slow and fast time. Jump on one foot, cross the arms, and while jogging, swing the rope from side to side with the handles in one hand.
2. *Beanbags.* Toss and catch while performing various locomotor movements. Use different tosses for a challenge.
3. *Hula hoops.* Rhythmically swing the hoop around different body parts. Perform different locomotor movements around and over hoops.
4. *Balls.* Bounce, toss, and dribble, and add locomotor movements while performing tasks.

Sample Routine

These aerobic movements are suggestions only. When students begin to fatigue, stop the aerobic fitness movements and work on developing flexibility and strength. This gives students time to recover aerobically.

Rhythmic run with clap

Bounce turn and clap

Rhythmic 4-count curl-ups (knees, toes, knees, back)

Rhythmic Crab Kicks (slow time)

Jumping Jack combination

Double knee lifts

Lunges (right, left, forward) with single-arm circles (on the side lunges) and double-arm circles (on the forward lunge)

Rhythmic trunk twists

Directional run (forward, backward, side, turning)

Rock side to side with clap

Side leg raises (alternate legs)

Rhythmic 4-count push-ups (If these are too difficult for students, substitute single-arm circles in the push-up position.)

Teaching Hints

1. Use music to stimulate effort. Any combination of movements can be used.
2. Keep the steps simple and easy to perform. Some students will become frustrated if the learning curve is steep.
3. Signs explaining the aerobic activities will help students remember performance cues.
4. Do not stress or expect perfection. Allow students to perform the activities as best they can.
5. Alternate bouncing and running movements with flexibility and strength development movements.

Partner Resistance and Aerobic Fitness Exercises

Partner resistance exercises combined with aerobic fitness routines make an excellent fitness activity. Partner resistance exercises develop strength but offer little aerobic benefit. Combining them with aerobic fitness routines offers a well-balanced program. The following exercises refer to partner resistance exercises (pages 268–269). Allot enough time for each partner to resist as well as exercise.

Sample Routine

Students find a partner and lead each other in aerobic activities. Partners switch leader and follower roles after each partner resistance exercise. See "Aerobic Fitness Routines" for descriptions of activities.

Bounce and Clap	25 seconds
Arm curl-up	45 seconds
Jumping Jack variations	25 seconds
Camelback	45 seconds
Lunge variations	25 seconds
Fist Pull-Apart	45 seconds
Directional Runs	25 seconds
Scissors	45 seconds
Rhythmic Running	25 seconds
Butterfly	45 seconds
Bounce with Body Twist	25 seconds
Push-Up with Resistance	45 seconds

Walk, stretch, and relax for 1 to 2 minutes.

Teaching Hints

1. Tape alternating segments of music and silence to signal duration of exercise. Music segments indicate aerobic activity (25 seconds); intervals of silence announce partner resistance exercises (45 seconds).
2. Teach the exercises first. A sign with aerobic activities on one side and partner resistance exercises on the other helps students remember the activities. The signs can be held upright by cones and shared by two to four students. Take 6 to 10 seconds to complete a resistance exercise.

Sport-Related Fitness Activities

Many sport drills can be modified to place fitness demands on students. An advantage of sport-related fitness activities is that many children are highly motivated by sport activities. Thoughtful planning and creative thinking can result in drills that teach sport skills and confer fitness benefits. Here are some examples of fitness adaptations of sport skills.

Baseball/Softball

1. *Base running.* Set up several diamonds on a grass field. Space the class evenly around the base paths. On signal, students run to the next base, round the base, take a lead, and run to the next base. Faster runners may pass on the outside.
2. *Most lead-up games.* Children waiting on deck to bat and those in the field perform selected activities (skill or fitness related) while waiting for the batter to hit.
3. *Position responsibility.* Start children at various positions on the field. On signal, children are free to move quickly to any other position. Upon reaching that position, students must display the movement most frequently practiced at that position (for instance, shortstop fields ball and throws to first base). Continue until all players have moved to each position.

Basketball

1. *Dribbling.* Each child has a basketball or playground ball. Assign one or more people to be "it." On command, everyone begins dribbling the ball and avoids being tagged by those who are it. A child who is tagged becomes a new tagger. A variation would be for the taggers to begin the game without a ball. Their objective would be to steal a ball from classmates.
2. *Dribbling, passing, rebounding, shooting, and defense.* Using the concept of a circuit, assign selected basketball skills to be performed at each station. Be sure that each station has ample equipment to keep all students active. Movement from one station to another should be vigorous and may include a stop for exercise.
3. *Game play.* Divide the class into four teams. Two teams take the court and play a game of basketball. The other teams line up along respective sidelines and practice a series of exercises. Upon completing the exercise sequence, playing teams change positions with exercising teams.

Football

1. *Ball carrying.* Divide the class into 4 to 6 squads. The first person in line carries the ball while zigzagging through preplaced boundary cones. The rest of the squad does a specific exercise. Upon completing the zigzag course, the first person hands off the ball to the next person in line. This handoff signals a change in exercise for the rest of the squad.
2. *Punting.* One child punts the ball to a partner. After catching the ball, the object is to see which child can get to the receiver's original starting position first (since the punt will more than likely move the receiver). Repeat, with the receiver becoming the punter.
3. *Forward passing.* Divide the children into groups of 4 or less. Children practice running pass patterns. Rotate the passing responsibility after every six throws.

Volleyball

1. *Rotating.* Place students in the various court positions. Teach them the rotational sequence. As they reach a new court position, have them do several repetitions of a specific exercise. On command, they rotate to the next position. Select activities that exercise components of fitness to enhance volleyball skill development.
2. *Serving.* Divide the class evenly among available volleyball courts. Starting with an equal number of children and several balls on each side of the net, have them practice the serve. After each successful serve, the children run (around the net standard) to the other side of the net, retrieve a ball, and serve.
3. *Bumping and setting.* Using the concept of the circuit, establish several stations for practicing the bump and set. Movement from station to station should be vigorous and may contain a special stop for exercise.

Soccer

1. *Dribbling.* With a partner, one child dribbles the ball around the playground as the partner follows close behind. On signal, the children reverse roles.
2. *Passing and trapping.* Devise routines for the players to move continuously (e.g., jogging, running in place, doing selected exercises while waiting to trap and pass the soccer ball) while working with partners or small groups.
3. *Game play.* Divide the class into teams of 3 or 4 players each. Organize the playground area to provide enough soccer fields for all teams to play. Make the fields as large as possible.

Sample Routine

Instructional Activities	Teaching Hints
Station 1: Soccer Lines Drill—Working with a beach ball, dribble the ball back and forth between two lines as quickly as possible. Use only dribbling skills; long kicks not allowed.	Place even numbers of students at each station so they can partner up for the sport activities.
Station 2: Push-Up challenges	Use intervals of music and silence to signal moves to the next station. Begin this routine with 60 seconds at the sport-related activities and 30 seconds at the strength and flexibility stations.

Station 3: Basketball Chest Pass—With a partner, practice the chest and bounce pass. If medicine balls are available, use them for strength development.	Ask students to store the equipment when the activity ends.
Station 4: Flexibility Activities	
Station 5: Volleyball Passing—Using a beach ball, practice passing and setting with a partner(s). Keep the ball in the air as long as possible using two-handed passes and sets.	
Station 6: Abdominal Challenges	
Station 7: Hockey Circle Passing—One partner is stationary while the other circles around and passes to his partner. Change roles after five passes.	
Station 8: Trunk Challenges	

Walking and Jogging

Jogging and walking, fitness activities for all ages, can lead to regular activity habits and a lifelong exercise program. *Jogging* is defined as easy, relaxed running at a pace that can be maintained for long distances without undue fatigue or strain. It is the first level of locomotion above walking. Jogging and walking are unique; they require no special equipment, can be done almost anywhere and anytime, are individual activities, and take relatively little time. For most people, this type of regular activity is an exercise in personal discipline that can enhance self-image and confidence.

Instructional Procedures

1. Let students find a friend to jog or walk with. This is usually a friend of similar ability level. A way to judge correct pace is to talk with a friend without undue stress. If students are too winded to talk, they are probably running too fast. The selected friend helps ensure that the experience is positive and within the student's aerobic capacity.
2. Allow children to jog and walk in any direction, so they cannot keep track of the distance covered. Doing laps on a track is one of the surest ways to discourage less able students. They always finish last and are open to chiding by the rest of the class.
3. Have children jog and walk for a specific time rather than a specific distance. Why should all students have to run the same distance? This goes against the philosophy of accommodating individual differences and varying aerobic capacities. Running or walking for a set amount of time allows less able children to move without fear of ridicule.
4. Do not be concerned about foot action, since children select the most comfortable gait. Arm movement should be easy and natural, with elbows bent. The head and upper body are held up and back. The eyes look ahead. The general body position in walking and jogging is erect but relaxed. Jogging on the toes should be avoided.
5. Do not turn jogging and walking into competitive, timed activities. Let students determine their own pace. Racing belongs in the track program. Another reason to avoid speed is that racing negates learning to pace during a run. For developing endurance and gaining health benefits, have children move for a longer time at a slower speed instead of running at top speed for a shorter distance.

13

Racetrack Fitness

Arrange five or six fitness activities in the center (the Pit) of a large circle outlined with marking spots (the racetrack). If desired, mark the pit stop area by placing tumbling mats in the center of the racetrack. Students work with a partner and alternate running (or doing other locomotor movements) around the racetrack and going to the pit to perform a strength or flexibility exercise. Have students do a different exercise each time, to vary the workout. Signal role changes by alternating 30 seconds of music with 10 seconds of silence. When the music stops, partner who was running the track goes to the pit to exercise, and vice versa.

Sample Routine

Instructional Activities	Teaching Hints
Here are some exercises that can be used for pit exercises. 1. Arm circles 2. Bend and Twist 3. Abdominal challenges 4. Knee-to-Chest Curl 5. Push-up challenges 6. Trunk Twist	Place exercise descriptions on signs in the pit area so students can easily see the sequence of activities and know how to perform the exercises. Place mats in the pit area to mark where students are to perform their exercises.

Instructional Activities	Teaching Hints
	To encourage students to do a variety of racetrack activities, post descriptions of different locomotor movements (e.g., jogging, sliding, skipping, and grapevine movements) at a corner of the track. Offer rope jumping as an alternative to running around the track.

Fitness Orienteering

Students work together as members of a team. Set up 8 to 10 stations randomly around the area. Give each squad a laminated "map" card of exercise stations. Each map shows the stations in different order, so only one squad is at a "landmark." Team members exercise together (at each child's own pace) and, on signal, "hunt" for the next exercise station listed on their map card. Upon completing a station activity, one squad member picks up a letter from the "checkpoint," and the team moves to the next station. The goal is to complete the fitness orienteering stations, pick up a letter at each station, and return to the original starting point to unscramble the "secret word." Intervals of music (30 seconds) and silence (15 seconds) signal when to exercise and when to change to a new station.

Here are some examples of checkpoint stations on the exercise map card:

1. Run to the northwest corner of the gym, and pick up your letter now. When the music starts, continue running to a different corner until the music stops.
2. Move to the individual mats and do push-up challenges until the music stops.
3. Run to the benches and do step-ups until the music stops. The step count is "up, up, down, down."
4. Move to the red marking spots and do two different stretches until the music stops.
5. Run and find the jump ropes. When the music starts, pick up the ropes and do some jump rope tricks you learned earlier.
6. Skip to the tumbling mats. When the music starts, do abdominal challenges.
7. As a group, jog to the three green marking spots and pick up your letter. Jog and try to touch at least five walls, two different red lines, and three different black lines. Stay together with your group.
8. Jog to the "jumping jacks" sign and do jumping jacks with at least four different variations in arm or foot patterns.

All-Around Jackpot Fitness

Around the teaching area, set up three different "jackpots" (boxes) filled with fitness exercises and activities. One jackpot has various strength development activities written on small index cards. A second jackpot holds flexibility activities. The third jackpot contains aerobic activities. Students can work individually or with a partner. They begin at any jackpot and randomly pick out an activity to perform. If with a partner, they take turns selecting the card from the box. The only rules are that they must rotate to a different jackpot each time, and they cannot select an activity they did earlier. If they draw an activity they have already performed, they return it to the jackpot and select another. A music interval of 30 seconds signals the duration of fitness activity, followed by a 10- to 15-second interval for selecting a new activity from a different jackpot. Instruct students to do as many repetitions as possible while the music is playing.

Here are some activities for the jackpot:

Aerobic Jackpot

1. Do the carioca around the basketball court.
2. Perform a "mirror drill" with your partner for 30 seconds.
3. Jump rope using both slow and fast time.
4. Do Tortoise and Hare/Running in Place.
5. March with high steps around the area.

Strength Jackpot

1. Perform abdominal challenges.
2. Perform push-up challenges.
3. Do the Treadmill exercise.
4. Do as many Power Jumps as possible.
5. Perform as many Crab Kicks as possible.

Flexibility Jackpot

1. Perform the Bend and Twist exercise.
2. Stretch using the sitting stretch.
3. Stretch using the lower leg stretch.
4. Do the Standing Hip Bend.
5. Improve your flexibility performing the Body Twist.

Partner Interval Fitness

Students pair up with a partner and perform these activities. The activities are designed so that one partner performs aerobic activity while the other is stretching or doing strength development activities. Use timed intervals of 30 seconds of music and 10 seconds of silence to signal changing positions (or activity). Have students perform all the activities.

1. *High Fives.* One partner runs around the area and gives as many "high fives" as possible to others who are running. The other partner remains stationary and performs push-up challenges. On signal, they switch roles. Various locomotor movements can be used as well as different high-five styles.
2. *Over and Around.* One partner makes a bridge on the floor while the other moves over and around the bridges of other students. To ensure that one child is moving (working) while the other is resting, they continue until a signal is given to change positions. Have students try different types of bridges and movements to vary the activity.
3. *Jump Rope and Exercise.* Each partner has a jump rope. One partner jumps the rope while the other partner folds the rope and does strength or stretching activities. On signal, partners switch roles. An example of a stretching activity is to fold the rope in half and hold it overhead while stretching from side to side and to the toes. See pages 365–375 for other rope exercises.
4. *Stick and Stretch.* One partner tries to stick like glue to her partner, who tries to move as far away as possible. All movements are controlled. On signal, the other partner leads a stretching or strength development (resting) activity. On the next signal, the partners switch roles.
5. *Partner Swing and Exercise.* During the first music interval, partners swing each other under control. On the next music interval, one partner leads the other in a stretching or strength development activity. The partners swing again and then the other partner leads a stretching or strength development activity.

Interval Training

All fitness routines in this chapter are based on interval training principles. Interval training is effective for elementary school children because they fatigue and recover quickly. Interval training involves alternating work and recovery intervals. Intervals of work (large-muscle movement dominated by locomotor movements) and recovery (dominated by nonlocomotor activity or walking) are alternated at regular timed intervals. Teachers can use all the activities just described in "Partner Interval Fitness" as well as the following motivating activity.

Rubber Band

Students move throughout the area. On signal, they time a move to the center of the area. Upon reaching the center simultaneously, they jump upward and let out a loud "yea!" or similar yell and resume running throughout the area. The key to the activity is to synchronize the move to the center. After several runs, students take a rest and stretch, or walk.

After all work intervals, students participate in recovery intervals characterized by strength development or stretching activities. Using a series of timed intervals of music and silence is an effective approach for motivating students.

Partner Fitness Challenges

Partner challenges are fitness activities that can be used with intermediate-grade students to develop aerobic endurance, strength, and flexibility. Another advantage of partner challenges is that they can be done indoors as a rainy-day activity. Try to pair students with someone of similar ability and size. Telling students to pair up with a friend usually means they will select a partner who is caring and understanding. Emphasize continuous movement and activity. The following partner activities are challenging and enjoyable.

Circle Five

Partner 1 stands stationary in the center of the circle with one palm up. Partner 2 runs in a circle around 1 and gives a "high five" when passing the upturned palm. Students should see how many touches they can make in 15 seconds. They reverse roles on signal.

13

Knee Tag

Partners stand facing each other. On signal, they try to tag their partner's knees. Students score 1 point each time they make a tag. Have them play for a designated amount of time.

Mini Merry-Go-Round

Partners face each other with their feet nearly touching and their hands in a double-wrist grip. Partners slowly lean backward while keeping the feet in place until the arms are straight. Then they spin around as quickly as possible. It is important for partners to be of similar size.

Around and Under

One partner stands with the feet spread shoulder width apart and hands held overhead. The other partner goes between the standing partner's legs, stands up, and slaps the partner's hands. They continue the pattern for a designated time.

Ball Wrestle

Both partners grasp an 8-inch playground ball and try to wrestle it away from each other.

Sitting Wrestle

Partners sit on the floor facing each other and grasp hands. The legs are bent and feet are flat on the floor with toes touching. The goal is to pull the partner's bottom off the floor.

Upset the Alligator

One partner lies facedown on the floor. On signal, the other partner tries to turn the "alligator" over. The alligator tries to avoid being turned over.

Seat Balance Wrestle

Partners sit on the floor facing each other with their knees raised and feet off the floor. If desired, they place their hands under their thighs to help support their legs. They start with the toes touching. Each student tries to tip the other backward using the toes.

Head Wrestle

Partners hold each other's left wrists with their right hands. On signal, they try to touch their partners' heads with their left hands, then switch the handhold and try to touch with the opposite hand.

Pull Apart

One partner stands with the feet spread, arms bent at the elbows in front of the chest, with the fingertips touching. Partner 2 holds the other's wrists and tries to pull the fingertips apart. Jerking is not allowed; the pull must be smooth and controlled.

Pin Dance

Partners hold hands, facing each other, with a bowling pin (spot or cone) between them. On signal, each student tries to make the other touch the pin.

Finger Fencing

Partners face each other with their feet one in front of the other in a straight line. The toes of each partner's front foot should touch. Partners lock index fingers and try to make the other move either foot from the beginning position.

REFLECTION AND REVIEW

HOW AND WHY

1. Why is America's youth perceived as being unfit and inactive?
2. Why must physical education teachers understand various concepts related to physical fitness?
3. Should fitness testing awards be used?
4. Why do so many students fail fitness tests? Defend your answer.
5. How can teachers make fitness fun?
6. Should physical education teachers be physically fit? Explain.

CONTENT REVIEW

1. Discuss several major conclusions of the Surgeon General's report on physical activity and health.
2. Differentiate between health-related fitness and skill-related fitness, and identify the components of each.
3. Indicate whether American children are fit. Explain your answer.
4. Identify the purpose of physical fitness testing and the steps to implementing a fitness test battery. Include descriptions of several fitness tests and the fitness component each measures.
5. Describe methods for fostering positive attitudes toward physical fitness.
6. Discuss guidelines for promoting fitness for children.
7. Cite several harmful exercises.
8. Create a developmentally appropriate fitness routine. Be sure to identify the developmental level that will use the routine.
9. Describe or demonstrate numerous activities and exercises designed to improve the fitness of children.

FOR MORE INFORMATION

REFERENCES AND SUGGESTED READINGS

AAHPER. (1976). *AAHPER youth fitness test manual.* Reston, VA: Author.

AAHPERD. (1987). *Youth fitness test manual.* Reston, VA: Author.

American College of Sports Medicine. (2005). *ACSM's guidelines for exercise testing and prescription* (7th ed.). Philadelphia: Lippincott, Williams, & Wilkins.

Bailey, R. C., Olson, J., Pepper, S. L., Porszaz, J., Barstow, T. J., & Cooper, D. M. (1995). The level and tempo of children's physical activities: An observational study. *Medicine and Science in Sport and Exercise, 27*(7), 1033–1041.

Bersma, D., & Visscher, M. (2003). *Yoga games for children: Fun and fitness with postures, movements and breaths.* Alameda, CA: Hunter House.

Blair, S. N., Kohl, H. W., Paffenbarger, R. S., Clark, D. G., Cooper, K. H., & Gibbons, L. W. (1989). Physical fitness and all-cause mortality: A prospective study of healthy men and women. *Journal of the American Medical Association, 17*, 2395–2401.

Bouchard, C. (1999). Heredity and health related fitness. In C. B. Corbin & R. P. Pangrazi (Eds.), *Toward a better understanding of physical fitness & activity* (pp. 11–18). Scottsdale, AZ: Holcomb Hathaway.

Bouchard, C., Dionne, F. T., Simoneau, J., & Boulay, M. (1992). Genetics of aerobic and anaerobic performances. *Exercise and Sport Sciences Reviews, 20*, 27–58.

Brown, C. (2004). *The Pilates program for every body.* Pleasantville, NY: Reader's Digest with Tucker Slingsby Ltd.

Cooper Institute. (2008). *Fitnessgram test administration manual* (3rd ed.). Champaign, IL: Human Kinetics.

Corbin, C. B., & Lindsey, R. (2007). *Fitness for life—updated* (5th ed.). Champaign, IL: Human Kinetics.

Corbin, C. B., Lindsey, R., & Welk, G. (2000). *Concepts of physical fitness and wellness: A comprehensive lifestyle approach.* Boston: McGraw-Hill.

Corbin, C. B., Lovejoy, P. Y., Steingard, P., & Emerson, R. (1990). Fitness awards: Do they accomplish their intended objectives? *American Journal of Health Promotion, 4*, 345–351.

Corbin, C. B., Lovejoy, P. Y., & Whitehead, J. R. (1988). Youth physical fitness awards. *Quest, 40*, 200–218.

Corbin, C. B., & Pangrazi, R. P. (1992). Are American children and youth fit? *Research Quarterly for Exercise and Sport, 63*(2), 96–106.

———. (1998). Physical activity pyramid rebuffs peak experience. *ACSM's Health & Fitness Journal, 2*(1), 12–17.

Corbin, C. B., Welk, G. J., Corbin, W. R., & Welk, K. A. (2008). *Concepts of physical fitness and wellness: A comprehensive lifestyle approach* (7th ed.). Boston: McGraw-Hill.

Glasser, W. (1976). *Positive addiction.* New York: Harper & Row.

Harter, S. (1978). Effectance motivation revisited. *Child Development, 21*, 34–64.

Hedley, A. A., Ogden, C. L., Johnson, C. L., Carroll, M. D., Curtin, L. R., & Flegal, K. M. (2004). Prevalence of overweight and obesity among U.S. children, adolescents, and adults, 1999–2002. *Journal of the American Medical Association, 291*(23), 2847–2850.

Heymsfield, S. B., Lohman, T., Wang, Z., & Going, S. B. (2005). *Human body composition* (2nd ed.). Champaign, IL: Human Kinetics.

Horvat, M., Block, M. E., & Kelly, L. E. (2007). *Developmental and adapted physical activity assessment.* Champaign, IL: Human Kinetics.

Howley, E. T., & Franks, B. D. (2007). *Fitness professional's handbook* (5th ed.). Champaign, IL: Human Kinetics.

Locke, E. A., & Lathan, G. P. (1985). The application of goal setting to sports. *Journal of Sport Psychology, 7*, 205–222.

Macfarlane, P. A. (1993). Out with the sit-up, in with the curl-up. *Journal of Physical Education, Recreation, and Dance, 64*(6), 62–66.

Mann, M., & Lloyd, E. (2005). *Discover Pilates*. Valencia, CA: Top That Publishing.

National Association for Sport and Physical Education. (2004). *Physical activity for children: A statement of guidelines* (2nd ed.). Reston, VA: Author.

———. (2005a). *Physical best activity guide* (2nd ed.). Champaign, IL: Human Kinetics.

———. (2005b). *Physical education for lifelong fitness* (2nd ed.). Champaign, IL: Human Kinetics.

Pangrazi, R. P. (2010). *Dynamic physical education curriculum guide: Lesson plans for implementation* (16th ed.). San Francisco: Benjamin Cummings.

Pangrazi, R. P., & Corbin, C. B. (1990). Age as a factor relating to physical fitness test performance. *Research Quarterly for Exercise and Sport, 61*(4), 410–414.

Pate, R., Corbin, C. B., & Pangrazi, R. P. (1998). Physical activity for young people. *Physical Fitness and Sports Research Digest, 3*(3), 1–8.

Pate, R. R., Dowda, M., & Ross, J. G. (1990). Association between physical activity and physical fitness in American children. *American Journal of Diseases of Children, 144*, 1123–1129.

Pate, R. R., & Ross, J. G. (1987). Factors associated with health-related fitness. *Journal of Physical Education, Recreation, and Dance, 58*(9), 93–96.

Payne, V. G., & Morrow, J. R., Jr. (1993). Exercise and VO_{2max} in children: A meta-analysis. *Research Quarterly for Exercise and Sport, 64*(3), 305–313.

Plowman, S. A. (1993). Physical fitness and healthy low back function. *Physical Activity and Fitness Research Digest, 1*(3), 1–8.

President's Council on Physical Fitness and Sports. (2008). *The President's Challenge handbook.* Washington, DC: Author.

Reiff, G. G., Dixon, W. R., Jacoby, D., Ye, X. Y., Spain, C. G., & Hunsicker, P. A. (1987). *The President's Council on Physical Fitness and Sports 1985 national school population fitness survey.* Washington, DC: U.S. Department of Health and Human Services.

Ross, J. G., & Gilbert, G. G. (1985). The national children and youth fitness study: A summary of findings. *Journal of Physical Education, Recreation, and Dance, 56*(1), 45–50.

Ross, J. G., Pate, R. R., Caspersen, C. J., Damberg, C. L., & Svilar, M. (1987). Home and community in children's exercise habits. *Journal of Physical Education, Recreation, and Dance, 58*(9), 85–92.

Rowland, T. W. (1990). *Exercise and children's health.* Champaign, IL: Human Kinetics.

Shaw, J. M., & Snow-Harter, C. (1995). Osteoporosis and physical activity. *Physical Activity and Fitness Research Digest, 2*(3), 1–8.

Slaughter, M. H., Lohman, T. G., Boileau, R. A., Horswill, C. A., Stillman, R. J., & Van Loan, M. D., et al. (1988). Skinfold equations for estimation of body fatness in children and youth. *Human Biology, 60*, 709–723.

Smith, L. L., Brunetz, M. H., Chenier, T. C., McCammon, M. R., Hourmard, J. A., & Franklin, M. E., et al. (1993). The effects of static and ballistic stretching on delayed onset muscle soreness and creatine kinase. *Research Quarterly for Exercise and Sport, 64*(1), 103–107.

U.S. Department of Health and Human Services (USDHHS). (1996). *Physical activity and health: A report of the Surgeon General.* Atlanta, GA: Centers for Disease Control and Prevention, National Center for Chronic Disease Prevention and Health Promotion.

Weing, M. (2003). *Yoga kids: Education the whole child through yoga.* New York: La Martiere Group.

Welk, G. J., & Meredith, M. D. (Eds.). (2008). *Fitnessgram/Activitygram Reference Guide.* Dallas, TX: Cooper Institute.

Whitehead, J. R., & Corbin, C. B. (1991). Effects of fitness test type, teacher, and gender on exercise, intrinsic motivation, and physical self-worth. *Journal of School Health, 61*, 11–16.

Williams, D. P., Going, S. B., Lohman, T. G., Harsha, D. W., Webber, L. S., & Bereson, G. S. (1992). Body fatness and the risk of elevated blood pressure, total cholesterol and serum lipoprotein ratios in children and youth. *American Journal of Public Health, 82*, 358–363.

Winnick, J., & Short, F. (1999). *The Brockport physical fitness test.* Champaign, IL: Human Kinetics.

WEBSITES

Physical Activity and Fitness Assessment

http://cooperinst.org/ourkidshealth/fitnessgram/index.cfm
www.presidentschallenge.org/home_kids.aspx

Physical Activity, Fitness, and Children

www.americanheart.org
www.cdc.gov/HealthyYouth/publications/index.htm
www.nlm.nih.gov/medlineplus/exerciseforchildren.html

Physical Activity Reports

www.cdc.gov/nccdphp/dnpa/physical/recommendations/index.htm
www.health.gov/healthypeople
www.actionforhealthykids.org

Teaching Fitness Concepts

http://pe4life.com
www.eatsmartmovemorenc.com

14 Active and Healthy Schools

ESSENTIAL COMPONENTS OF QUALITY PROGRAMS

- I. Organized around content standards
- II. Student-centered and developmentally appropriate
- III. Physical activity and motor skill development form the core of the program
- IV. Teaches management skills and self-discipline
- V. Promotes inclusion of all students
- VI. Focuses on process over product
- VII. Promotes lifetime personal health and wellness
- VIII. Teaches cooperation and responsibility and promotes sensitivity to diversity

NATIONAL STANDARDS FOR PHYSICAL EDUCATION*

1. Demonstrates competency in motor skills and movement patterns needed to perform a variety of physical activities.
2. Demonstrates understanding of movement concepts, principles, and tactics as they apply to the learning and performance of physical activities.
3. Participates regularly in physical activity.
4. Achieves and maintains a health-enhancing level of physical fitness.
5. Exhibits responsible personal and social behavior that respects self and others in physical activity.
6. Values physical activity for health, enjoyment, challenge, self-expression, and/or social interaction.

*National Association for Sport and Physical Education (NASPE), 2004.

Weight management problems have increased rapidly over the past two decades. The need to promote active and healthy behaviors in youth led to the new My Pyramid for Kids and to passage of the Child Nutrition and WIC Reauthorization Act of 2004. This act highlights the importance of developing solutions that increase children's physical activity, provide nutrition education, and ultimately teach them healthy eating and activity habits that last a lifetime. A sound physical education program is a necessity in schools; however, it is not enough. Even in a daily physical education program, children receive only a 30-minute period of instruction offering about 15 minutes of daily physical activity. The total school environment needs to change in a way that encourages children to be active and develop nutritional eating habits. This chapter shows how to change the structure of a typical school and create an active, healthy school.

Outcomes

- Discuss the recommendations of the Child Nutrition and WIC Reauthorization Act of 2004.
- Explain the importance of schools in promoting active, healthy behaviors.
-  Discuss each component of an Active and Healthy School Program.
- Explain how to implement ideas in schools to increase students' activity level.
- Describe the requirements for implementing and maintaining an Active and Healthy School Program.

IT IS 7:00 A.M. on a cold Wednesday morning. School does not start until 8:00, but already the gym has 15 students jumping rope and playing basketball while a third-grade teacher supervises. At 7:45, students in the "walking to school" program start arriving at school, led by a parent. During the day, the classroom teachers take a quick activity break every hour. Teachers integrate nutrition concepts into the physical education lessons. Today, the physical education teacher is teaching students about "sometimes" foods and "everyday" foods. Several other classroom teachers are teaching students phonics through movement. Immediately after school, several parents, the physical education teacher, and a county health agent meet in the physical education office to discuss an upcoming Health Festival. Right outside the door, children enrolled in the after-school program are learning to estimate their steps using pedometers. At 6:30 P.M. that night, the physical education teacher starts the second of four physical education demonstration nights held during the year. This one is for first graders, who get to show off what they are learning in physical education. The event ends at 7:30, and so does another day at an active and healthy elementary school.

You have just read some examples of the many opportunities available for increasing children's activity at school. The environment at that school was modified to ensure that students receive enough activity to promote health and active learning. This chapter shows you the many possibilities for changing the school environment to give children opportunities to accumulate adequate activity and learn about nutrition, proper eating habits, and sun safety.

Why schools and physical activity? The health of youth (and adults) in the United States is a national matter of concern. Schools have long been seen as pivotal players in influencing children's health. This is one reason students must have routine physicals before entering school, and it is why school districts have school nurses. A particular concern for students today are data showing that U.S. youth are more overweight now than ever—and the problem is increasing rapidly. All students can increase their physical activity levels and positively affect their risk factors for cardiovascular disease. Schools can play an important role in children's health by offering opportunities for increased physical activity. To abate the childhood obesity epidemic and improve programs for children, the Child Nutrition and WIC Reauthorization Act of 2004 was enacted. This act highlights the importance of developing solutions that increase children's physical activity, provide nutrition education, and ultimately teach youth healthy eating and activity habits that last a lifetime. In short, the law requires all school districts with a federally funded school meals program (i.e., nearly all public schools) to develop and implement wellness policies that address nutrition and physical activity. The policies were required to be in place by the start of the 2006–07 academic school year. Now that the wellness policies are in place, it is hoped that most districts will continually evaluate and revise their program each year. The Reauthorization Act recommends (but does not mandate) that schools implement some of the following points in an effort to meet the wellness policy plan:

- Make recess and lunchtime active settings for all students.
- Offer regularly scheduled activity breaks in the classroom. These breaks last 3 to 5 minutes and give students a respite from long periods of sitting.
- Design school walking programs that are buddy based or small group based.
- Develop activity contracts for students that teach them to monitor their daily activity patterns.
- Facilitate programs for parents; share information with parents through newsletters and school-based programs.
- Place point-of-decision prompts in classrooms to encourage healthy eating, physical activity, and other healthy behaviors.

- Encourage students to participate in after-school activities.
- Maintain and strengthen nutritional service programs.

Another important emphasis of the Reauthorization Act is to balance the effects of childhood obesity while maintaining local control for the states and schools. This means that the federal government does not dictate the content of wellness policies used by local school districts. The government does, however, recommend that wellness policies address issues—such as physical activity and nutrition—that affect childhood obesity. Since each school district develops its own program, wellness policies are strongly influenced by local demographics.

The WIC Reauthorization Act heightened schools' awareness of, and role in, promoting physical activity. More recently, the American Heart Association called on schools to take the lead in promoting physical activity (Pate et al., 2006). It was recommended that schools take a multifaceted approach to promoting physical activity, including physical education, classroom physical activity, recess, and school staff wellness. Similarly, the National Association for Sport and Physical Education (NASPE) "recommends that all PK–12 schools implement a comprehensive school physical activity program" (NASPE, 2008). This NASPE position statement suggests schools use quality physical education as the foundation for the program while creating an active school environment (classroom physical activity, recess, activity breaks, active transport, and out-of-school programs) that fosters community, parental, and staff involvement. As these sources demonstrate, school-based physical activity is being advocated by leading experts and organizations in the field.

Although health benefits are the primary reason for promoting school-based physical activity, schools often need a more convincing rationale. In the era of No Child Left Behind, schools are focusing on standardized test scores. Any ideas or programs interfering with that goal are often not implemented. This educational climate has led scholars to examine the role of physical activity in schools. Researchers want to know if physically active children learn better and perform better academically than physically inactive children do. Several studies examining the effects of increased physical activity on academic performance have found that allowing more time for physical activity neither increased nor decreased academic performance (Ahamed et al., 2007; Coe et al., 2006; Sallis et al., 1999). In a statistical review of many studies on children, Sibley and Etnier (2003) concluded that physical activity and cognition are positively related and that physical activity may aid in cognitive development. Tomporowski (2003) suggests that physical activity may improve cognitive performance. This article also suggests that behavior improves following activity bouts. Others have found that when physical activity is spread throughout the day, it may improve children's attention, concentration, and behavior (Azrin, Ehle, & Beaumont, 2006; Caterino & Polak, 1999; Mahar et al., 2006; Pellegrini, Huberti, & Jones, 1995). It is important to note that classroom teachers often report lack of concentration and misbehavior as common barriers to student learning. A relatively new line of research is examining the effects of physical activity on brain function. Although this research is in its infancy, the findings are encouraging and suggest physical activity does positively affect the brain and a person's ability to learn (Ratey, 2008). In sum, encouraging evidence is beginning to mount that either directly or indirectly, physical activity contributes to academic learning. This information can be used to further convince administrators to make physical activity a part of every child's school day.

If schools are to take the lead in promoting physical activity, it is essential for each school to appoint a leader. In schools seeking to implement a physical activity program as part of the wellness policy, the first choice for a director of physical activity should be the physical education teacher (Castelli & Beighle, 2007). If the physical educators are not sought, they should at least ask to be a part of the wellness policy committee. As committee members, physical education teachers absolutely must be familiar with the requirements of the law. Further, physical education teachers need an action plan that meets the requirements and addresses childhood obesity issues in their districts. These teachers can coordinate and direct the development of an Active and Healthy School Program (AHSP). The primary purpose of an AHSP is to improve the health and wellness of students through various strategies that modify the overall school environment. Because every school is different, the AHSP focuses on changing the school environment so that students are naturally encouraged to increase physical activity levels and make healthier choices such as healthy eating habits and sunscreen use.

The rest of this chapter presents suggested components of an AHSP and offers many strategies for implementing them. Again, these are simply recommended strategies. Not all strategies are likely to be effective at a particular school. However, by selecting and implementing effective strategies, reflecting on their effectiveness, and making adjustments, schools can create a dynamic AHSP that evolves over time.

COMPONENTS OF AN ACTIVE AND HEALTHY SCHOOL

QUALITY PHYSICAL EDUCATION

In most cases, physical education teachers should serve as the physical activity coordinators in a school, specifically in an AHSP. Although they may not actively participate in an event or strategy, these teachers probably will have input into virtually every physical activity-based strategy in an AHSP. For example, a physical education teacher may organize and teach an after-school aerobics class for teachers. He also may coordinate a group of teachers who supervise a before-school physical activity club for students. Physical education teachers are essential to AHSP success; without them, physical activity is highly unlikely to be an integral part of the school day.

One note here: If the physical educator chooses not to be involved in the AHSP, it is important to identify another person (e.g., a classroom teacher or other specialist) to assume the responsibility. The point is that someone must take the lead in ensuring that her school promotes active and healthy behaviors. In the model school program created in the Mesa, Arizona, public schools, the physical education teacher is released a half day a week to carry out AHSP program administrative duties. As with most effective programs, positive things happen when quality people direct them.

A quality physical education program is important for maintaining and increasing student involvement. If students do not enjoy physical education, it is difficult to imagine them wanting to participate in AHSP activities. For example, if a typical physical education lesson consists of calisthenics and sitting on the sidelines while half the class plays soccer, not many students will want to join an after-school program. Children might be thinking, "You want me to stay after school for more of the same?" For increased participation as well as a quality physical education program, a physical activity coordinator is the basis of an AHSP.

ACTIVE LEARNING IN THE CLASSROOM

Many teachers have heard that people remember 10% of what we read, 20% of what we hear, 20% of what we see, and 90% of what we say and do. Elementary classrooms are full of students who learn by doing or experiencing. Besides, as mentioned earlier, studies show that physical activity is related to the learning process. With these ideas in mind it follows that, when possible, teaching through movement is beneficial in the classroom. Not every classroom lesson, or even most of the lessons, has to be movement based; but when possible, integrating movement into instruction can offer students another medium for learning and increase their activity levels. To successfully implement this plan, schools must overcome two major barriers: Some classroom teachers do not feel comfortable teaching students in an active setting, and they do not know how to integrate movement into their lessons.

Physical education teachers have the luxury of using a large, open space for movement and must consider the issues of space and noise when designing activities for classroom teachers to implement. First, how much space is available? In most classrooms, space is at a premium. Strategies for addressing this issue include (1) having students (in upper grades) move their desks to the perimeter of the room; or (2) using activities that students can perform without moving desks. Second, the teacher must consider what is happening in the class next door. Children can be reminded to keep their voices down, but a classroom full of students making a reasonable amount of noise while being active can irritate nearby teachers and their students. The problem can be solved by teaching students to participate under control and quietly and avoiding highly active games. Scheduling when classes are away at music or PE may be another alternative.

In designing effective activities for classroom teachers, the physical educator first must develop an understanding of the standards, objectives, or concepts the classroom teachers are teaching. In an era of accountability, most teachers will not implement an activity unless it is aligned with a specific state standard. Next, ask how the concept is being taught. If a classroom teacher is using a particular strategy, his students may be confused by an activity that uses another strategy. Finally, learn each classroom teacher's "comfort zone." Would she be willing to do a dance with students? Is he an outdoors person? Does she like team sports? With this information, physical educators can work with classroom teachers to create effective and active classroom-based learning experiences for students.

Developing activities from scratch can be difficult, especially because physical educators have their own lessons to develop. Fortunately, many teachers and curriculum developers have created and marketed programs designed for classroom teachers to integrate physical activity into lessons that are aligned with standards. Many of these programs can be found online, and they include materials such as sample videotapes, lesson plans, equipment needed, and teaching strategies. When choosing a program and discussing options with classroom teachers, physical educators must be sure these teachers understand that activity in the classroom is not a physical education program. Rather, the goal is to offer classroom-based strategies for teaching some academic concepts through movement.

OUT-OF-SCHOOL PROGRAMS

Due to the sedentary nature of the school day, it is no surprise that students receive most of their physical activity outside of school hours (Morgan, Pangrazi, & Beighle, 2003; Tudor-Locke et al., 2006). In many schools, the

YMCA or local recreation department uses the gymnasium for after-school programs. These programs are usually activity-based; students play in the gym, on the playground, or in a grassy space. After-school programs offer an excellent opportunity to teach students about healthy foods and other healthy behaviors. They also can provide tutoring for students needing extra assistance. Before-school hours present another opportunity for students to be active. Opening the school grounds and offering activities for students who arrive before school has great potential. At many schools, parents trying to get to work on time often drop off students early. Without before-school programs, these students often just sit and wait outside the school.

Implementing effective extracurricular activities often requires overcoming barriers. The most prevalent barrier is cost. With the emphasis on standardized testing and childhood obesity, funding for programs that offer tutoring for physical activity and nutrition education is often available if teachers just ask. Other sources include private businesses, the PTA, and external grants. Most districts have resources to assist teachers who are seeking grants. Another barrier is transportation. Often the success of a program, particularly an after-school program, is strongly influenced by the availability of student transportation (Jago & Baranowski, 2004). Attendance in such programs can be limited because students who are bused to school have to leave immediately after school. If the additional transportation is a burden for parents, they may not allow their child to participate. Ideas for clearing this hurdle vary from school to school. Some school districts provide transportation in the form of an after-school bus for students participating in district-sponsored after-school activities. Lastly, liability is sometimes a barrier to after-school activities. Districts are often reluctant to allow students in the gym outside of school hours due to increased insurance costs. Many schools are developing community–school programs in which parks are built next to schools so the two institutions can work together to provide maximum use of both public facilities. Regardless of the roadblocks, they must be overcome for the good of all students.

ACTIVITY BREAKS

Elementary schools offer activity breaks in three forms: recess, lunchtime activity time, and mini-breaks throughout the school day. Students need at least two 15-minute activity breaks (recess) per day. *Note that there is strong emphasis on renaming recess an* "activity break." This new terminology indicates that a break has an educational purpose (to promote activity) rather than being a recess from learning. During this time, teachers should encourage students to be active. Providing equipment and organized games supervised by the playground attendant has been shown to increase physical activity during activity breaks (Jago & Baranowski, 2004). One study found that girls average almost 1,200 steps and boys 1,400 steps during a 15-minute activity break (Tudor-Locke et al., 2006). In just 15 minutes, children can accumulate approximately 10% of the daily physical activity award threshold for the President's Active Lifestyle Award (PCPFS, 2005).

Lunchtime also offers an excellent opportunity for physical activity. This time differs from activity breaks because children use the allotted time for eating and activity. Tudor-Locke and colleagues (2006) found that during a 40-minute lunch break, boys averaged 2,521 steps and girls 1,913 steps each day. No data are available regarding how much time students spent eating and how much they spent playing, but the study clearly indicates that children also use lunchtime to be active. Just as with activity breaks, teachers need to encourage students to be active during the lunch break. Nutritionists recommend that students be active first and then eat lunch, so they do not eat quickly to have more time for play. There also is some evidence that children who eat after being active waste less food. However, this approach is controversial because it lengthens the lunch hour (decreasing the physical education teacher's time to use the multipurpose room for classes). Also, some schools question whether having less playtime and eating more food is the direction we want children to pursue.

Mini–activity breaks in the classroom allow students to accumulate physical activity in small bouts throughout the day. Typically, a mini-break lasts 3 to 5 minutes and may or may not involve leaving the classroom. Pellegrini, Huberty, and Jones (1995) found that offering activity breaks every hour decreased behavior issues and problems with inattentive students. Other research has found that activity breaks, along with journaling activity from the previous day, are effective in increasing daily physical activity levels of children, particularly girls (Ernst & Pangrazi, 1999; Pangrazi et al., 2003). Unlike activity and lunch breaks, which occur once per day, mini-breaks can be offered much more frequently (up to six times per day). These short breaks provide a great source of physical activity and minimize long disruptions to classroom activities. With practice, students are soon quick and efficient at starting mini-breaks and immediately resuming class work afterward.

SUN SAFETY PROGRAM

One way of increasing students' activity is to have them spend more time outdoors, where they are more active. This strategy presents an additional risk—skin damage caused by the sun. In the United States, one in five people will develop skin cancer. Children are of particular concern because overexposure to the sun at a young age increases the risk of skin cancer throughout life. About 80%

of a person's sun exposure occurs before age 18 (Stern, Weinstein, & Baker, 1986). Blistering sunburns during childhood significantly increase the risk of developing skin cancer later in life (American Academy of Pediatrics, 1999). Children should know the risks associated with sun exposure and learn how they can protect themselves. Arizona is the first U.S. state to mandate a sun safety course for teachers.

Schools can improve their sun safety in several ways. Teachers can encourage or require children to wear long-sleeved clothes, hats, and sunglasses (these prevent cataracts from forming later in life) when playing outside. Some schools provide sunscreen for children who do not have their own, but this strategy requires collaboration with the school nurse in case of allergies. Activity breaks can be scheduled to avoid peak sun hours of 10:00 A.M. and 2:00 P.M. Newsletters can be sent home to notify parents of the measures being taken at school and encourage them to take similar precautions at home. Lastly, as a part of health education, teachers can present classroom lessons on the importance of sun safety, risks of sun exposure, and strategies for maximizing sun safety. The U.S. Environmental Protection Agency sponsors The Sunwise School Program, designed for educators. Sunwise is a comprehensive program that provides lesson plans, brochures and letters for parents, and workbooks for students. The materials suggest various active games that teach children about sun safety and include information on how to become a Sunwise school (available at www.epa.gov/sunwise). A study of the Sunwise Program (Kyle et al., 2008) showed that if the program were continued until 2015, it would avert more than 11,000 skin cancer cases and 50 premature deaths.

Safety Tip

Encourage or require children to wear sunscreen. The cost of sunscreen can be a barrier to some families, so explore buying it in gallon jugs for all children to use before going outside. Be sure to consult with the school nurse in case of allergies.

Another strategy for sun safety is to offer children shade from the sun. An examination of playgrounds often reveals a lack of shade for play. In Arizona, sun shades are becoming common playground structures. They also protect teachers and students during physical education classes. Teachers must allow students to wear hats (full brimmed, not baseball), during outdoor activity. Sending students outside during the peak sun hours of the day without sunscreen, hats, and dark glasses is a practice that needs to stop sooner rather than later.

POINT-OF-DECISION PROMPTS

Point-of-decision prompts are simply signs placed in areas around the school where students and faculty will be making choices regarding healthy behaviors. This strategy has been proven effective for increasing physical activity behavior in communities (Heath, 2003). A classic example is placing a sign directly above the "up" button on an elevator in an office building. The sign informs the elevator rider about the health benefits of taking the nearby stairs rather than taking the elevator.

Elementary schools can post signs on the playground to encourage students to be active. Signs can simply say, "Be Active," or they can suggest games for students to play during activity breaks (Figure 14.1). Nutrition-based point-of-decision prompts, such as signs reminding students of healthy food choices, can be placed in the cafeteria (Figure 14.2). Making signs that remind students to be sun safe, active, and choose healthy foods can be a classroom project or an art project, and classes can post their work throughout the school.

TEACHER INVOLVEMENT

Encouraging faculty to improve their own health through school-based activities is another strategy to consider when developing an AHSP. Students see teachers as models. If they see their teacher eating healthier foods and being active during activity breaks, these seemingly small acts can have

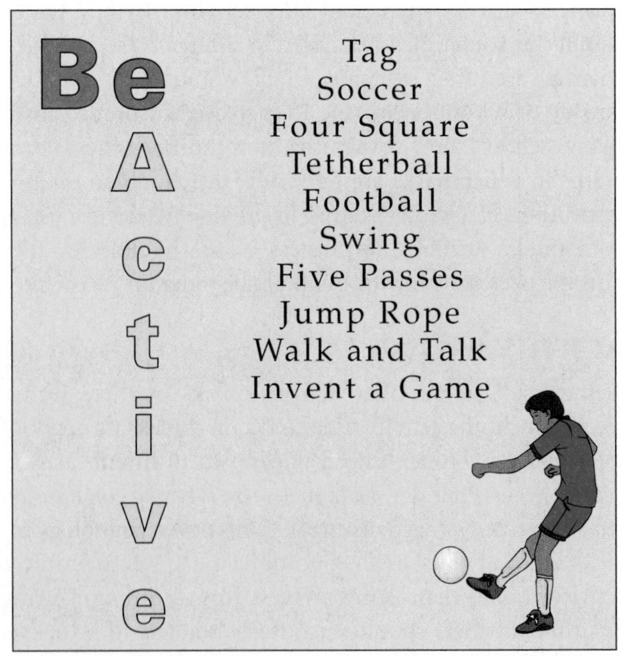

FIGURE 14.1 Example of a point-of-decision prompt sign for the playground.

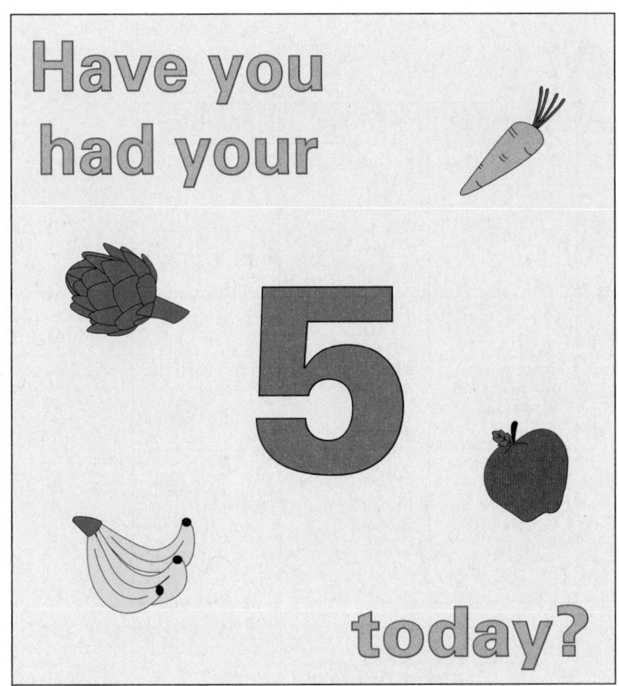

FIGURE 14.2 Example of a nutrition point-of-decision prompt sign for the school cafeteria.

tremendous potential impact. Physical educators can coordinate walking clubs, after-school aerobics, brief nutrition education presentations at faculty meetings, or even a friendly "steps" competition among teachers. In fact, step competitions are an effective way to introduce pedometers, particularly if a school has only a few pedometers. Seeing a few teachers wearing pedometers and discussing their steps often interests other teachers, who then want a pedometer. Students also begin asking about pedometers and become intrigued. Some companies sell pedometers at a discount for schools to resell for profit. Schools can then purchase class sets of pedometers for use during physical education. Selling pedometers is a much healthier fund-raising activity than selling candies, cookie dough, and the like. For an example of a shareware program, see www.walk4life.com.

WALKING-TO-SCHOOL EVENTS

Walking-to-school programs are increasingly popular. Local, state, and national events are held throughout the country. Even more important, these programs offer a safe, active, and enjoyable source of physical activity for students. Schools can develop a walking-to-school program by using the procedure outlined here. For more information about this topic, see the Centers for Disease Control and Prevention website (www.cdc.gov/nccdphp/dnpa/kidswalk).

1. *Generate interest.* Newsletters, conversations with parents, parent surveys, and discussions with local agencies such as the fire department, police department, or health department will attract interest and provide helpful feedback during the initial planning phase of the program.
2. *Organize.* During this phase of the program, recruit volunteers and hold meetings to work out program details and logistics. It is always helpful for important personnel such as the principal, crossing guards, key district administrators, parent volunteers, and representatives from the police department to serve on the planning committee. Topics to be covered include:
   a. Safe, practical routes for students to walk to school
   b. Traffic management
   c. Collecting contact information and addresses of families who are interested in participating as well as obtaining parental consent
   d. Location and scheduling of personnel during the event
   e. Time line of the event
   f. Media contacts and marketing of the event
3. *Implement and reflect.*
   a. After carrying out the plan and holding a walking-to-school event, it is important to call a planning committee meeting.
   b. At the meeting, members can talk openly about what they found successful and what they feel needs to be modified for the next event.
   c. If members cannot be present, encourage them to present their ideas in writing.

PARENTAL INVOLVEMENT

For elementary students, parents/guardians are the most significant adults in their lives. Parents substantially affect their child's attitude toward physical activity and their physical activity level (Welk, Wood, & Morss, 2003). Programs that involve parents and encourage them to be active with their children can help promote physical activity for an entire family. Here are some ideas that can be included in an AHSP to help foster parental involvement.

Activity Calendars

An activity calendar can challenge children and their families to participate in activities listed by day (Figure 14.3 on page 294). When families reach a certain goal (e.g., active 75% of the days), put their name on the Active Family Wall of Fame posted in the gym.

PE Nights/Demonstration Nights

On PE nights, students and parents participate in physical education activities together. Parents see what their

February

Sunday	Monday	Tuesday	Wednesday	Thursday	Friday	Saturday
1 *Active families stay healthy*	2	3 Play football with a friend	4	5 Play basketball for 10 minutes	6	7
8	9 Make a snowman	10 How many times can you jump rope without stopping?	11	12 Create a dance and practice it for 20 minutes	13 NO SCHOOL! BE ACTIVE ALL DAY!	14 Be kind to your heart . . . be active.
15 *Children should be active at least 60 minutes per day*	16 Teach someone your favorite stretch	17 Teach a family member a PE game	18 Do extra chores as a favor to your parents	19 Jump rope for a total of 10 minutes	20 Invent a new exercise	21 Shovel snow
22	23 Do your favorite fitness challenge	24 Play a new game at recess	25	26	27 Start a game of tag in your neighborhood	28

If you want to do an activity other than the one on the calendar, GREAT! Write the new activity on your calendar. Mrs. Panko may even put your activity on the calendar as an activity next month.

How many minutes of activity should you do a day? ____________

What types of activities are cardiovascular activities? ____________

Name three lifetime activities. ____________ ____________ ____________

What is a locomotor skill? ____________

FIGURE 14.3 Example of a family physical activity calendar.

children are learning in physical education, and they discover activities they can do at home with their children. Demonstration nights involve parents watching their children participate in physical education activities. Typically the grand finale involves parents and students participating in activities together. In a larger school, these events will need to be held for specific grade levels to prevent overcrowding and allow for safe activity. Most parents leave these programs thinking, "I wish PE was like that when I was younger," or "PE sure has changed."

Fun Days

Sometimes called Field Days or Play Days, these events are generally planned as a year-end celebration. They can also be held in September to kick off the school year. On Field Days, teachers set up several stations, and classes move from station to station and participate in the activities. Stations can offer the usual physical education activities as well as novel activities that are simply safe and fun. Parents are great resources to serve as station attendants and as planning committee members to help coordinate the event. For primary-age student activities, upper-level elementary students can also serve on the planning committee, help set up the event, and supervise the stations.

Charity Events

Charity events give families opportunities to be active together. Events can vary from a walk/run race, a walkathon, Chores for Change, or even a Physical Activity Festival whose proceeds go to a charity. The charity can be an outside organization or a local family, or support for the physical education program. Like any program, charity events require extensive planning and coordination. Collaborating with the school's parent organization or other school-based organizations may help divide the labor needed for planning.

COMMUNITY INVOLVEMENT

Every community is full of valuable resources for an AHSP. These resources may include people experienced in planning events, working with other community organizations, collaborating with schools, or simply generating program funding.

Physical educators should constantly seek collaborative, creative involvement from the community. Organizations unable to donate money may have a program that encourages employees to volunteer in the community or some other useful resource. Also, members of the AHSP committee should be open to volunteering for events held by other community organizations. Building such relationships can have considerable long-term benefit.

Early in the process of developing an AHSP, potential community resources must be identified. The following organizations may be interested in partnering with physical education teachers. Consider inviting personnel from these organizations to participate in the AHSP.

- *YMCAs, recreation centers, Boys and Girls Clubs.* These organizations are all interested in physical activity and youth. Further, they are all involved in before-school, after-school, and even during-school programs. One strategy is for the physical education teacher to offer training for their program staff. This allows the physical education teacher to teach the staff what is happening during physical education.
- *County health agencies.* Many county health departments and agents are already involved with health-related programs in the schools. This makes them an excellent resource and potential collaboration partner in developing an AHSP. County health agents may provide sun safety, nutrition education, tobacco education, and other lessons. Some departments, along with the physical education teacher, also can work with classroom teachers in efforts to increase classroom physical activity.
- *Businesses.* Most businesses—particularly health-related businesses such as hospitals, insurance companies, bicycle shops, fitness centers, and doctor clinics—near a school or within a school district have a vested interest in contributing to the lives of youth in their community. Businesses may also be willing to donate funds to purchase physical education equipment in exchange for posting a banner in the gym or having their logo on physical education newsletters.
- *Youth sports.* Youth sports offer an excellent opportunity for students to be active. To maximize this experience, be sure that parents and coaches receive training, so all parties involved agree on what is good for children. Physical educators are the experts at teaching skills and motivating youth in a fun environment. Why not share that knowledge with coaches? One Saturday morning per season could be set aside so that parents and coaches can come together to learn how to teach skills and gain an understanding of how all adults must work together for the good of the children.

SCHOOL NUTRITION ENVIRONMENT

When developing an AHSP, physical educators rightfully emphasize the importance of physical activity in managing weight; after all, physical activity is what they are trained to do. But they must also consider the other side of the equation—calories consumed, or diet. Although physical education teachers are not trained to make decisions regarding school food services, they most certainly can become involved and influence the school nutrition environment.

Schools realize that to stay healthy, children must have access to ample amounts of good, nutritious food (Anspaugh & Ezell, 2004). Many students eat both breakfast and lunch at school; thus, the school provides at least 67% of their meals. Schools that provide two meals per day also know that healthy students perform better academically (Hanson et al., 2005). To help their students form lifelong habits of eating well, schools also must provide nutrition education.

Physical educators can play a supportive role in enhancing the quality of nutrition in the schools. For example, the U.S. Department of Agriculture (USDA) recently released the new children's food guide pyramid, called MyPyramid for Kids, which offers accompanying tips, lesson plans, and coloring sheets designed to explain healthful eating to children (www.MyPyramid.gov/kids/index.html). Post the pyramid where students will see it every day. The advanced version (Figure 14.4 on page 296) contains the basic principles of nutrition and physical activity. Here are some strategies physical education teachers can advocate to improve the school nutrition environment.

1. Ensure that all students have access to nutritious foods. Because hungry children cannot perform well academically, schools must develop programs to ensure students receive a nutrient-dense breakfast and lunch.
2. If vending machines are on campus, be sure they offer only nutritious, healthy choices.
3. In the classrooms, do not give foods as a reward. Many teachers hand out candy bars, gum, or other sweet treats as rewards for correct answers, good behavior, and so on. To prevent this practice, the principal must develop policies for rewarding students in other ways (e.g., stickers, pencils, and other items). Another alternative is to ensure that when teachers give food to students, it is nutritious. Think of the positive message children receive

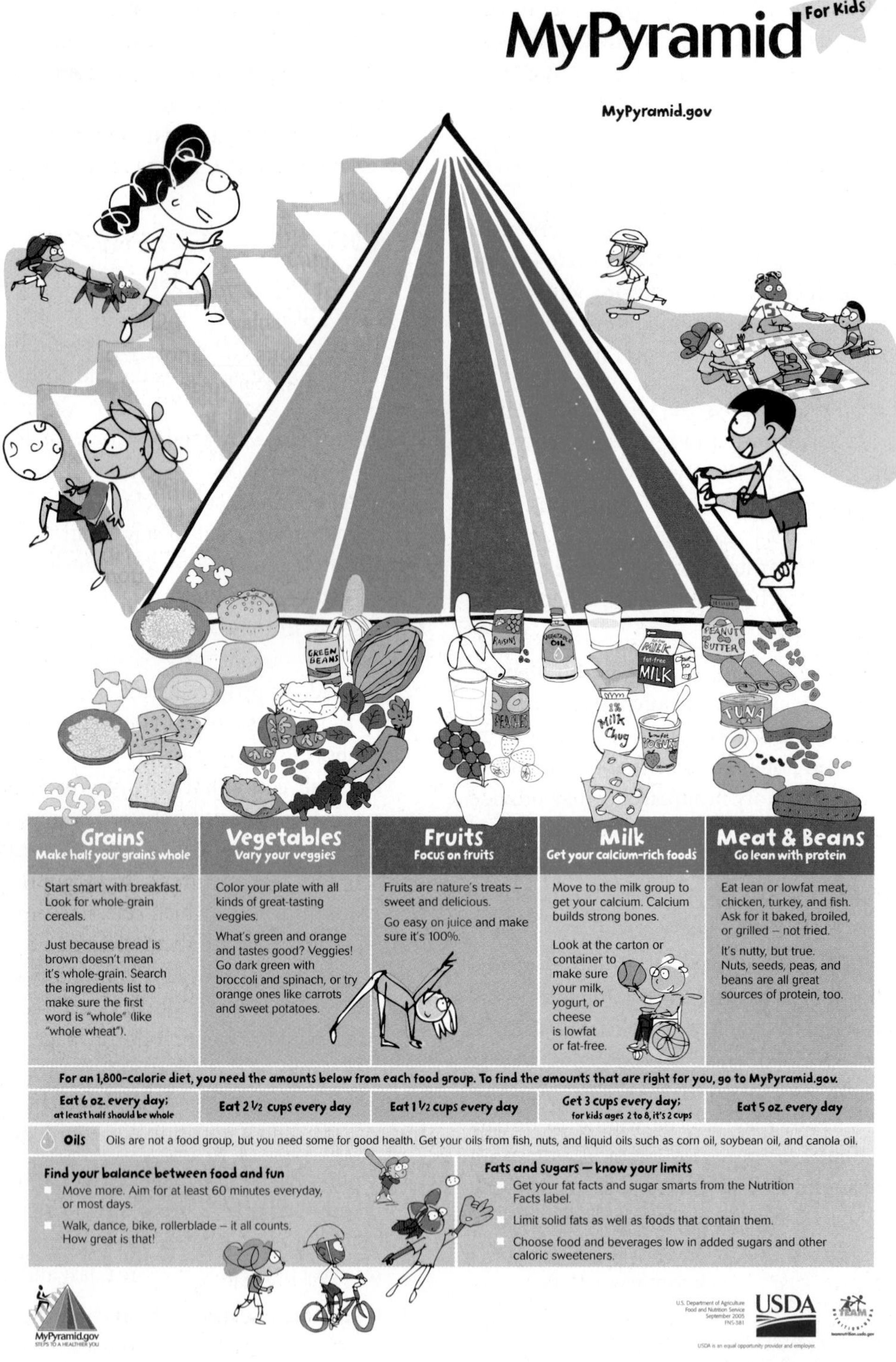

FIGURE 14.4 MyPyramid for Kids.

about eating healthy foods if an apple is their reward for a correct answer—they will start thinking of apples as a treat. This method works particularly well when used during a child's first few years of school.

4. Offer children nutrient-dense meals. This means the empty calories of french fries and cupcakes cannot make up even a small part of the calories. Recommendations for nutrition standards and instructional materials are available from the USDA at www.nutrition.gov.
5. Allow school clubs to sell only nutritious foods.
6. Provide a clean, safe, and attractive eating environment.

7. Serve lunch as close to noon as possible. More and more schools are serving lunch to students as early as 10 A.M.
8. Use bulletin boards and signs in the cafeteria to complement the nutrition education, sun safety, and physical activity being promoted throughout the school.
9. Integrate nutrition education and other health content into physical education activities. See the "Health Activities" section of Chapter 11.
10. Gather feedback from parents and other community members regarding their feelings about the nutrition environment at the school or the changes being made.

GETTING STARTED

When initiating any project, one of the toughest tasks is getting started. Great ideas may get lost because physical educators do not know where to begin and end up discarding them. Because people often see projects as a huge task that cannot be accomplished, many great ideas remain on the shelf. The key to starting any project, whether it is a paper for school or the organization of an AHSP, is to develop a series of manageable tasks. Remember that implementing and sustaining an AHSP program requires knowledge about physical activity promotion, advocacy, public relations, and marketing (McKenzie, 2007). The following suggestions can help make creating and maintaining an AHSP a series of steps that can be accomplished systematically.

FORM AN AHSP COMMITTEE

The physical educator should take on the role of the AHSP coordinator. Without support from others, however, an AHSP is difficult to achieve. When forming the committee, consider key personnel in the program. Teachers, school administrators, district administrators, parents, students, university faculty, fire department representatives, local business owners, community leaders, and community organizations are just a few potential partners. Invite all of these people to a kickoff meeting. At the meeting, be sure to encourage members of the AHSP committee to invite other people who might be important resources. Figure 14.5 gives some tips for recruiting potential AHSP committee members and collaborators. This is an opportunity for AHSP coordinators to use their public relations skills.

DEVELOP AN IMPLEMENTATION PLAN

The AHSP committee's first task is to develop a plan. As the coordinator, the physical education teacher should provide the committee with some background information, the components of an AHSP, and a larger vision for the school. After brainstorming for ideas, the committee needs to prioritize them and develop short- and long-term objectives. Lastly, to prevent overwhelming teachers, students, and communities, it is important for the AHSP to start small. The first AHSP activity might be to give a short presentation about the program at the school's open house. Also at the open house, they can set up a booth at the front door to provide fliers and survey parents. After surveying parents, AHSP members can develop the next steps. Another school might begin by sending fliers home and handing them out during school drop-off and pickup hours, while the physical education teacher begins using pedometers in his lessons. The key is to keep the tasks manageable and aligned with the goals. Over time, the AHSP will evolve into various activities with subcommittees having their own set of objectives related to the program's original purpose.

REFLECT, EVALUATE, AND PROGRESS

The AHSP should be viewed as an evolving program that will continue to progress and become more effective. Committee members must meet, examine where they have been and where they are going, and adjust the program. For instance, some events may have low attendance. Was it because the event was not attractive to children and

- *Network.* Talk to other teachers, administrators, parents, friends, and family. One person cannot have all of the appropriate contacts. People who are not able to provide what is needed may be able to give you names of those who can.
- *Introduce Yourself.* Be sure to introduce yourself to as many people in the school community as possible. When meeting people for the first time, take the time to get to know them if time permits. The first meeting is generally not an appropriate time to seek resources. Let the individual know about the AHSP.
- *Get Involved.* Parent organizations, youth sports, and local youth clubs are always looking for volunteers. Offer to help or ask someone on the AHSP committee to help out at an event held by these organizations. The best way to get others to help you is to help them.
- *Be Persistent.* During the process of starting an AHSP and seeking resources, you will hear "No" or "Not right now" regularly. Keep moving forward, knowing that what you are working toward is what is best for kids.
- *Ask Others to Help.* When one person agrees to get involved, ask him for names of anyone else who may be interested in helping. Find out his background. He may have excellent suggestions for getting others involved or may have great contacts.

FIGURE 14.5 Tips for recruiting an Active and Healthy School Program committee.

families? Was the event marketed well? Was the event on the same day as Little League opening day? Without thoughtful reflection and honest evaluation, an AHSP runs the risk of becoming stale, dormant, and, possibly, nonexistent. With quality reflection, programs can continue evolving to meet school and community needs. Information gathered through evaluation also helps when seeking funding from outside organizations.

MEET WITH OTHER SCHOOLS

Another strategy in developing and maintaining a quality AHSP is to meet with other schools with similar programs. "No sense reinventing the wheel" applies here. Your committee can benefit by learning what other schools have found successful. Remember that school demographics may affect the success of some activities; an activity that was not effective at Franklin Elementary may succeed at Monroe Elementary, and vice versa. While working with other schools, keep an open mind, collect as much information as possible, and allow the committee to discuss future directions based on the experiences of other schools.

When all is said and done, an AHSP demands a whole approach to the school environment. Schools, families, and communities must cooperate to create a setting that educates children physically as well as academically. The saying, "It takes a village to raise a child" could not be truer. No longer can we afford to believe that making children sit in class for long periods will improve their academic performance. Most adults know only too well that even they can sit and concentrate for only a finite amount of time. After that, the process becomes nonproductive. Let's make sure our schools excel in promoting activity and academic performance. The old saying, "A healthy mind lives in a healthy body" must drive the environment of today's schools.

REFLECTION AND REVIEW

HOW AND WHY

1. Why are Active and Healthy Schools Programs (AHSPs) important?
2. How can physical educators contribute to an active, healthy school?
3. How can community involvement improve the effectiveness of an AHSP?
4. Why is it important to develop an AHSP committee?

CONTENT REVIEW

1. Explain what the Child Nutrition and WIC Reauthorization Act means to physical education teachers.
2. Present several recommendations made by the Child Nutrition and WIC Reauthorization Act.
3. Discuss the purpose of an AHSP.
4. List and describe the components of an AHSP.
5. Describe how a physical education teacher can go about starting an AHSP.

FOR MORE INFORMATION

REFERENCES AND SUGGESTED READINGS

Ahamed, Y., MacDonald, H., Reed, K., Naylor, P., Liu-Ambrose, T., & McKay, H. (2007). School-based physical activity does not compromise children's academic performance. *Medicine and Science in Sports and Exercise, 39,* 371–376.

American Academy of Pediatrics. (1999). Ultraviolet light: A hazard to children. *Pediatrics, 104,* 328–333.

Anspaugh, D. J., & Ezell, G. (2004). *Teaching today's health.* San Francisco: Benjamin Cummings.

Azrin, N. H., Ehle, C. T., & Beaumont, A. L. (2006). Physical exercise as a reinforcer to promote calmness of an ADHD child. *Behavior Modification, 30*(5), 564–570.

Castelli, D. M., & Beighle, A. (2007). The physical education teacher as school activity director. *JOPERD, 78*(5), 25–28.

Caterino, M. C., & Polak, E. D. (1999). Effects of two types of activity on the performance of 2nd-, 3rd-, and 4th-grade students on a test of concentration. *Perceptual Motor Skills, 89,* 245–248.

Coe, D. P., Pivarnik, J. M., Womack, C. J., Reeves, M. J., & Malina, R. M. (2006). Effect of physical education and activity levels on academic achievement in children. *Medicine and Science in Sports and Exercise, 38,* 1515–1519.

Ernst, M. P., & Pangrazi, R. P. (1999). Effects of a physical activity program on children's activity levels and attraction to physical activity. *Pediatric Exercise Science, 11,* 393–405.

Hanson, T. L., Muller, C., Austin, G., & Lee-Bayha, J. (2005). Research findings about the relationship between student health and academic achievement. In California Department of Education, *Getting results: Developing safe and healthy kids update 5.* Sacramento: CDE Press.

Heath, G. W. (2003). Increasing physical activity in communities: What really works? *President's Council on Physical Fitness and Sports Research Digest, 4*(4), 1–8.

Jago, R., & Baranowski, T. (2004). Non-curricular approaches for increasing physical activity in youth: A review. *Preventive Medicine, 39*(1), 157–163.

Kyle, J. W., Hammitt, J. K., Lim, H. W., Geller, A. C., Hall-Jordan, L. H., Maibach, E. W., et al. (2008). Economic evaluation of the U.S. Environmental Protection Agency's Sunwise program: Sun protection education for young children. *Pediatrics, 121,* e1074–e1084.

Mahar, M. T., Murphy, S. K., Rowe, D. A., Golden, J., Shields, A. T., & Raedeke, T. D. (2006). Effects of a classroom-based program on physical activity and on-task behavior. *Medicine and Science in Sports and Exercise, 38,* 2086–2094.

McKenzie, T. L. (2007). The preparation of physical educators: A public health perspective. *Quest, 59*(4), 345–357.

Morgan, C. F., Pangrazi, R. P., & Beighle, A. (2003). Using pedometers to promote physical activity in physical education. *Journal of Physical Education, Recreation, and Dance, 74*(7), 33–38.

National Association for Sport and Physical Education (NASPE). (2008). Comprehensive school physical activity programs: A position statement from the National Association for Sport and Physical Education. Reston, VA: Author.

Pangrazi, R. P., Beighle, A., Vehige, T., & Vack, C. (2003). Evaluating the effectiveness of the State of Arizona's Promoting Lifestyle Activity for Youth program. *Journal of School Health, 73*(8), 317–321.

Pate, R. R., Davis, M. G., Robins, T. N., Stone, E. J., McKenzie, T. L., & Young, J. C. (2006). Promoting physical activity in children and youth: A leadership role for schools. *Circulation: Journal of the American Heart Association, 114*, 1214–1224.

Pellegrini, A. D., Huberty, P. D., & Jones, I. (1995). The effects of recess timing on children's playground and classroom behaviors. *American Educational Research Journal, 32*(4), 845–864.

President's Council on Physical Fitness and Sports. (2005). *The President's Challenge handbook*. Washington, DC: Author.

Ratey, J. J. (2008). *Spark: The revolutionary new science of exercise and the brain*. London: Little, Brown.

Sallis, J. F., McKenzie, T. L., Kolody, B., Lewis, M., Marshall, S., & Rosengard, P. (1999). Effects of health-related physical education on academic achievement: Project SPARK. *Research Quarterly for Exercise and Sport, 70*, 127–134.

Sibley, B. A., & Etnier, J. L. (2003). The relationship between physical activity and cognition in children: A meta-analysis. *Pediatric Exercise Science, 15*(3), 243–256.

Stern, R. S., Weinstein, M. C., & Baker, S. G. (1986). Risk reduction for nonmelanoma skin cancer with childhood sunscreen use. *Archives of Dermatology, 122*, 537–545.

Tomporowski, P. D. (2003). Cognitive and behavioral responses to acute exercise in youths: A review. *Pediatric Exercise Science, 15*, 348–359.

Tudor-Locke, C., Lee, S. M., Morgan, C. F., Beighle, A., & Pangrazi, R. P. (2006). Children's pedometer-determined physical activity patterns during the segmented school day. *Medicine and Science in Sports and Exercise, 38*(10), 1732–1738.

Welk, G. J., Wood, K., & Morss, G. (2003). Parental influences on physical activity in children: An exploration of the potential mechanisms. *Pediatric Exercise Science, 15*(1), 19–33.

WEBSITES

Arizona Sunwise Program
www.azdhs.gov/phs/sunwise/pdf/activities_k-2.pdf

Centers for Disease Control and Prevention Walk to School Program
www.cdc.gov/nccdphp/dnpa/kidswalk

Children's Food Pyramid
www.MyPyramid.gov/kids/index.html

Comprehensive School Physical Activity
http://aahperd.org/naspe/pdf_files/CSPAP_Online.pdf

Environmental Protection Agency Sunwise Program
www.epa.gov/sunwise

Gopher Sports Active and Healthy School Program
www.activeandhealthyschools.com

Nutrition.gov
www.nutrition.gov

School Nutrition Association
www.asfsa.org

U.S. Department of Agriculture
www.usda.gov

U.S. Department of Health and Human Services
www.os.hhs.gov

15 Movement Concepts and Themes

ESSENTIAL COMPONENTS OF QUALITY PROGRAMS

- I. Organized around content standards
- II. Student-centered and developmentally appropriate
- III. Physical activity and motor skill development form the core of the program
- IV. Teaches management skills and self-discipline
- V. Promotes inclusion of all students
- VI. Focuses on process over product
- VII. Promotes lifetime personal health and wellness
- VIII. Teaches cooperation and responsibility and promotes sensitivity to diversity

NATIONAL STANDARDS FOR PHYSICAL EDUCATION*

1. Demonstrates competency in motor skills and movement patterns needed to perform a variety of physical activities.
2. Demonstrates understanding of movement concepts, principles, and tactics as they apply to the learning and performance of physical activities.
3. Participates regularly in physical activity.
4. Achieves and maintains a health-enhancing level of physical fitness.
5. Exhibits responsible personal and social behavior that respects self and others in physical activity.
6. Values physical activity for health, enjoyment, challenge, self-expression, and/or social interaction.

*National Association for Sport and Physical Education (NASPE), 2004.

This chapter is designed to help teachers and students understand movement concepts—the classification and vocabulary of movement. Teachers learn about body awareness, space awareness, qualities of movement, and relationships. This level emphasizes the process of moving rather than the product of correctly performing a skill. Students' creativity is rewarded, and ingenuity is reinforced. Movement themes are designed to integrate the concepts into actual activities on the floor.

Outcomes

- Explain how movement themes are used to develop an understanding of movement concepts.
- Define the four major categories of human movement concepts.
- Explain the purpose of movement themes.
- Define the qualities of movement.
- Teach a variety of movement themes.
- Design a unique movement theme using the four-step approach.
- Specify individual cooperative partner activities and group activities to develop educational movement.

PHYSICAL EDUCATION emphasizes skill development in the elementary school years. It is important to learn fundamental skills in the early years because they are the building blocks for more sophisticated skills. This chapter explains the vocabulary and classification of human movement and offers teachers a framework for designing lessons that help students understand the relationship between their bodies and movement. In learning the movement concepts, teachers will consider three major components:

1. Know the classification scheme for movement.
2. Understand how to design effective movement themes for instruction.
3. Use movement themes to bring the concepts of movement to life. This step integrates concepts and activities aimed at developing a "movement educated" youngster.

Chapters 15 through Chapters 18 cover development of fundamental motor skills. This section forms the foundation for developing a physically educated youngster. These chapters explore movement concepts, fundamental motor skills, manipulative skills, and body management skills. Even though all the skills and concepts are learned simultaneously, for the sake of organization and reference, they are listed in separate chapters. Figure 15.1 on page 302 shows the movement concepts and skills addressed in each chapter.

With Developmental Level I children (ages 4 to 9), the emphasis is on developing an understanding of movement concepts and learning the vocabulary of movement. Skill technique and correct performance of skills receive less emphasis. Lessons are designed to help students understand and physically experience the classification of movement concepts, including body awareness, space awareness, qualities of movement, and relationships. Instructional objectives are designed to show children how movements are classified and how movement themes can turn concepts into concrete movements. Activities emphasize the process of moving rather than the product of correctly performing a skill.

Movement themes form the foundation of movement experiences necessary for developing more specific fundamental skills. Through this process, children develop an increased awareness and understanding of the body as a vehicle for movement, and they acquire a personal vocabulary of movement skills. This text presents movement themes in the major classifications of body awareness, space awareness, qualities of movement, and relationship.

CLASSIFICATION OF HUMAN MOVEMENT CONCEPTS

The movement concept categories of body awareness, space awareness, qualities of movement, and relationship offer structure and direction for planning new movement experiences. As youngsters experience movement, they learn the vocabulary of movement so they are able to discuss and understand the unlimited possibilities for creative and productive movement.

BODY AWARENESS

This category defines *what* the body can perform; the shapes it can make, how it can balance, and the transfer of weight to different body parts. Using these categories to develop challenges adds variety to movement.

1. *Shapes the body makes.* Many shapes can be formed with the body, such as long or short, wide or narrow, straight or twisted, stretched or curled, symmetrical or asymmetrical.
2. *Balance or weight bearing.* Different parts of the body support the weight or receive the weight. Different numbers of body parts can be involved in the movements and used as body supports.
3. *Transfer of body weight.* Body weight can be moved from one body part to another, such as in walking, leaping, rolling, and so on.
4. *Flight.* Unlike transfer of body weight, flight is explosive movement that involves lifting the body weight from the floor or apparatus for an extended period. The amount of time off the floor distinguishes flight from transfer of weight. Examples include running, jumping onto a climbing rope, and hanging.

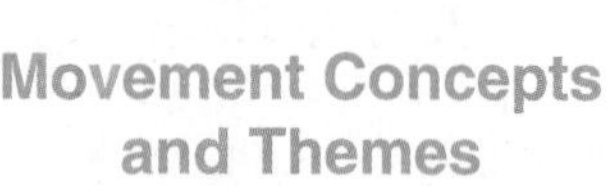

FIGURE 15.1 The components of movement concepts and fundamental motor skills.

SPACE AWARENESS

Space awareness defines *where* the body can move. The spatial qualities of movement related to moving in different directions and at different levels are the focus. Youngsters learn to use space effectively when moving. Space can be modified and used in movement experiences in the following ways:

1. *General or personal space. Personal space* is the limited area individual children use in most cases reserved for that individual only. *General space* is the total space that is used by all youngsters.
2. *Direction.* The desired route of movement, whether straight, zigzag, circular, curved, forward, backward, sideways, upward, or downward.
3. *Level.* The relationship of the body to the floor or apparatus, whether low, high, or in between.
4. *Pathways.* The path a movement takes through space. Examples are squares, diamonds, triangles, circles, and figure eights.
5. *Planes.* Somewhat specific pathways defined as circular, vertical, and horizontal, usually restricted in elementary school to performing simple activities in a specified plane.

QUALITIES OF MOVEMENT

The qualities of movement define *how* the body moves. Rather than dealing with specific movements, the focus is on how movements are performed—for example, with speed or great force or lightly. These qualities can be applied to many different skills and activities.

1. *Time or speed.* Children learn to move at varying speeds and to control speed throughout a variety of

movements. They should learn the relationship between body shape and speed and be able to use body parts to generate speed. The time factor may be varied by using different speeds—moving to a constant rhythm, accelerating, and decelerating.

2. *Force.* The effort or tension generated in movement. Force can be used effectively to aid in executing skills. Learning how to generate, absorb, and direct force is an important outcome. Force qualities may be explored by using words such as *light, heavy, strong, weak, rough,* and *gentle.*
3. *Flow.* How movements are purposefully sequenced to create continuity of movement. Most often this quality is discussed in terms of interrupted (bound) or sustained (free) flow. *Interrupted flow* stops at the end of a movement or part of a movement. *Sustained flow* involves smoothly linking different movements or parts of a movement.

RELATIONSHIP

This movement category defines with whom and/or to what the body relates. A *relationship* is defined as the position of the performer to a piece of apparatus or to other performers. Examples of relationships are near–far, above–below, over–under, in front–behind, on–off, and together–apart. In activities with other people, students can explore relationships such as leading–following, mirroring–matching, and unison–opposites. Additionally, relationships can define the body parts of a single performer, such as arms together–apart or symmetrical–asymmetrical.

TEACHING MOVEMENT SKILLS AND CONCEPTS

Four steps are suggested for creating lessons that teach movement skills and concepts incorporating the problem-solving style. These steps include many specific ideas for developing movement tasks that promote a diversity of responses.

STEP ONE: SET AND DEFINE THE MOVEMENT TASK

Define a movement task for students so they know what to solve. The task should include one or more of the following:

1. *What to do.* An action word directs the activity. Are children to move a certain way, go over and under, explore alternatives, or experiment with some nonlocomotor movement? Direct them to run, jump, or use a fundamental skill.
2. *Where to move.* What space is to be used—personal or general? What directional factors are to be employed—path or level?
3. *How to move.* What are the force factors (light–heavy)? What elements of time are involved (even–uneven, acceleration–deceleration, sudden–sustained)? What are the relationships (over–under–across, in front of–behind)? What body parts are involved for support? For locomotion?
4. *With whom or what to move.* With whom are children to work—by themselves, with a partner, or as a member of a group? Is there a choice involved? With what equipment or on what apparatus are they to perform?

When initiating movement patterns, use the following partial sentences to frame the task. Unlimited movement tasks can be developed for students to solve.

Develop a Task to Solve

1. Show me how a ______ moves. (Show me how an alligator moves.)
2. Have you seen a ______? (Have you seen a kangaroo jump?)
3. What ways can you ______? (What ways can you hop over the jump rope?)
4. How would you ______? How can you ______? (How would you dribble a ball, changing hands frequently?)
5. See how many different ways you can ______. (See how many different ways you can hang from a ladder.)
6. What can you do with a ______? What kinds of things can you ______? (What can you do with a hoop?)
7. Can you portray a ______? (Can you portray an automobile with a flat tire?)
8. Discover different ways you can ______. (Discover different ways you can volley a ball against a wall.)
9. Can you ______? (Can you keep one foot up while you bounce the ball?)
10. Who can ______ a ______ so that ______? (Who can bounce a ball so that it keeps time with the tom-tom?)
11. What does a ______? (What does a cat do when it is wet?)
12. Show ______ different ways to ______. (Show four different ways to move across the floor.)

STEP TWO: EXPERIMENT AND EXPLORE

After defining the movement task, encourage youngsters to accomplish it through experimentation and exploration. Variety can also be achieved by setting limitations and by asking youngsters to develop the task in a different way. Present tasks in the form of questions or statements that elicit and encourage variety, depth, and extent of movement. Using contrasting terms is another way to increase the depth and variety of movement. Some examples follow.

Phrases that Encourage Exploration and Variety

1. Try it again another way. Try to ______. (Try to jump higher.)
2. See how far (many times, high, close, low) ______. (See how far you can reach with your arms.)
3. Find a way to ______ or find a new way to ______. (Find a new way to jump over the bench.)
4. Apply ______ to ______. (Apply a heavy movement to your run.)
5. How else can you ______? (How else can you roll your hoop?)
6. Make up a sequence ______. (Make up a sequence of previous movements, changing smoothly from one movement to the next.)
7. Now try to combine a ______ with ______. (Now try to combine a locomotor movement with your catching.)
8. Alternate ______ and ______. (Alternate walking and hopping.)
9. Repeat the last movement and add ______. (Repeat the last movement and add a body twist as you move.)
10. See if you can ______. (See if you can do the movement with a partner.)
11. Trace (draw) a ______ with ______. (Trace a circle with your hopping partner.)
12. Find another part of the body to ______. Find other ways to ______. (Find another part of the body to take the weight.)
13. Combine the ______ with ______. (Combine the hopping with a body movement.)
14. In how many different positions can you ______? (In how many different positions can you carry your arms while walking the balance beam?)
15. How do you think the ______ would change if ______? (How do you think the balance exercise we are doing would change if our eyes were closed?)
16. On signal, ______. (On signal, speed up your movements.)

Contrasting Terms to Stimulate Variety

Another way to increase the variety of movement responses is to use terms that stress contrasts. Instead of challenging children to move quickly, ask them to contrast a quick movement with a slow movement. Table 15.1 includes many common sets of contrasting terms for use in describing ways to move.

Some of the terms may be grouped more logically in sets of three contrasts (such as forward–sideways–backward, up–down–in between, or over–under–through). Word meanings also can be emphasized according to rank or degree (as in near–nearer–nearest, or low–lower–lowest).

TABLE 15.1 Ways to move

- Above–below, beneath, under
- Across–around, under
- Around clockwise–around counterclockwise
- Before–after
- Between–alongside of
- Big–little, small
- Close–far
- Crooked–straight
- Curved–flat, straight
- Diagonal–straight
- Fast–slow
- Forward–back, backward
- Front–back, behind
- Graceful–awkward
- Heavy–light
- High–low
- In–out
- In front of–behind, in back of
- Inside–outside
- Into–out of
- Large–small
- Near–far
- On–off
- On top of–under, underneath
- Over–under, through
- Reach down–reach up
- Right–left
- Round–straight
- Separate–together
- Short–long, tall
- Sideways–forward, backward
- Smooth–rough
- Standing upright–inverted
- Sudden–sustained
- Swift–slow
- Tight–loose
- Tiny–big, large
- Top–bottom
- To the right of–to the left of
- Up–down
- Upper–lower
- Upside down–right side up
- Upward–downward
- Wide–narrow, thin
- Zigzag–straight

STEP THREE: OBSERVE AND DISCUSS VARIOUS SOLUTIONS

In this step, allow youngsters to observe some of the patterns created by others. Achievement demonstrations stimulate effort because children enjoy showing what they have put together. Focus discussions on how to put together different movements into flow and continuity. This also can be a time to point out that movement tasks can be solved in many ways.

STEP FOUR: REFINE AND EXPAND SOLUTIONS TO THE MOVEMENT TASK

The final step involves integrating various ideas students have developed and expanding their ideas into new solutions. Students can work together to develop cooperative partner and small-group skills. Make problems realistic, and allow opportunity for discussion and decision making between partners. Here are some activities that can be cooperatively developed:

1. One child is an obstacle, and the partner devises ways of moving around the positions the "obstacle" takes

FIGURE 15.2 Going around a partner.

(Figure 15.2). To increase the challenge, have one partner hold a piece of equipment such as a wand or hoop to expand movements.

2. One partner partially supports the other's weight, or the two work together to form different kinds of figures or shapes.
3. One child does a movement and the partner copies or provides a contrasting movement.
4. One child moves, and the partner attempts to shadow (do the same movements). Do it slowly with uninterrupted flow predominating.
5. One partner does a movement. The other partner repeats the movement and adds another. The first child repeats both movements and adds a third, and so on. Some limit on the number of movements can be set.
6. Children form letters or figures with their bodies on the floor or in erect positions.
7. Children practice copying activities. One child sets a movement pattern, and the rest copy the actions.

MOVEMENT SKILLS AND CONCEPTS LESSON PLANS

The accompanying text, *Dynamic Physical Education Curriculum Guide: Lesson Plans for Implementation*, 16th ed. (Pangrazi, 2010), contains lesson plans for teaching movement skills and concepts. Each lesson plan contains four or five parts presenting a variety of experiences in movement concepts and skills. This variety of activities offers children a broad spectrum of challenges and ensures a balance of experiences.

1. *Movement themes.* Two or more themes are developed to focus on teaching the concepts of movements. Locomotor and nonlocomotor movements are used as the medium for developing a movement vocabulary. Movement themes focus on a movement quality around which children build patterns and sequences. Exploration is emphasized so children develop body awareness and an understanding of movement concepts.
2. *Fundamental skills.* This section presents a wide variety of fundamental skills. Locomotor skills covered include walking, running, galloping, skipping, sliding, leaping, hopping, and jumping. Nonlocomotor skills covered are bending, rocking, swinging, turning, twisting, stretching, pushing, and pulling. Emphasis is on developing proper technique and using the skill in novel situations.
3. *Manipulative skills.* Manipulative skills are presented in each lesson using a variety of equipment. Skills practiced include throwing, kicking, striking, catching, bowling, and rolling.

TEACHING MOVEMENT THEMES

Children use the concept of movement themes to create various movement patterns and sequences. Some themes involve only a single principle or factor, while others involve two or more. Themes in this chapter focus on exploring different concepts of movement. In practice, however, isolating a particular factor is difficult. For example, in exploring balance, movement possibilities are expanded through the application of body shape, level, and time factors. The following themes are classified into four major groups or concepts of human movement: body awareness, space awareness, qualities of movement, and relationship.

15

BODY AWARENESS THEMES

Body Shapes (Figure 15.3)

FIGURE 15.3 Forming different shapes.

"Let's try making shapes and see whether we can name them. Make any shape you wish and hold it. What is the name of your shape, John? [Wide.] Try to make different kinds of wide shapes. Show me other shapes you can make. What is the name of your shape, Susie? [Crooked.] Show me different kinds of shapes that are crooked. Make yourself as crooked as possible."

"Make yourself wide and then narrow. Now tall and then small. How about tall and wide, small and narrow, tall and narrow, and small and wide? Work out other combinations."

"Select three different kinds of shapes, and move smoothly from one to another. This time I will clap my hands as a signal to change to a different shape."

"Select four different letters of the alphabet. On the floor, one after the other, make your body shape like each of these letters. Try it with numbers. Make up a movement sequence that spells a word of three letters. Show us a problem in addition or subtraction."

"Use your jump rope and make a shape on the floor. Make a shape with your body alongside the rope."

"Pretend to be as narrow as an arrow or telephone pole. Pretend to be as wide as a house, store, or hippopotamus."

"Squeeze into a tiny shape; now grow slowly into the biggest shape you can imagine. Travel to a different spot on the floor, keeping the big shape. Quickly change to the tiny shape again."

"Move around the room in groups of three. On signal, form a shape with one person standing, one kneeling, and one sitting."

"Pretend you are at a farm. Make a barn with your body."

"Jump upward, making a shape in the air. Land, holding that shape. Begin with a shape, jump upward with a half turn, and land in another shape."

"What body shapes can you make while standing on one foot?"

"Show me what body shapes you can make with your stomach touching the floor."

"Look to see where your personal space is within the general space. When I say 'Go,' run in general space. On the next signal, return to your personal space and sit down."

Balancing: Supporting Body Weight (Figure 15.4)

"Explore different ways you can balance on different surfaces of your body. Can you balance on three different parts of your body? On two? On one? Put together sequences of three or four balance positions by using different body parts or different numbers of body parts."

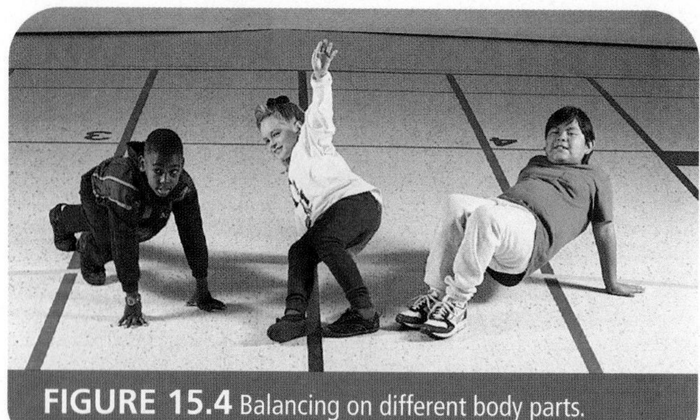

FIGURE 15.4 Balancing on different body parts.

"Can you balance on a flat body surface? What is the smallest part of the body you can balance on? Support the body on two parts that are not alike. On three parts that are not alike. Support the body on different combinations of body flats and body points."

"Use two parts of the body far away from each other to balance. Shift smoothly to another two parts."

"Who can balance on one foot with their arms stretched overhead? Out to the side?"

"Stand with feet together and eyes closed. Keep your balance while using different arm positions. Balance on one foot for 10 counts."

"From a standing position, raise one leg, straighten the leg in front of you, and swing the leg to the side and back without losing your balance."

"Move from a narrow, unstable base to a wide, stable base."

"Balance on parts of the body to form a tripod." (Explain the term.)

"Show different balance positions with part of your weight supported by the head."

"In a hands-and-knees position [crab position] balance on the right arm and right leg, the left arm and left leg, the right arm and left leg, the left arm and right leg."

"Stand on your toes and balance, using different arm positions."

"Place a beanbag on the floor. How many different ways can you balance over it? Try with a hoop. How many different ways can you balance inside the hoop?"

"When I call out a body part or parts, you balance for 5 seconds on that part or part combination." (Use knees, hands, heels, flats, points, and a variety of combinations.)

"Keep your feet together and sway in different directions without losing your balance. Can you balance on one foot with your eyes closed? Bend forward while balancing on one foot? Lift both sets of toes from the floor and balance on your heels? Now sit on the floor. Can you lift your feet and balance on your seat without hand support? Can you balance on your tummy without your feet or hands touching the floor?"

"In a standing position, lift one leg out sideways and balance on the other foot."

"Make a sequence by balancing on a narrow surface, changing to a wide surface, and changing back again to a different narrow surface."

Bridges (Figure 15.5)

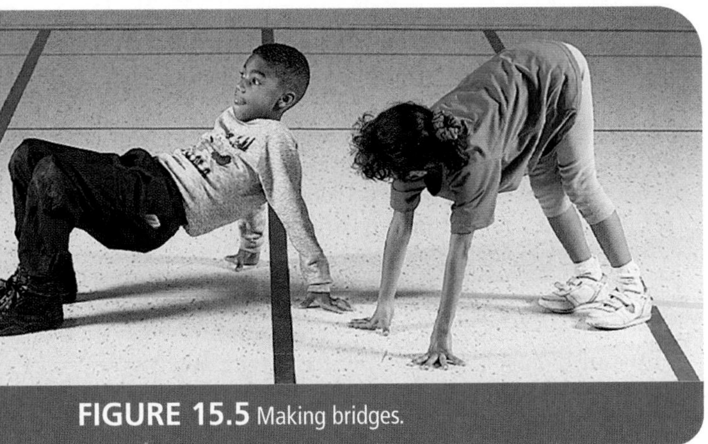

FIGURE 15.5 Making bridges.

"Show me a bridge made by using your hands and feet. What other kinds of bridges can you make? Can you make a bridge using only three body parts? Only two?"

"Show me a wide bridge. A narrow one. A short bridge. A long one. How about a high bridge? A low one? Can you make a bridge that opens when a boat goes through? Get a partner to be the boat, and you be the bridge. If you are the boat, choose three ways of traveling under a bridge. Each time the boat goes under the bridge, change the kind of bridge."

"As I touch you, go under a bridge and make another bridge."

"Show how you would make London Bridge fall down."

"With a partner, alternate going under a high bridge and going over a low bridge."

"Can you move one end of the bridge, keeping the other end still?"

"Make a bridge with one side of your body facing upward. Change to the other side."

"Show me a twisted bridge. A curved bridge."

"Be an inchworm and start with a long, low bridge. Walk the feet to the hands. Walk the hands forward while keeping the feet in one place."

"Make a bridge with three points of contact."

"Show me a bridge at a high level. At a low level. In between."

"Make up a sequence of bridge positions, going smoothly from one to the next."

Flight

"Show me three different ways you can go through space. Try again, using different levels. Lead with different parts of your body."

"See how high you can go as you move through space. What helps you get height?"

"Practice various combinations for takeoff and landing. See if you can work out five different possibilities for taking off and landing, using one or both feet." (Possibilities are same to same [hop]; one foot to the opposite [leap]; one-foot takeoff, two-foot landing; two-foot takeoff, two-foot landing [jump]; two-foot takeoff, one-foot landing.)

"Run and jump or leap through the air with your legs bent. With your legs straight. With one leg bent and the other straight. Try it with your legs spread wide. With your whole body wide. With your whole body long and thin through the air."

"Project yourself upward, beginning with the feet together and landing with the feet apart. Run, take off, and land in a forward stride position. Repeat, landing with the other foot forward."

"With a partner, find ways to jump over your partner as he or she changes shape."

"Using your arms to help you, run and project yourself as high as possible. Practice landing with bent knees."

Moving with the Weight Supported on the Hands and Feet (Figure 15.6)

"Pick a spot away from your personal space and travel to and from that spot on your hands and feet. Try moving with your hands close to your feet. Far away from your feet. Show me bilateral, unilateral, and cross-lateral movements. Build up a sequence."

"Move from your personal space for 8 counts. Do a jump turn (180 degrees) and return to your space using a different movement."

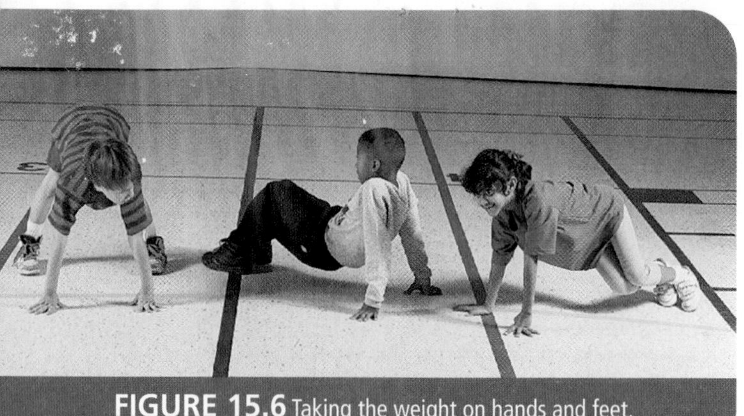

FIGURE 15.6 Taking the weight on hands and feet.

"Lie on your stomach. Move using only your hands."

"Experiment with different hand–foot positions. Begin with a narrow shape and with hands and feet as close together as possible. Extend your hands from head to toe until they are as far apart as possible. Extend the hands and feet as wide as possible and move. Now try with the hands wide and the feet together. Reverse."

"Practice traveling so that both hands and feet are off the ground at the same time. Go forward, backward, sideways."

"With your body straight and supported on the hands and feet [push-up position], turn the body over smoothly and face the ceiling. The body should remain straight throughout. Turn to the right and left. Return to your original position."

"What kinds of animal movements can you imitate? Move with springing types of jumps. What shapes can you make while you move?"

Receiving and Transferring Weight

"Support the weight on two different body parts and then transfer the weight smoothly to another pair of parts. Add another pair of unlike parts if you can."

"Take a deep breath, let out the air, relax, and drop to the floor, transferring the weight from a standing position to a position on the floor. Can you reverse the process?"

"Show in walking how the weight transfers from the heel to the ball of the foot with a push-off from the toes. In a standing position, transfer the weight from the toes, to the outside of the foot, to the heel, and back to the toes. Reverse the order."

"Using three different parts, transfer weight from one to another in a sequence."

"Travel with a jump or a leap and then lower yourself gently to your back after landing. Repeat, only lower yourself smoothly to your seat."

"From a standing position, bend forward slowly and transfer the weight partially to both hands. Lift one foot into the air. Return it to the ground gently. Repeat with the other foot. Lift a hand and a foot at the same time and return them smoothly."

"Lower yourself in a controlled way to take the weight on your tummy. Can you turn over and take the weight on your seat with your hands and feet touching the floor?"

"Move from lying on your back to a standing position without using your arms."

"Select a shape. See if you can lower yourself to the ground and return to your original position, keeping the shape."

"Try some jump turns, quarter and half. What is needed to keep your balance as you land?"

"Project yourself into the air and practice receiving your weight in different ways. Try landing without any noise. What do you have to do? See how high you can jump and still land lightly."

"See how many different ways you can transfer weight smoothly from one part of your body to another. Work up a sequence of three or four movements and go smoothly from one to another, returning to your original position."

Stretching and Curling

"In your own space, stretch out and curl. What different ways can you find to do this? Let's go slowly from a stretch to a curl and back to a stretch in a smooth, controlled movement. Curl your upper body and stretch your lower body. Now curl your lower body and stretch your upper body. Work out a smooth sequence between the two combinations."

"Show different curled and stretched positions on body points and on body flats. Go from a curled position on a flat surface to a stretched position supported on body points. Explore how many different ways you can support your body in a curled position."

"Stand in your personal space and stretch your arms at different levels. Lift one leg and stretch it to the front, side, and back. Repeat with the other leg."

"Stretch with an arm and a leg until it pulls you over."

"In a sitting position, put your legs out in front. Bend your toes forward as far as possible. Bend them backward so that your heels are ahead of your toes. Turn both toes as far as you can inward. Turn them outward."

"Lie on the floor on your back. Stretch one leg at a time in different ways in space."

"Stand. Stretch to reach as far as you can with your hand. Try reaching as far as possible with your toe."

"Show how you can travel on different body parts, sometimes stretched, sometimes curled."

"Jump and stretch as high as possible. Now curl and roll on the floor." (Repeat several times.)

Taking the Weight on the Hands (Figure 15.7)

FIGURE 15.7 Taking the weight on the hands.

Establishing proper hand positioning for taking the weight on the hands (and later for the headstand) is important.

"Put your hands about shoulder width apart, with fingers spread and pointed forward. With knees bent, alternate lifting the feet silently into the air, one foot at a time. Pick a point ahead of your hands (two feet or so), and watch it with your eyes. Keep from ducking your head between your arms."

"Place both hands on the floor. Kick up like a mule. Can you kick twice before coming down?"

"Take the weight on your hands. Make one foot go past the other while in the air."

"Do as many movements as you can while keeping your hands on the floor."

"See whether you can take the weight on your hands for a brief time. How do you get your body into the air? What different movements can you make with your feet while your weight is on your hands? See how long you can keep your feet off the ground. Repeat, and try to get your hips above your hands. Now add a twist at the waist to return your feet to the floor at a different spot."

"Try again, but shift the weight to one hand and land both feet at a different spot."

"Begin in a standing position and try to keep your feet over your head for as long as possible. Begin with the arms and hands stretched overhead, and repeat. Kick up one leg and then the other."

SPACE AWARENESS THEMES (WHERE THE BODY MOVES)

Moving in General Space

Besides developing movement competence, these movement experiences should enhance the ability to (a) share space with other children, (b) move through space without bumping anyone, and (c) develop consideration for the safety of others.

"Run lightly in the area, changing direction without bumping or touching anyone until I call 'Stop.' Raise your hand if you were able to do this without bumping into anyone."

"Let's try running zigzag fashion in the area without touching anyone. This time, when I blow the whistle, change your direction and change the type of movement."

"Run lightly in general space and pretend you are dodging someone. Can you run toward another runner and change direction to dodge?"

"Get a beanbag and drop it to mark your personal space. See how lightly, while under control, you can run throughout the area. When I give the signal, run to your spot, pick up your beanbag, put it on your head, and sit down [or give some other challenge]. Try this skipping."

"We are going to practice orienteering. [Explain the term.] Point to a spot on the wall, and see if you can run directly to it in a straight line. You may have to stop and wait for others to pass so as not to bump into anyone, but you cannot change direction. Stay in a straight line. When you get to your spot, pick another spot, and repeat."

"What happens when general space is decreased? You had no problem running without touching anyone in the large space. Now let's divide the area in half with cones. Run lightly within this area so as not to touch or bump anyone. Now it's going to get more difficult. I'm going to divide the space in half once more, but first let's try walking in the new area. Now, run lightly." (Decrease the area as feasible.)

"Get a beanbag and mark your personal space. Run around the beanbag until you hear a 'bang,' and then explode in a straight direction until I call 'Stop.' Return to your personal space."

"From your beanbag, take five [or more] jumps [hops, skips, gallops, slides] and stop. Turn to face home, and return with the same number of movements. Take the longest steps you can away from home, and then return home with tiny steps."

"Show me how well you can move with these combinations in general space: run–jump–roll, skip–spin–collapse. Now you make up a series of any three movements and practice them."

"Today our magic number is 5. Can you move in any direction with five repetitions of a movement? Change direction and pick another movement to do five times. Continue."

"Blow yourself up like a soap bubble. Can you huff and puff? Think of yourself as a big bubble that is floating around. When I touch you, the bubble breaks, and you collapse to the ground. This time, blow up your bubble and float around. When you are ready, say, 'Pop,' so the bubble bursts."

"I am going to challenge you on right and left movements. Show me how you can change to the correct direction when I say either 'Right' or 'Left.' Now begin running lightly."

"This time, see whether you can run rapidly toward another child, stop, and bow to each other. Instead of bowing, shake hands and say, 'How do you do.'"

"From your personal space, pick a spot on a wall. See whether you can run to the spot, touch it, and return without bumping anyone. This time, it's more difficult. Pick spots on two different walls, touch these in turn, and return."

Exploring Personal Space

Personal space is space that can be reached from a fixed base. Youngsters can take this personal space with them when they are moving in general space. A graphic way to illustrate personal space is to have youngsters take an individual jump rope and double it. From a kneeling position, they swing it in a full arc along the floor. It should not touch another child or rope.

"Show us how big your space is. Keeping one foot in place, outline how much space you can occupy. Sit cross-legged and outline your space. Support your weight on different parts of your body and outline your space."

"Make yourself as wide [narrow, small, large, low, high] as possible. Try these from different positions—kneeling, balancing on the seat, and others. Show us what kinds of body positions you can take while you stand on one foot. While you lie on your stomach. On your seat. Try the same with one foot and one hand touching the floor."

"Stand tall in your space. To the beat of a drum, move beat by beat to a squat position. Reverse."

"Move from a lying position to a standing position without using your arms or hands. Return to lying."

"Can you stay in one place and move your whole body but not your feet? Sway back and forth with your feet together and then with your feet apart. Which is better?"

"Sitting in your personal space, bend your toes forward; now backward. Bend your feet so that your heels move ahead of your toes."

"While lying on your back, move your arms and legs from one position slowly and then move them back quickly to where you started. Explore other positions."

"Keeping one part of your body in place, make as big a circle as you can with the rest of your body."

"Explore different positions while you keep one leg [foot] higher than the rest of your body. Work out a smooth sequence of three different positions."

"Pump yourself up like a balloon, getting bigger and bigger. Hold until I say, 'Bang!'"

"In your personal space, show me how a top spins. Keep your feet together in place. With your arms wide to the sides, twist and make your feet turn."

Circles and the Body (Figure 15.8)

FIGURE 15.8 Forming circles.

"Can you form full circles with your hands and arms at different joints—wrist, elbow, and shoulder? Now what circle can you make with your legs and feet?

Try this lying on your back. Use other body joints to make circles."

"Travel in general space by skipping [running, hopping, sliding]. Stop on signal and make moving, horizontal [vertical, inclined] circles with an arm. Repeat, but on signal lie down immediately on your back and make the [specified] circle with one foot."

"Show how swimmers make circles with their arms when doing the backstroke. Alternate arms and also move them together. Reverse the arm direction to make the crawl stroke. Make vertical circles with one arm and both arms across the body."

"With one hand, make a circle on your tummy. At the same time, use your other hand to pat the top of your head. Reverse hands."

"Keep one foot fixed and make a circle with the other foot by turning completely around."

"Select a partner. Match the arm circles your partner makes."

"Can you keep two different circles going at the same time? Make a circle turning one way, and another circle turning the other way. Repeat, using twisting actions of the body parts making the circles."

Planes of Movement

"Show me a variety of movements in a horizontal plane. In a vertical plane. In a diagonal plane. Put together combinations so that you go in sequence from one type of movement to another."

"Here's a challenge. When I call out a plane of movement, respond with a movement in the correct plane. Ready?" (Specify the plane of movement.)

"Using a jump rope doubled in one hand, make circles in the different planes. Try the same with a hula hoop."

"Crouch at a low level, spin upward toward the ceiling, and come back to the floor. Spin in the other direction."

Levels

"Choose one way of traveling at a high level and another at a low level. Again, move at a high level and stop at a low level. Move at a low level and stop at a high level. Choose one way of traveling at a medium level and add this somewhere in your sequence—beginning, middle, or end."

"Select three different kinds of traveling movements with the arms at a high, medium, and low level. Link these movements together in a smooth sequence."

"Travel around the room, raising your arms as high as possible. Travel on your tiptoes. Repeat with your arms as low as possible."

"Run at different levels. Run as high as you can. Run as low as possible. Run at a medium level."

"When I clap my hands, change direction and level."

"Move on all fours with your body at a high level, a medium level, and then as low as possible. Try these movements with your face turned to the ceiling."

"Use a jump rope or a line or board in the floor as your path to follow. Begin at the far end. Show me a slow, low-level movement down and back. What other ways can you go down and back slowly and at a low level? Change to a fast, high-level movement. On what other levels can you move?"

"Combine a low, fast movement down the path with a high, slow movement on the way back. Explore other combinations. Make different movements by leading with different parts of your body."

Moving in Different Ways

"Discover different ways you can make progress along the floor without using your hands and feet. See whether you can walk with your seat. Let your heels help you."

"What ways can you move sideways or backward? What rolling movements can you make? Look carefully before you move to make sure you have a clear space."

"Use large movements and travel through general space. Make your body into a straight line and move in straight lines, changing direction suddenly. With your body in a curved shape, move in a curved pathway."

"Each time you change direction, alternate a straight body and a straight path with a curved body shape and a curved path."

"Find ways of moving close to the floor with your legs stretched. Now move with your legs bent, keeping at a low level."

"As you travel forward, move up and down. As you travel backward, sway from side to side."

"Travel, keeping high in the air. Change direction and travel at a low level. Continue to alternate."

"Counting the four limbs [two arms, two legs], travel first on all four, then on three, next on an arm and a leg, and then on one leg. Now reverse the order."

"With your hands fixed on the floor, move your feet in different ways. Cover as much space as possible. With your feet fixed, move your hands around in different ways as far away from the body as you can. Move around general space the way a skater does. The way a person on a pogo stick does. Choose other ways. Change body direction as you move, but keep facing in the original direction."

QUALITIES OF MOVEMENT THEMES (HOW THE BODY MOVES)

Time (Speed)

Speed involves the pace of action, which can be slow, fast, or any degree in between. Speed involves acceleration and deceleration; that is, the time factor can be constant, or it can speed up or slow down. Time also can be even or uneven.

"With your arms, do a selected movement slowly and then quickly. Move your feet slowly and then as rapidly as you can. Change your support base and repeat."

"In turn, stretch a part of your body slowly and then return it to place quickly, like a rubber band snapping. Stretch the entire body as wide as possible and snap it back to a narrow shape."

"Travel through the area without touching anyone. Speed up when there is an open area and slow down when it is crowded."

"Choose a way of traveling across the floor quickly and then do the same movement slowly. Do a fast movement in one direction and, on signal, change to a slow movement in another direction."

"Select a magic number between 10 and 20. Do that many slow movements and then do the same number of fast movements."

"Choose a partner. With your partner a little bit away from you, begin moving quickly toward your partner and decelerate as you get close. Move away by beginning slowly and accelerate until you return to where you started. Repeat. Select the kinds of movement you wish to use together."

"Staying in your own personal space, begin with some kind of movement and accelerate until you are moving as fast as you can. Reverse by beginning with a fast movement and then slowing down until you are barely moving. Put together a sequence of two movements by beginning with one and accelerating, then changing to another movement and decelerating. Try doing two different body movements at the same time—one that accelerates and one that decelerates."

Contrasting Movements

Contrasting movements have wide and frequent applications in the development of other themes. See Table 15.1 on page 304 for examples of contrasting words.

"Show me a fast movement. Now a slow one. Show me a smooth movement. Now a rough, jerky movement."

"Find three ways to rise from the floor and three ways to sink to the floor. Choose one way to rise and one way to sink. Try to do this three times very smoothly."

"Make yourself as tall as possible. Now, get as short as you can."

"Move with a small and delicate skip. Change to a large skip."

"Show me a wide shape. Now, an opposite one. A crooked shape. Now, its opposite. Show me a high-level movement and its contrast. Can you do a balanced movement? What is its opposite?" (Use light–heavy and other contrasts as well.)

"Pick two contrasting movements. When I clap my hands, do one, and change to the other when I clap again. What movements did you do?"

Force

"Show me different kinds of sudden movements. Do a sudden movement and then repeat it slowly. Put together a series of sudden movements. Put together a series of sustained movements. Mix sudden and sustained movements."

"Pick a partner and do a quick, strong movement followed by a quick, light movement."

"Take five strong, slow jumps, changing your body for each jump."

"When the drum beat is loud, walk heavily. When the drum beat is soft, walk lightly."

"Reach in different directions with a forceful movement. Crouch down as low as you can and explode upward. Try again, exploding forward. Move as if you were pushing something very heavy. Pretend you are hitting a heavy punching bag."

"What kinds of movements can you do that are light movements? Can you make movements light and sustained? Light and sudden? Heavy and sustained? Heavy and sudden? Which is easier? Why?"

"Try making thunder [big noise with hands and feet] and then lightning [same movements without any noise], timing each movement with 5 slow counts."

"Can you combine heavy movements in a sequence of sudden and sustained movements? Can you make one part of your body move lightly and another part heavily?"

Tension and Relaxation

"Make yourself as tense as possible. Now slowly relax. Take a deep breath and hold it tight. Let out the air and relax."

"Hug yourself hard! Now, harder. Follow this by relaxing your body. Shake your hands."

"Reach as high as possible with both hands, relax slowly, and drop to the floor. Tense one part of your body and relax another. Slowly shift the tension to the relaxed part, and vice versa."

"Run forward, stop suddenly in a tensed position, and then relax. Run in a tensed manner, change direction, and then run in a relaxed manner."

"Walk forward with tight, jerky movements. Change direction and walk with loose, floppy movements. Pretend you are a boxer by using short, tense movements. Now move your arms like a floppy rag doll."

RELATIONSHIP THEMES (TO WHOM AND WHAT THE BODY RELATES)

Moving Over, Under, Around, and Through Things

This theme is flexible and can use any available equipment as obstacles to go over, under, around, and through. It can be used effectively in a rotating station system. Equipment can be already arranged, or the children can set it up themselves.

"Using the equipment, explore different ways you can go over, under, around, or through what you have set up. Lead with different parts of the body."

"Three youngsters with jump ropes form a triangle, a square, and a rectangle on the floor. Move in, out, and around the three figures."

"Toss your beanbag in the air. When I call out a body part, sit down quickly, and put the beanbag on that part."

Symmetrical and Asymmetrical Movements

Symmetrical movements are identical movements using similar body parts on opposite sides of the body. *Asymmetrical* movements are different movements using similar body parts on opposite sides of the body. Symmetry increases stability because the two body halves are counterbalanced. Asymmetry, with the body weight distributed unequally, leads to quick starts and easier sequential flow. Balancing on a balance beam with both arms to the side is a symmetrical movement. The arms are extended symmetrically to increase stability and balance. Running while alternately flexing and extending the legs is an asymmetrical movement.

"Show me different kinds of symmetrical movements. Now asymmetrical movements. Put together sequences of symmetrical and asymmetrical movements."

"Taking the weight on your hands, show symmetrical and asymmetrical movements of your legs."

"Run and jump high in the air, and place your limbs symmetrically in flight."

"Perform different movements like throwing, skipping, running, long jumping, and leaping and identify whether they are symmetrical or asymmetrical movements."

Relative Location of Body Parts

"We are going to try some special ways of touching. Raise your right hand as high as you can—now down. Raise your left hand as high as you can—now down. Touch your left [or right] shoulder [elbow, knee, hip, ankle] with the right [or left] hand." (Try many combinations.)

"Now, point to a door [window, ceiling, basket] with an elbow [thumb, toe, knee, nose]. Let's see if you can remember right and left. Point your left [or right] elbow to the window." (Try different combinations.)

"When I name a body part, let's see if you can make this the highest part of your body without moving from your place."

"Now, the next task is a little harder. Move in a straight line for a short distance and keep the body part named above all the other body parts. What body parts would be difficult to keep above all the others?" (Possibilities are the eyes, both ears, both hips.)

"Touch the highest part of your body with your right hand. Touch the lowest part of your body with your left hand."

"Let's see if you can locate some of the bones in your body. When I name a bone, hold that bone, move and touch a wall, and return to your spot." (These challenges depend on bones that the children can identify. The same procedure can be used to identify selected muscles.)

"Now move around the room, traveling any way you wish." (The movement can also be limited.) "The signal to stop will be a word describing a body part. Can you stop and immediately put both hands on that part or parts?" (Or, "On 'Stop,' hide the body part.") "You are to move around the room again. When I call out a body part, find a partner and place the body parts together."

"This time, when I call out a body part, you are to move around the room as you wish, while holding with one hand a named body part. When I name another body part, change the type of movement and hold that part with the other hand as you move. Now I will call out two body parts. Have the parts touch each other."

Leading with Different Parts of the Body (Figure 15.9)

FIGURE 15.9 Leading with a foot.

"As you move between your beanbags [lines, markers], explore ways that different parts of your body can lead movements. Add different means of locomotion. Work at different levels."

"Have a partner make a bridge and you go under, leading with different parts of the body. Can you find five different ways to go under with different body parts leading? Now try finding five ways to go over or around."

"What body parts are difficult to lead with?"

FOR MORE INFORMATION

REFERENCES AND SUGGESTED READINGS

Cone, T. P., & Cone, S. (2005). *Teaching children dance* (2nd ed.). Champaign, IL: Human Kinetics.

Gallahue, D. L., & Donnely, F. C. (2007). *Developmental physical education for all children* (4th ed.). Champaign, IL: Human Kinetics.

Graham, G., Holt/Hale, S. A., & Parker, M. (2007). *Children moving: A reflective approach to teaching physical education* (7th ed.). Boston: McGraw-Hill.

Joyce, M. (1994). *First steps in teaching creative dance to children* (3rd ed.). Mountain View, CA: Mayfield.

Laban, R., & Lawrence, F. (1947). *Effort.* London: Union Brothers.

McGreevy-Nichols, S., Scheff, H., & Sprague, M. (2005). *Building dances: A guide to putting movements together* (2nd ed.). Champaign, IL: Human Kinetics.

Pangrazi, R. P. (2010). *Curriculum guide: Lesson plans for dynamic physical education* (16th ed.). San Francisco: Benjamin Cummings.

Thompson, M. A. (1993). *Jump for joy! Over 375 creative movement activities for young children.* Englewood Cliffs, NJ: Prentice Hall.

Weikart, P. S. (2007). *Teaching movement and dance* (6th ed.). Ypsilanti, MI: High Scope Press.

WEBSITES

General Physical Education

www.pelinks4u.org/index.htm
www.pecentral.org
www.pe4life.org

Movement Activities for Young Children

www.happalmer.com/articlepg1.htm
www.southernearlychildhood.org/position_arts.html
www.edselect.com/fundamen.htm

Fundamental Motor Skills and Introductory Activities

16

ESSENTIAL COMPONENTS OF QUALITY PROGRAMS

- ▶ I. Organized around content standards
- ▶ II. Student-centered and developmentally appropriate
- ▶ III. Physical activity and motor skill development form the core of the program
- IV. Teaches management skills and self-discipline
- V. Promotes inclusion of all students
- ▶ VI. Focuses on process over product
- VII. Promotes lifetime personal health and wellness
- VIII. Teaches cooperation and responsibility and promotes sensitivity to diversity

NATIONAL STANDARDS FOR PHYSICAL EDUCATION*

- ▶ 1. Demonstrates competency in motor skills and movement patterns needed to perform a variety of physical activities.
- ▶ 2. Demonstrates understanding of movement concepts, principles, and tactics as they apply to the learning and performance of physical activities.
- ▶ 3. Participates regularly in physical activity.
- 4. Achieves and maintains a health-enhancing level of physical fitness.
- 5. Exhibits responsible personal and social behavior that respects self and others in physical activity.
- 6. Values physical activity for health, enjoyment, challenge, self-expression, and/or social interaction.

*National Association for Sport and Physical Education (NASPE), 2004.

This chapter focuses on fundamental skills and introductory activities. Fundamental skills in this chapter include two major categories: locomotor and nonlocomotor skills. These skills are the basis of nearly all physical activities students will participate in throughout life. Locomotor skills define the many ways the body can move through space. Nonlocomotor movements generally do not require moving through space; these skills are learned by repetition and refinement, offering many variations to keep students motivated.

The second part of the chapter presents introductory activities, which are based on locomotor movement. Teachers can use these activities to start a lesson and get students warmed up and motivated for the rest of the lesson.

Outcomes

- Understand that teaching fundamental movement is synonymous with providing instruction designed to learn a specific skill.
- Describe the differences between locomotor and nonlocomotor skills.
- Cite stress points, instructional cues, and suggested movement patterns to enhance the learning of locomotor and nonlocomotor skills.
- Specify activities designed to develop locomotor and nonlocomotor motor skills.
- Describe the rationale for including introductory activities in the lesson plan.
- Characterize various features of the opening phase of the lesson.
- Develop an introductory activity that meets established criteria for preparing children physiologically and psychologically.
- Describe the fundamental skills used in introductory activities.

FUNDAMENTAL SKILLS

Fundamental skills, sometimes called *basic* or *functional* skills, are the skills children need to function effectively in the environment. Fundamental skills are basic human movements usually identified by a single verb, such as *walking, twisting, running, jumping,* or *stretching.* Learning physical skills develops from general to specific movements. This chapter focuses on general motor skills involving the large muscles. Fundamental skills are the tools most adults use when participating in leisure activities. Without a learned set of fundamental skills and a positive feeling about being able to perform in activity settings, many people resign themselves to a lifetime of inactivity.

Learning fundamental skills requires practicing the basic locomotor and nonlocomotor skills through many repetitions. Repeating these skills over a wide range of activities helps assure that children can perform them in varying conditions. To help students learn the skills correctly and quickly, this chapter presents important stress points and instructional cues. Since all locomotor movements are rhythmic, that section also includes rhythmic activities. The skills are grouped for ease of teaching and ease of comprehension by students. The skills are presented here individually, but they are most often performed in a seemingly infinite number of combinations, depending on the sport or activity.

LOCOMOTOR SKILLS

Locomotor skills are used to move the body from one place to another or to project the body upward. They include walking, running, skipping, galloping, leaping, sliding, jumping, and hopping. They form the foundation of gross motor coordination and involve large muscle movement.

NONLOCOMOTOR SKILLS

Nonlocomotor skills are performed without appreciable movement from place to place. These skills are not as well defined as locomotor skills. They include bending and stretching, pushing and pulling, twisting and turning, rocking, swaying, and balancing, among others.

LOCOMOTOR SKILLS

The locomotor skill descriptions include stress points to help teachers present correct techniques. Also included are instructional cues—short, concise phrases for reminding students how to perform activities correctly. Suggested learning activities fall into two categories: (1) basic activities, consisting of movement-oriented sequences that do not require rhythm; and (2) rhythmic activities consisting of movements with rhythmic accompaniment.

WALKING

When walking, each foot moves alternately, with one foot always touching the ground or floor. The stepping foot touches the ground before the other foot is lifted. Body weight is transferred from the heel to the ball of the foot and then to the toes for push-off. The toes point straight ahead, and the arms swing freely from the shoulders in opposition to the feet. The body is erect, and the eyes focus straight ahead and slightly below eye level. The legs swing smoothly from the hips, with knees bent enough to clear the feet from the ground. Marching is a precise type of walk, accompanied by lifted knees and swinging arms.

Basic Activities

Stress Points

1. Toes are pointed reasonably straight ahead.
2. Arm movement is natural. The arms do not swing too far.
3. The head is up and the eyes focus ahead.
4. Stride length is not excessive. Avoid unnecessary up-and-down motion.

Instructional Cues

1. Head up, eyes forward.
2. Point toes straight ahead.
3. Nice, easy, relaxed arm swing.
4. Walk quietly.
5. Hold tummy in, chest up.
6. Push off from the floor with the toes.

Suggested Movement Patterns

1. Walk in different directions, changing direction on signal.
2. While walking, lift each knee and slap with the hands on each step.
3. Walk on the heels, toes, and sides of feet.
4. Gradually lower your body while walking (going downstairs), and rise again slowly (going upstairs).
5. Walk with a smooth, gliding step.
6. Walk with a wide base of support on the tiptoes and rock from side to side.
7. Clap the hands alternately in front and behind. Clap the hands under the thighs while walking.
8. Walk slowly, and gradually increase speed. Reverse the process.
9. Take long strides. Take tiny steps.
10. On signal, change levels (high, low, etc.).
11. Walk quickly and quietly. Walk heavily and slowly.
12. Change direction on signal, but keep facing the same way.
13. Walk gaily, angrily, happily. Show other moods.
14. Hold the arms in different positions. Make an arm movement with each step.
15. Walk in different patterns—circle, square, triangle, figure eight.
16. Walk through heavy mud. On ice or a slick floor. Walk on a rainy day. Walk in heavy snow.
17. Walk like a soldier on parade, a giant, a robot.
18. Duck under trees or railings while walking.
19. Point your toes in different directions—in, forward, and out.
20. Walk with high knees. Stiff knees. One stiff knee. A sore ankle.
21. Walk to a spot, turn in place while stepping, and go in another direction.
22. Practice changing steps while walking.
23. Walk and change direction after taking the magic number of steps (selected by a student).
24. Tiptoe around the area and through puddles of water.
25. Walk as if you are on a balance beam. Walk across a tightrope.
26. Walk as if you are sneaking up on someone.
27. Walk with funny steps, as if you are a clown.
28. Take heel-and-toe steps forward. Without turning around, walk heel-and-toe backward.

Rhythmic Activities

When using rhythmic accompaniment, teach students to hear the phrasing in the selection. Have children use one kind of walk during a phrase and then use another kind of walk during the next phrase.

1. Walk forward one phrase (8 counts) and change direction. Continue to change at the end of each phrase.
2. Use high steps during one phrase and low steps during the next.
3. Walk forward for one phrase and sideways during the next. The side step can be a draw step, or a grapevine step. To do a grapevine, step to the left, lead with the left foot, stepping directly to the side. Cross the right foot behind the left, and then cross the right foot in front of the left on the next step with that foot. The pattern is step left, cross right (behind), step left, cross right (in front), and so on.
4. Find a partner. Face each other and join hands. Pull your partner by walking backward as your partner resists a little (8 counts). Reverse roles. Now stand behind your partner and place your hands on your partner's shoulders. Push your partner by walking forward as your partner resists (8 counts). Reverse roles.
5. Walk slowly, then gradually increase the tempo. Now begin fast and decrease. (Use a drum for this activity.)
6. Walk in various directions while clapping your hands alternately in front and behind. Try clapping hands under a thigh at each step, or clap hands above the head in time with the beat.

7. Walk forward four steps, and turn completely around in four steps. Repeat, but turn the other way the next time.
8. While walking, lift each knee and slap with the hands on each step in time with the beat.
9. On any one phrase, take four fast steps (1 count to each step) and two slow steps (2 counts to each step).
10. Walk on the heels or toes or with a heavy tramp. Change every 4 or 8 beats.
11. Walk with a smooth, gliding step, or walk silently to the beat.
12. Walk to the music, accenting the first beat of each measure. Now sway your body to the first beat of the measure. (Use a waltz with a strong beat.)

RUNNING

Running (Figure 16.1), in contrast to walking, is moving fast so that both feet briefly leave the ground. Running varies from trotting (a slow run) to sprinting (a fast run for speed). The heels can take some weight in distance running and jogging. Running is done with the body leaning slightly forward. The knees are flexed and lifted, while the arms swing back and forth from the shoulders with a bend at the elbows. The track, field, and cross-country running unit gives more pointers for sprinting (see Chapter 29).

FIGURE 16.1 Running.

Basic Activities

Stress Points

1. The balls of the feet are used when sprinting.
2. The faster you want to run, the higher you must lift the knees. For fast running, bend the knees more.
3. For distance running, use less arm swing than when sprinting for speed. For greater comfort, less body lean is used in distance running. The weight is absorbed on the heels and transferred to the toes.

Instructional Cues

1. Run on the balls of the feet when sprinting.
2. Head up, eyes forward.
3. Bend your knees.
4. Relax your upper body and swing the arms forward and backward, not sideways.
5. Breathe naturally.

Suggested Movement Patterns

1. Run lightly throughout the area, changing direction as you wish. Avoid bumping anyone. Run zigzag throughout the area.
2. Run and stop on signal. Change direction on signal.
3. Run, turn around with running steps on signal, and continue in a new direction. Alternate turning direction.
4. Pick a spot away from you, run to it, and return without touching or bumping anyone.
5. Run low, gradually increasing the height. Reverse.
6. Run in patterns. Run between and around objects.
7. Run while slapping the knees.
8. Run with different steps—tiny, long, light, heavy, crisscross, wide.
9. Run with your arms in different positions—circling, overhead, stiff at your sides.
10. Run free, concentrating on good knee lift.
11. Run at different speeds.
12. Touch the ground at times with either hand while running.
13. Run backward, sideways.
14. Run with exaggerated arm movements. Run with a high bounce.
15. Run forward 10 steps and backward 5 steps. Repeat in another direction. (Other tasks can be imposed after the 10 steps.)
16. Run forward; then make a jump turn in the air to face in a new direction. Repeat. Be sure to use both right and left turns. Make a full reverse (180-degree) turn.
17. Run the Tortoise and Hare sequence (page 329) and Ponies in the Stable (page 329).
18. Run with knees turned outward. Run high on your toes.
19. Show how quietly you can run. Pretend you are running through high weeds.
20. Run to a wall and back to place. Run and touch two walls.
21. Run lightly twice around your spot. Then explode (run quickly) to another spot.

Rhythmic Activities

Many of the walking patterns apply equally to running patterns. Here are some additional suggestions for running.

1. Walk during a phrase of music and then run for an equal length of time.
2. Run in different directions, changing direction on the sound of a heavy beat (or on a signal).
3. Lift the knees as high as possible while running, keeping time to the beat.
4. Do European Rhythmic Running (pages 331) to supplement the running patterns described earlier.

HOPPING

Hopping involves propelling the body up and down on the same foot. The body lean, the other foot, and the arms help balance the movement. Students can practice hopping in place or try it as a locomotor movement.

Basic Activities

Stress Points

1. To increase height of the hop, swing arms rapidly upward.
2. Hop on the ball of the foot.
3. Small hops are used to start, and the height and distance of the hop increase gradually.

Instructional Cues

1. Hop with good forward motion.
2. Stay on your toes.
3. Use your arms for balance.
4. Reach for the sky when you hop.
5. Land lightly.

Suggested Movement Patterns

1. Hop on one foot and then on the other, using patterns such as 1rf–1lf, 2rf–2lf, 3rf–3lf; 2rf–1lf, 1rf–2lf, 3rf–2lf, 2rf–3lf; and so on (rf = right foot; lf = left foot). Have children practice each combination for 10 to 20 seconds.
2. Hop, increasing height. Reverse.
3. See how much space you can cover in two, three, or four hops.
4. Hop on one foot and do a heel-and-toe pattern with the other. Now change to the other foot. Try to follow a consistent pattern.
5. Make a hopping sequence by combining hopping in place with hopping ahead.
6. Hop forward, backward, sideways. Then hop in different patterns on the floor.
7. Hop while holding the free foot in different hand positions.
8. Hold the free foot forward or sideways while hopping. Explore other positions.
9. Hop with the body in different positions—try leaning forward, backward, sideways.
10. Hop lightly, so that no one can hear you. Then hop heavily.
11. While hopping, touch the floor with the hands—first one and then both.
12. Hop back and forth over a line, moving down the line as you hop.
13. Trace out numbers or letters by hopping.
14. Turn around while hopping in place.
15. Hop forward and then backward according to a magic number (selected by a student). Repeat in another direction. Now add sideward hopping instead of going backward.

Rhythmic Activities

Because students tire rapidly, combining rhythm with hopping patterns is harder than walking, running, or skipping to rhythm. The suggested patterns combine other locomotor movements with hopping.

1. Walk four steps, hop three times, and rest 1 count.
2. Walk four steps, then hop four times as you turn in place. Repeat in a new direction.
3. Hop eight times on one foot (8 counts) and then eight times on the other.
4. Hop forward and backward over a line to the rhythm, changing feet each phrase (8 counts).
5. Combine skipping, sliding, or galloping with hopping.
6. Practice the step-hop to music. (In 2 counts, the child steps and then hops on the same foot.)

JUMPING

Jumping requires taking off with both feet and landing on both feet (Figure 16.2 on page 320). The arms move forward with an upswing, and body movement combined with force of the feet helps lift the weight. Jumping can be done in place or as a locomotor activity to cover ground.

Basic Activities

Stress Points

1. Knees and ankles are bent before takeoff to get more force from muscle extension.
2. Landing is on the balls of the feet, with knees bent to absorb the impact.

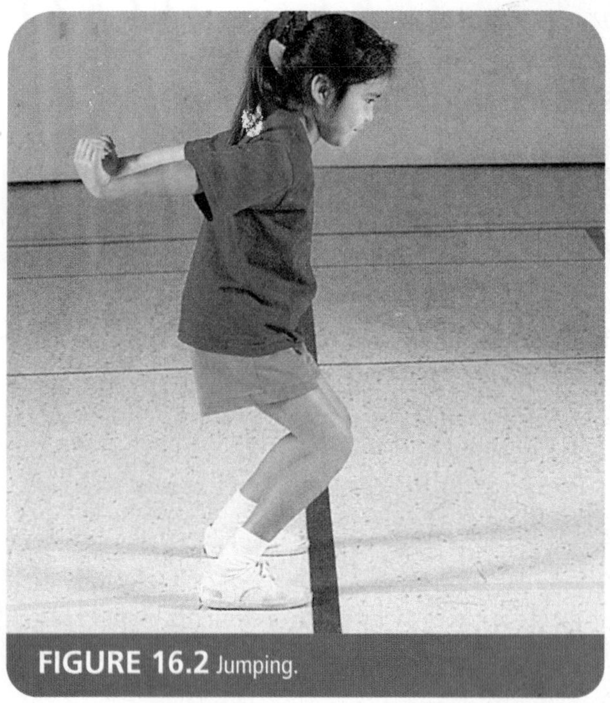
FIGURE 16.2 Jumping.

3. Arms swing forward and upward at takeoff to add momentum to the jump and to gain distance and height.
4. Legs must be bent after takeoff, or the feet will touch the ground too soon.

Instructional Cues

1. Swing your arms forward as fast as possible.
2. Bend your knees.
3. On your toes.
4. Land lightly with bent knees.
5. Jump up and try to touch the ceiling.

Suggested Movement Patterns

1. Jump up and down, trying for height. Try small and high jumps. Mix in patterns.
2. Choose a spot on the floor. Jump forward over the spot. Now backward and then sideways.
3. Jump with your body stiff and arms held at your sides. Jump like a pogo stick.
4. Practice jump turns in place—quarter, half, three-quarter, full.
5. Increase and decrease jumping speed. Increase and decrease jump height.
6. Land with feet apart and then together. Alternate with one foot forward and one backward.
7. Jump and land quietly. How is this done?
8. Jump, crossing and uncrossing the feet.
9. See how far you can go in two, three, and four consecutive jumps. Run lightly back to place.
10. Pretend you are a bouncing ball.
11. Clap hands or slap your thighs while in the air. Try different arm positions.
12. Begin a jump with your hands touching the floor.
13. Jump in various patterns on the floor.
14. Pretend you are a basketball center jumping at a jump ball. Jump as high as you can. Jump from a crouched position.
15. Combine a jump for distance with one for height.
16. Jump and click heels in the air. Try two clicks.
17. Jump like a kangaroo. A rabbit. A frog.
18. Combine opposite jumps: forward and backward. Big and little. Right and left. Light and heavy.
19. Try different ways of doing a jumping jack.
20. Jump and clap hands in front. Behind you. Overhead.
21. First swing your arms three times and then jump forward.
22. Jump. While in the air, touch your heels. Touch both knees. Touch both toes in front.
23. Half of the class is on the floor in selected positions. The other half jumps over those on the floor. Have the children switch positions.

Rhythmic Activities

Most of the activities suggested for hopping to rhythm are suitable for jumping. Other suggestions follow.

1. Begin jumping slowly to the drumbeat and then speed up. Then jump fast and slow down to the beat.
2. Toss a ball upward and jump in time to the bounce. (The ball must be a lively one.)
3. Do varieties of the jumping jack. First move your feet without moving your arms. Now lift arms to shoulder height; then lift arms straight overhead. Finally, add body turns and different foot patterns.
4. Take a forward stride position. As you jump, switch feet back and forth to the rhythm.

SLIDING

Sliding is similar to a gallop, but it is done with the body moving sideways in a 1-count movement; the leading foot steps to the side, and the other foot follows quickly. Slide on the balls of the feet while shifting weight from the leading to the trailing foot. Body bounce during the slide is minimal.

Basic Activities

Stress Points

1. Stress the sideways movement. Students may move forward or backward, which is actually galloping.
2. Slide in both directions, so each leg can lead as well as trail.
3. The slide is smooth and graceful, stressing balance and stability.

Instructional Cues

1. Move sideways.
2. Do not bounce.
3. Slide your feet.

Suggested Movement Patterns

1. Go in one direction a specific number of slides, do a half turn in the air, and continue the slide by leading with the other leg in the same direction. (A four-plus-four combination is excellent.)
2. Begin with short slides and increase length. Reverse.
3. Slide in a figure-eight pattern.
4. Change levels while sliding. Slide so that the hands touch the floor with each slide.
5. Slide quietly and smoothly.
6. Pretend to be a basketball defensive player, and slide with good basketball position.
7. Do three slides and a pause. Change the leading foot and repeat.
8. In circle formation, facing in, the whole class does 10 slides one way and then pauses. Repeat, going in the other direction.

Rhythmic Activities

With proper accompaniment, many of the above movement patterns can be set to rhythm. Use music phrases to signal a change of direction or issue another challenge.

GALLOPING

Galloping is similar to sliding, but the body faces forward. One foot leads and the other moves rapidly forward to it. The body has more upward motion than it does in sliding. Teach the gallop by having children hold hands and slide in a circle, responding to either verbal cues or a drumbeat. Ask the class to gradually face the direction the circle is moving. This takes them naturally from a slide into a gallop.

Basic Activities

Stress Points

1. The movement is smooth and graceful.
2. Give each foot a chance to lead.

Instructional Cues

1. Keep one foot in front of the other.
2. Now lead with the other foot.
3. Make high gallops.

Suggested Movement Patterns

1. Do a series of eight gallops with the same foot leading; then change to the other foot. Change after four gallops. Change after two gallops. (Later in the rhythmic program, the gallop is used to teach the polka, so it is important for children to learn to change the leading foot.)
2. Change the length of the gallops.
3. Gallop in a circle with a small group.
4. Pretend to hold reins and use a riding crop.
5. Gallop backward.
6. Gallop like a spirited pony. Like a heavy draft horse.

Rhythmic Activities

Because galloping is essentially rhythmic, many of the patterns described above can be done to rhythm. Use music phrases to signal a change in the lead foot. Check previous sections on locomotor movements for other rhythmic movement suggestions.

LEAPING

Leaping is an elongated step used to cover distance or move over low obstacles. It is usually combined with running, since a series of leaps is difficult to do alone (Figure 16.3). Suggested movement patterns use combinations of running and leaping.

FIGURE 16.3 Leaping.

Basic Activities

Stress Points

1. Strive for height and graceful flight.
2. Landing is light and relaxed.

Instructional Cues

1. Push off and reach.
2. Up and over, landing lightly.
3. Use your arms to help you gain height.

Suggested Movement Patterns

1. Leap in different directions.
2. See how high you can leap.
3. Leap and land softly.
4. Vary your arm position when leaping. Clap hands as you leap.
5. Leap with the same arm and leg forward. Try the other way.
6. Try leaping in slow motion.
7. Leap and turn backward.
8. Leap over objects or across a specified space.
9. Practice by playing Leap the Brook (page 543).
10. Leap and move into a balanced position.

Rhythmic Activities

Because a leap is an explosive movement through space, and children must gather themselves when preparing to leap, rhythm cannot easily be applied to this movement.

SKIPPING

Skipping is a series of step-hops done with alternate feet. To teach skipping, first have children do a step-hop on one foot and then a step-hop on the other. Skipping is done on the balls of the feet with arms swinging to shoulder height alternately with feet. Another way to teach skipping is to have children hold a large ball (9 inches or more) in front at waist height. Have them take a step with one foot and then raise the other knee to touch the ball. This movement stimulates the hop. Repeat with the other foot and opposite knee.

Basic Activities

Stress Points

1. Smoothness and rhythm, not speed and distance, are goals in skipping.
2. Weight is transferred from one foot to the other on the hop.
3. The arms swing alternately with the legs.

Instructional Cues

1. Step-hop.
2. Swing your arms.
3. Skip smoothly.
4. On your toes.

Suggested Movement Patterns

Many of the suggested movement patterns for walking and running can be applied to skipping, particularly those for changing direction, stopping, making floor patterns, and moving at different speeds.

1. Skip with exaggerated arm action and lifted knees.
2. Skip backward.
3. Clap as you skip.
4. Skip with a side-to-side motion.
5. Skip twice on one side (double skip).
6. Skip as slowly as possible. Skip as fast as possible.
7. Skip so lightly that your partner cannot hear the movement.
8. Skip to a chosen spot in as few skips as you can.

Rhythmic Activities

Most of the combinations suggested for walking and running are good for skipping movements, and many skipping, walking, and running combinations are possible. "Pop Goes the Weasel" is great skipping music. On the "pop," specify a movement challenge.

NONLOCOMOTOR SKILLS

Nonlocomotor skills include bending, twisting, turning (in place), moving toward and away from the center of the body, raising and lowering parts of the body, and other movements done in place. Flexibility, balance, and other movements leading to effective body control are important goals.

BENDING

Bending is movement at a joint. Teach students how the body bends, why it needs to bend, and how to combine bends in various movements.

Basic Activities

Stress Points

1. Bending as far as possible to increase flexibility and range of movement is a key goal.
2. Explore the bending possibilities of many joints.
3. Timing can be introduced in slow and rapid bending.

Instructional Cues

1. Bend as far as possible.
2. Bend one part while holding others steady.

Suggested Movement Patterns

1. Bend your body down and up.
2. Bend forward and backward, left and right, north and south.
3. Bend as many ways as possible.
4. Bend as many body parts as you can below your waist. Above your waist. Bend with your whole body.
5. Sit down and see if you can bend differently from the ways you bent when standing.
6. Try to bend one body part quickly while bending another part slowly.
7. Lie down and bend six body parts. Can you bend more than six? Now bend fewer.
8. Make a familiar shape by bending two body parts. Add two more parts.
9. Think of a toy that bends; see if you can bend like that.
10. Find a partner and bend together. Have your partner make big bends while you make tiny bends.
11. Show how you would bend to look funny. To look happy or sad. Bend slowly or quickly.
12. Bend your largest part. Your smallest part.
13. Begin by bending one body part. While returning this part to its original position, bend another part.
14. Bend your fingers one at a time. Bend all of them at once.
15. Bend your knees while standing, sitting, and lying. What other joint has to bend in a standing position?

ROCKING AND SWAYING

Rocking occurs when the center of gravity shifts fluidly from one body part to another. In rocking, the body is rounded where it touches the floor. Swaying is a slower movement and is somewhat more controlled than rocking.

Basic Activities

Stress Points

1. Rocking is done best on a rounded body surface. Arm movements and movements of other body parts can facilitate the motion.
2. Rocking is done smoothly and in a steady rhythm.
3. Rocking can begin with small movements and increase in extent, or vice versa.
4. Rocking and swaying are done to the full range of movement.
5. Swaying maintains a stable base.

Instructional Cues

1. Rock smoothly.
2. Rock in different directions. At varying speeds.
3. Rock higher (farther).
4. Sway until you almost lose your balance.

Suggested Movement Patterns

1. Rock in as many different ways as you can.
2. Show how you can rock slowly. Quickly. Smoothly.
3. Sit cross-legged with arms outstretched to the sides, palms facing the floor. Rock from side to side until the hands touch the floor.
4. Lie on your back and rock. Now point your arms and legs toward the ceiling as you rock.
5. Lie on your tummy with arms stretched overhead and rock. Hold your ankles and make giant rocks.
6. Try to rock while standing.
7. Rock and twist at the same time.
8. Lie on your back, lift your knees, and rock from side to side.
9. Show me two ways to have a partner rock you.
10. While standing, sway back and forth. Right and left. Try different foot positions. Sway slowly and rapidly. What effect does rapid swaying have?
11. Repeat swaying movements from a kneeling position.
12. Start with a little rocking motion and make it bigger and bigger.
13. Choose three (or more) ways of rocking and try to change smoothly between them.
14. Rock like a cradle. A rocking horse.
15. Sway like a tree in a heavy wind.

SWINGING

Swinging involves moving body parts somewhat like a swinging rope or clock pendulum. Most swinging movements involve the arms and legs.

Basic Activities

Stress Points

1. Swinging is a smooth, rhythmic action.
2. The body parts involved in swinging are relaxed and loose.

3. The extent of the swing movement is the same on both sides of the swing.
4. Swinging movements are as full as possible.

Instructional Cues

1. Loosen up; swing easy.
2. Swing fully; make a complete movement.
3. Swing in rhythm.

Suggested Movement Patterns

1. Explore different ways to swing your arms and legs.
2. Make up swinging patterns with the arms. Combine them with a step pattern, forward and back.
3. Swing the arms back and forth, and go into full circles at times.
4. With a partner, work out different swinging movements (Figure 16.4). Add circles.
5. Develop swinging sequences with swinging and full-circle movements (best done to waltz music with a slow or moderate tempo).
6. Swing like a clock pendulum. A cow's tail.

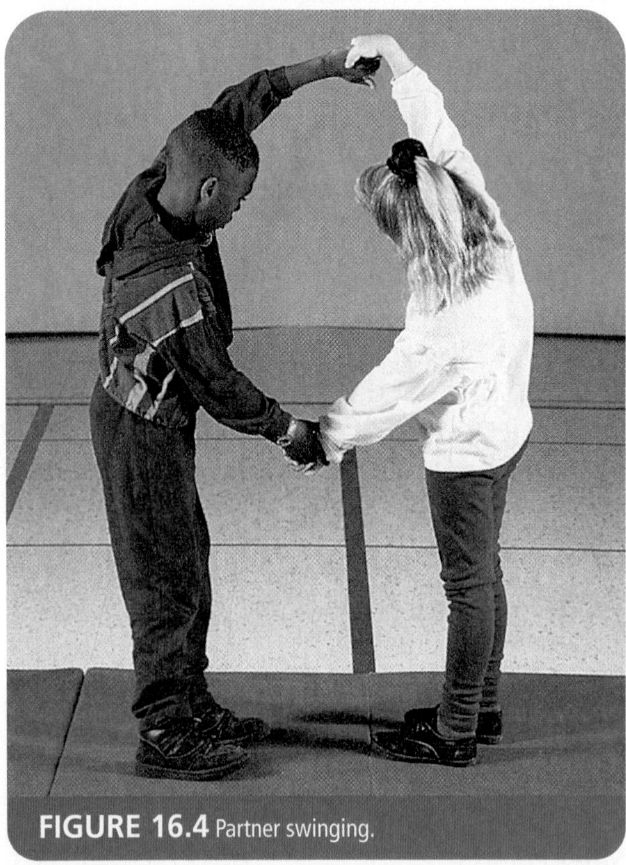

FIGURE 16.4 Partner swinging.

TURNING

Turning is rotating around the long axis of the body. *Turning* and *twisting* are sometimes used interchangeably to designate the movements of body parts, but *turning* refers to moving the body as a whole. Most turns begin with a twist. In the movements suggested here, action involves moving the entire body. Movements of body parts are discussed in the Twisting section.

Basic Activities

Stress Points

1. Maintaining balance and body control is important.
2. Turning is tried in both right and left directions.
3. Standing turns can be made by jumping, hopping, or shuffling with the feet.
4. Most turns are made in multiples of quarter turns. Students should practice multiples.
5. Turns are practiced in body positions other than standing—seated, on the tummy or the back, and so on.

Instructional Cues

1. Keep your balance.
2. In jump turns, land loosely with the knees relaxed.
3. Be precise in your movement, whether it is a quarter, half, or full turn.

Suggested Movement Patterns

1. While standing, turn your body to the left and right, clockwise and counterclockwise.
2. Turn to face north, east, south, west. (Post directions on the wall.)
3. Stand on one foot and turn around slowly. Now turn around quickly. Now turn with a series of small hops. Try to keep good balance.
4. Show me how you can cross your legs with a turn and sit down. Can you get up again in one movement?
5. Every time you hear the signal, see if you can turn around once, moving slowly. Can you turn two, three, or four times slowly on signal?
6. Lie on your tummy on the floor, and turn your body slowly in an arc. Turn over so you are on your back. Turn back to your tummy again.
7. Find a friend and see how many different ways you can turn each other. Take turns.
8. Play Follow the Leader with a partner. Take turns being the leader.
9. Begin with a short run, jump into the air, and turn to land facing in a new direction. Practice both right and left turns. Can you make a full reverse (180-degree) turn?
10. Lie on your back, turn, and rest on your side. Return. Repeat on the other side.

11. Lie on your back and turn over onto your stomach. Return. Turn over the opposite way.
12. Find a partner and see how many ways you can rotate each other.
13. Walk in general space and turn completely around on signal.
14. With your hands outstretched to the sides, pretend you are a helicopter.

TWISTING

Twisting is rotating a selected body part around its own long axis (Figure 16.5). Various joints can be used in twisting: spine, neck, shoulders, hips, ankles, and wrists.

FIGURE 16.5 Twisting movements.

Basic Activities

Stress Points

1. Twists extend as far as possible with good control.
2. The body parts the twist is based on are stabilized.
3. A twist in one direction is countered by a reverse twist.
4. Some joints are better for twisting than others. (Explain why.)

Instructional Cues

1. Twist as far as possible.
2. Twist the other way.
3. Hold the supporting parts firm.

Suggested Movement Patterns

1. Glue your feet to the floor. Can you twist your body to the left and right? Can you twist your body slowly? Quickly? Can you bend and twist at the same time? How far can you turn your hands back and forth?
2. Twist two or more parts of your body at once.
3. Twist one body part in one direction and another in the opposite direction.
4. Try twisting the lower half of your body without twisting the upper half.
5. What body parts can you twist while sitting on the floor?
6. Try to twist one body part around another part. Can you twist together even more parts?
7. Stand on one foot and twist your body. Can you bend and twist at the same time?
8. Show me some different shapes you can make by twisting your body.
9. Try to twist like a spring. Like a cord on a telephone.
10. Try to move and twist at the same time.
11. With the weight on your feet, twist as far as you can in one direction. Now take the weight on your hands and move your feet.
12. Twist like a pretzel. Like a licorice stick.
13. Twist like you are hitting a home run with a baseball bat.
14. Twist like you are hitting a golf ball.

STRETCHING

Stretching moves body parts away from the body center. Stretching sometimes involves moving a joint through the range of movement. Stretching is necessary for maintaining and increasing flexibility.

Basic Activities

Stress Points

1. Stretching is extended to the full range of movement.
2. Stretching exploration involves many body parts.
3. Stretching is done in many positions.
4. Stretching can be combined with opposite movements, such as curling.
5. Stretching is done slowly and smoothly.
6. Hold full stretching position for 10 seconds.

Instructional Cues

1. Stretch as far as possible. Make it hurt a little.
2. Find other ways to stretch the body part (joint).
3. Keep it smooth. Do not jerk.

Suggested Movement Patterns

1. Stretch as many body parts as you can.

2. Stretch your arms, legs, and feet in as many different directions as possible.
3. Try to stretch a body part quickly. Slowly. Smoothly.
4. Bend a body part and say which muscle or muscles are being stretched.
5. See how many ways you can stretch while sitting on the floor.
6. Lie on the floor and see if you can stretch two, three, four, or five body parts at once.
7. Try to stretch one body part quickly while stretching another part slowly.
8. While kneeling, see if you can stretch to a mark on the floor without losing your balance.
9. Stretch your right arm while curling your left arm.
10. Find a friend and see how many ways you can help each other stretch.
11. Try to stretch and become as tall as a giraffe. (Name other animals.)
12. Stretch and make a wide bridge. Find a partner to go under, around, and over your bridge.
13. Bend at the waist and touch your toes with your fingers. See if you can keep your legs straight while stretching to touch the toes.
14. Combine stretching with curling. With bending.
15. Stretch the muscles in your chest, back, tummy, ankles, wrists, fingers.
16. Make a shape with your body. Now stretch the shape to make it larger.
17. While moving at a low level, curl and stretch your fingers.
18. Find a position in which you can stretch one side of the body.
19. Find a position in which you can stretch both legs far apart in the air. Now make the legs as narrow as possible.
20. Stretch like a rubber band. When I say, "Snap!" move quickly back to original position.

PUSHING

Pushing is a controlled, forceful action against an object to move the body away from the object or to move the object in a desired direction by applying force to it (Figure 16.6).

Basic Activities

Stress Points

1. A forward stride position is used to broaden the base of support.
2. The body's center of gravity is low.
3. The line of force is directed toward the object.

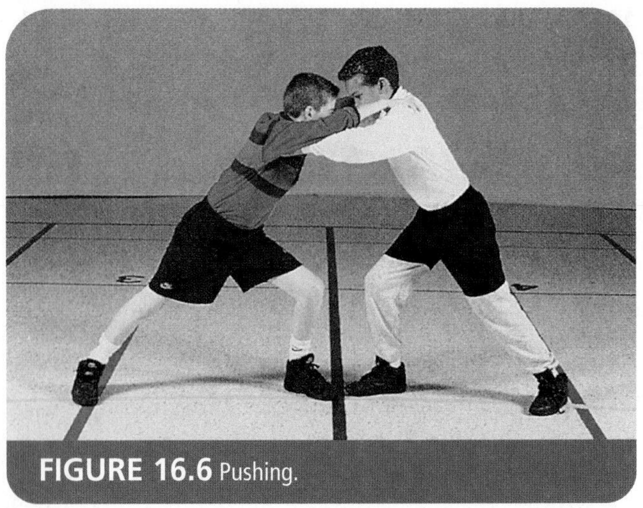

FIGURE 16.6 Pushing.

4. The back is in reasonable alignment, and the body forces gather for a forceful push. Do not bend the waist.
5. The push is controlled and steady.

Instructional Cues

1. Broaden your foot base.
2. Use all your body forces.
3. Push steadily and evenly.
4. Lower yourself for a better push.

Suggested Movement Patterns

1. Stand near a wall and push it from an erect position; then push with the knees bent and one foot behind the other. In which position can you push harder?
2. Pretend you are pushing something very light. Now pretend to push something heavy.
3. Try to push a partner who is sitting on a jumping box; then try to push a partner who is sitting on a scooter. How does your body position change?
4. Push an object with your feet without using your arms or hands.
5. Sit down and push a heavy object with your feet. Can you put your back against the object and push it? See how many different ways you can find to push the object.
6. Find a friend and try to push each other over a line in turn.
7. Sit back-to-back with your partner and take turns seeing if you can push each other backward.
8. Lie on the floor and push your body forward, backward, and sideward.
9. Lie on the floor and push yourself with one foot and one arm.
10. Put a beanbag on the floor and push it with your elbow, shoulder, nose, or other body part.

11. Move in crab position and push a beanbag.
12. Show how you can push a ball to a friend.

Safety Tip

During the introductory activity is an excellent time to introduce any safety precautions that are necessary in the lesson. These precautions can be reviewed for emphasis throughout the lesson.

PULLING

Pulling is a controlled, forceful action that moves an object closer to the body or the body closer to an object. If the body moves while pulling an object, the object follows the body.

Basic Activities

Stress Points

1. For forceful pulling, the base of support is broad and the body's center of gravity is low.
2. The body's vertical axis provides a line of force away from the object.
3. Pulling is a controlled movement with little jerking and tugging.
4. Hand grips must be comfortable if pulling is to be efficient. Gloves or other padding can help.
5. Pulling movements can be isolated in the body, with one part of the body pulling against the other.

Instructional Cues

1. Get your body in line with the pull. Lower yourself.
2. Widen your base of support.
3. Gather your body forces and pull steadily.

Suggested Movement Patterns

1. Reach for the ceiling, and pull an imaginary object toward you quickly. Pull it slowly and smoothly.
2. Use an individual tug-of-war rope and practice pulling against a partner. Try it with your hands and arms at different levels.
3. From a kneeling position, pull an object.
4. Try to pull with your feet while sitting on the floor.
5. Pretend to pull a heavy object while lying on the floor.
6. Clasp your hands together and pull as hard as you can.
7. Try pulling an object while standing on one foot.
8. Hold hands with a partner, and pull slowly as hard as you can.
9. Have your partner sit down, and then see how slowly you can pull each other. Take turns.
10. With your partner sitting on the floor, take turns seeing if you can pull each other to your feet.
11. Pull with different body parts.
12. Pull your partner by the feet as your partner sits on a rug square.
13. Reach for the stars with both hands and pull one hand back to you.
14. Balance on one foot. Try to pull something. What happens?

PUSHING AND PULLING COMBINATIONS

Combinations of pulling and pushing movements should be arranged in sequence. Musical phrases can signal changes from one movement to the other. Balance beam benches are excellent for practicing pulling and pushing techniques. Partner tug-of-war ropes provide effective pulling experiences. Partner resistance exercises (pages 268–269) are also useful pulling and pushing experiences.

FLEEING, CHASING, AND TAGGING

Many physical education games involve fleeing, chasing, and tagging. Speed and reaction are essential in dodging, for both the person being chased and the chaser responding to the target child's movements.

Basic Activities

Stress Points

1. Run under control.
2. The fleeing child is in a moderate crouch position with feet wider than usual. This position enables moving quickly from side to side.
3. The fleeing child becomes adept at faking—moving briefly in one direction before going another way.
4. All runners move on the balls of their feet.
5. The chaser maneuvers the fleeing child into a confined area to facilitate tagging.
6. Eyes are focused on the center of the dodger's body to avoid falling for a fake.
7. The tag is a gentle yet firm touch between the knees and shoulders.

Instructional Cues (Chaser)

1. Run under control.
2. Move on the balls of the feet, and stay slightly crouched when approaching the dodger.
3. Focus on the dodger's waistline.
4. Tag gently but firmly.

Suggested Movement Patterns

1. Run in general space toward other classmates and then dodge at the last moment. Avoid contact. To vary the activity, change direction on signal.
2. In general space, run and stop on signal.
3. In partners, have one person run and the other shadow (follow closely). Runners should change direction often. Switch roles.
4. Move into squads, with the leader 10 yards away from and facing the rest of the squad column. All members of the squad take turns running and dodging around a passive captain. Replace the squad captain regularly.
5. Partners mark a small area (12 feet by 12 feet) with cones. Chase and dodge within this area. Try it with two chasers and one dodger.

INTRODUCTORY ACTIVITIES

An introductory activity occurs during the first 2 or 3 minutes of the lesson. It is students' first movement experience when entering the teaching area. Such activities involve vigorous fundamental motor skills and minimal instruction. They help children warm up physiologically and prepare them for the physical activity to follow. A truism in teaching is, "A lesson that starts well, ends well."

Introductory activities are inherently upbeat and active, and they will overly arouse a poorly managed class. Try the excellent "rule of three freezes" to check the students' disposition and prepare them for instruction. Have the class enter the teaching area on the move and then freeze on signal. Move the children a second time and privately correct off-task behavior (while students are on the move). Freeze the class two more times to correct off-task behavior and see if students are ready to learn. If the class is still not with you after three corrective episodes, it is usually best to not teach the introductory activity; rather, focus on a management activity such as moving and freezing on signal.

Introductory activities are used for several reasons:

1. Offer students immediate activity when entering the gym. This satisfies their desire to move and helps teachers establish a positive learning attitude (purposeful movement done under control) for the class.
2. Help children warm up physiologically and prepare them for the activity to follow.
3. Practice management skills to be used in other parts of the lesson. For example, if partners or small groups will be used, the introductory activity could be finding partners quickly and getting a new partner each time.

Have students do introductory activities slowly at first, for safety reasons and to warm up. For example, if you are using Rhythmic Running, have children begin by walking. As the class warms up, increase the pace to a run. If you are using Curl and Around (page 333), begin by having students move around each other at moderate speed. After a short warm-up period, have them do the activity at full speed.

INTRODUCTORY ACTIVITIES USING LOCOMOTOR MOVEMENTS

The locomotor movements will involve the body as a whole and change abruptly from one movement pattern to another. A routine can begin with running and then change to another movement pattern either specified by the teacher or chosen by students. Supply signals for change with a voice command, whistle, drumbeat, or handclap. Children enjoy being challenged by having to change with the signal. Continue each part of a routine long enough for good body challenge and involvement, but not so long that it becomes tiresome.

Running is the basis of many gross movement activities, but other vigorous activities can be used. The suggested activities are classified roughly according to type and whether they are individual, partner, or group oriented.

Free Running

Students run in any direction, changing direction at will.

Running and Changing Direction

Children run in any direction, changing direction on signal. As a progression, specify the type of angle (right, obtuse, 45-degree, or 180-degree). Alternate right and left turns.

Running and Changing Level

Children run high on their toes and change to a lower level on signal. Instruct runners to touch the floor sometimes when at the lower level.

Running and Changing the Type of Locomotion

On signal, runners change from running to free choice or to a specific type of locomotion (walking, jumping, hopping, skipping, sliding, or galloping).

Running and Stopping

Students run in various directions and, on signal, freeze. Stress stopping techniques and an immobile position. On signal, have children stop running and assume a statue pose.

Move and Perform Athletic Movements

Students move and stop on signal. They then perform an athletic skill move, such as a basketball jump shot, leaping football pass catch, volleyball spike, or soccer kick. Have students focus on correct form and timing. Students can move with a partner and throw a pass on signal, punt a ball, or shoot a basket. The partner catches the ball or rebounds the shot.

Tortoise and Hare

The teacher calls out, "Tortoise," and the children run slowly in general space. On the command "Hare," they change to a rapid, circular run. Stress good knee lift during the run.

Ponies in the Stable

Each child has a stable—a place on the floor marked with a beanbag or hoop. On the first signal, children gallop lightly (like ponies) in general space. On the next signal, they trot lightly to their stable and continue trotting in place.

High Fives

Students move in different directions throughout the area. On signal, have them run toward a partner, jump, and give a "high five" (slap hands) while moving. Stress timing, so that the "high five" occurs at the top of the jump. Develop combinations of changing the level as well as speed of the movement.

Move and Perform a Task on Signal

Students move and perform a task on signal. During a signaled stop, they can perform several fitness challenges. Another variation is to perform individual or partner activities. Examples are Seat Circles, Balances, Wring the Dishrag, Partner Hopping, Twister, and Back-to-Back Get-Up (see Chapter 20).

Run, Stop, and Pivot

Students run, stop, and then pivot. This is an excellent activity for developing game skills. Children enjoy it especially when asked to imagine they are basketball or football players.

Triple-S Routine

The triple S's are *speed*, *style*, and *stop*. Children are in scatter formation throughout the area. On the command "Speed," they run in general space rapidly while avoiding contact with others. On "Style," all run with style (easy, light, loose running) in a large, circular, counterclockwise path. On the command "Stop," all freeze quickly under control. Repeat as necessary.

Agility Run

Pick two lines or markers 5 to 10 yards apart. Students run (or use other locomotor movements) back and forth between the lines for a specific time (10, 15, or 20 seconds). Students can challenge themselves by seeing how many times they can move back and forth in the given time limit.

Moving on Twos and Fours

Students begin with a movement in upright position and change to one on all fours.

Secret Movement

From a stack of cards, each naming various movements, the teacher selects one and says, "I want you to show me the secret movement." Students decide on a movement and keep doing it until signaled to stop. The teacher then identifies students who did the movement on the card. Those children demonstrate the movement, and all do it together. If no one does the movement, repeat the activity by asking the children to try other movements.

Airplanes

The class pretends to be airplanes. When told to take off, they zoom with arms out, swooping, turning, and gliding (Figure 16.7). When told to land, they drop to the floor facedown, simulating a plane at rest. To start their engines and take off, they can do a series of push-ups and move up and down while simulating engine noise.

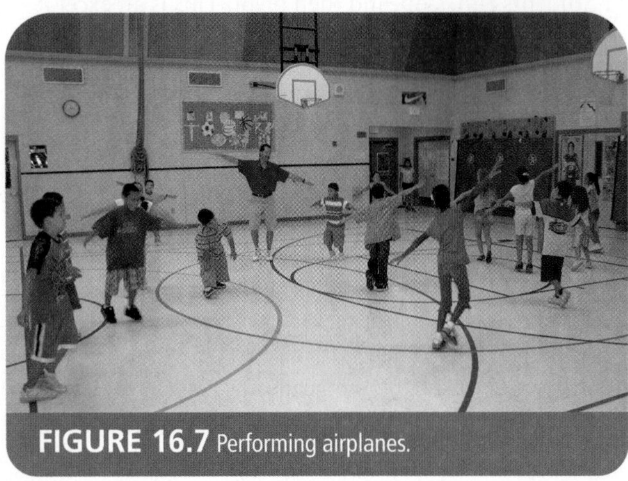

FIGURE 16.7 Performing airplanes.

Combination Movements

Combination movements can involve specified movements or allow some choice. The limitation might be to run, skip, and roll, or to jump, twist, and shake. Try setting a number for the sequence and letting the children select the activities. Say, "Put three different kinds of movements together in a smooth pattern."

Countdown

The teacher and class do a countdown to blastoff: "10, 9, 8, 7, 6, 5, 4, 3, 2, 1—blastoff!" The children are scattered during the countdown, and each makes an abrupt, jerky movement on each count. On the word *blastoff*, they jump up in the air and run in different directions until signaled to stop.

Magic-Number Challenges

The teacher issues a challenge like this: "10, 10, and 10." Children then put together three movements, doing 10 repetitions of each. Or the teacher could say, "Today we are going to play our version of Twenty-One." Twenty-one becomes the magic number to be fulfilled with three movements, each done seven times.

Crossing the River

Set up a "river" as the space between two parallel lines about 40 feet apart, or use the crosswise area in a gym. Each time the children cross the river, they use a different locomotor movement. Encourage them not to repeat a movement. Play is continuous over 1 minute or so.

Four-Corners Movement

Lay out a square with a cone at each corner. As students pass each corner, they change to a different locomotor movement with an agility emphasis. Challenge students with some sport agility movements (backward running, leaps, grapevine step, front crossover, back crossover, high knees, and slide steps), or change the qualities of movement (i.e., soft, heavy, slow, fast, etc.). Students doing faster movements can pass to the outside of the area.

Jumping and Hopping Patterns

Each child has a home spot. The teacher provides jumping and hopping sequences to take children away from and back to their spot. The teacher could say, "Move with three jumps, two hops, and a half turn. Return to place the same way." Have on hand a variety of sequences. Action can go beyond simply jumping and hopping.

Leading with Body Parts

Students move throughout the area, with some body part leading. Try using various body parts (elbow, fingers, head, shoulder, knees, and toes). Try the same exercise with different body parts trailing. Try leading or trailing with two and then three different body parts. Children can jog with some body part leading or trailing. On signal, have them make a different body part lead or trail.

Move, Rock, and Roll

Each child takes a mat and places it on the floor. Challenge students to move around, over, and on the mats. On signal, children move to a mat and try different ways of rocking and rolling. Specify rocking on different parts of the body, and suggest various body rolls. As another challenge, tell the children to rock or roll (or both) on a mat, get up and run to another mat, and repeat the sequence. Older children enjoy seeing how many mats they can move to in the allotted time.

RHYTHMIC INTRODUCTORY ACTIVITIES

European Rhythmic Running

In many European countries, Rhythmic Running opens the daily lesson. The European style is light, rhythmic running to the beat of a drum or tambourine. Skilled runners do not need the beat, but keep time with a leader. Much of the running is circular (Figure 16.8), but it can be done in scatter formation. To introduce a group of children to Rhythmic Running, have them clap to the drumbeat. Next, as they clap, have them shuffle their feet in place, keeping time. Then have them run in place without clapping. Finally, the class can run in single file. The running is light, bouncy, and in step with the beat. When running in single file, children stay behind the person in front, maintain proper spacing, and lift the knees in a light, prancing step.

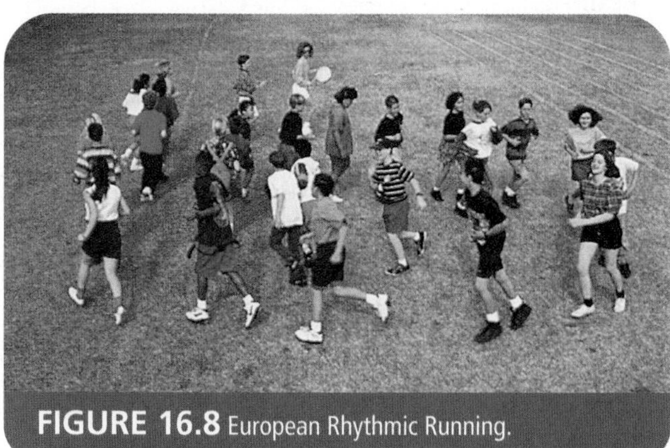

FIGURE 16.8 European Rhythmic Running.

Other movements can be combined with rhythmic running.

1. On signal (a whistle or double drumbeat), runners freeze in place. They resume running when the regular beat begins again.
2. On signal, runners make a full turn in four running steps, lifting the knees high while turning.
3. Children clap hands every fourth beat as they run. Instead of clapping, runners call a brisk, "Hey!" on the fourth beat, raising one arm with a fist at the same time.
4. Children run in squads, following their leader.
5. On signal, children run in general space, being careful not to bump into each other. Again on signal, they return to running in a circle.
6. Students alternate between running with high knee action and regular running.
7. Runners change to a light, soundless run and back to a heavier run. The drum tone controls the quality of the movement.
8. Students use Rhythmic Running while handling a parachute.
9. On the command, "Center," children run four steps toward the center, turn around (four steps), and run outward four steps to resume the original circular running pattern.
10. On signal, runners go backward, changing the direction of the circle.
11. Students carry a beanbag or a ball. Every fourth step, they toss the item up and catch it while running.
12. A leader moves the class through various formations. An enjoyable and challenging task is crossing two lines of children, alternating one child from one line in front of one child from the other line.
13. On signal, the class moves into various shapes (e.g., a square, rectangle, triangle, or pentagon). Rhythmic Running continues as students move into position.
14. On signal, each class member changes position with another student and then resumes the activity. For example, students opposite each other in the circle change places.
15. Because the movement is rhythmic, students can practice certain skills, such as a full turn. The turn can be done to a 4-count rhythm and is more deliberate than a quick turning movement.
16. When the beat stops, children scatter and run at random. When the beat resumes, they return to circular formation and proper rhythm.

Musical Relaxation

Conduct musical relaxation with a drum or appropriate recorded music. Children run in time to the rhythm. When the rhythm stops, all children lie on their backs, close their eyes, and relax until the music begins again.

Moving to Rhythm

Rhythm has many possibilities for guiding locomotor movements. Tempo changes can be part of the activity, and sound intensity can be translated into light or heavy movements.

Moving to Music

Pieces like the "Bleking" song (page 419) and "Pop Goes the Weasel" (page 424) can be a basis for creative movement. These are two-part pieces, so students can do a nonlocomotor movement in the first part and a locomotor movement in the second.

Folk Dance Movement

Use a CD or tape recording to stimulate different types of rhythmic movement such as polka, schottische, and two-step. Have students move around the room while practicing the steps.

INTRODUCTORY ACTIVITIES WITH EQUIPMENT

Individual Rope Jumping

Each child runs with rope in hand. On the signal to change, the child stops and begins to jump.

Hoop Activities

Each child runs while holding a hoop. On signal, students either start hula-hooping or put the hoop on the floor and use it for hopping and jumping patterns.

Wand Activities

Wands can be used in movements similar to those done with jump ropes and hoops. After running and stopping, students do wand stunts.

Milk Carton Fun

Each child has a milk carton stuffed with crumpled newspapers and taped shut. Students kick the cartons in different directions for 1 minute.

Ball Activities

Students dribble balls as in basketball or as in soccer. On signal they stop, balance on one leg, and pass (or kick) the ball under the other leg, around the back, and overhead, keeping both control and balance. Suggest other challenges involving both movement with the ball and manipulative actions performed in place.

Beanbag Touch-and-Go

Beanbags are spread throughout the area. On signal, students move and touch as many beanbags as possible with their hands. Specify different body parts for children to use in touching. Select different colors of beanbags, and issue commands such as "Touch as many blue beanbags as possible with your elbow."

Children can also move to and around a beanbag. Movement can be varied; for example, they might skip around the yellow beanbags with the left side leading. Change the movement as well as the direction and leading side of the body. Another enjoyable activity is to trace a shape (e.g., triangle, circle, square) while moving from beanbag to beanbag.

> *VARIATION:* **Vanishing Beanbags.** Students move around the beanbags as described above. While they are moving, the teacher or a student picks up one or two bags. On signal, students move to a beanbag and sit on it. The goal is not to be left out. Repeat, with all students participating each time.

Long-Rope Routine

Students begin in a loose column of four, all holding a single long jump rope in their right hands at waist level. The teacher gives a series of four signals. (1) Students jog lightly in a column. (2) The group shifts the rope overhead from the right to left side of the body while jogging. (3) The two inside students release the rope and begin jumping when the two students at the end of the rope start turning the rope. (4) The turners become jumpers, and vice versa. Repeat the series several times.

Disappearing Hoops

Each child gets a hoop and places it on the floor. Give challenges like "Move through five blue hoops, jump over four yellow hoops, and skip around six green hoops." On signal, the children move to a hoop and balance inside it. As they move, take away two or three hoops. At the signal, some students will not find a hoop. Those left out then offer the class the next movement challenge. Specify different challenges and stunts inside the hoops.

PARTNER AND SMALL-GROUP INTRODUCTORY ACTIVITIES

Marking

Each child has a partner about equal in ability. Under control, one partner runs, dodges, and tries to lose the other, who must stay within 3 feet of the runner. On signal, both stop. Chasers must be able to touch their partners to say they have marked them. Partners then change roles.

Following Activity

One partner leads and does various kinds of movements. The other partner must do the same movements. This idea can be extended to squad organization.

Fastest Tag in the West

Every player is a tagger. The object is to tag other players without being tagged. Players who are tagged must sit or kneel and await the next game (start new games frequently). If two or more players tag each other simultaneously, they are all "out."

Medic Tag

Three or four students are designated as taggers who try to tag other students. When tagged, a student kneels as if injured. Another child (not one of the taggers) can "rehabilitate" the injured student with a touch, so the student can resume play.

Hospital Tag

Every player is a tagger. Any player who is tagged must cover with one hand the body area that was touched. Students may be tagged twice but must be able to hold both tagged spots and keep moving. A student who is tagged three times must freeze. Restart the game when most of the students are frozen.

Curl and Around

Half of the class is scattered. Each child is in a curled position, facedown. The other half of the class moves around these children (Figure 16.9). On signal, reverse the groups quickly. Instead of being curled, challenge the students to form arches or bridges, with the moving children going around them. Try having the children on the floor alternate between curled and bridge positions; if a moving child goes around the curled position, the floor child changes immediately to a bridge. Another challenge: Ask the moving half of the class to move backward and sideways using different locomotor movements.

FIGURE 16.9 Curl and around.

Living Obstacles

This activity is similar to Group Over and Around, except the children on the floor are in a bridged position and moving. The children moving over and around must move quickly, as the obstacles are moving. Change positions after a designated time.

Popcorn

Half the class is scattered throughout the area and assumes the push-up position. The other half moves and "pops the popcorn." This is done by moving over and around the students who are in push-up position. When a student moves around a child doing a push-up, that child lowers to the floor. When a student moves over a child lying on the floor, that child raises to the push-up position. Moving students change places with those on the floor after a designated time.

Pyramid Power

Students move throughout the area. On signal, they find a partner and build a simple pyramid or partner stand. Examples are the hip–shoulder stand, double-crab stand, double-dog stand, and shoulder stand. Caution students to select a partner of similar size and to stand on the proper points of support.

Bridges by Threes

Three children in a group can set up an interesting movement sequence using bridges. Two of the children make bridges, and the third child goes under both bridges and sets up a bridge. Each child in turn goes under the bridges of the other two. Teachers can specify different kinds of bridges, and arrange the bridges so that a change in direction is made. An over-and-under sequence also is interesting. The child vaults or jumps over the first bridge and then goes under the next bridge before setting up the third bridge.

Rubber Band

Students gather around the teacher in the center of the area. On signal, students move away from the teacher with a specific movement such as run, hop sideways, skip backward, double-lame dog, or grapevine step. On signal, they sprint back to the central point, jump, and shout.

New Leader Movements

Squads or small groups run around the area, following a leader. On signal, the last person goes to the head of the line to lead. Groups of three are ideal for this activity.

Manipulative Activities

Each child has a beanbag. They move around the area, tossing the bags up and catching them. On signal, they drop the bags to the floor and jump, hop, or leap over as many bags as possible. On the next signal, they pick up a nearby bag and resume tossing it to themselves. Having one fewer beanbag than children adds to the fun. Hoops can also be used this way. Children begin by using hoops in rope-jumping style or for hula-hooping. On signal, they place the hoops on the floor and jump in and out of as many hoops as they can. Next, they pick up a nearby hoop and resume the original movement pattern. The activity also can be done with jump ropes.

Body Part Identification

Enough beanbags for the whole class are scattered on the floor. Students either run between or jump over the beanbags. When a body part is called out, the children place that body part on the nearest beanbag.

Drill Sergeant

The drill sergeant leads the squad, which marches in line. At will, the drill sergeant commands the squad to do a specific movement sequence: "Walk, jump twice, land, and roll." "Run, jump-turn, and freeze (pose)." "Shake, jump-turn, land, and roll." "Seal Walk, Log Roll, and jump." The sergeant can be given cards indicating suggested patterns. For more realism, the sergeant can call the squad members to attention, give them the command, and then call, "March!"

CREATIVE INTRODUCTORY ACTIVITIES

Another interesting approach is to give children creative and exploratory opportunities at the beginning of a lesson. Some examples follow.

1. Set out a variety of equipment (hoops, balls, wands, beanbags) and have each child take one piece to explore. This can be open exploration, or the movement can follow the trend of a prior lesson, thus extending the lesson.
2. Set out some manipulative items. Children select any item they wish and decide whether to play alone, with a partner, or as part of a small group.
3. Provide a range of apparatus, such as climbing ropes, climbing apparatus, mats, boxes, balance beams,

balance boards, and so on. Manipulative items also can be part of the package. Students decide where they want to participate.

TAMBOURINE-DIRECTED ACTIVITIES

The tambourine can signal changes of movement because it makes two different sounds: the tinny noise made by vigorous shaking and the percussive sound made by striking the instrument. Signal movement changes by going from one sound to the other.

Shaking Sound

1. The children remain in one spot but shake all over. These are gross movements.
2. The children shake and gradually drop to the floor.
3. The children scurry in every direction.
4. The children run lightly with tiny steps.

Drum Sound

1. Students make jerky movements to the percussive beat.
2. They jump in place or through space.
3. Students do locomotor movements in time with the beat.
4. Responding to three beats, the children collapse on the first beat, roll on the second, and form a shape on the third.

Combinations

To form a combination of movements, select one from each category above (shaking or percussive). When the shaking sound is made, the children perform that movement. When the drum sound is made, the children react accordingly.

GAMES AND MISCELLANEOUS ACTIVITIES

Selected games are quite suitable for introductory activities if they keep all children active, are simple, and require little teaching. To minimize teaching time, use one of these familiar games:

- Addition Tag (page 551)
- Back-to-Back Tag (page 549)
- Barker's Hoopla (page 564)
- Circle Touch (page 565)
- Couple Tag (page 555)
- Loose Caboose (page 559)
- One, Two, Button My Shoe (page 546)
- Squad Tag (page 561)
- Touchdown (page 571)
- Whistle Mixer (page 563)
- European Rhythmic Running (page 331)
- Airplanes (page 330)
- Curl and Around (page 333)

FOR MORE INFORMATION

REFERENCES AND SUGGESTED READINGS

Gabbard, C. P. (2008). *Lifelong motor development* (5th ed.). San Francisco: Benjamin Cummings.

Gallahue, D. L., & Donnely, F. C. (2007). *Developmental physical education for all children* (4th ed.). Champaign, IL: Human Kinetics.

Gallahue, D. L., & Ozmun, J. C. (2006). *Understanding motor development: Infants, children, adolescents, adults* (6th ed.). Boston: McGraw-Hill.

Haywood, K. H. (2005). *Lifespan motor development* (4th ed.). Champaign, IL: Human Kinetics.

Magill, R. A. (2007). *Motor learning: Concepts and applications* (8th ed.). Boston: McGraw-Hill.

Payne, G. V., & Isaacs, L. D. (2008). *Human motor development: A lifespan approach* (7th ed.). Boston: McGraw-Hill.

Wickstrom, R. L. (1983). *Fundamental movement patterns.* Philadelphia: Lea & Febiger.

WEBSITES

Fundamental Motor Skills

www.ptsd.k12.pa.us/motor_skills.htm
www.learning.gov.ab.ca/physicaleducationonline
http://rubistar.4teachers.org/index.php

General Physical Education

www.pelinks4u.org/index.htm
www.pecentral.org
http://pe4life.com

17 Manipulative Skills

ESSENTIAL COMPONENTS OF QUALITY PROGRAMS

I. Organized around content standards
II. Student-centered and developmentally appropriate
III. Physical activity and motor skill development form the core of the program
IV. Teaches management skills and self-discipline
V. Promotes inclusion of all students
VI. Focuses on process over product
VII. Promotes lifetime personal health and wellness
VIII. Teaches cooperation and responsibility and promotes sensitivity to diversity

NATIONAL STANDARDS FOR PHYSICAL EDUCATION*

1. Demonstrates competency in motor skills and movement patterns needed to perform a variety of physical activities.
2. Demonstrates understanding of movement concepts, principles, and tactics as they apply to the learning and performance of physical activities.
3. Participates regularly in physical activity.
4. Achieves and maintains a health-enhancing level of physical fitness.
5. Exhibits responsible personal and social behavior that respects self and others in physical activity.
6. Values physical activity for health, enjoyment, challenge, self-expression, and/or social interaction.

*National Association for Sport and Physical Education (NASPE), 2004.

Activities in this chapter develop manipulative skills. A *manipulative skill* is one in which a child handles an object with the hands, feet, or other body parts. Manipulative skills are basic to the development of sport skills. Jump-rope activities develop specialized motor skills, particularly visual–tactile coordination. Rope-jumping activities in this chapter progress from individual movements using rope patterns to long-rope jumping with turners to individual rope-jumping challenges. Rhythmic gymnastic activities combine rhythmic and manipulative skills using a particular piece of manipulative equipment while moving to accompaniment.

Outcomes

- Demonstrate the various stages of development associated with throwing, catching, kicking, and striking.
- Identify instructional procedures related to different types of manipulative skills.
- Identify objects that can be used to help children succeed in manipulative skills.
- Outline skill progressions, activities, and instructional hints associated with using balloons, beanbags, balls, paddles, Frisbees, hoops, jump ropes, parachutes, and other objects to teach manipulative skills.
- Identify beginning, intermediate, and advanced rope-jumping skills and routines using individual and long ropes.
- List progressions to use when teaching rope jumping.

MANIPULATIVE SKILLS involve using some type of implement, often with the hands but also with the feet or other body parts. Manipulative activities develop both hand–eye and foot–eye coordination as well as dexterity. Using equipment such as balloons, hoops, wands, beanbags, balls, tug-of-war ropes, Lummi sticks, Frisbees, and scoops, students can develop manipulative skills in many different settings. Activities with jump ropes are important in the program because they offer many possibilities for practicing multiple skills such as manipulative skills, rhythmic skills, and locomotor movements.

Balloons, beanbags, and yarn balls are used to teach throwing and catching activities for younger children. Soft, slow-moving objects reduce younger children's fear of being hurt while catching. Start children with an activity that allows all to achieve success. Based on that success, gradually increase the challenge of skills and experiences. Most activities begin with individual practice and then move to partner activity.

MANIPULATIVE SKILLS

Manipulative skills are basic to a number of specialized sport skills—catching, throwing, striking, and kicking, among others. These are complex motor patterns for which general developmental stages have been identified, from initial stages through mature performance patterns. Most complex skills should be practiced at normal speed. Whereas locomotor skills can be dramatically slowed down to promote learning, doing so with complex skills such as throwing, striking, or kicking destroys the rhythm of the skills. Provide the proper type of equipment and enough space for children to try these skills with maximum force. The following skills are listed by developmental stages rather than age, due to the wide maturity differences among children of similar ages. Major manipulative skills are described here and followed by many instructional activities, organized by equipment type, later in the chapter.

THROWING

In throwing, an object is thrust into space and accelerated using arm movement and total body coordination to generate force. Young children often go through two preliminary tossing stages before entering the stages of throwing. The first toss is a two-handed underhand throw involving little foot movement. A large ball, such as a beach ball, is best for teaching this type of throw, which begins with the ball held in front of the body at waist level. The toss is completed using only the arms. The second preliminary toss is a one-handed underhand throw. In this toss, which resembles pitching a softball, body torque is generated and weight shifts from the rear to the front foot. This toss requires a smaller object such as a beanbag, fleece ball, or small sponge ball.

Safety Tip

Children often have difficulty maintaining balance when encouraged to throw a ball for distance. To avoid too many trips or collisions, begin with proper form instead of distance or accuracy.

The following stages of skill analysis consider overhand throwing only. Velocity, not accuracy, is the primary goal in developing mature patterns characterized by a full range of motion and speed. Throwing for accuracy is practiced only after a mature form of the skill is in place.

Stage One

Stage one throwing is generally seen between the ages of 2 and 3 years. This stage is restricted to moving the arm from

FIGURE 17.1 Throwing form, stage one.

the rear toward the front of the body. The feet are stationary and positioned at shoulder width, and little or no trunk rotation occurs (Figure 17.1). Most of the movement force originates from flexing the hip, moving the shoulder forward, and extending the elbow.

Stage Two

Stage two throwing develops between the ages of 3 and 5 years. Some rotary motion is developed in an attempt to increase the amount of force. This stage is characterized by a lateral fling of the arm while rotating the trunk (Figure 17.2). Some children step into the throw, although many keep their feet stationary. This throwing style sometimes looks like a discus throw rather than a baseball throw.

FIGURE 17.2 Throwing form, stage two.

Stage Three

Typically, stage three is seen in children at ages 5 and 6 years. The starting position is similar to that of stages one and two because the body is facing the target area, the feet are parallel, and the body is erect. In this stage, however, the child steps toward the target with the foot on the same side of the body as the throwing arm. This allows the body to rotate and the body weight to shift forward as the step occurs. The arm action is closer to overhand throwing than is the fling of stage two, and hip flexion increases. Many students never mature beyond this stage without ample opportunity for practice in throwing.

Stage Four

Stage four is a mature form of throwing; more force is applied to the object being thrown. The thrower uses the rule of opposition in this stage, stepping into the throw with the leg opposite the throwing arm. This develops maximum body torque. Beginning with the weight on the back leg, the movement sequence is as follows: (a) step toward the target, (b) rotate the upper body, and (c) throw with the arm (Figure 17.3). Use the cue phrase, "Step, turn, and throw." The elbow leads the way in the arm movement, followed by forearm extension and a final snapping of the wrist. Have students practice this pattern frequently to develop total body coordination. Through a combination of sound instruction and practice, most children can develop a mature pattern of throwing by age 8 or 9 years.

FIGURE 17.3 Throwing pattern, stage four.

Stress Points

1. Stand with the nonthrowing side of the body facing the target. The throwing arm side of the body is away from the target.
2. Step toward the target with the leg opposite the throwing arm.

Teaching Hints

1. Offer a variety of objects during throwing practice, so students understand how varying weight and diameter affects throwing distance and speed.
2. When children are learning to throw, stress distance and velocity. Throwing for accuracy discourages the development of a mature throwing form. Tell students to "throw as hard as possible."
3. It is ineffective to work on throwing and catching at the same time. Many children's throws will be inaccurate and hard for a partner to catch. Have them practice throwing against a wall (velocity) or on a large field (distance).
4. Use carpet squares or circles drawn on the floor to teach children proper foot movement (stepping forward and off the square or out of the circle).
5. Beanbags and yarn balls are excellent for developing throwing velocity because they do not bounce.

3. Rotate the hips as the throwing arm moves forward.
4. Bend the arm at the elbow. The elbow leads the forward movement of the arm.
5. Body weight remains on the rear foot (away from the target) during early phases of the throw. Just before moving the arm forward, shift weight from the rear leg to the forward leg (nearer the target).

CATCHING

Catching uses the hands to stop and control a moving object. Catching is harder to learn than throwing, because children must track the object while moving into its path. Catching is also hard to master due to the fear of being hurt by an oncoming object. When teaching the early stages of catching, use balloons, fleece balls, and beach balls—they move slowly, make tracking easier, and usually do not hurt if they hit a child in the face.

Stage One

In stage one of catching, the child holds the arms in front of the body, with elbows extended and palms up, until the ball makes contact. The elbows are then bent in a trapping movement, and the arms press the ball against the chest (Figure 17.4). Children often turn their heads away or close their eyes because of the fear response. Encourage them to focus on the object rather than the thrower.

FIGURE 17.4 Catching form, stage one.

Stage Two

Stage two catching is much like that in stage one. Rather than waiting for the ball to contact the arms, however, the child makes an anticipatory reaching movement and cradles the ball somewhat.

Stage Three

In stage three, the child prepares for the catch by lifting the arms and bending them slightly. The chest is used as a backstop for the ball. During this stage, the child makes contact with the hands first and then guides the object to the chest (Figure 17.5 on page 340).

Stage Four

In the fourth and final stage of catching, which occurs at about age 9 years, the child catches with the hands.

17

FIGURE 17.5 Catching form, stage three.

Encourage this skill by decreasing the size of the ball. Teach "giving" with the arms (reaching and bringing the ball to the body, thus absorbing force) while catching. The legs bend, and the feet move in anticipation of the catch.

Stress Points

1. Maintain visual contact with the projectile.
2. Reach for the projectile and absorb its force by bringing the hands into the body. This "giving" makes catching easier by reducing the chance for the object to bounce out of the hands.
3. Place the feet in a stride position rather than a straddle position. A fast-moving object can cause a loss of balance if feet are in the straddle position.
4. Align the body with the object rather than reaching to the side of the body to make the catch.

KICKING

Kicking is a striking action made with the feet. Types of kicking include punting (dropping the ball from the hands and kicking before it touches the ground) and placekicking (kicking the ball in a stationary position on the ground). A third type, soccer kicking, may be the most difficult of all kicking skills because the ball is moving before the kick is executed.

Stage One

In stage one the body is stationary, and the kicking foot is flexed to prepare for the kick. The kicking motion is carried out with a straight leg and little or no flexing at the knee. There is little movement of the arms and trunk, and concentration is on the ball.

Stage Two

In the second stage of kicking, the kicking foot swings backward by flexing at the knee. Usually, the child displays opposition of the limbs. When the kicking leg goes forward, the opposite arm moves forward. Unlike the first stage, in stage two, the kicking leg moves farther forward in the follow-through.

Stage Three

In stage three, movement toward the object to be kicked is added. The leg moves a greater distance, coupled with a

Teaching Hints

1. It is natural to dodge an object that may cause harm. Remove the fear factor by using projectiles that will not hurt children, such as foam balls, yarn balls, beach balls, and balloons.
2. Use smaller projectiles as students improve their catching skills. Larger objects move more slowly and are easier to track visually.
3. Prepare students for a catch by asking them to focus on the ball while it is in the thrower's hand. Use a verbal cue such as "Look (focus), ready (for the throw), catch (toss the ball)."
4. Balls and background colors should strongly contrast to increase visual perception.
5. Throwing the projectile at a greater height offers the child more opportunity to track it successfully. Beach balls move slowly throughout a high trajectory, giving children time to focus and move into the path of the oncoming object.
6. Bounce objects off the floor so children learn to judge the rebound angle of a projectile.

movement of the upper body to counterbalance the leg movement.

Stage Four

Mature kicking styles involve a preparatory extension of the hip to increase the range of motion. The child runs to the ball and takes a small leap to get the kicking foot in position. While swinging the kicking foot forward, the child leans backward and then takes a small step forward on the support foot to regain balance (Figure 17.6).

FIGURE 17.6 Kicking a soccer ball, stage four.

Stress Points

1. Students need to step forward with the nonkicking leg. Have them stand behind and slightly to the side of the ball. Keep the eyes on the ball (head down) throughout the kick.
2. Practice kicking with both feet.
3. Use objects that will not hurt children. For example, regulation soccer balls, which are heavy and hard, hurt young children's feet. Foam balls and beach balls are excellent objects for kicking practice.
4. Encourage kickers to move their leg backward in preparing for the kick. Beginners often fail to move the leg backward, making it difficult for them to generate kicking force.
5. Arms move in opposition to the legs during the kick.
6. After children develop kick speed and velocity, focus on altering the force of the kick. Many children learn to kick only with velocity; activities like soccer demand both soft "touch" kicks and kicks of maximum velocity.

STRIKING

Striking is hitting an object with an implement. Common forms of striking are hitting a softball with a bat, using a racket for striking in tennis and racquetball, and striking a ball with the hand as in volleyball.

Stage One

In this stage, the child's feet are stationary and the trunk faces the direction of the oncoming object (or ball on a tee). The elbows are fully flexed, and force is generated by extending them downward. Little body force is generated because there is no trunk rotation and the motion is from back to front. The striking force comes from the arms and wrists.

Stage Two

In stage two, the child's upper body generates force. The trunk is turned to the side in anticipation of the ball. The weight shifts from the rear foot to the forward foot before contacting the ball. The child's trunk and hips rotate into the ball during the swing. The elbows are less flexed, and force is generated by extending the flexed joints. Trunk rotation and forward movement are in an oblique plane.

Stage Three

In stage three, mature striking skills, the child stands parallel to the path of the oncoming object. Weight shifts to the rear foot and the hips rotate, followed by a weight shift toward the ball as it approaches the hitter. Striking occurs with the arms extended in a long arc. The swing ends with weight on the forward foot. Mature striking involves a swing through the full range of motion and a smooth transfer of weight from the rear to the front plane of the body.

Teaching Hints

1. When teaching kicking skills, focus on velocity and distance rather than accuracy. Students who are asked to kick accurately will poke at the ball rather than develop a full kicking style.
2. Ensure that all students have a ball to kick. Beach balls (for primary grades) and foam balls are excellent because they do not travel far and children can kick and retrieve them quickly.
3. Stationary balls are easier to kick than moving balls. Use this progression when teaching beginners to kick.
4. Teach various types of kicks: the toe kick, instep kick, and side-of-the-foot kick.

Stress Points

1. Track the ball as soon as possible, and keep tracking until it is hit. (It is impossible to see the racket hit the ball, but this is an excellent teaching hint.)
2. Grip the bat with the hands together. For right-handed hitters, the left hand is on the bottom (near the small end of the bat).
3. Keep the elbows away from the body. Emphasis is on making a large swing and extending the elbows as the ball is hit.
4. Swing the bat in a horizontal (parallel to the ground) plane. Beginners tend to strike downward in a chopping motion.

MANIPULATIVE SKILL ACTIVITIES

Manipulative skills come into play when children handle an object, usually with their hands and feet. Other parts of the body can also be used. These skills lead to better hand–eye and foot–eye coordination, which are particularly important for tracking items in space. Manipulative skills are basic to many game skills. Throwing, batting, kicking, and catching objects are important skills that can be taught by using beanbags and various balls. Rebounding or redirecting an object in flight (such as a volleyball) is another useful manipulative skill. Continuous control of an object, such as a wand or hoop, is also a manipulative activity.

INSTRUCTIONAL ACTIVITIES

Instructional activities for each unit progress from easiest to most difficult and are organized by major skill groups. This structure helps teachers focus on desired objectives. For example, the first group of skills to practice in beanbag activities is Tossing to Self in Place. The teacher can take either of two approaches: Develop the first group in depth, exhausting all of the possibilities, or select two or more activities from several groups. In the latter case, when repeating the lesson the following day, use the same groups of activities but pose different challenges. By working within groups of activities, students focus on the same type of skill; but they stay motivated because of the many different challenges being offered. This approach offers random practice opportunities (see page 46). Random practice results in better retention because students are mentally generating solutions and are less likely to get bored.

Why work on group activities around equipment rather than skills? It is certainly possible to create random practice sessions by using different types of equipment to practice the same skills. However, this makes most lessons equipment intensive. Teachers often avoid units that demand too much equipment due to the difficulty of moving it to and from the instructional area. For example, if a teacher is working with first-graders and sixth-graders during the same time period and has to move equipment outside, twice as much equipment has to be moved. The same goal can be accomplished (random practice sessions) by bringing out one type of equipment and modifying the activities that focus on a single skill. The result will be effective and challenging random practice sessions.

STUDENT-DEVELOPED GAMES

Skills can be reinforced and enhanced through games that students create involving the skills just learned. For example, ask students to create a game using a certain skill for which they are to select the equipment needed, outline the game space, specify the number of participants, and set the rules, including scoring. If desired, the teacher can outline certain conditions, such as using two hoops and two bowling pins, limiting space to two lines 20 to 30 feet apart, and having competing sides of two against two. Within those parameters, students create and play a game.

Creative games can be designed for individuals, partners, or small groups. Keep the groups small, so each

✔ Teaching Hints

1. Striking is done with maximum force and bat velocity when the focus of instruction is on developing a mature striking form.
2. Practice hitting stationary objects before progressing to moving objects. Batting tees and balls suspended on a string are useful for beginners.
3. In the early stages of striking practice, use slow-moving objects such as balloons and beach balls. They are easier to track when moving.
4. As skill in striking increases, decrease the size of the projectile and bat (or racket).
5. To enhance visual perception, ensure that the ball contrasts with the background.
6. Use rubber footprints to help children learn to step into the ball.

child's input is considered. Specify different kinds of equipment (such as mats, wands, goals, or benches). Later, the new games can be demonstrated to the rest of the class. When students are in the learning phase of skill development, the games should focus on applying the skills rather than serious competition. Competition may reduce students' performance level if they focus on winning the game rather than correctly performing the skill.

ACTIVITIES WITH BALLOONS AND BEACH BALLS

Balloons provide interesting movement experiences and emphasize hand–eye coordination. Students who are not ready for faster-moving ball skills can achieve success with balloons. Beach balls are larger, and they move more slowly and predictably. Both objects are harmless, so students can learn to catch without fear of being hurt. These objects move slowly, so students have ample time to learn proper footwork—preparing for a volley, catching, and striking, for example.

INSTRUCTIONAL PROCEDURES

1. Use the following instructional cues when teaching balloon and beach ball skills:
   a. Catch and control with the fingertips.
   b. Keep your eyes on the object.
   c. Move your body into the path of the oncoming object.
   d. Reach, catch, and move the object to the body (giving).
2. After blowing up each balloon, do not tie a knot in the neck of the balloon. Fix it with a twist tie used to close plastic bags, so the balloon can be deflated easily and reused.
3. Beach balls last longer and are easier to control if they are a bit underinflated. Beach balls 16 to 20 inches in diameter are best for most students and can be used with older students for lead-up games in volleyball and soccer.

RECOMMENDED PROGRESSION

1. Begin with free exploration, having children play under control with their balloon (Figure 17.7). The objective is to have the children gain a sense of the balloon's flight.
2. Introduce specific hand, finger, and arm contacts. Include using alternate hands; contacting at different levels (low, high, in between); jumping and making high contact; using different hand contacts (palm, back, side, and different fist positions); using different finger combinations (two fingers, index finger, thumb only); and using arms, elbows, and shoulders.

FIGURE 17.7 Batting balloons from different body positions.

3. Establish contact sequences with three or four body parts. Use various levels and body shapes. Make some flash cards with names of body parts. Students must take their eyes off the balloon to see the named body part. This is an excellent challenge to help young children learn to track a moving object.
4. Bat from various body positions—kneeling, sitting, lying.
5. Use an object to control the balloon (Lummi stick, ball, stocking paddle).
6. Restrict movement. Keep one foot in place. Keep one or both feet within a hoop or on a mat or carpet square.
7. Work with a partner by alternating turns, batting the beach ball back and forth, employing follow-the-leader patterns, and so on.
8. Introduce some aspects of volleyball technique, including the overhand pass, underhand pass, and dig pass. Begin with a volleyball serve. Make this informal and on a "let's pretend" basis. Check the volleyball unit (see Chapter 30) for technique suggestions.
9. Toss a balloon up. Pick up a hoop from the floor, pass it around the balloon, place the hoop on the floor, and keep the balloon from touching the ground.

10. Have four to six children sit on the floor in a small circle. Each circle gets two balloons to be kept in the air. Children's seats are "glued" to the floor. If a balloon hits the floor, it is out of play. Play for a specific time (30 to 60 seconds). Increase the challenge by using beach balls.

ACTIVITIES WITH BEANBAGS

Beanbag activities provide valuable learning experiences for elementary school children at all levels. Challenging partner activities—juggling, different and unique methods of propulsion, and the Split-Vision Drill (page 346)—are suitable activities for older students.

INSTRUCTIONAL PROCEDURES

1. Use these instructional cues when teaching beanbag activities:
    a. Catch the beanbag softly by giving with the hands, arms, and legs. "Giving" involves the hands going out toward the incoming beanbag and bringing it in for a soft landing.
    b. Keep your eyes on the beanbag when catching.
    c. When tossing and catching, toss slightly above eye level.
2. Make sure that beanbags are about 6 inches square. This size balances well and can be controlled on various parts of the body for a greater challenge to intermediate-level children.
3. Throwing and catching skills involve many intricate elements. Stress the principles of opposition, eye focus, weight transfer, and follow-through. Stress tracking the object being caught and focusing on the target when throwing.
4. Stress laterality and directionality when teaching throwing and catching skills. Teach children to throw, catch, and balance beanbags with both the left and right sides of their body. Have them learn to catch and throw at different levels.
5. Children throw at chest height to a partner, unless teachers specify a different type of throw. Teach all types of return: low, medium, high, left, and right.
6. In partner work, keep distances between partners reasonable, especially in introductory phases. A good starting distance is 15 feet or so.
7. In partner work, emphasize skillful and varied throwing, catching, and handling of the beanbag. Throwing too hard or out of range, to make the partner miss, should be avoided.

Most activities are classified as individual or partner activities. A few activities are for groups of three or more.

INDIVIDUAL ACTIVITIES

Tossing to Self in Place

1. Toss with both hands, with right hand only, and with left hand only. Catch the same way. Catch with the back of the hands.
2. Toss the beanbag progressively higher, then progressively lower.
3. Hold the beanbag in one hand and make large arm circles (imitating a windmill). Release the bag so it flies upward and then catch it.
4. Toss from side to side, right to left (reverse), front to back (reverse), and around various body parts in different combinations.
5. Toss upward and catch with hands behind the back. Toss upward from behind the body and catch in front. Toss upward and catch on the back, knees, toes, and other body parts.
6. Hold the bag at arm's length in front of the body, with palms up. Withdraw hands quickly from under the bag, and catch it from on top in a palms-down stroke before it falls to the floor.
7. Toss upward and catch as high as possible. As low as possible. Work out a sequence of high, low, and in between.
8. Toss upward and catch with the body off the floor. Try tossing as well as catching with the body off the ground.
9. Toss in various ways while seated and while lying down.
10. Toss two beanbags upward and catch a bag in each hand.

Adding Stunts in Place

1. Toss overhead to the rear, turn around, and catch. Toss, do a full turn, and catch.
2. Toss, clap hands, and catch. Clap hands more than once. Clap hands around various body parts.
3. Toss, do pretend activities (e.g., comb hair, wash face, brush teeth, shine shoes), and catch.

4. Toss, touch different body parts with both hands, and catch. Touch two different body parts, calling out the name of the parts. Touch two body parts, clap hands, and catch.
5. Toss, kneel on one knee, and catch. Try this going to a sitting or lying position. Reverse the position, going from lying or sitting to standing to catch.
6. Toss, touch the floor, and catch. Explore with other challenges. Use heel clicks or balance positions.
7. Bend forward, reach between the legs, and toss the bag onto the back or shoulders.
8. Reach one hand over the shoulder, drop the beanbag, and catch it with the other hand behind the back. Reverse the hands. Drop the beanbag from one hand behind the back and catch it with the other hand between the legs. Put the beanbag on the head, lean back, and catch it with both hands behind the back. Catch it with one hand.

Locomotor Movements

1. Toss to self, moving to another spot to catch. Toss forward, run, and catch. Move from side to side. Toss overhead to the rear, run back, and catch.
2. Add various stunts and challenges described earlier. Vary with different locomotor movements.

Balancing the Beanbag on Various Body Parts

1. Balance the beanbag on the head. Move around, keeping the beanbag in place. Sit down, lie down, turn around, and so on.
2. Balance the beanbag on other parts of the body and move around. Balance on top of the instep, between the knees, on the shoulders, on the elbows, under the chin. Use more than one beanbag.

Propelling with Various Body Parts

1. Toss to self from various parts of the body: elbow, instep, knees, shoulders, between the feet, between the heels.
2. Sit and toss the bag from the feet to the hands. Practice tossing while lying on the back. While lying down, pick up the bag between the toes and place it behind the head, using a full curl position. Go back and pick it up, returning it to its original place.

Juggling

1. Begin with two bags and juggle them in the air. (See pages 351–355 for instructions on juggling.)
2. Juggle three bags.

Other Activities

1. From a standing wide straddle, place the beanbag on the floor and push it between the legs as far back as possible. Jump in place with a half turn and repeat.
2. Take the same position as above. Push the beanbag back as far as possible between the legs, bending the knees. Without moving the legs, turn to the right and pick up the beanbag. Repeat to the left.
3. Stand with feet apart and hold the beanbag with both hands. Reach as high as possible (with both hands), bend backward, and drop the beanbag. Reach between the legs, and pick up the beanbag.
4. On all fours, put the beanbag in the small of the back. Wiggle and force the beanbag off the back without moving the hands or knees from place.
5. In crab position, place the beanbag on the stomach, and try to shake it off. On all fours, put it on the back and do a Mule Kick (see Figure 20.43 on page 479).
6. Push the beanbag across the floor with different body parts such as the nose, shoulder, or knee.
7. Each student drops a beanbag on the floor. See how many different ways students can move over, around, and between the beanbags. For example, jump three beanbags, crab-walk around two others, and cartwheel over one more.
8. Spread the legs about shoulder width. Bend over and throw the beanbag between the legs and onto the back. Next, throw the beanbag all the way over the head, and catch it.

PARTNER ACTIVITIES

Tossing Back and Forth

1. Begin with various kinds of two-handed throws: underhand, overhead, side, and over the shoulder. Change to one-handed tossing and throwing.
2. Throw at different levels, at different targets, right and left.
3. Throw under the leg, around the body, as a center in football. Try imitating the shot put and the discus throw. Try the softball (full arc) throw.
4. Have partners sit cross-legged about 10 feet apart. Throw and catch in various styles.
5. Use follow activities, in which one partner leads with a throw and the other follows with the same kind of throw.
6. Jump, turn in the air, and pass to partner.
7. Stand back-to-back and pass the beanbag around both partners from hand to hand as quickly as possible. Try moving the beanbag around and through various body parts.
8. Toss in various directions to make partner move and catch.
9. Run around partner in a circle, tossing the beanbag back and forth.
10. Toss two beanbags back and forth. Each partner has a beanbag, and the beanbags go in opposite directions at the same time. Try having one partner toss both beanbags at once in the same direction, using various types of throws. Try to keep three beanbags going at once.

Propelling with Various Body Parts

1. From a sitting position, toss the beanbag to a partner with foot or toes, from on top of the feet, and from between the feet, with elbow, shoulder, head, and any other body part.
2. With back to partner, take a bunny-jump position. Hold the beanbag between the feet and kick it back to partner. Try kicking with both feet from a standing position.
3. Partners lie faceup on the floor with heads pointing toward each other, about 6 inches apart. One partner has a beanbag between the feet and places it between the partners' heads. The other partner picks up the beanbag with the feet (by reaching over the head) and places it on the floor by the feet after returning to original position. With both partners in a backward curl, try to transfer the beanbag directly from one partner to the other with the feet.

GROUP ACTIVITIES AND GAMES

Split-Vision Drill

This split-vision drill from basketball is adapted to beanbags. An active player faces two partners about 15 feet away. They stand side by side, not far apart. The active player holds a beanbag, and one of the partners holds a beanbag. The active player tosses to the open partner and at the same time catches the bag tossed by the other partner. The two bags move back and forth between the active player and the other two, alternately (Figure 17.8). After a while, change positions.

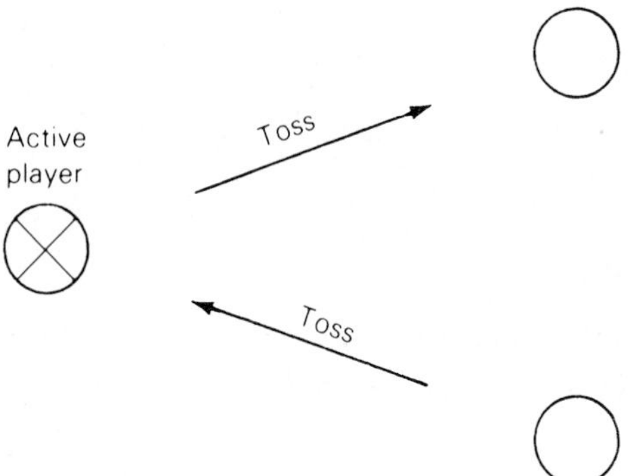

FIGURE 17.8 Split-vision drill for beanbags.

Target Games

Wastebaskets, hoops, circles drawn on the floor, and other objects can be used as targets for beanbag tossing. Target boards with holes cut out are available from commercial sources. Holes can be triangles, circles, squares, and rectangles, thus stressing form concepts.

Beanbag Quoits

This game is played like horseshoes. Draw a court by marking two spots (e.g., with masking tape) on the floor about 1 inch in diameter and 20 feet apart. Each competitor has two beanbags, a different color for each player. Players toss from behind one spot to the other spot. The object is to get one or both beanbags closer to the mark than the opponent does. If a beanbag completely blocks out the spot, as viewed from directly overhead, the player scores 3 points. Otherwise, the bag nearest the spot scores 1 point. Games are played to 11, 15, or 21 points. In each round, the player winning the previous point tosses first.

Other Games

Children enjoy playing One Step (page 560). Teacher Ball (page 550) is also readily adaptable to beanbags.

ACTIVITIES WITH BALLS

This section focuses on ball skills in which the child handles balls without using other equipment, such as a bat or paddle. Ball skills are mostly of two types: (a) hand–eye skills, including throwing, catching, bouncing, dribbling (as in basketball), batting (as in volleyball), and rolling (as in bowling); and (b) foot–eye skills, including kicking, trapping, and dribbling (as in soccer).

TYPES OF BALLS

For younger children, sponge rubber, yarn, and fleece balls are all excellent for introductory throwing and catching, because they help overcome the fear factor. (Chapter 10 gives instructions on making balls from yarn.) Innovative teachers can develop other suitable objects, such as crumpled-up newspaper balls wrapped with tape, papier-mâché balls, stitched rolls of socks, and stuffed balloons.

The whiffle ball, a hollow plastic ball with holes, is also useful. Scoops, either commercial or home constructed, are an extension of whiffle-ball activities. Another useful ball is a soft softball, a much softer version of the regular softball. It is suitable for catching and throwing but does not hold up well if batted.

The inflated rubber playground ball (8.5-inch size) should be used for most ball-handling experiences. Inflate the balls so that they bounce well, but do not overinflate, which makes them difficult to catch and distorts their shape.

Eight-inch foam balls last longer and have more utility for children. Foam balls are easier to catch and pass and do not hurt students who are accidentally hit by one. Many types of foam are used to make these balls, so it is important to make sure that the balls are dense and will bounce well. Many of the cheaper styles are extremely light and do not bounce. An even better (but more expensive) alternative is the foam "tough-skin" ball. These foam balls have a tough plastic coating that makes the balls bounce better and protects the soft foam. In the long run, these tough-skin balls may be the best buy because they do not leak or develop punctures like the standard playground ball. Bright-colored balls add contrast to the background, making it easier for children to track and catch.

TYPES OF ORGANIZATION

Instruction with younger children begins with individual work and progresses to partner and group activities. When propelling the ball back and forth, partners go from rolling the ball to throwing with one bounce to throwing on the fly. Be sure that partners with different skill levels can work well together.

Distance between partners is short at first and then lengthens gradually. Introduce the concept of targets by directing children to throw the ball to specific points. Later, to maintain progression, change from a stationary target to a moving target. Group activities are confined to small groups (of three to six), so that each child can be active, and they include activities not possible in individual or partner activity.

INSTRUCTIONAL PROCEDURES

1. Use these instructional cues when teaching ball skills.
   a. Keep your eyes on the ball.
   b. Catch and dribble the ball with the pads of the fingers.
   c. Use opposition and weight transfer when passing the ball.
2. When catching, receive the ball softly by "giving" with the hands and arms. The hands reach out to receive the ball and then cushion the impact by bringing the ball in toward the body in a relaxed way.
3. To catch a throw above the waist, hold the hands so the thumbs are together. To catch a throw below the waist, keep the little fingers toward each other and rotate the thumbs outward.
4. When throwing to a partner, unless otherwise specified, try to reach the partner at about chest height. At times, teachers can specify different target points—high, low, right, left, at the knee, and so on.
5. Begin with basic skills within all children's reach and progress to more challenging activities.
6. Laterality is an important consideration. Have students practice on right and left sides of the body in turn.
7. Incorporate split vision in bouncing and dribbling. Encourage students to look forward, rather than at the ball, when bouncing and dribbling.

Tossing and Catching on the Move

1. Toss the ball upward and forward. Run forward and catch it after one bounce. Toss the ball upward in various directions (forward, sideward, backward), run under it, turn, and catch it on the fly.
2. Add various stunts and challenges, such as touching the floor, clicking the heels, or turning around.

Batting on the Move

With first the right and then the left hand, bat the ball upward in different directions, and catch it on the first bounce or on the fly.

Practicing Foot Skills on the Move

Dribble the ball (soccer style) forward and in other directions. Dribble around an imaginary point. Make various patterns while dribbling, such as a circle, square, triangle, or figure eight.

Dribbling on the Move

1. Dribble (basketball style) forward using one hand, and dribble back to place with the other. Change direction on a signal. Dribble in various directions, describing different pathways. Dribble around cones, milk cartons, or chairs.
2. Place a hoop on the floor. Dribble inside the hoop until a signal is sounded, then dribble to another hoop and continue the dribble inside that hoop. Avoid dribbling on the hoop itself.

Practicing Locomotor Movements While Holding the Ball

1. Holding the ball between the legs, perform various locomotor movements.
2. Try holding the ball in various positions with different body parts.

PARTNER ACTIVITIES

Rolling in Place

Roll the ball back and forth to a partner. Begin with two-handed rolls and proceed to one-handed rolls. When partner rolls the ball, pick it up with the toes and snap it up into the hands.

Throwing and Catching in Place

1. Toss the ball to a partner with one bounce, using various kinds of tosses. Practice various kinds of throws and passes to partner.
2. Throw to specific levels and points: high, low, right, left, at the knee, and so on. Try various throws: from under the leg, around the body, backward tosses, and centering as in football.
3. Throw and catch over a volleyball net.
4. Work in a threesome, with one person holding a hoop between the two partners playing catch. Throw the ball through the hoop, held at various levels. Try throwing through a moving hoop.

Batting in Place (Volleyball Skills)

1. Toss the ball upward to self and bat it two-handed to a partner, who catches and returns it in the same way. Serve as in volleyball to partner. Partner makes a return serve. Toss the ball to partner, who makes a volleyball return. Keep distances short and control the ball. Try to keep the ball going back and forth as in volleyball.
2. Bat the ball back and forth on one bounce. Bat it back and forth over a line, wand, jump rope, or bench.

Kicking in Place

1. Practice different ways of controlled kicking between partners and different ways of stopping the ball (trapping).
2. Practice a controlled punt, preceding the kick with a step on the nonkicking foot. Place the ball between the feet and propel it forward or backward to a partner.
3. Practice foot pickups. One partner rolls the ball, and the other hoists it to self with extended toes.

Throwing in Place from Various Positions

1. Practice different throws from a kneeling, sitting, or lying position. (Allow the children to be creative in selecting positions.)

2. Using two balls, pass back and forth, with balls going in opposite directions.

Follow Activities in Place

Throw or propel the ball in any manner desired. Partner returns the ball in the same way.

Throwing and Catching Against a Wall

Alternate throwing and catching against a wall. Alternate returning the ball after a bounce, as in handball.

Throwing on the Move

1. One child stays in place and tosses to the other child, who is moving. The moving child traces different patterns, such as back and forth between two spots or in a circle around the stationary child. (Spatial judgments must be good to anticipate where the moving child will be to receive the ball. Moderate distances are maintained between children.)
2. Practice different kinds of throws and passes as both children move in different patterns. (Considerable space is needed for this type of work.) Practice foot skills of dribbling and passing.
3. Partners hold the ball between their bodies without using the hands or arms. Experiment with different ways to move together.
4. Carrying a ball, run in different directions while partner follows. On signal, toss the ball upward so that the child following can catch it. Now change places and repeat the activity.

JUGGLING

Juggling is a novel and exciting task for elementary school children. Learning to juggle demands practice and repetition. An excellent medium for teaching beginners is sheer, lightweight scarves from 18 to 24 inches square. Scarves move slowly, allowing children to track them visually. Juggling with scarves teaches children correct patterns of object movement. However, this skill does not transfer easily to juggling with faster-moving objects such as fleece balls, tennis balls, rings, and hoops. Therefore, two distinct sections for juggling are offered: a section that deals with learning to juggle with scarves and a second section that explains juggling with balls.

Most of the class will succeed at juggling with scarves. Students who have mastered the scarves can move to balls and other objects. When acquiring this skill, students will experience many misses. Because children tire quickly if they are not having success, it may be desirable to play a game and then return to juggling practice.

JUGGLING WITH SCARVES

Scarves are held by the fingertips near the center. To throw the scarf, lift and pull it into the air above eye level. Scarves are caught by clawing, a downward motion of the hand, and grabbing the scarf from above as it is falling. Scarf juggling should teach proper habits (for example, tossing the scarves straight up in line with the body rather than forward or backward). Many instructors remind children to imagine they are in a phone booth or large refrigerator box—to emphasize tossing and catching without moving.

Cascading

Cascading is the easiest pattern for juggling three objects. The following sequence can be used to learn this basic technique.

1. *One scarf.* Hold the scarf in the center. Quickly move the arm across the chest and toss the scarf with the palm out. Reach out with the other hand and catch the scarf in a straight-down motion (clawing). Toss the scarf with this hand using the same motion, and claw it with the opposite hand. Continue, repeating the tossing and clawing sequence. The scarf moves in a figure-eight pattern as shown in Figure 17.9 on page 352.
2. *Two scarves—two hands.* Hold a scarf with the fingertips in each hand. Toss the first one across the body as described in step 1. When it reaches its peak, look at it, and toss the second scarf across the body in the opposite direction. The first scarf thrown is clawed by the hand throwing the second scarf, and vice versa (Figure 17.10 on page 352). Verbal cues such as "Toss, claw, toss, claw" are helpful.
3. *Two scarves—one hand.* Students must learn this sequence before trying to juggle three scarves. Start with both scarves in one hand (hold them as described below in three-scarf cascading). The important skill to learn is the sequence: tossing the first scarf, then the second scarf, and then catching the first and the

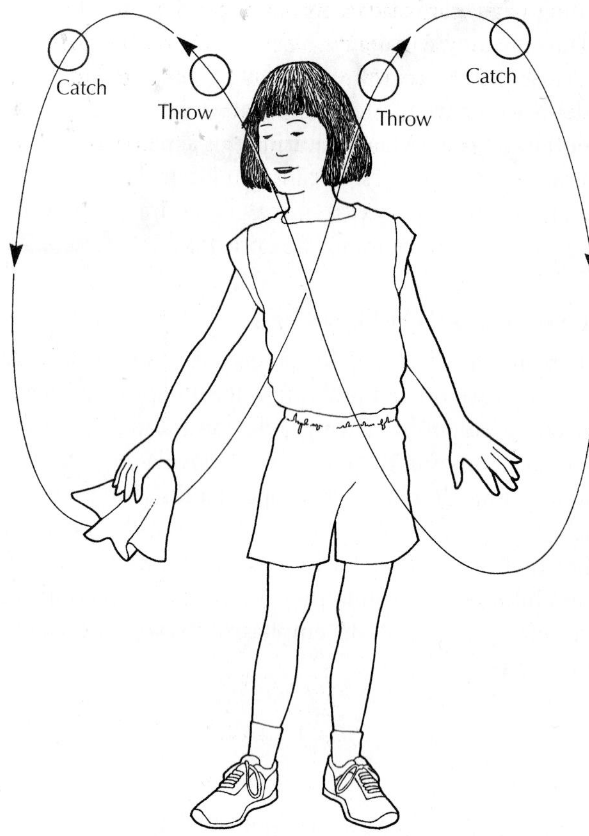

FIGURE 17.9 Clawing a scarf.

second. Verbal cues to use are "Toss, toss, catch, catch." If students cannot toss two scarves before catching one, they cannot master juggling with three scarves. Practice tossing skills with both hands.

FIGURE 17.10 Tossing and clawing with two scarves.

4. *Three-scarf cascading.* Hold a scarf in each hand by the fingertips, as described in step 2. Hold the third scarf with the ring and little fingers against the palm of one hand. Toss the first scarf from the hand that is holding two scarves. Toss this scarf from the fingertips across the chest as learned earlier. When scarf one reaches its peak, toss scarf two from the other hand and across the body. As this hand starts to come down, it catches scarf one. When scarf two reaches its peak, toss scarf three in the same path as that of scarf one. To complete the cycle, as the hand comes down from throwing scarf three, it catches scarf two. Repeat the cycle by tossing scarf one with the opposite hand. Figure 17.11 illustrates the figure-eight motion used in cascading. Tosses always alternate between left and right hands with a smooth, even rhythm.

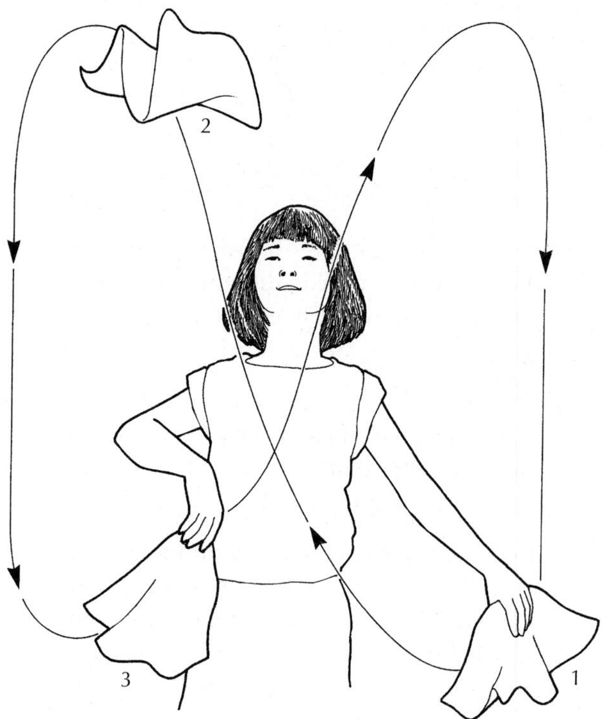

FIGURE 17.11 Three-scarf cascading.

Reverse Cascading

Reverse cascading involves tossing the scarves from waist level to the outside of the body and allowing the scarves to drop down the midline of the body (Figure 17.12).

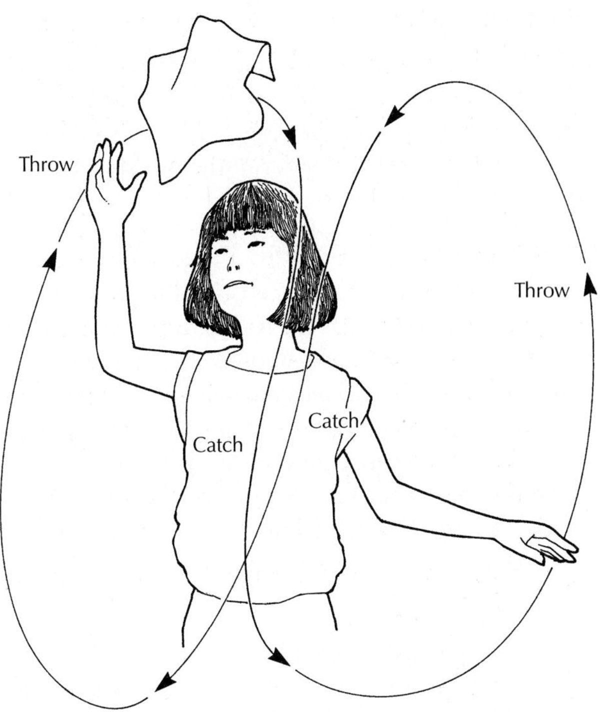

FIGURE 17.12 Reverse cascading.

1. *One scarf.* Begin by holding the scarf as described earlier. The throw goes away from the midline of the body over the top, releasing the scarf so that it falls down the center of the body. Catch it with the opposite hand and toss it in similar fashion on the opposite side of the body.
2. *Two scarves.* Begin with a scarf in each hand. Toss the first scarf as described in step 1. When it begins to fall, toss the second scarf. Catch the first scarf, then the second, and repeat the toss, toss, catch, catch pattern.
3. *Reverse cascading with three scarves.* Think of a large funnel at eye level directly in front of the juggler. The goal is to drop all scarves through this funnel so they drop straight down the center of the body. Begin with three scarves as described for three-scarf cascading. Toss the first scarf from the hand holding two scarves.

Column Juggling

Column juggling is so named because the scarves move straight up and down, as if they were inside a large pipe or column, and do not cross the body. To perform three-scarf column juggling, begin with two scarves in one hand and one in the other hand. From the hand that has two scarves, toss a scarf straight up the midline of the body and overhead. When this scarf reaches its peak, toss the other two scarves upward along the sides of the body (Figure 17.13). Catch the first scarf with either hand and toss it upward again. Catch the other two scarves and toss them upward, continuing the pattern.

FIGURE 17.13 Column juggling.

17

Showering

Showering is more difficult than cascading because the hands move rapidly and there is less time for catching and tossing. The scarves move in a circle following each other. For maximum challenge, students can practice in both directions

Start with two scarves in the right hand and one in the left. Begin by throwing the first two scarves from the right hand. Toss the scarves in a large circle away from the midline of the body and overhead as high as possible. As soon as the second scarf is released, toss the scarf across from the left hand to the right and then toss the scarf in the opposite hand and catch the first scarf with this hand also. Finish by tossing the last scarf (Figure 17.14 on page 354). All scarves are caught with the left hand and passed to the right hand.

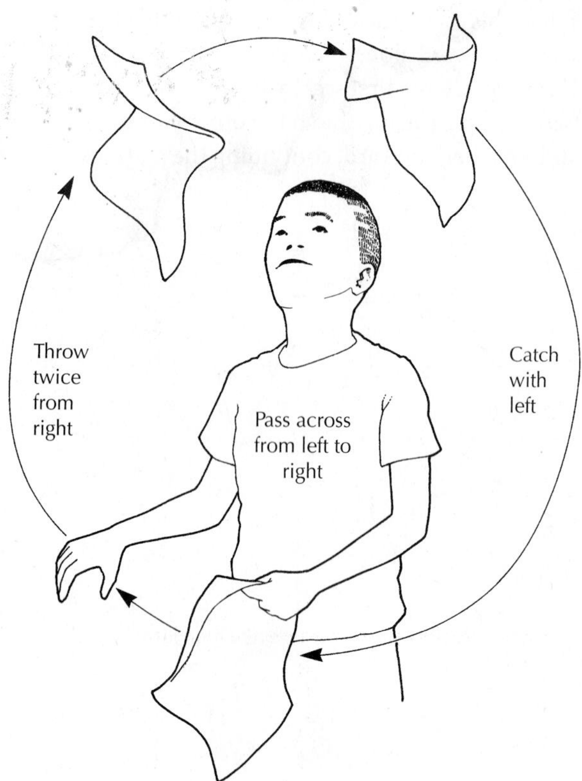

FIGURE 17.14 Showering with scarves.

Juggling Challenges

1. While cascading, toss a scarf under one leg.
2. While cascading, toss a scarf from behind the back.
3. Instead of catching one of the scarves, blow it upward with a strong breath of air.
4. Begin cascading by tossing the first scarf into the air with a foot. Lay the scarf across the foot and kick it into the air.
5. Try juggling three scarves with one hand. Do not worry about establishing a pattern, just catch the lowest scarf each time. Try both regular and reverse cascading as well as column juggling.
6. While doing column juggling, toss up one scarf, hold the other two, and make a full turn. Resume juggling.
7. Juggle three scarves while standing alongside a partner with inside arms around each other. (This is actually easy to do, because it is regular three-scarf cascading.)
8. Try juggling more than three scarves (up to six) with a partner.

JUGGLING WITH BALLS

Two balls can be juggled with one hand, and three balls can be juggled with two hands. Balls can be juggled using *cascading,* or they can be juggled using *showering.* Cascading, considered the easier of the two styles, should be the first one attempted.

Instructional Procedures

1. Juggling requires accurate, consistent tossing, which is the first emphasis. Toss the ball to the same height on both sides of the body—about 2 to 2.5 feet upward and across the body, since the ball is tossed from one hand to the other. Practice tossing the ball parallel to the body; the most common problem in juggling is that the balls are tossed forward and the juggler has to move forward to catch them.
2. Use the fingers, not the palms, when tossing and catching. Stress relaxed wrist action.
3. Instruct students to look upward and watch the balls at the peak of their flight, rather than watching the hands. Focus on where the ball peaks, not on the hands.
4. The balls are caught about waist height and released a little above this level.
5. Two balls must be carried in the starting hand, and the art of releasing only one must be mastered.
6. Students progress from working successively with first one ball, then two balls, and finally three balls (Figure 17.15).

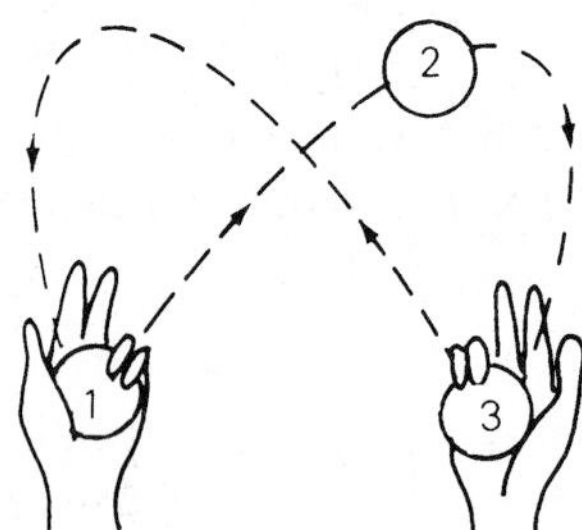

FIGURE 17.15 Cascading with three balls.

Recommended Progression for Cascading

1. Using one ball and one hand only, toss the ball upward (2 to 2.5 feet), and catch it with the same hand. Begin with the dominant hand, and later practice with the other. Toss quickly, with wrist action. Then handle the ball alternately with right and left hands, tossing from one hand to the other.
2. Now, with one ball in each hand, alternate tossing a ball upward and catching it in the same hand so that one ball is always in the air. Begin again with a ball in each hand. Toss across the body to the other hand. To

keep the balls from colliding, toss under the incoming ball. After acquiring some skill, try alternating the two kinds of tosses by doing a set number (four to six) of each before shifting to the other.

3. Hold two balls in the starting hand and one in the other. Toss one of the balls in the starting hand, toss the ball from the other hand, and then toss the third ball.

Recommended Progression for Showering

1. The showering motion is usually counterclockwise. Hold one ball in each hand. Begin by tossing with the right hand on an inward path and then immediately toss the other ball from the left directly across the body to the right hand. Continue this until the action is smooth.
2. Now, hold two balls in the right hand and one in the left. Toss the first ball from the right hand on an inward path and immediately toss the second on the same path. At about the same time, toss the ball from the left hand directly across the body to the right hand (Figure 17.16).

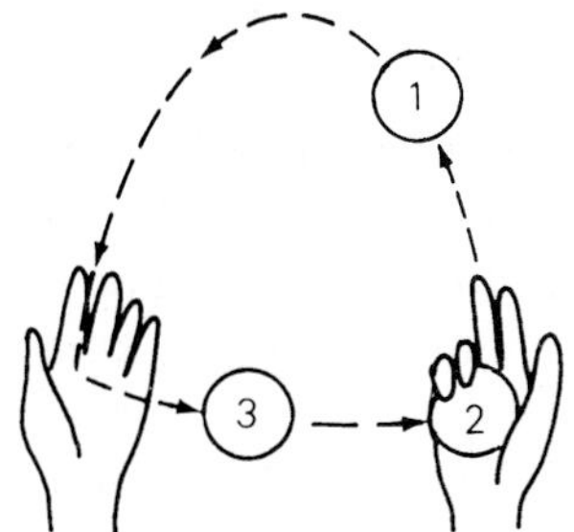

FIGURE 17.16 Showering with three balls.

3. A few children may be able to change from cascading to showering, and vice versa. This skill is quite a challenge.

ACTIVITIES WITH SCOOPS AND BALLS

Scoops can be purchased (Figure 17.17) or made with bleach bottles or similar containers (see Chapter 10). They are excellent for practicing catching and tossing skills using an implement rather than the hands. The following activities are recommended.

INDIVIDUAL ACTIVITIES

1. Put the ball on the floor and pick it up with the scoop. Toss the ball up and catch it with the scoop. Throw the ball against a wall and catch it in the scoop. Put the ball in the scoop, throw it in the air, and catch it. Throw the ball against a wall with the scoop, and catch it with the scoop.

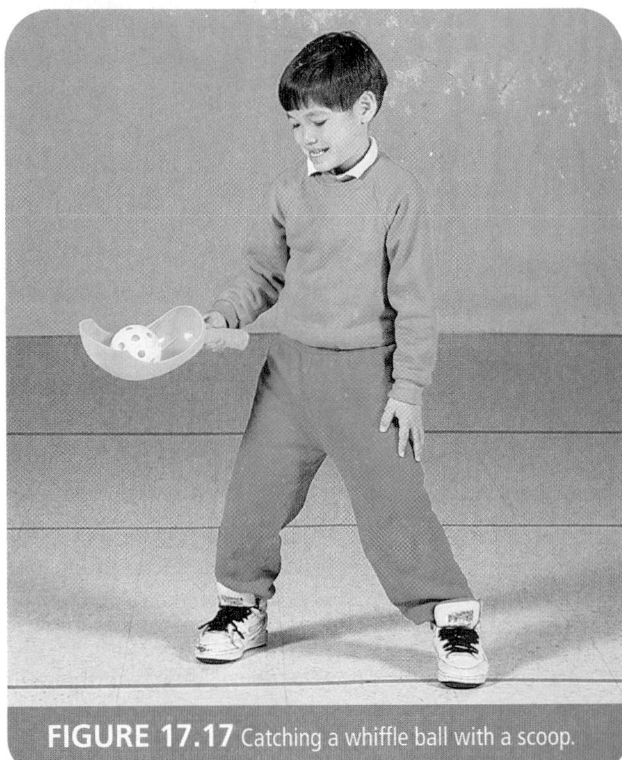

FIGURE 17.17 Catching a whiffle ball with a scoop.

2. Throw the ball, switch the scoop to the opposite hand, and catch in the scoop. Use the scoop to toss the ball up, do a stunt such as a heel click or a body turn, and catch the ball in the scoop.
3. Toss the ball up and catch it as low as possible. As high as possible. Toss it a little higher each time, and catch it in the scoop. Tell students to toss the ball so they have to stretch to catch it. (Most activities should begin with a toss from the free hand and later add a toss from the scoop.)

17

PARTNER ACTIVITIES

1. One partner rolls the ball on the floor, and the other catches it in the scoop. Partners throw the ball back and forth and catch it in the scoop. Challenge students to play One Step (page 560) while playing catch.
2. One partner tosses the ball from the scoop, and the other partner catches. Throw the ball from the scoop at different levels and catch it at different levels. Throw and catch from various positions, such as sitting, back-to-back, prone, and kneeling.
3. Work with more than one partner, with more than one ball, and with a scoop in each hand.

GAMES AND RELAYS

Many games and relays can be played using scoops. Modified lacrosse can be played using the scoops and a whiffle ball. Set up a lesson in which children devise games for themselves using the scoop and a ball.

BOWLING ACTIVITIES

Before bowling, younger children should practice informal rolling. As they mature, begin to emphasize bowling skills. Bowling skills begin with a two-handed roll and progress to one-handed rolls, alternating between the right and left hand. Various targets can be used—bowling pins, milk cartons, small cones, blocks, and even people.

The 8.5-inch foam or playground ball is excellent for teaching bowling skills. Volleyballs and soccer balls also can be used. Stress moderate speed in rolling the ball. The ball should roll off the fingertips with good follow-through.

The four-step approach is the accepted form for tenpin bowling, and it can be set in class work. Here is the technique, in brief, for a right-handed bowler.

Starting position: Stand with the feet together and the ball held comfortably in both hands in front of the body.
Step one: Step forward with the right foot, pushing the ball forward with both hands and a little to the right.
Step two: Step with the left foot, allowing the ball to swing down alongside the leg on its way into the backswing.
Step three: Step with the right foot. The ball reaches the height of the backswing with this step.
Step four: Step with the left foot and bowl the ball forward.

For instructional cues, the teacher can call out this four-step sequence: "Out," "Down," "Back," and "Roll."

Bowling activities are organized mostly as partner or group work. When using targets, have two children stand near the target end. One child resets the target, while the other recovers the ball. The following are partner activities unless otherwise noted. A fine game for rounding off the activities is Bowling One Step (page 560).

Recommended Activities

1. Use a wide-straddle stance, and begin with two-handed rolls from between the legs.
2. Roll the ball first with the right and then with the left hand. The receiver can use the foot pickup, done by hoisting the ball to the hands using the extended toes.
3. Practice putting different kinds of spin (English) on the ball. (For a right-handed bowler, a curve to the left is called a hook ball, and a curve to the right is a backup ball.)
4. Get into groups of three and use human straddle targets. Using a stick 2 feet long, make marks on the floor for the target child, who stands between the two bowlers. The target child stands with the inside edges of the shoes on the marks, thus standardizing the target spread. (Targets must keep their legs straight and motionless during the bowling. Otherwise, they can make or avoid contact with the ball and upset the scoring system.) Start from a moderate distance (15 to 20 feet), and adjust as proficiency increases. Scoring can be 2 points for a ball that goes through the legs without touching and 1 point for a ball that goes through but touches the leg.
5. Use milk cartons or bowling pins as targets. Begin with one and progress to two or three. (Plastic bowling pins are available. Other targets might be a wastebasket lying on its side—the ball is rolled into it—or a 3-pound coffee can for a smaller ball.)

ACTIVITIES WITH WANDS

Wands have been used in physical education programs for many years and now offer a wide variety of interesting and challenging activities. Wands can be made from 3/4-inch maple dowels or from broom and mop handles. If two lengths are chosen, make them 36 and 42 inches. If only one size is to be used, a length of 1 meter is recommended. Wands are more interesting when painted with imaginative designs—this can be a class project. Wands are noisy when they hit the floor. Gluing rubber crutch tips on the ends of a wand alleviates most of the noise and makes it easier to pick up.

INSTRUCTIONAL PROCEDURES

1. Because wands are noisy when dropped, have the children hold their wands with both hands or put them on the floor during instruction.
2. Many wand activities require great flexibility, which means that not all children are able to do them. Girls usually perform better than boys at flexibility stunts.
3. Give each child adequate space because wand stunts demand room.
4. To avoid injuries, do not allow children to misuse wands (or other potentially dangerous equipment).

Recommended Activities

Wands can be used for challenge activities that offer a relatively unstructured approach. Here are some of the many possible challenges.

1. Can you reach down and pick up your wand without bending your knees?
2. Try to balance your wand on different body parts. Watch the top of the wand for cues on keeping it balanced.
3. Can you hold your wand against the wall and move over and under it?
4. Let's see if you can hold the wand at both ends and move through the gap.
5. Can you spin the wand and keep it going like a windmill?
6. See how many different ways you can move over and around your wand when it is on the floor.
7. Put one end of the wand on the floor and hold the other end. How many times can you run around your wand without getting dizzy?
8. Place one end of the wand against a wall. Holding the other end and keeping the wand against the wall, duck under it. Place the wand lower and lower on the wall and go under.
9. Place the wand between your feet and hop around as though you are on a pogo stick.
10. Throw your wand into the air and catch it.
11. Hold the wand vertically near the middle. Can you release your grip and catch the wand before it falls to the floor?
12. Have a partner hold a wand horizontally above the floor. Jump, leap, and hop over the wand. Gradually raise the height of the wand.
13. Put your wand on the floor and try making different kinds of bridges over it.
14. Place the wand on the floor. Curl your body into a ball alongside it, just touching it. Curl your body at one end of the wand.
15. Balance the wand vertically on the floor. Release the wand and try some stunts—clap hands, do a heel click, touch different body parts—before the wand falls to the floor.
16. Put the wand on the floor and see how many ways you can push it, using different body parts.

INDIVIDUAL WAND STUNTS

Wand Catch

Stand a wand on one end and hold it in place with the fingers on the tip. Loop the foot quickly over the stick, letting go of the wand briefly but catching it with the fingers before it falls. Do this with the right and left hand for a complete set. Try to catch the wand with just the index finger.

Thread the Needle (V-Seat)

Maintaining a V-seat position, with the wand held in front of the body with both hands, bend the knees between the arms and pass the wand over them and return, without touching the wand to the legs. Try with the ankles crossed.

Thread the Needle (Standing)

Holding the wand in both hands, step through the space, one leg at a time, and return without touching the wand. Step through again, but this time bring the wand up behind the back, over the head, and down in front. Reverse. Try from side to side with the stick held front and back.

Grapevine

Holding the wand near the ends, step with the right foot around the right arm and over the wand inward, toward the body (Figure 17.18). Pass the

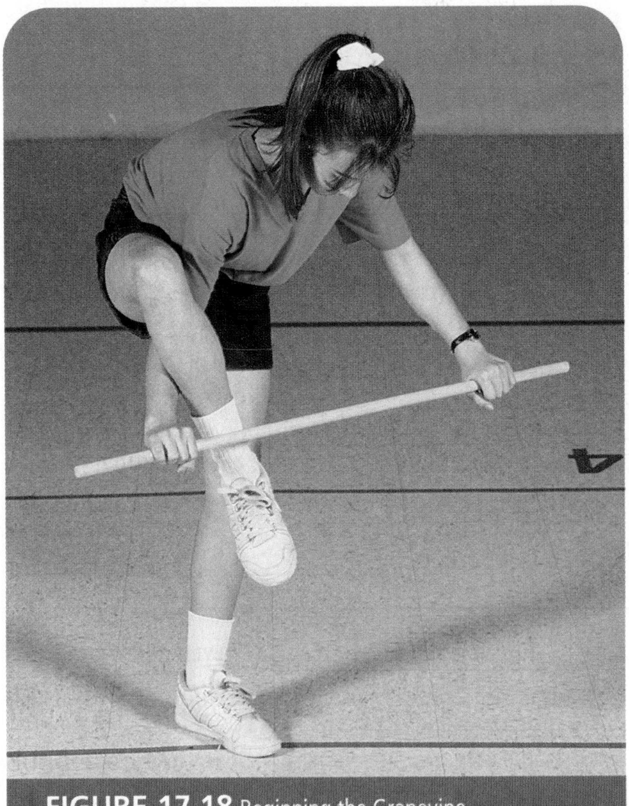

FIGURE 17.18 Beginning the Grapevine.

17

wand backward over the head and right shoulder (Figure 17.19), and continue sliding the wand down the body until you are standing erect with the wand between the legs. Reverse the process. Try with the left foot leading.

FIGURE 17.19 Grapevine, second stage (head ducks under, and wand is pressed down the back).

Back Scratcher

Hold the wand with an underhand grip (palms up), arms crossed in front of the body (Figure 17.20). Bend the elbows so the wand can go over and behind the head. Try to pass the wand down the length of the body from the back of the shoulders to the heels. Do not release the grip on the wand. The wand is worked down behind the back while the arms stay in front of the body.

Wand Whirl

Stand the wand upright in front of the body. Turn around quickly and grasp the wand before it falls. Do the movement both right and left. Try making two full turns and still catching the wand before it falls.

Twist Under

Grasp the upright wand with the right hand. Twist around under the right arm without letting go of the wand, taking it off the floor, or touching the knee to the floor. Repeat, using the left arm.

Jump Wand

Holding the wand in front of the feet with the fingertips of both hands, jump over it. Jumping back is not recommended, because the wand can hit the heels and cause an awkward fall. (If children are having difficulty, replace the wand with a rope or a towel.)

Balancing the Wand

Balance the wand vertically with one hand. Experiment with different hand and finger positions. Walk forward, backward, and sideward. Sit down, lie down, and move into other positions while keeping the wand balanced. Keep the eyes on the top of the wand. Balance the wand horizontally

FIGURE 17.20 Back Scratcher (wand has been passed overhead and is now being forced down the back).

on the hands, arms, feet, and thighs. Balance it across the back of the neck. In crab position, balance it across the tummy.

The Sprinter

Get into a sprinter's position, with the wand on the floor, between the feet, and perpendicular to the direction of the sprint. Change the feet rapidly, alternating over the wand. Try moving both feet together forward and backward over the wand.

Crab Leap

Place the wand on the floor. Get into crab position and attempt to move the feet back and forth over the wand without touching it. Try this with alternating feet.

Long Reach

Stand with legs extended and feet spread about 12 inches apart. Hold a wand in the left hand, and use it like a third limb. With a piece of chalk in the right hand, reach forward as far as possible and make a mark. Use the wand as a support and see if the mark can be bettered.

Wand Bridge

On a mat, start in a straddle stance with legs straight. Hold a wand near one end, with the other end above the head and pointed toward the ceiling. Bend backward, place the wand on the mat behind you, and walk the hands down the wand. Return to standing position.

Wand Twirl

Children in the class who have baton-twirling experience can show the class some points of technique.

PARTNER WAND STUNTS

Partner Catch

Partners face each other a short distance (5 feet) apart, each holding a wand in the right hand. On signal, each throws the wand to the partner with the right hand and catches the incoming wand with the left. Distances can be increased somewhat.

Partner Change

Partners face each other a short distance (5 feet) apart. Each has a wand standing upright, held on top by the right hand. On signal, each runs to the other's wand and tries to catch it before it falls. This can also be done in the same way as the Wand Whirl, with each whirling to the other's wand. Try with a small group of five or six. On signal, all move to the next wand.

Wring the Dishrag

Partners face each other and grasp a wand. When ready, they perform a dishrag turn.

Jump the Wand

One partner moves the wand back and forth along the floor, while the other partner jumps over it. To add challenge, partners can change the tempo and raise the wand.

Wand Reaction

One partner holds the wand horizontally. The other partner places one hand directly above the wand, palm down. When the first partner drops the wand, the second partner tries to catch it before it strikes the floor.

Cooperative Movements

Holding a wand between them, partners stand toe-to-toe and circle either way with light foot movements. Together, partners squat down and stand up. Sit down and come up. Kneel and hold the wand overhead as they face each other. Bend sideways and touch the wand to the floor.

ISOMETRIC EXERCISES WITH WANDS

The isometric exercises (muscle contractions without movement) with wands presented here are mainly grip exercises. Have children use a variety of grips. With the wand horizontal, use either the overhand or underhand grip. With the wand vertical, grip with the thumbs pointed up, down, or toward each other. Repeat each exercise with a different grip. Exercises can also be repeated with the wand in different positions: in front of the body (either horizontal or vertical), overhead, or behind the back. Hold each exercise for 8 to 12 seconds.

Pull the Wand Apart

Place the hands 6 inches apart near the center of the wand. With a tight grip to prevent slippage and with arms extended, try to pull the hands apart. Change grip and position.

Push the Wand Together

Hold the wand as previously, except attempt to push the hands together.

Wand Twist

Hold the wand with both hands about 6 inches apart. Twist the hands in opposite directions.

Bicycle

Holding the wand horizontally using an overhand grip, extend the wand out and down. Bring it upward near the body, completing a circular movement. On the downward movement, push the wand together; and on the upward movement, pull the wand apart.

Arm Spreader

Hold the wand overhead with hands spread wide. Attempt to compress the stick. Reverse force, and attempt to pull the stick apart.

Dead Lift

Partially squat and place the wand under the thighs. Place the hands between the legs and try to lift. Try also with hands on the outside of the legs.

Abdominal Tightener

From a standing position, place the wand behind the buttocks. With hands on the ends of the wand, pull forward and resist with the abdominal muscles.

STRETCHING EXERCISES WITH WANDS

Wands are useful for stretching, bending, and twisting movements.

Side Bender

Grip the wand and extend the arms overhead with feet apart. Bend sideways as far as possible, maintaining straight arms and legs. Recover, and bend to the other side.

Body Twist

Place the wand behind the neck, with arms draped over the wand from behind. Rotate the upper body first to the right as far as possible and then to the left. The feet and hips stay in position. The twist is at the waist.

Body Twist to Knee

Assume body twist position. Bend the trunk forward and twist so that the right end of the wand touches the left knee (Figure 17.21). Recover, and touch the left end to the right knee.

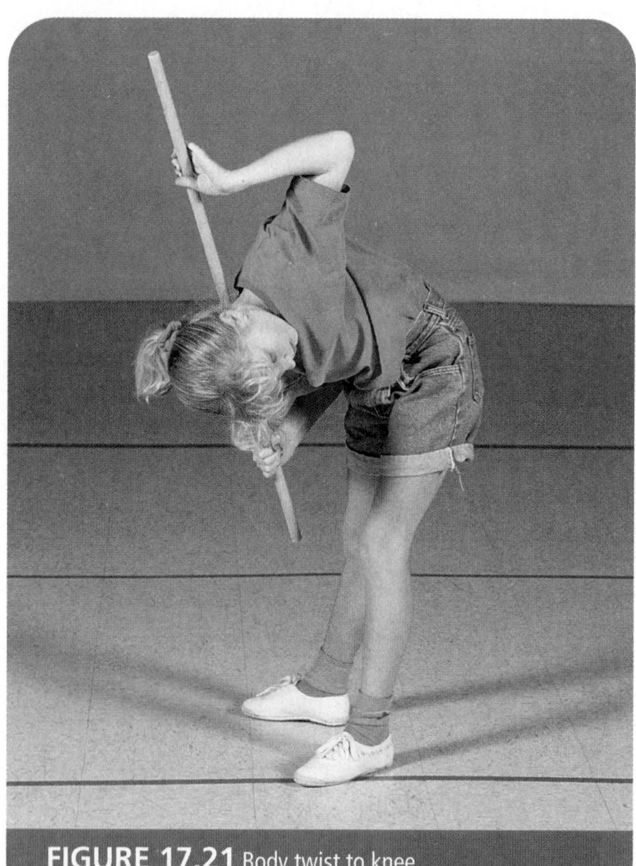

FIGURE 17.21 Body twist to knee.

Shoulder Stretcher

Grip the wand at the ends in a regular grip. Extend the arms overhead and rotate the wand, arms, and shoulders backward until the stick touches the back of the legs. Keep the arms straight. Those who find the stretch too easy can move their hands closer to the center of the wand.

Toe Touch

Grip the wand with the hands about shoulder width apart. Bend forward, reaching down as far as possible without bending the knees. The movement is slow and controlled. Try the same activity while sitting.

Over the Toes

Sit down, flex the knees, pass the wand over the toes, and rest it against the middle of the arch on the bottoms of the feet. Grip the stick with the fingers at the outside edge of the feet. Slowly extend the legs forward, pushing against the stick and trying to fully extend the legs.

ACTIVITIES WITH HOOPS

Most hoops made in the United States are plastic, but Europeans sometimes use wooden ones. Plastic hoops are less durable but more versatile. Extra hoops are needed because some breakage will occur. The standard hoop is 42 inches in diameter, but smaller hoops (36 inches) are best for primary-grade children.

INSTRUCTIONAL PROCEDURES

1. Hoop activities are quite noisy. Have the children lay their hoops on the floor when they are to listen.
2. Hoops can be a creative medium for children. Give them free time to explore their own ideas.
3. Give the children enough space in which to perform, for hoops require much movement.
4. In activities that require children to jump through hoops, instruct the holder to grasp the hoop lightly, so as not to cause an awkward fall if a performer hits it.
5. Hoops can serve as a "home" for various activities. For instance, the children might leave their hoops to gallop in all directions and then return quickly to the hoop on command.
6. Hoops are good targets. To make a hoop stand up, place an individual mat over its base.
7. When teaching the reverse spin with hoops, have the students throw the hoop up, in place, rather than forward along the floor. After learning the upward throw, they can progress to the forward throw for distance.

Recommended Activities

Hoops as Floor Targets

Each child has a hoop, which is placed on the floor. Various movement challenges can give direction to the activity.

1. Show the different patterns you can make by jumping or hopping in and out of the hoop.
2. Do a Bunny Jump and a Frog Jump into the center and out the other side.
3. Show the ways you can cross from one side of the hoop to the other by taking the weight on your hands inside the hoop.
4. What kinds of animal walks can you do around your hoop?
5. On all fours, show the kinds of movements you can do with your feet inside the hoop and your hands outside. With your hands inside the hoop and your feet outside. With one foot and one hand inside, and one foot and one hand outside.
6. (Set a time limit of 15 to 30 seconds.) See how many times you can jump in and out of your hoop during this time. Now try hopping.
7. Balance on and walk around the hoop. Try to keep your feet from touching the floor.
8. Curl your body inside the hoop. Bridge over your hoop. Stretch across your hoop. See how many different ways you can move around the hoop.
9. Pick up your hoop and see how many different machines you can invent. Let your hoop be the steering wheel of a car. What could it be on a train or a boat?
10. Jump in and out of the hoop, using the alphabet. Jump in on the vowels and out on the consonants. Use odd and even numbers in the same way. Vary the locomotor movements.
11. Get into the hoop by using two different body parts. Move out by using three parts. Vary the number of body parts used.
12. Get organized in squads or comparable groups, and divide the hoops. Arrange the hoops in various formations, and try different locomotor movements, animal walks, and other ways of maneuvering through the maze. (When the children are more experienced, this can become a follow-the-leader activity.)

Hoop Handling

1. Spin the hoop like a top. See how long you can make it spin. Spin it again, and see how many times you can run around it before it falls to the floor.
2. Hula-hoop using various body parts such as the waist, legs, arms, and fingers. While hula-hooping on the arms, try to change the hoop from one arm to the other. Lie on the back with one or both legs pointed toward the ceiling, and explore different ways the legs can twirl the hula hoop. Hula-hoop with two or more hoops.
3. Jump or hop through a hoop held by a partner. For a greater challenge, vary the height and angle of the hoop.
4. Roll the hoop and run alongside it. On signal, change direction.
5. Hula-hoop on one arm. Throw the hoop in the air and catch it on the other arm.
6. Hold the hoop and swing it like a pendulum. Jump and hop in and out of the hoop.
7. Use the hoop like a jump rope. Jump forward, backward, and sideward. Do a crossover with the hands.
8. Roll the hoop with a reverse spin to make it return to you. The key to the reverse spin is to pull down (toward the floor) on the hoop as it is released. Roll the hoop with a reverse spin, jump over it, and catch it as it returns. Roll the hoop with a reverse spin; as it returns, hoist it with the foot and catch it. Roll the hoop with a reverse spin, kick it up with the toe, and go through the hoop. Roll the hoop with a reverse spin, run around it, and catch it. Roll the hoop with a reverse spin, pick it up, and begin hooping on the arm—all in one motion.
9. Play catch with a partner. Try with two or more hoops.
10. Hula-hoop. Attempt to change hoops with a partner.
11. Have one partner roll the hoop with a reverse spin and the other attempt to crawl through the hoop. (This is done most easily just after the hoop reverses direction and begins to return to the spinner. Some children can go in and out of the hoop twice.)
12. Tell partners to spin the hoops like tops and see who can keep theirs spinning longer.

GAMES WITH HOOPS

Cooperative Musical Hoops

Hoops, one per student, are placed on the floor. Give players a locomotor movement to do. On signal, they cease the movement, find a hoop, and sit cross-legged in the center of it. Music can be used, with the children moving to the music and seeking a hoop when the music stops. The teacher can remove some hoops, challenging students to share hoops with each other. This can continue until all students are in three or four hoops.

Around the Hoop

Divide the class into groups of three, with children in each group numbered 1, 2, and 3. Each threesome sits back-to-back inside a hoop. Their heels may need to be outside the hoop. The leader calls out a direction (right or left) and names one of the numbers. The child with that number immediately gets up, runs in the indicated direction around the hoop, then runs back to place and sits down. The winner is the first group sitting in good position after the child returns to place.

Hula-Hoop Circle

Four to six children hold hands in a circle, facing in, with a hoop dangling on one pair of joined hands. They move the hoop around the circle and back to the starting point. This requires all bodies to go through the hoop. Hands can help the hoop move, but grips cannot be released.

Hula-Hoop Relay

Relay teams of four to six players, each with a hoop, are placed in line or circle formation. The hoop must be held upright with the bottom of the hoop touching the floor. On signal, designated starters drop their hoops and move through the hoops held by squad members. Repeat the sequence until every player has moved through the hoops.

Bumper Car Tag

Divide the class into pairs. Each pair stands inside a hoop held at waist level—the "bumper car." Three or more sets of partners are declared to be "it." The

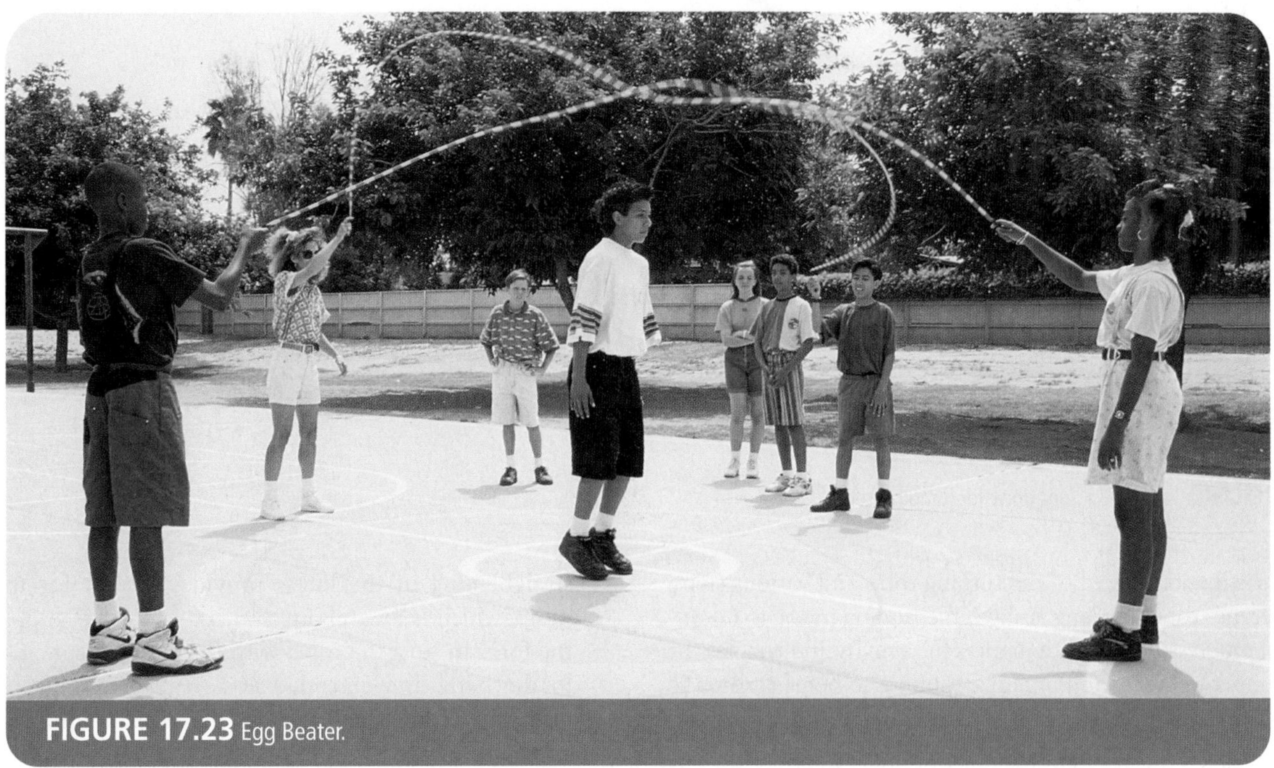

FIGURE 17.23 Egg Beater.

closed position. Straddle jumps are performed facing away from the turners.

4. *Scissors Jump.* Jump to a stride position with the left foot forward and the right foot back, about 8 inches apart. Each jump requires reversing the position of the feet.
5. *Jogging Step.* Run in place with a jogging step. Increase the challenge by circling while jogging.
6. *Hot Peppers.* Use the Jogging Step and gradually increase the speed of the ropes.
7. *Half-Turn.* Perform a half-turn with each jump. Remember to lead the turn with the head and shoulders.
8. *Ball Tossing.* Toss and catch a beanbag or playground ball while jumping.
9. *Individual Rope Jumping.* Enter Double Dutch with an individual rope and jump. Face the turner and decrease the length of the individual jump rope.
10. These activities are interesting variations for reviving motivation:
    a. *Double Irish.* Two ropes are turned in the reverse directions used in Double Dutch. The left hand turns counterclockwise and the right hand clockwise. Entry is made when the near rope hits the floor. Jumpers time their entry by following the near rope on its downward swing.
    b. *Egg Beater.* Two long ropes are turned at right angles simultaneously by four turners (Figure 17.23). Entry is at the quadrant where both ropes are turning front doors. The number of ropes being turned can be increased to three or four. This activity is easier than jumping Double Dutch since the jumping action is similar to single-rope jumping. It is an excellent activity for building confidence in jumping more than one long rope.

FORMATION JUMPING

For formation jumping, four to six long ropes with turners can be placed in various patterns, with tasks specified for each rope. Ropes can be turned in the same direction, or the turning directions can be mixed. Several formations are illustrated in Figure 17.24 on page 370.

INDIVIDUAL ROPE JUMPING

Individual rope jumping should stress establishing basic turning skills and letting children create personal routines. Individual rope jumping is particularly valuable as part of the conditioning process for certain sports. It lends itself to prescribed doses based on number of turns, length of

17

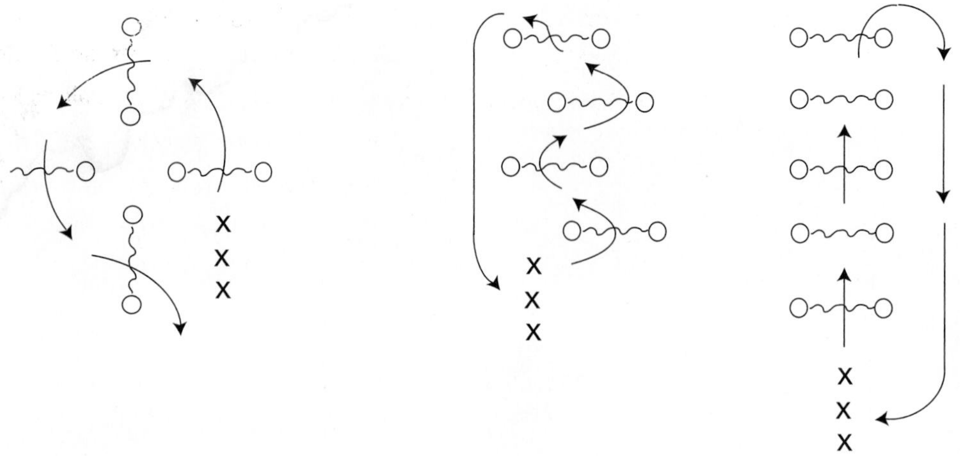

FIGURE 17.24 Formations for jumping rope.

participation, speed of the turning rope, and various steps. Because rope jumping is rhythmic, adding music is a natural progression. Music enhances the activity and enables the jumper to create and organize routines to be performed to the musical pieces. The most effective approach is probably a combination of experiences with and without music.

Several types of jump ropes are on the market. All of them are satisfactory, depending on the instructor's likes and dislikes. The most popular appear to be the solid plastic speed (often called licorice) ropes and the beaded or segmented ropes. The speed rope is excellent for rapid turning and doing tricks. It does not maintain momentum as well as the segmented ropes do, which can be important for beginners. Beaded ropes are heavier and seem easier to turn for beginning jumpers, but these ropes hurt when they hit another student. Also, if the segments are round, the rope rolls easily on the floor and children may fall when they step on it. An ideal situation would be to have a set of each type of rope. Sash cord is economical, but it has no handles and does not wear well on blacktop or cement.

INSTRUCTIONAL PROCEDURES

1. The rope length depends on the jumper's height. It should be long enough so that the ends reach to the armpits (Figure 17.25) or slightly higher when the child stands on its center. Preschool children generally use 6-foot ropes, and the primary-level group needs mostly 7-foot ropes, with a few 6- and 8-foot lengths. Grades 3 through 6 need a mixture of 7-, 8-, and 9-foot ropes. A 9- or 10-foot rope serves well for tall students and most instructors. Ropes or handles should be color-coded for length.
2. Posture is an important consideration in rope jumping. The body should be in good alignment, with the head up and the eyes looking straight ahead. The jump is made with the body held erect. A slight straightening of the knees provides the lift for the jump, which is low (about 1 inch). The wrists supply the force to turn the rope, with the elbows kept close to the body and extended at a 90-degree angle. A pumping action and lifting of the arms is unnecessary. Jumpers land on the balls of the feet, with the knees bent slightly to cushion the shock. Usually, the feet, ankles, and legs are kept together, except when a specific step calls for a different position.
3. The rope is held by the index finger and thumb on each side, and the hands make a small circle. The elbows are

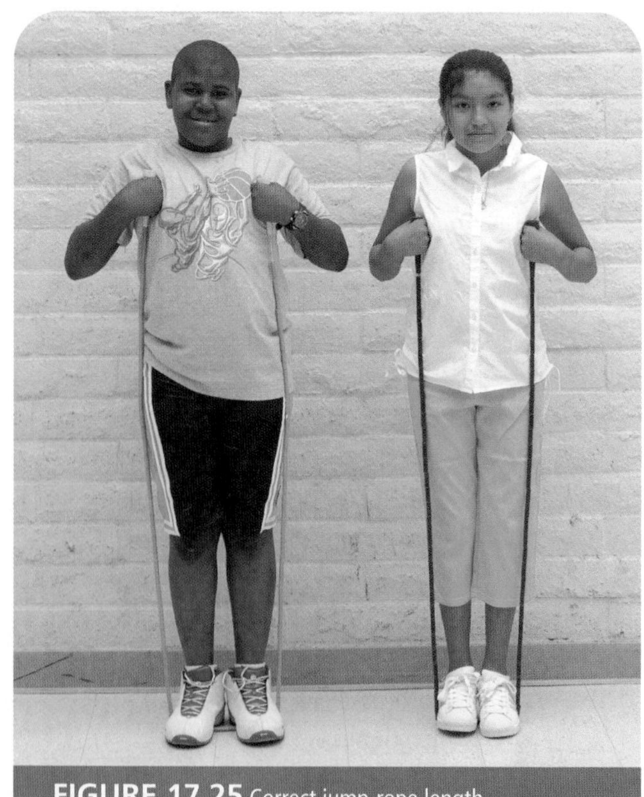

FIGURE 17.25 Correct jump-rope length.

held near the sides to avoid making large arm circles with the rope.

4. Introducing and teaching students individual rope-jumping skills can be accomplished by following these steps:
   a. Students first jump without the rope until they learn the correct rhythm and footwork. For slow time, this is a jump and then a rebound step. Children can pretend they are turning the rope. Remember that rope jumping involves learning two separate skills: jumping a rope and turning a rope. Students who have difficulty need to practice the parts separately before trying them together.
   b. Students turn the rope overhead and catch it with the toes.
   c. The jumper holds the rope stationary in front of the body. Jump forward and backward over the rope. To increase the challenge, swing the rope slightly. Gradually increase the swing until a full turn of the rope is made.
   d. Hold the rope to one side with one or both hands, swing the rope forward, and jump each time the rope hits the floor. If swinging the rope is a problem, practice without jumping first.
5. When jumpers have learned the first stages of jumping, add music to motivate them to continue jumping.
6. In the primary-level group, some children cannot jump. By the third grade, nearly all children who have some experience can jump. Children who cannot jump may be helped by the pendulum swing of the long rope, or by another student jumping with them inside an individual rope. Give cues such as "Jump" or "Ready–jump."
7. Most steps can be done with either rhythm: slow time or fast time. In slow-time rhythm, the child jumps over the rope, rebounds, and then does the second step (or repeats the original step) on the second jump. The rebound is simply a hop in place as the rope passes overhead. Better jumpers bend the knees only slightly, without actually leaving the floor on rebound. The rebound carries the rhythm between steps. The rope rotates slowly, passing underfoot on every other beat. The feet also move slowly, since there is rebound between each jump.

   In fast-time rhythm, the rope rotates in time with the music, one turn per beat (120 to 180 turns per minute, depending on the tune's tempo), and the student does a step only when the rope is passing underfoot.
8. Instructional cues for improving jumping technique:
   a. Keep the arms at the sides of the body while turning. (Many children lift the arms to shoulder level, trying to move the rope overhead. This makes it impossible for the child to jump over the elevated rope.)
   b. Turn the rope by making small circles with the wrists.
   c. Jump on the balls of the feet.
   d. Bend the knees slightly to absorb the force of the jump.
   e. Make a small jump over the rope.
9. To collect ropes after a rope-jumping activity, have two or three children act as monitors. They put both arms out to the front or to the side at shoulder level. The other children then drape the ropes over their arms (Figure 17.26). The monitors return the ropes to the correct storage area.

FIGURE 17.26 Collecting the ropes.

BASIC STEPS

The basic steps presented here can be done in slow or fast time. After children have mastered the first six steps in slow time, teachers can introduce fast time. The Alternate-Foot Basic Step and Spread Legs Forward and Backward are two steps that work well for introducing fast-time jumping.

Side Swing

Swing the rope, held with both hands to one side of the body. Switch and swing the rope on the other side of the body.

Double Side Swing and Jump

Swing the rope once on each side of the body. Follow the second swing with a jump over the rope. The sequence should be swing, swing, jump.

Two-Foot Basic Step

Jump over the rope with feet together as it passes underfoot, then take a preparatory rebound while the rope is overhead.

Alternate-Foot Basic Step

As the rope passes underfoot, shift the weight alternately from one foot to the other, raising the free foot in a running position.

Bird Jumps

Jump with the toes pointed in (pigeon walk) and with the toes pointed out (duck walk). Alternate toes in and toes out.

Swing-Step Forward

This step is the same as the Alternate-Foot Basic Step, except that the free leg swings forward. The knee is kept loose, and the foot swings naturally.

Swing-Step Sideways

This step is the same as the Swing-Step Forward, but the free leg swings to the side. The knee is kept stiff. The sideways swing is about 12 inches.

Rocker Step

In this step, one leg is always forward in a walking-stride position. As the rope passes underfoot, the weight shifts from the back foot to the forward foot. The rebound is on the forward foot while the rope is overhead. On the next turn of the rope, the weight shifts from the forward foot to the back foot, repeating the rebound on the back foot.

Spread Legs Forward and Backward

Start in a stride position (as in the Rocker) with weight equally distributed on both feet. As the rope passes underfoot, jump into the air and reverse the position of the feet.

Straddle Jump

Alternate a regular jump with a straddle jump. The straddle jump is performed with the feet shoulder width apart.

Cross Legs Sideways

As the rope passes underfoot, spread the legs in a straddle position (sideways) to take the rebound. As the rope passes underfoot on the next turn, jump into the air and cross the feet with the right foot forward. Then repeat with the left foot forward and continue alternating feet.

Toe-Touch Forward

Swing the right foot forward as the rope passes underfoot and touch the right toes on the next count. Then alternate, landing on the right foot and touching the left toes forward.

Toe-Touch Backward

This step is similar to the Swing-Step Sideways, except that the toes of the free foot touch to the back at the end of the swing.

Shuffle Step

Push off with the right foot and sidestep to the left as the rope passes underfoot. Land with the weight on the left foot and touch the right toes beside the left heel. Repeat the step in the opposite direction.

Skier

This is a double-foot jump similar to a technique used by skiers. The jumper stands on both feet to one side of a chalked or painted line. Jumping is done sideways from side to side over the line. Have children try jumping forward and backward also.

Heel-Toe

As the rope passes underfoot, jump with the weight landing on the right foot while touching the left heel forward. On the next turn of the rope, jump, land on the same foot, and touch the left toes beside the right heel. This pattern is then repeated with the opposite foot bearing the weight.

Leg Fling

On the first jump, bring the right leg up so that it is parallel to the floor with the knee bent. On the second jump, kick the same leg out and up as high as possible. Try with the other leg.

Heel Click

Do two or three Swing-Steps Sideways, in slow time, in preparation for the Heel Click. When the right foot swings sideways, instead of a hop or rebound when the rope is above the head, raise the left foot to click the heel of the right foot. Repeat on the left side.

Step-Tap

As the rope passes underfoot, push off with the right foot and land on the left. While the rope is turning overhead, brush the sole of the right foot forward and then backward. As the rope passes underfoot for the second turn, push off with the left foot, land on the right, and repeat.

Skipping

Do a step-hop (skip) over the rope. Start slowly, and gradually increase the rope speed.

Schottische Step

This step can be done to double-time rhythm, or it can be done with a varied rhythm. The pattern is step, step, step, hop (repeat), followed by four step-hops. In varied rhythm, three quick turns in fast time are made for the first three steps and then double-time rhythm prevails. Students practice the step first in place and then in general space. Schottische music is introduced.

Bleking Step

Turn the rope in the pattern slow-slow, fast-fast-fast. The Bleking Step begins with a hop on the left foot with the right heel forward, followed by a hop on the right with the left heel forward. Repeat this action with three quick changes: right, left, right. Start the sequence again, this time hopping on the right foot with the left heel extended. If music for the Bleking dance (page 419) is used, students do four Bleking steps. The second part of the music (the chorus) allows the children to create their own routine. They must listen for changes in the music.

CROSSING ARMS

After mastering the basic steps, children can try this interesting variation. Crossing the arms while turning the rope forward is easier than crossing them while turning backward. Crossing and uncrossing can be done at predetermined points after a specific number of turns. Crossing can be used during any of the routines.

DOUBLE TURNING

The double turn of the rope is also interesting. The jumper does a few basic steps in preparing for the double turn. As the rope approaches the feet, give an extremely hard flip of the rope from the wrists, jump from 6 to 8 inches in height, and let the rope pass underfoot twice before landing. The jumper must bend forward at the waist somewhat, which increases the speed of the turn. Challenge advanced rope jumpers to see how many consecutive double-turn jumps they can do.

SHIFTING FROM FORWARD TO BACKWARD JUMPING

To switch from forward to backward jumping without stopping, use any of these techniques.

1. As the rope starts downward in forward jumping, rather than allowing it to pass underfoot, the performer swings both arms to the left (or right) and makes a half-turn of the body in that direction (i.e., facing the rope). On the next downward swing, the jumper spreads the arms and starts turning in the opposite direction. This method also works for shifting from backward to forward jumping.
2. When the rope is directly overhead, the jumper extends both arms, causing the rope to hesitate momentarily, at the same time making a half-turn in either direction and continuing to skip with the rope turning in the opposite direction.
3. From a crossed-arm position, as the rope is going overhead, the jumper may uncross the arms and turn simultaneously. This starts the rope turning and the jumper going in the opposite direction.

SIDEWAYS SKIPPING

In sideways skipping, the rope is turned laterally with one hand held high and the other extended downward. The rope is swung around the body sideways. To accomplish this, the jumper starts with the right hand held high overhead and the left hand extended down the center of the body. Swing the rope to the left, at the same time raising the left leg sideways. Usually the speed is slow time, taking the rebound on each leg in turn. Later, better jumpers may progress to fast-time speed. The rope passes under the left leg, and the jumper then is straddling the rope as it moves around his body behind him. Take the weight on the left foot, raising the right foot sideways. A rebound step on the left as the rope moves to the front brings the jumper back to the original position.

COMBINATION POSSIBILITIES

Many combinations of steps and rope tricks are possible in rope jumping. Here are some ideas.

1. Make changes in the speed of the turn—between slow time and fast time. Children should be able to shift from one speed to another, particularly when the music changes.
2. Developing expertise in various foot patterns and steps is important. Have children practice changing from one foot pattern to another.
3. Try the crossed-hands position both forward and backward. Many of the basic steps can be combined with crossed-hands position to add challenge.
4. Practice moving from a forward to a backward turn and returning. Perform the turn while doing a variety of basic steps.
5. Double turns combined with basic steps look impressive and are challenging. A few children may be able to do a triple turn.
6. Have children try to move forward, backward, and sideways, employing various basic steps.
7. Backward jumping is exciting, as it is a different skill than forward jumping. Most basic steps can be done backward or modified for the backward turn.
8. Practice doing speedy turns (Hot Peppers). Have children see how fast they can turn the rope for 15 or 30 seconds.

INDIVIDUAL ROPE JUMPING WITH PARTNERS

Many interesting combinations are possible when one child turns the individual rope and one or more children jump it. For routines that call for a child to run into a jumping pattern, it may be more effective to begin with the child already in position, before proceeding to the run-in stage.

1. The first child turns the rope and the other stands in front, ready to enter.
   a. Run in and face partner, and both jump (Figure 17.27).
   b. Run in and turn back to partner, and both jump.
   c. Decide which steps are to be done; then run in and match steps.

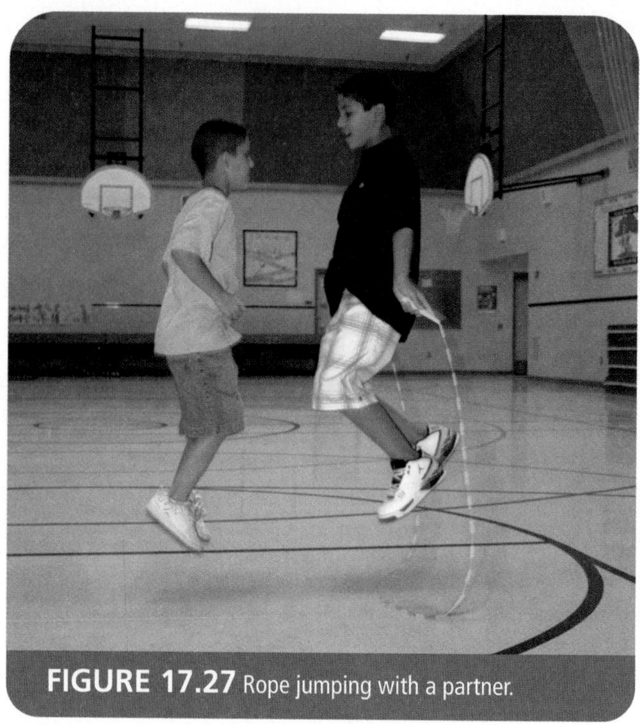

FIGURE 17.27 Rope jumping with a partner.

   d. Repeat with the rope turning backward.
   e. Run in with a ball and bounce it during the jumping.
2. Partners stand side by side, clasp inside hands, and turn the rope with outside hands.
   a. Face the same direction and turn the rope.
   b. Face opposite directions, clasp left hands, and turn the rope.
   c. Face opposite directions, clasp right hands, and turn the rope.
   d. Repeat routines with inside knees raised.
   e. Repeat routines with elbows locked. Try other arm positions.
3. The first child turns the rope while the second is to the rear, ready to run in. The second child runs in and grasps the first child's waist or shoulders, and they jump together (engine and caboose).
4. The children stand back-to-back, holding a single rope in the right hand.
   a. Turn in one direction—forward for one and backward for the other.
   b. Reverse direction.
   c. Change to left hands, and repeat.
5. Three children jump. One turns the rope forward; one runs in, in front; and one runs in behind. All three jump. Try with the rope turning backward.

6. Two jumpers, each with a rope, face each other and turn both ropes together, forward for one and backward for the other, jumping over both ropes at once. Turn the ropes alternately, jumping each rope in turn.
7. One partner jumps in a usual individual rope pattern. The other jumps to the side. The turning partner hands over one end of the rope, and the other maintains the turning rhythm and then hands the rope back.
   a. Try from the other side.
   b. Turn the rope backward.
8. Using a single rope held in the right hand, partners face each other and turn the rope in slow time. With the rope overhead, one partner makes a turn to the left (turning in) and jumps inside the rope, exiting by turning either way. See if both can turn inside.

MOVEMENT SEQUENCES TO MUSIC

Opportunities for creative movement sequences performed to music are unlimited. Music must have a definite beat and a bouncy quality. Pieces with a two-part format (verse and chorus) are excellent. The change from the verse to the chorus signals changes in rope-jumping pattern. Many of the recordings listed in Chapter 19 are suitable for rope jumping to music. Schottisches, marches, and polkas provide good background. Popular rock music motivates children if it has a strong, even rhythm. Special selections for rope jumping also are available from commercial sources. Suggested recordings include

"The Muffin Man" (page 412)

"Looby Loo" (page 412)

"Bleking" (page 419)

"Pop Goes the Weasel" (page 424)

Schottische (page 448)

Polka (page 444)

Devising Sequences to Music

Devising jumping sequences allows children to create their own routines to selected music. Simple changes from slow time to fast time can introduce this activity. Later, students can try different steps, add crossing and uncrossing of arms, and vary the turning direction. Partner rope-jumping stunts can also be adapted to music. Suggestions for incorporating different steps in the sequences follow.

1. "Pop Goes the Weasel" has a definite verse and chorus change. Children can switch from slow-time jumping to fast-time jumping on the chorus.
2. Bleking music offers an interesting change in rope speed. The rhythm is slow-slow, fast-fast-fast (four times). The rope is turned with each beat. Later, the Bleking step can be added.
3. Using schottische music, children can do the schottische step in place twice and four moving step-hops in different directions during the chorus.
4. To "Little Brown Jug," students can do a four-part routine to four rounds of the music.

   First verse: Two-Foot Basic Step (slow time)

   Chorus: Two-Foot Basic Step (fast time)

   Second verse: Alternate-Foot Basic Step (slow time)

   Chorus: Alternate-Foot Basic Step (fast time)

   Third verse: Swing-Step Forward (slow time)

   Chorus: Swing-Step Forward (fast time)

   Fourth verse: Swing-Step Sideways (slow time)

   Chorus: Swing-Step Sideways (fast time)

ASSESSMENT OF INDIVIDUAL ROPE JUMPING

Individual rope-jumping stunts, because of their specificity and individuality, can be adapted easily to learning packages and contract teaching. Skill assessment can be based on completing a stated maneuver in so many turns of the rope. The assessment can be organized progressively or grouped by beginning, intermediate, and advanced tests. An example of a beginning test follows. All test items are done first in slow time and then in fast time.

1. *Two-Foot Basic Step:* 10 turns
2. *Alternate-Foot Basic Step:* 10 turns
3. *Turning Rope Backward:* 10 turns
4. *Alternate Crossing Arms:* 10 turns
5. *Running Forward:* 20 turns

Intermediate and advanced tests can be organized similarly.

17

FOOTBAG ACTIVITIES

A footbag is a specifically designed object used for footbag skills and games. Although the construction varies, most footbags are leather spheres about 2 inches in diameter and weighing about 1 ounce. These soft, flexible balls are stitched internally for durability and do not bounce. The object of the activities is to keep the bag in the air by means of foot contact.

The kicking motion used for footbag activities is new to most participants because of the lift, which is done by lifting the foot upward, not away from the body. The lifting motion directs the footbag upward to permit controlled, consecutive kicks and passes.

Several points contribute to successful footbag work. Start with the basic athletic stance (ready position): feet are about shoulder width apart and point straight ahead. Knees are bent slightly, so body weight is lowered.

Use both feet equally for lifting and kicking. The standing foot is important for maintaining balance and keeping the body in a crouched position. Eye focus on the footbag is essential. Kicking speed is slow; most beginners kick too quickly. Kicking speed is about that of the descending footbag. *Slow* and *low* are the key words in kicking.

Use the arms and upper body for balance and control. For the outside and back kicks, an outstretched arm, opposite to the kicking foot and in line with it, aids in maintaining balance. The near arm is carried behind the body so as not to restrict the player's vision. For inside kicks, the arms are relaxed and in balanced position.

To begin, start with a hand toss to self or with a courtesy toss from another player. Touching the footbag with any part of the body above the waist is a foul and interrupts any sequence of kicks. Three basic kicks are recommended.

1. *Inside kick.* Used when the footbag falls low and directly in front of both shoulders. Use the inside of the foot for contact by turning the instep and the ankle upward to create a flat striking surface. Curling the toes under aids in creating a flat striking surface. Contact with the footbag is made at about knee level.
2. *Outside kick.* Used when the footbag falls outside of either shoulder. Use the outside of the foot by turning the ankle and knee in to create a flat striking surface. With the kicking foot now parallel to the playing surface, use a smooth lifting motion, striking the footbag at approximately knee level. Pointing the toes up aids in creating a flat surface.
3. *Back kick.* Somewhat similar to the outside kick; used when the footbag goes directly overhead or is approaching the upper body directly. Rotate the hips and body parallel to the flight direction to enable the footbag to pass while still maintaining constant eye contact. Lean forward in the direction of the footbag's flight and allow it to pass by before executing the kick.

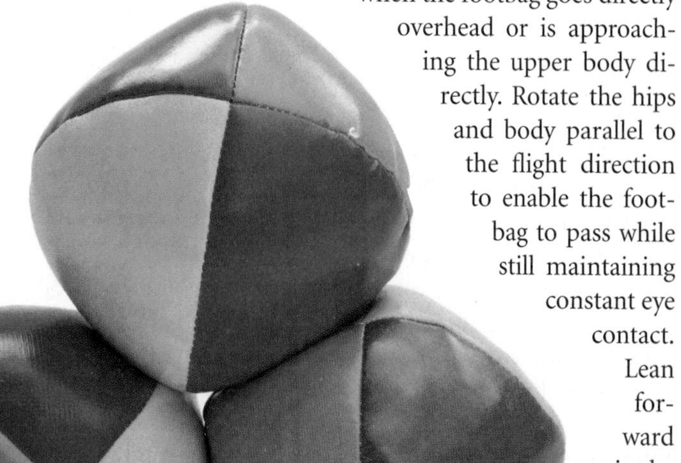

Play can take different forms.

1. *Individual play.* Individuals attempt to see how long they can keep the footbag in play. Score 1 point for each kick.
2. *Partner play.* Partners alternate kicking the footbag. Score 1 point for each alternate successful kick.
3. *Group play.* A circle of four or five individuals is the basic formation. Rules governing consecutive kicks are (a) all members of the circle must have kicked the footbag for a consecutive run to count, and (b) return kicks are prohibited; that is, kickers may not receive return kicks from the person to whom they kicked the footbag.

Footbag play is an enjoyable activity, but the skills are not easily learned. Persistence and patience are needed. Students will have many misses before slowly gaining control. Many physical education suppliers carry footbags; for further sources and information, write to World Footbag Association, P.O. Box 775208, Steamboat Springs, CO 80477; (800)-878-8797, http://worldfootbag.com.

RHYTHMIC GYMNASTICS

Rhythmic gymnastics became popular in the United States during the 1970s and was then accepted as an official sport competition in the 1984 Summer Olympic Games. The activities are varied and merit much more explanation than can be presented in this context. Essentially, rhythmic gymnastics involves routines done to music by a performer using a particular type of manipulative equipment. The routine can be individual, partner, or team competition. Equipment used includes balls, jump ropes, hoops, ribbons, and clubs. Wands, flags, and scarves are sometimes used, but not in national or international competition. The elements of competition are not discussed here.

Many movement qualities—balance, poise, grace, flow of body movement, coordination, rhythm, and kinesthetic sense—grow out of serious participation in rhythmic gymnastics. Fitness qualities of agility, flexibility, and proper posture are also developed. Furthermore, skill in handling the various pieces of manipulative equipment is enhanced, because these skills must be mastered before they can be organized into a routine set to music.

Participants, after developing the necessary skills, work with music. In competitive situations the music is restricted to one instrument. In the school setting the music should be instrumental, light, lively, and enjoyable to the gymnast. Most companies dealing in music for physical education stock specialized recordings for gymnastic movement, including specific selections for various pieces of equipment. Most of these recordings contain directions for suggested routines. There is no substitute, however, for teacher ingenuity in helping children expand and create their routines.

This is an excellent unit for developing group routines in which a class works together. Routines can be used for physical education demonstrations, back-to-school presentations, and at halftimes of athletic events. The routines are impressive and do not require a high level of skill. All children are capable of participating and will enjoy the opportunity to be involved in a "team" event.

ORGANIZING THE PROGRAM

The activities presented here focus on balls, jump ropes, hoops, and ribbons—all ordinarily covered in the elementary program. The club is a difficult hand apparatus to use and is not included in elementary school programs.

Rhythmic gymnastics strives for continuous body movement with the selected piece of equipment. Composition goals are originality, variety of movement, use of the performing area, performance presentation, and smoothness of transition. Harmony of movement with the music, the apparatus, and execution factors are also important. An individual competitive routine is 1 to 1.5 minutes long, but performing time should be shorter for children. Group routines last 2 to 3 minutes and may involve one or two types of equipment. The primary goal is the personal satisfaction that students receive from participating in the program. Introducing students to these activities is more important than having them compete.

A practical way to include rhythmic gymnastics in the curriculum is a dual approach. Teach the basic skills to all children in physical education classes, so they can express themselves by composing creative routines. More refined work can take place through the intramural program or a sport club. Students can choose to participate in competition. Instructors often lack background in these activities. This problem may be solved by bringing in dance instructors from private clubs to introduce the activities.

DEVELOPING ROUTINES

Routines for the elementary level should be uncomplicated and based on learned skills. Aesthetics, although important as skill develops, is of secondary emphasis. Ballet, jazz, and modern dance movements, along with basic dance steps, are normally included in high-level competition.

In developing routines to music, remind children that most music is based on units of 8 or 16 counts. Movements are performed in the sagittal, frontal, and horizontal planes. These terms are used when developing routines and should be learned by children. The *sagittal plane* is an imaginary division of the body into right and left halves. Movements "in the sagittal" are performed parallel to this plane on either side of the body. The *horizontal plane* involves movements that are parallel to the floor. The *frontal plane* divides the body into front and rear halves. Movements in this plane are performed parallel to this plane either in front of or in back of the body.

An effective way to form a routine is to teach the beginning of a routine and then let students create the rest. For example, perform the following movements using ribbons. End each series with the hands in front of the waist.

Sagittal forward circles on the right side (6 counts)

Sagittal forward circles on the left side (6 counts)

Elevator (page 473) (4 counts)

This routine could consist of a number of 16-count units, each concluding with the Elevator (4 counts). Students can develop additional units. For any one piece of apparatus, certain skill areas can be specified. It is then up to the participant to include these skills at some point in the routine.

Rhythmic Gymnastic Ball Skills

The ball should be large enough that it cannot be grasped by the hand but must rest in the hand and be controlled by balance. For elementary school children, use either a 6-inch or an 8.5-inch ball, moderately inflated.

In handling the ball, the fingers are closed and slightly bent, with the ball resting in the palm. In throwing, the ball can roll from the fingertips. After catching, the ball returns immediately to the palm.

Here are some ball skills that can be combined to develop a routine:

1. In a sitting position, try these activities: Roll the ball under the legs and around the back; around the body; down the legs; down the arms; down the legs, lift legs and toss the ball off the toes into the air and catch.
2. Combine basketball dribbling drills with graceful body movements; execute locomotor dance-type movements while bouncing.
3. Toss and catch the ball employing different body positions.
4. Add locomotor movements to tosses and catches.

5. Perform body waves with the ball.
6. Throw and/or bounce the ball in a variety of ways.
7. Make swinging movements (also circular movements). Swinging movements are more difficult than they seem. The ball must be kept in the palm while doing the movements.
8. Try different balancing movements. These are spirals, curls, and other balances inherent to rhythmic gymnastics.
9. Allow opportunity for student exploration combining several of these activities.

Figure 17.28 is an example of a simple routine using balls. The numbers refer to the floor area in the figure where each activity is performed.

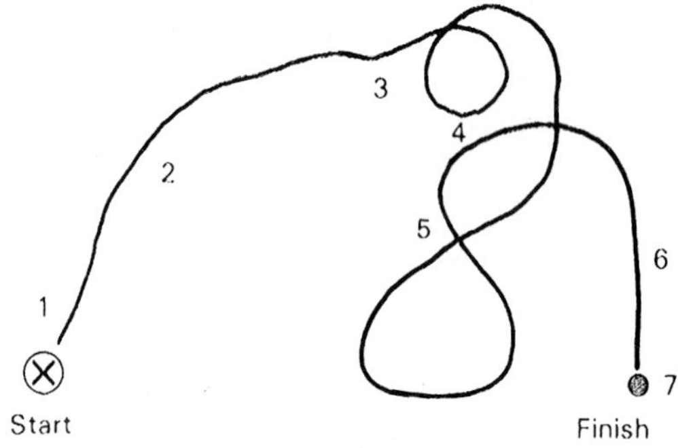

FIGURE 17.28 Floor pattern for routing using balls.

1. Bounce the ball in place.
2. Bounce the ball while moving forward slowly.
3. Run forward while making swing tosses from side to side.
4. Bounce the ball and make a full turn.
5. Run in a figure-eight pattern.
6. Toss the ball up and catch it with one hand.
7. Finish with a toss and catch behind the back.

Rhythmic Gymnastic Rope Routines

As with ball routines, jump-rope routines can be used in various ways. Most important is that the participant excels in the basic jumps. Ropes can be full length, folded in half, or folded in fourths. Knotting the end of the rope makes it easier to handle. Proper length is determined by standing on the center of the rope with one foot and extending the rope ends to the outstretched hands at shoulder level. Handles are not appropriate. Most rope jumping is done with the hands far apart. The rope should not touch the floor, but should pass slightly above it. Jumping techniques used for rhythmic gymnastics obviously differ from those taught in the physical education class. Here are some movements that can be performed using jump ropes.

1. Try single and double jumps forward and backward.
2. Circle the rope on each side of the body, holding both ends of the rope.
3. Make figure-eight swings by holding both ends of the rope or by holding the center of the rope and swinging the ends.
4. Swing the rope like a pendulum and jump it.
5. Run or skip over a turning rope. Try forward and backward.
6. Do a schottische step over a turning rope.
7. Holding the ends and center of the rope, kneel and horizontally circle the rope close to the floor. Stand and circle the rope overhead.
8. Perform a body wrap with the rope. (Hold one end on the hip, and wrap the rope around the body with the other hand.)
9. After jumping over a backward-turning rope, toss the rope with both ends into the air and catch.
10. Run while holding both ends of the rope in one hand and circling the rope sagittally backward at the side of the body. Toss the rope and catch it while running.
11. While performing a dance step, toss and catch the rope.
12. Hold both ends of the rope and swing it around the body like a cape.
13. Perform leaps while circling the rope sagittally at one side of the body.
14. Try different balance movements. Balance movements add variety and permit the performer to catch her breath. These involve held body positions, with the rope underneath the foot or hooked around a foot.

15. Hold the rope around the foot and make shapes with the body and foot–rope connection.
16. Explore and combine a number of the activities described.

Rhythmic Gymnastic Hoop Movements

The basic hoop stunts and challenges (pages 361–363) should first be mastered. The same hoop used in physical education classes is suitable for these routines. The hoop may be held, tossed, or caught in one or both hands and with a variety of grips (Figure 17.29). Hoops may turn forward or backward. Some suggested rhythmic movements with hoops follow.

FIGURE 17.29 Rhythmic gymnastic movements using hoops.

1. *Swinging movements.* A variety of swinging movements are possible. The swinging movement is very large. Good alignment between body and hoop is important. Hoops can be swung in a frontal, sagittal, or horizontal plane. Do the movements in place or while moving. Suggestions:
   a. Swing across the body.
   b. Swing with body lean.
   c. Swing around the body, changing hands.
   d. Swing across the body, changing hands.
   e. Swing overhead, change hands, and swing downward.
   f. Swing in a figure-eight pattern.
2. *Spinning movements.* Turn the hoop, usually with both hands but sometimes with one. The hoop also can be spun on the ground. Suggestions:
   a. Spin in front of the body.
   b. Spin on the floor.
   c. Spin and kick one leg over the hoop. Add a full body turn after the kickover.
3. *Circling movements.* These are the movements most characteristic of hoop activities. Hoops can be twirled by the hand, wrist, arm, leg, or body (hula-hooping). Changes are made from one hand or wrist to the other. Suggestions:
   a. Extend the arm in front of the body. Circle on the hand between the thumb and first finger in the frontal plane.
   b. Circle the hoop while swaying from side to side.
   c. Circle the hoop horizontally overhead.
   d. Hold both sides of the hoop and circle it in front of the body.
   e. Circle the hoop around different parts of the body.
4. *Tossing and catching movements.* Toss the hoop high in the air with one or both hands. Catch it one-handed, between the thumb and index finger. Most tosses grow out of swinging or circling movements. Suggestions:
   a. Try with one- and two-handed catches.
   b. Toss the hoop in different directions.
   c. Toss overhead from hand to hand.
   d. Circle the hoop on the hand, toss into the air, and catch.
5. *Rolling movements.* Roll the hoop on the floor—either forward or reverse (return) rolling—or roll it on the body in diverse ways. If the hoop is rolled along the floor, various jumps can be executed over it. Suggestions:
   a. Roll the hoop and run alongside it.
   b. Roll the hoop and move through it.

c. Roll the hoop and jump over it.

d. Roll the hoop along one arm to the other, on the front or the back of the body.

6. *Jumping movements.* Use the hoop, turned forward or backward, like a jump rope.

Rhythmic Gymnastic Ribbon Movements

Ribbon movements are spectacular and make fine demonstrations. Official ribbon length is around 21 feet with the first 3 feet doubled. For practical purposes, shorter lengths are used at the elementary school level.

Ribbons can be made easily in many colors. A rhythmic flow of movement is desired, featuring circular, oval, spiral, and wavelike shapes. A light, flowing movement is the goal, with total body involvement. The dowel or wand to which the ribbon is attached should be an extension of the hand and arm. Laterality is also a consideration. The following are basic ribbon movements.

1. *Swinging movements.* The entire body should coordinate with these large, swinging motions:

   a. Swing the ribbon forward and backward in the sagittal plane.

   b. Swing the ribbon across and in front of the body in the frontal plane.

   c. Swing the ribbon overhead from side to side.

   d. Swing the ribbon upward and catch the end of it.

   e. While holding both ends of the ribbon, swing it upward, around, and over the body.

2. *Circling movements.* Large circles involve the whole arm; smaller circles involve the wrist. Make circles in the frontal, sagittal, and horizontal planes.

   a. Circle the ribbon at different levels.

   b. Circle the ribbon horizontally, vertically, or diagonally.

   c. Circle the ribbon in front of the body, around the body, and behind the body.

   d. Run while circling the ribbon overhead; leap as the ribbon is circled downward and under the legs.

   e. Add dance steps and turns while circling the ribbon.

3. *Figure-eight movements.* Figure eights are also made in the three planes. The two halves of the figure eight should be the same size and on the same plane level. Make the figure with long arm movements or with movements of the lower arm or wrist. While doing a figure eight, hop through the loop when the ribbon passes the side of the body.

4. *Zigzag movements.* Make these in the air or on the floor. Use continuous up-and-down hand movements, primarily with the wrist.

   a. Execute the zigzag in the air in front, around, and behind the body.

   b. Run backward while zigzagging the ribbon in front of the body. Perform at different levels.

   c. Run forward while zigzagging behind the body at different levels.

5. *Spiral movements.* The circles in the spiral can be the same size or in an increasing or decreasing progression. Make spirals from left to right or the reverse.

   a. Execute spirals around, in front of, or beside the body while performing locomotor dance steps.

   b. Execute spirals while performing forward and backward rolls.

6. *Throwing and catching movements.* These are difficult skills, usually combined with swinging, circling, or figure-eight movements. Toss the ribbon with one hand and catch it with either the same hand or the other hand.

7. *Exchanges.* During group routines, hand or toss the ribbon to a partner.

FOR MORE INFORMATION

REFERENCES AND SUGGESTED READINGS

Bibaud, R. (2008). *Complete fundamentals of rope jumping: A teaching guide* (DVD edition). Champaign, IL: Human Kinetics.

Cassidy, J., & Rimbeaux, B. C. (2007). *Juggling for the complete klutz.* Palo Alto, CA: Klutz Press.

Fujimoto, M. (1996). *Rhythmic gymnastics.* Los Angeles: Price Stern Sloan.

Hackett, P., & Owen, P. (1997). *The juggling book.* New York: Lyons & Burford.

Lee, B. (2003). *Jump rope training.* Champaign, IL: Human Kinetics.

Loredo, E. (1996). *The jump rope book (classic games).* New York: Workman Publishers.

Marrott, B. (1997). *Getting a jump on fitness.* New York: Barricade Books.

Mitchelson, M. (1997). *The most excellent book of how to be a juggler.* Brookfield, CT: Copper Beech Books.

Palmer, H. C. (2003). *Teaching rhythmic gymnastics: A developmentally appropriate approach.* Champaign, IL: Human Kinetics.

WEBSITES

Footbag
http://worldfootbag.com

Frisbees
www.upa.org
www.ultimatehandbook.com/uh

General Physical Education Sites
www.pelinks4u.org/index.htm
www.pecentral.org

Jump Rope
www.worldofropejumping.com
www.aahperd.org

18 Body Management Skills

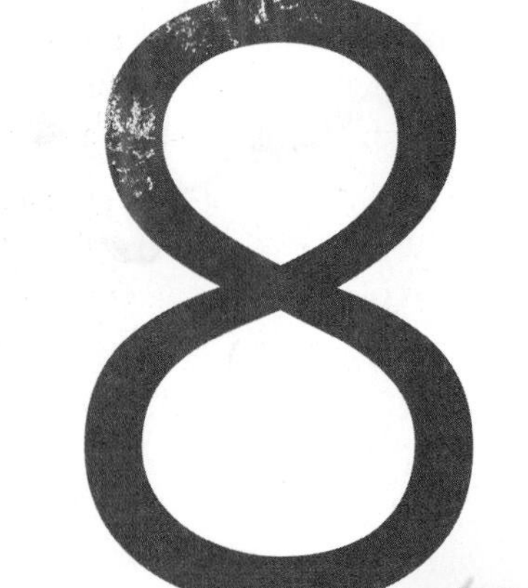

ESSENTIAL COMPONENTS OF QUALITY PROGRAMS

I. Organized around content standards

II. Student-centered and developmentally appropriate

III. Physical activity and motor skill development form the core of the program

IV. Teaches management skills and self-discipline

V. Promotes inclusion of all students

VI. Focuses on process over product

VII. Promotes lifetime personal health and wellness

VIII. Teaches cooperation and responsibility and promotes sensitivity to diversity

NATIONAL STANDARDS FOR PHYSICAL EDUCATION*

1. Demonstrates competency in motor skills and movement patterns needed to perform a variety of physical activities.
2. Demonstrates understanding of movement concepts, principles, and tactics as they apply to the learning and performance of physical activities.
3. Participates regularly in physical activity.
4. Achieves and maintains a health-enhancing level of physical fitness.
5. Exhibits responsible personal and social behavior that respects self and others in physical activity.
6. Values physical activity for health, enjoyment, challenge, self-expression, and/or social interaction.

*National Association for Sport and Physical Education (NASPE), 2004.

Body management skills are usually large muscle activities required for controlling the body in various situations. Body management skills integrate agility, coordination, strength, balance, and flexibility. Activities in this chapter help students learn to control their bodies while using a wide variety of apparatus. This chapter offers organizational hints, instructional strategies, and activities for helping students develop body management skills.

Outcomes

- Help students develop body management skills using large and small apparatus.
- Apply proper instructional procedures to a wide variety of apparatus activities.
- Design a safe environment when teaching large apparatus activities.
- Teach a variety of activities on large apparatus, including climbing ropes, benches, balance beams, and jumping boxes.
- Teach activities using small apparatus, including magic ropes, individual mats, tug-of-war ropes, and gym scooters.

BODY MANAGEMENT skills are an important component of movement competency. Efficient movement demands integration of agility, balance, strength, flexibility, and coordination. Students also must learn how to control their bodies while on large apparatus such as beams, benches, and jumping boxes.

This chapter focuses on developing body management skills using large and small apparatus. The first half of this chapter describes large apparatus activities such as climbing ropes, benches, balance beams, and jumping boxes. Large apparatus activities enable students to learn body management skills while free of ground support. The second half of the chapter focuses on small apparatus activities, including magic ropes, individual mats, and gym scooters. Small apparatus activities help develop body control in space and on the ground.

SAFE AND EFFECTIVE USE OF APPARATUS

Many of the body management skills require large apparatus. Have the apparatus in place before a class arrives, if possible. To ensure a safe environment, tell students they are not to use the equipment until the teacher gives approval. Establish procedures for setup, storage, and safe use of apparatus and mats. Here are guidelines for using apparatus in the instructional setting.

1. *Use tumbling mats to absorb shock.* Position tumbling mats for safety in dismounting and where falls are possible—for example, under all climbing ropes.
2. *Students must carry, not drag, apparatus.* Teach students how to lift and carry the apparatus. For the pieces that require cooperation, designate the number of children and the means of carrying. Discuss proper setup and storage of apparatus and have students practice the procedures.
3. *Activity on apparatus occurs only when directed by teachers.* Instruct children to stay away from all apparatus in the area that has been positioned for later use.
4. *Instruction precedes activity on all apparatus.* Improper use of apparatus can result in injury. Signs emphasizing proper use can be placed on cones near individual pieces of equipment.
5. *Use return activities to increase the movement potential of apparatus.* Return activity requires children to do a movement task (jumping, hopping, skipping, animal walks, etc.) after performing on the apparatus. This reduces the time children stand in line waiting for another turn after completing their task on the apparatus. To increase the amount of time children are actively engaged, increase the distance they have to travel. Return activities demand little supervision. For example, when teaching balance-beam activities, give the children this task: Walk across the beam, do a straddle dismount, and crab-walk (the return activity) to a cone and back to place.
6. *Have students move slowly when working on apparatus.* Many of the activities require balance and agility. Instruct students to aim for controlled and sustained movements.

ACTIVITIES WITH CLIMBING ROPES

Climbing ropes offer high-level developmental possibilities for the upper trunk and arms as well as training in coordination of different body parts (Figure 18.1 on page 384). Adequate grip and arm strength are prerequisites for climbing. Becoming accustomed to the rope and gaining confidence are important early goals. Climbing rope sets can be purchased from Gopher Sport, 220 24th Avenue NW, P.O. Box 998, Owatonna, MN 55060-0998 (1-800-533-0446 or www.gophersport.com).

INSTRUCTIONAL PROCEDURES

1. Place tumbling mats under all ropes.
2. The hand-over-hand method is used for climbing and the hand-under-hand method for descending.
3. Caution the children not to slide; sliding can cause rope burns on the hands and legs.

FIGURE 18.1 Rope climbing on an eight-rope set.

4. A climber who becomes tired should stop and rest. Proper rest stops are taught as part of the climbing procedure.
5. Teach children to go no higher than their strength allows. Marks to limit the climb can be put on the rope with adhesive tape. A height of 8 to 10 feet above the floor is reasonable until a child demonstrates proficiency. A maximum height of 14 to 16 feet is plenty for elementary school children.
6. Use spotters for activities in which the body is inverted.
7. Rosin in powdered form and magnesium chalk aid in gripping. They are particularly important when the rope becomes slippery.
8. Instruct children to make sure other children are out of the way before swinging on the ropes.

PRELIMINARY ACTIVITIES

Progression is important in rope climbing. Teachers should follow these fundamental skill progressions.

Supported Pull-Ups

In supported pull-up activities, a part of the body remains in contact with the floor. The pull-up is hand-over-hand, and the return is hand-under-hand.

1. Kneel directly under the rope. Pull up to the tiptoes and return to kneeling position.
2. Start in sitting position under the rope. Pull up; weight is on the heels. Return to sitting position.
3. Start in a standing position. Grasp the rope, rock back on the heels, and lower the body to the floor. Keep a straight body. Return to standing position.

Hangs

To do a hang, pull up the body in one motion and hold for a length of time (5, 10, or 20 seconds). Progression is important.

1. From a seated position, reach up as high as possible and pull the body from the floor, except for the heels. Hold.
2. Same as step 1, but pull the body completely off the floor. Hold.
3. From a standing position, jump up, grasp the rope, and hang. This is a Bent-Arm Hang, with the hands about even with the mouth. Hold.
4. Repeat step 3, but add leg movements—one or both knees up, bicycling movement, Half Lever (one or both legs up, parallel to the floor), Full Lever (feet up to the face).

Swinging and Jumping

Use a bench, box, or stool as a takeoff point. The child reaches high and jumps to a bent-arm position. Landing is with bent knees.

1. Swing and jump. Add half turns and full turns.
2. Swing and return to the perch. Add single and double knee bends.
3. Jump for distance, over a high-jump bar or through a hoop.
4. Swing and pick up a bowling pin and return to the perch.
5. Carry objects (beanbags, balls, or deck tennis rings). A partner, standing to the side away from

the takeoff bench, can put articles to be carried back on the takeoff perch by placing each article between the knees or feet.

6. Not using a takeoff device, run toward a swinging rope, grasp it, and gain momentum for swinging.

Pull-Ups

Repeatedly raise and lower the body. At the highest point of the Pull-Up, the chin touches the hands. Start by challenging students to accomplish one Pull-Up in the defined position and then slowly increase the number of repetitions. All the activities described for hangs are adaptable to Pull-Ups.

Inverted Hang

Both hands reach up high, and the rope hangs to one side. Jump to a bent-arm position, at the same time bringing the knees up to the nose to invert the body, which is now in a curled position. In a continuation of the motion, bring the feet up higher than the hands, and lock the legs around the rope. The body should now be straight and upside down. In the learning phase, teachers should spot.

FIGURE 18.2 Scissors Grip.

CLIMBING THE ROPE

Scissors Grip

Approach the rope and reach as high as possible, standing with the right leg forward of the left. Raise the back leg, bend at the knee, and place the rope inside the knee and outside the foot. Cross the forward leg over the back leg, and straighten the legs with the toes pointed down (Figure 18.2). This should give a secure hold. The teacher can check the position.

To climb using the Scissors Grip, raise the knees up close to the chest, the rope sliding between them, while supporting the body with the hand grip. Lock the rope between the legs and climb up, using the hand-over-hand method and stretching as high as the hands can reach. Bring the knees up to the chest and repeat the process until you have climbed halfway. Later, strive for a higher climb.

Leg-Around Rest

Wrap the left leg completely around the rope, keeping the rope between the thighs (Figure 18.3 on page 386). The bottom of the rope then crosses over the instep of the left foot from the outside. The right foot stands on the rope as it crosses over the instep, providing pressure to prevent slippage. For additional pressure, release the hands and wrap the arms around the rope, leaning away from the rope at the same time.

To climb using the Leg-Around Rest, proceed as in climbing with the Scissors Grip, but loosen the grip each time and grasp higher up on the rope.

18

DESCENDING THE ROPE

There are four ways to descend the rope. The only differences are in the use of the leg locks, because the hand-under-hand is used for all descents.

Scissors Grip Descent

From an extended Scissors Grip position, lock the legs and lower the body with the hands until the knees are against the chest. Hold with the hands, and lower the legs to a new position.

FIGURE 18.3 Leg-Around Rest.

Leg-Around Rest Descent

From the Leg-Around Rest position, lower the body until the knees are against the chest. Lift the top foot, and let the feet slide to a lower position (see Figure 18.3). Secure with the top foot and repeat.

Instep Squeeze Descent

Squeeze the rope between the insteps by keeping the heels together. Lower the body while the rope slides against the instep.

Stirrup Descent

Have the rope on the outside of the right foot and carry it over the instep of the left. Pressure from the left foot holds the position. To get into position, let the rope trail along the right leg, reach under, and hook it with the left instep. When the pressure from the left leg is reduced, the rope slides smoothly while the descent is made with the hands.

OTHER CLIMBING ACTIVITIES

Climbing for Time

This activity requires a stopwatch and a distinct mark on the rope. The height of the mark depends on the children's skill and capacity. Each child gets three trials (but not in succession) and the best time is recorded. Children start from a standing position with hands reaching as high as desired. The descent is not included in the timing, because attempting a speedy descent may cause the children to drop and may promote rope burns.

Climbing Without Using the Feet

This strenuous activity should be attempted only by the most skilled climbers. During early sessions, do not set the mark too high. Climbers start from a sitting position. The activity can be timed.

Organizing a Climbing Club

The teacher can put a marker at the top limit of the rope. Each child who climbs to and touches the marker becomes a member of the Climber's Club. Form a Super-Climber's Club for those who can climb to the marker without using their feet. Climbers must start from a sitting position on the floor.

STUNTS USING TWO ROPES

Two ropes hanging close together are needed for the following activities.

Straight-Arm Hang

Jump up, grasp one rope with each hand, and hang with the arms straight.

Bent-Arm Hang

Do this like the Straight-Arm Hang, but bend the arms at the elbows.

Arm Hangs with Different Leg Positions

1. Do single and double knee lifts.
2. Do a Half Lever. Bring the legs up parallel to the floor and point the toes.
3. Do a Full Lever. Bring the feet up to the face and keep the knees straight.
4. Do a Bicycle. Pedal as on a bicycle.

Skin the Cat

From a bent-arm position, kick the feet overhead and continue the roll until the feet touch the mat. Return to the starting position. A more difficult stunt is to start from a higher position with the feet not touching the mat. Reverse to original position.

Pull-Ups

Do a Pull-Up the same way as on a single rope, except that each hand grasps a rope.

Inverted Hangs

1. Hang with the feet wrapped around the ropes.
2. Hang with the feet against the inside of the ropes.
3. Hang with the toes pointed and the feet not touching the ropes (Figure 18.4).

Climbing

1. Climb up one rope, transfer to another, and descend.
2. Climb halfway up one rope, cross over to another rope, and keep climbing to the top.
3. Climb both ropes together without using the legs. This is difficult and requires climbers to slide one hand at a time up the ropes without completely releasing the grip.
4. Climb as on a single rope, with hands on one rope and feet on the other rope.

ACTIVITY SEQUENCES

Rope-climbing activities offer sequences that help the child progress. The following sequence indicates the kind of progressive challenges that can be met.

FIGURE 18.4 Spotting an Inverted Hang on two ropes. (Holding the performer's hands ensures confidence and safety.)

1. Jump and hang (10 seconds).
2. Pull up and hold (10 seconds).
3. Scissors climb to blue mark (10 feet).
4. Scissors climb to top (15 feet).
5. Demonstrate Leg-Around Rest (10 feet).
6. Do an Inverted Hang, with body straight (5 seconds).

18

ACTIVITIES ON BALANCE BEAMS

Balance-beam activities contribute to control in both static and dynamic balance situations (Figure 18.5 on page 388). The balance-beam side of a balance-beam bench is ideal for such activities, with its 2-inch-wide and 12-foot-long beam. Balance-beam benches can be purchased from Gopher Sport, 220 24th Avenue NW, P.O. Box 998, Owatonna, MN 55060-0998 (1-800-533-0446 or www.gophersport.com). Balance beams come in many other sizes, however, and can be built from common lumber materials (see Chapter 10). Some teachers prefer a wider beam for kindergarten and first-grade children and, in particular, for special education children. Students graduate to the narrower beam as

FIGURE 18.5 Walking on a balance-beam bench.

soon as they are no longer challenged by activities on the wider beam.

Other ideas for balance equipment are also interesting. A pole with ends shaped to fit the supports can be substituted for the flat balance beam and is more challenging. Another idea is building a beam that goes from 2-inches wide to 1-inch wide at the other end. Beams of varying widths (from 1 to 4 inches) can also be used. Children progress from the wider to the narrower beams. For children with disabilities, provide a variety of widths.

INSTRUCTIONAL PROCEDURES

1. Children should move with controlled, deliberate movements. Speed is not a goal. Advise students to recover their balance before taking another step or making another movement.
2. Observing the principle of control, children should step slowly on the beam, pause momentarily in good balance at the end of the activity, and dismount with a small, controlled jump from the end of the beam upon completing the routine.
3. Place tumbling mats at the end of the bench to cushion the dismount and allow for rolls and stunts after the dismount.
4. Visual focus is important. Tell children to look straight ahead rather than down at the feet. Eye targets can be marked on or attached to walls to assist in visual focus. This focus allows balance controls other than vision to function more effectively. From time to time, have children do movements with the eyes closed, entirely eliminating visual control of balance.
5. Direct children to step off the beam immediately if they think they are losing their balance, rather than teetering and falling off awkwardly. Allow the child to step back on the beam and continue the routine.
6. Success in a balance-beam activity can be based on two levels. The lower level allows the child to step off the beam once during the routine. The higher level requires the child to remain on the beam throughout. For both levels, ask students to pause in good balance at the end of the beam before dismounting.
7. Both laterality and directionality are important. Give the right and left feet reasonably equal treatment. For example, if a student does steps leading with the right foot, the next effort is made leading with the left foot. Give equal weight to directions right and left. A child naturally uses the dominant side and direction but must be encouraged to perform with both sides.
8. The child next in line begins when the performer ahead is about three-quarters of the distance across the beam.
9. Return activities (see page 383) are a consideration for enhancing the breadth of activity.
10. A child or the teacher can assist the performer. The assistant holds the hand palm up, ready to help the performer if and when help is needed.

ACTIVITY SEQUENCES

Activities for the balance beam are presented as a progression of movement themes. The teacher can fully develop all activities and possibilities within a theme before proceeding to the next theme, or can take a few activities from each theme and cover more ground.

Activities on Parallel Beams

Activities on two parallel beams are presented first as lead-up practice for the single-beam tasks. The beams are placed about 10 to 30 inches apart. The parallel-beam activities can be done alone or with a partner when more security is desired.

1. With a partner, join inside hands and walk forward, backward, and sideways. Walk sideways, using a grapevine step (step behind, step across). Hold a beanbag in the free hand.
2. Without a partner, do various animal walks, such as the Crab Walk, Bear Walk, Measuring Worm, and Elephant Walk.
3. With one foot on each beam, walk forward, backward, and sideways.

4. Step to the opposite beam with each step taken.
5. Progress the length of the beams with hands on one beam and feet on the other.
6. Progress to the middle of the beams and do various turns and stunts, such as picking up a beanbag, moving through a hoop, and stepping over a wand.

Movements Going the Full Length of a Single Beam

1. Do various locomotor tasks, such as walking, follow steps, heel-and-toe steps, side steps, tiptoe steps, the grapevine step, and so on.
2. Follow different directions—forward, backward, sideways.
3. Use different arm and hand positions—on the hips, on the head, behind the back, out to the sides, pointing to the ceiling, folded across the chest.
4. Move across the beam while assuming different shapes.
5. Balance an object (beanbag or eraser) on various body parts—on the head, on the back of the hands, on the shoulders. Try balancing two or three objects at once.

Half-and-Half Movements

These movements repeat the movements, arm positions, and balancing stunts described previously, except the performer goes halfway across the beam using a selected movement and then changes to another type of movement on the second half of the beam.

Challenge Tasks or Stunts

The performer moves halfway across the beam with a selected movement, does a particular challenge or stunt at the center, and finishes the movements on the second half of the beam. Suggestions:

1. Balances: Forward Balance (page 472), Backward Balance (page 472), Stork Stand (page 471), Seat Balance (page 486).
2. Stunts: Leg Dip (page 486), Finger Touch (page 487).
3. Challenges: Make a full turn, pick up a beanbag at the center, do a push-up.

More Difficult Movements Across the Beam

1. Hop the length of the beam—forward, sideways, backward.
2. Do the Cat Walk (page 463), Rabbit Jump (page 466), Lame Dog Walk (page 467), Seal Crawl (page 478), or Crab Walk (page 467).
3. Do various locomotor movements with the eyes closed.
4. Walk to the center of the beam and do a Side-Leaning Rest. Try on the other side as well.
5. Walk to the center and do a complete body turn on one foot only.

Activities with Wands and Hoops

1. Carry a wand or hoop. Step over the wand or through the hoop in various fashions.
2. Step over or go under wands or hoops held by a partner.
3. Twirl a hula-hoop on the arms or around the body while moving across the beam.
4. Balance a wand on various body parts while moving across the beam.
5. Balance a wand in one hand and twirl a hoop on the other hand and proceed across the beam.

Solo Manipulative Activities

1. Using one or two beanbags, toss to self in various fashions—over the head, around the body, under the legs.
2. Using a ball, toss to self. Circle the ball around the body, under the legs.
3. Bounce a ball on the floor. On the beam. Dribble on the floor.
4. Roll a ball along the beam.

Partner Manipulative Activities

With a partner standing beyond the far end of the beam, throw a beanbag or ball back and forth. Have partner toss for a volleyball return. Bat the ball (as in a volleyball serve) to partner.

Stunts with a Partner

1. Do a Wheelbarrow (page 493) with the supporting performer keeping the feet on the floor.
2. Partners start on opposite ends of the beam and move toward each other with the same kind of movement, do a balance pose together in the center, and return to their respective ends of the beam.
3. Partners start on opposite ends of the beam and attempt to pass each other without losing their balance and without touching the floor. Find different ways to pass.

ACTIVITIES ON BENCHES

The balance-beam bench is effective in developing strength and balance. Bench activities are challenging to children and offer a variety of movement possibilities.

INSTRUCTIONAL PROCEDURES

1. Divide all activities on the benches into three parts: approaching and mounting the bench, doing the bench activity, and dismounting from the bench.
2. Place tumbling mats at each end of the bench to facilitate the dismount and various rolls and stunts done after dismounting.
3. Position benches either horizontally or inclined. For more variety and challenge, combine bench activities with other equipment.
4. Limit the number of children using a bench to four to five.
5. The child next in turn begins when the performer ahead is about three-quarters of the way across the bench.
6. Return activities add to the activity potential.
7. Speed is not a goal in bench activities. Students move deliberately and carefully, paying attention to body control.
8. Students should also focus on laterality and directionality. For example, if a child hops on the right foot, the next move is made on the left foot. In jump turns, both right and left movements are used.

ACTIVITY SEQUENCES

Animal Walks

Do various animal walks on the bench, such as the Seal Crawl (page 478), Cat Walk (page 463), Lame Dog Walk (page 467), and Rabbit Jump (page 466).

Locomotor Movements

Do various locomotor movements along the length of the bench, such as stepping or jumping on and off the side of the bench, hopping on and off the side of the bench, or skipping and galloping on the bench.

Pulls

Pull the body along the bench, using different combinations of body parts. Use the arms only, the legs only, the right leg and the left arm, or the left leg and the right arm. Use the following positions:

1. Prone position (head first and feet first; Figure 18.6)

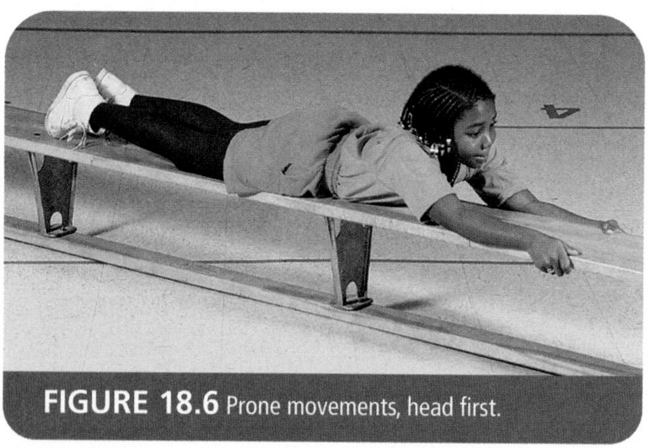

FIGURE 18.6 Prone movements, head first.

2. Supine position (head first and feet first; Figure 18.7)
3. Side position (head first and feet first)

Have students use various leg positions (such as legs up in a half-lever position, knees bent, and

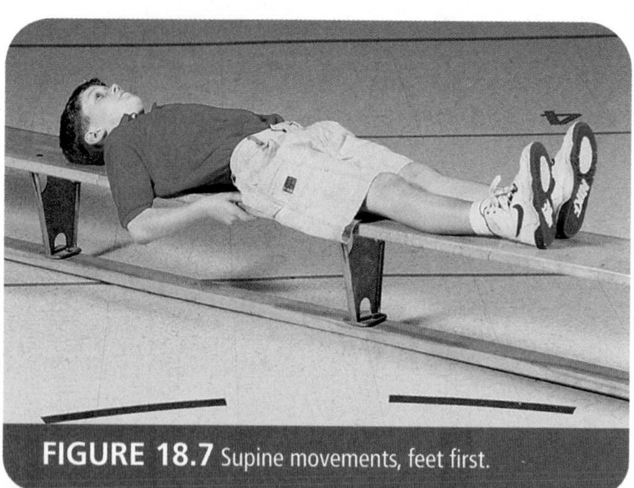

FIGURE 18.7 Supine movements, feet first.

so on) when doing pulls and pushes. Body parts not used in pulling can carry a piece of manipulative equipment (a beanbag, ball, or wand). Try different body shapes, like the Submarine (one foot in the air like a periscope).

Pushes

Push the body along the bench, using different parts of the body as discussed for pulls. Use the following positions:

1. Prone position
2. Supine position
3. Side position

Movements Along the Side of the Bench

Move alongside the bench in the following positions. Keep the hands on the bench and the feet on the floor as far from the bench as possible.

1. Prone position
2. Supine position
3. Turn over (move along the bench, changing from prone to supine position).

Repeat these positions with the feet on the bench and the hands on the floor as far from the bench as possible.

Scooter Movements

Sit on the bench and move along it without using the hands. Suggestions:

1. Do a Scooter. Move with the feet leading the body. Try to pull the body along with the feet.
2. Do a Reverse Scooter. Move with the legs trailing and pushing the body along the bench.
3. Do a Seat Walk. Move forward by walking on the buttocks. Use the legs as little as possible.

Crouch Jumps

Place both hands on the bench and jump back and forth over it. Move the length of the bench by placing the hands forward a few inches after each jump.

1. Do a regular Crouch Jump (Figure 18.8). Use both hands and both feet. Jump as high as possible.
2. Do a Straddle Jump. Straddle the bench with the legs, take the weight on the hands, and jump with the legs as high as possible.
3. Use one hand and two feet. Do a Crouch Jump, but use only one hand.
4. Use one hand and one foot. Do the Crouch Jump, using only one hand and one foot.
5. Stand to one side, facing the bench, with both hands on it. With stiff arms, try to send the seat as high as possible into the air. Add the Mule Kick (page 479) before coming down.

FIGURE 18.8 Crouch Jump.

Basic Tumbling Stunts

Basic tumbling stunts can be incorporated into bench activities: the Back Roller (pages 468–469), Backward Curl (page 469), Forward Roll (page 468; Figure 18.9 on page 392), Backward Roll (page 481), and Cartwheel (page 483).

Dismounts

All bench activities in which the child moves from one end of the bench to the other should end with a dismount. Many stunts can be used. Suggestions:

1. Single jump (forward or backward; Figure 18.10 on page 392).
2. Jump with turns (half turn, three-quarter turn, full turn).
3. Jackknife. Jump, kick up the legs, and touch the toes with the fingertips. Keep the feet together.

FIGURE 18.9 Preparing to do a Forward Roll on the bench.

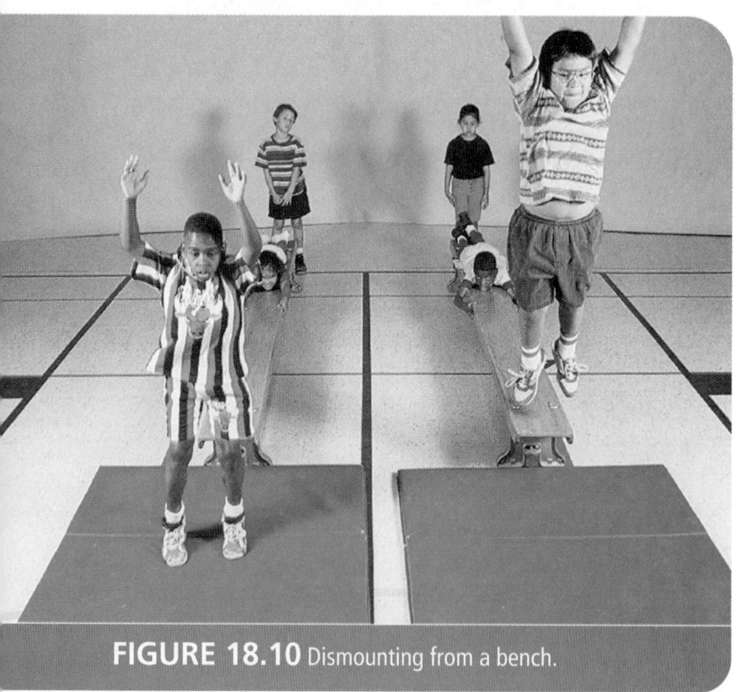

FIGURE 18.10 Dismounting from a bench.

4. Jackknife Split. Same as the Jackknife but spread the legs as far as possible.
5. Jump to a Forward Roll.
6. Backward jump to a Backward Roll.
7. Side jump to a Side Roll (page 468).
8. Judo Roll.
9. Jump with combinations of the stunts noted in this list.

ADDITIONAL EXPERIENCES ON BENCHES

1. Extend the range of activities by adding balls, beanbags, hoops, and wands. Use wands and hoops as obstacles to go over, under, around, or through. Use balls and beanbags to incorporate basic balance and manipulative skills into the activity.
2. Two can perform at once, each child near an opposite end of the bench, doing different balance positions on the bench.
3. Children like to go over and under a row of benches arranged in a kind of obstacle course.
4. A bench can be supported by two jumping boxes and used as a vaulting box. Each bench is long enough to accommodate three children. They can jump off it, Mule Kick on it, and vault over it.
5. Four benches can be placed in a large rectangle (Figure 18.11), with a squad standing at attention on top of each bench. On signal, each squad gets off its bench, runs around the outside of the other three benches, and then runs back to its own bench. The first squad back and at attention on the bench is the winner.
6. Place benches in a square formation, so children can move around the square and try a different movement on each bench.
7. Place one end of the bench on a jumping box or on another bench. Children can practice jumping by running up the incline and striving for jump height at the end of the bench.
8. Benches are appropriate for some partner activities. Partners can start on each end and pass through or around each other, reversing original positions. Wheelbarrow Walks are also suitable.

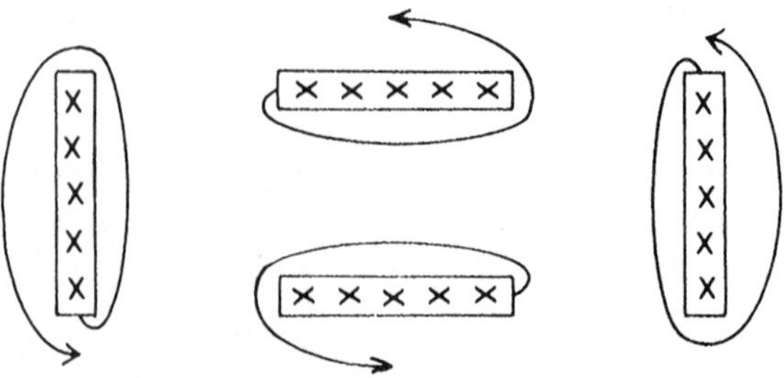

FIGURE 18.11 Rectangular bench activities.

9. Another enjoyable activity is arranging the benches in a course as illustrated in Figure 18.12. Have one student lead the squad or class through the challenge course. A different activity must be done at each bench.

ACTIVITIES WITH JUMPING BOXES

Jumping boxes give children opportunities to jump from a height and propel the body through space. Activities with jumping boxes are generally confined to the primary grades. Boxes can be of varying heights; 8 inches and 16 inches are suggested. Place a rubber floor pad under the box to protect the floor and prevent sliding. Jumping boxes can be built or purchased; Chapter 10 includes plans for building boxes.

INSTRUCTIONAL PROCEDURES

1. Have students focus on landing in proper form. Stress lightness, bent-knee action, balance, and body control.
2. Use tumbling mats to cushion the landing.
3. Emphasize exploration and creativity; there are few standard stunts in jumping box activities.
4. Assign no more than four or five children to each series of boxes.
5. Incorporate additional challenges by using hoops, wands, balls, and the like. Rolling stunts after the dismount extend the movement possibilities.
6. Return activities work well with boxes.
7. Children should strive for height and learn to relax as they go through space.

ACTIVITY SEQUENCES

The following activities can be augmented easily. Let the children help expand the activity.

Various Approaches to the Boxes

Vary the approach to the boxes by using movements like these.

1. Fundamental locomotor movements: run, gallop, skip, and hop
2. Animal walks: Bear Walk, Crab Walk, and so on
3. Moving over and under various obstacles: jumping over a bench, moving through a hoop held upright by a mat, doing a Backward Roll on the mat
4. Rope-jumping to the box: students try to continue jumping while mounting and dismounting the box

Mounting the Box

Students can use many different combinations to get onto the box.

1. Practice stepping onto the box (mounting) by taking the full weight on the stepping foot and holding it for a few seconds. This develops a sense of balance and stabilizes the support foot.
2. Mount the box, using locomotor movements such as a step, jump, leap, or hop. Do various turns—quarter, half, three-quarter, and full—while jumping onto the box.
3. Use a Crouch Jump to get onto the box.
4. Back up to the box and mount it without looking at it.
5. Mount the box while a partner tosses you a beanbag.

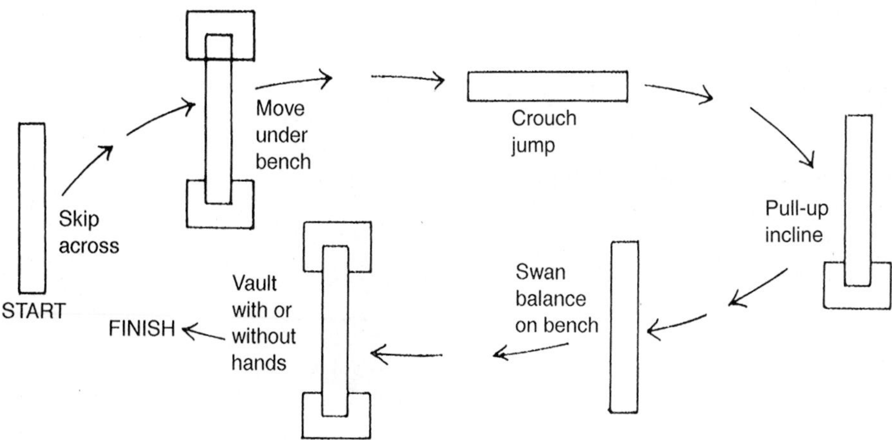

FIGURE 18.12 Challenge course using benches.

6. Make various targets on top of the box with a piece of chalk, and try to land on the spot when mounting.

Dismounting the Box

Use the following dismounts to develop body control.

1. Jump off with a quarter turn, half turn, or full turn.
2. Jump off with different body shapes: stretching, curling up in a ball, jackknifing.
3. Jump over a wand or through a hoop.
4. Jump off, and do a Forward Roll or a Backward Roll.
5. Change the foregoing dismounts by substituting a hop or a leap in place of the jump.
6. Increase the height and distance of the dismount.
7. Dismount in various directions, such as forward, backward, sideways, northward, and southward.
8. Jump off using a jackknife or wide straddle.
9. Do a balance stunt on the box and then dismount.

After the class has learned the basic movements used with jumping boxes, teachers can incorporate continuous squad motion. The squad captain is responsible for leading the group through different approaches, mounts, and dismounts. The same activity cannot be used twice in succession.

Addition of Equipment

Various pieces of equipment enhance box activities. Suggestions:

1. Toss beanbags up while dismounting, or try to keep one on your head while mounting or dismounting the box.
2. Try to dribble a playground ball while doing the box routine.
3. Jump through a stationary hoop held by a partner while dismounting, or use the hoop as a jump rope and see how many times you can jump through it while dismounting.
4. Jump over or go under a wand.

Box Combinations

Arrange boxes in a straight line and in other patterns. Children do a different movementover each box as though running a challenge course.

ACTIVITIES WITH INDIVIDUAL MATS

Individual mat activities originated in England and are the basis for many exploratory and creative movements. The mat serves as a base of operation or as an obstacle to go over or around. Mats vary in size, with the most popular being 24 inches by 48 inches. Standard thickness is three-quarters of an inch, but can vary. The mat should have rubber backing to prevent slipping. Rubber-backed indoor– outdoor carpeting makes excellent mats; commercial mats also are available.

INSTRUCTIONAL PROCEDURES

1. Educational movement techniques are important in mat work.
2. Stress body management and basic skills of locomotor and nonlocomotor movement.
3. Place the mats far enough apart to allow free movement around them.
4. Each child should have a mat.

ACTIVITY SEQUENCES

The sequence presented here is a suggestion only. The activities are quite flexible and require only fundamental skills.

Command Movements

In command movements, children change movement on command. Try these:

- *Stretch:* Stretch out your body in all directions as wide as possible.
- *Curl:* Curl into a tight little ball (Figure 18.13).
- *Balance:* Form some kind of balanced position.
- *Bridge:* Make a bridge over the mat.
- *Reach:* Keeping the toes of one foot on the mat, reach out as far as possible across the floor in a chosen direction.
- *Rock:* Rock on any part of the body.

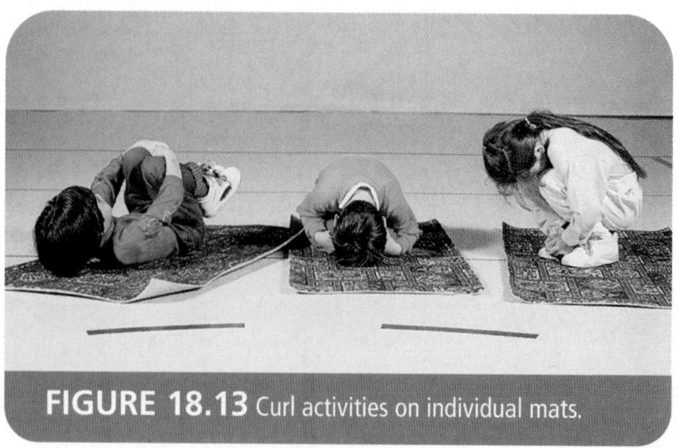

FIGURE 18.13 Curl activities on individual mats.

- *Roll:* Do some kind of roll on the mat.
- *Twist:* Make a shape with a part of the body twisted.
- *Shake:* Shake all over, or shake designated parts of the body.
- *Melt:* Sink down slowly into a little puddle of water on the mat.
- *Fall:* Fall to the mat.
- *Collapse:* The movement is similar to a fall but follows nicely after a bridge.
- *Prone:* Lie facedown on the mat.

Sequencing can be established in several ways. The children can emphasize flow factors by changing at will from one movement to another, or changes can be made on a verbal signal or on the beat of a drum. Magic-number challenges can be used, too.

Another means of exploration is selecting one of the movement challenges—say, Stretch—and changing from one type of stretch position to another. If Balance is selected, the movement sequence can begin with a balance on six body parts; then the number can be reduced by one on each signal until the child is balancing on one body part. Have students explore different kinds of shapes.

Movements On and Off the Mat

Children do different locomotor movements on and off the mat in different directions. Turns and shapes can be added (Figure 18.14).

1. Take the weight on the hands as you go across the mat.
2. Lead with different body parts as you go on and off the mat. Move on and off the mat and land by using a specific number (1 to 5) of body parts.
3. Jump backward, forward, sideways. Make up a rhythmic sequence. Move around the area, jumping from mat to mat.

FIGURE 18.14 Movements on and off the mat.

Movements Over the Mat

These movements are similar to the preceding movements, but the child goes completely over the mat each time.

Movements Around the Mat

Locomotor movements around the mat are done both clockwise and counterclockwise.

1. Do movements around the mat, keeping the hands on the mat. Now do movements around, keeping the feet on the mat.
2. Change to one foot and one hand on the mat. Vary with the Crab position.
3. Work out combinations of stunt movements and locomotor activities, going around the mats. Reverse direction often.
4. Move throughout the area, running between the mats. On signal, jump over a specific number of mats.

Activities Using Mats as a Base

1. Stretch and reach in different directions to show how big the space is.
2. Do combination movements away from and back to the mat. For example, do two jumps and two hops or six steps and two jumps.
3. Use the magic-number concept.
4. See how many letters you can make. Find a partner, put your mats together, and make your bodies into different letters and numbers.

Mat Games

Each child sits on a mat. On signal, each rises and jumps over as many different mats as possible. On the next signal, each child sits on the nearest mat. The last child to sit can pay a penalty. The game can also be played by eliminating one or two mats so one or two children are left without a home base. The teacher can stand on a mat or turn over mats to put them out of the game. To control roughness, make a rule that the first child to touch a mat gets to sit on it.

VARIATION: Have each child touch at least 10 mats and then sit cross-legged on the 11th, or have them alternate touching a mat and jumping over the next mat until reaching a total of 10. Challenge students: "See how many mats you can cartwheel or jump over in 10 seconds." Change the challenge and try again.

Developmental Challenges

1. Experiment with curl-ups (partial or full). (This can be done informally or as a challenge.)
2. From a sitting position on the mat, pick up the short sides of the mat and raise the feet and upper body off the floor. Try variations of the V-Up (page 500).

Manipulative Activities

Keeping one foot on the mat, maintain control of a balloon in the air, either with a hand, a nylon-stocking paddle, or a Lummi stick. Try the same activity with a stocking paddle and a paper ball. Children can count the number of touches, or strokes. Try with both feet on the mat.

ACTIVITIES WITH MAGIC ROPES

Magic rope activities originated in Germany. Each rope is similar to a long rubber band. Magic ropes can be made by knitting wide rubber bands together, or they can be made from ordinary 3/4-inch elastic tape available in most fabric stores. Children place their hands through loops on each end and grasp the rope. Ropes should be long enough to stretch to between 30 and 40 feet (see Chapter 10). A major advantage of the magic rope is its flexibility; children have no fear of hitting it or tripping on it while performing. Ropes should be stretched tight, with little slack.

INSTRUCTIONAL PROCEDURES

1. Two or more children are rope holders while the others are jumping. Teachers can develop a rotation plan for holders.
2. By changing the height or raising and lowering opposite ends of the ropes, many variations are possible.
3. The jumping activities are strenuous; alternate them with activities that involve crawling under the ropes.
4. Have students focus on not touching the rope. The magic rope can help develop body perception in space if treated as an obstacle to be avoided.
5. Better use can be made of the rope by using an angled approach, which involves starting at one end of the rope and moving to the other end by using jumping and hopping activities. In comparison, the straight-on approach allows the child to jump the rope only once.
6. From 8 to 12 ropes, 2 for each squad, are needed for a class. Squads are excellent groups for this activity because the leader can control the rotation of the rope holders.
7. The child next in turn begins when the child ahead is almost to the end of the rope.

ACTIVITY SEQUENCES

Activities with Single Ropes

Start the ropes at a 6-inch height and gradually raise them to add challenge.

1. Jump over the rope.
2. Hop over the rope.
3. Jump and do various body turns while jumping.
4. Make different body shapes and change body size while jumping.
5. Crawl or slide under the rope.
6. Crouch-jump over the rope.
7. Hold the rope overhead and have others jump up and touch it with their foreheads.
8. Gradually lower the rope, and do the limbo under it without touching the floor with the hands.
9. Jump over the rope backward without looking at it.
10. Do a Scissors Jump over the rope.

Activities with Double Ropes

Vary the height and spread of the ropes.

1. Do these activities with the ropes parallel to each other.
   a. Jump in one side and out the other (Figure 18.15).
   b. Hop in one side and out the other.

FIGURE 18.15 Jumping in and out of two magic ropes.

c. Crouch-jump in and out.

d. Do various animal walks in and out of the ropes.

e. Do a long jump over both of the ropes.

f. Do a stunt while jumping in between the two ropes. Possible stunts are the Heel Click, body turn, and Straddle Jump.

g. Jump or leap over one rope and land on the other rope.

2. With the ropes crossed at right angles to each other, try these activities:

   a. Do various movements from one area to the next.

   b. Jump into one area and crawl into another.

3. With one rope above the other to resemble a fence, do these activities. Vary the height of the ropes and their distance apart. Challenging children not to touch the "barbed-wire fence" adds much excitement to the activity.

   a. Step through the ropes without touching.

   b. Crouch-jump through.

Miscellaneous Activities with Magic Ropes

Give students time to create their own ideas with the ropes and other pieces of equipment.

1. Do the various activities with a beanbag balanced on the head. Try them while bouncing a ball.
2. Use four or more ropes to create various floor patterns.
3. Add variety with a follow-the-leader activity.
4. Create a challenge course with many ropes for a relay.

ACTIVITIES WITH PARTNER TUG-OF-WAR ROPES

A partner tug-of-war rope is about 6 feet long with a loop on each end. (See Chapter 10 for instructions on making partner tug-of-war ropes.) Tug-of-war activities develop strength, because students must use most of their strength. These strength demands may continue over a short period of time.

INSTRUCTIONAL PROCEDURES

1. It is important to start and stop the tugging with clear signals. Tugging bouts should last no more than 5 to 7 seconds. Problems occur when students become tired and one partner gets pulled around. Tell students not to pull until someone falls down, but to have a good tug and stop.
2. Contests are between partners of comparable ability, so each child has a chance to win.
3. Plan a system of rotation so children meet different partners. If students stay with the same partner, the same person keeps winning.
4. Caution students not to let go of the rope. If the grip is slipping, they should ask the other student to stop pulling, renew the grip, and start over.
5. Individual ropes are excellent for partner resistance activities. Have students practice some of these activities each time they use the ropes.
6. Use a line on the floor, perpendicular to the direction of the rope, to signal a win. When one child pulls the other over the line, the contest ends. Another signal for a win could be for children to back up, while pulling, until they can pick up an object behind them.

PARTNER ACTIVITIES

The tug-of-war rope offers good possibilities in movement exploration. Have partners try the following ways of pulling. Let them devise other ways to pull against each other.

1. Pull with the right hand only, the left hand only, both hands.
2. Grasp with the right hand, with the body supported on three points (the left hand and the feet). Change hands.
3. Pull with backs toward each other, with the rope between the legs, holding with one hand only.
4. Partners get down on all fours, with feet toward each other. Hook the loops around one foot of each partner. Each contestant pulls using both hands and the foot still on the floor.
5. Partners get into Crab position and pull the rope by hooking a foot through the loop (Figure 18.16).

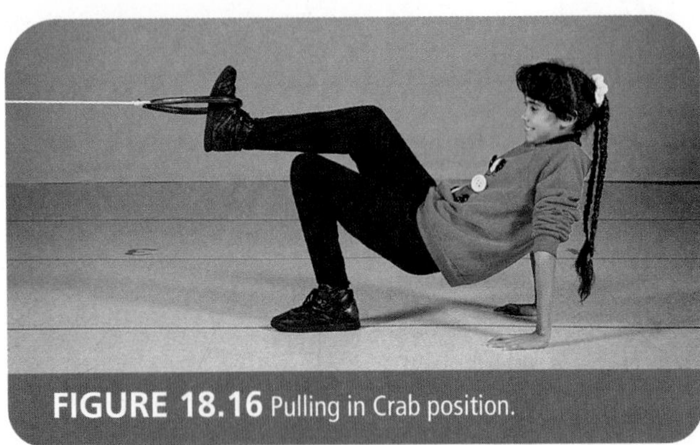

FIGURE 18.16 Pulling in Crab position.

6. Partners face each other and stand on one foot only. Students try to pull each other off balance without losing their own balance. If the raised foot touches the floor, the other person wins.
7. Partners stand with opposite sides toward each other. They hold a tug-of-war rope with opposite hands and move apart until the rope is taut. By pulling and giving on the rope, they try to make the other person move the feet. The legs must be kept straight, and only the arms can be used in the contest.
8. Students stand 10 feet away from the rope, which is on the floor. On signal, they run to the rope, pick it up, and have a tug-of-war. Students can start from different positions, such as push-up, curl-up, or Crab.
9. Instead of pulling each other across a line, each partner tries to pull the other toward a peg or bowling pin placed behind them and pick up the object.
10. Tie two individual ropes together at the center so four loops are available for pulling. Use four cones to form a large square; four children stand inside it and compete to see who can pick up a cone first.
11. Two children pull against two others. Be sure the rope loops are big enough so two students can hold each end. They can use right hands only or left hands only.
12. For Frozen Tug-of-War, two children hold a rope, each with both hands on a loop. The children stand close enough together to give the rope some slack. A third child grasps the rope to make a 6-inch bend at the center, and the contestants then pull the rope taut so there is no slack (Figure 18.17). On "Go," the third child drops the loop, and the opponents try to pull each other off balance. The feet are "frozen" to the floor; the player who moves either foot loses.

FIGURE 18.17 Frozen Tug-of-War.

13. Hawaiian Tug-of-War uses two parallel lines about 20 feet apart. The game is between two people; as many pairs as are in a class can play. Lay a partner tug-of-war rope on the floor at right angles to, and midway between, the two lines. Each player stands about 1 foot from one end of the rope. On signal, they pick up the rope and pull against each other. The goal is to pull the other child far enough to be able to touch the line behind. Children must not reach down and pick up the rope until the teacher says, "Hula!" To trick the students, the teacher can use other commands, such as "Go" and "Begin!"
14. Group contests are possible. (See Figure 10.28 on page 197 for rope arrangements suitable for groups.)

PARTNER RESISTANCE ACTIVITIES

In partner resistance activities, students follow exercise principles of using sufficient force (near maximum), maintaining resistance through the full range of motion for 8 to 10 seconds, and stabilizing the base so the selected part of the body is exercised. The force is a controlled pull, not a tug. The partner should not be compelled to move out of position. Much of the exercise centers on the hands and arms, but other parts of the body come into play as braces. Partners work together, both in the same position.

As in other activities, grip can be varied. The upper grip (palms down) and the lower grip (palms up) are usually used. Occasionally, a mixed grip—one hand palm down and one hand palm up—is used. Be sure the right and left sides of the body receive equal treatment.

Partners Standing with Sides Toward Each Other

1. Use a lower grip. Do a flexed-arm pull, with elbows at right angles.
2. Use an upper grip. Extend the arm from the side at a 45-degree angle. Pull toward the side.
3. Use a lower grip. Extend the arm completely overhead. Pull overhead.
4. Loop the rope around one ankle. Stand with feet apart. Pull with the closer foot.

Partners Standing, Facing Each Other

1. Use a lower grip. Do a flexed-arm pull, with one and then both hands.
2. Use an upper grip. Extend the arms at the side or down. Pull toward the rear.
3. Use an upper grip. Pull both hands straight toward chest.
4. Use an upper grip. Extend the arms overhead. Pull backward.

Partners Sitting, Facing Each Other

1. Repeat the activities described for standing position (Figure 18.18).
2. Hook the rope with both feet. Pull.

Partners Prone, Facing Each Other

1. Use an upper grip. Pull directly toward the chest.
2. Use a lower grip. Do a flexed-arm pull.

Partners Prone, Feet Toward Each Other

1. Hook the rope around one ankle. With knee joint at a right angle, pull.
2. Try with both feet together.

FIGURE 18.18 Partner resistance activity in sitting position.

ACTIVITIES WITH GYM SCOOTERS

When used properly, gym scooters are excellent for developmental activity. The minimum number is one scooter for two children, unless the scooters are used for relays only. In that case, four or six scooters suffice for an average-sized class. Children can work individually or in pairs. A child working alone can do many different combinations by varying the propulsion method and the method of supporting the body. Children can propel the scooter with their feet, their hands, or both. They can kneel, sit, or lie prone, supine, and even sideways. Body weight can be wholly or partially supported on the scooter. The variation of space factors, particularly direction, adds interest.

When children work in pairs, one child rides and the other pushes or pulls. The rider's weight may be wholly supported by the scooter or partially supported by the scooter and partially supported by the partner. Educational movement methodology is applicable to scooter work, but teachers must ensure that scooter activities are developmental and not just a free play session.

FOR MORE INFORMATION

WEBSITES

Body Management Skills

www.learning.gov.ab.ca/physicaleducationonline
http://rubistar.4teachers.org/index.php
www.extension.iastate.edu/Publications/PM1359B.pdf
www.uen.org/Lessonplan/preview.cgi?LPid=945
www.mpsaz.org/tafttest/programdescrip.html

General Physical Education

www.pelinks4u.org/index.htm
www.pecentral.org
http://pe4life.com

19 Rhythmic Movement Skills

ESSENTIAL COMPONENTS OF QUALITY PROGRAMS

I. Organized around content standards
II. Student-centered and developmentally appropriate
III. Physical activity and motor skill development form the core of the program
IV. Teaches management skills and self-discipline
V. Promotes inclusion of all students
VI. Focuses on process over product
VII. Promotes lifetime personal health and wellness
VIII. Teaches cooperation and responsibility and promotes sensitivity to diversity

NATIONAL STANDARDS FOR PHYSICAL EDUCATION*

1. Demonstrates competency in motor skills and movement patterns needed to perform a variety of physical activities.
2. Demonstrates understanding of movement concepts, principles, and tactics as they apply to the learning and performance of physical activities.
3. Participates regularly in physical activity.
4. Achieves and maintains a health-enhancing level of physical fitness.
5. Exhibits responsible personal and social behavior that respects self and others in physical activity.
6. Values physical activity for health, enjoyment, challenge, self-expression, and/or social interaction.

*National Association for Sport and Physical Education (NASPE), 2004.

Activities in this chapter are selected expressly for developing rhythmic movement skills. The activities progress from easy to more complex and from Developmental Level I to III. Students develop social skills and a positive self-concept when rhythmic activities are taught in a sensitive, educational way. Schedule rhythmic activities as you would other phases of the yearly physical education program. Most dances use skills and steps that children learn in sequence.

Outcomes

- Know where to find sources of rhythmic accompaniment.
- Understand the inherent rhythmic nature of all physical activity.
- Outline components of the yearly rhythmic movement program, and identify accompanying activities and skill progressions.
- Describe instructional procedures and ideas to facilitate implementation of rhythmic movements into the yearly program.
- Cite creative rhythms, movement songs, folk dances, and other dance activities that are used as learning experiences in physical education.
- Describe dance progressions appropriate to the various levels of children's development.

RHYTHM is the basis of music and dance. Rhythm in dance is simply expressive movement either with or without music. All body movements tend to be rhythmic—from the beating of the heart to swinging a tennis racket, wielding a hammer, and throwing a ball. Most movements in physical education class also contain elements of rhythm. Movement to rhythm begins early in the child's school career and continues throughout. Rhythmic activities are particularly appropriate for younger children. Much of the Developmental Level I program focuses on such activities. One problem in incorporating rhythmic activities is the vast amount of material available; teachers must judiciously make hundreds of choices to present a broad, progressive program. Another problem is that many teachers are hesitant about the subject area. But if you prepare properly, you soon will become comfortable with rhythmic activities and find that they are a favorite among children.

Early experiences center on functional and creative movement forms. Locomotor skills are inherently rhythmic in execution, and adding rhythm can enhance students' development of these skills. An important component of children's dance is fundamental rhythms. Instruction begins with and capitalizes on locomotor skills that children already possess—walking, running, hopping, and jumping.

Rhythmic activities are a vehicle for expressive movement. These activities offer opportunity for broad participation and personal satisfaction for all, as children personalize their responses to a movement, and create unique rhythmic responses within action songs and dances.

IMPLEMENTING THE RHYTHMIC MOVEMENT PROGRAM

The rhythmic program should be balanced and include activities from each category of rhythmic movement. Table 19.1 shows recommended types of rhythmic activities for each developmental level.

SKILL PROGRESSIONS

Another factor in program construction is the progression of basic and specific dance steps. Dances employing the following skills and steps appear in each of the respective developmental level programs.

Developmental Level I

Children in Developmental Level I focus on creative rhythms and movement songs. Students learn simple folk dances and mixers with a focus on one or two locomotor movements. They also use simple mixers in learning to find new partners and move rhythmically. At this level, teachers focus on activities requiring a minimum of instruction while giving students a positive experience with rhythms.

TABLE 19.1 Types of rhythmic activity

	Developmental Level		
Activity	**I**	**II**	**III**
Creative rhythms	X		
Folk dances	X	X	X
Line dances		X	X
Mixers	X	X	X
Aerobic dancing		X	X
Square dancing			X
Rope jumping to music	S	X	X
Musical games	S	S	S
Rhythmic gymnastics (refer to Chapter 17)			

Note: X means that the activity is an integral part of the program. S means that the activity receives only minor emphasis.

Developmental Level II

At this level, greater practice on folk dances and line dances includes combinations of locomotor skills, such as the step-hop and the grand right and left. Marching, basic tinikling steps, and introductory square dancing steps are taught as skill improves. All the activities are taught with an emphasis on mastering simple locomotor skills rather than performing the dances perfectly.

Developmental Level III

Developmental Level III students begin to learn more difficult steps such as the grapevine step, schottische, polka, intermediate tinikling steps, two-step, advanced tinikling steps, square dancing, and all steps introduced at earlier levels. Developmentally, these students are not yet comfortable moving with partners of the opposite sex, so activities are modified to allow for individual activity.

UNDERSTANDING RHYTHMIC ACCOMPANIMENT

Music has essential characteristics that children should recognize, understand, and appreciate. These characteristics are also present to varying degrees in other purely percussive accompaniment.

Tempo is the speed of the music. It can be constant, show a gradual increase (acceleration), or decrease (deceleration).

Beat is the underlying rhythm of the music. Some musicians refer to the beat as the pulse of the music. The beat can be even or uneven. Music with a pronounced beat is easier to follow.

Certain notes or beats in a rhythmic pattern receive more force than others, and this defines *accent*. Accent is generally expressed by a more forceful movement in a sequence of movements.

A *measure* is a group of beats made by the regular occurrence of a heavy accent. Usually the accent is applied to the first beat of a measure. A measure represents the underlying beat enclosed between two adjacent bars on a musical staff.

The *intensity* of music can be loud, soft, light, or heavy. Mood is related to intensity but carries the concept deeper into human feelings. Music can reflect many moods—happiness, sadness, gaiety, fear, or stateliness.

A *phrase* is a natural grouping of measures. Phrases of music are put together into rhythmic *patterns*. Children should learn to recognize when a pattern repeats or changes.

SOURCES OF RHYTHMIC ACCOMPANIMENT

Essential to any rhythmic program is accompaniment that encourages desired motor patterns and expressive movement. Children are more likely to move to a rhythm that is stimulating, appropriate for the expected responses, and appealing. Skillful use of a drum or tambourine adds much to rhythmic experiences. A major use of the drumbeat is to guide the movement from one pattern to another by signaling tiny increments of change with light beats that control the flow. The motion in striking is essentially a wrist action, not an arm movement.

Each school and teacher should build a collection of recorded music. Sets created especially for physical education movement patterns and dance are available from various sources (see information on Wagon Wheel Records on page 406). Physical education teachers should store their CDs or tapes in the physical education facility rather than the school library. Arrange storage so that each recording has its assigned place and is readily available.

CREATIVE RHYTHMS

Creativity should be part of all dance and rhythmic activities, and the scope of the activity will determine the degree of freedom. Creative rhythms, however, are a special program area in which creativity is the goal and functional movement is secondary. The emphasis is on the process, not the movement outcomes.

Creativity manifests itself in the opportunity for each child to respond expressively within the scope of the movement idea, which can range from total freedom to stated limits. Teachers must respect children's judgment, and look for original interpretations. Guide the movement patterns by suggestions, questions, encouragement, and challenges that help children structure their ideas and add variety. Careful guidance is necessary to fan the spark of self-direction; freedom alone does not automatically develop creativity.

INSTRUCTIONAL PROCEDURES

1. Provide appropriate music or rhythmic background; otherwise, movement can become stilted. Establish an atmosphere of creative freedom, making the class comfortable and relaxed.
2. When analyzing the setting, ask, "What is the basic idea? What expressive movements can be expected? What are the guidelines or boundaries of movement? What space are the children to use?"
3. Listening is an important element, because children must understand the mood or sense of the rhythmic background. Some questions for the children are, "What does the music make us think of?" and "What does the music tell us to do?" If the movement or interpretation is preselected, waste no time in starting. Provide enough music so children can grasp the effect. Have them clap the beat if necessary and then move into action.

4. Use action-directing statements such as, "Let's pretend we are . . .," "Let's try being like . . .," "Try to feel like a . . .," and "Make believe you are. . . ."
5. In some lessons, the initial focus may be on selecting appropriate rhythmic background. In this instance children formulate a creative rhythm of the dramatic type and then seek suitable music for their dance.
6. Give children time to develop and try their ideas. This is an open-ended process with a variety of solutions. Coaching and guidance are important aspects at this stage. Application of time, space, force, flow, and body factors is essential. Encourage large, free movement of all body parts. Use the entire area, and fill in the empty places in general space. Allow time for exploration.

EXPRESSIVE MOVEMENT

Children can express moods and feelings and show reactions to colors and sounds by improvising dances or movements that demonstrate different aspects of force, or gestures that depict different feelings. After playing a piece of music, discuss its qualities and ask the children how it makes them feel. Children may interpret the music differently. Moods can be described as happy, lighthearted, sad, brave, fearful, cheerful, angry, solemn, silly, stately, sleepy, funny, cautious, bold, or nonchalant.

Identification

There are endless sources for identification and interpretation. Children can assume the identity of a familiar character, creature, or object. These ideas may be useful.

1. Animals—elephants, ducks, seals, chickens, dogs, rabbits, lions, and others
2. People—soldiers, firefighters, sailors, nurses, various kinds of workers, forest rangers, teachers, and cowboys and cowgirls
3. Play objects—seesaws, swings, rowboats, balls, various toys, and other common articles
4. Make-believe creatures—giants, gnomes, witches, trolls, dragons, pixies, and fairies
5. Machines—trains, planes, jets, rockets, automobiles, bicycles, motorcycles, tractors, and elevators
6. Circus characters—clowns, trained animals, trapeze artists, tightrope walkers, jugglers, acrobats, and bands
7. Natural phenomena—fluttering leaves, grain, flowers, rain, snow, clouds, wind, tornadoes, hurricanes, and volcanoes

Dramatization

Dramatization and rhythm are useful vehicles for group activity. Suitable background music or rhythmic accompaniment is required. Excellent recordings are available, from short numbers lasting 1 or 2 minutes to more elaborate productions such as those found in the Dance-a-Story series (RCA Victor).

Here are some useful ideas for dramatic rhythms.

1. Build a house, garage, or other structure.
2. Make a snowman, throw snowballs, go skiing.
3. Fly a kite, go hunting or fishing, go camping.
4. Act out stories about astronauts, cowboys and cowgirls, firefighters, explorers.
5. Interpret familiar stories, such as "Sleeping Beauty," "The Three Bears," or "Little Red Riding Hood."
6. Do household tasks such as chopping wood, picking fruit, mowing the lawn, cleaning the yard, washing dishes, and vacuuming.
7. Celebrate holidays such as Halloween, the Fourth of July, Thanksgiving, or Christmas; or dramatize the seasons.
8. Play sports such as football, basketball, baseball, track and field, swimming, tennis, and golf.
9. Divide the class in groups of 3 or 4, and assign each group a sport other than one of the major sports. Have them develop a series of movements dramatizing that sport to the class. Have the remaining groups guess which sport is being presented. Slow-motion movements add to this activity.
10. Plan a trip through a haunted house. Use Halloween music for this activity.
11. Have the children make a motor. One student starts by getting into a position of choice in the middle of the floor and by putting one body part in motion. The motion should be a steady, rhythmic movement. The remaining students, one at a time, attach onto the first person, and each person puts one body part in motion. After all are attached, a machine with many moving parts is the result.
12. Act out the children's favorite parts in popular movies. Having the children perform to the original soundtrack makes the performance more realistic.
13. Select a favorite poem ("Old Mother Hubbard," "Pat-a-Cake," "The Giant") and design a sequence of activities to fit the meaning of the poem. Stories have excellent appeal.

To learn how an idea can be exploited for a lesson on creative rhythm, consider an activity called "The Wind and the Leaves." One or more children are chosen to be the wind, and the other children are the leaves. Two kinds of rhythm are needed; a tambourine can be used. The first rhythm is high, fast, and shrill, indicating the blowing of the wind. The intensity and tempo illustrate the speed and force of the wind. The second rhythm is slow, measured, and light, to represent the leaves fluttering in the still air and finally coming to rest at various positions on the ground. During the first rhythm, children representing the wind act out a heavy gust. While this is going on, the leaves show what it is like to be blown about. During the second rhythm, the wind is still and the leaves flutter to the ground. Other characterizations can be added. For example, street sweepers can come along and sweep up the leaves.

Another lesson strategy is to divide the class into groups and ask each group to develop and act out an idea with percussive accompaniment. Each group then performs for the others. After each group performs, the other groups guess what they interpreted. In this game, keep the interpretations brief.

FOLK DANCES

A *folk dance* is defined as a traditional dance of a particular culture. In this concept, a definite pattern or dance routine is usually specified and followed. Folk dancing is one phase of a child's education that can assist in bringing about international understanding. A country's folk music often reflects its way of life and many other habits. From these dances, children gain an understanding of why people from certain countries act and live as they do, even though modern times may have changed their lifestyle from that of days gone by.

Folk dances in Developmental Level I consist of fundamental locomotor skills, either singly or in combination. Dances with more specialized steps, such as the two-step, polka, and schottische, are found in Developmental Levels II and III. The first consideration when teaching folk dance is to determine whether children know the basic skills required for the dance. If a skill needs to be taught, it can be handled in one of two ways. The first is to teach the skill separately, before teaching the dance. The second is to teach the dance in its normal sequence, giving specific instructions when the skill appears. The first method is often best, because children can concentrate solely on learning the skill.

Rhythmic movements require students to be aware of other students in their area. This should be reinforced throughout the lesson.

TEACHING NEW DANCES

Learning to move rhythmically is the underlying goal of folk dancing. Unfortunately, many students (often boys) develop negative attitudes and feelings of failure about rhythmic activities. Effective teachers have long recognized the need to modify sport activities to ensure that students learn skills correctly and experience success. Modifications, such as using smaller balls, lower baskets, and slower-moving objects, are now commonplace in most elementary school physical education activities. Interestingly, when teaching rhythmic activities, teachers often discard this approach. Dances are taught with precision and emphasis on "doing it right," instead of modifying them so they are appealing and easier to learn. Here are some guidelines for modifying rhythmic activities to increase the likelihood of success.

1. *Slow down the music.* Children's first contact with the activity must be successful. No student wants to be embarrassed because he or she is out of step. If students are still not doing well, stop the music and walk them through it. If the footwork is difficult, repeat the steps a number of times. Start from the beginning each time, so students who are lost can begin anew.
2. *In general, if the dance is short, use the whole-teaching approach.* If the dance is longer and has several parts, use the part–whole method and teach one part at a time. For example, have children learn half of a two-part dance or one-third of a three-part dance and then put that part to music. After learning all the parts, students can try the complete dance.
3. *When introducing a new dance, place students in scatter formation.* Circles and formations make some students feel as if others are looking directly at them. If they are self-conscious about their ability, a circle formation may be intimidating. A scattered formation allows these children to move to an area where fewer peers can see them perform.
4. *Avoid the use of partners when teaching a new activity.* Because using partners makes many dances more complex, add them only after students master the basic steps. Also avoid forcing intermediate-grade students to choose a partner of the opposite sex unless they wish to do so. Let students who do not want to dance with a partner perform the steps alone.
5. *Avoid the left-right and clockwise-counterclockwise orientation when introducing a new dance.* Anytime students are asked to move in a specified direction, it increases the possibility of error. Let students choose the direction they would like to move when learning new steps. Later, when students master the steps, teachers can add various orientations and formations.

6. *To avoid stressing students, perform a dance once or twice in a daily lesson.* Presenting several dances, rather than one or two in depth, allows students who are having difficulty to start with a clean slate on a new dance. Come back to a difficult dance and practice it in a later lesson. Some students panic when they experience difficulty, and the increased stress limits their ability to learn.
7. *Teach rhythmic activities in the same way sport skills are taught.* Teachers expect that students will make mistakes, regardless of their ability level; baskets are missed and passes are dropped. Treat rhythmic activities like sport skills, and know that perfection is virtually impossible to reach. Use rhythmic activities to teach students to move rhythmically, not to showcase one or two dances learned perfectly. If teachers accept student errors, students learn that rhythms are fun and worth trying.
8. *Dances that emphasize strong movements such as hand clapping and foot stomping appeal to boys.* Since boys are often "hard to sell" on rhythmic activities, it makes sense to introduce them to some activities that include strong, bold physical movements.

MODIFYING RHYTHMIC ACTIVITIES

Folk dances are traditional rhythmic activities people have done for generations. The traditional music and style may not appeal to some children in a school setting, but with a few modifications, the dances are easier to learn. Table 19.2 shows how some common folk dances can be modified to increase student interest and increase the ease of learning.

Another way to motivate students is to use current music and change traditional dances into line dances. Line dances can motivate students to learn new steps without worrying about a partner. Here are some folk and popular dances that can be done as line dances.

- Popcorn, page 434
- Jiffy Mixer, page 435
- Cotton-Eyed Joe, page 443
- Jessie Polka, page 446
- Teton Mountain Stomp, page 443
- Alley Cat, page 445

TABLE 19.2 Examples of dance modifications

Dance	Skills	Modifications	Formation
The Bird Dance	Skipping or walking, elbow swing or star	Good introductory dance for all levels	Scattered
Shortnin' Bread	Sliding, turning with a partner, clapping	Slow music; practice without partner	Scattered first, then with partner
Jump Jim Jo	Jumping, running, draw step	No partner; move in any direction	Scattered
Eins Zwie Drie	Walking, heel-toe step, sliding	No partner, no numbering; slide any direction; play giant cymbals	Scattered, then facing center of area
Wild Turkey Mixer	Walking, elbow swing	Groups of three—scattered; center person with pinny; do not mix when learning	Scattered first, then circle formation
Irish Washerwoman	Walking, swinging, promenade position	No partners; swing and promenade the closest partner or move to the center for a partner; emphasize clapping and stomping	Facing center
Oh, Susanna	Walking, promenade, grand right and left	Half of class with pinnies; use a wild grand right and left; go to center and find partner if left without one	Facing center
Jessie Polka	Step and touch, two-step or polka	Slow down music; no partners; practice step and touch first	Scattered, students can hook on if they desire
Limbo Rock	Touch step, swivel step, jump-clap-clap	Slow down music; teach steps and add together	Scattered
Inside-Out Mixer	Wring the dishrag, walk, change partners	Practice without music; no mixing until learned	Groups of three
Teton Mountain Stomp	Walking, two-step	Do individually; emphasize clapping; move in any direction; no side car or banjo position	Scattered

ARRANGING FOR PARTNERS

Arranging for partners can be deeply hurtful or embarrassing for some children. To be acceptable, a method of arranging for partners must prevent any children from being rejected or overlooked. Some suggestions follow.

1. Dancing boy-girl fashion in the traditional way is not necessary. When starting a dance program with students who are uncomfortable with each other, allow students to dance with a partner of their choice. If this places boys with boys and girls with girls, allow that arrangement. Refer to the partners as number 1 and number 2, or have one partner in each pair wear a colored pinny. Instead of giving directions for the girls or for the boys, call it out as "The students in red on the outside of the circle do . . . ." Change partners frequently; sooner or later the children will dance with members of the opposite sex. This chapter uses the designations "Partner A" and "Partner B" for the leading and following positions. Gender references alternate by example.
2. In a follow-the-leader approach, put on some brisk marching music and begin walking among the students, who are scattered in general space. As you pass students, tap them on the shoulder and ask them to "fall in" behind you. Subsequent students go to the end of the line when tagged until all students are chosen. You can then either arrange students as desired, or separate those who do not work well together.
3. Boys join hands in a circle formation, and each girl steps behind a boy. Reverse the procedure and have girls make the circle, or have half of the class wear red pinnies and form the circle.
4. Girls stand in a circle facing counterclockwise, while boys form a circle around them facing clockwise. Both circles move in the direction they are facing and stop on signal. The girl takes the boy nearest her as her partner.
5. For square dances, take the first four couples from any of the previous formations to form a set. Continue until all sets are formed.

CDS AND CASSETTE TAPES FOR FOLK DANCES

Quality recordings are difficult to find. Wagon Wheel Records is a reliable source of music accompaniment for all the dances included in this chapter. You can order CDs, video, books, and supplies from the following address or website:

Wagon Wheel Records
16812 Pembrook Lane
Huntington Beach, CA 92649
Phone/Fax:(714) 846-8169
Website: www.wagonwheelrecords.net
E-mail: info@wagonwheelrecords.net

Each dance in this chapter includes a code indicating whether it is in CD (WWCD) or cassette (WWC) format, with a catalog number (e.g., -7054) identifying the source for ordering.

FORMATIONS FOR FOLK DANCES

Figure 19.1 illustrates the formations used for folk dances in this chapter. Each folk dance description begins by listing the records, skills, and formation to be used. If you are unsure about how the class should be arranged, consult Figure 19.1, which shows four types of formations: single-circle, double-circle, triple-circle, and others.

DANCE POSITIONS

In most dance positions, Partner A holds a hand or hands palms up and Partner B joins the grip with a palms-down position. The following dance positions or partner positions are common to many dances.

Partners Facing Position

In partners facing position, as the name suggests, the partners are facing. Partner A extends hands forward with palms up and elbows slightly bent. Partner B places hands in A's hands.

Side-By-Side Position

In side-by-side position (Figure 19.2, page 408), Partner A always has Partner B to the right. Partner A offers the right hand, held above the waist, palm up. B places the left hand in A's raised hand.

Closed Position

Closed position is the social dance position. Partners stand facing each other, shoulders parallel, and toes pointed forward. Partner A holds Partner B's right hand in A's left hand out to the side, at about shoulder level, with elbows bent. Partner A places the right hand on B's back, just below the left shoulder blade. B's left arm rests on A's upper arm, and B's left hand is on A's right shoulder.

Open Position

To go from closed to open position, Partner A turns to the left and Partner B to the right. Their arms stay in about the same position. Both face in the same direction and are side by side.

Promenade Position

Promenade position (Figure 19.3, page 408) is a crossed-arm position in which dancers stand side by side, facing the same direction. The partners hold each other's right hand in their right hand, and left hand in their left.

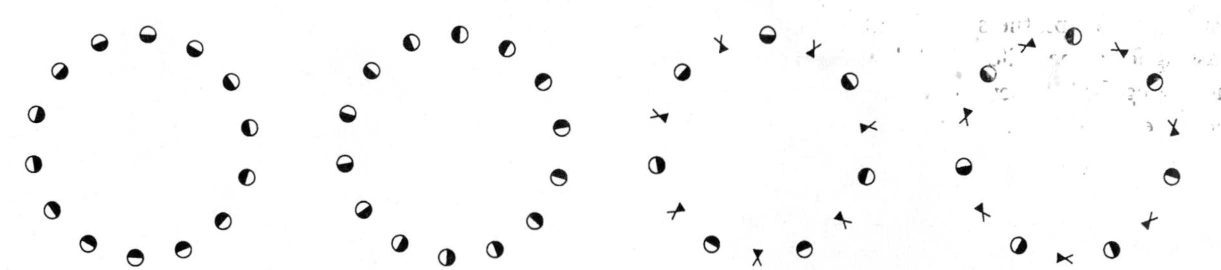

1. All facing center, no partners
2. All facing counterclockwise
3. By partners, all facing center
4. By partners, with partners facing

DOUBLE–CIRCLE FORMATIONS

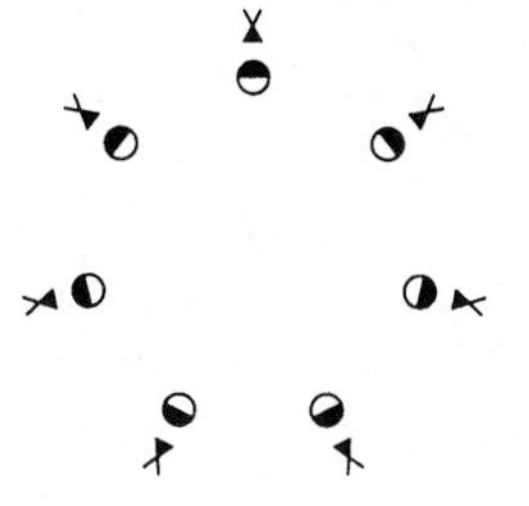

5. Partners facing each other

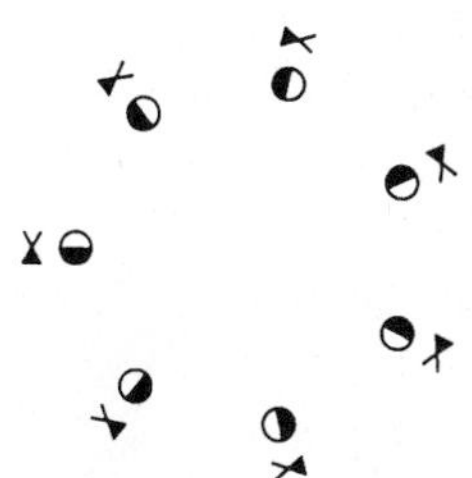

6. Partners side by side, facing counterclockwise

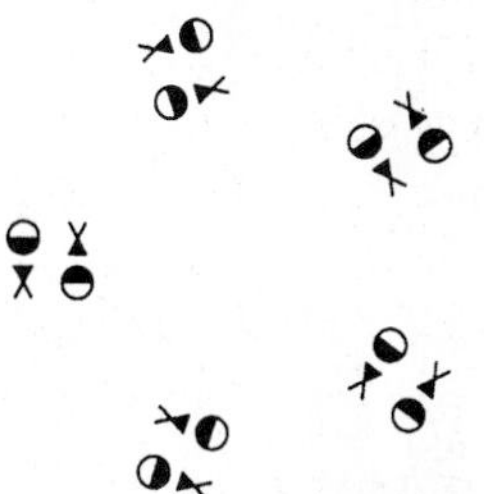

7. Sets of four, couples facing with girl on partner's right

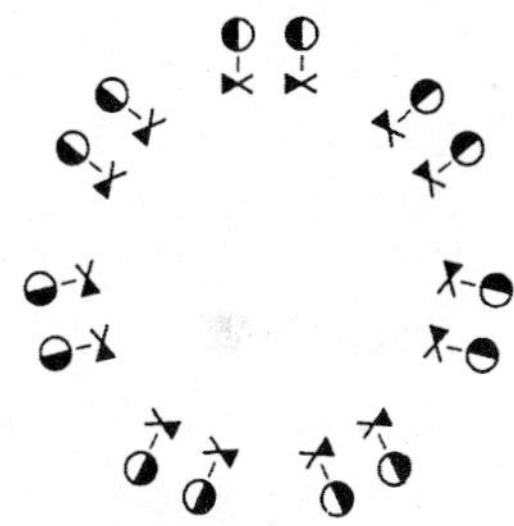

8. Sets of four, all facing counterclockwise

TRIPLE–CIRCLE FORMATIONS

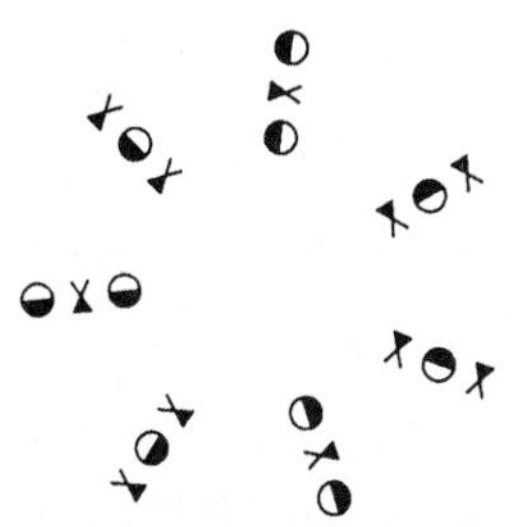

9. Standing side by side

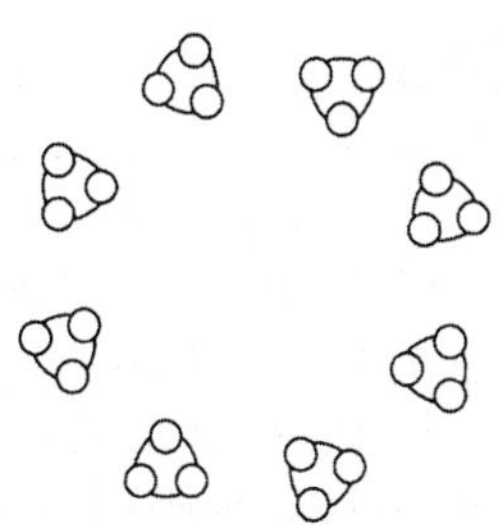

10. In small circles

OTHER FORMATIONS

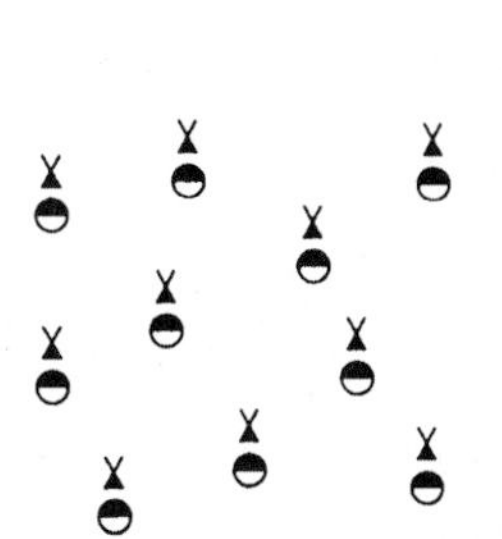

11. Partners in scattered formation

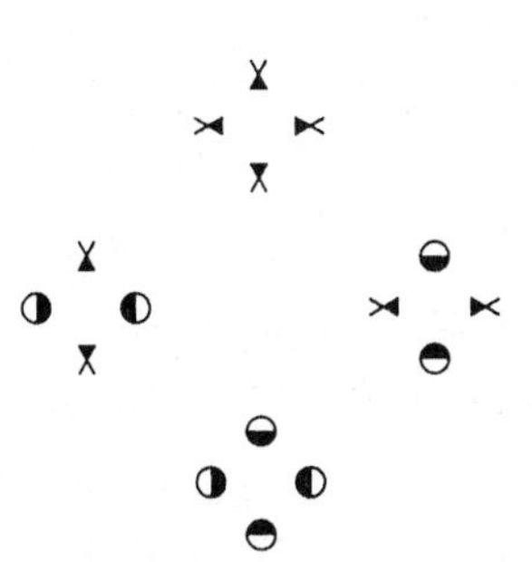

12. Groups of four, partners facing each other

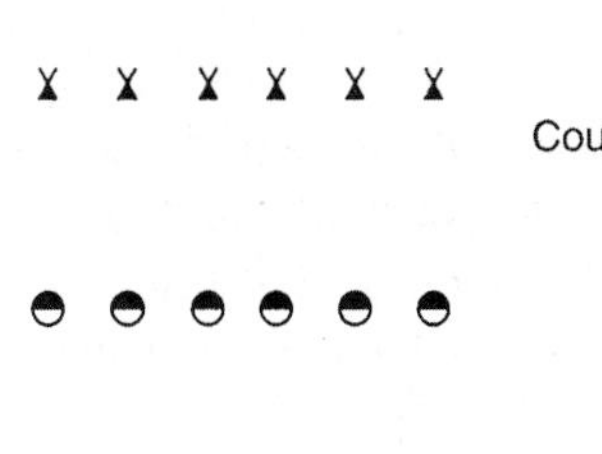

13. Longways set

Couple 1

Couple 2

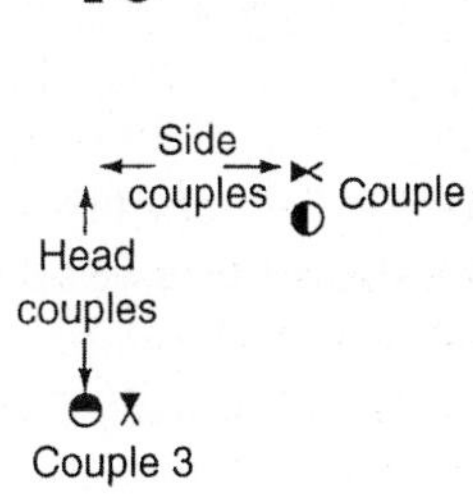

14. Square dance formation

FIGURE 19.1 Dance formations.

19

FIGURE 19.2 Side-by-side position.

FIGURE 19.3 Promenade position.

Varsouvienne Position

Partners stand side by side and face the same direction. Partner B is slightly in front and to the right of Partner A. A holds B's left hand in his or her left hand in front and at about shoulder height. B brings the right hand directly back over the right shoulder, and A reaches behind B at shoulder height and grasps that hand with his or her right hand.

PROGRESSION OF FOLK DANCES

The dances in this section start with the easiest and end with the most difficult. Dances are grouped into the three developmental levels to give you the widest possible latitude in selecting dances that fit the students' maturity and skills. For a quick and clear overview of the total dance program, see Table 19.3 (pages 409–411), which lists all dances in alphabetical order by developmental level, notes skills required for the dance, and includes page numbers for quick reference.

Regarding level of difficulty, teachers must be aware that if a group of students lacks a rhythmic background, some dances at their developmental level may be too difficult. For example, a sixth-grade class that lacks dance skills may need to begin with Developmental Level II dances. On the other hand, avoid boring a class by starting children on material below their maturity level.

DEVELOPMENTAL LEVEL I DANCES

Dances in this section contain introductory movement songs and folk dances using simple formations and uncomplicated changes. The movements are primarily basic locomotor skills and hand gestures or clapping sequences. There are dances both with and without partners. As the dances increase in difficulty, patterns become more definite, and more folk dances are included. Movements are still primarily of the simple locomotor type, with additional and varied emphasis on more complicated patterns.

Movin' Madness (American)

MUSIC SOURCE: WWCD-1044

SKILLS: Keeping time, creativity

FORMATION: Scattered

DIRECTIONS: The music is in two parts.

PART I: The tempo is slow, slow, fast-fast-fast. The children do any series of movements of their choice to fit this pattern, repeated four times. The dance involves large motor movements.

PART II: During the second part (chorus) of the music, the children do any locomotor movement

TABLE 19.3 Alphabetical listing of folk dances by Developmental Level

Dance	Skills	Page
	Developmental Level I	
Ach Ja	Walking, sliding	414
Ballin' the Jack	Sliding, do-si-do	413
Bleking	Bleking step, step-hop	419
Bombay Bounce	Hesitation step, side step	418
Carousel	Draw step, sliding	418
Children's Polka	Step-draw	416
Chimes of Dunkirk (Var. 1)	Turning in a small circle with a partner, changing partners	415
Chimes of Dunkirk (Var. 2)	Turning with a partner, skipping	417
Circassian Circle	Walking, skipping, promenade	421
Clapping Out	Rhythmic clapping	413
Danish Dance of Greeting	Running or sliding, bowing	414
Did You Ever See a Lassie?	Walking at $^{3}/_{4}$ time, creativity	411
Eins Zwei Drei	Walking, sliding	417
Hitch Hiker, The	Chug step, skipping	421
Hokey Pokey	Body identification, nonlocomotor movements	412
How D'Ye Do, My Partner?	Bowing, curtsying, skipping	413
Jingle Bells (Var. 1)	Elbow swing, skipping, sliding	420
Jolly Is the Miller	Marching	418
Jump Jim Jo	Jumping, running, draw step	416
Little Liza Jane	Marching, rope jumping, galloping	412
Looby Loo	Skipping or running, body identification	412
Movin' Madness	Keeping time, creativity	408
Muffin Man, The	Jumping, skipping	412
Nixie Polka	Bleking step	419
Patty Cake Polka	Heel and the polka step, sliding, elbow swing, skipping	421
Rhythm Sticks—It's a Small, Small World	Rhythmic tapping and manipulation of sticks	422
Seven Jumps	Step-hop, balance, control	414
Seven Steps	Running, hopping	422
Shoemaker's Dance	Skipping, heel and toe	416
Shortnin' Bread	Sliding, turning with a partner	415
Skip to My Lou	Skipping, changing partners	413
Turn the Glasses Over	Walking, wring the dishrag	420

(continued)

TABLE 19.3 Alphabetical listing of folk dances by Developmental Level (Continued)

Dance	Skills	Page
	Developmental Level I (Continued)	
Yankee Doodle	Walking, galloping, sliding, bowing	417
	Developmental Level II	
Apat Apat	Walking, star hold	432
Bingo	Walking, right-and-left grand	426
Bird Dance, The (Chicken Dance)	Skipping or walking, elbow swing or star	423
Crested Hen	Step-hop, turning under	430
Csebogar (Csehbogar)	Skipping, sliding, draw step, elbow swing	423
E-Z Mixer	Walking, elbow swing, or swing in closed position	429
Grand March	Controlled walking, marching, grand march figures	426
Green Sleeves	Walking, star formation, over and under	428
Gustaf's Skoal	Walking (stately), skipping, turning	431
Irish Washerwoman	Walking, elbow swing, promenade	429
Jiffy Mixer	Heel-and-toe step, chug step	435
Jingle Bells (Var. 2)	Skipping, promenade position, sliding, elbow swing	428
La Raspa	Bleking step, running, elbow swing	425
Los Machetes	Marching, rhythmic clapping	434
Lummi Sticks	Rhythmic movements	436
Oh, Susanna	Walking, promenade position, grand right and left	430
Pata Pata	Toe touches, knee lifts, quarter turns	433
Polly Wolly Doodle	Sliding, turning, walking	425
Pop Goes the Weasel	Walking, skipping, turning under	424
Popcorn	Toe touches, knee lifts, jumps	434
Red River Valley	Walk, buzz swing	434
Savila Se Bela Loza	Running step, crossover step, hop	433
Shoo Fly	Walking	432
Sicilian Circle	Walking, two-hand swing, wheel turn	435
Tinikling	Tinikling steps	437
Troika	Running step, turning under	431
Ve David	Walking, pivoting, buzz-step turn	429
Wild Turkey Mixer	Walking, elbow swing, partner change	425
	Developmental Level III	
Alley Cat	Grapevine step, touch step, knee lifts	445
Alunelul	Step behind step, grapevine step, stomping	449
Big Sombrero Circle Mixer	Circling, do-si-do, swing	451

TABLE 19.3 (Continued)

Dance	Skills	Page
	Developmental Level III (Continued)	
Circle Virginia Reel	Star, swing, do-si-do, promenade	451
Cotton-Eyed Joe	Heel-toe, two-step	443
D'Hammerschmiedsgselln	Clapping routine, step-hops	446
Doudlebska Polka	Polka step, walking, clapping pattern	447
Hora	Stepping sideways, step-swing	440
Horse and Buggy Schottische	Schottische step	448
Inside-Out Mixer	Wring the dishrag, walking, changing partners	446
Jessie Polka	Step and touch, two-step or polka step	446
Jugglehead Mixer	Two-step, elbow turn (forearm grasp)	442
Kalvelis	Polka step, swing, clapping pattern, grand right and left	447
Klumpakojis	Walking, starts, polka step	444
Korobushka	Schottische step, balance step, cross-out-together step, walking step	449
Limbo Rock	Touch step, swivel step, jump clap step	445
Oh Johnny	Shuffle step, swing, allemande left, do-si-do, promenade	450
Shindig in the Barn	Walking, do-si-do, swinging, sliding	450
Ten Pretty Girls	Walking, grapevine	445
Teton Mountain Stomp	Walking, banjo position, sidecar position, two-step	443
Trio Fun Mixer	Walking, do-si-do, star	451
Virginia Reel	Skipping, arm turn, do-si-do, sliding (sashay), reeling	441

in keeping with the tempo. They can use a step-hop or a light run with the tempo of Part II.

Have students clap the rhythm. They should pay particular attention to the tempo in Part I. The music is Bleking, a dance presented later. The music for "I See You" is also suitable, but note that the movements in Part I are repeated twice instead of four times.

Did You Ever See a Lassie? (Scottish)

MUSIC SOURCE: WWCD-7054; WWC-7054

SKILLS: Walking at 3/4 time, creativity

FORMATION: Single circle, facing halfway left, hands joined; one child in the center

DIRECTIONS:

MEASURES	ACTION
1–8	All walk (one step per measure) to the left in a circle with hands joined. (Walk, 2, 3, . . ., 8.) The child in the center gets ready to demonstrate some type of movement.
9–16	All stop and copy the movement suggested by the child in the center.

As the verse starts over, the center child selects another to do some action in the center and changes places with him or her.

19

Looby Loo (English)

MUSIC SOURCE: WWCD-7054; WWC-7054

SKILLS: Skipping or running, body identification

FORMATION: Single circle, facing center, hands joined

DIRECTIONS: The chorus is repeated before each verse. During the chorus, all children skip around the circle to the right. On the verse part of the dance, the children stand still, face the center, and follow the directions of the words. On the words "and turn myself about," they make a complete turn in place and get ready to skip around the circle again. Movements are definite and vigorous. On the last verse, they jump forward and then backward, shake vigorously, and then turn about.

Make the dance more fun and vigorous by changing the tasks. Try these: Right side or hip, left side or hip, big belly, backside.

Hokey Pokey (American)

MUSIC SOURCE: WWC-9126

SKILLS: Body identification, nonlocomotor movements

FORMATION: Single circle, facing center

DIRECTIONS: During the first four lines, the children act out the words. During lines 5 and 6, they hold their hands overhead with palms forward and do a kind of hula while turning around in place. During line 7, they stand in place and clap their hands three times.

The basic verse is repeated by substituting, successively, the left foot, right arm, left arm, right elbow, left elbow, head, right hip, left hip, whole self, and backside.

Teaching Hint

Encourage the students to make large, vigorous motions during the Hokey Pokey portions and during the turn around. This adds to the fun. The children should sing lightly while following the directions in the song.

Little Liza Jane (American)

MUSIC SOURCE: WWCD-FFD

SKILLS: Marching, rope jumping, galloping

FORMATION: Single circle, facing center

DIRECTIONS: Students do a different movement every 32 counts. After each movement, they perform the chorus.

MEASURES	ACTION
1–4	Introduction: Listen to the rhythm.
1–16	Feet together and bend the knees up and down.
17–32	Swing arm overhead like swinging a lasso (16 counts in each hand).
33–48	March eight steps to the center and eight steps back (repeat).
49–64	Jump rope for 32 counts.
65–80	Do arm circles (16 forward and 16 backward).
81–96	Gallop around the circle (16 gallops in each direction).
97–112	Join hands and circle (16 steps in each direction).

CHORUS: After each movement above, students perform the chorus. Roll the hands four times in front, then touch both hands to the knees, clap hands together, and push palms forward. Sing, "Roll Little Liza, Little Liza Jane" while performing the hand pattern. Perform this movement in 8 counts (roll, 2, 3, 4, knees, clap, palms for 2). Repeat the chorus four times.

The Muffin Man (American)

MUSIC SOURCE: WWCD-YR002; WWC-YR002

SKILLS: Jumping, skipping

FORMATION: Single circle, facing center, hands at sides. One child, the Muffin Man, stands in the circle, in front of another child of the opposite gender.

DIRECTIONS:

Verse 1: The children stand still and clap their hands lightly. The Muffin Man and his partner join hands and jump lightly in place while keeping time to the music. On the first beat of each measure, the partners take a normal jump, followed by a bounce in place (rebound) on the second beat.

Verse 2: The Muffin Man and his partner then skip around the inside of the circle individually and, near the end of the verse, each stands in front of a child, thus choosing a new partner.

Verse 1 is then repeated, with two sets of partners doing the jumping. During the repetition of verse 2, four children skip around the inside of the circle and choose partners. This procedure continues until all children have partners.

Let the children choose the name of a street to put in the verses.

Clapping Out (American)

MUSIC SOURCE: WWCD-FFD

SKILLS: Clapping hands rhythmically

FORMATION: Single circle, facing center

DIRECTIONS:

MEASURES	ACTION
Short introduction (8 counts)	
1–4	Hand pattern 1: Two hands touch own thighs, then touch knees of the person on the right, clap own knees, then touch knees of the person on the left. Repeat four times for 16 counts.
5–8	Hand pattern 2: Clap own knees; cross hands and clap own knees; uncross hands and clap own knees; clap out hands to the right and left of the person next to you at the same time. Other person's hands can pass over or underneath. Repeat four times for 16 counts.
9–12	Hand pattern 3: Clap own knees; clap own hands; snap fingers twice while bumping hips from side to side. Repeat four times.
13–16	Hand pattern 4: Clap own knees; clap own hands; snap fingers twice while bumping hips from side to side. Repeat four times.
17–32	Repeat entire dance with only the rhythm section of the music playing.
33–48	Repeat entire dance again. This time there is no music for hand patterns 1–3. The group continues clapping without accompaniment. On hand pattern 4, the music starts. If the group has maintained the correct rhythm, they are right in time with the music.

Skip to My Lou (American)

MUSIC SOURCE: WWCD-7054; WWC-7054

SKILLS: Skipping, changing partners

FORMATION: Scattered with a partner

DIRECTIONS: During the chorus, partners skip around the area. At the verse, everyone finds a new partner and continues skipping.

Ballin' the Jack (American)

MUSIC SOURCE: WWCD-FFD

SKILLS: Sliding, do-si-do

FORMATION: Double circle, partners facing each other

DIRECTIONS:

MEASURES	ACTION
1	Each person slaps own thighs twice.
2	Each person claps hands twice.
3	Each person does a scissors movement with hands twice (with palms down, slide right hand over left, then left hand over right).
4	Each person touches partner's hands twice.
5–16	Repeat the sequence above three more times.
17–18	Holding hands, slide four steps (step-close) to the outside circle person's right.
19–20	Slide four steps (step-close) and return to the original position.
21	Slide two steps (step-close) to the outside circle person's right.
22	Slide two steps (step-close) and return to the original position.
23–26	Drop hands and do-si-do, passing right shoulders for 8 counts back to the original position or partner.

VARIATION: To change partners after the do-si-do, outside people return to their original position. Inside circle partners move one space to the right after the do-si-do. On the last two beats of the do-si-do, move to the right diagonally to face a new partner.

How D'Ye Do, My Partner? (Swedish)

MUSIC SOURCE: WWCD-1041; WWC-07042

SKILLS: Bowing, curtseying, skipping

FORMATION: Double circle, partners facing, Partner A on inside

DIRECTIONS: Words in parentheses are teacher cues.

MEASURES	ACTION
1–2	Partners A bow to their partner. (Bow.)
3–4	Partners B bow. (Bow.)
5–6	A offers the right hand to B, who takes it with the right hand. (Join right hands.) Both turn to face counterclockwise. (Face counterclockwise.)
7–8	Couples join left hands in promenade position, preparing to skip when the music changes. (Join left hands.)
9–16	Partners skip counterclockwise in the circle, slowing down on measure 15. (Skip.) On measure 16, Bs stop and As move ahead to secure a new partner. (New partner.)

Danish Dance of Greeting (Danish)

MUSIC SOURCE: WWCD-1041; WWC-07042

SKILLS: Running or sliding, bowing

FORMATION: Single circle, all face center. Partner A stands to the left of Partner B.

DIRECTIONS:

MEASURES	ACTION
1	All clap twice and bow to partner. (Clap, clap, bow.)
2	Repeat, but turn your back to partner and bow to neighbor. (Clap, clap, bow.)
3	Stamp right, stamp left. (Stamp, stamp.)
4	Turn around in four running steps. (Turn, 2, 3, 4.)
5–8	Repeat the action of measures 1–4.
9–12	All join hands and run to the left for four measures. (Run, 2, 3, . . ., 16.)
13–16	Repeat the action of measures 9–12, taking light running steps in the opposite direction. (Run, 2, 3, . . ., 16.)

VARIATION: Instead of a running step, use a light slide.

Ach Ja ("Oh Yes"; German)

MUSIC SOURCE: WWCD-0860; WWC-0860

SKILLS: Walking, sliding

FORMATION: Double circle, partners facing counterclockwise, Partners A on the inside, inside hands joined

DIRECTIONS:

MEASURES	ACTION
1–2	Partners walk eight steps in the line of direction. (Walk, 2, 3, . . ., 8.)
3	Partners drop hands and bow to each other. (Bow.)
4	Each A then bows to the B on the left, who returns the bow. (Bow.)
5–8	Measures 1–4 are repeated.
9–10	Partners face each other, join hands, and take four slides in the line of direction. (Slide, 2, 3, 4.)
11–12	Partners take four slides clockwise. (Slide, 2, 3, 4.)
13	Partners bow to each other. (Bow.)
14	A bows to the B on the left, who returns the bow. (Bow.) To start the next dance, A moves quickly toward this B, who is the next partner.

Seven Jumps (Danish)

MUSIC SOURCE: WWCD-1043; WWC-3528

SKILLS: Step-hop, balance, control

FORMATION: Single circle, hands joined

DIRECTIONS: The dance involves seven jumps, each preceded by an action.

MEASURES	ACTION
1–8	The circle moves to the right with seven step-hops, one to each measure. On measure 8, all jump high in the air and reverse direction. (Step-hop, 2-hop, 3-hop, . . ., 7-hop, change direction.)
9–16	Circle to the left with seven step-hops. Stop on measure 16 and face the center. (Step-hop, 2-hop, 3-hop, . . ., 7-hop, face center.)

17	All drop hands, put their hands on hips, and lift the right knee with the toes pointed downward. (Knee up.)
18	All stamp the right foot to the ground on the signal note, then join hands on the next note. (Stamp.)
1–18	Repeat measures 1–18, but do not join hands.
19	Lift the left knee, stamp, and join hands.
1–19	Repeat measures 1–19, but do not join hands.
20	Put the right foot back and kneel on the right knee. Stand and join hands.
1–20	Repeat measures 1–20; do not join hands.
21	Kneel on the left knee. Stand and join hands.
1–21	Repeat measures 1–21; do not join hands.
22	Put the right elbow to the floor with the cheek on the fist. Stand and join hands.
1–22	Repeat measures 1–22; do not join hands.
23	Put the left elbow to the floor with the cheek on the fist. Stand and join hands.
1–23	Repeat measures 1–23; do not join hands.
24	Put forehead on the floor. Stand, join hands.
1–16	Repeat the first measures.

Teaching Hint

Danish men originally performed this dance as a competition. Those who made unnecessary movements or mistakes were eliminated.

VARIATION: To increase motivation, have students perform the dance with a parachute. Dancers hold the parachute taut with one hand during the step-hops. They use both hands to keep the chute taut for all jumps except the last, when they drop the chute to the floor and touch it with their foreheads.

Chimes of Dunkirk, Var. 1 (French–Belgian)

MUSIC SOURCE: WWCD-1042; WWC-07042

SKILLS: Turning in a small circle with a partner, changing partners

FORMATION: Double circle, partners facing

DIRECTIONS:

MEASURES	ACTION
1–2	Stamp three times in place, right-left-right. (Stamp, 2, 3.)
3–4	Clap hands three times overhead (chimes in the steeple). (Clap, 2, 3.)
5–8	Partner A places both hands on Partner B's hips; B places both hands on A's shoulders. Taking four steps, they turn around in place. (Turn, 2, 3, 4.) On the next 4 counts, Partner B (on the outside) moves one person to the left with four steps. (Change, 2, 3, 4.) Repeat the sequence from the beginning.

VARIATION: Instead of the turn described, students can do an elbow turn by linking right elbows.

Shortnin' Bread (American)

MUSIC SOURCE: WWCD-7050; WWC-7050

SKILLS: Sliding, turning with a partner

FORMATION: Scattered with partner

DIRECTIONS:

MEASURES	ACTION
1–2	Clap own hands.
3–4	Slap partner's hands, palms together.
5–6	Clap own hands.
7–8	Slap own thighs.
9–16	Repeat measures 1–8.
17–20	Couples slide to the right holding hands.
21–24	Circle holding hands.
25–32	Repeat measures 17–24, moving to the left.

Children's Polka (German)

MUSIC SOURCE: WWCD-07042; WWC-07042

FORMATION: Single circle of couples, partners facing

SKILLS: Step-draw

DIRECTIONS:

MEASURES	ACTION
1–2	Take two step-draw steps toward the center of the circle, ending with three steps in place. (Draw, draw, step, 2, 3.)
3–4	Take two step-draw steps away from the center, ending with three steps in place. (Draw, draw, step, 2, 3.)
5–8	Repeat the pattern of measures 1–4.
9	Slap own knees once with both hands; clap own hands once. (Slap, clap.)
10	Clap both hands with partner three times. (Clap, 2, 3.)
11–12	Repeat the pattern of measures 9 and 10.
13	Hop, placing one heel forward, and shake the forefinger at partner three times. (Scold, 2, 3.)
14	Repeat the "scolding" pattern with the other foot and hand. (Scold, 2, 3.)
15–16	Turn once around in place with four running steps and stamp three times in place. (Turn, 2, 3, 4; stamp, 2, 3.)

Shoemaker's Dance (Danish)

MUSIC SOURCE: WWCD-1042; WWC-07042

SKILLS: Skipping, heel and toe

FORMATION: Double circle, partners facing, with Partner A's back to the center of the circle

DIRECTIONS:

MEASURES	PART I ACTION
1	With arms bent and at shoulder height, and with hands clenched to form fists, circle one fist over the other in front of the chest. (Wind the thread.)
2	Reverse the circular motion and wind the thread in the opposite direction. (Reverse direction.)
3	Pull the elbows back vigorously twice. (Pull and tighten the thread.)
4	Clap own hands three times. (Clap, 2, 3.)
5–7	Repeat the pattern of measures 1–3.
8	Tap own fists three times to drive the nails. (Tap, 2, 3.)
	PART II ACTION
9–16	Partners face counterclockwise, inside hands joined. Skip counterclockwise, ending with a bow. (Skip, 2, 3, . . ., 15, bow.)

VARIATION: Dancers can try this variation of Part II.

9	Place the heel of the outside foot forward (counts 1 and), and point the toe of the outside foot to the back (2 and).
10	Take three running steps forward, starting with the outside foot and pausing on the last count.
11–12	Repeat the pattern of measures 9–10, starting with the inside foot.
13–16	Repeat the pattern of measures 9–12, entire "heel and toe and run, run, run" pattern dance, four times while singing Part II verse.

Jump Jim Jo (American)

MUSIC SOURCE: WWCD-1041

SKILLS: Jumping, running, draw step

FORMATION: Double circle, partners facing, both hands joined

DIRECTIONS:

MEASURES	ACTION
1–2	Do two jumps sideways, progressing counterclockwise, followed by three quick jumps in place. (Slow, slow, fast-fast-fast.)
3–4	Release hands and turn in place once, using four jumps (two jumps per measure). Finish facing partner and rejoin hands. (Jump, turn, 3, 4.)

5	Take two sliding steps sideways, moving counterclockwise. (Slide, slide.)
6	Partners face counterclockwise with inside hands joined and tap three times with the toe of the outside foot. (Tap, tap, tap.)
7–8	Take four running steps forward; then face partner, join both hands, and end with three jumps in place. (Run, 2, 3, 4; Jump, 2, 3.)

Yankee Doodle (American)

MUSIC SOURCE: WWCD-FDN

SKILLS: Walking, galloping, sliding, bowing

FORMATION: Scattered or open circle, facing counterclockwise

DIRECTIONS:

MEASURES	ACTION
1–4	All gallop eight steps. (Gallop, 2, . . ., 8.)
5–8	All stop, face center, point to cap and bow on word *macaroni.* (Stop, point, bow.)
9–12	All join hands, take six slides to the right, and stamp feet two times on word *dandy.* (Slide, 2, 3, . . ., 6; stamp, stamp.)
13–16	All slide six times to the left and clap hands two times on the word *candy.* (Slide, 2, 3, . . ., 6; clap, clap.)

VARIATION: Change the locomotor movements to fit the group's age and interests. Have the class create new movement patterns.

Eins Zwei Drei ("One, Two, Three"; German)

MUSIC SOURCE: WWCD-1042

SKILLS: Walking, sliding

FORMATION: Single circle of couples (Partner B to Partner A's right) facing the center and numbered alternately couple 1, 2, 1, 2

DIRECTIONS:

MEASURES	PART I ACTION
1–2	Couples 1 take three steps toward the center of the circle as they clap their hands by brushing them vertically like cymbals. (Forward, 2, 3, pause.)
3–4	Couples 1 repeat measures 1–2, walking backward to place. (Back, 2, 3, pause.)
5–8	Couples 1 face, join both hands, and take four slides toward the center of the circle and four slides back to place. Partner A starts with the left foot, Partner B with the right. (Slide, 2, 3, 4.)
9–16	Couples 2 repeat measures 1–8.
	PART II ACTION
17	Partner A turns and touches the right heel sideways while shaking the right index finger at partner. Partner B does the same with the left heel and left index finger. (Scold, 2, 3.)
18	Repeat measure 17 with the corner, reversing footwork and hands. (Scold, 2, 3.)
19–20	Repeat measures 17 and 18.
21–24	All join hands and circle left with eight slides. (Slide, 2, 3, . . ., 8.)
25–32	Repeat measures 17–24, reversing the direction of the slides. (Slide, 2, 3, . . ., 8.)

VARIATION: To facilitate learning, practice all steps individually in a scattered formation.

Chimes of Dunkirk, Var. 2 (French–Belgian)

MUSIC SOURCE: WWCD-1042

SKILLS: Turning with a partner, skipping

FORMATION: Single circle of couples, partners facing

DIRECTIONS:

MEASURES	ACTION
1–2	Stamp three times in place. (Stamp, 2, 3.)
3–4	Clap own hands three times. (Clap, 2, 3.)

5–8	Do a two-hand swing with partner. Join both hands with partner and turn once clockwise with eight running or skipping steps. (Swing, 2, 3, . . ., 8.)
	CHORUS ACTION
1–8	Circle left, singing, "Tra, la, la, la, la, ..." All join hands and circle left with 16 running or skipping steps, ending with a bow. (Run, 2, 3, . . ., 15; bow.)

Teaching Hints

1. Use this dance as a mixer by having all Partner Bs advance one partner to the left. Instead of a two-hand swing with partner, have dancers use the shoulder–waist position. A places a hand on B's waist, and B places both hands on A's shoulders.
2. To facilitate forming the circle for the chorus, use a 4-step turn instead of an 8-step turn on measures 5–8. This gives the dancers 4 counts to get ready for the circle formation and 4 counts to make the circle.

Bombay Bounce

MUSIC SOURCE: Any music with a definite, moderately fast beat

SKILLS: Hesitation step, side step

FORMATION: Scattered, all facing forward

DIRECTIONS:

PART I (16 counts): Perform a hesitation step to the left by taking a short step to the left and touching the right foot near the left while standing on the left foot. Do a hesitation step to the right by taking a step to the right and touching the left foot near the right. Start the dance by doing eight hesitation steps in place and a hand clap on each touch. (Left, touch and clap; right, touch and clap.) Repeat four times.

PART II (16 counts): Take two side steps to the left, then two to the right. Clap on counts 4 and 8. (Left, close; left, close and clap; right, close; right, close and clap.) Repeat the pattern.

PART III (16 counts): Take four side steps left and four side steps right. Clap only on count 8. (Left, close, left, close, left, close, left, close and clap.) Repeat to the right.

PART IV (16 counts): Take four steps forward and four steps backward, four steps forward and four steps backward. Clap on counts 4, 8, 12, and 16. (Forward, 2, 3, 4 and clap; backward, 2, 3, 4 and clap; forward, 2, 3, 4 and clap; backward 2, 3, 4 and clap.)

VARIATION: In Part IV, instead of four steps, use three steps and a kick (swing).

Carousel (Swedish)

MUSIC SOURCE: WWCD-1041

SKILLS: Draw step, sliding

FORMATION: Double circle, facing center. The inner circle, representing a merry-go-round, joins hands. The outer players, representing the riders, place their hands on the hips of the partner in front.

DIRECTIONS:

MEASURES	VERSE ACTION
1–16	Moving to the left, children take 12 slow draw steps and stamp on the last 3 steps. (Step, together, 2, 3, . . ., 12; stamp, stamp, stamp, rest.)
MEASURES	CHORUS ACTION
17–24	Moving left, speed up the draw step until it becomes a slide or gallop. Sing the chorus. (Slide, 2, 3, . . ., 8.)
25–32	Repeat measures 17–24 while moving to the right. (Slide, 2, 3, . . ., 8.)

During the chorus, the tempo increases and the movement changes to a slide. Have children take short, light slides to keep the circle in control.

VARIATION: Students can do this dance while holding the edge of a parachute.

Jolly Is the Miller (American)

MUSIC SOURCE: WWC-317

SKILLS: Marching

FORMATION: Double circle, partners face counterclockwise, A partners on the inside with inside hands joined. A "miller" is in the center of the circle.

DIRECTIONS: All sing. Students march counterclockwise, with inside hands joined. During the second line, when "the wheel goes round," the dancers turn their outside arm in a circle to form a wheel. Children change partners at the line "right steps forward and the left steps back." The miller then tries to get a partner. The child left without a partner becomes the next miller.

Bleking (Swedish)

MUSIC SOURCE: WWCD-1044; WWC-07042

SKILLS: Bleking step, step-hop

FORMATION: Single circle, partners facing, both hands joined; Partners A face counterclockwise and Partners B clockwise.

DIRECTIONS:

PART I: The Bleking Step—Cue by calling "Slow-slow, fast-fast-fast."

MEASURES	ACTION
1	Hop on the left foot and extend the right heel forward with the right leg straight. At the same time, thrust the right hand forward. Hop on the right foot, reversing the arm action and extending the left foot to rest on the heel. (Slow, slow.)
2	Repeat the action with three quick changes—left, right, left. (Fast-fast-fast.)
3–4	Beginning on the right foot, repeat the movements of measures 1 and 2. (Slow, slow, fast-fast-fast.)
5–8	Repeat measures 1–4.

PART II: The Windmills—Partners extend their joined hands sideways at shoulder height.

MEASURES	ACTION
9–16	Partners turn in place with a repeated step-hop. At the same time, the arms move up and down like a windmill. They turn clockwise, with A starting on the right foot and B on the left. After doing the step-hops (16), the partners are in their original places ready for Part I again. (Step-hop, 2-hop, 3-hop, . . ., 16-hop.)

VARIATIONS:

1. Change from original positions to a double circle, partners facing, A partners with back to the center. Part I is as described. For Part II, all face counterclockwise, and partners join inside hands. Partners do the basic schottische of "step, step, step, hop" throughout Part II (page 448).
2. An excellent variation is to do the dance with partners scattered. Part I is as described. In Part II, the children leave their partners and step-hop in various directions around the dancing area. Just before the music changes back to Part I, performers find a partner wherever they can and repeat the dance.
3. Bleking music is excellent for creative dance. Instruct the children to follow the Bleking rhythm of "slow, slow, fast-fast-fast" during Part I and do any kind of movement in place. In Part II, let them do a locomotor or other movement at will.

Nixie Polka (Nigarepolska; Swedish)

MUSIC SOURCE: WWCD-1041; WWC-572

SKILLS: Bleking step

FORMATION: Single circle, all facing center, with one or more children scattered inside the circle. There is 1 child in the center for each 12 dancers.

DIRECTIONS:

MEASURES	PART I ACTION
1–4	Bleking step: With hands joined, all spring lightly onto the left foot and extend the right foot forward, heel to ground, toe up. Next, spring lightly onto the right foot and extend the left foot forward. Do four slow Bleking steps. (Slow, slow, slow, slow.)
5–8	All clap hands once and shout, "Hey!" The center child then runs around the inside of the circle, looking for a partner and finally selecting one. They join both hands and run lightly in place until the music ends. This refrain is repeated, giving the children time to return to the center of the circle. (Clap, run.)
	PART II ACTION
1–4	The center dancer and partner, with both hands joined, repeat the action of measures 1–4. All dancers in the circle also repeat the action of measures 1–4. (Slow, slow, slow, slow.)

5–8	On count 1, all clap hands, shouting, "Hey!" The center dancer then about-faces and puts both hands on the shoulders of partner, who becomes the new leader. In this position, both shuffle around the inside of the circle, looking for a third person to dance with. The music is repeated again so partners can return to the center. (Clap, run.)
	PART III ACTION
1–4	The action of measures 1–4 is repeated, with the new dancer facing the circle and the two others facing the new dancer. (Slow, slow, slow, slow.)
5–8	On count 1, all clap hands, shouting, "Hey!" The two people in the center then about-face. All three now face the center to form a line of three dancers with a new leader, who looks for a fourth dancer. The music is repeated. (Clap, run.)

Students repeat the entire dance, accumulating dancers with each repetition.

Turn the Glasses Over (American–English)

MUSIC SOURCE: WWCD-W0F1

SKILLS: Walking, wring the dishrag

FORMATION: Single circle of couples in promenade position. Extra students are in the center.

DIRECTIONS:

MEASURES	VERSE ACTION
1–16	The couples walk forward, singing the verse. At the phrase "turn the glasses over," they raise their arms, keeping the hands joined, and turn under the raised arms, making one complete outward "dishrag" turn. Dancers must anticipate the turn and start in time to complete the movement by the end of the phrase.

MEASURES	CHORUS ACTION
1–16	Dancers in the outer circle continue walking while those in the inner circle turn and walk in the opposite direction. An extra dancer(s) joins one of the circles and continues with the group. At the phrase "girl in the ocean," students take the nearest person for a new partner. Those without a partner move to the center.

Jingle Bells, Var. 1 (Dutch)

MUSIC SOURCE: Any version of Jingle Bells or WWCD-FFD

SKILLS: Elbow swing, skipping, sliding

FORMATION: Double circle, partners facing, with both hands joined

DIRECTIONS:

MEASURES	ACTION
1–2	Partners take eight slides counterclockwise. (Slide, 2, 3, . . ., 8.)
3–4	Partners turn so they are back-to-back, and take eight more slides in the same direction. This move is best made by dropping the front hands and swinging the back hands forward until the dancers are standing back-to-back. They rejoin the hands that are now in back, making this move without losing rhythm. (Slide, 2, 3, . . ., 8.)
5–6	Repeat the action of measures 1 and 2. To get back to the face-to-face position, let go of the back hands and swing the front hands backward, allowing the bodies to pivot and face again. (Slide, 2, 3, . . ., 8.)
7–8	Repeat measures 3 and 4. (Slide, 2, 3, . . ., 8.)
	CHORUS ACTION
1	Clap own hands three times. (Clap, 2, 3.)
2	Clap both hands with partner three times. (Clap both, 2, 3.)
3	Clap own hands four times. (Clap, 2, 3, 4.)

4	Clap both hands with partner once. (Clap both.)
5–8	Right elbow swing with partner. Partners hook right elbows and swing clockwise with eight skips. (Swing, 2, 3, . . ., 8.)
9–12	Repeat clapping sequence of measures 1–4.
13–16	Left elbow swing with partner for eight skips, finishing in the original starting position, ready to repeat the entire dance with the same partner. Or, left elbow swing with partner for four skips, which is once around; then all children in the inner circle skip forward to the outer dancer ahead and repeat the entire dance from the beginning with a new partner. (Swing, 2, 3, . . ., 8.)

The Hitch Hiker (American)

MUSIC SOURCE: WWCD-FDN

SKILLS: Chug step (a short backward jump with the feet together on the floor), skipping

FORMATION: Double circle, partners facing each other with boys on inside facing out

DIRECTIONS:

MEASURES	ACTION
1–2	Introduction (no movement.)
1–2	Take two chugs away from partner and clap hands on each step. Jerk right thumb over right shoulder while twisting right foot with heel on the floor. Repeat. (Chug, chug, right, right.)
3–4	Same as measures 1–2 except use left thumb and foot. (Chug, chug, left, left.)
5–6	Same as measures 1–2 except use both thumbs and feet. (Chug, chug, both, both.)
7–8	Skip diagonally forward and to the right toward a new partner with four skips; continue with four more skips around your new partner with right hands joined and get ready to repeat the dance. (Skip, 2, 3, 4; around, 2, 3, 4.)

Repeat the sequence eight times.

Patty Cake (Heel-and-Toe) Polka (International)

MUSIC SOURCE: WWCD-FDN

SKILLS: Heel-and-toe polka step, sliding, elbow swing, skipping

FORMATION: Double circle, partners facing, A in the inner circle with back to the center. Partners join both hands. A's left foot and B's right foot are free.

DIRECTIONS:

MEASURES	PART I ACTION
1–2	Heel-toe twice with A's left and B's right foot. (Heel, toe, heel, toe.)
3–4	Take four slides sideways to A's left, moving counterclockwise. Do not transfer the weight on the last count. Finish with A's right and B's left foot free. (Slide, 2, 3, 4.)
5–8	Repeat the pattern of measures 1–4, starting with A's right and B's left foot, moving clockwise. Finish with the partners separated and facing. (Heel, toe, heel, toe; slide, 2, 3, 4.)
	PART II ACTION
9	Clap right hands with partner three times. (Right, 2, 3.)
10	Clap left hands with partner three times. (Left, 2, 3.)
11	Clap both hands with partner three times. (Both, 2, 3.)
12	Slap own knees three times. (Knees, 2, 3.)
13–14	Right elbow swing with partner. Partners hook right elbows and swing once around with four walking steps, finishing with A's back to center. (Swing, 2, 3, 4.)
15–16	Move to the left toward a new partner with four walking steps. (Left, 2, 3, 4.)

Repeat the entire dance with the new partner.

Circassian Circle (English)

MUSIC SOURCE: WWCD-FDN

SKILLS: Walking, skipping, promenade

FORMATION: Large single circle of couples, facing center with all hands joined

DIRECTIONS:

MEASURES	ACTION
1–2	Introduction (no movement.)
1–2	All walk four steps forward to center and four steps backward to starting place. (Walk 2, 3, 4; back, 2, 3, 4.)
3–4	Repeat measures 1 and 2. (Walk 2, 3, 4; back, 2, 3, 4.)
5–6	Girls walk four steps forward and four steps backward. (Girls, 2, 3, 4; back, 2, 3, 4.)
7–8	Boys walk four steps forward and then do a half-turn left and walk diagonally clockwise four steps to a new partner. (Boys, 2, 3, 4; move to new partner.)
9–10	Using a crossed-arm grip, new partners lean away from each other and skip eight steps clockwise once around each other. (Skip, 2, 3, . . ., 8.)
11–12	Without dropping hands, couples promenade counterclockwise for eight steps. They take the last two steps to stop and face the center, ready to do the dance again. (Promenade, 2, 3, . . ., 6; face center.)

Students repeat the dance four times.

Seven Steps (Austrian)

MUSIC SOURCE: WWCD-FDN

SKILLS: Running, hopping

FORMATION: Double circle, couples facing counterclockwise with inside hands joined

DIRECTIONS:

MEASURES	ACTION
1–2	Introduction (no movement.)
1–2	Start with outside foot and run seven steps forward counterclockwise, and then pause with weight on outside foot on count 8. (Run, 2, 3, . . ., 7, pause.)
3–4	Start with inside foot and run seven steps backward (clockwise), and then pause with weight on inside foot count 8. (Run, back, 3, 4, . . ., 7, pause.)
5	Release hands, turn away from partner; starting with the outside foot, run three steps away from partner and hop on the outside foot on count 4. (Away, 2, 3, hop.)
6	Turn and face partner; starting with the inside foot, run three steps toward partner and then hop on the inside foot on count 4. (Back, 2, 3, hop.)
7–8	Partners join right hands and run once around each other with eight running steps clockwise. (Swing, 2, 3, . . ., 8.)
9	Release hands, and turn away from partner. Starting with the outside foot, run three steps away from partner; on count 4, hop and turn on the outside foot to face diagonally toward new partner. (Apart, 2, 3, hop.)
10	Take three running steps to a new partner (inside partner moves counterclockwise forward diagonally toward new partner; outside partner moves clockwise backward diagonally to next partner). Then hop on count 4.
11–12	New partners join left hands and run once around each other with eight running steps counterclockwise. Finish in starting position with inside hands joined.

Perform the dance a total of five times.

Rhythm Sticks—It's a Small, Small World (American)

Rhythm sticks or Lummi sticks are 12 to 15 inches long. Activities may be done individually or in partners. This routine is done individually. Students hold the sticks with the thumb and the forefinger at about the bottom third of the stick.

MUSIC SOURCE: WWCD-2015; WWC-2015

SKILLS: Rhythmic tapping and manipulation of sticks

FORMATION: Children sitting cross-legged individually scattered around the area

DIRECTIONS:

MEASURES	CALL	ACTION
1–2	Down, cross, down, cross	Tap ends of both sticks on the floor, and then cross the arms over, tapping the sticks on the floor again.
3–4	Down, cross, down, cross	Repeat.
5–6	Down, cross, down, cross	Repeat.
7–8	Chorus: It's a small, small world.	Lean forward, touching head to knees. (Curl forward.)
9–10	Tap, tap, knees, knees.	Tap sticks two times in front of the chest and then lightly tap the knees twice.
11–12	Tap, tap, knees, knees	Repeat
13–14	Tap, tap, knees, knees	Repeat
15–16	Chorus: It's a small, small world.	Lean forward, touching head to knees. (Curl forward.)

Repeat the sequence several times with touches to the toes, shoulders, head, and nose.

VARIATION: Students can face a partner and tap both of their sticks to their partner's sticks.

DEVELOPMENTAL LEVEL II DANCES

Developmental Level II activities focus clearly on folk dance. Locomotor skills are still the basis of the movement patterns; but in most dances, the patterns are more difficult than those in Developmental Level I. At this level, each dance always has at least two parts and may have three or more. Because the movement patterns are longer, at this level you will use the part–whole teaching method more often. These are vigorous, fast-moving dances that are exciting for children to perform.

Tinikling and Lummi sticks add challenge and novelty to the progression. Emphasize participation and enjoyment rather than perfection. Normal progress through the rhythms program will assure children's success.

Teaching Hint

Have students perform the following Chicken Dance individually, with everyone moving to find a new partner on the skipping sequence. Vary the locomotor movements to include sliding or galloping.

The Bird Dance (Chicken Dance)

MUSIC SOURCE: WWC-9126

SKILLS: Skipping or walking, elbow swing or star

FORMATION: Circle or scatter formation, partners facing

DIRECTIONS:

MEASURES	PART I ACTION
1	Four snaps—thumb and fingers, hands up.
2	Four flaps—arms up and down, elbows bent.
3	Four wiggles—hips, knees bent low.
4	Four claps.
5–16	Repeat action of measures 1–4 three times.
	PART II ACTION
1–8	With a partner, do either a right-hand star with 16 skips or 16 walking steps, or an elbow swing. (Skip, 2, 3, . . ., 15; change hands.)
9–16	Repeat with the left hand. On the last 4 counts of the last swing, everyone changes partners. If dancing in a circle formation, partners B advance forward counterclockwise to the next partner A. If dancing in a scattered formation, everyone scrambles to find a new partner. (Skip, 2, 3, . . ., 12; change partners.)

Csebogar (Hungarian)

MUSIC SOURCE: WWCD-1042

SKILLS: Skipping, sliding, draw step, elbow swing

FORMATION: Single circle, partners facing center, hands joined with partners B on the right

DIRECTIONS:

PART I:

MEASURES	ACTION
1–4	Take seven slides to the left. (Slide, 2, 3, . . ., 7, change.)
5–8	Take seven slides to the right. (Back, 2, 3, . . ., 7, stop.)
9–12	Take three skips to the center and stamp on count 4. Take three skips backward to place and stamp on count 8. (Forward, 2, 3, stamp; Backward, 2, 3, stamp.)
13–16	Hook right elbows with partner and turn around twice in place, skipping. (Swing, 2, 3, . . ., 8.)

PART II: Partners face each other in a single circle with hands joined.

MEASURES	ACTION
17–20	Holding both of partner's hands, take four draw steps (step, close) toward the center of the circle. (Step-close, 2-close, 3-close, 4-close.)
21–24	Take four draw steps back to place. (Step-close, 2-close, 3-close, 4-close.)
25–26	Go toward the center of the circle with two draw steps. (In-close, 2-close.)
27–28	Take two draw steps back to place. (Out-close, 2-close.)
29–32	Hook elbows and repeat the elbow swing, finishing with a shout and facing the center of the circle in the original formation. (Swing, 2, 3, 4, 5, "Csebogar!")

✔ Teaching Hint

Instead of an elbow swing, partners can use the Hungarian turn. Partners stand side by side, put their right arms around the partner's waist, and lean away from partner. They hold their left arms out to the side with the elbow bent, the hand pointing up, and the palm facing the dancer.

Pop Goes the Weasel (American)

MUSIC SOURCE: WWCD-1043; WWCD-FDN

SKILLS: Walking, skipping, turning under

FORMATION: Double circle of sets of four; couples facing with Partner B on Partner A's right. Couples facing clockwise are number 1 couples; couples facing counterclockwise are number 2 couples.

DIRECTIONS:

MEASURES	ACTION
1–4	Join hands in a circle of four and circle left, once around, with eight skipping or sliding steps. (Circle, 2, 3, . . ., 8.)
5–6	Take two steps forward, raising the joined hands, and two steps backward, lowering the hands. (Forward, 2; back, 2.)
7–8	"Ones" pop the "Twos" under: Couples number 1 raise their joined hands to form an arch and pass the number 2 couples under. All walk ahead to meet a new couple. (Forward; pop through.)

Repeat as desired.

VARIATIONS:

1. Dancers are in sets of three, all facing counterclockwise. Each forms a triangle with one child in front and the other two with joined hands forming the base. The front dancer reaches back and holds the outside hands of the other two dancers. The groups of three are in a large circle formation.

MEASURES	ACTION
1–2	Sets of three dancers skip forward four times. (Forward, 2, 3, 4.)
3–4	Sets of three skip backward four times. (Backward, 2, 3, 4.)
5–6	Sets of three skip forward four times. (Forward, 2, 3, 4.)
7–8	On "Pop goes the weasel," the two back dancers raise their joined hands, and the front dancer backs up underneath to the next set. This set, meanwhile, has "popped" its front dancer back to the set behind it. (Raise and pop under.)

2. "Pop Goes the Weasel" is excellent for stimulating creative movement. The music actually

consists of a verse and a chorus part. During the verse, children can slide, gallop, or skip until the "Pop" line, when they make a half or full turn in the air. During the chorus, they can do jerky nonlocomotor movements. Other options include ball routines, in which children dribble in time to the music during the verse and pass the ball around various parts of the body during the chorus. Another variation has children carry a jump rope while skipping, sliding, or galloping. During the chorus, they jump in time to the music, and on "Pop," they try to do a double jump.

Wild Turkey Mixer

MUSIC SOURCE: WWC-FFD or any music with a definite rhythm

SKILLS: Walking, elbow swing, partner change

FORMATION: Trios abreast, facing counterclockwise around the circle

DIRECTIONS:

MEASURES	ACTION
1–8	In lines of three, with the right and left person holding the near hand of the center person, all walk 16 steps forward. (Walk, 2, 3, . . ., 16.)
9–12	The center person (Wild Turkey) turns the right-hand person once around with the right elbow. (Turn, 2, 3, . . ., 8.)
13–16	The Wild Turkey turns the left-hand person with the left elbow and then moves forward to repeat the dance with the two new people ahead. (Turn, 2, 3, 4; forward, 2, 3, 4.)

The same dance can be adapted to other pieces of music. With a faster tempo, dancers do elbow swings while skipping instead of walking.

La Raspa ("The Rasp"; Mexican)

MUSIC SOURCE: WWCD-05117

SKILLS: Bleking step, running, elbow swing

FORMATION: Partners facing, couples scattered around room

DIRECTIONS: These dance movements are supposed to represent a rasp or file in action. Directions are the same for both partners.

PART I: To begin, the partners face each other, Partner B with hands at sides and Partner A with hands behind the back.

MEASURES	ACTION
1–4	Beginning right, take one Bleking step (page 419). (Slow, slow, fast-fast-fast.)
5–8	Turn slightly counterclockwise away from partner (right shoulder to right shoulder) and, beginning with a jump on the left foot, repeat measures 1–4. (Slow, slow, fast-fast-fast.)
9–12	Repeat action of measures 1–4, facing opposite direction (left shoulder to left shoulder). (Slow, slow, fast-fast-fast.)
13–16	Repeat action of measures 1–4, facing partner. (Slow, slow, fast-fast-fast.)

PART II: Partners hook right elbows; left elbows are bent and left hands point toward the ceiling.

MEASURES	ACTION
1–4	Do a right elbow swing, using eight running or skipping steps. Release and clap the hands on count 8. (Swing, 2, 3, . . ., 7, clap.)
5–8	Do a left elbow swing, using eight running or skipping steps. Release and clap the hands on count 8. (Swing, 2, 3, . . ., 7, clap.)
9–16	Repeat the actions of measures 1–8.

VARIATIONS:

1. Face partner (all are in a single-circle formation for this version) and do a grand right and left around the circle. Repeat Part I with a new partner.
2. All face center or face a partner and do the Bleking or raspa step. On each pause, clap own hands twice.

Polly Wolly Doodle (American)

MUSIC SOURCE: WWCD-1041

SKILLS: Sliding, turning, walking

FORMATION: Double circle, partners facing with both hands joined, Partner A with back to center of circle

DIRECTIONS:

MEASURES	PART I ACTION
1–4	All slide four steps—A partners to left, Bs to right, counterclockwise. (Slide, 2, 3, 4.)

5–8	Drop hands and all turn solo circle, A partners to left, Bs to right, with five stamps in this rhythm: 1-2-1, 2, 3. (Stamp on the word *Polly*, stamp the other foot on the word *doodle*, and do three quick stamps on the word *day*.) (Turn, 2, stamp, 2, 3.)
9–16	Repeat measures 1–8, but in the opposite direction, A partners moving to right and Bs to left. (Slide, 2, 3, 4; turn, 2, stamp 2, 3.)

PART II ACTION

1–4	Both bow to each other, A partners with hands on hips, Bs with hands at sides. (A bows; B bows.)
5–8	With four walking steps (or skipping steps), both move backward, away from each other. (Back, 2, 3, 4.)
9–12	Both move diagonally forward to own left to meet a new partner. (Diagonal, 2, 3, 4.)
13–16	With the new partner, elbow swing in place using a skipping step. (Swing, 2, 3, 4.) Repeat the dance from the beginning with the new partner.

Bingo (American)

MUSIC SOURCE: WWCD-FDN

SKILLS: Walking, grand right and left

FORMATION: Double circle, partners side by side and facing counterclockwise, Partners A on the inside and inside hands joined

NOTE: "Bingo" is a favorite of young people. The singing must be brisk and loud. The dance is in three parts.

DIRECTIONS:

PART I: Partners walk counterclockwise around the circle, singing the refrain. (Walk, 2, 3, . . . , 15; face center.)

PART II: All join hands to form a single circle, Partner B on Partner A's right. They sing (spelling out) with these actions.

ACTION:

All take four steps into the center.

All take four steps backward.

All take four steps forward again.

Take four steps backward, drop hands, and face partner.

PART III: Shake right hands with the partner, calling out *B* on the first heavy note. All walk forward, passing their partner, to meet the oncoming person with a left handshake, calling out *I* on the next chord. Continue to the third person with a right handshake, calling out *N*. Pass on to the fourth person, giving a left handshake and a *G*. Instead of a handshake with the fifth person, face each other, raise the arms high above the head, shake all over, and call out a long, drawn-out *O*. The fifth person becomes the new partner, and the dance is repeated.

Teaching Hint

Adapt this dance to use a parachute. At the end of Part II (the end of the line "And Bingo was his name"), Partners A face the chute and hold it with both hands, lifting it to shoulder level. Partners B drop their hands from the parachute and get ready to move clockwise. On each of the letters *B-I-N-G-O*, they move inside the first A, outside the next, and so on, for five changes. They then take a new place as indicated and get ready to repeat the dance. The next sequence can have Partners B remaining in place, holding the chute, while Partners A move counterclockwise.

Grand March (American)

MUSIC SOURCE: WWCD-W0F-2 or any good march or square dance music

SKILLS: Controlled walking, marching, grand march figures

FORMATION: Partners B are on the left side of the room, facing the end, and Partners A are on the right side, facing the same end. This is the foot of the hall. The teacher or caller stands at the other end of the room, the head of the hall. An alternative formation is to put half of the class on each side of the room and have each half wear different-colored pinnies.

Teaching Hint

The leaders (couples 1 and 2) should maintain an even, steady pace and not hurry, or the march becomes a race. When one set of couples forms arches (as in movements 5 and 6) for the other set of couples to tunnel under, the arches should be made with the inside arms, and the couples should continue marching while they form the arches.

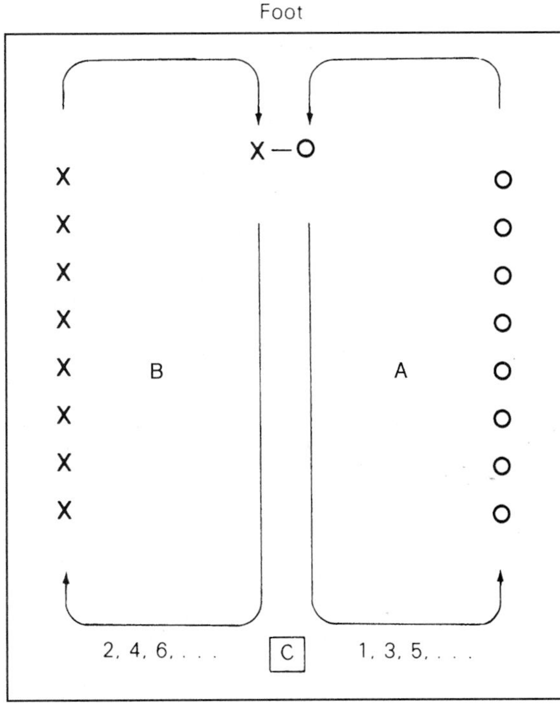

FIGURE 19.4 Formation and action for Grand March.

DIRECTIONS:

CALL	ACTION
Down the center by twos.	The lines march forward to the foot of the hall, turn the corner, meet at the center of the foot of the hall, and march in couples toward the caller (Figure 19.4), with inside hands joined. The Bs' line should be on the proper side so that, when the couples come down the center, A is on B's left. Odd couples are numbered 1, 3, 5, and so on. Even couples are numbered 2, 4, 6, and so on.
Twos left and right.	The odd couples go left and the even couples go right around the room and meet at the foot of the hall.
Down the center by fours.	The couples walk down the center, four abreast.
Separate by twos.	When they approach the caller, odd couples go left and even couples right. They meet again at the foot of the hall.
Form arches.	Instead of coming down the center, odd couples form arches and even couples tunnel under. Each continues around the sides of the hall to meet at the head.
Other couples arch.	Even couples arch, and odd couples tunnel under. Each continues around the sides of the room to the foot.
Over and under.	The first odd couple arches over the first even couple, then ducks under the second even couple's arch. Each couple goes over the first couple and under the next. Continue around to the head of the hall.
Pass right through.	As the lines come toward each other, they mesh and pass through each other in the following fashion: All drop handholds. Each B walks between the A and B of the opposite couple and continues walking to the foot of the hall.
Down the center by fours.	Go down the center four abreast.
Fours left and right.	The first four go left around the room, and the second four go right. The fours meet at the foot of the hall.
Down the center by eights.	Go eight abreast down the center.
Grapevine.	All persons in each line join hands and keep them joined. The leader takes either end of the first line and starts around the room with the line trailing. The other lines hook on to form one long line.
Wind it up.	The leader winds up the group in a spiral formation, like a clock spring. The leader makes the circles smaller and smaller until he or she is in the center.

Reverse (unwind).	The leader turns and faces in the opposite direction and walks between the lines of winding dancers. The leader unwinds the line and leads it around the room.
Everybody swing.	After the line is unwound, everybody does a square dance swing.

Green Sleeves (English)

MUSIC SOURCE: WWCD-1042

SKILLS: Walking, star formation, over and under

FORMATION: Double circle with couples in sets of four, facing counterclockwise. Two couples form a set and are numbered 1 and 2. Inside hands of each couple are joined.

DIRECTIONS:

MEASURES	CALL	ACTION
1–8	Walk	Walk forward 16 steps.
9–12	Right-hand Star	Each member of couple 1 turns individually to face the couple behind. All join right hands and circle clockwise (star) for eight steps.
13–16	Left-hand Star	Reverse direction and form a left-hand star. This should bring couple 1 back to place facing in the original direction.
17–20	Over and under	Couple 2 arches, and couple 1 backs under four steps while couple 2 moves forward four steps. Couple 1 then arches, and couple 2 backs under (four steps for each).
21–24	Over and under	Repeat the action of measures 17–20.

Jingle Bells, Var. 2 (Dutch)

MUSIC SOURCE: Any version of Jingle Bells or WWCD-FFD

SKILLS: Skipping, promenade position, sliding, elbow swing

FORMATION: Single circle of couples facing counterclockwise, Partner B on Partner A's right. Promenade position: hands crossed in front, right hands joined over left, right foot free.

DIRECTIONS:

MEASURES	PART I ACTION
1–2	Take four skips forward and four skips backward, starting with the right foot free. (Forward, 2, 3, 4; Back, 2, 3, 4.)
3–4	Repeat the pattern of measures 1 and 2. (Forward 2, 3, 4; Back, 2, 3, 4.)
5	Do four slides to the right, away from the center of the circle. (Out, 2, 3, 4.)
6	Now do four slides left, toward the center. (In, 2, 3, 4.)
7–8	Skip eight times, making one turn counterclockwise, with Partner A pivoting backward and Partner B moving forward. Finish in a double circle, partners facing, with As back to the center. (Skip, 2, 3, . . ., 8.)
	PART II ACTION
1	Clap own hands three times. (Clap, 2, 3.)
2	Clap both hands with partner three times. (Both, 2, 3.)
3	Clap own hands four times. (Clap, 2, 3, 4.)
4	Clap both hands with partner once. (Both.)
5–8	Right elbow swing with partner. Partners hook right elbows and swing clockwise for eight skips. (Swing, 2, 3, . . ., 8.)
9–12	Repeat clapping pattern of measures 1–4.
13–16	Left elbow swing with partner using eight skips and finishing in the original starting position to repeat the

entire dance with the same partner; or left elbow swing with partner once around, then all children in the inner circle skip forward to the outer dancer ahead and repeat the entire dance with a new partner. (Swing, 2, 3, . . ., 8.)

E-Z Mixer

MUSIC SOURCE: WWC-FFD or any music with a definite rhythm

SKILLS: Walking, elbow swing, or swing in closed position

FORMATION: Single circle, couples in promenade position, inside hands joined, facing counter-clockwise

DIRECTIONS:

MEASURES	ACTION
1–2	With Partner B on the right, walk forward four steps. (Forward, 2, 3, 4.) Back out to face center in a single circle. (Circle, 2, 3, 4.)
3–4	Partners B walk to the center. (In, 2, 3, 4.) Back out of the center. (Out, 2, 3, 4.)
5–6	Partners A take four steps to the center and do a half turn to the left on count 4. (In, 2, 3; turn left.) They take four steps toward the corner. (Out, 2, 3, 4.)
7–8	Partners A swing the corner B twice around, opening up to face counter-clockwise, back in starting position, to begin the dance again. (Swing, 2, 3, open.)

Any piece of music with a moderate 4/4 rhythm is appropriate for this basic mixer.

Ve David (Israeli)

MUSIC SOURCE: WWCD-FFD; WWC-RM3

SKILLS: Walking, pivoting, buzz-step turn

FORMATION: Double circle, couples facing counter-clockwise, Partner B on Partner A's right. Inside hands joined, right foot free.

DIRECTIONS:

MEASURES	PART I ACTION
1–2	All walk forward and form a ring. Take four walking steps forward, starting with the right foot and going counter-clockwise; then back out, taking four walking steps to form a single circle, facing center, with all hands joined. (Walk, 2, 3, 4; single, circle, 3, 4.)
3–4	All forward and back. Four steps forward to center and four steps backward, starting with the right foot. (Forward, 2, 3, 4; back, 2, 3, 4.)
	PART II ACTION
1–2	B partners forward and back; A partners clap. Partners B, starting with the right foot, walk four steps forward to the center and four steps backward to place while Partners A clap. (Bs in, 2, 3, 4; out, 2, 3, 4.)
	PART III ACTION
1–2	Partners A forward, circle to the right, and move to a new partner; all clap. A partners, clapping hands, walk four steps forward to the center, starting with the right foot. They do an about-face right on the last "and" count and walk forward four steps, passing their original partner and moving forward to the next. (A partners in, 2, 3, 4; Turn to new partner.)
3–4	Swing the new partner. The A and the new Partner B swing clockwise with right shoulders adjacent, right arms around each other across in front, and left arms raised—pivoting with right foot for an 8-count "buzz-step" swing. (Swing, 2, 3, . . ., 8.)

Repeat the entire dance.

Irish Washerwoman (Irish)

MUSIC SOURCE: WWCD-1043

SKILLS: Walking, elbow swing, promenade

FORMATION: Single circle, couples facing center, Partner B to the right, hands joined

DIRECTIONS: Dancers follow the call.

ACTION:

Beginning left, take four steps to the center. (Center, 2, 3, 4.)

Stamp four times in place. (Stamp, 2, 3, 4.)

Take four steps backward to place. (Back, 2, 3, 4.)

Swing the corner and promenade in the line of direction. (Swing, 2, 3, promenade.)

Dancers keep promenading until they hear the call again to repeat the pattern.

Oh, Susanna (American)

MUSIC SOURCE: WWCD-1043

SKILLS: Walking, promenade position, grand right and left

FORMATION: Single circle, all facing center, Partner B on the right

DIRECTIONS:

MEASURES	PART I ACTION
1–4	Partners B walk forward four steps and back four, as Partners A clap hands. (Forward, 2, 3, 4; back, 2, 3, 4.)
5–8	Reverse, with A walking forward and back, and B clapping time. (Forward, 2, 3, 4; back, 2, 3, 4.)
	PART II ACTION
1–8	Partners face each other, and all do a grand right and left by grasping the partner's right hand and passing to the next person with a left-hand hold. Continue until reaching the seventh person, who becomes the new partner. (Face, 2, 3, . . ., 8.)
	CHORUS ACTION
1–16	All join hands in promenade position with the new partner and walk counterclockwise around the circle for two full choruses. (Promenade, 2, 3, . . ., 16.)

Repeat the dance from the beginning, each time with a new partner. For variety in the chorus, skip instead of walk, or walk during the first chorus and swing the partner in place during the second chorus.

Crested Hen (Danish)

MUSIC SOURCE: WWCD-1042

SKILLS: Step-hop, turning under

FORMATION: Sets of three; one child is designated the center child.

DIRECTIONS:

PART I:

MEASURES	ACTION
1–4	Dancers in each set form a circle. Starting with a stamp with the left foot, each set circles to the left, using step-hops. (Stamp-and, 2-and, 3-and, 4-and, 5-and, 6-and, 7-and, stop.)
5–8	The figure is repeated. Dancers reverse direction, beginning again with a stamp with the left foot and following with step-hops. The dancers change direction vigorously and quickly, with the left foot crossing over the right. At the end of the sequence, two dancers release each other's hands to break the circle and stand on either side of the center person, forming a line of three while retaining joined hands with the center dancer. (Stamp-and, 2-and, 3-and, 4-and, 5-and, 6-and, 7-and, line.)

PART II: During this part, the dancers use the step-hop continuously while making the pattern figures.

MEASURES	ACTION
9–10	The dancer on the right moves forward in an arc to the left and dances under the arch formed by the other two. (Under-and, 2-and, 3-and, 4-and.)
11–12	After the right dancer has gone through, the two forming the arch turn under (dishrag), to form once again a line of three. (Turn-and, 2-and, 3-and, 4-and.)
13–16	The dancer on the left then repeats the pattern, moving forward in an arc under the arch formed by the other two, who turn under to unravel the line. (Under-and, 2-and, 3-and, 4-and; turn-and, 2-and, 3-and; circle.)

As Part II ends, dancers again join hands in a small circle. The entire dance is repeated. Another of the three can be designated the center dancer.

Troika (Russian)

MUSIC SOURCE: WWCD-3528; WWC-3528

SKILLS: Running step, turning under

FORMATION: Trios face counterclockwise. Start with hands joined in a line of three. The body weight is on the left foot; the right foot is free.

DIRECTIONS:

MEASURES	PART I ACTION
1	Take four running steps diagonally forward right, starting with the right foot. (Forward, 2, 3, 4.)
2	Take four running steps diagonally forward left, starting with the right foot. (Diagonal, 2, 3, 4.)
3–4	Take eight running steps in a forward direction, starting with the right foot. (Forward, 2, 3, . . ., 8.)
5–6	The center dancer and the left-hand partner raise joined hands to form an arch and run in place. Meanwhile, the right-hand partner moves counter-clockwise around the center dancer with eight running steps, goes under the arch, and back to place. The center dancer unwinds by turning under the arch. (Under, 2, 3, 4; turn, 2, 3, 4.)
7–8	Repeat the pattern of measures 5 and 6, with the left-hand partner running under the arch formed by the center dancer and the right-hand partner. (Under, 2, 3, 4; turn, 2, 3, circle.)
	PART II ACTION
9–11	The trio joins hands and circles left with 12 running steps. (Run, 2, 3, . . ., 12.)
12	Three stamps in place (counts 1–3), pause (count 4). (Stamp, 2, 3, pause.)
13–15	The trio circles right with 12 running steps, opening out at the end to re-form in lines of three facing counterclockwise. (Run, 2, 3, . . ., 8, open, 10, 11, 12.)
16	The center dancer releases each partner's hand and runs under the opposite arch of joined hands to advance to a new pair ahead. Right- and left-hand partners run in place while waiting for a new center dancer to join them in a new trio. (Stamp, 2, line, pause.)

Teaching Hint

Practice the running steps in groups of three. Then introduce turning under the arch and finish by practicing the running circle with accent stamps.

Gustaf's Skoal (Swedish)

MUSIC SOURCE: WWCD-1044CD; WWCD-FDN

SKILLS: Walking (stately), skipping, turning

FORMATION: Similar to a square dance set of four couples, each facing center. Partner A is on Partner B's left. Couples join inside hands; outside hand is on the hip. Two of the couples facing each other are the head couples. The other two couples, also facing each other, are the side couples.

DIRECTIONS: The dance has two parts. Part I music is slow and stately; dancers move with dignity. Part II music is light and represents fun.

MEASURES	PART I ACTION
1–2	Head couples, inside hands joined, walk forward three steps and bow to the opposite couple. (Forward, 2, 3, bow.)
3–4	Head couples take three steps backward to place and bow to each other (meanwhile, side couples hold their places). (Back, 2, 3, bow.)
5–8	Side couples repeat action of measures 1–4; head couples hold their places. (Forward, 2, 3, bow; back, 2, 3, bow.)
9–16	Dancers repeat measures 1–8.
	PART II ACTION
17–22	Side couples raise joined hands to form an arch. Head couples skip forward four steps, release partners' hands, join inside hands with opposite person, and skip under the nearest arch with new partner. After going under the arch,

	they drop hands and head back home to their original partner. (Head couples: Skip, 2, 3, 4; under, 2, 3, 4; around, 2, 3, 4.)
23–24	All couples join both hands with partners and swing once around with four skipping steps. (Swing, 2, 3, 4.)
25–30	Head couples form arches; side couples repeat the action of measures 17–22. (Side couples: Skip, 2, 3, 4; under, 2, 3, 4; around, 2, 3, 4.)
31–32	All couples then repeat the movements in measures 23–24. (Swing, 2, 3, 4.)

VARIATION: During the first action sequence of Part I (the dancers take three steps and bow), dancers can shout "Skoal!" and raise their right fists high overhead as a salute. The word *skoal* is a toast. (Partners release hands when raising their fists.)

Shoo Fly (American)

MUSIC SOURCE: WWCD-FDN

SKILLS: Walking

FORMATION: Single circle, couples facing the center with all hands joined; about six couples to a circle

DIRECTIONS:

MEASURES	PART I ACTION
4	Introduction (no movement)
1–4	All walk four steps to the center and four steps back to place. (Center, 2, 3, 4; back, 2, 3, 4.)
5–8	Repeat action of measures 1–4. (Center, 2, 3, 4; back, 2, 3, 4.)
9–12	Partners turn each other clockwise with a right forearm grasp using eight walking steps. (Turn, partner, 3, 4, . . ., 8.)
13–16	Partners turn each other counterclockwise with a left forearm grasp using eight walking steps. (Turn, partner, 3, 4, . . ., 8)
	PART II ACTION
1–8	Repeat action of measures 1–8 in Part I.
9–12	Keep hands joined. Choose a leading couple to form an arch by lifting inside joined hands and then move toward the center of the circle. The couple opposite the leading couple pulls the continuous circle through the arch using eight steps. (Through, arch, 3, 4, . . ., 8.)
13–16	When all have passed through the arch and are facing out, the leading couple turns under their joined arms to turn the circle inside out. (Inside, out, 3, 4, . . ., 8.)
	PART III ACTION
1–8	Repeat the action of measures 1–8 in Part I, but all walk backward four steps to the center and then forward four steps back to place. Repeat. (Backward, 2, 3, 4, forward, 6, 7, 8; Repeat.)
9–12	Leading couple release joined hands (others keep joined hands) and separate, pulling dancers attached to them by joined hands around the circle with eight walking steps. (Release, 2, 3, . . ., 8.)
13–16	Continue following leaders with eight walking steps until in original places facing the center. Lead couple joins hands to form a circle again. (Circle, 2, 3, . . ., 8.)

Perform the dance twice.

Apat Apat (Philippines)

MUSIC SOURCE: WWCD-572; WWC-572

SKILLS: Walking; star hold

FORMATION: Double circle, partners facing counterclockwise with inside hands joined

DIRECTIONS:

MEASURES	ACTION
Introduction	No movement
1	All face counterclockwise with inside hands joined and walk forward four steps. On count 4, release hands and do a half turn right to face clockwise. (Walk, 2, 3, turn.)

2	Take four walking steps forward clockwise. Release hands on the fourth step and face partner. (Walk, 2, 3, face.)
3	Walk four steps backward away from partner. (Away, 2, 3, 4.)
4	Walk four steps forward toward partner with each partner taking a quarter turn to the right on count 4. Partners now face opposite directions. (Forward, 2, 3, right turn.)
5	Walk forward four steps with partners moving in opposite directions. (Forward, 2, 3, 4.)
6	Walk backward four steps to meet partner. (Backward, 2, 3, 4.)
7	Face partner. With right-hand star (join right hands with elbows bent), walk clockwise around partner four steps in place. (Star, 2, 3, 4.)
8	Release hands; dancers inside circle walk forward four steps counterclockwise to meet next partner. Dancers outside circle do a half turn in place to wait for new partner.

Repeat the dance.

Pata Pata (African)

MUSIC SOURCE: WWCD-3528; WWC-3528

SKILLS: Toe touches, knee lift, quarter turns

FORMATION: Single lines facing in one direction

DIRECTIONS:

MEASURES	ACTION
1–2	Start with feet together; touch right foot sideways right and return next to left foot. (Right touch, together.)
3–4	Same as above with left foot. (Left touch, together.)
5	With feet together, move toes out, keeping heels on the ground. (Toes out.)
6	Turn heels out, keeping toes on the ground. (Heels out.)
7	Turn heels in, keeping toes on the ground. (Heels in.)
8	Turn toes in, keeping heels on the ground. The feet are now together. (Toes in.)
9–12	Raise right knee diagonally in front of the body and then touch right foot next to left foot. Repeat for counts 11–12. (Lift, touch, lift, touch.)
13–16	Kick left foot forward while doing a quarter turn to the right with weight on the right foot. Step backward left, right, left. Feet are together at the end of count 16. (Kick, left, right, left.)

Repeat the dance.

Teaching Hint

After learning the footwork, students enjoy adding some arm movements to the dance. At count 5, with elbows close to the body, raise hands up and straight out, palms up. Count 6—turn palms down with elbows out. Count 7—turn palms up. Count 8—turn palms down.

Savila Se Bela Loza ("Grapevine Twined in Itself"; Serbian)

MUSIC SOURCE: WWCD-572; WWC-572

SKILLS: Running step, crossover step, hop

FORMATION: Broken circle or line; joined hands held down

DIRECTIONS: *Savila se bela loza* is pronounced "SAH-vee-lah say BAY-lah LOH-zah."

MEASURES	PART I ACTION
Introduction	No movement
1–20	Face slightly to right; move right starting with the right foot, taking 18 small running steps forward. Do a step-hop on steps 19 and 20. (Run, 2, 3, . . ., 18, step, hop.)
21–40	Face slightly left and repeat above action starting with the left foot. Finish with a step-hop on the left foot. (Run, 2, 3, . . ., 18, step, hop.)
	PART II ACTION
41–44	With right foot, take one schottische step moving right (this is a step to the right sideways on the right foot, a step

	with the left foot behind the right, and then a step-hop on the right foot). (Right, left, right, hop.)
45–48	With left foot, take one schottische step to the left (step to the left sideways on left foot, step with the right foot behind the left, and do a step-hop on the left foot). (Left, right, left, hop.)
49–64	Repeat the action of counts 41–48 two more times.

Repeat the dance. During the music for Part I, the leader may lead the line anywhere, winding or coiling it like a grapevine.

Los Machetes (Mexico)

Central America and parts of Mexico are largely covered with dense jungle, and the workers (macheteros, both men and women) must clear the trails with machetes. Macheteros often do this dance at fiestas.

MUSIC SOURCE: WWCD-FFD

SKILLS: Marching, rhythmic clapping

FORMATION: Two lines of partners facing forward

DIRECTIONS:

MEASURES	ACTION
Introduction	No movement
1–4	March forward 16 steps while clapping or clicking sticks.
5–8	Do an about-face and march back 16 steps.
9–12	The two lines face each other. Partners walk backward four steps and bow on count 4. (One, 2, 3, bow.) An alternative to the bow is to click Lummi sticks on count 4. Walk forward to original position and clap on count 4.
13–16	Repeat measures 9–12.
17–18	Clapping sequence facing partner. Clap own hands once (1); clap right hand to partner's right hand (2); clap own hands once (3); clap left hand to partner's left hand (4); clap own hands once (5); clap both hands to partner's hands (6); clap own hands together three times fast (7–8).
19–20	Repeat clapping sequence (measures 17–18).
21–28	With partner, do a right-hand star for 8 counts; do a left-hand star for 8 counts. Repeat.
29–84	Repeat the entire dance two more times.

Popcorn (American)

MUSIC SOURCE: WWCD-RM7; WWC-RM7

SKILLS: Toe touches, knee lifts, jumps, quarter turns

FORMATION: Single lines of students; no partners

DIRECTIONS:

COUNTS	ACTION
1–24	Wait 24 counts; gently bounce up and down by bending the knees during the introduction.
1–4	Touch right toe in front and return; repeat. (Right, together, right, together.)
5–8	Touch left toe in front and return; repeat. (Left, together, left, together.)
9–12	Touch right toe in back and return; repeat. (Back, together, back, together.)
13–16	Touch left toe in front and return; repeat. (Back, together, back, together.)
17–20	Lift right knee up in front of left knee and return; repeat. (Knee up, return, knee up, return.)
21–24	Lift left knee up in front of right knee and return; repeat. (Knee up, return, knee up, return.)
25–26	Lift right knee up in front of left knee and return. (Knee up, return.)
27–28	Lift left knee up in front of right knee and return. (Knee up, return.)
29–30	Clap both hands together once. (Clap.)
31–32	Jump and do a quarter turn to the right. (Jump and turn.)

Repeat entire dance to the end of the music.

Red River Valley (American)

MUSIC SOURCE: WWCD-FDN

SKILLS: Walk, buzz swing, do-si-do

FORMATION: Triple circle with three dancers side by side in sets of six dancers—two trios facing each other. Half the trios face counterclockwise and half face clockwise.

DIRECTIONS:

MEASURES	PART I ACTION
Introduction	No movement
1–4	Middle child in each trio leads partners forward to right to meet on coming trio using eight walking steps. (Walk, 2, 3, . . ., 8.)
5–8	Join hands with oncoming trio and circle to the left (clockwise) four walking steps; reverse direction and circle right using four walking steps. (Circle, left, 3, 4; circle, right, 3, 4.)
9–12	Middle child swings around with child on left using eight buzz steps (shuffling). (Swing, 2, 3, . . ., 8.)
13–16	Middle child swings around with child on right using eight buzz steps (shuffling). (Swing, 2, 3, . . ., 8.)
	PART II ACTION
1–8	Repeat action of measures 1–8 in Part I. (Walk, 2, 3, . . ., 8.)
9–12	The four outside students form a right-hand star in the center of the set and walk around once to starting point using eight walking steps. (Star, 2, 3, . . ., 8.)
13–16	The two middle students do-si-do around each other, returning to own place using eight walking steps. (Do-si-do, 2, 3, . . ., 8.)
	PART III ACTION
1–8	Repeat action of measures 1–8 in Part I. (Walk, 2, 3, . . ., 8.)
9–12	The two left-hand outside students change places diagonally across using eight walking steps. (Left, diagonal, 3, . . ., 8.)
13–16	The two right-hand outside students change places diagonally across using eight walking steps. The middle child now has different partners. (Right, diagonal, 3, . . ., 8.)

Repeat the entire dance twice.

Jiffy Mixer (American)

MUSIC SOURCE: WWCD-FDN

SKILLS: Heel-and-toe step, chug step

FORMATION: Double circle, partners facing

DIRECTIONS: The music includes an introduction. Directions are for Partners A; B's actions are opposite.

MEASURES	INTRODUCTION
1–4	Wait, wait, balance apart (push away on the left foot and touch the right). Balance together (forward on the right and touch the left).
	ACTION
1–4	Strike the left heel diagonally out and return to touch the toe near the right foot. Repeat. Do a side step left with a touch. (Heel-toe, heel-toe, side-close, side-touch.)
5–8	Repeat while moving in the opposite direction, beginning with the right foot. (Heel-toe, heel-toe, side-close, side-touch.)
9–12	Take four chug steps backward, clapping on the upbeat. (Chug-clap, chug-clap, chug-clap, chug-clap.)
13–16	Starting with the left foot, take four slow, swaggering steps diagonally to the right, moving to a new partner. (Walk, 2, 3, 4.)

The chug step is done by jumping and dragging both feet backward. The body is bent slightly forward.

Teaching Hint

Introduce the dance by having all join hands in a single circle, facing inward. There are no partners and no progressions to new partners.

Sicilian Circle (American)

MUSIC SOURCE: WWCD-FDN

SKILLS: Walking, two-hand swing (either walking or buzz turn), wheel turn

FORMATION: Double circle, groups of two couples facing each other with partners side by side. Couples are numbered 1 and 2; number 1 couples move counterclockwise and number 2 couples clockwise.

DIRECTIONS:

MEASURES	ACTION
Introduction	No movement
1–4	The sets of two couples join hands and walk eight steps to the left, ending where they started, and drop hands. (Circle, left, 2, 3, . . ., 8.)
5–8	Partners join both hands and swing once around to the left using eight walking or buzz steps. (Swing, left, 2, 3, . . ., 8.)
9–12	Couples move toward each other and pass right shoulders through to opposite's place using four walking steps. As soon as they are across, couples do a wheel-turn with partner on the left, walking backward four steps and moving into place on partner's left, who turns in place using four steps. If desired, left partner can take partner's left hand in their left and put their right arm around partner's waist. Hands are dropped. (Pass, through, 3, 4; wheel, turn, 3, 4.)
13–16	Couples pass through again as described in measures 9–12. (Back, through, 3, 4; wheel, turn, 3, 4.)
17–20	Right-hand partners advance toward each other, join right hands briefly, pass each other by right shoulders, drop hands, and join left hand with opposite left partner using four steps. The opposite left partner does a wheel turn as described in measures 9–12 using four steps. (Right partner, chain, 3, 4; wheel, turn, 3, 4.)
21–24	Right-hand partners chain back again and turn as in measures 17–20 using eight steps and end with left hands joined with partner. (Chain, back, 3, 4; wheel, turn, 3, 4.)
25–28	Partners join hands in promenade position and advance four steps toward opposite and four steps backward to place. (Forward, 2, 3, 4; back, 2, 3, 4.)
29–32	Each couple with hands in promenade position advances to the left of the opposite couple to the next couple using eight steps. (New couple, 2, 3, . . ., 8.)

Repeat the dance three times.

Lummi Sticks

MUSIC SOURCE: WWCD-2015 or 2014; WWC-2000

SKILLS: Rhythmic tapping, flipping, and catching of sticks

FORMATION: Couples scattered throughout the area

Lummi sticks are smaller versions of wands; they are 12 to 15 inches long. Some believe that the Lummi Indians in northwest Washington first used these sticks; others credit South Pacific cultures. Their actual origin remains obscure.

Most Lummi stick activities use partners, although some can be done individually. Each child sits cross-legged, facing a partner at a distance of 18 to 20 inches. Children adjust this distance as the activities demand. They hold the sticks in the thumb and fingers (not the fist) at about the bottom third of the stick.

Routines are based on sets of six movements; each movement is completed in 1 count. Many different routines are possible, but only the basic ones are presented here. Use the following 1-count movements to make up routines.

Vertical tap: Tap both sticks upright on the floor.

Partner tap: Tap partner's stick (right stick to right stick, or left to left).

End tap: Tilt the sticks forward or sideways and tap the ends on the floor.

Cross-tap: Cross hands and tap the upper ends to the floor.

Side tap: Tap the upper ends to the side.

Flip: Toss the stick in air, giving it a half turn, and catch other end.

Tap together: Hold the sticks parallel and tap them together.

Toss right (or left): Toss the right-hand stick to partner's right hand, at the same time receiving partner's right-hand stick.

Pass: Lay the stick on the floor and pick up partner's stick.

Toss right and left: Toss stick to partner quickly, right to right and left to left, all within 1 count.

The following routines incorporate the basic movements and are listed in order of difficulty. Partners do each routine four times to complete the 24 beats of the chant.

1. Vertical tap, tap together, partner tap right, vertical tap, tap together, partner tap left.
2. Vertical tap, tap together, pass right stick, vertical tap, tap together, pass left stick.
3. Vertical tap, tap together, toss right stick, vertical tap, tap together, toss left stick.
4. Repeat routines 1–3, but substitute an end tap and flip for the vertical tap and tap together. Perform the stated third movement (i.e., end tap, flip, partner tap right, end tap, flip, partner tap left).
5. Vertical tap, tap together, toss right and left quickly, end tap, flip, toss right and left quickly.
6. Cross-tap, cross-flip, vertical tap (uncross arms), cross-tap, cross-flip, vertical tap (uncross arms).
7. Right flip side—left flip in front, vertical tap in place, partner tap right. Left flip side—right flip in front, vertical tap in place, partner tap left.
8. End tap in front, flip, vertical tap, tap together, toss right, toss left.
9. Vertical tap, tap together, right stick to partner's left hand, toss own left stick to own right hand. Repeat. This is the circle throw.
10. Same as routine 9, but reverse the circle.

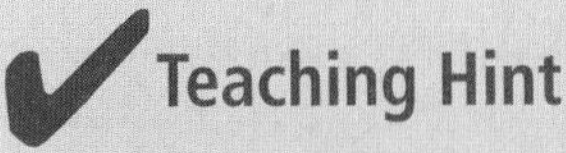

The activity can be done by four children with a change in the timing. One set of partners begins at the start, and the other two start on the third beat. All sing together. In this way, the sticks are flying alternately.

Tinikling (Philippine Islands)

MUSIC SOURCE: WWC/CD-8095; WWC/CD-9015

SKILLS: Tinikling steps

FORMATION: Sets of fours scattered around the room. Each set has two strikers and two dancers (Figure 19.5).

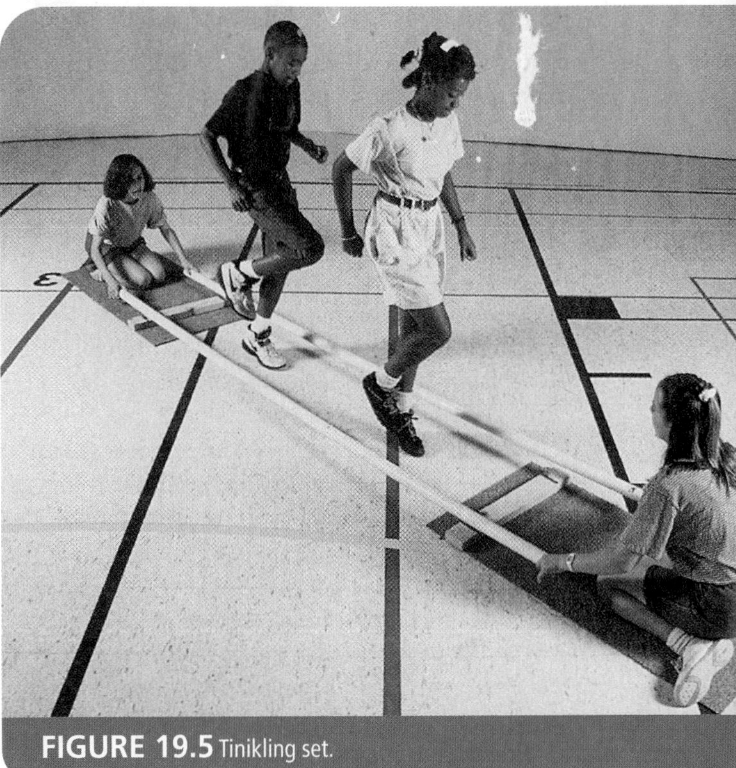

FIGURE 19.5 Tinikling set.

NOTE: The dance represents a rice bird as it steps, with its long legs, from one rice paddy to another. The dance is popular in many countries in Southeast Asia, where different versions are seen.

DIRECTIONS: Two 8-foot bamboo poles and two crossbars on which the poles rest are needed for the dance. A striker kneels at each end of the poles; both strikers hold the end of a pole in each hand. The music is in waltz meter, 3/4 time, with an accent on the first beat. The strikers slide and strike the poles together on count 1. On the other two beats of the waltz measure, strikers open the poles about 15 inches apart, lift them an inch or so, and tap twice on the crossbars in time to counts 2 and 3. The rhythm "close, tap, tap" continues throughout the dance, each sequence taking a measure.

Basically, the dance requires students to step outside the poles on the close (count 1) and two steps inside the poles (counts 2 and 3) when the poles are tapped on the crossbars. Many step combinations have been devised.

Have students practice the basic tinikling step until they master it. The step is done singly, although two dancers can perform at once. The dancers stand at opposite ends with their right sides to the poles.

Count 1: Step slightly forward with the left foot.

Count 2: Step with the right foot between the poles.

Count 3: Step with the left foot between the poles.

Count 4: Step with the right foot outside poles to dancer's own right.

Count 5: Step with the left between the poles.

Count 6: Step with the right between the poles.

Count 7: Step with the left outside to the original position.

The first step (count 1) is used only to get the dance started. The last step (count 7) to original position is actually the beginning of a new series (counts 7–12).

Because some tinikling dances and records guide the dancers with a different rhythm (tap, tap, close), they require adjusting the steps and patterns in these descriptions.

Tinikling steps also can be adjusted to 4/4 rhythm (close, close, tap, tap), so the poles are closed on 2 counts and open on the other 2. The basic foot pattern is two steps outside the poles and two inside. For consistency, this text presents all routines in the original 3/4 time (close, tap, tap).

Dancers can go from side to side or can return to the side from which they entered. The dance can be done singly, with the two dancers moving in opposite directions from side to side, or the dancers can enter from and leave toward the same side. Dancers can do the same step patterns or different ones. They can dance as partners and move side by side with inside hands joined, or they can face each other with both hands joined.

✔ Teaching Hint

First have students practice steps with stationary poles, with lines drawn on the floor, or with jump ropes laid on the floor. Students handling the poles must concentrate on watching each other rather than the dancer to avoid becoming confused by the dancer's feet.

To gain a sense of the movement pattern for 3/4 time, slap both thighs with the hands on the "close," and clap the hands twice for movements inside the poles. For 4/4 time, slap the right thigh with the right hand, then the left thigh with the left hand, and clap two times. This routine should be done to music, with the poles closing and opening as indicated. Getting the feel of the rhythm is important.

Other Tinikling Steps and Routines

STRADDLE STEP: Dancers do a straddle jump outside the poles on count 1 and do two movements inside the poles on counts 2 and 3. Let the dancers explore the different combinations. Jump turns are possible.

JUMP STEP: Dancers begin the side jump with their side toward the poles. They can do the jump from either side.

MEASURE 1:

Count 1: Jump lightly in place.

Counts 2 and 3: Jump twice between the poles.

MEASURE 2:

Count 1: Jump lightly in place (other side).

Counts 2 and 3: Jump twice between the poles.

Dancers keep the feet close together to fit between the poles. They can exit to the same side they entered from or alternate sides. Another way to enter and exit is by facing the poles and jumping forward and backward rather than sideways. When jumping sideways, dancers can keep one foot ahead of the other in a stride position. On the second jump inside the poles, they can reverse this position.

ROCKER STEP: For the rocker step, dancers face the poles and begin with either foot. As they step in and out (forward and backward), they make a rocking motion with the body.

CROSSOVER STEP: The crossover step is similar to the basic tinikling step, but the dancer begins with the right foot (forward step) and steps inside the poles with the left foot, using a cross-foot step. Each time, the dancer must step in or out using a cross-step.

CIRCLING POLES: For circling the poles, dancers position themselves as in the basic tinikling step (Figure 19.6) and execute the following movements:

MEASURE 1:

Count 1: Step slightly forward with the left foot.

Count 2: Step with the right foot between the poles.

Count 3: Step with the left foot between the poles.

MEASURE 2:

Count 1: Step with the right foot outside the poles to the right.

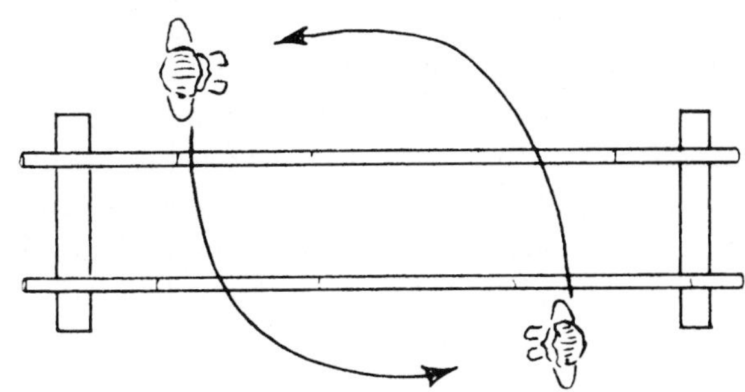

FIGURE 19.6 Circling poles for tinikling.

Counts 2 and 3: With light running steps, make a half circle to a position for the return movement.

MEASURES 3 AND 4:

Dancers return to their original position using the same movements as in measures 1 and 2.

FAST TINIKLING TROT: The fast tinikling trot is similar to circling the poles, but the step goes twice as fast and thus requires only two sets of 3 counts. Instead of having the side of the body to the poles, as in the basic tinikling step, the dancers face the poles. They do the following steps:

MEASURE 1:

Count 1: Shift the weight to the left foot and raise the right foot.

Count 2: Step with the right foot between the poles.

Count 3: Step with the left foot outside the poles and begin turning to the left.

MEASURE 2:

Count 1: Step with the right foot outside the poles, completing the left turn to face the poles again.

Count 2: Step with the left foot inside the poles.

Count 3: Step outside with the right foot.

Dancers do the next step with the left foot to begin a new cycle. The movement is a light trot with quick turns. Note that the step outside the poles on count 3 in each measure is made with the poles apart.

CROSS-STEP: To do the cross-step, dancers begin with the basic tinikling position and use the following sequence:

MEASURE 1:

Count 1: Cross-step across both poles with the left foot, hopping on the right side.

Counts 2 and 3: Hop twice on the right foot between the poles.

MEASURE 2:

Count 1: Hop on the left foot outside the poles to the left.

Counts 2 and 3: Hop twice again on the right foot between the poles.

LINE OF POLES: Place three or more sets of poles about 6 feet apart. The object is to dance down the sets, make a circling movement (as in Circling Poles), and return down the line in the opposite direction (Figure 19.7). Dancers keeps their right sides toward the poles throughout.

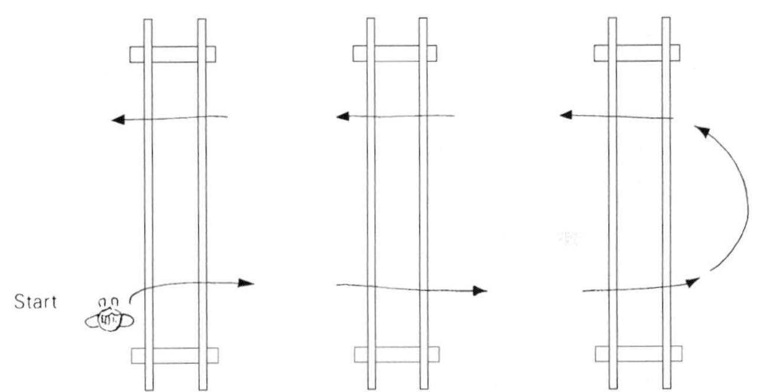

FIGURE 19.7 Movement through line of poles for tinikling.

During measure 1 (3 counts), dancers do a basic tinikling step, finishing on the right side of the first set of poles. During measure 2 (3 counts), they do three light running steps to position themselves for the tinikling step at the next set of poles. Upon reaching the end, dancers circle in three steps to get in position for the return journey.

SQUARE FORMATION: Four sets of poles can be placed in a square formation for an interesting dance sequence (Figure 19.8). Four dancers are positioned as shown. During measure 1, each dancer does a

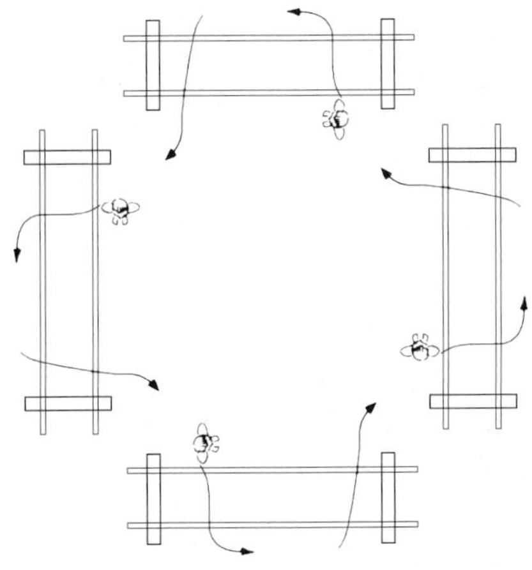

FIGURE 19.8 Square formation for tinikling.

tinikling step, crossing to the outside of the square. On measure 2, the dancers circle to position for a return tinikling step. During measure 3, the dancers do a tinikling step, returning to the inside of the square. On measure 4, they rotate counterclockwise to the next set of poles with three running steps.

Tell the dancers to look ahead (not at the poles), so they learn by thinking and doing and not by gauging the pole distances visually.

FOUR-POLE SET: This arrangement features two longer crossbars, on which two sets of poles rest, leaving a small space between the poles when the sets are open. Four strikers control the poles. Two dancers begin by facing each other and straddling a set of poles on opposite ends. They can change foot patterns every 16 measures, which for most selections is a full pattern of music. Here are some suggested routines.

1. Straddle, jump, jump, exiting on measure 16 to the left.
2. Do the basic tinikling step, exiting on the left foot.
3. Do the basic tinikling step, first on one's own set of poles and then on the other set of poles. As the dancer comes out of the first set of poles with the right foot, she makes a half turn to do the tinikling step through the other poles. On the return, she makes another half turn in the middle to face and return to her original position. Repeat the sequence twice.
4. Do routine 3, but move diagonally, passing the oncoming dancer with right shoulder to right shoulder, in effect changing places. (Do not use half turns.) Turn around in six steps and return to position. Repeat.
5. Jump to a straddle position with one foot in each of the pole openings. On "close," jump to the space between the sets. On measure 16, the dancer jumps out to the left on both feet.
6. Two-footed step: Jump twice with both feet inside the first set of poles, to the space between, twice inside the second set, and out. Return. Repeat twice.

DEVELOPMENTAL LEVEL III DANCES

Children at Developmental Level III are adept dancers, especially if they have participated in rhythmic activities for several years. If students do not have a well-developed dance background, have them start by learning dances from Developmental Levels I and II. Developmental Level III dances include patterns that students must perform with skill and finesse. At this level, patterns are longer and require more concentration and memorization. The schottische, polka, and two-step first appear at this level. The difficulty level ranges from a dance that is performed in a circle and introduces square dance moves, to dances featuring the two-step, polka step, and schottische.

Hora ("Hava Nagila"; Israeli)

MUSIC SOURCE: WWCD-3528; WWC-3528

SKILLS: Stepping sideways, step-swing

FORMATION: Single circle, facing center, hands joined. The circle can be partial.

NOTE: The hora is regarded as the national dance of Israel. It is a simple dance that expresses joy. The traditional hora is done in circle formation, with the arms extended sideways and the hands on the neighbors' shoulders. It is easiest to introduce the dance step individually. After learning the step, students can join hands and practice the circle formation counterclockwise or clockwise. The clockwise version is presented here.

Israelis perform an old and a new hora. The new hora is more energetic; dancers spring high in the air and whirl around with shouts of ecstasy. The hora can be danced to many tunes, but "Hava Nagila" (meaning "Come, let us be happy!") is the favorite.

DIRECTIONS—OLD HORA:

MEASURES	ACTION
1–3	Step left on the left foot. Cross the right foot in back of the left, keeping weight on the right. Step left on the left foot and hop on it, swinging the right foot forward. Step-hop on the right foot and swing the left foot forward. Repeat the same step over and over. (Side, behind, side, swing; side, swing.)

The circle also may move to the right; dancers use the same step, beginning with the right foot.

DIRECTIONS—NEW HORA:

MEASURES	ACTION
1–3	Face left and run two steps. Jump in place. Hop on the left foot, swinging the right foot forward. Take three quick steps in place. Continue in the same way, moving to the left. (Run, run, jump, hop-swing, step, step, step.)

The hora often begins with the dancers swaying in place from left to right as the music builds. Gradually, the dance increases in pace and intensity. Shouts accompany the dance as the participants call to each other across the circle.

Virginia Reel (American)

MUSIC SOURCE: WWCD-05114

SKILLS: Skipping, arm turn, do-si-do, sliding (sashay), reeling

FORMATION: Six couples in a longways set of two lines facing. Partners on one end of the set are designated the head couple.

DIRECTIONS:

MEASURES	CALL	ACTION
1–4	All go forward and back.	Take three steps forward, curtsey or bow. Take three steps back and close.
5–8	Right hands around.	Move forward to partner, turn once in place using a right forearm grasp and return to position.
9–12	Left hands around.	Repeat measures 5–8 with a left forearm grasp.
13–16	Both hands around.	Partners join both hands, turn once in a clockwise direction, and move backward to place.
17–20	Do-si-do your partner.	Partners pass each other right shoulder to right shoulder and then back-to-back and move backward to place.
21–24	All go forward and back.	Repeat the action of measures 1–4.
25–32	Head couple sashay.	The head couple, with hands joined, takes eight slides down to the foot of the set and eight slides back to place.
33–64	Head couple reel.	The head couple begins the reel with linked right elbows and turns $1\frac{1}{2}$ times to face the next couple in line. Each member in the head couple then links left elbows with the person facing and turns once in place. The head couple meets again in the center and turns once with a right elbow swing. The next dancers down the line are turned with a left elbow swing and then the head couple returns to the center for another

Teaching Hints

1. Versions of this dance vary. Some allow time at the beginning for a do-si-do after the "both hands around" (measures 13–16); others do not. Check the music for phrasing before presenting the dance to the class.
2. Technically, the dance is written for eight couples in each set. For the head couple to reel all couples in the set, they must not miss one beat of the music or they will be behind the phrasing for the reel section. When introducing the dance to a class for the first time, having only six couples in each set is helpful. Then, if a couple gets behind the music for the reeling section, they still can stay in time to the music and finish before the "casting off" section begins.

		right elbow turn. The head couple thus progresses down the line, turning each dancer in order. After the head couple has turned the last dancers, they meet with a right elbow swing, turn halfway around, and sashay (slide) back to the head of the set.
65–96	Everybody march.	All couples face toward the head of the set with the head couple in front. The person on the right turns to the right; the person on the left turns to the left and goes behind the line, followed by the other dancers. When the head couple reaches the foot of the set, they join hands and make an arch for all other couples to pass under. The head couple is now at the foot of the set, and the dance is repeated with a new head couple.

Repeat the dance until each couple gets to be the head couple.

TEACHING THE TWO-STEP

Children can learn the forward two-step simply by moving forward on the cue "Step, close, step," starting on the left foot and alternating thereafter. The close-step is made by bringing the toe of the closing foot to a point even with the instep of the other foot. All steps are almost slides, a kind of shuffle step.

The two-step just described is nothing more than a slow gallop, alternating the lead foot. One way to help students learn the step-close-step pattern is to put them in a single circle and have them gallop forward. Instruct them to start on the left foot and move forward eight slow gallops. Stop the class and have them put their right foot forward and repeat the gallops. Continue this pattern, and have students change from galloping with their left foot forward to galloping with their right foot forward without stopping. When making this change, students bring the right foot forward in a walking step, keeping their weight on the left foot. Reverse the procedure when moving the left foot forward. The movement is very smooth. When students master this pattern, repeat the sequence, but have them do four gallops with each foot forward. After they master this pattern, repeat the pattern with two gallops on each foot. Students who can do this are performing the forward two-step.

Next, arrange the children by couples in a circle formation, Partners A on the inside, all facing counterclockwise. Repeat the instruction, with both partners beginning on the left foot. Practice the two-step with a partner, with Partner A beginning on the left foot and Partner B starting on the right. In the next progression, the children move face-to-face and back-to-back.

Jugglehead Mixer (American)

MUSIC SOURCE: Any music with a definite, steady beat

SKILLS: Two-step, elbow turn (forearm grasp)

FORMATION: Double circle, facing counterclockwise in promenade position

DIRECTIONS: Actions described are for partners on the inside circle; directions are opposite for partners on the outside circle.

MEASURES	CALL	ACTION
1–4	Two-step left and two-step right. (Walk-2-3-4.)	Do a two-step left and a two-step right, and take four walking steps forward.
5–8	Two-step left and two-step right. (Walk-2-3-4.)	Repeat measures 1–4.
9–10	Turn your partner with the right.	Inside partner takes the outside partner's right hand and walks around to face the person behind.
11–12	Now turn your corner with your left.	Inside partner turns the person behind with the left hand.

13–14	Turn your partner all the way around.	Inside partner turns partner with the right hand going all the way around.
15–16	And pick up the forward lady.	Inside partner steps up one place to the outside person ahead, who becomes the new partner.

Teton Mountain Stomp (American)

MUSIC SOURCE: WWCD-FDN

SKILLS: Walking, banjo position, sidecar position, two-step

FORMATION: Form single circle of partners in closed dance position, Partners A facing counterclockwise, Partners B facing clockwise.

DIRECTIONS:

MEASURES	ACTION
1–4	Step to the left toward the center of the circle on the left foot, close right foot to the left, step again to the left on the left foot, stomp right foot beside the left but leave the weight on the left foot. Repeat this action, but start on the right foot and move away from the center. (Side, close; side, stomp; side, close; side, stomp.)
5–8	Step to the left toward the center on the left foot; stomp the right foot beside the left. Step to the right away from the center on the right foot, and stomp the left foot beside the right. In "banjo" position (modified closed position with right hips adjacent), Partner A takes four walking steps forward while Partner B takes four steps backward, starting on the right foot. (Side, stomp, side, stomp; walk, 2, 3, 4.)
9–12	Partners change to sidecar position (modified closed position with left hips adjacent) by each making a one-half turn to the right in place, A remaining on the inside and B on the outside. A walks backward while B walks four steps forward. Partners change back to banjo position with right hips adjacent by each making a left-face one-half turn; then they immediately release from each other. A walks forward four steps to meet the second B approaching, while B walks forward four steps to meet the second A approaching. (Change, 2, 3, 4; new partner, 2, 3, 4.)
13–16	New partners join inside hands and do 4 two-steps forward, beginning with A's right foot and B's left. (Step, close, step; repeat four times.)

Cotton-Eyed Joe (American)

MUSIC SOURCE: WWCD-FDN

SKILLS: Heel-toe, two-step

FORMATION: Double circle of couples with Partner B on the right, holding inside hands and facing counterclockwise. Varsouvienne position can also be used.

DIRECTIONS:

MEASURES	ACTION
1–2	Starting with the left foot, cross the left foot in front of the right foot, kick the left foot forward. (Cross, kick.)
3–4	Take one two-step backward. (Left, close, left.)
5–6	Cross the right foot in front of the left foot; kick the right foot forward. (Cross, kick.)
7–8	Do one two-step backward. (Right, close, right.)
9–16	Repeat measures 1–8.
17–32	Perform 8 two-steps counterclockwise beginning with the left foot. (Step, close, step; Repeat eight times.)

19

Teaching Hint

If the dancers are skillful enough, use the following action for measures 13–16 of the Teton Mountain Stomp: New partners take the closed dance position and do four turning two-steps, starting on A's left (B's right) and make one complete right-face turn while moving in the specified direction.

TEACHING THE POLKA STEP

Like the two-step, the polka has a step-close-step pattern. The two-step is simply step-close-step, but the polka is step-close-step-hop. Technically, the polka is usually described as hop-step-close-step (or hop-step-together-step). However, the first description is probably more helpful when working with beginning students.

The polka step involves four movements: (1) step forward left; (2) close the right foot to the left, bringing the toe up and even with the left instep; (3) step forward left; and (4) hop on the left foot. The series begins with the weight on the right foot.

Several methods can be used to teach the polka:

1. *Step-by-step rhythm approach.* Analyzing the dance slowly, have the class walk through the steps together in even rhythm. The cue is "Step, close, step, hop." Accelerate the tempo to normal polka time and add the music.
2. *Gallop approach.* Many elementary instructors prefer the gallop approach. Use the same approach as in "Teaching the Two-Step," but add the polka hop and increase the tempo. When moving the right foot forward, students hop on the left foot. When moving the left foot forward, they hop on the right foot.
3. *Two-step approach.* Students begin with the left foot and two-step with the music, moving forward in the specified direction in a single circle. Accelerate the tempo gradually to a fast two-step, and have students take smaller steps. Without stopping, have students change to a polka rhythm by following each two-step with a hop. Use polka music for the two-step, but slow it down considerably to start.
4. *Partner approach.* After learning the polka step individually by one of the three methods, children can practice the step with partners in a double-circle formation, Partners A on the inside and all facing counterclockwise, with inside hands joined. Partners A begin with the left foot and Partners B with the right.

Klumpakojis (Swedish)

MUSIC SOURCE: WWCD-1042

SKILLS: Walking, stars, polka step

FORMATION: Couples in a circle, side by side, all facing counterclockwise, with Partner B to the right

DIRECTIONS:

MEASURES	PART I ACTION
1–4	With inside hands joined, free hand on hip, all walk briskly around the circle for eight steps counterclockwise. (Walk, 2, 3, . . ., 7; turn.)
5–8	Turn individually to the left, reverse direction, change hands, and walk eight steps clockwise. (Walk, 2, 3, . . .,7; turn.)
	PART II ACTION
9–12	Face partner and make a star by joining right hands (be sure the right elbow is bent). The left hand is on the hip. With partner, walk around clockwise for eight walking steps. Change hands and repeat the eight steps, reversing direction. (Star, 2, 3, . . ., 8; reverse, 2, 3, . . ., 8.)
	PART III ACTION
13–16	Listen to the musical phrase, then stamp three times on the last 2 counts. Listen to the phrase again, then clap own hands three times. (Listen, listen, stamp, 2, 3; listen, listen, clap, 2, 3.)
17–20	Shake the right finger in a scolding motion at partner. (Scold, 2, 3.) Shake the left finger. (Scold, 2, 3.)
21–24	Turn solo to the left, clapping partner's right hand once during the turn. Use two walking steps to make the turn, and finish facing partner. (Turn, 2; stamp, 2, 3.)
25–32	Repeat the action of measures 13–24.
	PART IV ACTION
33–40	With inside hands joined, do 16 polka steps (or two-steps) forward, moving counterclockwise. (Later, as the dance is learned, change to the promenade position.) On polka steps 15 and 16, Partner A moves forward to take a new Partner B while handing the original Partner B to the A in back. New couple joins inside hands. (Step, close, step, hop; step, close, step, hop; repeat for a total of 16 polka steps.)

Alley Cat (American)

MUSIC SOURCE: WWCD-9126; WWC-RM3

SKILLS: Grapevine step, touch step, knee lifts

FORMATION: None, although all should face the same direction during instruction

DIRECTIONS:

MEASURES	ACTION
1–2	Do a grapevine left and kick: Step sideways left, step right behind left, step left again, and kick. Repeat to the right. (Left, behind, left, kick; right, behind, right, kick.)
3–4	Touch the left toe backward, bring the left foot to the right, touch the left toe backward again, bring the left foot to the right, taking the weight. Repeat, beginning with the right toe. (Left-and, left-and; right-and, right-and.)
5–6	Raise the left knee up in front of the right knee and repeat. Raise the right knee up twice, similarly. (Left-and, left-and; right-and, right-and.)
7–8	Raise the left knee and then the right knee. Clap the hands once and make a jump quarter turn to the left. (Left-and, right-and, clap-and, jump.)

After repeating the routine three times, each dancer will be facing in the original direction.

Ten Pretty Girls (American)

MUSIC SOURCE: WWCD-1042

SKILLS: Walking, grapevine

FORMATION: Circle of groups of any number, with arms linked or hands joined, all facing counter-clockwise

DIRECTIONS:

MEASURES	ACTION
1–2	Starting with the weight on the right foot, touch the left foot in front, swing the left foot to the left and touch, swing the left foot behind the right foot and put the weight on the left foot, step to the right, close the left foot to the right. (Front, side, back-side, together.)
3–4	Repeat, starting with the weight on the left foot and moving to the right. (Front, side, back-side, together.)
5–6	Take four walking or strutting steps forward, starting on the left foot. (Walk, 2, 3, 4.)
7–8	Swing the left foot forward with a kicking motion; swing the left foot backward with a kicking motion; stamp left, right, left, in place. (Swing, swing, stamp, stamp, stamp.)

Repeat the entire dance 11 times, starting each time with the alternate foot. The dance can be used as a mixer when performed in a circle by groups of three. On measures 7–8, have the middle person move forward to the next group during the three stamps.

Limbo Rock

MUSIC SOURCE: WWCD-9126

SKILLS: Touch step, swivel step, jump clap step

FORMATION: Single circle or scattered

DIRECTIONS:

MEASURES	PART I ACTION
1–2	Touch left foot in. Touch left foot out. Three steps in place. (In, out, left, right, left.)
3–4	Repeat measures 1 and 2 beginning with opposite foot. (In, out, right, left, right.)
5–8	Repeat measures 1–4.
	PART II ACTION
9–10	Swivel toes right, swivel heels right. Repeat and straighten feet. (Swivel, 2, 3, straighten.)
11–12	Repeat beats 1 and 2 beginning with swivel toes left.
13–14	Jump in, clap; jump out, clap. (Jump, clap, jump, clap.)
15–16	Repeat measures 13 and 14.

Teaching Hint

An easier version involves walking eight steps right during measures 9–16.

Jessie Polka (American)

MUSIC SOURCE: WWCD-RM8

SKILLS: Step and touch, two-step, or polka step

FORMATION: Single circle, couples facing counterclockwise with inside arms around each other's waist

DIRECTIONS:

MEASURES	PART I ACTION
1	Beginning left, touch the heel in front, then step left in place. (Left heel, together.)
2	Touch the right toe behind. Then touch the right toe in place, or swing it forward, keeping the weight on the left foot. (Right toe, touch.)
3	Touch the right heel in front, then step right in place. (Right heel, together.)
4	Touch the left heel to the left side, sweep the left foot across in front of the right. Keep the weight on the right. (Left heel, crossover.)
	PART II ACTION
5–8	Take 4 two-steps or polka steps forward in the line of direction. (Step, close, step; step, close, step; step, close, step; step, close, step.)

VARIATIONS: The dance may be done as a mixer by having Partner B turn out to the right on the last 2 two-steps and come back to the A behind her. Partners A keep moving forward on the last 2 two-steps, making it easier to meet the B coming toward them. Another variation is to perform this activity as a line dance. Students place their hands on the waist or shoulders of the dancer in front of them.

Inside-Out Mixer

MUSIC SOURCE: Any music with a pronounced beat suitable for walking at a moderate speed

SKILLS: Walking, wring the dishrag, change partners

FORMATION: Triple circle (three children standing side by side), facing counterclockwise, inside hands joined. Children in the center of each trio can wear pinnies.

DIRECTIONS:

MEASURES	ACTION
1–4	Take eight walking steps forward. (Forward, 2, 3, . . ., 8.)
5–8	Form a small circle and circle left in eight steps back to place. (Circle, 2, 3, . . ., 8.)
9–12	The center child walks forward under the raised arms opposite, pulling the other two under to turn the circle inside out. (Inside-out, 2, 3, . . ., 8.)
13–16	The trio circles left in eight steps, returning to place. When almost back to place, drop hands. The center child walks forward counterclockwise, and the other two walk clockwise (the way they are facing) to the nearest trio for a change of partners. (Circle, 2, 3, 4; mix, 6, 7, 8.)

D'Hammerschmiedsgselln ("The Journey Blacksmith"; Bavarian)

MUSIC SOURCE: WWCD-FFD; WWC-TC1

SKILLS: Clapping routine, step-hops

FORMATION: Circle of four

DIRECTIONS:

MEASURES	ACTION
1–16	First opposites do a clapping pattern beginning on the first count of measure 1, while the other pair does a clapping pattern beginning on the first count of measure 2. The 6-count pattern follows: With both hands, slap own thighs (count 1), slap own chest (count 2), clap own hands (count 3), clap right hands (count 4), clap left hands (count 5), and clap opposite's hands (count 6). (Thighs, chest, together, right, left, both.) Repeat the 6-count pattern seven more times.
	PART I
17–24	Join hands and circle left with eight step-hops. (Step-hop, 2-hop, . . ., 8-hop.)
25–32	Circle right in the same way. (Step-hop, 2-hop, . . ., 8-hop.)
33–48	Repeat the chorus action.

PART II—STAR

49–56	Right-hand star with eight step-hops. (Step-hop, 2-hop, . . ., 8-hop.)
57–64	Left-hand star in the same manner. (Step-hop, 2-hop, . . ., 8-hop.)
65–80	Repeat the chorus action.

PART III—BIG CIRCLE

81–88	Circles of four open to form one large circle, and circle left with eight step-hops. (Step-hop, 2-hop, . . ., 8-hop.)
89–96	Reverse direction, continuing with eight step-hops. (Step-hop, 2-hop, . . ., 8-hop.)

VARIATION: As a mixer, try the following sequence.

MEASURES	ACTION
1–16	Use the chorus clapping pattern described.
17–24	As in Part I or II, circle left, or do a right-hand star with step-hops (or simple walking steps).
25–32	Do eight step-hops with the corner in general space or in any comfortable position, moving anywhere.

Repeat the entire sequence with a new foursome.

Kalvelis ("Little Blacksmith"; Lithuanian)

MUSIC SOURCE: WWCD-WOF3

SKILLS: Polka step, swing, clapping pattern, grand right and left

FORMATION: Single circle of couples facing center, Partner B on Partner A's right, all hands joined in a single circle with the right foot free.

DIRECTIONS:

MEASURES	PART I ACTION
1–8	Circle right with seven polka steps, ending with three stamps. (Circle-and, 2-and, 3-and, . . ., 7-and; stamp, stamp, stamp.)
9–16	Circle left with seven polka steps, ending with three stamps. (Circle-and, 2-and, 3-and, . . ., 7-and; stamp, stamp, stamp.)

CHORUS ACTION

1–2	Clap own hands four times, alternating, left hand onto own right, then right hand onto own left. (Clap, 2, 3, 4.)
3–4	Right elbow swing with four skips. (Swing, 2, 3, 4.)
5–6	Repeat the clapping pattern of measures 1 and 2. (Clap, 2, 3, 4.)
7–8	Left elbow swing with four skips. (Swing, 2, 3, 4.)
9–16	Repeat the pattern of measures 1–8.

PART II ACTION

1–8	Partners B dance three polka steps forward toward the center, ending with three stamps. They turn to face their partner and return to place with three polka steps forward, ending with three stamps, facing center again. (Step-close-step-hop; step-close-step-hop; step-close-step-hop; stamp, stamp, stamp.)
9–16	Partners A repeat the pattern of measures 1–8, but dance more vigorously, stamping on the first beat of each measure. (Step-close-step-hop; step-close-step-hop; step-close-step-hop; stamp, stamp, stamp.)

CHORUS ACTION

1–16	As described.

PART III ACTION

1–16	Grand right and left around the circle with 16 polka steps, meeting a new partner on the last measure. (Step-close-step-hop; repeat 16 times.)

CHORUS ACTION

1–16	As described, but with a new partner.

Doudlebska Polka (Czechoslovakian)

MUSIC SOURCE: WWCD-572; WWC-572

SKILLS: Polka step, walking, clapping pattern

FORMATION: Either one large circle or several smaller circles scattered around the floor. The directions are for one large circle.

DIRECTIONS:

MEASURES	PART I ACTION
1–16	Partners assume the varsouvienne position and do 16 polka steps around the circle, one couple following another. (Polka, 2, 3, . . ., 16.)
	PART II ACTION
17–32	Partner A puts his right arm around Partner B's waist as they stand side by side, while B puts her left hand on A's right shoulder. A puts the left hand on the shoulder of the A in front. This closes the circle. Partners A move sideways to the center to catch up with the A ahead. In this position, all march forward counterclockwise and sing loudly, "La, la, la," and so forth. This takes 32 walking steps. (Walk, 2, 3, . . ., 32.)
	PART III ACTION
33–48	Partners A face the center, and Partners B drop behind their partner. Bs turn to face the other way, clockwise, and polka around the circle (around the A partners) with their hands on hips. At the same time, A partners, who face center, clap a rhythm as follows: Clap hands twice, then extend both hands, palms outward, toward the neighbor on each side, and clap hands once with the neighbor. Repeat this pattern over and over. For variation, A partners may slap a thigh occasionally, or duck down, or cross their arms when clapping the neighbor's hand. (A: Clap, clap, out; repeat 16 times.) (B: Polka, 2, 3, . . ., 16.)

At the end of Part III, Partners A turn around, each taking the Partner Bs behind them, and start the dance from the beginning. Children who are looking for a partner move to the center to find one.

Extra children can enter the dance during the clapping part for Partners A, and some can join the ring to polka around the outside. Those left without a partner wait for the next turn. When the group is large, form several circles; it is perfectly fine for unpartnered children to steal into another circle. The polka in this case is done anywhere around the room. During the march, circles can have any number of people.

TEACHING THE SCHOTTISCHE STEP

The schottische is actually a light run; but when students are learning, have them practice it as a walking step. (This is also true in polka instruction.) Lively music will quicken the step later. The cue is "Step, step, step, hop; step, step, step, hop; step-hop, step-hop, step-hop, step-hop." A full schottische pattern, then, is three steps and a hop, repeated once, followed by four step-hops. Partner A starts on the left foot and Partner B on the right. The step can be learned first in scattered formation, then in a single circle, and practiced later by couples in a double circle. The "Horse and Buggy Schottische" is a good introduction to this step.

Horse and Buggy Schottische (American)

MUSIC SOURCE: WWCD-1046

SKILLS: Schottische step

FORMATION: Couples in sets of four in a double circle, facing counterclockwise. Couples join inside hands and join outside hands with the other couple (Figure 19.9).

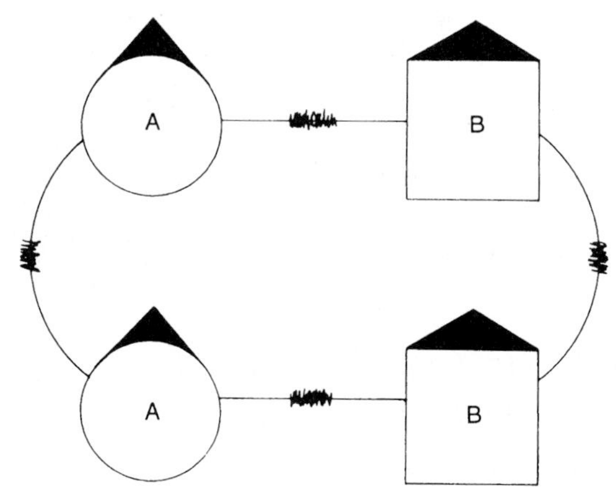

FIGURE 19.9 Horse and Buggy Schottische formation.

DIRECTIONS:

MEASURES	ACTION
1–2	Moving forward, perform two schottische steps. (Step, step, step, hop; step, step, step, hop.)
3–4	Progress in specified direction, performing four step-hops. (Step-hop, 2-hop, 3-hop, 4-hop.)

During the four step-hops, dancers can do one of three movement patterns.

1. The lead couple drops inside hands and step-hops around the outside of the back couple,

who move forward during the step-hops. The lead couple then joins hands behind the other couple, and the positions are reversed.

2. The lead couple continues to hold hands and move backward under the upraised hands of the back couple, who untwist by turning away from each other.
3. Alternate 1 and 2.

Alunelul ("Little Hazelnut"; Romanian)

MUSIC SOURCE: WWCD-FFD; WWC-TC1

SKILLS: Step-behind step, grapevine step, stomping

FORMATION: Single circle, hands on shoulders to both sides, arms straight ("T" position)

DIRECTIONS: The Romanians are famous for rugged dances. In this dance, the stomping action represents the breaking of hazelnuts. The title is pronounced "ah-loo-NAY-loo."

MEASURES	PART I ACTION
1–2	Sidestep right, step left behind right, sidestep right, step left behind right, sidestep right, stomp left foot twice. (Side, back, side, back, side, stomp, stomp.)
3–4	Beginning with the left foot, repeat the action but with reverse footwork. (Side, back, side, back, side, stomp, stomp.)
5–8	Repeat the action of measures 1–4.
	PART II ACTION
9–10	Sidestep right, left behind right, sidestep right, stomp. (Side, back, side, stomp.)
11–12	Sidestep left, right behind left, sidestep left, stomp. (Side, back, side, stomp.)
13–16	Repeat the action of measures 9–12.
	PART III ACTION
17–18	In place, step right, stomp left; step left, stomp right; step right, stomp left twice. (Side, stomp, side, stomp, side, stomp, stomp.)
19–20	In place, step left, stomp right; step right, stomp left; step left, stomp right twice. (Side, stomp, side, stomp, side, stomp, stomp.)
21–24	Repeat action of measures 17–20.

Teaching Hint

Stomps are made close to the supporting foot. When teaching the dance, scatter the dancers in general space so they can move individually.

Korobushka (Russian)

MUSIC SOURCE: WWCD-572; WWC-572

SKILLS: Schottische step, balance step, cross-out-together step, walking step

FORMATION: Double circle, Partner A's back to the center with partners facing and both hands joined. A's left and B's right foot are free.

DIRECTIONS:

MEASURES	PART I ACTION
1–2	Take one schottische step away from the center (Partner A moving forward, Partner B backward) starting with A's left and B's right foot. (Out, 2, 3, hop.)
3–4	Repeat the pattern of measures 1 and 2, reversing direction and footwork. (In, 2, 3, hop.)
5–6	Repeat the pattern of measures 1 and 2, ending on the last count with a jump on both feet in place. (Out, 2, 3, jump.)
7–8	Hop on the left foot, touching the right toes across in front of the left foot (count 1). Hop on the left foot, touching the right toes diagonally forward to the right (count 2). Jump on both feet in place, clicking the heels together (count 1), pause, and release the hands (count 2). (Across, apart, together.)
	PART II ACTION
9–10	Facing partner and beginning with the right foot, take one schottische step right, moving sideways away from partner. (Side, back, side, hop.)
11–12	Facing partner and beginning with the left foot, take one schottische step left, returning to partner. (Side, back, side, hop.)

13–14	Joining right hands with partner, balance forward and back: Step forward on the right foot (count 1), pause (count 2), rock back on the left foot in place (count 3), pause (count 4). (Forward, hop; back, hop.)
15–16	Take four walking steps forward, starting with the right foot, and change places with partner. (Walk, 2, 3, 4.)
17–24	Repeat the pattern of measures 9–16, returning to place.

Teaching Hint

To use the dance as a mixer, during measures 19 and 20, move left to the person just before partner and continue with this new partner. Practice the schottische steps in different directions before trying the dance as a whole.

Oh Johnny (American)

MUSIC SOURCE: WWCD-05114; WWC-57

SKILLS: Shuffle step, swing, allemande left, do-si-do, promenade

FORMATION: Single circle of couples facing inward with Partner B on the right

DIRECTIONS: A shuffle step is used throughout this dance.

ACTION:

All join hands and circle for eight steps.

All stop and swing with partner.

A partners turn to their left and swing the corner B.

Swing with partner again.

A partners turn to their left and do an allemande left with their corner.

A partners turn to their right and do-si-do with their partner.

A partners promenade with the corner B, who becomes the new partner for the next repetition.

Teaching Hint

To simplify the dance, begin in scattered formation and teach each call with students changing from partner to corner using any nearby person. Since this is a fast-moving dance, slow down the music until students have learned it.

Shindig in the Barn (American)

MUSIC SOURCE: WWC-FFD

SKILLS: Walking, do-si-do, swinging, sliding

FORMATION: Contra style (two lines with partners facing each other). The music is for seven couples.

DIRECTIONS:

MEASURES	ACTION
2 (8 counts total)	Introduction (no movement).
1–2	Everybody walk forward four steps and back four steps. (Forward, 2, 3, 4; back, 2, 3, 4.)
3–4	All pass through to the other side by walking forward four steps toward partner, do a half turn while passing right shoulder of partner, and walk four steps backward. (Walk, 2, 3, 4; turn, 6, 7, 8.)
5–6	Everybody forward and back—repeat measures 1–2 above. (Forward, 2, 3, 4; back, 2, 3, 4.)
7–8	Everybody pass through to the other side with eight steps—repeat measures 3–4 above. (Walk, 2, 3, 4; turn, 6, 7, 8.)
9–10	All couples do-si-do by passing right shoulders and back. (Do-si-do, 2, 3, . . ., 8.)
11–12	All couples do a two-hand swing once around to the left in eight steps. After the swing, all couples except the head couple go back to their original position. Head couples remain in the middle with their hands joined and face each other. (Swing, 2, 3, . . ., 8.)

13–14	The head couple takes eight sliding (sashay) or skipping steps to the foot of the line. All the other couples clap to the beat and watch. (Slide, 2, 3, . . ., 8.)
15–16	Head couple does a right elbow swing at the foot of the line for 8 counts and remains at the foot of the line, creating a new head couple. (Swing, 2, 3, . . ., 8.)

Repeat dance to the end of the music.

Big Sombrero Circle Mixer (American)

MUSIC SOURCE: WWC-FFD

SKILLS: Circling, do-si-do, star, swing

FORMATION: Sicilian circle; couples facing couples clockwise and counterclockwise around the circle.

DIRECTIONS:

MEASURES	ACTION
2 (8 counts total)	Introduction (no movement).
1–2	Join hands with the facing couple and circle left using eight walking steps. (Circle, 2, 3, . . ., 8.)
3–4	Keeping hands joined, circle right using eight walking steps. (Circle right, 2, 3, . . ., 8.)
5–6	Face partner and do-si-do using eight walking steps. (Do-si-do, 2, 3, . . ., 8.)
7–8	Face opposite and do-si-do using eight walking steps. (Opposite, 2, 3, . . ., 8.)
9–10	All four circle while doing a right-hand star using eight walking steps. (Star, 2, 3, . . ., 8.)
11–12	All four circle while doing a left-hand star using eight walking steps. (Star, 2, 3, . . ., 8.)
13–14	Swing partner by linking right elbows and swinging once or twice. (Swing, 2, 3, . . ., 8.)
15–16	Pass through the opposite couple, passing right shoulders, and walk to the next couple using eight steps. (Pass, through, 3, 4, . . ., 8.)

Repeat the dance to the end of the music. Dancers return to starting positions after every 8-count movement.

Trio Fun Mixer (American)

MUSIC SOURCE: WWC-FFD

SKILLS: Walking, do-si-do, star

FORMATION: Single large circle with lines of three facing lines of three

DIRECTIONS:

MEASURES	ACTION
1–4	Facing threesomes (six dancers) join hands and circle left one time around back to place. (Circle, 2, 3, . . ., 16.)
5–6	Center students in each threesome do a do-si-do with each other. (Do-si-do, 2, 3, . . ., 8.)
7–8	Right students in each threesome move diagonally to do-si-do with each other. (Do-si-do, 2, 3, . . ., 8.)
9–10	Left students in each threesome move diagonally to do-si-do with each other. (Do-si-do, 2, 3, . . ., 8.)
11–12	Center student in each threesome faces the child on the right and turns that child with a right-hand star and then turns the child on the left with a left-hand star and goes back to place. (Star, 2, 3, 4; Left, 2, 3, 4.)
13–14	Lines of three go forward 4 counts and back 4 counts. (Forward, 2, 3, 4; Back, 2, 3, 4.)
15–16	Lines of three walk forward, passing right shoulders, and move forward to the next group of three. (Forward pass, 2, 3, . . ., 8.)

Repeat to the end of the music.

Circle Virginia Reel (American)

MUSIC SOURCE: WWCD-57; WWC-57

SKILLS: Star, swing, do-si-do, swing, promenade

FORMATION: Couples facing in a double circle with dancers about 4 feet apart

DIRECTIONS:

MEASURES	ACTION
1–4	Partners walk forward four and backward four steps; repeat. (Forward, 2, 3, 4; back, 2, 3, 4; forward, 2, 3, 4; back, 2, 3, 4.)

5–8	Partners make a star by joining right hands (with bent elbows) and circling around once clockwise in eight steps. Reverse direction and star with left hands back to place in eight steps. (Right star, 2, 3, . . ., 8; left star, 2, 3, . . ., 8.)
9–10	Partners join hands with bent elbows held chest high and circle clockwise back to place in eight steps. (Circle, 2, 3, . . ., 8.)
11–12	Partners walk forward and do-si-do, passing right shoulders and stepping to the right when passing back-to-back. After passing, each partner moves diagonally (veers) to the right to end in front of a new partner. (Do-si-do, 2, 3, 4; veer, 2, 3, 4.)
13–16	Facing a new partner and joining hands, inside partner begins with left foot and outside partner begins with right foot, doing two heel-toe steps and four slide steps counterclockwise. Repeat to the other side, sliding clockwise. (Heel-toe, heel-toe, slide, slide, slide, slide; heel-toe, heel-toe, slide, slide, slide, slide.)
17–20	Partners do a right elbow swing in place for 12 counts using a walking step and use 4 counts to end in promenade position. (Swing, 2, 3, . . ., 12; promenade position 15, 16.)
21–24	In promenade position, partners walk forward counterclockwise 16 steps and end facing each other. (Promenade, 2, 3, . . ., 16.)

INTRODUCTORY SQUARE DANCE

When teaching introductory square dance, do not expect elementary school children to become finished, accomplished square dancers. Instead, emphasize enjoyment and learning the basics within the students' maturity capabilities. Some dancers, however, will acquire considerable skill and polish. Square dancing is a varied, colorful activity with many figures, patterns, and dances. The abundance of materials (introductory, intermediate, and advanced) poses a selection problem given the limited amount of program time for the activity.

Square dance fun begins with an effective caller, and calling takes practice. Although a few children can develop into satisfactory callers, teachers may want to select square dance music that includes some selections with calls and some with the music only. Directions are usually supplied with the CDs. Choose singing calls that an individual, a group, or the entire class can use. Singing calls are fun to dance to because they tell children what is coming next.

Square dance instruction can begin modestly in the fourth grade, with increased focus in the fifth and sixth grades. This method does not rule out using square-dance–related figures in folk dances taught earlier. Square dance as a specialized dance activity requires an appropriate method. Some teaching suggestions follow.

1. In early figure practice or patter calls, pairing off by gender is not important. Let boys dance with boys and girls with girls. Avoid labeling one position for boys and one for girls. In a couple, one partner becomes the left partner and the other the right. The goal is, however, to have boys and girls dance together. In the following section, calls are given in their traditional forms, and gender references, where they appear, correspond with the traditional calls.
2. Use the shuffle step rather than the skipping or running step for beginners. The shuffle step makes a smoother and more graceful dance, has better carryover to other dancing, and conserves energy. It is a quick walk, almost a half glide, in time to the music and is done by reaching out with the toes in a gliding motion. Dancers have good posture and do not bounce up and down on each step.
3. Teach the dancers to listen to the call. They can have fun, but they must be quiet enough to hear the call.
4. Dancers must follow the caller's directions and not move too soon. Instruct children to be ready for the call and then move at the proper time.
5. Generally, the caller explains the figures, has the children walk through the patterns, and then

calls the figures. It is important for children to know what the call means.

6. When teaching, remember there are many different ways to do different turns, swings, hand positions, and so on—and as many opinions on how they should be done. Settle on good principles and stick with them.
7. When a set becomes confused, have each couple return to home position and try to pick up from that point. Otherwise, have them wait until the dance is over or a new sequence starts.
8. Change partners at different times during the dancing. Have each Partner A move one place to the right and take a new partner, or have all of the A partners (or Bs) keep their positions and have their partners change to another set.

THE INDIVIDUAL APPROACH TO SQUARE DANCE

Many square dance terms can be taught using an individual approach. Students scatter in general space, and there are no boy or girl roles. A piece of country and western music with a strong beat is played. Anytime students hear the call, they perform it with the person nearest to them. Dancers use a two-handed swing instead of the regular buzz-step swing.

Two calls are basic. "Hit the lonesome trail" directs students to promenade individually in general space in diverse directions. Use this call at any time to move the students in new directions. The other basic call is, "Stop where you are and keep time to the music." Students stop and beat time to the music with light claps. Here are some other calls.

1. *Right (or left) arm round.* With a forearm grasp, turn your partner once around and return to place.
2. *Honor your partner, honor your corner.* Bow to one person, then bow to another.
3. *Do-si-do your partner, do-si-do your corner.* Pass around one person, right shoulder to right shoulder, and go back to place. Repeat with another person.
4. *Right- (or left-) hand star.* Place indicated hands (palm to palm with fingers pointed upward) about shoulder height with elbow somewhat bent. The next call indicates how far to turn the star.
5. *Two-hand swing.* Partners grasp both hands, lean away from each other, and circle clockwise once around.
6. *Go forward and back.* Move forward with three steps and a touch toward another person, who is moving toward you the same way. Move back to place with three steps and a touch.

Another teaching strategy is to divide the class into groups of four. Use a call such as, "Circle up, four hands round." Groups of four circle clockwise. There are usually extra children. If there are three extras, one child can pretend to have a partner. Rotate the extras in and out.

Circle fours until all groups are formed. With the call, "Break and swing," the fours separate into pairs within the foursome. Position the pairs so they face each other. Call "left partner" and "right partner" instead of "boy" and "girl." If convenient when there are mixed pairs, the girl is on the right.

These figures can be practiced in fours.

1. *Circle to the left (or right).* Join hands and circle once around as indicated.
2. *Form a right- (or left-) hand star.* Hold right hands at about shoulder height and turn clockwise. A left-hand star turns counterclockwise.
3. *Swing your opposite and swing your partner.* Left partners walk toward their right partner opposite and swing. They walk back to their own partner and swing. The call can be reversed.
4. *Birdie in the cage and three hands round.* One child (the birdie) goes to the center, while the other three join hands and circle left once around.
5. *The birdie hops out and the crow hops in.* The birdie joins the circle and another child goes in the center.
6. *Go into the middle and come back out; go into the middle and give a little shout.* This figure is done from a circle-right or circle-left formation. The dancers face center and come together. Repeat, but with a light shout.
7. *Round and round in a single file; round and round in frontier style.* Circle left (or right), drop hands and move into a single file.
8. *Dive for the oyster, dig for the clam.* Usually after circling left once around, one couple goes partially under the raised joined hands of the other couple. The other couple repeats the same maneuver. (In, 2, 3, touch; out, 2, 3, touch.)

19

SQUARE DANCE FORMATION

Each couple's position is numbered, going counterclockwise around the set. It is important for couples to know their position. The couple with their backs to the music is generally couple 1, or the head couple. The couple to their right is number 2, and so on. While the head couple is number 1, the term *head couples* includes both couples 1 and 3; couples 2 and 4 are the *side couples*.

For any one left-hand partner (gent), the following terms are used in traditional calls (adjust references to gender as necessary):

Partner: The other (right-hand) dancer of the couple

Corner or corner lady: The right-hand partner on the left

Right-hand lady: The right-hand partner in the couple to the right

Opposite or opposite lady: The right-hand partner directly across the set

Callers also use these terms:

Home: The couple's original or starting position

Active or leading couple: The couple leading or visiting the other couples for different figures

After introducing the square dance formation, have children practice the figures and patter calls in the full formation of four couples. Some of this material is presented in "The Individual Approach to Square Dance," but the following figures merit discussion regarding square dance formation.

AMERICAN SQUARE DANCE FIGURES

Here are some common square dance figures:

1. *Honor your partner.* Partners bow to each other.
2. *Honor your corner.* Left-hand dancer bows to corner, who returns the bow.
3. *Shuffle step.* Dancers do a light walking step on the ball of the foot, holding the body upright and moving in time with the music.
4. *Do-si-do your partner (or corner).* Partners face and pass each other right shoulder to right shoulder, move around each other back-to-back, and return to the original position facing their partner.
5. *Promenade.* The couple walks side by side, right hand joined to right hand and left to left in a crossed-arm promenade position. They walk around the square once and return to home position.
6. *Circle right (or left).* All eight dancers join hands and circle. The caller can add, "Into the center with a great big yell!" Dancers can break circle with a swing at home place.
7. *Grand right and left.* All face their partner, join right hands, walk past the partner, and join left hands with the next person in the ring, and so on down the line. This causes left-hand partners to go in one direction (counterclockwise) around the circle and right-hand partners to go in the other direction, alternately touching right and left hands until partners meet again. Grand right and left starts with your partner and ends with your partner, and then the another call is given.
8. *Allemande left.* Left-hand dancer faces corner, grasps corner with a left-forearm grip, walks around corner, and returns to partner.
9. *Arm swing.* Left-hand dancer turns partner with a right-arm swing, using a forearm grasp.
10. *Swing your partner (or corner).* Partners stand side by side with right hip against right hip. The dancers are almost in social dance position, but the left-hand partner's right arm is more around to the side than back at the shoulder blade. The dancers walk around each other with a slight lean away from each other until reaching their starting position.
11. *Do paso.* Starting position is a circle of two or more couples. Partners face, grasp left forearms, and turn each other counterclockwise until facing the corner. Turn corner with right forearm grasp until facing partner. Take partner with the left hand; left-hand partner turns the other with a courtesy turn.
12. *All around your left-hand lady, seesaw your pretty little taw.* Corners move one time around each other in a loop pattern, left-hand dancer starting behind the corner, on moving around corner and back to place, right-hand dancer starting in front of corner and moving around back to place. Repeat with partner to complete the other half of the loop.
13. *Ladies chain.* From a position with two couples facing each other, the girls cross over to the opposite boy, touching right hands as they pass each other. Upon reaching the opposite boy, they join left hands with him. At the same time, each boy places his right arm around the girl's waist and turns her once around to face the other couple. On "Chain right back," the girls cross back to their partner in a similar figure.
14. *Right-and-left through (and back).* Two couples face each other. Dancers join right hands and pull past opposite, passing right shoulder to right shoulder. Couples are back-to-back. Courtesy turn to face again and repeat to original place.

SELECTING SQUARE DANCES AND MUSIC

In the past, elementary students learned traditional square dances using a patter call. Today, square dancing is a popular form of adult recreation. Singing calls and modern music help make square dancing popular among adults, but more important is the change from traditional to modern calls. In traditional square dancing, everyone knew what the next call was. In modern square dancing, only the caller knows the next call.

Two popular series of albums with different developmental levels and proper progression are the Wagon Wheel Fundamentals of Square Dancing, Levels 1, 2, and 3, and Square Dance Party for the New Dancer, No. 1 and No. 2. Both series feature the calling of Bob Ruff. They can be ordered from the following source:

Wagon Wheel Records

16812 Pembrook Lane

Huntington Beach, CA 92649

Phone/Fax:(714) 846-8169

Website: www.wagonwheelrecords.net

E-mail: info@wagonwheelrecords.net

CULMINATING EVENTS FOR THE RHYTHMS UNIT

When students in all grade levels are reasonably accomplished dancers, the school can sponsor a culminating event. Here are a few suggestions.

COUNTRY-WESTERN DAY

On country-western day, teachers and students wear country-western clothing all day. For the last hour of the school day, the student body attends a square dance. It is important to include activities that everyone, from third graders to sixth graders, can do together. The movement approach presented earlier can help achieve this goal.

MAY FESTIVAL

In the spring, as the rhythm program draws to a close, it is exciting to hold a May festival featuring all of the dances learned. This activity includes everyone; each class or grade level presents a dance. Have an announcer describe the history and background of each dance (consult specialty dance books for a description of the various dances). End the festival with the entire school performing the Maypole Dance.

FOR MORE INFORMATION

WEBSITES

Dance Ideas
www.pecentral.org

Dances of Mexico
www.alegria.org/rgndance.html

Multicultural Dances
www.activevideos.com/multicultural.htm
www.centralhome.com/ballroomcountry/video_store.htm

Music Sources
www.wagonwheelrecords.net

Square Dancing
www.dosado.com

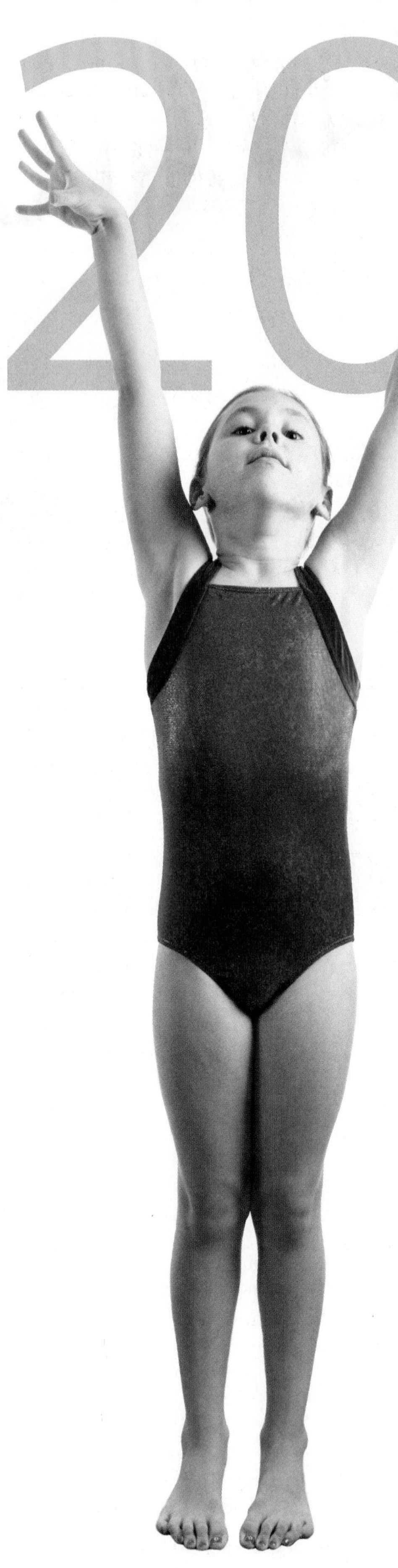

20 Gymnastic Skills

ESSENTIAL COMPONENTS OF QUALITY PROGRAMS

- I. Organized around content standards
- II. Student-centered and developmentally appropriate
- III. Physical activity and motor skill development form the core of the program
- IV. Teaches management skills and self-discipline
- V. Promotes inclusion of all students
- VI. Focuses on process over product
- VII. Promotes lifetime personal health and wellness
- VIII. Teaches cooperation and responsibility and promotes sensitivity to diversity

NATIONAL STANDARDS FOR PHYSICAL EDUCATION*

1. Demonstrates competency in motor skills and movement patterns needed to perform a variety of physical activities.
2. Demonstrates understanding of movement concepts, principles, and tactics as they apply to the learning and performance of physical activities.
3. Participates regularly in physical activity.
4. Achieves and maintains a health-enhancing level of physical fitness.
5. Exhibits responsible personal and social behavior that respects self and others in physical activity.
6. Values physical activity for health, enjoyment, challenge, self-expression, and/or social interaction.

*National Association for Sport and Physical Education (NASPE), 2004.

Gymnastic activities contribute significantly to the overall physical education experience for elementary school children. Gymnastic activities develop body management skills without the need for equipment and apparatus. Participating in gymnastics enhances children's flexibility, agility, balance, strength, and body control. Students learn specialized motor skills such as body rolling, balance skills, inverted balances, and tumbling skills. Various partner and group activities offer opportunity for social interaction and cooperation. Positive learning experiences in gymnastic activities depend on progression. Enjoyable teaching activities, developing a positive attitude, and overcoming students' personal limitations are more important than performing with perfect technique. Safety is foremost in the gymnastic program.

Outcomes

- List progressions and specify developmental levels for gymnastic activities.
- Understand the techniques of spotting when teaching gymnastic activities.
- Organize a comprehensive lesson of gymnastic activities, including the six basic groups: (1) animal movements; (2) tumbling and inverted balances; (3) balance stunts; (4) individual stunts; (5) partner and group stunts; and (6) partner support activities.
- Identify effective management techniques when teaching gymnastic activities.
- Cite safety considerations essential to the gymnastic program.
- Describe appropriate tumbling activities for elementary school children.

GYMNASTIC ACTIVITIES are an important part of every child's physical education experience, and they can contribute significantly to physical education goals. The gymnastics program helps strengthen children's dedication and perseverance, for stunts are seldom mastered quickly. Because much of the work is individual, students face challenges and have the opportunity to develop resourcefulness, self-confidence, and courage. When children master a challenging stunt, satisfaction, pride in achievement, and a sense of accomplishment can improve their self-esteem. Students benefit from social interplay, cooperating in various partner and group stunts. Through an educationally sound methodology, teachers nurture the social attributes of tolerance, helpfulness, courtesy, and appreciation for the ability of others.

Important physical values also emerge from a gymnastics program. Teachers offer body management opportunities for students to enhance coordination, flexibility, and agility. Many activities give children an opportunity to practice balance. By holding positions and executing stunts, students develop strength and power in diverse parts of the body. Many stunts demand support—wholly or in part—by the arms, and thus develop the often weak musculature of the arm–shoulder girdle.

PROGRESSION AND DEVELOPMENTAL LEVEL PLACEMENT

Progression is important in the gymnastics program. This book presents activities in progression within the three developmental levels. To avoid safety problems, the order of these activities should be reasonably maintained. Adhering to a developmental level is secondary to the principle of progression. If children have little or no experience in these activities, start them on activities specified in a lower developmental level.

Activities in this chapter are in six basic groups: (1) animal movements; (2) tumbling and inverted balances; (3) balance stunts; (4) individual stunts; (5) partner and group stunts; and (6) partner support activities. This arrangement allows teachers to pick activities from each group for a well-balanced lesson. Often, too much time is spent on tumbling activities, and children become bored and fatigued. Choosing activities from all the categories will help children who do not like tumbling activities find something they enjoy. At the heart of a gymnastic program are the standard tumbling activities, such as rolls, stands, springs, and related stunts. As your students perform these activities, emphasize exposure and overcoming fear. Perfect technique is less important than developing positive approach behaviors. Here is the suggested progression of basic activities for each developmental level.

DEVELOPMENTAL LEVEL I

- Log Roll
- Side Roll
- Forward Roll (Tuck Position)
- Back Roller
- Forward Roll (Straddle Position)
- Backward Curl
- Backward Roll (Handclasp Position)
- Climb-Up
- Three-Point Tip-Up
- Mountain Climber—Handstand Lead-Up Activity
- Switcheroo—Handstand Lead-Up Activity

DEVELOPMENTAL LEVEL II

- Forward Roll (Pike Position)
- Backward Roll (Regular)
- Frog Handstand (Tip-Up)
- Half Teeter-Totter—Handstand Lead-Up Activity
- Cartwheel
- Forward Roll to a Walkout
- Forward Roll Combinations
- Backward Roll Combinations
- Headstand Practice and Variations
- Teeter-Totter—Handstand Lead-Up Activity
- Handstand

DEVELOPMENTAL LEVEL III

- Forward and Backward Roll Combinations
- Back Extension
- Headstand Variations
- Handstand against a Wall
- Freestanding Handstand
- Cartwheel and Round-Off
- Judo Roll
- Forward and Backward Roll Combinations
- Developing Gymnastic Routines
- Straddle Press to Headstand
- Headspring
- Walking on the Hands
- Walk-Over

The Developmental Level I program relies on simple stunts, with a gradual introduction to tumbling stunts classified as lead-ups or preliminaries to more advanced stunts. Stunts requiring exceptional body control, critical balancing, or substantial strength are best for higher levels of development. The Developmental Level II and III programs are built on activities and progressions developed earlier. Emphasis is on learning more standard gymnastic activities. Most stunts at Developmental Level I have a wide range of acceptable performance; at Developmental Levels II and III, increasing conformance to correct technique is desirable. In general, the upper developmental level activities place higher demands on strength, control, form, agility, balance, and flexibility.

Most students can do the activities at Developmental Level I, at least in some fashion; but certain activities at Developmental Levels II and III may be too challenging for some students. Design lessons to include a variety of activities ranging from to easy to moderately challenging to very challenging.

INSTRUCTIONAL METHODOLOGY FOR GYMNASTICS

WARM-UP AND FLEXIBILITY ACTIVITY

Normal introductory activity and fitness development activity are usually sufficient as a warm-up for the gymnastics lesson. If additional stretching seems warranted, instruct students to take a wide straddle position with their feet about 3 feet apart and toes pointed ahead. With arms out to the sides, bend, twist, and generally stretch in all directions. Next, touch the floor with the hands to the front, sides, and back, with some bending of the knees.

Extra flexibility may be required in the wrists, ankles, and neck. Have students do these activities before participating in gymnastic activities.

Wrists

1. Extend one arm forward. With the other hand, push the extended hand down, thus stretching the top of the wrist and forearm muscles. Hold the position for 8 counts. Next, pull the hand backward and hold for 8 counts to stretch the wrist flexor muscles.
2. Clasp the fingers of both hands in front of the chest. Make circles with both hands, and stretch the wrists.

Ankles and Quadriceps

1. Kneel and sit on both feet. Smoothly and gently lean backward over the feet, using the arms to support the body.
2. In a sitting position, cross one leg over the other. Use the hands to help rotate each foot through its full range of motion. Reverse legs and repeat.

Neck

1. In a sitting position, slowly circle the head in both directions through the full range of motion.
2. In the same position, hold the chin against the chest for 8 counts. Repeat with the head looking backward as far as possible. Look to each side and hold for 8 counts.

Lower Back and Shoulders

Begin in a supine position. Raise both arms overhead; bend elbows and place the hands facing backward on the mat with fingers pointing toward the toes. Form a bridge by extending the arms and legs. While in the bridge position, slowly rock back and forth.

EFFECTIVE CLASS MANAGEMENT

Here are some guidelines for keeping children engaged during a gymnastics class.

1. Whenever possible, all children should be active and performing. Activities not requiring mats can be done anywhere in the gymnasium. Use individual mats for simple balances and rolling stunts, particularly at Developmental Level I. When larger mats are required, be more ingenious. Ideally, provide one mat for each group of three students. When students in groups of three are doing return activities, few children are standing around.
2. When the number of mats is limited, students can perform sideways on them. An 8-foot-long mat is large enough for three performers at the same time. This arrangement allows for single rolls but does not rule out an occasional series of rolls lengthwise on the mat. Use the ends of the mats as a cushion for various headstands, as long as children are aligned so they do not fall toward each other.
3. Consider station teaching if equipment is limited. Make plans that ensure the experience stresses progress and diligence. You can include a few tumbling and inverted balance stations as well as other stations featuring less demanding activities. Wall charts listing the activities in progression provide excellent guidance.

FORMATIONS FOR TEACHING

For best effect in a particular lesson, choose from these standard formations.

1. *Squad formation.* Mats are laid end to end, and squads line up behind the mats. Each child takes a turn and then goes to the end of the squad line as the others move up. An alternative method is for each child to perform and then return to a seated position.
2. *Semicircular formation.* Students and mats are positioned in a semicircular arrangement. This formation directs attention toward the teacher, who stands in the center.
3. *U-shaped formation.* The mats are placed in a large U shape. This formation offers an excellent view for the teacher and allows children to see what their classmates are doing.
4. *Demonstration mat.* One mat is placed in a central position and used exclusively for demonstrations. Little student movement is necessary to see demonstrations.

DESCRIPTION AND DEMONSTRATION OF NEW GYMNASTIC ACTIVITIES

To enhance student learning when presenting an activity, try the three-step approach:

1. *Significance of the name.* Most activities have a characteristic name that students should learn. If the stunt is of an imitative type, briefly discuss the animal or character represented.
2. *Description of the activity.* Most stunts have three parts: starting position, execution, and finishing position. Most stunts have a defined starting position, which is part of the performance. First tell students how to assume the starting position. Next, teach the key points in properly executing the activity. Technical points include how far to travel, how long to balance, and how many times to do a movement. In some gymnastic activities, a definite finishing position or action is part of the stunt. Balancing stunts require performers to return to standing (or some other) position without losing balance and moving the feet.
3. *Demonstration of the activity.* Three levels of demonstration are recognized: (a) minimal demonstration in the form of the starting position; (b) slow, step-by-step demonstration of the entire stunt, with an explanation of what is involved; and (c) execution of the stunt as it is normally done. Remember that children need to analyze and solve problems. Because too much demonstration defeats this process, cover just a few points in your explanation. Show only the points necessary to get the activity going. Add further details and refinements as the activity progresses.

Opportunities for Practice and Improvement

The character of each stunt determines the amount of practice needed and the number of times the stunt should be performed. Analyze the stunt thoroughly enough to explain the points necessary for proper performance. Practice and repetition are essential in establishing effective movement patterns. To maximize activity and minimize standing in line, allow time for the class to practice the activity. On signal, the class stops whatever they are doing without returning to formation. Upon receiving directions for the next activity, the class resumes practicing. This method decreases the amount of management time spent waiting for each squad to finish and return to formation.

SAFETY CONSIDERATIONS

Safety is a foremost consideration in the gymnastic program. The inherent hazards of an activity must be emphasized in the instructional procedures.

SPOTTING

You will have to decide whether you feel qualified and confident enough to teach activities that require spotting; if you do not, it is probably best to avoid spotting children. You can still teach tumbling and inverted balances, but offer them as choices for more advanced students. Because tumbling and inverted balance activities make up only about 10% of the activities in this chapter, you can offer many other stunts and balance activities to teach students body management skills. To avoid the potential for serious injuries, do not force children to participate in tumbling and inverted balance activities. This chapter offers spotting techniques for competent teachers who are knowledgeable about stunts and tumbling.

The purpose of spotting is twofold. First and foremost is assisting the performer, helping support the body weight, and preventing a hazardous fall. Second is guiding the performer through the stunt to help develop proper body awareness.

Teachers often have two major questions about spotting.

1. *Should teachers spot students?* In most cases, a child who has to be spotted for a basic tumbling or balance activity should not be asked to do the activity. A better alternative is to let students choose one of several activities. For example, allow children to choose between the forward roll and a log roll. Students who are fearful or do not want to do a forward roll can still have a successful and enjoyable experience.

   Because teachers can spot only one child at a time, many children will be standing around waiting for a turn. Teachers also have to be aware that some children do not want an adult's hands on them. Finally, some children, because of their strength or other physical limitations, may never be able to do a forward roll, backward roll, or headstand. Fortunately, there are many other ways to physically educate these students.

2. *Should students spot their peers?* If an accident were to occur while a student was spotting, who would be liable? Legal authorities might try to show that you were not supervising the spotting carefully or that students are too young and not responsible enough to fulfill the duties of correct spotting. If your only recourse is to have students spot each other, avoid teaching those activities. Rarely are students able to perform quality spotting.

INSTRUCTIONAL PROCEDURES

1. Mats are not needed for some stunts, but it is wise to include stunts requiring mats in every lesson. Children like to perform on mats, and rolling stunts using mats are vital to the gymnastic program.
2. Many partner stunts work best when partners are about the same size. If the stunt requires partner support, be sure the support child is strong enough to hold the other's weight.
3. No two children are alike. Respect individual differences, and allow for different levels of success.
4. Relating new activities to those learned earlier is important. An effective approach is to review the lead-up stunt for an activity.
5. When a stunt calls for a position to be held for a number of counts, use a standard counting system (e.g., "One thousand one, one thousand two, ...").
6. When appropriate, have children work in pairs, with one child performing and the second providing a critique.
7. Shifting of mats should not be necessary during the instruction. When arranging a gymnastic routine for a day's lesson, group the mat stunts. The tumbling mats should be bordered with Velcro for fastening them together.

START-AND-EXPAND TECHNIQUE

When feasible, use the start-and-expand technique to teach stunts. Consider this example for teaching a simple Heel Click (page 474).

1. *Start.* "Let's see all of you jump high in the air and click your heels together before you come down."
2. *Expand.* "Now, to do the stunt properly, you will jump into the air, click your heels, and land with your feet apart with a nice bent-knee action to absorb the shock." To expand further, have students add a quarter or half turn before landing, clap the hands overhead while clicking the heels, or click the heels twice before landing.

The start is generally simple, so that all children can experience some success. The instruction then expands to other elements of the stunt, adding variations and refining movements.

BASIC MECHANICAL PRINCIPLES

Certain mechanical principles are basic to gymnastic techniques. Teaching children to build on these principles can facilitate learning.

1. Momentum needs to be developed and applied, particularly for rolls. Tucking, starting from a higher point, and preliminary raising of the arms are some ways to increase momentum.
2. The center of weight must be positioned over the center of support in balance stunts, particularly in the inverted stands.
3. In certain stunts, such as the Headspring, the hips should be projected upward and forward to raise the center of gravity for better execution.
4. When hands wholly or partially support the body, proper hand position is essential to effective performance. The hands should be approximately shoulder width apart, the fingers spread and pointed forward.

BASIC GYMNASTIC POSITIONS

Teach your students to recognize and demonstrate the basic positions unique to gymnastics. At the elementary level, children focus on learning the basic form of the activity rather than pure technique.

Tuck Position

Perform the tuck with the legs bent and the chin tucked to the chest. Cue students to "curl up like a ball." There are three different tuck positions, and students should know all of them: Sitting Tuck (Figure 20.1), Standing Tuck, and Lying Tuck.

Pike Position

Perform the pike by bending forward at the hips and keeping the legs straight. The three basic pike positions are the Sitting Pike (Figure 20.2), Standing Pike, and Lying Pike.

Straddle Position

Perform the straddle position by bending forward at the hips and spreading the legs to the sides as far as possible. Keep the legs straight. Variations of the straddle position are the sitting piked Straddle (Figure 20.3), standing piked Straddle, and lying piked Straddle.

Front-Support Position

This position is similar to the push-up position. Hold the body straight and the head up (Figure 20.4 on page 462).

Back-Support Position

This is an inverted push-up position. Keep the body as straight as possible (Figure 20.5 on page 462).

FIGURE 20.1 Tuck position.

FIGURE 20.2 Pike position.

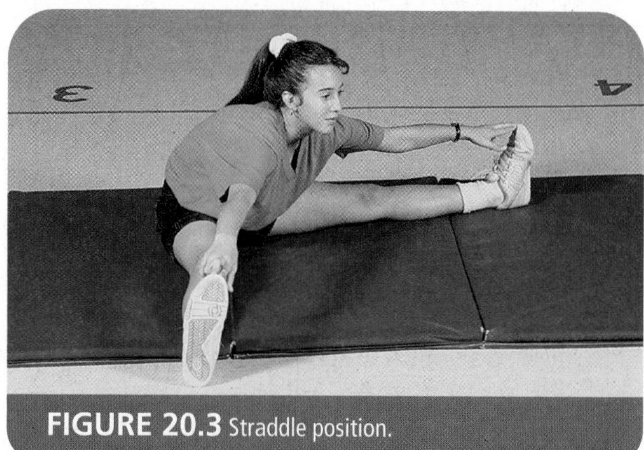

FIGURE 20.3 Straddle position.

20

GYMNASTIC DANCE POSITIONS

Attitude

Assume this position by supporting the body weight on one leg while lifting the other leg and bending it at the knee. Hold the arm on the side of the lifted leg overhead, and extend the other arm to the side (Figure 20.6 on page 462).

FIGURE 20.4 Front-support position.

FIGURE 20.5 Back-support position.

FIGURE 20.6 Attitude.

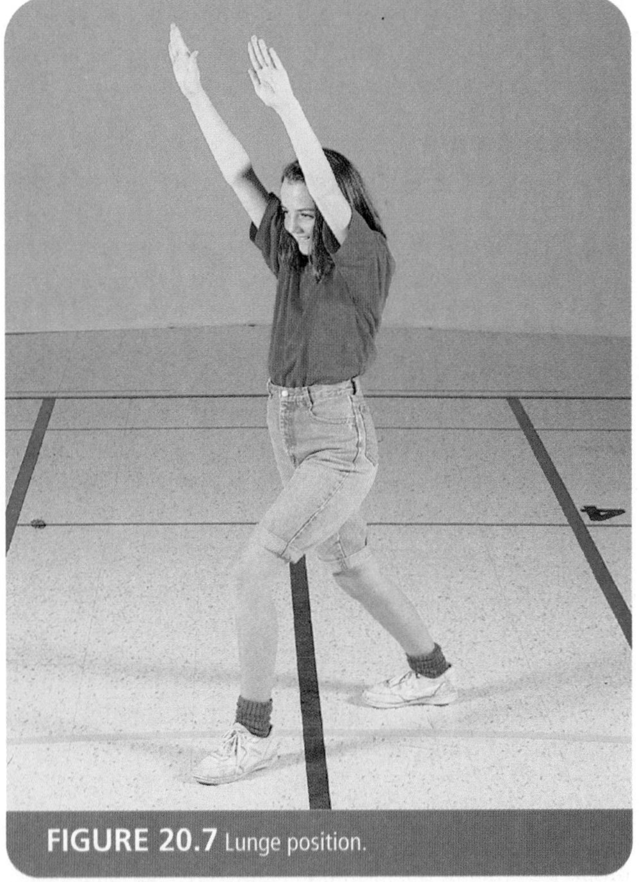

FIGURE 20.7 Lunge position.

Lunge Position

Perform the lunge by straightening the rear leg and bending the forward, supporting leg at the hip and knee. Most of the weight is on the forward leg. Extend the arms, and keep the head up with eyes forward (Figure 20.7).

Plié

Plié ("plee-AY") means "a bending of the knees." Bend both knees, extend the arms at right angles to the sides, and tuck the seat to hold the abdomen flat. There are different plié positions; but in gymnastic instruction, the plié is used to teach landing with grace and control.

Relevé

The relevé ("rell-uh-VAY") is an extension movement from the plié position. The movement goes from the plié (knees bent) position to the extended position (legs straight). Extension is complete through all of the joints, stretching upward from the balls of the feet.

Arabesque

Perform the Arabesque by supporting the weight on one leg while extending the other leg to the rear. Keep the extended leg with the toe pointed, and hold the torso erect (Figure 20.8). The Back Extension and the Cartwheel are often brought to completion with an Arabesque.

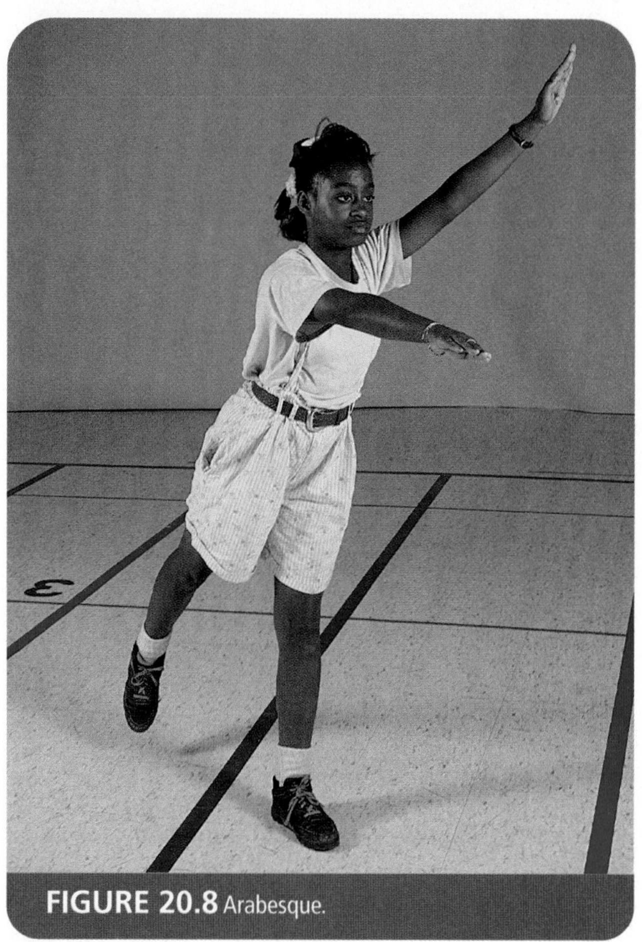
FIGURE 20.8 Arabesque.

Jumps

Gymnastic dance commonly uses three jump variations: the Tuck Jump, Pike Jump, and Straddle Jump. These jumps are simply a jump with the prescribed position added. The arms are raised in a lifting motion to increase the height of the jump and to enhance balance. The impact of the landing is absorbed at the ankles and knee joints.

Chassé

The chassé ("shah-SAY") is a slide. This basic locomotor movement involves one leg chasing the other out of position. It is done close to the floor with a light spring in the step.

STUNTS AND TUMBLING ACTIVITIES

This chapter presents the stunts and tumbling activities, in order of difficulty, within three developmental levels. Table 20.1 (pages 464–466) lists all the activities in each of the levels and offers a page reference to descriptions of each activity. A brief discussion of each developmental level follows.

DEVELOPMENTAL LEVEL I ACTIVITIES

Developmental Level I activities consist primarily of imitative walks and movements, plus selected balance stunts and rolls. The Forward Roll is practiced but refined only in later levels. The Back Roller is a prelude to the Backward Roll.

ANIMAL MOVEMENTS

Alligator Crawl

Lie facedown on the floor with elbows bent. Move along the floor like an alligator, keeping the hands close to the body and the feet pointed out (Figure 20.9). First, use unilateral movements—that is, right arm and leg moving together—then change to cross-lateral movements.

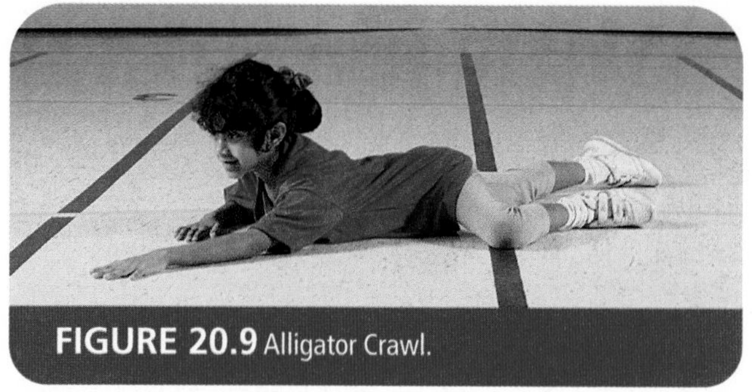
FIGURE 20.9 Alligator Crawl.

Kangaroo Jump

Carry the arms close to the chest with the palms facing forward. Place a beanbag or ball between the knees. Move in different directions by taking small jumps without dropping the object.

Puppy Dog Run

Place the hands on the floor, bending the arms and legs slightly. Walk and run like a happy puppy. Look straight ahead. Keep the head up, in good position, to strengthen the neck muscles. Go sideways, backward, and so on. Turn around in place.

VARIATIONS:

1. *Cat Walk.* Use the same position to imitate a cat. Walk softly. Stretch at times like a cat. Be smooth and deliberate.
2. *Monkey Run.* Turn the hands and feet so that the fingers and toes point in (toward each other).

TABLE 20.1 Stunts and tumbling activities

Activity	Page
Developmental Level I	
Animal Movements	
Alligator Crawl	463
Kangaroo Jump	463
Puppy Dog Run	463
Cat Walk	463
Monkey Run	463
Bear Walk	466
Gorilla Walk	466
Rabbit Jump	466
Elephant Walk	466
Siamese Twin Walk	467
Tightrope Walk	467
Lame Dog Walk	467
Crab Walk	467
Tumbling And Inverted Balances	
Log Roll	468
Side Roll	468
Forward Roll	468
Back Roller	468
Forward Roll (Straddle Position)	469
Backward Curl	469
Backward Roll (Handclasp Position)	469
Climb-Up	470
Three-Point Tip-Up	470
Mountain Climber	470
Switcheroo	470
Balance Stunts	
One-Leg Balance	470
Double-Knee Balance	471
Head Touch	471
Head Balance	471
One-Leg Balance Stunts	471
Kimbo Stand	471
Knee-Lift Stand	471
Stork Stand	471
Balance Touch	472
Single-Leg Balances	472
Forward Balance	472
Backward Balance	472
Side Balance	472
Hand-and-Knee Balance	472
Single-Knee Balance	472
Individual Stunts	
Directional Walk	473
Line Walking	473
Fluttering Leaf	473
Elevator	473
Cross-Legged Stand	473
Developmental Level I (Continued)	
Individual Stunts (Continued)	
Walking in Place	473
Jump Turns	473
Rubber Band	474
Pumping Up the Balloon	474
Rising Sun	474
Heel Click	474
Lowering the Boom	474
Turn-Over	474
Thread the Needle	474
Heel Slap	475
Pogo Stick	475
Top	475
Sitting Stand	476
Push-Up	476
Crazy Walk	476
Seat Circle	476
Partner And Group Stunts	
Bouncing Ball	476
Seesaw	477
Wring the Dishrag	477
Partner Toe Toucher	477
Double Top	477
Roly Poly	478
Developmental Level II	
Animal Movements	
Cricket Walk	478
Frog Jump	478
Seal Crawl	478
Reverse Seal Crawl	478
Elbow Crawl	478
Measuring Worm	479
Mule Kick	479
Walrus Walk	479
Double-Lame Dog	479
Turtle	480
Walrus Slap	480
Reverse Walrus Slap	480
Tumbling and Inverted Balances	
Forward Roll to a Walkout	480
Backward Roll (Regular)	481
Headstand	481
Headstand Climb-Up	481
Headstand Kick-Up	482
Headstand Practice and Variations	482
Frog Handstand (Tip-Up)	482

TABLE 20.1 (Continued)

Activity	Page
Developmental Level II (Continued)	
Half Teeter-Totter	483
Cartwheel	483
Forward Roll (Pike Position)	483
Forward Roll Combinations	483
Backward Roll Combinations	484
Teeter-Totter	484
Handstand	484
Balance Stunts	
One-Leg Balance Reverse	484
Tummy Balance	485
Leg Dip	486
Balance Jump	486
Seat Balance	486
Face-to-Knee Touch	486
Finger Touch	487
Individual Stunts	
Reach-Under	487
Stiff Person Bend	487
Coffee Grinder	487
Scooter	488
Hip Walk	488
Long Bridge	488
Heelstand	488
Wicket Walk	488
Knee Jump to Standing	489
Individual Drops or Falls	489
Knee Drop	489
Forward Drop	489
Dead Body Fall	490
Stoop and Stretch	490
Tanglefoot	490
Egg Roll	490
Toe Touch Nose	491
Toe-Tug Walk	491
Partner And Group Stunts	
Partner Hopping	491
Partner Twister	492
Partner Pull-Up	492
Back-to-Back Get-Up	492
Rowboat	493
Leapfrog	493
Wheelbarrow	493
Wheelbarrow Lifting	493
Camel Lift and Walk	494
Dump the Wheelbarrow	494
Dromedary Walk	494
Centipede	494
Double Wheelbarrow	494
Partner Support Stunts	
Double Bear	495
Table	495
Statue	495
Lighthouse	496
Hip–Shoulder Stand	496
Developmental Level III	
Tumbling and Inverted Balances	
Forward and Backward Roll Combinations	497
Back Extension	497
Headstand Variations	497
Handstand Against a Wall	497
Freestanding Handstand	497
Cartwheel and Round-Off	497
Judo Roll	498
Advanced Forward and Backward Roll Combinations	499
Straddle Press to Headstand	499
Handstand Variations	499
Headspring	499
Walking on the Hands	500
Walk-Over	500
Balance Stunts	
V-Up	500
Push-Up Variations	500
Flip-Flop	500
Long Reach	501
Toe Jump	501
Handstand Stunts	501
Front Seat Support	501
Elbow Balance	501
Individual Stunts	
Wall Walk-Up	501
Skier's Sit	502
Rocking Horse	502
Heel Click (Side)	502
Walk-Through	502
Jump-Through	503
Circular Rope Jump	503
Bouncer	503
Pretzel	503
Jackknife	504
Heel-and-Toe Spring	504
Single-Leg Circle (Pinwheel)	504

(continued)

TABLE 20.1 Stunts and tumbling activities (Continued)

Bear Walk

Bend forward and touch the ground with both hands. Travel forward slowly by moving the hand and foot on the same side together (that is, first the right hand and foot, then the left hand and foot) (Figure 20.10). Make deliberate movements.

FIGURE 20.10 Bear Walk.

VARIATION: Lift the free foot and arm high while the support is on the other side.

Gorilla Walk

Bend the knees and carry the trunk forward. Let the arms hang at the sides. Touch the fingers to the ground while walking.

VARIATION: Stop and beat on the chest like a gorilla. Bounce up and down on all fours with hands and feet touching the floor simultaneously.

Rabbit Jump

Crouch with knees apart and hands placed on the floor. Move forward by reaching out with both hands and then bringing both feet up to the hands. Look straight ahead.

Tell students that this is a jump rather than a hop because both feet move at once. Note that the jump is a bilateral movement.

VARIATIONS:

1. Try with knees together and arms on the outside. Try alternating with knees together and apart on successive jumps. Go over a low hurdle or through a hoop.
2. Experiment with taking more weight on the hands before the feet move forward. To do this, raise the seat higher in the air when the hands move forward.

Elephant Walk

Bend well forward, clasping the hands together to form a trunk. Swing the end of the trunk close to the ground. Walk slowly and deliberately, keeping the legs straight and swinging the trunk from side to side (Figure 20.11). Stop and throw water over the back with the trunk. Recite the following verse while walking, and move the trunk appropriately.

The elephant's walk is steady and slow,

His trunk like a pendulum swings to and fro.

But when there are children with peanuts around,

He swings it up and he swings it down.

VARIATION: With a partner, decide who is the *mahout* (elephant keeper) and who is the elephant. The mahout walks to the side and a

FIGURE 20.11 Elephant Walk.

little in front of the elephant, with one hand touching the elephant's shoulder. She leads the elephant around during the first two lines of the poem. During the last two lines, the mahout walks to a spot in front of the elephant and tosses it a peanut when the trunk sweeps up. She returns to the elephant's side and repeats the action.

Siamese Twin Walk

Stand back-to-back with a partner. Lock elbows (Figure 20.12). Walk forward, backward, and sideways in unison.

Tightrope Walk

Select a line, board, or chalked line on the floor as the high wire. Pretend to be on the high wire and do various tasks, exaggerating loss and control of balance. Add tasks such as jumping rope, juggling balls, and riding a bicycle. Pretend to hold a parasol or a balancing pole while performing. Children can give good play to the imagination. The teacher can set the stage by discussing what a circus performer on the high wire might do.

Lame Dog Walk

Walk on both hands and one foot. Hold the other foot in the air as if injured. Walk a distance and change feet. The eyes should look forward. Move backward and in other combinations. Try moving with an injured front leg.

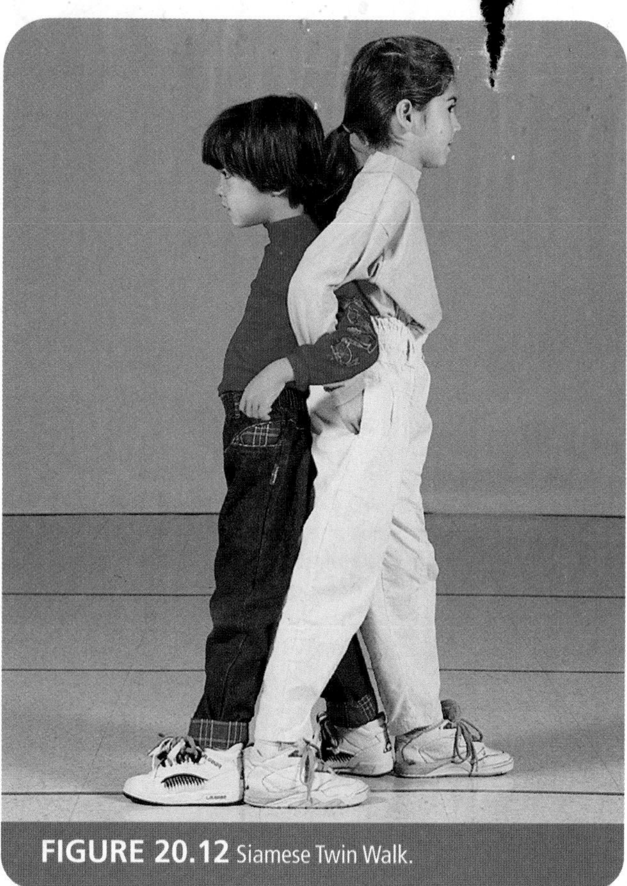
FIGURE 20.12 Siamese Twin Walk.

Crab Walk

Squat down and reach back, putting both hands on the floor without sitting down. With head, neck, and body level, walk forward, backward, and sideways (Figure 20.13). Because children tend to lower the hips, emphasize keeping the body in a straight line.

FIGURE 20.13 Crab Walk.

VAR[torn]ONS:

1. As [torn]ach step is taken with one hand, slap the chest or seat with the other.
2. Move the hand and foot on the same side simultaneously.
3. Try balancing on one leg and the opposite hand for 5 seconds.

TUMBLING AND INVERTED BALANCES

Safety Tip

To avoid risk of injuries, never encourage or force children to perform an activity they are uncomfortable with. If a child lacks the neck and shoulder-girdle strength to do tumbling or inverted balances, substitute an alternate activity. Spotting techniques are offered for teachers who feel capable of helping children who can perform the activities. Spot only children who can and want to perform an activity.

Log Roll

Lie on the back with arms stretched overhead (Figure 20.14). Roll sideways the length of the mat. The next time, roll with the hands pointed toward the other side of the mat. To roll in a straight line, keep the feet slightly apart.

VARIATION: Alternately curl and stretch while rolling.

FIGURE 20.14 Log Roll.

Side Roll

Start on the hands and knees, with one side toward the direction of the roll. Drop the shoulder, tuck both the elbow and the knee, and roll over completely, returning to the hands-and-knees position. Momentum is needed to return to the original position. Practice rolling back and forth from one hand-and-knee position to another.

Forward Roll

Stand facing forward, with the feet apart. Squat and place the hands on the mat, shoulder width apart, with elbows against the inner thighs. Tuck the chin to the chest and make a rounded back. A push-off with the hands and feet provides the force for the roll (Figure 20.15). Carry the weight on the hands, with the elbows bearing the weight of the thighs. By keeping the elbows against the thighs and bearing the weight there, the force of the roll transfers easily to the rounded back. Try to roll forward to the feet. Try with knees together and no weight on elbows.

FIGURE 20.15 Forward Roll.

Spotting: The spotter kneels beside the child and places one hand on the back of the child's head and the other under the thigh (Figure 20.16). As the child moves through the roll, the spotter lifts upward on the back of the neck to assure the neck does not absorb the body's weight. Use this technique for all forward roll variations.

Back Roller

Begin in a crouched position with knees together and hands resting lightly on the floor. Roll backward, gaining momentum by bringing the knees to the chest and clasping them with the arms (Figure 20.17). Roll back and forth rhythmically. On the backward movement, go well back on the neck

FIGURE 20.16 Spotting the Forward Roll. (One hand is on the back of the head and one is under the thigh.)

and head. Try to roll forward to original position. If students have difficulty rolling back to original position, have them cross the legs and roll to a crossed-leg standing position. (This stunt is a lead-up to the Backward Roll.)

FIGURE 20.17 Back Roller.

Forward Roll (Straddle Position)

Start with the legs spread in the straddle position. Bend forward at the hips, tuck the head, place the hands on the mat, and roll forward. To return to the standing position, students must push with the hands at the end of the roll.

Forward Roll Practice and Variations

Review the Forward Roll (tucked), with spotting and assistance as necessary. Work on coming out of the roll to the feet. Grasping the knees at the end of the roll helps.

VARIATIONS:

1. Roll to the feet with ankles crossed.
2. Try to roll with knees together.

Backward Curl

Approach this activity in three stages. The first stage begins in a sitting position with the knees drawn up to the chest and the chin tucked. Clasp the hands and place behind the head, holding the elbows out as far as possible. Gently roll backward until the weight is on the elbows (Figure 20.18). Roll back to starting position.

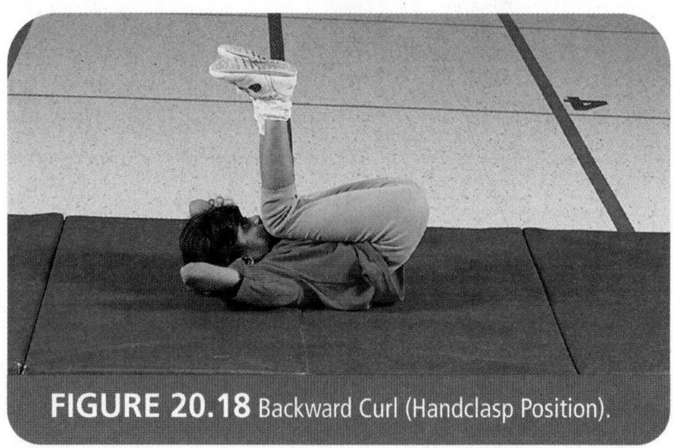

FIGURE 20.18 Backward Curl (Handclasp Position).

In stage two, perform the same action as before, but place the hands beside the head on the mat while rolling back. Point the fingers in the direction of the roll, with palms down on the mat. (A good cue is, "Point your thumbs toward your ears and keep your elbows close to your body.")

For stage three, perform the same action as in stage two, but start in a crouched position on the feet with the back facing the direction of the roll. Gain momentum by sitting down quickly and bringing the knees to the chest. This, like the Back Roller, is a lead-up to the Backward Roll. Teach children to push against the floor to take pressure off the back of the neck.

Backward Roll (Handclasp Position)

Clasp the fingers behind the neck, holding the elbows out to the sides (Figure 20.19 on page 470). From a crouched position, sit down rapidly, bringing the knees to the chest for a tuck to gain momentum. Roll completely over backward, taking much of the weight on the forearms (Figure 20.20 on page 470). This method, which protects the neck, brings children early success in learning the backward roll. Remind children to keep their elbows back and out to the sides to ensure maximum support and minimal neck pressure. This is a lead-up activity to the regular backward roll. Allow children who cannot roll over to practice rocking back and forth with the elbows out. In no case should another person apply force to a child's hips in attempting to force him over.

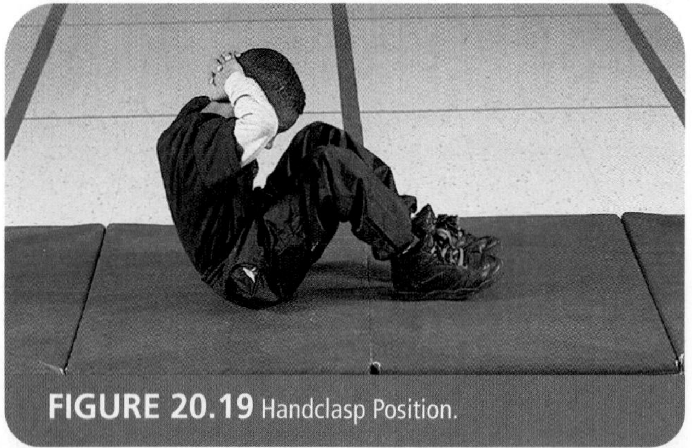
FIGURE 20.19 Handclasp Position.

FIGURE 20.20 Backward Roll.

Climb-Up

Begin on a mat in a kneeling position, with hands about shoulder width apart and the fingers spread and pointed forward. Place the head in front of the hands, so that the head and hands form a triangle on the mat. Walk the body weight forward so that most of it rests on the hands and head. Using the knees, climb to the top of the elbows. (This stunt is a lead-up to the Headstand.) Overweight children or those lacking strength may need to perform an alternate activity.

VARIATION: Lift the knees off the elbows.

Three-Point Tip-Up

Squat down on the mat, placing the hands flat with fingers pointing forward. The elbows are inside and pressed against the inner part of the lower thighs. Lean forward, slowly transferring body weight to the bent elbows and hands until the forehead touches the mat (Figure 20.21). Return to starting position.

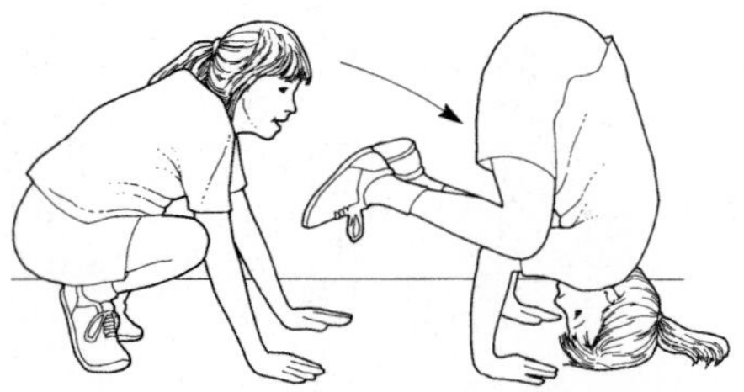
FIGURE 20.21 Three Point Tip-Up.

The Three-Point Tip-Up ends in the same general position as the Climb-Up, but with the elbows held inside the thighs. Some children may have better success by turning the fingers in slightly, thus making the elbows point outward more and offering better support at the thigh contact point. This stunt is a lead-up to the Headstand and the Handstand done at later levels.

VARIATION: Tuck the head and do a Forward Roll as an alternative finishing act.

Mountain Climber

This activity is similar to the Treadmill. Take the weight on the hands with one foot forward and one foot extended back, similar to a sprinter's start. When ready, switch foot position by moving both feet simultaneously. As a lead-up to the Handstand, this activity teaches children to support the body weight briefly with the arms.

Switcheroo

This Handstand lead-up activity begins in the front lunge position with the arms overhead. In one continuous movement, bend forward at the hips, place the hands on the mat, and raise the legs overhead. Scissor the legs in the air, and then reverse the position of the feet on the mat. Repeat in a smooth and continuous motion.

BALANCE STUNTS

One-Leg Balance

Lift one leg from the floor. Later, bring the knee up. The arms are free at first and then assume specified positions: folded across the chest, on the hips, on the head, or behind the back.

Double-Knee Balance

Kneel on both knees, with feet pointed to the rear. Lift the feet from the ground and balance on the knees. Experiment with different arm positions.

Head Touch

On a mat, kneel on both knees, with feet pointed backward and arms outstretched backward for balance. Lean forward slowly and touch the forehead to the mat. Recover to original position (Figure 20.22). Vary the arm position.

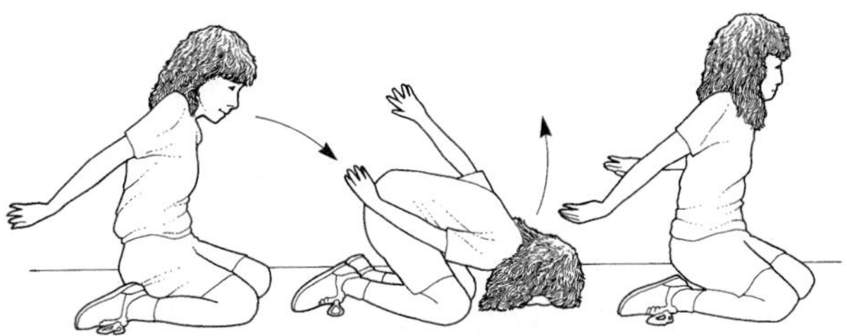

FIGURE 20.22 Head Touch.

Head Balance

Place a beanbag, block, or book on the head (Figure 20.23). Walk, stoop, turn around, sit down, get up, and so on. Maintain good upper-body posture while balancing the object. Keep the hands out to the sides for balance. Later, vary the position of the arms—fold across the chest, place behind the back, or hold down at sides. Link together a series of movements.

FIGURE 20.23 Head Balance.

One-Leg Balance Stunts

Try each of these stands with different arm positions, starting with the arms out to the sides and then folded across the chest. Have children devise other arm positions.

Have students hold each stunt first for 3 seconds and then for 5 seconds. Later, they can close the eyes during the count. Children should recover to original position without losing balance or moving excessively. Repeat these stunts, using the other leg.

1. *Kimbo Stand.* Keeping the left foot flat on the ground, cross the right leg over the left until the right foot points partially down and the toe touches the ground.
2. *Knee-Lift Stand.* From a standing position, lift one knee up so that the thigh is parallel to the ground and the toe points down. Hold. Return to starting position.
3. *Stork Stand.* From a standing position, shift all of the weight to one foot. Place the other foot so that the sole is against the inside of the knee and thigh of the standing leg (Figure 20.24). Hold. Recover to standing position.

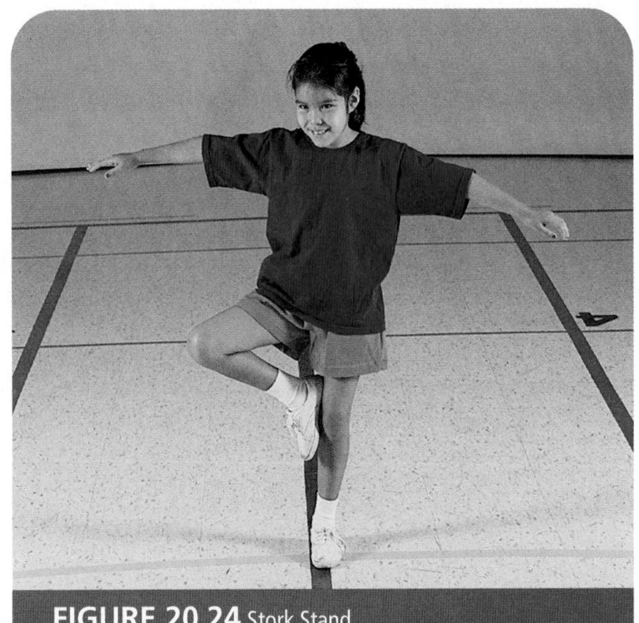

FIGURE 20.24 Stork Stand.

Balance Touch

Place an object (block, beanbag) 1 yard away from a line. Balancing on the line on one foot, reach out with the other foot, touch the object (without placing weight on it; Figure 20.25), and recover to the starting position. Reach sideways, backward.

FIGURE 20.25 Balance Touch.

VARIATION: Try placing the object at various distances. On a gym floor, count the number of boards to establish the distance for the touch.

Single-Leg Balances

1. *Forward Balance.* Extend one leg backward until it is parallel to the floor. Keeping the eyes forward and the arms out to the sides, bend forward, balancing on the other leg (Figure 20.26). Hold for 5 seconds without moving. Reverse legs. (This is also called a Forward Scale.)
2. *Backward Balance.* With knee straight, extend one leg forward, with toes pointed. Keep the arms out to the sides for balance. Lean back as far as possible. Bend back far enough to look at the ceiling.
3. *Side Balance.* Standing on the left foot, bend to the left until the right (top) side of the body is parallel to the floor. Put the right arm alongside the head and in line with the rest of the body. Reverse, standing on the right leg (students may need support briefly to get into position).

FIGURE 20.26 Forward Balance.

Hand-and-Knee Balance

Start on all fours and take the weight on the hands, knees, and feet (toes point backward). Lift one hand and the opposite knee (Figure 20.27). Keep the free foot and hand from touching during the hold. Reverse hand and knee positions.

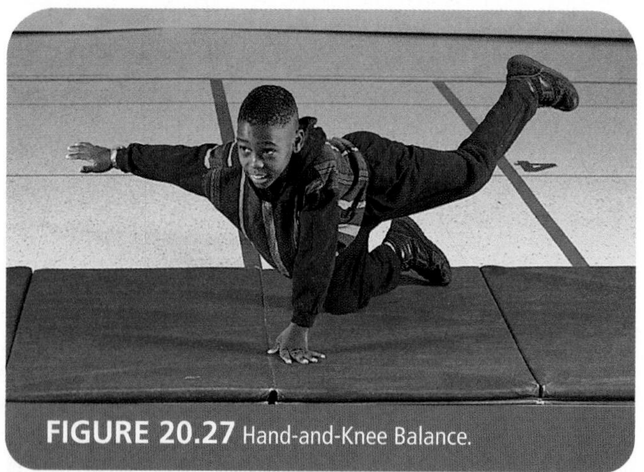

FIGURE 20.27 Hand-and-Knee Balance.

Single-Knee Balance

Perform the Hand-and-Knee Balance, this time balancing on one knee (and leg) with both arms outstretched to the sides (Figure 20.28). Use the other knee.

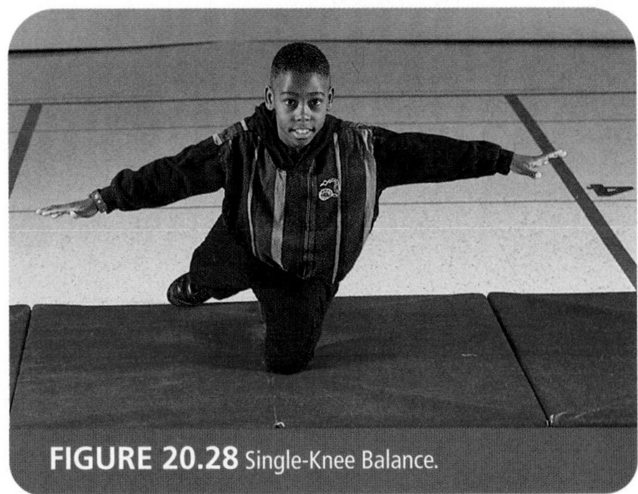
FIGURE 20.28 Single-Knee Balance.

INDIVIDUAL STUNTS

Directional Walk

For a left movement, begin in standing position (feet together). Do all of these actions simultaneously: Take a step to the left, raise the left arm and point left, turn the head to the left, and state crisply, "Left." Return to standing position. Take several steps left and then reverse. The Directional Walk is designed to aid in establishing right–left concepts. Definite and forceful simultaneous movements of the arm, head (turn), and leg (step) coupled with crisply stating the direction are the ingredients of this stunt.

Line Walking

Use a line on the floor, a chalked line, or a board. Walk forward and backward on the line as follows. First, take regular steps. Next, try follow steps—the front foot moves forward and the back foot moves up. The same foot always leads. Then do heel-and-toe steps, bringing the back toe up against the front heel on each step. Finally, hop along the line on one foot. Change to the other foot. The eyes look forward.

Fluttering Leaf

Keeping the feet in place and the body relaxed, flutter to the ground slowly, like an autumn leaf. Swing the arms back and forth loosely to accentuate the fluttering.

Elevator

With arms out level at the sides, pretend to be an elevator going down. Lower the body bit by bit, bending the knees but keeping the upper body erect and eyes forward. Return to position. Add a body twist to the downward movement. (Use a drum to signal movements.)

Cross-Legged Stand

Sit with the legs crossed, and bend the body partially forward. Respond appropriately to these six commands.

"Touch the right foot with the right hand."

"Touch the left foot with the right hand."

"Touch the right foot with the left hand."

"Touch the left foot with the left hand."

"Touch both feet with the hands."

"Touch the feet with crossed hands."

Vary the sequences of these commands. Students must remember that their right foot is on the left side, and vice versa. If this seems too difficult, have children start with the feet in normal position (uncrossed).

VARIATION: Do the stunt with a partner, one child giving the commands and the other following.

Walking in Place

Pretend to walk vigorously, using the same movements as in walking but not making any progress. This is done by sliding the feet back and forth. Exaggerated arm movements are made. (Children can gain or lose a little ground. Two children can walk alongside each other, with first one and then the other going ahead.)

Jump Turns

Do jump turns (use quarter turns and half turns) right and left, as directed. Keep the arms outstretched to the sides. Land lightly without a second movement. Jump turns reinforce directional concepts. Teachers can use jump turns to develop number concepts. Call out the number as a preparatory command and then say, "Move." Number cues are "One" for a left quarter turn, "Two" for a right quarter turn, "Three" for a left half turn, and "Four" for a right half turn. Give children a moment after calling the number and before giving the "Move" command.

Rubber Band

Start in a squat position and clasp the hands and arms around the knees. On the command "Stretch, stretch, stretch," stretch as tall and as wide as possible. On the command "Snap," snap back to original position.

> VARIATION: *Pumping Up the Balloon.* One child, the pumper, is in front of the other children, who are the balloons. The pumper pretends to use a bicycle pump to inflate the balloons, making a "shoosh" sound for every pumping motion. The balloons get larger and larger until the pumper shouts, "Bang!" The balloons then collapse to the floor.

Rising Sun

Lie on the back. Using the arms for balance only, rise to a standing position.

> VARIATION: Fold the arms over the chest. Experiment with different foot positions: crossed, spread wide, both to one side, and so on.

Heel Click

Stand with the feet slightly apart, jump up, and click the heels, coming down with the feet apart (Figure 20.29). Try with a quarter turn right and left.

VARIATIONS:

1. Clap the hands overhead while clicking the heels.
2. Join hands with one or more children. Count, "1, 2, **3!**" and jump on the third count.
3. Begin with a cross-step to the side; then click the heels. Try both right and left.
4. Try to click the heels twice before landing. Land with the feet apart.

FIGURE 20.29 Heel Click.

Lowering the Boom

Start in push-up (front-leaning rest) position. Lower the body slowly to the floor. Control the movement, keeping the body rigid.

VARIATIONS:

1. Pause halfway down.
2. Go down in stages, inch by inch. (Show children what you mean by an inch.)
3. Go down slowly, accompanied by a noise that simulates air escaping from a punctured tire. Try representing a blowout, starting with an appropriate sound.
4. Go down in stages by alternating lowering the right and left arms.
5. Vary the stunt with different hand-base positions, such as fingers pointed in, thumbs touching, and others.

Turn-Over

From a front-leaning rest position, turn over so the back is to the floor. The body does not touch the floor. Continue the turn until the original position is reassumed. Reverse the direction. Turn back and forth several times. Keep the body as rigid as possible while turning.

Thread the Needle

Touch the fingertips together in front of the body. Step through with one foot at a time, keeping the fingers in contact (Figure 20.30). Step back

FIGURE 20.30 Thread the Needle.

to the original position. Next, lock the fingers in front of the body and repeat the stunt. Finally, step through the clasped hands without touching them.

Heel Slap

From an erect position with hands at the sides, jump upward and slap both heels with the hands (Figure 20.31).

FIGURE 20.31 Heel Slap.

VARIATION: Use a one-two-three rhythm with small preliminary jumps on the first and second counts. Make a quarter or half turn in the air. During a jump, slap the heels twice before landing.

Pogo Stick

Pretend to be on a pogo stick by keeping a stiff body and jumping on the toes. Hold the hands in front as if grasping the stick (Figure 20.32). Move in various directions. (Teachers: Stress upward propelling action by the ankles and toes, keeping the body stiff, particularly at the knees.)

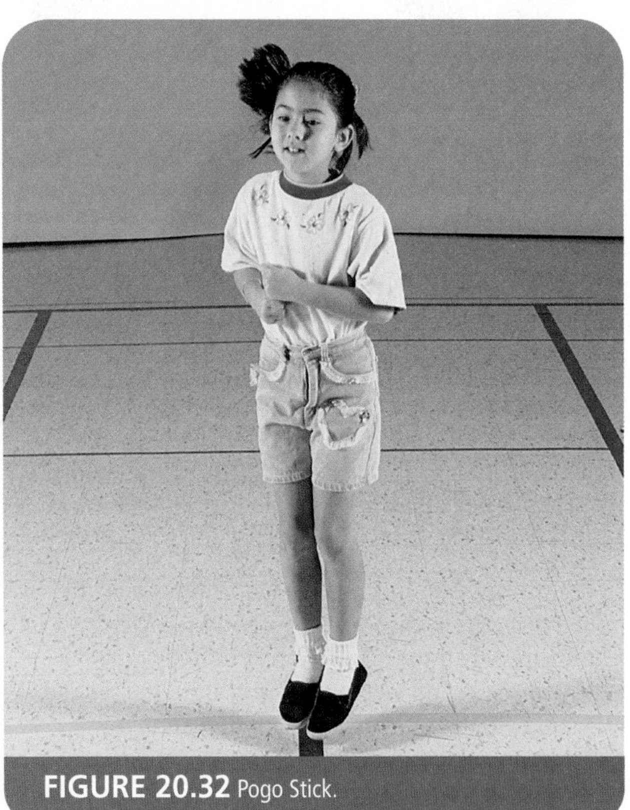
FIGURE 20.32 Pogo Stick.

Top

From a standing position with arms at the sides, try jumping and turning to face the opposite direction, turning three-quarters of the way around, or making a full turn to face the original direction. Land in good balance with hands near the sides. Do not move the feet after landing. Turn both right and left. (Stress number concepts by having children do half turns, three-quarter turns, and full turns.)

VARIATION: Fold the arms across the chest.

Sitting Stand

Stand with feet apart and arms folded in front. Pivot on the balls of both feet, and face the opposite direction. The legs are now crossed. Sit down in this position. Reverse the process. Get up without using the hands for aid, and uncross the legs with a pivot to face in the original direction. The feet do not move much (Figure 20.33).

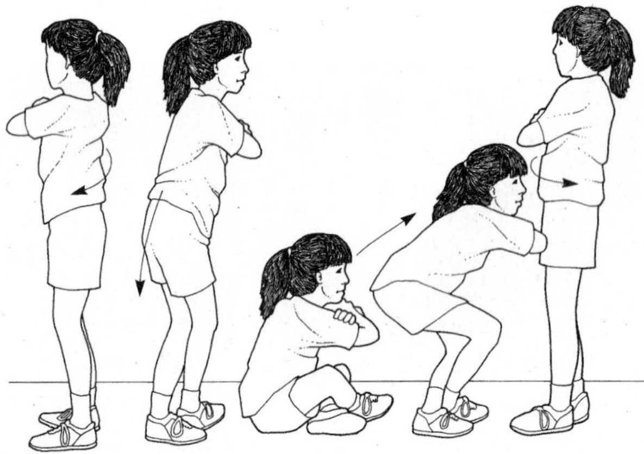

FIGURE 20.33 Sitting Stand.

Push-Up

From a front-leaning rest position, lower the body and push up, back to original position. Focus on moving only the arms, and keep the body rigid. (Because the Push-Up is used in many exercises and testing programs, it is important for children to learn proper execution early.)

VARIATION: Stop halfway down and halfway up. Go up and down by inches.

Crazy Walk

Move forward in an erect position by bringing one foot behind and around the other to gain a little ground each time (Figure 20.34). (Teachers can set a specified distance and see which children cover the distance in the fewest steps.)

VARIATION: Reverse the movements and go backward. This means bringing the foot in front and around to gain distance in back.

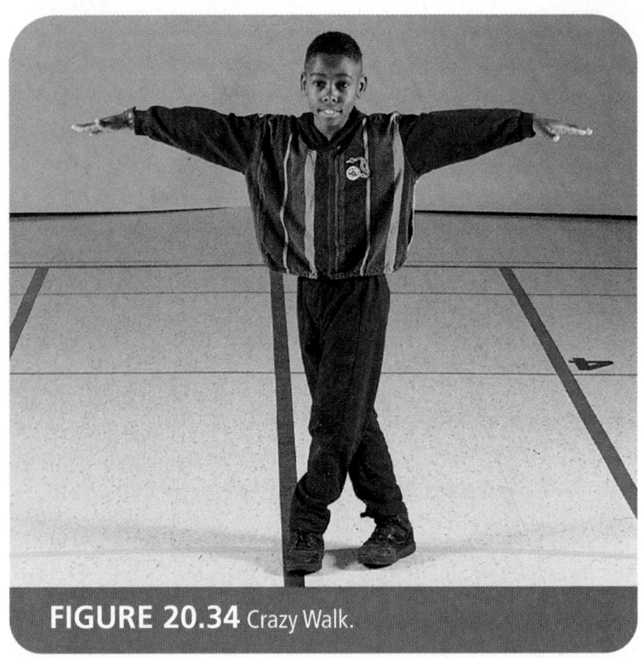

FIGURE 20.34 Crazy Walk.

Seat Circle

Sit on the floor with knees bent and hands braced behind. Lift the feet off the floor, and push with the hands so the body spins in a circle with the seat as a pivot (Figure 20.35). Spin right and left.

FIGURE 20.35 Seat Circle.

VARIATION: Place a beanbag between the knees or on the toes and spin without dropping it.

PARTNER AND GROUP STUNTS

Bouncing Ball

Toss a lively utility ball into the air and watch how it bounces lower and lower until coming to rest on the floor. From a bent-knee position with the upper body erect, imitate the ball by beginning with a high bounce and gradually lowering the height of the jump to simulate the ball coming to rest. Have children push off from the floor with the hands to gain additional height and absorb part of the body weight with their hands as well. Toss a real ball into the air and move with the ball.

VARIATION: Try this with a partner, one partner serving as the bouncer and the other as the ball (Figure 20.36). Reverse positions. Try having one partner dribble the ball in various positions.

FIGURE 20.36 Bouncing Ball.

Seesaw

Face and join hands with a partner. Move the seesaw up and down, one child stooping while the other rises. Recite the words to this version of "Seesaw, Margery Daw."

Seesaw, Margery Daw,

Maw and Paw, like a saw,

Seesaw, Margery Daw.

VARIATION: Jump upward at the end of the rise each time.

Wring the Dishrag

Face a partner and join hands. Raise one pair of arms (right for one and left for the other) and turn under, continuing a full turn until back to original position. Take care not to bump heads. Reverse.

VARIATION: Try the stunt using a crouched position.

Partner Toe Toucher

Partners of about the same height lie on their backs with heads near each other and feet in opposite directions. They join arms, using a hand-wrist grip, and bring the legs up so their toes touch. They stay high on the shoulders and touch the feet high (Figure 20.37). Partners should strive to reach the high shoulder position, which is the most difficult.

FIGURE 20.37 Partner Toe Toucher.

VARIATION: One child carries a beanbag, a ball, or similar object between the feet. She transfers the object to the partner, who lowers it to the floor.

Double Top

Face a partner and join hands. Experiment to see which type of grip works best. With straight arms, lean away from each other while moving the toes close to partner's (Figure 20.38 on page 478). Spin around slowly in either direction, taking tiny steps. Increase speed.

VARIATIONS:

1. Use a stooped position.
2. Instead of holding hands, hold a wand and increase the body lean backward. Try the stunt while standing right side to right side.

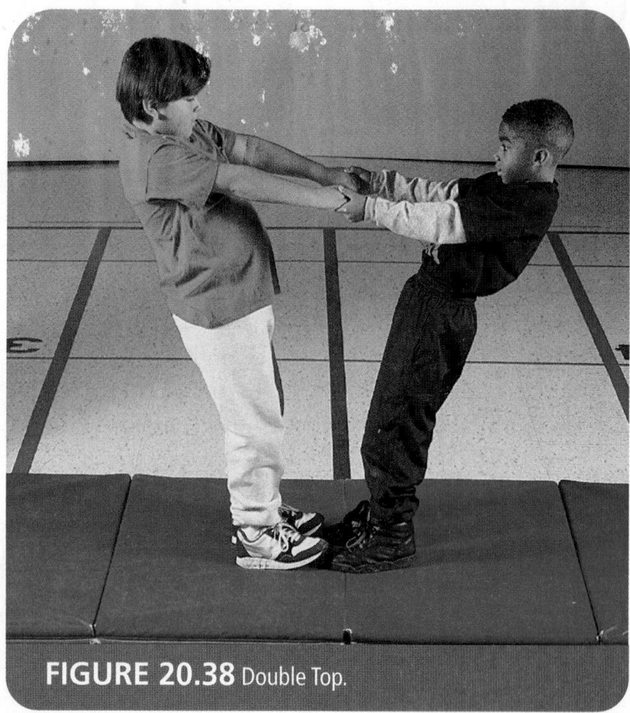

FIGURE 20.38 Double Top.

Roly Poly

Review the Rolling Log. Four or five children lie face-down on the floor, side by side. The last child does a Rolling Log over the others and then takes a place at the end. Continue until all have rolled twice.

DEVELOPMENTAL LEVEL II ACTIVITIES

Developmental Level II activities focus more on form and quality of performance than do those at Level I. Stunts such as the Frog Handstand, Mule Kick, Teeter-Totter, and Handstand give children experience in taking the entire weight on the hands. Partner support stunts are introduced. Flops or falls are another addition.

ANIMAL MOVEMENTS

Cricket Walk

Squat. Spread the knees. Put the arms between the knees and grasp outsides of the ankles with the hands. Walk forward or backward. Chirp like a cricket. Turn around right and left. What happens when both feet are moved at once?

Frog Jump

From a squatting position, with hands on the floor slightly in front of the feet, jump forward a short distance, landing on the hands and feet simultaneously (Figure 20.39). Note the difference between this stunt and the Rabbit Jump. Emphasis eventually is on both height and distance. The hands and arms absorb part of the landing impact to prevent excessive strain on the knees.

FIGURE 20.39 Frog Jump.

Seal Crawl

Start in the front-leaning rest position, with the weight on straightened arms and toes. Keeping the body straight, walk forward, using the hands for propelling force and dragging the feet (Figure 20.40). Keep the body straight and the head up.

FIGURE 20.40 Seal Crawl.

VARIATIONS:

1. Crawl forward a short distance and then roll over on the back, clapping the hands like a seal, with appropriate seal barks.
2. Crawl with the fingers pointed in different directions, out and in.
3. *Reverse Seal Crawl.* Turn over and attempt the crawl, dragging the heels.
4. *Elbow Crawl.* Assume the original position, but with weight on the elbows. Crawl forward on the elbows (Figure 20.41).
5. Use the crossed-arm position for a more challenging stunt.

FIGURE 20.41 Elbow Crawl.

Measuring Worm

From a front-leaning rest position, keeping the knees stiff, inch the feet up as close as possible to the hands. Regain position by inching forward with the hands. Keep the knees straight, and bend at the hips as necessary (Figure 20.42).

Mule Kick

Stoop down and place the hands on the floor in front of the feet. The arms are the mule's front legs. Kick out with the legs while briefly supporting the weight on the arms (Figure 20.43). Taking the weight on the hands is important. Students can learn the stunt in two stages: (1) practice taking the weight momentarily on the hands; (2) add the kick.

VARIATION: Make two kicks before the feet return to the ground.

Walrus Walk

Begin in a front-leaning rest position, with fingers pointed outward. Progress by moving both hands forward at the same time (Figure 20.44 on page 480). Try to clap the hands with each step. Before doing this stunt, review the similar Seal Crawl (Figure 20.40) and its variations.

VARIATION: Move sideways so the upper part of the body describes an arc while the feet hold position.

Double-Lame Dog

Support the body on one hand and one leg (Figure 20.45 on page 480). Move forward in this position, maintaining balance. Keep the distance short (5 to 10 feet) because this stunt is strenuous. Have students try different leg–arm combinations, such as

FIGURE 20.42 Measuring Worm.

FIGURE 20.43 Mule Kick.

FIGURE 20.44 Walrus Walk.

FIGURE 20.45 Double-Lame Dog.

cross-lateral movements (right arm with left leg and left arm with right leg).

VARIATION: Keep the free arm on the hip.

Turtle

Hold the body in a wide push-up position with the feet and hands widely spread (Figure 20.46). From this position, move in various directions, keeping the body always about the same distance from the floor. Move the hands and feet only in small increments.

Walrus Slap

From the front-leaning rest position, push the body up in the air quickly by force of the arms, clap the hands together, and recover to position. Before doing this stunt, review the Seal Crawl and the Walrus Walk.

FIGURE 20.46 Turtle.

VARIATIONS:

1. Try clapping the hands more than once.
2. Move forward while clapping the hands.
3. *Reverse Walrus Slap.* Turn over and do a Walrus Walk while facing the ceiling. Clapping the hands in this position is not easy; only the more skilled students should try it while on a mat.

TUMBLING AND INVERTED BALANCES

Safety Tip

To prevent risk of injuries, never encourage or force children to perform an activity they are uncomfortable with. If a child lacks the neck and shoulder-girdle strength to do tumbling or inverted balances, substitute an alternate activity. Spotting techniques are offered for teachers who feel capable of helping children who can perform the activities. Spot only children who can and want to perform an activity.

Forward Roll to a Walkout

Perform the Forward Roll as described earlier, but walk out to a standing position. The key to the Walkout is to develop enough momentum to enable a return to the feet. Bend the leg that first absorbs the weight while keeping the other leg straight.

Spotting: Same as the Forward Roll (Figure 20.15).

Backward Roll (Regular)

Begin in the Forward Roll squat position, but with the back to the direction of the roll. Push off quickly with the hands, sit down, and start rolling over onto the back. Bring the knees to the chest, tucking the body and thus increasing momentum. Quickly bring the hands up over the shoulders, with palms up and fingers pointed backward. Continue rolling backward with knees close to the chest. The hands touch the mat at about the same time as the head. At this point, push hard with the hands to release pressure on the neck. Continue rolling over and pushing off the mat until the roll is completed (Figure 20.47). Teachers can emphasize proper hand position by having children point their thumbs toward their ears and spread their fingers for better push-off control.

FIGURE 20.47 Regular Backward Roll.

Spotting: Rather than spotting a child who is having trouble doing the Backward Roll, have him try an activity like the Log Roll. If you choose to spot this activity, never push a child at the hips or buttocks, thus forcing the roll. This puts undue pressure on the back of the neck. The proper way to aid a child who has difficulty with the stunt is as follows: The spotter stands in a straddle position, with the near foot alongside the spot where the student's hands and head will make contact with the mat (Figure 20.48). The other foot is one stride in the direction of the roll. The critical point is for the spotter to lift the hips just as the child's head and hands contact the mat. This is done by taking the back hand and reaching across to the child's far hip, getting under the other hip with the near hand. Apply the lift on the front of the hips and just below the beltline to ensure pressure on the neck is released.

FIGURE 20.48 Spotting the Backward Roll. (The lift is at the child's hips. Lift the student rather than forcing her over.)

Headstand

Two approaches are suggested for the Headstand: (1) relate the Headstand to the Climb-Up; and (2) go directly into a Headstand, using a kick-up to achieve the inverted position. In either case, maintaining the triangle position of the hands and the head is essential.

In the final inverted position, the legs are straight with feet together and toes pointed. The weight is evenly distributed among the three points—the two hands and the forward part of the head. The body is as straight as possible.

The safest way to come down from the inverted position is to return to the mat in the same direction used in going up. To ease recovery, bend at the waist and the knees. In the case of overbalancing, have students tuck their heads under and go into a Forward Roll. When presenting the instructional sequence, explain both methods of recovery from the inverted position.

Headstand Climb-Up

Take the inverted position of the Climb-Up (page 470) and move the feet slowly upward to the headstand position (Figure 20.49 on page 482).

Spotting: The spotter stands directly in front of the performer and steadies the performer as needed. The spotter must be alert to moving out of the way when the performer goes into a Forward Roll to come out of the inverted position.

FIGURE 20.49 Headstand based on the Climb-Up.

Headstand Kick-Up

Keeping the weight on the forward part of the head and maintaining the triangle base, walk the feet forward until the hips are high over the body (similar to the Climb-Up position). Keep one foot on the mat, bending the knee of that leg and extending the other leg backward. Kick the back leg up to the inverted position, following quickly with a push by the other leg, thus bringing the two legs together in the inverted position (Figure 20.50). The timing is a quick one–two movement.

FIGURE 20.50 Headstand based on the Kick-Up.

Emphasize the importance of forming a triangle with the hands and the head as well as centering the weight on the forward part of the head. Most difficulties with the Headstand come from an incorrect head–hand position. The correct positioning has the head placed the length of the performer's forearm from the knees and the hands placed at the knees. To help children form the proper triangle, mark the three spots on the mat with chalk.

Spotting: When learning, students can try the stunt with a spotter on each side. Each spotter kneels,

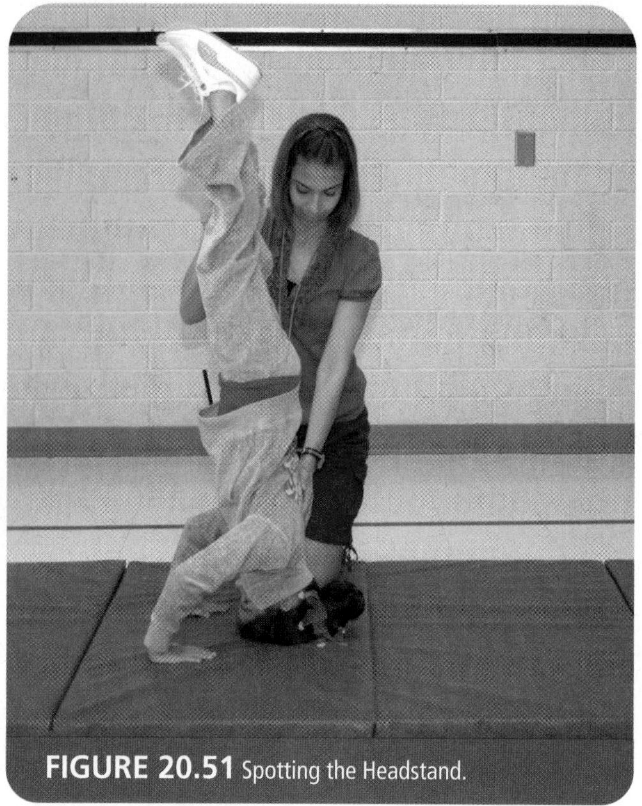

FIGURE 20.51 Spotting the Headstand.

placing the near hand under the performer's shoulder. The performer then walks the weight above the head and kicks up to position. The spotter on each side supports by grasping a leg (Figure 20.51). It is the performer's responsibility to get into the inverted position.

Headstand Practice and Variations

Continue work on the Headstand. Try the following variations. (Spot as needed.)

1. Clap the hands and recover. The weight shifts momentarily to the head for the clap. (Some children will be able to clap the hands twice before recovery.)
2. Use different leg positions (Figure 20.52)—legs split sideways, legs split forward and backward, and knees bent.
3. Holding a utility ball or a beanbag between the legs, go into the Headstand, retaining control of the ball.

Frog Handstand (Tip-Up)

Squat down on the mat, placing the hands flat, with fingers pointing forward and elbows inside and pressed against the inner knees. Lean forward, using

FIGURE 20.52 Headstand Variation.

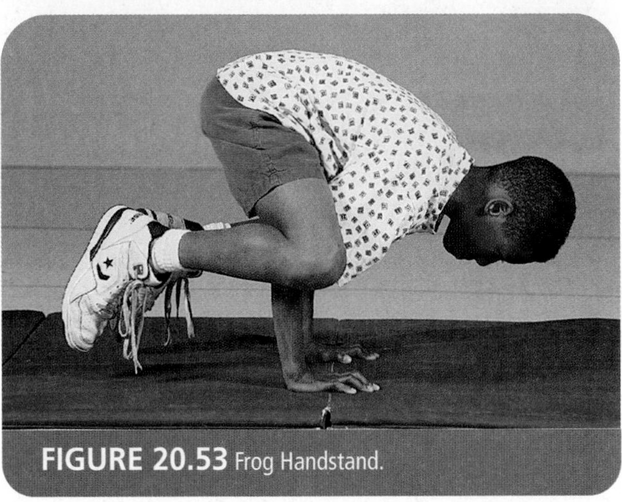

FIGURE 20.53 Frog Handstand.

the leverage of the elbows against the knees, and balance on the hands (Figure 20.53). Hold for 5 seconds. Return to position. The head does not touch the mat at any time. The hands may be turned in slightly if this makes better contact between the elbows and the insides of the thighs. (This stunt follows from the Three-Point Tip-Up.)

Half Teeter-Totter

This activity is part of the continued lead-up for the Handstand. Begin in the lunge position and shift the weight to the hands. Kick the legs up in the air to a 135-degree angle; then return to the feet. This activity is similar to the Switcheroo, but the feet are kicked higher without switching foot position.

Cartwheel

Start with the body in an erect position, arms outspread and legs shoulder width apart. Bend the body to the right and place the right hand on the floor. Follow this, in sequence, by the left hand, the left foot, and the right foot (Figure 20.54). Each body part touches the floor at evenly spaced intervals. The body is straight and extended when in the inverted position. The entire body stays in the same plane throughout the stunt, and the feet pass directly over the head.

FIGURE 20.54 Cartwheel.

Instruct children who have difficulty with the Cartwheel to concentrate on taking the weight of the body on the hands in succession. They need to learn to support their weight and later concentrate on getting the body into proper position. After the class has had some practice in doing Cartwheels, add a running approach with a skip before takeoff.

Forward Roll (Pike Position)

Begin the piked Forward Roll in a standing pike position. Keep the legs straight and bend forward at the hips. Place the hands on the mat, bend the elbows, and lower the head to the mat. Keep the legs straight until nearing the end of the roll. Bend at the knees to facilitate returning to the feet.

Forward Roll Combinations

Review the Forward Roll, focusing on proper form. Introduce some of these combinations:

1. Do a Forward Roll preceded by a short run.
2. Do two Forward Rolls in succession.
3. Do a Leapfrog (page 493) plus a Forward Roll.

4. Do a Forward Roll to a vertical jump in the air, and repeat.
5. Do a Rabbit Jump plus a Forward Roll.
6. Hold the toes while doing a Forward Roll.

Backward Roll Combinations

Review the Backward Roll. Continue focusing on the Push-Off with the hands. Teach students these combinations:

1. Do a Backward Roll to a standing position. Push strongly with the hands to create enough momentum to land on the feet.
2. Do two Backward Rolls in succession.
3. Do a Crab Walk into a Backward Roll.
4. Add a jump in the air at the end of a Backward Roll.

Teeter-Totter

The Teeter-Totter is the final lead-up activity for the Handstand. It is performed like the Half Teeter-Totter, but the feet are held together for a moment in the handstand position before returning to the standing position.

Safety Tip

To prevent serious injuries when attempting all headstands and handstands in this chapter, never encourage or force children to perform an activity they are uncomfortable with. If a child lacks the neck and shoulder-girdle strength to do an inverted balance, substitute an alternate activity. Spotting techniques are offered for teachers who feel capable of helping children who can perform the activities. Spot only children who can and want to perform an activity.

Handstand

Start in the lunge position. Do a Teeter-Totter to the inverted position. The body extends in a straight line from the shoulders through the feet, and the head is down. It is helpful to teach the correct position first in a standing position with the arms overhead and the ears between the arms.

Spotting: The Handstand can be done with double or single spotting. In double spotting, the spotters stand on both sides of the performer. Each spotter uses one hand in a firm grip beneath the performer's shoulder. The other hand can assist the lift by pressing upward on the thigh (Figure 20.55). The performer walks the hips forward until they are over the hands and then kicks up with one foot, pushing off with the other and raising that leg to join the first in the inverted position (Figure 20.56). The rhythm is a one-two count.

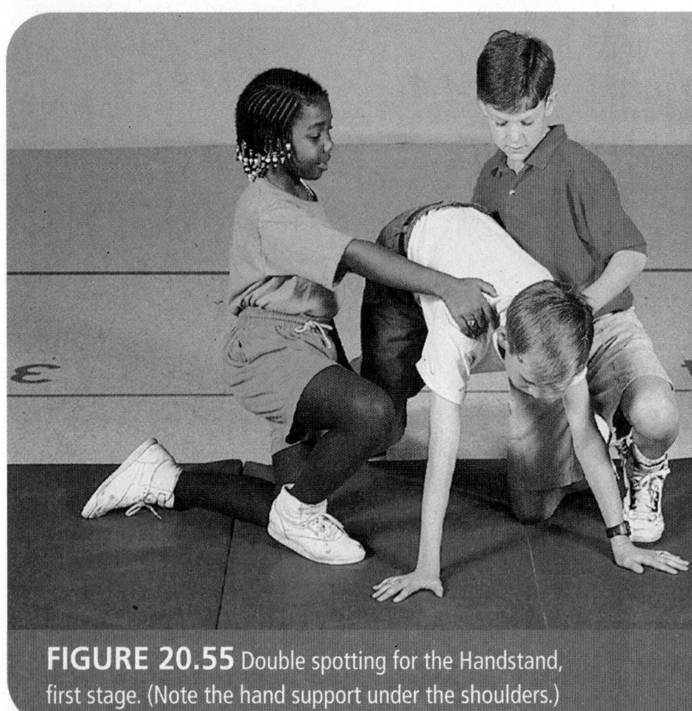

FIGURE 20.55 Double spotting for the Handstand, first stage. (Note the hand support under the shoulders.)

In single spotting, the spotter takes a stride position, with the forward knee bent somewhat (Figure 20.57). The performer's weight is transferred over the hands, and the body goes into the handstand position with a one-two kick-up. The spotter catches the legs and holds the performer in an inverted position (Figure 20.58).

BALANCE STUNTS

One-Leg Balance Reverse

Assume a forward balance position (page 472). Moving quickly to gain momentum, swing the free leg down and change to the same forward balance position facing in the opposite direction (a 180-degree turn; Figure 20.59). No unnecessary movement of the supporting foot occurs after completing the turn. The swinging foot does not touch the floor.

FIGURE 20.56 Double spotting for the Handstand, second stage.

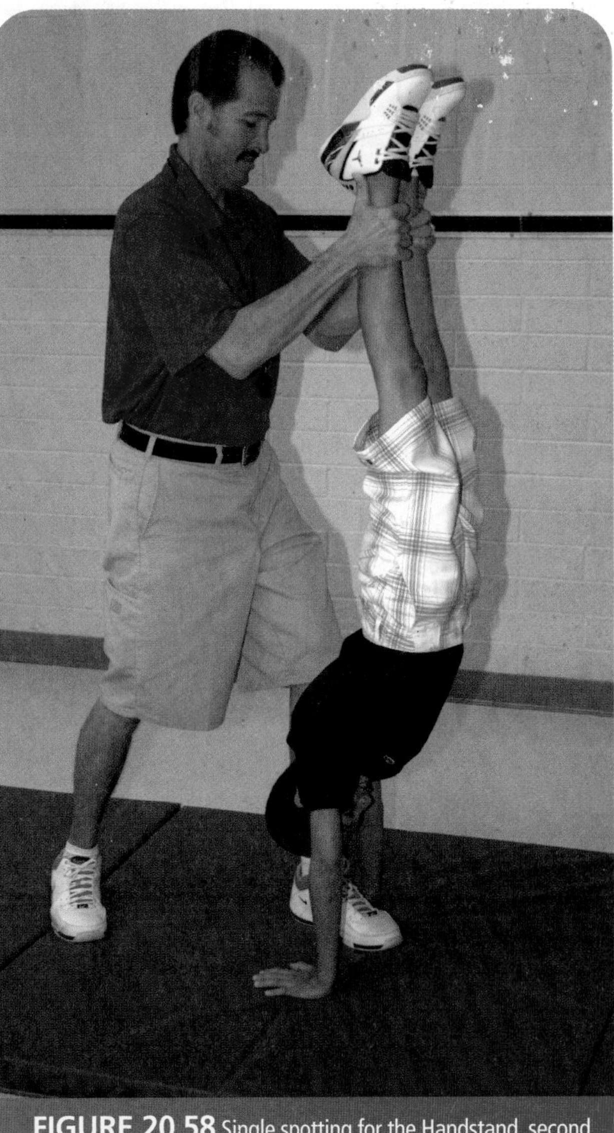
FIGURE 20.58 Single spotting for the Handstand, second stage. (Note knee pressure against performer's shoulder.)

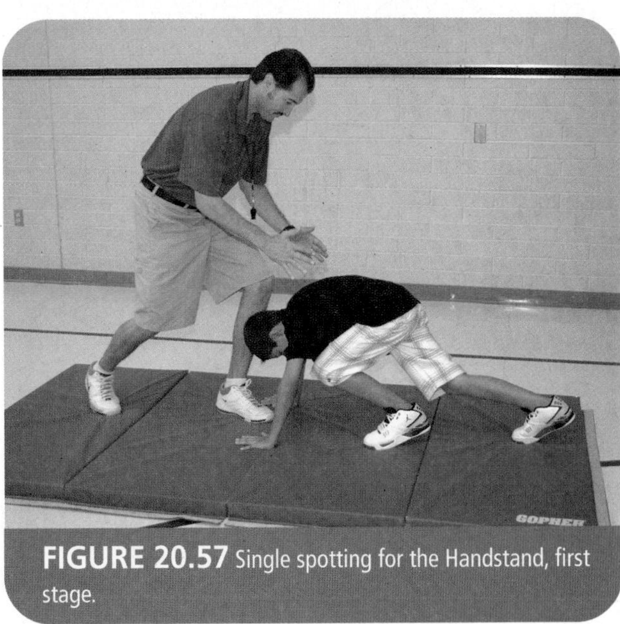

FIGURE 20.57 Single spotting for the Handstand, first stage.

FIGURE 20.59 One-Leg Balance Reverse.

Tummy Balance

Lie prone on the floor with arms outstretched forward or to the sides, with palms down. Raise the arms, head, chest, and legs from the floor and balance on the tummy (Figure 20.60 on page 486). Keep the knees straight.

FIGURE 20.60 Tummy Balance.

Leg Dip

Extend both hands and one leg forward, balancing on the other leg. Lower the body to sit on the heel and return without losing the balance or touching the floor with any part of the body. Try with the other foot. (Another child can assist from the back by pressing upward on the performer's elbows.)

Balance Jump

With arms out to the sides and body parallel to the ground, extend one leg back and balance the weight on the other leg (Figure 20.61). Quickly change to the other foot, and balance in the initial position (Figure 20.62). Keep the body parallel to the ground when switching legs. Try with arms outstretched forward. Working in pairs might be helpful. One student critiques the other's performance to ensure that the arms and body are straight and parallel to the floor.

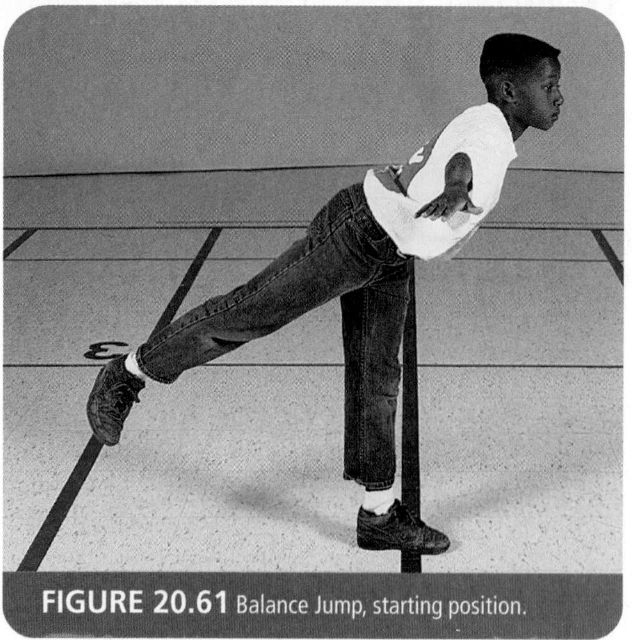
FIGURE 20.61 Balance Jump, starting position.

FIGURE 20.62 Balance Jump.

Seat Balance

Sit on the floor, holding the ankles in front, with elbows inside the knees. The feet are flat on the floor, and the knees are bent at almost a right angle. Raise the legs (toes pointed) so the knees are straight (Figure 20.63), and balance on the seat for 5 seconds.

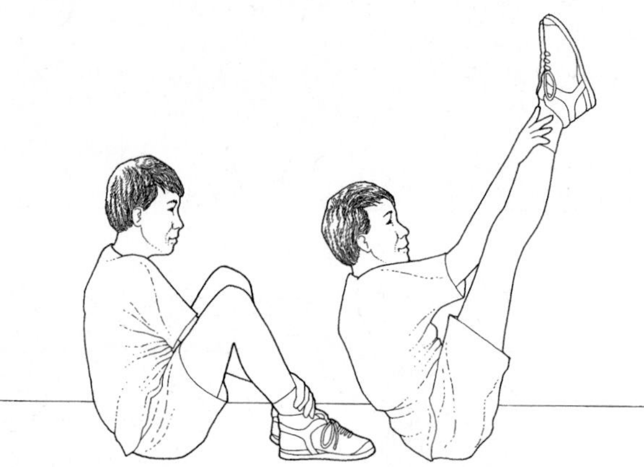
FIGURE 20.63 Seat Balance.

Face-to-Knee Touch

Begin in a standing position with feet together. Placing the hands on the hips, balance on one foot, with the other leg extended backward. Bend the trunk forward and touch the knee of the supporting leg with the forehead (Figure 20.64). Recover to original position.

Teachers can have children begin by keeping the arms away from the sides for balance and then try the hands-on-hips position later. In the learning stages, assist a student from behind by supporting the leg extended backward, or have students place one hand against a wall.

FIGURE 20.64 Face-to-Knee Touch.

Finger Touch

Put the right hand behind the back with the index finger straight and pointed down. Grasp the right wrist with the left hand. From an erect position with the feet about 6 inches apart, squat down and touch the floor with the index finger (Figure 20.65). Regain the erect position without losing balance. Reverse hands. (In the learning stages, teachers can use a book or the corner of a mat to decrease the distance and make the touch easier.)

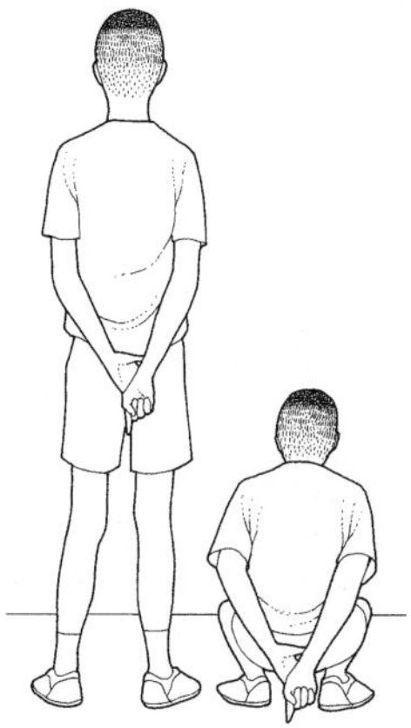

FIGURE 20.65 Finger Touch.

INDIVIDUAL STUNTS

Reach-Under

Take a position with the feet pointed ahead (about 2 feet apart) and toes against a line or a floorboard. Place a beanbag two boards in front of, and midway between, the feet. Without changing the foot position, reach one hand behind and between the legs to pick up the beanbag. Now pick up with the other hand. Repeat, moving the beanbag a board farther away each time.

VARIATION: Allow the heels to lift off the floor. Use the other hand.

Stiff Person Bend

Stand with feet about shoulder width apart and pointed forward. Place a beanbag a few inches behind the right heel. Grasp the left toes with the left hand, thumb on top. Without bending the knees, reach the right hand outside the right leg and pick up the beanbag without releasing the hold on the left toes. Gradually increase the distance of the reach. Reverse sides (Figure 20.66).

FIGURE 20.66 Stiff Person Bend.

Coffee Grinder

Put one hand on the floor and extend the body to the floor on that side in a side-leaning rest position. Walk around the hand, making a complete circle and keeping the body straight (Figure 20.67 on page 488). The stunt is done slowly, with controlled movements.

20

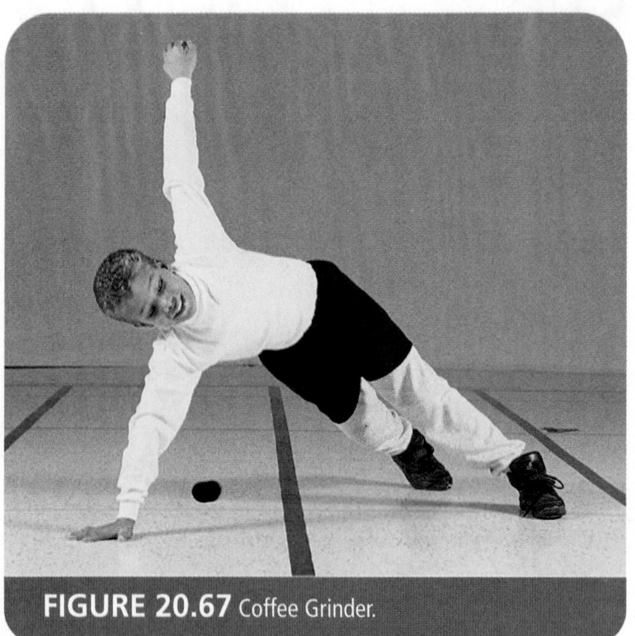

FIGURE 20.67 Coffee Grinder.

Scooter

Sit on the floor with legs extended, arms folded in front of the chest, and chin held high. To scoot, pull the seat toward the heels, using heel pressure and lifting the seat slightly (Figure 20.68). Extend the legs forward again and repeat the process. (This is an excellent activity for abdominal development.)

Hip Walk

Sit in the same position as for the Scooter, but with arms in thrust position and hands making a partial fist. "Walk" by using alternate leg–seat movements. Arm–leg coordination is unilateral.

Long Bridge

Begin in a crouched position with hands on the floor and knees between the arms. Push the hands forward a little at a time until reaching an extended push-up position (Figure 20.69). Return to original position. (Teachers: Challenge children to extend as far as they can in this position.)

VARIATIONS:

1. Begin with a forward movement; then change to a sideways movement, spreading as wide as possible.
2. Work from a crossed-hands position.

Heelstand

Begin in a full squat with the arms dangling at the sides. Jump upward to full leg extension with the weight on both heels and fling the arms out diagonally. Hold momentarily, then return to original position (Figure 20.70). Several movements can be done rhythmically in succession.

Wicket Walk

Bend over and touch the floor with the weight evenly distributed on the hands and feet, thus forming a wicket. Walk the wicket forward,

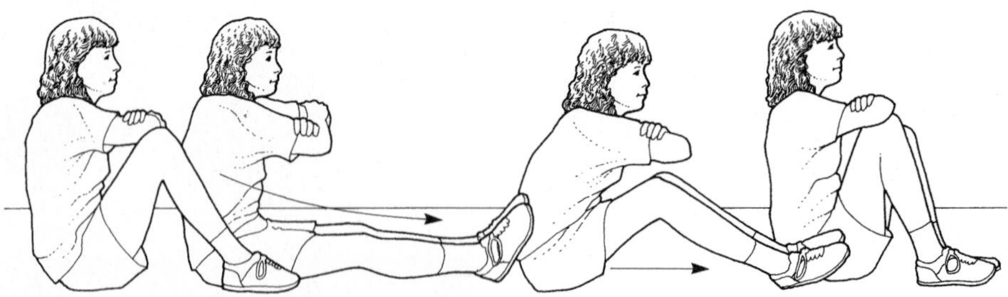

FIGURE 20.68 Scooter.

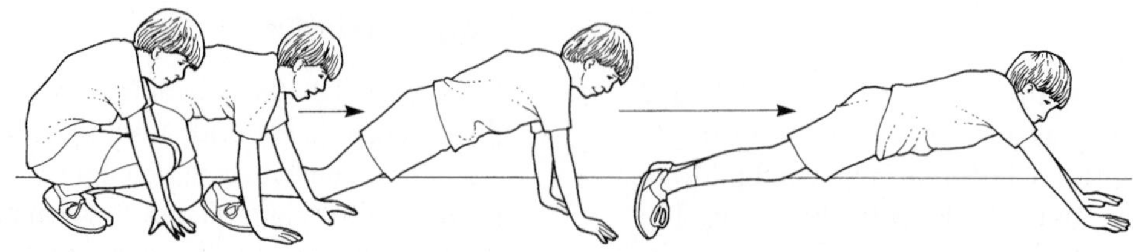

FIGURE 20.69 Long Bridge.

FIGURE 20.70 Heelstand.

backward, and sideways. Keep the arms and legs as nearly vertical as possible (Figure 20.71). This stunt loses much of its flexibility value if students bend their knees too much. A common error in the execution of this stunt is to place the hands too far forward of the feet. (The stunt is named for the child's body position, which resembles a wicket in a croquet game.)

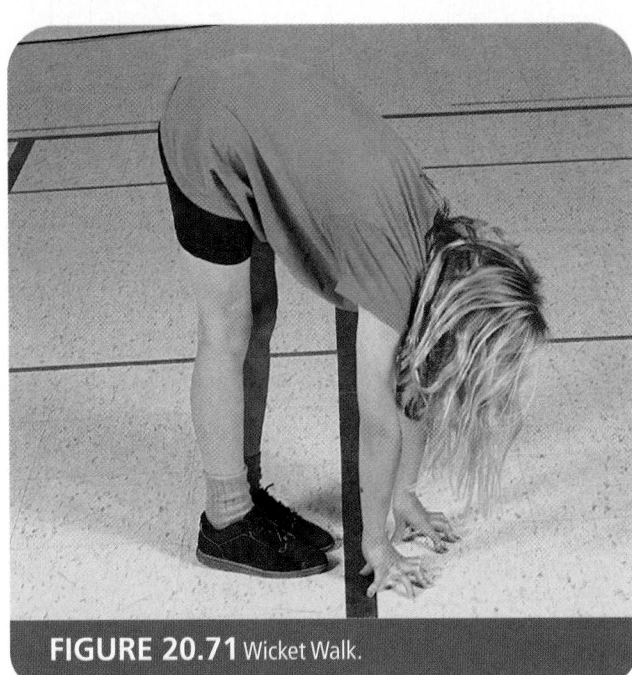

FIGURE 20.71 Wicket Walk.

Knee Jump to Standing

Kneel, with seat touching the heels and toes pointing backward (shoelaces against the floor). Jump to a standing position with a vigorous upward swing of the arms (Figure 20.72). It is easier to jump from a smooth floor than from a mat, because the toes slide more readily on the floor.

FIGURE 20.72 Knee Jump to Standing.

VARIATION: Jump to a standing position, doing a quarter turn in the air in one quick motion. Try a half turn.

Individual Drops or Falls

Drops, or falls, can challenge children to achieve good body control. Mats must be used. The hands and arms absorb the impact of a forward fall. During the fall, keep the body in a straight-line position. Little change in body angles occurs, particularly at the knees and waist.

Knee Drop

Kneel on a mat, with the body upright. Raise the feet up, off the floor, and fall forward, breaking the fall with the hands and arms (Figure 20.73).

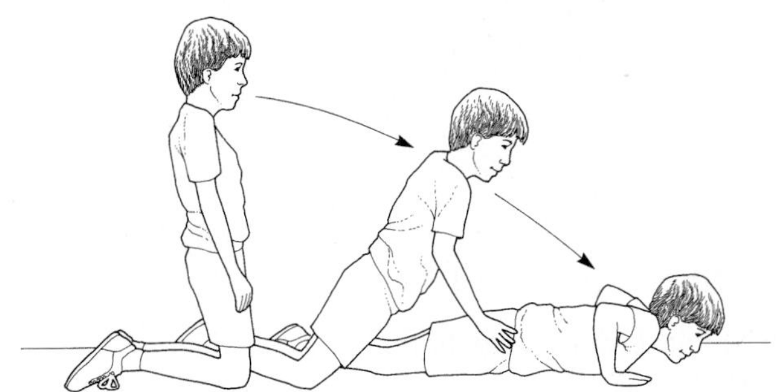

FIGURE 20.73 Knee Drop.

Forward Drop

From a forward balance position, on one leg with the other leg extended backward and the arms extended forward and up, lean forward slowly, bringing the arms toward the floor. Continue to drop forward slowly until overbalanced; then let the hands and arms break the fall (Figure 20.74). The head is up and the extended leg is raised high; knee joints are reasonably straight. Repeat, changing position of the legs.

FIGURE 20.74 Forward Drop.

Dead Body Fall

Fall forward from an erect position to a down push-up position (Figure 20.75). A slight bend at the waist is permissible, but keep the knees straight and do not move the feet forward.

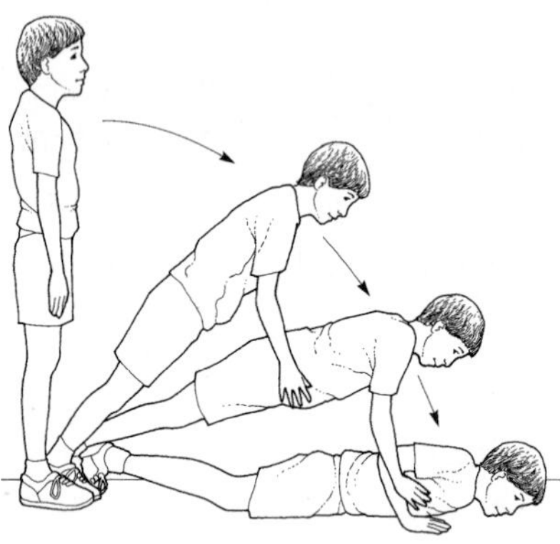

FIGURE 20.75 Dead Body Fall.

Stoop and Stretch

Hold a beanbag with both hands. Stand with heels against a line and feet about shoulder width apart. Keeping the knees straight, reach between the legs with the beanbag and place it as far back as possible. Reach back and pick it up with both hands.

VARIATIONS:

1. Bend at the knees, using more of a squatting position during the reach.
2. Use a piece of chalk instead of a beanbag. Reach back and make a mark on the floor. Try writing a number or drawing a small circle or some other shape.

Tanglefoot

Stand with heels together and toes pointed out. Bend the trunk forward and wrap arms between the knees and around behind the ankles. Bring the hands around the outside of the ankles from behind and touch the fingers to each other (Figure 20.76). Hold for 5 seconds.

FIGURE 20.76 Tanglefoot.

VARIATION: Instead of touching, clasp the fingers in front of the ankles. Hold this position in good balance for 5 seconds without releasing the hands.

Egg Roll

While sitting, assume the same clasped-hands position as for Tanglefoot. Roll sideways over one shoulder, then to the back, then to the other shoulder, and finally back up to the sitting position (Figure 20.77). Repeat the movements in turn to make a full circle back to original position. The key to performing this stunt is a vigorous sideways movement to gain initial momentum. If mats are used, place two

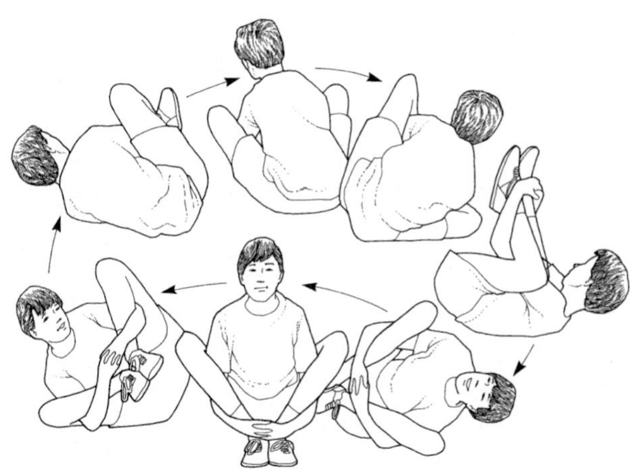

FIGURE 20.77 Egg Roll.

side by side to cushion the entire roll. (Some children can do this stunt better from a crossed-ankle position.)

Toe Touch Nose

While sitting on the floor, touch the toes of either foot to the nose with the help of both hands. First do one foot and then the other. More flexible students will be able to place the foot on top of the head or even behind the neck. Although this is a flexibility exercise, caution students not to force the leg too far.

VARIATION: Perform from a standing position. Touch the toes to the nose and return the foot to original position without losing balance. Try the standing version with eyes closed.

Toe-Tug Walk

Bend over and grasp the toes with thumbs on top (Figure 20.78). Keep the knees bent slightly and the eyes forward. Walk forward without losing the grip on the toes. Challenge students to walk backward and sideways. Walk in various geometric patterns, such as a circle, triangle, or square. (Teachers can introduce an easier version of this stunt by having children grasp the ankles, thumbs on the insides, and perform the desired movements.)

VARIATION: Try doing the walk with the right hand grasping the left foot, and vice versa.

FIGURE 20.78 Toe-Tug Walk.

PARTNER AND GROUP STUNTS

Depending on the maturity and nature of the class, it may be more effective to separate boys and girls for some of the partner and group stunts. Students enjoy these activities, but some of the requisite touching may cause problems for some classes.

Partner Hopping

Partners coordinate hopping movements for short distances and in different directions and turns. Three combinations are suggested.

1. Stand facing each other. Extend the right leg forward to be grasped at the ankle by partner's left hand. Hold right hands and hop on the left leg (Figure 20.79 on page 492).
2. Stand back-to-back. Lift the leg backward, bending the knee, and have partner grasp the ankle. Hop as before.
3. Stand side by side with inside arms around each other's waist. Lift the inside foot from the floor and move by hopping on the outside foot.

If either partner begins to fall, the other releases the leg immediately. Reverse foot positions.

FIGURE 20.79 Partner Hopping.

to return to the original face-to-face position. Partners need to duck to avoid being kicked during the leg swings.

VARIATION: Introduce the stunt by having students grasp a wand instead of holding hands.

Partner Twister

Partners face and grasp right hands as if shaking hands. One partner swings the left leg over the other's head and turns around, taking a straddle position over partner's arm (Figure 20.80). The other swings the right leg over the first partner, who has bent over, and the partners are now back-to-back. First partner continues with the right leg and faces in the original direction. Second partner swings the left leg over the partner's back

FIGURE 20.80 Partner Twister.

Partner Pull-Up

Partners sit facing each other in a bent-knee position, with heels on the floor and toes touching. Pulling cooperatively, they come to a standing position (Figure 20.81).

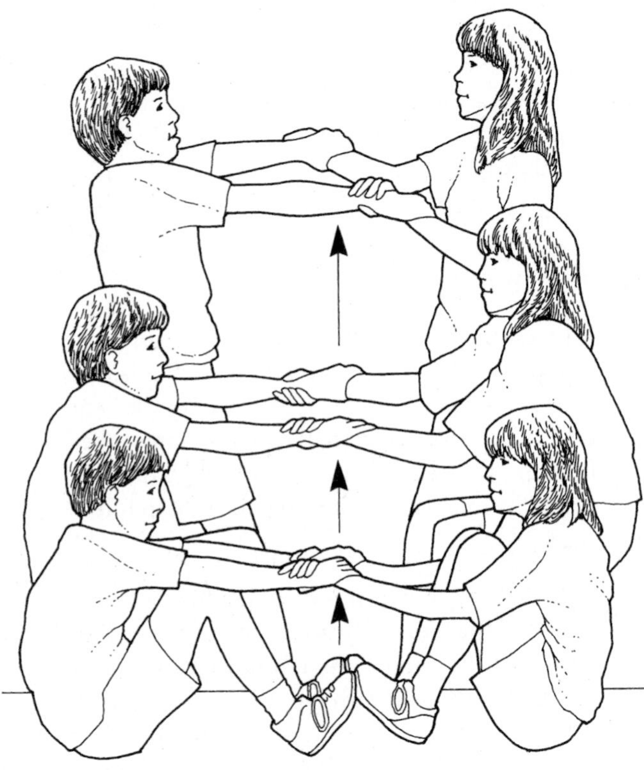

FIGURE 20.81 Partner Pull-Up.

VARIATION: Try with feet flat on the floor.

Back-to-Back Get-Up

Partners sit back-to-back and lock arms. From this position, they try to stand by pushing against each other's back (Figure 20.82). They sit down again. If the feet are sliding, do the stunt on a mat.

VARIATIONS:

1. Try with three or four children.
2. Try from a halfway-down position, and move like a spider.

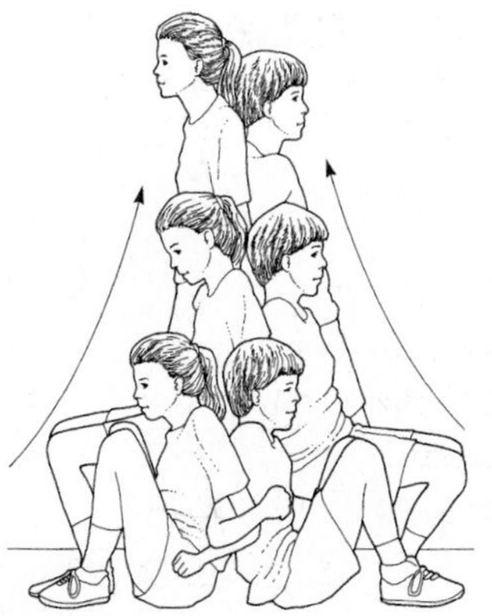

FIGURE 20.82 Back-to-Back Get-Up.

FIGURE 20.83 High, medium, and low Leapfrog positions.

Rowboat

Partners sit on the floor or on a mat, facing each other with legs apart and feet touching. Both grasp a wand with both hands and pretend to row a boat. Seek a wide range of movement in the forward–backward rowing motion. (The stunt can be done without a wand by having children grasp hands.)

Leapfrog

One student bends over forward, forming a base. A leaper takes a running start, lays hands flat on the back at the shoulders, and vaults over the first student. Bases are formed at various heights (Figure 20.83). To form a low base, crouch down on the knees, curling into a tight ball with the head tucked well down. To form a medium base, reach down the outside of the legs from a standing position and grasp the ankles. The feet are moderately spread and the knees straight. The position must be stable to absorb the shock of the leaper. To form a high base, stand stiff-legged, bend over, and brace arms against the knees. The feet are spread, the head down, and the body braced to absorb the vault.

Leapfrog is a traditional physical education activity, but the movement is actually a jump-and-vault pattern. The takeoff is made with both feet. At the height of the jump, the chest and head are held erect to avoid falling forward. Teachers should emphasize a forceful jump to achieve height, coordinated with light hand pressure to vault over the back. Landing is light and under good control, with a bent-knee action.

VARIATIONS:

1. Work in pairs. Alternate leaping and forming the base while moving around the room.
2. Have more than one base for a series of jumps.
3. Using the medium base, vault from the side rather than from the front. The vaulter's legs must be well spread, and the base must keep the head well tucked down.
4. Following the Leapfrog, do a Forward Roll on a mat.

Wheelbarrow

One partner gets down on the hands with feet extended to the rear and legs apart. The other partner (the pusher) grasps partner's legs about halfway between the ankles and the knees. The wheelbarrow walks forward on the hands, supported by the pusher (Figure 20.84 on page 494). Movements should be under good control.

Children tend to grasp the legs too near the feet. The pusher must not push too fast. The wheelbarrow holds the head up and looks forward. Fingers are pointed forward and well spread, with the pads of the fingers supporting much of the weight. The pusher carries the legs low and keeps the arms extended.

20

Wheelbarrow Lifting

Partners assume the wheelbarrow position. The pusher lifts partner's legs as high as possible without changing the hand position. The pusher must lift the legs enough so that the lower child's body is about at a 45-degree angle to the floor.

VARIATION: The pusher brings the legs up to the level described, changes the handgrip to a pushing one, and continues raising the lower child toward a

FIGURE 20.84 Wheelbarrow.

handstand position. The lower child keeps arms and body straight.

Camel Lift and Walk

In the wheelbarrow position, the wheelbarrow raises the seat as high as possible, forming a camel. Camels can lower themselves or walk in the raised position.

Dump the Wheelbarrow

Get into the wheelbarrow position. Walk the wheelbarrow over to a mat. The lower child ducks the head (chin to waist), raises the seat (bending at the waist), and exits from the stunt with a Forward Roll. The pusher gives a little push and a lift of the feet to help create momentum.

Dromedary Walk

One child (the support) gets down on the hands and knees. The other child sits on the support, facing the rear, and fixes the legs around the support's chest. The top child leans forward, to grasp the back of the support's ankles. The top child's arms are reasonably extended (Figure 20.85). The support takes the weight off the knees and walks forward with the top child's help.

FIGURE 20.85 Dromedary Walk.

Centipede

A strong, large child gets down on hands and knees. The other child faces the same direction, places the hands about 2 feet in front of the support's, and places her legs and body on top of the support. The knees are spread apart and the heels locked together. The centipede walks with the top child using hands only and the supporting child using both hands and feet. The support gathers the legs well under while walking and is not on the knees.

VARIATION: More than two can do this stunt (Figure 20.86). After getting into position, the players keep step by calling out "Right" and "Left."

Double Wheelbarrow

Two children form a Centipede, but the support child extends his legs to the rear and spreads his feet apart. A third child stands between the support's legs, reaches down, and picks them up (Figure 20.87). The Double Wheelbarrow moves forward with right and left arms moving together. Three children usually do this stunt, but it can be done by more.

PARTNER SUPPORT STUNTS

Several considerations are important for partner support stunts at this level. The lower child (the support) needs to keep the body as level as possible. This means widening the hand base to make the shoulders more nearly level with the hips. The support child must be strong enough to handle the support chores. Spotters are needed, particularly

FIGURE 20.86 Centipede.

FIGURE 20.87 Double Wheelbarrow.

FIGURE 20.88 Double Bear.

when the top position involves a final erect or inverted pose. The top child must avoid stepping on the small of the support's back. In the Lighthouse and the Hip–Shoulder Stand, the top performer can remove his shoes, making the standing position more comfortable for the support. When holding the final pose, the top child fixes his gaze forward and relaxes as much as possible while maintaining the position.

Another consideration is the students' size. Avoid obvious mismatches, and try to ensure that students of nearly equal size are partnered. Some students may be designated as bases only, since their size restricts their ability to be supported by others. Also, in some settings, it is best to pair students of the same sex to avoid the touching issues when performing these activities.

Double Bear

The bottom child gets down on the hands and knees. The top child assumes the same position directly above the support, with hands on the shoulders and knees on the hips of the support (Figure 20.88). Improve the final position by holding heads up and backs straight.

Table

The bottom performer assumes a crab position. The top performer straddles this base, facing the rear, and positions the hands on the base's shoulders, fingers pointing toward the ground. The top child then places the feet on top of base's knees, forming one crab position on top of another (Figure 20.89 on page 496). As a final touch, the performers look up toward the ceiling and lift their seats so their backs are straight.

Statue

The first child gets down in crab position. The second child straddles either foot, facing the first child. With a spotter's help, the second child mounts the base child's knees and stands erect (Figure 20.90 on page 496). Hold the position for a few seconds. The top child must not mount with back toward the base child. (Spotters are important; students must use them until they master the stunt.)

FIGURE 20.89 Table.

FIGURE 20.90 Statue.

Lighthouse

The support gets down on the hands and knees. The top child completes the figure by standing on the support's shoulders and facing in the same direction. The lighthouse stands erect with arms out to the sides (Figure 20.91).

FIGURE 20.91 Lighthouse.

VARIATION: The support turns around in a small circle, while the partner keeps the standing balance.

Hip–Shoulder Stand

The support child is on the hands and knees, with hands spread out to make the back level. The top child faces to the side and steps up, first with one foot on support's hips and then with the other on the shoulders (Figure 20.92). A spotter stands on the opposite side and aids in the mounting. Caution the top child to avoid stepping on the small of the support's back.

DEVELOPMENTAL LEVEL III ACTIVITIES

It is unrealistic to expect all children to accomplish the entire list of stunts at this level. In fact, it is unrealistic to think some children will ever become outstanding at the tumbling and inverted stunts. Such activities are difficult for students who are heavier and less strong. Some children at this level will become skillful at both the Forward and the Backward Rolls. The Judo Roll, Cartwheel with Round-Off, and Double Roll continue the tumbling activities. Improvement in the Headstand is expected. Such

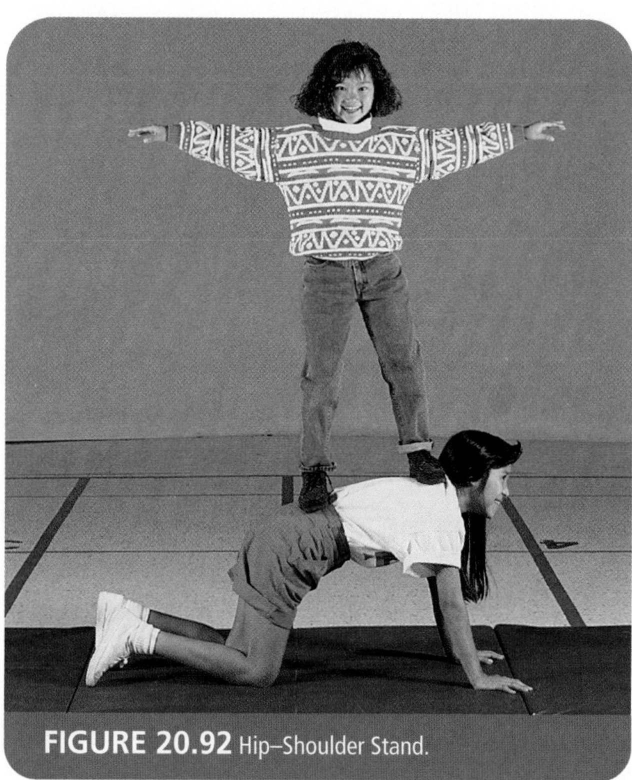

FIGURE 20.92 Hip–Shoulder Stand.

stunts as the Headspring, Front Seat Support, Elbow Balance, Straddle Press to Headstand, and Walk-Over provide sufficient breadth for even the most skilled.

TUMBLING AND INVERTED BALANCES

Safety Tip

To prevent serious injuries, never encourage or force children to perform an activity they are uncomfortable with. If a child lacks the neck and shoulder-girdle strength to do tumbling or inverted balances, substitute an alternate activity. Spotting techniques are offered for teachers who feel capable of helping children who can perform the activities. Spot only children who can and want to perform an activity.

Forward and Backward Roll Combinations

Have students review combinations from Developmental Level II. The following routines can be added.

1. Begin with a Forward Roll, coming to a standing position with feet crossed. Pivot the body to uncross the feet and to bring the back in the line of direction for a Backward Roll (Figure 20.93 on page 498).
2. Hold the toes, heels, ankles, or a wand while rolling. Use different arm positions, such as out to the sides or folded across the chest. Use a wide straddle position for both the Forward Roll and the Backward Roll.

Back Extension

Carry the Backward Roll to the point where the feet are above and over the head. Push off vigorously with the hands, shoot the feet into the air, and land on the feet.

Headstand Variations

Review the various aspects of the Headstand, using the single-spotter technique as needed. Vary with different leg positions. Add the two-footed recovery. After holding the headstand, a student recovers by bending at the waist and knees, pushing off with the hands, and landing on the feet in the original position.

Handstand Against a Wall

Using a wall as support, do a Handstand. The arms must be kept straight, with the head between the arms (Figure 20.94 on page 498). Some performers like to bend the knees and place the soles of the feet against the wall.

A critical point in the Handstand against a Wall is to position the hands the correct distance from the wall. It is better to be too close than too far. Being too far can cause the performer to collapse before the feet gain the support of the wall. Use spotters and a mat in the preliminary stages.

Freestanding Handstand

Perform a Handstand without support. Students must learn to turn the body when a fall is imminent, so that they land on the feet. (Use spotters to prevent an awkward fall.) Move the hands to help control the balance.

Cartwheel and Round-Off

Practice the Cartwheel, adding a light run with a skip for a takeoff. To change to a Round-Off, place

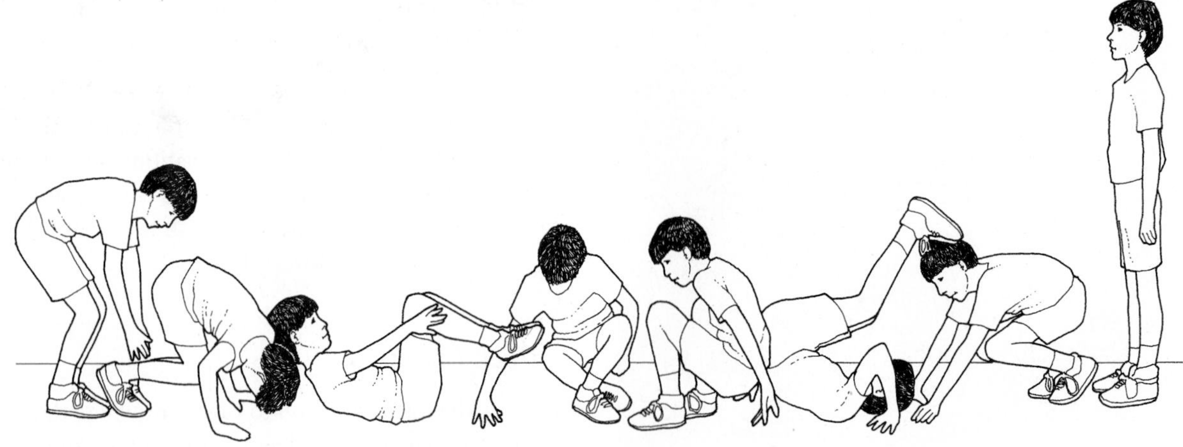

FIGURE 20.93 Alternating Forward and Backward Rolls.

FIGURE 20.94 Handstand against a wall.

the hands somewhat closer together during the early Cartwheel action. Bring the feet together and make a quarter turn to land on both feet, with the body facing the starting point. The Round-Off can be followed by a Backward Roll.

Judo Roll

For a left Judo Roll, stand facing the mat with the feet well apart and the left arm extended at shoulder height. Bring the arm down and throw the left shoulder toward the mat in a rolling motion, making the roll on the shoulder and upper part of the back (Figure 20.95). Reverse for a right Judo Roll. Practice the rolls on both sides. Later, start the Judo Roll with a short run and a two-footed takeoff. The Judo Roll is a basic safety device to prevent injury from tripping and falling. Rolling and taking the fall lessen the chances of injury. The Judo Roll is essentially a Forward Roll with the head turned to one side. The point of impact is the back of one shoulder and the finish is a return to the standing position.

FIGURE 20.95 Judo Roll.

VARIATIONS:

1. Roll to the feet and to a ready position.
2. Place a beanbag about 3 feet in front of the toes and go beyond the bag to start the roll.

Advanced Forward and Backward Roll Combinations

Develop different combinations of Forward Rolls and Backward Rolls. Emphasize choice, exploration, and self-discovery. Variations can involve different approaches, execution acts, and finishes. Try these variations of the Forward Roll.

1. Roll while holding the toes, heels, ankles, or a wand.
2. As above, but cross the hands.
3. Roll with hands on the knees or with a ball between the knees.
4. Roll with arms at the sides, folded across the chest, or on the back of the thighs.
5. Press forward from a front-leaning rest position and go into the roll.

Try these suggestions with the Backward Roll.

1. Begin with a Stiff-Legged Sitdown and go into the roll.
2. Push off into a Back Extension, landing on the feet.
3. Roll to a finish on one foot only.
4. Roll with hands clasped behind the neck.
5. Roll with a ball between the knees.
6. Walk backward using a Crab Walk and then roll.

Finally, try combining Forward Rolls with Backward Rolls in various ways.

Straddle Press to Headstand

Begin by placing the hands and head in the Triangular Headstand position. The feet are in a wide straddle and the hips are up. Raise the hips slowly by pressing to a point over the base of support. Slowly raise the legs to a straddle position and finish with the legs brought together in regular Headstand position. All movement is done as a slow, controlled action. (This stunt is more difficult than a regular Headstand.)

Handstand Variations

Review the first two stages of the Handstand, done with double spotting and then single spotting with knee support (page 484). Progression can then follow this order.

1. Single spotting, without knee support
2. Handstand against a wall
3. Freestanding Handstand
4. Walking on the hands
5. Stunts against a wall

Spotting: For single spotting without knee support, the performer and the spotter face each other at 4 to 5 feet apart. The performer lifts both arms and the left leg as a preliminary move; the weight shifts to the right leg. The lifted arms and forward leg come down forcefully to the ground, as the weight shifts first to the left leg and then to the arms. For momentum, the performer kicks the right leg backward and upward, followed quickly by the left leg. The downward thrust of the arms, coupled with the upward thrust of the legs, inverts the body to the handstand position. The performer's hands are about 2 feet in front of the spotter, who reaches forward and catches the performer between the knees and the ankles.

Headspring

With forehead and hands on the mat and knees bent, lean forward until almost overbalanced. As the weight begins to overbalance, raise the feet sharply and snap forward, pushing with the hands. As the feet begin to touch the ground, snap the body to a bent-knee position (Figure 20.96). Keep control of balance and rise to a standing position.

Spotting: Use two spotters, one on each side of the performer. Each spotter places one hand under the performer's back and the other hand under a

FIGURE 20.96 Headspring.

shoulder. The spotters give the performer a slight lift under the shoulders to help in snapping to the standing position.

Walking on the Hands

Walk on the hands in a forward direction, bending the knees slightly, if desired, for balance. (Walking can be done first with a spotter supporting, but this support should be minimal.)

VARIATION: Walk on the hands, using a partner. The performer does a Handstand and the partner catches the feet. The performer then walks the hands forward until they are on the partner's feet. The two walk cooperatively.

Walk-Over

Do preliminary movements as if for the Handstand. Let the legs continue beyond that position and contact the floor with a one-two rhythm. Keep the body well arched as the leading foot touches the floor. Push off with the hands and walk out.

Spotting: The spotter supports the small of the performer's back.

BALANCE STUNTS

V-Up

Lie on the back, with arms overhead and extended. With the knees straight and feet pointed, bring the legs and upper body up at the same time to form a V shape. The entire weight balances on the seat (Figure 20.97). Hold for 5 seconds. This exercise, like the Curl-Up, is excellent for developing the abdominal muscles. It is much like the Seat Balance, except for the starting position.

VARIATION: Place the hands on the floor in back for support. (This makes the stunt easier for some students.)

FIGURE 20.97 V-Up.

Push-Up Variations

Begin the development of Push-Up variations by reviewing proper Push-Up techniques. The only movement is in the arms. The body does not quite touch the floor. Explore the following variations.

MONKEY PUSH-UP. Point the fingers toward each other. Next, bring the hands close enough for the fingertips to touch.

CIRCLE-O PUSH-UP. Form a circle with each thumb and forefinger.

FINGERTIP PUSH-UP. Get up high on the fingertips.

DIFFERENT FINGER COMBINATIONS. Do a Push-Up using the thumb and three (or two) fingers only.

EXTENDED PUSH-UP. Extend the position of the hands progressively forward or to the sides.

CROSSED PUSH-UP. Cross the arms. Cross the legs. Cross both.

ONE-LEGGED PUSH-UP. Lift one leg from the floor.

ONE-HANDED PUSH-UP. Use only one hand, with the other outstretched or on the hip.

EXPLORATORY APPROACH. Try creating other types of Push-Ups or combinations.

Flip-Flop

From a push-up position, propel the body upward with the hands and feet, doing a Turn-Over (Figure 20.98). Flip back. Do this stunt on a mat. (Review the Turn-Over on page 474 before students try this stunt.)

FIGURE 20.98 Flip-Flop.

Long Reach

Place a beanbag about 3 feet in front of a line. Keeping the toes behind the line, lean forward on one hand and reach out with the other hand to touch the beanbag (Figure 20.99). Recover in one clean, quick movement to the original position, lifting the supporting hand off the floor. Increase the distance of the bag from the line.

FIGURE 20.99 Long Reach.

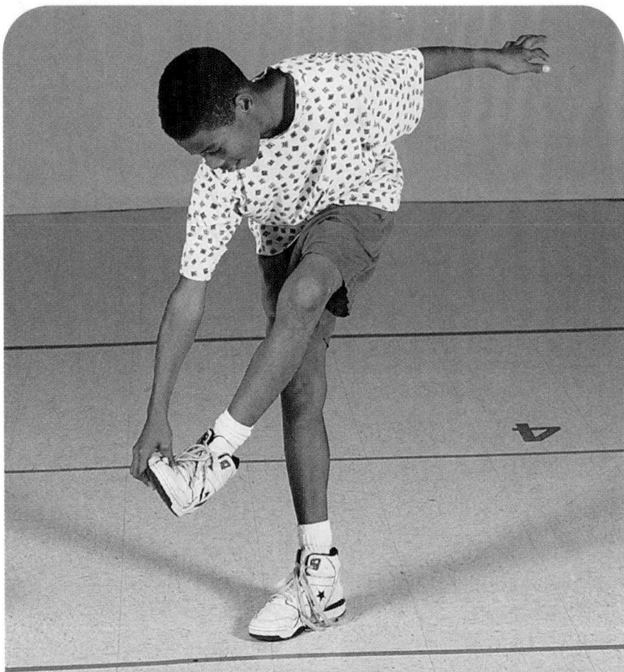

FIGURE 20.100 Toe Jump.

Toe Jump

Hold the left toes with the right hand (Figure 20.100). Jump the right foot through without losing the grip on the toes. Try with the other foot. (Teachers: Do not be discouraged if only a few students can do this stunt; it is quite difficult.)

Handstand Stunts

Try these challenging activities from the handstand position against a wall.

1. Turn the body in a complete circle, maintaining foot contact with the wall throughout.
2. Shift the support to one hand and hold for a moment.
3. Do an Inverted Push-Up, lowering the body by bending the elbows and then returning to handstand position by straightening the elbows.

Front Seat Support

Sit on the floor, with the legs together and forward. Place the hands flat on the floor, somewhere between the hips and the knees, with fingers pointed forward. Push down so the hips come off the floor, with the weight supported on the hands and heels. Next, lift the heels and support the entire weight of the body on the hands for 3 to 5 seconds. (Someone can help the performer get into position by giving slight support under the heels.)

Elbow Balance

Balance the body facedown horizontally on two hands, with elbows supporting the body in the hip area. To get into position, support the arched body with the toes and forehead. Work the forearms underneath the body for support, with fingers spread and pointed backward. Try to support the body completely on the hands for 3 seconds, with elbows providing the leverage under the body (Figure 20.101 on page 502). (Slight support under the toes can be provided.) The Elbow Balance is quite challenging. The teacher should take time to discuss the location of the center of gravity. The elbow support point should divide the upper and lower body mass.

INDIVIDUAL STUNTS

Wall Walk-Up

From a push-up position with feet against a wall, walk up the wall backward to a handstand position (Figure 20.102 on page 502). Walk down again.

FIGURE 20.101 Elbow Balance.

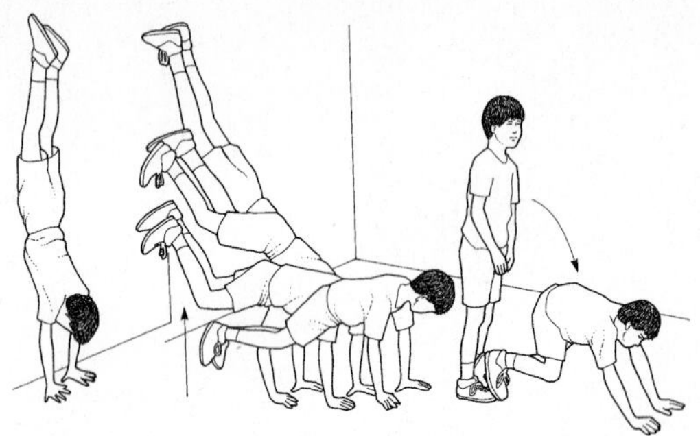
FIGURE 20.102 Wall Walk-Up.

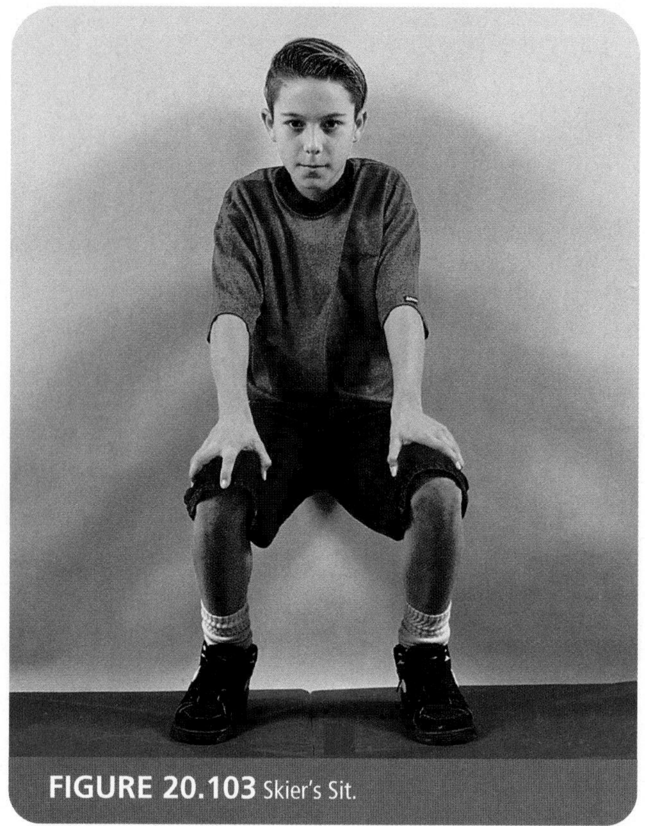
FIGURE 20.103 Skier's Sit.

Skier's Sit

Assume a sitting position (as if in a chair) against a wall with the thighs parallel to the floor and the knee joints at right angles. Place the hands on the thighs with the feet flat on the floor and the lower legs straight up and down (Figure 20.103). Try to sit for 30 seconds, 45 seconds, and 1 minute. The Skier's Sit is an isometric activity and is excellent for developing the knee extensor muscles. Skiers use it to develop the muscles used in skiing.

VARIATION: A more difficult stunt is to support the body on one leg and extend the other leg.

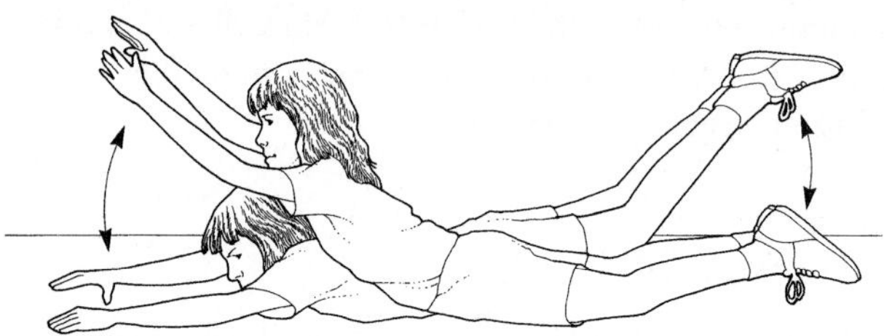
FIGURE 20.104 Rocking Horse.

Rocking Horse

Lie facedown on a mat with arms extended overhead, palms down. Arch the back and rock back and forth (Figure 20.104). (Some children may need someone to start them rocking.)

VARIATION: Reach back and grasp the insteps with the hands. (The body arch is more difficult to maintain in this position.) Also try rocking from a side position.

Heel Click (Side)

Balance on one foot with the other out to the side. Hop on the supporting foot, click the heels, and return to balance. Try with the other foot. Good form dictates recovering to the one-footed balance position with little foot movement.

VARIATIONS:

1. Take a short step with the right foot leading. Follow with a cross-step with the left and then a hop on the left foot. During the hop, click the heels together. To hop on the right foot, reverse these directions.
2. Jump as high as possible before clicking the heels.
3. Combine right and left clicks.

Walk-Through

From a front-leaning rest position, walk the feet through the hands, using tiny steps, until the body is fully extended with the back to the floor (Figure

20.105). Return to original position. The hands are on the floor throughout.

FIGURE 20.105 Walk-Through.

Jump-Through

Starting in a front-leaning rest position, jump the feet through the arms in one motion. Reverse with another jump and return to original position. The hands must push off sharply from the floor, so the body is high enough off the floor to allow the legs to jump under. (Students may find it easier to swing a little to the side with one leg, going under the lifted hand, as indicated in Figure 20.106.)

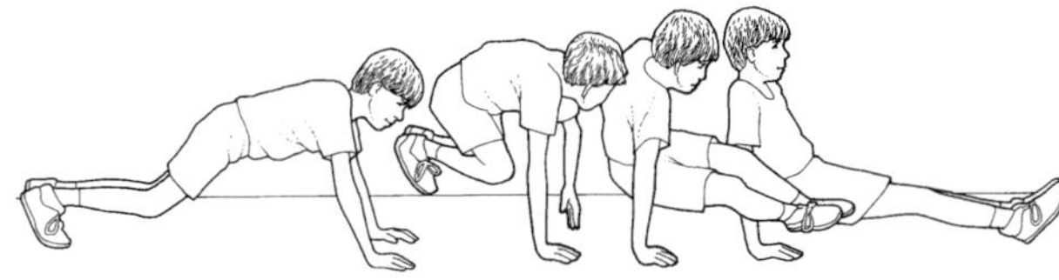

FIGURE 20.106 Jump-Through.

Circular Rope Jump

Crouch down in a three-quarter knee bend, holding a folded jump rope in one hand. Swing the rope under the feet in a circular fashion, jumping it each time (Figure 20.107). Reverse the direction of the rope. Work from both right and left sides, turning the rope either counterclockwise or clockwise.

VARIATIONS:

1. Perform the rope jump with a partner.
2. Jump using different foot patterns (one foot or alternate feet) and using slow and fast time.
3. Establish standards for declaring a class champion in different areas, such as maximum number of turns in 30 seconds, most unique routine, and most jumps without a miss.

Bouncer

Start in a push-up position. Bounce up and down with the hands and feet leaving the ground at the

FIGURE 20.107 Circular Rope Jump.

same time. Try clapping while doing this. Move in various directions. Turn around.

Pretzel

Touch the back of the head with the toes by raising the head and trunk and bringing the feet to the back of the head (Figure 20.108). First try to get the toes within a hand span (the distance between the thumb and little finger when spread) of the head. If this

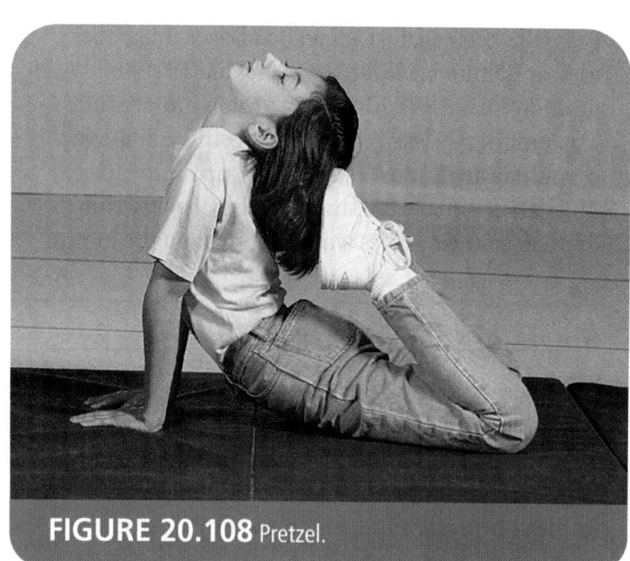

FIGURE 20.108 Pretzel.

FIGURE 20.127 Side Stand.

FIGURE 20.128 Pyramid Formation.

recommended at this developmental level. To decrease potential for accidents, have students practice stunts using only one performer or pair before trying to make pyramids with three students.

DEVELOPING GYMNASTIC ROUTINES

Teachers can design sequences of stunts and other movements and present them as movement problems. The problems might be structured as follows.

1. Specify the number and kind of stunts and movements to be done and the sequence to be followed. For example, tell the child to do a balance stunt, a locomotor movement, and a rolling stunt.
2. Arrange the mats in some prescribed order to provide the key to the movement problems. For example, place two or three mats in succession, three or four in a U shape, or four in a hollow square. Leave some space between mats, depending on the problem. You could present the problem like this: "On the first mat, do a Forward Roll variation and then a movement to the next mat on all fours. On the second mat, do some kind of balance stunt, and then proceed to the next mat with a jumping or hopping movement. On the third mat, you choose the activity." You can also state the problem in more general terms, and children can do a different stunt or variation on each mat and a different movement between mats.
3. Have partners design a series of stunts. Ensure that paired children are of equal size and strength, so they can alternate as the support. If children are of different sizes, the larger child can provide support for the smaller, and a third child may act as a spotter. After practicing for awhile, each pair demonstrates the routines they have created.

FOR MORE INFORMATION

REFERENCES AND SUGGESTED READINGS

Bizley, K. (1999). *Gymnastics.* Des Plaines, IL: Heineman Library.

Hacker, P., Malmbert, E., & Nance, J. (1996). *Gymnastics fun & games.* Champaign, IL: Human Kinetics Publishers.

Malmburg, E. (2003). *Kidnastics: A child-centered approach to teaching gymnastics.* Champaign, IL: Human Kinetics.

Mattern, J. (1999). *Gymnastics.* Vero Beach, FL: Rourke Corporation.

Mitchell, D., Davis, B., & Lopez, R. (2002). *Teaching fundamental gymnastic skills.* Champaign, IL: Human Kinetics.

Readhead, L. (1997). *The fantastic book of gymnastics.* Brookfield, CT: Copper Beech Books.

Werner, P. H. (2004). *Teaching children gymnastics* (2nd ed.). Champaign, IL: Human Kinetics.

WEBSITES

www.usa-gymnastics.org

Cooperative Skills

21

ESSENTIAL COMPONENTS OF QUALITY PROGRAMS

I. Organized around content standards

II. Student-centered and developmentally appropriate

III. Physical activity and motor skill development form the core of the program

IV. Teaches management skills and self-discipline

V. Promotes inclusion of all students

VI. Focuses on process over product

VII. Promotes lifetime personal health and wellness

VIII. Teaches cooperation and responsibility and promotes sensitivity to diversity

NATIONAL STANDARDS FOR PHYSICAL EDUCATION*

1. Demonstrates competency in motor skills and movement patterns needed to perform a variety of physical activities.
2. Demonstrates understanding of movement concepts, principles, and tactics as they apply to the learning and performance of physical activities.
3. Participates regularly in physical activity.
4. Achieves and maintains a health-enhancing level of physical fitness.
5. Exhibits responsible personal and social behavior that respects self and others in physical activity.
6. Values physical activity for health, enjoyment, challenge, self-expression, and/or social interaction.

*National Association for Sport and Physical Education (NASPE), 2004.

Cooperative activities teach students to work together for their group's common good. The activities in this chapter give students opportunities to learn cooperative skills and apply them in a rewarding activity. By participating in these activities, students can learn the skills of listening, discussing, thinking as a group, group decision making, and sacrificing individual wants for the common good. The activities also offer students unique challenges. The parachute activities in this chapter demand an entire class work together to accomplish desired outcomes with the parachute. Students have many opportunities to learn cooperative skills while using the parachute to perform various fundamental motor and fitness skills.

Outcomes

- Understand the role of cooperative activities in physical education.
- Understand the steps involved in teaching cooperative activities.
- Communicate the importance of questioning and discussion following cooperative activities.
- Describe several group challenges appropriate for elementary school children.
- Discuss various parachute activities and explain their role as cooperative activities.

THE ROLE OF COOPERATIVE ACTIVITIES

In physical education terms such as *team building, cooperative learning, cooperative,* and *adventured education* are used interchangeably to describe a variety of activities. Each term has subtle differences, but most of them focus primarily on teaching cooperation. This chapter uses the term *cooperative activities* to describe such activities.

Two primary objectives guide the teaching of cooperative activities. First, cooperative activities allow students to apply a variety of fundamental motor skills in a unique setting. Students are typically asked to perform motor skills in a specific way, such as "skip in general space" or "balance on one foot and one elbow." Rarely are students asked to skip with their hands on the shoulders of someone in front of them, or walk with big steps while placing their feet on small spots, or walk across an area blindfolded while someone directs their moves. Due to the uniqueness of such experiences, students also enjoy cooperative activities.

Second, cooperative activities teach children personal and social skills necessary to function in daily life. Often, cooperation is thought of as conforming to group norms. For example, consider Scott, who is seen as cooperative because he does not speak out in class until asked. This is a form of cooperation, and it is seen in cooperative activities, but a more advanced form of cooperation is also apparent. This type of cooperation, which may require students to sacrifice what they want to do in order to help the group, is best exemplified by a simple parachute activity. The first-grade class is challenged to get a tennis ball to fall through the hole in the center of the chute. After trying many different approaches, the class decides to have everyone raise the chute above their heads and watch the ball fall through the hole. Barbara would rather make waves with the chute by her waist. But, when she does that, the ball rolls to her and not into the hole. She decides to raise her hands above her head and help the class make the ball fall through the chute.

Cooperative activities also teach other social skills. In many classes, students become members of cliques and rarely interact with other students, even in their own class. Effectively implemented cooperative activities require all students to work together. By working together, students learn that all students are important, that everyone has similarities and differences, and that all students can contribute to the group's effort to accomplish a common goal. Obvious roles include leader and follower, but other student roles, such as being responsible for organizing a plan, keeping the group focused, and remembering specific rules, will emerge. With their varied roles and unique tasks, most cooperative activities allow all students to contribute and experience success. This outcome is especially helpful for less physically skilled students, who often benefit greatly from enhanced self-confidence. In summary, cooperative activities teach social skills such as teamwork, communication, decision making, and conflict resolution while using fundamental motor skills in unique situations.

TEACHING COOPERATIVE ACTIVITIES

It is a common misconception that teaching cooperative activities and skills simply means providing students with the appropriate activities. In fact, presenting the activities without adequately introducing and summarizing them can do more harm than good. Without a series of concluding questions or effective teacher monitoring, negative outcomes may emerge. The usual role of quiet, less skilled students—"stay in the back and don't be embarrassed"—may be reinforced as dominant students continue to control the activities while learning nothing about group dynamics and cooperation. Explaining what cooperative skills the group will be using before the activity can also limit its effectiveness. By doing so, you may cause students to begin focusing on specific skills, preventing them from learning other skills that may present themselves. Students who are told the activity requires them to communicate will focus on listening and talking, but may lose sight of the different roles other students are assuming to help accomplish the goal. Similarly, telling the group what they learned after the cooperative activity may diminish its effectiveness. For example, after students have participated in an activity that requires discussion about methods of accomplishing a task, the teacher says, "In that activity you had to think and then explain your ideas to your teammates. That is communication, which is important in cooperation." But one student may have figured out that he had to listen to his group more, or that he did not explain himself clearly. As with all education, remember that all children are individuals who approach challenges differently. To encourage individuality and maximize the effectiveness of cooperative activities in teaching cooperative skills, teachers can use the following steps.

Many of the activities used to teach cooperative skills place students in situations they are not accustomed to being in. For this reason, students must move with caution and be aware of the safety of those around them.

STEPS TO TEACHING COOPERATIVE ACTIVITIES

1. *Set the stage.* The teacher's job is to sell the activity by giving students the following information:

    What is the challenge?

    What are the rules?

    What are the consequences for breaking the rules?

    Do any safety issues need to be addressed?

    During this step, provide only the information needed to get the group going. This information is best presented in the form of a descriptive and often imaginary story. For example, rather than framing a challenge as getting the entire group to go through a hoop hanging from a basketball basket, place the students in an imaginary jungle where they find a time-traveling cell. They are lost and their only way out of the jungle is to get everyone in the group through the cell. But when anyone touches the cell, it pushes out everyone who is already through, and they have to start over. These types of stories pique students' interest and help them exercise imagination and creativity.

2. *Facilitate.* After setting the stage, the teacher must step back and let the students work. Many teachers find this step difficult because they want to tell students how to accomplish the task or at least give them a few hints. However, it is best simply to answer questions and monitor the group's safety. Many teachers answer questions vaguely to avoid giving too much information or too much of a hint. This approach forces students to improve their questioning skills to get the answers they need. While monitoring the class, teachers must make physical and emotional safety the highest priorities. If students get frustrated and begin making disrespectful remarks, stop or refocus the activity immediately and offer a fresh beginning. It is not critical for the group to accomplish the task. Often, time may run out before the class has time to complete the challenge. In cooperative activities, success does not always mean accomplishing the task; learning to cooperate is more important. Much can be learned and gained from simply working on the task. However, teachers must allow time for the final step—debriefing.
3. *Debrief.* This may be the most important step in effectively implementing cooperative activities. So far, little has been said about cooperation. This step of the cooperative activity process allows students to share their experiences and gives teachers the opportunity to meet their own objectives (e.g., to discuss listening) and to connect what was learned to daily living.

    The foundation of debriefing is open-ended questions. Questions like, "Did that work?" or "Would you do that again?" require a yes or no response and do not foster discussion. Here are some examples of open-ended questions:

    What did you have to do to accomplish the goal?

    What does *communicate* mean?

    What happened that was positive?

    What happened that could have been better?

    How could you have changed things?

    What does it mean to be patient?

    How can you compromise?

    What would you have done differently? The same?

During the debriefing, it is important to discuss how students can use the skills learned in the activity outside of PE class. Again, open-ended questions—"When would you have to be patient outside of PE?" or "How would good communication skills help you at home?"—are helpful in discussing these ideas.

GROUP CHALLENGES

Group challenges are designed to place students in an unfamiliar situation that requires some form of cooperation. The activities and rules are created in such a way that students cannot complete the tasks alone; they must cooperate. Many of these activities are most effective with small groups and can be taught in one of three ways:

1. The entire class works on the same task or activity, such as Pig Ball (see page 520).
2. All groups work independently on the same task. For example, Groups A and B can work on Group Juggling in separate areas. Teachers using this approach must ensure that the activities do not become races. This is best accomplished by downplaying the speed and stressing cooperation. When a team accomplishes a task, challenge them with another. For example, if a team performed the Group Juggle five times without dropping the ball, have them try to better their own record, thus creating a continuous challenge for all groups. Many teaching tips for the group challenge activities address this goal.
3. Teach through stations, and provide one station per team. Each team reports to a station and begins the challenge by reading the task card. Task cards allow teachers to integrate reading into physical education without sacrificing physical education time. They also allow for a more efficient, active lesson because the teacher does not have to explain every challenge. For more difficult challenges, teachers can first get the teams engaged and then quickly stop the entire class and explain the activity. Depending on the challenge, groups can work at each station for 5 to 10 minutes and then rotate. Because some groups will not get to all challenges, encourage students to work on them—particularly those requiring few pieces of equipment—at recess.

Group challenges in this chapter are designed for Developmental Levels II and III. In Developmental Level I, students learn basic cooperative skills—sharing, listening, and individual or partner decision making—throughout the curriculum. These skills are further taught and reinforced throughout the curriculum for older students. The following cooperative activities specifically focus on basic as well as more advanced cooperative skills such as group decision making and group communication.

Lifeboats

FORMATION: Groups of 8 to 12 students

SUPPLIES: Two to three individual mats or hoops, two scooters, and one long jump rope per group

Teams stand on one side of the gym (a slowly sinking ship). Each team has a scooter (lifeboat) and a long jump rope. The objective is to get the entire team from the sinking ship to the mainland (the other side of the gym) using only the lifeboat. Spaced randomly between the ship and mainland are three individual mats or hoops (islands in the ocean). Any students who touch the gym floor (water) must return to the starting point or island they were on (if hoops are used as islands, inside the hoop counts as land). All students must stay on a mat at all times unless they are traveling across the ocean in a lifeboat (scooter). Students may be pulled with the jump rope, but they may not be pushed. Students who reach the mainland must stay there; they cannot return to the island or lifeboats. But, if they step into the water when trying to rescue a teammate, they must return to the final island. Figure 21.1 is a poster for the lifeboat station.

Mat Folding

FORMATION: Groups of 4 to 5 students

SUPPLIES: One tumbling mat for each group

Give each team one tumbling mat and instruct them to stand on it. While keeping their feet on the mat at all times, teams work on the following challenges:

1. Rotate the mat 360 degrees.
2. Move the mat 15 feet.
3. Without using any hands, fold the mat into fourths.
4. Unfold the mat without using any hands.

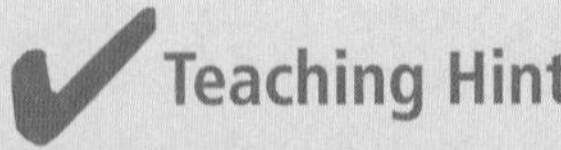

Teaching Hint

This is an enjoyable activity to use at the end of a gymnastics lesson.

Lifeboats

The Challenge

Save the entire group by getting everyone to the mainland using only the lifeboats, islands, and tug rope

Your Equipment:
Lifeboats—Scooters
Tug rope—Long Jump Rope
Islands—Tumbling Mats

Rules:

1. Anyone that touches the ocean (gym floor) must return to the starting point.
2. Lifeboats may only be pulled.
3. Once you make it to the mainland you must stay there unless you step in the water.
4. Only one person on the lifeboat at a time.

FIGURE 21.1 Station sign for Lifeboats.

Attached at the ...

FORMATION: Partners

SUPPLIES: One beanbag or ball for each set of partners

Partners stand on one side of the activity area. Challenge them to get to the other sideline or end line while attached at the hip, head, back, ankle, elbow, hamstring, and so on. Locomotor movements can be specified for moving across the area. For a more difficult activity, instruct the students to hold a beanbag or ball between the "attached" body parts.

To add difficulty after students complete partner tasks, challenge them to work in groups of 3, 4, or more.

Moving Together

FORMATION: Groups of four students

SUPPLIES: None

Teams stand on the sidelines of the teaching area. The objective is for the team to move to the other sideline with the following stipulations:

1. Six feet touching the floor and all team members touching an ankle.
2. Eight body parts (no heads) touching the ground at all times.
3. Half of the team at a high level and half the team at a low level.
4. Every foot touching one other foot.
5. Only four feet can touch the ground.
6. Four feet and one hand must be on the ground.
7. Move with the fewest number of feet possible touching the floor.
8. Move with the most hands and fewest feet touching the floor.

Teaching Hint

Pose additional challenges by having the teams carry different pieces of equipment while attempting the challenges. To minimize competition and ensure continuous activity, give each team its own list of challenges. After completing a challenge, teams choose a new challenge from their list.

Balance Beam Mixer

FORMATION: Groups of 8 to 10 students

SUPPLIES: One low balance beam or bench per group

Students stand shoulder-to-shoulder on a low balance beam or bench (for younger students) with mats alongside the beam for safety (Figure 21.2). Challenge groups, while remaining on the balance beam or bench, to get in order based on these criteria:

1. Alphabetical order by first name from left to right
2. Alphabetical order by first name from right to left
3. Tallest to shortest
4. Month of birth date (January to December, or vice versa)

FIGURE 21.2 Balance Beam Mixer.

Quiet Cooperation

FORMATION: Groups of 10 to 12 students

SUPPLIES: One marking spot for each student

Students stand in a line, shoulder-to-shoulder, with a marking spot under their feet. Without talking, making any noise, or touching the gym floor, students get in order using these criteria:

1. Number of pets (fewest to most)
2. Alphabetical by first name (or father's, mother's, or pet name)
3. Alphabetical by last name
4. Month of birthday (January to December, or vice versa)
5. Shortest to tallest

All Aboard

FORMATION: Entire class scattered, hoops spread throughout area

SUPPLIES: 15 hoops

Challenge students to get as many students as possible into one hoop placed on the ground. A person is considered "on board" when one foot touches the ground inside of the hoop and no body parts touch the floor outside the hoop.

Teaching Hint

A lead-up to All Aboard is to play "musical hoops" Scatter hoops throughout the gym and play some music. When the music stops, students move to a hoop, placing at least one foot inside the hoop. More than one student can be in a hoop. Each time the music plays, the teacher removes one or two hoops until only enough hoops remain for all students to be aboard.

Human Spelling Bee

FORMATION: Groups of 5 to 6 players

SUPPLIES: None

Challenge teams with spelling out words, letter by letter, with their bodies while lying on the floor. All team members must be in the letter, and the team's result must differentiate between the top and bottom of the letter. Physical education terms or spelling words may be used. Also, teams can spell out answers to questions asked by the teacher. Teams could also write mathematical equations (i.e., $7 \times 7 = 49$), one number and symbol at a time.

Moving the World

FORMATION: Entire class, scattered throughout area

SUPPLIES: One large cageball

Using a cageball or other large ball as the world, challenge the class to move the world to different locations in the gym. The ball may not be kicked, thrown, or struck, and all class members must be involved:

1. No hands can touch the ball.
2. Only feet can touch the ball.
3. Half of the team must be lying on their backs.
4. Only backs can touch the ball.

5. Only elbows can touch the ball, and no talking is allowed (Figure 21.3).
6. Students must crabwalk.

Teaching Hint

Use directions such as "move the ball 30 feet northwest" or "move the world 25 feet in the same direction you would travel from Arcanum to Pittsburgh."

FIGURE 21.3 Moving the World.

FIGURE 21.4 Group Juggling.

Group Juggling

FORMATION: Groups of 5 to 6 students

SUPPLIES: One ball or beanbag for each student

Each student in every team has a ball or beanbag. Using a variety of balls makes this activity more exciting. On signal (e.g., "1, 2, ready, toss"), each team member tosses his ball to another teammate and then catches a ball tossed to him (Figure 21.4). The goal is to see how many successful tosses can be made in unison. Often, students will toss to the same person each time. A successful juggle occurs when all team members catch the ball tossed to them. After several tosses, the teacher gives each team the responsibility of selecting one member to give the signal for their team.

Stranded

FORMATION: Groups of 5 to 6 students

SUPPLIES: One tumbling mat, three hoops (or volleyball standards), two scooters, and one long jump rope per team

In this challenge, all team members must get from a capsized but floating boat (represented by a tumbling mat), across the river via three islands, and onto the shore (a line on the opposite side of the area). Islands (the hoops) are about 15 feet apart, and one team member is placed on each island. These students' other team members are on the boats. The students on the boat have two scooters and a 16- to 20-foot-long jump rope. While on the scooters, students may not be pushed by other students or pulled using the rope; they must find a way to move without touching the "water." Any student touching the water must return to the boat.

Scoop Ball

FORMATION: Groups of 6 to 8 students

SUPPLIES: Four basketballs, one hoop, four tinikling poles (or 10- to 15-foot sections of PVC pipe), and two scoops for every team

Using tinikling poles and scoops, the teams try to move four basketballs about 50 feet. Without touching the basketballs with any body parts, they must place the balls into a hoop. The following rules apply:

1. If a ball touches the floor or a student, the ball must be returned to the starting point.

2. Players may not walk with the balls.
3. The balls may not be thrown, kicked, or passed.
4. Balls that roll or bounce out of the hoop must be returned to the starting point.
5. Students are permitted to hold only one scoop at a time.

Centipede

FORMATION: Entire class, shoulder-to-shoulder

SUPPLIES: None

All students stand on a sideline, facing the same direction, with feet touching the person next to them. The entire class must move to the other sideline without breaking the chain of touching feet. If the chain breaks, the class must take three steps back. Students may put their arms around each other if desired.

Some classes may require a progression starting with partners, then small groups, and finally the entire class.

Flippers

FORMATION: Entire class, divided into two teams

SUPPLIES: 30–40 flying disks

Spread the flying disks throughout the teaching area. Instruct one team to flip the disks faceup; instruct the other team to flip the disks facedown. After a practice game, add the following stipulations.

1. No hands
2. Feet only
3. Students must crabwalk or bear crawl
4. Feet only, and only one foot can touch the disk at a time
5. Knees only
6. Heel only

Circle Up

FORMATION: Groups of 6 to 8 students in circle formation

SUPPLIES: Three or four hoops per group

Students in each team join hands or wrists to close the circle. Two students release hands, and the teacher places a hoop between them. The students then rejoin hands inside the hoop. Without releasing hands, teams must pass the hoop around the circle. That is, each student must pass through the hoop without letting go of their neighbors' hands. Once the students get the hang of going through the hoop, add more hoops. If a slightly smaller hoop is available, have team members pass it in the opposite direction.

When teaching Circle Up, give teams one or two hoops, and time them to see how fast they can pass the hoop around the circle. After letting the teams briefly discuss how to move the hoop faster, challenge them to beat their own record. Emphasize that this is not a race.

Is It Raining?

FORMATION: Entire class in a circle

SUPPLIES: None

This activity works well at the end of a vigorous lesson. Standing in the circle, the teacher initiates a movement that makes a sound; then the child immediately to her right imitates the movement, and so on, like a wave at a stadium. When the "wave" gets back to the teacher, another movement is started. The students keep making the previous sound until the next one gets around to them. The movements can be any sounds that mimic those heard in nature during a storm:

- Clapping
- Snapping
- Patting quadriceps
- Stamping
- Patting the chest
- Rubbing the hands on the legs

- Rubbing the hands together
- Clucking the tongue
- Making hollow whistles
- Making "shhhhh" sounds

Teaching Hint

Allow students to create movements and lead the changes. Instruct students to close their eyes and rely on their hearing to listen for the sound to come around while trying to figure out what the new movement is.

FIGURE 21.5 Be Careful.

Be Careful

FORMATION: Groups of 6 to 8 students

SUPPLIES: For each group of 8 students: 4 blindfolds, 10 beanbags, 10 yarn balls, 8 poly spots, 8 cones, and 3 jump ropes

Mark off a 10- by 10-foot area with four cones. Next, scatter the beanbags, yarn balls, poly spots, jump ropes, and remaining cones inside the area so there are no straight paths from any one side to another. In partners, students decide who will be the walker and who will be the driver. Roles will be reversed later. The walker is blindfolded and tries to get from one side of the area to the opposite side without touching any of the equipment. The driver stands on the opposite side giving directions such as, "Walk forward" to the walker (Figure 21.5). Thus, the walker must trust the driver and follow strict directions. The team gets 1 point for each piece of equipment the walker touches. The goal is to get to the other side with no points. As students experiment with the activity, directions will become more specific.

Teaching Hint

For an advanced activity, start one walker on each side of the square and add 1 point for each walker who is touched. To motivate each set of partners to move faster, allow them to time how long it takes to cross. Then multiply the number of items touched by 10, and add their time in seconds. For example, if a team touches two items and takes 30 seconds to cross, their score is $2 \times 10 + 30 = 50$. These partners would then attempt to cross and achieve a better score.

Zap

FORMATION: Groups of 4 to 10 students

SUPPLIES: One tumbling mat, one magic rope or jump rope, two volleyball standards or device to attach the ropes

Attach the rope on either side of the mat, about 3 to 4 feet off the ground (height depends on the children's age). Challenge students to get their entire team over the rope and to the other side without touching, or getting "zapped" by, the rope. However, to enhance the challenge and keep it safe, do not permit students to jump over the rope. In addition, to start, each team forms a circle and joins hands to form a "closed chain." This chain must remain closed throughout the challenge. If anyone is zapped by the rope or the chain is broken (two people release hands), the entire team must go back to the other side and start over.

Keep It Floating

FORMATION: Groups of 4 to 8 students

SUPPLIES: For each group, two balloons, one beach ball, and one hoop for every two students

Students form a circle and join hands. Their challenge is to keep a balloon up for as many hits as possible without releasing hands (Figure 21.6 on page 520). After a few rounds, add another balloon to increase the difficulty. Finally, add a beach ball and one balloon.

FIGURE 21.6 Keep It Floating.

VARIATION: For advanced classes, place one hoop between each team. Team members must keep one foot in each hoop on either side of them. This advanced challenge is best with only one balloon. To integrate other academic content, have the teams do the following while participating in the basic challenge:

1. State a different fruit or vegetable with each hit.
2. Count in a foreign language.
3. Count by twos, threes, fours, etc.
4. Try to strike the balloon with a different bone or muscle each time, and call out the name of that body part.
5. Call out a different lifetime activity with each hit.

Teaching Hint

Students tie their shoes in several different ways. For this reason, some partners may become frustrated simply because their method of tying shoes is different. This is a great teachable moment for dealing with frustration and learning the importance of communication.

Shoe Tying

FORMATION: Partners

SUPPLIES: Shoes with shoelaces

This is a great activity for the end of a highly active lesson. Partners sit side by side and untie one shoe. That is, of the four shoes, only one should be untied. Each partner then puts one hand behind her back. Using both remaining hands cooperatively, the partners must then tie the shoe. After tying the shoe, the partners must try using the other hand. Finally, still using only one hand each, have them try to tie the shoe with their eyes closed.

Pig Ball

FORMATION: Two equal teams

SUPPLIES: A rubber pig (If a pig is not available, use a deflated playground ball.)

This activity is a continuous version of Alaskan Baseball. Team A stands in single file with the last person in line holding the pig. That child starts the game by throwing the pig anywhere in the teaching area (the teacher marks this area). Team B then hustles to the pig and stands in single file behind the first child to reach the pig. They pass the pig to the back of the line, alternating between passing it overhead and between the legs. This part is best described as "over and under, over and under." While Team B is doing this, the child who threw the pig hustles around her team, which is still in single file. Each time she passes an end of the line, her team scores 1 point. This part allows all children to score at least 1 point for their team. When the pig gets to the last child on Team B, the team yells, "PIG!" and that child throws the pig anywhere in the teaching area. The child who threw the pig then begins running around his teammates, who stay in single file. At the same time, Team A hustles to the pig and begins the over-and-under passing. The game continues for as long as desired.

Teaching Hint

Because this game is very rigorous, stop after three to four rounds and give students some type of instruction. You might talk about cardiovascular health and why the heart is beating faster, why Pig Ball is cooperative, or a strategy for the game. However, students soon will be ready to resume play. This time, have all students use a specific locomotor movement or animal movement when running around their teammates.

Pretzel

FORMATION: Groups of 6 to 10 students

SUPPLIES: None

Students stand shoulder-to-shoulder in a circle with arms extended in front. Each student must grasp two other hands, one in each hand. The hands that each student grasps cannot be of the same child, and they cannot be of the child beside them. The team must then undo the pretzel they have just created and form a circle—without releasing hands. Once the pretzel unravels, some children may be facing toward the center and some away from the center. Figure 21.7 is a poster for a Pretzel station.

PRETZEL
CHALLENGE
Untangle the group pretzel you create to form a circle, with each person standing next to the person they are holding hands with.
DIRECTIONS
1. Make a circle standing shoulder to shoulder.
2. Put your hands in the middle.
3. Join hands with two different people.
4. You may not join hands with the person next to you.
RULES
Hands must stay together.

FIGURE 21.7 Station sign for the Pretzel.

Who's Leading?

FORMATION: Entire class in a circle

SUPPLIES: None

The entire class stands shoulder-to-shoulder in a circle. One student volunteers to go into the middle and cover her eyes. The teacher then selects a volunteer to lead the class in movements while remaining in the circle. This must be done quietly so the child in the middle does not know who the leader is. The teacher suggests some movements to the leader (jogging or skipping in place, bicep curls, jumping jacks, etc.), and instructs him to change activities every few seconds. The child in the middle then opens her eyes and watches the movements. She must stay in the middle but may scan the entire class in an effort to find the leader as he changes movements.

Teaching Hint

To add difficulty, encourage the leader to make small changes in movements. For example, start with normal jumping jacks, move to skier jacks, then to skiers with no arm movements, and finally to walking in place. Also, suggest that the guesser watch only half of the circle. If the activity changes and she does not see anyone do it first, the leader is probably in the other half of the circle. Remind followers to not give the leader away by staring at him.

How Are We Alike?

FORMATION: Partners

SUPPLIES: None

This is a great activity for the physical education orientation held at the beginning of the school year, when students are getting to know each other and the teacher. Students join with a partner and discuss, "How are we alike?" The teacher provides a few categories—such as appearance, family, favorite activities, and birthdays—and then lets students talk. Before grouping students with a different partner or a group of four to repeat the activity, allow volunteers to share their findings.

Teaching Hint

After "How are we alike?" have students find out "How are we different?" This sets the tone for a physical education setting in which children understand that we all have similarities and differences, and that is okay. It is important for students to understand early on that respecting similarities and differences is crucial to working with others.

Lily Pads

FORMATION: Groups of 6 to 15 students

SUPPLIES: One poly spot per child

Students begin by standing on their poly spots, or lily pads, in a straight line. The lily pads are about 12 inches apart. The team's challenge is to reverse their order so that the two students on the end switch places, the second to last switch places, and so on (see visual explanation). The catch is that each team member must have at least one foot on a lily pad at all times. If this rule is broken, the team must start over in the original order.

Teaching Hint

If poly spots are not available, use a line or a long piece of tape for this activity. Simply make the rule that all team members must keep one foot on the tape at all times.

START	FINISH
1 2 3 4 5 6 7 8	8 7 6 5 4 3 2 1

The Cell

FORMATION: Groups of 5 to 6 students

SUPPLIES: One tumbling mat and one hula hoop suspended from a basketball hoop. The hoop should be about 2 to 4 feet above the mat at its lowest point.

Students are charged with the task of getting everyone on the team through the hoop, or cell. No team member may touch the hoop. Jumping through the hoop is not allowed. Students may step through, or the group may "hand" team members through.

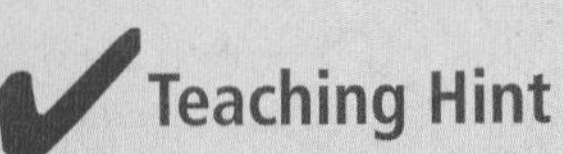

Teaching Hint

The height of the hoop determines the difficulty of the challenge. For an additional challenge, require all team members to hold hands throughout the activity.

Dot Bridge

FORMATION: Groups of 5 to 6 students

SUPPLIES: One poly spot per player plus one additional poly spot

The challenge is for students to get from one side of the "river" (teaching area) to the other, but they cannot touch the "water" (the floor). The only tools they have are their floating dots (the poly spots). If anyone touches the water, the entire team must start over.

VARIATIONS: To add difficulty and prevent teams from moving straight across, place hazards (hoops, cones, etc.) that the students must avoid throughout the river. Also, add the rule that if at any time a dot is not being touched, it sinks and can no longer be used.

ACTIVITIES WITH PARACHUTES

Parachute play can be enjoyed by children of all ages while learning a variety of skills, including cooperation skills. Unless all students work together, many of the tasks are difficult to accomplish. Activities must be selected carefully for younger children, since some of the skills required are difficult for them. One parachute about 24 to 32 feet in diameter is generally suitable for a class of 30 children. Each parachute has an opening near the top to allow trapped air to escape and to keep the parachute shaped properly. Most parachutes are constructed of nylon. A parachute should stretch tight and not sag in the middle when pulled on by children spaced around it. One that sags has limited usefulness.

VALUES OF PARACHUTE PLAY

For most adults and children, parachute activities rank high on the scale of all-time enjoyable physical education activities. Besides being enjoyable, parachute play holds many educational opportunities. Students learn movement concepts and practice fundamental motor skills. Teachers can incorporate and reinforce levels of movement, speed, weight transfer, force, direction, balancing, pulling, bending, twisting, and all locomotor movements.

Parachutes are also an interesting way to accomplish physical fitness goals: developing strength, agility, coordination, and endurance. Strength development is focused especially on the arms, hands, and shoulder girdle. At times, however, strength demands are made on the entire body. Parachute play offers various movement possibilities, some of them rhythmic. Teachers can use the tom-tom or appropriate music can guide students' locomotor movements. Lastly, parachute play is effective in teaching cooperation. The success and enjoyment gained from many parachute activities depend on group and individual cooperation. All students must work together to complete the tasks successfully; for example, if one child decides to not sit on his part of the chute to make the dome, the air escapes and the dome collapses.

GRIPS

Students can handle the parachute with grips similar to those used in hanging activities on an apparatus. Grips can be with one or two hands, overhand (palms facing away), underhand (palms facing toward), or mixed (one hand underhand and the other overhand). Design activities requiring students to use various grips.

INSTRUCTIONAL PROCEDURES

1. Carefully explain the terms relating to parachute activity. Define words such as *inflate, deflate, float, dome,* and *mushroom* the first time they are used.
2. For preliminary explanations, spread out the parachute on the ground in its circular pattern. Have the children sit around the parachute, just far enough away so that they cannot touch it. Allow students to hold the parachute during later explanations, but instruct them to hold it lightly, letting the center drop to the ground. Teach children to exercise control and not to manipulate the parachute while listening to explanations.
3. Explain the activity, demonstrating as needed. If there are no questions, start the activity with a command such as "Ready—begin!"
4. Teams can be used to form the parachute circle, with each team occupying a quarter of the chute's circumference. Teams are useful for competitive units in game activity.
5. Be sure to watch for fatigue, particularly with younger children.

This section presents activities by type, along with variations and tips for supplementary activities. Unless otherwise specified, activities begin and halt on signal. Children's suggestions can broaden the scope of activity.

EXERCISE ACTIVITIES

Exercises are done vigorously and with enough repetitions to challenge the children. Teachers also can adapt other exercises to parachute play.

Toe Toucher

Sit with feet extended under the parachute and hold the chute taut with a two-hand grip, drawing it up to the chin. Bend forward and touch the grip to the toes. Return parachute to stretched position.

Abdominal Curl-Up (Good Morning and Good Night)

Extend the body in supine position under the parachute in curl-up position, so that the chute comes up to the chin when held taut. Do Curl-Ups, returning each time to the stretched chute position. Students say, "Good morning!" when rising to the sitting position and "Good night!" when returning to the supine position.

Dorsal Lift

Lie prone, with head toward the parachute and feet pointed back, away from it. Grip the chute and slide it toward the feet until there is some tension on the chute. Raise the chute off the ground with a vigorous lift of the arms, until head and chest rise off the ground. Return.

V-Sit

Lie supine, with head toward the chute. Do V-Sits by raising the upper and lower parts of the body simultaneously into a V-shaped position. Keep the knees straight.

Backward Pull

Face the parachute and pull back, away from its center. Pulls can be made from a sitting, kneeling, or standing position.

Other Pulls

With arm flexed, do Side Pulls with either arm. Devise other variations of pulling.

Hip Walk and Scooter

Begin with the parachute taut. Move forward with the Scooter (page 488) or Hip Walk (page 488). Move back to place with the same movement until the chute is taut again.

Elevator

Begin with the chute taut and at ground level. On the command "Elevator up," lift the chute overhead while keeping it stretched tight. On the command "Elevator down," lower the chute to starting position. Lowering and raising are done quickly or in increments. Levels can also bring in body part identification; have children hold the chute even with their head, nose, chin, shoulders, chest, waist, thighs, knees, ankles, and toes.

Running in Place

Students run in place while holding the chute at different levels.

Isometrics

Hold the chute taut at shoulder level and try to stretch it for 10 seconds. Many other isometric exercises can be performed with the parachute to develop all body parts.

DOME ACTIVITIES

To make a dome, children begin with the parachute on the floor, holding with two hands and kneeling on one knee. To trap air under the chute, children stand up quickly, thrusting their arms overhead (Figure 21.8), and then return to starting position (Figure 21.9). Some or all of the children can move inside of the chute on the down movement. Try making domes while moving in a circle.

Students Under the Chute

Specify tasks to do under the chute, such as turning a certain number of turns with a jump rope, throwing and catching a beanbag, or bouncing a ball a number of times. Place the needed objects under the chute before making the dome.

Number Exchange

Children are numbered from 1 to 4. The teacher calls a number as the dome is made, and those whose number is called must get under the chute before it comes down. Locomotor movements can be varied.

Punching Bag

Children make a dome and stand on the edges. They then punch at the chute while slowly and gently walking the edges of the chute toward the center.

Tidal Wave or Bubble

Students create a dome and then stand on the edges. The teacher then pushes the chute to the left while still standing on the edges. The child to the teacher's left follows and pushes the parachute to the left. Each child then continues pushing the parachute in the same direction immediately after the child

FIGURE 21.8 Making a dome.

FIGURE 21.9 Holding the air inside a dome.

before them while keeping his feet on the edges. After a few rounds a bubble, or wave, of air will begin quickly circulating around the chute.

Blooming Flower

Children make a dome and kneel with both knees on the edge of the chute. Students hold hands around the chute and lean in and out to represent a blooming flower opening.

Lights Out

While making a dome, the children take two steps toward the center and sit inside the chute. The chute can be held with the hands at the side or by sitting on it.

Class Picture

After making a dome, students carefully move to their knees and then to their stomach. While lying on their stomach and with the parachute in their hands, students bring their hands to their shoulders. This leaves only their head inside the chute.

Mushroom Activities

To form a mushroom, students begin with the chute on the ground, kneeling on one knee and holding with two hands. They stand up quickly, thrusting the arms overhead. Keeping the arms overhead, each child walks forward three or four steps toward the center. Students hold their arms overhead until the chute deflates.

Mushroom Release

All children release the chute at the peak of inflation and either run out from under it or move to the center and sit down. The chute descends over them.

Mushroom Run

Children make a mushroom. Upon moving into the center, they release the chute and run once around the inside, counterclockwise, back to place.

FIGURE 21.10 Popping popcorn.

ACTIVITIES WITH EQUIPMENT

Ball Circle

Place a basketball or a cageball on the raised chute. Make the ball roll around the chute in a large circle, controlling it by raising or lowering the chute. Try the same with two balls. A beach ball is also excellent.

Popcorn

Place from 6 to 10 beanbags on the chute. Shake the chute to make the bags rise like corn popping (Figure 21.10).

Cageball Elevator

Place a 2-foot cageball on the chute. On signal, the class lifts the chute and makes a mushroom. Just before the chute with the ball on it reaches its apex, students snap the chute to the floor. If the "elevator" works correctly, the cageball rises up to the ceiling.

Team Ball

Divide the class in half, and have each team defend half of the chute. Put from 2 to 6 balls of any kind on the chute. Teams try to bounce the balls off their opponents' side and score 1 point for each ball.

Poison Snake

Divide into two teams. Place from 6 to 10 jump ropes on the chute. Shake the chute and try to make the ropes hit players on the other side. Each time a rope touches a team member, 1 point is scored against that team. The lowest-scoring team wins.

Circular Dribble

Each child has a ball suitable for dribbling. The object is to run around the chute counterclockwise, holding onto it with the left hand and dribbling with the right hand while retaining control of the ball. As an equalizer for left-handers, try the dribbling clockwise. Students start the dribble first and then, on signal, they start to run. Children who lose a ball must recover it and try to hook on at their original place.

Hole in One

Use four or more plastic whiffle balls the size of golf balls (half of the balls in one color, half in another color). Divide the class into two teams on opposite sides of the chute. Each team tries to shake the other team's balls into the hole in the center of the chute.

OTHER ACTIVITIES

Merry-Go-Round Movements

Merry-Go-Round movements, in which children rotate the chute while keeping the center hole over the same spot, offer many opportunities for locomotor movements, either free or to the beat of a tom-tom. European Rhythmic Running is particularly suitable. Also appropriate are fundamental movements, such as walking, running, hopping, skipping, galloping, sliding, draw steps, and grapevine steps. Have students hold the parachute at different levels, using one- or two-handed grips.

Shaking the Rug and Making Waves

Shaking the Rug involves rapid movements of the parachute, either light or heavy. Making Waves involves large movements to send billows of cloth up and down. Waves can be small, medium, or high. Children can make different types of waves by alternating their up-and-down motions, or by working in small groups around the chute. These small groups take turns showing what they can do. For a more demanding activity, children can perform locomotor movements while shaking the rug.

Chute Crawl

Half the class, either standing or kneeling, stretches the chute at waist level parallel to the ground. The other children crawl under the chute to the opposite side from their starting position.

Kite Run

The class holds the chute on one side with one hand. The leader points in the direction they are to run while holding the chute aloft like a kite.

Running Number Game

The children around the chute count off by fours; then they run lightly, holding the chute in one hand. The teacher calls out one of the numbers. Children with that number immediately release their grip on the chute and run forward to the next place vacated. They must use a burst of speed to move ahead.

FIGURE 21.11 Parachute Tug-of-War.

Routines to Music

Like other routines, parachute activities can be adapted to music. Base each sequence on 8 counts, and design the routine for an appropriate number of sequences.

Tug-of-War

For team tug-of-war, divide the class into halves. On signal, teams pull against each other and try to reach a line located behind them (Figure 21.11 on page 527). Primary-age children often enjoy pulling individually, in any direction they desire.

Action Songs and Dances

Children can perform many action songs, games, and dances while holding onto a parachute. Here are some suggestions: Carousel (page 418), Bingo (page 426), and Seven Jumps (page 414).

FOR MORE INFORMATION

REFERENCES AND SUGGESTED READINGS

Dyson, B., & Rubin, A. (2003). Implementing cooperative learning in elementary physical education. *JOPERD, 74*(1), 48–53.

Gabbei, R. (2004). Generating effective facilitation questions for team-building/personal-challenge activities. *JOPERD, 75*(9), 20–24, 49.

Hall, H. (2002). Team building made easy. *Strategies, 15*(6), 27–29.

Le Fevre, D. N. (2002). *Best new games.* Champaign, IL: Human Kinetics.

Midura, D. W., & Glover, D. R. (1999). *The competition-cooperation link—Games for developing respectful competitors.* Champaign, IL: Human Kinetics.

———. (2005). *Essentials of team building—Principles and practices.* Champaign, IL: Human Kinetics.

Orlick, T. (2006). *Cooperative games and sports—Joyful activities for everyone* (2nd ed.). Champaign, IL: Human Kinetics.

Rogers, K. (2004). Team building for young students. *Strategies, 17*(4), 17–19.

Rohnke, K., & Butler, S. (1995). *Quicksilver: Adventure games, initiative problems, trust activities and a guide to effective leadership.* Dubuque, IA: Kendall/Hunt.

WEBSITES

PE Central Cooperative Lessons
www.pecentral.org/lessonideas/searchresults.asp?subcategory=cooperative+learning

Project Adventure
www.pa.org

Team-Building Activities
www.corporategames.com
www.wilderdom.com/games/InitiativeGames.html
www.teachingideas.co.uk/pe/contents.htm

Game Skills

ESSENTIAL COMPONENTS OF QUALITY PROGRAMS

- I. Organized around content standards
- II. Student-centered and developmentally appropriate
- III. Physical activity and motor skill development form the core of the program
- IV. Teaches management skills and self-discipline
- V. Promotes inclusion of all students
- VI. Focuses on process over product
- VII. Promotes lifetime personal health and wellness
- VIII. Teaches cooperation and responsibility and promotes sensitivity to diversity

NATIONAL STANDARDS FOR PHYSICAL EDUCATION*

1. Demonstrates competency in motor skills and movement patterns needed to perform a variety of physical activities.
2. Demonstrates understanding of movement concepts, principles, and tactics as they apply to the learning and performance of physical activities.
3. Participates regularly in physical activity.
4. Achieves and maintains a health-enhancing level of physical fitness.
5. Exhibits responsible personal and social behavior that respects self and others in physical activity.
6. Values physical activity for health, enjoyment, challenge, self-expression, and/or social interaction.

*National Association for Sport and Physical Education (NASPE), 2004.

Games are excellent activities for developing social skills. Students can be taught to display interactive skills such as leading, following, and making decisions. To reach common goals, students need cooperative skills—following directions, accepting individual differences, and participating in a teamwork situation. Game situations offer many scenarios for teaching sportsmanship behavior. Teachers need to eliminate games that involve only a few children, allow some children to dominate, or offer little opportunity for skill development. Children must have the opportunity to create and modify games to meet their needs. Safety is a primary concern when selecting and presenting game activities.

Outcomes

- Explain various ways to create or modify games.
- Understand safety precautions associated with the teaching of games.
- Cite various ways to teach games effectively.
- Identify games that offer maximum participation and ample opportunity to develop skills.
- List games that can be explained and implemented quickly.
- Classify various games according to developmental levels.

GAMES make a valuable contribution to children's growth and development. Through games, children can experience success and accomplishment. They can develop interpersonal skills, understand rules and limitations, and learn how to behave in various competitive and cooperative situations. Games are a laboratory where children can apply physical skills in a gamelike setting. Many games help develop large-muscle groups and enhance the child's ability to run, dodge, start, and stop under control while sharing space with others. By applying strategy in games, children learn the importance of alertness and the mental aspect of participation.

As an important part of the physical education program, games must be scrutinized and evaluated based on what they offer children. Many traditional games can be modified to make a meaningful contribution to the program. Offering students a chance to create and modify games helps them understand that they can change game components to improve the play experience for all.

EVALUATING GAMES

Factors affecting the worth of games include the physical skills required, number of participants, complexity of rules, and amount of strategy involved. Successful participation demands that students have learned required skills in a practice setting. But unless they learn the skills, players cannot apply them in a game setting. Children may be able to throw with proper form, but throwing accurately in a game setting is different. They may be able to hit a stationary object but not a moving target.

Students also have to learn how to cooperate with teammates and compete against peers. The greater the number of teammates and competitors, the more difficult the game becomes. Cooperating with teammates is just as difficult as competing in a meaningful way. Moving from partners to a small group to team games is a natural progression and a formula for success. Many games are more effective when played in small groups because the players handle objects more often and get more chances to actively contribute.

The rules and strategies for a game increase its difficulty. Developmental Level I children find it difficult (and uninteresting) to play a game that has many rules. If cognitive strategy is required, these students must learn (overlearn) the required physical skills previously so they can concentrate on the mental aspects of the game rather than the skills. Most elementary school children cannot concentrate on skill performance and strategy simultaneously. Complex games require team members to play specific roles, some of which (i.e., goalkeeper or line positions) may not appeal to many children. In contrast, many of the more popular games are spontaneous and demand little concentration on strategy.

Be sure that children receive positive feedback from game experiences. The younger children are, the less willing they are to wait for the outcome; feedback must be immediate. Children become bored and tire of playing long games. Fatigue is also a factor in children's interest level; watch carefully for such signs.

Games require a combination of skills. Games that call for children to sequence many skills may result in failure or frustration for many. Lead-up games are developed expressly to limit the number of skills needed to participate successfully. Evaluate the skills required, and build a progression of games that gradually increases the use of skill combinations.

CREATING OR MODIFYING GAMES

Students, working with your help or individually, can modify games and create new variations. For example, after noticing that a specific game is not meeting the desired objectives, you may decide to modify or change it to facilitate skill development. Stop the class and ask them to think of a way to make the game better. Students can suggest alternatives and then test the newly created activity to see if it is more effective. With Developmental Level II and III students, you can offer some parameters for developing a game and then give the class time to create and test the activity. Establish ground rules that facilitate group dynamics. For example, suggest voting on a rule change or specify a maximum number of changes allowed per period.

To make meaningful modifications, you and your students must understand how to analyze a game. The most recognized elements of game structure are desired outcomes, skills, equipment, rules or restrictions, number of players, and scheme of organization. Morris and Stiehl's (1999) approach to game analysis may be helpful if you are interested in modifying games. Students need to learn how and what to modify, and they need to practice the process. Here are some suggestions to start children thinking:

1. Change the distance to be run by decreasing or increasing it. For example, in Star Wars, go around once instead of twice.
2. Change the means of locomotion. Use hopping, walking, skipping, or galloping instead of running.
3. Play the game with one or more partners. The partners can move and act as if they were a single person.
4. Change the method of tagging in simple tag games. Call out "Reverse" to signal that the chaser is to become the tagger, and vice versa.
5. Make goals or restricted areas larger or smaller. In Over the Wall, modify the restraining area size, or change its shape.
6. Vary the boundaries of the game by making them larger or smaller, as dictated by the number of players.
7. Change the formation in which the game is played. For example, play Circle Kickball in a square or triangular shape.
8. Change the requirements necessary for scoring. In Hand Hockey, require players to make four passes before taking a shot.
9. Increase the number of players, taggers, or runners. Also try increasing the amount of equipment. For example, in Nine Lives, the more fleece balls used, the more practice students get in throwing at a moving target.
10. Change the rules or penalties of the game. For example, set a maximum of three dribbles, or allow players to hold the ball for no more than 3 seconds.

COOPERATION AND COMPETITION

Without cooperation, there would be no game activities. If participants chose not to follow the rules and play with teammates, it would be impossible to structure games. Clearly, games require cooperation before competition can be an outgrowth of an activity. *Cooperation* involves two or more children working together to achieve a common goal. *Competition* is characterized by opponents working against each other as each person tries to reach a goal or reward. Since cooperation precedes competition and is more difficult for students to learn, focus on this phase of game activity. Through games, players can develop a spirit of working together, a concern for teammates, and an appreciation for the collective skills of the group.

Safety Tip

Many games involve fast movements. Teach students that their safety and the safety of their classmates are much more important than winning a game.

Achieving a balance between offense and defense helps participants understand that both phases are important. In tag and capture games, offer opportunities to remain safe as well as a challenge to be at risk and elude capture. Evaluate game components continually, and modify them to ensure an enjoyable experience. Because children's motivation fades when they have no chance to succeed, teachers must ensure that teams are somewhat equal. Rotate students regularly so they have a chance to play with different classmates and be on a winning team. Emphasizing cooperation reinforces the need to play with all classmates regardless of ability level. Include children with disabilities in all rotation plans.

SAFETY

Safety is a primary consideration in game situations. Check the play area for dangerous objects and hazards. Tables, chairs, equipment, and apparatus can become dangerous during a high-speed game. Teach children to move in a controlled way, using the entire playing area to avoid collisions. Learning to stop play immediately when a signal is given prepares students for games with referees and assures safety. This is an important prerequisite for later sports experiences.

TEACHING GAMES EFFECTIVELY

1. *Put students in the formation they are going to use before presenting a new game to a class.* If students can sit in game formation, they will more easily understand instructions. Make directions as brief as possible, and

begin the game quickly. Give minimal instruction and gradually add more subtle rules. Try the game first before answering any questions students may have. This gives them some idea of how the game is played and answers many questions without taking more time and boring students who already understand.

2. *Use a trial period (no scoring) when students are first learning a game.* This prevents children from feeling resentful about losing a point or being caught off guard because they did not understand the activity.

3. *Do not use games that isolate one child.* Games like these may create a negative experience for students who have low self-esteem. The common sport lead-up game called Birdies in the Cage traditionally puts one child in the center of the circle and requires him to intercept or touch passes made by circle players. A child who reacts slowly or is overweight may never succeed, and this game makes his failure especially public. Placing several students in the center makes it a team game and spreads the responsibility among more players.

4. *Develop a rotation plan to give all children equal time to play.* Avoid letting winners stay on the court while the losers sit out, receiving much less practice than better players get. Likewise, do not play elimination games until only one or two children remain. The least skilled students are eliminated early and have to sit the longest. Remember that games are played to keep students involved in physical activity. Sitting out does not contribute to physical education goals.

5. *Give all children an equal chance to participate in games that require taking turns.* For games where numbers are called, write the numbers on a card so no one is left out. If a game eliminates children from play, have them sit out for only one or two turns so they can get back in the game quickly.

6. *Plan carefully before teaching a new game.* Identify safety hazards, anticipate difficult concepts, and adapt the game to the class and the situation. Make physical preparations before teaching. Mark boundaries, and have equipment ready for distribution. The children's skill and age usually dictate the size of the playing area. If you plan to do some instruction during a game, make the playing area smaller so students are closer to you.

7. *When playing low-organized and sport lead-up games, avoid using the out-of-bounds rule.* Instead, make a rule that whoever gets to the ball first gains possession. This speeds up the game and offers a strong incentive for quickly getting the ball back into play. If the game involves a goal line or running to a line, establish a safety zone. Instead of using the wall or a line near the wall as the goal, draw safety lines 10 feet from the wall to allow for deceleration. Mark the deceleration zone with cones or spots. Try to play as many games as possible.

8. *Change the makeup of the teams often, and play relatively short games.* Nobody likes to lose all the time. Playing short games means more games can be played, so more children can be winners. If a team wins twice in a row, that is usually a signal to form new teams. This gives everybody a fresh start and keeps more students motivated.

9. *To identify teams, use pinnies, crepe paper armbands, colored shoulder loops, or team belts worn around the waist.* Have a standing rule that the team that puts on the pinnies gets the ball first. Students usually dislike wearing pinnies, and this gives them some incentive.

10. *Games are an excellent vehicle for learning social skills.* Encourage children to call infractions or penalties on each other and on themselves. Teach them to accept calls made by officials as an integral part of any game situation. When disagreements occur, adopt the role of arbitrator, rather than taking one side or the other. Encourage players to learn negotiation skills and resolve differences rather than having a teacher decide each issue.

11. *Help students understand that learning to perform skills correctly is more important than winning the game.* Continue instruction throughout the early phases of a game. Look for opportunities to stop the game briefly and offer instruction or correction. Give coaching hints to improve skill techniques.

12. *Use the "rule of three" as a way of simplifying rules.* Apply the "rule of three" to mean students can only hold the ball for 3 seconds, or take three steps, or miss three catches, and so on. This reduces the number of rules students have to remember and makes games easier to play. It also seems to diminish the disagreements children have about rules.

SELECTION OF GAMES

The games selected for this chapter require minimal skill and offer activity for all children. Analyze the skills children must practice before playing. Drills and skill practice become more meaningful when children know they will use the skill in a game situation. Games are sorted by difficulty and placed into three developmental levels. Table 22.1 (pages 533–536) lists each of the games alphabetically by developmental level and gives its page number in text. The table also describes the skills required for successful play. Games in Developmental Level I do not require competency in sport

TABLE 22.1 Alphabetical listing of games by Developmental Level

Games	Skills	Page
	Developmental Level I Games	
Animal Tag	Imagery, running, dodging	536
Aviator	Running, locomotor movements, stopping	538
Ball Passing	Object handling	538
Blindfolded Duck	Fundamental locomotor movements	539
Bottle Bat Ball	Batting, retrieving balls	539
Bottle Kick Ball	Kicking, trapping	539
Cat and Mice	Running, dodging	539
Change Sides	Body management	540
Charlie over the Water	Skipping, running, stopping, bowling (rolling)	540
Circle Stoop	Moving to rhythm	540
Circle Straddle Ball	Ball rolling, catching	541
Colors	Color or other perceptual concepts, running	541
Corner Spry	Light, silent walking	541
Firefighter	Running	542
Flowers and Wind	Running	542
Forest Ranger	Running	542
Freeze	Locomotor movements to rhythm	543
Hill Dill	Running, dodging	543
Hot Potatoes	Object handling	543
Jack Frost and Jane Thaw	Running, dodging, holding position	543
Leap the Brook	Leaping, jumping, hopping, turning	543
Marching Ponies	Marching, running	544
May I Chase You?	Running, dodging	544
Midnight	Running, dodging	544
Mix and Match	Fundamental locomotor movements	545
Mousetrap	Skipping, running, dodging	545
Musical Ball Pass	Passing and handling	545
One, Two, Button My Shoe	Running	546
Popcorn	Curling, stretching, jumping	546
Red Light	Fundamental locomotor movements, stopping	546
Right Angle	Rhythmic movement, body management	547
Rollee Pollee	Ball rolling, dodging	547
The Scarecrow and the Crows	Dodging, running	547
Sneak Attack	Marching, running	548
Soap Bubbles	Body management	548
Squirrel in the Trees	Fundamental locomotor movements	548
Statues	Body management, applying force, balance	549
Stop Ball	Tossing, catching	549

(continued)

TABLE 22.1 Alphabetical listing of games by Developmental Level (Continued)

Games	Skills	Page
	Developmental Level I Games (Continued)	
Tag Games (Simple)	Fundamental locomotor movements, dodging	549
Back-to-Back		549
Bowing		549
Frozen		549
Locomotor		549
Nose-and-Toe		549
Skunk		549
Stoop		549
Stork		549
Turtle		549
Teacher Ball (Leader Ball)	Throwing, catching	550
Toe-to-Toe	Fundamental locomotor movements	550
Tommy Tucker's Land	Dodging, running	550
Twins (Triplets)	Body management	550
Up Periscope	Fundamental locomotor movements	551
Where's My Partner?	Fundamental locomotor movements	551
	Developmental Level II Games	
Addition Tag	Running, dodging	551
Alaska Baseball	Kicking, batting, running, ball handling	552
Arches	Moving rhythmically	552
Bat Ball	Batting, running, catching, throwing	552
Beach Ball Bat Ball	Batting, tactile handling	553
Bird Catcher	Chasing, fleeing, dodging	553
Bounce Ball	Throwing, ball rolling	553
Box Ball	Running, ball handling	554
Busy Bee	Fundamental locomotor movements	554
Cageball Kick-Over	Kicking	554
Club Guard	Throwing	555
Competitive Circle Contests	Throwing, catching	555
Circle Club Guard		555
Touch Ball		555
Couple Tag	Running, dodging	555
Crows and Cranes	Running, dodging	556
Fly Trap	Fundamental locomotor movements	556
Follow Me	All locomotor movements, stopping	557
Fox Hunt	Running, dodging	557
Galloping Lizzie	Throwing, dodging, running	557
Hand Hockey	Striking, volleying	557
Home Base	Reaction time, locomotor movements, body management	558

TABLE 22.1 (Continued)

Games	Skills	Page
	Developmental Level II Games (Continued)	
Indianapolis 500	Running, tagging	558
Jump the Shot	Rope jumping	558
Keep 'em Movin'	Body management, cooperation	559
Loose Caboose	Running, dodging	559
Nine Lives	Throwing, dodging	559
Nonda's Car Lot	Running, dodging	560
One Behind	All locomotor and nonlocomotor movements	560
One Step	Throwing, catching	560
Partner Stoop	Marching rhythmically	561
Ricochet	Rolling	561
Squad Tag	Running, dodging	561
Steal the Treasure	Dodging	562
Trades	Imagery, running, dodging	562
Trees	Running, dodging	562
Whistle March	Moving rhythmically	563
Whistle Mixer	All basic locomotor movements	563
Wolfe's Beanbag Exchange	Running, dodging, tossing, catching	563
	Developmental Level III Games	
Air Raid	Throwing	563
Barker's Hoopla	Running	564
Cageball Target Throw	Throwing	564
Chain Tag	Running, dodging	564
Circle Touch	Dodging, body management	565
Clean-Up	Throwing	565
Fast Pass	Passing, catching, moving to an open area	565
Flag Chase	Running, dodging	565
Four Square	Batting a ball	572
Galactic Empire and Rebels	Chasing, fleeing, dodging	565
Guess the Leader	Body management	566
Jolly Ball	Kicking	566
Jump-the-Shot Variations	Rope jumping	567
Mushrooms	Rolling, throwing	567
Octopus	Maneuvering, problem solving	567
One-Base Tagball	Running, dodging, throwing	567
Over the Wall	Running, dodging	568
Pacman	Fleeing, reaction time	568
Partner Dog and Cat	Chasing, fleeing, dodging	568

(continued)

TABLE 22.1 Alphabetical listing of games by Developmental Level (Continued)

Games	Skills	Page
	Developmental Level III Games (Continued)	
Pin Knockout	Rolling, dodging	569
Right Face, Left Face (Streets and Alleys)	Running, dodging	569
Scooter Kickball	Striking with various body parts	569
Star Wars	Running	570
Strike the Pins	Throwing	570
Sunday	Running, dodging	571
Team Handball	Running, dribbling, passing, throwing, catching	573
Tetherball	Batting a ball	574
Touchdown	Running, dodging	571
Triplet Stoop	Moving rhythmically	571
Two Square	Batting a ball	574
Volley Tennis	Most volleyball skills	574
Whistle Ball	Passing, catching	572

skills. Most use basic locomotor skills and offer children opportunities to practice and participate successfully. You can easily modify these games so all children will enjoy them.

Many of the games in Developmental Levels II and III require specialized sport skills. Ball-handling and movement skills, emphasizing agility, are important for success in many of these games. Give children opportunities to practice required game skills before they start to compete.

SPORT LEAD-UP GAMES

Games in Developmental Levels II and III are separated into two categories: sport lead-up games and low-organization games. This chapter includes low-organization games only; however, sport lead-up games can also be integrated into the games program. Sport lead-up games limit the number of skills required for successful participation, thus helping children experience success in a sport setting. For example, Five Passes is a game designed to develop passing skills. Children do not have to perform other skills (such as dribbling or shooting) required by the regulation sport to achieve success. Table 22.2 (pages 537–538) lists all sport-related lead-up games presented in Chapters 24 to 30. If you are teaching soccer skills and want to finish the lesson with a lead-up game, consult this table to find an appropriate activity. Many of the lead-up games are excellent choices for skill development, particularly with Developmental Level III students.

DEVELOPMENTAL LEVEL I

Games in the early part of Developmental Level I feature individual games and creative play. Few of these games emphasize team play or have scoring systems. The games are simple, easily taught, and not demanding of skills. Many games feature dramatic elements, and others help establish number concepts and symbol recognition. As children mature, they enjoy running, tag, and ball games. Ball games at this level require the skills of throwing and catching.

Animal Tag

SUPPLIES: None

SKILLS: Imagery, running, dodging

FORMATION:

```
X |            | O
X |            | O
X |            | O
X |            | O
X |            | O
X |            | O
X |            | O
X |            | O
X |            | O
X |            | O
X |            | O
```

TABLE 22.2 Lead-up games from sport Chapters 24 to 30*

Basketball (Chapter 24)	
Developmental Level II	**Page**
Circle Guard and Pass	616
Basketball Tag	616
Dribblerama	617
Birdies in the Cage	617
Captain Ball	617
Around the Key	618
Five Passes	619
Captain Basketball	619
Developmental Level III	**Page**
Quadrant Basketball	619
Sideline Basketball	620
Twenty-One	620
Lane Basketball	620
Freeze Out	621
Flag Dribble	621
Through the Maze	622
One-Goal Basketball	622
Basketball Snatch Ball	622
Three-on-Three	622
Basketrama	622
Paper Clip Basketball	623
Football (Chapter 25)	
Developmental Level II	**Page**
Football End Ball	632
Five Passes	633
Speed Football	634
Developmental Level III	**Page**
Kick-Over	634
Fourth Down	634
Football Box Ball	635
Flag Football	635
Pass Ball	637
Hockey (Chapter 26)	
Developmental Level II	**Page**
Stick-Handling Competition	647
Circle Keep-Away	647
Five Passes	648
Star Wars Hockey	648
Lane Hockey	648
Modified Hockey	649
Developmental Level III	**Page**
Goalkeeper Hockey	649
Sideline Hockey	649
Regulation Elementary Hockey	650

Soccer (Chapter 27)	
Developmental Level II	**Page**
Circle Kickball	664
Soccer Touch Ball	664
Diagonal Soccer	665
Dribblerama	665
Bull's-Eye	665
Pin Kickball	666
Sideline Soccer	666
Kick Bowling	667
Soccer Golf	667
Developmental Level III	**Page**
Manyball Soccer	667
Addition Soccer	667
Over the Top	667
Lane Soccer	668
Line Soccer	668
Mini-Soccer	669
Six-Spot Keep-Away	669
Regulation Soccer	670
Softball (Chapter 28)	
Developmental Level II	**Page**
Throw-It-and-Run Softball	683
Two-Pitch Softball	683
Hit and Run	684
Kick Softball	684
In a Pickle	685
Beat Ball	685
Steal a Base	685
Developmental Level III	**Page**
Five Hundred	685
Batter Ball	686
Home Run	687
Tee Ball	687
Scrub (Work-Up)	688
Slow-Pitch Softball	688
Babe Ruth Ball	689
Hurry Baseball (One Pitch)	689
Three-Team Softball	690
Volleyball (Chapter 30)	
Developmental Level II	**Page**
Beach Ball Volleyball	710
Informal Volleyball	710
Shower Service Ball	710

(continued)

TABLE 22.2 Lead-up games from sport Chapters 24 to 30* (Continued)

Volleyball (Chapter 30)			
Developmental Level III	**Page**	**Developmental Level III (Continued)**	**Page**
Pass and Dig	711	Three-and-Over Volleyball	713
Mini-Volleyball	711	Rotation Volleyball	713
Rotation Mini-Volleyball	712	Four-Square Volleyball	713
Regulation Volleyball	712	Wheelchair Volleyball	713

*Many of these games are used as culminating activities with sport lesson plans.

Mark off two parallel lines about 40 feet apart. Divide children into two groups, each standing along one of the lines. Children in one team get together with their leader and decide what animal they wish to imitate. After choosing the animal, they move over to within 5 feet or so of the other team's line. There they imitate the animal, and team 2 tries to identify the animal correctly. Upon doing so, team 2 chases team 1 back to its line, trying to tag as many opponents as possible. Those caught must go over to the other team. Team 2 then selects an animal, and the roles are reversed. If the guessing team cannot guess the animal, however, the performing team gets another try. To avoid confusion, children must raise their hands to take turns at naming the animal. Otherwise, many false chases will occur. If children have trouble guessing, the leader of the performing team can give the initial of the animal.

Aviator

SUPPLIES: None

SKILLS: Running, locomotor movements, stopping

FORMATION:

ATC

Players are parked (in push-up position) at one end of the playing area. The air traffic controller (ATC) is in front of the players and calls out, "Aviators aviators, take off!" Students take off and move like airplanes to the opposite side of the area. The first person to move to the other side and land the plane (get into push-up position facing the ATC) becomes the new ATC.

If the ATC yells out some type of stormy weather, all planes must return to the starting line and resume the parked position. Examples of stormy weather commands are lightning, thunder, hurricane, and tornado. Each ATC is allowed to give stormy weather warnings once.

Ball Passing

SUPPLIES: Five or six different kinds of balls for each circle, a whistle

SKILL: Object handling

FORMATION: Circles with 15 or fewer in each circle

Divide the class into two or more circles, with no more than 15 children in any one circle. Each circle consists of two or more teams, but team members need not stand together.

The teacher starts a ball around the circle; it passes from player to player in the same direction. The teacher introduces more balls until five or six are moving around the circle at the same time and in the same direction. If a child drops a ball, he must retrieve it, and a point is scored against his squad. After a specific time, a whistle is blown, and the points against each team are totaled. The team with the lowest score wins. Beanbags, large blocks, or softballs can be substituted for balls.

Blindfolded Duck

SUPPLIES: A wand, broomstick, cane, or yardstick

SKILLS: Fundamental locomotor movements

FORMATION:

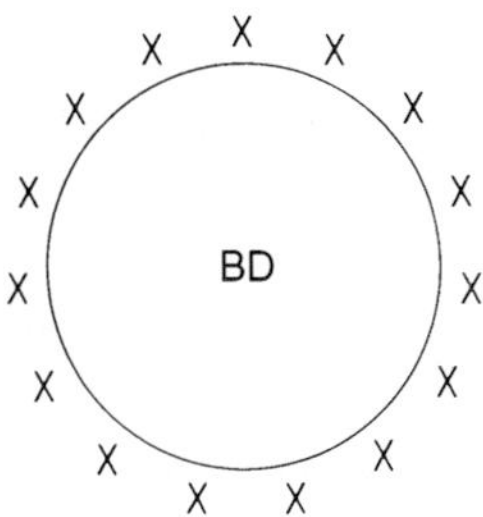

One child, designated the duck (Daisy if a girl, Donald if a boy), stands blindfolded in the center of a circle and holds a wand or similar article. She taps on the floor and tells children to hop (or do some other locomotor movement). Children in the circle act accordingly, all moving in the same direction. Daisy then taps the wand twice on the floor to signal all children to stop. She moves forward with her wand, still blindfolded, to find a child in the circle. She asks, "Who are you?" The child responds, "Quack, quack." Daisy tries to identify this student. If she is correct, that child becomes the new duck. If she is wrong, Daisy must take another turn. After two unsuccessful turns, choose another child to be the duck.

Bottle Bat Ball

SUPPLIES: A plastic bottle bat, whiffle ball, batting tee (optional), home plate, base marker

SKILLS: Batting, retrieving balls

FORMATION: Scattered

Batters get three pitches (or swings if a batting tee is used) to hit a fair ball, or they are out. The pitches are easy (as in slow-pitch softball), so the batter has a chance to hit the ball. The batter hits the ball and runs around the base marker and back to home. If the ball is returned to the designated pitcher's mound before the batter reaches home, the batter is out. Otherwise, the batter has a home run and bats again. One fielder other than the pitcher is needed, but another can be used. The running distance to first base is critical. It can either remain fixed or be made progressively (one step) longer, until it grows so long that the fielders are heavily favored.

Teaching Hint

Use a plastic bottle bat and whiffle ball. Establish a rotation system for players after an out is made. Limit the number of home runs per at bat to three.

Bottle Kick Ball

SUPPLIES: Plastic gallon jugs (bleach or milk containers), 8-inch foam balls

SKILLS: Kicking, trapping

FORMATION:

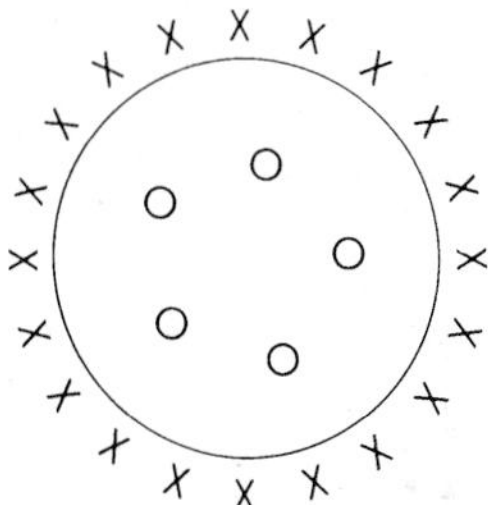

Players form a large circle around 10 to 12 plastic gallon jugs (bowling pins) standing in the middle of the circle. Students kick the balls and try to knock over the bottles. Use as many foam balls as necessary to keep all children active. If the group is large, make more than one circle of players.

Cat and Mice

SUPPLIES: None

SKILLS: Running, dodging

FORMATION:

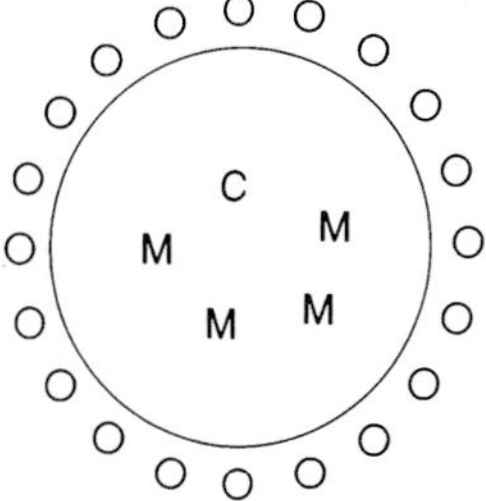

Form a large circle. Two or three children are the cats, and four others are the mice. The cats and mice cannot leave the circle. On signal, the cats chase the mice inside the circle. As they are caught, the mice join the circle. The last three mice caught become the cats for the next round. Start at one point in the circle and go around the circle selecting mice, so each child gets a chance to be in the center. Sometimes, children have difficulty catching the last mouse or any of the mice. If this happens, children forming the circle can take a step toward the center, thus constricting the running area. Regardless, cut off any prolonged chase sequence.

Change Sides

SUPPLIES: None

SKILL: Body management

FORMATION:

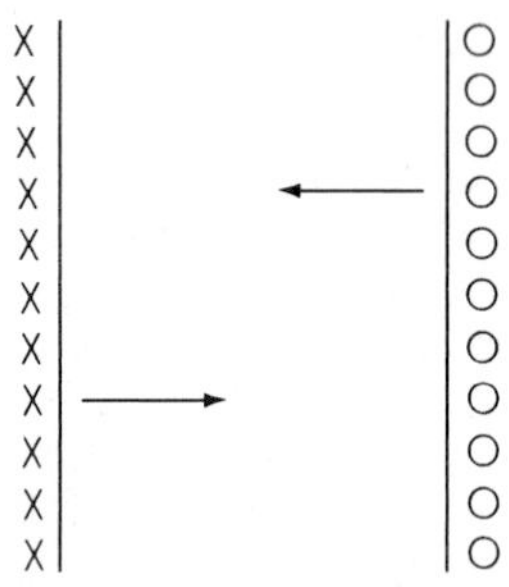

Establish two parallel lines 30 feet apart. Half of the class stands on each line. On signal, all players cross through to the other line, face the center, and stand at attention. The first group to do all three things correctly wins a point. Caution children to use care when passing through the opposite group. They should be spaced well along each line, allowing room to move through each group. Vary the locomotor movements used by specifying skipping, hopping, long steps, sliding, and other movements. The final position also can be varied.

Charlie over the Water

SUPPLIES: Volleyballs or playground balls

SKILLS: Skipping, running, stopping, bowling (rolling)

FORMATION: Single large circle

Place two or more children in the center of the circle, each holding a ball. Introduce one of the center players as Charlie (or Sally). The class skips around the circle, reciting this chant:

Charlie over the water,

Charlie over the sea,

Charlie caught a bluebird,

But can't catch me!

On the word *me*, the center players toss their balls in the air while the rest of the class runs and scatters throughout the area. When Charlie catches his ball, he shouts, "Stop!" All of the children stop immediately and must not move their feet. Each center player rolls their ball and tries to hit one of their scattered classmates. When a ball is rolled into a scattered player, he becomes a new Charlie. If center players miss, they remain in the center, and the game is repeated. If a center player misses twice, however, he or she joins the circle and picks another child as a replacement.

Circle Stoop

SUPPLIES: Music or tom-tom

SKILLS: Moving to rhythm

FORMATION:

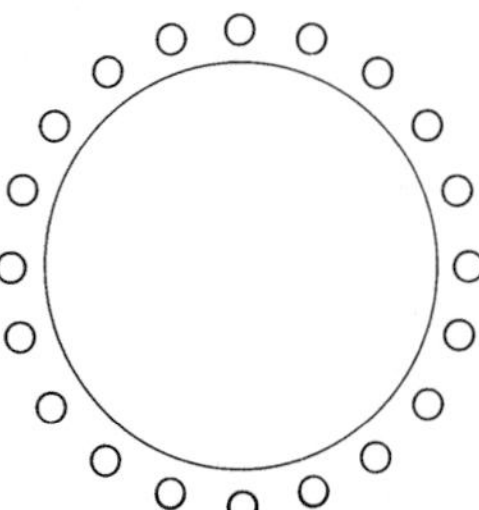

Children are in a single circle, facing counterclockwise. Use a march or similar music, or a tom-tom beat, to signal movement. The class marches until the music stops and then they stoop and touch both hands to the ground without losing balance. The last child to touch both hands to the ground, and the children who lost balance, pay a penalty by going into the mush pot (the center of the circle) for one turn. Vary the length of the music so children cannot anticipate the signal.

VARIATIONS:

1. Using suitable music, have children try different locomotor movements, such as skipping, hopping, or galloping.

2. Vary the stopping position. Instead of stooping, use positions such as the push-up, Crab, Lame Dog, balancing on one foot, or touching with one hand and one foot.

Circle Straddle Ball

SUPPLIES: Two or more 8-inch foam balls

SKILLS: Ball rolling, catching

FORMATION: Circles of 10–15 students, facing in

Each player stands in a wide straddle with the side of each foot against their neighbors'. Their hands are on the knees. The object of the game is to roll a ball between another player's legs before that player can get hands down to stop the ball. Keep the circles small to give students more ball-handling opportunities. Players must catch and roll the ball, rather than batting it. They must keep their hands on their knees until a ball is rolled at them. After some practice, try the following variation.

VARIATION: Two or more children are in the center, each with a ball. The other children are in the same formation as before. The center players try to roll the ball through any child's legs, masking intent by using feints and changes of direction. Any child allowing the ball to go through becomes it.

Colors

SUPPLIES: Colored paper (construction paper) cut in circles, squares, or triangles for markers

SKILLS: Color or other perceptual concepts, running

FORMATION:

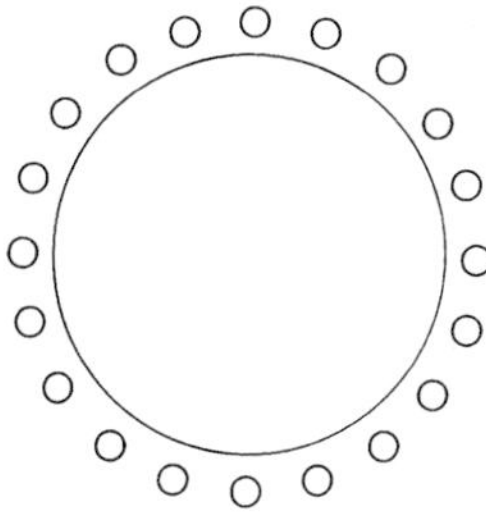

Use 5 or 6 different-colored markers, so several children have the same color. Children stand or sit in a circle, each with a marker in front of them. The teacher (or another player) calls out a color. Everyone having that color runs counterclockwise around the circle and back to place. The first player seated upright and motionless is declared the winner. Specify different kinds of locomotor movement, such as skipping, galloping, walking, and so on. After playing for awhile, the children leave the markers on the floor and move one place to the left.

VARIATION: Use shapes (circles, triangles, squares, rectangles, stars, and diamonds) instead of colors, or try numbers and other articles or categories, such as animals, birds, or fish.

Corner Spry

SUPPLIES: Blindfold

SKILLS: Light, silent walking

FORMATION:

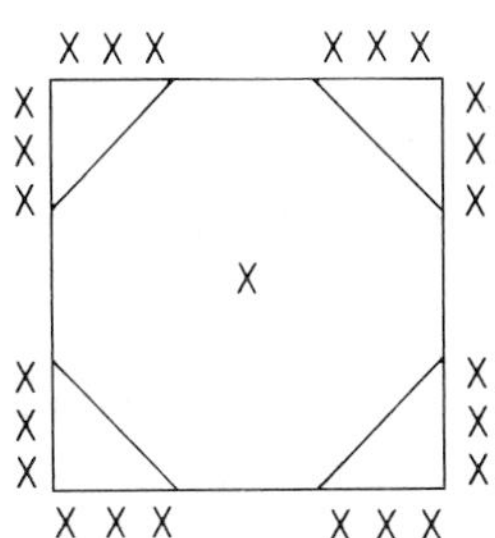

One person is blindfolded and stands in the center of the square. The other players are scattered in the corner areas. On signal, they travel as quietly as possible from corner area to corner area. The blindfolded person, when ready (less than 20 seconds), calls out "Corner Spry!" All players finish their trips to the corner nearest them. The blindfolded person then picks (by pointing) a corner, trying to select the one with the most players. A new player is then selected to be blindfolded.

VARIATION: Number the corners 1, 2, 3, and 4, and have the blindfolded person call out the corner number. The blindfolded child can also start class movement by naming the locomotor movement to be used.

Mark off a brook across the floor as shown in the diagram. Children line up on one side of the area. On the signal, "Cross the Brook!" players pick a challenge and try to jump across the brook. The wider the brook, the greater the challenge. Use different styles of locomotor movements such as hopping, jumping, and leaping over the brook. The distances are arbitrary and can be changed if unsuitable for your group of children.

VARIATION: Use different types of turns while jumping the brook, such as right or left; quarter, half, three-quarter, or full. Use different body shapes, different arm positions, and so on.

Marching Ponies

SUPPLIES: None

SKILLS: Marching, running

FORMATION:

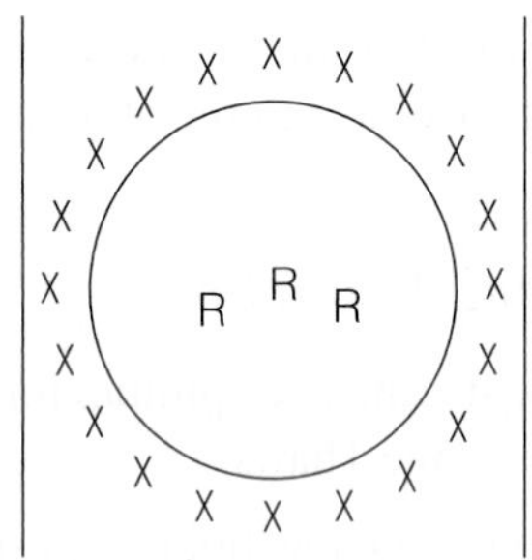

Two or three children are ringmasters who crouch in the center of a circle of ponies formed by the rest of the class. Two goal lines on opposite sides of the circle are established as safe areas. The ponies march around the circle in step, counting as they do so. At a predetermined number (the teacher whispers it to the ringmasters), the ringmasters jump up and try to tag the others before they can reach the safety lines. Anyone tagged joins the ringmasters in the center and helps catch others. Reorganize the game after 6 to 8 children have been caught. Try other characterizations, such as lumbering elephants, jumping kangaroos, and the like.

May I Chase You?

SUPPLIES: None

SKILLS: Running, dodging

FORMATION:

The class stands behind a line long enough to accommodate all. Two or three runners stand about 5 feet in front of the line. The class asks, "May I chase you?" One of the runners (designated by teacher) replies, "Yes, if you are wearing . . . " and names a color, an article of clothing, or a combination of the two. All who qualify immediately chase the runners until one is tagged. New runners are chosen and the game is repeated. Encourage players to think of other ways to identify those who run.

Midnight

SUPPLIES: None

SKILLS: Running, dodging

FORMATION:

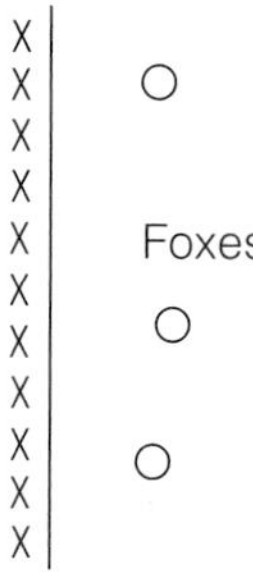

Mark off a safety line about 40 feet from a den in which two or three players, the foxes, are standing. The others stand behind the safety line and ask, "What time is it, Mr. Fox?" Chose one of the foxes to answer in various ways, such as "1 o'clock," "4 o'clock," and so on. When the fox says a certain time, the class walks forward that number of steps. For example, if the fox says, "6 o'clock," the class has to move forward six steps. The fox continues to draw the players toward him. Eventually, the fox answers the question by saying, "Midnight," and chases the others back to the safety line. Any player who is caught becomes a fox in the den and helps to catch others.

> *VARIATION:* **Lame Wolf.** The wolf is lame and advances in a series of three running steps and a hop. Other children taunt, "Lame Wolf, can't catch me!" or "Lame Wolf, tame wolf, can't catch me!" The wolf may give chase at any time. Children who are caught join the wolf and must also move as if lame.

Mix and Match

SUPPLIES: None

SKILLS: Fundamental locomotor movements

FORMATION:

Mark off a line through the middle of the area. Half of the children stand on each side. Two or three extra children stand on one side of the line. The teacher signals children to move as directed on their side of the line. Instruct them to run, hop, skip, or make some other movement. On signal, players run to the dividing line and reach across to join hands with a player on the opposite side. The goal is to find a partner and not be left out. Children may reach over but cannot cross the line. The players left out move to the opposite side, so that players left out come from alternating sides of the area. To speed up the process, encourage students to raise their hands if they need a partner.

> *VARIATION:* Try playing the game to music or a drumbeat. Players rush to the centerline to find partners when the rhythm stops.

Mousetrap

SUPPLIES: None

SKILLS: Skipping, running, dodging

FORMATION:

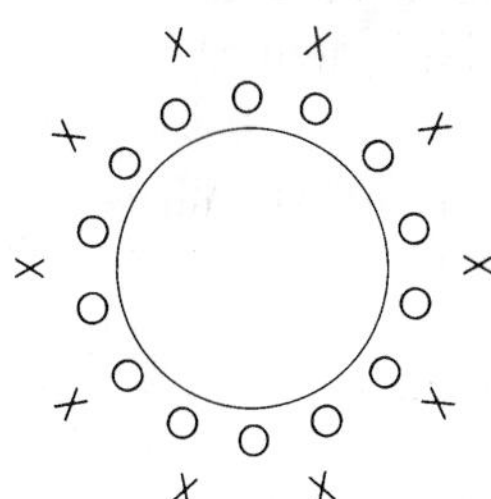

Half of the class forms a circle, joining hands and facing the center. This is the trap. The other children, the mice, are on the outside of the circle. The game involves three signals (word cues or other signals). On the first signal, the mice skip around, outside the circle, playing happily. On the second signal, the trap opens (players in the circle raise their joined hands to form arches). The mice run in and out of the trap. On the third signal, the trap snaps shut (the arms come down). All mice caught inside join the circle. The game is repeated until most of the mice are caught. The players then exchange places, and the game begins anew.

Musical Ball Pass

SUPPLIES: One or two playground balls per group, music

SKILLS: Passing, handling

FORMATION:

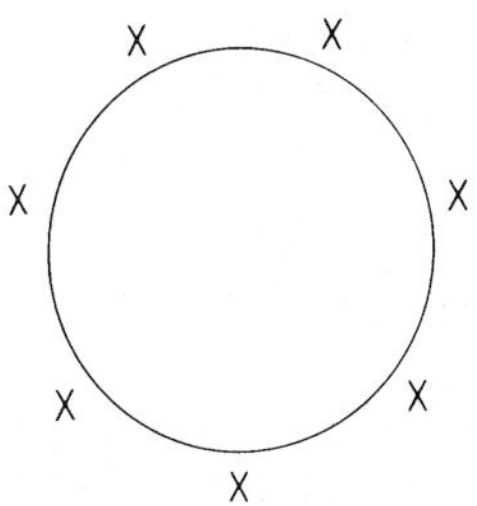

Break the class into small groups (6 to 7 players) in circle formation facing the center. Each team receives a ball and passes it around their circle when the music starts. When the music stops, the player with the ball (or the last player to touch the ball) takes the ball and moves to another circle. To avoid arguments, a player must move to the next circle if the ball is in her hands or on the way to her. Try using more than one ball.

One, Two, Button My Shoe

SUPPLIES: None

SKILL: Running

FORMATION:

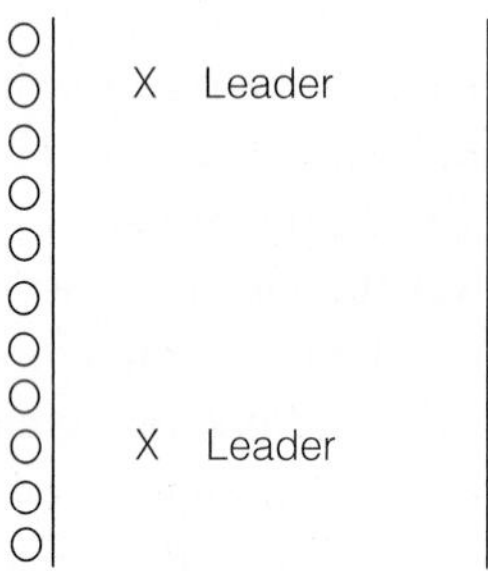

Mark off two parallel lines on opposite sides of the playing area. Choose two or three players to be leaders and stand in front of the class. The rest of the class stands behind one of the lines. When the leaders say, "Ready," the following dialogue begins.

Children:	One, two.
Leader:	Button my shoe.
Children:	Three, four.
Leader:	Close the door.
Children:	Five, six.
Leader:	Pick up sticks.
Children:	Seven, eight.
Leader:	Run, or you'll be late!

As children carry on the conversation with the leaders, they toe the line, ready to run. When the leaders say the word *late*, players run to the other line and return. Choose new leaders after each run. The leaders can give the last response ("Run, or you'll be late!") in any timing desired—pausing or dragging out the words. No player can leave before hearing the word *late* spoken.

Popcorn

SUPPLIES: None

SKILLS: Curling, stretching, jumping

FORMATION:

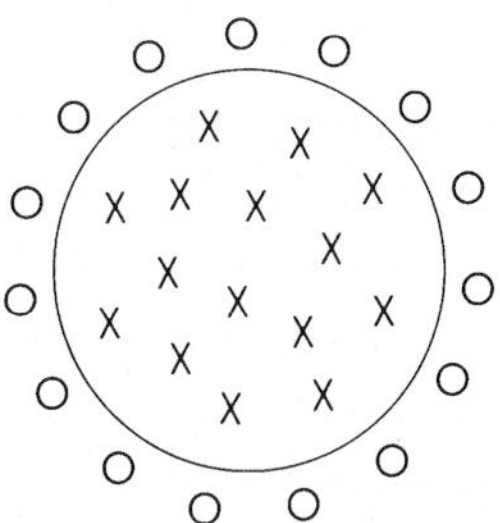

Choose half of the class is to be popcorn; they crouch down in the center of the circle formed by the rest of the class. Children in the circle also crouch to represent the heat. Choose one of them to be the leader, whose actions will guide the other children. Children in the circle gradually rise to a standing position, extend their arms overhead, and shake them vigorously to indicate the intensifying heat. In the meantime, the popcorn in the center starts to pop. This begins slowly and increases in speed and height as the heat is applied. In the final stages, children are popping up rapidly. After a time, the groups change places and repeat the game.

Red Light

SUPPLIES: None

SKILLS: Fundamental locomotor movements, stopping

FORMATION:

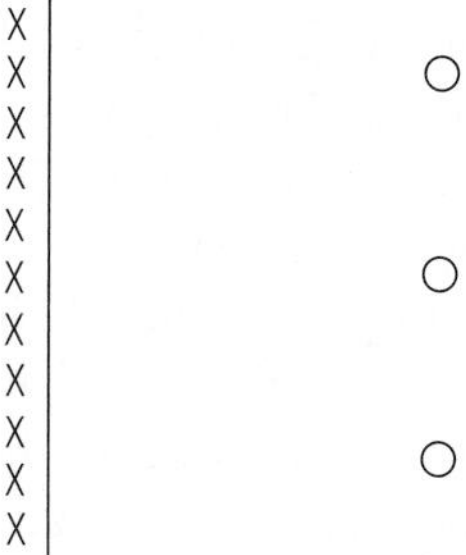

Mark off a goal line at one end of the area. The object of the game is to move across the area successfully without getting caught. Two or three players are leaders and stand on the goal line. The leaders turn away from the players. One of the leaders claps five times. All leaders turn around on the fifth clap. Meanwhile, the players move toward the goal line, timing their movements to end on the fifth clap. If any of the leaders catch any child moving, that child returns to the starting line and begins anew. After the clapper turns away, she can turn back immediately to catch any movement. Once she begins clapping, however, she has to clap five times before turning around. The first child to reach the goal line successfully without being caught moving is the winner. Choose new leaders for the next game.

VARIATIONS:

1. An excellent variation of the game is to have the leaders face the oncoming players. The designated leader calls out "Green light" for them to move and "Red light" for them to stop. When the leader calls other colors, the players should not move.
2. Explore different types of locomotion. The leader names the type of movement (e.g., hop, crawl, skip) before turning her back to the group.
3. Have the leader specify how those caught must go back to place—walk, hop, skip, slide, crawl.
4. Divide the area into quadrants and have four games with one or two leaders.

Teaching Hint

In the original game of Red Light, the leader counts rapidly, "1, 2, 3, 4, 5, 6, 7, 8, 9, 10—red light," instead of clapping five times. This has proved impractical in most gymnasiums, however, because children moving forward cannot hear the counting. Clapping, which provides both a visual and an auditory signal, is preferable.

Right Angle

SUPPLIES: Music

SKILLS: Rhythmic movement, body management

FORMATION: Scattered

To provide the rhythm for this activity, use a tom-tom. Children quickly change direction at right angles on each heavy beat or change of music. The object of the game is to make the right-angle change on signal and not to bump into other players.

Rollee Pollee

SUPPLIES: Many 8-inch foam balls

SKILLS: Ball rolling, dodging

FORMATION:

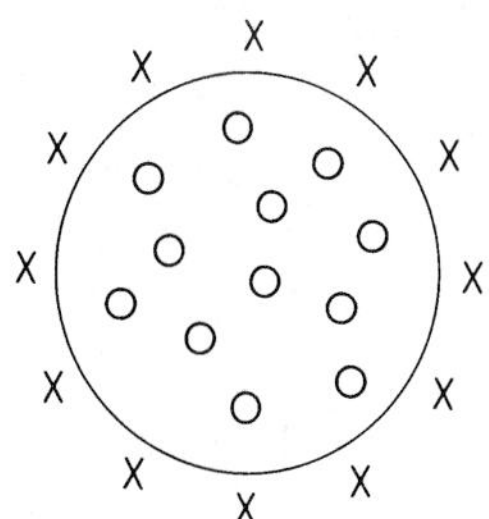

Half of the class forms a circle; the other half is in the center. Give balls to the players forming the circle. These players roll the balls at the feet and shoes of the center players, trying to touch them with a ball. The center players move around to avoid the balls. A center player who is touched leaves the center and joins the circle. After a specific time, or when all of the children have been touched, the teams trade places.

Teaching Hint

The instructor can have the children practice rolling a ball first. Balls that stop in the center are dead and must be taken back to the circle before being put into play again. The preferable procedure is to have players who recover balls roll them to a teammate rather than return to place with the ball.

The Scarecrow and the Crows

SUPPLIES: None

SKILLS: Dodging, running

FORMATION:

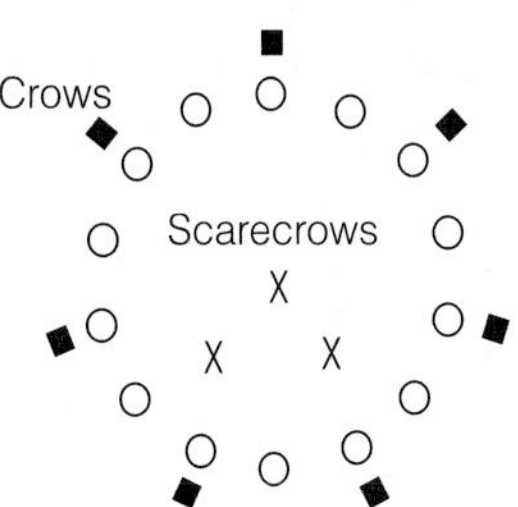

Children form a large circle to outline the garden, which is guarded by two or three players who are the scarecrows. Six to eight crows scatter on the outside of the circle, and the scarecrows assume a

22

characteristic pose inside the circle. Players in the circle raise their joined hands and let the crows run through, into the garden, where they pretend to eat. The scarecrows try to tag the crows. The circle children help the crows by raising their joined hands and allowing them to leave the circle, but they try to hinder the scarecrows. If the scarecrows run out of the circle, all the crows immediately run into the garden and start to nibble at the vegetables while the circle children hinder the scarecrows' reentry.

When the scarecrows have caught one or two crows, choose new players. If, after a reasonable time, the scarecrows fail to catch any crows, change players.

Sneak Attack

SUPPLIES: None

SKILLS: Running

FORMATION:

Draw two parallel lines about 60 feet apart. Divide the class into two teams. Team 1, the chasers, stands along one line with their backs to the area. Team 2, the sneak team, is on the other line, facing the area. The sneak team moves forward on signal, moving toward the chasers. When they get reasonably close, a signal is given, and the sneak team turns and runs back to its line, chased by the other team. Anyone tagged before reaching the line becomes a chaser. The game is then repeated, with the roles exchanged.

Soap Bubbles

SUPPLIES: Cones to delineate space, music

SKILLS: Body management

FORMATION: Scattered

Use four cones to mark off the movement area. Each player is a soap bubble floating throughout the area. Call out a locomotor movement for students to perform while moving within the four cones. As the game progresses, move the cones toward the center of the area to make it smaller. The object of the game is not to touch or collide with another bubble. When this occurs, both bubbles burst and sink to the floor, making themselves as small as possible. Keep making the area smaller, until only a few players have not been touched. Players who are broken bubbles can go to the area outside of the cones and move. This game teaches the concept of moving in general space without touching.

Squirrel in the Trees

SUPPLIES: None

SKILLS: Fundamental locomotor movements

FORMATION:

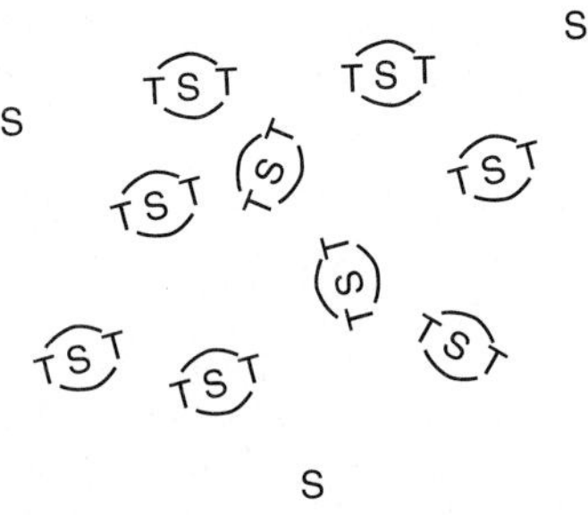

Form several trees by having two students face each other and hold hands or put hands on each other's shoulders. A squirrel is in the center of each tree, and one or two extra squirrels are outside. On signal, the trees open up and let the squirrels move around the area. The trees stay together and also move throughout the area. On signal, the trees freeze in place and the squirrels find any available tree. Only one squirrel is allowed in a tree. Quickly begin another game to avoid drawing attention to those who did not find a tree.

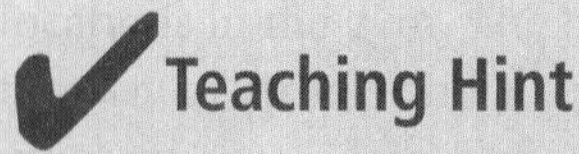

Teaching Hint

Rotate students so everyone gets to be a squirrel. Once the squirrels are in a tree, ask them to face one of the tree players. The child they are facing becomes their partner for a tree; the other child becomes a new squirrel.

Statues

SUPPLIES: None

SKILLS: Body management, applying force, balance

FORMATION: Scattered in pairs

One partner in each pair is the swinger and the other the statue. The teacher calls a directive, such as "Pretty," "Funny," "Happy," "Angry," or "Ugly." The swinger takes the statue by one or both hands, swings it around in a small circle two or three times (the teacher specifies), and releases it. The statue then takes a pose that follows the directive, and the swinger sits on the floor.

A committee of children can decide on the best statues. Statues must hold the position without moving or be disqualified. After the winners are announced, the partners reverse positions. Caution students to use control when swinging their partners.

VARIATION: In the original game, partners swing until they hear the directive. The swinger then immediately releases the statue, who takes the pose as called. This gives the statue little time to react. Statues are more creative if the directive is given earlier.

Stop Ball

SUPPLIES: A ball

SKILLS: Tossing, catching

FORMATION:

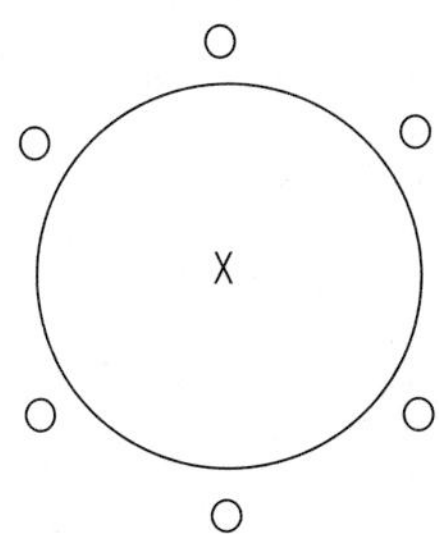

Divide the class into small circles of 5 to 7 players. One player, with hands over the eyes, stands in the center of each circle. Players toss a ball clockwise or counterclockwise around the circle. When she chooses, the center player calls, "Stop!" The player caught with the ball (or the ball coming to her) takes the ball to the next circle and plays with a new team. Give the center players 3 or 4 turns each.

Tag Games (Simple)

SUPPLIES: None

SKILLS: Fundamental locomotor movements, dodging

FORMATION: Scattered

Tag has many variations. The following are "give up the tag" games; a player is no longer "it" after tagging another child, who then becomes it. Children are scattered, and several players are taggers. When making a tag, that player says, "You're it." The new tagger can chase any player other than the person who tagged him (no tagbacks). Eliminating tagbacks keeps students from always being it because they are slower than the child who tagged them.

VARIATIONS:

1. Touching a specific object (such as wood or iron), color, or the floor can make a runner safe.
2. Children can be safe by doing a particular action or by striking a certain pose.
   a. *Stoop Tag.* Players touch both hands to the ground.
   b. *Stork Tag.* Players stand on one foot. (The other cannot touch.)
   c. *Turtle Tag.* Players get on their backs, feet pointed toward the ceiling.
   d. *Bowing Tag.* Players bow with forehead to the ground.
   e. *Nose-and-Toe Tag.* Players touch the nose to the toe.
   f. *Back-to-Back Tag.* Players stand back-to-back with any other child.
   g. *Skunk Tag.* Players reach an arm under one knee and hold the nose.
3. *Locomotor Tag.* The child who is it says how the others should move—skipping, hopping, jumping. The tagger must use the same kind of movement.
4. *Frozen Tag.* Two children are it. The rest are scattered over the area. When tagged, they are "frozen" and must keep both feet in place. Any free player can tag a frozen player and thus release her. The tagger's goal is to freeze all players. Frozen players can be required to hop in place until released.

Teacher Ball (Leader Ball)

SUPPLIES: A volleyball or rubber playground ball

SKILLS: Throwing, catching

FORMATION:

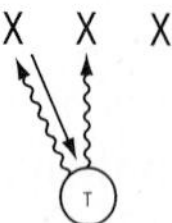

One child, the "teacher," stands about 10 feet in front of three other students, who are lined up facing the teacher. The object of the game is to move up to the teacher's spot by not making bad throws or missing catches. The teacher throws to each child in turn, beginning with the child on the left, who must catch and return the ball. Any child making a throwing or catching error goes to the end of the line, on the teacher's right. Those in the line move up, filling the vacated space.

A teacher who makes a mistake goes to the end of the line, and the child at the head of the line becomes the new teacher. Teachers score 1 point by remaining in position for three rounds (three throws to each child). After scoring a point, the teacher goes to the end of the line, and the first child becomes the teacher.

> ***VARIATION:*** The "teacher" can suggest specific methods of throwing and catching, such as "Catch with the right hand only" or "Catch with one hand and don't let the ball touch your body."

Toe-To-Toe

SUPPLIES: None

SKILLS: Fundamental locomotor movements

FORMATION: Scattered

Students perform a locomotor movement around the area. On signal, each child must find a partner and stand toe-to-toe (one foot only) with that person. An important skill is to take the nearest person for a partner instead of searching for a particular friend. Students who cannot find a partner in their immediate area must run quickly to the center of the area (marked with a spot or cone) to find one. The goal is to find a nearby partner as quickly as possible and avoid being the last pair formed. If the number of students playing is uneven, the teacher can join in and play. Change locomotor movements often.

Tommy Tucker's Land

SUPPLIES: About 10 beanbags for each game

SKILLS: Dodging, running

FORMATION:

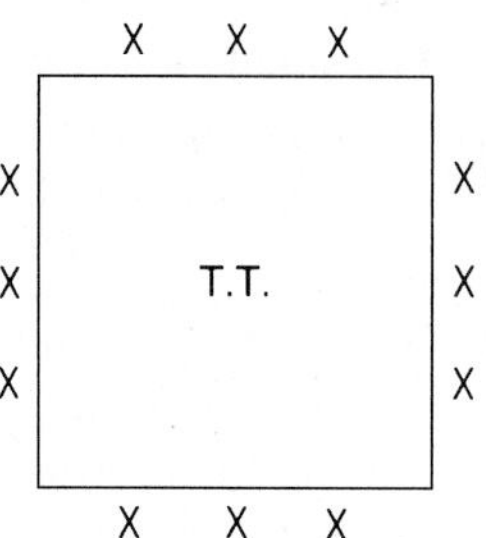

Two or three students, Tommy and Tammy Tucker, stand in the center of a 15-foot square, within which the beanbags are scattered. The Tuckers are guarding their land and treasure. The other children chant,

> I'm on Tommy Tucker's land,
>
> Picking up gold and silver.

Children try to pick up as much of the treasure as they can while avoiding being tagged by the Tuckers. Any child who is tagged must return the treasure and retire from the game. The game ends when only one child is left, or when all beanbags are successfully filched. The teacher may wish to stop the game earlier if it reaches a stalemate. In that case, select new Tuckers.

Twins (Triplets)

SUPPLIES: None

SKILLS: Body management, running

FORMATION: Scattered with partner

Have students pair with a partner (twin). The teacher gives commands such as "Take three hops and two leaps" or "Walk backward four steps and three skips." When the pairs are separated, the teacher says, "Find your twin!" Players find their twin and stand frozen toe-to-toe. The goal is to not be the last pair to find each other and freeze. Make sure students move away from each other when following commands. One alternative is to find a new twin each time. Another variation is to separate twins in opposite ends of the playing area.

VARIATION: For greater challenge, have students play in groups of three (triplets). For this variation, children select new partners each time.

Up Periscope

SUPPLIES: None

SKILLS: Fundamental locomotor movements

FORMATION: Scattered

Children move around the area pretending to be ships. Remind the ships to not contact another ship and stay as far away as possible. When the teacher says, "Submarines," players quickly lower their bodies and move at a low level. On "Up periscope," students move to their backs and put one leg in the air to imitate a periscope. On "Double periscope," they raise both legs to imitate two periscopes. While students are in double periscope position, the teacher can quickly give the previous commands to keep students moving. When the teacher says, "Surface," the students resume moving through the area as ships.

Where's My Partner?

SUPPLIES: None

SKILLS: Fundamental locomotor movements

FORMATION:

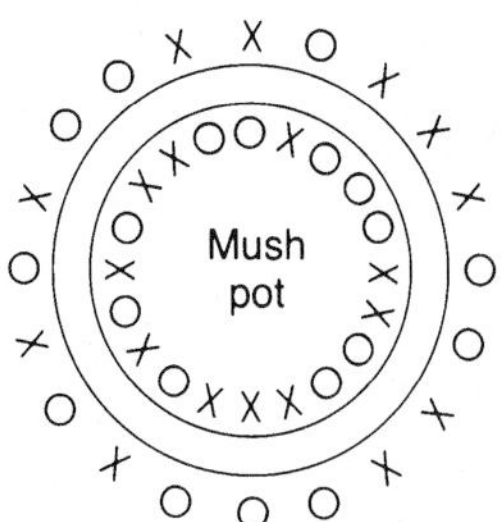

Children are in a double circle by couples, with partners facing. The inside circle has two or three more players than the outside. On signal, the circles skip (or walk, run, hop, gallop) to the right. This means they are skipping in opposite directions. On the command "Halt," the circles face each other to find partners. The players left without a partner go to the mush pot (the center area of the circle) for one turn. The circles are reversed after a time.

VARIATION: Play the game to music or a drumbeat. When the music stops, the players seek partners.

DEVELOPMENTAL LEVEL II

Compared with the games in Developmental Level I, the games program in Level II is distinctly different. Chase and tag games are more complex and demand more maneuvering. Introductory lead-up games make an appearance. Children become more interested in games with a sports slant, and kicking, throwing, catching, batting, and other sport skills start to mature.

Addition Tag

SUPPLIES: None

SKILLS: Running, dodging

FORMATION:

Two or more pairs are it, and each stands with inside hands joined. These are the taggers. The other children run individually. The pairs move around the area, trying to tag with the free hands. The first child tagged joins the couple, making a trio. The three then chase until they catch a fourth. After catching a fourth child, the four divide and form two pairs, adding another set of taggers to the game. This continues until most of the players are tagged.

Teaching Hint

If pairs are having problems catching the runners, establish some area restrictions. For a faster game, start with more pairs. A tag is legal only when the pair or trio keeps their hands joined.

Alaska Baseball

SUPPLIES: A volleyball or soccer ball

SKILLS: Kicking, batting, running, ball handling

FORMATION:

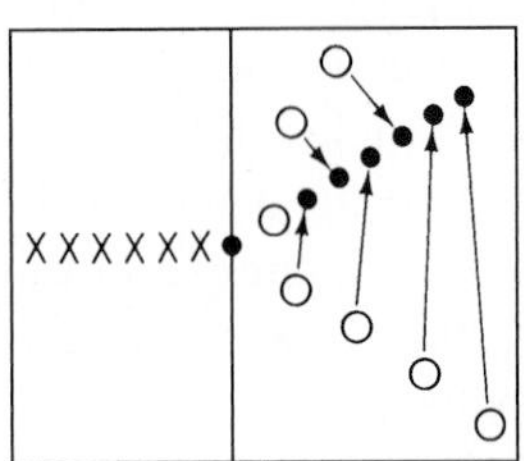

Players form two teams; one is at bat and the other is in the field. A straight line is the only out-of-bounds line. The team at bat is behind this line at about the middle. The other team scatters around the fair territory. One player propels the ball, either by batting a volleyball or kicking a stationary soccer ball. Teammates are in a close file behind the batter. Upon sending the ball into the playing area, the batter starts running around the line of teammates. Each time the runner passes the head of the file, the team gives a loud count.

There are no outs. The first fielder to get the ball stands still and starts passing the ball back overhead to the nearest teammate, who moves directly behind to receive it. The rest of the field players must run to the ball and form a file behind it. Teammates pass the ball back overhead, and each player handles the ball. When the last field player in line has a firm grip on it, she shouts "Stop!" A count is then made of the number of times the batter ran around her team. To score more closely, count half rounds. When five batters (or half of the team) has batted, the teams change places. This is better than having an entire team bat before changing to the field, because players in the field tire from many consecutive runs.

> ***VARIATION:*** Set up regular bases for the batters to run. Score points whether or not the batter makes a home run; or have the batter continue around the bases, scoring 1 point per base.

Arches

SUPPLIES: Music

SKILLS: Moving rhythmically

FORMATION:

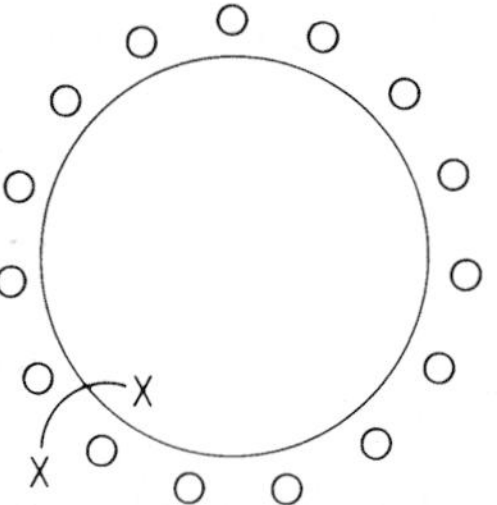

The game is similar to London Bridge. In the playing area, two students form an arch by facing one another with hands joined and arms raised. When the music starts, the other players move in a circle, passing under the arch. Suddenly, the music stops, and the arch comes down as the two students drop hands. All players caught in the arch immediately pair off to form other arches, staying in a general circle formation. If a caught player has no partner, he waits in the center of the circle until one is available. The last players caught (or left) form arches for the next game. Warn the arches not to bring down their hands and arms so forcefully that they hit children passing under.

> ***VARIATION:*** Try using different types of music, and have children move to the pattern of each piece.

Bat Ball

SUPPLIES: An 8-inch foam ball

SKILLS: Batting, running, catching, throwing

FORMATION:

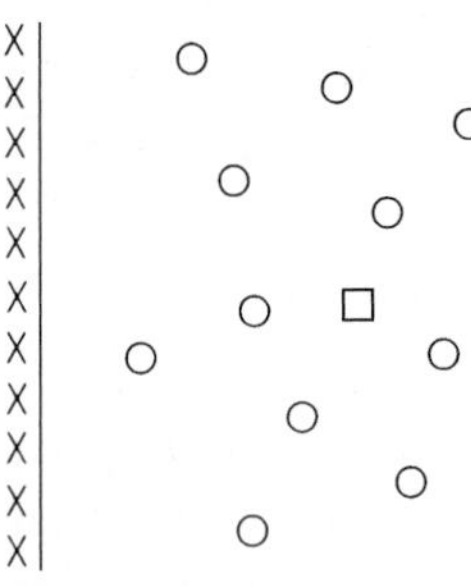

Mark off a serving line across one end of the field, and set up a 3-by-3-foot base about 50 feet from the serving line. Divide children into two teams. Team 1 is scattered over the playing area. Team 2 is behind the serving line, with one player at bat. The batter puts the ball into play by batting it with a hand into the playing area. To be counted as a fair ball, the ball must land in the playing area or be touched by a member of Team 1. As soon as the ball is hit, the batter runs to the base and back across the serving line. In the meantime, Team 1 fields the ball and tries to complete five passes before the Team 2 runner gets back across the line.

Fielders may not run with the ball. It must be passed from fielder to fielder. A pass may not be returned to the fielder it was received from. Violation of any of these rules constitutes a foul.

A run is scored each time the batter hits a fair ball, touches the base, and gets back to the serving line. A run is also scored if the fielding team commits a foul.

The batter is out when the ball is caught on the fly. Two consecutive foul balls also put the batter out. The batter is out when hit by a thrown ball in the field of play. Sides change when three outs are made.

Beach Ball Bat Ball

SUPPLIES: Four to six beach balls

SKILLS: Batting, tactile handling

FORMATION:

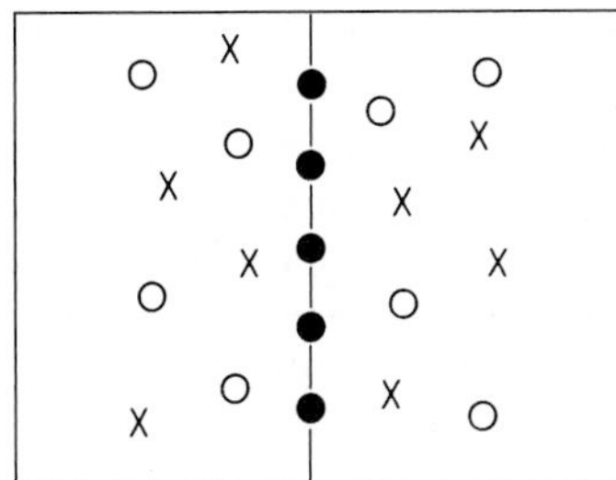

Divide players into two teams. Begin the game by placing the balls on the centerline of the court area. All beach balls are in play at the same time. Players score by batting a ball over the endline. Balls that cross the endline are dead. Players use the remaining balls in play. Balls on the floor are picked up and batted into play. Balls may never be carried. The game ends when all four balls score. Teams then switch places and start a new game.

Bird Catcher

SUPPLIES: Hoops or cones

SKILLS: Chasing, fleeing, dodging

FORMATION: Class in line formation with 2 to 4 players in the bird nest

Choose 2 to 4 players to be bird catchers and stand in the center of the teaching area. One child is the mother/father bird and stands on an endline. (Or, use cones to mark the bird's nest.) The rest of the class stands on the other endline. Students on the endline quickly choose the type of bird they will be for the game. On signal, the mother/father bird commands a specific type of bird to fly—for example, "Cardinals fly." All students who are cardinals then try to reach the bird's nest without being tagged by a bird catcher. Students who are tagged help the bird catcher until the game ends.

Teaching Hint

Expedite the game by suggesting various types of birds.

Bounce Ball

SUPPLIES: Volleyballs or rubber playground balls of about the same size

SKILLS: Throwing, ball rolling

FORMATION:

Children form two teams. Each team occupies half of the court and has several balls. Two players from each team are assigned to retrieve balls behind their own endlines. Teams try to bounce or roll the ball over their opponents' endline. A ball thrown across the line does not count. Two scorers are needed, one at each endline. Players can move wherever they wish in their own area but cannot cross the centerline. After the starting signal, students bounce and roll the balls back and forth at will.

Box Ball

SUPPLIES: A sturdy box, 2 feet square and about 12 inches deep; four volleyballs (or similar balls)

SKILLS: Running, ball handling

FORMATION:

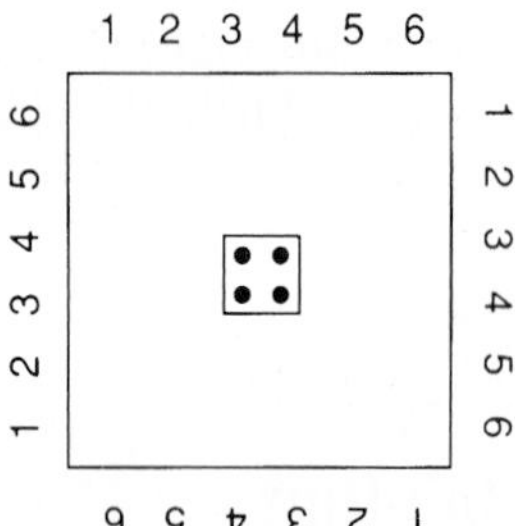

Divide the class into four even teams of 6 to 10 players. Each team stands along one side of a hollow square at an equal distance from the center. Players face inward, and each team numbers off consecutively from right to left. Place a box containing four balls into the center. When the teacher calls a number, the player from each team who has that number runs forward to the box, takes a ball, and runs to the head of her line, taking the place of Player 1. Meanwhile, the players in the line have moved to the left just enough to fill in the space left by the runner. On reaching the head of the line, the runner passes the ball to the next child, and so on down the line to the end child. The last child runs forward and returns the ball to the box. The first team to return the ball to the box scores a point.

Runners must not pass the ball down the line until they are in place at the head of the line. Each child must receive and then pass the ball. Teams failing to follow these rules are disqualified. Runners stay at the head of the line, retaining their original number. The lines do not stay in consecutive number sequence.

Busy Bee

SUPPLIES: None

SKILLS: Fundamental locomotor movements

FORMATION:

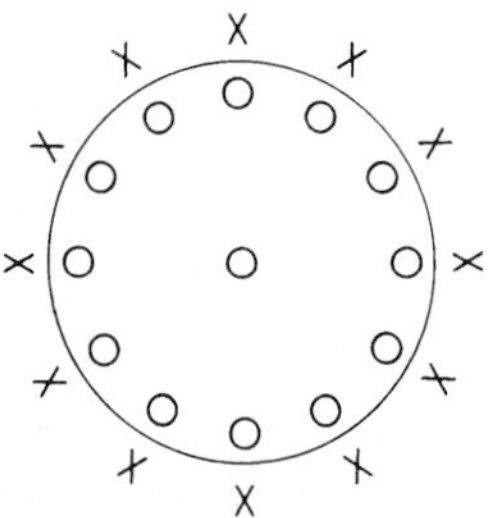

Half of the students form a large circle, facing in, and are the stationary players. The other students seek partners from this group, and stand in front of the stationary players. An extra child in the center is the busy bee. The bee calls out directions such as "Toe-to-toe," "Face-to-face," "Shake hands," "Kneel on one knee [or both]," and "Hop on one foot." All the children in the double circle follow these directions. When the bee calls out, "Busy bee," stationary players stand still. Their partners seek new partners, while the bee also tries to get a partner. The child without a partner becomes the new busy bee.

Teaching Hint

Teach students various movements they can call out if they become the busy bee. When changing partners, children must select a child other than the stationary player next to them. After a specific time, rotate the active and stationary players.

Cageball Kick-Over

SUPPLIES: An 18-, 24-, or 30-inch cageball

SKILL: Kicking

FORMATION:

Players are divided into two teams and sit facing each other, with legs outstretched and soles of the feet about 6 to 12 feet apart. All players support their weight on the hands, which are placed slightly to the rear. The teacher rolls the cageball between the two teams. Players try to kick the ball over the other team and score a point. When a team scores, the teacher rolls the ball into play again. Rotate players by having a player on the left side of the line take a place on the right side after a point is scored, thus moving all players one position to the left. If players kick the ball out at either end, no score results. The teacher returns the ball into play.

Teaching Hint

Let children use their hands to stop the ball from going over them.

Club Guard

SUPPLIES: A juggling club or bowling pin, foam rubber ball

SKILL: Throwing

FORMATION:

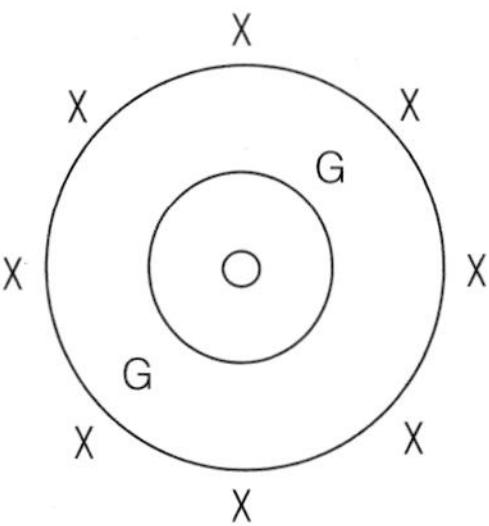

Draw a circle about 15 feet in diameter. In the center of that circle, draw an 18-inch circle and place the club in it. Two or three students guard the club. The other players stand outside the large circle, which is the restraining line for them. The circle players throw the ball at the club and try to knock it down. The guards try to block the throws with the legs and body but must stay out of the small inner circle. The circle players pass the ball around rapidly so that one of the players can get an opening to throw as the guards maneuver to protect the club. Rotate in new guards after a short time (15–20 seconds). The guards are disqualified if they step into the small circle.

Teaching Hints

1. Place more than one club in the center.
2. Play multiple games to increase the activity level for all players.

Competitive Circle Contests

SUPPLIES: Volleyballs or 8-inch foam rubber balls, two bowling pins

SKILLS: Throwing, catching

FORMATION: Two circles with the same number of students in each

Two teams arranged in separate circles compete against each other. Draw lines on the floor to ensure that the circles are the same size. Consecutively number each team's players, using the same numbers for both teams. Two consecutively numbered players go to the center of the opponents' circle to compete for their team in one of the following activities.

1. *Circle Club Guard.* The two center players guard a bowling pin. Players roll the ball at the club. The team that knocks down the club first wins a point. They must pass the ball to three different players before rolling it at the club.
2. *Touch Ball.* The circle players pass the ball from one to another while the two center players try to touch it. The center player who touches the ball first wins a point for her team. If neither player can touch the ball within a reasonable time, stop the action without awarding a point.

After all players have competed, the team with the most points wins.

Couple Tag

SUPPLIES: None

SKILLS: Running, dodging

FORMATION:

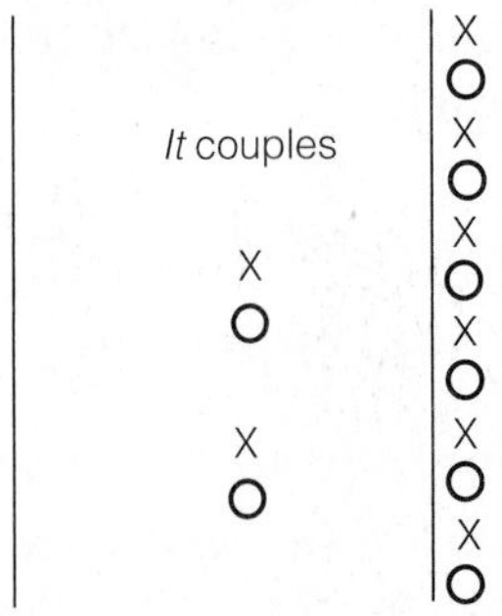

It couples

Mark two goal lines on opposite sides of an area. Players run in pairs, with inside hands joined. All pairs, except two, line up on one of the goal lines. The pairs in the center are it. When they call "Come," all pairs, with hands joined, run to the other goal line. The pairs in the center, also keeping hands joined, try to tag any other pair. As soon as a couple is caught, they help the center couples. The game continues until all are caught. The last two couples caught are it for the next game.

VARIATION: **Triplet Tag.** Try playing the game with sets of threes. Tagging is done with any pair of joined hands. If a triplet breaks joined hands, it is caught.

Crows and Cranes

SUPPLIES: None

SKILLS: Running, dodging

FORMATION:

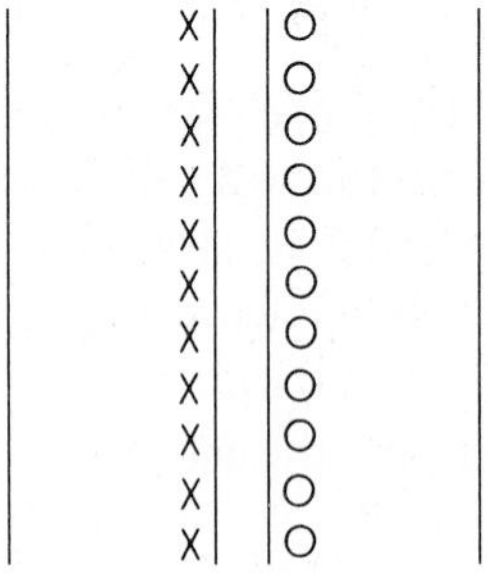

Establish two goal lines on opposite sides of an area. The class is divided into two groups—crows and cranes. The groups face each other at the center of the area, about 5 feet apart. The leader calls out either "Crows" or "Cranes," using a cr-r-r-r-r-r sound at the start of either word to mask the result. If "Crows" is the call, the crows chase the cranes to the goal line. If "Cranes" is the call, then the cranes chase. Any player caught goes over to the other side and becomes a member of that group. The goal is to capture the most players.

VARIATIONS:

1. *Toe-to-Toe.* Instead of facing each other, children stand back-to-back, about a foot apart, in the center.
2. *Red and Blue.* Instead of using calls, throw a piece of cardboard (red on one side and blue on the other) into the air between the teams. If red comes up, the red team chases, and vice versa.
3. *Nouns and Verbs.* When the leader calls out any verb, the nouns team chases, and vice versa.
4. *Odd and Even.* Throw large foam rubber dice in the air. If they come up even, the even team chases. If they come up odd, the odd team chases.
5. *Blue, Black, and Baloney.* On the command "Blue" or "Black," the game proceeds as described. On the command "Baloney," no one is to move. The caller draws out the bl-l-l-l sound in giving one of the three commands.
6. Have a leader tell a story using as many words beginning with *cr–* as possible (e.g., *crazy, crunch, crust, crown, crude, crowd, crouch, cross, croak, critter*). Each time the leader says one of these words, he lengthens the beginning with a drawn-out *cr-r-r-r* sound. No one may move on any of the words except crows or cranes.

Fly Trap

SUPPLIES: None

SKILLS: Fundamental locomotor movements

FORMATION:

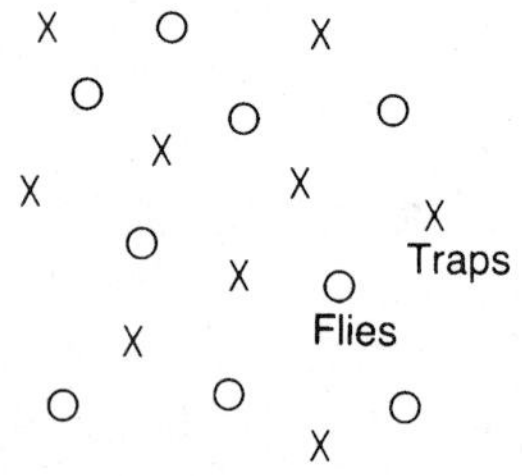

Traps

Flies

Half of the class is scattered around the playing area, sitting cross-legged on the floor. These children form the trap. The rest of the players are the flies, and they buzz around the seated children. On signal, the flies must freeze where they are. If any of the traps can touch a fly, that fly sits down at that spot and becomes a trap. The traps must keep their seats glued to the floor. The game continues until all flies are caught. To add realism, have the flies make buzzing sounds and move their arms like wings.

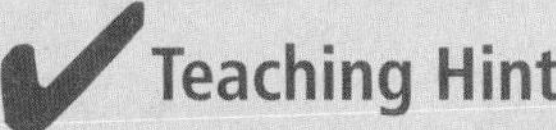

Teaching Hint

Some experience with the game helps you determine how far apart to place the seated children. When most of the flies are caught, the groups trade places. Occasionally change the method of locomotion.

Follow Me

SUPPLIES: A marker for each child (use squares of cardboard or plywood; individual mats or beanbags also work well)

SKILLS: All locomotor movements, stopping

FORMATION:

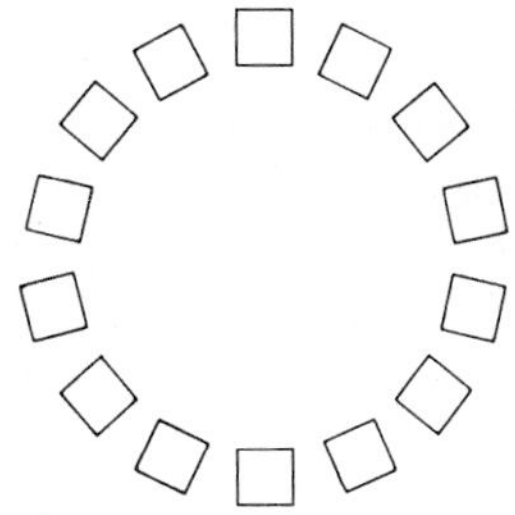

Arrange the class in a rough circle, each child standing or sitting with one foot on a marker. Two extra players are guides. They move around the circle, pointing at different players and asking them to follow until all players are selected. Each player chosen falls in behind the guide who pointed at him or her. The guides then take their group on a tour, and each group member does just what the guide does. The guide may hop, skip, and do stunts or other movements; the group following must do the same. At the signal "Home," all run for places with a marker. Two players will be left without a marker. They can become guides or choose other guides.

Fox Hunt

SUPPLIES: None

SKILLS: Running, dodging

FORMATION:

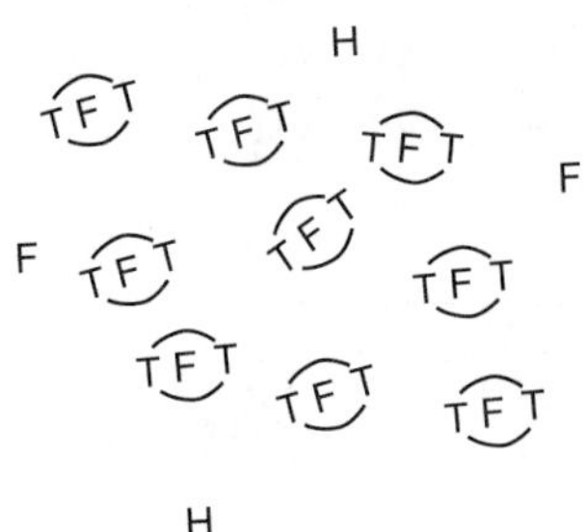

Pairs of players form trees by facing each other and holding hands. A third member of each group is a fox and stands between the hands of the trees. Two players are foxes without trees, and two players are hounds. The hounds try to tag foxes who are not in trees. The extra foxes may move to a tree and displace the fox who is in that tree. The foxes in trees may leave the safety of their trees at any time. If the hound tags a fox, their roles are reversed immediately.

Stop the game at regular intervals to allow the players who are trees to change places with the foxes and hounds. Vary the game by specifying different locomotor movements.

Galloping Lizzie

SUPPLIES: A beanbag or fleece ball

SKILLS: Throwing, dodging, running

FORMATION: Scattered

Two or more players are it and have beanbags. The other players are scattered around the playground. The players with the beanbags run after the others and try to hit other players below the waist with the beanbag. The person hit becomes it, and the game continues. Taggers must throw the beanbag, not just touch another child with it.

Hand Hockey

SUPPLIES: 8-inch gray foam ball

SKILLS: Striking, volleying

FORMATION:

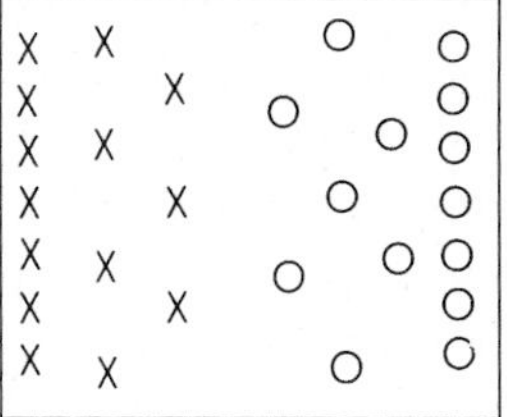

Players are divided into two teams. Half of the players on each team are guards and stand on the goal line as defenders. The other half are active players and are scattered throughout the playing area in front of their goal line.

The ball is put into play by being rolled into the center of the field. The object of the game is to bat or push the ball with either hand so that it crosses the goal line defended by the other team. Players may move the ball as in hockey but may not throw, hoist, or kick it. Defensive goal line players are limited to one step into the playing field when playing the ball. When a team scores, or after a specific period, guards become active players, and vice versa. An out-of-bounds ball goes to the opposite team and is put into play by being rolled from the sidelines into the playing area. If the ball is entrapped among players, the teacher stops play and puts the ball into play again.

Players must play the ball and not resort to rough tactics. Players who use unnecessary roughness or illegally handle the ball must go to the sidelines (as in hockey) and stay in the penalty area until the players change positions. Players should scatter and try to pass to each other rather than bunch around the ball. Once students learn the game, increase the activity by adding more balls.

> *VARIATION:* **Scooter Hockey.** The active center players from each team are on gym scooters. Specify the position (e.g., kneeling, sitting, on tummy) each child takes on the gym scooter, or allow a free choice. Because scooters require a hard surface, this version is usually played indoors on a basketball court.

Home Base

SUPPLIES: Cones to delineate the area, four pinnies

SKILLS: Reaction time, locomotor movements, body management

FORMATION: Groups of 5 or 6, in single file

Place several marking spots on the floor throughout the area. Each team quickly lines up behind one child who stands on a marking spot. This child is the team captain. When the teacher calls out a locomotor movement, all players do this movement throughout the area. When the teacher calls, "Home base," the captains quickly find the closest spot and their respective team members line up behind them. The first team to return to proper position (standing in a straight line) is the winner.

Teaching Hint

Avoid calling "Home base" until the students are thoroughly mixed. You can specify many different formations for teams to assume upon returning to home base.

Indianapolis 500

SUPPLIES: None

SKILLS: Running, tagging

FORMATION:

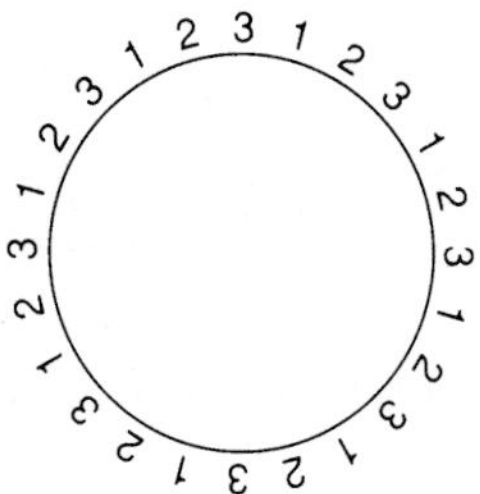

Children start in a large circle and are numbered off by threes or fours. A race starter says "Start your engines," and then calls a number. Children with the corresponding number run the same way around the circle and try to tag players in front of them. If the starter yells, "Pit stop," all runners have to stop and return to their original position. If the starter calls, "Car wreck," all runners change direction and keep running until they hear "Pit stop" called. Change the starter often.

Jump the Shot

SUPPLIES: Jump-the-shot ropes

SKILL: Rope jumping

FORMATION:

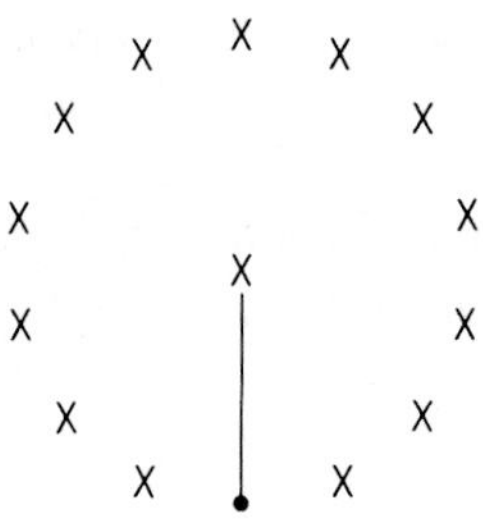

Divide the class into 4 or 5 small circles. One player with a long rope stands in the center. Tie a soft object

to the free end of the rope to give it some weight. A deflated ball or beanbag makes a good weight (use duct tape to keep it from becoming untied). The center player turns the rope for the circle players, who must jump over it. A player who touches the rope with the feet must move up to the next group.

VARIATIONS:

1. Change the center player after one or two misses. Caution center players to keep the rope along the ground. The rope speed can be varied. A good way to turn the rope is to sit cross-legged and turn it overhead. Students can do different tasks such as hopping, jumping and turning, or jumping and clapping.
2. Teams line up in spoke formation. Each member does a specified number of jumps (3 to 5) and then exits. The next team member in line must come in immediately without missing a turn of the rope. Players score a point for the team by coming in on time, jumping the prescribed number of turns, and exiting successfully. The team with the most points wins.
3. Couples line up in the same formation. They join inside hands and stand side by side when jumping.

Keep 'em Movin'

SUPPLIES: Tennis balls, whiffle balls, foam balls

SKILLS: Body management

FORMATION: Scattered throughout the teaching area

Scatter many tennis balls and/or whiffle balls (10 to 15 more than there are students) throughout the teaching area. On signal, students begin tapping the tennis balls with their feet or hands to get them moving or "alive." Balls may not be picked up or kicked. While the students try to keep all balls moving, the teacher looks for balls that are stationary. Upon seeing three different balls not moving, the teacher yells, "Dead bugs," and all students move to their backs with their arms and legs up and moving like a bug. After several seconds, the teacher signals for the game to resume.

Loose Caboose

SUPPLIES: None

SKILLS: Running, dodging

FORMATION:

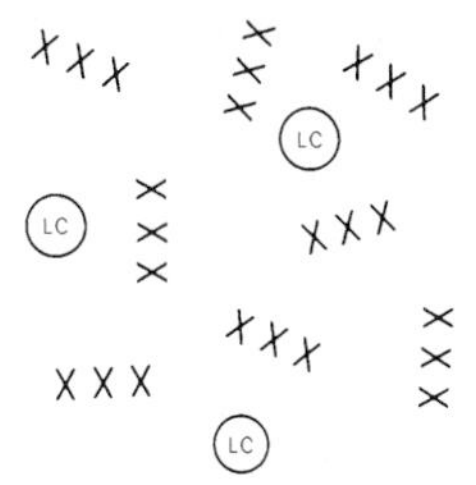

XXX XXX XXX LC LC XXX XXX XXX XXX XXX LC

Choose 2 or 3 children to be loose cabooses that try to hook onto a train. Trains are formed by 3 or 4 children standing in single file with their hands on the shoulders of the child immediately in front. The trains, by twisting and turning, try to keep the caboose from hooking on. Should the caboose manage to hook on, the front child in the train becomes the new caboose. Each train also tries to keep together. If a train breaks while being chased, it goes to the side and counts to 25 before reentering.

Nine Lives

SUPPLIES: Fleece balls

SKILLS: Throwing, dodging

FORMATION: Scattered

Any number of fleece balls can be used—the more the better. On signal, players get a ball and hit as many children below waist level as possible. Players who are hit nine times leave the game and stay out of bounds until they have counted to 25. Players may run anywhere with a ball or to get a ball, but may possess only one ball at a time. All throwers who hit players in the head are out.

Teaching Hint

Children often cheat about the number of times they are hit. A few words about fair play may be necessary, but high activity is the important part of the game.

VARIATIONS:

1. Players who catch a ball on the fly may deduct a specific number of hits.
2. Specify either left- or right-hand throwing.

Nonda's Car Lot

SUPPLIES: None

SKILLS: Running, dodging

FORMATION:

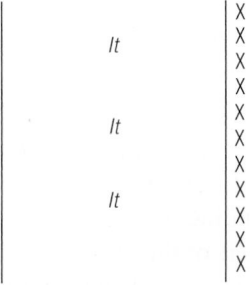

It X X X X
It X X X X
It X X X

Two or three players are it and stand in the center of the area between two lines at opposite ends of the playing area. The class selects four brands of cars (e.g., Honda, Corvette, Toyota, Cadillac). Each student then selects a car from the four but keeps it a secret.

One of the taggers calls out a car name. All students who chose that name try to run to the other line without getting tagged. The tagger calls out the cars until all students have run. Children (cars) that are tagged must sit down at the spot of the tag. They cannot move but may tag other students who run too near. When a tagger calls out, "Car lot," all of the cars must go. Change taggers often.

One Behind

SUPPLIES: None

SKILLS: All locomotor and nonlocomotor movements

FORMATION: Scattered

Students are instructed to watch a leader's activities and stay one move behind. As the leader begins an activity, the children watch. After 10–15 seconds, the leader changes movements and the students begin the first leader movement. Each time the leader changes movements, the students do the "one behind." The leader can trick students by doing an activity with her eyes closed. Thus, when the students begin this activity, they have no way of knowing when to change activities or what the next leader activity is.

Teaching Hint

Use this activity for any skills or with any piece of equipment.

One Step

SUPPLIES: A ball or beanbag for each pair of children

SKILLS: Throwing, catching

FORMATION:

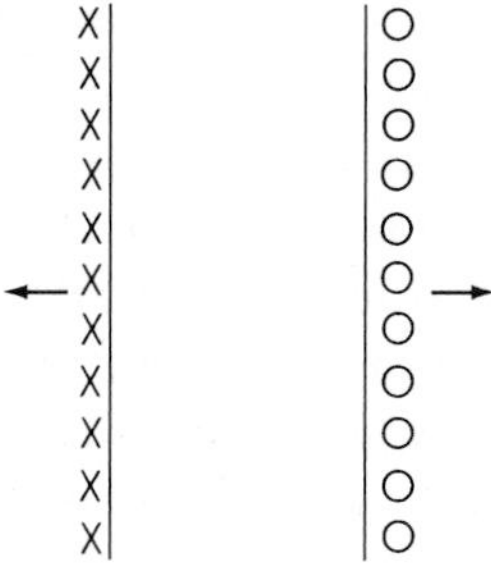

Two children stand facing each other about 3 feet apart. One has a ball or a beanbag. The object of the game is to throw or toss the item in the specified way so the partner can catch it without moving the feet on or from the ground. After successfully completing the throw, the thrower takes one step backward and waits for the throw from her partner. Children can try to increase their distance to an established line, or the two children who move the greatest distance apart can be declared the winners. When either child misses, moves the feet, or fails to follow directions, the partners move forward and start over. Variables offering interest and challenge are type of throw, type of catch, and kind of step. Throwing can be underhand, overhand, two-handed, under one leg, around the back, and so on. Catching can be two-handed, left-handed, right-handed, to the side, and so on. The step can be a giant step, a tiny step, a hop, a jump, or a similar movement.

VARIATION: **Bowling One Step.** In groups of 4 to 6, each of the players in turn gets a chance to roll the ball at a bowling pin. Use a minimal distance (5 to 10 feet), so most bowlers can hit the pin on the first try. Players take a step backward each time the pin is knocked down, and keep rolling until they miss. The winner is the child who moves the farthest from the pin.

Partner Stoop

SUPPLIES: Music, a whistle

SKILLS: Marching rhythmically

FORMATION:

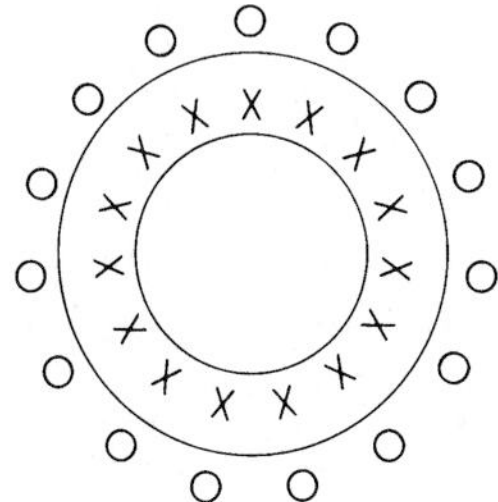

The game follows the same basic principle of stooping as in Circle Stoop, but is played with partners. The group forms a double circle, with partners facing counterclockwise; one partner is on the inside, one on the outside. When the music begins, all march in the line of direction. After a short period of marching, and on signal (whistle), the inside circle reverses direction and marches the other way—clockwise. The partners are thus separated. When the music stops, the outer circle stands still, and the partners making up the inner circle walk to rejoin their original partners. As soon as children reach their partner, they join inside hands and stoop without losing balance. The last couple to stoop and those who lose balance go to the center of the circle and wait out the next round. Start the game with walking and gradually increase the speed of movements when the class moves under control.

Ricochet

SUPPLIES: Foam balls, fleece balls

SKILLS: Ball rolling

FORMATION: Circle

Place several foam balls in the center of a large circle of students. Also give the class several fleece balls. On signal, the class begins rolling the fleece balls at the foam balls, trying to move them out of the circle. Children may move outside of the circle to retrieve fleece balls but may not enter the circle. The game is over when all or most of the foam balls are out of the circle.

Teaching Hints

1. Time the students and challenge them to beat their best class time.
2. Play several games at once.
3. Use beach balls rather than foam balls.

Squad Tag

SUPPLIES: Pinnies or markers for one squad, stopwatch

SKILLS: Running, dodging

FORMATION:

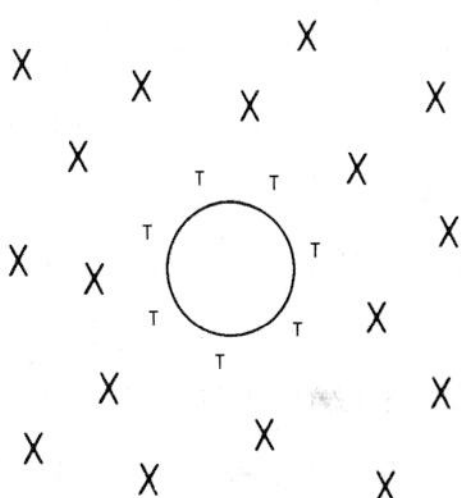

Mark the running area with cones. An entire squad acts as taggers. The object is to see which squad can most quickly tag the remaining class members. The tagging squad, which is marked, stands in a football huddle in the center of the area with their heads down. The rest of the class scatters at will throughout the area. On signal, the tagging squad scatters and tags the other class members. A class member who is tagged stops in place and remains there. Time is recorded when the last person is tagged. Each squad gets a turn at tagging.

Teaching Hint

Caution children to move under control, because there is much chasing and dodging in different directions. Definite boundaries are needed.

Steal the Treasure

SUPPLIES: A bowling pin

SKILL: Dodging

FORMATION:

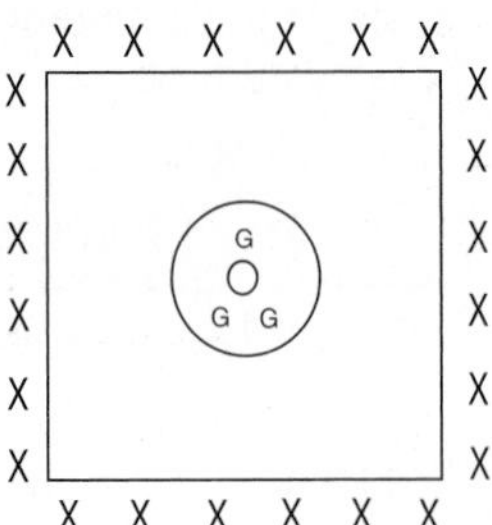

Outline a playing area about 20 feet square, with a small circle (hula hoop) in the center. Inside the hula hoop is a bowling pin—the treasure. Choose two or more guards to protect the treasure. The guards can move as far from the treasure as they like to tag a player. Anyone tagged is out until the next game. To successfully steal the treasure, a player must pick it up cleanly without being tagged. The guards tag players who come too near. If the treasure is knocked over by a player trying to steal it, that player must also wait out a turn. The guards must find the balance between being too far from the treasure and staying too near the treasure and never tagging anyone. If the guards tag all players, they are declared billionaires.

> *VARIATION:* **Bear and Keeper.** Instead of a treasure, a bear (seated cross-legged on the ground) is protected by two keepers. Anyone who touches the bear without being tagged becomes the new keeper.

Trades

SUPPLIES: None

SKILLS: Imagery, running, dodging

FORMATION:

Divide the class into two teams of equal number, each team with a goal line on opposite sides of the area. One team, the chasers, stays behind its goal line. The other team, the runners, approaches from its goal line, marching to the following dialogue:

Runners: Here we come.
Chasers: Where from?
Runners: New Orleans.
Chasers: What's your trade?
Runners: Lemonade.
Chasers: Show us some.

Runners move up close to the other team's goal line and begin acting out a selected occupation or a specific task. The opponents try to guess what the pantomime represents. On a correct guess, the running team must run back to its goal line chased by the others. Any runner tagged must join the chasers. The game is repeated with roles reversed. The team ending with the most players wins.

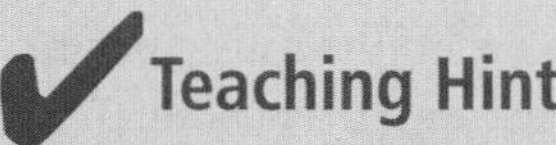

Teaching Hint

If a team has trouble guessing the pantomime, the other team should provide hints. Encourage teams to choose several activities so they take little time in choosing the next activity to be pantomimed.

Trees

SUPPLIES: None

SKILLS: Running, dodging

FORMATION:

Two parallel lines are drawn at opposite ends of the playing area. All players, except two or three taggers, are on one side of the area. On the signal "Trees," the players run to the other side of the area. The taggers try to tag as many players as possible. Any player tagged becomes a tree, stopping where tagged and keeping both feet in place. Trees cannot move their feet but can tag any runners who come close enough. The taggers keep chasing the players as they cross on signal until only a few remain. New players are selected to be taggers.

Whistle March

SUPPLIES: Music, a whistle

SKILL: Moving rhythmically

FORMATION: Scattered

Use brisk marching music for this game. Children are scattered around the room, walking in various directions and keeping time to the music. When the teacher blows a whistle several times, players form lines of that exact number of children. To form the lines, children stand side by side with locked elbows. As soon as players form a line of the proper number, they begin marching to the music counterclockwise around the room. Any children left over go to the center of the room and stay there until the next signal. On the next whistle signal (a single blast), the lines break up, and all walk individually around the room in various directions.

Before children form new lines, instruct them not to use the same players as in the previous line.

Whistle Mixer

SUPPLIES: A whistle

SKILLS: All basic locomotor movements

FORMATION: Scattered

Children are scattered throughout the area. To begin, they walk around in any direction they wish. The teacher blows several short, sharp whistle blasts. Children then form small circles with the number in the circles exactly equal to the number of whistle blasts. The goal is not to be left out or caught in a circle with an incorrect number of students. Encourage players to move to the center of the area and raise their hands to find others without a group. When the circles are formed, the teacher calls "Walk," and the game continues.

VARIATION: This game can be played with the aid of a tom-tom. Different beats indicate different locomotor movements—skipping, galloping, slow walking, normal walking, running. The teacher still uses a whistle to signal the number for each circle.

Wolfe's Beanbag Exchange

SUPPLIES: One beanbag per child

SKILLS: Running, dodging, tossing, catching

FORMATION: Scattered

Identify 5 or 6 children as taggers. The remaining children start scattered throughout the area, each with a beanbag in hand. The taggers chase the players with beanbags. Tagged players must freeze, keeping their feet still and beanbag in hand. To unfreeze a player, a nonfrozen player can exchange his beanbag with one held by a frozen player. If two frozen players are within tossing distance, they can thaw each other by exchanging their beanbags through the air using a toss and catch. Both tosses have to be caught, or the players must retrieve the beanbags and try again.

VARIATION: After students have learned the game, tell the taggers they may interfere with the tossing of beanbags between two frozen players by batting them to the floor. This forces the toss to be tried again, and the players are frozen until both players make successful catches.

DEVELOPMENTAL LEVEL III

Games at Developmental Level III are more complex and organized. Greater cooperation is needed to make the activities enjoyable. Strategy is important for successful play at this level, thus encouraging cognitive development.

Air Raid

SUPPLIES: Four to eight tumbling mats, fleece balls, foam balls

SKILLS: Throwing

FORMATION: Class divided into two teams

Two teams are in opposite halves of the teaching area. Each team has two tumbling mats that are fastened together and set on end to form an upright cylinder or target. The target is then placed near the back wall in the center of the gym (if baskets are obstructing the flight of balls, move the cylinder). Teams also have fleece balls and foam balls to throw. On signal, teams try to throw as many balls into the target as possible. The team with the most balls in at the end of the game wins.

VARIATIONS:

1. Use two targets for each side.
2. Place the target in a corner, and score 2 points for balls that ricochet in.
3. Have the students decide where to place the target.
4. Allow students to guard their target. This may require setting cones around the target to keep guards from colliding with it.

The team with the most beanbags in their home base is the winner.

Cageball Target Throw

SUPPLIES: A cageball (18- to 30-inch), 12 to 15 smaller balls of various sizes

SKILL: Throwing

FORMATION:

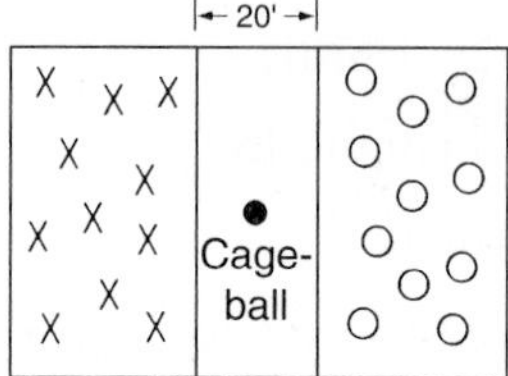

Mark an area about 20 feet wide across the center of the playing area, and set a cageball in the center. Form two teams whose players must throw the smaller balls against the cageball, thus forcing it across the line in front of the other team. Players may come up to the line to throw, but they may not throw while inside the cageball area. A player may enter the area, however, to recover a ball. No one is to touch the cageball at any time or with any object (such as a ball). If the cageball seems to roll too easily, deflate it slightly. The throwing balls can be of almost any size (e.g., soccer balls, volleyballs, or playground balls).

Barker's Hoopla

SUPPLIES: Hoops, beanbags

SKILL: Running

FORMATION:

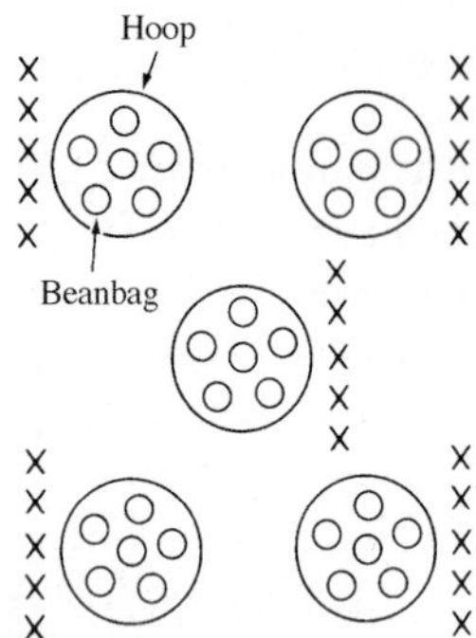

Arrange five hoops as illustrated. Use any distance between hoops (25 to 30 feet is a challenge). Place 5 or 6 beanbags in each hoop. Divide the class into five equal teams; one team is near each hoop, which is their home base. The teams then try to steal beanbags from other hoops and return them to their own home base. Here are the rules:

1. Players can take only one beanbag at a time. They must take the beanbag to their team's home base before returning for another one.
2. Beanbags cannot be thrown or tossed to the home base. Players must set each bag on the floor in the hoop.
3. No player can protect the home base or its beanbags with any defensive maneuver.
4. Beanbags may be taken from any hoop.
5. When signaled to stop, every player must freeze immediately and release any beanbags in possession. Any follow-through of activities to get a better score is penalized.

Chain Tag

SUPPLIES: None

SKILLS: Running, dodging

FORMATION:

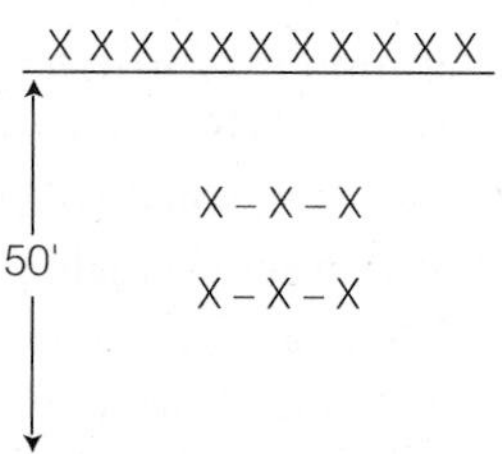

Mark two parallel lines at opposite ends of the playing area. Two groups of three players form a chain with joined hands and occupy the center. The players with free hands on either end of the chain do the tagging. All other players line up on one of the parallel lines. The center players call, "Come on over,"

and children cross from one line to the other. The chains try to tag the runners. Anyone caught joins the chain. When the chain grows to six players, it divides into two groups of three players.

VARIATION: **Catch of Fish.** The chain catches runners by surrounding them like a fishing net. The runners cannot run under or through the links of the net.

Circle Touch

SUPPLIES: Yarn balls, marking spots

SKILLS: Dodging, body management

FORMATION:

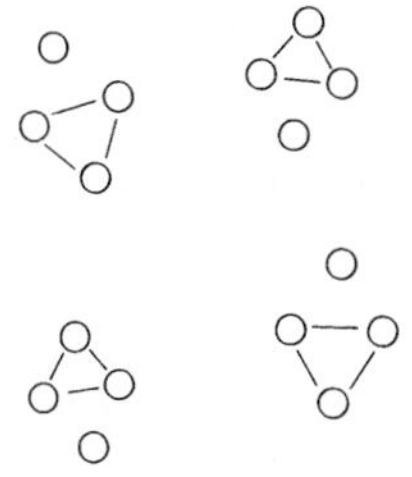

One child plays against three others, who form a small circle with joined hands. The object of the game is for the lone child to touch a designated child (on the shoulders) in the circle with a yarn ball. The other two children in the circle, by moving side to side, try to keep the tagger away from the third member of the circle. The circle players may circle in any direction but must not release hand grips. The circle cannot move across the floor; they must circle back and forth around a marking spot. The tagger, in trying to touch the protected circle player, must go around the outside of the circle. He cannot go underneath or through the joined hands of the circle players. To avoid roughness, play the game in short, 7-second bouts and then rotate in a new tagger.

VARIATION: **Grab the Flag.** A piece of cloth, a handkerchief, or a flag is tucked into the belt in back of the protected child. The fourth child, the tagger, tries to pull the flag from the belt.

Clean-Up

SUPPLIES: Volleyball net or magic rope, fleece balls, and/or foam balls

SKILL: Throwing

FORMATION: Scattered in two large groups

Use a volleyball net to divide the gym in half, and place one team on each side of the net. Scatter many fleece balls around each side of the gym (the more balls the better). On signal, students begin throwing balls over the net one at a time. After throwing one ball, students quickly find another ball and throw it over the net. This process continues until the game is stopped. The team with the fewest balls on their side of the gym is the winner.

VARIATION: Track scoring individually, awarding children 1 point for each ball they throw over the net. Balls that hit the back wall are worth 2 points.

Fast Pass

SUPPLIES: One 8-inch foam rubber ball, pinnies

SKILLS: Passing, catching, moving to an open area

FORMATION: Scattered

One team begins with the ball. The object is to make five consecutive passes without letting the ball touch the floor. The team without the ball tries to intercept it or recover an incomplete pass. Each time a pass is caught, that team shouts the number of consecutive passes completed. Each time a ball touches the floor or is intercepted, the count starts over.

Players may not contact each other. Emphasize spreading out and using the entire court area. If players do not spread out, break the area into quadrants and restrict players to one quadrant.

Flag Chase

SUPPLIES: Flags, stopwatch

SKILLS: Running, dodging

FORMATION: Scattered

One team wears flags tucked in the back of the belt. The flag team scatters throughout the area. On signal, the chasing team tries to capture as many flags as possible in a specific amount of time. Players give the flags to the teacher or place them in a box. Players cannot use their hands to ward off a chaser. Roles are reversed. The team pulling the most flags is the winner.

Galactic Empire and Rebels

SUPPLIES: None

SKILLS: Chasing, fleeing, dodging

COURT MARKINGS:

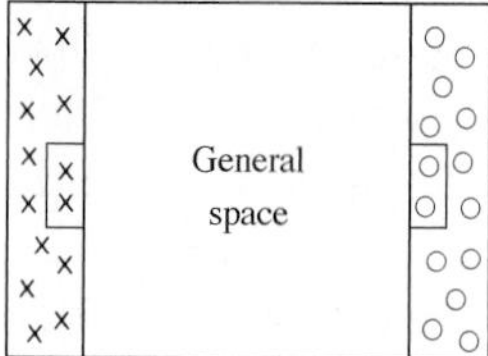

This game can be played indoors or outdoors in a square that is about 100 feet on each side. Each team's spaceport is behind the endline, where the single space fighters are stationed, waiting to emerge against the enemy. To begin, one or more space fighters from either team move from their spaceport to entice enemy flyers for possible capture. A flyer leaving the spaceport may capture only opposing flyers who previously have left their respective spaceport. This is the basic rule of the game. A flyer may go back to her spaceport and be eligible immediately to emerge again to capture an opponent who was already in general space. The technique of the game is to entice enemy flyers close to the spaceport so that fellow flyers can go out and capture (tag) an opposing flyer.

Here is an example of how the game proceeds: Rebel flyer 1 moves into general space to entice Empire flyer 1 so that he can be captured. Rebel flyer 1 turns back and heads for her spaceport, chased by Empire flyer 1. Rebel flyer 2 now leaves her spaceport and tags Empire flyer 1 before the Empire flyer can tag Rebel flyer 1. The Empire flyer is now a prisoner.

A player captured by an opposing flyer goes to the tagger's prison—both captor and captive have free passage to the prison. In prison, the captives form a chain gang, holding hands and extending the prisoners' line toward their own spaceport. The last captive is always at the end of the prisoners' line with one foot in the prison. Captives can be released if a teammate can get to them without being tagged. The released prisoner (only the end one) is escorted back to her own spaceport, and both players are given free passage.

The game becomes one of capturing opposing flyers and freeing captured teammates. Flyers stepping over the sideline automatically become prisoners. Assign 1 or 2 players in the spaceport to guard the prison. Set a time limit of 10 minutes, and declare the team with the most prisoners the winner.

Guess the Leader

SUPPLIES: None

SKILLS: Body management

FORMATION:

The class forms a large circle and chooses 2 or 3 students, the guessers, to be in the middle. While the guessers have their eyes closed, a leader in the circle is chosen. After this child leads the class in an exercise, the guessers open their eyes and try to guess who the leader is. As the guessers watch the class, the leader continues to lead the class in various exercises. The guessers are watching for the student who changes first (the leader). The guessers have three chances to identify the leader. A new leader is then chosen.

Jolly Ball

SUPPLIES: A cageball 24 inches or larger (or a 36- to 48-inch pushball)

SKILL: Kicking

FORMATION:

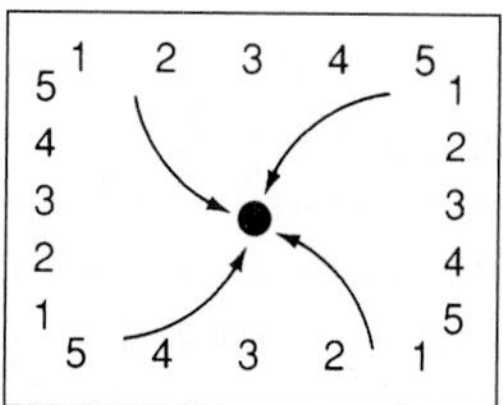

Organize four teams, each forming one side of a hollow square. Children sit down, facing in, with hands braced behind them (crab position). Consecutively number each team's members. Children wait until their number is called. Four active players (one from each team) move in crab position and try to kick the cageball over any one of the three opposing teams. Sideline players can also kick the ball. Allow players to use their hands when learning the game; later, the hands are not used.

A point is scored against a team that allows the ball to go over its line. A ball that goes out at the corner between teams is dead and must be replayed. When a point is scored, the active players return to their teams and the teacher calls another number. The team with the fewest points wins the game. This game is strenuous for the active players, so rotate them after a reasonable length of time when there is no score.

VARIATION: Call two active players from each team.

Jump-the-Shot Variations

SUPPLIES: A jump-the-shot rope

SKILL: Rope jumping

FORMATION:

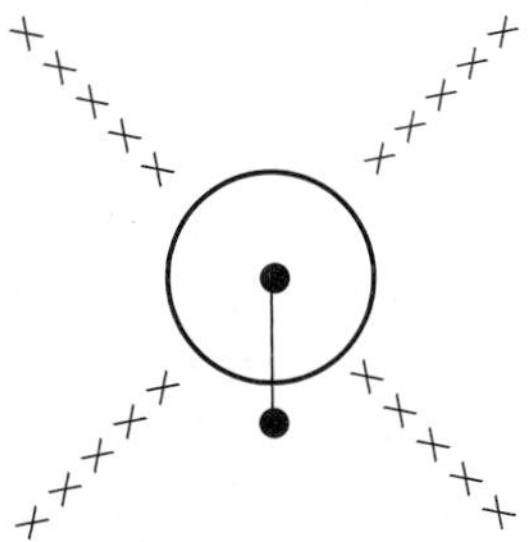

Before students try these variations, have them review the Jump-the-Shot routines and variations listed earlier (pages 558–559).

1. Two or more teams are in file formation facing the rope turner. Each player runs clockwise (against the turn of the rope), jumping the rope as often as necessary to return to the team.
2. Each player runs counterclockwise and tries to run around the circle before the rope catches up with him. If this happens, he must jump to allow the rope to go under him. The best time to start the run is just after the rope passes.
3. Players can try some stunts in which the hands and feet are on the ground, to see if they can have the rope pass under them. The Rabbit Jump, push-up position, Lame Dog, and others are possibilities.

Mushrooms

SUPPLIES: 10–16 cones, 10–16 Frisbees, fleece balls (or foam balls)

SKILL: Rolling, throwing

FORMATION: Class divided into two equal teams; scattered formation

Each team occupies half of the gym. On the endline of each half are 5 to 8 cones with a Frisbee balanced on top of the cone (to resemble mushrooms). Each team member has a foam ball. On signal, team members try to roll (or throw) their balls and knock off the Frisbees. Students may not guard the cones, and any Frisbee knocked off has to stay off, even if touched by a team's member. The game ends when all Frisbees are knocked off.

Octopus

SUPPLIES: None

SKILLS: Maneuvering, problem solving

FORMATION: Groups of 6 to 9, holding hands, tangled

This game gets its name from the many hands joined together. Children stand shoulder-to-shoulder in a tight circle. Everyone thrusts the hands forward and reaches through the group of hands to grasp the hands across the circle. Players must make sure that they do not hold both hands of the same player. Players also may not hold the hand of an adjacent player. The object is to untangle the mess created by the joined hands by going under, over, or through fellow players. No one is permitted to release a hand grip during the unraveling. What is the end result? Perhaps one large circle or two smaller connected circles.

Teaching Hint

If, after a while, the knotted hands do not seem to unravel, call a halt and administer "first aid." The teacher and group can decide where the difficulty is and allow a change in position of those hands until the knot is dissolved. This is a cooperative game that demands teamwork.

One-Base Tagball

SUPPLIES: A base (or standard), a volleyball (8-inch foam ball for younger children)

SKILLS: Running, dodging, throwing

FORMATION:

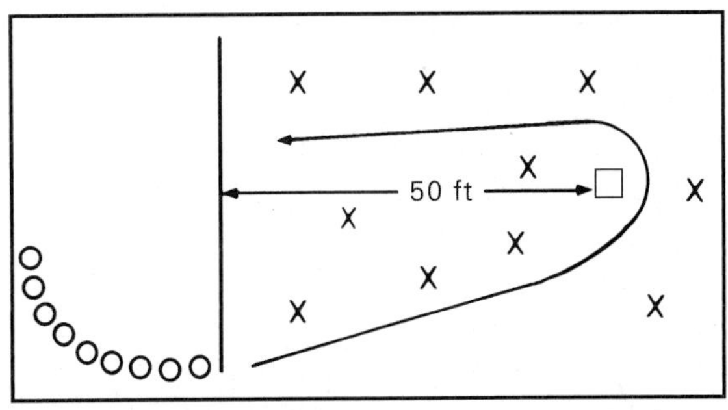

Draw a home line at one end of the playing space. Place a base or standard about 50 feet in front of the

22

home line. Use two teams, one scattered around the fielding area (whose boundaries are determined by the number of children). Have the other team form a single file behind the home line. The object of the game is for the fielding team to tag the runners with the ball. Two runners at a time try to round the base and head back for the home line without being tagged. The game is continuous—as soon as a running team player is tagged or crosses the home line, another player starts immediately.

The fielding team may run with the ball and pass it from player to player, trying to tag one of the runners. The running team scores a point for each player who runs successfully around the base and back to the home line. When the game begins, the running team has two players ready at the right side of the home line. The others on the team are in line, waiting for a turn. The teacher throws the ball anywhere in the field, and the first two runners start toward the base. They must run around the base from the right side. After all players have run, the teams exchange places. The team scoring the most points wins.

Teaching Hint

To facilitate tagging a runner, instruct the fielding team players to pass the ball to a child close to the runner. They must be alert, because two children at a time are running. The next player on the running team must watch carefully and start the instant one of the two active runners is back behind the home line or has been hit.

Over the Wall

SUPPLIES: None

SKILLS: Running, dodging

FORMATION:

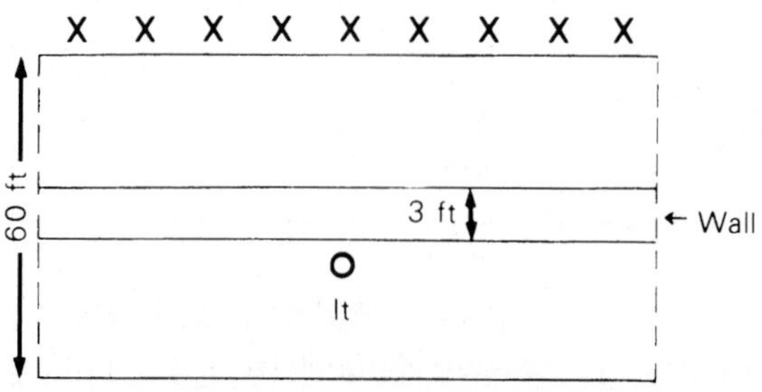

Mark off two parallel goal lines about 60 feet apart. In the middle of the game area, lay out two parallel lines about 3 feet apart. This is the wall. Two or three players are it and stand on, or behind, the wall. All other players are behind one of the goal lines. One of the taggers calls, "Over the wall." All of the players must then run across the wall to the other goal line. The taggers try to tag any crossing players. Anyone caught helps catch the others. Taggers can step on or run through the wall at will, but other players who step on the wall are caught. They must clear it with a leap or a jump and cannot step on it anywhere, including on the lines. After crossing over to the other side safely, players wait for the next call. For a more difficult game, make the wall wider.

Pacman

SUPPLIES: Markers in the shape of Pacman

SKILLS: Fleeing, reaction time

FORMATION:

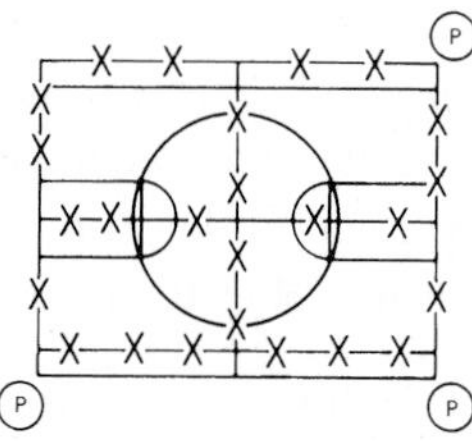

Three students are it and carry the Pacman marker. The rest of the class scatters throughout the area, standing on a floor line. Players can move only on a line. Begin the game by placing the three taggers at the corners of the perimeter lines. Play is continuous; a player who is tagged takes the marker and becomes a new tagger. If a player leaves a line to escape being tagged, that player must secure a marker and become an additional tagger. Tagbacks are not allowed—players cannot tag the person who tagged them.

Partner Dog and Cat

SUPPLIES: None

SKILLS: Chasing, fleeing, dodging

FORMATION: Partners

Partners stand toe-to-toe on a line in the center of the area. Partner A begins the game by saying

"Dog." Partner B can then say "Dog" or "Cat." If Partner B says "Cat," Partner A chases her to a designated line. If Partner A tags her, he gets a point and the game starts over.

Teaching Hint

Try varying the number of "Dogs" partners must say before they can call "Cat." Using four or five "Dogs" makes the game more enjoyable.

Pin Knockout

SUPPLIES: Many playground balls, 12 bowling pins

SKILLS: Rolling, dodging

FORMATION:

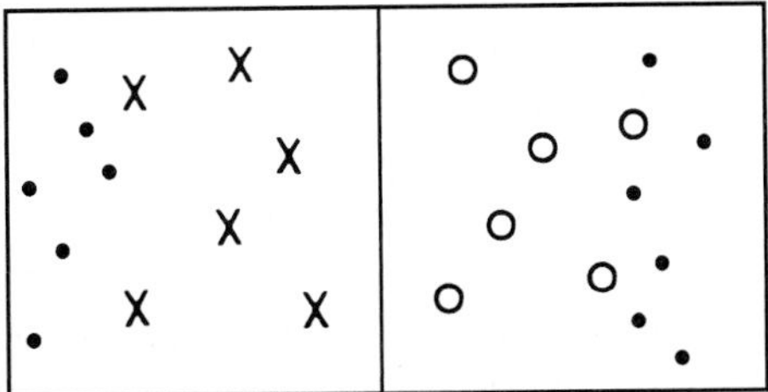

Two teams of equal number play the game on a court 30 by 60 feet or larger (its size depends on the number of players). Each team has many playground balls and six bowling pins. The object of the game is to knock down all of the opponents' bowling pins. The balls are used for rolling at the opposing team's pins. Each team stays in its half of the court.

Players are eliminated in these cases:

1. Being touched by any ball at any time, regardless of the situation (other than picking up a ball)
2. Stepping over the centerline to roll or retrieve a ball (Any opposing team member hit because of such a roll is not eliminated.)
3. Trying to block a rolling ball with a ball in their hands and being touched by the rolling ball in any way

A foul is called when a player holds a ball longer than 10 seconds without rolling it at the opposing team. Play stops, and the ball goes to the opposing team.

The bowling pins are put anywhere in the team's area. Players may guard the pins but must not touch them. When a pin is down, even if a defending team member knocked it over unintentionally, it is removed immediately from the game. The game is over when all pins on one side have been knocked down.

Right Face, Left Face (Streets and Alleys)

SUPPLIES: None

SKILLS: Running, dodging

FORMATION:

X X X X
X X X X
X X X X
X X X X

Children stand in rows, aligned from front to rear and from side to side. Two runners and two chasers are chosen. Players all face the same way and join hands with the players on either side. The chasers try to tag the runners, who run between the rows with the restriction that they cannot break through or under the arms. The teacher helps the runners by calling, "Right face" or "Left face" at various times. On command, the children drop hands, face the new direction, and join hands with the players on each side, thus making new passages available. When runners are caught or when children become tired, choose new runners and chasers.

VARIATIONS:

1. Use directions (north, south, east, west) instead of right-left commands.
2. *Streets and Alleys.* The teacher calls, "Streets" and the children face in one direction. He calls, "Alleys" and they face the other way.
3. Give the command, "Air raid" and children drop to their knees and make themselves into small balls, tucking their heads and seats down. This gives taggers and runners unlimited movement.

Scooter Kickball

SUPPLIES: A cageball, gym scooters for active players

SKILL: Striking with various body parts

FORMATION:

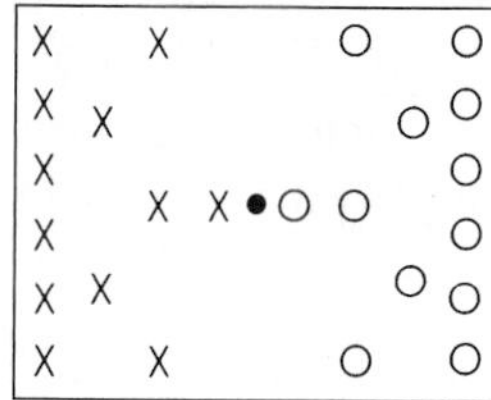

Divide each team into active players (on scooters) and goal defenders. The active players sit on the scooters, and the goal defenders sit on the goal line with feet extended. The object of the game is to kick the cageball over the goal line defended by the opposite team. The players are positioned as shown above. The game starts with a face-off of two opposing players on scooters at center court. The face-off is also used after a goal is scored. The players on scooters propel the ball mainly with their feet. Touching the ball with the hands is a foul and results in a free kick by the opposition at the spot of the foul. Players also may use the head and body to stop and propel the ball.

The goal defenders may not use their hands either; but they can use the feet, body, and head. (If scoring seems too easy, allow the defenders to use their hands.) Defenders must remain seated at the goal line and cannot enter the field of play to propel or stop the ball.

Teaching Hint

The number of scooters determines the number of active players. The game works well if half of the players from each team are in the center on scooters and the other half are goal defenders. After a goal or after a specific time, active players and goal defenders exchange places. Active players must be seated on the scooter before propelling the ball.

VARIATION: If every child has a scooter, the game can be played like soccer. Use standards to mark a more restricted goal (perhaps half of the endline). A goalie defends this area. All other players are active and can move anywhere on the floor. The area must be large enough to allow some freedom of play.

Star Wars

SUPPLIES: Four bowling pins

SKILL: Running

FORMATION:

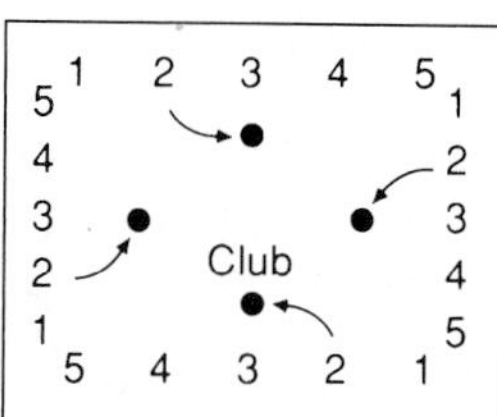

Four teams, each occupying one side facing in, form a hollow square about 10 yards on each side. Each team's members are numbered consecutively from right to left; thus, four players (one on each team) have the same number. At the center of the square, place four bowling pins, one in front of each team and spaced to keep players from colliding.

When the teacher calls their number, four children run to the right, around the outside of the square, and through their own vacated space to the center of the square. The first child to lay the team bowling pin on its side is the winner.

Keep score by using letters in the words *Star Wars.* The player who puts the pin down first gets two letters; the second player gets one. The first team to spell *Star Wars* wins and a new game begins. Since numbers are not called in order, be sure to call every number.

Strike the Pins

SUPPLIES: 8 to 12 bowling pins per team, 15 to 20 foam rubber balls

SKILL: Throwing

FORMATION:

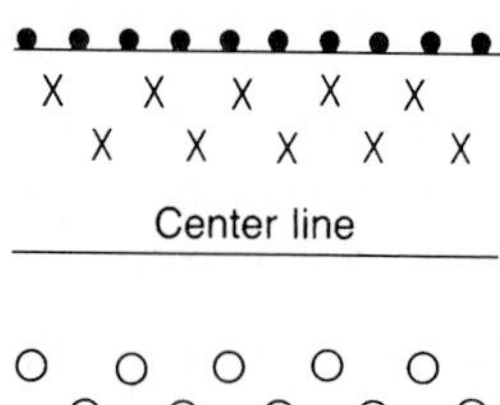

Divide the floor into two courts, each occupied by one team. Each court has another line, 25 feet from the centerline, where each team spaces its bowling

pins. Each team has at least five balls. The object of the game is to knock over the other team's pins by rolling the balls. Players roll the balls back and forth but cannot cross the centerline. Remove pins that are knocked over by a ball or player (accidentally or not). The team with the most pins standing at the end of the game is the winner. Out-of-bounds balls can be recovered but must be rolled from inside the court.

VARIATION: Pins can be reset instead of removed. Two scorers, one for each pin line, are needed.

Sunday

SUPPLIES: None

SKILLS: Running, dodging

FORMATION:

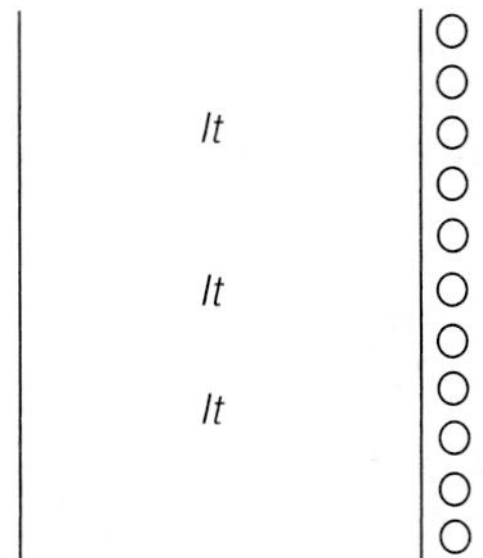

Three or more players are it and stand in the center of the area between the two parallel lines. The rest of the class is on one of the two lines. The object is to cross to the other line without being tagged or making a false start.

All line players stand with their front foot on the line. The line players must run across the line immediately when the tagger calls, "Sunday." Anyone who does not run immediately is caught. The tagger can call other days of the week to confuse the runners. Players cannot make a start if another day of the week is called.

Clearly define "making a start." To begin, define it as a player moving either foot. Later, when children get better at the game, define it as any forward movement of the body.

Touchdown

SUPPLIES: A small object (coin, thimble) that can be concealed in the hand

SKILLS: Running, dodging

FORMATION:

X | | O
X | | O
X | | O
X | | O
X | | O
X | | O
X | | O
X | | O
X | | O
X | | O
X | | O

Two teams face each other, each standing on one of the parallel lines in the playing area. One team (offensive) huddles as the members choose a player to carry an object to the opponent's goal line. The offensive team moves out of the huddle and spreads out along the line. On the signal "Hike," the offensive players move toward the opponent's goal line, each player holding the hands closed as if carrying the object. The opponents (defense) also run forward and try to tag the players. On being tagged, players must stop immediately and open both hands to show whether they have the object. If the player carrying the object reaches the goal line without being tagged, that player calls "Touchdown!" and scores 6 points. The defensive team then goes on the offense.

Triplet Stoop

SUPPLIES: Music

SKILL: Moving rhythmically

FORMATION:

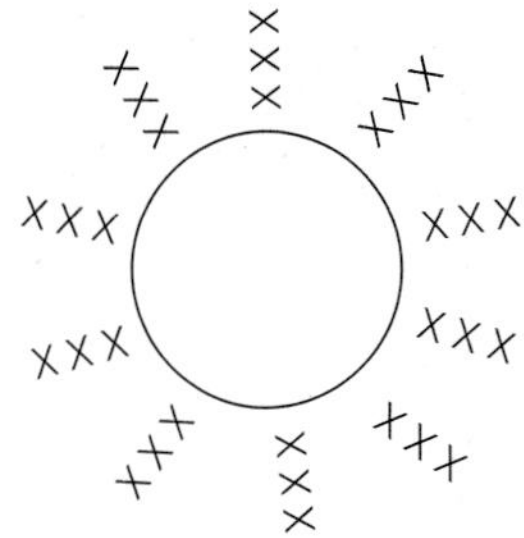

The game is played in groups of three players, who march abreast in the same direction. On signal, the outside player of the three continues marching in the same direction. The middle player stops and marches in place. The inside player reverses direction. When the music stops, the groups of three try to reunite at the spot where the middle player stopped. The last three to join hands and stoop move to the center to wait out one turn.

Whistle Ball

SUPPLIES: A ball for each group of 6 to 8 players

SKILLS: Passing, catching

FORMATION: Circles of 6 to 8

Eight or fewer children stand in circle formation. They pass a ball rapidly back and forth among them in any order. The object is to stay in the game as long as possible. A player sits down in place after making any of these errors:

1. Either holding the ball or catching it as the stop signal occurs (Signal time intervals with music on–music off, in 5- to 15-second segments.)
2. Making a poor throw, or not catching the ball after a catchable throw
3. Passing the ball back to the player who threw it

Another way to control the time intervals is to appoint a child as timer. Give her a list of the intervals, a whistle, and a stopwatch. Caution her not to indicate when she will blow the whistle. So no one sits out for too long, restart the game when 4 or 5 players are left standing.

MISCELLANEOUS PLAYGROUND GAMES

The following playground games are useful only for small groups, but children do enjoy playing them.

Four Square

(Developmental Levels II and III)

SUPPLIES: 8-inch playground ball or volleyball

SKILL: Batting a ball

COURT MARKINGS:

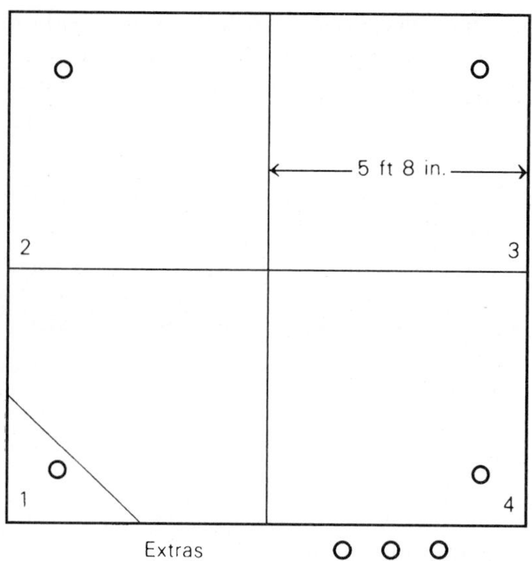

Lines are drawn as shown above. The squares are numbered 1, 2, 3, and 4. A service line is drawn diagonally across the outer corner of square 1. The player in this square always serves and must stay behind the line when serving.

Serve the ball by dropping and hitting it underhanded from the bounce. If the serve hits a line, the server is out. The server can hit the ball after it has bounced once in his square. The receiver directs it to any other square with an underhand hit. Play continues until one player fails to return the ball or commits a fault. Any of the following constitutes a fault:

1. Hitting the ball sidearm or overhand
2. Landing a ball on a line between the squares (A ball landing on an outer boundary is considered good.)
3. Stepping into another square to play the ball
4. Catching or carrying a return volley
5. Letting the ball touch any part of the body except the hands

A player who misses or commits a fault goes to the end of the waiting line, and all players move up. The player at the head of the waiting line moves into square 4.

VARIATIONS:

1. Draw a 2-foot circle at the center of the area. Hitting the ball into the circle constitutes a fault.
2. Change the game by varying the method of propelling the ball. The ball can be hit with

a partially closed fist, the back of the hand, or the elbow. A foot or knee also can be used to return the ball. The server calls, "Fisties," "Elbows," "Footsies," or "Kneesies" to set the pattern.

3. *Chain Spelling.* The server names a word, and each player returning the ball must add the next letter in the sequence.
4. For Developmental Level I students, use cooperative scoring. Players see how many consecutive hits they can make without missing.

Team Handball

SUPPLIES: Team handball, foam rubber ball, or volleyball; cones; pinnies

SKILLS: Running, dribbling, passing, throwing, catching

COURT MARKINGS:

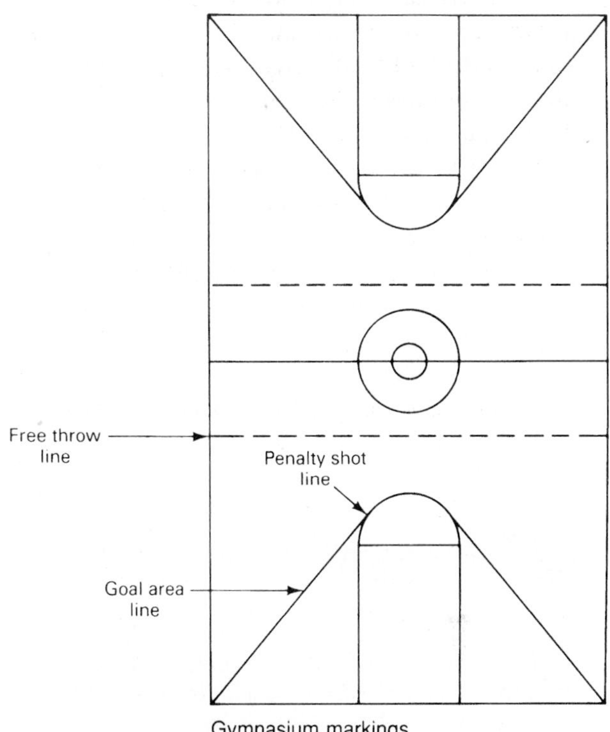

Gymnasium markings

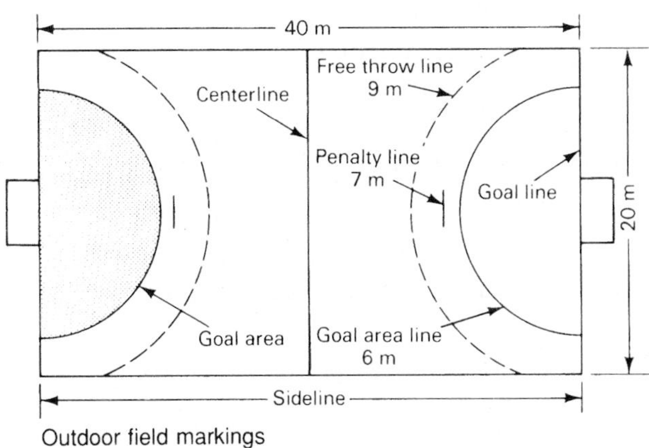

Outdoor field markings

The regulation handball court is shown above. Only the goalie occupies the goal area inside the 6-meter line. Players use the 7-meter line for a major penalty shot and the 9-meter line for a minor penalty shot. Boundary cones, tape on the wall, rope through a chain-link fence, soccer goals, or field hockey goals can be substituted for actual team handball goals. For indoor play, modify a basketball court for team handball by running a line from the corners of the court to the top of the key.

The object of the game is to move a small soccer ball down the field by passing and dribbling and then throw the ball into a goal area 3 meters wide by 2 meters high. In regulation play, each team has six court players and one goalie. The six court players cover the entire court. A player is allowed three steps before and after dribbling the ball. There is no limit on the number of dribbles. Dribbling is, however, discouraged because passing is more effective. A double dribble is a violation. Players can hold the ball for 3 seconds only before passing, dribbling, or shooting. Only the goalie can kick the ball.

One point is awarded for a goal. Violations and penalties are similar to those in basketball. Free throws are taken from the point of the violation, and defense must stay 3 meters away from that player while protecting the goal. A penalty throw is awarded from the 7-meter line for a major violation, such as fouling an offensive player who is inside the 9-meter line in a good shooting position. During a penalty throw, all players must be behind the 9-meter line.

For more in-depth coverage of rules, order a teaching resource kit from USA Team Handball, One Olympic Plaza, Colorado Springs, CO 80909 (www.usateamhandball.org).

The offensive team starts the game with a throw-on from the center line. A throw-on also starts play after each goal. All six offensive players line up at the centerline, and a teammate throws the ball to a teammate. The defense is in position, using either a zone or person-to-person defense.

Offensive strategy is similar to basketball with picks, screens, rolls, and movement to open up shots on the goal. With a zone defense, players make short, quick passes in an overloaded portion of the zone.

The defensive strategy is also similar to basketball, commonly using person-to-person and zone defense. Beginning players should start with the person-to-person defense and learn how to stay with an offensive player. In zone defense, the back players in the zone are back against the goal line, and front players are just inside the 9-meter line. The zone rotates with the ball as passes are made around the court.

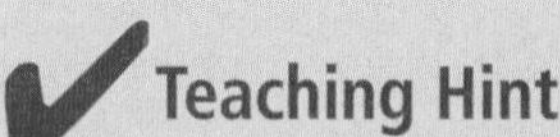

Set up learning stations for passing, shooting, goal tending, dribbling, and defensive work. Performance objectives are useful for structuring practice time at each station. Students can use nerf balls, playground balls, and volleyballs to practice goal attempts while helping goalies perfect their skills. Group drills from basketball apply to team handball defense, offense, passing, and dribbling. Include various instructional devices for targets in passing, timing for dribbling through cones, or narrowing the goal area for shots to the corners. Have students practice penalty shots. Competitive drills are enjoyable and motivating for most students.

VARIATION: **Sideline Team Handball.** Try this game when space is limited and the class is large. Extra team members spread out a long each sideline (one team on each side). These sideline players can receive passes from teammates and help pass the ball downcourt. Sideline members can only pass the ball, however, and the 3-second rule applies to them. A challenging variation might have different team members on each sideline. This distribution forces the active players to sharpen their passing skills.

Tetherball

(Developmental Levels II and III)

SUPPLIES: A tetherball assembly (pole, rope, ball)

SKILL: Batting a ball

COURT MARKINGS:

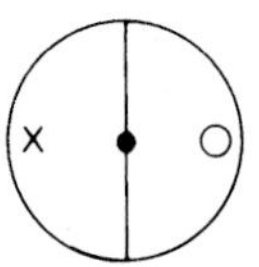

The first server is picked by lot. One player stands on each side of the pole. The server puts the ball into play by tossing it into the air and hitting in the direction he chooses. The opponent must not strike the ball on the first swing around the pole. On its second swing around the pole, she hits the ball back in the opposite direction. Each player tries to hit the ball so that the rope winds completely around the pole in the direction they are hitting the ball. The winner is the player who succeeds in doing this or whose opponent forfeits the game by making a foul. A foul is any of the following:

1. Hitting the ball with any part of the body other than the hands or forearms
2. Catching or holding the ball during play
3. Touching the pole
4. Hitting the rope with the forearms or hands
5. Throwing the ball
6. Winding the ball around the pole below the 5-foot mark

After the opening game, the winner of the preceding game serves. Winning four games wins the set.

Two Square

(Developmental Levels II and III)

SUPPLIES: A playground ball or volleyball

SKILL: Batting a ball

The basic rules and lines are the same as for Four Square, but only two squares are used. If players are waiting for a turn, the active player who misses or fouls can be eliminated as in Four Square. If only two players wish to play, they can keep score. The ball must be served from behind the baseline.

Volley Tennis

SUPPLIES: A volleyball

SKILLS: Most volleyball skills

FORMATION: Scattered

The game can be played as a combination of volleyball and tennis. The net touches the ground, as in tennis, and the ball is put into play with a serve. It may bounce once or be passed directly to a teammate. Players must hit the ball three times before sending it over the net. Spiking is common because of the low net. A point is scored when the ball cannot be returned over the net to the opposing team.

FOR MORE INFORMATION

REFERENCES AND SUGGESTED READINGS

Barbarash, L. (1997). *Multicultural games.* Champaign, IL: Human Kinetics.

Byl, J. (2004). *101 fun warm-up and cool-down games.* Champaign, IL: Human Kinetics.

Dowson, A., & Morris, K. (2005). *Fun and games 1—Sport-related activities for ages 5–16.* Champaign, IL: Human Kinetics.

Kasser, S. L. (1995). *Inclusive games: Movement fun for everyone.* Champaign, IL: Human Kinetics.

Lichtman, B. (1999). *More innovative games.* Champaign, IL: Human Kinetics.

Pangrazi, R. P., Beighle, A., & Pangrazi, D. L. (2009). *Promoting physical activity and health in the classroom.* San Francisco: Benjamin Cummings.

Stiehl, J., Morris, D., & Sinclair, C. D. (2008). *Teaching physical activity—Change, challenge, and choice.* Champaign, IL: Human Kinetics.

23 Lifetime Activities

ESSENTIAL COMPONENTS OF QUALITY PROGRAMS

- I. Organized around content standards
- II. Student-centered and developmentally appropriate
- III. Physical activity and motor skill development form the core of the program
- IV. Teaches management skills and self-discipline
- V. Promotes inclusion of all students
- VI. Focuses on process over product
- VII. Promotes lifetime personal health and wellness
- VIII. Teaches cooperation and responsibility and promotes sensitivity to diversity

NATIONAL STANDARDS FOR PHYSICAL EDUCATION**

1. Demonstrates competency in motor skills and movement patterns needed to perform a variety of physical activities.
2. Demonstrates understanding of movement concepts, principles, and tactics as they apply to the learning and performance of physical activities.
3. Participates regularly in physical activity.
4. Achieves and maintains a health-enhancing level of physical fitness.
5. Exhibits responsible personal and social behavior that respects self and others in physical activity.
6. Values physical activity for health, enjoyment, challenge, self-expression, and/or social interaction.

**National Association for Sport and Physical Education (NASPE), 2004.

Lifetime activities can be used to maintain an active lifestyle throughout the life span. Too often, curriculums are limited in scope and do not offer activities that students can use as they become adults. This chapter is designed to introduce students to various activities they can perform alone or in small groups. These activities can be played in highly competitive situations or enjoyed in recreational settings. Rather than creating outstanding performers, this chapter focuses on introducing students to activities not always found in elementary school settings.

Outcomes

- Explain why lifetime physical activities should be taught in physical education.
- Identify characteristics of lifetime physical activities.
- Discuss the importance of teaching walking in elementary schools.
- Design an orienteering course for students, and list the skills students will need to know before attempting the course.
- List a variety of racket skills and lead-up games involving rackets.
- Discuss various Frisbee activities that can be taught in elementary schools.

LIFETIME physical activities can be enjoyed throughout the life span. A primary role of physical education is to promote lifetime physical activity for all students. Thus, it is important for physical education teachers to firmly understand what is popular in other schools and in the general community (such as health clubs). When thinking of lifetime activities, most people immediately envision activities for the elderly. After all, such activities are participated in throughout life, including when elderly. Since the elderly typically engage in less intense activities, the thought process might go something like this: "An 80-year-old woman can walk for exercise; therefore, walking is a lifetime activity" or "Basketball requires large amounts of intense running, so you probably can't play if you are in your seventies; therefore, it's not a lifetime activity." Although this is logical thinking, it is not entirely accurate. Lifetime activities usually meet all or most of these criteria:

- They offer opportunity for participation at various intensities, including low and vigorous.
- They can be noncompetitive; they are enjoyable even if competition is not the focus of participation.
- They can be done alone or with a partner or teammates.
- They can contribute to the participant's overall health.

As most of us grow older, our desire and ability to engage in intense physical activity decrease. Thus, the physical activities we enjoy will change. At age 20, we may like playing football and rugby, but after age 25, we do not typically choose to play these games. In fact, we do not think of most traditional team sports as lifetime activities because they are usually quite vigorous. Further, team sports, in their purest form, do not meet the criteria of being a lifetime activity. Physical education traditionally has focused on team sports, but new data suggest that the types of activities adults participate in are not team sports. The National Sporting Goods Association (2003) reports that of the top 20 activities participated in by adults, only 2 are team sports: basketball is 10th and baseball 19th. As Table 23.1 shows, not all of the top 20 activities are appropriate for elementary children or the physical education setting. Also, the data do not suggest that these are the only activities that should be included in physical education; they are merely the most popular.

The feasibility of including physical activity in a typical day also plays a role in lifetime activity. Most adults work an 8-hour day, care for children, and run errands—leaving little time for physical activity. Those who deem physical activity important must work it into their schedules when time permits. Trying to find a group of 6 to 8 adults who can work physical activity into their schedules at the same time and on the same day is even more difficult, although it

TABLE 23.1 Top 20 physical activities for adults

1. Exercise walking
2. Camping
3. Exercising with equipment
4. Swimming
5. Bowling
6. Fishing
7. Bicycle riding
8. Billiards/Pool
9. Aerobic exercising
10. Basketball
11. Weight lifting
12. Golf
13. Hiking
14. Boating
15. Running/Jogging
16. Hunting
17. Target shooting
18. Roller skating
19. Baseball
20. Backpacking

Source: Data from *Sports Participation in 2003: Series I*, 2003, Mt. Prospect, IL: National Sporting Goods Association.

can be done. For example, at universities, small groups of faculty and staff often participate in sports during lunch. But most adults do not work on a campus that has facilities such as gyms and fields. For these scheduling and logistics reasons, most lifetime physical activities require only one or two participants.

The role of physical education is to promote lifetime physical activity for all students. Because all students have unique needs and desires, it is important to offer a variety of activities. Using the four criteria given earlier, virtually all activities, with a few modifications, qualify as lifetime activities. Thus, physical educators should teach students a variety of activities—gymnastics, rhythms, traditional sports, and lifetime activities—via a balanced curriculum.

WALKING

Walking is by far the most popular physical activity for adults (National Sporting Goods Association, 2006). It requires minimal equipment, causes few injuries, and can be enjoyed alone or in small groups. For these reasons, walking is likely the activity most physical education students will engage in as adults. Walking is an often overlooked, but important, component of any physical education curriculum designed to promote lifetime physical activity.

INSTRUCTIONAL PROCEDURES

1. Delineate the walking route with cones.
2. Emphasize appropriate posture and technique: head up, eyes forward, and smooth arm swing.
3. Check the course before student use.
4. If an outside course is used, emphasize safety.
   a. Use crosswalks.
   b. Watch for irregular sidewalks.
   c. Walk on the left, looking toward oncoming traffic.
5. During the walking lessons, emphasize the excellent health benefits gained from walking.
6. Students can participate in walking activities alone, with a partner, or in small groups. For most activities, encourage students to walk with a friend. Being able to socialize is a great motivator for children.
7. Teach "Pace, don't race." Many students will want to start out fast, even jogging, only to tire out quickly. Pacing is a difficult concept for some students to grasp and thus must be taught.
8. Avoid counting laps and having children walk in the same direction. Doing so conveys the message that winning, finishing last, and lap counting are important.
9. Let students walk in any direction they choose within the marked course.
10. Use time as the workload rather than laps. Have students walk for a set number of minutes. This helps minimize the ridicule many slower students face.
11. Some students may enjoy walking with a piece of equipment, such as a beanbag, hoop, jump rope, or basketball.
12. After the walking activity, let students choose an activity such as basketball, hopscotch, jump rope, or Four Square.

Thoroughly investigate designated walking routes to ensure that each seems entirely safe and is difficult to stray from. Are there sidewalks or wide shoulders on the road? Is it a low-traffic area? Are there aggressive dogs? Are there obvious distractions that would tempt students to stray from the route?

WALKING ACTIVITIES

Move to the Beat

PLAYING AREA: Gymnasium and/or outside teaching area

PLAYERS: Individuals

SUPPLIES: Cones, one tambourine or drum

SKILLS: Walking, pacing

Begin with students walking in general space to the beat of the drum. When the drumbeat is fast, students walk fast; when the drumbeat slows, students slow down. Next, have students walk around the perimeter (marked by cones) of the teaching area to the drumbeat (Figure 23.1). Directions such as "Take a step with each beat" help students learn to move at the correct pace.

Once students have grasped the concept of fast, medium, and slow walking, you can introduce the concept of pacing. Explain that the goal is to get from one cone to the next in a designated number of steps, reaching each cone neither before nor after the last beat, but "just in time." Give the signal "Go," and begin a steady beat; the students step in time, stopping on the designated beat. They should be right at the next cone. If not, they move to the closest cone and you begin another set of beats. Many students will take one step per beat, which may or may not be the correct pace. Some students will need time to adjust. Once students learn this pacing, you can increase or decrease the tempo. Each time, ask students, "Is this a slower beat (tempo) or a faster beat (tempo)?" Finally, take students outside on a larger walking path. It does not have to be symmetrical or on a track. Start students at different places on a path marked by cones, and repeat this activity.

FIGURE 23.1 Move to the Beat.

✔ Teaching Hint

Challenge students to move from cone to cone in a specific amount of time by using a beat per second and then ultimately removing the beat. Progressively increase the distance students move by increasing the number of cones they have to pass.

Walking Interviews

PLAYING AREA: Gymnasium or outside walking course

PLAYERS: Partners

SUPPLIES: 4- by 6-inch index cards with interview questions

SKILLS: Walking, communication, pacing

Children choose a partner. Give each set of partners an index card with a series of questions. For this activity, students simply walk with their partner and interview them using the questions provided

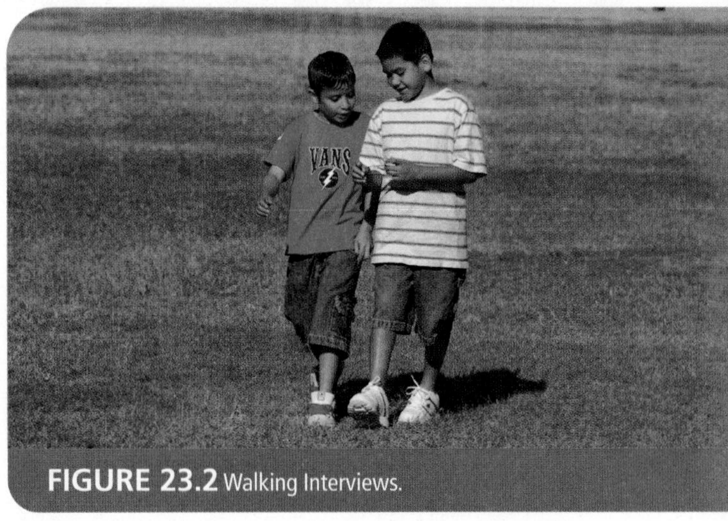

FIGURE 23.2 Walking Interviews.

(Figure 23.2). After the first partner's interview, the partners switch roles using the questions on the back side of the card. Here are some possible interview questions:

- What is your favorite physical activity? Why?
- What is your favorite movie and why?
- How many people are in your family?
- What do you usually do after school?
- What is your favorite subject in school?
- Who was your teacher last year?
- What is your favorite fruit or vegetable?

✔ Teaching Hint

Use just a few interview questions, so students can change partners often and get to know other children. Another motivating idea is to let students create their own questions.

Bank Walk

PLAYING AREA: Gymnasium or outside walking trail

PLAYERS: Individuals or partners

SUPPLIES: Cones, fake money or other tokens

SKILLS: Walking, pacing, counting money, communication

Students choose a partner and begin walking a planned route. The teacher walks the route in the opposite direction. Each time the students meet the teacher, they receive money. After a set amount of time, students then count their money. Next, they give the money back to the teacher and begin again, this time trying to beat the total they earned the first time.

To promote politeness, pay extra to students who are polite (e.g., say "please" and "thank you"). So students do not say "thank you" just to get money, keep this bonus a secret by *not* telling the class what it is for until after the lesson.

Giant Map Construction

PLAYING AREA: Gymnasium or defined teaching area

PLAYERS: Groups of 2 or 3 students

SUPPLIES: One sheet of paper and a pencil for each set of partners

SKILLS: Walking, map reading, cooperation

In an activity setting marked by cones, each set of partners maps a route they will walk together. They can use shapes, words, or letters as routes. They then walk the route with their partner. For example, a spelling word for the week may be *intensity*. Using the entire activity area as their "mapping area," the partners walk and spell out the word *intensity* from left to right.

The key to this activity is to get students to use the entire teaching area for the route they will map and walk. If pedometers are used, have students guess the number of steps it will take one or both partners to finish the route. Sets of partners can test the number of steps or amount of activity time it takes to walk the route and then swap maps with another group.

New Engineer

PLAYING AREA: Gymnasium or defined activity area

PLAYERS: Groups of 6 to 8 students

SUPPLIES: A small piece of equipment (beanbag or baton) for a group of 4 to 6 students

SKILLS: Walking, pacing

Teams of students stand in single-file and begin walking with the leader (engineer) holding the piece of equipment and leading the group throughout the teaching area. On signal, the leader hands the piece of equipment to the second person, who hands it to the third, and so on. This is all done while the line is still walking. When the equipment gets back to the last person (caboose), the caboose speed-walks to the front of the line and becomes the new engineer.

Challenge students to walk briskly. At different intervals, stop and change the makeup of the teams to provide renewed interest.

Just Walk

PLAYING AREA: Outside walking area

PLAYERS: Groups of 1 to 4 students

SUPPLIES: Cones

SKILLS: Walking, pacing

Use cones to set up a walking course. If desired, draw a map of the path directions for students. With the map, this activity is a precursor to an orienteering lesson presented later. Students can walk alone, with a partner, or in groups. The only rules are (1) they must keep moving, and (2) they must stay on the course for a predetermined time. This activity is not intended to take an entire period; 10 to 15 minutes is sufficient. It is an excellent opportunity for teachers to walk with students and get to know them as individuals.

Walking Club

Walking clubs are great for getting youth moving both in and out of school. They can be conducted before school, after school, and even during recess. This provides more opportunities for participation. After a motivating walking unit, students may be excited to start walking whenever possible. Physical educators can create school walking courses, changing them often to add excitement. Emphasize safety when starting a walking club; Figure 23.3 offers walking safety tips. Careful planning helps ensure the success of a walking club. Programs that are hastily put together tend to disappear quickly. Here are some steps for starting a walking club.

1. Envision what a walking club should look like at the elementary level.
   a. How many students will participate?
   b. What grades will be invited?
   c. When will the club meet?
   d. Who will be responsible for administering the program?
2. Discuss the possibilities and options with the principal.
3. Recruit other teachers who may be interested in co-supervising the club.
4. Develop an inclement weather plan. Most schools have hallways or a gym/cafeteria where students could walk in case of rain, snow, and the like. It is important for the club to meet even during long stretches of poor weather.
5. Create and post a schedule. The schedule will depend on the number of supervisors and participants. It may be necessary to rotate grades—with one or two participating each day—especially for before- and after-school clubs. Starting with one grade level, or even one classroom, may also help work out any problems before taking the club school-wide.
6. Advertise the club with school announcements, during physical education lessons, in a physical education newsletter to parents, and at open houses. As the first club meeting approaches, letters home inviting parents to participate will help in recruiting participants.
7. Create a system for tracking participation. Sheets can be designed to track laps or minutes of participation. Given the number of laps that equal 1 mile, students can track their progress on a map of their city, state, or country. Devise a similar system for minutes of movement. For example, 12 minutes of walking equals 1 mile. Granted, each child's pace affects this formula, but the idea is simply to get students moving.
8. Consider calling your club a "Physical Activity Club" (PAC for short), and include a variety of activities, either structured or unstructured. You can thus address the interests of a variety of students, especially those who may not enjoy walking.
9. Approach local businesses about sponsoring the club. Hosting a Family Walk-a-Thon is another great fund-raiser and public relations event for the physical education program.
10. If funds are available, buy pedometers for club use. Also purchase walking club T-shirts for all club members. Local sporting good stores may be willing to help with T-shirts.
11. Using activities from the following section, teachers and students can create challenging orienteering courses for the walking club.

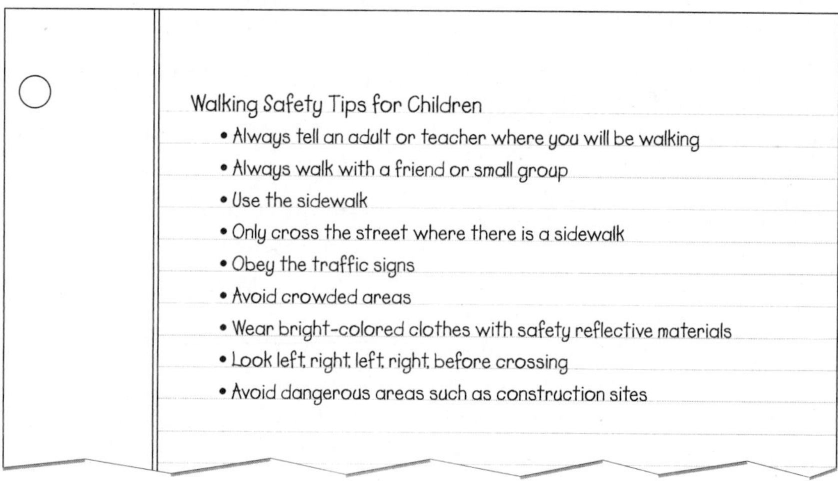

FIGURE 23.3 Walking safety tips.

ORIENTEERING

Orienteering is a navigation and sport activity that incorporates walking or jogging, determining directions, and map reading. The object of the activity is to use a map and compass to locate specific points in a given area. Competitive orienteering can involve skills such as skiing, mountain biking, compass readings, and point tracking, while navigating a wilderness course designed to test participants' skills. At the elementary level, orienteering focuses on teaching students basic concepts such as recognizing directions (north, south, east, west) and map reading. Orienteering can also be integrated with walking, Frisbee golf, challenge courses, or other activities that involve map reading. Students will actively learn the skills necessary to navigate an area such as the gymnasium, a classroom, the school, the playground, or a local park.

INSTRUCTIONAL PROCEDURES

1. Introduce map directions by placing a large N, S, E, and W on the appropriate walls.
2. Refer to the walls as the east wall or the north wall when giving directions. For example, "When I say *go*, hustle to the red line closest to the east wall."
3. To introduce directional travel, use small instructional bouts such as, "If we run from this wall (pointing to the east wall) to that wall (pointing to the west wall), what direction are we moving?" Presenting this information in a variety of lessons leading up to orienteering will help set the stage for those lessons. For example, if working on basketball passing with a partner, you might say, "When I say *go*, work on your overhead pass with one partner facing north and one facing south."
4. Introduce students to basic symbols used to designate landmarks and controls. *Controls* refer to the specific locations students are challenged to find on an orienteering course. See Figures 23.4 and 23.5 for examples of maps with symbols.
5. If pencils are needed, for safety reasons have students carry their materials (maps, pencils, etc.) in a pencil box or folder.

ORIENTEERING SKILLS

Determining Directions

Many students have difficulty with learning directions. One strategy is to mark the gym walls with *N, S, E,* and *W* to identify compass directions. This allows students to learn the relationship of each direction (e.g., when they face east, north is to the left). Another strategy is to mark landmarks on the school grounds—paint an *S* on the slide on the south side of the playground; paint or hang an *E* on the fence on the east side of the school grounds. These strategies allow teachers to teach directions inside and outside. Teach older children to determine directions by looking at the sun. The sun always rises in the east. Thus, if students are looking at the sun in the morning, west is always behind them. Another way to teach this concept is to know that in the morning, shadows point west. Next, students can transfer what they learned in the gym and know that if they face east, then north is to the left and south is to the right. Conversely, in the afternoon, when students face the sun, their shadows point east; north is to the right and south is to the left. Students will need time to process and understand this information. Since most physical education classes are at the same time each day, students can learn one method before going on to another.

Reading a Map

Most classrooms have maps and globes that help students understand the idea of map reading. Reading a map involves determining landmarks and directions. For elementary students in a gym, this could be recognizing symbols such as doors, the clock, or posters on a wall when shown a map of the gym. Figure 23.4 shows a gymnasium map with symbols. Students will ultimately read the map to find specific locations called *controls*.

Before reading a map, students must orient it. This involves turning the map until it matches what the students are facing in the gym. For example, using Figure 23.4, students may be standing in the southeast corner of the gym facing the side door on the west wall. They would then turn the map until the southeast corner of the gym on the map is closest to them and the west wall is farthest away. Teachers can give instruction such as "Standing where you are, orient your map to the clock." Students can also learn to keep their thumb where they are on the map and move their thumb as they move. This is called *thumbing*.

ORIENTEERING ACTIVITIES

Gymnasium Orienteering

PLAYING AREA: Gymnasium or designated teaching area

PLAYERS: Individuals, partners, or small groups (3 or 4 students)

SUPPLIES: Map of the gymnasium, cones, poly spots

SKILLS: Map reading, problem solving, cooperation

Because orienteering is likely a new activity for most students, it is best to begin map reading and learning to find controls in a controlled environment like the gym. It is also important to introduce concepts like map reading and compass

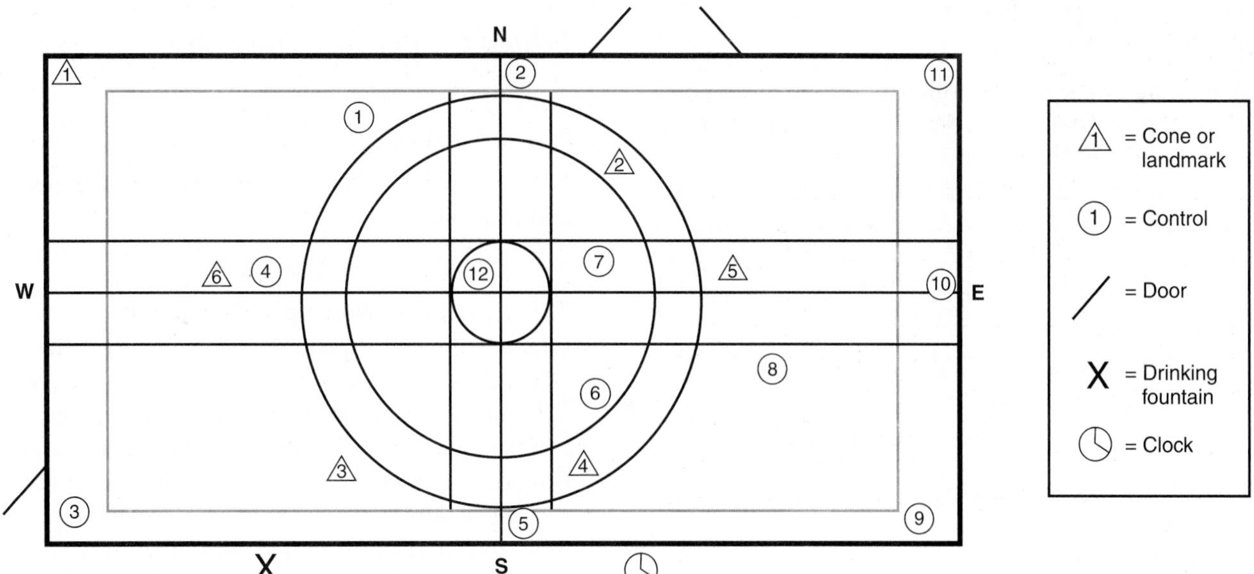

FIGURE 23.4 Gymnasium orienteering map.

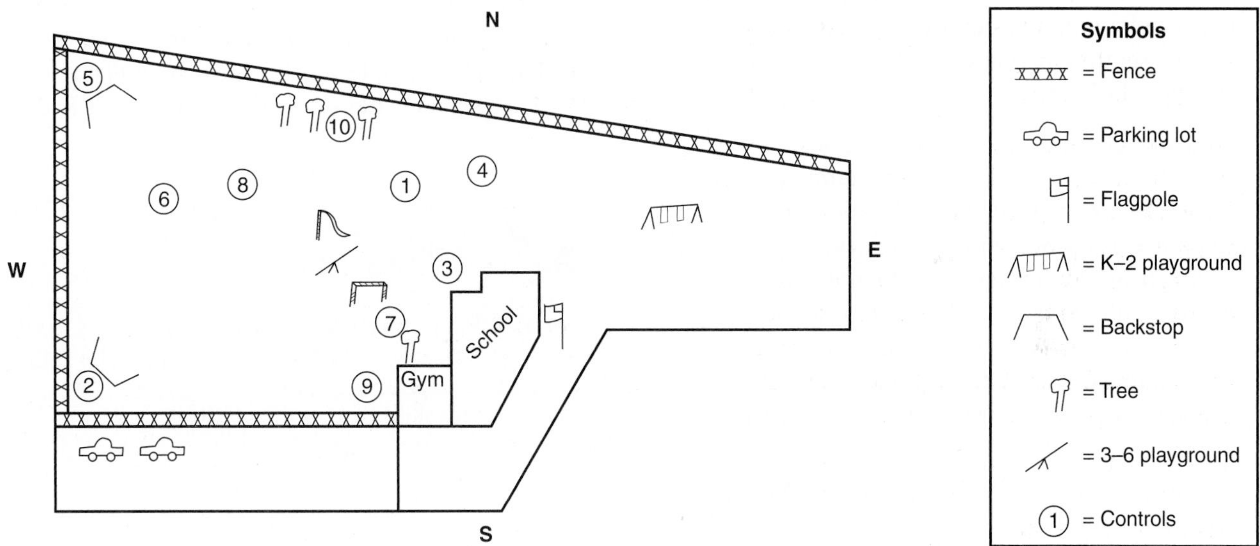

FIGURE 23.5 School grounds orienteering map.

directions in short pieces leading up to orienteering activities. For example, when teaching circuit training, give students a simple map of the stations and ask them to find their stations when prompted. Or, use poster board and draw a large map that students can see from a distance. This activity introduces students to map reading while searching for controls. These steps will aid in planning this activity.

1. Get a drawing of the gym and lay out an orienteering course on paper (see Figure 23.4). Be sure to mark *N*, *S*, *E*, and *W* on the map. Figure 23.4 uses numbered circles to designate control points and numbered triangles to designate cones or landmarks. If a gym has few landmarks, add some numbered cones. Poly spots (also numbered) represent controls.
2. Next develop a set of instructions (Figure 23.6 on page 584) that students will follow to get to the next control point. Print each set of instructions, cut it into individual instructions, and tape each one to the appropriate control marker or poly spot (e.g., tape instructions for finding control number 2 on control number 1).
3. After writing the instructions, use the map to walk through them and ensure they are accurate.

At Control:	Instructions:
1	Move directly east to find Control 2.
2	To find Control 3, go to the southwest corner of the gym.
3	Control 4 is close to Landmark 6.
4	Find Control 5 in the middle of the south wall.
5	Control 6 is just north of Landmark 4.
6	To find Control 7, walk directly north of Control 6.
7	You will find Control 8 directly south of Landmark 5.
8	Control 9 is in the southeast corner of the gym.
9	Walk directly north of Control 9 to find Control 10.
10	To find Control 11, go to the northeast corner of the gym.
11	Control 12 is in the middle of the gym.
12	Control 1 can be found by walking northwest from Control 12.

FIGURE 23.6 Gym orienteering instructions.

4. On the day of instruction, be sure to have the correct number of cones with numbers on them and the correct number of poly spots, or controls, with numbers on them. Using the map, set the cones and control points in their proper locations.

Divide the class into teams. Give each team a map and instruct them to report to any numbered control. Review concepts that have been taught leading up to this lesson. For example, ask, "If I am walking from the south wall to the north wall, in what direction am I traveling?" A refresher on map orienting may also be helpful. Signal the teams to begin, following the instructions at their control. This way, all teams are searching for a different control.

Teaching Hints

1. To add difficulty, remove the control numbers from the map. This forces students to use the directions on the control and the map, rather than just the map.
2. At each control, place a pencil box. After finding each control and before moving on to the next, students draw a line from the previous control to the current one. With some extra planning, these lines could form an object, make a letter, or spell a short word.
3. Each control also could present a trivia question, a skill to perform, or a fitness challenge. Orienteering is thus integrated with other physical education lessons.

School Grounds Orienteering

PLAYING AREA: School grounds

PLAYERS: Individuals or groups of 2 to 4 students

SUPPLIES: Map of school grounds with landmarks and controls

SKILLS: Map reading, cooperation

This activity is a follow-up to Gymnasium Orienteering, so the planning process is identical. Depending on students' familiarity with finding *N*, *S*, *E*, and *W* outside, the instructions may change. For example, instead of reading, "Move northwest from control number 7 to find control number 8," the instruction may say, "From control number 7, move toward the slide to find control number 8." Figure 23.5 on page 583 is an example of a school grounds orienteering map. Notice that the teacher can see all controls—and thus all students—from anywhere on the grounds. Before starting this activity, give students instructions about the area they will use. For example, if using the map in Figure 23.5, tell students there are no controls on the K–2 playground or in front of the school.

Teaching Hint

For additional challenge, remove the numbers from each control. Just as with Gymnasium Orienteering, students will have to use the instructions and their map-reading skills to find the controls.

Scavenger Hunt

PLAYING AREA: Entire gymnasium or designated teaching area

PLAYERS: Individuals, partners, or small groups of 3 to 4

SUPPLIES: An orienteering map, instructions, an envelope for each control, a clue for each control

SKILLS: Map reading, problem solving

Devise an orienteering course similar to those shown earlier. This activity is taught and participated in like an orienteering course; but at each control, students find a clue that is part of a series to be collected at each control. At the end of the course, each team uses the clues to solve the puzzle. Here are some possible puzzles to be solved.

- At each control, students collect an index card with a single letter. Together, the letters spell out O-R-I-E-N-T-E-E-R-I-N-G.
- Paste a picture onto stiff paper and cut it into the same number of pieces as there are controls. At each control, teams collect a piece of the puzzle that they will assemble into a picture after completing the course.
- At each control, students find an index card bearing one word. When put together, the words form a question such as, "What is an important part of a healthy lifestyle?" for teams to answer. Each team will probably come up with a different answer, such as "physical activity," "a balanced diet," or "not smoking."
- On separate index cards, print the letters used in two or three of a class's spelling words. Students must then unscramble the letters to spell the words. This is an excellent way to reinforce classroom content without sacrificing physical education objectives.

TENNIS

Tennis is a popular activity worldwide. Because it can be played at varying levels and intensities, it is a lifetime activity that many older adults enjoy. Tennis is played on a regulation court (Figure 23.7) with concrete, grass, clay, or synthetic flooring. At the elementary level, most students have not experienced many racket activities and have only basic skills. Thus, the role of physical education is to present modified activities that expose students to using a tennis racket to strike the ball. Such activities allow children to explore the game of tennis and give them a chance to successfully use a racket. Practice in tennis should move from individual to partners as quickly as is feasible.

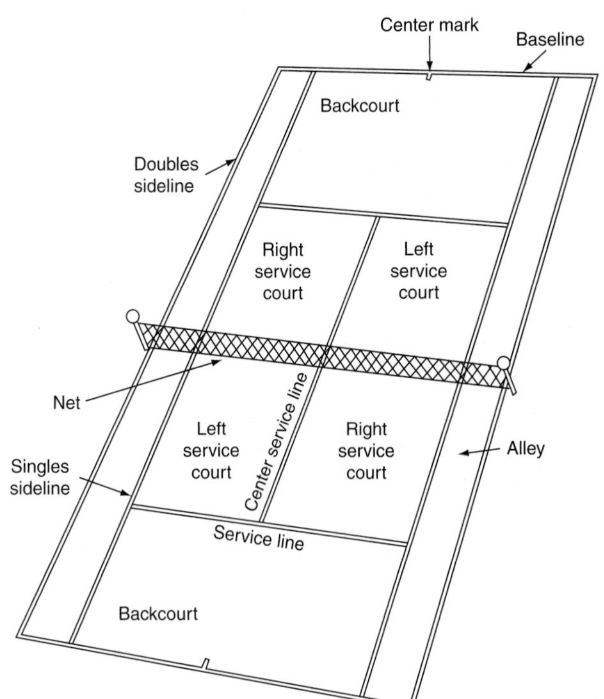

FIGURE 23.7 Regulation tennis court.

TENNIS SKILLS

Grip

An easy method for teaching the grip is to have the student hold the paddle perpendicular to the floor and "shake hands" with it (Figure 23.8). Young people tend to revert to the inefficient hammer grip, so named because it is similar to the grip used on a hammer. Students should practice picking up their racket using a handshake grip. Spinning the racket and stopping in a handshake grip is excellent practice.

FIGURE 23.8 Handshake grip.

Ready Position

Getting ready to hit is the first step to successful tennis strokes. This skill is often overlooked because it is usually missed by spectators who are watching the other player hit the ball. Preparing to hit involves being in a solid athletic position with heels slightly raised (just enough to get a piece of paper under the heels) and ready to move. The racket is gripped in the handshake grip with the other hand just below the strings. This position enables students to move quickly to the ball. Use these instructional cues to aid skill development:

1. Athletic position.
2. Paper under your heels.
3. Racket in front.
4. Little jump.

Forehand

The forehand shot is the most frequently used tennis shot and the easiest for most people to learn. For this reason, many students will want to make every shot a forehand. Be sure to encourage students to try other shots as their skills improve. For the forehand stroke, the body is turned sideways; for a right-handed player, the left side points in the direction of the hit. Contact is made slightly before the ball reaches the body. Instructional cues for a proper forehand shot follow.

1. Ready position.
2. Opposite side to target.
3. Racket back.
4. Watch the ball.
5. Step and swing through the ball with a stiff wrist.
6. Ready position.

Backhand

The backhand is a more difficult stroke to learn than the forehand. Forehand resembles other motions students often perform, such as throwing and swinging a baseball bat, but backhand is just the opposite. It thus feels unnatural and must be practiced before it feels comfortable. For the backhand stroke, the thumb is placed against the racket handle for added support and force, and the body turns sideways so the shoulder on the side of the racket hand points in the direction of the stroke. The racket strikes the ball even with, or slightly before, it reaches the front leg (Figure 23.9).

1. Ready position.
2. Same side to target.
3. Both hands back.
4. Watch the ball.
5. Step and swing through the ball.
6. Follow through high.
7. Ready position.

Serve

The serve is a difficult skill for children to perform accurately. When teaching serving, begin by allowing any serve that crosses the net to be played, regardless of location. With beginners, the goal of playing activities is to maximize repetitions and refinement. Instruct your students to put the ball into play with a bounce and forehand or backhand stroke.

Volley

A volley is made with a sort of punch stroke. The hitter faces in the direction of the hit, pushing the racket forward rather than stroking. In modified courts and activities, children often use this stroke. For many, it is their primary stroke. Provide these skill cues to help develop the volley:

1. Ready position.
2. Step and push the racket toward the ball.
3. Back to ready position.

INDIVIDUAL TENNIS DRILLS

Racket Spin

Stand the racket on its frame with the grip up. On signal, spin the racket like a top; quickly grab and turn it until it is in a handshake grip.

Racket Roll

All students place a ball on their racket. On signal, they begin rolling the ball around the racket while sitting, standing, or walking. The challenge is for the ball to touch every hole on the racket. After a short time, have students let the ball bounce off the floor

FIGURE 23.9 Tennis backhand sequence.

once and catch it on the other side of the racket. If the ball falls, they simply catch it, turn the racket over so the other side of the hand is up, and place the ball on the racket.

Bounce-Downs

In scattered formation, each child has a racket and a tennis ball. They use the racket to dribble the ball on the ground, trying to bounce the ball waist high. This is similar to dribbling a basketball with a tennis racket. Instruct students to switch hands periodically. Bouncing the ball and catching can also be allowed.

Bounce-Ups

As the name suggests, this activity is the opposite of bounce-downs. Each student has a ball and bounces the ball into the air. Instruct students to keep the ball "eye high." After a short time, students switch hands. Challenge students to bounce the ball up several times and then catch the ball on their racket.

Edgies

In scattered formation, each child has a ball and racket. On signal, they begin bouncing the ball, either up or down, using the edge of the racket. Encourage them to switch hands and try using different edges of the racket.

Flip-Flops

Every student starts with a racket and a ball in scattered formation. Using bounce-ups, students rally the ball with alternating sides of the racket. Notice the positioning of the hand in Figures 23.10 and 23.11. If necessary, the ball can bounce on the floor. Instruct students to switch hands often.

Invent-a-Bounce

Once players are comfortable with basic bouncing, encourage them to invent different ways of bouncing the ball. First offer some examples such as around the back, under the leg, using the handle, or balancing on one foot. To modify an activity, students develop a dribbling routine such as two bounce-downs, two bounce-ups, two edgies, and two flip-flops.

FIGURE 23.10 Tennis flip.

FIGURE 23.11 Tennis flop.

Racket Stunts

Each student has a ball and racket. When instructed, they hit the ball into the air and try to touch the floor—or do a heel click, clap their hands, or turn around—before the ball hits the floor. Emphasize controlled rackets and bounces. For this activity, students can use beanbags rather than balls. If they use balls, once the ball hits the floor, have students try to absorb the force of the bounce by dribbling the ball back down until it is rolling on the racket. Once the ball is rolling, have them try another stunt.

Self-Rally

With a ball and racket, students try to rally the ball for as many times as possible. Bounce-ups, bounce-downs, edgies, and flip-flops can be used. Students can also choose if they want to allow a bounce. The primary goal is for students to develop personal challenges and try to better previous self-rally scores.

Pick It Up

All students start with the racket in hand and the ball on the floor. The challenge is to get the ball on the racket without touching it with the other hand. One strategy is to scoop up the ball with the racket. An easier alternative is to get the ball rolling by tapping it with the racket and then scooping it up. Students may also choose to trap the ball between the outside of their foot and the racket. They then lift the foot and racket, raising the ball to a level where it can be dropped. The ball then bounces, and they try to balance it on the racket. Lastly, students can start dribbling the ball, gradually bouncing it higher and higher. They can then catch the ball on the racket by placing the racket under the ball and "giving" with the knees as the ball touches the racket.

Wall Rally

Introducing the forehand and backhand by using Wall Rally allows students many repetitions. Standing with their opposite side to the wall, students bounce the ball with their "other" hand and lightly tap the ball to the wall. Stop the class periodically to introduce the next cue. You might say, "If you want to continue working on bringing your racket back, that's great. If you are ready, go ahead and work on stepping toward the wall when you hit the ball. Remember, watch the ball. Go."

Wall Rally can be used to teach every tennis stroke, with instruction progressing to students counting the number of times they can rally the ball without missing. Emphasize a controlled, soft racket.

PARTNER TENNIS DRILLS

Racket Grab

Partners stand about 3 feet apart with their racket on its frame with the grip standing up. On signal, partners let go of their racket and move forward toward their partner's racket. The goal is to grab the partner's racket before it hits the ground and quickly take a handshake grip. With each success, partners take one step back.

Partner Toss

One partner has a racket, and the other partner stands about 8 feet away with the ball. The partner with the racket takes the ready position. The partner with the ball lightly tosses the ball to the other partner's forehand side. The racket partner quickly turns with the opposite side to the target and lightly hits the ball back to the partner. Be sure to emphasize the importance of the toss. After five hits, partners switch roles. Challenge each pair of partners to see how many times they can execute a toss to the forehand side followed by a correct forehand hit. This activity can be used for backhand and volley strokes as well. As the students' skills progress, increase the distance and use a line in the area as the net.

Partner Rally

Players are paired up, each with a racket and one ball. The partner with the ball bounces it and hits a forehand or backhand shot. After striking the ball, that player returns to the ready position. Meanwhile, the receiving partner moves from the ready position to a striking position and hits a forehand or backhand shot. This activity teaches players to return to ready position after stroking the ball. To increase the challenge, have students find a line on the floor and use it as a net.

Step Back

This drill is like Partner Rally, with one exception. For every four consecutive hits, each player takes one step back. Be sure all students are in a formation that allows them to step back without getting in the others' way. Figure 23.12 shows where partners might be during a Step Back game.

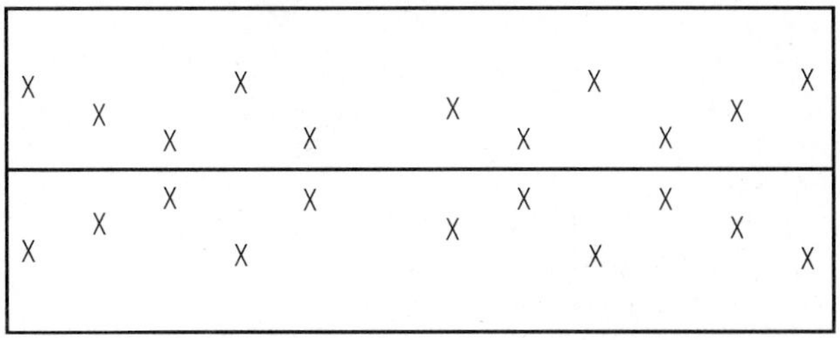

FIGURE 23.12 Step Back formation. Partners are across the line from each other and are the same distance from the line.

Juggle Rally

Each set of partners has two rackets and one ball. The partner with the ball starts the rally with two individual drills. This could be two bounce-downs, or an edgie and a bounce-up. After the two hits, the third hit is to her partner. The partner then receives the ball with one hit, executes another individual activity, and then hits it back to his partner. Children may choose to use floor bounces, the wall, or any other creative idea. The only rule is to hit the ball three times during each rally.

Toss and Catch

Partners stand about 8 feet apart, one with a racket and one with a ball. The partner with the ball tosses the ball to the partner with the racket, who uses his hand and racket to catch the ball against the racket strings. He then tosses the ball back to the tosser, and they repeat the drill. The object of this activity is to teach students to move to the ball. The tosser attempts to move the catcher forward, backward, left, and right.

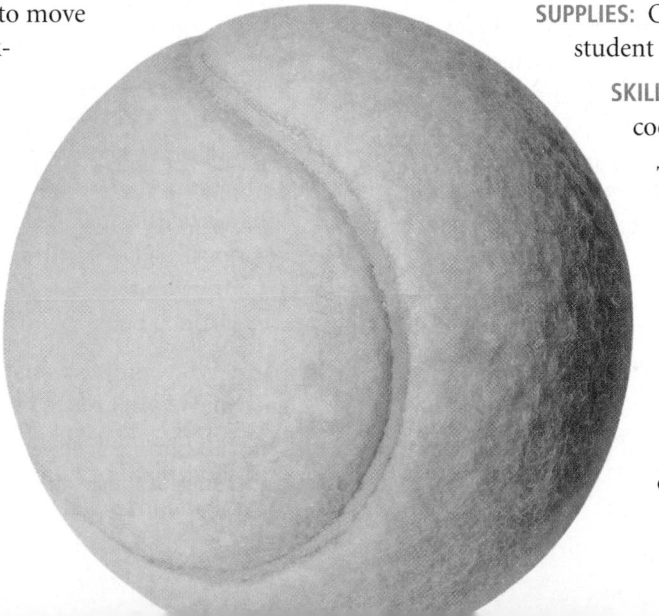

Toss, Hit, Catch

One partner starts with a ball and the other with a racket. The partner with the ball tosses the ball to the partner with the racket, who hits it back; the tosser then tries to catch the ball. As a variation, the tosser can have a racket and try to trap the ball against the racket with the nondominant hand. The game can also be changed to Hit, Hit, Catch, or ultimately Hit, Hit, Hit, which is essentially a tennis rally.

TENNIS ACTIVITIES

Racket Roll Tag

PLAYING AREA: Gymnasium or specified playing area

PLAYERS: Entire class

SUPPLIES: One racket and ball per student

SKILLS: Racket awareness, dodging, fleeing

Every player has a racket with a ball balanced on it. Designate 2 to 4 students as taggers. All players must move with the ball balanced on their racket. If tagged by a tagger, that person becomes "it," and the previous tagger is no longer it. If the ball falls off, the child quickly grabs the ball, places it on the racket, and continues. The tagger's ball must be on his or her racket when tagging someone. Before beginning, define how students may be tagged (e.g., only tapped on the shoulder with the hand not holding the racket). Stop and start the game often to keep students from getting frustrated if they cannot tag someone or if they keep getting tagged.

Racket Red Light

PLAYING AREA: Gymnasium or specified playing area

PLAYERS: Entire class

SUPPLIES: One racket and ball per student

SKILLS: Racket awareness, cooperation

This game is played like regular Red Light (see page 546), with two twists. The traffic controller holds a red piece of paper and a green piece of paper. Rather than yell "red light" to stop students' movement or "green light" to start

them, the controller holds up the red or green paper. This forces students to keep their eyes up and not focused on the ball. If this is too challenging, use the traditional method of calling out commands. Also, all players must have their ball balanced on their racket. If the ball falls off, they must return to the starting line. As in the original game, the first person to reach the line the traffic controller is standing on becomes the traffic controller. Another variationis to command left turn, right turn, and caution.

Wall Rally

PLAYING AREA: Gymnasium or playing area with wall sections of 5 to 6 feet for each group

PLAYERS: Groups of 2 to 4 students

SUPPLIES: One racket per child, one ball for each group, masking tape to mark off wall space

SKILLS: Forehand, backhand, court movement

Assign each group to a section of wall designated with tape. For this activity, students in all teams on the court are working together to see how many times they can consecutively rally without the ball being called dead. One player puts the ball in play by bouncing it and hitting a forehand or backhand (Figure 23.13). After the ball hits the wall, the second player must return the ball to the same section. However, there is no limit to the number of hits or the number of bounces allowed before the ball is hit back to the wall. Encourage students to hit it back after the first bounce. To keep the rally going, allow even rolls. Each team's players must also maintain the order in which they hit the ball to the wall (first player, second player, third player, etc.). However, remind players that they are all a team and can help each other. For example, Player 1 hits the ball off the wall and Player 2 is unable to reach it, but Player 3 can. Player 3 can stop the ball with his racket and set it up for Player 2. The only thing Player 3 cannot do is hit it to the wall until after Player 2 does. The rally is over if:

1. The ball stops rolling.
2. The ball is hit toward the wall and is not between the tape lines.
3. The ball is hit to the wall but not in the correct order of players.

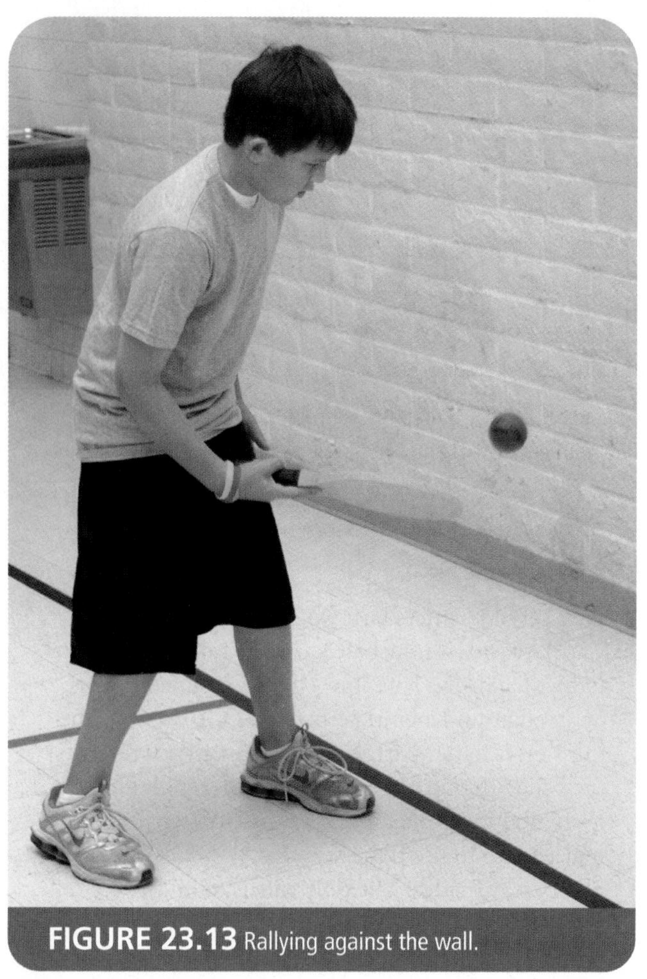

FIGURE 23.13 Rallying against the wall.

One-Wall Tennis

PLAYING AREA: Gymnasium or playing area with wall sections of 5 to 6 feet for every group (Figure 23.14)

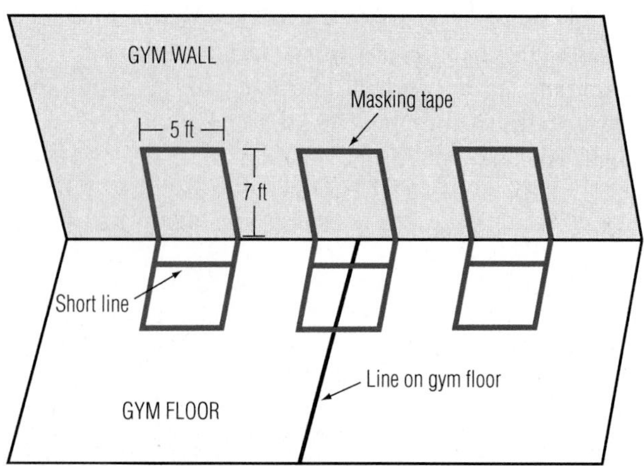

FIGURE 23.14 One-Wall Tennis setup.

PLAYERS: Groups of 2 to 4 students

SUPPLIES: One racket per child, one ball for each group, masking tape to mark off wall space

SKILLS: Forehand, backhand, score keeping, court movement

Player 1 serves the ball to the wall. The ball must hit the wall and come off the wall past the short line. The short line is 3 feet from the wall. Player 2 then must return the ball to the wall before it bounces twice and before her third hit. Thus, after Player 1 hits it off the wall, Player 2 can let it bounce once, hit it in the air, let it bounce again, and then hit it to the wall. Emphasize using short strokes. Do not allow spiking and hitting the ball downward. Score points as follows:

- If the ball bounces more than twice before being returned to the wall.
- If the ball is hit more than twice before returning to the wall.
- If the ball hits the wall, but not in the space designated by tape.
- If the ball hits the wall, but does not come back past the short line.

Tennis Volleyball

PLAYING AREA: Volleyball court

PLAYERS: Two teams of 8 to 10 students

SUPPLIES: One training ball, one racket per child, a net

SKILLS: Forehand, backhand, volley, score keeping

A Team 1 player puts the ball in play by hitting it to Team 2's half of the court. After the ball hits the floor on Team 2's side, all Team 2 players can hit the ball. They can hit the ball to their teammates or directly over the net to Team 1's side. Teams can hit the ball any number of times before hitting it back over the net. The opposing team scores a point each time the ball is not hit back to them. Bounces are unlimited, but a rolling ball is considered dead. No boundaries, other than the net, are used. Students play to 11 points and then start over. As in most games, frequently change the makeup of teams.

Tennis over the Line

PLAYING AREA: Teaching area divided into 5- by 10-foot squares with masking tape

PLAYERS: Partners

SUPPLIES: One training ball, one racket for each student, one line, strips of masking tape

SKILLS: Forehand, backhand, volley

Before class, mark off the teaching area using masking tape and existing lines to create two 5-feet squares with a common middle line. One child stands in one square and her opponent stands in the other. The game is a combination of two square and tennis. Only underhand shots are permitted. Player 1 puts the ball in play by dropping the ball and hitting a forehand or backhand off of the bounce into Player 2's square. Before the ball bounces twice, Player 1 must return the ball, again using only an underhand stroke, to Player 2's square. If a player cannot return the ball into her opponent's square or does not hit the ball before it bounces twice, her opponent scores 1 point. Player 1 serves five times in a row, regardless of scoring, and then Player 2 serves.

USA School Tennis

PLAYING AREA: Gymnasium divided so there is one court per 6 students

PLAYERS: 3 students per team

SUPPLIES: One racket per student; one training ball per group of 6; tumbling mats, stretched magic rope or other equipment to use as a net for each court (Figure 23.15 on page 592)

SKILLS: Forehand, backhand, volley, score keeping

This is a team game of tennis with no more than three players on a side. The focus of the game is controlled swings. All balls must move upward when leaving the racket, and no spiking is allowed. Again, racket control is important. Each game is played to 5 points, by ones. Scoring is as follows:

- If the ball rolls, it is dead; the other team scores.
- If the first bounce after the ball crosses the net is out-of-bounds, the other team scores.
- If the ball is spiked, the other team scores.

Start play with a drop serve—one player drops the ball and hits a forehand or backhand over the net. If players are having difficulty with spacing and staying in their own area, divide the halves of the court into three equal areas, and instruct all players to stay in their area. Teams can hit the ball any number of times before sending it back to the other side. Similarly, bounces are unlimited. A modification of the game allows a rolling ball to be in play. This requires students to scoop the ball up and continue play.

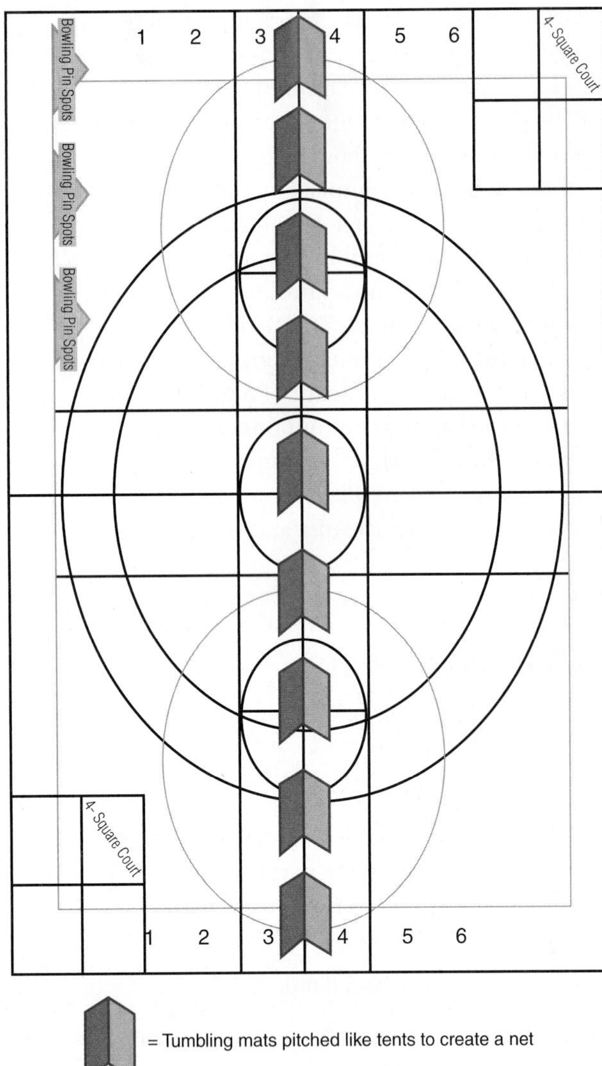

FIGURE 23.15 USA School Tennis diagram.

BADMINTON

People around the world enjoy playing badminton. Although this sport is less popular in the United States, it still ranks as one of students' favorite activities in many physical education programs. The game is played with a shuttlecock, or birdie, rackets (Figure 23.16), and a net. Its regulation court is unique to badminton (Figure 23.17). Badminton is considered a lifetime activity because it can be played at a fast pace when at competitive levels or at a slower pace as a recreation or leisure activity. The basic badminton strategy is not necessarily hitting the birdie as hard as possible. In fact, finesse and moving the opponent up, back, and side-to-side is an effective strategy. At the elementary level, the goal is exposing students to striking a birdie with a badminton racket. For this reason, teachers focus on skills and strokes that will enable students to successfully participate in modified badminton games. To increase children's success, several equipment manufacturers now offer larger birdies. Also, students can use smaller paddles or rackets at first and then progress to the longer badminton rackets. After learning this skill, students will experience greater success in other skills, and they can enjoy badminton as a lifetime activity.

FIGURE 23.16 Birdie and badminton racket.

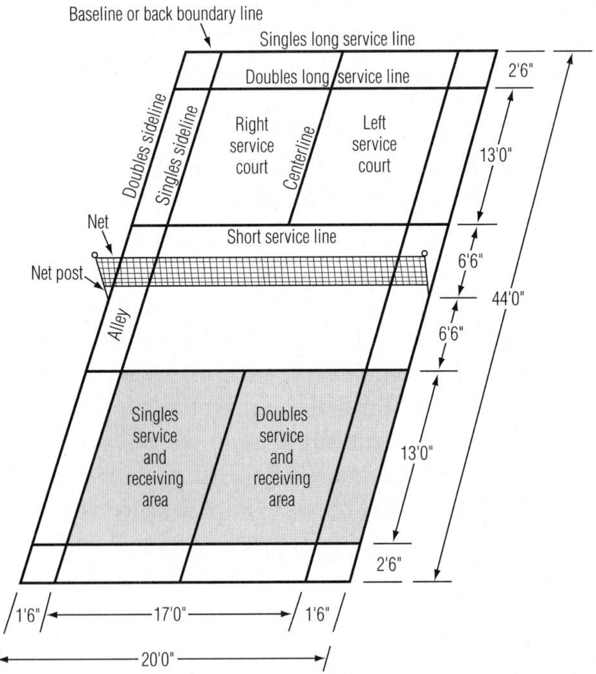

FIGURE 23.17 Regulation badminton court.

BADMINTON SKILLS

Serve

For beginners, the most appropriate serve is the underhand forehand serve (Figure 23.18). This serve can be used for long and short serves. It is useful to teach this skill first,

FIGURE 23.18 Badminton serve sequence.

for two reasons: (1) for children to succeed early and learn the basic underhand motion, they must drop the birdie to themselves; and (2) to progress to partner rallying, students must be able to put the birdie into play. The easiest way to do this is the underhand serve.

For this serve, the child begins with the opposite foot forward; his dominant foot is back with the weight shifted to the back foot. In his nondominant hand, he holds the birdie by the tip in front of his body. The racket goes straight back in the backswing. As he swings the racket forward, he shifts his weight to the front foot, drops the birdie, and makes contact about at knee level. He hits through the birdie and stops when his arm is parallel to the ground. Here are instructional cues for the serve:

1. Favorite foot back with weight on back foot.
2. Birdie by tip and out in front.
3. Backswing, shift weight, drop, swing.
4. Racket follows birdie.

Forehand Underhand Clear

The underhand clear on the forehand side is a common shot in badminton and an easy stroke to learn. The major difference between this forehand and forehands in other racket activities is the step. For the forehand underhand clear, the player reaches with the dominant foot and the dominant hand, which has the racket in it. This allows for a greater reach for the birdie. The shot begins with the student in ready position. After seeing that the birdie will fall in front on the dominant side, she quickly steps toward the birdie. If necessary, she takes a few shuffles or slide steps. She then swings with an upward motion with the palm of the hand up. Here are teaching cues for the forehand underhand clear:

1. Ready position.
2. Move toward birdie with dominant side.
3. Reach with dominant hand and foot.
4. Swing low to high.
5. Back to the ready position.

Forehand Overhead Clear

The forehand overhead clear uses a similar motion to throwing. When the player sees that the serve is a high one that he can return, he moves into position as if to make a throw with the nonstriking side closest to the net. He draws back the racket as if scratching the back. Next he swings forward, trying to contact the birdie as high as possible. The follow-through is down to the waist. The trajectory of this shot is either straight or upward. These instructional cues will help develop this skill:

1. Ready position.
2. Opposite side to net.
3. Scratch your back.
4. Swing high to low.
5. Back to the ready position.

Backhand Underhand Clear

The backhand underhand clear shot is executed when the birdie is on the nondominant side and cannot be hit above the head. The shot starts with the player stepping with the dominant foot toward the birdie and placing her side or back to the net. As this is taking place, she shifts her thumb from the handshake grip to on top of the racket. Next, she reaches back and swings to strike the birdie using an upward motion. Here are some useful cues for teaching this skill:

1. Ready position.
2. Step with dominant foot toward birdie.

3. Back to net.
4. Swing low to high.
5. Back to the ready position.

Backhand Overhead Clear

The backhand overhead clear is the most difficult shot taught at the elementary level. Much of this difficulty is due to the uniqueness of the movement. The shot begins much like the underhand backhand clear. However, once the player gets his back to the net, he raises the dominant elbow and swings the racket down toward his nondominant hip. The player then looks up and over his dominant shoulder. The swing is actually a lean or shift of weight onto the tiptoes and a snapping up of the racket to straighten the arm in an effort to contact the birdie as high as possible. The arm then follows around and down to the player's side. Cues for this skill include the following:

1. Ready position.
2. Step with dominant foot toward birdie.
3. Back to net.
4. Elbow high, racket on stomach.
5. Climb to tiptoes and snap racket high.
6. Racket down to side.
7. Back to the ready position.

INDIVIDUAL BADMINTON DRILLS

Cradle the Birdie

Beginning with the racket in hand and the birdie on the ground, each student tries to scoop up the birdie from the ground using only the racket. The goal is to get the birdie on the racket and balanced. Once this happens, the child drops the birdie and does this activity again. Combine this activity with Birdie Balance and Bird Bounce, below.

Birdie Balance

Each student has a racket and a birdie. When instructed, students place the birdie on their racket and move around the teaching area using various locomotor skills. At first, most students will place the birdie on the racket with feathers down. Next, instruct students to put the birdie on its side and continue moving. Challenge students to jump, jump while turning, sit down, lie down, stand up, and do other movements while balancing the birdie.

Bird Bounce

Each student begins with a racket and birdie. On signal, they begin bouncing the birdie with their racket. They can start by standing still and then progress to moving. Challenge students to make each bounce with alternating sides of the racket. Also encourage students to try using their nondominant hand, and to switch hands between bounces. As a lead-up to other activities, ask students to catch the birdie in the nondominant hand after every third hit.

Flip and Catch

With a birdie and a racket, students balance the birdie on the racket by standing it on its feathers. Next they toss the birdie into the air with the racket and catch it with the other hand. Have them practice this skill with the racket in the nondominant hand as well. Next, students toss the birdie in the air and catch it on the racket. Remind them that "giving" with the birdie, by bending their knees, creates a "soft" racket and helps with catching. Do not encourage high flips, which make catching more difficult. Have students stand in hoops to emphasize safe, controlled flips.

Flip and Hit

This drill is a continuation of Flip and Catch. Rather than catch the birdie, the student tries to hit it using the appropriate stroke. This is an excellent opportunity to review the best strokes for use in particular situations. To ensure that students have ample space and remember the importance of safe, low tosses, have them stand inside a hoop while flipping and hitting.

PARTNER BADMINTON DRILLS

Hit and Catch

Birdies move differently from balls and tend to drop at a steeper angle, so players must learn to track their flight. For this activity, one partner has a birdie and a racket. She uses an underhand serve to hit it to her partner, who then tracks the birdie and catches it with her hands. Encourage all the serving partners to hit high shots, low shots, short shots, and long shots. After 5 to 10 serves, partners reverse roles. Next, the receiving partner gets a racket and traps the birdie with one hand and the racket. Finally, the receiver tries to catch the birdie with just the racket.

Bounce, Bounce, Hit

Both partners have rackets, and they get one birdie. The first partner bounces the birdie twice on his racket, just as in Birdie Bounce. After the second bounce, he hits it to his partner. The partner receives the birdie and tries to bounce it twice before hitting it back. The partners try to see how many times they can hit the birdie back and forth in this way.

Partner Rally

Partners begin with a racket each and one birdie. The partner with the birdie begins the rally with an underhand serve. The receiving partner sends the birdie back to her partner with one stroke. The partners try to see how many times they can hit it back and forth, or rally, without a mistake. A line on the floor can be used to simulate a net. The birdie must also pass over the line in order to count. Once teams reach 20–25 times, challenge them to use two birdies—each partner starts with a birdie and serves at the same time. From then on, each partner strikes the birdie at about the same time and then quickly finds the returning birdie.

BADMINTON ACTIVITIES

Badminton Conveyer

PLAYING AREA: Gymnasium or designated teaching area

PLAYERS: Groups of 8 to 10 students

SUPPLIES: One racket per student, one birdie, one cone

SKILLS: Racket awareness, cooperation

Students, with racket in hand, begin in a line on one end of the teaching area. Their challenge is to get the birdie to the other end of the teaching area and set it on the cone. These rules apply:

1. The birdie must be touching a racket at all times.
2. The birdie cannot be touching more than two rackets at a time.
3. The birdie may touch rackets only until it is set on a cone.
4. If the birdie is on your racket, your feet may not move.

If students pick up on this activity quickly, they can move the cone as a group. Encourage them to experiment by putting the racket in their nondominant hand, or even by blindfolding them so they must communicate to move the birdie.

Shuttle Shuttle

PLAYING AREA: Courts, 8 by 20 feet

PLAYERS: 6 per court

SUPPLIES: One racket per student, one birdie per court, nets or lines, lines or tape for boundaries

SKILLS: Forehand strokes, backhand strokes, serving, court movement

Three players are on each side of their court. One player from each side is in bounds, and the other two wait by the back line (Figure 23.19). The first player puts the birdie in play by serving to the other side. Immediately after striking the birdie, he quickly runs out of bounds, around the net or line, and to the other side, quickly getting in line behind the two players out of bounds. The receiving player

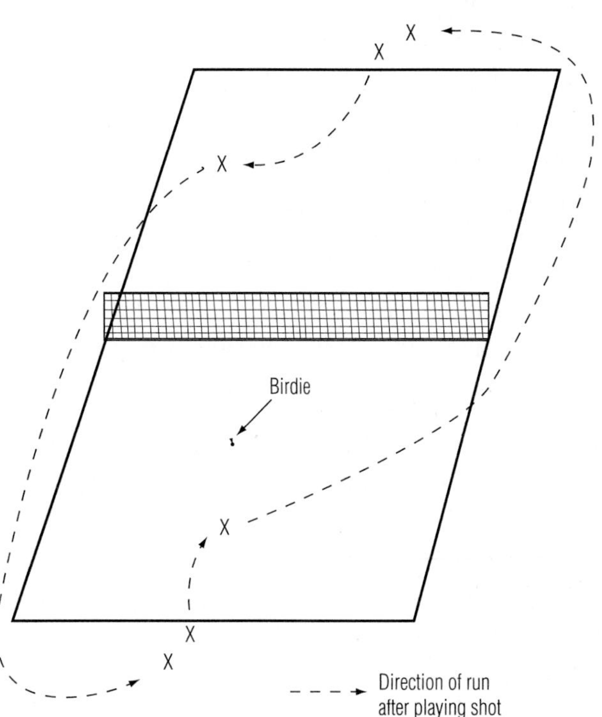

FIGURE 23.19 Shuttle Shuttle diagram. Each X represents a student.

returns the birdie and hustles over to stand behind the players on the side he just hit it to. All players on the court work together to see how many times they can rally the birdie in this way. The rally is over if the birdie hits the ground. Double hits are allowed.

Badminton 500

PLAYING AREA: Gymnasium or designated teaching area

PLAYERS: Groups of 2 to 4 students

SUPPLIES: One racket per student, one birdie

SKILLS: Serving, tracking

One student is the server, and the other students are scattered about 20 feet in front of him. The server serves the birdie to the other students, who try to catch the birdie with their racket for points. For safety and order, students either alternate turns catching or let the first player to call it attempt the catch. Students score points as follows:

- Clean catch with the racket with no hands and no bounces = 100
- Catch with no hands and one bounce = 75
- Catch with no hands and two bounces = 50
- Catch using racket and the other hand or more than two bounces = 25

Each catcher quickly serves the birdie back to the server for another round. The first player to earn 500 points becomes the server.

FRISBEES

Frisbee activities are popular with children of all ages. Basic skills are used for Frisbee Golf, Frisbee Bowling, and Ultimate Frisbee, which is a popular sport. Manipulating a Frisbee is a novel skill for elementary school children, and they will require considerable guidance to develop skills.

INSTRUCTIONAL PROCEDURES

1. Allow students to individually toss and catch the disk first. Otherwise, students spend more time chasing than they do throwing and catching.
2. Use these instructional cues:
   a. Release the disk parallel to the ground. Tilting it results in a curved throw.
   b. Step toward the target and follow through on releasing the disk.
   c. Snap open the wrist and make the Frisbee spin.
3. If space is limited, have students throw all Frisbees in the same direction. They can line up on each side of the area and throw across to each other.
4. To maximize practice time, give each child a disk at first. Later, most activities are best practiced by pairs of students using one disk.
5. Children can develop both sides of the body by learning to throw and catch with either hand. Design the activities so that students get both right-hand and left-hand practice.
6. Because a disk is somewhat different from other objects that children usually throw, devote some time to teaching form and style in throwing and catching. Avoid drills that reward speed in throwing and catching.

FRISBEE SKILLS

Backhand Throw

The backhand grip is used most often. The thumb is on top of the disk, the index finger along the rim, and the other fingers underneath. To throw the Frisbee with the right hand, stand sideways with the right foot toward the target. Step toward the target, and throw the disk in a sideways motion across the body, snapping the wrist and trying to keep the disk flat on release.

Underhand Throw

The underhand throw uses the same grip as in the backhand throw, but the thrower faces the target and holds the Frisbee at the side of the body. Step forward with the leg opposite the throwing arm while bringing the disk forward. When the throwing arm is out in the front of the body, release the disk. The trick to this throw is learning to release the disk so that it is parallel to the ground.

Thumb-Down Catch

The thumb-down catch is used for catching the Frisbee at waist level or above. The hand is shaped like a *C* with the thumb pointing toward the ground. To see any tilt on the disk that may cause it to curve, the catcher tracks the disk from the thrower's hand.

Thumb-Up Catch

The thumb-up catch is used when the Frisbee is received below waist level. The thumb points up, and the fingers are spread. As with the thumb-down catch, the hand forms a *C* and then clamps the disk (Figure 23.20).

Sandwich Catch

The catcher holds one hand at chin level and the other at stomach level. As the Frisbee approaches and the catcher can see where it will arrive, she moves her hands closer to that spot. She catches the disk by sandwiching it between both hands (one above and one below the disk).

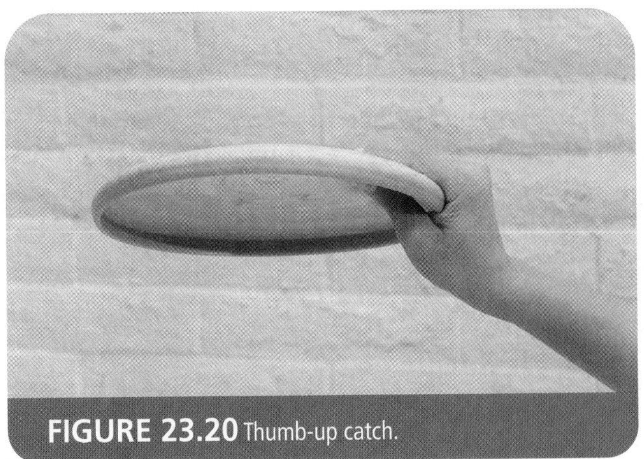

FIGURE 23.20 Thumb-up catch.

Trick Catches

Frisbees can be caught in different positions. The two most popular trick-catch positions are behind the back and between the legs. The behind-the-back catch uses the thumb-up technique; the disk is caught with the arm farthest away from the thrower. The between-the-legs catch also uses the thumb-up catch; the catcher can lift one leg to facilitate the catch.

INDIVIDUAL FRISBEE DRILLS

Throw and Catch

Each with a Frisbee, students practice the appropriate throws and catches individually. They toss the disk into the air using the backhand grip and the underhand throw. Throwers must release the disk at a sharp angle to get it to boomerang back. This activity offers an excellent chance to try the thumb-up, thumb-down, and sandwich catches. Also challenge students to throw and catch the disk with their nondominant hand. Students can try more difficult stunts such as throwing the disk under their leg or behind their back, doing a trick while the disk is in the air, and catching the disk under the leg, on the foot, and so on. Throughout this activity, emphasize controlled throwing.

Throw to a Wall

Each student has a Frisbee and practices a soft underhand throw to a wall about 3 feet away. This activity allows students many repetitions and prevents them from having to spend most of their time chasing the disk. Early on, lots of repetitions in throwing are important.

Outside Throwing and Catching

If outside, students can move through the Throw and Catch activity just described and then try other drills. Have them throw the Frisbee like a boomerang. Also challenge students to throw the disk into the air and then run and catch it. Each time, they can increase the throwing distance and still try to make the catch before the disk touches the ground.

PARTNER AND SMALL GROUP FRISBEE DRILLS

Tossing and Catching

After practicing Frisbee grips and catches individually, these drills allow students to practice the skills more authentically. Each set of partners has one disk and is about 15 to 20 feet apart. Offer these challenges:

- Throw the disk at different levels to a partner.
- Catch the disk, using various catching styles and hand positions.
- Throw a curve by tilting the disk. Try curving it to the left, right, and upward. Throw a slow curve and then a fast slider.
- Throw a bounce pass to a partner. Throw a low, fast bounce. Throw a high, slow bounce.
- As the catcher, do various stunts after the disk leaves the partner's hand. Examples are a full turn, heel click, handclap, or touching the ground.
- Throw the disk with the nondominant hand. Try to throw for accuracy first, and then strive for distance.
- Have the partner hold a hoop as a target. See how many times you can throw the disk through the hoop. Play a game of One Step, in which you move back a step each time you throw the disk through the hoop. When you miss twice in a row, your partner gets a turn.
- Place a series of hoops on the ground. Different-colored hoops can signify different point values. Challenge your partner to see who earns more points in five throws.
- Play catch while both partners are moving. Try to throw the disk so your partner does not have to break stride to catch it.
- Throw for distance. Try to throw farther than your partner by adding up a series of four throws.

- Throw for both distance and accuracy. Using a series of four or more throws, try to reach a goal that is a specific distance away. Many different objects can be used as goals, such as basket standards, fence posts, and trees. (This could be the start of playing Frisbee Golf, which is becoming a popular recreational sport.)
- Set a time limit of 30 seconds. Within this time, students see how many successful throws and catches they can make. Partners must stand a set distance apart, and missed catches do not count as throws.
- Working in groups of three, students try to keep the disk away from the person in the middle. Let them make their own rules about when someone else must move to the middle.
- In groups of three, with one child in the middle, students try to throw the disk through the middle child's legs (which are spread to shoulder width). A point is scored each time the disk is thrown through the legs without touching.

FRISBEE ACTIVITIES

Frisbee Keepaway

PLAYING AREA: Gymnasium, 10 by 10 feet

PLAYERS: Groups of 4 to 5 students

SUPPLIES: One Frisbee per group

SKILLS: Throwing, catching

Two players start on defense. The other players spread out around the designated area and are the offense. Use cones to establish boundaries if necessary. The players on offense try to make three consecutive throws. Defensive players try to break up the consecutive throws by knocking the disk down or catching it. Once the disk is caught, it cannot be taken away or knocked to the ground. If the disk is caught or knocked from the air to the ground, the player who threw the disk becomes a member of the defense, and the defensive player who knocked the disk down or caught it is on offense. After making three consecutive throws, two players from offense switch with the defensive players and the game continues.

Step Back

PLAYING AREA: Gymnasium or designated activity area

PLAYERS: Partners

SUPPLIES: One Frisbee per set of partners

SKILLS: Throwing, catching

Partners begin standing 1 to 2 feet apart with the gym's center line between them. The partner who makes a successful catch gets to take one step backward. If either partner drops the disk, they return to the center line and begin again.

Frisbee Bowling

PLAYING AREA: Gymnasium or outside, in 8- by 15-foot lanes

PLAYERS: Groups of 3 students

SUPPLIES: Two Frisbees and 6 to 10 bowling pins (rectangular blocks or plastic 2-liter soda bottles will work) per group

SKILLS: Throwing

Each group gets two Frisbees, a bowling lane, and 6 to 10 bowling pins. Two students take on the role of pin setters and stand beside the pins. The third student is the bowler. She stands 15 feet from the pins and has two throws to knock down as many pins as possible. After the first throw, the setters remove only the disk. All pins are left as they are. After the second throw, the setters quickly tell the bowler how many pins were knocked down. One setter then collects both disks and reports to the bowling line while the other setter sets up the pins. At first the pins are set to form a triangle; later, allow the students to choose the pin setup. The only rule is that they must use the same setup for each bowler. When the pins are set, the next bowler begins. The game continues until every student rotates to each role. Setters can also retrieve errant throws when they see they are not going to hit the pins. Give students safety reminders throughout this activity—students must look before throwing and before stepping in front of someone on the bowler's end of the lane.

Frisbee Golf

PLAYING AREA: Large outside playing area

PLAYERS: Groups of 2 to 4 students

SUPPLIES: One Frisbee per child, 8 to 10 hoops, 8 to 10 cones

SKILLS: Throwing

Frisbee Golf is played exactly like golf except players throw the disk rather than hitting a ball with a club. Before students play, give them an overview of golf. Explain that they must get their Frisbee from the cone (called the tee) to the hoop (the hole) in the fewest number of throws. To minimize waiting after each hole, assign each group a starting tee. One at a time, each child in the group throws his disk. Students then hustle to their disk for the second throw. The child farthest from the hole goes first. For safety reasons, remind all group members to watch the throw. This process continues until all players have thrown the disk into the hoop. The next tee is near the previous hole. Teach students to move to hole 2 after playing hole 1, or to hole 6 after playing hole 5. If they start on hole 6, then hole 5 is the end of their course. Students can track their own score or use a scorecard. Do not have students carry pencils, which creates a safety hazard; instead, place pencils at each tee. Before starting the next hole, they record their score from the previous hole. Students must wait until the group in front of them is finished and has moved on to the next hole. If desired, make inexpensive flags (see Figure 23.21) with 1-inch PVC pipe or wands and plastic triangles and put them into cones. The flags help students locate the hole. To integrate orienteering with Frisbee activities, give students a map of the course (Figure 23.22). It may be easiest to print the scorecard on the back of the map.

FIGURE 23.21 Frisbee Golf tees and flags.

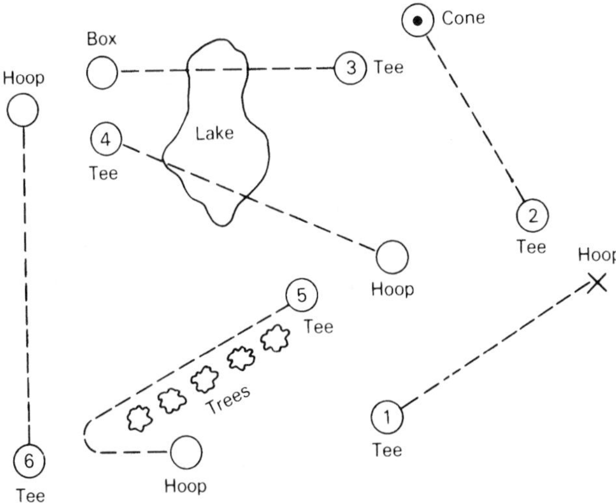

FIGURE 23.22 Frisbee Golf course.

Ultimate Frisbee

PLAYING AREA: Gymnasium or outside area, 40 by 50 feet

PLAYERS: Teams of 8 to 10 students

SUPPLIES: One Frisbee, cones to mark boundaries, pinnies

SKILLS: Throwing, catching, moving to open spaces, cooperation

Ultimate Frisbee is a combination of basketball, soccer, and football, played with a Frisbee. At the elementary school level, rules are minimized and activity emphasized. Teams try to move the disk down the field or court by throwing it to teammates. These rules apply:

1. The disk can be stolen only when it is in the air; it cannot be taken from someone's hands.
2. The player with the disk can take only three steps.
3. The player with the disk can hold it for only 5 seconds.
4. If the disk is dropped or hits the ground after a throw, it goes to the other team.
5. A point is scored when the disk is thrown across a team's endline and caught by an opposing player.

After each score, the scoring team quickly throws the disk downfield. The opposing team either catches

Skills instruction for basketball is introduced primarily during the intermediate grades after children have mastered the basic prerequisite skills. The teaching of rules and strategies for basketball should be an integral part of the instructional process. Using proper progression is a key to success when teaching fundamental skills and lead-up games associated with basketball. Lead-up games provide an opportunity to emphasize development of selected basketball skills in a setting compatible with children's ability.

Outcomes

- Structure learning experiences efficiently by using appropriate formations, progressions, and coaching techniques.
- Know the basic rules of basketball.
- Develop a unit plan and lesson focus for basketball.
- Identify safety precautions associated with teaching basketball.
- Describe essential elements for a successful lead-up game.
- Cite assessment procedures for evaluating basketball skills.

BASKETBALL is an activity enjoyed by many boys and girls. The thrill of making a basket and the exhilaration of running up and down the court makes it an attractive game. Along with the joy of playing, its positive effects on children's cardiorespiratory systems make basketball a strong contributor to the total curriculum. Basketball instruction in the elementary school focuses on developing skills and competence so students can participate later in life. Often, elementary basketball programs focus on developing future high school stars with little concern for less talented students. Emphasize lead-up games so all students can experience success and enjoyment.

The physical education setting, which emphasizes instruction and skill development, allows little time for regulation basketball during school hours. More skilled and interested students should be given additional opportunities through intramural programs, recreational leagues (such as the Youth Basketball Association), or an educationally sound interschool competitive league.

Modifying equipment used by elementary school children is important. Smaller balls and lower baskets help develop technically correct patterns, increase students' success, and maintain motivation. Children cannot practice the ball control drills if the ball is too large for their hands.

INSTRUCTIONAL EMPHASIS AND SEQUENCE

Table 24.1 shows the sequence of basketball activities, divided into two developmental levels. In most cases, children are not ready to participate in this chapter's activities until age 8.

DEVELOPMENTAL LEVEL II

Little emphasis is placed on regulation basketball at Developmental Level II. Teaching focuses on the fundamental skills of passing, catching, shooting, and dribbling. Lead-up games such as Birdies in the Cage, Circle Guard and Pass, and Basketball Tag allow students to learn skills in a setting that offers both enjoyment and success. Movement of players is somewhat limited, increasing the opportunity for a positive experience. As children mature at this level, a goal is to develop a range of skills, including passing, catching, dribbling, and shooting. Have them work on the layup shot and the one-hand push shot. Captain Ball adds elements of simple defense, jump balls, and accurate passing.

DEVELOPMENTAL LEVEL III

Several lead-up activities are introduced at Developmental Level III. Shooting games, such as Twenty-One and Freeze-Out, become favorites. Sideline Basketball and Captain Basketball offer meaningful competition. To ensure a good base of motor development, have students continue practicing fundamental skills. Drills to enhance skill performance and rules for regulation basketball are presented. Teach officiating so students can learn to appreciate the importance and difficulty of refereeing. Allow players to conduct some games through self-officiating.

BASKETBALL SKILLS

Basketball skills at the elementary level are divided into the following categories: passing, catching, dribbling, shooting, defending, stopping, pivoting, and feinting.

PASSING

All passes have some common elements. For firm control, handle the ball with the thumb and finger pads, not with the palms of the hands. Step forward in the direction of the receiver while extending the arms and wrists. After releasing the pass, the palms face the floor.

Instructional Cues

1. Fingers spread with thumbs behind the ball.
2. Elbows in; extend through the ball.
3. Step forward, extend arms, and rotate hands slightly inward.
4. Throw at chest level to the receiver.

TABLE 24.1 Suggested basketball program

Developmental Level II	Developmental Level III
Skills	
Passing	
Chest pass One-hand push pass Bounce pass Two-hand overhead pass	All passes to moving targets Two-hand overhead pass Long passes Three-player weave
Catching	
Above the waist Below the waist	While moving
Dribbling	
Standing and moving Down and back Right and left hands	Figure eight Pivoting Individual dribbling skills
Shooting	
One-hand (set) push shot Layup, right and left	Free-throw shot Jump shot
Defending and stopping	
Pivoting Feinting	Parallel stop Stride stop
Developmental Level II	**Developmental Level III**
Knowledge	
Dribbling Violations Traveling Out-of-bounds Double dribbling	Held ball Personal fouls Holding Hacking Charging Blocking Pushing Conducting the game Officiating
Activities	
Circle Guard and Pass Basketball Tag Dribblerama Birdies in the Cage Captain Ball Around the Key Five Passes Captain Basketball	Quadrant Basketball Sideline Basketball Twenty-One Lane Basketball Freeze-Out Flag Dribble Through the Maze One-Goal Basketball Basketball Snatch Ball Three-on-Three Basketrama Paper Clip Basketball
Skill Tests	
Straight Dribble	Figure-eight dribble Wall pass test Baskets per minute Free throws

5. For bounce passes, bounce the ball past the halfway point closer to the receiver.

Chest (or Two-Hand) Pass

For the chest, or two-hand, pass, place one foot ahead of the other, with the knees flexed slightly. Release the ball at chest level, with the fingers spread on each side of the ball. Pass the ball by extending the arms and snapping the wrists as one foot moves toward the receiver (Figure 24.1).

FIGURE 24.1 Chest pass.

One-Hand Push Pass

For the one-hand push pass, support the ball with the left hand, and place the right hand behind the ball. Using the right hand, push the ball forward with a quick wrist snap.

Bounce Pass

Any of the preceding passes can be adapted to a bounce pass. The object is to get the pass to the receiver on the first bounce, with the ball coming to the receiver's outstretched hands at about waist height. Some experimentation determines the distance. Bounce the ball a little more than halfway between the two players to make it come efficiently to the receiver.

Two-Hand Overhead Pass

The two-hand overhead pass is effective against a shorter opponent. The passer is in a short stride position, holding the ball overhead (Figure 24.2). The momentum of the pass comes from a forceful wrist and finger snap. The pass should take a slightly downward path.

CATCHING

When catching, the receiver moves toward the pass with the fingers spread and relaxed, reaching for the ball with elbows bent and wrists relaxed. To absorb the ball's force, the hands give as the ball comes in.

FIGURE 24.2 Two-hand overhead pass.

Instructional cues for catching:

1. Move to the ball.
2. Spread the fingers and catch with the fingertips.
3. Reach for the ball.
4. Give with the ball (bring the ball to the chest).

DRIBBLING

Use dribbling to advance the ball, break for a basket, or maneuver out of a difficult situation. The dribbler's knees and trunk are slightly flexed (Figure 24.3), with hands and eyes forward. Peripheral vision is important. The dribbler looks beyond the ball and sees it in the lower part of the visual area. Dribble the ball using the fingertips and a downward wrist action. Younger children tend to slap at the ball rather than push it. Have students practice dribbling with both hands.

Instructional cues for dribbling:

1. Push the ball to the floor. Don't slap it.
2. Push the ball forward when moving.
3. Keep the hand on top of the ball. (Carrying the ball is illegal.)
4. Keep eyes forward and head up.

FIGURE 24.3 Dribbling.

SHOOTING

Shooting is an intricate skill, and students need to develop consistent and proper technique rather than be satisfied when the ball happens to drop into the basket.

1. Good body position is important. Both the toes and the shoulders are facing the basket. The weight is evenly distributed on both feet. When preparing to shoot, hold the ball between shoulder and eye level.
2. A comfortable grip, with fingers well spread and the ball resting on the pads of the fingers, is essential. The palms of the hand do not touch the ball. The shooting elbow is held near the side, so the hand moves up through the ball toward the basket.
3. When shooting, focus on the front of the rim for the entire shot.
4. As the shot starts, cock the wrist.
5. The follow-through gives the ball a slight backspin. The arms are fully extended, the wrist is completely flexed, and the hand drops down toward the floor ("make a swan's neck"). The arc should be 45 degrees or a little higher.

Instructional cues for shooting:

1. Use the pads of the fingers. Keep the fingers spread.
2. Keep the shooting elbow in (near the body).
3. Shoot through the ball by extending the elbow.
4. Bend the knees and use the legs for more force.
5. Release the ball off the fingertips.

One-Hand Shot

The one-hand shot is usually a jump shot at short distances and a set shot at longer distances for young children. Most elementary school children cannot shoot a jump shot. The one-hand set shot can be a prelude to the jump shot as students mature. At the beginning level, stress proper technique rather than accuracy. Hold the ball at shoulder–eye level with both hands; keep the body erect and the knees slightly flexed in preparation for a jump. For a jump shot, the shooter executes a vertical jump, leaving the floor slightly (Figure 24.4). (In a set shot, the shooter rises on the toes.) The supporting (nonshooting) hand stays in contact with the ball until the top of the jump is reached. The shooting hand then takes over with fingertip control, and the ball rolls off the center three fingers. The hand and wrist follow through.

FIGURE 24.4 One-hand push shot.

Layup Shot

The layup is a short shot, taken when going to the basket, either after receiving a pass or at the end of a dribble. In a shot from the right side, the player takes off with the left foot, and vice versa. The ball is carried with both hands early in the shot and then shifted to one hand for the final push. The ball, guided by the fingertips, should gently rebound off the backboard with a minimum of spin.

Free-Throw Shot

The one-hand set shot is the shot of choice for free throws. Some players find it helpful to bounce the ball several times before shooting. Others like to take a deep breath and exhale completely just before shooting. The mechanics of the shot are the same as those of any shot at a comparable distance. Smoothness and consistency are important.

Jump Shot

The jump shot has the same upper-body mechanics as the one-hand shot described earlier. The main difference is the jump height. The jump is straight up, rather than at a forward or backward angle. The ball is released at the height of the jump (Figure 24.5). Because the legs cannot increase the force applied to the ball, the jump shot is difficult for most elementary school children. It may be best to avoid teaching this type of shot to children who lack the strength to shoot the ball correctly and thus resort to throwing it. If the jump shot is taught, move the basket to the lowest level and use a junior-sized basketball to develop proper shooting habits. Another way to practice proper form with the jump shot is to use foam balls and cardboard boxes or garbage cans for goals. The balls are light and easy to shoot. Concentrate on proper form rather than on making baskets. Reinforce students who use proper technique.

DEFENDING

Defending involves a characteristic stance. The defender, with knees bent slightly and feet comfortably spread (Figure 24.6 on page 608), faces the opponent at a distance of about 3 feet. Distributing body weight evenly on both feet allows for movement in any direction. Sideways movement is done with a sliding motion; the feet do not cross. The defender can wave one hand to distract the opponent

FIGURE 24.5 One-hand jump shot.

24

played. If the score is still tied after this period, the next team to score (1 or 2 points) wins. Some teachers alter the rules to offer more scoring opportunities: teams can score 1 point for hitting the backboard, 2 points for hitting the basket (rim), and 3 points for making a basket.

SUBSTITUTES

Substitutes must report to the official scorer and await a signal from the referee or umpire before entering the game. The scorer will indicate when the ball is not in play, so the official on the floor can signal the player to enter the game. In physical education classes, involve all students in multiple games so they all have equal opportunity to learn.

BASKETBALL DRILLS

Drills should simulate actual game situations. Teach students that practice is ineffective unless it is purposeful and correct. For drills, instructors should use the technique suggestions for the skill being practiced and apply movement principles. The drills presented here cover both individual skills and combinations of skills.

BALL-HANDLING DRILLS

Ball-handling drills are practiced continuously for about 30 seconds. The ball is handled with the pads of the fingers. The drills are listed in order of difficulty.

Around-the-Body Drills

1. *Around the waist.* Hold the ball in the right hand, circle it behind the back, and transfer to the left-hand. The left hand carries it to the front of the body for a transfer to the right hand. Start with the left hand and move the ball in the opposite direction.
2. *Around the head.* With shoulders back, circle the ball around the head much as described above. Try it in both directions.
3. *Triple play.* First circle the ball around the head; then circle at waist level and knee level. Try it in the opposite direction.

Figure Eight

1. Begin by squatting with the ball in the right hand. Move the ball around the leg to the right, and bounce the ball between the legs to the left hand. Circle the ball around the left leg, through the legs to the right hand.
2. Bounce the ball through the legs front to back, followed by the figure-eight pattern.

Speed Drill

Place the feet shoulder width apart. Hold the ball between the legs with one hand in front and the other behind the back in contact with the ball. In a quick motion, flip the ball slightly upward and reverse the hand positions. Using a quick exchange of the hands, make a series of rapid exchanges. The ball will appear to be suspended between the legs (Figure 24.9).

FIGURE 24.9 Speed drill.

Double-Circle Drill

Start with the ball in the right hand. Go around both legs, with an assist from the left hand. When the ball returns to the right hand, move the left foot away from the right foot. With the ball moving in the same direction, circle the right leg. Move the leg back to the starting position and circle both legs; then move the legs apart and circle the left leg (Figure 24.10). In short, circle both legs; circle the right leg; circle both legs; circle the left leg. Try moving the ball in the opposite direction.

Two-Hand Control Drill

Start from a semi-crouch with the feet shoulder width apart. Hold the ball with both hands between the legs in front of the body (Figure 24.11). Let go of the ball, move the hands behind the body, and catch the ball before it hits the floor. It may be helpful to flip the ball upward slightly. Reverse the action, moving the hands to the front of the body. Perform continuously.

Changing Hands Control Drill

Begin with the ball in the right hand. Move the ball around the back of the right leg and catch it

FIGURE 24.10 Double-circle drill.

FIGURE 24.11 Two-hand control drill.

with both hands. The right hand is in front and the left hand behind. Drop the ball and quickly change position of the hands on the ball after it has bounced once (Figure 24.12). Immediately after the catch, bring the ball to the front of the body with the left hand and switch the ball to the right hand. Repeat continuously. Try moving the ball in the opposite direction.

INDIVIDUAL DRIBBLING DRILLS

Students can practice dribbling only, or combine it with other skills. Here are some individual drills.

Hoop Dribbling Drill

Each child has a ball and hula hoop. Place the hoop on the floor and practice dribbling the ball inside the hoop while walking outside the hoop. Dribble counter clockwise using the left hand and clockwise using the right hand. Repeat by dribbling outside the hoop while walking inside the hoop.

Random Dribbling

Each child has a ball. Dribble in place, using the left and then right hand. Develop a sequence of body positions (standing, kneeling, lying on the side, on two feet and one hand). Encourage players to develop a sequence by dribbling a certain number of times in each selected position. Dribble with each hand.

One-Hand Control Drill

Hold the ball in the right hand. Make a half circle around the right leg to the back. Bounce the ball between the legs (back to front), catch it with the

FIGURE 24.12 Changing hands control drill.

right hand, and move it around the body again (Figure 24.13). Try the drill with the left hand.

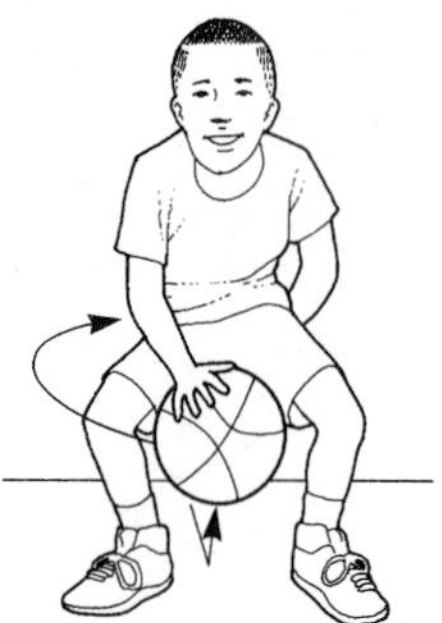

FIGURE 24.13 One-hand control drill.

Figure-Eight Dribbling Drill (Speed)

Start with either hand. Dribble outside the respective leg, between the feet, and continue in front with the opposite hand in figure-eight pattern. Begin slowly and gradually increase dribbling speed.

Figure-Eight Dribbling Drill (One Bounce)

Stand in a semi-crouch with feet shoulder width apart. Start with the ball in the right hand and bounce it from the front of the body between the legs. Catch it with the left hand behind the legs (Figure 24.14). Bring the ball to the front of the body with the left hand and start the sequence over with that hand.

FIGURE 24.14 Figure-eight dribbling drill (one bounce).

Figure-Eight Dribbling Drill (Two Bounces)

Begin in the same position as described in the preceding drill. Using the right hand, take one dribble outside the right leg (angled toward the back) and a second dribble between the legs to the left hand in front of the body (Figure 24.15). Repeat, starting with the left hand.

FIGURE 24.15 Figure-eight dribbling drill (two bounces).

GROUP DRIBBLING DRILLS

Children can practice these drills in groups of various sizes.

File Dribbling

Players dribble forward around an obstacle (such as a bowling pin, a cone, or a chair)and back to the line, where the next player starts the drill (Figure 24.16). A variation has each player dribbling down with one hand and back with the other.

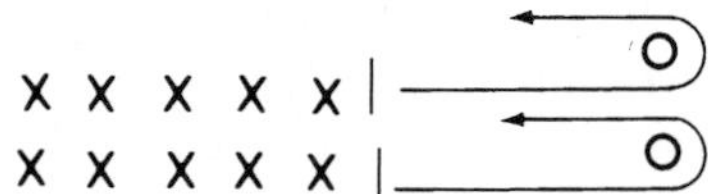

FIGURE 24.16 File dribbling.

Shuttle Dribbling

Students stand in files. The head player dribbles across to another file and hands the ball off to the player at the head of the second file. The first player then takes a place at the end of that file (Figure 24.17). The player receiving the ball dribbles back to the first file. Various shuttles can be arranged for dribbling cross ways over a basketball court.

FIGURE 24.17 Shuttle dribbling.

Obstacle, or Figure-Eight, Dribbling

Position three or more obstacles about 5 feet apart. The first player at the head of each file dribbles in and around each obstacle, changing hands so that the hand opposite the obstacle is the one always used (Figure 24.18).

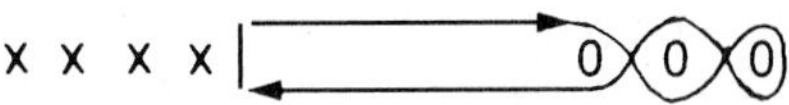

FIGURE 24.18 Obstacle, or figure-eight, dribbling.

DRIBBLING AND PIVOTING DRILLS

Dribbling and pivoting drills focus on stopping and turning.

File Drill

Each player in turn dribbles forward to a designated line, stops, pivots, faces the file, passes back to the next player, and runs to a place at the end of the line (Figure 24.19). The next player repeats the pattern.

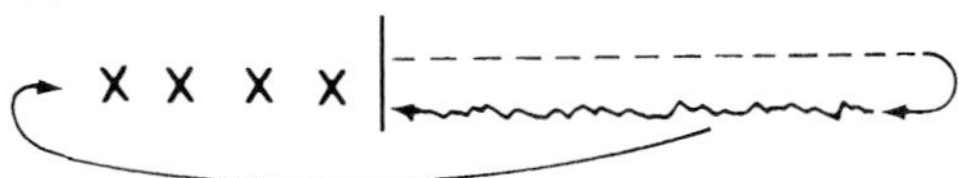

FIGURE 24.19 File drill.

Dribble-and-Pivot Drill

Players scatter in pairs around the floor (Figure 24.20). Each pair has one ball. On the first whistle, the front player of the pair dribbles in any direction. On the second whistle, the player stops and pivots back and forth; on the third whistle, he or she dribbles back and passes to the partner, who immediately dribbles forward, repeating the drill.

FIGURE 24.20 Dribble-and-pivot drill.

PASSING DRILLS

In passing practice, make regular use of the various movement and shuttle formations (Chapter 3): two-line, circle, circle-and-leader, line-and-leader, shuttle turn-back, and so on.

Safety Tip

When dribbling a basketball, students should be taught to keep their head up. This lets them see other players around them and prevents them from running into others.

Slide Circle Drill

A circle of four to six players slides around a person in the center. The center person passes to and receives from the sliding players. After the ball has gone around the circle twice, another player takes the center position.

Circle-Star Drill

This drill is particularly effective for five players, and it works well as a relay. Players pass to every other player, and the path of the ball forms a star (Figure 24.21). Any odd number of players ensures that the ball goes to everyone so they all receive equal practice.

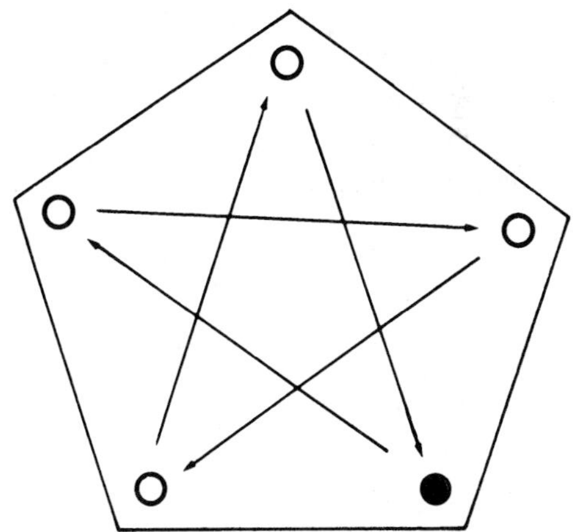

FIGURE 24.21 Circle-star drill formation.

Triangle Drill

Four to eight players can participate in this drill. The ball begins at the head of a line and is passed forward to a player away from the line. This player then passes to a teammate out at a corner, who then passes back to the head of the line (Figure 24.22 on page 614). Players take turns passing and then moving to the spot where they passed the ball, thus constantly changing positions.

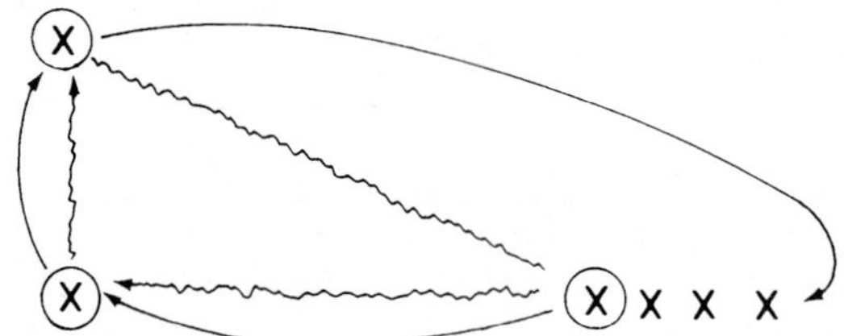

FIGURE 24.22 Triangle drill formation.

Squad Split-Vision Drill

This drill requires two basketballs. The center player holds one ball; player 1 (Figure 24.23) has the other. The center player passes the ball to player 2 while receiving the other ball from player 1. The center player now passes to player 3 and receives the other ball from player 2 until the balls move completely around the semicircle. To rotate players, the player with the ball moves to the center; the first center player becomes player 1. All other players shift one space to the right.

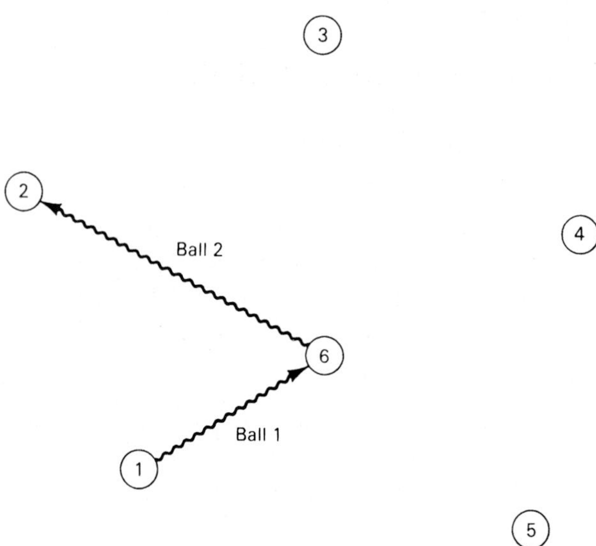

FIGURE 24.23 Squad split-vision drill.

Three-Lane Rush

This drill leads up to the three-player weave, which is difficult for elementary school children. Students are in three lines across one end of the area. The first three players move in parallel down the court, passing the ball back and forth to each other. As they near the basket, one player can try a layup.

Three-Player Weave

This drill requires practice and should be learned at slow speed. Walking students through the drill sometimes helps. If it is too difficult for a class, do not use it. The player in the center always starts the drill. She passes to another player coming across in front and then goes behind that player. As soon as she goes behind and around the player, she heads diagonally across the floor until she receives the ball again. The pass from the center player can start to either side.

SHOOTING DRILLS

Shooting drills may involve only shooting or a combination of shooting and other skills.

Simple Shooting Drill

In one simple shooting drill, players form files of no more than four people and take turns shooting a long and then a short shot or some other prescribed series of shots.

File-and-Leader Drill

The first player in each file has a ball and is the shooter. He passes the ball to the leader, who returns the ball to the spot that the shooter has selected for the shot (Figure 24.24).

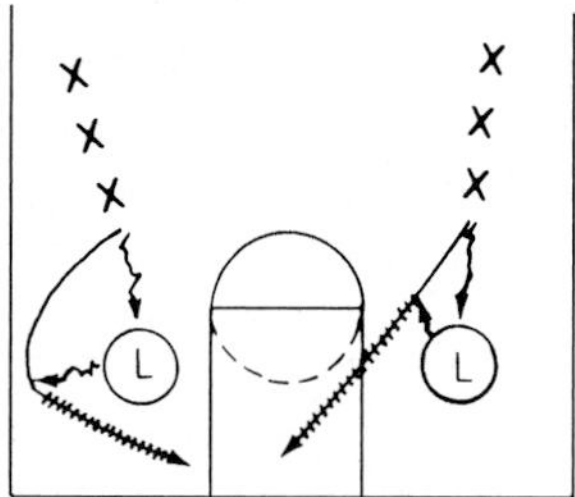

FIGURE 24.24 File-and-leader drill.

Dribble-and-Shoot Drill

Students form two files at one end of the floor. One file has a ball. The first player dribbles in and shoots a layup. A member of the other file recovers the ball and passes it to the next player (Figure 24.25). As each person in turn either shoots or retrieves, she goes to the rear of the other file. When students develop some proficiency in the drill, two balls can be used to provide more shooting opportunities.

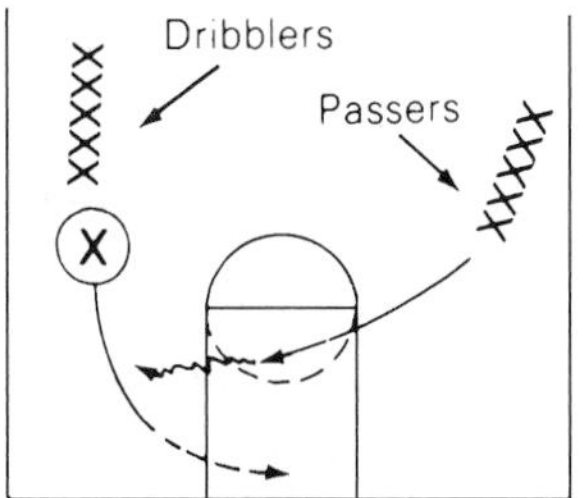

FIGURE 24.25 Dribble-and-shoot drill.

Shoot-and-Rebound Drill

Players are scattered an equal distance around the basket in a semicircle. Have them stand close enough to the basket so they can shoot accurately. All shooters have a ball and must rebound their own shots. Inject a bit of competition by allowing successful shooters to take one step back for the next shot.

Layup Drill

This drill is a favorite. One line passes to the other line for layup shots (Figure 24.26). Shooters come in from the right side first (this is easier), then from the left, and finally from the center. Each player goes to the end of the other line.

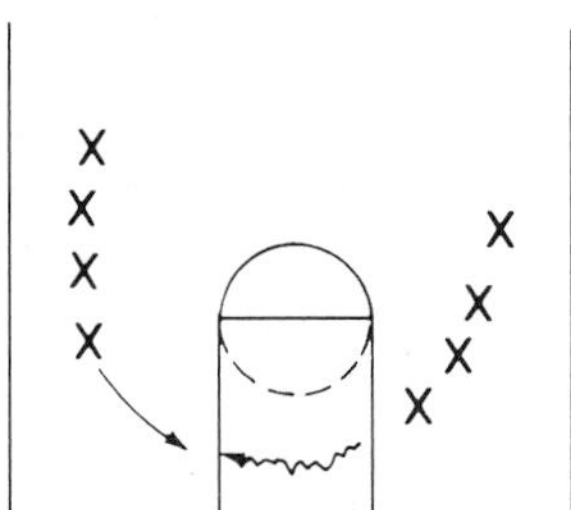

FIGURE 24.26 Layup drill.

Jump-Shot Drill

This drill is like the layup drill, except the incoming shooter receives the ball from a passer, stops, and takes a jump shot. The line of shooters should move back to allow room for forward movement to the shooting spot. As soon as the passer releases the ball to the shooter, he moves to the end of the shooter's line. The shooter goes to the passer's line after shooting (Figure 24.27).

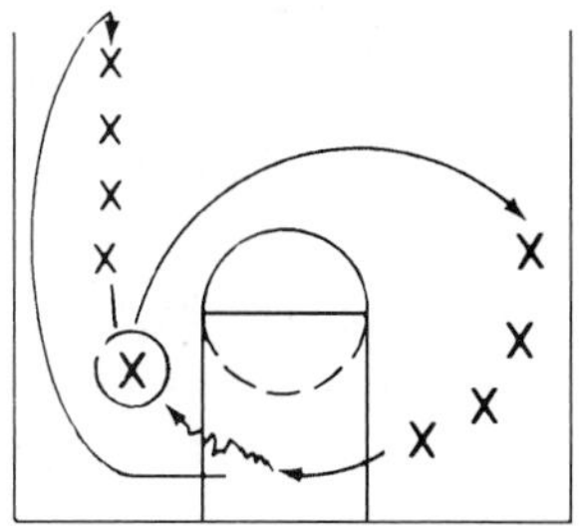

FIGURE 24.27 Jump-shot drill.

One extension of this drill is to allow a second jump shot when a shooter makes the first. In this case, the incoming passer throws to the shooter taking a second shot as well as to the next shooter. Another extension, which simulates a game situation, is having both the shooter and the incoming passer rebound when the shot is missed. As soon as the follow-up shot is made or the followers make three misses, the passer throws the ball to the new shooter. Encourage children to practice shooting from different spots.

OFFENSIVE AND DEFENSIVE DRILLS

Group Defensive Drill

The entire class is scattered on a basketball floor, facing one of the sides (Figure 24.28). The instructor or the student leader stands on the side, near the center. The drill can be done in several ways.

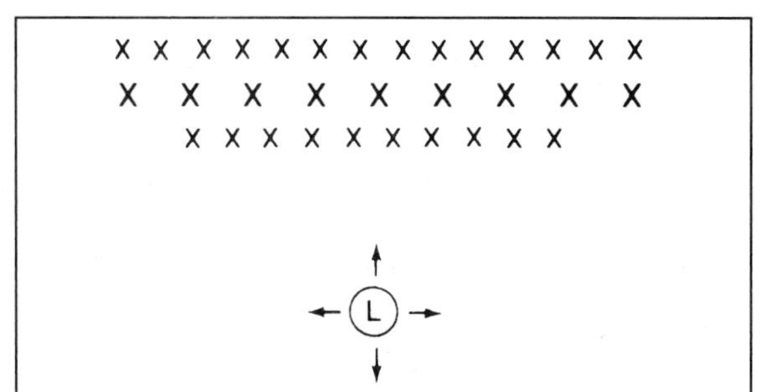

FIGURE 24.28 Group defensive drill.

1. The leader points in one direction (forward, backward, or to one side) and gives the command "Move." When the students have moved a short distance, the leader commands, "Stop." Players keep good defensive position throughout.

2. Commands can be changed so that movement is continuous. Commands are "Right," "Left," "Forward," "Backward," and "Stop." The leader must watch that players do not move so far in any one direction that they run into obstructions. Commands can be given in order and be accompanied by pointing.
3. The leader is a dribbler with a ball, who moves forward, backward, or to either side, with the defensive players reacting accordingly.

It is important to stress good defensive position and movement. Movement from side to side should be a slide. Movement forward and backward is a two-step, with one foot always leading.

Offensive–Defensive Drill with a Post

This drill consists of an offensive player, a defensive player, and another player acting as a passing post. The post player usually stands still and receives the ball from and passes to the offensive player. The player on offense tries to maneuver around or past the defensive player to find a good shot (Figure 24.29). Players can be confined to one side of an offensive basket area so two drills can occur at the same time on one end of the court. If there are side baskets, many drills can occur at once. After a basket attempt, all players, including any waiting player, rotate.

The defensive player's job is to cover the offensive player well enough to prevent shots in front of her. The drill is nonproductive when players' skill levels are not well matched.

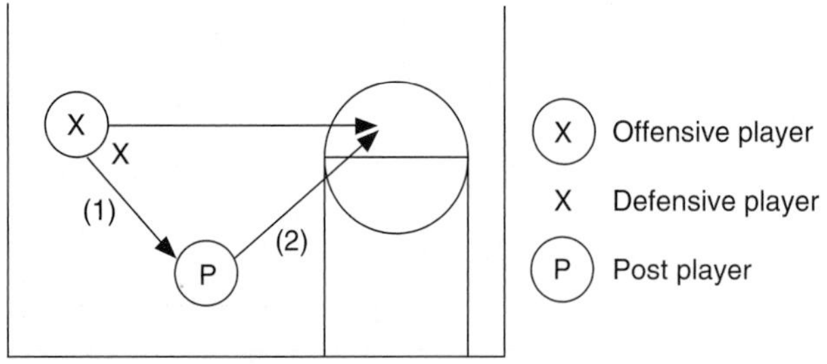

FIGURE 24.29 Offensive–defensive drill with post.

BASKETBALL ACTIVITIES

DEVELOPMENTAL LEVEL II

Games at this level focus on the basic skills of passing, catching, shooting, and dribbling.

Circle Guard and Pass

PLAYING AREA: Any smooth surface with circle markings

PLAYERS: 8 to 10 per team

SUPPLIES: A basketball or playground ball

SKILLS: Passing, catching, guarding

The offensive team is in formation around a large (30-foot diameter) circle. Two or more offensive players move into the center. The defensive team is positioned around a smaller (20-foot) circle inside the larger circle. On signal, the offensive team tries to pass the ball to the center players. They may pass the ball around the circle to each other before making an attempt to the center. The defensive team tries to bat the ball away but cannot catch it. After a specific time (1 minute), offensive and defensive teams trade positions. If score is kept, 2 points are awarded for each successful pass.

> *VARIATION:* Use more than one ball, and specify different types of passes. The defensive team also can earn points for each time a team member touches the ball.

Basketball Tag

PLAYING AREA: Gymnasium or playground area, 30 by 50 feet

PLAYERS: 8 to 10 per team

SUPPLIES: A foam rubber basketball, pinnies

SKILLS: Catching, passing, dribbling, guarding

This game has two versions. In the easier version, 3 to 5 students are "its" and wear pinnies. The rest of the class may only pass the ball and use it in trying to tag one of the players who is "it." Players may move as desired when they do not have the ball. When they have the ball, they may not move or dribble. More than one ball can be used.

The more difficult version allows dribbling and tagging with the hands. Two or more players from each team are "its" and wear pinnies. The goal is to tag the "its" with a hand when they have the ball. The players who are "it" may move only by walking. The rest of the players can move only when dribbling or not holding the ball. The "its" try to avoid moving near the ball; the other players pass and dribble while trying to get close enough to tag the roving "its."

✔ Teaching Hints

1. Play two or more games simultaneously so students get to handle the ball more often.
2. Designate two teams to play each other. Both teams have "its" who wear different-colored pinnies. They are "it" when their team does not have the ball. When their team has the ball, they play offense with their teammates.

Dribblerama

PLAYING AREA: Any smooth surface with a large circle or square, clearly outlined

PLAYERS: Entire class

SUPPLIES: One basketball for each player

SKILLS: Dribbling and protecting the ball

The playing area is a large circle or square. Dribblerama can be played at three levels of difficulty.

Level 1: All players dribble throughout the area, controlling their ball so it does not touch another ball. If a touch occurs, both players go outside the area and dribble around the area. Once students have completed dribbling around the area, they reenter the game.

Level 2: The area is divided in half and all players move to one of the halves. While dribbling and controlling a ball, each player tries to make other players lose control of the ball. Players who lose ball control take their ball and move to the opposite half of the area. Play continues against other players who have lost control. When 5 or 6 players remain, bring all players back into the game and start over.

Level 3: The class is divided into four teams, and the area is divided into equal quadrants. Each of the four teams goes to one of the quadrants. Upon losing ball control, players move to the next quadrant and begin play. This variation is more controlled and keeps students involved continuously.

Birdies in the Cage

PLAYING AREA: Any smooth surface with circle marking

PLAYERS: 8 to 15 per team

SUPPLIES: A soccer ball, basketball, or volleyball

SKILLS: Passing, catching, intercepting

Players stand in circle formation with two or more children in the center of the circle. The goal is for the center players to try to touch the ball while circle players are passing it. After 15–20 seconds, choose new players to enter the circle. If scoring is desired, center players can count the number of touches they made. The ball should move rapidly. Passing to a neighboring player is not allowed. Play can be limited to a specific type of pass (bounce, two-hand, push).

Captain Ball

PLAYING AREA: Playground or gymnasium area, about 30 by 40 feet

PLAYERS: 7 or more on each team

SUPPLIES: A basketball, pinnies, mats or spots

SKILLS: Passing, catching, guarding

Two games can be played crosswise on a basketball court. A centerline is needed (Figure 24.30); otherwise, normal boundary lines are used. Use spots to mark where forwards and captains must stay. Each team has a captain, three or more forwards, and three or more guards. The guards are free to move in their half of the playing area and try to keep the ball from being thrown to the opposing captain.The captain and forwards are each assigned to their respective spots and must always keep one foot on their assigned spot.

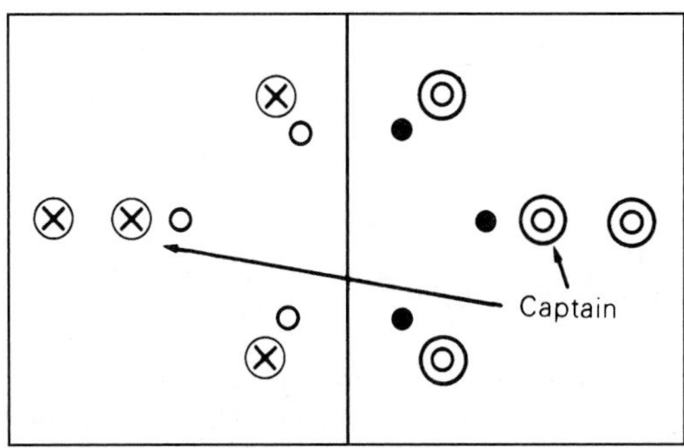

FIGURE 24.30 Formation for Captain Ball.

The game starts with a tip-off jump at the centerline by two guards from opposing teams. Guards can roam in their half of the court but may not touch the opposing forwards. Once points are scored by getting the ball to the captain, an opposing guard immediately puts the ball into play with an in-bounds throw. Guards try to throw the ball to their forwards, who maneuver to be open while keeping a foot on their spot. The forwards can throw the ball to their guards and forwards or to the captain. Score 3 points when two forwards handle the ball and it is passed to the captain. Score 2 points when the ball is passed to the captain but has not been handled by two forwards. No points are scored when a guard throws the ball to the captain.

Stepping over the centerline is a foul. It is also a foul if a guard steps on a forward's marking spot or makes personal contact with a player on a spot. The penalty for a foul is a free throw. For a free throw, an unguarded forward gets the ball and has 5 seconds to pass successfully to the guarded captain. If the throw succeeds, score 1 point. If it does not, the ball is in play. Rotate free-throw shooting among all the forwards.

As in basketball, when the ball goes out-of-bounds, it is awarded to the team that did not make it go out. If a forward or a captain catches a ball without a foot touching her spot, the ball is taken out-of-bounds by the opposing guard. For violations such as traveling or kicking the ball, the ball is awarded to an opposing guard out-of-bounds. No score may be made from a ball that is thrown in directly from out-of-bounds.

VARIATIONS:

1. Try a five-spot formation like that on a die. Each team has 9 players: 4 forwards, 4 guards, and 1 captain. Depending on space and the size of the courts, teams can have even more players.
2. Use more than one captain on each side to make scoring easier.

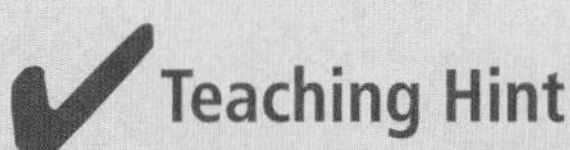

Teaching Hint

An effective offensive formation places guards spaced along the centerline (Figure 24.31—only the offensive team is diagrammed). By passing the ball back and forth among the guards, the forwards have more opportunity to be open, since the passing makes the guards shift position. To advance the ball, guards may dribble—but only three times. The forwards and captain may shift back and forth to become open for passes, but must keep one foot on the spot. Short and accurate passing uses both chest and bounce passes. Forwards and centers may jump for the ball, but must come down with one foot on their spot.

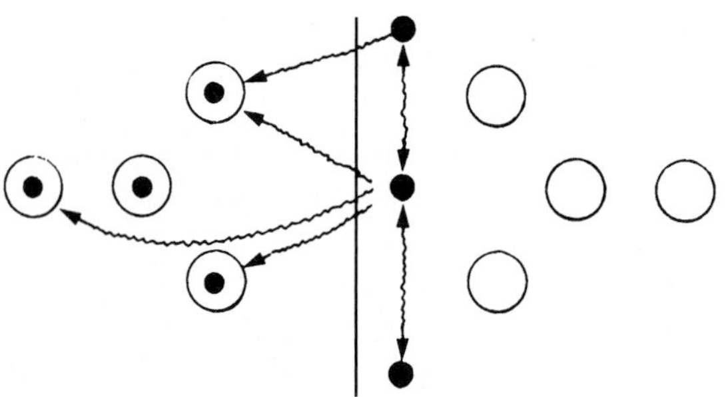

FIGURE 24.31 An effective offensive formation in Captain Ball.

Around the Key

PLAYING AREA: One end of a basketball floor

PLAYERS: 3 to 8

SUPPLIES: A basketball

SKILLS: Shooting

Spots are arranged for shooting as indicated in Figure 24.32. A player begins at spot 1 and continues around the key, shooting from each spot. When he misses, he can stop and wait for the next opportunity, starting from the spot where he missed. Rather than waiting, he can risk taking another shot immediately from that spot. If he makes the shot, he continues. If he misses, he must start from spot 1 on the next turn. The winner is the player who either completes the key first or makes the most progress.

VARIATIONS:

1. Each child shoots from each spot until a basket is made. Limit players to three shots from any one spot. The child finishing the round of eight spots after taking the lowest number of shots is the winner.

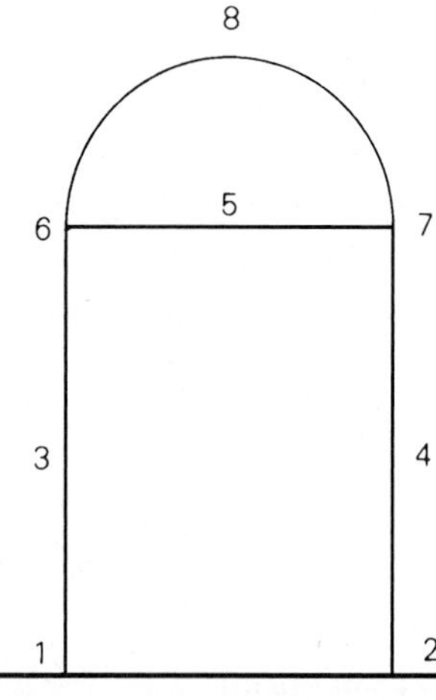

FIGURE 24.32 Shooting positions for Around the Key.

2. Change the order of the spots. Players can start on one side of the key and move back along the line, around the free-throw circle, and down the other side of the key.

Five Passes

PLAYING AREA: Half of a basketball floor

PLAYERS: 5 or more on each team

SUPPLIES: A basketball, pinnies

SKILLS: Passing, guarding

Two teams play. Divide the area into smaller areas so many teams can play at once. The goal is to complete five consecutive passes, which scores a point. The game starts with a jump ball at the free-throw line. The teams observe regular basketball rules for ball handling, traveling, and fouling. The team with the ball counts out loud as a pass is completed.

The ball may not be passed back to the person who threw it. No dribbling is allowed. If the ball is fumbled and recovered or improperly passed, a new count begins. After a team scores, the other team gets the ball. A foul draws a free throw, which can score a point. Teams are well marked to avoid confusion.

VARIATION: After each successful point (five passes), the team is awarded a free throw, which can score an additional point.

Captain Basketball

PLAYING AREA: A basketball court with centerline

PLAYERS: 6 or more on each team

SUPPLIES: Basketballs, pinnies

SKILLS: All basketball skills except shooting

Lay out a captain's area by drawing a line (or placing a mat) between the two foul lines 4 feet out from the end line. The captain must keep one foot in this area. Captain Basketball is more like regulation basketball than Captain Ball. Captain Ball limits the movements of the forwards. Captain Basketball allows more natural passing and guarding situations without restricting the forwards.

A team typically includes three forwards, one captain, and four guards. The captain must keep one foot in the area under the basket. The game starts with a jump ball, after which the players advance the ball as in basketball. No player may cross the centerline, however. The guards must bring the ball up to the centerline and throw it to one of their forwards. The forwards maneuver and try to pass successfully to the captain. A throw by one of the forwards to the captain scores 2 points; a free throw scores 1 point.

Fouls are the same as in basketball. Players stepping over the centerline, or guards stepping into the captain's area, draw a foul. After a foul, a forward gets the ball at the free-throw line. The player is unguarded and has 5 seconds to pass successfully to the captain, who is guarded by one player. The ball is in play if the free throw is unsuccessful.

Teaching Hint

Using a folding mat to designate the captain's area at each end of the court discourages intrusion by guards. Instruct players to move freely in their own half of the court. Stress short, quick passes, which are more effective in this game. Captain Basketball offers the chance for practicing proper guarding techniques.

DEVELOPMENTAL LEVEL III

Games at this level give students lead-up practice in all basketball skills.

Quadrant Basketball

PLAYING AREA: Basketball court divided into four equal areas

PLAYERS: At least 8 per team with a minimum of 2 in each area

SUPPLIES: A basketball, pinnies

SKILLS: Passing, catching, dribbling, guarding, shooting

Divide the court by its length and width into four equal areas with markers. Start play either with a jump ball or by giving the ball to one team. Two offensive and two defensive players are in each quadrant. Players may not leave their quadrant during the course of play. Use normal basketball rules, but limit dribbles to three. The goal is to teach students to remain spaced throughout the area. Rotate players to different quadrants so they can try playing offense and defense.

VARIATION: To encourage passing to other areas, limit the number of passes consecutively made in one quadrant. Encourage passing by allowing players to hold the ball for only 5 seconds.

Sideline Basketball

PLAYING AREA: Basketball court

PLAYERS: Entire class

SUPPLIES: A basketball, pinnies

SKILLS: All basketball skills

Divide the class into two teams, each lined up along one side of the court and facing the other. Three or four active players from each team enter the court to play regulation basketball. The other players, who stand on the sideline, can catch and pass the ball to the active players. Sideline players may not shoot or enter the court. They must keep one foot completely out of bounds at all times.

The active players play regulation basketball, but may not shoot until they pass and receive the ball three times from sideline players. Sideline players may pass to each other, but must pass back to an active player after three sideline passes. The team that was scored on takes the ball out of bounds under its own basket. Play continues for a specific period (30 seconds to 1 minute). Teams do not change after a score; only at the end of the period. The active players then go to the end of their line, and three new active players come out from the front. All other players move down and adjust to fill the space left by the new players.

No official out-of-bounds on the sides is called. Players on that side simply put the ball into play with a quick pass to an active player. Out-of-bounds on the ends is the same as in regular basketball. If any sideline player enters the court and touches the ball, it is a violation; the ball is awarded out-of-bounds on the other side to a sideline player of the other team. Active players who are fouled get free throws.

Teaching Hint

Use a modified scoring system so all students can help win the game. Hitting the backboard: 1 point; hitting the rim: 2 points; making a basket: 3 points.

Twenty-One

PLAYING AREA: One end of a basketball court

PLAYERS: 3 to 8 in each game

SUPPLIES: A basketball

SKILLS: Shooting

Players are in file formation by teams. Each player attempts a long shot (from a specified distance) and a follow-up shot. The long shot, if made, is 2 points; the follow-up shot is 1 point. Players must shoot the follow-up shot from where they recovered the ball after the first shot. Allow the normal one- to two-step rhythm on the follow-up shot.The first player scoring a total of 21 points is the winner. Players who miss the backboard and basket altogether on the first shot must take their second shot from the corner.

Teaching Hint

The rules above are for regulation Twenty-One. For more activity time and practice in rebounding, use this modified version. Score 1 point for hitting the backboard, 2 points for hitting the rim, and 3 points for a made basket. Players who make the basket or hit the rim get a free long shot that must make a basket to count. If the shooter misses, the player who gets the rebound tries to score. If that shot misses, the shooter gets 1 point for hitting the backboard or 2 points for hitting the rim, and play continues. Because players are learning these skills, standing and waiting for long shots seldom occurs.

VARIATIONS:

1. Start with a simpler game that permits dribbling before the second shot.
2. Let players shoot until they miss. Players who make both the long and the short shot go back to the original position for a third shot. Count all shots made.
3. Use various combinations and types of shots.

Lane Basketball

PLAYING AREA: Basketball court divided into six or more lanes

PLAYERS: 5 per team

SUPPLIES: A basketball, pinnies, cones to mark zones

SKILLS: All basketball skills

Divide the court into six lanes as shown in Figure 24.33. Players must stay in their lane and cannot cross the midcourt line. Regular basketball rules prevail, but players cannot dribble more than three times. Play starts with a jump ball. At regular intervals, players rotate to the next lane so they get to play offense and defense.

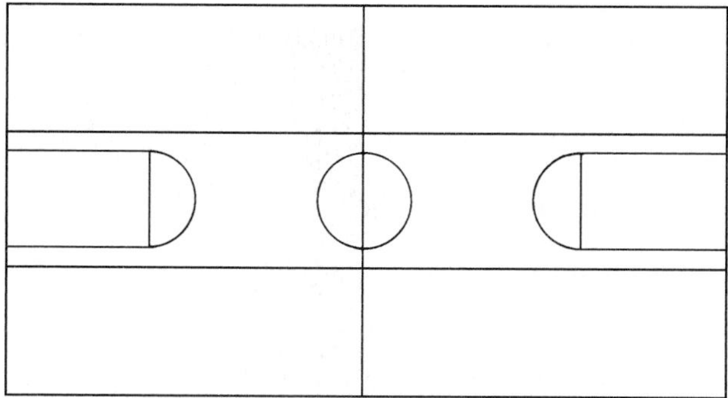

FIGURE 24.33 Court markings for Lane Basketball.

To change the game's focus, teachers can adapt the rules. For example, require three passes before shooting may occur. Also, for increased activity, permit students to move the entire length of the floor within their lane.

Freeze-Out

PLAYING AREA: One end of the basketball court

PLAYERS: 4 to 8

SUPPLIES: A basketball

SKILLS: Shooting under pressure

There are many types of freeze-out shooting games. This is an interesting game that ends quickly and allows players back into the game with little waiting time. Each player gets three misses before being out. After the first miss, the player gets an O; after the second, a U; and after the third, a T. This spells OUT and puts the player out. The last player remaining is the winner.

The first player shoots a basket from any spot desired. If the basket is missed, there is no penalty and the next player shoots from any spot desired. If the basket is made, the next player must make a basket from the same spot or it is scored as a miss (and a letter).

Flag Dribble

PLAYING AREA: One end of a basketball floor or a hard-surfaced area outside with boundaries

PLAYERS: 10 to 20

SUPPLIES: A basketball and a flag for each player

SKILLS: Dribbling

The goal is to eliminate other players and avoid being eliminated. Players are eliminated for losing control of the ball, having their flag pulled, or going out-of-bounds. Keeping control of the ball by dribbling means continuous dribbling without missing a bounce. A double dribble (both hands) is regarded as losing control.

Start the game with players scattered around the area near the sidelines. Each has a ball, and all have flags tucked in the back of their belts. On signal, all players begin dribbling in the area. While controlling the dribble and staying in bounds, they try to pull a flag from any other player's belt. Players who lose control must move to the perimeter of the area and practice their dribbling skills. When the game is down to a few players, start again. Sometimes two players lose control of their basketball at about the same time. In this case, both are eliminated.

VARIATIONS:

1. If using flags is impractical, play the game without them. The goal is then to knock aside or deflect the other basketballs while keeping control of one's own ball.
2. Flag Dribble can be played with clearly marked teams or squads.

Through the Maze

PLAYING AREA: Basketball court

PLAYERS: Two teams of 5 to 7

SUPPLIES: One ball for each player on offense

SKILLS: Dribbling, ball control, guarding, tackling

One team is on offense and one on defense, placed according to Figure 24.34. Defensive players stay in their assigned areas. On signal, all offensive players try to dribble through the three areas without losing their ball. A player whose ball is either recovered by a defensive player or goes out-of-bounds is eliminated. The offensive team scores 1 point for each ball dribbled across the opposite end line. Reverse roles and give the other team a chance to score. Use several marking spots to identify where the defensive players must stay. A variation is to put neutral zones between the active zones.

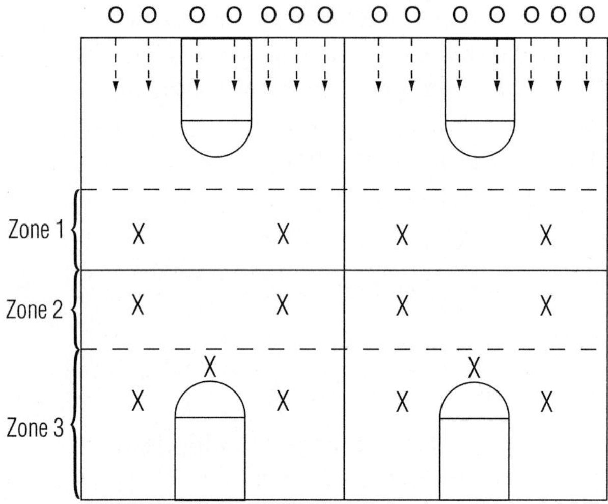

FIGURE 24.34 Through the Maze.

One-Goal Basketball

PLAYING AREA: An area with one basketball goal

PLAYERS: 2 to 4 on each team

SUPPLIES: A basketball, pinnies (optional)

SKILLS: All basketball skills

This is an excellent class activity if four or more baskets are available. The game is played by two teams using basketball rules, but with these exceptions:

1. A defensive player who recovers the ball, either from the backboard or on an interception, must take the ball out past the foul-line circle before starting offensive play and attempting a goal.
2. After a basket is made, the ball is again taken to the center of the floor, where the other team starts offensive play.
3. Regular free-throw shooting can be used after a foul, or the offended team can take the ball out-of-bounds.
4. An offensive player who is tied up in a jump ball loses the ball to the other team.
5. Individuals are responsible for calling fouls on themselves.

Basketball Snatch Ball

PLAYING AREA: Basketball court

PLAYERS: 6 to 20 on each team

SUPPLIES: Two basketballs, two hoops

SKILLS: Passing, dribbling, shooting

Two teams line up on opposite sides of a basketball floor. Number each team's players consecutively from the right-hand end of the line. Place two balls inside two hoops, one on each side of the centerline. The teacher calls three or more numbers (in any-order), and players from each team whose numbers were called run to the ball assigned to them. These players pass and dribble to the basket on their right and try to make a basket. They must make three passes, and all players must handle the ball before shooting a basket. After making a basket, the players pass and dribble back and put the ball in the hoop. The first players to make a basket and return the ball score 1 point for their team. Use a system for calling the numbers so all children have a turn.

Three-On-Three

PLAYING AREA: Half of a basketball court

PLAYERS: Many teams of 3 players each

SUPPLIES: Basketballs

SKILLS: All basketball skills

Three teams of three are assigned to a basket. The offensive team stands at the top of the key, facing the basket. The defensive team starts at the free-throw line. The third team waits their turn beyond the end line. Use regular basketball rules. The offensive team plays until they score or the defense steals the ball. The defensive team then moves to the center of the floor and becomes the offensive unit. The waiting team moves onto the floor and plays defense. The first offensive team goes to the end of the line of waiting players. All teams keep their own score. A team wins by scoring 3 points. Winning teams can rotate to games at other baskets. Many games can go on at once, depending on the baskets available.

Basketrama

PLAYING AREA: Area around one basket

PLAYERS: Usually 2

SUPPLIES: A basketball for each player

SKILLS: Shooting under pressure

On signal, two players each begin shooting their basketball as fast as possible, taking any kind of shots they wish, until one scores 10 baskets to become the winner. Players must handle their own basketball and must not impede or interfere with the other's ball. Naturally, the balls do collide at times; but players who deliberately knock the other ball out of the way or kick it are disqualified.

To avoid arguments over ownership, mark the balls with chalk or tape (or use different types of basketballs). Players can count out loud each basket they make, or another student can keep score for them.

Paper Clip Basketball

PLAYING AREA: Basketball court

PLAYERS: Entire class

SUPPLIES: Basketballs, hula hoops, paper clips, Frisbees

SKILLS: Shooting, passing, dribbling

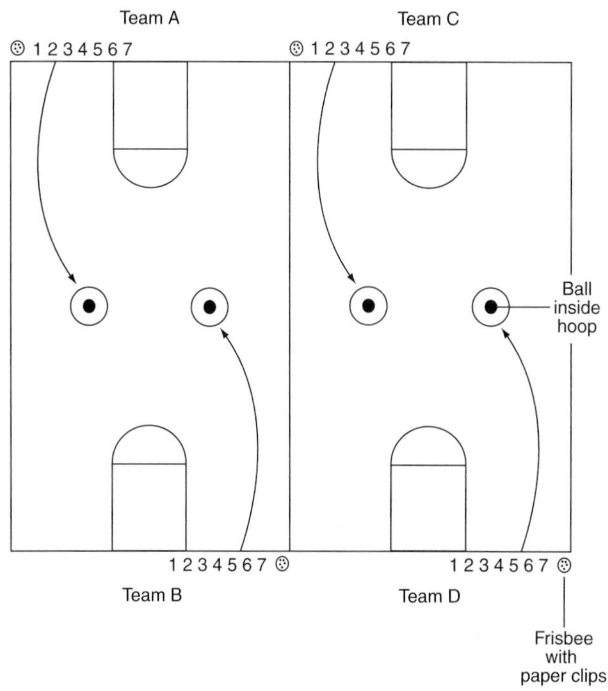

FIGURE 24.35 Paper Clip Basketball.

Form four equal teams, each standing on the sideline of one quadrant of the basketball floor (Figure 24.35). Each team has a basketball and a hoop that has been placed near the center of the gym. Allow enough room between the hoops so players do not collide. On signal, the first three players for each team must hustle for their ball, then pass and dribble toward one basket. Each player must receive the ball before that group can shoot. After making a basket, or after three tries, the players return the ball to their team's hoop, return to their sideline, and give a "high five" to the next three players. These three players repeat the process, moving toward the other basket. On the sideline, each team also has a Frisbee and several paper clips. If any of the three players makes a basket, the team places one paper clip into the Frisbee upon returning to the sideline. The game continues for several minutes, after which the team with the most paper clips in their Frisbee is the winner. So different combinations of players can work together, use team numbers not divisible by three.

BASKETBALL SKILL TESTS

Tests in basketball cover dribbling, passing, shooting, and making free throws. The first four tests presented here are timed, so a stopwatch is needed.

STRAIGHT DRIBBLE

Place a marker 15 yards down the floor from the starting point. The dribbler must dribble around the marker

or backward to qualify as a lateral. It is tossed with an easy motion, not trying to make it spiral like a forward pass.

CATCHING

In catching, the receiver keeps both eyes on the ball and catches with the hands with a slight give (Figure 25.4). Upon being caught, the ball is tucked into the carrying position. The little fingers are together for most catches.

FIGURE 25.4 Catching a pass.

These instructional cues help students focus on catching technique:

1. Keep eyes on the ball.
2. Thumbs together for a high pass (above shoulder level).
3. Thumbs apart for a low pass (below shoulder level).
4. Reach for the ball, catch with the hands, and bring it to the body.

HANDING OFF THE BALL

Children enjoy making plays in which one player gives the ball to another, as for a reverse. The reverse play starts as the player with the ball goes one direction and then hands the ball to another player heading the opposite way. The ball can be handed backward or forward. The player with the ball holds the ball with both hands but always makes the exchange with only the inside hand—the one near the receiving player. When the receiver is about 6 feet away, the carrier shifts the ball to the hand on that side, with the elbow bent partially away from the body. The receiver comes toward the carrier with the near arm bent and carried in front of the chest, the palm down. The other arm is about waist high, with the palm up (Figure 25.5). As the ball is handed off (not tossed), the receiver clamps down on the ball to secure it. As quickly as possible, the receiver then changes to a normal carrying position.

A fake reverse, sometimes called a *bootleg*, is made when the ball carrier pretends to make the exchange but the quarterback keeps the ball instead and briefly hides it behind one leg.

CARRYING THE BALL

Carry the ball with the arm on the outside and the end of the ball tucked into the notch formed by the

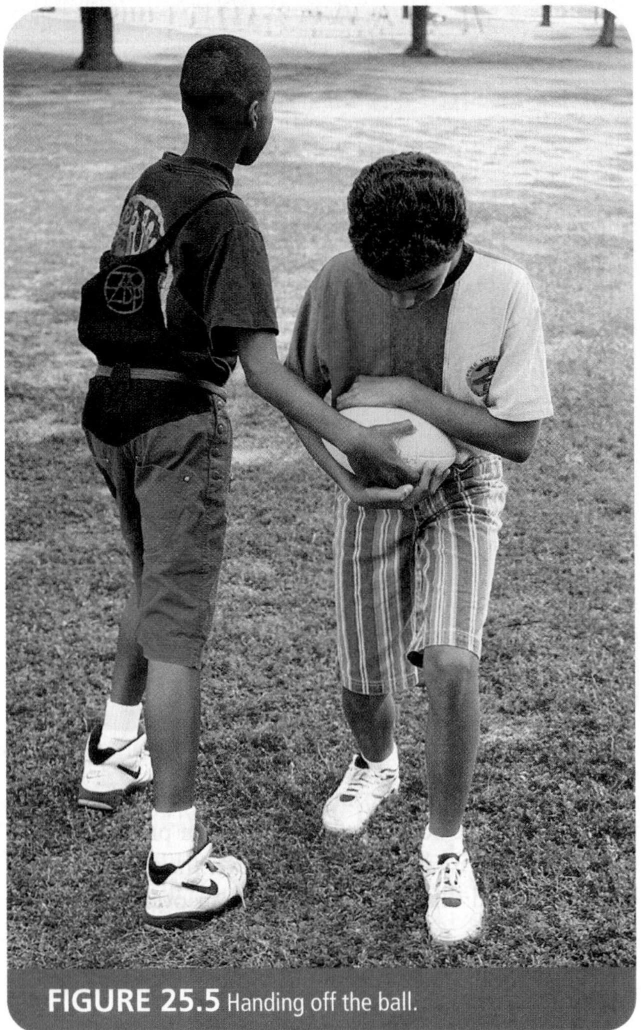

FIGURE 25.5 Handing off the ball.

elbow and arm. The fingers add support for the carry (Figure 25.6).

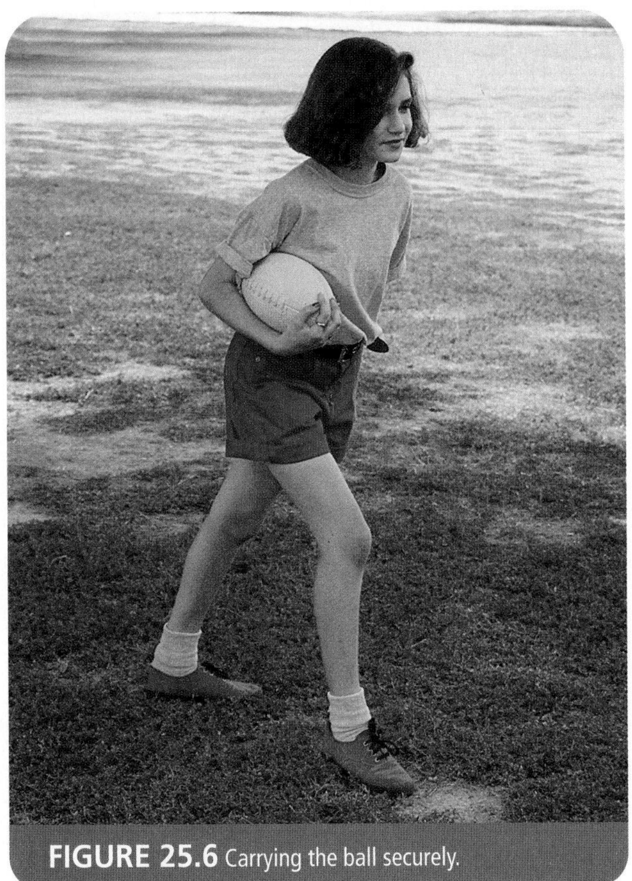

FIGURE 25.6 Carrying the ball securely.

CENTERING

Centering involves transferring the ball, on signal, to the quarterback. Elementary schools most often use the shotgun formation. This requires snapping the ball a few yards backward to the quarterback. In a direct snap, the quarterback holds her hands under the center's buttocks. The center lifts the ball, rotates it a quarter turn, and snaps it into the quarterback's hands.

The centering player bends his knees with the feet well spread and toes pointed straight ahead. He is close enough to the ball to reach it with a slight stretch. The right hand takes about the same grip as is used in passing. The other hand is on the side near the back of the ball and merely acts as a guide (Figure 25.7). On signal from the quarterback, the center extends his arms backward through the legs and hands the ball to the quarterback.

Here are some instructional cues for centering:

1. Keep legs spread and toes straight ahead.
2. Reach forward for the ball.
3. Snap the ball with the dominant hand.
4. Guide the ball with the nondominant hand.

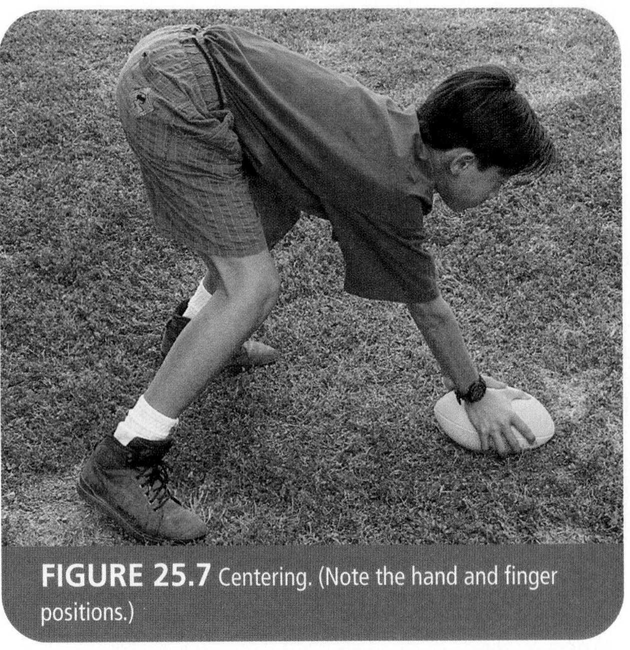

FIGURE 25.7 Centering. (Note the hand and finger positions.)

STANCE

The three-point stance is the offensive stance most generally used in Flag Football. The feet are about shoulder width apart and the toes point straight ahead, with the toes of one foot even with the heel of the other. The hand on the side of the back foot is used for support; the knuckles rest on the ground. The player looks straight ahead and always takes the same stance (Figure 25.8).

FIGURE 25.8 Offensive three-point stance.

Some players prefer the parallel stance, in which the feet, instead of being in the heel-and-toe position, are lined up evenly. In this case, players can use either hand for support. Some defensive players like to use a four-point stance with both hands in contact with the ground (Figure 25.9 on page 630).

FIGURE 25.9 Defensive four-point stance.

These instructional cues help students learn proper stance:

1. Bend the knees; keep the back parallel to the ground.
2. Keep most of the weight on the legs.
3. Do not lean forward or backward.

BLOCKING

Blocking requires the player to maintain balance and not fall to the knees. The elbows are out, and the hands are held near the chest. The block is more of an obstruction than a takeout and is set with the shoulder against the opponent's shoulder or upper body (Figure 25.10). Making contact from the rear in any direction is a penalty (clipping) because it could cause injury.

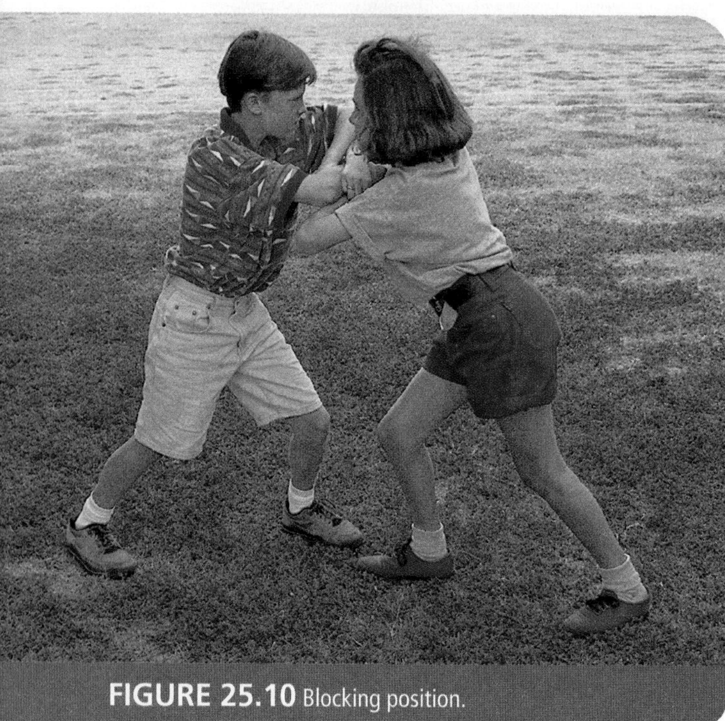

FIGURE 25.10 Blocking position.

These instructional cues help students learn to block:

1. Keep feet spread and knees bent.
2. Keep head up.
3. Stay in front of the defensive player.
4. Move your feet; stay on the balls of the feet.

PUNTING

The kicker stands with the kicking foot slightly forward. The fingers extend in the direction of the center. The eyes are on the ball from the time it is centered until it is kicked—the kicker should actually see the foot kick the ball. After receiving the ball, the kicker takes a short step with the kicking foot and then a second step with the other foot. She swings the kicking leg forward and, at impact, straightens the leg to create maximum force. The toes are pointed, and the long axis of the ball makes contact on the top of the instep. The leg follows through well after the kick (Figure 25.11). Emphasize dropping the ball properly. Beginners tend to throw it in the air, making the punt more difficult.

FIGURE 25.11 Punting.

These instructional cues help students learn to punt:

1. Drop the football; do not toss it upward.
2. Keep the eyes focused on the ball.
3. Kick upward and through the ball.
4. Contact the ball on the outer side of the instep.

PLACE KICKING

The kicker stands 5 to 7 feet behind the ball and slightly to the left (if a right-footed kicker). The ball is held upright by a teammate or a kicking tee. As when kicking a long soccer pass, the kicker approaches the ball at an angle and sets her opposite foot beside the ball. At this point, the kicking leg is at the height of its backswing. The kicker's head is down as the kicking foot comes forward, making ball contact with the inside part of the shoelaces. To create loft, the kicker leans back slightly and strikes the ball below the middle, close to the ground. The kicking foot continues up and forward after contact (Figure 25.12).

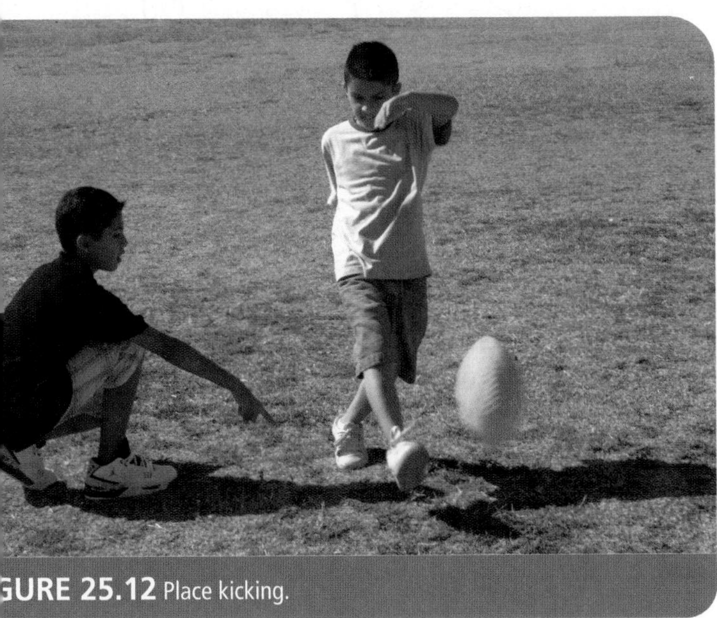

GURE 25.12 Place kicking.

Here are instructional cues for place kicking:

1. Approach and plant.
2. Foot back, knee bent.
3. Head down and lean back.
4. Swing through the ball.

INSTRUCTIONAL PROCEDURES

1. All children need the opportunity to practice all football skills. To ensure this, set up a rotation system.
2. Drills should be performed with attention to proper form, and they should approximate game conditions. For example, when students practice going out for passes, have them start the pattern in the proper stance.
3. Use junior-sized or foam footballs. Provide at least 6 to 8 footballs for football drills. The best teaching situation is to have one football for each pair of children.
4. Control roughness and unfair play by supervising play and strictly enforcing rules.

Safety Tip

In order to avoid rough contact and decrease the possibility of injuries, flag belts or soft touching (with the back of the hand on the shoulder) should be the method used to "down" students during football lessons.

FOOTBALL DRILLS

Ball Carrying

FORMATION: Scattered

PLAYERS: Four to six students

SUPPLIES: A football, a flag for each player, cones to mark the zones

The ball carrier stands on the goal line ready to run. At 20-yard intervals, three defensive players wait; each one is stationed on a zone line of a regular Flag Football field, facing the ball carrier (Figure 25.13). Each defender is assigned to the zone she is facing and must down the ball carrier by pulling a flag while the carrier is still in the zone. The ball carrier runs and dodges, trying to get by each defender in turn without having her flag pulled. If the flag is pulled, the runner continues, and the last defender uses a two-handed touch to down the ball carrier. After completing the run, the ball carrier goes to the end of the defender's line and rotates to a defending position.

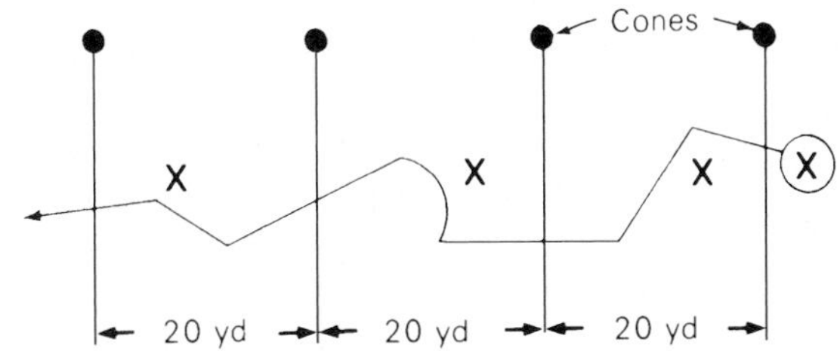

FIGURE 25.13 Ball carrying drill.

Ball Exchange

FORMATION: Shuttle, with the halves about 15 yards apart

PLAYERS: 4 to 10 students in two files

SUPPLIES: A football

25

The two halves of the shuttle face each other across the 15-yard distance. A player at the head of one of the files has a ball and carries it over to the other file, where he makes an exchange with the player at the front of that file (Figure 25.14). The ball is carried back and forth between the shuttle files. Receiving players do not start until the ball carrier is almost up to them. A player, after handing the ball to the front player of the other file, continues around and joins that file. A simpler way to practice ball exchanges is to use scatter formation where half the class has a ball and the other half does not. On signal, students without a ball run toward those who have a ball. Handoffs continue as students alternate handing off with taking the handoff.

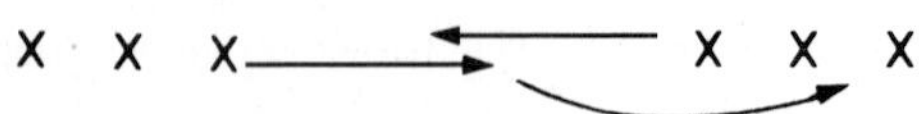

FIGURE 25.14 Ball exchange drill.

Combination

FORMATION: Regular offensive formation with passer, center, end, and ball chaser

PLAYERS: 4 to 8 students

SUPPLIES: A football

This drill combines passing, centering, and receiving skills. Each player, after her turn, rotates to the next spot. At least 4 players are needed. The center player centers the ball to the passer; the passer passes the ball to the end; the end receives the pass; the ball chaser retrieves the ball if missed by the end, or takes a pass from the end (if she caught the ball) and carries the ball to the center spot, which is her next assignment (Figure 25.15).

The rotation follows the path of the ball—the rotation system moves from center to passer to end to ball chaser to center. Extra players are stationed behind the passer waiting their turns.

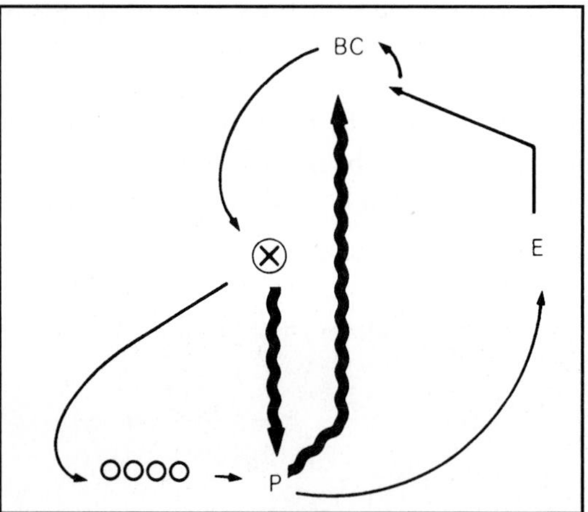

FIGURE 25.15 Combination drill.

One-on-One Defensive Drill

FORMATION: Center, passer, end, defender

PLAYERS: 8 to 10 students

SUPPLIES: A football

This drill is as old as football itself. A defensive player stands about 8 yards back, waiting for an approaching end. The passer tries to complete the pass to the end while the defender tries to break up the pass or intercept the ball. One defender practices against all the players and then rotates (Figure 25.16). The passer must be able to pass well, or this drill has little value.

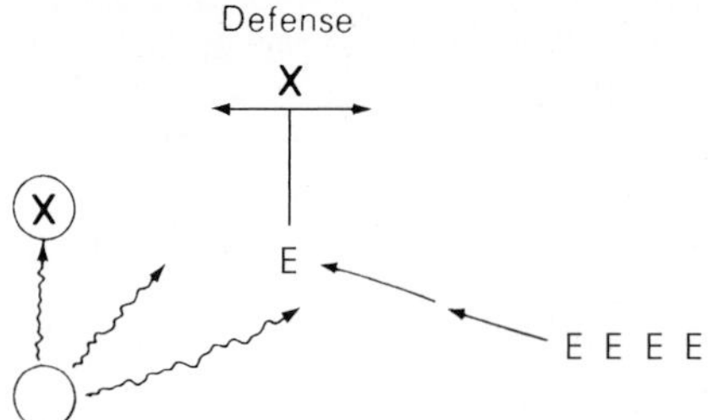

FIGURE 25.16 One-on-one defensive drill.

VARIATION: Play the drill with two ends and two defenders. The passer throws to the end who seems the most unguarded.

Punt Return

FORMATION: Center, kicker, two lines of ends, receivers

PLAYERS: 10 to 20 students

SUPPLIES: A football, a flag for each player

In this drill, the receiver must catch a punted ball and return it to the line of scrimmage while two ends try to pull a flag or make a tag. Two ends are ready to run downfield. The center snaps the ball to the kicker, who punts the ball downfield to the punt receiver. The ends cannot cross the line of scrimmage until the ball has been kicked. Each end makes two trips downfield as a "tackler" before rotating to the punt-receiving position.

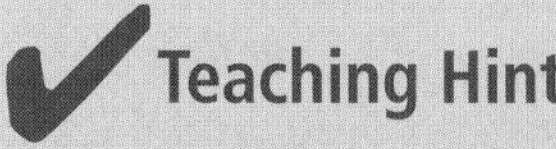

Teaching Hint

This drill requires an effective punter. It is also important for the ends to wait until the ball is kicked, or they will be downfield too soon for the receiver to have a fair chance of making a return run.

Stance

FORMATION: Squads in extended file formation

PLAYERS: 6 to 8 students in each file

SUPPLIES: None

The first player in each file performs the drill and then goes to the end of his file. On the command "Ready," the first child in each file assumes a football stance. The teacher can correct and make observations. On the command "Hike," the players charge forward for about 5 yards (Figure 25.17). The new player at the head of each line gets ready.

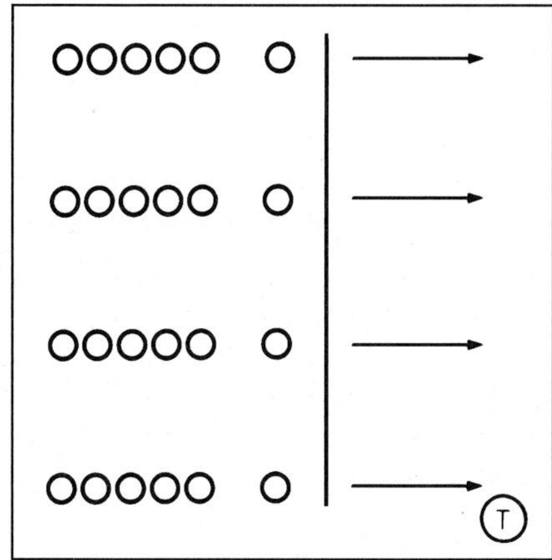

FIGURE 25.17 Stance drill.

FOOTBALL ACTIVITIES

DEVELOPMENTAL LEVEL II

Football End Ball

PLAYING AREA: Court 20 by 40 feet

PLAYERS: Two teams of 9 to 12 students each

SUPPLIES: Footballs

SKILLS: Passing, catching

The court is divided in half by a centerline. End zones are marked 3 feet wide, completely across the court at each end. Divide players on each team into three groups: forwards, guards, and ends. The object is for a forward to throw successfully to one of the end-zone players. Position players from each team as shown in Figure 25.18. End-zone players take positions in one of the end zones. Their forwards and guards then occupy the half of the court farthest from this end zone. The forwards are near the centerline, and the guards are back near the end zone of their half of the court.

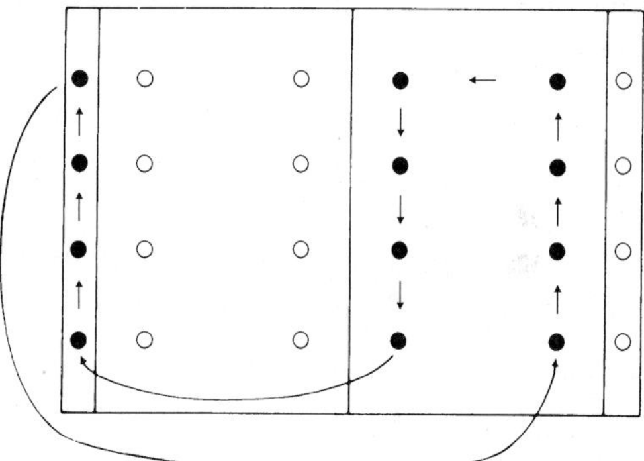

FIGURE 25.18 Player positions for Football End Ball.

When a team gets the ball, the forwards try to throw over the heads of the opposing team to an end-zone player. To score, a player with both of her feet inside the end zone must catch the ball. No players may move with the ball. After each score, resume play with a jump ball at the centerline.

A penalty results in loss of the ball to the other team. Penalties are assessed for these actions:

1. Holding a ball for more than 5 seconds
2. Stepping over the endline or stepping over the centerline into the opponent's territory
3. Pushing or holding another player

In case of an out-of-bounds ball, the ball belongs to the team that did not cause it to go out. The nearest player retrieves the ball at the sideline and returns it to a player of the proper team.

VARIATION: Using more than one ball increases activity and throwing repetitions, but also requires a different rotation system. When a throw is completed to an end, he switches with the forward who threw the ball. Throughout the game, play is stopped as forwards and ends quickly become guards while guards become forwards and ends.

Encourage fast, accurate passing. Players in the end zones must practice jumping high to catch the ball yet land with both feet inside the end-zone area. A rotation system is desirable. After making a score, players on that team can rotate one player (see Figure 25.18).

To outline the end zones, some instructors use folding mats (4 by 7 feet or 4 by 8 feet). Three or four mats for each end zone define the area and eliminate the problem of defensive players (guards) stepping into the end zone.

Five Passes (Football)

PLAYING AREA: Football field or other defined area

PLAYERS: 6 to 10 students on each team

SUPPLIES: A football, pinnies or other identification

SKILLS: Passing, catching

Players scatter on the field. The object is for one team to make five consecutive passes to five different players without losing control of the ball. This scores 1 point. The defense may play the ball only and cannot make personal contact with opposing players. No player can take more than three steps when in possession of the ball. More than three steps is called *traveling*, and the ball is awarded to the other team.

The ball is given to the opponents at the nearest out-of-bounds line for traveling, minor contact fouls, after a point has been scored, and for causing the ball to go out of bounds. No penalty is assigned when the ball hits the ground. It remains in play, but the five-pass sequence is interrupted and must start again. Jump balls are called when the ball is tied up or when there is a pileup. Players should call out the pass sequence.

Speed Football

PLAYING AREA: Football field 30 by 60 yards, divided into three equal sections

PLAYERS: Entire class divided into two teams

SUPPLIES: A football, flag for each player

SKILLS: Passing, catching, running with ball

The ball is kicked off or started at the 20-yard line. The object is to move the ball across the opponent's goal by running or passing. If the ball drops to the ground or if a player's flag is pulled when carrying the ball, it is a turnover and the ball is set into play at that spot. Interceptions are turnovers, and the intercepting team moves on offense. Teams must make at least four complete passes before being eligible to move across the opponent's goal line. No blocking is allowed. To speed up the game, a team can immediately (without waiting for the opponents to set up) kick or throw off after the other team scores. This motivates all players to hustle after a score.

VARIATION: So more students can be actively involved, use smaller fields and let your class play more than one game at a time. Students also enjoy playing this game with Frisbees.

DEVELOPMENTAL LEVEL III

Kick-Over

PLAYING AREA: Football field with a 10-yard end zone

PLAYERS: 6 to 10 students on each team

SUPPLIES: A football

SKILLS: Kicking, catching

Teams are scattered on opposite ends of the field. The object is to punt the ball over the other team's goal line. If the ball is caught in the end zone, no score results. A ball kicked into the end zone and not caught scores a goal. If the ball is kicked beyond the end zone on the fly, a score is made whether or not the ball is caught.

Play is started by one team with a punt from 20 to 30 feet in front of its own goal line. On a punt, if the ball is not caught, the team must kick from the spot of recovery. If the ball is caught, players can take three long strides to advance the ball for a kick.

Teaching Hint

The player kicking next should move quickly to the area where the ball is to be kicked. Players are numbered and kick in rotation. If the players do not kick in rotation, one or two aggressive players will dominate the game.

Fourth Down

PLAYING AREA: Half of a football field or equivalent space

PLAYERS: 6 to 8 students on each team

SUPPLIES: A football, pinnies

SKILLS: Most football skills, except kicking and blocking

Every play is a fourth down—the play must score or the team loses the ball. No kicking is permitted, but players may pass at any time from any spot and in any direction. A series of passes can occur on any play, either from behind or beyond the line of scrimmage.

The teams line up in an offensive football formation. To start the game, the ball is placed at the center of the field; a coin toss decides which team has the chance to put the ball into play. The ball is put into play by centering. The back receiving the ball runs or passes to any of his teammates. The one receiving the ball has the same privilege. No blocking is permitted. After each touchdown, the ball is brought to the center of the field, and the team that did not score puts the ball into play.

Players can down a runner or pass receiver by making a two-handed touch above the waist. The back first receiving the ball from the center has immunity from tagging, providing she does not try to run. All defensive players must stay 10 feet away unless she runs. The referee waits for a reasonable length of time for the back to pass or run. If the player holds the ball beyond that time, the referee calls out, "Ten seconds." The back must then throw or run within 10 seconds or be rushed by the defense.

Defensive players scatter to cover the receivers. They can use either a one-on-one defense, with each player covering an offensive player, or a zone defense.

Because the team with the ball loses possession after each play, use the following rules to determine where the ball is placed when the other team takes possession.

1. If a ball carrier is tagged with two hands above the waist, the ball goes to the other team at that spot.
2. If an incomplete pass is made from behind the line of scrimmage, the ball is given to the other team at the spot where the ball was put into play.
3. When a player beyond the line of scrimmage makes an incomplete pass, the ball is brought to the spot from which it was thrown.

Teaching Hint

The team in possession must pass by the count of 10, because children tire from running around to become free for a pass. The defensive team can score by intercepting a pass. Because passes can be made at any time, on interception, the player should look down the field for a pass to a teammate.

VARIATION: The game can be called Third Down, and the offensive team then has two chances to score.

Football Box Ball

PLAYING AREA: Football field 50 yards long

PLAYERS: 8 to 16 students on each team

SUPPLIES: A football, pinnies

SKILLS: Passing, catching

Five yards beyond each goal is a 6- by 6-foot square, which is the box. Teams are marked so they can be distinguished. The game is similar to End Ball because the teams try to make a successful pass to the captain in the box.

To begin the play, players are onside (on opposite ends of the field). The team losing the toss kicks off from its own 10-yard line to the other team. The game then becomes a kind of keep-away—teams try to secure or retain possession of the ball until a successful pass can be made to the captain in the box. The captain must catch the ball on the fly and still keep both feet in the box. This scores a touchdown.

A player may run sideways or backward when in possession of the ball. Players may not run forward but are allowed momentum (two steps) if receiving or intercepting a ball. The penalty for illegal forward movement while in possession of the ball is loss of the ball to the opponents, who take it and immediately begin play.

The captain is changed after three unsuccessful attempts or when a goal is scored. If either occurs, another player is rotated into the box. On any incomplete pass or failed attempt to get the ball to the captain, the team loses the ball. If a touchdown is made, the team brings the ball back to its 10-yard line and kicks off to the other team. If the touchdown attempt is not successful, the other team receives the ball out-of-bounds on the end line.

Any out-of-bounds ball is put into play by the team that did not send it out-of-bounds. No team can score from a throw-in from out-of-bounds.

In case of a tie ball, a jump ball is called at the spot. The players face off as in a jump ball in basketball.

Players must play the ball and not the individual. For unnecessary roughness, a player is sidelined until a pass is thrown to the other team's captain. The ball is awarded to the offended team out-of-bounds.

On the kickoff, all players must be onside (behind the ball when it is kicked). If the kicking team is called offside, the ball goes to the other team out-of-bounds at the centerline. After the kickoff, players may move to any part of the field. On the kickoff, the ball must travel 10 yards before either team can recover it. A kickoff outside or over the endline is treated like any other out-of-bounds ball.

A ball hitting the ground remains in play as long as it is inbounds. Players may not bat or kick a free ball. The penalty is loss of the ball to the other team out-of-bounds.

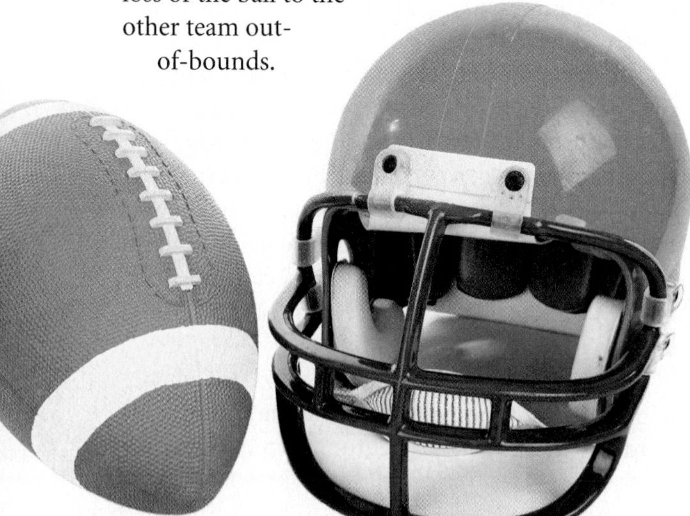

Falling on the ball also means loss of the ball to the other team.

Teaching Hint

Use a folding tumbling mat (about 4 by 7 feet) as the box where the captain must stand to catch the ball for a score.

Flag Football

PLAYING AREA: Field 30 by 60 yards

PLAYERS: 6 to 9 students on a team

SUPPLIES: A football, two flags per player (about 3 inches wide and 24 inches long), pinnies

SKILLS: All football skills

Divide the field into three zones by marking off lines at 20-yard intervals. Also mark two end zones, from 5 to 10 yards wide, defining the area behind the goal where passes may be caught. Flag Football is played with two flags on each player. The flag is a length of cloth hanging from the side at each player's waist. Opposing players can down (stop) a player with the ball by pulling one of the flags.

Avoid playing Flag Football with 11 players on a side. This results in a crowded field and leaves little room to maneuver. If 6 or 7 are on a team, 4 players must stand on the line of scrimmage. For 8 or 9 players, 5 offensive players must be on the line.

The game consists of two halves. Each half involves 25 plays. All plays count in the 25, except the try for the point after a touchdown and a kickoff out-of-bounds.

The game begins with a kickoff. The team winning the coin toss can either select the goal it wishes to defend or choose to kick or receive. The loser of the toss takes the option not chosen by the first team. The kickoff is from the goal line, and all players on the kicking team must be onside. The kick must cross the first zone line, or it does not count as a play. A kick that flies out-of-bounds (and is not touched by the receiving team) must be kicked again. A second consecutive kick out-of-bounds gives the ball to the receiving team in the center of the field. The kicking team cannot recover the kickoff unless the receivers catch and then fumble it.

A team has four downs to move the ball into the next zone, or they lose the ball. If they legally advance the ball into the last zone, the team has four downs to score. A ball on the line between zones is considered to be in the more forward zone, and the team with the ball may continue to advance it.

Time-outs are permitted only for injuries or when called by the officials. Unlimited substitutions are permitted. Each substitute must report to the official.

The team in possession of the ball usually huddles to make up the play. After any play, the team has 30 seconds to put the ball into play after the referee gives the signal.

Blocking is done with the arms close to the body. Blocking must be done from the front or side, and blockers must stay on their feet.

A player is down if one of her flags has been pulled. The ball carrier must try to avoid the defensive player and is not permitted to run over or through the defensive player. The tackler must focus on making physical contact with the flags, not with the ball carrier. Good officiating is needed, because defensive players may try to hold or grasp the ball carrier until they can remove one of her flags.

All forward passes must be thrown from behind the line of scrimmage. All players on the field are eligible to receive and intercept passes.

All fumbles are dead at the spot of the fumble. The first player who touches the ball on the ground is ruled to have recovered the fumble. When the ball is centered to a back, she must gain definite possession of it before a fumble can be called. She is allowed to pick up a bad pass from the center when she does not have possession of the ball.

All punts must be announced. Neither team can cross the line of scrimmage until the ball is kicked. Kick receivers may run or use a lateral pass. They cannot make a forward pass after receiving a kick.

A pass caught in an end zone scores a touchdown. The player must have control of the ball in the end zone. A ball caught beyond the end zone is out-of-bounds and is considered an incomplete pass.

A touchdown scores 6 points, a completed pass or run after touchdown scores 1 point, and a safety scores 2 points. A point after touchdown is made from a distance of 3 feet from the goal line. One play (pass or run) is allowed for the extra point. Any ball kicked over the goal line is ruled a touchback and is brought out to the 20-yard line to be put into play by the receiving team. A pass intercepted behind the goal line can be a touchback if the player does not run it out, even if she is tagged behind her own goal line.

A penalty of 5 yards is assessed for these actions:

1. Being offside
2. Delaying the game (too long in huddle)
3. Failure of substitute to report to the official
4. Passing from a spot not behind line of scrimmage (also results in loss of down)
5. Stiff-arming by the ball carrier, or not avoiding a defensive player
6. Failing to announce intention to punt
7. Shortening the flag in the belt, or playing without flags in proper position
8. Faking the ball by the center, who must center the pass on the first motion

The following infractions are assessed a 15-yard loss:

1. Holding, illegal tackling
2. Illegal blocking
3. Unsportsmanlike conduct (also can result in disqualification)

Teaching Hint

Specifying 25 plays per half eliminates the need for timing and avoids arguments about a team's taking too much time in the huddle. Using the zone system makes the first-down yardage point definite and eliminates the need for a chain to mark off the 10 yards needed for a first down.

Pass Ball

PLAYING AREA: Field 30 by 60 yards

PLAYERS: 6 to 9 students on a team

SUPPLIES: A football, flags (optional), pinnies

SKILLS: All football skills, especially passing and catching

Pass Ball is a more open game than Flag Football, but the rules are similar except for these differences.

1. The ball may be passed at any time. It can be thrown at any time beyond the line of scrim-

mage, immediately after an interception, during a kickoff, or during a received kick.

2. Four downs are given to score a touchdown.
3. Players use a two-handed touch on the back instead of pulling a flag. Flags can be used, however.
4. If the ball is thrown from behind the line of scrimmage and results in an incomplete pass, the ball is down at the previous spot on the line of scrimmage. If the pass originates otherwise and is incomplete, the ball is placed at the spot from which this pass was thrown.
5. Because the ball can be passed at any time, no downfield blocking is permitted. A player may screen the ball carrier but cannot make a block. *Screening* is defined as running between the ball carrier and the defense.

FOOTBALL SKILL TESTS

Tests for football skills cover centering, passing, and kicking (punting).

CENTERING

Each player is given five trials to center at a target. The target is stationed 6 yards behind the center. Some suggestions for targets follow.

1. Suspend an old tire so that the bottom of the tire is about 2 feet above the ground. Players score 2 points for centering the ball through the tire. They score 1 point for hitting the tire but not going through it. Possible total: 10 points.
2. Use a baseball pitching target from the softball program. Scoring is the same as with the tire target.
3. Have a player hold a 2- by 3-foot piece of plywood at the target line in front of his body, keeping the target's upper edge even with the shoulders. The target is not to be moved during the centering. Players score 1 point for hitting the target. Possible total: 5 points.

PASSING FOR ACCURACY

To test accuracy in passing, each player attempts five throws from a minimum distance of 15 yards at a tire suspended at about shoulder height. (To stabilize the tire, suspend it from goal posts or volleyball standards.) As skill increases, increase the distance.

Players score 2 points for throwing through the tire and 1 point for hitting the tire but not passing through. Possible total: 10 points.

PASSING FOR DISTANCE

Each player is allotted three passes to determine how far she can throw a football. Measure the longest throw to the nearest foot. Reserve the test for a relatively calm day, because the wind can be quite a factor (for or against the player) in this test.

The passes are made on a field marked off in 5-yard intervals. Use markers made from tongue depressors to indicate the first pass distance. If a later throw is longer, move the marker to that point. When individual markers are used, team members can complete the passing turns before measuring.

KICKING FOR DISTANCE

Punting, place kicking, and drop kicking can be measured for distance by using techniques similar to those described for passing for distance.

FLAG FOOTBALL FORMATIONS

Figures 25.19 and 25.20 illustrate various offensive formations for Flag Football, including the T-formation. The T-formation has limited use in Flag Football, because the passer (the quarterback) is handicapped by being too close to the center. Emphasize using a variety of formations including spread formations, with flankers and ends positioned out beyond normal placement.

Balanced (tight ends):

E O X O E

Unbalanced right (tight ends):

E X O O E

Line over right (tight end):

X E O O E

Right end out (can be one or both):

E O X O (5 yards) E

Right end wide (can be one or both):

E O X O (15 yards) E

Right end wide, left end out (can be reversed):

E (5 yards) O X O (15 yards) E

Spread (3 to 5 yards between each line position):

E O X O E

FIGURE 25.19 Offensive line formations.

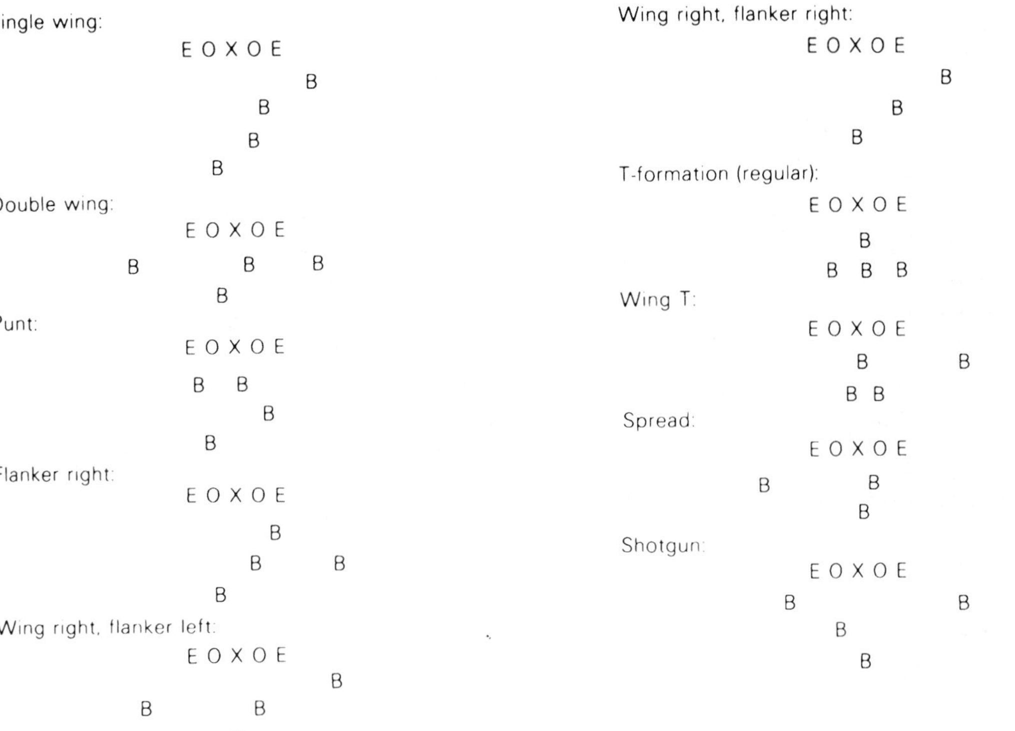

FIGURE 25.20 Offensive backfield formations.

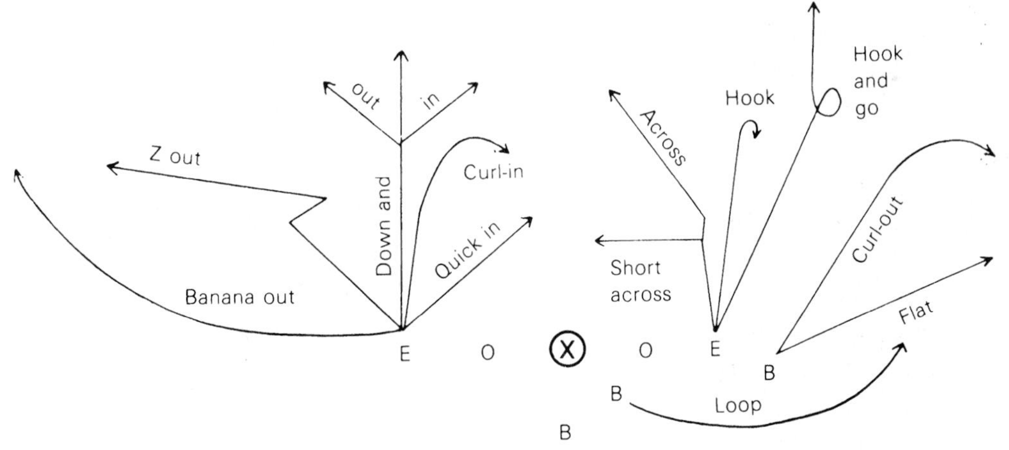

FIGURE 25.21 Pass patterns.

The following formations are based on a 9-player team (4 in the backfield and 5 on the line). The formations will vary if the number on each team is decreased. Presenting a variety of formations to players makes the game more interesting. Backfield formations can be right or left (see Figure 25.20).

OFFENSIVE LINE FORMATIONS

Figure 25.19 depicts only formations to the right. The center is indicated by an X, backs by B, ends by E, and line positions by O.

OFFENSIVE BACKFIELD FORMATIONS

The formations diagrammed in Figure 25.20 can be combined with any of the offensive line formations. For clarity, however, the illustrations for all formations show a balanced line with tight ends.

PASS PATTERNS

The pass patterns illustrated in Figure 25.21 may be run by the individual pass catcher, whether he occupies a line position or is a back. The patterns are particularly valuable in practice, when the pass receiver informs the passer of his pattern.

sideline, with their right sides facing their team's goal. Players simultaneously hit the ground three times with their sticks (on their side of the base). After the third hit on the ground, the ball is played, and each player tries to control the ball or pass it to a teammate. The right hand can be moved down the stick to facilitate a quick, powerful movement. Another method of starting action is for a referee to drop the ball between the players' sticks.

GOALKEEPING

The goalie may kick the puck, stop it with any part of the body, or let it rebound off his body or hand. He may not, however, hold the puck or throw it toward the other end of the playing area. The goalkeeper is positioned in front of the goal line and moves between the goal posts. When a puck is hit toward the goal, the goalie tries to move in front of the puck and keep the feet together. This allows the body to block the puck should the stick miss it. After the block, the goalie immediately passes the puck to a teammate.

INSTRUCTIONAL PROCEDURES

1. For many children, hockey is a new experience. Few have played the game, and many may never have seen a game. Showing a film of a hockey game may be helpful.
2. Since few children have had the opportunity to develop skills elsewhere, teach the basic skills in sequence and give students ample practice sessions.
3. Hockey is a rough game if children do not learn the proper methods of stick handling. Remind them often to use caution and good judgment when handling hockey sticks.
4. Ample equipment increases individual practice time and facilitates skill development. Try to provide each child with a stick and a ball or puck.
5. If hockey is played on a gym floor, use a plastic puck or yarn ball. If played on a carpeted area or outdoors, use a whiffle ball. An 8-foot folding mat set on end makes a satisfactory goal.
6. Hockey is a team game that is more enjoyable for all when the players pass to open teammates. Discourage excessive control of the ball by one player.

HOCKEY DRILLS

STICK-HANDLING DRILLS

1. *Phantom stick handling.* Successful hockey play demands good footwork and proper stick handling. To develop these skills, spread players on the field, carrying the stick in proper position, in a group mimetic drill. On command, players move forward, backward, and to either side. Quick reactions and footwork are the focus.
2. *Direction stick handling.* Each player with a ball practices handling it individually. Practice first at controlled speeds and increase speed as skill develops. On signal, players change direction while maintaining control of the ball.
3. *Change-of-direction stick handling.* Players are spread out on the field, each with a ball. On command, they carry the ball left, right, forward, and backward. On the command "Change direction," the players move away from an imaginary tackler. Players should concentrate on ball control and dodging in all directions.
4. *Down, around, and pass.* Players can practice in pairs, with partners standing about 20 feet apart. One player carries the ball toward a partner, goes around the partner, and returns to the starting spot (Figure 26.8). The ball is then passed to the partner, who moves in a similar manner. A shuttle type of formation can be used with three players.

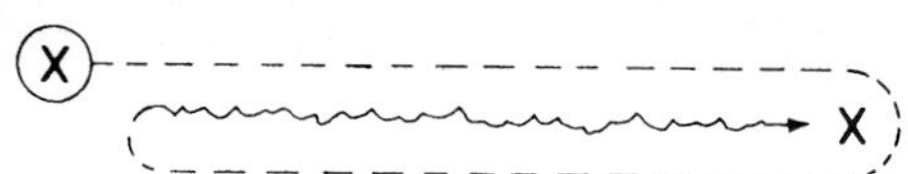

FIGURE 26.8 Down, around, and pass drill.

PASSING AND RECEIVING DRILLS

1. *Partner passing.* In pairs, about 20 feet apart, players pass the ball quickly back and forth. Emphasize passing immediately after receiving the ball. Cue phrase: "Receive and pass."
2. *Pass and carry.* One player passes the ball to a partner, who carries the ball a few steps left or right and passes it back to the other. Players can try receiving passes from various angles and from the right and left sides.
3. *Sliding circle drill.* In this drill, a circle of 4 to 6 players skates around a player in the center. The center player passes to and receives from the skating players. After the puck has gone around the circle twice, another player takes the center position.
4. *Triangle drill.* From 4 to 8 players can participate in this drill. The puck begins at the head of a line and is passed forward to a player off to one side of the line. This player then passes to a teammate out at a corner, who then passes back to the head of the line. Each player passes and then moves to the spot to where he passed the puck, thus making a continual change of positions. *Note:* This drill replicates the motion of cycling the puck.

5. *Circle-star drill.* This drill is particularly effective for 5 players. Players pass to every other player, and the path of the puck forms a star. Any odd number of players will cause the puck to go to all participants, assuring that all receive equal practice.
6. *Downfield drill.* This drill is useful for polishing passing and receiving skills while moving. Three files of players start at one end of the field. One player from each file moves downfield, passing to and fielding from the others until she reaches the other end of the field. She can make a goal shot at this point. Players remain close together for short passes until they reach a higher skill level.
7. Practice driving for distance and accuracy with a partner.

DODGING AND CHECKING DRILLS

1. *Cone dodge.* Three players form the drill configuration (Figure 26.9). Player 1 has the puck in front, approaches the cone (which represents a defensive player), dodges around the cone, and passes to Player 2, who repeats the dodging maneuver in the opposite direction. Player 2 passes to Player 3, and the drill continues.

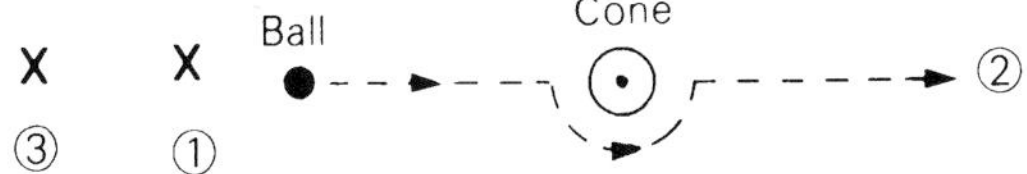

FIGURE 26.9 Cone dodge drill.

2. *Partner stick checks.* Players work in pairs. One partner dribbles toward the other, who tries to make a stick check. Reverse the roles at regular intervals. Have students start by practicing this drill at moderate speeds.
3. *Three on three.* A three-on-three drill affords practice in many skill areas. Three players are on offense and three are on defense. The offense can concentrate on passing, stick handling, and dodging, while the defense concentrates on checking. The offense scores 1 point for reaching the opposite side of the field. Reverse offensive and defensive roles at set times.

SHOOTING DRILLS

1. *Give-and-go drill.* Each player has a partner. The first partner has a puck and is the shooter. She passes the puck to the wing (partner), who passes the puck to the spot the shooter has selected for the shot. *Note:* To increase difficulty, have players try one-timers.
2. *Three-player rush.* For this drill, establish three lines of players at one end of the ice. One line has a puck. One player from each line moves down the ice, passing to the other two players. As the players near the goal, one of the players shoots on goal. The other players retrieve the puck, and all three players hustle back to the starting point and start again.

HOCKEY ACTIVITIES

DEVELOPMENTAL LEVEL II

Stick-Handling Competition

PLAYING AREA: Any clearly defined area

PLAYERS: Entire team

SUPPLIES: A stick and puck (or ball) for each player

SKILLS: Stick handling and protecting the puck

This activity can be played at two levels of difficulty.

Level 1: All players stick-handle throughout half of the area, controlling their puck so that it does not touch another puck. If a touch occurs, both players go to the other half of the area and stick-handle around its perimeter. After stick-handling around the second area, these players reenter the game.

Level 2: Divide the area and have all players move to one of the halves. While stick-handling and controlling a puck, each player tries to make another player lose control of his puck. Players who lose control take their puck and move to the other area. Play continues against other players who have lost control. When 5 or 6 players remain in the first area, all players return to the game and start over.

Circle Keep-Away

PLAYING AREA: A 20- to 25-foot circle

PLAYERS: 8 to 10 students

SUPPLIES: One stick per player, a puck or ball

SKILLS: Passing, receiving

Players are spaced evenly around the circle, with two or more players in the center. The object is to keep the players in the center from touching the puck. Players pass the puck back and forth, focusing on accurate passing and receiving. Center players see how many touches they can make during their turn. Change the center players after a set time so all students get to be center players.

Illegal touching, sideline violations, and other minor fouls result in loss of the ball to the opposition. Players who commit roughing fouls and illegal striking are sent to the sideline until the game period ends.

✔ Teaching Hint

Try to encourage team play and passing strategies rather than having all players charge and swarm the puck. An effective rule is to require active players to make three passes to their sideline teammates before taking a shot on goal. This makes all players an important part of the game.

Regulation Elementary Hockey

PLAYING AREA: Hockey field or gymnasium area, approximately 40 to 50 feet by 75 to 90 feet

PLAYERS: Teams of 6 or more students each

SUPPLIES: One stick per player, a puck or ball

SKILLS: All hockey skills

In a small gym, use the walls as boundaries. In a large gym or on an outdoor field, mark off the playing area with traffic cones. Divide the area in half, with a 12-foot restraining circle centered on the midline. Play begins here at the start of a period, after goals, or after foul shots. The official goal is 2 feet high by 6 feet wide, with a restraining area 4 by 8 feet around the goal to protect the goalie (Figure 26.13). Each team has a goalkeeper, who stops shots with her hands, feet, or stick; a center, who is the only player allowed to move full court and who leads offensive play (the center's stick is striped with black tape); two guards, who cannot go beyond the centerline into the offensive area and are responsible for keeping the ball or puck out of their defensive half of the field; and two forwards, who work with the center on offensive play and cannot go back over the centerline into the defensive area.

A game consists of three periods of 8 minutes each, with a 3-minute rest between periods. Play begins with a face-off by the centers at midcourt. Other players cannot enter the restraining circle until the ball has been hit by the centers. The clock starts when the ball is put into play and runs continuously until a goal is scored or a foul is called. Substitutions can be made only when the clock is stopped. If the ball goes out-of-bounds, the team that did not hit it last puts it back into play.

Whenever the ball passes through the goal on the ground, 1 point is scored. If, however, the ball crosses the goal line while in the air, it must strike against the mat or back wall to count for a score. Under no circumstances can a goal be scored on a foul. The ball can deflect off a player or equipment to score, but it cannot be kicked into the goal.

The goalkeeper may use her hands to clear the ball away from the goal, but she may not hold it or throw it toward the other end of the playing area. She is charged with a foul for holding the ball. The goalkeeper may be pulled from the goal area but cannot go beyond the centerline. No other player may enter the restraining area without being charged with a foul.

The following actions are fouls that are penalized by losing the ball at the spot of the foul:

1. Illegally touching the ball with the hands
2. Swinging the stick above waist height (called "high sticking")
3. Guards or forwards moving across the centerline
4. Player other than the goalie entering the restraining area

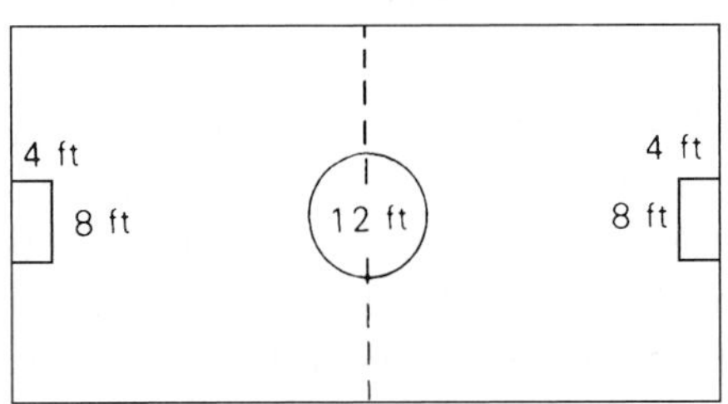

FIGURE 26.13 Regulation elementary hockey playing field.

5. Goalie throwing the ball
6. Holding, stepping on, or lying on the ball

Defenders must be 5 yards back when the ball is put into play after a foul. If the spot where the foul occurred is closer than 5 yards to the goal, only the goalkeeper may defend. The ball is then put into play 5 yards directly out from the goal.

Personal fouls include any action or rough play that endangers other players. A player committing a personal foul must retire to the sidelines for 2 minutes. The following are personal fouls:

1. Hacking or striking with a stick
2. Tripping with either the foot or the stick
3. Pushing or blocking

HOCKEY SKILL TESTS

PASSING FOR ACCURACY

In passing for accuracy, the player has five attempts to pass the puck or ball into a 3- by 3-foot target. Draw or tape the target on the wall, or use a 3-foot square of cardboard. The player must pass from a distance of 30 feet. He can approach the 30-foot restraining line in however he chooses. Each successful pass scores 2 points.

RECEIVING

Three players are designated as passers and pass from different angles to a student being tested for receiving. The puck must be definitely stopped and controlled. The teacher can judge whether the pass was a fair opportunity for the player to field. Six passes, two from each angle, are given, and players score 1 point for each successful field.

STICK HANDLING FOR SPEED

To test carrying for speed, line up three cones 8 feet apart. The first cone is 16 feet from the starting line. The player carries the puck around the cones in a figure-eight pattern to finish at the original starting line. Use a stopwatch for timing, and record scores to the nearest tenth of a second. Players get two trials, and the faster trial is recorded as the score.

SHOOTING FOR DISTANCE

Test shooting for distance outdoors only. Use a restraining line as a starting point. Give each player five trials to see how many goals can be scored from an established distance. Adjust the distance to the goal depending on the players' ability level. Line up players in four or five squads behind the restraining line. After taking their five trials, players can exchange places with someone who is returning pucks.

FOR MORE INFORMATION

REFERENCES AND SUGGESTED READINGS

American Sports Education Program. (2006). *Coaching youth hockey* (2nd ed.). Champaign, IL: Human Kinetics.

Anders, E. (2008). *Field hockey: Steps to success* (2nd ed.). Champaign, IL: Human Kinetics.

Callighen, B., & Chipperfield, R. (1996). *Mastering in-line hockey.* Chicago: Triumph Books.

Chambers, D. (1995). *The incredible hockey drill book.* New York: McGraw-Hill.

Fronske, H. (2005). *Teaching cues for sport skills* (3rd ed.). San Francisco: Benjamin Cummings.

Mood, D. P., Musker, F. F., & Rink, J. E. (2007). *Sports and recreational activities* (14th ed.). New York: McGraw-Hill.

Schmottlach, N., & McManama, J. (2006). *The physical education handbook* (11th ed.). San Francisco: Benjamin Cummings.

Siller, G. (1998). *Roller hockey.* New York: McGraw-Hill.

Trimble, R. M. (1997). *The ultimate hockey drill book.* Indianapolis, IN: Masters Press.

United States Field Hockey Association. (Current ed.). *Rulebook for outdoor and indoor hockey.* Colorado Springs, CO: Author.

Whitney, M. G. (Ed.). *Eagle, Official Publication of the United States Field Hockey Association Inc.* Colorado Springs, CO: USFHA (periodical).

WEBSITES

Field Hockey Information
www.fieldhockey.com

Hockey News and Information
www.letsplayhockey.com

In-line Hockey
www.usahockey.com/Template_USAHockeyInLine.aspx
www.inlinehockey.net/forums/

In-line Hockey Drills
www.whockey.com/work/cirsa/drillbook/

International Field Hockey
www.planetfieldhockey.com

United States Field Hockey Association
www.usfieldhockey.com

United States Hockey
www.usahockey.com

27 Soccer

ESSENTIAL COMPONENTS OF QUALITY PROGRAMS

I. Organized around content standards
II. Student-centered and developmentally appropriate
III. Physical activity and motor skill development form the core of the program
IV. Teaches management skills and self-discipline
V. Promotes inclusion of all students
VI. Focuses on process over product
VII. Promotes lifetime personal health and wellness
VIII. Teaches cooperation and responsibility and promotes sensitivity to diversity

NATIONAL STANDARDS FOR PHYSICAL EDUCATION*

1. Demonstrates competency in motor skills and movement patterns needed to perform a variety of physical activities.
2. Demonstrates understanding of movement concepts, principles, and tactics as they apply to the learning and performance of physical activities.
3. Participates regularly in physical activity.
4. Achieves and maintains a health-enhancing level of physical fitness.
5. Exhibits responsible personal and social behavior that respects self and others in physical activity.
6. Values physical activity for health, enjoyment, challenge, self-expression, and/or social interaction.

*National Association for Sport and Physical Education (NASPE), 2004.

Skills instruction for soccer begins during the intermediate grades after children have mastered basic prerequisite skills. Teaching the rules and strategies for soccer is an integral part of the instructional process. Proper progression is the key to successfully teaching fundamental skills and lead-up games associated with soccer. Lead-up games allow teachers to emphasize development of selected soccer skills in a setting compatible with their students' abilities.

Outcomes

- Structure learning experiences efficiently using appropriate formations, progressions, and coaching techniques.
- Develop a unit plan and a lesson focus for soccer.
- Identify safety precautions associated with teaching soccer.
- Describe instructional procedures used for directing a successful lead-up game.
- Cite assessment procedures used for evaluating soccer skills.

SOCCER is the most popular—and probably the most active—sport in America for youth. Effective soccer instruction stresses position play, in contrast to a group of children chasing the ball. To improve their playing ability, students must have organized practice that involves handling the ball as often as possible. Offer students many opportunities on offense to kick, control, dribble, volley, and shoot the ball and many opportunities on defense to mark, guard, tackle, and recover the ball. Success in soccer depends on how well individual skills are coordinated in team play.

MODIFICATIONS OF SOCCER FOR CHILDREN

A regulation soccer ball is too large and heavy for young soccer players who are learning the sport. Many students avoid contact with the regulation ball for fear of injury. Several manufacturers produce smaller-sized soccer balls that move and rebound exactly like regulation balls. Using foam balls covered with a tough plastic skin that looks like a soccer ball can calm players' fear of being hurt. Beach balls are excellent for teaching beginning skills because they move slowly and do not hurt when they strike someone. A beach ball is an excellent and painless way to learn heading skills.

To give students more chances to practice skills, use fewer players per game. The 11-person team is not suitable for beginning players, but Mini-Soccer is an excellent game with 6 or 7 players per team. Two games can be played crosswise on a regulation soccer field, and only a penalty area and the out-of-bounds lines are marked. The regulation soccer goal (24 feet wide by 8 feet high) is too large for elementary school play. Modify the size to give teams a reasonable chance of scoring as well as preventing a score. The suggested size is from 18 to 21 feet wide by 6 to 7 feet high. Depending on the game, the goal size can be even smaller.

INSTRUCTIONAL EMPHASIS AND SEQUENCE

Table 27.1 on page 654 shows the sequence of soccer activities divided into two developmental levels. Based on the skills children have acquired through community sports programs, the actual sequence may differ in certain areas and communities.

DEVELOPMENTAL LEVEL II

The two basic soccer skills are (1) controlling or stopping the ball with the foot so that the ball is in a position to be kicked and (2) passing the ball with the foot to another player or to a target. Activities at Developmental Level II stress games and drills that facilitate practicing and using basic skills. To maximize involvement, provide one ball for every two players.

DEVELOPMENTAL LEVEL III

To enhance control of the ball, dribbling skills are introduced in Developmental Level III. Students are taught to control the ball with other body parts, such as the thigh and chest. Lessons continue to focus on passing, and teachers can introduce games with 2 to 5 players per team. Players learn the basic goalkeeping skills of catching low and high balls. Further development of basic skills is recommended, along with instruction on shooting, tackling, heading, jockeying, and the concept of two-touch soccer for more advanced players. Students learn the basics of team and positional play as well as regular soccer rules. A unit of study focusing on soccer as an international game is valuable because few U.S. children realize how important this game is in other countries.

SOCCER SKILLS

Offensive skills taught in the elementary grades are passing, kicking, controlling, dribbling, volleying (including heading), and shooting. *Shooting* is defined as taking a shot at the goal with the intent to score. Defensive skills include marking, guarding, jockeying, tackling, and recovering the ball.

TABLE 27.1 Suggested soccer program

Skills	
Developmental Level II	**Developmental Level III**
Dribbling	Dribbling
Inside-the-foot pass	Outside-the-foot pass
Long pass	Ball control (trapping)
Foot trap	Passing
Passing	Tackling
Goalkeeping	Kicking goals
Defensive maneuvers	Kickoff (placekicking)
Soccer rules	Punting Volleying Heading with beach balls Ball control and passing The game of soccer Team play and strategy
Activities	
Developmental Level II	**Developmental Level III**
Circle Kickball	Manyball Soccer
Soccer Touch Ball	Addition Soccer
Diagonal Soccer	Over the Top
Dribblerama	Lane Soccer
Bull's-Eye	Line Soccer
Pin Kickball	Mini-Soccer
Sideline Soccer	Six-Spot Keep-Away
Kick Bowling	Regulation Soccer
Soccer Golf	
Skill Tests	
Developmental Level II	**Developmental Level III**
Controlled passing	Figure-eight dribbling
Kicking for accuracy	Controlling (three types)
Placekicking	Punting for distance Penalty kicking

DRIBBLING

Dribbling involves moving the ball with a series of taps or pushes to cover ground while still retaining control. It allows a player to change direction quickly and avoid opponents. The best contact point is the inner side of the foot, but the outer side of the foot is used at faster running speeds. Players must keep the ball close to maintain control. Use these instructional cues to emphasize proper dribbling form:

1. Keep the head up in order to see the field.
2. Move on the balls of the feet.
3. Contact the ball with the inside, outside, or instep of the foot.
4. Keep the ball near the body so it can be controlled. (Do not kick it too far in front of the body.)
5. Dribble the ball with a controlled tap.

PASSING

Balance and timing are the keys to accurate passing. Players use passes to advance the ball to a teammate and to shoot on goal. Occasionally, teams use a pass to send the ball downfield so they can regroup—though their opponents have an equal chance to recover the ball. Here are instructional cues to enhance accurate passing:

1. Place the nonkicking foot alongside the ball.
2. Keep the head down and the eyes focused on the ball during contact.
3. Spread the arms for balance.
4. Follow through with the kicking leg in the intended direction of the ball.
5. Make contact with the outside or inside of the foot rather than with the toe.
6. Practice kicking with both the left and right foot.

Inside-the-Foot Pass (Push Pass)

The inside-the-foot pass is used for accurate passing over distances of up to 15 yards. Because of the technique used, this pass is sometimes known as the *push pass.* The passer places the nonkicking foot well up alongside the ball. As he draws back the kicking foot, he turns the toe out. During the kick, the toe remains turned out, keeping the inside of the foot perpendicular to the line of flight. The sole stays parallel to the ground. At contact, the knee of the kicking leg is well forward, over the ball, and both knees are slightly bent (Figure 27.1).

Outside-the-Foot Pass (Flick Pass)

The player's nonkicking foot is more to the side of the ball than it is for the inside-the-foot kick, and the kicking leg approaches directly behind the ball. The kicking foot is fully extended, and contact with the ball is on the outside of the foot between laces and sole line. This pass is useful for running without breaking stride, or for flicking the ball to the side.

The Long Pass (Shoelace Kick)

The long pass is the power pass in soccer, used to kick for distance or to kick the ball past a goalie. Rather than the top of the foot (shoelace area), beginners often use the toes

FIGURE 27.1 The inside-the-foot pass.

when making this pass; this can cause injury or an inaccurate kick. For a long pass, the player approaches the ball in a full running stride at an angle to the line of flight. As she sets the nonkicking foot alongside the ball, her kicking leg is cocked in the backswing. Just before contact, the ankle of the kicking foot is fixed with the toes pointed down. As with all passes, the head is down and the eyes focus on the ball. Contact is made at the shoelace area of the foot. The passer crisply snaps the lower leg forward at the knee, completing the pass with a normal follow-through in the direction of the pass. To lift the ball, the passer contacts the ball below the midline, close to the ground, with the body leaning slightly backward. The nonkicking leg is to the side and slightly behind the ball so the kicking foot makes contact just as the leg begins its upswing. The lofted pass is aimed over the heads of opposing players.

Safety Tip

When teaching students the long pass, ample spacing should be provided in setting up as students who are learning the activity often have difficulty controlling the location of the pass.

BALL CONTROL (TRAPPING)

Learning to receive a ball and get it into the ideal position for making a pass or shot is vital. In fact, one of the best measures of skilled players is how quickly they can bring the ball under control with the feet, legs, or torso. Advanced players achieve control in one smooth movement with one touch of the ball. The second touch occurs when the pass is made.

For efficient control, present a large surface of the body to the ball. On contact, briefly withdraw the surface to produce a spongelike or shock-absorbing action that decelerates the ball and allows it to drop into an ideal position about a yard in front of the body. Then make the pass or shot. These instructional cues will help students develop ball control skills:

1. Move in line with the path of the ball.
2. Reach to meet the ball and give with the contact.
3. Stay on the balls of the feet.
4. Keep the eyes on the ball.

Inside-the-Foot Trap

This is the most common method of control; it is used when the ball is either rolling along the ground or bouncing up to knee height. Present the full surface of the foot, from heel to toe, alongside the ball (Figure 27.2).

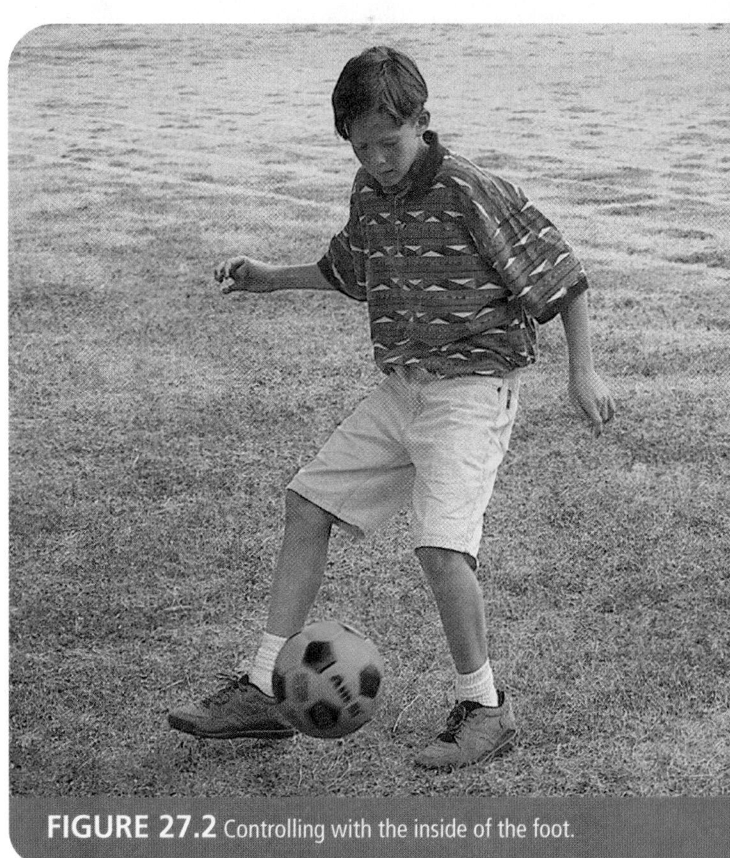

FIGURE 27.2 Controlling with the inside of the foot.

Chest and Thigh Traps

Soccer players also use the chest and inner thigh to deflect the ball downward when it is bouncing high. For the chest trap, the player aligns his body with the path of the ball (Figure 27.3). On contact, he draws back the chest and waist so his body leans forward and the ball drops directly to the ground in front of him. For the thigh trap, the player turns his body sideways to the flight of the ball. He contacts the ball with the inner thigh, which he then relaxes and draws backward. This action absorbs the force of the ball, which drops to the ground ready to be played.

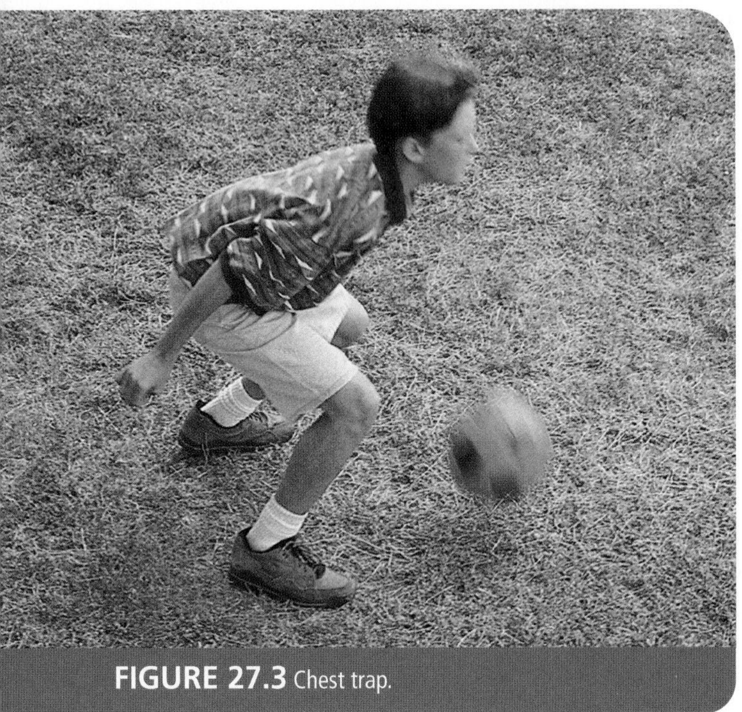

FIGURE 27.3 Chest trap.

Sole-of-the-Foot Trap

This method of control, sometimes called *trapping the ball*, is used occasionally to stop the ball. For beginners, it is less successful than the inside-the-foot trap, because the ball can roll easily under the foot. Players also use the sole to roll the ball from side to side in dribbling and to adjust for a better passing position.

HEADING

Heading is a special kind of volleying in which players change the ball's path by hitting it with the head. Recent research has shown that heading might cause some brain damage. With this in mind, use beach balls—and most especially, avoid regulation soccer balls—if teaching heading skills. Beach balls also move slowly, giving beginners time to get into proper position.

In heading, teach players to use the neck muscles to help reduce the impact of the blow. When executing the header, students must keep their mouths shut to avoid chipping teeth or biting their tongue. The eyes must be kept on the ball until the moment of impact. The point of contact is the top of the forehead at the hairline. In preparing to contact the ball with the head, the player stands in stride position, with knees relaxed and trunk leaning backward at the hips. At the moment of contact, the trunk moves forward abruptly, driving the forehead into the ball. Advanced heading is achieved in midair and is especially useful in beating other players to the ball. Midair heading can be done by using a running one-footed takeoff or a standing two-footed jump.

DEFENSIVE MANEUVERS

Tackling is a move to take the ball away from an opponent who is dribbling. The most common tackle is the front block, which involves contacting the ball with the inside of the foot just as the opponent touches it. The tackler presents a firm instep to the ball, his weight behind it. The stronger the ball contact, the better the chance of controlling it. Body contact is avoided since it may constitute a foul. Other tackles may be made when running alongside the player with the ball.

How much tackling should be taught in elementary school programs? In most cases, it is probably best to teach tackling skills that involve the defensive player remaining upright. Methods like the hook slide and split slide have little value in elementary school programs.

JOCKEYING

Knowing when to make a tackle, and when not to, is one of the most difficult skills to learn. A failed tackle may mean that an attacker breaks through with a free shot on goal. Often, defenders keep jockeying until defensive support arrives. This means backing off while staying close enough to pressure the advancing player. Defenders stay on their toes, watching the ball rather than the opponent's feet and staying within 1 or 2 yards of the ball.

THROW-INS

The throw-in is the only time field players can handle the ball with their hands. Players must closely follow throw-in rules to avoid a turnover to the other team. The rules are as follows:

1. Both hands must be on the ball.
2. The ball must be released from over the thrower's head.
3. The thrower must face the field.
4. The thrower cannot step onto the field until after the throw-in.

5. Both feet must be in contact with the ground until the ball is released.
6. The thrower cannot play the ball until another player on the field touches it.

The throw-in from out-of-bounds (see Figure 27.20 on page 664) may be executed from a standing or running position. Teach beginning players how to make the throw without a running start. The feet often are placed one behind the other, with the rear toe trailing along the ground. Delivery of the ball is from behind the head, using both arms equally. Release is in front of the forehead with arms outstretched. Instructional cues to help students perform correctly are "Drag your back foot" and "Follow through with both hands pointing toward the target."

SHOOTING

Scoring is the purpose of the game, and players need to practice shooting skills while stationary as well as on the run. As with passing, players can use the inside, outside, and top of the foot.

GOALKEEPING

Goalkeeping involves blocking shots by catching, stopping, or otherwise deflecting the ball. Goalkeepers should become adept at catching low-rolling balls, diving on rolling balls, catching airborne balls at waist level and below (Figure 27.4), and catching airborne balls at waist height and above.

FIGURE 27.4 Goalie catching a ball below waist level.

Have students practice catching low-rolling balls much like a baseball outfielder does. The goalie gets down on one knee, with her body behind the ball to act as a backstop, and catches the ball with both hands, fingers pointing toward the ground.

When catching a ball below the waist, goalies point the thumbs outward as the arms reach for the ball; the body and arms give while bringing the ball into the abdomen. For balls above waist level, the goalie's thumbs turn inward as the arms reach to meet the ball and give while guiding it to the midsection. When diving for the ball, the goalie always tries to throw his body behind it and cradle it with his hands. Drills for goalies should offer opportunities to catch different shots. All students should receive goalkeeping practice.

PUNTING

The punt, used by the goalkeeper only, can be stationary or done on the run. The ball is held in both hands at waist height in front of the body and directly over the kicking leg. For the stationary punt, the kicking foot is forward. A short step is taken with the kicking foot, followed by a full step with the other foot. With the knee bent and the toe extended, the kicking foot swings forward and upward. As contact is made with the ball at the instep, the knee straightens, and additional power is secured from the other leg through a coordinated rising on the toes or a hop (Figure 27.5).

FIGURE 27.5 Punt.

The goalkeeper who can develop a strong punt has an advantage. Distance and accuracy are important in setting up the next attack. Over shorter distances, throwing underhand or overhand can be more accurate than kicking. In those cases, goalies must use a straight arm for rolling or throwing the ball to players.

INSTRUCTIONAL PROCEDURES

1. In practices, emphasize controlling the ball and passing. Organize drills and activities to keep all children involved and active. One ball is needed per two children.
2. Include many combination drills featuring both offense and defense. Enjoyment is the key to continued learning. Use drills and lead-up activities to make the

skills challenging, but be sure all activities are appropriate to the players' developmental level.

3. Use small-group games (2 to 5 players per team) to ensure maximum activity. As players' skill improves, use larger teams.
4. Lead-up games are designed to use the skills practiced in drills. For example, if long passing is the skill of the day, have students play lead-up games requiring and rewarding long passing. In the early stages of teaching soccer, it may be best to prohibit tackling.
5. The grid system is useful when organizing drills, activities, and small-sized games. With cones or chalk, mark a grid system of 10-yard squares on the playing field. The number of squares needed depends on class size, but at least one square for every three students is recommended (Figure 27.6 shows two layouts). Use the squares as boundaries for tackling, keeping possession, and passing diagonally or sideways. Drill and game areas can be defined easily, allowing several small-sized games to be played simultaneously.
6. Use balls smaller and lighter than the regulation soccer ball. An excellent alternative for novices is the tough-skin foam rubber training ball. It withstands heavy usage and does not hurt students on impact. Another alternative is a beach ball. They are light and move slowly, making them an excellent choice for unskilled players. Junior-sized soccer balls (number 4) are also excellent but more expensive. The key to soccer practice is to have plenty of balls available.
7. Soccer, with its attack and defense, can be a rough game. Control rough play such as pushing, shoving, kicking, and tripping. Teachers need to strictly enforce rules.
8. Modify the scoring to make the activity more enjoyable for more children. Scoring must be a challenge—neither too easy nor too difficult. To avoid arguments when the ball is to be kicked through a line of children, limit the height of the kick to shoulder level or below. Mark goal outlines with cones and designated spots. Regulation soccer goals are not needed for an elementary school program.

SOCCER DRILLS

Teachers typically use two types of soccer drills: (1) players practice technique without opposition from any defense; and (2) players practice skills in a drill involving both offensive and defensive players and perhaps a target. In skill-type drills, the goal is to outmaneuver the opponent. Some drills begin by practicing technique and then move to using skills. Individual practice is excellent, particularly with dribbling techniques, but most practice is best accomplished in combinations of 2 or 3 players and small groups.

The playing surface greatly affects the quality of soccer practice. Grass is the most desirable surface, but some schools have only hard-top surfaces. In that case, deflate the balls slightly to simulate how they travel on grass. When space is restricted, outline areas with cones, beanbags, jugs, or boundary boards.

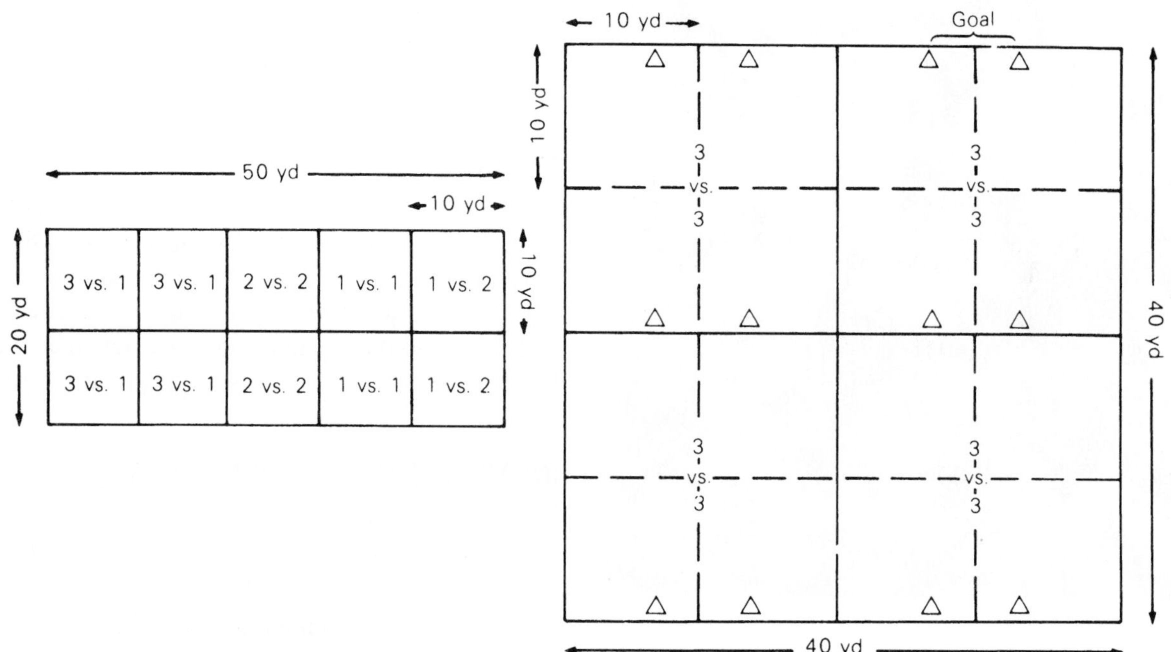

FIGURE 27.6 Examples of grid layouts and usage.

Individual Work

Dribbling practice is best done individually. Activity can begin by having students dribble in various directions and signaling them to make right and left turns. As a variation, teach children signals: One whistle means turn left, two means turn right, and three means reverse direction. Scatter some cones around the area and have players dribble around one cone clockwise and around the next cone counterclockwise.

Have students practice heading skills by tossing a beach ball overhead and heading it. Alternate heading with a short period of dribbling practice. To teach trapping skills, drop a ball and show students how to smother it with a foot. Another drill is to have players toss the ball into the air, let it bounce, and then kick it to themselves with an instep (inside-the-foot) pass. Yet another activity is to toss the ball high and use the instep kick to control the ball.

Rebounding to oneself continuously, although not actually used in the game of soccer, is an excellent way to learn ball control. (This is sometimes called *foot juggling.*) Students begin by dropping the ball so that it bounces to waist height, and then practice the following skills:

1. Rebound the ball with alternating feet, letting it bounce between contacts.
2. Play the ball twice with one foot, let it bounce, and then play it twice with the other foot.
3. Toss the ball so it can be handled with the thigh and then catch it. Add successive rebounds with the thigh.
4. Play ball with the foot, thigh, head, thigh, foot, and catch it.

The foot pickup is another skill that can be taught in two ways. The first is to have students put the ball between their feet, jump up, and hoist the ball so it can be caught. The second is the toe pickup. Students put a toe on top of the ball and pull the toe back and down so that the ball spins up the instep, from which it can be hoisted to the hands. Another bit of individual work is toe changing on top of the ball. Students put the ball of the foot on top of the ball. On signal, they change feet.

Drills for Two Players

Many introductory drills are best practiced with a partner. The grid system, mentioned earlier, is a fine way to organize partner drills. The distance between the grid lines depends on the skills to be practiced. Partners position themselves opposite each other, thus forming two lines of players and giving the teacher a clear view of the class in action (Figure 27.7). This approach is recommended for introducing all new skills, such as passing with both sides of the foot and ball control. Skill combinations can be used, such as throw-ins by one partner and control-and-pass by the other. Within the grids, partners can work on passing, dribbling, keep-away, and one-on-one games.

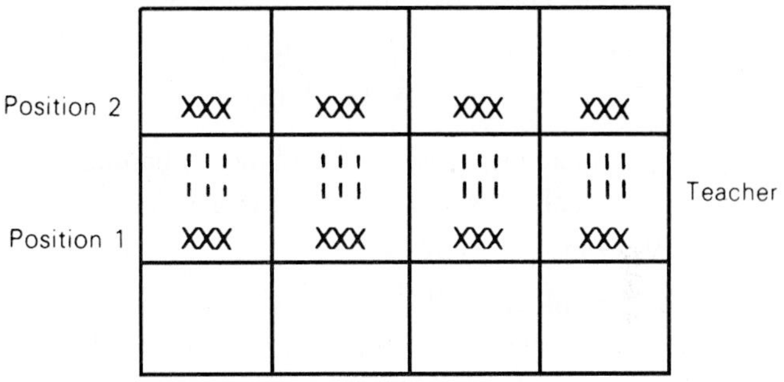

Position 2 XXX XXX XXX XXX
Teacher
Position 1 XXX XXX XXX XXX

FIGURE 27.7 Class organized along grid lines.

Here are some drills that can be used in partner formation.

1. *Dribbling, marking, and ball recovery.* Pairs are scattered, and one player in each pair has a soccer ball. That player dribbles in various directions as the second player tries to stay close to the first (marking). As skill improves, the defensive players try to recover the ball from the dribblers. If they succeed, roles are reversed.
2. *Dribbling.* One player of the pair has a ball and dribbles in different directions. On signal, she passes to her partner, who repeats the dribbling, continuing until another signal is given.
3. *Dribbling, moving, and passing.* Two lines of paired children face each other across a 40- to 60-foot distance (Figure 27.8 on page 660). Each child in one of the lines has a ball and works with a partner directly across from him. The teacher calls one of the following challenges, and a player with a ball from line A moves forward to perform it. When he moves near his partner, he passes to him, and the partner (line B) repeats the same maneuver back to line A. Both players are then in their starting places.

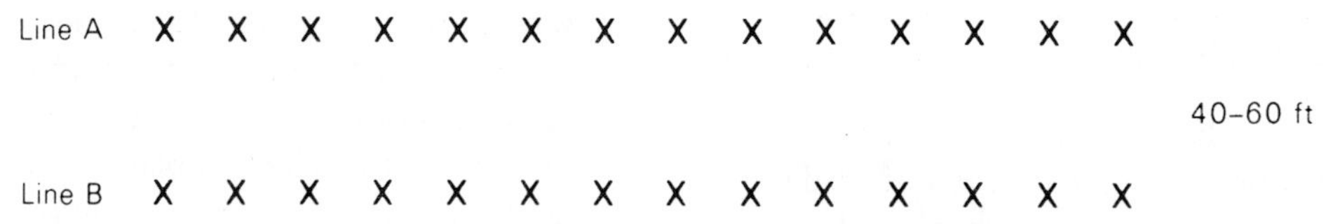

Line A X X X X X X X X X X X X X X

40–60 ft

Line B X X X X X X X X X X X X X X

FIGURE 27.8 Dribbling, moving, and passing.

a. Dribble across to partner, using the outside of either foot.

b. Gallop across, handling the ball with the front foot only. On return, lead with the other foot.

c. Skip across, dribbling at the same time.

d. Slide across, handling the ball with the back foot. On return, lead with the other foot.

e. Hop across, using the lifted foot to handle the ball. Be sure to change feet halfway across.

f. Dribble the ball to a point halfway across. Stop the ball with the sole of the foot and leave it there. Continue to the other line. Meanwhile, the partner from line B moves forward to dribble the ball back to line A.

g. Player A dribbles to the center and passes to Player B. Player A now returns to line A. Player B repeats and returns to line B.

4. *Volleying and controlling.* Pairs of players are scattered. One player in each pair has a ball and acts as a feeder, tossing the ball to practice various receptive skills including different kinds of volleying and controlling balls in flight. Controlled tossing is essential to this drill.

Drills for Three Players

With one ball for three players, many of the drills suggested for pairs are still possible. Drills for three players require fewer balls.

1. *Passing and controlling.* The trio of players sets up a triangle with players about 10 yards apart. They practice controlled passing and ball control.

2. *Volleying and controlling.* One player acts as a feeder, tossing to the other two players, who practice volleying and controlling in-flight balls.

3. *Dribbling and passing.* Structure a shuttle-type drill as shown in Figure 27.9. Players continuously go back and forth. Player 1 has the ball and dribbles to Player 2, who dribbles the ball back to Player 3, who in turn dribbles to Player 1. Players can dribble the entire distance, or dribble partway and then pass the ball to the end player. Obstacles can be set up to challenge players to dribble through or around each obstacle.

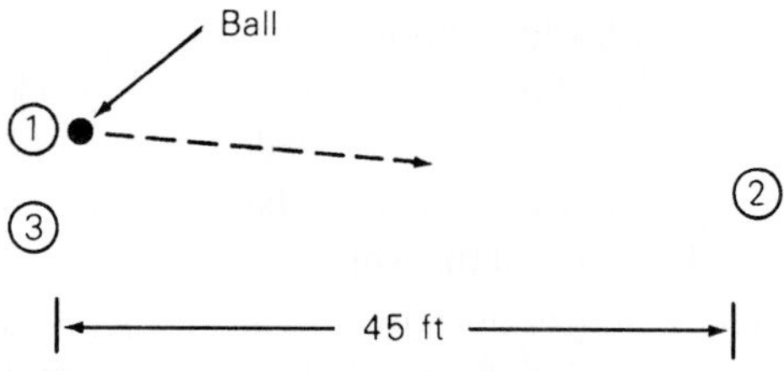

FIGURE 27.9 Shuttle-type dribbling drill.

4. *Dribbling and stopping the ball.* Three dribblers are in line, each with a ball. The leader moves in various directions, followed by the other two players. On signal, each player controls her ball. The leader circles around to the back ball, and the other two move one ball forward. The dribbling continues for another stop. A third stop returns the players to their original positions.

5. *Passing.* Players stand in three corners of a 10-yard square. After passing, a player moves to the empty corner of the square, which may be a diagonal movement (Figure 27.10).

6. *Passing and defending.* One player is the feeder and rolls the ball to either player. Upon rolling the ball, she tries to block or tackle the player receiving the ball to prevent a pass to the third player, who—if the pass is completed—tries to pass back (Figure 27.11).

Drills for Four or More Players

Organize drills for four or more players using a rotation system that gives all players an equal chance to practice skills.

1. *Dribbling.* Four players are in line, as in Figure 27.12. Each player in front has a ball. Both front players dribble to the center, where they exchange

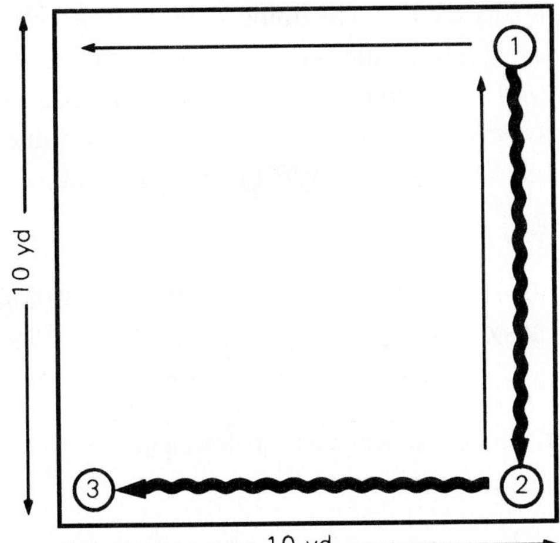

FIGURE 27.10 Passing drill.

Note: The following symbols are used in soccer game formation diagrams:

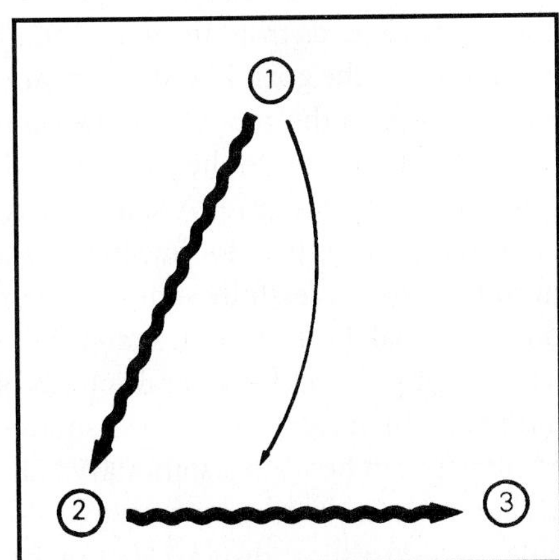

FIGURE 27.11 Passing and defense drill.

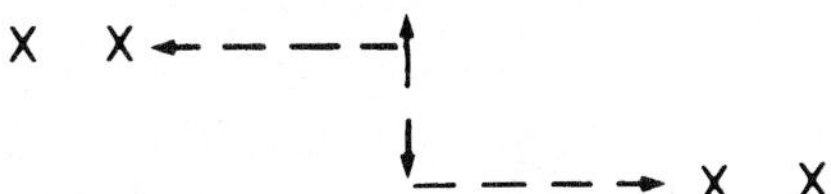

FIGURE 27.12 Dribble exchange drill.

balls and continue dribbling to the other side. The next players do the same. A variation is to have the two players meet at the center, exchange balls, and dribble back to their starting point. Action is continuous.

2. *Passing, guarding, and tackling.* Four players occupy the four corners of a square (Figure 27.13). One player has a ball. Practice begins with one player rolling the ball to the player in the opposite corner, who, in turn, passes to either of the other two players. The player rolls the ball twice per round, so that passes are made both ways. The next progression calls for the player who rolled the ball to move forward rapidly to block the pass to either side. She gets several tries before another player takes over the rolling duties.

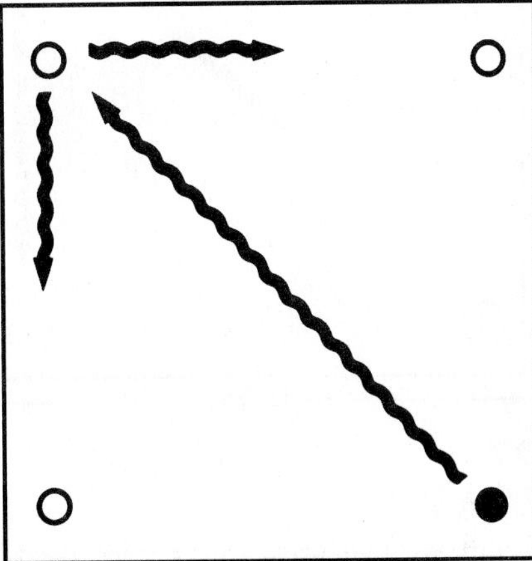

FIGURE 27.13 Passing, guarding, and tackling drill.

3. *Shooting, goalkeeping, and defense.* A shooting drill against defense can be coordinated with four players and a 15-foot goal set off with cones or other markers (Figure 27.14). One player has the ball. He advances and tries to maneuver around a second player so he can shoot past the goalkeeper guarding the goal. A fourth player acts as the retriever. Rotate positions.

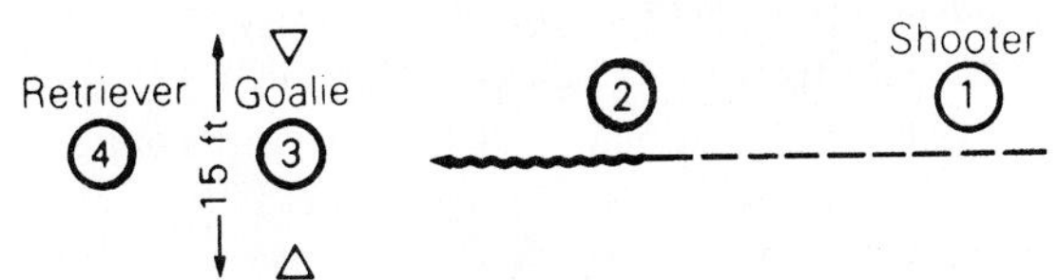

FIGURE 27.14 Shooting, goalkeeping, and defense.

4. *Dribbling.* Four or five players, each with a ball, form a line. A "coach" stands about 15 yards in front of the line. Each player, in turn, dribbles up to the coach, who indicates with a thumb in which direction the player should dribble. The coach gives the direction at the last possible moment.

5. *Passing, controlling, and defense.* Four players stand in the four corners of a square, 10 yards on a side. Two defensive players are inside the square. The corner players stay in place within square. The corner players stay in place within the square and try to pass the ball between them

while the two defenders try to recover the ball (Figure 27.15). After a set time, another two players take over as defenders.

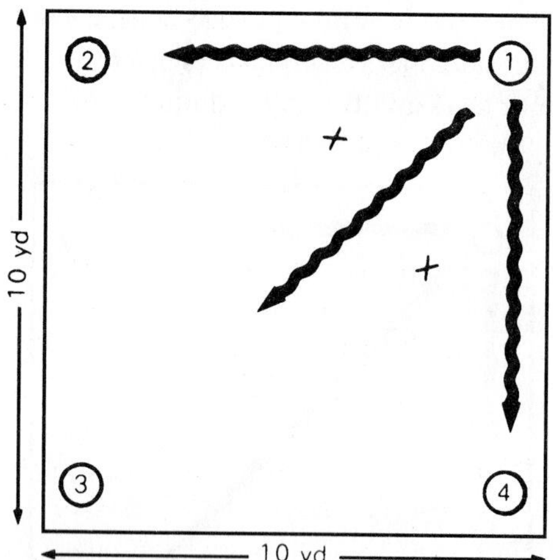

FIGURE 27.15 Passing, controlling, and defense.

6. *Shooting.* For two-way goal practice, use two teams of 2 to 6 players and assign each team to one side of the goal. The goal width can vary, depending on the players' skill. Players practice two types of shooting: (a) kicking a stationary ball from 10 to 20 yards out and (b) preceding a kick with a dribble. The second type requires a restraining line 12 to 15 yards out. Mark this line with cones, as in Figure 27.16. Use at least four balls for this two-way drill. After a period of kicking, the groups change sides. Ball chasers are the players at the end of each line.
7. *Shooting and goalkeeping.* Players can also practice scoring with a goalkeeper (Figure 27.17). Players use a stationary ball from 12 yards out (penalty distance) by doing kicks preceded by a dribble. The goalie and the chaser complete one round and then rotate. Having a second ball to play with saves time because play can continue while the chaser recovers the previous ball.

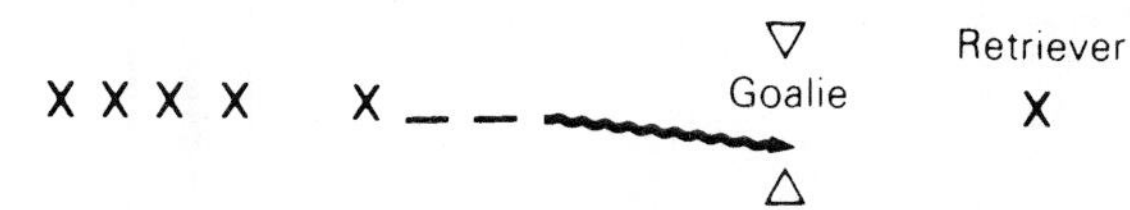

FIGURE 27.17 Shooting and goalkeeping.

8. *Kicking and trapping.* This is an excellent squad drill. About 8 players form a circle 15 yards in diameter. They pass two balls back and forth independently. Passes are kept low, using primarily the side-of-the-foot kick. Players can try using three balls.
9. *Passing and shooting.* The drill can be done with 4 to 6 players and two balls. A passer stands about 15 yards from the goal, and a retriever is behind the goal. The shooters are in line, 20 yards from the goal and to the right. The first shooter passes to the passer and then runs forward. The passer returns the ball to the shooter. The shooter tries to time her run forward so that she successfully shoots the pass through the goal. Both the passer and the retriever stay in position for several rounds of shooting and then rotate to become shooters. The first pass can be from a stationary ball. Later, however, the kicker can be allowed to dribble forward a short distance before making the first pass. Reverse the field and practice

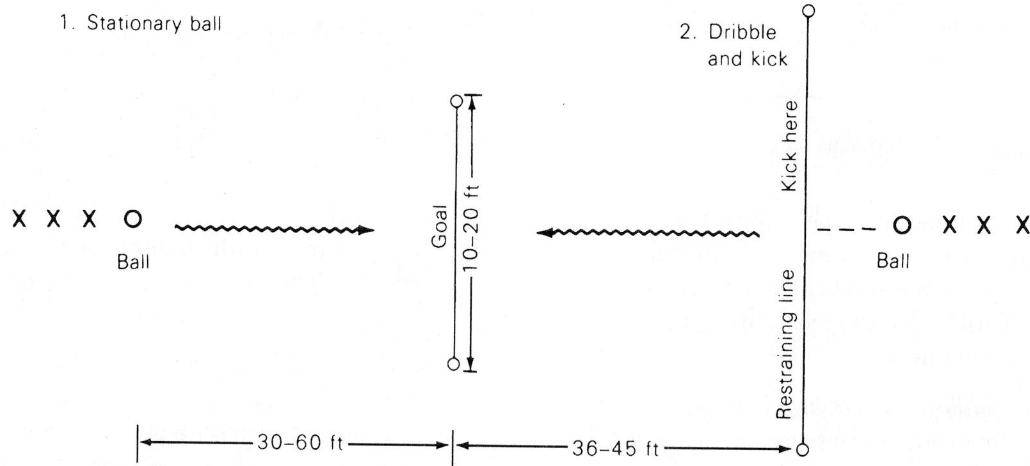

FIGURE 27.16 Shooting drill.

from the left, shooting with the nondominant leg (Figure 27.18).

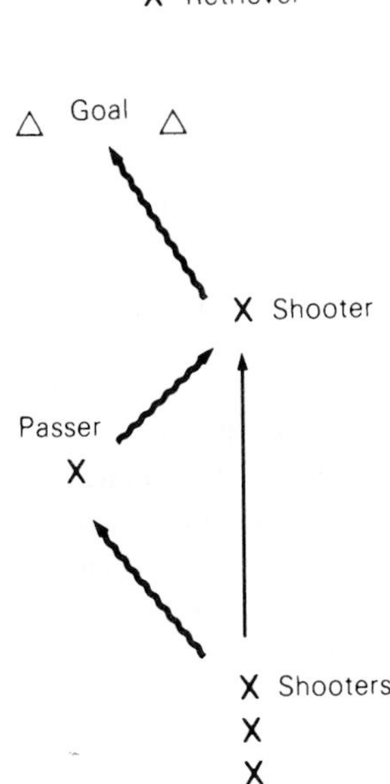

FIGURE 27.18 Passing and shooting.

10. *Tackling and ball handling.* A defender is restricted to tackling in the area between two parallel lines spaced 1 yard apart. The field is 20 by 40 yards (Figure 27.19). Four to six players can practice this drill. Player 1 advances the ball by dribbling and tries to maneuver past the defender. After evading the defender, he passes to Player 2 and takes his place at the other side of the field. Player 2 repeats the routine, passing the ball off to the next player in the line. If the ball goes out of control or is stopped by the defender, it is rolled to the player whose turn is next. Play is continuous, with the defender maintaining her position for several rounds.

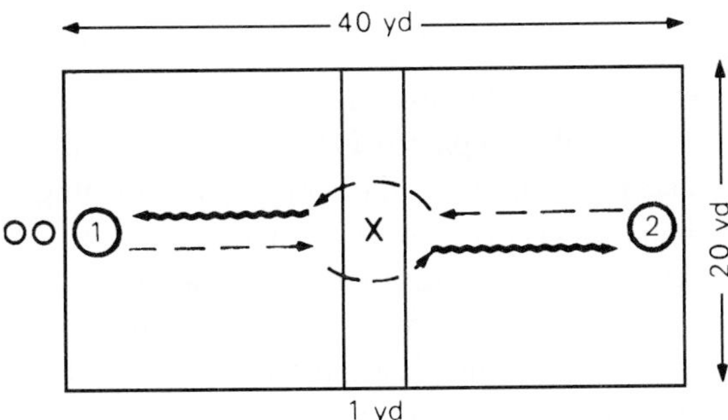

FIGURE 27.19 Tackling and ball-handling drill.

BASIC SOCCER RULES FOR LEAD-UP GAMES

Teach players not to handle the ball deliberately with the hands or arms; but in the early stages, ignore incidental or unintentional handling of the ball. Eventually, a violation leads to a direct free kick—the ball is placed on the ground with the opposition a specific distance away (10 yards on a full-sized field). A goal can be scored directly from this type of kick.

The goalkeeper is allowed to handle the ball within her area by catching, batting, or deflecting with the hands. If the goalie has caught the ball, opponents cannot charge her. While the goalie is holding the ball, official rules limit her to four steps. In elementary school play, teachers should insist on the goalkeeper getting rid of the ball immediately by throwing or kicking. This removes the temptation to rough up the goalie. In some lead-up games, several students may have the same ball-handling privileges as the goalie. The rules need to be clear, and ball handling is done within a specific area.

All serious fouls—tripping, kicking a player, holding, or pushing—result in a direct free kick. If a defender commits one of these fouls or handles a ball in his own penalty area, the other team gets a penalty kick. Only the goalkeeper may defend against this kick, which is shot from 12 yards out. All other players must be outside the penalty area until the ball is kicked. In lead-up games, devise rules for penalty fouls committed in a limited area near the goal by the defensive team. Award the attacking team a kick or an automatic goal.

The ball is out of play and the whistle blown when the ball crosses any of the boundaries, when a goal is scored, or when a foul is called. The team that last touched the ball or sent it out-of-bounds on the side of the field loses possession. The ball is put into play with an overhead throw-in using both hands (Figure 27.20 on page 664).

If the attacking team causes the ball to go over the endline, the defending team is awarded a kick from any point chosen near the endline of that half of the field. If the defense last touched the ball going over the endline, the attacking team gets a corner kick. The ball goes to the corner on the side where the ball went over the endline, where the player takes a direct free kick and may score a goal.

The game is normally started by a kickoff with both teams onside. In lead-up games, the ball can be dropped for a free ball. In some games, the teacher may decide simply to award the ball for a free kick in the backcourt to the team not making the score.

Lead-up games can continue for a specific time (by halves) or until one team reaches a predetermined score. In a regular soccer game, the play is timed.

FIGURE 27.20 Throwing in, from out-of-bounds.

When the ball is ensnarled by several players or when someone has fallen, a quick whistle is needed. Put the ball into play by dropping it between players of the opposing teams.

The offside rule has little value in elementary school play, but children should understand the rule and the reasons for it. It prevents the "cheap" goal (i.e., a player on offense waits near the goal to take a pass behind the defenders and score easily against the goalie). Although the concept of *offsides* involves various details, it basically means that a player on offense who is ahead of the ball must have two defensive players between her and the goal when the ball is kicked forward. One of these players is, of course, the goalie. The offside rule does not apply when the player receives the ball directly from an attempted goal kick or from an opponent, on a throw-in or corner kick, or when the player is in her own half.

Instruct players not to raise their feet high or show the soles or cleats of their shoes when other players are nearby. This constitutes dangerous play, and the other team receives an indirect free kick.

SOCCER ACTIVITIES

DEVELOPMENTAL LEVEL II

Circle Kickball

PLAYING AREA: Playground or gymnasium

PLAYERS: 10 to 20 students

SUPPLIES: Two beach balls or 8-inch foam rubber balls

SKILLS: Blocking (goalie skills), kicking

Players are in circle formation. Using the sides of their feet, players kick the balls back and forth inside the circle. The object is to kick the ball out of the circle beneath the shoulder level of the other players. Circle players can use their hands and feet to block the ball since they are goalies. All players score 1 point if a ball leaves the circle between them. If, however, a lost ball is clearly one player's fault, then only that player scores a point. Any player who kicks a ball higher than the shoulders of the circle players scores a point. Players scoring the fewest points win. A player is not penalized if she leaves the circle to recover a ball and the second ball goes through the vacated spot.

Teaching Hint

Specify the types of kicks players may use.

Soccer Touch Ball

PLAYING AREA: Playground or gymnasium

PLAYERS: 8 to 10 students

SUPPLIES: Soccer balls, beach balls, or 8-inch foam rubber balls

SKILLS: Kicking, controlling

Players are spaced around a circle 10 yards in diameter with two players in the center. The object is to keep the players in the center from touching the ball. The ball is passed back and forth as in soccer. If a center player touches the ball with a foot, he is awarded a point. To keep the game moving, rule that no player may contain or hold the ball longer than 3 seconds. Rotate two new players into the center after 15 to 30 seconds.

Diagonal Soccer

PLAYING AREA: A square about 60 by 60 feet

PLAYERS: 20 to 30 students

SUPPLIES: Soccer ball, beach ball, or 8-inch foam rubber ball and pinnies (optional)

SKILLS: Kicking, passing, dribbling, some controlling, defending, blocking shots

Mark off two corners with cones 5 feet from the corners on both sides, outlining triangular dead areas. Each team lines up (Figure 27.21) and tries to protect two adjacent sides of the square. To start play, three students from each team move into the playing area in their own half of the space. These active players may roam anywhere in the square. Only active players may score; the other players act as goalkeepers.

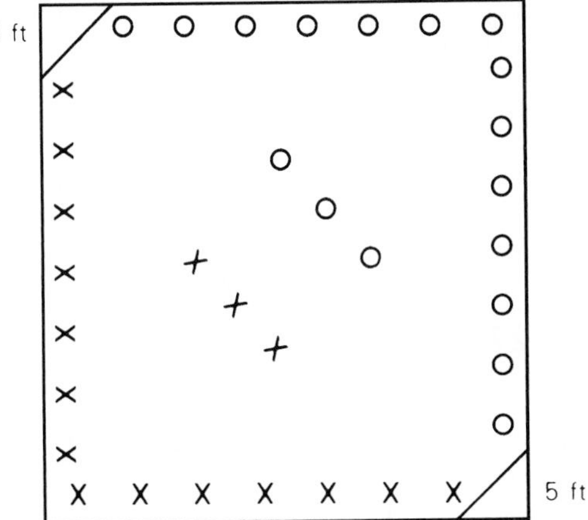

FIGURE 27.21 Formation for Diagonal Soccer.

The object is for active players to kick the ball through the opposing team's line (beneath shoulder height) to score. After 30 to 45 seconds, active players rotate to the sidelines and new players take their place. Players on the sidelines may block the ball with their bodies and use their hands. The team that was scored against starts the ball for the next point. Scoring is much the same as in Circle Kickball—the opponents score 1 point when any of these actions occur:

1. A team allows the ball to go through its line below the shoulders.
2. A team touches the ball illegally.
3. A team kicks the ball over the other team above shoulder height.

Dribblerama

PLAYING AREA: Playground

PLAYERS: 10 to 20 students

SUPPLIES: Soccer ball or 8-inch foam rubber ball for each player

SKILLS: Dribbling, protecting the ball

The playing area is a large circle or square, clearly outlined. All players dribble within the area. The game is played on three levels.

Level 1: Each player dribbles throughout the area, controlling the ball so it does not touch another ball. If a touch occurs, both players go outside the area and dribble around the area. After dribbling one lap, these players may reenter the game.

Level 2: Mark off two equal playing areas. All players start in one of the areas. While dribbling and controlling the ball, each player tries to kick any other ball out of the area. When a ball is kicked out, the player owning that ball takes it to the other area and dribbles. As more players move to the second area, a second game ensues. Players in this area move back to the opposite side. This keeps all players actively involved in the games.

Level 3: Start with one game on each half of the teaching area. When a player is out, he moves to the other game. Or he takes one lap dribbling and then joins the other game. Or, divide the area into quadrants and play four games; players can choose another game to move to when ousted from a game.

Bull's-Eye

PLAYING AREA: Playground

PLAYERS: 6 to 10 students

SUPPLIES: Soccer ball or 8-inch foam rubber ball for each player

SKILLS: Dribbling, protecting the ball

The playing area is a large outlined shape—circle, square, or rectangle. One player holds a ball in her hands, which serves as the bull's-eye. The other players dribble within the area. The player with the bull's-eye tries to throw her ball (basketball push shot) at any other ball. The player whose ball is hit becomes the new bull's-eye player. The old bull's-eye player becomes one of the dribblers. A new bull's-eye cannot hit back immediately at the old bull's-eye. If the group is large, have two bull's-eyes. No score is kept and no one is eliminated.

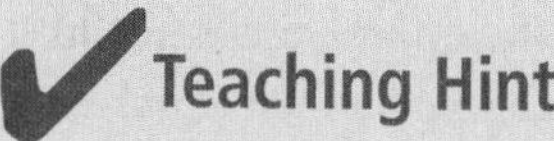

Teaching Hint

Specify that the bull's-eye must keep one foot on a marking spot.

Pin Kickball

PLAYING AREA: Playground or gymnasium

PLAYERS: Teams of 7 to 10 students each

SUPPLIES: 10 or more pins (cones or bowling pins), many soccer or foam rubber balls

SKILLS: Kicking, controlling

Two teams start about 20 yards apart, facing each other. At least 10 pins are placed between the two lines of players. Each team has several balls at the start of the kicking (Figure 27.22). Kicks must be made from behind each team's line. Each knocked-down pin scores a point for that team. After knocking down all of the pins, the teams reset them, and the game resumes.

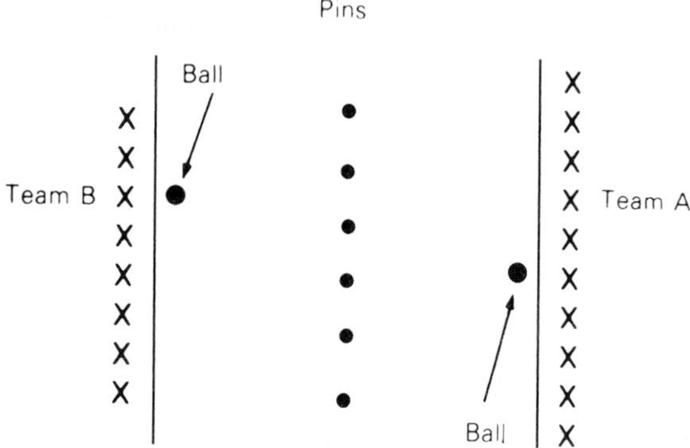

FIGURE 27.22 Formation for Pin Kickball.

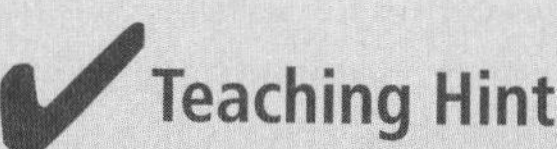

Teaching Hint

This is a flexible game; the number of pins, balls, and players can be varied easily. You can specify the type of kick or let the players choose. As accuracy improves, increase the distance between the teams.

Sideline Soccer

PLAYING AREA: Rectangle about 60 by 100 feet

PLAYERS: Teams of 10 to 12 students each

SUPPLIES: A soccer or foam rubber ball, four cones, pinnies (optional)

SKILLS: Most soccer skills, competitive play

Teams line up on the sidelines of the rectangle. Call 3 or 4 active players from the end of each team's line (Figure 27.23). These players remain active until a point is scored; then they rotate to the other end of the line. The object is to kick the ball between cones (goals) that define the scoring area. The active players on each team compete against each other, aided by their teammates on the sidelines.

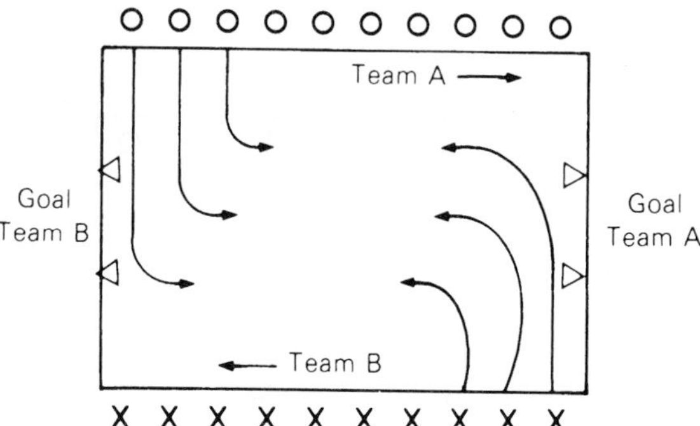

FIGURE 27.23 Formation for Sideline Soccer.

To start play, give the ball to one team or drop it between two opposing players at the center of the field. Only active players can score a goal—by kicking the ball through the goal at or below shoulder height. A goal counts as 1 point. Sideline players can pass to other sideline players or an active teammate, but they cannot score.

Regular soccer rules generally prevail, with special attention to restricting pushing, holding, tripping, or

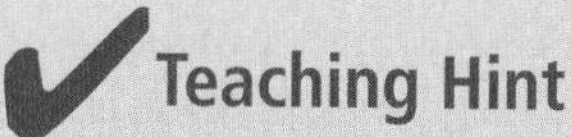

Teaching Hint

Rotate in a new set of active players after 30 to 45 seconds; use more active players when the class is large. Rule that sideline players must receive a set number of passes before active players can take a shot on goal. When players become more skilled, make the goal area narrower. If the ball goes over the endline but not through the goal area, a defender puts the ball into play with a kick.

other rough play. Rough play is a foul; the other team receives 1 point. For an out-of-bounds ball, the team on that side of the field gets a free kick near that spot. No score can result from a free kick. Violation of the touch rule also results in a free kick.

Kick Bowling

PLAYING AREA: Playground or soccer field

PLAYERS: Groups of 4 players

SUPPLIES: Soccer balls or 8-inch foam rubber balls and bowling pins

SKILLS: Kicking

Kick Bowling is played like bowling, except that students kick rather than roll the ball at pins. Students are in groups of four: one is the kicker, one is the pinsetter, and the other two are ball retrievers.

Soccer Golf

PLAYING AREA: Playground or soccer field

PLAYERS: Groups of 3 or 4 students

SUPPLIES: One soccer ball per student, hoops to mark each hole, cones to mark tees

SKILLS: Kicking, knowledge of golf rules

This game is played like golf, but students kick a soccer ball rather than hitting a golf ball. Before the lesson, set up a course similar to a Frisbee golf course (pages 598–599) using trees, boxes, and other equipment as obstacles.

DEVELOPMENTAL LEVEL III

Manyball Soccer

PLAYING AREA: Soccer field

PLAYERS: Entire class

SUPPLIES: Six foam rubber or soccer balls, cones, pinnies

SKILLS: All soccer skills

Players are divided into two teams and begin in the defensive half of the field. Players can freely roam the entire field except for the two goalie boxes, which are marked with cones. Only the goalie is allowed in the goalie box, and only goalies can touch the ball with their hands. Goalies try to keep the balls from going between the cones and can return the ball to play by punting or throwing. To make scoring more difficult, use several goalies.

The object is to kick one of the six balls through the goal. If a ball goes through the goal, the player who scored (not the goalie) retrieves the ball and returns it to the midline for play. All balls are in play at once except when being returned after a goal. Basic soccer rules (pages 663–664) control the game.

Addition Soccer

PLAYING AREA: Playground

PLAYERS: 10 to 15 students

SUPPLIES: One soccer ball per player

SKILLS: Dribbling, ball control

Select five or more players to defend against the other players. The other players dribble throughout the area, trying to keep the defenders from touching any ball with their feet. When a player's ball is touched, she rolls it to the side of the playing area and joins hands with the defender to become his partner. They operate as a twosome and must keep their hands joined while trying to touch other balls. When another player's ball is touched, he takes it to the side and joins hands with one of the other defenders. This twosome becomes defenders also, adding their efforts to those of the first twosome. Play continues until all defenders have touched a ball and gained a partner, or for 1 minute, whichever occurs first. The game then starts over. If partners break joined hands in touching a ball, the touch does not count. The game is similar to Addition Tag (page 551).

Over the Top

PLAYING AREA: Playground

PLAYERS: Two teams of 5 to 7 students each

SUPPLIES: A ball for each player on offense

SKILLS: Dribbling, ball control, guarding, tackling

One team is on offense and the other is on defense, placed as in Figure 27.24 on page 668. Defensive players stay in their respective areas. On signal, all offensive players dribble through the three areas. A player is eliminated if her ball is recovered by a defensive player or goes out-of-bounds. The offensive team scores 1 point for each ball dribbled across

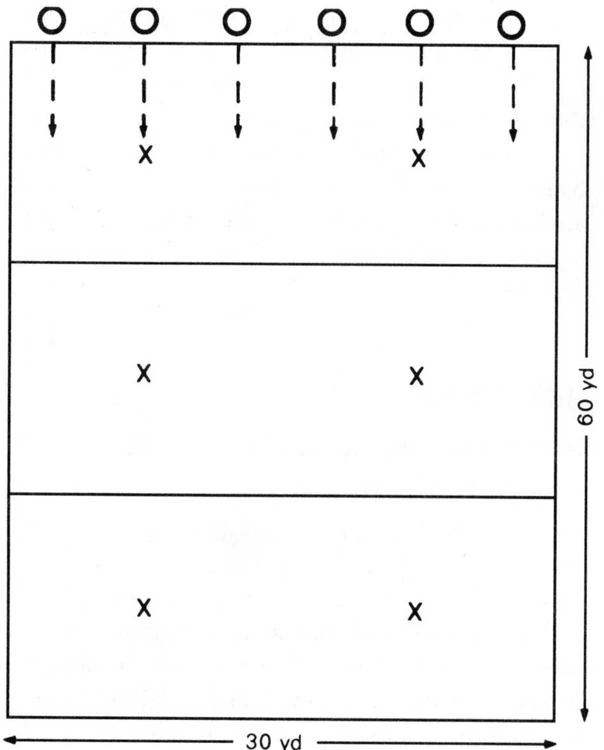

FIGURE 27.24 Over the Top.

the far endline. Have the teams reverse roles to give the other team a chance to score. Field markings need to be definite to keep the defensive players in their respective zones. A variation is to use neutral zones between the active zones.

Lane Soccer

PLAYING AREA: Soccer field

PLAYERS: 9 students per team

SUPPLIES: Soccer, foam rubber, or beach balls; pinnies

SKILLS: All soccer skills

Divide the field into four lanes (eight equal sections), as in Figure 27.25. Place a defensive and an offensive player in each of the eight areas. A goalkeeper guards each goal per regulation soccer rules. At least two passes must be made before taking a shot on goal. Basic soccer rules guide play. Only the goalie can handle the ball with the hands. Players who were fouled by an opponent get a free kick. Failing to stay within a lane also results in a free kick. Players must rotate after a goal is scored or a specific time has elapsed. This rotation enables all students to play four positions: defense, midfield defense, midfield offense, and offense.

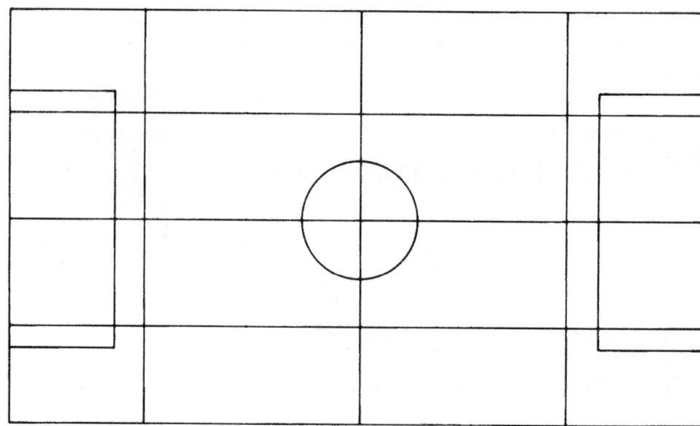

FIGURE 27.25 Field markings for Lane Soccer.

Teaching Hint

Vary the number of lanes depending on the number of players and the field size. Allow players to choose an opponent for their lane. Usually, they will choose an opponent of equal ability. Increase the number of balls, goals, and goalies.

Line Soccer

PLAYING AREA: Soccer field

PLAYERS: Teams of 8 to 10 students each

SUPPLIES: A soccer, foam rubber, or beach ball; four cones; pinnies

SKILLS: Most soccer skills, competitive play

Each team stands on, and defends, one of two goal lines drawn 80 to 120 feet apart. A restraining line is drawn 15 feet in front of and parallel to each goal line. Field width can vary from 50 to 80 feet. The referee stands in the center of the field and holds a ball (Figure 27.26). At the whistle, three players (more if the teams are large) run from the right side of each line to the center of the field and become the six active players. The referee drops the ball to the ground, and the players try to kick it through the team defending the goal line. The players in the field may advance by kicking only.

A team scores 1 point when an active player kicks the ball through the opposing team and over the endline (the kick must be made from outside the restraining line). Place cones at the field corners to define the goal line. Teams score 1 point for kicking the ball over the opponent's goal line below shoulder level. A team is awarded 1 point in the case of a personal foul involving pushing, kicking, tripping, and so on.

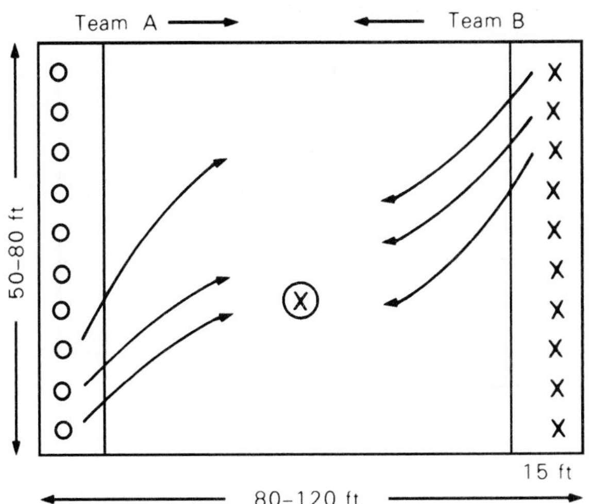

FIGURE 27.26 Line Soccer.

Line players act as goalies and are allowed to catch the ball. Upon catching the ball, however, the goalie must put it down immediately and either roll or kick it. It cannot be punted or drop-kicked.

For illegal touching by the active players, the opposing team gets a direct free kick from a point 12 yards in front of the penalized team's goal line. All active players on the defending team must stand to one side until the ball is kicked. Only goalies can defend. An out-of-bounds ball is awarded to the opponents of the team last touching it. Use the regular soccer throw-in from out-of-bounds. If the ball goes over the shoulders of the defenders at the endline, any endline player may retrieve the ball and put it into play with a throw or kick.

Set a time limit of 1 minute for any group of active players. When time is up, stop play and rotate the players so that all participants get to play.

Mini-Soccer

PLAYING AREA: Any large area 100 by 150 feet, with goals

PLAYERS: Two teams of 7 students each

SUPPLIES: A soccer ball, pinnies or colors to mark teams, four cones for the corners

SKILLS: All soccer skills

Each end of the field has a 21-foot-wide goal marked by jumping standards. A 12-yard semicircle on each end outlines the penalty area. The center of the semicircle is at the center of the goal (Figure 27.27).

The game follows the general rules of soccer, with one goalie for each side. One new feature, the corner kick, is incorporated in this game. This kick

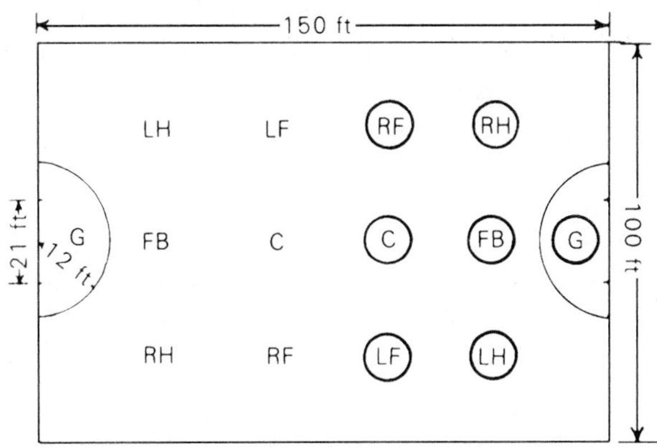

FIGURE 27.27 Formation for Mini-Soccer.

is used when the ball, last touched by the defense, goes over the endline but not through the goal. The ball is taken to the nearest corner for a direct free kick, and a goal can be scored from the kick. In a similar situation, if the attacking team last touched the ball, the goalkeeper kick is awarded. The goalie puts the ball down and placekicks it forward.

The players are designated as center, right-forward, left-forward, right halfback, left halfback, fullback, and goalie. Players should rotate positions. The forwards play in the front half of the field, and the guards play in the back half. Neither position, however, is restricted to these areas entirely; all players may cross the centerline without penalty.

A foul by the defense within its penalty area (semicircle) results in a penalty kick, taken from a point 12 yards distant, directly in front of the goal. Only the goalie is allowed to defend. The ball is in play, with others waiting outside the penalty area.

Teaching Hint

Emphasize position play, and encourage the lines of three to spread out and stay in their area. The number of players can vary; games may use as few as three on a side in a more restricted area.

Six-Spot Keep-Away

PLAYING AREA: Playground, gymnasium

PLAYERS: Two teams, one with 6 offensive players and one with 3 defensive players

SUPPLIES: A soccer ball, stopwatch

SKILLS: Passing, ball control, guarding

Five offensive players stand in a pentagon formation, with the sixth player in the center (Figure 27.28). The pentagon is about 20 yards across. The game begins with the ball in possession of the center player. Three defenders from the other team enter the pentagon and try to interrupt the offensive team's passing the ball from one to another. Offensive players should stay reasonably in position. Players may not pass the ball back to the player who passed it to them.

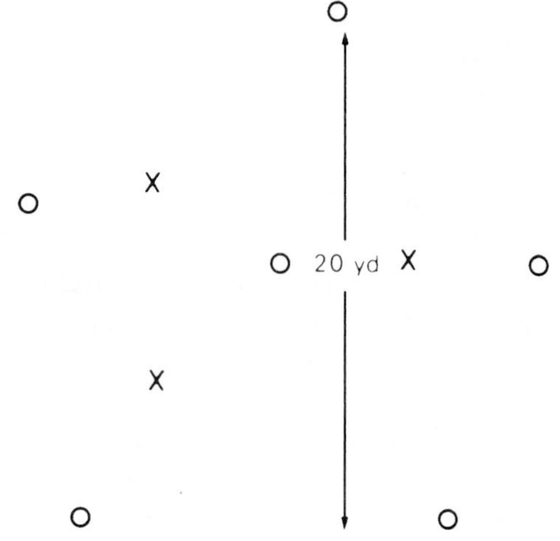

FIGURE 27.28 Six-Spot Keep-Away.

The object is to make as many good passes as possible against the three defenders. After 1 minute, three offensive players become defensive players and repeat the activity. One more rotation occurs so that all players have been on defense. The threesome scoring the most points is the winner.

Regulation Soccer

PLAYING AREA: Soccer field (Figure 27.29)

PLAYERS: 11 students on each team

SUPPLIES: A soccer ball, pinnies

SKILLS: All soccer skills

A team usually consists of three forwards, three midfield players, four backline defenders, and one goalkeeper. Teams can have more players, depending on class size. Forwards are the main line of attack and focus primarily on scoring. Midfield players need good passing and tackling skills as well as good cardiovascular fitness. Defenders work to keep the opponent from scoring. They try to keep the ball away from their own penalty area and avoid dribbling or passing toward their own goal unless it is absolutely safe to do so. Goalkeepers are usually quick, agile, and have good ball-handling skills.

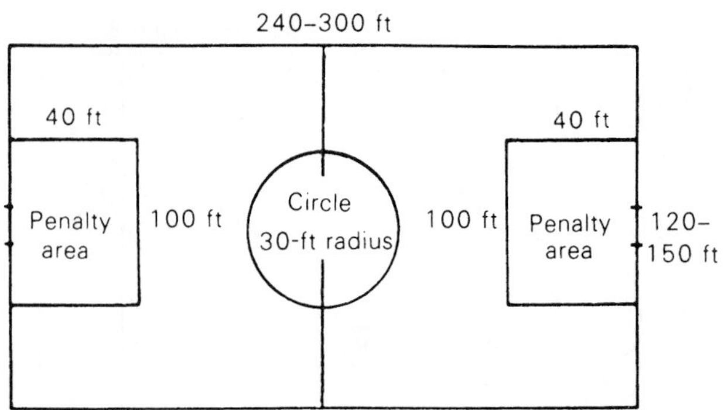

FIGURE 27.29 Regulation soccer field.

After a coin toss, the winning team gets to kick off or choose a goal to defend. The loser exercises the option not selected by the winner.

On the kickoff, the ball must travel forward at least 1 yard, and the kicker cannot touch it again until another player has kicked it. The defensive team must be 10 yards away from the kicker. After each score, the team not winning the point gets to kick off. Both teams must be onside at the kickoff. The defensive team must stay onside and out of the center circle until the ball is kicked. Regular soccer rules call for scoring by counting the number of goals made.

Elementary school children usually play 6-minute quarters, but this time can vary depending on the players' skill. Provide a rest period of 1 minute between quarters and 10 minutes between halves.

When the ball goes out-of-bounds on the sideline, it is put into play with a throw-in from the spot where it crossed the line. A goal may not be scored nor may the thrower play the ball a second time until another player has touched it. All opponents are to be 10 yards back at the time of the throw.

If the attacking team causes the ball to go out-of-bounds on the endline, a goal kick is awarded. The ball is placed in the goal area and kicked beyond the penalty area by a defending player, who may not touch the ball twice in a row. If a player touches the ball before it goes out of the penalty area, it is not yet in play and is kicked again.

If the defensive team sends the ball out-of-bounds over the endline, the other team gets a corner kick. The ball is placed 1 yard from the corner of the field and kicked into the field of play by an attacking player. The 10-yard restriction also applies to defensive players.

If two opponents touch the ball at the same time and it goes out-of-bounds, a drop ball is called. The referee drops the ball between two opposing players, who cannot kick it until it touches the ground. A drop ball is also called when the ball is trapped among downed players.

If a player is closer to the opponent's goal line than to the ball when the ball is played in a forward direction, it is an offside infraction. Exceptions exist, and a player is not offside when he is in his half of the playing field, when two opponents are nearer their goal line than the attacking player at the moment the ball is played, or when the ball is received directly from a corner kick, a throw-in, or a goal kick.

Personal fouls involving unnecessary roughness are penalized. Tripping, striking, charging, holding, pushing, and jumping an opponent intentionally are forbidden.

It is a foul for any player, except the goalkeeper, to handle the ball with the hands or arms. The goalkeeper is allowed only four steps and must then get rid of the ball. After the ball has left his possession, the goalkeeper may not pick it up again until another player has touched it. Players are not allowed to screen or obstruct opponents, unless they are in control of the ball.

Penalties are as follows:

1. A direct kick is awarded for all personal fouls and handled balls. A goal can be scored from a direct free kick. Examples of infringements are pushing, tripping, kicking a player, and holding.
2. A penalty kick is awarded if a defender in his penalty area commits direct free-kick infringements.
3. An indirect free kick is awarded for offsides, obstruction, dangerous play such as high kicking, a goalkeeper's taking more than four steps or repossessing the ball before another player has touched it, and playing the ball twice after a dead-ball situation. A second player must touch the ball before a goal can be scored. A referee signals if the kick is indirect by pointing one arm upward vertically.

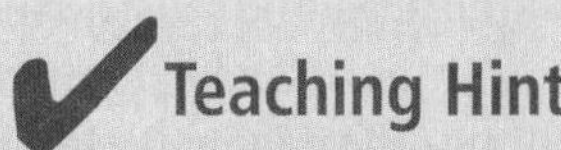

Encourage players to use the space on the field to the best advantage. When a team is in possession of the ball, players should try to find a position where they can pass either behind the player with the ball to give support, or toward the goal to be in a better position to shoot. When a team is forced into defense, the defenders should get "goalside" of attackers (between the attackers and their own goal) to prevent them from gaining an advantage.

From an early stage, players must learn to give information to each other during the game. Valuable help can be given by shouting instructions such as "Man on," "You have time," or "Player behind," and by calling for the ball when in position to receive a pass.

SOCCER SKILL TESTS

The tests for soccer skills cover various kinds of kicks, dribbling, and controlling. An excellent use of the skill tests is to set up self-testing stations. Signs will tell students how to test themselves. If desired, the teacher can formally test students at one of the stations. Students rotate from station to station after a designated amount of time.

PASSING AGAINST A WALL

Players pass the ball from behind a line drawn 5 to 10 yards away from a wall. Encourage students to control the ball before kicking. The score consists of the number of passes made from behind the line in 1 or 2 minutes. This is an excellent test of general ball control and short passing skill.

FIGURE-EIGHT DRIBBLING

For a figure-eight dribbling test, arrange three obstacles or markers in a line, 4 yards apart, with the first marker 4 yards from the starting line. The finish line is 4 yards wide. Using a stopwatch, time the players to the nearest tenth of a second.

Each player gets three trials, and the fastest trial is recorded. On each trial, the player dribbles over the figure-eight course and finishes by kicking or dribbling the ball over the 4-yard finish line, and the watch is then stopped. The test is best done on a grass surface. If a hard surface must be used, deflate the ball somewhat so players can control it.

CONTROLLING

For the controlling test, the formation is a file plus one. A thrower stands 15 to 20 feet in front of the file and rolls or bounces the ball to the player at the head of the file. Players get three trials each for sole-of-the-foot control, foot control, and body control. The ball must be definitely stopped and controlled. The highest possible total score is 9 points.

The thrower should adopt one type of throw for all controls and for all players. If the scorer judges that the roll was not a good opportunity, the trial is taken over. Five trials can be allowed.

PUNTING AND PLACEKICKING FOR DISTANCE AND ACCURACY

To test punting for distance, a football field or any other field marked in gridiron fashion at 5- or 10-yard intervals is needed. One soccer ball is required, but using three saves considerable time. A measuring tape (25 or 50 feet) and individual markers complete the supply list.

Each player takes three kicks from behind a restraining line. One child marks the kick for distance, and one or two others act as ball chasers. Each player's marker is left at the spot of their longest kick. This is determined by marking where the ball first touched the ground after the kick.

Kicks are measured to the nearest foot, and each student in the small group should kick before the distances are measured. The punt must be from a standing, not a running, start. If a child crosses the line during the kick, it counts as a trial and is not marked.

Placekicking for distance is tested in the same way as punting for distance, with two exceptions. First, the ball is kicked from a stationary position and must be laid on a flat surface and not elevated by dirt, grass, or other means. Second, the child gets credit for the entire distance of the kick, including the roll. Kicking should be done on a grassy surface, because the ball will roll indefinitely on a smooth, hard surface. If the surface presents a problem, the test can be limited to the distance the ball has traveled in flight.

PENALTY KICKING AND SHORT PASSING ACCURACY

In the penalty-kicking test, the kicker faces a target area from a point 12 yards out, where the ball has been placed. The target area is formed by a rope stretched tight 6 feet above the ground. Four ropes, set 5 feet apart, are dropped from the stretched rope. This outlines three target areas 6 feet high and 5 feet wide. The center target area scores 1 point, and the side areas score 2 points (Figure 27.30). (This reflects the principle that a penalty kick should be directed away from a goalkeeper and toward either corner of the goal.) Each child is allotted five kicks at the target. Possible score: 10 points.

The same target is used for kicking for accuracy, but the center area scores 2 points and the side areas score 1 point each. A chalk line is about 20 feet from the target, and the child stands back another 20 feet for the start. She dribbles the ball forward and must kick the ball as it is moving and before it crosses the chalk line. Five trials are given. Possible score: 10 points.

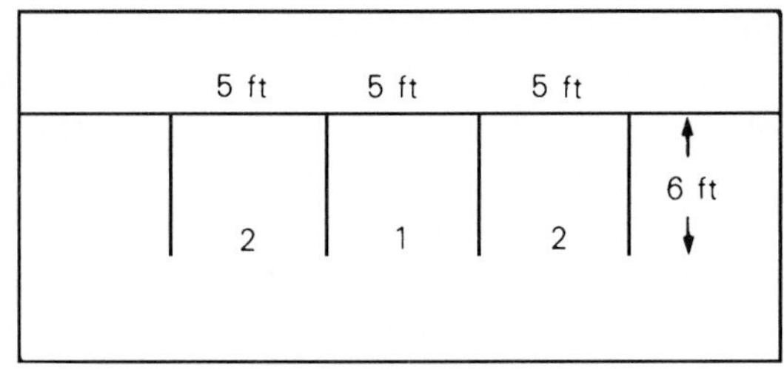

FIGURE 27.30 Penalty-kicking target area.

FOR MORE INFORMATION

REFERENCES AND SUGGESTED READINGS

Beswick, B. (2001). *Focused for soccer.* Champaign, IL: Human Kinetics.

Bungsbo, J., & Peitersen, B. (2000). *Soccer systems and strategies.* Champaign, IL: Human Kinetics.

Fronske, H. (2005). *Teaching cues for sport skills* (3rd ed.). San Francisco: Benjamin Cummings.

Garland, J. (2003). *Youth soccer drills* (2nd ed.). Champaign, IL: Human Kinetics.

Hanlon, T. (2004). *The sports rule book* (2nd ed.). Champaign, IL: Human Kinetics

Luxbacher, J. (2005). *Soccer: Steps to success* (3rd ed.). Champaign, IL: Human Kinetics.

Mood, D. P., Musker, F. F., & Rink, J. E. (2007). *Sports and recreational activities* (14th ed.). New York: McGraw-Hill.

National Soccer Coaches Association of America (T. Schum, Ed.). (1996). *Soccer skills and drills.* Indianapolis, IN: Masters Press.

Schmottlach, N., & McManama, J. (2006). *The physical education handbook* (11th ed.). San Francisco: Benjamin Cummings.

Wein, H. (2000). *Developing youth soccer players.* Champaign, IL: Human Kinetics.

WEBSITES

Soccer America Magazine
www.socceramerica.com

Soccer Information
www.soccercoachinginternational.com
www.soccerhelp.com
www.gotsoccer.com

U.S. Soccer Federation
www.ussoccer.org

Women's United Soccer Association
www.wusa.com

Youth Soccer
www.usyouthsoccer.org
www.SaySoccer.org

Softball

28

ESSENTIAL COMPONENTS OF QUALITY PROGRAMS

- I. Organized around content standards
- II. Student-centered and developmentally appropriate
- III. Physical activity and motor skill development form the core of the program
- IV. Teaches management skills and self-discipline
- V. Promotes inclusion of all students
- VI. Focuses on process over product
- VII. Promotes lifetime personal health and wellness
- VIII. Teaches cooperation and responsibility and promotes sensitivity to diversity

NATIONAL STANDARDS FOR PHYSICAL EDUCATION*

1. Demonstrates competency in motor skills and movement patterns needed to perform a variety of physical activities.
2. Demonstrates understanding of movement concepts, principles, and tactics as they apply to the learning and performance of physical activities.
3. Participates regularly in physical activity.
4. Achieves and maintains a health-enhancing level of physical fitness.
5. Exhibits responsible personal and social behavior that respects self and others in physical activity.
6. Values physical activity for health, enjoyment, challenge, self-expression, and/or social interaction.

*National Association for Sport and Physical Education (NASPE), 2004.

Skills instruction for softball begins during the intermediate grades after children have mastered basic prerequisite skills. Teaching the rules and strategies for softball is an integral part of the instructional process. Using proper progression is key to successful teaching of fundamental skills and lead-up games associated with softball. Lead-up games allow teachers to emphasize development of selected softball skills in a setting compatible with their students' abilities.

Outcomes

- Structure learning experiences efficiently using appropriate formations, progressions, and coaching techniques.
- Develop a unit plan and lesson focus for softball.
- Identify safety precautions associated with teaching softball.
- Describe instructional procedures used for directing a successful lead-up game.
- Cite assessment procedures used for evaluating softball skills.

CHILDREN enjoy softball, and a good program makes use of this drive. The focus in softball is on instruction and lead-up games. Children have adequate opportunity during recess, at the noon hour, and at other times to play the regulation game.

INSTRUCTIONAL EMPHASIS AND SEQUENCE

Table 28.1 shows the sequence of softball activities divided into two developmental levels. The activities are listed in progression. Students can practice many softball skills but may not be ready to participate in this chapter's activities until age 8.

DEVELOPMENTAL LEVELS I AND II

Developmental Levels I and II emphasize the basic skills of batting, throwing, and catching. Batting receives much attention, for softball is little fun unless children can hit. Proper form and technique in all three basic skills are parts of the instruction, paying attention to the how as well as the why. Lead-up games introduce students to the basic rules of the game. As children mature, lessons focus on specific skills for pitching, infield play, base running, and batting.

DEVELOPMENTAL LEVEL III

Children at Developmental Level II acquire the background to play the game of regulation softball. Tee Ball offers an opportunity for developing all softball skills except pitching and catching. Home Run and the ever-popular Scrub (Work-Up) provide a variety of experiences, and Batter Ball stresses hitting skills. Students practice batting, throwing, catching, and infield play. Teachers add new pitching techniques, situation play, and double-play work. Slow-Pitch offers lots of action. Babe Ruth Ball emphasizes selective hitting.

SOFTBALL SKILLS

Children can find many ways to execute softball skills effectively, by trial and error and through instruction. Do not try to mold every child into a prescribed form. Work toward making the most of each child's movement patterns.

GRIPPING THE BALL

The standard softball grip, which is difficult for elementary school children, calls for the thumb on one side, the index and middle fingers on top, and the other fingers supporting the ball along the other side (Figure 28.1 on page 676). Children with small hands can use a full-hand grip, spacing the thumb and fingers rather evenly (Figure 28.2 on page 676). Regardless of the grip used, the pads of the fingers control the ball.

THROWING (RIGHT-HANDED)

Softball requires accurate throwing. To play softball well, players must develop proper throwing technique. Of all the team sports, softball is probably the most difficult for children because of the fine motor coordination required. Use these instructional cues to help students develop proper throwing technique:

1. Place the throwing-arm side of the body away from the target.
2. Step toward the target with the foot opposite the throwing hand.
3. Rotate the hips as the throwing arm moves forward.
4. Bend and raise the arm at the elbow. Lead with the elbow.
5. Shift the weight from the rear foot to the front foot (nearest the target) before the arm moves forward.

Overhand Throw

To prepare for throwing, the child firmly grips the ball, raises the throwing arm to shoulder height, and brings the elbow back. For the overhand throw, the hand with the ball then moves back over the head until it is well behind the shoulder at about shoulder height. The left side of the body turns in the direction of the throw, and the left arm is raised in front of the body. The weight is on the back (right) foot, with the left foot advanced and the toe touch-

TABLE 28.1 Suggested softball program

Developmental Level II	Developmental Level III	Developmental Level II	Developmental Level III
Skills		**Knowledge, Rules**	
Throwing		Strike zone	Pitching rule
Gripping the ball	Throw-in from outfield	Foul and fair ball	Position
Overhand throw		Safe and out	Illegal pitches
Underhand toss		Foul tip	Infield fly
Around the bases		Bunt rule	Keeping score
		When batter is safe or out	Base running
			Situation quiz
Catching and Fielding		**Activities**	
Catching thrown balls	Catching flies from fungo bat	Throw-It-and-Run Softball	Five Hundred
Catching fly balls	Infield practice	Two-Pitch Softball	Batter Ball
Grounders		Hit and Run	Home Run
Fielding grounders in infield		Kick Softball	Tee Ball
Sure stop for outfield		In a Pickle	Scrub (Work-Up)
Batting		Beat Ball	Slow-Pitch Softball
Simple skills	Different positions at plate	Steal a Base	Babe Ruth Ball
Tee batting	Bunting		Hurry Baseball (One-Pitch Softball)
Fungo hitting			Three-Team Softball
Fielding Positions		**Skill Tests**	
Infield practice	Backing up other players	Throwing for distance	Pitching
How to catch	Double play	Throwing for accuracy	Circling the bases
Base Running			Fielding grounders
To first base and turn	Fast start off base		
Circling the bases	Tagging up on fly ball		
	Sacrifice		
Pitching			
Simple underhand	Target pitching		
Application of pitching rule	Slow pitches		

ing the ground. The arm comes forward with the elbow leading, and the ball is thrown with a downward snap of the wrist (Figure 28.3 on page 676). The body weight is brought forward into the throw, shifting to the front foot. The player follows through so that the palm of the throwing hand faces the ground after the throw. The eyes are on the target throughout, and the arm is kept free and loose during the throw.

Underhand Throw

For the underhand throw, the player draws back the throwing hand and arm—with the ball in her palm, facing up—in a downward swing. The elbow is bent slightly; weight is mostly on the back foot. The arm comes forward in a bowling motion, and she tosses the ball. The weight shifts to the front foot during the toss. The flight of the ball stays low and arrives at about waist height.

PITCHING

Official rules call for the pitcher to have both feet in contact with the pitcher's rubber, but few elementary schools have one. Instead, the pitcher can stand with both feet about even, facing the batter, and hold the ball briefly in front with both hands. The pitcher takes one hand from the ball, extends the right arm forward, and brings it back in a pendulum swing, positioning the ball well behind the body. A normal stride taken with the left foot toward the

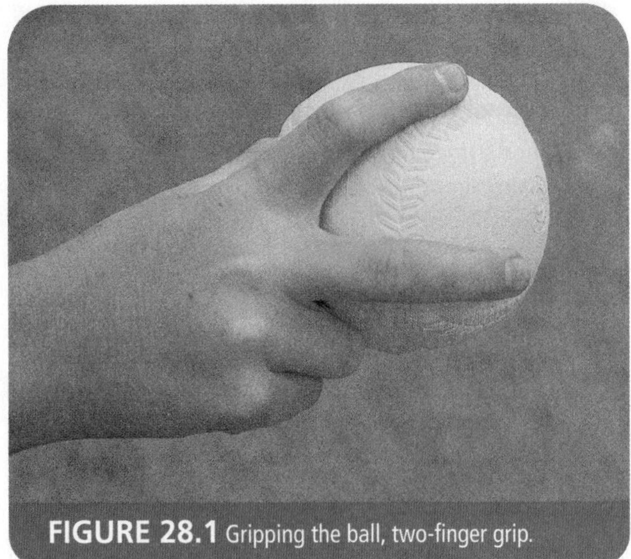

FIGURE 28.1 Gripping the ball, two-finger grip.

FIGURE 28.2 Gripping the ball, full grip. (The little finger supports on the side.)

FIGURE 28.3 Throwing overhand.

batter begins the throwing sequence for a right-handed pitcher. The arm swings forward with an underhanded slingshot motion, and the weight shifts to the leading foot. Only one step is permitted. The follow-through motion is important (Figure 28.4).

FIGURE 28.4 Pitching.

The windmill is an alternate pitching motion in which the arm makes a full arc overhead, moving behind the body and then forward toward the batter. The arm goes into full extension on the downward swing in the back, gathering momentum as the forward motion begins. The pitch is otherwise the same as the normal motion. The windmill is generally difficult for students to master. Here are instructional cues for pitching:

1. Face the plate.
2. Keep your eyes on the target.
3. Swing the pitching arm backward and step forward.
4. Keep the pitching arm extended.

FIELDING

Infielders should assume the ready position—a semi-crouch, with legs shoulder width apart, knees bent slightly, and hands on or in front of the knees (Figure 28.5). As the ball is delivered, the weight shifts to the balls of the feet. The outfielder's position is a slightly more erect semi-crouch. Here are instructional cues for fielding:

1. Move into line with the path of the ball.
2. Give when catching the ball.
3. Use the glove to absorb the force of the ball.
4. For grounders, keep the head down and watch the ball move into the glove.

Fly Balls

There are two ways to catch a fly ball. For a low ball, the fielder keeps the fingers together and forms a basket with

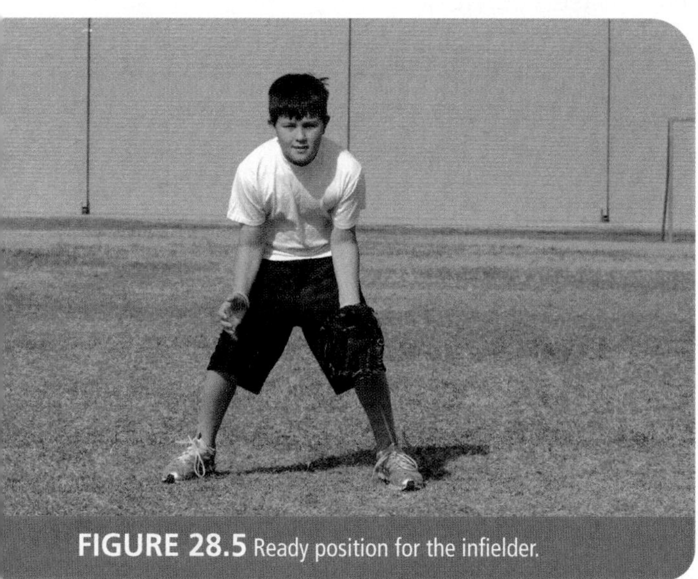

FIGURE 28.5 Ready position for the infielder.

the hands (Figure 28.6). For a higher ball, the thumbs are together, and the ball is caught overhead (Figure 28.7). The fielder must give with the hands, and be careful with a spinning ball to squeeze it enough to stop the spinning. The eye is on the ball continually until the ball hits the glove or hands. The knees are flexed slightly when receiving and aid in giving when the ball is caught.

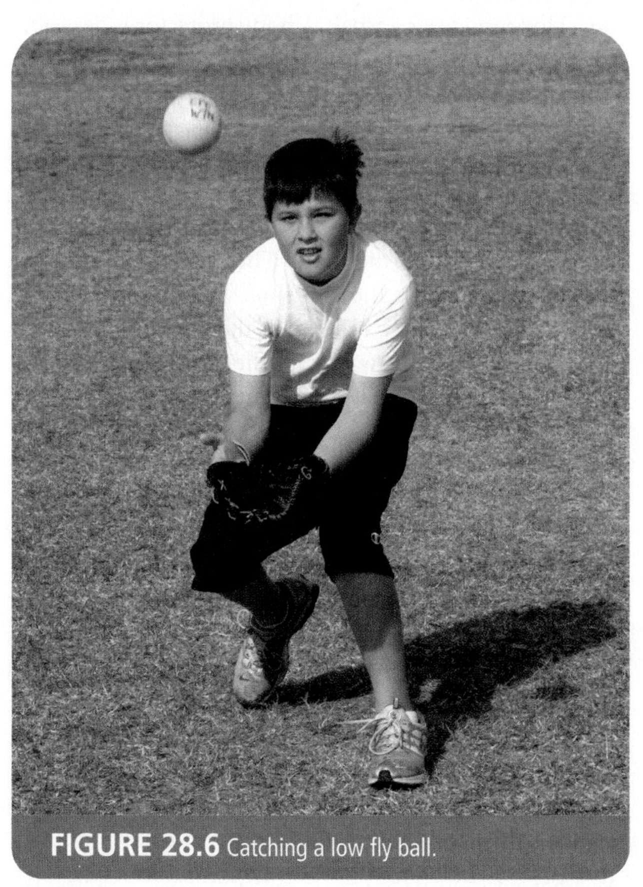

FIGURE 28.6 Catching a low fly ball.

FIGURE 28.7 Catching a high fly ball.

Grounders

To field a grounder, the fielder moves as quickly as possible into the path of the ball (Figure 28.8) and then moves forward to play the ball on a good hop. The eyes focus on the ball, following it into the hands or glove. The feet are spread, the seat stays down, and the hands are held low and in front (Figure 28.9 on page 678). Weight is on the balls of the feet or on the toes, and the knees are bent to

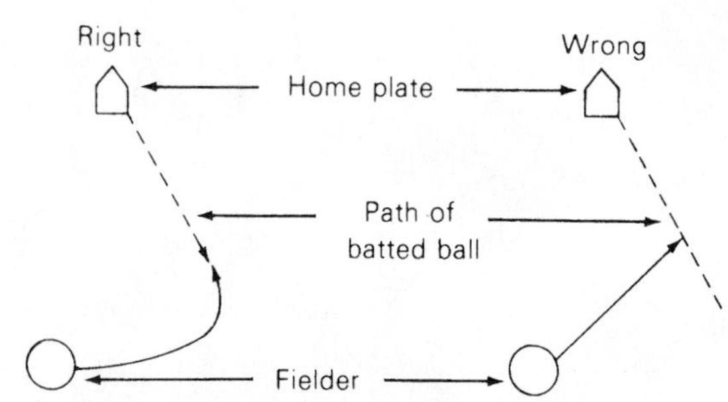

FIGURE 28.8 Fielding a grounder correctly.

28

FIGURE 28.9 Fielding a grounder.

lower the body. Upon catching the ball, the fielder straightens up, takes a step in the direction of the throw, and makes the throw.

Sure Stop for Outfield Balls

To keep the ball from going through the hands and thus allowing extra bases, the outfielder can use her body as a barrier. She turns halfway to the right and lowers one knee to the ground at the point toward which the ball is traveling (Figure 28.10). The hands catch the rolling ball; but if they miss, the body generally stops it.

FIGURE 28.10 Sure stop.

First-Base Positioning

When a ball is hit to the infield, the first-base player moves to the base until his foot is touching it. He then judges the path of the ball, stepping toward it with the left foot (if right-handed) and stretching forward. The right foot remains in contact with the base (Figure 28.11).

FIGURE 28.11 First-base player stretching for a catch.

Catcher's Position

The catcher crouches with the feet about shoulder width apart and the left foot slightly ahead of the right. He must use a glove and wear a mask. A body protector is desirable. The catcher is positioned just beyond the swinging range of the bat (Figure 28.12).

BATTING (RIGHT-HANDED)

The batter stands with the left side of the body toward the pitcher. The feet are spread and weight is on both feet. The body faces the plate. The bat is held over the right shoulder (with the trademark up), pointing both back and up. The left hand grasps the bat below the right hand. The elbows are away from the body (Figure 28.13). The swing begins with a hip roll and a short step toward the pitcher. The bat is then swung level with the ground at the height of the pitch. The eyes focus on the ball until it is hit.

Batters should avoid the following habits: lifting the front foot high off the ground, stepping back with the rear foot, dropping the rear shoulder, chopping down on the ball, golfing, dropping the elbows, and crouching or bending forward. Failing to keep the eyes on the ball is a serious error. Players should practice the choke grip, the long grip, and the middle grip. In all three, the grip is relaxed. Beginning batters can start with the choke grip. Here are instructional cues for batting:

1. Keep the hands together.
2. Swing the bat horizontally.

FIGURE 28.12 Catcher's position.

FIGURE 28.13 Batter's position.

3. Swing through the ball.
4. Hold the bat off the shoulder.
5. Watch the ball hit the bat.

Safety Tip

Students should be taught to never swing a bat unless they have looked all around them and they are standing in the area designated for swinging the bat. Similarly, students should be taught to never walk in the designated bat swinging area unless no one in the area is holding a bat.

BUNTING (RIGHT-HANDED)

To bunt, the batter turns to face the pitcher, setting the right foot alongside home plate. As the pitcher releases the ball, the batter runs his upper hand about halfway up the bat. He holds the bat loosely in front of the body and parallel to the ground to meet the ball (Figure 28.14). Bunts can be directed down the first- or third-base line.

The surprise, or drag, bunt is done without squaring around to face the pitcher. The batter holds the bat in a choke grip. When the pitcher lets go of the ball, the batter runs the right hand up the bat and directs the ball down either foul line, keeping it as close as possible to the line in fair territory.

FIGURE 28.14 Regular bunt position.

BASE RUNNING

A batter who hits the ball runs hard and purposefully toward first base, no matter what kind of hit it is. The runner runs past the bag, touching it in the process, and steps on the foul-line side of the base to avoid colliding with the first-base player.

Because a runner on base must hold the base position until the pitcher releases the ball, quickly leaving the base is essential. With either toe touching the base, the runner leans her body, keeping her weight on the ball of the leading foot and eyes on the pitcher. After the pitch, the runner takes a few steps away from the base in the direction of the next base.

INSTRUCTIONAL PROCEDURES

1. Safety is of the utmost importance. Teachers must take these precautions:
   a. Throwing the bat is a constant danger. Have members of the batting team stand well back from the baseline, preferably behind a fence or in a dugout if available.
   b. Try these techniques for teaching batters not to throw the bat:

      Have the batter touch the bat to the ground before dropping it.

      Call the batter out if the bat is thrown.

      Have the batter carry the bat to first base.

      Have the batter change ends of the bat before dropping it.

      Have the batter place the bat in a 3-foot circle before running.
   c. Sliding can lead to injury and destruction of clothing. With unskilled players, it is best to forbid sliding.
   d. A catcher who stands close behind the plate while catching must wear a mask. A body protector is also recommended.
   e. To avoid collisions while running for a fly ball, teach players to call for the ball and stay out of another player's area.
   f. When changing fields at the beginning of an inning, the batting team stays on the first-base side of the infield. The fielding team goes to bat via the third-base side of the infield.
   g. Use soft softballs, particularly in the early stages of development. Fleece balls are excellent for introductory fielding skills. Because many children fear batted balls, using balls that will not hurt them is a necessity.
2. Emphasize batting skills. There is no more an ego-shattering experience for a child than standing at the plate and showing an ineptness that draws scorn and ridicule from peers. Make sure that students know the correct stance and proper mechanics of batting. Improved hitting will come with practice.
3. The spoiler of many softball games is the pitcher–batter duel. If this becomes prolonged, the other players become justifiably bored while standing around. To eliminate the problem, have a member of the batting team pitch or give each batter only two or three swings.
4. Players should rotate positions often. In physical education classes, have everyone—including the pitcher—rotate to another position at the start of each inning.
5. The distance between bases greatly affects the game. Adjust the distance according to the game and the players' abilities.
6. Appoint umpires, or have the team at bat umpire. A convenient method is to appoint the person who made the last out of the previous inning as the umpire for the next inning. Teach all students how to umpire.
7. Encourage players to recognize and give approval and support to less skillful players. Because students vary widely in ability, take the opportunity to teach tolerance. It is important not to let an error become a tragedy to a player.
8. Have each player run out a hit, no matter how hopeless it seems.
9. Analyze the purpose of lead-up games. Have students practice needed skills before using them in a game.
10. Players must learn to respect officials and accept the umpire's judgment. Do not allow the disreputable practice of baiting the umpire to be a part of children's softball experiences.

ORGANIZING FOR INSTRUCTION

Students must develop skills in softball and acquire knowledge about the various phases of the game. The amount of field space and the equipment available determine the instructional organization. To cover the various phases of the game, a multiple-activity or station pattern is effective. Here are some guidelines for instruction:

1. Give children many opportunities to practice different skills. Even with rotation, use as many small groups as possible. For example, two children can practice throwing and fielding grounders.
2. Address differences in ability. Because some players have practiced more, they are often more skilled than

others in the class. Teachers can use skillful players (first giving them sufficient direction) in various phases of instruction.

3. Carefully plan and communicate to all students the activities and procedures to be followed at each station. Covering appropriate softball rules in meetings with captains and other helpers is valuable.
4. Complete rotation of stations is not necessary at each class session. During a class session, teams may practice at one station for part of the time and use the remaining time to participate in an appropriate lead-up game.
5. Provide directions at each station to help students make the most of the skill development opportunities. Post signs offering instructional strategies on cones at each station.
6. Using the rotational station system does not rule out whole-class activities. Mimetic drills (i.e., drills without equipment) help establish basic movement patterns for most skills. Have students practice batting, pitching, throwing, and fielding without worrying about results.
7. Station teaching offers an excellent opportunity for older students to help. In some school systems, high school students routinely visit elementary schools for observation and educational experiences.
8. Having students move from one station to another gives them encouragement, correction, coaching, and motivation for learning.
9. Motivate players by comparing the rotational system to varsity or major league practices. This gives the activity an adult flavor.
10. Let students choose from the list of lead-up games, particularly for team or small-group activities.

BASIC SOFTBALL RULES

Most sporting goods establishments have copies of the official softball rules, which students should use when learning the game. This section describes the basic rules.

The official diamond has 60-foot baselines and a pitching distance of 46 feet. Elementary school students should use a diamond with baselines no longer than 45 feet and a pitching distance of 35 feet or less. The nine players on a softball team are the catcher; the pitcher; first-, second-, and third-base players; the shortstop; and left, center, and right fielders. The right fielder is the outfielder nearest first base.

BATTING ORDER

Players may bat in any order, but having them bat according to their positions in the field can be convenient in class. Once established, the batting order cannot be changed, even if the player changes to another position in the field.

PITCHING

The pitcher must face the batter with both feet on the pitching rubber, holding the ball in front with both hands. The pitcher can take one step toward the batter and must deliver the ball during that step. The ball must be pitched underhanded. The pitcher cannot fake a pitch or make any motion toward the plate without delivering the ball. It is illegal to roll or bounce the ball to the batter. No quick return is allowed before the batter is ready. To be called a *strike*, a pitch must be over the plate and between the batter's knees and shoulders. A *ball* is a pitch that does not go through this area.

BATTING

The bat must be a softball bat. The batter cannot cross to the other side of the plate when the pitcher is ready to pitch. If a player bats out of turn, she is out. A bunt that goes foul on the third strike is an out. A pitched ball that touches or hits the batter entitles the batter to first base if she does not strike or bunt at the ball.

STRIKING OUT

A batter who misses the ball on the third strike is out. This is called *striking out*.

BATTER SAFE

A batter who reaches first base before the fielding team can field the ball and throw it to first is safe.

FAIR BALL

A fair ball is any batted ball that settles on fair territory between home and first base and home and third base. A ball that rolls over a base or through the field into fair territory is a fair ball. Fly balls (including line drives) that drop into fair territory beyond the infield are fair balls. Foul lines are in fair territory.

FOUL BALL

A foul ball is a batted ball that settles outside the foul lines between home and first or between home and third. A fly ball that drops into foul territory beyond the bases is a foul.

FLY BALL

Any fly ball (foul or fair), if caught, is an out. A foul fly, however, must rise over the batter's head or it is ruled a foul tip. A foul tip caught on the third strike, then, puts the batter out.

BASE RUNNING

Base runners cannot lead off. On penalty of being called out, the runner must stay on base until the ball leaves the pitcher's hand. On an overthrow when the ball goes into foul territory and out of play, runners advance one base beyond the one they were headed toward when the overthrow occurred. On an overthrow at second base, when the ball rolls into center field, the runners may advance as far as they can. The runner may try to avoid being tagged on a baseline but must stay within 3 feet on either side of a direct line from base to base. A runner hit by a batted ball while off the base is out. The batter, however, is entitled to first base. Base runners must touch all bases. If a runner fails to touch a base, it is an *appeal play*—the fielding team must call the oversight to the umpire's attention before she will rule on the play.

Runners may overrun first base without penalty. On all other bases, however, the runner must maintain contact with the base or be tagged out. To score, the runner must make contact with home plate.

SCORING

A run is scored when the base runner makes the circuit of the bases (i.e., first, second, third, and home) before the batting team has three outs. If the third out is a force out, no run is scored, even if the runner crossed home plate before the out was actually made.

The situation needing the most clarification occurs when a runner is on base with one out and the batter hits a fly ball that is caught, making the second out. If the runner does not return to the base previously occupied before the ball reaches that base, she, too, is out. If she makes the third out by failing to return to the base in time, no run is scored.

SOFTBALL DRILLS

Softball drills lend themselves to a station setup. For a regular class of 30 students, four squads of 7 or 8 students each are suggested. Activities at each station can emphasize a single skill or a combination of skills. Situational drills can also be incorporated. Remind children that constant repetition is necessary to develop, maintain, and sharpen softball skills.

The multitude of softball skills to be practiced allows for many different combinations and setups. Here are some examples for use in station teaching:

1. Batting can be organized in many ways. Ensure that each child has many opportunities to hit the ball successfully.
   a. Have the students use a batting tee. For each station, two tees are needed, with a bat and at least two balls per tee. Assign 3 to 5 children to each station: a batter, a catcher to handle incoming balls, and fielders. When only three children are in a unit, omit the catcher. Give each batter a certain number of swings before rotating to the field. The catcher becomes the next batter, and a fielder moves up to catcher.
   b. Organize informal hitting practice. A batter, a pitcher, and fielders are needed. Assign two batting groups to each station. A catcher is optional.
   c. Have the students practice hitting a foam rubber ball thrown underhand. The larger ball is easier to hit.
   d. Have the students practice bunting in groups of three: a pitcher, a batter, and a fielder.
2. Have students practice throwing and catching using these drills:
   a. Throw back and forth, practicing various throws.
   b. Throw ground balls back and forth for fielding practice.
   c. A player acting as a first-base player, throws grounders to the other infielders and receives the put-out throw.
   d. Throw flies back and forth.
   e. Hit flies, with two or three fielders catching.
   f. Establish four bases and throw from base to base.
3. Have players use proper pitching and catching form for pitching practice.
   a. Pitch to another player over a plate.
   b. Call balls and strikes. One player is the pitcher, the second is the catcher, and the third is the umpire. A fourth player can be a stationary batter to offer a more realistic pitching target.
   c. Pitch toward pitching targets—either a wooden target (see page 690) or a similar area outlined on a wall.
4. For infield drills, place children at normal infield positions—behind the plate, at each base, and at shortstop. One child acts as the batter and gives directions. The play begins with practice in throwing around the bases in either direction. Next, the batter can roll the ball to the different infielders, starting at third base and continuing in turn around the infield, with each player throwing to first to retire an imaginary runner. A skillful batter can hit the ball instead of rolling it to infielders, thus making the drill more realistic. Using a second softball saves time when the ball is thrown or batted past an infielder, because players do not have to wait for the ball to be retrieved before continuing play. After the ball is thrown to first base, other throws around the infield can take place. The drill also can be done with only a partial infield.
5. Organize various situations for practicing base running.
   a. Bunt and run to first base. A pitcher, a batter, an infielder, and a first-base player are needed. The pitcher serves the ball up for a bunt, and the batter, after bunting, takes off for first base. A fielding play can be made on the runner.

b. Bunt and run to second base. The batter bunts the ball and runs to first base and then on to second, making a proper turn at first.

6. Play Pepper. (This is one of the older skill games in softball.) A line of 3 or 4 players stand about 10 yards in front of and facing a batter. The players toss the ball to the batter, who tries to hit controlled grounders back to them (Figure 28.15). The batter stays at bat for a specified time and then rotates to the field.

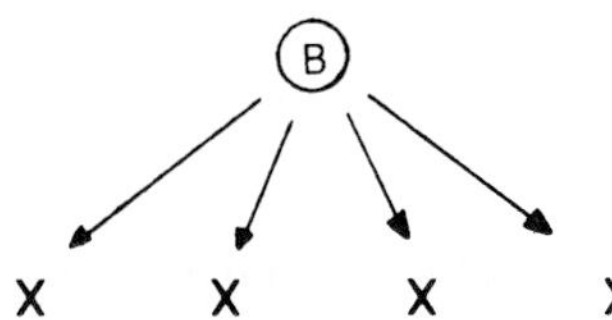

FIGURE 28.15 Play Pepper.

7. At stations, schedule some game-type activities like Batter Ball, In a Pickle, Five Hundred, and Scrub. Stations might be organized as follows. (Numbers and letters refer to the drills just listed. The page number refers to an activity not yet discussed.)

Station 1: Batting (see 1a)

Station 2: Throwing and fielding grounders (see 2c)

Station 3: Base running—In a Pickle (see page 685)

Station 4: Bunting and base running (see 5a)

Here is another example of station arrangement:

Station 1: Batting and fielding—Pepper (see 6)

Station 2: Pitching and umpiring (see 3b)

Station 3: Infield practice (see 4)

Station 4: Batting (see 1b)

Stations might also be arranged as follows:

Station 1: Fly ball hitting, fielding, and throwing (see 2e)

Station 2: Bunting and fielding (see 1d)

Station 3: Pitching to targets (see 3c)

Station 4: Batting (see 1a and 1b)

SOFTBALL ACTIVITIES

DEVELOPMENTAL LEVEL II

Throw-It-and-Run Softball

PLAYING AREA: Softball diamond reduced in size

PLAYERS: Two teams of 7 to 11 (usually 9) students each

SUPPLIES: A softball or similar ball

SKILLS: Throwing, catching, fielding, base running

Throw-It-and-Run Softball is played like regular softball, with one exception: With one team in the field at regular positions, the pitcher throws the ball to the batter, who, instead of batting the ball, catches it and immediately throws it into the field. The ball is then treated as a batted ball, and regular softball rules prevail. No stealing is permitted, however, and runners must hold their bases until the batter throws the ball. A foul ball is an out.

VARIATIONS:

1. *Under-Leg Throw.* Instead of throwing directly, the batter can turn to the right, lift the left leg, and throw the ball under the leg into the playing field.
2. *Beat-Ball Throw.* The fielders, instead of playing by regular softball rules, throw the ball directly home to the catcher. The batter, in the meantime, runs around the bases. He scores 1 point for each base he touches before the catcher receives the ball. A ball caught on the fly means no score. Similarly, a foul ball does not score points but counts as a turn at bat.

Two-Pitch Softball

PLAYING AREA: Softball diamond

PLAYERS: Two teams of 7 to 11 students each

SUPPLIES: A softball, bat

SKILLS: Most softball skills, except regular pitching

Two-Pitch Softball is played like regular softball, but with these changes:

1. A member of the team at bat pitches. Set up a rotation system that gives every child a turn as pitcher.
2. The batter has only two pitches in which to hit the ball, and she must hit a fair ball on one of these pitches or is out. The batter can foul the first ball, but if she fouls the second, she is out. Do not call balls or strikes.
3. The pitcher does not field the ball. A member of the team in the field acts as the fielding pitcher.
4. If the batter hits the ball, teams follow regular softball rules. Stealing is not allowed.

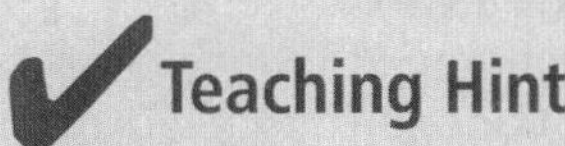

Teaching Hint

To help the pitcher throw a ball that batters can hit, shorten the pitching distance. The instructor can act as the pitcher.

VARIATION: **Three Strikes.** In this game, the batter gets three pitches (strikes). Otherwise, the game proceeds as in Two-Pitch Softball.

Hit and Run

PLAYING AREA: Softball field or gymnasium

PLAYERS: Two teams of 6 to 15 students each

SUPPLIES: A volleyball, soccer ball, or playground ball; home plate; base markers

SKILLS: Catching, throwing, running, dodging

One team is at bat, and the other is scattered in the field. Boundaries are established, but the area does not have to look like a baseball diamond. The batter stands at home plate with the ball. In front of the batter, 12 feet away, is a short line over which the ball must be hit to be in play. In the center of the field, about 40 feet away, is the base marker.

The batter bats the ball with the hands or fists so that it crosses the short line and lands inside the area. He then tries to run down the field, around the base marker, and back to home plate without being hit by the ball (Figure 28.16). The other team's members field the ball and try to tag the runner. The fielders may not run or walk with the ball but may throw to teammates closer to the runner.

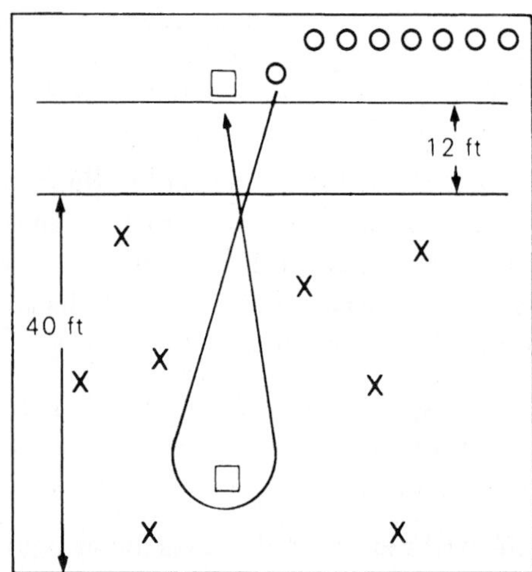

FIGURE 28.16 Hit and Run.

A run is scored each time a batter runs around the marker and back to home plate without getting tagged by the ball. A run is also scored if a foul is called on the fielding team for walking or running with the ball.

The batter is out in any of these situations:

1. A fly ball is caught.
2. The ball is not hit beyond the short line.
3. The team touches home plate with the ball before the runner returns. (This out is used only when the runner stops in the field and does not continue.)

The game can be played in innings of three outs each, or teams can change positions after all members of one team have batted. Depending on players' abilities, you may have to adjust the distance from home plate to the base marker.

VARIATION: **Five Passes.** The batter is out when a fly ball is caught—or when the ball is passed among five different players of the fielding team, with the last pass to a player at home plate beating the runner to the plate. Passes must not touch the ground.

Kick Softball

PLAYING AREA: Regular softball field with a 3- by 3-foot home base

PLAYERS: Two teams of 7 to 11 students each

SUPPLIES: A soccer ball or another ball to be kicked

SKILLS: Kicking a rolling ball, throwing, catching, running bases

The batter stands in the kicking area, a 3-foot-square home plate. The batter kicks the ball rolled on the ground by the pitcher. The ball is rolled at moderate speed. An umpire calls balls and strikes. A strike is a ball that rolls over the 3-foot square. A ball rolls outside this area. Strikeouts and walks are called as in regular softball. The number of foul balls allowed should be limited. No base stealing is permitted. Otherwise, the game is played like softball.

VARIATIONS:

1. The batter kicks a stationary ball. This saves time, as there is no pitching.
2. *Punch Ball.* The batter can hit a volleyball as in a volleyball serve or punch a ball pitched by the pitcher.

In a Pickle

PLAYING AREA: Any flat surface with 60 square feet of room

PLAYERS: 3 or more students

SUPPLIES: A softball, two bases 45 to 55 feet apart

SKILLS: Throwing, catching, running down a base runner, tagging

A base runner who gets caught between two bases and is in danger of being run down and tagged is "in a pickle." To begin, both fielders are on bases, and one has a ball. The runner is on the base path, 10 to 15 feet away from the fielder who has the ball. The two fielders throw the ball back and forth in an effort to run down and tag the runner between the bases. A runner who escapes and secures a base gets to try again. Otherwise, a system of rotation is established, including any sideline (waiting) players. No sliding is permitted.

Beat Ball

PLAYING AREA: Softball diamond, bases approximately 30 feet apart

PLAYERS: Two teams of 5 to 12 students each

SUPPLIES: Soft softball, bat, batting tee (optional)

SKILLS: All softball skills

One team is at bat, and the other team is in the field. The object is to hit the ball and run around the bases before the fielding team can catch the ball, throw it to first base, and then throw it to the catcher at home plate. If the ball beats the hitter home or a fly ball is caught, it is an out. If the hitter beats the ball to home plate, a run is scored. All players on a team bat once before switching positions with the fielding team. The ball must be hit into fair territory before the hitter can run. Each hitter gets three pitches.

✔ Teaching Hints

1. Depending on the players' maturity, a batting tee may be used. Give hitters the option of using the batting tee or hitting a pitched ball.
2. Select the pitcher from the batting team. This ensures that the player will try to make pitches that can be hit.
3. Vary the distance so that hitters have a fair opportunity to score. If hitters score too easily, add another base.

Steal a Base

PLAYING AREA: Any 40- by 20-foot flat area, or larger with more skilled students

PLAYERS: 6 to 10 students

SUPPLIES: Hoops, softball, gloves (optional)

SKILLS: Throwing, catching, tagging, running

Space the hoops about 20 feet apart in a rectangular shape. Hoops are used as bases to prevent collisions. One player, serving as a fielder, stands at each hoop to begin the game. All other players are on a base; more than one runner is permitted on a base. On signal, runners begin accumulating runs by running to another base without being tagged. Fielders work together to tag as many runners as possible. Fielders may leave their base and chase runners if necessary. If a fielder leaves his base, other fielders may rotate to the vacant base. Fielders and runners change positions every 2 to 3 minutes.

VARIATION: Runners may not move to an adjacent base.

DEVELOPMENTAL LEVEL III

Five Hundred

PLAYING AREA: Field big enough for fungo hitting

PLAYERS: 3 to 12 (or more) students

SUPPLIES: A softball, bat

SKILLS: Fungo batting, catching flies, fielding grounders

There are many versions of the old game Five Hundred. A batter stands on one side of the field and bats the ball to several fielders, who are scattered. The fielders try to become the batter by reaching a score of 500. Fielders earn 200 points for catching a ball on the fly, 100 points for catching a ball on the first bounce, and 50 points for fielding a grounder cleanly. When the batter changes, all fielders lose their points and must start over. Let players hit the ball off a batting tee if fungo hitting is too difficult.

VARIATIONS:

1. The fielder's points must total exactly 500.
2. Points are subtracted from the fielder's score for mishandling a ball. Fielders who drop a fly ball, for example, lose 200 points.

Batter Ball

PLAYING AREA: Softball diamond

PLAYERS: Two teams of 8 to 12 students each

SUPPLIES: A softball, bat, mask

SKILLS: Slow-pitching, hitting, fielding, catching flies

Batter Ball involves batting and fielding but no base running. It is much like batting practice but adds the element of competition. A line is drawn directly from first to third base (Figure 28.17). This is the balk line, over which a batted ball must travel to be fielded. Another line is drawn from a point on the foul line 3 feet behind third base to a point 5 feet behind second base and in line with home plate. Another line connects this point with a point on the other baseline 3 feet behind first base. The shaded area in the diagram is the infield.

Each batter receives three pitches from a teammate and tries to hit the ball into fair territory across the balk line. The pitcher may stop any ground ball before it crosses the balk line. The batter then gets another turn at bat.

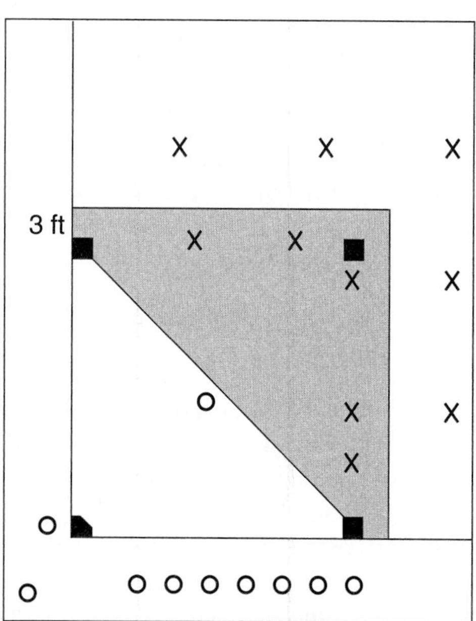

FIGURE 28.17 Field for Batter Ball.

Scoring is as follows:

1. A successful grounder scores 1 point. A grounder is successful when an infielder fails to handle it cleanly within the infield area. Only one player may field the ball. If the ball is fielded properly, the batter is out.
2. A line drive in the infield area scores 1 point if not caught. It can be handled for an out on any bounce. Any line drive caught on the fly is also an out.
3. A fly ball in the infield area scores 1 point if not caught. For an out, the ball must be caught legally by the first player touching it.
4. A two-bagger scores 2 points. Any fly ball, line drive or not, that lands fairly in the outfield area without being caught scores 2 points. If the ball is caught, the batter is out.
5. A home run scores 3 points. Any fly ball driven over the head of the farthest outfielder in that area scores a home run.

Three outs can constitute an inning, or all batters on a team can take one turn at bat and then change places with the other team. Use a new set of infielders for each inning. The old set goes to the outfield. Limit the pitchers to one inning. They also take a turn at bat.

Teaching Hints

1. Many games of this type require special fields, either rectangular or narrowly angled. This game is included because it uses a regular softball field with the added lines, which can be drawn with a stick or marked using regular methods.
2. The pitcher decides whether to stop the ball. If the ball goes beyond the restraining line, it is in play even if the pitcher touched it.

VARIATION: Batter Ball can be modified for use as a station in rotational teaching, with the emphasis on individual batting and team organization. One team member would be at bat and get a definite number of chances (e.g., five) to score. She keeps her own point total. The other team members occupy the necessary game positions.

Home Run

PLAYING AREA: Softball diamond (only first base is used)

PLAYERS: 4 to 10 students

SUPPLIES: A softball, bat

SKILLS: Most softball skills, modified base running

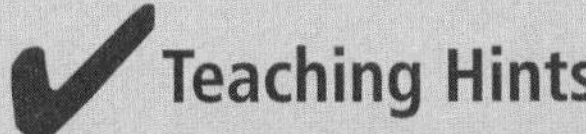

1. To keep skillful players from staying too long at bat, make a rule that, after a certain number of home runs, the batter automatically moves to the field. Devise a rotation (work-up) system. The batter goes to right field, moves to center, and then goes to left field. The rotation continues through third base, shortstop, second base, first base, pitcher, and catcher. The catcher is the next batter. Naturally, the number of positions depends on the number of players in the game. If there are enough players, an additional batter can be waiting to take a turn.
2. The game can be played with only 3 students and no catcher. With only one fielder, the pitcher covers home plate. Make the first-base distance far enough away to be a challenge but close enough so that a well-hit ball scores a home run. The distance depends on the number playing and the players' abilities.

The crucial players are a batter, a catcher, a pitcher, and one fielder. Any other players are fielders; some can take positions in the infield. The batter hits a regular pitch and on a fair ball must run to first base and back home before the ball can be returned to the catcher.

The batter is out in these situations:

1. A fly ball (fair or foul) is caught.
2. The batter strikes out.
3. On a fair ball, the ball beats the batter back to home plate.

VARIATIONS:

1. This game can be played like softball—allowing the batter to stop at first base if another batter is up.
2. A fielder who catches a fly ball goes directly to bat. The preceding batter then goes to the end of the rotation, and the other players rotate up to the position of the fielder who caught the ball. This rule has one drawback—it may cause children to scramble and fight for fly balls, which is not desirable in softball. The ball belongs to the player in whose territory it falls.
3. *Triangle Ball.* First and third bases are moved toward each other, thus narrowing the playing field. Second base is not used. The game gets its name from the triangle formed by home plate and the two bases. The batter must circle first and third bases and return home before the ball reaches home plate. This game can be played with as few as three players, with the pitcher covering home plate.

Tee Ball

PLAYING AREA: Softball field

PLAYERS: Two teams of 7 to 11 students each

SUPPLIES: A softball, bat, batting tee

SKILLS: Most softball skills (except pitching and stealing bases), hitting a ball from a tee

Tee Ball has many advantages. There are no strikeouts, every child hits the ball, there is no dueling between pitcher and batter, and fielding opportunities abound.

This game follows softball rules, with these exceptions:

1. Instead of hitting a pitched ball, the batter hits the ball from a tee. The catcher sets the ball on the tee. After the ball is hit, the play is the same as in regular softball. With no pitching, there is no stealing. A runner stays on the base until the ball is hit by the batter.
2. A fielder, who occupies the position normally held by the pitcher, fields bunts and ground balls and backs up the infielders on throws.

Teams can play regular innings for three outs or switch to the field after each player on the batting team has a turn at bat.

You can purchase a tee or make one from a radiator hose. An improvised batting tee is shown in Figure 28.18. (For another type of tee, see page 191.) If the tee is not adjustable, provide three different sizes. The batter stands far enough behind the tee so that, as she steps forward to swing, the ball is slightly in front of the midpoint of her swing.

FIGURE 28.18 Improvised batting tee.

Slow-Pitch Softball

PLAYING AREA: Softball diamond

PLAYERS: Two teams of 10 students each

SUPPLIES: A softball, bat

SKILLS: Most softball skills

The major difference between regular softball and Slow-Pitch Softball is in the pitching, but there are other differences. With slower pitching, players make more hits and thus create more action on the bases and in the field. Outfielders are an important part of the game, because many long drives are hit. Official softball rules are modified as follows:

1. The pitch must be a slow-pitch. Any other pitch is illegal and is called a ball. The pitch must have an arc of 1 foot but must not rise over 10 feet from the ground. Pitch legality depends on the umpire's call.
2. The game uses 10 players instead of 9. The extra one, called the roving fielder, plays in the outfield and handles line drives hit just over the infielders.
3. The batter must take a full swing at the ball and is out if he chops at the ball or bunts.
4. If the batter is hit by a pitched ball, she is not entitled to first base. The pitch is merely called a ball. Otherwise, balls and strikes are called as in softball.
5. The runner must stay at his base until the pitch has reached or passed home plate. No stealing is permitted.

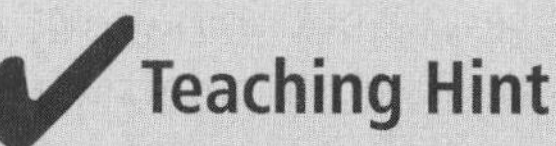

Teaching Hint

Shortening the pitching distance somewhat may be desirable. Much of the game's success depends on pitching the ball over the plate.

Scrub (Work-Up)

PLAYING AREA: Softball field

PLAYERS: 7 to 15 students

SUPPLIES: A softball, bat

SKILLS: Most softball skills

The main feature of Scrub is player rotation. The game follows regular softball rules, with individuals more or less playing for themselves. There are at least two batters—and generally three. A catcher, a pitcher, and a first-base player are essential. The remaining players assume the other positions. A batter who is out goes to a position in right field. All other players move up one position, with the catcher becoming the batter. The first-base player becomes the pitcher, the pitcher moves to catcher, and all others move up one place. You could also add a rule that if a fly ball is caught, the fielder and batter exchange positions.

Babe Ruth Ball

PLAYING AREA: Softball diamond

PLAYERS: 5 students

SUPPLIES: A bat, ball, four cones or other markers

SKILLS: Batting, pitching, fielding

The three outfield zones—left, center, and right field—are separated by four cones. It is helpful if foul lines have been drawn, but cones can define them (Figure 28.19). The batter calls the field where he intends to hit. The pitcher throws controlled pitches so that the batter can hit easily. The batter remains in position as long as he hits to the designated field. Field choices must be rotated. The batter gets only one swing to make a successful hit. He can let a ball go by; but if he swings, it counts as a try. There is no base running. Players rotate.

Teaching Hint

Using a variety of rules, children play this game informally on sandlots. Here are some possibilities to consider: What happens when a fly ball is caught? What limitations should be made on hitting easy grounders? Let the players discuss these points and others not covered by the stated rules.

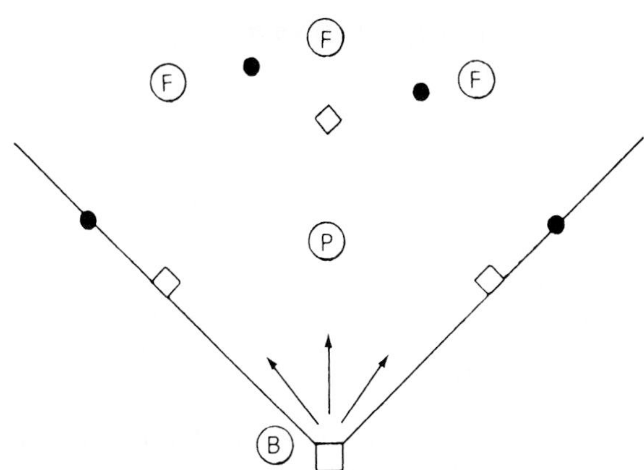

FIGURE 28.19 Babe Ruth Ball.

Hurry Baseball (One-Pitch Softball)

PLAYING AREA: Softball diamond

PLAYERS: Two teams of 8 to 12 students each

SUPPLIES: A softball, bat

SKILLS: Slow-pitching, most softball skills except stealing bases and bunting

Hurry Baseball demands rapid changes from batting to fielding, and vice versa. The game is like regular softball, with these exceptions:

1. The pitcher is from the team at bat and must not interfere with, or touch, a batted ball on penalty of the batter's being called out.
2. The team coming to bat does not wait for the fielding team to get set. It has its own pitcher, who gets the ball to the batter just as quickly as the batter can grab a bat and get ready. The fielding team has to hustle to get out to their places.
3. Each batter gets only one pitch. She must hit a fair ball, or she is out. The pitch is made from about two-thirds of the normal pitching distance.
4. No stealing is permitted.
5. No bunting is permitted.

The batter must take a full swing. The game offers much activity in the fast place changes that must be made after the third out. Teams in the field learn to make the next hitter a catcher, so he can bat immediately when the third out is made. Batters must bat in order. Scoring follows regular softball rules.

Three-Team Softball

PLAYING AREA: Softball diamond

PLAYERS: 12 to 15 students

SUPPLIES: A mask, ball, bat

SKILLS: All softball skills

Three-Team Softball works well with 12 players, a number considered too small to divide into two effective fielding teams. The players are instead divided into three teams. Softball rules apply, with these exceptions:

1. One team is at bat, one team covers the infield (including the catcher), and the third team consists of the outfielders and the pitcher.
2. The team at bat must bat in a definite order. This means that due to the small number of batters on each side, the person due to bat may sometimes be on base. To take a turn at bat, the runner must be replaced by a player not on base.
3. After three outs, the teams rotate; the outfield moves to the infield, the infield takes a turn at bat, and the batters go to the outfield.
4. An inning is over when all three teams have batted.
5. The pitcher is limited to one inning only. A player may repeat as pitcher only after all members of that team have had a chance to pitch.

SOFTBALL SKILL TESTS

THROWING FOR ACCURACY

To test accuracy in throwing, make a target on a wall. Draw three concentric circles of 54, 36, and 18 inches. Scoring is

1, 2, and 3 points, respectively, for the circles. Five trials are allowed, for a possible score of 15. Balls hitting a line score the higher number.

Instead of the suggested target, hang a tire. Scoring allows 2 points for a throw through the tire and 1 point for simply hitting the tire. Highest possible total: 10 points.

THROWING FOR DISTANCE

In the test of throwing for distance, give each child three throws, and record the longest throw on the fly.

FIELDING GROUNDERS

A file of players stands behind a restraining line. A thrower is about 30 feet in front of this line. Each player in turn tries to field five ground balls. The score is the number of balls fielded cleanly. Inconsistencies will occur in the throw and bounce of the ground balls served up for fielding. If a throw is obviously not fair, give the child another chance.

CIRCLING THE BASES

Runners are timed as they circle the bases. A diamond with four bases and a stopwatch for timing are needed. Two runners can run at once by starting from opposite corners of the diamond; two stopwatches are needed with this system. The batter can bunt a pitched ball and run around the bases. The timing starts with the bunt and ends when the batter touches home plate.

PITCHING

Pitching is one of the easier skills to test in softball and certainly one of the most popular with children. Testing is done in two basic ways. In the first, each child makes a certain number of pitches at a target. Scoring is based on the number of strikes thrown. In the second, each child pitches regularly—as if to a batter—and balls and strikes are counted. Batters are either struck out or walked. The score is the number of batters the child is able to strike out from a given number at bat. This score is recorded as a percentage.

Both methods require a target. It should be 19 inches wide and 42 inches high. The bottom of the target should be about 18 inches above the ground or floor. If the target is made from plywood or wood, it will need to be supported or hung up. A target also can be outlined temporarily on a wall with chalk or paint. Balls that hit the edges of the target count as strikes. Use a normal pitching distance (35 feet), and observe regular pitching rules.

"Old Woody" is the name of a pitching target in the form of a stand that can be moved from school to school (Figure 28.20). A sturdy frame holds the target and allows it to be used almost anywhere.

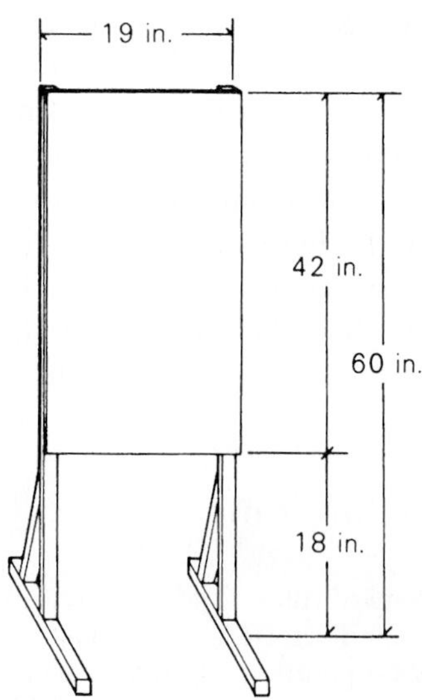

FIGURE 28.20 Old Woody pitching target.

FOR MORE INFORMATION

REFERENCES AND SUGGESTED READINGS

Amateur Softball Association of America. (2005). *Official rules of softball.* Oklahoma City, OK: ASA.

American Sport Education Program. (2007). *Coaching youth softball* (4th ed.). Champaign, IL: Human Kinetics.

Clumper, R. (2003). *Sports progressions.* Champaign, IL: Human Kinetics.

Fronske, H. (2005). *Teaching cues for sport skills* (3rd ed.). San Francisco: Benjamin Cummings.

Garman, J. (2001). *Softball skills and drills.* Champaign, IL: Human Kinetics.

Mood, D. P., Musker, F. F., & Rink, J. E. (2007). *Sports and recreational activities* (14th ed.). New York: McGraw-Hill.

Noren, R. (2005). *Softball fundamentals.* Champaign, IL: Human Kinetics.

Potter, D. L., & Johnson, L. V. (2007). *Softball: Steps to success.* (3rd ed.). Champaign, IL: Human Kinetics.

Schmottlach, N., & McManama, J. (2006). *The physical education handbook* (11th ed.). San Francisco: Benjamin Cummings.

U.S. Olympic Committee Sport Series. (2001). *A basic guide to softball.* Torrance, CA: Griffen.

Walker, K. (2007). *The softball drill book.* Champaign, IL: Human Kinetics.

WEBSITES

Amateur Softball Association
www.softball.org

Coaching Youth Softball
www.coachsoftball.com

Softball Manitoba
www.softball.mb.ca

Softball Skills by Howard Kabota
www.softballskills.com

USA Softball
www.usasoftball.org

Track, Field, and Cross-Country Running

29

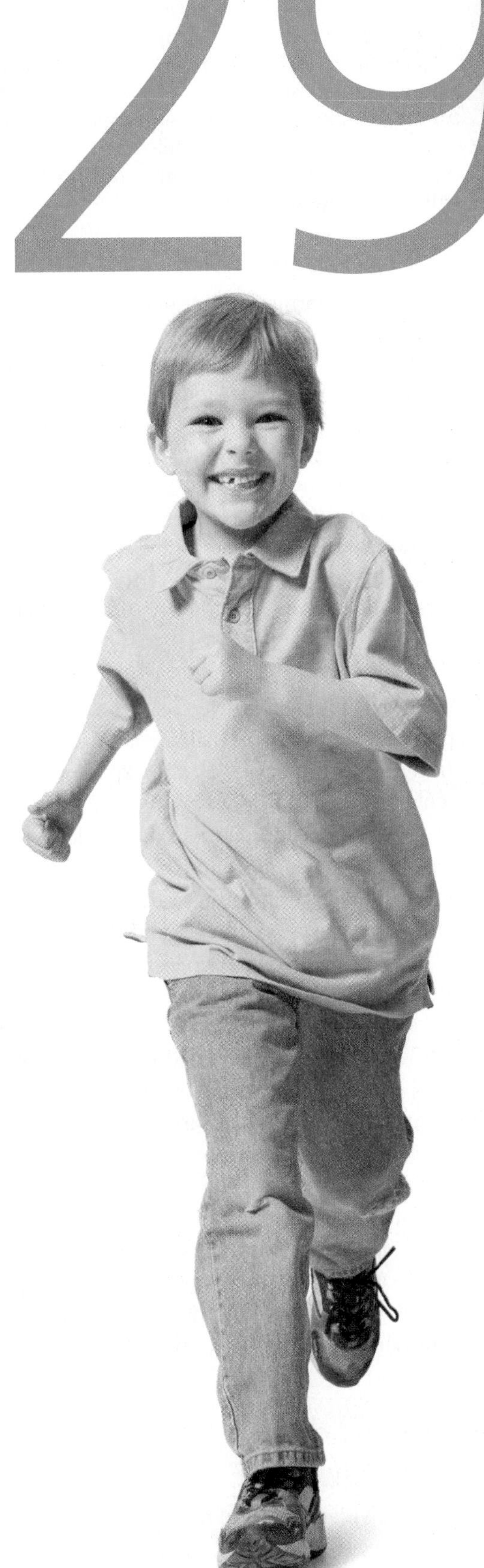

ESSENTIAL COMPONENTS OF QUALITY PROGRAMS

- I. Organized around content standards
- II. Student-centered and developmentally appropriate
- III. Physical activity and motor skill development form the core of the program
- IV. Teaches management skills and self-discipline
- V. Promotes inclusion of all students
- VI. Focuses on process over product
- VII. Promotes lifetime personal health and wellness
- VIII. Teaches cooperation and responsibility and promotes sensitivity to diversity

NATIONAL STANDARDS FOR PHYSICAL EDUCATION*

1. Demonstrates competency in motor skills and movement patterns needed to perform a variety of physical activities.
2. Demonstrates understanding of movement concepts, principles, and tactics as they apply to the learning and performance of physical activities.
3. Participates regularly in physical activity.
4. Achieves and maintains a health-enhancing level of physical fitness.
5. Exhibits responsible personal and social behavior that respects self and others in physical activity.
6. Values physical activity for health, enjoyment, challenge, self-expression, and/or social interaction.

*National Association for Sport and Physical Education (NASPE), 2004.

Skills instruction for track, field, and cross-country running begins during the intermediate grades after students have mastered basic prerequisite skills. Teaching the rules and strategies for track, field, and cross-country running is an integral part of the instructional process. Using proper progression is vital to successful teaching of fundamental skills and lead-up games associated with track, field, and cross-country running. Lead-up games allow teachers to emphasize development of selected track, field, and cross-country running skills in a setting compatible with their students' abilities.

Outcomes

- Structure learning experiences efficiently using appropriate formations, progressions, and coaching techniques.
- Develop a unit plan and lesson focus for track, field, and cross-country running.
- Identify safety precautions associated with teaching track, field, and cross-country running.
- Describe instructional procedures used for directing a successful lead-up game.
- Cite assessment procedures used for evaluating track, field, and cross-country running skills.

TRACK AND FIELD is a diverse sport that allows students to apply a wide variety of skills. For this reason, students can find an activity they enjoy and experience success. The elementary track and field program consists of short sprints (40 to 100 yards); running and standing long jumps, high jumps, and hop-step-and-jumps; and relays. Jogging and distance running are encouraged throughout the program. The primary focus is on practice and personal accomplishment, but modified competition in cross-country running is acceptable. Hurdling can be included when the equipment is available.

Children should experience the differences between walking, sprinting, running, striding (for pace), and jogging. Sprinting techniques are particularly important, with instruction centering on correct form for starting, accelerating, and sprinting. Speed and quickness are important attributes affecting the degree of success in many play and sport activities. Teach the rules for different events. Because few elementary schools have a permanent track, laying out and lining the track (see page 699) each year are valuable educational experiences.

INSTRUCTIONAL EMPHASIS AND SEQUENCE

Table 29.1 divides track and field activities into two developmental levels. The activities are listed in progression. Because many track and field skills involve locomotor movements, students of all ages can enjoy and participate in these activities.

TABLE 29.1 Suggested track, field, and cross-country program

Track and Cross-Country Skills	
Developmental Levels I and II	**Developmental Level III**
40- to 60-yard sprints	50- to 100-yard sprints
Standing start	Distance running
Sprinter's start	Relays
Jogging and cross-country running	Hurdling
	Baton passing
Field Skills	
Developmental Levels I and II	**Developmental Level III**
Standing long jump	High jump
Long jump	Hop-step-and-jump

DEVELOPMENTAL LEVELS I AND II

Because children can easily master running and jumping, these skills are introduced in Developmental Level I. Early experiences at this level stress running short distances, learning different starting positions, and participating in the two types of long jump. Some running for distance is included, and cross-country meets are introduced. Relays offer exciting experiences and involve many students in a quasi team activity.

Safety Tip

Encourage students to move at their own pace during running events to avoid accidents and injuries.

DEVELOPMENTAL LEVEL III

More serious efforts to achieve proper form begin at Developmental Level III. The scissors style of high jumping can be introduced, and students can be encouraged to experiment with other styles. Students should begin to use check marks with the running long jump. Running for distance and cross-country activities are emphasized. Hurdling using modified hurdles is an exciting event. In the high jump, students learn critical points of the Straddle Roll and the Western Roll. Teachers encourage developing pace in distance running without strong elements of competition. The hop-step-and-jump extends the range of jumping activities. Relays and baton passing receive increased coverage at this level.

TRACK AND FIELD SKILLS

STARTING

Standing Start

Have students practice the standing start because it has several uses in physical education activities. Many children find it more comfortable than the sprinter's start. As soon as is practical, however, children should accept the sprinter's start for track work.

In the standing start, the feet are in a comfortable half-stride position. An extremely long stride is to be avoided. The body leans forward with the center of gravity forward. Weight is on the toes, and the knees are flexed slightly. The arms can be down or hanging slightly back (Figure 29.1).

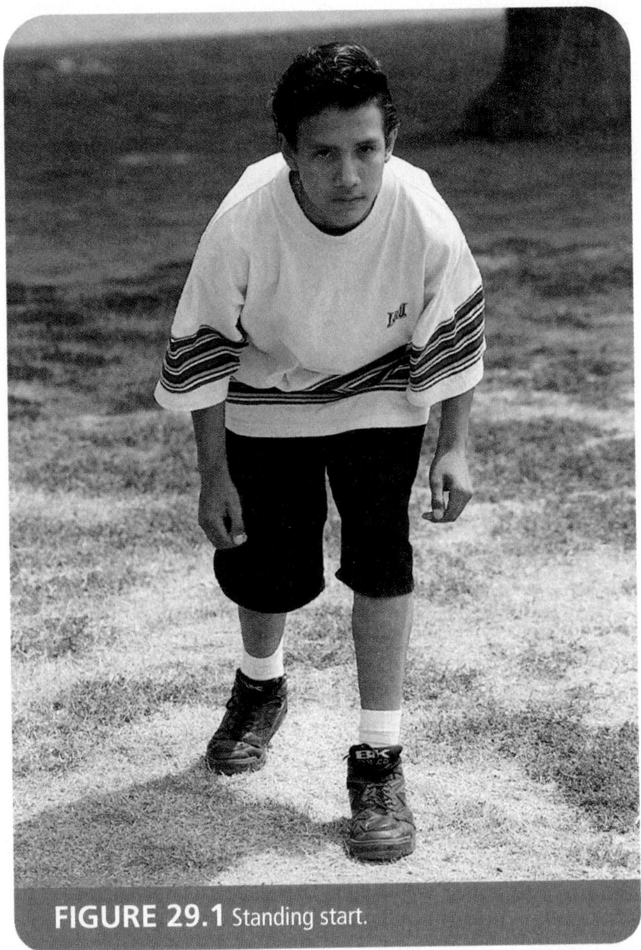

FIGURE 29.1 Standing start.

Norwegian Start

The Norwegians use the standing start in a novel way. On the command "On your mark," the runner takes a position at the starting line with the right foot forward. On "Get set," the left hand is placed on the right knee and the right hand is carried back for a thrust (Figure 29.2). On "Go," the right hand comes forward, coupled with a drive by the right foot. The advantage claimed for this start is that it forces the body to lean and uses the forward thrust of the arm coordinated with stepping off on the opposite foot.

FIGURE 29.2 Norwegian start.

Sprinter's Start

The kinds of sprinter's starts vary, but teachers are advised to concentrate on a single one. The "On your mark" position places the toe of the front foot from 4 to 12 inches behind the starting line. The thumb and first finger are just behind the line, with other fingers adding support. The knee of the rear leg is placed just opposite the front foot or ankle (Figure 29.3 on page 694).

For the "Get set" position, the seat lifts so that it is nearly parallel to the ground. The knee of the rear leg raises off the ground, and the shoulders move forward over the hands. Weight is evenly distributed over the hands and feet (Figure 29.4 on page 694). The head is not raised; the runner should be looking at a spot a few feet in front of the starting line.

On the "Go" signal, the runner pushes off sharply with both feet, with the front leg straightening as the back leg comes forward for a step. The body rises gradually rather than pops up suddenly. Teachers should watch for a stumbling action on the first few steps. This results from too much weight resting on the hands in the "Get set" position.

FIGURE 29.3 Sprinter's start—"On your mark."

FIGURE 29.4 Sprinter's start—"Get set!"

RUNNING

SPRINTING

In proper sprinting form, the body leans forward, with the arms swinging in opposition to the legs. The arms are bent at the elbows and swing from the shoulders in a forward and backward plane, not across the body (Figure 29.5). Forceful arm action aids sprinting. The runner lifts her knees sharply forward and upward and brings them down

FIGURE 29.5 Proper sprinting form.

with a vigorous motion, followed by a forceful push from the toes. Sprinting is a driving and striding motion, as opposed to the inefficient pulling action displayed by some runners.

DISTANCE RUNNING

In distance running, as compared with sprinting, the body is more erect and arm motion is less pronounced. Pace is an important consideration. Runners should try to concentrate on the qualities of lightness, ease, relaxation, and looseness. Good striding action, a slight body lean, and good head position are also important. Encourage runners to strike the ground with the heel first and then push off with the toes (Figure 29.6).

FIGURE 29.6 Proper running form.

RELAYS

Children's track and field programs generally include two types of relays. Instruction in baton passing is incorporated into relay activity. On the track, students always run in a counterclockwise direction.

Circular (Pursuit) Relays

Circular relays occur on the regular circular track. The baton exchange technique is important, and students need to practice it. On a 220-yard or a 200-meter track, relays can be organized in various ways, depending on how many runners are spaced for one lap. Four runners can do a lap, each running one-fourth of the way; two can do a lap, each running one-half of the distance; or each runner can complete a whole lap. In these races, each member of the relay team runs the same distance. A medley relay allows for individual differences because members of the team run different distances (e.g., the first person runs 100 meters, the second 200 meters, etc.).

Shuttle Relays

Because children are running toward each other, one great difficulty in running shuttle relays is controlling the exchange. In the excitement, the next runner may leave too early, and the tag or exchange is then made ahead of the restraining line. A high-jump standard or cone can be used to prevent early exchanges. The next runner awaits the tag with an arm around the standard or a hand on a cone.

Baton Passing

Two methods of baton passing are commonly used. The first, known as the right- to left-hand method, is used in longer-distance relays. It is the best choice for elementary school children because it is easy and offers a consistent passing method. This pass allows the receiver to face the inside of the track while waiting to receive the baton in the left hand. The oncoming runner holds the baton in the right hand like a candle when passing it to a teammate. The receiver reaches back with the left hand, fingers pointing down and thumb to the inside, and begins to run as the runner comes to within 3 to 5 yards. The receiver grasps the baton and shifts it from the left to the right hand while moving. A dropped baton must be picked up, or the team is disqualified. An alternative way to receive the baton is to reach back with the hand facing up; however, the fingers-down method is considered more suitable for sprint relays.

The second style of passing, the alternating handoff, is often used in the 400- and 800-meter relays. The first exchange is right to left, the second exchange is left to right, and the third exchange is right to left, a method that prevents the runner from having to switch the baton from hand to hand while sprinting. This method is used in high-level competition in short distances but is less effective with elementary-age children.

Receivers can look over their shoulders to see the oncoming runner or can look forward in the direction of the run. Looking backward is called a *visual pass* and is slower than passing while looking forward (a *blind pass*). However, the chance of error increases when the receiver is not looking backward and at the baton during the pass. The visual pass is recommended for elementary school children.

HORIZONTAL JUMPING

For both the standing and the running long jump, distance is measured from the front of the takeoff board or line to the nearest point (from takeoff) on the ground touched by the jumper. To help children improve their jump distances, teach them the importance of not falling or stepping backward after making a jump.

Standing Long Jump

In the standing long jump, the child toes the line with feet flat on the ground and fairly close together. He brings his arms forward in a preliminary swing and then swings down and back (Figure 29.7). He jumps with both feet while swinging his arms forcibly forward to assist in lifting his body upward and forward. In the air, he brings his knees upward and forward while holding his arms forward for balance.

FIGURE 29.7 Standing long jump. (Note position of hands and arms.)

Long Jump

The running long jump begins with a short run. The run ends when the toes of the runner's jumping foot contact the board in a natural stride. She takes off from one foot and strives for height. She lands on both feet after bringing the knees forward. A proper landing is in a forward direction, not sideways.

Using a checkpoint results in more efficient jumping. Set up the checkpoint about halfway down the run. Competitors can help each other mark checkpoints. Each jumper should know the number of steps from the checkpoint to the takeoff board. In running for the jump, the student hits the mark with the appropriate foot (right or left) so as to reach the board with the correct foot in a normal stride for the jump. He should arrive at the checkpoint at full speed. The last four strides taken before the board should be relaxed in readiness for the takeoff. The last stride can be shortened somewhat (Figure 29.8).

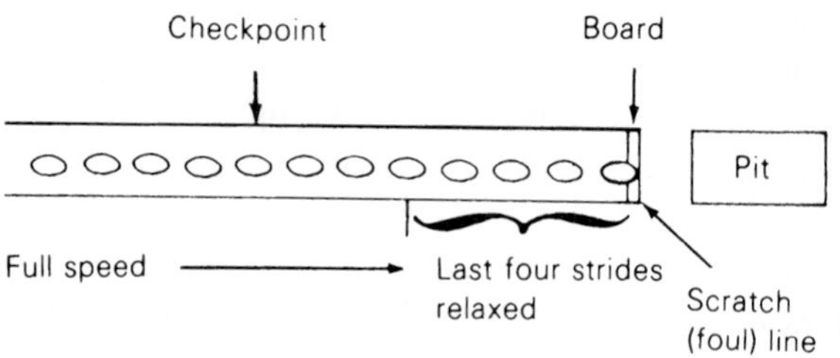

FIGURE 29.8 Long jump.

A fair jump takes off behind the scratch line. A foul (scratch) jump is called if the jumper steps beyond the scratch line or runs into or through the pit. Each contestant gets a certain number of trials (jumps). A scratch jump counts as a trial. Distance is measured from the scratch line to the nearest point of touch.

Hop-Step-and-Jump

The hop-step-and-jump event is gaining popularity, particularly because it is now included in Olympic competition. A takeoff board and a jumping pit are needed. Place the takeoff board close enough to the pit so that all jumpers can reach the pit. Like the running long jump, this event typically begins with a run; but beginners should start from a standing, stationary position. They can then progress from standing to a walking approach and then to the running approach. Regardless of the approach, the sequence of skills is the same. The jumper takes off with one foot and must land on the same foot to complete the hop. He then takes a step (skilled performers take a leap) followed by a jump. He ends by landing on both feet, as in the long jump (Figure 29.9). Left-handers can change the pattern to begin with the left foot. This event also uses a checkpoint.

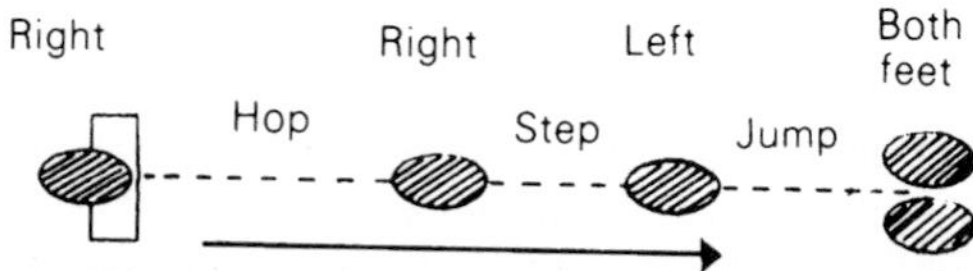

FIGURE 29.9 Hop-step-and-jump.

To avoid fouling, the jumper must not step over the takeoff board in the first hop. Distance is measured from the front of the takeoff board to the closest place the body touches. This is usually a mark made by one of the heels, but it could be a mark made by an arm or another part of the body if the jumper landed poorly and fell backward.

HIGH JUMPING

High-jump techniques are developed by practice. Place the bar at a height that challenges students but allows them to focus on technique rather than height. Too much emphasis on competition for height quickly eliminates the poorer jumpers, who need the most practice. Safety is of utmost importance. Prevent injury by using a flexible elastic rope as a crossbar and having the students avoid any type of flop. Children often want to use the Fosbury Flop technique. But if not taught and performed correctly, this technique can result in a neck or back injury. Include it only if taught by a knowledgeable instructor and supervised closely. Use a crash pad to absorb the force of the landing for Straddle Roll and Western Roll techniques.

Scissors Jump

In the Scissors Jump, the student approaches the high-jump bar from a slight angle. The takeoff is by the leg farthest from the bar. The near leg is lifted and goes over, followed quickly by a looping movement of the far leg. Students should focus on an upward kick with the front leg and an upward thrust of the arms. The knees should be straightened at the highest point of the jump. The landing is made on the lead foot followed by the rear foot.

Straddle Roll

In the Straddle Roll (Figure 29.10), the jumper approaches from the left side at an angle of no more than 45 degrees. The jump has four key parts to be coached:

1. *Gather.* The last three steps are fast and vigorous, with the body leaning back a bit. The takeoff is on the left foot.
2. *Kick.* The right leg is kicked vigorously as the jumping foot is planted.
3. *Arm movement.* Both arms are quickly lifted, and the left arm reaches over the bar as the right arm moves straight up. This puts the jumper in a straddle position while going over.
4. *Back leg clearance.* The jumper clears the bar by straightening the body, rolling the hips to the right (over the bar), or dropping the right shoulder.

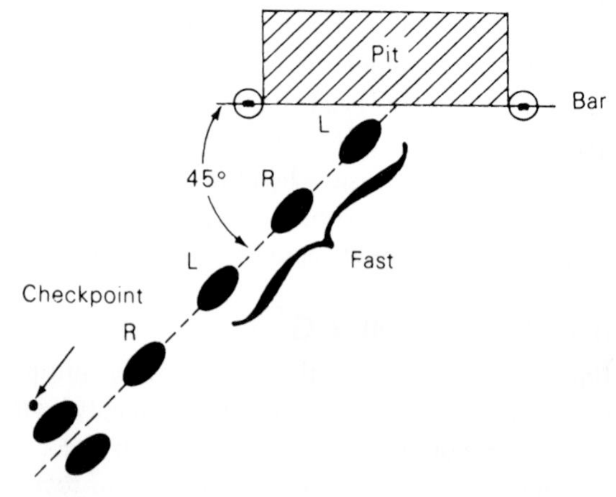

FIGURE 29.10 Straddle Roll.

Western Roll

In the Western Roll, the approach, gather, and kick are the same as for the Straddle Roll; but instead of being face-down, the jumper clears the bar by lying parallel to it on her side. The left arm points down at the legs while crossing the bar and then is lowered. The jumper's head is turned toward the pit after clearance, and she lands on both hands and the left (takeoff) foot.

HURDLING

For safety, students should use hurdles designed specifically for elementary schools. The hurdles should tip over easily when struck by runners. Children often want to jump hurdles in the wrong direction. This can cause a serious fall since the hurdles do not give when crossed from the wrong side. Hurdles can be made from electrical conduit pipe (see page 194 for a diagram). Wands supported on blocks or cones also can be used as hurdles. To begin, set hurdles at 12 inches high and increase to 18 inches. Place hurdles about 25 feet apart. Using six hurdles, you can set up a 60-yard (180-foot) course as shown in Figure 29.11.

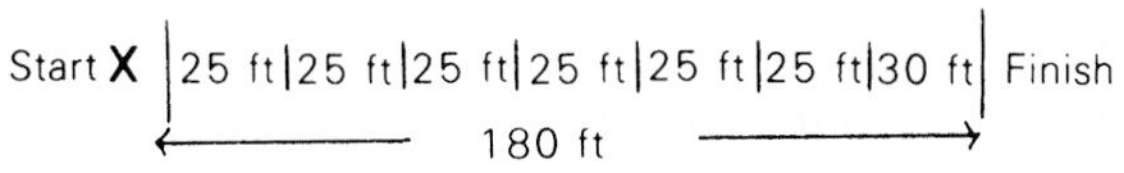

Start X | 25 ft | 25 ft | 25 ft | 25 ft | 25 ft | 25 ft | 30 ft | Finish
← 180 ft →

FIGURE 29.11 Hurdling course.

Several key points govern good hurdling technique. The runner must adjust his stepping pattern so that the takeoff foot is planted 3 to 5 feet from the hurdle. The lead foot extends straight forward over the hurdle; the rear (trailing) leg is bent, with the knee to the side. The lead foot reaches for the ground, quickly followed by the trailing leg. A hurdler may lead with the same foot over consecutive hurdles or may alternate the leading foot. Some hurdlers like to thrust both arms instead of a single arm forward. Encourage students to develop a consistent step pattern.

INSTRUCTIONAL PROCEDURES

1. Spiked running shoes are not permitted. They create a safety problem and give an unfair advantage to children whose parents can afford them.
2. Stress good form at all times, but make it appropriate to the individual. Encourage students to develop good technique within their own style. Observing participants in any event at a track meet proves that many individual styles are successful.
3. Be sure the program offers something for all boys and girls, the highly skilled and the less skilled, and those with physical problems. Children with weight problems need particular attention. They must be stimulated and encouraged to participate. Set special goals for overweight children, and establish special events and goals for children with disabilities.
4. Progressively increase the amount of activity, particularly distance work. A period of conditioning should precede any competition or all-out performance. If this procedure is followed, children will show few adverse effects.
5. Provide warm-up activities before track and field work, and design warm-ups to include jogging as well as bending and stretching exercises.
6. Ensure that pits for the long jump and the high jump are maintained properly. They should be filled with fresh sand of a coarse variety. For high jumping, commercial impact landing pads are necessary though expensive. If they are not available, restrict high jumping to the scissors style and use tumbling mats for the landing area.
7. A metal high-jump crossbar is economical in the long run, although it will bend. A satisfactory crossbar can be made of nylon cord with a weight on each end to keep it taut yet allow it to give. Magic ropes (rubberized stretch ropes) can be adapted for low-level jumping practice.
8. The use of a track starter signal is recommended. The clapboard track starter (page 199) approximates the sound of the usual starter's gun and does not have the drawback of requiring expensive ammunition.
9. Make the goal of the program to allow students to develop at their own rate. Instructional sessions should be strenuous enough to ensure some overload but not enough to make students discouraged or physically ill. Watch students closely to determine whether they are working too hard or too little. Pay special attention to students who seem disinterested, dejected, emotionally upset, or withdrawn.

ORGANIZING FOR INSTRUCTION

Track, field, and cross-country running differ from other areas of the elementary school program in that they require considerable preparation before the classes begin.

1. If the school has no permanent courses, a track or a cross-country course must be laid out. This can be done with marking lime. Sprinting lanes are useful but not absolutely required.
2. Outline a hurdling area (use marking lime) in an appropriate location.
3. Make separate pits for the running long jump, the high jump, and the hop-step-and-jump. Space the pits well apart to minimize interference.

4. Obtain the high-jump equipment. Standards with pins, crossbars (or cord substitutes), and cushioned landing pads are needed.
5. Be sure that takeoff boards for the long jump and the hop-step-and-jump are in place. Jumping without a takeoff board is not a satisfying experience.
6. Gather accessory materials including batons, starter clapboards, watches, hurdles, and yarn for the finish line.
7. Decide whether to use starting blocks (their value is debatable). Starting blocks add interest to the program, but elementary school students may find them difficult to use.

Organizing students is as important as organizing equipment. Children's height and weight affect the degree of physical performance in track, field, and cross-country activities. Grouping students by height and weight allows for more efficient instruction. They also can be arranged by gender. These groups may serve as a basis for instruction: (1) heavier and taller boys, (2) shorter and lighter boys, (3) heavier and taller girls, and (4) shorter and lighter girls. A simple way to form groups is to rank boys and girls separately according to the following formula, which yields a standard number: Score = 10 × age (to the nearest half-year) + weight (in pounds).

After ranking the boys, assign the upper 50% to group 1 and the rest to group 2. Do the same with the girls. You may have to make some decisions in borderline cases.

Some track and field skills can be practiced with a single-activity organization. Starting skills can be practiced with perhaps one-fourth of the children at a time. Four groups can practice baton passing skills at a time. Striding for distance can be practiced with each group running as a unit.

Station Teaching

The overall organization plan should include multiple activities. Four stations can make use of the selected group organization, but more stations are desirable. If eight stations are used, assign two stations to each group. Choose stations from these skill areas: (1) starting and sprinting, (2) baton passing, (3) standing and running long jump, (4) hop-step-and-jump, (5) high jump, (6) hurdles, (7) striding for distance and pace judgment, and (8) the Potato Shuttle Race.

It is generally not sound to have children practice at all stations in any one class session. They can complete the entire circuit during additional sessions. Posting written directions at each station is helpful. The directions can describe the activity and offer points of technique.

In later instruction, students can select the skills they want to practice. With guidance, the choice system could embrace the entire program and be used at every session. This system can be related to individualized or contract instruction.

TRACK AND FIELD DRILLS AND ACTIVITIES

Potato Shuttle Race

The Potato Shuttle Race is an adaptation of an old U.S. custom during frontier harvest celebrations. For each competitor, several potatoes were placed in a line at various distances. The winner was the one who brought in his potatoes first, one at a time. He won a sack of potatoes for the best effort.

The modern version of this race uses blocks instead of potatoes, and each runner runs the following course: A box is placed 15 feet in front of the starting line, followed by four blocks in individual circles set the same distance (15 feet) apart (Figure 29.12). The box is 12 by 12 inches, with a depth of 3 to 6 inches. The runner begins behind the starting line and brings the blocks, one at a time, back to the box. She can bring the blocks back in any order desired but must put all blocks inside the box. Blocks must be placed or dropped, not thrown, into the box.

FIGURE 29.12 Potato Shuttle Race.

The most practical way to organize competition in this race is to time each runner and then award places based on elapsed time, for the race is physically challenging. Competitors must understand that each child is running individually and that they are striving for their best time, regardless of position or place of finish in the race. Timers can act as judges to see that the blocks are not thrown into the box. A block that lands outside the box must be placed inside before going after another.

The race can be run as a relay: The first runner brings in all of the blocks, one at a time, and then tags the second team member, who returns the blocks, one at a time, to the respective spots. The third relay runner brings in the blocks again, and the fourth puts them out again. This race requires pie tins, floor tiles (9 by 9 inches), or some other items besides the box. When the second and fourth runners put out the blocks, they will place them precisely at these spots (e.g., pie tins) before going on to the next block.

Running for Pace

To learn pacing, children need some experience in running moderate distances. The running should be loose and relaxed. Distances up to 1,600 meters may be part of the work. To check his time, each runner needs a partner. Someone with a stopwatch loudly counts the elapsed time, second by second, and the partner notes the runner's time as he crosses the finish line.

Children can be motivated by estimating their pace and time. On a circular track, at a set distance, let the runners stipulate their own target time and see how close they can come to it.

Interval Training

Children should know the technique of interval training, which consists of running at a set speed for a specific distance and then walking back to the starting point. On the 1/8 mile track, children can run for 110 yards and then walk to the starting point, repeating this procedure several times. They can also run the entire 220 yards, take a timed rest, and then repeat. Allow the runners' breathing to return to near normal before they run the next 220-yard interval.

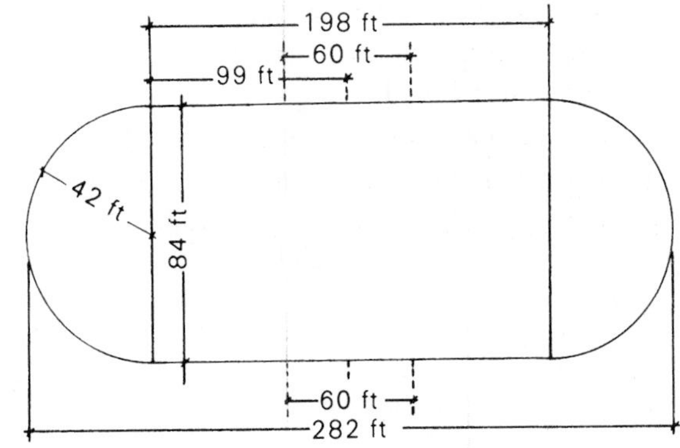

FIGURE 29.13 220-yard (1/8-mile) track.

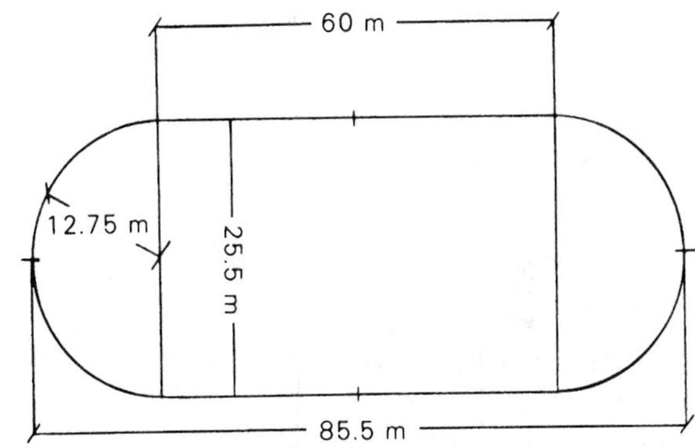

FIGURE 29.14 200-meter track.

SUGGESTED TRACK FACILITY

Having a track facility is a boon to any program. Few elementary schools have the funds or space for a quarter-mile track. A shorter track facility that can be installed permanently with curbs or temporarily with marking lime is suggested. Use discarded fire hoses to mark curbs; they can be installed each spring and fastened with spikes.

The short facility is 1/8 mile (220 yards) long and has a straightaway of 66 yards, which is ample for the 60-yard dash (Figure 29.13). It offers flexibility in relays, allowing for relay legs of 55, 110, and 220 yards. In keeping with international practice, a 200-meter track may be preferable (Figure 29.14). Running on a track is always counterclockwise.

CONDUCTING TRACK AND FIELD DAYS

Track and field days can range in organization from single-classroom competition to competition among several classes and from an all-school playday meet to a meet between neighboring schools or an areawide or all-city meet. In informal meets within a class or between a few classes, ensure that all children participate in one or more events. Each student can be limited to two individual events plus one relay event, with no substitutions permitted. An additional condition could be imposed that competitors for individual events enter only one track event and one field event.

For larger meets, two means of qualification are suggested:

1. At the start of the season, set qualifying times and performance standards. Any student meeting or bettering these times or performances is qualified to compete.
2. In an all-school meet, first- and second-place winners in each class competition qualify for entry. For a district or all-city meet, first- and second-place winners from each all-school meet become eligible.

Generally, competition is organized for each event by sex and grade or age. This does not preclude mixed teams competing against mixed teams in relays. Height and weight classifications can be used to equalize competition.

PLANNING THE MEET

Determine the order of events by the type of competition. Relays are usually last on the program. If preliminary heats are necessary, these relays are run off first. Give color-coded cards to the heat qualifiers. This helps get them into the correct final race.

The local track coach can give advice about details of organizing the meet. Helpers can be secured from among school patrons, secondary students, teacher-training students, and service clubs. Adequate and properly instructed help is essential. A list of key officials and their duties follows.

1. *Meet director.* The meet director records the winners and makes final decisions if there are any disputes. Position the meet director at a convenient point near the finish line, with a table on which all official papers are kept.
2. *Announcer.* The announcer is in charge of the public address system. Much of the meet's success depends on the announcer's abilities.
3. *Clerk of course.* The clerk of course is in charge of all entries and places the competitors in their proper starting slots.
4. *Starter.* The starter works closely with the clerk of course.
5. *Head and finish judges.* There should be one finish judge for each place awarded, plus one extra. In case of a disqualification, judges identify the first competitor "out of the money." The head judge casts the deciding vote if there is doubt about the first- and second-place winners.
6. *Timers.* Use three timers for first place, although fewer can be used. Another timer, if available, can time second place. Timers report their times to the head timer, who determines the correct winning time. Accurate timing is important if records are a factor.
7. *Messenger.* A messenger takes the entry card from the clerk of course to the finish judge, who records the correct finish places and the winner's time. The messenger then takes the final record of the race to the meet director's table.
8. *Field judges and officials.* Each field event should be managed by a sufficient crew, headed by a designated individual. Provide each crew head with a clipboard and full explanation of the rules of the particular event.
9. *Marshals.* Appoint several marshals to keep general order. They are responsible for keeping noncompetitors from interfering with the events. Competitors can be kept under better control if each unit has an assigned place, either in the infield or in the stands.

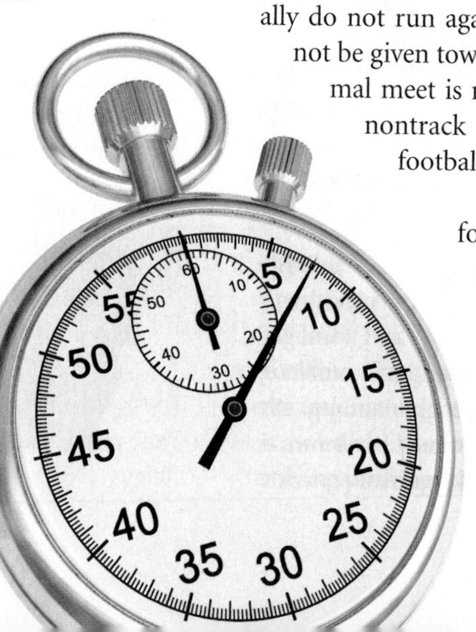

Ensure that only the assigned officials and competitors are at the scenes of competition. In smaller meets, first, second, and third places are usually awarded, with scoring on a 5-, 3-, and 1-point basis. Relays, because of multiple-student participation, should count double in the place point score. For larger meets, more places can be awarded, and the individual point scores can be adjusted.

Ribbons can be awarded to winners but need not be elaborate. The ribbon bears the meet title, the individual event, and the place. After each event, award blue ribbons for first place, red for second, and white for third. Awarding ribbons at the end of a large interschool meet is anticlimactic, because many spectators will have left.

An opening ceremony, including a salute to the flag, is desirable for larger meets. After introducing each group of competitors, the announcer can emphasize or clarify announcements and instructions. Holding the event on a school morning or afternoon gives status to the affair and allows all children to participate.

It is helpful for competitors to wear numbers. Use safety pins, not straight pins, to keep the numbers in place. Numbers can be made at the individual schools before the meet, following clear instructions for materials, colors, and sizes.

ORGANIZING THE COMPETITION

The overriding goal of elementary school competition is to have many children take part and experience some success. Determining individual champions and meet winners has lower priority. Track and field competition can take many forms.

In informal competition, competitors are assigned to different races and compete only in those races. There are no heats as such, nor is there advancement to a final race. Races are chosen so that individuals on the same team usually do not run against each other. Points may or may not be given toward an overall meet score. The informal meet is more like a playday and can include nontrack events such as the softball throw, football kick, and Frisbee throw.

Track and field competition can be focused on individuals or teams. In individual competition, there is no team scoring and only individuals are declared winners. Team competition results in individual as well as team winners. Points scored by individual winners, such as 5 points for first place, or 3 points for second place, are credited to respective teams. The team with the highest score wins. Different team winners can be determined for different grades and/or levels.

Relay competition is a carnival consisting of several relays. Performances can be combined for several individuals if field events are to be included. Few, if any, uncombined scores are considered. Some relays should be part of track and field days under any plan. Relays increase student participation. Mixed relays are another possibility.

CROSS-COUNTRY RUNNING

Many students are motivated by running laps around a track. Others soon tire of these circular efforts, however, and can be motivated by cross-country running. Students can run marked or unmarked courses and enjoy the competition. By focusing on improving personal time rather than on winning, all students have personalized goals and an ongoing incentive for running.

Cross-country courses can be marked with a chalk line and cones so that runners follow the course as outlined. Checkpoints every 220 yards offer runners a convenient reference point for accurately gauging how far they have run. Three courses of differing lengths and difficulty can be laid out. The beginning course can be 1 mile long, the intermediate 1.25 miles, and the advanced 1.5 miles. Including sandy or hilly areas in the course increases the challenge. When students run cross-country, they can select the course that challenges them appropriately.

Students who are running long distances need to learn pacing. One teaching method is to place cones at similar intervals and challenge students to run from cone to cone at a specified rate. A student or the instructor can call out the time at each cone, and students can adjust their running to the desired pace. Another method is to break down long-distance runs into smaller segments and times, thus helping students get a feel for how fast they must run the shorter distances to attain a certain cumulative time over the longer distance. Table 29.2 gives times for the 40- and 100-yard dashes.

TABLE 29.2 Times for 40- and 100-yard dashes

To run a mile in:	Runner has to run 40-yard dash 44 times—each dash run in:	Runner has to run 100-yard dash 17.6 times—each dash run in:
3:44 minutes (world record time)	5.18 seconds	12.95 seconds
5:00 minutes	6.81 seconds	17.04 seconds
6:00 minutes	8.18 seconds	20.45 seconds
7:00 minutes	9.55 seconds	23.87 seconds
8:00 minutes	10.90 seconds	27.25 seconds
10:00 minutes	13.62 seconds	34.08 seconds

TABLE 29.3 Suggested divisions for cross-country meets

Division	Age	Sex	Distance (in miles)
1	8–9	M	1
2	8–9	F	1
3	10–11	M	1.25
4	10–11	F	1.25
5	12–13	M	1.5
6	12–13	F	1.5

CROSS-COUNTRY MEETS

Cross-country meets provide a culminating activity for students involved in distance running. The attraction of cross-country competition is that it is a team activity, and its success depends on all team members. Runners should learn how to score a meet. Probably the easiest way to keep team scores is to assign seven (depending on class size) members to each team. Finishers receive points based on their placement in the race. For example, the first-place runner receives 1 point, the tenth-place runner receives 10 points, and so on. The points for all team members are totaled, and the team with the lowest score is declared the winner.

To equalize the teams, have students run the course before the meet and record their times. Form teams whose abilities are somewhat balanced. As a guideline, Table 29.3 offers suggested competitive divisions and distances to be run. Divisions 5 and 6 are classed as open divisions, which any child in the elementary school may enter, even if under age 12. Ages are defined by birthdays; that is, a child is classified as being a certain age until the next birthday.

A primary concern is for children to gauge their running pace so they can finish the race. Improving personal times should be the focus of the activity, and place at the end of the race a secondary goal. The timekeeper can voice the time as each runner finishes so children can evaluate their performance.

weight shifts to the back foot. The height of the toss is a matter of choice, but from 3 to 5 feet is suggested. As the ball drops, the server's striking arm comes forward, contacting the ball a foot or so above the shoulder. His weight shifts to the forward foot, which can take a short step forward. He contacts the ball with an open palm or with the fist. An effective serve is one that has no spin—a floater.

PASSING

In a formal game of volleyball, players typically use the forearm pass to receive the serve and pass the ball to a teammate for a set. The set is then used to pass the ball in preparation for an attack. At the elementary level, setting and attacking are rare; so players use both types of passes to send the ball to teammates and hit the ball over the net. When teaching these skills, use beach balls and trainer volleyballs so players have time to move into the volleyball's path instead of reaching. Proper footwork is critical to success in volleyball; using proper balls helps ensure that students learn correctly.

Forearm Pass

To prepare for the pass, the player must move rapidly to the spot where the ball is descending. Body position is important. The trunk leans forward and the back is straight, forming a 90-degree angle between the thighs and the back. The legs are bent, and the body is partially crouched with the feet shoulder width apart (Figure 30.3). The hands are clasped together so the forearms are parallel. The hands are relaxed, and the type of clasp is a matter of choice: (1) keeping the thumbs parallel and together, make a partial fist with the fingers of one hand and cup the fist with the fingers of the other hand; (2) cup both hands and turn them out a little, so that the thumbs are apart. In either case, turn the wrists downward and lock the elbow joints somewhat to form a "table." Hold the forearms at the proper angle to rebound the ball by slightly moving the shoulders, making contact with the fists or forearms between the knees while crouching. Here are cues for the forearm pass:

1. Move into the path of the ball.
2. Bend the knees.
3. Make a table with arms flat and shoulders stiff.
4. Guide the ball with your shoulders.
5. Contact ball with the forearms.

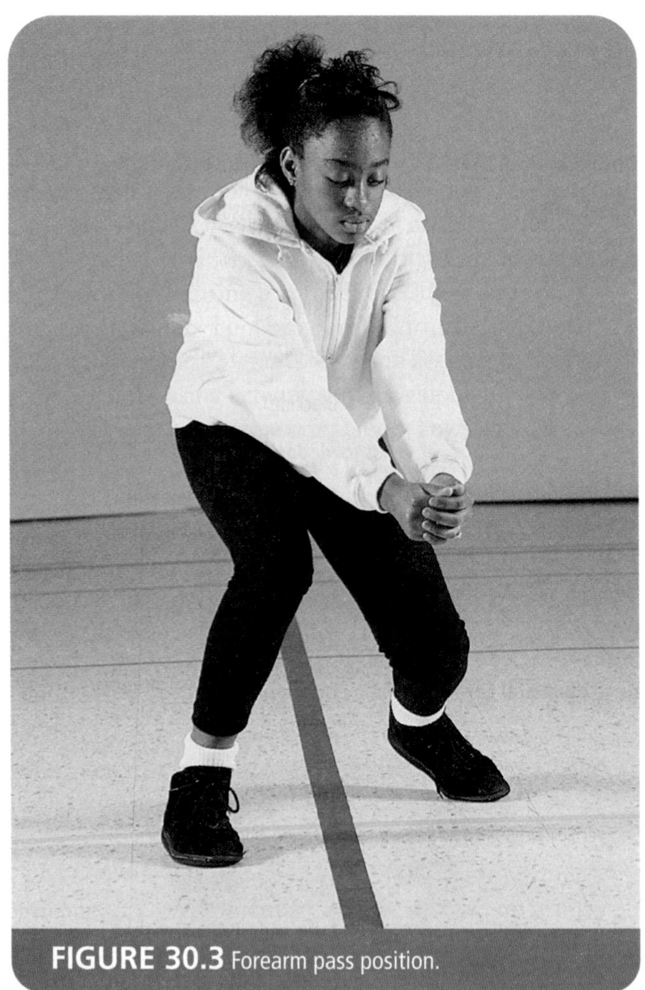

FIGURE 30.3 Forearm pass position.

Set

Elementary students often use the setting motion to return the ball to the other team. This skill is sometimes called an overhead pass. As players become more proficient, they use this skill to set up other teammates (thus, "the set"). To execute the set, the player moves underneath the ball and controls it with the fingertips. Her feet are in an easy, comfortable position, and her knees are bent. She cups her fingers so the thumbs and forefingers are close together and the other fingers are spread. The hands are held forehead high, with elbows out and level with the floor. The player, when in receiving position, looks ready to shout upward through her cupped hands (Figure 30.4).

The player contacts the ball above eye level and propels it with the force of spread fingers, not with the palms. At the moment of contact, she straightens her legs and the hands and arms follow through. The object is to raise the ball with a soft, easy pass to a position 1 or 2 feet above the net and about 1 foot away from it. The set is generally the second pass in a series of three. Here are teaching cues for the set:

1. Move to the ball.
2. Hands up and cupped with fingers spread.

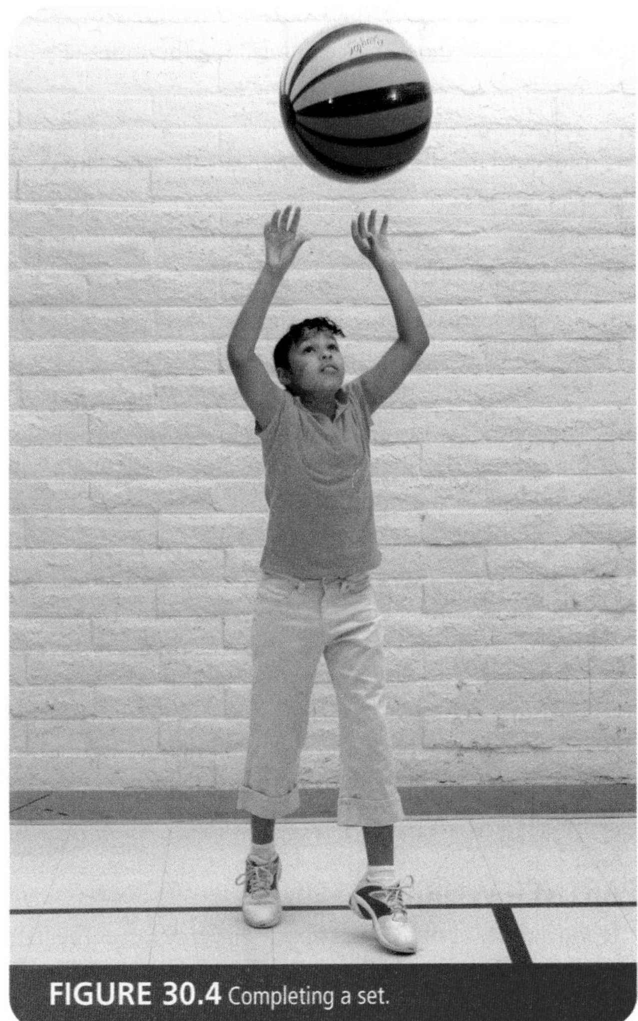
FIGURE 30.4 Completing a set.

3. Shoulders square to target and ready to shout.
4. Push with fingerpads through the ball.

ADVANCED VOLLEYBALL SKILLS

Attacking

The attack is the most effective play in volleyball; when properly done, it is extremely difficult to return. Its success depends a great deal on a teammate's ability to set properly. At the elementary school level, players should attack by jumping high in the air and striking the ball above the net, driving it into the opponent's court. Experienced players may back up for a short run, but they must jump straight up to avoid touching the net and to keep the striking hand from going over the net. Here are instructional cues for the attack:

1. Approach.
2. Knees bent, arms back, head up.
3. Jump with arms up.
4. Contact ball in front of body.
5. Follow through with hand to same-side hip.

Blocking

Blocking involves one or more defensive (receiving) team members, who form a screen of arms and hands near the net to block an attack. At the elementary school level, blocking is rarely used. To block a ball, a player jumps high with arms outstretched overhead, palms facing the net, and fingers spread. The jump must be timed with the attacker's jump, and the blocker must avoid touching the net. The blocker does not strike the ball; instead, it rebounds from his stiffened hands and arms.

INSTRUCTIONAL PROCEDURES

1. Most volleyball-type games begin with a serve, so a successful serve is critical. Regular volleyball rules call for one chance to serve the ball over the net without touching the net. Three modifications can ensure more successful serving: (a) serve from the center of the playing area instead of the back line; (b) allow another serve if the first is not good; and (c) allow an assist by a team member to get the ball over the net.
2. To save time, instruct players to roll the ball back to the server. Other players should let the ball roll to its destination without interception.
3. Effective instruction is possible only when players can rebound the balls from the hands and arms without pain. A heavy or underinflated ball takes much of the enjoyment out of the game. Beach balls and trainers are excellent for beginning players.
4. Focus the predominant instructional pattern on individual or partner work. For individual work, each child needs a ball.
5. Using the fist to hit balls on normal returns results in poor control and interrupts play. Players should use both hands when returning the ball. Make a rule that hitting with the fist will result in a loss of a point if the practice persists.
6. Introduce a rotation plan early, and use it in lead-up games. Figure 30.5 on page 708 shows two rotation plans.

ORGANIZING FOR INSTRUCTION

Practice sessions can be categorized as individual play, partner work, or group work. Teachers can preface these tasks with, "Can you . . ." or "Let's see if you can . . .". A skill to learn early is tossing to oneself to start a practice routine. This occurs when the practice directions call for a pass from a student to herself or to another student.

Two lines

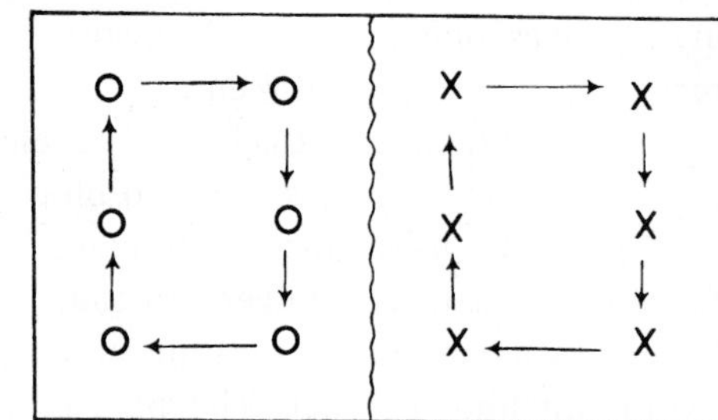

Three lines

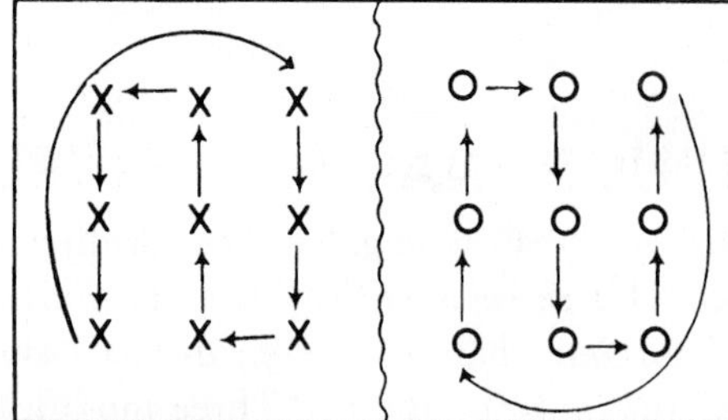

FIGURE 30.5 Rotation plans.

INDIVIDUAL PLAY

1. For wall rebounding, the player stands 6 feet away from a wall. He throws the ball against the wall and passes it to the wall. The player then catches and begins again. He should make two passes against the wall before making a catch. A further extension is for the player to pass the ball against the wall as many times as possible without making a mistake.
2. From a spot 6 feet in front of the wall, the player throws the ball against the wall and alternates an overhand pass with a forearm pass. The player then catches the ball.
3. In another wall-rebounding exercise, the player throws the ball to one side (right or left) and then moves to the side to pass the ball to the wall. She then catches the rebound.
4. The player passes the ball directly overhead and catches it. She should try making two passes before catching the ball. Later, she can alternate an overhand pass with a forearm pass and catch the ball. A further extension of the drill is for the player to keep the ball going 5 or 6 times with one kind of pass or with alternate passes. This is a basic drill and should be mastered before proceeding to others.
5. The player passes the ball 10 feet high and 10 feet forward, moves rapidly under the ball, and catches it. Later, he can try making additional passes without the catch.
6. The player passes the ball 15 feet overhead, makes a full turn, and passes the ball again. This should vary with other stunts such as touching the floor, making a half turn, clapping the hands at two different spots, and others. Allow choice in selecting the stunt.
7. Two lines 3 feet apart are needed. The player stands in front of one line, makes a backward pass overhead, moves to the other line, and repeats the procedure.
8. The player passes 3 feet or so to one side, moves under the ball, and passes it back to the original spot. The next pass should be to the other side.
9. The player passes the ball directly overhead. On the return, he jumps as high as possible to make a second pass. He makes as many passes as possible.
10. The player stands with one foot in a hoop. She passes the ball overhead and tries to keep passing while her foot stays in the hoop. She can then try it with both feet in the hoop.
11. The player stands about 15 feet away from a basketball hoop, either in front or to the side. He passes toward the hoop, trying to make a basket. He scores 3 points for making the basket, 2 points for no basket but for hitting the rim, and 1 point for hitting the backboard only. A further challenge is for the player to pass to himself first and then pass toward the hoop.

PARTNER WORK (PASSING)

1. Players are about 10 feet apart. Player A tosses the ball (controlled toss) to Player B, who passes the ball back to A, who catches the ball. This continues for several exchanges and then Player B becomes the change thrower. Another option is for Player B to make a pass straight overhead, catch the ball, and then toss to Player A. Yet another variation is to have one player toss the ball slightly to the side. Player B then passes to Player A. Player A can then toss the ball so that Player B must use a forearm return.
2. Two players are about 15 feet apart. Player A passes to herself first and then passes to Player B, who catches the ball and repeats the pattern. Player B can then return the ball to Player A.
3. Players A and B try to keep the ball in the air continuously.
4. Players are about 15 feet apart. Player A stands still and passes in such a way that Player B must move from side to side. An option is to have Player B move forward and backward.

5. Players are about 10 feet apart. Both have hoops and try to keep one foot in the hoop while passing. Then they try keeping both feet in the hoop.
6. Two players pass back and forth, contacting the ball while it is off the ground.
7. Players are about 15 feet apart. Player B is seated. Player A tries to pass to Player B. A second method is for both players to stand. Player A passes to Player B and then sits down quickly. Player B tries to pass the ball back to Player A, who catches it while seated.
8. Player A passes to Player B and does a complete turnaround. Player B passes back to Player A and also does a full turn. Other stunts can be used.
9. Player A stands near a basketball hoop, with Player B in the lane. Player A passes to Player B in the lane; Player B tries a pass to the basket. They score 3 points for a basket, 2 points for a miss that hits the rim, and 1 point for hitting the backboard only. Any pass from Player A that lands outside the center lane is void, and another chance is given.
10. Partners stand on opposite sides of a volleyball net. The object is to keep the ball in the air. The drill can include up to 6 players.

PARTNER WORK (SERVING AND PASSING)

1. Partners are about 20 feet apart. Partner A serves to Partner B, who catches the ball and returns the serve to Partner A.
2. Partner A serves to Partner B, who makes a pass back to Partner A. Then they switch so that Partner B serves.
3. *Service one-step.* Partners begin about 10 feet apart. Partner A serves to Partner B, who returns the serve with Partner A catching. If there is no error and if neither receiver moved the feet to catch, both players take one step back. This process is repeated each time no error or foot movement by the receivers occurs. If an error or some foot movement occurs, the players start over at the original distance of 10 feet.
4. A player stands at the top of the key on a basketball court. The object is to serve the ball into the basket. Scoring can be as in other basket-making drills: 3 points for a basket, 2 points for hitting the rim, and 1 point for hitting the backboard but not the rim. The partner retrieves the ball.

GROUP WORK

1. A leader stands in front of up to 4 other players, who are arranged in a semicircle. The leader tosses to each player in sequence around the circle, and they return the ball. After a round or two, another player comes forward to replace the leader.
2. For blocking, six players are positioned alongside the net, each with a ball. The players take turns on the other side of the net, practicing blocking skills. Each attacker tosses the ball to himself for attacking. A defensive player moves along the line to block a total of six attacks consecutively. The next step is to have 2 players move along the line to practice blocking by pairs.
3. Players can practice setting and spiking according to the drill shown in Figure 30.6. A back player tosses the ball to the setting player, who passes the ball properly for an attack. The entire group or just the attackers can rotate.

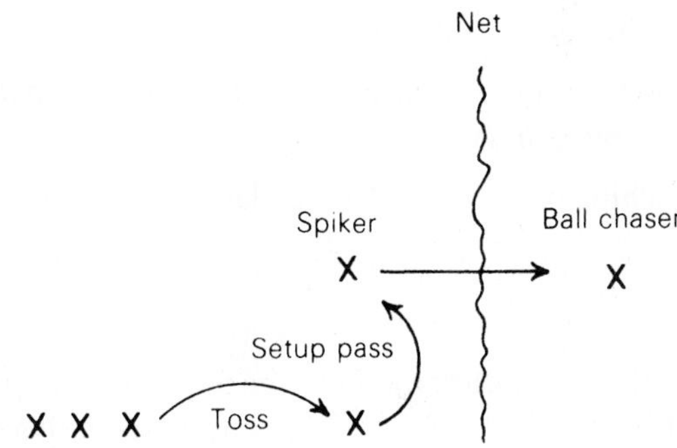

FIGURE 30.6 Setting and spiking drill.

4. Two groups of children stand on opposite sides of a net. They need from 8 to 10 balls to make this practice worthwhile. Players serve from behind the endline and recover balls coming from the other team. The action should be informal and continuous.

BASIC VOLLEYBALL RULES

Officially, 6 players make up a team; but any number from 6 to 9 is suitable in the elementary school program. Many official rules of volleyball have changed recently. Many of these changes result in a faster, more active game.

To begin, captains toss a coin for the order of choices. The winner can choose to serve or to select a court. The opposing captain takes the option not chosen by the winner of the toss. Upon finishing a game, the teams change courts and the losing side serves first.

To be in proper serving position, a player may stand anywhere behind the endline and must keep both feet behind the line during the serve. The server covers the right back position. A point is scored with each serve (rally scoring). The server retains the serve, scoring consecutive points, until her team loses a point; then the other team serves. Members of each team take turns serving, according to the rotation plan.

Official rules allow a player only one serve to get the ball completely over the net and into the opponent's court. If the ball touches the net and goes into the correct court, this is considered a good serve and play continues. The lines bounding the court are inbounds; that is, balls landing on the lines are counted as good. Any ball that touches or is touched by a player is considered to be inbounds, even if the player who touched the ball was clearly outside the boundaries at the time. The ball must be returned over the net by the third volley—that is, the team has a maximum of three volleys to make a good return.

These major violations result in a point for the other team and loss of serve if the violating team is serving:

1. Touching the net during play
2. Not clearly batting the ball—sometimes called *palming* or *carrying the ball*
3. Reaching over the net during play
4. Stepping over the centerline (Contact with the line is not a violation.)

A ball going into the net may be recovered and played if no player touches the net. The first team to reach a score of 25 points wins the game if the team is at least 2 points ahead. If not, play continues until one team secures a 2-point lead. Only players in the front line may attack, but all players may block. No player may volley the ball twice in succession.

VOLLEYBALL ACTIVITIES

DEVELOPMENTAL LEVEL II

Beach Ball Volleyball

PLAYING AREA: Volleyball court

PLAYERS: Teams of 6 to 9 students each

SUPPLIES: A beach ball 12 to 16 inches in diameter

SKILLS: Most passing skills, modified serving

Each team's players are in two lines on their own side of the net. As in regulation volleyball, the player on the right side of the back line serves. To ensure successful serves, the distance is shortened; players serve from the normal playing position on the court in the right back position. Scoring is as in regulation volleyball. Play continues until the ball touches the floor.

A team loses a point to the other team when it fails to return the ball over the net by the third volley, or when it returns the ball over the net but the ball hits the floor out-of-bounds without being touched by the opposing team. The server keeps serving as long as her team scores. Rotation is as in regulation volleyball.

Teaching Hint

Have servers stand as close to the net as possible while staying in the right back position on the court. Successful serving is an important part of an enjoyable game.

VARIATIONS:

1. In a simplified version of Beach Ball Volleyball, the ball is put into play by one player in the front line, who throws the ball into the air and then passes it over the net. Play continues until the ball touches the floor, but the ball may be volleyed any number of times before crossing the net. When either team scores 5 points, the front and back lines of both teams change. When the score reaches 10 for the leading team, the lines change back. The game is won at 15 points.
2. Any player in the back line may catch the ball as it first comes from the opposing team and may immediately make a little toss to a teammate. The player who catches the ball and bats it cannot send it across the net before a teammate has touched it.

Informal Volleyball

PLAYING AREA: Volleyball court, 6-foot net

PLAYERS: Teams of 6 to 8 students each

SUPPLIES: A trainer volleyball

SKILLS: Passing

This game is similar to regulation volleyball, but there is no serving. Each play begins with a student on one side tossing to herself and passing the ball high over the net. Points are scored for every play; there is no "side-out." When a point is scored, the nearest player takes the ball and immediately puts it into play. Otherwise, basic volleyball rules govern the game. When a team has scored 5 points, the front and back lines exchange places. Action is fast, and the scoring makes this game move rapidly.

Shower Service Ball

PLAYING AREA: Volleyball court

PLAYERS: Teams of 6 to 12 students each

SUPPLIES: 4 to 6 trainer volleyballs

SKILLS: Serving, catching

Mark the serving area by drawing a line parallel to the net through the middle of each court. Players are scattered in no particular formation (Figure 30.7). The game involves the skills of serving and catching. To start the game, each team gets 2 or 3 volleyballs that are handled by players in the serving area.

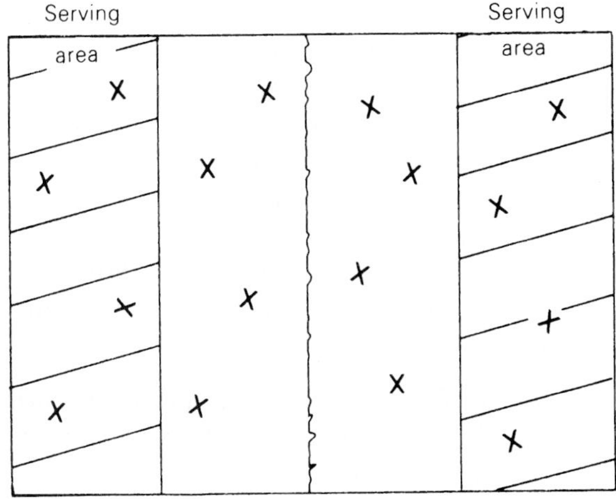

FIGURE 30.7 Formation for Shower Service Ball.

Balls may be served at any time and in any order by a server, who must be in the back half of the court. Any ball served across the net is to be caught by any player near the ball. The person catching or retrieving the ball moves quickly to the serving area and serves. Teams score 1 point whenever a served ball hits the floor in the other court or is dropped by a receiver. Two scorers are needed, one for each side. As children improve, have them make all serves from behind the baseline.

DEVELOPMENTAL LEVEL III

Pass and Dig

PLAYING AREA: Playground or gymnasium

PLAYERS: Teams of 5 to 8 students each

SUPPLIES: A trainer volleyball for each team

SKILLS: Overhand and forearm passes

Each team forms a small circle of up to 8 players. The object is to see which team can make the most passes in a specified time, or which team can keep the ball in the air while making the most consecutive passes without error.

On the signal "Go," a player starts the game with a volley. The following rules are in force:

1. Balls are passed back and forth with no specific order of turns, except that the ball cannot be returned to the last player who passed it.
2. A player may not pass a ball twice in succession.
3. Any ball touching the ground does not count and ends the turn.

Teaching Hint

Make players take responsibility for calling illegal returns on themselves and thus interrupting the consecutive pass count. Be sure the teams have equally good volleyballs, so one team cannot claim a disadvantage. Instruct teams to count the passes out loud to report their progress.

Mini-Volleyball

PLAYING AREA: Gymnasium or badminton court

PLAYERS: Teams of 3 students each

SUPPLIES: A volleyball or trainer volleyball

SKILLS: Most volleyball skills

Mini-Volleyball is a modified activity designed to provide successful volleyball experiences for children between ages 9 and 12. The playing area is 15 feet wide and 40 feet long. Many gyms are marked for badminton courts that are 20 by 44 feet with a spiking line 6.5 feet from the center. This is an acceptable substitute court.

Here are the modified rules for Mini-Volleyball:

1. Teams consist of 3 players. Two substitutions may be made per game.
2. Player positions for the serve call for two front line players and one back line player. After the ball is served, the back line player cannot attack the ball from the attack area or hit the ball into the attack area unless the ball is below net height.
3. Net height is 6 feet, 10 inches.
4. Players rotate positions when they receive the ball for serving. The right front line player becomes the back line player, and the left front line player becomes the right front line player.
5. The winner is the first team to score 15 points with a 2-point advantage over the opponent. A team wins the match when it wins two out of three games.

The back line player cannot attack and thus serves a useful function by allowing the front players to receive the serves while moving to the net to set up for the attackers.

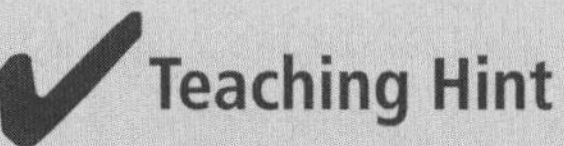

You can modify this game to suit your students' needs. Sponge training balls work well in the learning stages of Mini-Volleyball.

Rotation Mini-Volleyball

PLAYING AREA: Basketball or volleyball court

PLAYERS: Teams of 3 students each

SUPPLIES: A volleyball or trainer volleyball

SKILLS: All volleyball skills

Three games, involving 18 active players, can be played at the same time crosswise, on a regular basketball court. The remaining children, organized in teams of three, wait on the sideline with teams designated in a particular order. Whenever a team is guilty of a side-out, it leaves the game and the next team in line moves in. Each team keeps its own running score. If, during a single side-in, 10 points are scored against a team, that team leaves the game. Teams in this arrangement move from one court to another and play different opponents. The one or two extra players left over from team selection by threes can be substitutes; rotate them into play on a regular basis.

Regulation Volleyball

PLAYING AREA: Volleyball court

PLAYERS: Teams of 6 students each

SUPPLIES: A volleyball or trainer volleyball

SKILLS: All volleyball skills

Regulation volleyball can be played with one possible rule change: In early experiences, give the server a second chance if the first attempt fails to go over the net and into play. Apply this rule only to the first serve. Some instructors like to shorten the serving distance during the introductory phases of the game. It is important for the serving to be done well enough to keep the game moving. There should be some emphasis on team play. Encourage backcourt players to pass to frontcourt players rather than merely batting the ball back and forth across the net.

A referee should supervise the game. There are generally three calls:

1. *Side-out.* The serving team fails to serve the ball successfully to the other court, fails to return of a volley legally, or violates a rule.
2. *Point.* Either team fails to make a legal return or violates a rule.
3. *Double foul.* Both teams make fouls on the same play, in which case the point is replayed. No score or side-out results.

   VARIATION: The receiver in the backcourt is allowed to catch the serve, toss it, and propel it to a teammate. The catch is limited to the serve, and the pass must go to a teammate, not over the net. This variation solves the problem of children in the backcourt being unable to handle the serve to keep the ball in play if the served ball is spinning, curving, or arriving so fast that it is difficult to control.

Three-and-Over Volleyball

PLAYING AREA: Volleyball court

PLAYERS: Teams of 6 students each

SUPPLIES: A volleyball or trainer volleyball

SKILLS: All volleyball skills

The game Three and Over emphasizes the basic offensive strategy of volleyball. The game follows regular volleyball rules, except that players must pass the ball three times before going over the net. The team loses the serve or the point if they do not pass the ball three times.

Rotation Volleyball

PLAYING AREA: Volleyball court

PLAYERS: Variable

SUPPLIES: A volleyball or trainer volleyball

SKILLS: All volleyball skills

If four teams are playing in two contests at the same time, set up a rotation plan during any one class period. Divide the available class time roughly into three parts, less the time allotted for logistics. Each team plays against the other three teams on a timed basis. After a specified period, whichever team is ahead wins the game. A team may win, lose, or tie during any period, and the score is determined at the end of the period. The best win–loss record wins the overall contest.

Four-Square Volleyball

PLAYING AREA: Volleyball court

PLAYERS: Teams of 2 to 4 students each

SUPPLIES: A volleyball or trainer volleyball

SKILLS: All volleyball skills

Place a second net at right angles to the first net, dividing the playing area into four equal courts. The courts are numbered as in Figure 30.8. Four teams are playing, and an extra team can be waiting to rotate to court number 4. The object is to force one of the teams to make an error. Whenever a team makes an error, it moves down to court 4 or off the courts if a team is waiting. A team errs by not returning the ball to another court within the prescribed three volleys or by sending the ball out-of-bounds.

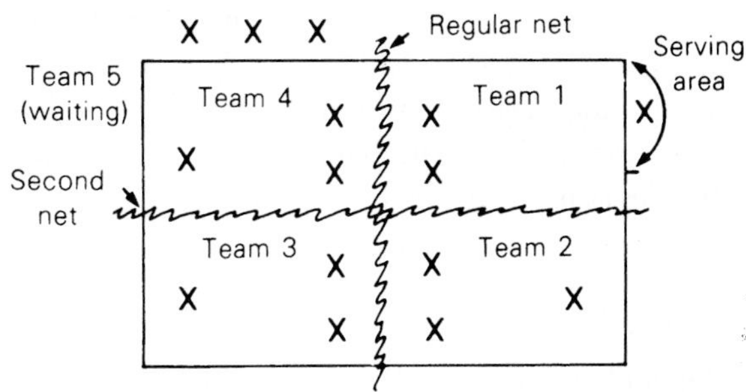

FIGURE 30.8 Four-Square Volleyball courts.

A Team 1 player always puts the ball in play with a serve from any point behind the team's endline. Players must rotate for each serve. The serve is made into court 3 or 4. Play proceeds as in regular volleyball, but the ball may be volleyed into any of the other three courts. No score is kept. The object is for Team 1 to retain its position.

Teaching Hint

The game seems to work best with five or more teams. With four teams, the team occupying court 4 is not penalized for an error, because it is already in the lowest spot.

Wheelchair Volleyball

Children in wheelchairs can participate successfully in some phases of volleyball. For example, a child confined to a wheelchair can compete one-on-one with another student when courts are laid out as shown in Figure 30.9. The size difference of the playing areas

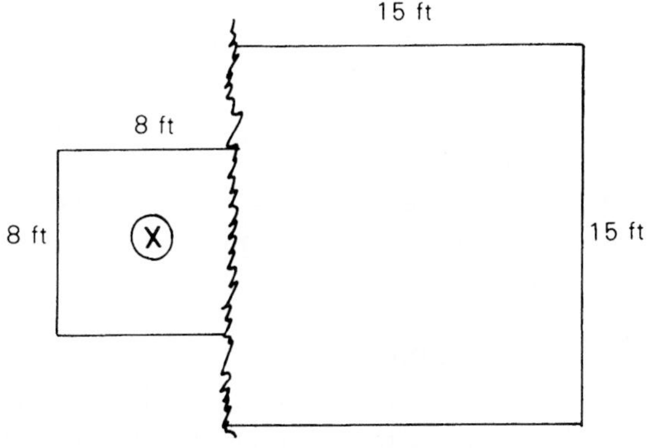

FIGURE 30.9 Court for Wheelchair Volleyball.

30

equalizes the mobility factor. Set the net about 6 feet in height and use a beach ball. The able child serves from behind the back line, and the child in a wheelchair serves with the wheels on the back line. Adjust the rules as necessary.

VOLLEYBALL SKILL TESTS

Serving and volleying are the skills to be tested in volleyball. Serving is tested in two ways: (1) with a simple serve and (2) with an accuracy score.

SIMPLIFIED SERVING

In the simplified serving test, the child to be tested stands in normal serving position behind the endline on the right side. He receives 10 trials in which to serve. The score is the number of successful serves out of 10 trials. The serve must clear the net without touching and must land in the opponent's court. A ball touching a boundary line is counted as good.

SERVING FOR ACCURACY

To test serving for accuracy, draw a line parallel to the net through the middle of one of the courts. Further divide each half into three equal areas by lines drawn parallel to the sidelines. This makes a total of six areas that correspond to the positions of the members of a volleyball team. Number the areas from 1 to 6 (Figure 30.10).

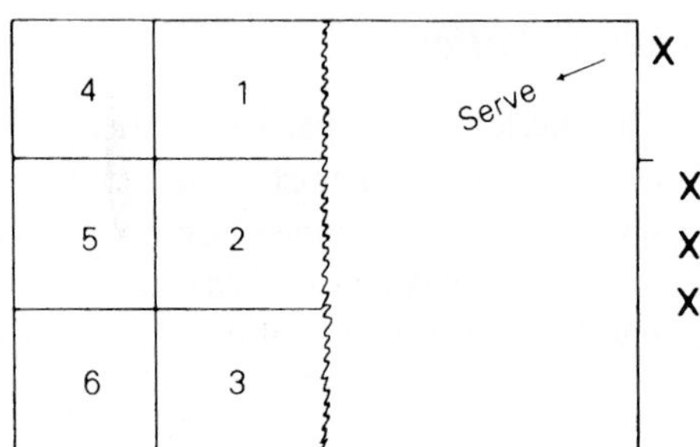

FIGURE 30.10 Court layout for service testing.

Each child is allowed one attempt to serve the ball into each of the six areas in turn. Players score 2 points for serving into the designated court area and 1 point for missing the designated area but landing in an adjacent area. No points are scored otherwise.

WALL VOLLEYING

For the wall volleying test, the player stands behind a restraining line 4 feet away from a wall. A line representing the net height of the net is drawn on the wall parallel to the floor and 6.5 feet up. Each player has 30 seconds to make as many volleys as possible above the line while staying behind the restraining line. Each testing station has a counter who records the total successive volleys. The child makes a short toss to herself for the first volley. If time permits, give players more than one 30-second period and use the best count as the score. A mat can mark the restraining line. Stepping onto the mat makes that volley illegal.

FOR MORE INFORMATION

REFERENCES AND SUGGESTED READINGS

American Sport Education Program. (2007). *Coaching youth volleyball* (4th ed.). Champaign, IL: Human Kinetics.

American Volleyball Coaches Association. (2006). *Volleyball skills & drills*. Champaign, IL: Human Kinetics.

Dearing, J. (2003). *Volleyball fundamentals*. Champaign, IL: Human Kinetics.

Fronske, H. (2005). *Teaching cues for sport skills* (3rd ed.). San Francisco: Benjamin Cummings.

Kenny, B., & Gregory, C. (2006). *Volleyball: Steps to success*. Champaign, IL: Human Kinetics.

Kluka, D. A., & Dunn, P. J. (2000). *Volleyball* (4th ed.). Dubuque, IA: McGraw-Hill.

Mood, D. P., Musker, F. F., & Rink, J. E. (2007). *Sports and recreational activities* (14th ed.). Boston: McGraw-Hill.

Schmottlach, N., & McManama, J. (2006). *The physical education handbook* (11th ed.). San Francisco: Benjamin Cummings.

WEBSITES

About Volleyball
http://volleyball.about.com/od/skillshowtosinfo

American Volleyball Coaches Association
www.avca.org

Youth Volleyball
www.youthvolleyball.net
www.usyvl.org

GLOSSARY

A

AAHPERD American Alliance for Health, Physical Education, Recreation and Dance

absorbing force Lessening the force of a projectile by bending the arms while catching it

accent Certain notes or beats in a rhythmic pattern that receive more force than others

act of God Defense that places the cause of injury on forces beyond the control of the teacher or the school; the defense is made that it was impossible to predict an unsafe condition, but through an act of God, the injury occurred

act of omission See *nonfeasance*

Active and Healthy School Program (AHSP) An approach that focuses on changing the environment of the school so students are naturally encouraged to increase their physical activity levels and make healthy choices, such as eating habits and sunscreen use

active listener One who convinces the speaker he/she is interested in what the speaker is saying; much of this is done through nonverbal behavior, such as eye contact, nodding the head in agreement, facial expressions, and moving toward the speaker

active sports This type of activity is typically more vigorous than lifestyle physical activity; sports often involve vigorous bursts of activity with brief rest periods; examples include basketball, tennis, soccer, and hiking

active supervision Supervision that involves moving among students and offering them personalized feedback

activity reinforcers Reinforcement that uses types of activities that children enjoy

aerobic activities Activities performed at a pace for which the body can supply adequate oxygen to meet the demands of the activity

aerobic capacity Maximum ability to use oxygen in the body for metabolic purposes

affective domain Deals with feelings, attitudes, and values; the major categories of learning in this area are receiving, responding, valuing, organization, and characterization

agility The ability of the body to change position rapidly and accurately while moving in space

anecdotal record sheet A record sheet that contains student names and has room for comments about student behavior that can be used to assess student progress

anticipatory set Pre-focuses on the skill and cognitive objectives of the lesson

arousal Level of excitement stress produces; level of arousal can have a positive or negative impact on motor performance

assessment The collection of information about student performance; traditionally directed at functions of compliance (i.e., participation, attendance, effort) and not on components that reflect student learning

asymmetrical movements Different movements using similar body parts on opposite sides of the body

attractive nuisance The legal concept of an *attractive nuisance* implies that some piece of equipment or apparatus, usually left unsupervised, was so attractive to children that they could not be expected to avoid it. When an injury occurs, even though students may have been using the apparatus incorrectly, teachers and school administration are often held liable because the attractive nuisance should have been removed from the area when unsupervised

B

balance The body's ability to maintain a state of equilibrium while remaining stationary or moving

ballistic stretching Strong bouncing movements; formerly was the most common stretching used, but this has been discouraged for many years because it was thought to increase delayed onset muscle soreness

baseline and goal-setting technique Approach that requires each individual to identify their average daily activity (baseline) level so that each individual has a reference point for setting a personal goal

basic urges An innate desire to do or accomplish something

baton passing The passing of batons during a relay race

batting Swinging at a ball that's pitched to you

beat The underlying rhythm of the music; some musicians refer to the beat as the pulse of the music

behavior contract A written statement specifying certain student behaviors that must occur to earn certain rewards or privileges; it is agreed upon and signed by the student and teacher

behavior games Strategy for changing class behavior in the areas of management, motivation, and discipline; use the shaping technique and are useful in changing whole-class behavior

blocked practice Practice where all the trials of one task are completed before moving on to the next task

body awareness Awareness of what the body can perform

body composition The proportion of body fat to lean body mass; it is an integral part of health-related fitness

body management skills Skills required for control of the body in a variety of situations; body management skills necessitate an integration of agility, coordination, strength, balance, and flexibility

breach of duty Failing to conform to the required duty; after it is established that a duty was required, it must be proved that such duty was not performed

C

cage ball A large canvas-covered ball that is 24 inches or more in diameter

cardiovascular endurance The ability of the heart, the blood vessels, and the respiratory system to deliver oxygen efficiently over an extended period of time

cardiovascular fitness Fitness that includes aspects of physiological function that promote cardiovascular endurance; activities are aerobic in nature

centering Involves transferring the football, on a signal, to the quarterback

closure Brought on by the closing activity; stressing and reinforcing skills learned, revisiting performance techniques, and checking cognitive concepts

cognitive domain Includes six major areas: knowledge, comprehension, application, analysis, synthesis, and evaluation; the focus of the cognitive domain for physical education is knowing rules, health information, safety procedures, and so on, and being able to understand and apply such knowledge

comparative negligence Under the doctrine of comparative negligence, the injured party can recover only if found to be less negligent than the defendant (the teacher). Where statutes apply, the amount of recovery is generally reduced in proportion to the injured party's participation in the circumstances leading to the injury

competition Characterized by opponents working against each other as each tries to reach a goal or reward

conceptual framework A series of statements that characterize the desired curriculum; directs the selection of activities and reflects beliefs about education and the learner

conflict resolution Cooperative approach to solving problems; can help students build positive feelings and learn to solve conflicts in a peaceful manner with no apparent losers

contrasting movements Movements that differ in their qualities, for example, smooth and jerky

contributory negligence Improper behavior by the injured party that causes the accident; harm that resulted from the injured party's contribution. This responsibility is directly related to the maturity, ability, and experience of the child

cooperation Involves two or more children working together to achieve a common goal

cooperative learning A style that focuses on the importance of people working together to accomplish common goals

coordination The ability of the body to perform smoothly and successfully more than one motor task at the same time

corrective feedback Feedback offered with the intent of correcting a problem

criterion-referenced health standards Standards that represent a level of fitness that offers some degree of protection against diseases resulting from sedentary living; represent good health instead of traditional percentile rankings

D

deadweight Fat; has a negative impact on motor performance because it reduces relative strength

demonstration mat One mat is placed in a central position and is used exclusively for demonstrations

Developmental Levels I–III Levels used to group activities and units of instruction because it allows for greater variation of skill development among students

direct style The most teacher-controlled approach to teaching; teacher provides instruction to either the entire class or small groups and guides the pace and direction of the class

dramatization Acting out an idea with music or rhythmic accompaniment

dribbling Moving the ball with a series of taps or pushes to cover ground and still retain control

due process guidelines Guidelines required so that parents and children are informed of their rights and have the opportunity to challenge educational decisions they feel are unfair or incorrect

duration recording Used to evaluate practice time; a student or fellow teacher observes the lesson and times when students are involved in practicing skills

duty Responsibility or obligation

E

ectomorph Identified as being extremely thin, with a minimum of muscle development, and is characterized as "skinny"; may be less able in activities requiring strength and power, but able to perform well in aerobic endurance activities such as jogging, cross-country running, and track and field

endomorph Characterized as soft and round, with an excessively protruding abdomen; may perform poorly in many areas, including aerobic and anaerobic skill-oriented activities

endurance training Exercises that increase one's endurance; examples include distance running, bicycling, and swimming

equipment Items that are more or less fixed in nature; has a relatively long lifespan, needs periodic safety checks, and requires planned purchasing

exploration style/free exploration The most child-centered style of learning; guidance by the teacher is limited to the selection of the instructional materials to be used and designation of the area to be explored

expulsion The act of removing a student from the class or school setting, usually as a punishment

extinction Method of reinforcement wherein the teacher ignores performance that does not meet the predetermined criterion

extrinsic reward Rewards offered to encourage performance; examples include trophies, published league standings, ribbons, and excessive parental involvement

F

face-off Used at the start of the hockey game, after a goal, or when the ball is stopped from further play by opposing players

fast twitch (FT) fibers Fast contracting fibers in skeletal muscle tissue; capable of bursts of intense activity but are subject to rapid fatigue. These fibers are well-suited to activities demanding short-term speed and power (for example, pull-ups, standing long jump, and shuttle run)

feedback Any kind of information about a movement performance; impacts what is to be learned, what should be avoided, and how the performance can be modified

fielding Catching balls when they're hit out to the infield or outfield

Fitnessgram Test used to measure health-related physical fitness and is the recommended test for the AAHPERD. The focus of the Fitnessgram is on teaching students about the importance of activity for good health

flexibility The range of movement through which a joint or sequence of joints can move

flexibility exercises Exercises done specifically to build the part of physical fitness called flexibility

folk dance A traditional dance of a particular culture

follow through The final phase of any skill performance. In most cases, the follow through occurs after maximum force has been generated

force The effort or tension generated in movement

forearm pass Underhand pass in volleyball

foreseeability The ability to foresee potentially harmful situations; courts expect trained professionals to predict and anticipate the danger of a harmful act or situation and to take appropriate measures to prevent it from occurring

foreseeable dangers Dangers that school district personnel predict or anticipate happening (so that they can prevent such problems from occurring)

formation jumping Rope jumping where four to six ropes with turners are placed in various patterns

fundamental motor skills Locomotor and nonlocomotor skills that form the foundation for nearly all physical activities

fundamental skills Basic or functional skills; requisite for children to function fully in the environment. Fundamental skills are divided into three categories: locomotor, nonlocomotor, and manipulative skills

G

galloping A movement similar to sliding, but progressing in a forward direction. One foot leads and the other is brought rapidly forward to it. There is more upward motion of the body than in sliding

game skills Games allow children to apply newly learned skills in a meaningful way; social objectives include development of interpersonal skills, acceptance of rule parameters, and a better understanding of oneself in a competitive and cooperative situation

general supervision Refers to broad coverage, when students are not under direct control of a teacher or a designated individual (for example, playground duty). A plan of supervision should be made, designating the areas to be covered and including where and how the supervisor should rotate

gross motor movements Often referred to as large muscle movements. Most often used to identify locomotor (skipping, walking, etc.) and non-locomotor movements (twisting, turning, etc.)

guided discovery Used when there is a predetermined choice or result that the teacher wants students to discover

gymnastic skills Help develop flexibility, agility, balance, strength, and body control; basic gymnastic skills include body rolling, balance skills, inverted balances, and tumbling

H

heading In soccer, a special kind of volleying in which the direction of flight of the ball is changed through an impact with the head

health-related fitness Can be integrated into regular everyday activities that are often characterized as lifetime activities; people who are generally unwilling to exercise at high intensities should aim for health-related fitness

healthy activity zone (HAZ) A suggested way to promote physical activity using pedometer step counts

healthy fitness zone (HFZ) Category that Fitnessgram uses to classify fitness performance; students are encouraged to score in the HFZ

Healthy People 2010 Document that addresses two major goals: (1) increasing the years of healthy life; and (2) eliminating health disparities; includes enabling goals concerned with promoting healthy behaviors, protecting health, achieving access to quality health care, and strengthening community prevention

hidden curriculum Implied messages sent to students through how the lesson is organized, the types of activities presented, how teachers view students who are less successful, and how children with disabilities are treated

hop-step-and-jump An event that begins with a run similar to that for the running long jump. The takeoff is with one foot, and the jumper must land on the same foot to complete the hop. He then takes a step followed by a jump. The event finishes like the long jump, with a landing on both feet

hopping Propelling the body up and down on the same foot

horizontal articulation See *scope*

human wellness An area where physical education can have a lifelong impact on students; wellness instruction teaches the principles of fitness, the importance of daily physical activity, and the benefits of physical fitness

I

IDEA Individuals with Disabilities Education Act; Public Law 105-17 has the objective of providing handicapped individuals with the least restrictive environment in the school setting—Physical education services must be made available to every child with a disability receiving a free appropriate public education

IEP Individualized Educational Program; a specific learning program for each disabled student as mandated by PL 94-142

individualized style Individualized curriculum that uses a variety of teaching strategies designed to allow students to progress at an individual rate; each student's needs are diagnosed and a program is prescribed to address those needs

indoor facilities Indoor space designated for play; gymnasium

institutional evaluation Program that involves examining the fitness levels of students to see if the institution (school) is reaching its desired objectives

instructional cues Keywords that quickly and efficiently communicate proper technique and performance of skills and movement tasks

instructional feedback Feedback given to students so that meaningful goals for improvement can be established

instructional time The amount of instruction offered to students

intensity The intensity of music can be loud, soft, light, or heavy. Mood is related to intensity but carries the concept deeper into human feelings

interrupted flow Motion that stops at the end of one movement or part of a movement before beginning another

intrinsic motivation Willingness to do something for the sake of doing it

introductory activities Activities used for starting a lesson that require little instruction and immediately immerse students in large muscle movements

J

jump shot For a jump shot, the shooter executes a vertical jump, leaving the floor slightly. The supporting (nonshooting) hand remains in contact with the ball until the top of the jump is reached. The shooting hand then takes over with fingertip control, and the ball rolls off the center three fingers. The hand and wrist follow through.

jumping box Boxes of varying heights; 8 inches and 16 inches are suggested

K

knowledge of performance Feedback that is verbal, extrinsic in nature, and occurs after the performance; relates to the process of the skill performance and refers to specific components

knowledge of results Extrinsic feedback given after a skill has been performed; usually verbal information about performance

L

large apparatus Climbing ropes, benches, balance beams, and jumping boxes; large apparatus activities offer an opportunity to learn body management skills while free of ground support

lead-up activities See *lead-up games*

lead-up games Games developed for the express purpose of limiting the number of skills needed for successful participation

leaping An elongated step designed to cover distance or move over a low obstacle

least restrictive environment Refers to the idea that not all individuals can do all of the same activities in the same environment; used to help determine the best placement arrangement of students with disabilities

liability The responsibility to perform a duty to a particular group; an obligation to perform in a particular way that is required by law and enforced by court action

lifestyle physical activities Activities that people can do as part of their regular everyday work or daily routine; examples include yard work and delivering the mail

locomotor movements Movements performed where the body travels through space

locomotor skills Skills used to move the body from one place to another or to project the body upward, as in jumping and hopping. These skills also include walking, running, skipping, leaping, sliding, and galloping

M

mainstreaming The practice of placing children with disabilities into classes with able youngsters

magic ropes Flexible ropes, similar to large rubber bands that stretch between 30 and 40 feet

malfeasance Act that occurs when a teacher does something improper by committing an act that is unlawful and wrongful, with no legal basis (often referred to as an *act of commission*)

management time Episodes that occur when students are moved into various formations, when equipment is gathered or put away, and when directions are given relative to these areas

manipulative skills Skills in which a child handles an object with the hands, feet, or other body parts

mastery learning An instructional strategy that takes a general program outcome and breaks it into smaller parts, providing a progression of skills

mental practice Involves practicing a motor skill in a quiet, relaxed environment—the experience involves thinking about the activity and its related sounds, color, and other sensations; used in combination with regular practice, not in place of it

mesomorph Characterized as having a predominance of muscle and bone and is often labeled "muscled;" in general, children who possess a mesomorphic body type perform best in activities requiring strength, speed, and agility

METS Resting metabolic rate; used to quantify activity

misfeasance Occurs when a teacher follows proper procedures but does not perform according to the required standard of conduct; based on performance of the proper action, but not up to the required standard. It is usually the sub par performance of an act that might have been otherwise lawfully done

mismatched opponents The mismatching of students on the bases of size and ability; just because the competitors are the same gender and choose to participate does not absolve the instructor of liability if an injury occurs

modeling Teachers exhibiting behaviors they expect of students

movement concepts The classification and vocabulary of movement

movement education Instruction and training in skills and concepts associated with fitness and physical education

movement themes Movements that are categorized in the major classifications of space awareness, body awareness, qualities of movement, and relationships

multicultural education Creates an educational environment in which students from a variety of backgrounds and experience come together to experience educational equality

muscular endurance The ability to exert force over an extended period; endurance postpones the onset of fatigue so that activity can be performed for lengthy periods

muscular strength The ability of muscles to exert force

MyPyramid for Kids The new children's food guide pyramid that was recently released by the USDA; it has accompanying tips, lesson plans, and coloring sheets designed to explain healthful eating to children

N

NASPE National Association for Sport and Physical Education

negative feedback Feedback that focuses on negative aspects of performance; should be avoided

negligence Defined by the courts as conduct that falls below a standard of care established to protect others from unreasonable risk or harm; several types of negligence can be categorized

nonfeasance Based on lack of action in carrying out a duty; this is usually an *act of omission* (i.e., the teacher knew the proper procedures but failed to follow them)

nonlocomotor movements Movements performed without the body traveling through space

nonlocomotor skills Skills performed in place, without appreciable spatial movement. They include bending and stretching, pushing and pulling, balancing, rolling, curling, twisting, turning, and bouncing

nonverbal behavior Another way to deliver feedback; nonverbal feedback is effective because it is easily interpreted by students and often perceived as more meaningful than words

nonverbal feedback Feedback that is given nonverbally

Norwegian Start On the command "On your mark," the runner takes a position at the starting line with the right foot forward. On "Get set," the left hand is placed on the right knee and the right hand is carried back for a thrust. On "Go," the right hand comes forward, coupled with a drive by the right foot

O

objectives Instructional goals designed and listed for the purpose of accomplishing standards

opposition Refers to throwing or kicking skills most often. For example, proper form implies stepping forward with the left foot when throwing with the right hand.

outdoor apparatus Outdoor equipment that help users develop various components of fitness; abstract in nature and can be manipulated and changed to suit the needs of users

outdoor facilities Outdoor area designated for play; the outdoor areas should include field space for games, a track, hard-surfaced areas, apparatus areas, play courts, age-group–specific play areas, covered play space, and a jogging trail

P

PACER Aerobic fitness test that can be administered indoors and does not require running to exhaustion; as a cardiovascular fitness measure, the PACER is as accurate as the mile run and produces much less emotional stress for participants

part practice Method that breaks down a skill into a series of parts and then combines the parts into the whole skill

partial mainstreaming Students participate in selected physical education experiences but do not attend on a full-time basis because they can be successful in only a few of the offerings; their developmental needs are usually met in special classes.

partner resistance activities Partner activities where each partner pulls against each other with a tug-of-war rope

partner tug-of-war ropes A rope that is about 6 feet long with a loop on each end

passing Advancing the ball to a teammate

pedometers Small devices that measure the quantity of physical activity; they are fastened to a belt or waistband

perceived competence How people feel about their ability level; becomes more specific as students mature

personal wellness Developing a personal lifestyle that is balanced in all phases with *moderation* the keyword

phrase A natural grouping of measures; phrases of music are put together into rhythmic patterns

physical activity Bodily movement that is produced by the contraction of skeletal muscle and that substantially increases energy expenditure; it is a process oriented outcome related to behavior and lifestyles

Physical Activity Pyramid A prescription model for good health that helps students understand how much and what type of activity they need

physical education Education through movement; it is an instructional program that gives attention to all learning domains: psychomotor, cognitive, and affective.

physical education specialist Teachers certified in physical education

physical fitness A set of attributes that people have or achieve relating to their ability to perform physical activity; it is a product outcome with an emphasis on achieving a higher state of being

pitching The act of throwing a softball to the catcher

placheck recording Placheck (planned activity check) recording is a technique used to observe group behavior at different times during a lesson; used to monitor behavior that is "yes or no" in nature

PL 94-142 Public Law 94-142 states that all youngsters have the right to a free and public education and must be educated in the least restrictive educational environment possible. Children with disabilities cannot be assigned to segregated classes or schools unless a separate environment is determined by due process to be in the child's best interest

point-of-decision prompts Signs placed in areas around the school where students and faculty will be making choices regarding healthy behaviors

posture Refers to the habitual or assumed alignment and balance of the body segments while the body is standing, walking, sitting, or lying

power The ability to transfer energy explosively into force

Premack principle Principle that states a highly desirable activity can be used to motivate students to learn an activity they enjoy to a lesser degree

problem solving Teaching style that involves input, reflection, choice, and response; the problem is structured so there is no one prescribed answer

process of learning outcomes Relates to the performance of movement patterns and skills with emphasis on correct technique; the form used to execute the movement is the point of assessment rather than the outcome of the skill performed

product outcomes Focus on performance in terms of measurable increments of what learners accomplish

progression Sequential presentation of skills

proximate cause Defense that attempts to prove that the accident was not caused by the negligence of the teacher

psychomotor domain This domain is the primary focus of instruction for physical educators; the seven levels in psychomotor domain taxonomy are movement vocabulary, movement of body parts, locomotor movements, moving implements and objects, patterns of movement, moving with others, and movement problem solving

punting Kicking in football

Q

qualities of movement How the body moves

R

random practice Method where the order of multiple task presentations is mixed and no task is practiced twice in succession

recreational activities Activities that involve playing games or sports for fun

reinforcement Positive behavior given when students perform acceptable behavior

relative strength Strength in relation to body size

reprimanding Approach used to decrease unacceptable behavior

resistance training The term is used here to denote the use of barbells, dumbbells, rubber bands, or machines as resistance

response latency The amount of time it takes for students to respond when commands or signals are given

responsible behavior Implies behaving in a manner that doesn't negatively impact on others; Includes behaving in an acceptable manner and assuming responsibility for the consequences of one's actions

return activities Activities that require children to perform a movement task (jumping, hopping, skipping, animal walks, etc.) after they have performed on an apparatus; this reduces the time children stand in line waiting for another turn after completion of their task on the apparatus

reverse mainstreaming Able students are brought into a special physical education class to promote intergroup peer relationships

rhythmic activities Activities performed to a rhythmic beat

rhythmic gymnastics Routines done to music by a performer using a particular type of manipulative equipment

rhythmic movement skills Skills involving motion with a regular and predictable pattern; can be attained through a rhythmic program that includes dance, rope jumping, and rhythmic gymnastics

S

scoliosis Lateral curvature in the spine

scope The yearly content of the curriculum; also referred to as the *horizontal articulation* of the curriculum

screening A process that involves all students in a school setting and is part of the "child find" process; screening tests may be administered without parental permission and are used to make initial identification of students who may need special services

self-concept A person's perception of self

self-control Level 1 of responsible behavior; the student does not participate in the day's activity or show much mastery or improvement; these students control their behavior enough so they do not interfere with other students' right to learn or the teacher's right to teach

self-responsibility Level 3 of responsible behavior; students take responsibility for their choices and for linking these choices to their own identities; they are able to work without direct supervision, eventually taking responsibility for their intentions and actions

semicircular formation Students are positioned in a semicircular arrangement; this formation directs attention toward the teacher, who stands in the center

sequence Defines the skills and activities to be covered on a year-to-year basis; also known as *vertical articulation*

shaping technique Using extinction and reinforcement to build new acceptable behavior

single standard goal Approach that is based on a single standard with the assumption that it is possible to set one goal that fits all types of youngsters regardless of age, gender, or health

skill refinement Teaching how to perform and/or refine skills properly; not synonymous with performance improvement

skill-related fitness Activities that helps improve performance in motor tasks related to sport and athletics; for people who can and want to perform at a high level because it requires training and exercising at high intensities

skipping A series of step-hops done with alternating feet

sliding A one-count movement done to the side, with the leading foot stepping to the side and the other foot following quickly; facilitate performance in the mile run or other endurance-oriented activities.

slow twitch (ST) fibers Slow contracting fibers in skeletal muscle tissue that have a rich supply of blood and related energy mechanisms; this results in a slowly contracting, fatigue-resistant muscle fiber that is well suited to endurance-type (aerobic) activities

small apparatus Magic ropes, individual mats, tug-of-war ropes, gym scooters; small apparatus activities help develop body control in space and on the ground

social reinforcers Praise, physical contact, and facial expressions to acknowledge acceptable behavior

social skills Ability to interact with others

somatotype Classification of body physique

space awareness Awareness of where the body can move

specialized motor skills Specialized skills used in various sports and other areas of physical education, including apparatus activities, tumbling, dance, and specific games; many of these skills have critical points of technique, and teaching emphasizes correct performance

specific feedback Feedback that identifies the student by name and reinforces an actual behavior; it also might be accompanied with a valuing statement

specific supervision Supervision that requires that the instructor be with a certain group of students (a class)

speed The ability of the body to perform movement in a short period of time; usually associated with running forward, speed is essential for the successful performance of most sports and general locomotor movement skills

spiking Jumping high in the air and striking the volleyball above the net, driving it into the opponent's court

sport skills Skills learned in a context of application, using an approach of teaching skills, drills, and lead-up activities

spotting A safety precaution that involves assisting a performer by helping support the body weight, and preventing a hazardous fall

squad formation Mats are placed in a line, with squads lined up behind the mats. Each child takes a turn and then goes to the end of the squad line, with the others moving up. An alternative method is for each child to perform and then return to a seated position.

static stretching Involves increasing the stretch to the point of discomfort, backing off slightly to where the position can be held comfortably, and maintaining the stretch for an extended time

strength training Weight training

striking Hitting an object with an implement, such as a bat or a hand

supplies Nondurable items that have a limited period of use

sustained flow Smoothly linking different movements or parts of a movement

symmetrical movements Identical movements using similar body parts on opposite sides of the body

T

tackling A move by a soccer player to take possession of the ball away from an opponent who is dribbling

teacher movement Moving into position to observe skill performance; enhances teacher's ability to improve student learning

tempo The speed of the music; can be constant or show a gradual increase (acceleration) or decrease (deceleration)

The Child Nutrition and WIC Reauthorization Act of 2004 This act highlights the importance of developing solutions that increase the physical activity of children, provide nutrition education, and ultimately teach youth healthy eating and activity habits that last a lifetime

time on task The amount of time students spend practicing skills that result in accomplishment of program objectives; also known as practice time or ALT-PE (Academic Learning Time in Physical Education)

time-out Equitable technique for dealing with unacceptable behavior that occurs randomly on an individual basis; it moves youngsters out of the class setting and places them into a predesignated area when they misbehave so that they have time to reconsider and redirect their misbehavior

Title IX Title IX of the Educational Amendments Act of 1972 rules out separation of sexes and calls for all offerings to be coeducational.

token enforcers Some type of token used as a reinforcer

tort In education, a tort is concerned with the teacher–student relationship and is a legal wrong that results in direct or indirect injury to another individual or to property. *Black's Law Dictionary* defines a tort as a private or civil wrong or injury, other than breach of contract, for which the court will provide a remedy in the form of an action for damages

trainability Ability of an individual to receive more benefit from training (regular physical activity) than others

trapping Method of ball control

trekking poles See *walking poles*

twisting The rotation of a selected body part around its own long axis

U

U-shaped formation The mats are placed in the shape of a large U. This formation offers an excellent view for the teacher, and children are able to see what their classmates are doing.

V

value orientation A set of personal and professional beliefs that provides a basis for determining curricular decisions

vertical articulation See *sequence*

W

waiver forms Forms that explain the risks involved in voluntary participation and discuss briefly the types of injuries that have occurred in the past during practice and competition; participants in extracurricular activities should be required to sign a responsibility waiver form

walking poles Poles that are used in conjunction with walking or a physical education program in order to motivate students, reduce joint injuries in overweight children and realize greater results from walking

wand A sticklike piece of equipment about ¾-inch thick and between 36 and 42 inches long

Western Roll For the Western Roll, the approach, gather, and kick are the same as for the Straddle Roll, but instead of being facedown, the jumper clears the bar by lying parallel to it on her side. The left arm is pointed down at the legs while crossing the bar and then is lowered. The head is turned toward the pit after clearance, and the landing is made on both hands and the left (takeoff) foot.

whole practice Method that refers to the process of learning the entire skill or activity in one dose

GENERAL INDEX

C

D

G

M

N

O

Q

R

GYMNASTIC ACTIVITIES

HEALTH ACTIVITIES

INTRODUCTORY ACTIVITIES (APPLYING FUNDAMENTAL MOTOR SKILLS)

JUMPING ACTIVITIES

LANGUAGE ARTS ACTIVITIES

LIFETIME PHYSICAL ACTIVITIES. *See* Orienteering Activities; Sports-Related Fitness Activities; Walking Activities

MATH ACTIVITIES

MULTICULTURAL ACTIVITIES

ORIENTEERING ACTIVITIES

PARACHUTE ACTIVITIES

PEDOMETER ACTIVITIES

PERSONAL CHALLENGE ACTIVITIES

RELAYS

RHYTHMIC ACTIVITIES (MOVEMENT)

PHOTO CREDITS

SECTION 1

Chapter 1 Opener: Jesus Cervantes/shutterstock; pair of sneakers: Allsop/shutterstock; Chapter 2 Opener: Photodisc/Getty Images; basketball: FeudMoth/shutterstock; bottle of water: Andresr/shutterstock.

SECTION 2

Chapter 3 Opener: Photodisc/Getty Images; clipboard: Morgan Lane Photography/shutterstock; soccer ball: Alessio Ponti/shutterstock; Chapter 4 Opener: Fotosearch; scoop with ball: dragon_fang/shutterstock; Chapter 5 Opener: Jason Lugo/iStockphoto; orange cone: Stephen Coburn/shutterstock; Chapter 6 Opener: iStockphoto; whistle: Feng Yu/shutterstock; Chapter 7 Opener: Rich Legg/iStockphoto; asthma inhaler: Nigel Carse/shutterstock.

SECTION 3

Chapter 8 Opener: Serhiy Kyrychenko/iStockphoto; Frisbee: Bruce Lonngren/iStockphoto; basketball with sneakers: Jeffrey M Horler/shutterstock; Chapter 9 Opener: Junial Enterprises/shutterstock; boy in football uniform: VanHart/shutterstock; red balloon: Michael Greenberg/Getty Images; Chapter 10 Opener: Paul Tessier/iStockphoto; girl on slide: Denise Kappa/iStockphoto; Chapter 11 Opener: Thomas Perkins/iStockphoto; ABC blocks: appler/shutterstock; Book bag: Graca Victoria/shutterstock.

SECTION 4

Chapter 12 Opener: Serhiy Kyrychenko/shutterstock; Chapter 13 Opener: Photodisc/Getty Images; measuring tape: Timothy Boomer/shutterstock; softball: R. Gino Santa Maria/shutterstock; Chapter 14 Opener: Vadim Ponomarenko/iStockphoto; dodgeball: Geoffrey Black/iStockphoto; apple: Alexpi/shutterstock.

SECTION 5

Chapter 15 Opener: sparkmom/Fotolia; jump rope: Graca Victoria/shutterstock; girl using hula hoop: Darren Baker/shutterstock; Chapter 17 Opener: Image Source/Jupiter Images; juggling balls: Brian Jackson/iStockphoto; girl dancing with ribbon: Paul Conrath/Getty Images; Chapter 18 Opener: Steven Errico/Getty Images.

SECTION 6

Chapter 19 Opener: Image Source/Getty Images; tambourine: Photos.com; children in conga line: Steve Gorton/Dorling Kindersley; Chapter 20 Opener: Chris Schmidt/iStockphoto; Chapter 21 Opener: Alan Bailey/Getty Images; white volleyball: Skip ODonnell/iStockphoto; Chapter 22 Opener: BLOOMimage/Getty Images; whiffle ball: Craig Veltri/iStockphoto; softball and mitt: Serghei Starus/shutterstock.

SECTION 7

Chapter 23 Opener: iStockphoto; tennis ball: chris scredon/iStockphoto; shuttlecocks: Auter/shutterstock; Chapter 24 Opener: Julian Rovagnati/iStockphoto; basketball and net: Alamy Images; basketball: Andresr/shutterstock; Chapter 25 Opener: Elena Milevska/iStockphoto; Fig. 25.12: kicking ball; football and helmet: Lisa F. Young/shutterstock; football: Denis Pepin/shutterstock; Chapter 26 Opener: bonnie jacobs/iStockphoto; hockey puck: Viktor Pravdica/iStockphoto; hockey stick: Flashon Studio/shutterstock; Chapter 27 Opener: Chris Fertnig/iStockphoto; black and white soccer ball: Ronald Sumners/shutterstock; Chapter 28 Opener: Lawrence Sawyer/iStockphoto; Chapter 29 Opener: iStockphoto; stopwatch: Slavoljub Pantelic/iStockphoto; Chapter 30 Opener: Nikolay Titov/iStockphoto; blue and white volleyball: Andres Peiro Palmer/iStockphoto.